OXFORD REFERENCE

A Dictionary of

SUPERSTITIONS

Iona Opie was the author, with her late husband Peter, of a number of admired works on the folklore of children. This dictionary of superstitions was one of the books they had planned in the adult field.

Moira Tatem is a linguist by profession and has taught in England, France, and Nigeria. Her interest in superstitions dates back to her childhood in the mining and seafaring community of South Shields.

A Dictionary of
SUPERSTITIONS

Edited by
IONA OPIE
and
MOIRA TATEM

Oxford   New York
OXFORD UNIVERSITY PRESS
1992

Oxford University Press, Walton Street, Oxford OX2 6DP

Oxford New York Toronto
Delhi Bombay Calcutta Madras Karachi
Petaling Jaya Singapore Hong Kong Tokyo
Nairobi Dar es Salaam Cape Town
Melbourne Auckland
and associated companies in
Berlin Ibadan

Oxford is a trade mark of Oxford University Press

First published 1989
First issued as an Oxford University Press paperback 1992

British Library Cataloguing in Publication Data
Data available
ISBN 0-19-282916-5

Library of Congress Cataloging in Publication Data
A dictionary of superstitions / edited by Iona Opie and Moira Tatem.
p.   cm.
Includes bibliographical references.
1. Superstition—Great Britain—Dictionaries. 2. Folklore—Great
Britain—Dictionaries. 3. Superstition—Ireland—Dictionaries.
4. Folklore—Ireland—Dictionaries. I. Opie, Iona Archibald.
II. Tatem, Moira.
001. 9'6'03—dc20   [BF1775.D53 1992] 91-20077
ISBN 0-19-282916-5

Printed in Great Britain by
Clays Ltd.
Bungay, Suffolk

Preface

THE vast subject of 'superstitions', taken by us to include divinations, spells, cures, charms, signs and omens, rituals, and taboos, has never before been systematically organized. In this dictionary we have assembled chiefly those superstitions from Great Britain and Eire which survived into the nineteenth and twentieth centuries, with a preponderance of the everyday, domestic beliefs with which most readers will be familiar. They have been arranged alphabetically according to their central idea or object, and illustrated with a selection of quotations chronologically ordered to show the history and development of each belief. The quotations are from a wide range of sources: diaries, letters, local histories and glossaries, works of literature, folklore publications, journals, and newspapers. They have been checked with their original sources, or occasionally, in the case of some early manuscripts, have been taken from reliable secondary sources. We have used quotations from early foreign sources such as St Augustine of Hippo and St John Chrysostom, the classics, and the Bible, to demonstrate the antiquity of a particular belief; and from the seminal fifteenth-century German work the *Malleus Maleficarum* to elucidate underlying principles.

It would have been wearyingly repetitious, as well as impractical, to have included every superstition we encountered, or every description we found of an individual superstition. The quotations have been chosen to reflect as far as possible the popularity of a belief or custom, its time span, and its geographical spread. Local variations have only been recorded where they have intrinsic significance.

There is a chronological unevenness in some of the entries, which is inevitable when one compares the fluctuating amount of attention paid to the subject over the centuries. Compare for example the meagre and incidental references from the rationalist eighteenth century with the superabundance of detailed observations from the nineteenth, the age when the word 'folklore' was invented.

It would not be possible to deal with all the ramifications and background of superstitious belief within the compass of a single volume. Hence witchcraft and the effects of the evil eye are only mentioned when they are the motive for a practice, or the original reason for a belief. We do not include fallacies that are straightforward misunderstandings of nature, or herbal remedies that have no magical element. Nor do we include wonders such as stones that grow or move, nor beliefs restricted to particular families or local features.

We have only admitted those calendar customs that have a magic purpose:

the carrying of a dead wren as an amulet for instance, but not the history of wren-hunting in mid-winter; the keeping of a piece of the Yule Log as a charm against bad luck in the New Year, but not the bringing in of the Log with its attendant ceremonies; the power of greenery in May, but not its wider manifestations as Jack in the Green and the Green Man.

The analytical index lists the unifying themes which connect the individual superstitions. It also contains the bulk of the cross-references which link the main entries with each other. Only when it seemed essential to compare one entry with another specifically resembling it did we make the comparison within the main text. The index must be seen as an integral part of the book, bringing the subject together into a coherent whole. When first encountered many superstitions seem disconnected or meaningless, but when the index is consulted most can be seen to be related to a pervasive and deeply rooted network of belief.

In the process of assembling the dictionary we have received some much appreciated help. Our particular thanks go to Anthony Davies of Gröningen University, who encouraged us to include pre-Chaucerian quotations and supplied many of them himself; Malcolm Jones, who directed our attention to some useful sources, as well as contributing to the text; Brian McConnell, of the *Daily Mirror*'s 'Live Letters' page; Samuel P. Menefee, who gave us good advice at the outset, supporting our decision to use literary sources such as plays and novels as well as folkloristic sources.

We are also grateful to Gillian Bennett, for orally collected contributions in the early stages of the work; to Win Bennett, who explored the resources of The Centre for English Cultural Tradition and Language at Sheffield University for us, and Professor J. D. A. Widdowson, the Centre's Director, who made this possible; to Tressillian Garner and Jean Henderson, who undertook extensive reading programmes for us; to the many other friends (and casual acquaintances on trains and buses) who willingly responded to our enquiries; to Jack Flavell and the other members of staff at the Bodleian Library, and the staff at the British Library, for their tireless and patient assistance; to Melissa Spielman, our editor at the Oxford University Press, without whose cheerful encouragement we should never have mastered the mysteries of the word-processor; and to The Folklore Society which, by voting us a grant even before we started work, demonstrated its faith in our project.

I.O. and M.T.

Liss, Hampshire
1989

Introduction

WHEN Henry Bourne, the Curate of the Parochial Chapel of All-Saints in Newcastle upon Tyne, wrote *Antiquitates Vulgares: or, the Antiquities of the Common People* in 1725, it was with the intention of saving his parishioners from opinions which, being 'the produce of heathenism' or 'the Inventions of the Devil', were drawing them away from a perfect trust in the providence of God. 'The Observations of Omens, such as the falling of Salt, a Hare crossing the Way, of the Dead-Watch, of Crickets, &c. are sinful and diabolical,' he said, 'For by such Observations as these, they [the parishioners] are the Slaves of Superstition and Sin.' He also, as would be appropriate at that time, blamed the Roman Catholic monks for forging 'many silly and wicked Opinions, to keep the World in Awe and Ignorance'.

The Church's view of superstition was based on such definitions as that of St Thomas Aquinas in the *Summa Theologica* (1266–73): 'A vice contrary to religion by excess, not that it offers more to the divine worship than true religion, but because it offers divine worship either to whom it ought not, or in a manner it ought not'.[1] Thus to the Christian Church the belief in any power but that of the Christian God was superstition; and practices such as divination, spells, charms, and magic cures were proscribed. As well as the deliberate acts of magic, there was a multitude of less heinous actions and beliefs, often termed 'vulgar errors' or 'superstitious practices', which were also frowned upon, and to as little effect. As John Melton put it in 1620, 'A whole Universitie of Doctors cannot roote these superstitious observances out' of people's minds. It was not until the middle of the nineteenth century that all these beliefs were referred to, in telescoped form, as 'superstitions'.

Nevertheless there appear to have been priests who had a sympathetic understanding of the wish for supplementary occult aid, and to have used the 'magic' of their own religion to alleviate anxiety and suffering. 'Some priests,' said Ælfric, 'keep the sacrament which was consecrated on Easter Day the whole year long for sick men.' And seven hundred or so years later Thomas Ady recounted, in *A Candle in the Dark*, 1656, how an old woman thought her butter-making charm especially efficacious 'for it was taught my Mother by a learned Church-man in Queen Maries days, when as Churchmen had more cunning and could teach people many a trick, that our Ministers now a days know not'.

The observances and appurtenances of the Christian faith continued to be

---

[1] 1922, pt. 2, 2nd pt., Quest. 92, art. 1.

used in an extra-mural fashion: Bibles were fanned in sick men's faces, communion wine was recommended for whooping cough, women bathed their sore eyes with baptismal water; and although people may no longer cross themselves when faced with an evil omen such as a magpie, they still cross their fingers to prevent bad luck. Church ceremonies themselves, some of the clergy feel, are still being used for superstitious reasons, as when non-churchgoing parents bring their babies to be christened, or children bring their animals to be blessed.

Folklore in general 'consists of all the knowledge traditionally passed on from one person to another which is not knowledge generally accepted or "officially" recognized',[1] and most superstitions can be seen to be based on unauthorized or out-moded religion. To the Christian Church pagan religion was superstitious; the fourteenth-century preacher John Bromyard called it 'This blyndnesse of old misbileve'. To the Protestant Church the use of rosaries and the Lady Psalter, and the details of Roman Catholic ritual, were superstitious; can children not be christened, asked Bishop Pilkington in 1563, 'without fontes, wythout crossinge, blowinge, censing, saltinge, spittinge, oyle and chreame?' To the Puritans the keeping of Christmas and the decking of houses with holly and ivy were superstitious. Today even a belief in God can be called superstitious.

In its widest sense, superstition seems to be an inherent part of the human mind—what Hugh Miller named 'the workings of that religion natural to the human heart'.[2] Most of us are awe-struck at coincidences; and when we look back at a fortunate chain of events we say they were 'meant', assigning their apparent predestination to the hand of fate rather than to the will of God. We take note of freakish occurrences, such as comets and unseasonable blossom, and the behaviour of certain birds and animals which seem to possess mystical knowledge, and many of us still believe that these things forecast our destiny, usually for the worse. As John Brand noticed, 'In all ages Men have been Self-Tormentors, the bad Omens fill a catalogue infinitely more extensive than that of the good'.[3] We have fears so deep they might be said to be instinctive: the fear of disobeying old taboos, of tempting fate, of retribution, of darkness and its denizens.

'Witchcraft' is nowadays probably thought of in terms of the seventeenth-century epidemic when, Kittredge says, 'The belief in witchcraft was practically universal . . . even among the educated [and] with the mass of the people it was absolutely universal'.[4] Although witchcraft is only included in the present work when it appears as the motive for a practice or the original reason for a belief, many more of the superstitions should be seen against this same malevolent background.

[1] Peter Opie, *Journal of the Royal Society of Arts*, vol. CI, p. 697.
[2] *Scenes of North Scotland*, 1835, p. 109.   [3] *Popular Antiquities*, 1813, II, pp. 449–50.
[4] *Witchcraft in Old and New England*, 1929, p. 372.

The deepest apprehensions of primitive man were largely connected with fears that his means of livelihood or his ability to reproduce his own kind would be harmed or destroyed. Hence many superstitions show that the farming population was constantly worried lest a witch should, for instance, steal the milk and butter by magical means; and others demonstrate that a wedding was a time of anxiety, when the young couple, fearing that a witch might secretly have tied knots in their clothing to frustrate their hopes of progeny, carefully loosened every knot about their persons before coming to the altar. The persistent dread of witchcraft also underlies the superstitions which warn against doing certain things, such as combing one's hair, hiving bees, or selling eggs, after dark when witches are known to be abroad and working their spells.

Some transactions are, indeed, dangerous at any time. Significant objects, such as pins, knives, and shoes, must not be accepted as gifts for fear of evil intent, though the gift can often be rendered harmless by converting it into a purchase. Lending is also fraught with danger, for if a witch is granted milk or butter from a cow, she gains control over that cow and may bewitch it; and if a fisherman is allowed to borrow anything from another man's boat he takes his luck as well—for 'the luck of the fishing' goes with the article.

The strains imposed upon human relationships by the belief in witchcraft must have been immense. If someone was suspected of being a witch, then precautions and countermeasures had to be taken; yet to be seen taking defensive action was an insult. Turning an object round was a common way of making magic; and turning a chair round has survived as a way of changing one's luck at cards. It is more than likely that this was once a method of neutralizing the evil power of a supposed witch, for one of Hone's correspondents reported in 1831, 'When talking thoughtlessly with a good woman, I carelessly turned a chair round two or three times; she was offended, and said it was a sign we should quarrel'.[1] Above all a witch had to be prevented from tampering with the domestic fire, and thus it is only after an acquaintanceship of seven years that someone outside the family is allowed to tend the fire—a superstition that has survived as a social pleasantry. Suspicions of witchcraft might, however, sometimes be allayed by the incomer, who could prove his or her goodwill by joining in any work of consequence that was in progress; the visitor could for instance put a hand to the butter churn, help bait the fishing line, or take a turn at stirring the Christmas pudding.

Some of our beliefs hark back to a time when human beings lived in closer proximity with nature than they do now, and believed in an 'anima mundi'. In those days the sun and moon, fire and water, flora and fauna were accorded a religious respect. With man and nature in harmony it would seem right to

---

[1] *Year Book*, 29 Feb.

stir one's food in the same direction as the course of the sun, and to sleep (or die) with one's bed not athwart the ceiling-beam or floorboards but in sympathy with the other woodwork in the room. Much the same feeling is found in the idea that plentiful berries in the autumn are a provision for the birds during a coming hard winter, rather than the result of the absence of frosts at blossom time; and in the belief that a house-fly which survives until January is lucky not so much because it is a rarity as because it seems to be under some kind of heavenly protection.

Other beliefs are characterized by a direct symbolism. A symbolic burial was, in the long distant past, believed to cure a patient by enacting his death and rebirth; a newborn baby was carried upstairs to signify that he would rise in the world; the eagle-stone was believed to ease childbirth because 'it conteyneth & bredith a nother stone wythin: lyke as it were a woman wyth chylde'; an overturned bowl was seen as a witch's attempt, through sympathetic magic, to overturn a ship. As Jung said, 'Who can doubt that the Flanders poppies are more than local flora?' Red petals are indeed taken to symbolize blood; and according to a firm present-day belief, red and white flowers taken to a patient in hospital symbolize blood and bandages.

Magic may be used for evil or for good. Witch knots on lengths of string were spells that could hinder a birth or cure a sprained wrist. A black cat could portend evil, or its blood could cure all manner of diseases. Some magic things may be converted from being potentially dangerous to being positively beneficial: the sacred white horse becomes lucky after one has spat at him; the black, Devil-like figure of the chimney-sweep, if propitiated with a kiss, becomes a bringer of good fortune.

Whereas death omens and other supernatural verdicts are accepted as unavoidable—the witnesses simply watching for a likely victim and being wise after the event—the mere threat of evil can be counteracted. If one meets the Devil in the form of a magpie or chimney sweep, or encounters his agent, a witch, either in human form or in the guise of a cat or hare; or if an unsanctified spirit is at large; or a piece of iron or money of dubious origin is found on the road, then various antidotes are available. These may be pagan in origin, such as spitting, or turning round, or throwing the thing feared backwards over the shoulder; or they may be Christian, as by making the sign of the cross. Other possible ways of disarming evil are by propitiation with gifts or courteous gestures; or by taking avoiding action—for instance when on a journey, by the simple expedient of going home and starting out again. Counter or preventive measures such as these are especially important on occasions when future happiness is at risk: for instance when a baby is taken on its first outing, when a bride is on her way to church, when a person wears new clothes for the first time, or when a journey or a piece of work is begun.

As rationalism grew during the seventeenth and eighteenth centuries, so superstitious belief declined; and by the middle of the eighteenth century it began to be looked upon with nostalgic regret. In about 1759 Lord Orrery was lamenting that 'not a crooked pin has been visible for these last score years. No croaking family Ravens foretell the death of the Esquire . . . Such Portents and omens made each person who beheld them imagine himself distinguished by Heaven, and cast if not in a sacred in an uncommon mould';[1] and in 1830 Mary Russell Mitford complained that 'Superstition has fallen woefully into decay in our enlightened country' and deplored the neglect of 'the old saws . . . which once formed a sort of supplement to the national faith'.[2]

In the present day the real significance of many of the superstitions has been forgotten. Omens that once foretold a death are now merely a matter of 'bad luck'; the serious ritual of throwing wheat over a bride 'in tokenyng of plentie and fruitfulnesse' has degenerated into a frolicsome throwing of paper rose petals. Nevertheless many people cherish superstitions that have been handed down in their families and, women being the traditional custodians of folklore, one often hears such phrases as 'My grandmother insisted that . . .' and 'As my mother used to say . . .'. Some superstitions are so popular that they have become part of our language, and we find ourselves saying 'Touch wood' or 'Cross fingers' without ever putting the words into action. These, and others such as the unfurling of an umbrella in the house, spilling salt, walking under a ladder, crossing knives, hanging up horseshoes, and dreading Friday the Thirteenth, remain as 'a sort of supplement to the national faith'.

[1] *The Orrery Papers*, II, App. p. 300.   [2] *Our Village*, IV, p. 298.

Notes to the Reader

QUOTATIONS from oral tradition (beginning for instance '1952 Girl, 14 [Helensburgh, Dunbarton.]') are from one of the following sources: (1) material collected by A. S. Macmillan through the columns of his paper *The Western Gazette* during the early 1920s; (2) the nationwide Opie survey amongst schoolchildren in the 1950s; (3) notes, newscuttings, and contributions from correspondents already in the Opie archive in 1982, and oral quotations collected especially for this work since that date; (4) material from The Centre for English Cultural Tradition and Language at Sheffield University, by courtesy of its Director, Professor J. D. A. Widdowson. A geographical provenance is given in square brackets for each of these quotations, or is apparent from the quotation itself.

In references for quotations from published sources: plays are referred to by act and scene; line numbers are given when the quotation is from a long poem; volumes are referred to by upper-case Roman numerals; chapters, 'letters', and similar sections of a book by small capital Roman numerals; page numbers in preliminary matter by lower case Roman numerals, omitting 'p.'; and pages by Arabic numbers only, omitting 'p.'

The quotations from Old English have been given in translation.

The following abbreviations have been used:

EETS	Early English Text Society
Gents Mag.	*The Gentleman's Magazine*, 1731–1907
N & Q	*Notes and Queries.* 1849–
Rel. Ant.	*Reliquiæ Antiquæ*, ed. T. Wright and J. O. Halliwell, 2 vols. 1841–3

So have I heard, and do in part believe.

Horatio, in *Hamlet*, *c.*1601

A whole Universitie of Doctors cannot roote these superstitious observations out of their minde.

John Melton, *Astrologaster*, 1620

The superstitious follies of our country are almost eradicated.

William Hayley, *Essay on Old Maids*, 1785

No one now likes to own a belief in evil spirits or witches, but considers it would be a pity to receive harm from neglecting so easy a precaution [as hanging up an old horseshoe.]

George Roberts, *History of Lyme Regis and Charmouth*, 1834

I love folklore and all festering superstition.

Margaret, in E. M. Forster's *Howard's End*, 1910

Freedom from superstition is not necessarily a form of wisdom.

Robert Lynd, *Solomon In All His Glory*, 1922

A

ADULTERER cures warts

1849 *Athenaeum* 911 [Black Isle, Ross.]
Warts are infallibly cured by rubbing
the part affected secretly against the
body of a man who has had the misfortune, after marriage, to become the
father of an illegitimate child. 1874
Journal Anthropological Inst. III 271
[Banff.] Let the warts be rubbed on a
man that is the father of an adulterous
child .. without the man's knowledge.

AFTERBIRTH, burning: divination

1686–7 AUBREY *Remaines* (1881, 73)
Midwives woemen have some custome,
of saving the after-birth, or burning of
it, in relation to the long or short life of
the new-borne Babe. 1940 *Folklore* 118.
In September 1936 I delivered a Mrs
J., High Wycombe [Bucks.] As I was
clearing up .. the handywoman told me
that the next door woman wanted to
burn the placenta. I asked, 'Why does
she want to do it?' and was told, 'To
find out by the number of pops how
many children she is going to have.'
1959 *Trans. Devon. Ass.* 200 [Newton
Abbot] The number of times it pops
indicates the number of future children
to be expected.

ALBATROSS

1798 COLERIDGE 'Ancient Mariner' I
st. 20, II st. 3. 'God save thee, ancyent
Marinere! From the fiends that plague
thee thus—Why look'st thou so?'—with
my cross bow I shot the Albatross ..
And I had done an hellish thing And it
would work 'em woe: For all averr'd, I
had kill'd the Bird That made the Breeze
to blow. 1929 E. MARJORIBANKS *Life of
Marshall Hall* 29. One day he did a
terrible thing: he repeated the sin of the
Ancient Mariner. 'Saturday, Sept. 20th
.. Shot .. an albatross measuring about
18 ft. from tip to tip.' 1934 *Daily Mail*
14 Apr. 34. Around the Dornoch Firth ..
the striking of a match on this particular
box [Swan Vestas] is regarded as an
omen of bad luck because the swan on

the matchbox symbolises the albatross
in the Ancient Mariner poem. 1956
Daily Express 7 July 5. Men sent out in
a boat could not spot him. Then they
saw the albatross swoop down—and a
moment later .. they spotted it perched
on Oakley's chest. He was floating, unconscious. Tonight he is recovering in
hospital. The albatross, mariners have
always said, is a bird of good luck.
1959 *Daily Telegraph* 7 July 1. The crew
complained they had had a series of
misfortunes since the albatross .. being
taken to a zoo in Germany, was brought
aboard.

AMBER cures/protects

AD 77 PLINY *Natural History* XXXVII XI,
XII (1857, VI 401, 404) At the present
day we see the female peasantry ..
wearing necklaces of amber, principally
as an ornament, no doubt, but on account of its remedial virtues as well ..
It is beneficial for infants also, attached
to the body in the form of an amulet.
c. AD 750 EGBERT *Penitential* VIII 4 (*Councils & Eccles. Doc.*, ed. A. W. Haddon &
W. Stubbs, III 424) They trust they
can protect themselves by .. hanging
diabolical amulets whether made from
grass or amber on their people or themselves. c.1240 BARTHOLOMAEUS *De Proprietatibus Rerum* (tr. Trevisa, XVI 48)
Gagate [amber] .. drawyth lyghte
strawe to itselfe .. It is sayd that this
stone helpyth for fantasyes: & ayenst
trauelynge fendys by nyghte .. Also
it helpyth ayenst wytche crafte: and
fordooth harde enchauntementes. 1650
J. B. VAN HELMONT *Ternary of Paradoxes*
(tr. Charleton, 37) A translucid piece of
Amber .. rubd to calefaction upon the
seven planetary pulses (those on the
jugular Arteries, on the handwrists, neer
the instep, and on the throne of the
heart) and hung about the neck ..
becomes the most certaine Amulet .. to
the fatall contagion of this plague. 1825
JAMIESON *Scottish Dict.* Suppl. *Lammer*.
In olden time, the present made by a

mother to her daughter on the night of her marriage, was a set of lammer beads, to be worn about her neck, that, from the influence of the bed-heat on the amber, she might smell sweet to her husband. It is not improbable that it was originally used as a charm. 1826 R. CHAMBERS *Popular Rhymes of Scotland* 277. Lammer bead . . Put[s] the witches to their speed! 1851 *N & Q* 1st ser. III 84. Lammer beads . . are almost always made of amber, and are considered as a charm to keep away evil of every kind; their touch is believed to cure many diseases, and they are still worn by many old people in Scotland round the neck. 1866 HENDERSON *Northern Counties* 113. I have myself . . handled a talisman from the Tweedside . . called a lammer-bead . . Wondrous were the cures it wrought, in the witch-woman's hands, when drawn over inflamed eyes or sprained limbs. 1911 *Folklore* 52. An amber bead, used as a charm in childbirth, was long preserved at Ennis [Co. Clare]. 1925 E. LOVETT *Magic in London* 13 [Soldier, 1914–18.] I carried that [amber bead] from the time I went out . . I reckon that thing saved my life. 1942 *Folklore* 98. Amber necklaces are still sold . . as cures for croup, whooping cough and asthma. 1955 *Folklore* 299 [overheard in antique amber shop] 'It's good for you to wear, Madam.' 'You mean it's lucky?' 'No, it is good for your health.'

AMBULANCE, seeing

*c.*1908 Finsbury Park (ROLPH *London Particulars* 55) The children . . would grasp their coat collars on seeing an ambulance . . and call out something like 'Grab your collar, don't swaller, Never catch the fever,' or 'There goes the fever-van, Never touch the mealy-man' . . Having seen an ambulance in the street, you must hold your breath and pinch your nose until you saw a black or brown dog. 1930 Child, 7 [London] 'Touch collar, Never swallow, Never catch the fever; Not for you, Not for me, Not for all the family.' 1953 Girl, 15 [Loughton, Essex] Hold your collar and don't swallow till you see a dog. If you don't do this, the person in the ambulance will die. 1954 Boy, 12

[London] When you see an ambulance it is the custom to hold your lapel until you see a four-legged animal. 1983 Girl, 14 [Maldon, Essex] If ever an ambulance passes me I always say the saying 'Touch your toes, touch your nose, Never go in one of those. Hold your collar do not swallow Until you see a dog.'

AMBULANCE, taking lift in

1953 Man, *c.*40 [London] In the flying club, the pilots would rather walk than take a lift back in the ambulance.

ANIMAL, buying and selling

1486 SPRENGER & KRAMER *Malleus Maleficarum* (tr. Summers, 223) A certain honest man was bargaining with a woman, and would not come to terms with her about the price of some article; so she angrily called after him, 'You will soon wish you had agreed' . . Then he, not unreasonably being angry with her, looked over his shoulder to see with what intention she had uttered those words; and behold! he was suddenly bewitched so that his mouth was stretched sideways as far as his ears in a horrible deformity. 1584 SCOT *Discoverie of Witchcraft* XVI VIII. You shall not heare a butcher or horsse-courser cheapen [make an offer for] a bullocke or a jade, but if he buie him not, he saith, God save him; if he doo forget it, and the horsse or bullocke chance to die, the fault is imputed to the chapman. 1861 C. C. ROBINSON *Dialect of Leeds* 296. A rather amusing superstition prevails in respect of a cow or a pig. It is unlucky either to set a price or bid a price for them, for if this is done the animals are sure to die; and, believe it or not, reader, we have known several such coincidences. A woman bid eighteen pounds for a cow while her husband was absent, and obtained it. When he came home, he found it to his liking, a fine, healthy-looking animal, but when she told him what she had *bid*, and given for it, he said, 'Wah it'll dee sure as thah's bowt it;' when, sure enough, immediately after, it did die. 'Ah told thuh it ad dee thah sees,' the husband said to her then. 1870 *N & Q* 4th ser. VI 567. It is a prevalent belief, in the north of Fife, that if a cow or other domestic animal has been anxiously sought in purchase by another, it will not thrive if it is withheld. The peasantry quote abundance of instances in proof of their belief. **1883** BURNE *Shropshire* 208. It is very unlucky to refuse a good offer for a horse. If you do, some accident will befall the animal shortly afterwards. **1899** *Newcastle Weekly Chronicle* 4 Feb. 7 [Jesmond] If a horse, cow, or sheep, be retained after a fair price has been offered, some accident is sure to happen to it. **1909** M. TREVELYAN *Folk-Lore of Wales* 213. A butcher living .. at Cadoxton-juxta-Barry, in South Glamorgan, was reported to be the son of a witch. Whenever he wished to buy stock of the neighbours the latter were obliged to sell to him, or the animals would surely die. **1957** D. CAMPION *Take Not Our Mountain* 161 [Snowdonia, Wales] It is considered unlucky in the mountains to be offered money for a working sheep-dog when he is not for sale.

Cf. BEES, buying and selling.

ANIMAL, four-legged: meeting

1898 BLAKEBOROUGH *Yorkshire Customs* 147. The fisherman near Staithes [thought it not] a good omen for a four-legged animal to cross their path when going to their boat or at any time. **1930** P. F. ANSON *East Coast of Scotland* 38. In Portknockie, even dogs were looked upon as 'ill-fitted'. Stories are told of more than one fisherman who met a dog when going down to the harbour, pursued it, and killed it for fear that the same animal might cross his path another morning.

Cf. FIRST-FOOT: animal or person first encountered.

APPLE BLOSSOM in house

1923 [Martock, Som.] Apple blossom— sure teller of sickness in the house. **1957** Boy, 12 [Langholm, Dumfries.] A branch of apple blossom is not to be brought into the house.

APPLE CROP

1862 *N & Q* 3rd ser. I 482. When it is a good apple year, it is a great year for twins.

Cf. NUTS plentiful: children likewise.

APPLE PEEL: divination

1714 GAY *Shepherd's Week* 36. This mellow Pippin, which I pare around, My Shepherd's Name shall flourish on the Ground. I fling th' unbroken Paring o'er my Head, Upon the Grass a perfect L is read. **1755** *Connoisseur* 20 Feb. I have, many is the time, taken great pains to pare an Apple Whole, and afterwards flung the Peel over my head; and it always falls in the shape of the first letter of his Sirname or Christian name. **1839** *Everlasting Fortune-Teller* 11–12 [Co. Durham] Take an apple, pare it whole, and take the paring in your right hand, and say .. 'St Simon and St Jude, on you I intrude, By this paring I hold to discover, Without any delay, to tell me this day, The first letter of my own true-lover.' Turn round three times and cast the paring over your left shoulder, and it will form the first letter of your future husband's surname. **1873** HARLAND & WILKINSON *Lancashire Legends* 230. She must peel an apple without breaking the rind, and hang the shred on a nail behind the door—the initials .. of the first gentleman who enters the house .. will be the same as those of the person she will marry. **1909** M. TREVELYAN *Folk-Lore of Wales* 235. An apple must be peeled in one unbroken strip .. This peel should be placed behind the front-door. The first person who enters .. will have the same Christian name as the future husband or wife. **1911** LAWRENCE *White Peacock* pt. I VIII. She stood up, holding up a long curling strip of peel. 'How many times must I swing it, Mrs Saxton?' 'Three times— but it's not All Hallows' Eve.' **1939** *N & Q* CLXXVI 333. The curling peel will fall into the shape of the initial letter of your lover's name. This was .. demonstrated by a young lady who had the gratification of seeing the correct initial formed. Is this an old fancy or a quite modern one? **1953** Girl, 15 [Loughton, Essex] Throw the apple peel over your left shoulder—it will fall as the initial of your lover's name.

APPLE PIPS, burning: divination

1849 HALLIWELL *Popular Rhymes* 224. I remember throwing apple-pips into the fire, saying 'If you love me, pop and fly,

If you hate me, lay and die,' addressing an imaginary love, or naming some individual whose affection was desired to be tested. 1850 *N & Q* 1st ser. II 4 [Suffolk] The maiden takes an apple-pip, and naming one of her followers, puts the pip in the fire. If it makes a noise in bursting from the heat, it is a proof of love; but if it is consumed without a crack, she is fully satisfied that there is no real regard towards her in the person named. 1873 HARLAND & WILKINSON *Lancashire Legends* 230–1. Place two pippins on the mouth of a pair of tongs, so as to touch each other. The lady .. gives her own name to the left-hand pippin, and that on the right must bear the name of the person whose intentions are being tested. The tongs must now be placed in a hollow portion of the fire .. and if both pippins fly off on the same side, the parties will be married; if on opposite sides, there will be no union; and if both burn together without flying off, the gentleman will never propose.

Cf. NUTS: divination: burning.

APPLE PIPS pressed on cheek/forehead: divination

1714 GAY *Shepherd's Week* 36–7. See from the Core two Kernels brown I take; This on my Cheek for Lubberkin is worn, And Boobyclod on t'other side is born. But Boobyclod soon drops upon the Ground, A certain Token that his love's unsound, While Lubberkin sticks firmly to the last; Oh were his Lips to mine but join'd so fast! 1755 *Connoisseur* 20 Feb. I am sure Mr Blossom loves me, because I stuck two of the Kernels upon my forehead, while I thought upon him and the lubberly squire my pappa wants me to have: Mr Blossom's Kernel stuck on, but the other dropt off directly.

APPLE PIPS, squeezing: divination

1844 BARNES *Poems in Dorset Dialect* 319–20 [fruit-pip kernel] Sometimes shot from between the thumb and forefinger by young folks after saying 'Kernel come kernel, hop over my thumb, And tell me which way my truelove will come, East, west, north, or south, Kernel jump into my true love's mouth.' 1870 *N & Q* 4th ser. VI 340 [Lancs.] The anxious inquirer moves round in a circle, squeezing an apple pippin between the finger and thumb, which, on pressure being employed, flies from the rind in the supposed and desired direction of the lover's residence. The following doggerel is repeated .. 'Pippin, pippin, paradise, Tell me where my true love lies: East, west, north, or south, Pilling brig, or Cocker-mouth.' 1909 M. TREVELYAN *Folk-Lore of Wales* 237–8. Even in the present day the girls in rural districts place an apple seed in the palm of the left hand and cover it with the right, meanwhile shaking both hands up and down .. repeating: 'Kernel, kernel of the apple-tree, Tell me where my true love be, East, west, north, or south? Pretty kernel, tell the truth' .. They examine the kernel, and whichever way the pointed end is found, from that direction the true love will come.

APPLE STALK: divination

1983 Woman, 21 [Yorks.] A girl can discover whom she will marry by twisting the stalk of an apple and going through the alphabet, a letter for each twist. The letter she has reached when the stalk comes off is the initial of the first name of the man she will marry. To find the initial of his second name she taps the apple with the stalk, going through the alphabet until the stalk pierces the skin of the apple.

APRON comes untied

1818 *Edinburgh Mag.* Nov. 410 [Angus: mishap at wedding of girl obstinate enough to marry in May] In walking to church, her apron-strings loosed, and it fell in the path before her. 1861 C. C. ROBINSON *Dialect of Leeds* 300. For a married woman's apron to fall off is a sign that something is coming to vex her; but when the apron of an unmarried female falls off, there is nothing surer than that she is thinking about her sweetheart. 1872 H. CULLWICK *Diary* 14 Sept. My apron string got loose as I stood in the station yard .. So I thought, Well the saying must be true, that 'When your apron comes untied of itself your sweetheart's thinking about you.' And I felt pretty sure M. was thinking about me then. 1895 S. O. ADDY *Household Tales* 100. If your apron falls off

somebody is thinking about you. **1940**
N & Q CLXXIX 302. I lately heard that
apron-strings unfastened mean either
'He loves you very much' or as a variation, 'Someone is thinking about you.'
1953 *Woman, c.*45 [Swansea, Glam.]
If your apron drops off somebody is
thinking of you.

Cf. GARTER comes untied.

ASCENSION DAY, egg laid on

1584 SCOT *Discoverie of Witchcraft* XII
XVIII. To hang an eg laid on ascension
daie in the roofe of the house, preserveth
the same from all hurts. **1934** *Times*
14 May 10. In Nottinghamshire it is
believed that an egg laid on Ascension
Day, if placed in the roof of a house,
will ward off fire, lightning, and other
calamities.

ASCENSION DAY, working on

1880 *Daily News* 7 May 6 [Bangor,
Caernarvon.] Ascension Day is always
rigorously observed by the men employed at the Bethesda Slate Quarries ..
consequent upon an old superstition ..
that working on that day will be attended with an accident .. Yesterday
the old custom was observed, and the
quarries were at a standstill. **1883**
BURNE *Shropshire* 218. Rooks are accounted pious as well as wise. At Core-
ley, in the Clee Hills, it is believed that
they never 'carry' (sticks to their nests,
understood) on Ascension Day, but sit
quietly on the trees and do no work.
1886 *N & Q* 7th ser. II 166. The whole
of Lord Penrhyn's slate quarrymen took
a holiday on Ascension Day, because of
the universally prevalent superstition
that a fatal accident will inevitably cut
off those who work during that day.
1934 *Times* 8 May 12. There is a curious
superstition in these parts [Gainsbor-
ough, Lincs.] among some of the older
people that if you hang out sheets on
Ascension Day, whether to dry or merely
to air them, there will be a death in the
family before the year is out.

ASCENSION DAY WATER

1806 R. C. HOARE *Itinerary through Wales*
I 133. On a spot called Nell's Point, is a
fine well, to which great numbers of
women resort on Holy Thursday, and

having washed their eyes at the spring,
each drops a pin into it. The landlord of
the boarding-house told me that on
cleaning out the well, he took out a pint
full of these votive pins. **1848** *Athenaeum*
142. Custom .. in the neighbourhood
of Banbury, in Oxfordshire .. of saving
the rain which may happen to fall on
Holy Thursday and bottling it as a specific remedy for sore eyes. **1854** *N & Q*
1st ser. IX 542. In the parish of Marston
St Lawrence, Northamptonshire, there is
a notion very prevalent, that rain-water
collected on Holy Thursday is of powerful efficacy in all diseases of the eye.
Ascension-day of the present year was
very favourable in this respect to these
village oculists, and numbers of the
cottagers might be seen in all directions
collecting the precious drops as they fell.
1875 *N & Q* 5th ser. III 465 [Shrops.]
Rain-water caught on Holy Thursday ..
is good for bad eyes .. Of course it must
be corked up in a clean bottle. **1905**
N & Q 10th ser. IV 447. At the village
of Shudy Camps, in Cambridgeshire, last
July, an old man told me that rain
caught on Holy Thursday was good to
heal sore eyes and cuts. He called it 'holy
water' and assured me that it 'don't
never stink'. **1932** WOMEN'S INSTITUTE
Worcestershire Book 33 [Elmley Castle]
As recently as five years ago, on Ascension Day basins were placed out of
doors to catch any rain that might fall.
This was put into bottles and used to
bathe inflamed eyes (considered a sure
cure).

Cf. MAY RAIN.

ASH TREE benign

1696 AUBREY *Miscellanies* (1890, 139)
Cut an ash of one, two, or three years
growth, at the very hour and minute of
the sun's entring into Taurus: a chip of
this applied will stop it [nosebleed] ..
When King James II was at Salisbury,
1688, his nose bled near two days; and
after many essays in vain, was stopped
by this sympathetick ash, which Mr
William Nash, a surgeon in Salisbury,
applied. **1709** *British Apollo* Supernumerary no. 10, Jan. 1708/9. Q. Gentlemen, A Friend of mine constantly
practiceth the cutting down Ash Trees,
a certain [astrological] Critical Minute

in the Year .. that he also cuts out into small Pocket-pieces, and gives gratis some Thousands Yearly for the general good; That indisputably have wrought great Cures, and are deem'd to Simpathize with Nature in all her deficiencies. *A.* We are not altogether ignorant of the Reputed Vertues of the Ashen-stick .. To cut this wood .. Midsummer-Day is the Time. 1846 *Athenaeum* 17 Oct. 106–8. 'If you are troubled with the ague, you go to a grafter of trees, and tell him your complaint (every grafter notices the first branch of a maiden ash). You must not give him any money, or there will be no cure. You go home, and in your absence the grafter cuts the first branch.' Upon this I asked her, 'How long it was before the patient felt any relief?' 'Relief!' said the old lady; 'why he is cured that instant that the branch is cut from the tree.' 1851 *N & Q* 1st ser. IV 380. The herd boys in the district of Buchan [Aberdeen.] always prefer a herding stick of ash to any other wood, as in throwing it at their cattle, it is *sure* not to strike on a vital part. 1899 W. DICKINSON *Dialect of Cumberland* 58. Since 1850, James Bunting of Cockermouth, a man of seventy, charmed a scorbutic sore on a carter named Telford. He took an ashen stick and burnt its end, and with it drew a circle round the sore. He said something to himself which Telford did not understand, 'bit it dud nea good'.

ASH TREE, child passed through

1776 WHITE *Selborne* 8 Jan. These trees, when young and flexible, were severed and held open by wedges, while ruptured children, stripped naked, were pushed through the apertures, under a persuasion that, by such a process, the poor babes would be cured of their infirmity. As soon as the operation was over, the tree, in the suffering part, was plastered with loam, and carefully swathed up. If the parts coalesced and soldered together, as usually fell out, where the feat was performed with any adroitness at all, the party was cured; but, where the cleft continued to gape, the operation, it was supposed, would prove ineffectual. 1784 J. CULLUM *History of Hawsted* 234 [Suffolk] A young ash was

each time selected, and split longitudinally about 5 feet: the fissure was kept wide open by my gardener; whilst the friend of the child, having first stripped him naked, passed him thrice through it, always head foremost. As soon as the operation was performed, the wounded tree was bound up with packthread; and as the bark healed, the child was to recover. The first of the young patients was to be cured of the rickets, the second of a rupture. 1785 *Gents Mag.* 600. It is probably owing to the remains of the Gothic veneration for this tree, that the country people, in the south-east part of the kingdom, split young ashes, and pass their distempered children through the chasm in hopes of a cure. 1804 *Gents Mag.* 909 [Warwicks.] Thomas Chillingworth, now about 34, was, when an infant .. passed through an (ash) tree, now perfectly sound, which he preserves with so much care .. for it is believed the life of the patient depends on the life of the tree .. These trees are left to close of themselves, or are closed with nails .. Instances of trees that have been employed in the cure are very common. 1846 *Athenaeum* 26 Sept. 988 [Shaugh, Devon, 1833] Two men drew the parts forcibly asunder until there was room enough to draw the child through, which was done by the mother three times. This .. was not alone considered effective; it was necessary that the child should be washed for three successive mornings in the dew from the leaves of the 'charmed tree'. 1912 LEATHER *Herefordshire* 80. A maiden ash was split and a child passed through it, from the father's hands into another man's, nine times. The father said 'The Lord giveth,' the other man replied, 'The Lord receiveth.' The tree was then carefully bound up, and if it grew together again, the patient would recover [from rupture]. 1913 E. M. WRIGHT *Rustic Speech* 236. An instance of the old practice of passing a child suffering from rupture through the split trunk of a growing ash-tree was reported to me from Devonshire last summer. 1935 *I Walked by Night* (ed. L. Rider Haggard, 15) [Norfolk] The Father wold go out and serch about till he found a strait young ash plant, wich he could put his knife through and split down. Then they wold .. draw the child through the split .. As the sapling grew together so the Child's rupture healed. I have seen several of these plants near the old People's houses but I canot say if the charm came true. **1945** *Folklore* 270 [Suffolk] To pass through a split tree is a cure for rupture.

ASH TREE: even ash-leaf: divination

1813 BRAND *Antiquities* I 302 n. [Wales] *Cyniver*. A play in which the youth of both sexes seek for an even-leaved sprig of the ash; and the first of either sex that finds one calls out Cyniver, and is answered by the first of the other that succeeds; and these two, if the omen fails not, are to be joined in wedlock. **1831** HONE *Year Book* 8 Oct. [Dorset] Pluck an even ash-leaf, and .. say, 'The even ash-leaf in my hand, The first I meet shall be my man.' Then, putting it into the glove, .. say,'The even ash-leaf in my glove, The first I meet shall be my love.' And, lastly, into the bosom, saying, 'The even ash-leaf in my bosom, The first I meet shall be my husband.' Soon after which the future husband will make his appearance. **1846** *Athenaeum* 106–8 [Wilts.] It was once the practice .. to pluck the leaf in every case where the leaflets were of equal number, and to say: 'Even ash, I do thee pluck, Hoping thus to meet good luck; If no luck I get from thee, I shall wish I'd left thee on the tree.' Ibid. **1142** [Wilts.] 'An even-ash, or a four-leaved clover, You'll see your true love before the day's over.' It was told to me in my childhood by my nurse, who never, I think, forgot it when we passed by an ash tree or through a clover-field. **1895** J. HARDY *Denham Tracts* 282 [Long Benton, Northumb., 1845] The leaf of the ash which has an equal number of divisions on each side, which is very difficult to obtain, is pulled with the following rhyme: 'Even, even, ash, I pull thee off the tree, The first young man that I do meet, My lover he shall be.' It is then placed in the *left* shoe. **1923** [Martock, Som.] 'White heather, even-ash, or four-leaved clover, You'll get good luck and see your love 'fore the day is over.' **1978** *Folklore* 156 [Dorset] Start at the bottom leaflet on the left-hand side and say: 'An even ash is in my hand The first I meet will be my man, If he don't speak and I don't speak, This even ash I will not keep.' As each word is said, count a leaflet around the leaf until the rhyme is completed .. When the rhyme is finished, continue by reciting the alphabet until the bottom right-hand leaflet is reached. The letter given to this leaflet gives the initial of your boyfriend.

ASH TREE, harming

1686 PLOT *Natural History of Staffordshire* 207. The common people believe that 'tis very dangerous to break a bough from the ash, to this very day.

ASH TREE: keys: divination

1830 FORBY *East Anglia* 406. A failure of the Crop of Ash-keys portends a death in the Royal Family .. The failure in question is certainly, in some seasons, very remarkable; and many an old woman believes that, if she were the fortunate finder of a bunch, and could get introduced to the king, he would give her a great deal of money for it. **1849** *Norfolk Archaeology* II 298. Mrs Lubbock asked .. whether there were any ash-keys; adding, that when they failed, there would be a change in the Government, and great disturbances. **1873** T. JACKSON *Recollections* 14 [Sancton, Yorks.] Some of the people every summer examined the ash trees .. to see whether or not they produced any seed; for the barrenness of the ash was said to be a sure sign of public calamity. It was a tradition among aged and thoughtful men, that the ash trees of England produced no seed during the year in which Charles the First was beheaded.

ASH TREE protects against snakes

AD **77** PLINY *Natural History* XVI XXIV (1855, III 365–6) So great .. are the virtues of this tree, that no serpent will ever lie in the shadow thrown by it .. We state the fact from ocular demonstration, that if a serpent and a lighted fire are placed within a circle formed of the leaves of the ash, the reptile will rather throw itself into the fire than encounter the leaves of the tree. **1578** DODOENS

Herball 749. They say that the Ashe is of so great force against poyson, that in the circutie or shadowe of the same there hath not bene knowen any maner of venemous beast to abyde. **1646** BROWNE *Vulgar Errors* II VI. That a Snake will not endure the shade of an Ashe we can deny. **1838** A. E. BRAY *Devonshire* I 95. The farmer says, "Tis a wisht old place .. and full of adders ..' but .. supplies a speedy remedy .. the ashen bough .. He tells me, that the moment I see an adder I have nothing to do but to draw a circle with an ash rod round it, and the creature will never go out of it. **1857** *N & Q* 2nd ser. IV 25 [Bodmin, Cornwall] For the Bite of an Ader. 'Bradgty, bradgty, bradgty, under the ashing leef,' to be repeated three times. (*Braggaty* is said to mean 'mottled, like an adder'.) **1865** R. HUNT *West of England* 2nd ser. 223. A child who was in the habit of receiving its portion of bread and milk at the cottage door, was found to be in the habit of sharing its food with one of the poisonous adders .. The mother .. was frequently, being a labourer in the fields, compelled to leave her child to shift for itself—she adopted the precaution of binding an 'ashen-twig' about its body. The adder no longer came near the child; but from that day forward the child pined, and eventually died. **1909** M. TREVELYAN *Folk-Lore of Wales* 171. The ash-tree is said 'to have a spite against snakes'.

ASH TREE protects against storm and witchcraft

1507 *Gospelles of Dystaues* pt. 3 VII. Whan some tempest doth aryse in the ayer we oughte anone to make a fyre of foure staues of an asshe tree in crosse wyse aboue the wynde and thenne afterwarde make a crosse vpon it, and anone the tempest shal torne a syde. **1852** DENHAM *North of England* (1895, 30) A bunch of Ash Keys carried in the hand preserves the bearer from Witchcraft.

ASHES, footprint in

1775 L. SHAW *History of Moray* 249. When the corpse is lifted, the bed-straw, on which the deceased lay, is carried

out and burnt in a place where no beast can come near it; and they pretend to find next morning, in the ashes, the print of the foot of that person in the family, who shall die first. **1845** J. TRAIN *Isle of Man* II 115–16. On New Year's Eve, in many of the upland cottages, it is yet customary for the housewife, after raking the fire for the night .. to spread the ashes smooth over the floor with the tongs in the hope of finding in it, next morning, the tract of a foot; should the toes of this ominous print point towards the door, then, it is believed, a member of the family will die in the course of that year; but should the heel of the fairy foot point in that direction, then, it is as firmly believed, that the family will be augmented within the same period. **1849** BRAND *Antiquities* I 193. On the eve of St Mark [24 Apr.] the ashes are riddled or sifted on the hearth. Should any of the family be destined to die within the year, the shoe will be impressed on the ashes; and many a mischievous wight has made a superstitious family miserable by slily coming down stairs after the rest of the family have retired to rest, and impressing the ashes with a shoe of one of the party. **1866** HENDERSON *Northern Counties* 34. After a death .. the straw or chaff from the bed of the departed is .. burned. Among its ashes the survivors look for a footprint .. whose foot fits the impression will be the next to die. **1881** W. GREGOR *North-East of Scotland* 160. The last thing done on the last day of the year was to .. cover up the live coals with the ashes. The whole was made as smooth and neat as possible. The first thing on New Year's morning was to examine if there was in the ashes any mark like .. a human foot with the toes pointing towards the door. If there was such a mark, one was to be removed from the family before the year was run. Some climbed to the roof of the house and looked down the 'lum' for the dreaded mark. **1883** J. R. TUDOR *Orkneys and Shetland* 174 [Shetland] The moment the funeral procession had started, the straw on which the corpse had been laid was burnt, and the ashes narrowly examined, to see if any footmarks could be seen .. If any were found, they were supposed to be those of the next person who would die in the house.

ASHES, pictures in

1664 J. WILSON *The Cheats* IV v. Why last New-Years Eve .. I swept up the Hearth, and smooth'd the Ashes, and next morning, found the print of a Wedding Ring and a Grave upon them. I am confident we shall have a Wedding, and a Burial, out of our house this year. 1688 AUBREY *Remaines* (1881, 95) On New Year's-eve night, sift (or smooth) the Ashes and leave it so when you goe to Bed; next morning looke and if you find there the likeness of a Coffin, one will dye: if a Ring one will be married. 1862 *N & Q* 3rd ser. II 62 [Devon] Raking out the fire on Midsummer Eve, sift the ashes fine, and leave them in a heap on the hearth .. The next morning .. if any object is represented on them, your future fortune will be foretold thereby. The person who related this said her mother tried it when young, and she saw in the ashes .. a waggon, waggoner, and team of horses. And sure enough it told true, for she afterwards married one of the waggoners of the late Lord Rolle of Bicton, Devon.

ASHES, streaks in

1648 HERRICK *Hesperides* 146 'New-yeares gift'. Of Ash-heapes, in the which ye use Husbands and Wives by streakes to chuse. 1686–7 AUBREY *Remaines* (1881, 24) When I was a Boy in North Wilts (before ye Civill-warres) the mayd-servants were wont at night (after supper) to make smoothe, the Ashes on the Hearth, and then to make streakes on it with a stick; such a streake signified

privately to her that made it such an unmarried man, such a one such a mayd: the like for men. Then the men and the mayds were to choose by this kind of way, their Husbands and wifes: or by this divination to know whom they should marry. *c.*1700 W. KENNETT Note to Aubrey's *Remaines* (1881, 24) This way of chusing valentines by making little furrows in the Ashes and imposing such and such names on each line or furrow is practist in Kent and many other parts.

AURORA BOREALIS (Northern Lights)

1784 PENNANT *Arctic Zoology* I xxviii [Shetland] [The aurora borealis] often put on the color of blood, and make a most dreadful appearance. The rustic sages become prophetic, and terrify the gazing spectators with the dread of war, pestilence, and famine. This superstition was not peculiar to the northern islands .. They appeared with great brilliancy in England, on March 6th, 1715/16 [when] the vulgar considered them as marking the introduction of a foreign race of princes. 1827 CLARE *Shepherd's Calendar* 111. With shooting North-lights, 'tokening bloody wars; She might know these, which, if 'tis sin to know, Then every body is a witch below. 1849 AYTOUN *Scottish Cavaliers* 'Edinburgh after Flodden' pt. 1. All night long the northern streamers Shot across the trembling sky: Fearful lights, that never beckon Save when kings or heroes die. 1871 *N & Q* 4th ser. VIII 506. I have heard speak of 'black northern lights' in Derbyshire. They are streamers which stream across the sky .. and are said to portend all manner of disasters to a country.

B

BABY: bringing home in car

1981 *Daily Express* 27 May 36. Princess Anne has been criticised for sitting in the front passenger seat of the car with her first baby. I remember leaving hospital in 1972 with my first baby, to be told by the sister, 'Oh you mustn't sit in the back, it's terribly bad luck.' Being slightly superstitious, what could I do? Cf. DOOR, front.

BABY carried upwards first

1695 CONGREVE *Love for Love* II i. I came up-stairs into the world; for I was born in a cellar. **1853** MRS GASKELL *Cranford* v. There was a letter to 'my dear, dearest Molly', begging her, when she left her room, whatever she did, to go *up* stairs before going *down*: and .. to wrap her baby's feet up in flannel. **1864** R. CHAMBERS *Book of Days* II 39 [Suffolk] When children first leave their mother's room, they must go upstairs before they go down-stairs, otherwise they will never rise in the world. Of course it frequently happens that .. the mother's room is the highest in the house. In this case the difficulty is met by the nurse setting a chair, and stepping upon that with the child in her arms as she leaves the room. **1866** HENDERSON *Northern Counties* 10. Nurses say that it is very important for an infant to go up in the world before it goes down .. For want of a flight of stairs, one of the gossips will take it in her arms, and mount a table, chair or chest of drawers. **1932** E. J. D. RADCLYFFE *Magic and Mind* 96. When Mr Baldwin was born [at Bewdley, Worcs., 1867], he was carried all the way upstairs by his nurse: at the top floor she got a chair and climbed on that, that the baby might rise in life. **1946** UTTLEY *Country Things* 125. Another custom still in use .. is to carry a baby upstairs on its first journey outside the room of birth. If there is no upper floor, then the child is carried up a pair of steps, or even lifted high on a chair.

'He will go up in the world now,' they say.

BABY, eating and drinking to

*c.*1816 Wilkie MS (HENDERSON *Northern Counties* 1866, 3) Throughout the Borderland, the birth of an infant is the signal for plenty of eating and drinking .. It is very unlucky to allow anyone to leave the house without his share. **1874** *N & Q* 5th ser. I 485 [Co. Durham] Each one who goes into a house on the occasion of a birth must drink a glass of spirit, else the child will not live. **1898** BLAKEBOROUGH *Yorkshire Customs* 106. From the day of its birth to that of its baptism, pepper cake, cheese and wine .. are offered to all those who cross the threshold. No one would think of refusing to 'tak a bite an' sup', to wish the little stranger all the happiness and good luck possible.

BABY, gifts to: on first visit

1778 W. HUTCHINSON *View of Northumberland* II app. 4. Children when first sent abroad in the arms of the nurse to visit a neighbour, are presented with an egg, salt, and fine bread. **1787** GROSE *Provincial Glossary* Superstitions 64. The first time a nurse brings a child to visit its parents or relations, it is unlucky to send it back without some gift, as eggs, salt, or bread. **1837** R. ROBINSON *Diary* 24 Jan. This being its first outing, the little Darling brought home an egg, rolls and salt. **1851** DENHAM *North of England* (1895, 25) The offering of an egg, a handful of salt, and a bunch of matches, to a young child, on its first visit to the house of a neighbour, is still very prevalent .. In the neighbourhood of Leeds, the ceremony is termed 'puddening', and the child is said to be 'puddened'. **1878** *N & Q* 5th ser. X 216. In Lincolnshire, at the first visit of a new baby at a friendly house, it is presented with 'an egg, both meat and drink; salt, which savours everything; bread, the staff of life; a match, to light it through the world; and a coin, that it may never want money'. **1879** J. NAPIER *West of Scotland* 33. In visiting any house .. for the first time, it was incumbent on the person whom they were visiting to put a little salt or sugar into baby's mouth, and wish it well: the omission of this was regarded as a very unlucky omen. **1888** S. O. ADDY *Sheffield Glossary* xxv. It is customary, after baptism, to give the baptised child an egg, a little salt, and a small silver coin, such as sixpence. **1923** [Bridgwater, Som.] The first visit to a house made by a baby, it is given an egg, salt, and sixpence. The egg is the sign of the Trinity, being made up of three, shell, white and yolk, also the egg comes to life again and therefore is the promise of immortality. Salt signifies salubrity of mind and body. Silver means money and the needful things of life. **1952** *Daily Express* 14 May 1 [Reporter visited home of Mrs Kate Campbell, South Uist, Outer Hebrides, who had just had triplets.] In a corner of the room was a pile of half-crowns. For by strong local custom, visitors from all parts of the island had crossed each baby's hand with silver. **1962** Girl, 13 [Cumnock, Ayr.] Give a new-born baby a match, a sweet, and a piece of silver. **1971** *Trans. Devon. Ass.* 268 [South Molton] Common to give silver to a new-born baby: if it grasps it, it will be rich. **1984** Woman, 56 [South Shields, Co. Durham] When I was a child—when we met a new baby for the first time, my mother always bent over the pram and put a shilling into the baby's hand. If the baby grasped it, it was a good sign. She called this 'handselling' the baby. **1985** Journalist, male, 57 [Percy Main, Northumb.] I am never introduced to a new baby without crossing its palm with silver.

BABY looks between legs
1982 Woman, 37 [Sheffield, Yorks.] If a baby looks at you from between its legs you will get pregnant.

BABY protected by clothes of opposite sex
1898 CLODD *Tom Tit Tot* 131. To this day, the peasants of Achill Island (on the north-west coast of Ireland) dress their boys as girls till they are about fourteen years old to deceive the boy-seeking devil. **1910** *N & Q* 11th ser. II 65. In Connemara [Eire], in some districts, a nurse has met with boys of twelve .. in petticoats. The mothers insist that the petticoats are worn to prevent the fairies from taking their boys. **1932** C. IGGLESDEN *Those Superstitions* 147–8. An elderly midwife .. said: 'Before the birth I always had a boy's nightshirt and a girl's nightgown quite ready .. If it was a boy I put on a girl's nightgown and if it was a girl I put on a boy's nightshirt .. And this is the reason .. The boy when he grew up would fascinate all girls, and a girl who had had a nightshirt put on her would have young men buzzing round her till she married.'

BABY protected by parent's garment
1866 HENDERSON *Northern Counties* 6. In Scotland the little one's safeguard is held to lie in the juxtaposition of some article of dress belonging to its father. **1874** W. GREGOR *Olden Time* 91 [NE Scotland] To guard the child from being forespoken [bewitched] it was passed three times through the petticoat or chemise the mother wore at the time of the accouchement. **1893** *Folklore* 359 [Eire] Women in childbirth often wear the trousers of the father of the child round the neck, the effect of which is supposed to be the lightening of the pains of labour. I have myself seen a case of this in Dublin about two years ago. **1911** J. CLAGUE *Manx Reminiscences* 177. When the child was born, if it was a boy, he was put into some part of the man's clothing, and if it was a girl, it was placed in some of the mother's clothing, very often a petticoat.

BABY protected by 'something old'
1659 LOVELACE *Lucasta* 28 'To a Lady with Child that ask'd an Old Shirt'. Since to Ladies 't hath a Custome been Linnen to send, that travail and lye in; To the nine Sempstresses .. I su'd .. the jolli'st .. Rent th' apron from her smock, and gave it me. **1912** LEATHER *Herefordshire* 111. An old-fashioned nurse told me she never liked to dress babies in new clothes for the first time, if she could avoid it. She always took an old flannel petticoat

with her, to be the first garment worn
by each baby she nursed. **1971** *Nursing
Times* 23 Dec. 1591. In most areas .. it
was believed very unlucky if the first
covering put upon a new baby was new.
First, he had to be wrapped in something
old .. The midwife normally brought
with her an old petticoat or similar
garment when she was called to the
confinement.

Cf. BRIDE'S CLOTHES: 'something old'.

BABY, referring to

1650 J. GREGORY *Opuscula* 'Assyrian Monarchy' 202. This Custom of offering
Cakes to the Moon .. our Ancestors may
seem not to have been ignorant of; to
this daie our women make Cakes at such
times, yea the childe it self is no sooner
born, but 'tis baptized into the names of
these Cakes; for so the women call their
babes Cake-bread. **1953** *Woman* 30 May
4. She [a very old Shropshire woman]
regarded it as very risky to speak openly
of an expected baby. No hint should be
given to the fairies of the child's coming,
lest they injure it before birth or come
to steal it immediately it was born. When
her grandchildren were expected, she
referred to each as a 'pot lid', explaining
that a pot lid was such a trivial thing,
no fairy would bother about it.

BABY, stillborn

1852 *N & Q* 1st ser. V 77 [Devonport,
Devon] When I was a young man it was
thought lucky to have a still-born child
put into any open grave, as it was
considered to be a sure passport to
heaven for the next person buried there.

BABY'S CLOTHES put over head

1867 *N & Q* 3rd ser. XII 185 [Dar-
lington, Co. Durham] When an infant is
first dressed, its clothes should never be
put on over its head (which is very
unlucky), but drawn over its feet. **1953**
Woman, c.60 [Bishop Auckland, Co.
Durham] Never put a baby's gown over
its head. Draw it up over its feet. **1987**
Woman, 83 [Acton, W. London] I noticed she pulled the baby's vest over its
head. We were always told not to put
the baby's clothes on over its head, but
to pull them up over its feet.

BABY'S CLOTHES/CRADLE given away

1864 R. CHAMBERS *Book of Days* II 322
[Suffolk] If a mother gives away *all* the
baby's clothes she has (or the cradle)
she will be sure to have another baby,
though she may have thought herself
above such vanities.

BABY'S HAND: first one used

*c.*1816 Wilkie MS (HENDERSON *Northern
Counties*, 1866, 12) Scotch nurses note
with which hand a child takes up a
spoon to sup. If it be the left you may
be sure that he will be an unlucky fellow
all his life. **1982** *Woman*, 20 [Cleveland,
Yorks.] Whichever hand a young child
uses to reach out for his spoon is supposed to dictate his future. The right
hand indicates good fortune and the left,
ill-fortune.

Cf. LEFT HAND.

BABY'S HANDS open when born

1644 BULWER *Chirologia* 62. There is a
tradition our Midwives have concerning
children borne open handed, that such
will prove of a bountifull disposition,
and franke-handed. **1832** *Gents Mag.*
pt. 2 492 [Lincs.] It is vulgarly believed
that if a childe be born with its hands *open*,
it is an indication of .. benevolence; but
if .. *closed*, the future individual will
assuredly prove a churl. **1970** *Farmers
Weekly* 9 Jan. 75 [Orkneys] A baby
whose hands were open, and who
stretched out his fingers, was expected
to grow up generous and open-handed;
whereas a baby whose fingers were
tightly curled would be tight-fisted.

BABY'S HANDS, washing

1866 HENDERSON *Northern Counties* 9.
One curious nursery practice exists ..
that of leaving an infant's right hand
unwashed .. that he may gather riches.
1923 [Somerset] Wash a newly born
baby's hand before it is twelve-months
old and they say you wash the baby's
fortune away. **1970** *Farmers Weekly* 9
Jan. 75 [Orkneys] When a new baby
was first bathed, it was necessary to
prevent water from touching the palms
of his hands, for this would wash away
his luck.

Cf. DIRT lucky.

BABY'S NAPPY: first

1768 A. ROSS *Fortunate Shepherdess* 6. The first hippen to the green was flung, And unko words thereat baith said an' sung. 1969 Woman, 43 [Liss, Hants.] Never wash the first nappy a baby dirties.

BABY'S NAPPY in moonlight

1952 Health visitor [Alton, Hants.] One of my mothers refused to hang her baby's nappies out in the moonlight for fear of bad luck.

Cf. MOONLIGHT, charm against; MOON-LIGHT, sleeping in.

BACHELOR'S BUTTON

1754 Z. GREY *Notes on Shakespeare* I 108. An antient custom amongst the country fellows, of trying whether they shall succeed with their mistresses by carrying the bachellour's buttons (a plant of the *lychnis* kind, whose flowers resemble a coat button in form) in their pockets. And they judged of their good, or bad success, by their growing, or not growing there. 1851 J. W. WARTER *Southey's Common Place Book* 4th ser. 244 n. Within my own recollection, both in Shropshire and Staffordshire, this old custom was common enough.

BALL, cowslip: divination

1889 *Dorset Field Club* 43 [repeated by children while playing with a cowslip ball] 'Tisty-tosty, tell me true, Who shall I be married to?' The names of A, B, C [etc.] are mentioned until the ball drops. Then 'Tisty [etc.] How many years shall I live hearty?' The numbers are .. called. 1890 *Bye-Gones* July 142. 'Tusball, tusball, tell unto me What my sweetheart's name shall be' [repeating letters of alphabet until ball falls]. 1912 LEATHER *Herefordshire* 63. Make a ball of cowslip blossom, and toss it .. to 'Tisty-tosty, tell me true, Who shall I be married to?' The names of actual or possible lovers are recited, until the ball falls. 1922 [Somerset] Tisty, Tosty, tell me true, Who shall I be married to? Tinker, tailor, soldier, sailor, Gentleman, farmer, 'pothecary, thief.

BALL: divination

1842 R. CHAMBERS *Popular Rhymes* 61. 'Stottie ba', hinnie ba', tell to me, How mony bairns am I to hae? Ane to leeve, and ane to dee, And ane to sit on the nurse's knee!' Addressed to a hand-ball by girls, who suppose that they will have as many children as the times they succeed in catching it. 1849 HALLIWELL *Popular Rhymes* 220–1. 'Cook [toss] a ball, cherry-tree; Good ball, tell me How many years I shall be Before my true love I do see? One and two, and that makes three; Thank'ee, good ball, for telling of me.' The ball is thrown against a wall, and the divination is taken from the number of rebounds it makes. 1866 G. TATE *History of Alnwick* I 436. A girl sent the ball against a tree and drove it back again as often as she could, saying the following rhymes, in order to divine her matrimonial future: 'Keppy ball, keppy ball, Coban tree Come down the long loanin' and tell to me, The form and the features, the speech and degree Of the man that is my true love to be .. How many years old I am to be One a maiden, two a wife, Three a maiden, four a wife, &c.' 1888 *N & Q* 7th ser. V 187 [Co. Durham] Keppy-ball, keppy-ball, Cobin tree, Come down and tell me, How many year old our Jenny [Johnny, etc.] shall be. 1952 Girl, 13 [Welshpool, Montgomery.] You pat the ball on the ground and say 'Bally, ally, tell me true, How many years shall I live now? One, two, three, etc.'

BALLAST

1881 W. GREGOR *North-East of Scotland* 198. In some of the villages .. a stone bored by the *pholas* [a shell-fish] was rejected [as ballast]. Such a stone bore the name of the 'hunger steen'. 1885 *Folklore* 180. In Broadsea [Aberdeen.] a stone, that has been used in building, and has still some of the mortar adhering, is rejected as ballast. In Portknockie, Banffshire, granite stones are avoided.

BASTARD lucky

c.1598 SHAKESPEARE *King John* I i. *Bastard.* Brother, adieu, good fortune come to thee, For thou wast got i' th way of honesty. 1942 *N & Q* CLXXXIII 355. Under Roman law they [natural children] were free from *patria potestas* [authority of father], which may be a basis for the notion they are lucky.

BAT

AD 77 PLINY *Natural History* XXIX XXVI
(1856, V 400) If one .. is carried alive,
three times round a house .. and then
nailed outside of the window with the
head downwards, it will have all the
effects of a countercharm. 1507 *Gospelles of Dystaues* pt. 5 XV. Whan one
seeth plente of backes flee aboute a house
it is good for to dyslodge þe tymes, for
it is a grete synge that fyre shall be put
in it shortly. 1630 HEYWOOD *Rape of
Lucrece* H^v–H2. The Bell doth towle, For
some but new Departing soule. And was
not that Some ominous fowle, The Batt
the Night-Crow, or Skreech-Owle.
*c.*1816 Wilkie MS (HENDERSON *Northern
Counties* 1866, 94) The bawkie-bird, or
bat .. is in Scotland connected with
witchcraft. If .. the bat is observed .. to
rise, and then descend again earth-
wards, you may know that the witches'
hour is come—the hour in which they
have power over every human being ..
not .. shielded from their influence.
1878 MRS HENRY WOOD *East Lynne* I 121–
2. 'What does all this mean, Wells?'
cried Mrs Mason, 'the bats must have
turned wild tonight .. Did you ever see
them so thick?' .. 'No, ma'am, nor so
near .. and I don't like to see them, for
it betokens no good .. I have heard ..
that it is a sure sign death is at the very
door of the house' .. Mrs Mason .. closed
the window .. and the nasty things
beat against it with their wings. 1879
JEFFERIES *Wild Life in a Southern County*
x. Occasionally a bat will come into the
sitting-room, should the doors be left
open on a warm summer evening. This
the old folk think an evil omen, and still
worse if .. it should chance to knock
against the candle and overturn or put
it out. They think, too, that a bat seen
in daytime is a bad sign. 1883 BURNE
Shropshire 214. At Pulverbatch it is
accounted very unlucky to bring a bat
into the house [and] at Baschurch it is
considered unlucky to kill a bat. 1923
[Taunton, Som.] A bat in your room, or
flying against the window, is a 'token'
and means death or misfortune. 1957
Boy, 12 [Shrewsbury, Shrops.] It is supposed to be lucky if you see a bat flying
in the daytime, but if you disturb them
and make them fly it brings you bad
luck. 1972 *Lore and Language* July 7
[Coalisland, Co. Tyrone] If .. a bat comes
into the house it's a sure sign of a death
in the family.

BAY/LAUREL protects

AD 77 PLINY *Natural History* II LVI (1857,
I 86) Thunder never strikes the laurel
.. sea-calf [nor] eagle. Ibid. XV XXXIX
(III 332) The laurel .. guards the portals
of our emperors and pontiffs: there suspended .. before the threshold. Ibid.
XV XL (III 335–6) Not even for the
propitiation of the divinities, should a
fire be lighted with [laurel] .. It is said
that when it thundered, the Emperor
Tiberius was in the habit of putting on
a wreath of laurel to allay his apprehensions of .. lightning. 1579 LUP-
TON *Thousand Notable Things* VI § 50.
Neyther falling syckness, neyther deuyll,
wyll infect or hurt one in that place:
wheras a Bay tree is. The Romaynes
calles it the Plant of the good Angell.
1591 T. LODGE *Diogenes* B2^v. You beare
.. Lawrell to escape lightning. 1634
Strange Metamorphosis of Man no. 37.
The Bay-tree .. so priviledged by nature,
that even Thunder and lightning, are
here even taxed of partiality, and will
not touch him for respects sake, as a
sacred thing. 1688 AUBREY *Remaines*
(1881, 89) We dresse our Houses at
Christmas, with Bayes .. 'tis obvious to
ghesse how 'tis derived downe to us.
1846 DENHAM *Proverbs* 4. He who carrieth a bay-leaf shall never take harm
from thunder. 1983 Girl, 12 [Maldon,
Essex] We have a bay tree outside our
house and it keeps away the witches
and very bad luck.

BAY/LAUREL withers

1587 HOLINSHED *Chronicles* (1807, II
850) Throughout all the realme of England, old baie trees withered, and ..
grew greene againe .. a strange sight,
and supposed to import some vnknowne
euent. 1595 SHAKESPEARE *Richard the
Second* II iv. 'Tis thought the King is
dead, we will not stay; The Bay-trees in
our Countrey all are wither'd.

BAY/LAUREL LEAVES: divination

1711 *Aristotle's Last Legacy* 49. Take
two Bay-leaves, sprinkle them with

Rose-water; the Evening of this Day, lay them a cross under your Pillow, when you go to Bed, putting on a clean Shift, and turning it wrong side outwards; and lying down, say . . 'Good Valentine be kind to me, In dreams let me my true Love see.' So crossing your Legs, and go to sleep . . you will see in a Dream the Party you are to Marry. **1755** *Connoisseur* 20 Feb. [St Valentine's Eve] I got five Bay-leaves, and pinned four of them to the four corners of my pillow, and the fifth to the middle, and then if I dreamt of my sweetheart, Betty said we should be married before the year was out. **1933** *Folklore* 280 [Gainsborough, Lincs.] On the eve of St Valentine's Day . . pin bay leaves to your pillow, one at each corner and one in the middle. You will then dream of . . the man you are to marry.

BEAN: divination

1787 GROSE *Provincial Glossary. Scadding [boiling] of Peas.* A custom in the North . . a bean, shell and all, is put into one of the peapods, whosoever gets this bean is to be first married. **1895** J. HARDY *Denham Tracts* II 282 [Longbenton, Northumb.] My mother has seen a bean placed in a pea swad, the receiver, whether male or female, is to be first married.

BEAN BLOSSOMS

1853 *N & Q* 1st ser. VII 152 [Leics.] Sleep in a beanfield all night if you want to have awful dreams, or go crazy. **1960** *Folklore* 205. Bean-blossoms . . have a bad reputation among miners. It is sometimes said that accidents in the pit occur more frequently when they are in bloom.

Cf. MAY BLOSSOM.

BED across floorboards or ceiling-beam

1846 *Athenaeum* 17 Oct. 1068. A clerical friend . . related to me that, in a village near Collumpton [Devon], he witnessed the death of a person, when the last moments seemed delayed by some unseen cause, and the relatives, in consequence, moved the bed, observing that over the place there was a beam concealed in the floor above [and] as they said, the sick man 'went off like a lamb'. **1871** *N & Q* 4th ser. VIII 322 [Cornwall] Granny . . were athurt the planchin', and could n' die till we did put her right along it. **1879** *N & Q* 5th ser. XI 125. An old gossip . . went up into the sick chamber, and observing that the position of the bedstead was *across* the planks, instead of being parallel with them, assigned that as the reason for the patient's lingering death. **1883** *Folklore* 196. My mother-in-law having been sick unto death for some weeks I have been earnestly entreated to move her bed 'as it must be under a cross beam or she would have passed away long ago, and then she will quickly pass away.' **1883** BURNE *Shropshire* 282. The position of the bed . . must sympathise with the other wood-work of the chamber, for if it is placed across the boards of the floor, it is said at Edgmond that it prevents sleep. And worse: some two years ago, a young lady wished . . to rearrange the furniture of her bed-chamber, but the servants . . remonstrated strongly . . If the bed were placed as she wished, it would stand across the boards, and . . there would certainly be a death in the family! **1923** [Ruishton, Som.] A dying man lying under the cross beam of a house will pass away in pain. **1923** *Folklore* 165 [Kingweston, Som.] His family charged the vicar's wife with his death, as she had insisted on his bed being moved out of the draught. The only other place where it could stand was under a cross-beam, and it was believed fatal for a sick person to lie under such a beam. **1953** *Man, c.*40 [London] It's unlucky to sleep across the joints of the bedroom floor. **1971** *Trans. Devon. Ass.* 268 [South Molton] To be sure of sleeping well, make sure the bed runs the same way as the floorboards. If it is placed across them, you have the Devil against you. **1978** N. MAYES *Nature Notebook* 88 [Cornwall] The dead were always left lying in the direction that the floorboards ran, never across them.

BED: foot towards door

1929 R. THORNDIKE *Sybil Thorndike* 43. We were each given an attic to ourselves, with full permission to alter the furniture about how we liked, so long as we .. didn't put the feet of our beds facing the door. A funeral superstition. Sybil did hers, just to see if she did, but she didn't. **1965** *Folklore* 46 [Portnahaven, Islay] In 1963 a wife was reproached by her husband for putting a bed in a room with the foot end to the door. It was explained that bodies in coffins were carried out feet first and orientating a bed in that direction was asking for trouble. **1972** *Lore and Language* July 7 [Coalisland, Co. Tyrone] Never sleep with your feet towards the door. Only corpses lie like that.

BED, getting out of: backwards

1695 CONGREVE *Love for Love* II i. I have had some omens: I got out of bed backwards too this morning, without premeditation; pretty good that too. **1777** BRAND *Antiquities* 94–5. Getting out of Bed backwards, without Premeditation [is] reckoned [a] good [omen]. **1826** G. M. HUDSON *Comic Songs* 14. Says Sam, 'No good luck shall I get, I got out o' bed backside first.' Says Tom .. 'Such old woman's sayings are stuff.' **1923** [Bridgwater, Som.] It is unlucky to get out of bed backwards.

BED, getting out of: on right side

1540 PALSGRAVE *Acolastus* 90. Howe happily rose I on my ryght syde to day, or blessed me well .. this happye or lucky day. **1627** W. HAWKINS *Apollo Shroving* 46. I thinke I rose not on the right side today. I haue rambled vp and downe, and can get no playfellowes. **1652** GAULE *Mag-astro-mances* 181. It is a vain observation .. to bode good or bad luck .. from the rising up on the right, or left side. **1824** SCOTT *Redgauntlet* XX. Why, brother Nixon, thou art angry this morning .. hast risen from thy wrong side, I think. **1894** BLACKMORE *Perlycross* XXXII. I have heard of people getting out of bed the wrong side; and you can't make it right all day. **1988** Woman, 35 [Dunmow, Essex] When somebody is crotchety you say to them, '*You've* got out of bed the wrong side, this morning.' I've always wondered what it means.

Cf. BOAT, right side of; LEFT FOOT unlucky.

BED, sitting on

1881 W. GREGOR *North-East of Scotland* 4. A woman giving suck [could not] seat herself on the edge of the bed of the lying-in woman, from the belief that such an action stopped the flow of the milk of the lying-in woman. **1940** *Folklore* 117 [Woolwich, London, 1936] Last week I was washing a patient in the district when a neighbour came in. I .. hastily put forward a chair. 'No fear of my sitting on the bed,' she said, 'or you know what happens. I'll be the next in bed!'

BED-MAKING interrupted

1892 *N & Q* 8th ser. II 189. In Scotland there is a belief that it is unlucky in making a bed to leave the work before it is completed. An interruption will cause the occupant of the bed to pass a sleepless night, or, it may be, some much worse evil will befall him.

BED-MAKING, sneezing during

late **18th c.** J. RAMSAY (*Scotland in the Eighteenth Century* II 456) Sneezing is .. deemed ominous. If it happens when one is making a bed, a little of the straw or heather is taken out and thrown into the fire, that so nothing may disturb the rest of such as sleep in it.

BED-MAKING: three people

1913 E. M. WRIGHT *Rustic Speech* 215. That if three people take part in making up a bed there is sure to be a death in the house within the year, is a superstition which I found was held to in my own house.

BED-MAKING: turning mattress/changing sheets at 'dangerous' times

1851 *N & Q* 1st ser. IV 98. It is very unlucky to turn a featherbed on a Sunday; my housemaid says she would not turn my bed on a Sunday on any account. **1852** *N & Q* 1st ser. VI 432 [Liverpool, Lancs.] An attendant was making a bed occupied by the mother of a child born a few days previously. When she attempted to turn it over .. the nurse energetically interfered, peremptorily forbidding her doing so till a month after the confinement, on the ground that it was decidedly unlucky. 1872 *N & Q* 4th ser. X 495. A friend of mine died a few Christmases ago. His cook told me she was not surprised, as his man had turned his mattress the day before. If it had been his feather-bed, indeed, it would not have mattered! 1878 *Folk-Lore Record* 11 [Fittleworth, Sussex] You must not turn a feather-bed on a Sunday, or the person who sleeps on it will have fearful dreams for the rest of the week. 1883 BURNE *Shropshire* 261. Maidservants consider it extremely unlucky to turn a feather-bed on a Sunday; if you do it, 'you'll sure to lose your sweetheart.' 1887 *N & Q* 7th ser. IV 246. 'Your mistress says that her bed last night was hard and full of lumps; I'm afraid you did not turn it yesterday.' 'Oh no, Ma'am! Yesterday was Friday: it would turn the luck.' 1913 E. M. WRIGHT *Rustic Speech* 215. The belief . . was held to in my own house . . that it is unlucky to turn a mattress on a Friday or Sunday. 1957 *W. Sussex Gazette* 17 Oct. 6. They always used to tell if you turned a feather bed of a Sunday you'd be hagridden all the week. No-one takes any notice nowadays. 1983 K. ROSE *King George V* IV. The King . . was less superstitious than his father, who would never allow his mattress to be turned on a Friday. 1983 Woman, 79 [Bentworth, Hants.] If you change the sheets on Friday the devil has control of your dreams for a week.

Cf. MAY, washing blankets in.

BEDSPREAD, making

1861 *N & Q* 2nd ser. XII 490. Patchwork quilt. If a lady completes one of these without assistance, she will never be married. 1923 [Ruishton, Som.] As long as there is an unfinished bedspread in the house, no one there will be married.

BEES, buying and selling

*c.*1720 LUPTON *Thousand Notable Things* (21st edn., 217) If you have no Stocks of Bees, but must buy them, I advise you first, not to give Money for them, but some other Commodity; for though there can be nothing in it but a su-

perstitious Observation, yet things often dishearten People that are apt to credit such Reports. 1750 W. ELLIS *Modern Husbandman* IV VI 182. It's commonly regarded for a fortunate Omen to buy a Hive of Bees, by exchanging a Commodity for it of its equal Value . . Or to give Gold for it. 1813 BRAND *Antiquities* II 202. A clergyman in Devonshire informed me that, when any Devonian makes a purchase of bees, the payment is never made in money, but in things (corn for instance) to the value of the sum agreed upon. 1846 DENHAM *Proverbs* 45 n. When you purchase a hive of bees, you should not pay for them in money, but in goods; for instance . . in wheat, oats, or barley, &c., and never presume to bring them home till Good-Friday following. 1854 *N & Q* 1st ser. IX 446 [Hants.] There is not one peasant I believe in this Village, man or woman, who would sell you a swarm of bees. To be guilty of selling bees is a grievous omen . . To barter bees is quite a different matter. If you want a hive, you may easily obtain it in lieu of a small pig, or some other equivalent. 1881 GREGOR *North-East of Scotland* 147. A bought swarm led but to disaster in bee-keeping. 1881 *N & Q* 6th ser. IV 396. In Essex, when I was a boy, it was a matter of faith that a swarm of bees ought always to be acquired as a gift, or else bought with gold. 1883 BURNE *Shropshire* 233–4. If you sell bees no silver must be used, the hand must be crossed with gold. 1904 E. V. LUCAS *Sussex* 76. If you wish your bees to thrive Gold must be paid for every hive; For when they're bought with other money There will be neither swarm nor honey. 1923 [Somerset] There are country people who will never take money for a swarm. They will exchange for ducks, chickens, or other farm produce, but will not take cash fearing the ill luck that will follow. 1948 Woman, *c.*30 [Weybourne, Surrey] If you buy bees, you *must* give silver for them.

Cf. ANIMAL, buying and selling.

BEES cross running water

1883 BURNE *Shropshire* 234. In removing a hive of bees, care must be taken not to carry them over any stream, for they will not live after crossing water.

BEES dislike bad behaviour

AD 77 PLINY *Natural History* XI xv (1855, III 15) It is particularly recommended .. that the person who takes the honey should be well washed and clean: bees have a particular aversion, too, to a thief and a menstruous woman. 1850 *N & Q* 1st ser. II 165 [Northants.] [Bees] will not thrive in a quarrelsome family. 1856 *Gents Mag.* 39. In Oxfordshire .. if a man and his wife quarrel, the bees will leave them. 1863 R. CHAMBERS *Book of Days* I 752 [Suffolk] Her next-door neighbour's hives, which had formerly been so prosperous, now seemed quite deserted .. 'Them bees couldn't du .. ' she said, 'There was words about them, and bees'll niver du if there's words about them.' 1883 BURNE *Shropshire* 234. Care must be taken that no one at any time uses bad language near the hives, as it disturbs and annoys the bees. 1904 *N & Q* 10th ser. II 27. No swarm of bees over which there has been any contention can possibly benefit either party.

BEES leave hive

1813 BRAND *Antiquities* II 202. A vulgar prejudice prevails in many places of England, that, when bees remove or go away from their hives, the owner of them will die soon after. 1887 'SPERANZA' WILDE *Superstitions of Ireland* II 64–5. When a swarm of bees suddenly quits the hive it is a sign that death is hovering near the house. But the evil may be averted by the powerful prayers and exorcism of the priest. 1923 [Somerset] If the bees desert their hives it means your luck will leave you.

BEES, lifting/turning

1621 P. CAMERARIUS *Historical Meditations* (tr. J. Molle, 283) Who would beleeue without superstition (if experience did not make it credible), that most commonly, all the Bees die in their hiues, if the master or the mistresse of the house chance to die, except the hiues be presently remooued into some other place? And yet I know this hath hapned to folke no way stained with superstition.

1790 *Argus* 13 Sept. (BRAND *Antiquities* 1813, II 202–3 n.) A superstitious custom prevails at every Funeral in Devonshire, of turning round the Bee-hives that belonged to the deceased, if he had any, and that at the moment the Corpse is carrying out of the House. At a Funeral some time since at Cullompton, of a rich old Farmer, a laughable circumstance of this sort occurred: for just as the Corpse was placed in the Herse, and the horsemen .. were drawn up in order for the procession of the Funeral, a person called out, 'turn the Bees', when a Servant who had no knowledge of such a Custom, instead of turning the Hives about, lifted them up, and laid them down on their sides. The Bees, thus hastily invaded, instantly attacked and fastened on the Horses and their Riders. It was in vain they gallopped off, the Bees as precipitately followed [and] a general Confusion took place, attended with loss of Hats, Wigs, &c. 1872 *Bye-Gones* 31 July 75 [nr. Oswestry, Shrops.] To lift the bee-hives a few inches clear of the bee bench when a funeral passes the house, is considered important to the well-being of the bees. 1883 BURNE *Shropshire* 236. In North Shropshire it is very common instead of—or as well as—telling the bees, to 'heave up' the hives, i.e. lift them a few inches from the stand and set them down again .. the hive and the coffin are both to be 'lifted' at the same moment. 1923 [Somerset] If the head of the house dies, the hive of bees should be turned round while the people are gone to the funeral, or the bees will die. 1948 Woman, c.30 [Weybourne, Surrey] Tap the hives three times and say to the bees 'Wake, browny, wake, Your old master's dead And a new one you must take,' and then move the hives.

BEES, news told to

c. AD 500 (*Oxford Book Greek Verse*, no. 678) When bees come hither in the fair springtide, Tell them, ye nymphs .. How on a wintry night Leucippus died. 1810 *Gents Mag.* pt. I 309 [Pamber, Hants.] When the head of a family who keeps bees, dies, it is usual .. to repair to the hives, and, gently tapping them, to say:

'Bees, bees, awake! Your Master is dead; And another you must take.' Otherwise the bees would either all die, or fly away. **1851** *N & Q* 1st ser. IV 308 [Bucks., *c.*1825] It is common .. for the nurse to go to all the bee-hives in the garden, and tap gently three times, each time repeating three times these words, 'Little brownie, little brownie, your master's dead;' when the bees, beginning to *hum*, show their consent to remain. **1867** *Trans. Devon. Ass.* 40. The bees must be informed, by tapping on the hive and whispering, of anything that takes place in the house, or if any of the family are ill, or going to, or returning from, a visit. **1870** *Stamford Mercury* 15 Apr. 6 [Stallingborough, Lincs., *c.*1840] A woman staying with the bereaved family asked the widow, 'Have the bees been told?' The reply being 'No', she at once took some spice cake and some sugar in a dish [for the bees] then, rattling a bunch of small keys (I suppose to attract the attention of the indwellers), she repeated this formula: 'Honey bees! honey bees! hear what I say! Your master, J.A., has passed away. But his wife now begs you will freely stay, And still gather honey for many a day. Bonny bees, bonny bees, hear what I say!' **1883** BURNE *Shropshire* 236. A woman at Meole Brace .. lately tapped the hive three times and said, 'The poor maister's dead, but yo mun work fur me,' in which phrase .. we have the key to the whole matter. **1906** KIPLING *Puck of Pook's Hill* IX. A maiden in her glory, Upon her wedding-day, Must tell her Bees the story, Or else they'll fly away. **1926** W. RAYMOND *Verity Thurston* XV. She .. passed behind the row of beehives and fastened a wedding favour on the top of each with a hairpin. Then .. she went down the front and told them .. in .. a little intimate confidential whisper at the entrance of each hive. 'I be to be married today to Cap'n Merman.' **1946** *Sussex N & Q* 60. The teller should rap on the outside of the hive with the front door key. **1955** *Sunday Times* 24 July 2 [Worcs., *c.*1925] She visited [the bees] many times a day .. When she had any important family news she would dress very carefully—even to gloves—and leave the house ceremoniously by the front door. For a death she wore her very formidable widow's weeds and carried two pieces of crape to tie on the hives. For a wedding she donned her gayest dress and carried white ribbon; for a birth the ribbon was pale blue or pink. **1959** *Woman's Day* 5 Sept. 2 [Shrops.] He was not superstitious, and did not tell the bees of a death in the family, but some time later he lost seven hives of bees, and it was not because of lack of winter feeding—he always fed them on barley sugar. **1961** *Shrewsbury Chronicle* 3 Mar. 1. Sam Rogers was devoted to his bees. And when he suddenly died .. his children .. walked round the 14 hives 'telling the bees'— to stop them, as legend has it, flying away. But as a memorial service was being held in the Shropshire village church of Myddle, the bees left their hives and settled in a great swarm all over the flowers on Sam's grave. **1969** S. MAYS *Reuben's Corner* 165 [Ashdon, Essex] Family letters with bad tidings should always be read to the bees, preferably those in hives, otherwise misfortune would continue. **1984** [Dulwich, London] My neighbour's son came round to say 'Have you heard, I'm getting married.' 'Has your father told his bees?' I asked. 'Of course,' he said.

Cf. ROOKS informed of a death.

BEES, swarm of: hiving after nightfall

1889 *Dorset Field Club* 29. It is .. considered very unlucky to 'pot' a swarm .. after nightfall.

BEES, swarm of: on dead wood

1714 GAY *Shepherd's Week* 49. When Blouzelind expir'd .. Swarm'd on a rotten stick the bees I spy'd. **1851** *N & Q* 1st ser. IV 436 [Sussex] Both him and his poor wife had been 'warned' .. by her going into the garden a fortnight before her confinement, and discovering that their bees, in the act of swarming, had made choice of a dead hedge stake for their settling-place. This is generally considered as an infallible sign of a death in the family. **1853** *N & Q* 1st ser. VIII 382 [Lincs.] If a swarm of bees alight on a dead tree, or on the dead bough of a living tree, there will be a death in the

family of the owner during the year.
1883 BURNE *Shropshire* 235. Should
[bees] settle on dead wood, or .. close
to the ground, it is a sign of death. **1922**
[Trowbridge, Wilts.] When your bees
swarm on rotten wood there will be a
death in the family before the year is
out.

BEES, swarming

1793 Correspondent [Brampton,
Cumb.] (J. HUNTER MS note in Brand's
Antiquities II 202) Bees *rising* and not
staying in a critical illness—certain in-
dications of death. **1856** *Gents Mag.*
pt. I 39 [Worcs.] If a swarm of bees
return to their old hive, it is believed
that a death will happen in the family
within the year. **1863** R. CHAMBERS *Book
of Days* I 752 [Suffolk] People *did* say
that if a stray swarm of bees came to a
house, and were not claimed by their
owner, there would be a death in the
family within the year. **1883** BURNE
Shropshire 235. If [the bees] settle on the
wall of a house, there will be a death in
that house before long. **1923** [Somerset]
If a swarm of bees come in the chimney
it is a sign of death in the family.

BEES take part in funeral/wedding

1837 S. TYMMS *Family Topographer* VI
49. The inhabitants of Cherry Burton
[Yorks.] believe in the necessity of clothing the bees in mourning at the death
of the head of a family, to secure the
prosperity of the hive. An instance occurred in July **1827** in a cottager's
family, when a black crape scarf was
appended to each hive, and an offering
of pounded funeral biscuit, soaked in
wine, was placed at the entrance with
great solemnity. **1849** *Athenaeum* 8
Sept. 911. At all weddings and funerals
they give a piece of the wedding-cake or
funeral biscuit to the bees, informing
them .. of the name of the party married
or dead. If the bees do not know of the
former they become very irate and sting
everybody within their reach; and if
they are ignorant of the latter they
become sick and many of them die.
1851 *N & Q* 1st ser. IV 390 [Bradfield,
Yorks.] When a death occurs, a person
is appointed to call the neighbours to
the funeral .. and .. the messenger is

instructed to address the same invitation
to the bees in their hives .. if this
compliment be omitted, the bees will die.
1863 R. CHAMBERS *Book of Days* I 752
[Suffolk] A neighbour of mine had
bought a hive of bees at an auction ..
The bees seemed very sickly .. when my
neighbour's servant bethought him that
they had never been put in mourning
for their late master; on this he got a
piece of crape and tied it to a stick,
which he fastened to the hive. After this
the bees recovered. **1864** *N & Q* 3rd ser.
V 393 [Yorks.] Last week, passing the
Hambleton Station on the railway between Milford and Selby, I observed
three bee-hives having pieces of crape
attached to them. On inquiring of a
fellow-passenger, he informed me that
some members of the station-master's
family had lately died, and that the
custom of putting the hives in mourning
.. was not uncommon. **1869** *N & Q* 4th
ser. IV 225–6 [Notts.] My nurse .. said
.. that in her village it is the custom ..
not only to inform the bees, but also to
give them a piece of the funeral cake ..
with beer. **1876** *Trans. Devon. Ass.*
51 [North Bovey] Mrs Blank when she
buried her husband forgot to give the
bees a bit of mourning and now, sir, all
the bees be dead. **1890** *N & Q* 7th ser.
X 312. I have seen in Derbyshire gardens
the whole of the hives each with a strip
of black material tied to the tip of the
thatch, and small plates on the ledge at
the mouth of the hives containing a little
wine and a small piece of cake. **1891**
J. C. ATKINSON *Forty Years in a Moorland Parish* 127 [nr. Colchester, Essex,
*c.*1825] I .. remember the key of the
main door of the house being taken,
together with sundry strips of some
black material .. the bearer of the key
proceeded to bind a black strip round
each hive—this was called 'putting the
bees into mourning'—and as each strip
was knotted, three taps with the key
were given, and each hive severally
informed that the master was dead.
1895 J. HARDY *Denham Tracts* II 213
[Northumb.] It is still customary to warn
the bees of the death of their master,
otherwise they will bring luck no longer.
One had seen a piece of the funeral cake
placed at the mouth of the hive, which

the inmates dragged within with a mournful noise. **1922** [Trowbridge, Wilts.] When there is a death in the family the beehives must be put in mourning with a strip of black material or the bees will sulk. **1986** Woman, *c*.50. In Southern Ireland, if anyone dies in the household they put mourning black crêpe on the hives. A young boy died [Killorglin, Co. Kerry] and they forgot about the bees, and they swarmed on the day of the funeral. They were found next day on the tomb a few miles away.

bees: also see BUMBLE BEE.

BEETLE cures
AD **77** PLINY *Natural History* XI xxxv (1855, III 34) These beetles [flying stag-beetles] are suspended from the neck of infants by way of remedy against certain maladies. *c*.**1040** MS Harl. 55 (COCKAYNE *Leechdoms* II 319–21) For wamb wark [bellyache] when thou seest a dung beetle .. throwing up mould, catch him .. along with his casting up, wave him strongly and say thrice, 'Remedium facio ad ventris dolorem;' then throw the beetle over thy back away; take care thou look not after it. **1866** *N & Q* 3rd ser. IX 319 [Brigg, Lincs.] A little girl came in with a small paper box in her hand, and said to the mistress of the cottage that her mother had sent her to request that, if she happened to find a black clock [beetle] she would save it for her and send it, at once, in the little box .. The mistress asked her what her mother wanted to do with the insect? Her reply was, 'To hing round sister Madelina's neck, who has got king cough, that as the clock decays away, her cough may go away too.'

BEETLE, killing: causes rain
1879 JEFFERIES *Wild Life in a Southern County* x. Slender beetles come forth from the cracks of the earth and run swiftly across the paths, glittering green and gold .. These are locally called sun-beetles, because they appear when the sun is brightest. Be careful not to step on or kill one; for if you do it will certainly rain, according to the old superstition. **1912** LEATHER *Herefordshire* 28. I once heard a servant say

'Oh, it'll be wet tomorrow, there's a black-beetle. *Please* don't kill it; it will be wetter if you do!' **1915** *Folklore* 210 [Oxford] A street urchin, seeing one of the writers tread on a large blackbeetle, remarked, 'Now we'll have rain.' **1952** Girl, 13 [Swansea, Glam.] 'Step on a black beetle, It will rain; Pick it up and bury it, The sun will shine again.' **1957** KIRKUP *Only Child* 20 [South Shields, Co. Durham, 1920s] Once I stamped on a black beetle when I had barely learned to walk, and was severely reprimanded by a group of big girls .. They told me solemnly that if you stamped on a beetle you would make it pour with rain, and .. a black beetle .. was the very worst sort. **1981** Farmer, *c*.45 [Woodborough, Wilts.] Stepping on a beetle will bring a storm.

BEGGAR, meeting
1652 GAULE *Mag-astro-mances* 181. A vain observation .. to bode good or bad luck .. from .. the meeting of a beggar .. the first in a morning.

BELLOWS as present
1923 [Ruishton, Som.] It is unlucky to give a pair of bellows as a wedding present.

BELLOWS, borrowing or lending
1865 R. HUNT *West of England* 2nd ser. 241. To borrow or lend a bellows is most unlucky, and many would rather give than lend one.

BELLOWS cure
1878 *Folk-Lore Record* 39 [Fittleworth, Sussex] A clergyman .. finding an old infirm woman seated on the very edge of her chair .. assured him that she was quite safe, and that she was sitting in that way .. to make room for the bellows behind her .. as the leaning against them was 'a fine thing for the rheumatis' .. they would, as she believed, charm away the malady.

BELLOWS on table
c.**1840** *Mother Bunch's Golden Fortune-Teller* 22. Bellows .. on a table .. is a sign of words in the domestic circle. **1869** *N & Q* 4th ser. IV 505 [Dublin serving-woman] If a pair of bellows be

placed on a table, there will be a fight
in the house. 1910 W. RAYMOND *English
Country Life* 194–5 [Somerset] 'Tis said,
an' have a-been proved hundreds o'
times, that if you should dap the bellices
down 'pon table, there'll be a death
in house afore the year's out. 1923
[Bridgwater, Som.] If you put the bellows
on the table you will make Satan
dance—there'll be quarrelling in the
house before the day is over.

BELT twisted

1953 Girl, 15 [Loughton, Essex] If you
wear your belt twisted, you are in love.
1961 Girl, 14 [Norwich, Norfolk] A
twisted belt is a sign that you will have
twins, and if it is twisted twice it is a
sign that you will marry a blackman.

BERRIES plentiful

1627 BACON *Sylva Sylvarum* § 737. It
is an Observation amongst Countrey-
People, that Yeares of Store of Hawes
and Heps, doe commonly portend Cold
Winters; And they ascribe it to Gods
Providence. 1788 MRS THRALE *Diary* 8
Sept. (ed. Balderston, II 720) Tis very
fine & very hot Weather still; Hips,
Haws, Blackberries &c. are in uncommon plenty: provision for the Birds
if chance a hard Winter is coming. 1814
Time's Telescope 351. White thorns and
dog-rose bushes. Wet summers are generally attended with an uncommon
quantity of seed on the shrubs: whence
the unusual fruitfulness is a sign of a
severe winter. 1842 R. CHAMBERS *Popular Rhymes* 37. Many hawes, Many
snaws. It is thus inferred that, when
there is a great exhibition of blossom on
the hedgerows, the ensuing winter will
be remarkable for snow-storms. It is said
that in this there is a providential object,
namely, to supply food for the birds in
the coming season. 1855 F. K. ROBINSON
*Whitby Glossary. Brummels or Bum-
melkites*, the fruit of the bramble, hedge
blackberries. An abundance in autumn
is said to denote a hard coming winter;
a prophecy also applying to the red fruit
of the hawthorn, called 'cat haws'; 'As
many haws, So many cold toes.' 1879
N & Q 5th ser. XII 327. Speaking to a
North Yorkshire farming man on the
quantity of haws on the thorn trees this

year, as indicative of a severe winter, he
mentioned [the] saying, 'Many haws,
cold toes.' 1892 C. M. YONGE *Old
Woman's Outlook* December. As to the
belief that their [holly berries'] number
foretells hard weather, it rather points
back to the absence of killing frosts at
their blossoming time in the spring.
1923 [Castle Cary, Som.] A good pigs-
berry [haw] year, a hard winter. 1971
Times 17 Apr. 23. Really, 1971 is proving a puzzler for gardeners as far as the
weather is concerned. The old myth of
a fine crop of berries foretelling a hard
winter misfired.

BETWEEN, coming

c. AD 396 ST AUGUSTINE OF HIPPO *De
Doctrina Christiana* I xx (tr. Robertson,
55–6) To these [superstitious things]
may be added a thousand vacuous observances to follow if .. a stone, dog, or
child comes between friends walking
arm in arm. The custom of kicking a
stone, as if it were a destroyer of friendship, is less obnoxious than that of
hitting an innocent child with the fist if
he runs between two people walking
together. And it is fitting that sometimes
children are avenged by dogs; for some
persons are so superstitious that they
even dare to hit a dog that has come
between them, and not without paying
for it. For sometimes the dog quickly
sends him who strikes him from a vain
remedy to a true physician. 1486
SPRENGER & KRAMER *Malleus Maleficarum*
(tr. Summers, 55) Of the obstruction to
marriage caused by witchcraft .. and
concerning the method by which such
obstruction is procured .. the devil,
being a spirit, has power over a corporeal
creature to cause or prevent a local
motion. Therefore he can prevent bodies
from approaching each other, either
directly or indirectly, by interposing
himself in some bodily shape. 1584
SCOT *Discoverie of Witchcraft* XI xv. It is
thought verie ill lucke of some, that a
child, or anie other liuing creature,
should passe betweene two friends as
they walke togither; for they say it
portendeth a division of freendship.
1636 Kirk-session, Kirkcaldy, Fife (*Stat.
Acc. Scotland* XVIII 660) When he was
to sail, the said Alison [on trial for

witchcraft] went betwixt him and the boat .. and that same voyage .. the sea came and took him away, and he died. **1652** GAULE *Mag-astro-mances* 181. To bode good or bad luck .. from .. the running in of a child betwixt two friends. **1721** KELLY *Scotish Proverbs* 330. The Swine's gone through it .. A superstitious Conceit, that if a Swine come between a Man and his Mistress, they will never be married. **1771** PENNANT *Tour in Scotland* 160. During the marriage ceremony, great care is taken that dogs do not pass between them [the couple]. **1823** GALT *Entail* LXVI. 'Get the swine driven through't, or it may work .. as his father's moonlight marriage did.' **1900** S. HEWETT *Nummits* 23 [Devon] Should .. a cat, dog, or hare pass between them [bride and groom] then terrible misfortunes will follow them. **1909** M. TREVELYAN *Folk-Lore of Wales* 270. Bride and bridegroom .. are to stand as closely as possible together, to prevent witches creeping in between them. **1923** [Somerset] Should a spider's web come between you and your 'young man' you will disagree. **1952** Girl, 15 [Aberdeen] If you are out with a friend and she walks one side of a lamp post and you go the other, it means there will be a quarrel. **1954** Woman, 35 [Oxford] If two friends have to walk either side of a lamp-post it means their friendship will be broken—but it's all right if they say 'Bread and butter' the other side of the lamp-post. **1962** *Scotsman* 9 May 11. Leave Towser at home with his white satin bow. It is considered an ill omen if a dog comes between the couple as they leave the church.

BIBLE as present

1869 *N & Q* 4th ser. IV 212 [Paisley, Renfrew.] It is considered unlucky for a young man to present a copy of the Bible to his sweetheart.

BIBLE, buying and selling

1932 A. G. STREET *Strawberry Roan* 75 [Wilts.] 'Which .. do you want to keep?' asked Mr Wheeler. 'I wants thic Bible. 'Tis bad luck to trade in they.'

BIBLE protects

1691 R. KIRK *Secret Commonwealth* (1815, 6) [Scottish-Irish] Tramontains to this Day put .. the Bible .. in Womens Bed when travelling [in labour], to save them [mother and child] from being .. stollen. **1703** M. MARTIN *Western Isles* 248 [Collonsay] My Landlord having one of his Family sick of a Fever, asked my Book as a singular favour for a few Moments; I was not a little surpriz'd at the honest Man's request, he being illiterate, and when he told me the reason of it, I was no less amazed, for it was to fan the Patient's Face with the Leaves of the Book; and this he did at Night: He sought the Book next Morning, and again in the Evening, and .. told me, the sick Person was much better by it, and thus I understood that they had an ancient Custom of fanning the Face of the Sick, with the Leaves of the Bible. **1811** A. GRANT *Highlanders of Scotland* I 166 [Before baptism] the bed, containing the mother and the infant, was drawn out on the floor, the attendant took a Bible, and went thrice round it, waving all the time the open leaves, and adjuring all the enemies of mankind .. to fly instantly to the Red Sea. **1879** J. NAPIER *West of Scotland* 40 [Glasgow] Early in the century, a labourer's wife .. became the mother of a very pretty baby .. The neighbours .. urged .. the necessity of carefulness and advised her .. never to leave the child without placing near it an open Bible. **1900** J. G. CAMPBELL *Superstitions of the Highlands* 36–7. The Bible was opened, and the breath blown across it in the face of the woman in childbed.

BIBLE, treatment of

1873 EWING *Flat Iron for a Farthing* (1894–6, 164) I .. picked up certain little quaint superstitions from Nurse Bundle .. Neither she nor I ever put anything on top of a Bible. **1923** [Trowbridge, Wilts.] Whoever tears a Bible will be unfortunate, and to let a Bible fall brings bad luck. It is also bad luck to burn or otherwise destroy a Bible, and when it is old, shabby and worn out it is difficult to know how to dispose of it.

BIBLE AND KEY: divination

1303 MANNYNG *Handlyng Synne* (EETS

119 Fr. l. 1092, Eng. l. 354) Si le sauter feites unques turner [if anyone turns the psalter] wycchëcraft men clepyn hyt al. **1584** SCOT *Discoverie of Witchcraft* XVI v. Popish preests .. doo practice with a psalter and a keie fastned upon the 49. psalme, to discover a theefe. And when the names of the suspected persons are orderlie put into the pipe of the keie, at the reading of these words of the psalme ['If thou sawest a theefe thou diddest consent unto him'] the booke will wagge, and fall out of the fingers of them that hold it, and he whose name remaineth in the keie must be the theefe. **1691** *Athenian Mercury* III no. 22. Quest. What is the reason (if any) that a Bible having a Key fastned in the middle, and being held between the two fore-fingers of two persons will turn round after some words said, as if one desires to find out a Thief, a certain verse taken out of a Psalm is to be repeated, and those who are suspected nominated, and if they are guilty, the Book and Key will turn, else not. **1830** FORBY *East Anglia* 398–9. The parties suspected are arranged round a table, on which is laid the bible, with the key upon it. The owner of the stolen goods then takes the key by the middle, and gives it a strong twirl .. The person, opposite to whom it stops, is the thief. Ibid. 399. The key is to be inserted .. exactly over the 6th and 7th verses of the last chapter of Solomon's Song. The person who makes the inquiry is then to tie the bible closely together with the garter taken from her right knee; and she and some other female are to suspend it, by placing each a finger under the bow of the key .. then repeat the two verses to every letter of the alphabet .. till she comes to the initial of her future husband's name. As soon as she pronounces this happy letter, the bible will turn round. **1831** HONE *Year Book* 29 Feb. A disagreeable woman had lost one of her husband's shirts, and, suspecting the thief to be in the house, was going to find it out by the Bible and key .. neither a Bible nor a key belonging to any person living in the house would do .. I found the people of the house assembled together, and a young boy and girl to hold the apparatus .. it can only be done properly by a bachelor and a maid. The key was bound into the Bible against the first chapter of Ruth and part of the seventeenth verse, 'the Lord do so to me and more also,' and strict silence and gravity were then enjoined .. The boy and girl placed their left hands behind their backs, and the key balanced on the middle fingers of their right hands: then, the woman .. said 'the Lord do so to me and more also, has he [or she] got my husband's shirt?' Nearly all the names of the people in the house had been repeated when .. the urchin who held the Bible suspended from the key gave his hand a slight motion—down went the Bible. The loser's husband came home and .. said he had removed the shirt himself. **1838** A. E. BRAY *Devonshire* II 294. Many old people when they have lost anything, and suspect it to be stolen, take the fore-door key of their dwelling .. and tie this key to the Bible, placing it very carefully on the eighteenth verse of the fiftieth psalm 'When thou sawest a thief, then thou consentedst with him' .. If the Bible moves, the suspected person is considered guilty. **1850** *N & Q* 1st ser. II 5 [Burnley, Lancs.] Having opened the Bible at the passage in Ruth which states, 'whither thou goest I will go,' &c., and having carefully placed the wards of the key upon the verses, she ties the book firmly with a piece of cord; and, having mentioned the name of an admirer, she very solemnly repeats the passage in question, at the same time holding the Bible suspended by joining the ends of her little fingers inserted under the handle of the key. If the key retain its position during the repetition, the person whose name has been mentioned is considered to be rejected; and so another name is tried, until the book turns round and falls through the fingers. **1866** HENDERSON *Northern Counties* 195–8 [long description]. **1871** KILVERT *Diary* 1 Feb. [Clyro, Radnor.] Mrs Jones declared two pairs of drawers and a 'shimmy' had been stolen, and her suspicions fell on some of the neighbours. She and her husband consulted the ordeal of the key and Bible .. The key said 'Bella Whitney'. **1888** *Bye-Gones* 79 [Welsh Border] If any thing had been stolen, and a person was suspected, she

could tell whether the suspicion was justifiable by 'turning the key on the Bible'. **1935** *I Walked by Night* (ed. L. Rider Haggard, 19–20) [Norfolk] Granny used to .. tell me .. the way to find out if a lover cared any thing about you. You must take the Door key and put it between the leaves of the Book of Ruth in the Bible, two people balancen the key by the bow on the midle finger of there hands .. Then these words must be repeated: 'Many Waters canot quence true love, neither can the floods drown it. Love is as strong as Death, but Jelousy is as cruele as the Grave, and burneth with a most vehiment flame. If a man should give all the substince of his house for love, it would be utterly consumed.' If the book turn to the left the lover will be false and ficcle, but if to the right the lover will be true. **1952** Woman, 80 [Wokingham, Berks.] The text was in the Song of Solomon, and the rhyme, 'If —— begins my true lover's name, May the Bible turn round and the key do the same.' **1952** *Trans. Devon. Ass.* 300 [Bideford fisherman, 63] A big key would be brought and all but its loop put into the Bible at the passage in Ruth 1, 16 ['Intreat me not to leave thee, or to return from following after thee: for whither thou goest I will go .. '] The Bible was then lashed up with twine .. then my sweetheart and I had to put the tips of our right forefinger under the loop and so hold the Bible suspended between us, whilst we recited the passage in unison. **1963** Teacher [Cumnock, Ayr.] Key and Bible was a craze with the 14-year-old girls a couple of years ago. They asked the Bible questions which it will answer 'yes' by turning one way, 'no' by turning the other. You can find out the name of your future boy-friend by going through the letters of the alphabet.

Cf. SIEVE AND SHEARS: divination.

BILLHOOK on table
1923 Girl, 11 [Taunton, Som.] It is unlucky to put a billhook on the table.

BIRCH TREE
1960 Woman, *c.*45 [Sheet, Hants.] We always crossed our fingers under birch trees and it became such a habit that I

still do. It was connected with witchcraft. **1970** J. MCPHEE *Crofter and Laird* 145 [Colonsay, Hebrides] You must always put birch branches over a baby's cradle or baby carriage to protect it from the fairies.

Cf. MAY BOUGHS AND FLOWERS.

BIRD, dead
1957 Boy, 13 [Stock, Essex] It is unlucky to see a dead pigeon. **1957** Girl, 13 [Canonbie, Dumfries.] When we see a dead bird lying on the road we spit on it so that we don't get it for our supper. **1967** R. LEHMANN *Swan in the Evening* pt. 2 v. A loud, sudden thud on one of the french windows .. A few moments later .. on the paved terrace .. a dark blot upon the stone—a dead bird .. On the instant of my seeing that lifeless shape a thud fell, leaden, upon my heart .. 'You know what it's supposed to mean: a death in the family.'

BIRD in house
1646 BROWNE *Vulgar Errors* I IV. His [Pythagoras'] injunction is, not to harbour Swallowes in our houses: Whose advice notwithstanding we doe not contemn, who daily admit and cherish them. **1652** GAULE *Mag-astro-mances* 181 [among omens] The Swallows falling down the Chymney. **1792** MRS SHERWOOD (*Life*, ed. Kelly, 111) A bird flew in and flew round the bed of the girl who had been first taken ill, and then out again. We, all the other pupils in the room, and the persons who nursed us, looked at each other, and from that moment we accounted the child as one doomed to die. Such was the force of superstition with us, and as we imagined, so it happened. **1850** *N & Q* 1st ser. II 435. It is said that for a bird to fly into a room, and out again, by an open window, surely indicates the decease of some inmate. Is this belief local? **1851** *N & Q* 1st ser. III 4 [Northants.] Omens of death and misfortune are .. drawn .. from .. the flying down the chimney of swallows. **1866** HENDERSON *Northern Counties* 33. The flight of jackdaws or swallows down the chimney is held to presage death. **1873** *N & Q* 4th ser. XI 275 [Edenderry, Co. Offaly] While the guests were seated

round the festive board, an old owl .. who had for many years been .. made a great pet of by .. the family .. flew in through the parlour door, and alighting on the back of the bride's chair .. for a few moments .. flew three times round the room, and out through the open window .. The circumstance was .. taken to be a foreshadowing of some disagreeable event .. but, of course nothing ever happened. **1901** N & Q 9th ser. VIII 288. Two years ago a young swallow flew into my bedroom in Devon, and on telling my hostess she remarked 'it was unlucky.' **1934** M. V. HUGHES *London Child* x [Cornwall] As for a funeral anywhere about .. she was sure to have heard .. a bird flutter in the chimney, and consequently knew that something would happen. **1935** *I Walked by Night* (ed. L. Rider Haggard, 18) [Norfolk] If a bird flew into a house and flew round three times, that denoted great trubble. **1941** F. THOMPSON *Over to Candleford* XXIII. The morning after a death in the hamlet would see them with serious faces discussing the signs which were supposed to have foretold it .. the beating of a bird's wings against the window. **1954** Girl, 14 [Newbridge, Monmouth.] The lady next door will not have a bird of any kind in the house. She says they will bring bad luck to all the family. **1964** Woman, c.70 [Whitby, Yorks.] I were just going to redecorate when my sister-in-law kem in an' saw t' paper. 'Get it out of 'ere,' she says. 'Nae birds. Birds is unlucky.' **1966** *News of the World* 20 Feb. 8. Finding an injured starling in my back yard I took it indoors until it was well enough to fly again. My wife insisted it was bad luck to keep a wild bird in the house even for a few days .. On the day we let the bird go, my wife fell ill and was in bed for over a week. **1973** Woman, 62 [Sheffield, Yorks.] When I had a hardware shop I would never stock cups, saucers, plates, dishes with a picture of a bird on them as I knew I wouldn't be able to sell them.

BIRD on ship

1958 *Daily Herald* 10 Apr. 4. The Queen Elizabeth ran into nothing but trouble, gale, delays, fog and storm-batterings ..

Joey (yes, he's a budgie) was escorted off the liner yesterday accused of the worst crime of the sea—being the ship's Jonah.

BIRD sings unseasonably

1846 DENHAM *Proverbs* 27. As long as the bird sings before Candlemas, it will greet [cry] after it. **1876** HARDWICKE *Science Gossip* XII 118. At Pomeroy, Co. Tyrone .. the saying .. is: 'Blackbird or Thrush which sings before Candlemas will be sure to mourn many days afterwards.' **1887** F. T. HAVERGAL *Herefordshire Words* 49. If the birds sing before Candlemas, they will cry before May.

Cf. COCK crows unseasonably.

BIRDS' EGGS in house

AD 77 PLINY *Natural History* X xv (1855, II 491) It is a vulgar belief .. that if the [ravens'] eggs are even so much as brought beneath the roof, a difficult labour will be the consequence. **1829** J. L. KNAPP *Journal of a Naturalist* 2nd edn. 228–9. Regarding these birds' eggs we have a very foolish superstition here [Glos.]; the boys may take them unrestrained, but their mothers so dislike their being kept in the house, that they usually break them .. under the idea that they bring bad luck, or prevent the coming of good fortune. **1831** HONE *Year Book* 29 Feb. Birds' eggs hung up in a house, are unlucky. **1851** STERNBERG *Northamptonshire* 172. Birds' eggs should never be kept in the house, they are very unlucky. **1870** N & Q 4th ser. V 370. In the vicinity of Manchester it used to be believed that it was unlucky to suspend strings of blown birds' eggs in a dwellinghouse, but good luck ensued from placing them in an outhouse. **1878** *Folk-Lore Record* 10 [Fittleworth, Sussex] There is a superstitious feeling that will not allow birds' eggs to be brought into a house, though long strings of them may generally be seen in Spring hanging up in out-houses. **1890** N & Q 7th ser. X 235 [Bucks./Berks.] Sixty years ago .. it was deemed unlucky to have strings of birds' eggs in a house. I can well remember my brothers and myself, our father being seriously ill, being compelled by our maiden aunt to remove our birds' eggs from the house and hang them up in the garden. **1953** Boy, 12 [Peterborough, Northants.] If you bring a bird's egg in the house you would have bad luck.

Cf. EGGSHELL, piercing or crushing.

BIRTH, breech

1874 *Journal Anthropological Inst.* III 271 [Banff.] Those .. who were born with their feet first possessed great power to heal all kinds of sprains, lumbago, and rheumatism, either by rubbing the affected part or by trampling on it. The greater virtue lay in the feet. **1895** J. HARDY *Denham Tracts* II 274 [Scottish Border] A popular remedy for sleep-walking, is the peculiar attribute of individuals born with their feet first. A benevolent and even sensible old lady, thus privileged 'in life's morning march' .. cured her grandchild .. by stamping nine times with her naked feet on his breast.

BIRTH, contact with

1838 W. HOWITT *Rural Life* I 320 [Yorkshire dales] When a sow litters, they allow her to champ oats out of a bee-hive to make the bees lucky. **1881** *N & Q* 6th ser. III 364 [Skateraw, Kincardine.] A cotter's wife had a cow which .. ceased to give milk .. she was told she must feed the cow with straw from the bed of a woman who had given birth .. but had not since that event been in church. **1920** *Folklore* 320 [Oxford] The first house a newly-delivered woman enters will shortly have a child. **1939** *Folklore* 185 [East Anglia] Any outsider who helps with the washing in a house where a birth has occurred will become pregnant if her age makes it possible; only old women assist with the household washing during a birth.

Cf. CHURCHING; PREGNANT WOMAN causes pregnancy.

BIRTH, day of: divination rhyme

1594 NASHE *Terrors of the Night* E4. I haue heard aged mumping beldams .. tell what luck euerie one should haue by the day of the weeke he was borne on. **1838** A. E. BRAY *Devonshire* II 287 [Tavistock] Here is a poetical adage .. common in our town: 'Monday's child

is fair in face, Tuesday's child is full of grace, Wednesday's child is full of woe, Thursday's child has far to go, Friday's child is loving and giving, Saturday's child works hard for its living; And a child that's born on a Christmas day, Is fair and wise, good and gay.' **1850** *N & Q* 1st ser. II 515. Born of a Monday, Fair in face; Born of a Tuesday, Full of God's grace; Born of a Wednesday, Merry and glad; Born of a Thursday, Sour and sad; Born of a Friday, Godly given; Born of a Saturday, Work for your living; Born of a Sunday, Never shall we want: So there ends the week, And there's an end on't. **1851** *N & Q* 1st ser. IV 98 [Devon] Born on a Sunday, a gentleman .. Monday, fair of face .. Tuesday, full of grace .. Wednesday, sour and grum .. Thursday, welcome home .. Friday, free in giving .. Saturday, work hard for your living. **1865** R. HUNT *West of England* 2nd ser. 237. Sunday's child is full of grace, Monday's child is full in the face, Tuesday's child is solemn and sad, Wednesday's child is merry and glad, Thursday's child is inclined to thieving, Friday's child is free in giving, And Saturday's child works hard for a living. **1923** [Taunton, Som.] Born on Monday, you'll have good health, Born on Tuesday, will make wealth, Born on Wednesday, born to power, Born on Thursday, many losses to endure, Born on Friday, loving and kind, Saturday's child lags far behind, Sunday's child has a contented mind. **1987** Woman, *c.*60 [Gt. Ayton, Yorks.] Our version is: 'Monday's child is fair of face; Tuesday's child is full of grace; Wednesday's child is full of woe; Thursday's child has far to go; Friday's child is loving and giving; Saturday's child works hard for its living; But the child that is born on the Sabbath day Is blithe and bonny, and good and gay.'

BIRTH: opening locks

1881 W. GREGOR *North-East of Scotland* 4. While the woman was in labour all locks in the house were undone. **1900** J. G. CAMPBELL *Superstitions of the Highlands* 36–7 n. [NW Argyll.] Various .. precautions were taken [at childbirth] .. the opening of every lock in the house.

Cf. DEATH: opening locks/doors and windows eases.

BIRTHDAY, crying on

1923 [Castle Cary, Som.] To cry on your birthday—to cry every day of the year. 1953 Girl, 10 [Ipswich, Suffolk] Many people say that if you cry on your birthday you will cry all the year round.
Cf. NEW YEAR: activities set precedent.

BLACK Devil's colour

c.20 BC VIRGIL Aeneid VI (tr. Dryden, ll. 336–60) The Prince .. Hastes to the neather World .. And here .. Four sable Bullocks, in the Yoke untaught, For Sacrifice the pious Heroe brought .. A Lamb to Hell and Night, (The sable Wool without a streak of white) Aeneas offers .. With Holocausts he Pluto's Altar fills. 1662 Witchcraft trial (R. PITCAIRN Criminal Trials of Scotland III 605–6) We took a threid of each cullor of yairne that wes in the .. litt-fatt [dying-vat], and did cast thrie knots on each threid, in the Divellis name; and did put the threidis in the fatt, withersones abowt in the fatt, in the Divellis name; and thairby took the heall strength of the fatt away, that it could litt nothing bot onlie blak, according to the culor of the Divell, in quhoes nam we took away the strength of the rycht culouris that wes in the fatt. 1834 DALYELL Darker Superstitions of Scotland 434. If black is a mystical colour in Scotland, it has been always in combination with the metamorphoses of Satan, or his imps, as a black dog, a black cat, or a black cock. 1858 DENHAM North of England (1895, 68) In Weardale .. it is supposed the victim can be saved by giving the fiend anything black when he appears to him; as a black hen, a black cat, dog, etc. 1885 Folklore 308–9 [Aberdeen./Banff.] Not many years ago J.M. .. was making a very poor herring fishing .. His son had a rabbit, and, what was still more serious, of a black colour. It was this black rabbit that was at the root of the evil .. So the .. rabbit had to die, and the fisherman secretly put it out of the way. This man I know. 1976 C. OMAN Oxford Childhood 141. We all gave her the presents we had made and she [the Scottish nanny] went off resignedly

saying she had known her stay would not be for long since she had seen a black pig at a station somewhere on her journey south.
Cf. CAT, black.

BLACK BEETLE

1855 Trans. Ossianic Soc. II 124 n. Daol [Devil] is the name for a small black reptile popularly supposed to be the darkest object in creation .. If you kill him with the thumb of your right hand before he cocks his tail, the seven deadly sins will be forgiven you. 1872 N & Q 4th ser. X 183. The Dharrig Dhael [Black Devil] is .. amongst the humble class in the south of Ireland .. looked on with horror by both old and young, as it has the credit of having informed on our Saviour .. My own servants were not over pleased at my bringing it [the beetle] into the house, saying it was very unlucky. 1972 Lore and Language July 7 [Coalisland, Co. Tyrone] Always kill a clock when you see one because they betrayed Christ, calling out to the soldiers: 'He went there,' i.e. towards Gethsemane.

BLACK MAN

1590 Witchcraft trial (R. PITCAIRN Criminal Trials in Scotland I pt. 2 239–40) At the Kirk of North Beruik .. abone ane hundreth persounes .. maid .. thair homage [to the Devil]. The Devill start vp him selff in the pulpett, lyke ane mekle blak man .. He had one him ane goun and ane hatt, quhilkis wer baith blak. 1662 (Ibid. III 603) I met with THE DIVELL .. in the Kirk of Aulderne .. He wes in the Reader's dask, and a blak book in his hand .. He wes a meikle, blak .. man. c.1700 (W. PAUL Aberdeenshire 18–19) Alex. Thomson, minister of Peterculter .. is guilty of superstitious observances .. saying that he knew some evil would befall that day that he fell and hurt his leg, for .. he went out without his hat, and saw a black man in the sun. 1958 G. PARRINDER Witchcraft 64. The devil was said frequently to appear as a black man .. The superstition still lingers in parts of England that if one meets a black man one must turn right round, to shake off the bad luck. 1963 S. PATTERSON Dark

Strangers 232 [Brixton] The widespread belief that to touch a Negro brings good luck.

Cf. CHIMNEY SWEEP, meeting: and actions to avert evil.

BLACK SHEEP

1878 *Folk-Lore Record* 8. One black sheep is regarded by the Sussex shepherd as an omen of good luck to his flock. 1887 'SPERANZA' WILDE *Superstitions of Ireland* II 64. If the first lamb of the season is born black, it foretells mourning garments for the family within the year. 1909 *N & Q* 10th ser. XII 484 [Stromness, Orkney] It is unlucky to see a black lamb as the first of the season. 1923 [Somerset] To keep a black ewe is supposed to bring luck to the flock—others say bad luck. 1932 C. IGGLESDEN *Those Superstitions* 105. In Kent a black lamb foretells good luck to the flock, but I am told that in Shropshire an exactly opposite fate befalls the farmer to whom a black lamb is born. 1946 UTTLEY *Country Things* 130 [Cromford, Derbys., c.1900] A black lamb was lucky, and we liked black horses and mares, preferably with a white star or white foot. When a black lamb was born, we children felt elated and excited as we spread the good news all around.

BLACKBERRIES not to be eaten after Michaelmas (29 Sept.)

1727 C. THRELKELD *Synopsis Stirpium Hibernicarum. Rubus Major Fructu Nigro* .. The Fruit of the Bramble is reputed infamous, for causing sore Heads .. but I look upon this as a vulgar Error, and that after Michaelmas the D---l casts his Club over them, which is a Fable: For the Earth is the Lord's, and the Fulness thereof. 1829 BROCKETT *North Country Words* 53. I have often been admonished, by the 'good old folks', never to eat these berries after Michaelmas day; because the arch-fiend .. was sure to pass his 'cloven foot' over them at that time. 1852 W. R. WILDE *Irish Popular Superstitions* 14 n. It is a popular belief .. that the pooca, as he rides over the country, defiles the blackberries at Michaelmas and Hollyeve. 1855 F. K. ROBINSON *Whitby Glossary* 22. Brambles in October are

pronounced out of season, for the devil, about that time, has waved his club over the bushes. 1905 *Folklore* 454. Repeated about the time of Rood Fair held at Dumfries in the end of September .. 'Oh weans, ho weans, the morn's the fair, Ye mana eat the brambles mair, This nicht the Deil gangs ower them a' Tae touch them wi' his pooshioned paw.' 1911 D. H. LAWRENCE *White Peacock* VI. The webs on the brambles were white; the devil throws his net over the blackberries as soon as September's back is turned, they say. 1943 F. THOMPSON *Candleford Green* 119. After Michaelmas blackberries were unfit for food because on Michaelmas Day the devil dragged his tail over them. 1985 *Woman,* 29 [Colchester, Essex] I wouldn't eat blackberries after the end of September, because the Devil has spat on them.

BLACKSMITH

1691 R. THORESBY *Diary* 1 Apr. [from Mr Sharp's sermon, at Leeds] We may condemn for presumers .. All you that place any confidence in any thing of your own .. devising, which is not instituted by God; as .. holding children over the smith's anvils for rickets. 1701 J. BRAND *Description of Orkney* 62. Other Charms .. they have .. when their Children are sick, by taking them to a Smith (without premonishing him) who hath had a Smith to his Father, and a Smith to his Grand-Father. 1866 HENDERSON *Northern Counties* 151. At Stamfordham a sickly child is .. brought to a blacksmith of the seventh generation, and laid naked on the anvil. The smith raises his hammer [and] brings it down gently on the child's body. This is done three times, and the child is sure to thrive. 1874 *Journal Anthropological Inst.* III 269–70 [cure for rickets] The child was taken before sunrise to a smithy in which three blacksmiths of the same name wrought. One of them bathed it in the water-trough of the smithy .. it was laid upon an anvil, and all the tools of the shop were passed over it, and the use of each was asked .. If a fee was exacted, the virtue of the lay was lost. 1911 *Folklore* 238 [Glos.] To cure shingles, wheat was placed on the blacksmith's anvil and then applied.

BLADE-BONE: divination

1188 GIRALDUS CAMBRENSIS *Itinerary through Wales* (1806, I 192) The husband purposely gave the shoulder-bone of the ram, properly cleaned, to his wife .. for her examination; when, having for a short time examined the secret marks, she smiled and threw the oracle down on the table. Her husband dissembling, earnestly demanded the cause of her smiling, and she answered, 'The man to whose fold this ram belongs, has an adulterous wife .. ' The husband, with a sorrowful countenance, replied, 'You deliver indeed an oracle supported by too much truth.' *c.*1395 CHAUCER Parson's Tale l. 602. Conjuracioun, as doon thise false .. nigromanciens .. in a shulder-boon of a sheep. **1480** CAXTON *Description of Britain* Ca15. It semeth of these men [the Flemings of W. Wales] a grete wondre that in a boon of a wethers right sholder whan the flessh is soden away and not rosted they knowe what haue be don, is don, & shall be don, as it were by a spirite of prophecie and a wonderfull craft, They telle what is don in ferre contreyes, tokenes of pees or of werre, the state of the royame, sleyng of men, and spousebreche, suche thinges they declare certainly of tokenes and signe that is in suche a sholdre boon. **1586** CAMDEN *Britannia* (tr. Gibson, II 380) They look through the blade-bone of a shoulder of mutton, when the meat is picked clean off; and, if they find a spot in any part, they think it portends a funeral out of that family. **1622** DRAYTON *Poly-Olbion* V ll. 263–8 (1961, IV 104) A divination strange the Dutch made-English have, Appropriate to that place [Pembrokeshire] (as though some Power it gave) By th' shoulder of a Ram from off the right side par'd, Which usuallie they boile, the spade-boane beeing bar'd: Which then the Wizard takes, and gazing there-upon, Things long to come fore-showes, as things done long ago. **1685** G. SINCLAIR *Satans Invisible World Discovered* 215 [Scottish Highlands] Others can lecture in a sheeps shoulder bone a death within the Parish, seven or eight days before it come. **1691** R. KIRK *Secret Commonwealth* (1815, 17) The minor Sort of Seers prognosticat many future events,

only for a Month's Space, from the Shoulder-bone of a Sheep on which a Knife never came .. By looking into the Bone, they will tell if Whoredome be committed in the Owners House; what Money the Master of the sheep had; if any will die out of that House for that Moneth. **1763** T. INSULANUS *Treatise on the Second Sight* 77. There is [a] kind of divination, by looking in the shoulder-blade of a sheep, goat, &c as in a book, by which some .. pretend to read future events, such as the death of some remarkable person .. foretell general meetings, battles, bloodsheds, &c .. And besides will describe what numerate money is to be found in the custody of the owner of the sheep. **1774** PENNANT *Voyage to Hebrides* 282. Molly Mac-leane (aged forty) has the power of foreseeing events through a well-scraped blade bone of mutton: some time ago she took up one and pronounced that five graves were soon to be opened; one for a grown person: the other four for children .. and so it fell out. **1775** L. SHAW *History of Moray* 249. They Divine by Bones; Having picked the flesh clean off a shoulder-blade of mutton, which no iron must touch, they turn towards the East, or the Rising Sun, and looking steadily on the transparent Bone, pretend to foretell deaths, burials, etc. **1895** *Folklore* 157 [Argyll.] The shoulder-blades of sheep are used in the Highlands for predicting of marriages, births, deaths, and funerals. Ibid. 167. In Lewis divination by means of the blade-bone .. was practised in the following manner. The shoulder-blade of a black sheep was procured by the inquirer into future events, and with this he went to some reputed seer, who held the bone lengthwise before him and .. began to read the bone from some marks he saw in it, and then oracularly declared what events .. were to happen. It is not very far distant that there were a host of believers in this method of prophecy.

BLADE-BONE medicates well-water

*c.*1390 CHAUCER *Tales* Pardoner's Prologue ll. 350–60. Thanne have I in latoun a sholder-boon Which that was of an hooly Jewes sheep .. 'If that this boon be wasshe in any welle, If cow, or calf, or sheep, or oxe swelle .. Taak water of that welle and wassh his tonge, And it is hool anon .. Of pokkes and of scabbe, and every soore Shal every sheep be hool that of this welle Drynketh a draughte.'

BLADE-BONE: spell

1839 *Everlasting Fortune-Teller* 7. Take a blade-bone of a shoulder of lamb and borrowing a penknife (but be sure not to mention for what purpose) on going to bed, stick the knife once through the bone, every night for nine nights .. repeating .. ''Tis not this bone I mean to stick, But my Lover's heart I mean to prick, Wishing him neither rest nor sleep, Until he comes to me to speak.' 1852 *N & Q* 1st ser. VI 312 [Hull, Yorks.] Take the blade-bone of a rabbit and stick nine pins in it, and then put it under your pillow, and you will be sure to see the object of your affections. 1861 C. C. ROBINSON *Dialect of Leeds* 302. [to dream about future husband] Take a blade-bone of mutton, stick it full of pins, and put it under your pillow, going backwards-way to bed. 1861 *N & Q* 2nd ser. XII 501 [Shrops.] Procure the blade-bone of a lamb, and prick it with a pen-knife at midnight, repeating .. ''Tis not this bone I mean to prick, But my love's heart I wish to prick; If he comes not, and speaks to-night, I'll prick, and prick, till it be light.' 1877 *N & Q* 5th ser. VII 86 [Ireland] The peasant girls seek on the hill sides .. the weather-bleached blade-bone of a sheep, which [is] kept till the moon is at the full, and stabbed with a knife at midnight, while the following conjuration is repeated .. 'It is not this bone I mean to stick, But my true love's heart I mean to prick, Wishing him neither rest nor sleep Until he comes with me to speak.' 1880 W. SIKES *British Goblins* 303. In Pembrokeshire a shoulder of mutton, with nine holes bored in the blade bone, is put under the pillow to dream on. At the same time the shoes of the experimenting damsel are placed at the foot of the bed in the shape of a letter T, and an incantation is said over them, in which it is trusted by the damsel that she may see her lover in his every-day clothes.

Cf. CANDLE, pricking: spell; SALT, burning: in spell.

BLEEDING, charm to staunch

1486 SPRENGER & KRAMER *Malleus Maleficarum* (tr. Summers, 181) There must be nothing in the words that is untrue; for if there is, the effect of them cannot be from God, who is not a witness to a lie. But some old women in their incantations use some such jingling doggerel as the following: 'Blessed Mary went a-walking Over Jordan river. Stephen met her, and fell a-talking, etc.' late 15th c. MS (*N & Q* 7th ser. IV 56) Ihu that was in Bethlem borne and baptizid was in floin iordun, and stynte the water up on the stoon. Stynte the blood of this man, & by yisuante forth the vertue of thin holy name + Ihu & of swete seynt Iohn. And sey this charme v tymes. With v p'r n'r [paternoster] in the worschyp of the v Woundes. 1584 SCOT *Discoverie of Witchcraft* XII XVIII. For a bloudie flux: 'In the bloud of Adam death was taken, In the bloud of Christ it was all too shaken, And by the same bloud I doo thee charge, That thou doo runne no longer at large.' 1610 MS book of physic (*Gents Mag.* 1835, pt. 2 31) To staunche bloude. 'There were three Maryes went over the floude; The one bid stande, the other stente bloude: Then bespake Mary that Jesus Christ bore, Defende gods forbod thou shouldeste bleede anye more.' 1692 *Athenian Mercury* VII 10 May. I know an Emperick in the Country who stops bleeding at the Nose, and stanches all manner of Haemoraghes .. only by saying over these following words, (either present with the Patient, or within some miles distance) In the Blood of Adam Sin was taken, In the Blood of Christ it was all to shaken. And by the same Blood I do thee charge, That the Blood of —— run no longer at large. 1804 MS charmer's book (LEATHER *Herefordshire* 73) Our blessed Lord and Saviour was baptised in the River Jordan; the waters was wild, the Child was mild the water was blest and still it stood sweet Jesus Christ in Charity stop this blood. 1851 *N & Q* 1st ser. III 259 [Launceston, Cornwall] Our Blessed Saviour was born in Bethlehem and baptized in the river Jordan. The waters were wild and rude, The child Jesus was meek, mild, and good. He put His foot into the waters, and the waters stopped, and so shall thy blood, in the Name, &c. 1854 *N & Q* 1st ser. X 221 [Orkneys] Three virgins came over Jordan's land, Each with a bloody knife in her hand; Stem, blood, stem—Letherly stand! Bloody nose (or mouth) in God's name mend. 1883 BURNE *Shropshire* 183. Here [is a charm] of which Sarah Mason's father is the owner .. 'Through the blood of Adam's sin Was taken the blood of Christ. By the same blood I do thee charge That the blood of A.B. run no more at large.' 1900 *Trans. Devon. Ass.* 92. The verse to stop nose-bleeding is the 6th verse of the 16th chapter of Ezekiel, which must be repeated by one of the opposite sex from the patient. 'And when I passed by thee, and saw thee polluted in thine own blood, I said unto thee when thou wast in thy blood, Live; yea, I said unto thee, when thou wast in thy blood, Live.' 1953 *Trans. Devon. Ass.* 219. The wise woman .. came—put her hand on the bleeding part, bleeding stopped. As sure as I sit here I saw it with my own eyes. She said something, I think it was a verse from the Bible, but I couldn't hear it.

BLIND MAN

1952 Girl, 11 [Lydney, Glos.] Lucky to see a blind man in the street. 1954 Girl, 10 [Alton, Hants.] Help a blind man brings you luck.

BLOOD, shedding: at funeral

1885 *Folklore* 281. In the Highlands of Scotland it used to be customary for the friends of a deceased person to fight at the funeral till blood was drawn (the drawing of blood was essential).

BLOOD, shedding first: brings success

1810 SCOTT *Lady of the Lake* v st. 13. Who spills the foremost foeman's life His party conquers in the strife. 1873 *N & Q* 4th ser. XI 10. To 'draw blood' is practised in .. fishing villages on the northeast coast of Scotland under the belief that success follows .. This act must be performed on New Year's Day, and the good fortune is his only who is the *first*

to shed blood .. There is quite a struggle which boat will reach the fishing ground first .. and thus make sure of one year's good fortune. 1886 *Folklore* 14. Two Crovie [Banff.] boats were, one spring not long ago, fishing in S. Uist. In the boat of one was caught a rat. The skipper of the other boat made the remark, 'This winna be a rich year fahtever [whatever], for we hinna gotten a beastie.' 1892 C. M. YONGE *Old Woman's Outlook* 176–7. It was considered 'lucky' if the child, just promoted to reaping, cut herself with the sickle. 1930 P. F. ANSON *East Coast of Scotland* 40–2. No Moray fisherman would ever be induced .. to go to sea at the beginning of the season, before blood had been shed .. At Burghead .. a fisherman should never go to sea after the New Year until he had shed blood. The first person who should draw blood in a quarrel was held to have fulfilled this obligation.

BLOSSOM unseasonable

1854 *N & Q* 1st ser. X 461 [Pembroke] Last year I was walking in the garden of a neighbouring farmer, aged seventy-one. We came up to an apple-tree, heavily laden with nearly ripe fruit; and perceived a sprig of very late bloom .. He told me, rather gravely, that in his boyhood this occurrence was invariably held to herald a death in the family. 1874 *N & Q* 5th ser. II 3 [Northants.] A bloom upon the apple when the apples are ripe Is a sure termination to somebody's life. 1892 C. M. YONGE *Old Woman's Outlook* December. Now and then a branch of pear tree, if it have been nipped in the summer, attempts to blossom, but it is considered 'unlucky'. 1910 *N & Q* 11th ser. II 199 [Worcester Park, Surrey] At Easter, 1909, I planted some apple trees, which flowered the same autumn. On a local gardener seeing them, he said that he never liked to see apple trees flower out of season, as it meant a death in the family before the year was out. 1962 Woman, *c.*50 [Petersfield, Hants.] I knew there was going to be a death in the family because there was some lovely blossom on one of the apple trees at the same time as the fruit. 1985 R. VICKERY *Unlucky Plants* 30–1 [Towcester, Northants.] My

Grandmother told me, when I was very young, that it was unlucky to take into the house or indeed pick a flower that was 'blooming out of season'. Quite often an odd sprig of cherry or plum will blossom in December . . because 'the devil has touched it' and he wants to bring his influence into the house.

BLUE protects

5th c. BC Numbers 15: 38. Speak unto the children of Israel, and bid them that they make them fringes in the borders of their garments throughout their generations, and that they put upon the fringe of the borders a ribband of blue. **c.1650** DR WREN Note in Browne's *Vulgar Errors* III XIII (1852, I 287) I have heard itt avowched by persons of great quality, contemporarye to the old Lord Burleigh . . that hee alwayes wore a blue ribbon (next his leg, garter-wise) studded (thick) with these shels of the grey snayles, to allaye the heate of the goute, and . . found manifest releef in itt. **1802** SCOTT *Minstrelsy of Scottish Border* II 214. Cattle which are suddenly seized with the cramp, or some similar disorders, are said to be elf-shot; and the approved cure is to chafe the parts affected with a blue bonnet, which, it may be readily believed, often restores the circulation. **c.1816** Wilkie MS (HENDERSON *Northern Counties* 1866, 12) Women . . of the Ale and Teviot have a singular custom of wearing round their necks blue woollen threads . . till they wean their children . . for the purpose of averting fevers. **1909** *The Hospital* 25 Dec. 351. Dr Lowry is medical inspector of schools at Wimbledon . . Thirty per cent of the children she inspected wear necklaces of blue beads or cheap coral as prophylactics against common colds and quinseys. **1925** E. LOVETT *Magic in London* 81 [E. London, 1914] An old lady who keeps a 'marine store' . . told me that she wore a necklace herself [of blue beads, for bronchitis] and that all her friends . . did the same . . They were worn beneath the . . collar of the dress . . and never taken off . . even at death. When a string breaks the beads are at once re-threaded . . and replaced round the neck. **1931** *N & Q* CLX 206. Blue beads are hung round children's necks,

generally, I think, under their clothes. At Long Itchington, Warwickshire, a woman told me her little girl wore them as a matter of course. **1979** P. MORTIMER *About Time* 39 [Wilts., 1899] A long series of illnesses, anaemia, rheumatic fever, abscesses, erythema . . The local doctor told her to wear a blue ribbon and live on onions.

Cf. BRIDE'S CLOTHES: 'something blue'.

BOAT, changing name of

1881 STEVENSON *Treasure Island* XI. He was hanged like a dog, and sun-dried like the rest, at Corso Castle. That was Roberts' men, that was, and comed of changing names to their ships—*Royal Fortune* and so on. Now, what a ship was christened, so let her stay, I say. **1932** C. IGGLESDEN *Those Superstitions* 118 [Folkestone, Kent] It were like this. Bill's first wife were named Bertha, and this 'ere boat were named *Bertha*—and quite right, too. But she died last year, and Bill married again—quite right too—but damned if 'e don't go and re-christen the boat *Beatrice*, 'cause that were the name of 'is fresh wife. It's all wrong—agin Providence—for ain't it true that you must never rename a boat or a ship? 'E tempted Providence, and e's boat's smashed. **1961** C. HOLE *Superstitions* 245. Sailors believe that it is unlucky to alter the name of a ship. Many tales are told of vessels which were lost after such a change. HMS *Victoria*, which sank in a tragic accident in 1893, was one of these; so was HMS *Cobra*. **1980** Sea captain's wife, 59 [South Shields, Co. Durham] When we buy a boat, we never change her name— it's very unlucky.

BOAT, new: delivery postponed

1886 *Folklore* II. It is accounted unlucky to go for a new boat, and come back without her. J. Watt, of Crovie [Banff.], went . . for a new boat. She was not finished, and he had to return empty-handed. He went for her some time after. [At first all went well but] when off Gamrie Mohr, a high headland, a gust of wind came down and sank the boat. One man was drowned.

BOAT, new: naming before launching

1965 P. F. ANSON *Fisher Folk-Lore* 94.

On the North East Coast of Scotland ..
there was the belief that it was unlucky
to name her [new boat] until she was
afloat.

Cf. NAMING baby before christening;
NAMING COWS.

BOAT, right side of

1887 'SPERANZA' WILDE *Superstitions of
Ireland* II 119 [Western Islands] Fishermen when going to sea must always
enter the boat by the right side, no
matter how inconvenient.

BOAT'S CREW, changing

1790 GROSE *Provincial Glossary* Superstitions 55. The fishermen every year
change their companions, for luck's
sake. 1880 W. JONES *Credulities* 117. At
Redcar, in Yorkshire, it was customary
every year to change a boat's crew for
'luck's sake'.

BOAT'S CREW: members related

1888 *N & Q* 7th ser. V 405–6. I have
just heard from a sailor friend .. that it
is unlucky for two relatives to sail together (as seamen) in the same vessel,
as one of them will certainly be drowned.
It is unnecessary to add that he was able
to give ample proof that such was the
case, and some of the coincidences he
mentioned were sufficiently startling to
confirm a superstitious person in the
belief.

BODY: locating in water

1586 T. HILL *Natural Conclusions* D3. To
finde a person drowned .. Take a white
loafe, and cast the same into the water,
neer ye suspected place, and it wil forthwith goe directly ouer the dead body,
and there abide. 1767 *Gents Mag.* 189
[Newbury, Berks.] After diligent search
had been made in the river .. a two-
penny loaf, with a quantity of quicksilver
put into it, was set floating from the
place where the child, it was supposed,
had fallen in, which steered its course
down the river upwards of half a mile
.. when the body happening to lay on
the contrary side of the river, the loaf
suddenly tacked about .. and gradually
sank near the child. 1866 HENDERSON
Northern Counties 43–4. A loaf weighted
with quicksilver, if allowed to float on

the water, is said to swim towards and
stand over .. the body .. When a boy,
I have seen persons endeavouring to
discover the corpses of the drowned in
this manner in the River Wear .. and ten
years ago, the friends of one Christopher
Lumley sought for his body .. by the aid
of a loaf of bread with a lighted candle
in it. 1885 *Folklore* 281 [Ayr.] About
drowning it is said that in a river or
pond a light is seen pointing out the
body. 1893 *Folklore* 357 [Co. Cork] A
drowned body is searched for by floating
a bundle of straws on the surface of the
water; it is supposed to stop and quiver
over the body. Ibid. 258 [Norfolk] A
middle-aged woman had been missing
.. Her friends .. alarmed about her ..
asked that the river .. be dragged. Instead .. recourse was had to a very
curious procedure .. The Navigation
Superintendent .. rowed down the river
accompanied by a policeman, who was
mildly and slowly beating a big drum.
It was stated that, if they came to any
part [where] there might be a dead body,
a difference in the sound of the drum
would be distinctly noticed. The experiment .. was a failure, and, later on,
it was reported that a person answering
to the description of the missing woman
was at Elvedon. This proved to be correct
.. to the great relief of her friends. 1925
Yorkshire Observer 5 May 14 [Amesbury,
Wilts.] The missing nursemaid .. was
last seen on the bridge over the Avon ..
and one of the theories .. is that she
may have got into the river .. It was
decided to carry out an experiment ..
The method .. an old custom .. had
been used with success at Bristol some
years ago .. Mercury was placed in a
loaf of bread .. attached to a long line.
The idea is that the bread, floating over
.. a body, would hover there .. Heavy
rains apparently interfered with the experiment, for no result was obtained.
1972 Woman, 71 ['The Potteries',
Staffs.] They used to try to locate a
drowned person by throwing a brown
loaf into the water with mercury inside
it. It always came to rest over the body.

BOILING continues off fire

1507 *Gospelles of Dystaues* pt. 2 IX. Whan
pesen dothe boyle in a pot after it is

taken of y[e] fyre, knowe for a trouthe that in that same house is no wytches. **1953** Girl, 15 [Ipswich, Suffolk] If your soup continues to boil after it has been drawn back from the fire, the cook will live to a good old age.

BOILING WATER spills over

1755 *Connoisseur* 13 Mar. I heard one of my cousins tell the cook-maid that she boiled away all her sweethearts, because she had let her dish-water boil over. **1923** [Wellington, Som.] If you let boiling water fall on the carpet it is a sign of a quarrel.

BONE: side-bone of fowl

1866 HENDERSON *Northern Counties* 21. It is very important that the bride should receive the little bone called 'hug ma close' (*anglice* 'sidesman', or side-bone), for she who gets it on her wedding-day is sure to be happy in her husband.

BONES, burning

1507 *Gospelles of Dystaues* pt. 2 XIII. He that dothe not caste, or suffreth not to caste bones in the fyre shall not haue the tooth ache for y[e] honour of saynt Laurens. *c.*1840 *Mother Bunch's Golden Fortune-Teller* 22. Burning beef bones— brings sorrow through poverty; and to cast those of pork or veal into the fire, inflicts pains in the bones of the person so improvident. **1883** BURNE *Shropshire* 278. If you burn bones, you will be burnt yourself. **1885** *Folklore* 183 [Aberdeen.] Fisher-folks will on no account burn the bones of the fish they use as food and the shells of the mussels employed for bait. Hence the rhyme . . 'Roast me weel, or boil me weel, Bit dinna burn ma behns, An ye'll get plenty o' fish Aboot yir fire-stehns.' **1923** [Bridgwater, Som.] It is very unlucky to burn bones. **1960** Man, 45 [Wrecclesham, Surrey] Mother's grandmother used to tell her not to put bones on the fire as otherwise 'you'll always have your bones ache.' **1965** P. F. ANSON *Fisher Folk-Lore* 12. Fisher taboos and superstitions [from the NE coast of Scotland] have been absorbed into my system during the past forty-five years. Even today at the age of seventy-five nothing would induce me to throw fish bones on the fire.

BONES, sleeping on

1864 R. CHAMBERS *Book of Days* II 39 [Suffolk] It is not good for children to sleep upon bones—that is, upon the lap. **1899** *Newcastle Weekly Chronicle* 4 Feb. 7 [Jesmond] To allow children to sleep on bones, i.e. the knee . . is unlucky.

BOOK: opening at random

c. AD **397** ST AUGUSTINE OF HIPPO *Confessions* IV v (tr. Pusey, 54) When a man by hap-hazard opens the pages of some poet, who sang and thought of something wholly different, a verse sometimes fell out, wonderfully agreeable to the present business. **1584** SCOT *Discoverie of Witchcraft* XI x. Lots comprised in verses, concerning the lucke ensuing, either of Virgil, Homer, or anie other, wherein fortune is gathered by the sudden turning unto them. **1595** SIDNEY *Apologie for Poetrie* (1907, 5–6) Among the Romans a Poet was called *Vates*, which is as much as a Diuiner, Fore-seer, or Prophet . . And so farre were they carried into the admiration thereof, that they thought in the chaunceable hitting vppon any such verses great fore-tokens of their following fortunes were placed. Whereupon grew the worde of *Sortes Virgilianae*, when, by suddaine opening *Virgil's* booke, they lighted vpon any verse of hys making: whereof the histories of the Emperors are full, as of *Albinus*, the Gouernour of our Iland, who in his childehood mette with this verse, *Arma amens capio nec sat rationis in armis* [I madly take up arms, nor have I enough reason to take up arms] and in his age performed it. **1688** AUBREY *Remaines* (1881, 90) Sortes Biblicae . . These divinations are performed after this manner, viz.: the Party that has an earnest desire to be resolved in such an Event takes a pinne; an thrusts it between the leaves of one of y[e] above said bookes [Homer, Virgil, the Bible] and choose w[ch] of the pages she or he will take, and then open the booke and begin to read at the beginning of y[t] period. The booke at the prickinge is held in another's hand. **1783** MRS THRALE *Diary* 28 Mar. (ed. Balderston, I 560) I walked into Robson's Shop the other Day, and seeing a very fine Virgil was tempted to open it with something of Superstitious Intention by way of trying the *Sortes Virgilianae*. **1807** BLAKE *Memoranda* South Molton Street. Sunday, Aug. 1. My Wife was told by a Spirit to look for her fortune by opening by chance a book which she had in her hand; it was Bysshe's Art of Poetry. **1821** *Queen Bee* 468. Mr Lackington, the great bookseller, when young, was locked up .. to prevent his attendance at a Methodist meeting in Taunton .. in a fit of superstition, he opened the Bible for directions what to do. The .. first words he hit upon were .. 'He shall give his angels charge concerning thee, and in their hands they shall bear thee up' .. 'This,' says he, 'was quite enough for me .. and out of the window I leaped.' **1830** FORBY *East Anglia* 400. On the morning of New Year's-day before breakfast .. the bible is laid on the table unopened, and the parties who wish to consult it are then to open it in succession. They .. must open it at random .. and place [their] finger on any chapter .. It is believed that .. the ensuing year will in some way or other be described and foreshewn by the contents of the chapter. **1861** *N & Q* 2nd ser. XII 303 [Oxon.] She .. stared wildly at me, and exclaimed .. 'New Year's Day! and I have never dipped' .. I gathered from her that it was customary to dip into the Bible before twelve o'clock on New Year's Day, and the first verse that meets the eye indicates the good or bad fortune of the inquirer through the ensuing year. **1872** KILVERT *Diary* 10 Sept. When I opened the Testament this morning, the first passage my eye fell on was this, 'And falling into a place where two seas met they ran the ship aground .. ' The next passage .. was this, 'There came down a great storm of wind upon the lake .. ' When my Mother heard of this ominous conjunction she doubted whether we had better go [in a steam boat down the channel]. **1930** T. F. POWYS *Kindness in a Corner* IX. The Holy Bible .. Mr Dottery took the book into his hands and opened it at random, hoping to find counsel there. **1933** D. L. MOORE *E. Nesbit* IX [Laurence Housman agrees to take part in a tableau.] I couldn't decide myself, so I asked the Holy Bible to come and help me. I shut

my eyes and let my fingers go at random. This, when I looked, is what I read. 'He made a pit, and digged it, and is fallen into the ditch which he made' .. so now I'm in for it.

BOOTS on shoulder

1923 P. S. JEFFREY *Whitby Lore* 137 [Staithes, Yorks., 1885] If a fisher sends his son to fetch his sea-boots, the bearer must be careful to carry them under his arm. Should he inadvertently place them on his shoulder, his father will inevitably refuse to put out to sea that day.

Cf. SPADE etc.: on shoulder in house.

BOOTS toppled over

1910 *Folklore* 226 [Yorks.] A Featherstone miner who finds his boots toppled over in the morning will not work in the pit that day for fear of disaster.

BORROWING AND LENDING

1486 SPRENGER & KRAMER *Malleus Maleficarum* (tr. Summers, 189–90) When witches wish to deprive a cow of milk they .. beg a little of the milk or butter which comes from that cow, so that they may .. bewitch the cow; therefore women should take care, when they are asked by persons suspected of this crime, not to give away the least thing to them .. Women who, when they have been turning a churn .. to no purpose, and if they suspect .. some witch, procure .. butter from that witch. Then they make that butter into three pieces and throw them into the churn, invoking the Holy Trinity .. so all witchcraft is put to flight .. The butter must be borrowed from the suspected witch. **1881** W. GREGOR *North-East of Scotland* 200. When a boat was leaving home for another fishing station, as during the herring season, some had the habit of borrowing an article of trifling value from a neighbour, but with the intention of not returning it. The luck of the fishing went along with the article; those who were aware of the fact refused to lend. **1898** *Aberdeen Weekly Free Press* 29 Oct. 3. It was believed in certain fishing villages that tackle stolen from a friend or neighbour brought better luck than that bought with money. **1900** S.

HEWETT *Nummits* 58 [Devon] Fishermen
.. would never .. lend anything from
one boat to another. 1909 M. TREVELYAN
Folk-Lore of Wales 210. If a thing is
bewitched, burn it, and immediately
afterwards the witch will come to borrow something of you. If you give what
she asks, she will go free; if you refuse
it, she will burn, and a mark will be on
her body the next day. 1910 T. SHARPER
KNOWLSON *Superstitions* 233. He who
lends money at play [card play] will
lose; he who borrows money at play
will win.

Cf. BRIDE'S CLOTHES: 'something borrowed'; FIRE not allowed out of house.

BOWL overturned

1869 *N & Q* 4th ser. IV 131 [Scar-
borough, Yorks.] No sailor will set out
on a voyage if he finds his earthenware
basin turned upside down in the morning when he is about to have breakfast.
The boys sometimes turn their basins
upside down purposely when they wish
to have a day's play. 1916 *N & Q* 12th
ser. I 154. Ashore [the sailors] would be
careful to observe all signs of coming
ill-luck. An overturned bowl—how
could anything .. foreshadow more
plainly an upturned boat?

Cf. BUCKET upturned.

BRAMBLE ARCH cures

*c.*1040 MS Harl. 55 (COCKAYNE *Leechdoms* II 291–3) Against dysentery, a
bramble of which both ends are in the
earth; take the newer root, delve it up,
cut up nine chips into the left hand, and
sing three times the Miserere .. then
take mugwort and everlasting, boil ..
the worts and the chips, in milk .. then
let the man sip at night fasting a good
dish full. 1607 MARKHAM *Cavelarice*
VII 80. If your horse be shrew-runne
[paralysed by a shrew], you shall looke
for a briere which growes at both endes,
and draw your horse thorow it and he
will be well. 1627 DRAYTON *Nimphidia*
ll. 401–4. Thrice under a Bryer doth
creepe, Which at both ends was rooted
deepe .. Her Magicke much avayling.
1686–7 AUBREY *Remaines* (1881, 187)
For ye Chin-cough. Mdm. to creep under
a Bramble that rootes again in the
ground at the other end. 1831 HONE

Year Book 29 Feb. There are dames in
the country who, to cure the whooping
cough, pass the afflicted child three times
before breakfast under a blackberry
bush, both ends of which grow into the
ground. 1850 KINGSLEY *Alton Locke* XXI.
When my vather's cows was shrew-
struck, she made un be draed under a
brimble as growed together at the both
ends. *c.*1860 *Practical Housewife* 25. A
mother will say, with great self-esteem
in her look and tone, 'I have taken out
my child fasting for nine mornings, and
put him through a bramble three times
every morning; but his cough isn't no
better.' 1875 C. H. POOLE *Stafford* 37.
Find a briar growing in the ground both
ends, pass the child under and over it
nine times, for three mornings, before
sunrise, repeating: 'Under the briar, and
over the briar, I wish to leave the chin-
cough here.' The briar must be cut, and
made into the form of a cross, and worn
on the breast. 1879 JEFFERIES *Wild Life
in a Southern County* x. There is an old
superstition about these arches of brier
hung out along the hedgerow: magical
cures of whooping-cough and some
other diseases of childhood can, it is
believed, be effected by passing the child
at sunrise under the brier facing the
rising sun. 1883 W. G. BLACK *Folk-
Medicine* 70. To crawl under a bramble
which has formed a second root .. is
said to cure rheumatism, boils [etc.] The
arch must be complete. If it is a child
suffering from whooping-cough, who is
thus symbolically to be re-born, he is
passed seven times from one side to the
other, while the operators repeat .. 'In
bramble, out cough, Here I leave the
whooping-cough.' 1912 LEATHER *Herefordshire* 82. They say the Lord's Prayer,
while passing the patient nine times
under the briar arch; he must be eating
bread and butter meanwhile. On returning, the bread and butter must be given
to some bird or other creature ('not a
Christian'); the bird will die, and the
cough will be cured. 1937 *Folklore* 53–
4 [Gwent] In the forest a child was cured
of whooping cough by making him pass
nine times under the arch formed by a
long bramble branch which had thrown
itself on to the roadside and rooted there.

Cf. GREENERY, circle of: cures.

BREAD, burning

1889 *Folklore* 196 [N. Scotland] Old people looked with much reverence on 'bread', as well as meal . . It was believed that any one guilty of casting meal or bread into the fire, or in any way destroying either the one or the other, would assuredly sooner or later come to want. 1901 *N & Q* 9th ser. VIII 383 [Worksop, Notts.] Seldom heard in this time of the big, cheap loaf . . 'If you throw crumbs in the fire you are feeding the devil.' 1923 [Trowbridge, Wilts.] To throw crusts of bread on the fire brings ill luck. 1982 Woman, 20 [Cleveland, Yorks.] It is thought to be unlucky to burn bread and a friend from Scarborough maintains that this is because to do so is to feed the devil.

BREAD cures and protects

1499 'Cardinal Morton's Register' (R. W. SETON-WATSON *Tudor Studies*, 72) [advice from a witch living near Bury St Edmunds, Suffolk] If you are willing to give your horse holy bread (*panem benedictum*) and holy water, your horse would not be stolen. 1537 R. WHITFORDE *Werke for Housholders* C. The charmer . . taketh here a pece of whyte brede, and sayth ouer that breade nothynge: but onely the Pater noster, and maketh a crosse vpon the breade . . than doth he nothynge els but ley that pece of breade vnto the toth that aketh, or vnto any other sore . . and so is the persone healed. 1587 GIFFORD *Subtill Practises of Devilles* G2ᵛ. They had holy bread . . that he [the Devil] could rest no where. 1648 HERRICK *Hesperides* 336 'Charmes'. Bring the holy crust of Bread, Lay it underneath the head; 'Tis a certain Charm to keep Hags away, while Children sleep. Ibid. 383 'Another'. In your Pocket for a trust, Carrie nothing but a Crust: For that holy piece of Bread, Charmes the danger, and the dread. 1691 R. KIRK *Secret Commonwealth* (1815, 6) [Scottish-Irish.] Tramontains to this Day put Bread . . in Womens Bed when travelling [in labour], to save them [mother and baby] from being stollen. 1882 *Folk-Lore Record* 83 [Co. Wexford] If an infant is carried out after dark a piece of bread is wrapped in its bib or dress, and this protects it from any witchcraft or evil. 1887 'SPERANZA' WILDE *Superstitions of Ireland* II 117. When a servant leaves her place, if her mistress gives her a piece of bread let her put by some of it carefully, for as long as she has it good luck will follow her. 1911 *Folklore* 58 [Co. Clare] In Kilnaboy . . meal used to be tied up in a corner of an infant's clothes for luck when it was taken to baptism.

BREAD, cutting or pricking

1790 GROSE *Provincial Glossary* Superstitions 45 [Wilts.] If a bread cake be taken out of the oven, and cut, all the rest of that batch will be heavy. 1876 *N & Q* 5th ser. VI 397 [Weardale, Co. Durham] Should the good wife cut the first cake from the oven, all the rest will be heavy; the first cake must be broken. 1883 BURNE *Shropshire* 278. I have been accustomed to see the cross-mark on bread made with a *fork*, but at Pulverbatch and Ruyton old-fashioned people say it must be done with a skewer, for 'She that pricks bread with fork or knife Will never be happy, maid or wife.' 1902 *N & Q* 9th ser. IX 514 [Derbys.] When quite a child, I was told that the reason why it was more proper to break bread rather than cut or bite it was because bread was broken by Christ on the occasion of the Last Supper. 1912 LEATHER *Herefordshire* 88. Bread must not be cut with a knife while the next baking is in the oven, though it may be broken. No exact reason is given, it is 'unlucky'.

Cf. KNIFE, toasting on.

BREAD, hole in

1909 *N & Q* 10th ser. XII 155 [Yorks./ Lincs.] A hollow in a loaf is called a grave, and is held to signify death. Ibid. In Pembrokeshire . . they say [a hollow loaf] foretells a birth. More than that, they say, 'Mrs *Baker* is going to have a child.' 1926 *Folklore* 297 [Colwall, Herefords.] If the bread rises too much, so that the loaf has big holes in it, it is a sign that the woman who baked it is going to have a baby. 1932 WOMEN'S INSTITUTE *Worcestershire Book* 37 [Lenches] A big hole in a loaf of bread is regarded as the sign of a grave. 1955 Girl, 14 [Swansea, Glam.] My grandmother says that if, when you are cutting bread, you come upon a hole in the loaf, that is a grave for someone. **1966** [Liss, Hants.] Cottage loaves have a hole in the top, which used to be made by the baker's elbow. Mr Nun Smith, the baker, says that if the hole was still deep when the loaf came out of the oven they reckoned the baker's wife was in the family way.

BREAD, kneading

1912 LEATHER *Herefordshire* 88. It is said that if a maid kneading up bread rub her 'doughy' hand over a boy's face, he will never have any whiskers.

BREAD: loaf, cake, etc. breaks

1866 HENDERSON *Northern Counties* 89. If a loaf parts in the hand while you are cutting it, it bodes dissension in the family: you part man and wife. **1879** *Times* 23 Jan. 6 [Priorslee, Cheshire] During the day his wife had been baking, and after she had gone out he went to take the bread out of the oven. There he found 'one of the loaves cracked right across', and he immediately knew that something had happened to his wife. **1893** *Dorset Field Club* 186. If a cake on being cut breaks in two [sign of death]. **1922** JOYCE *Ulysses* (1960, 911) It brings a parting and the last plumpudding too split in 2 halves. **1923** [Trowbridge, Wilts.] The breaking of a Christmas pudding on taking up or turning out of its basin is a very evil omen, and indicates the death of one of the heads of the household.

BREAD: loaf upside-down

1830 FORBY *East Anglia* 414. If you overturn a loaf of bread in the oven, you will have a death in the house. **1861** C. C. ROBINSON *Dialect of Leeds* 296. When a loaf is laid the wrong side up, it is a saying that 'the devil's in the house'. **1866** HENDERSON *Northern Counties* 89. Along the coast, they say, that for every loaf so turned [upside down] a ship will be wrecked. **1887** *Folk-Lore Record* 190 [Cornwall] Sailors regard many things as bad omens, such as 'a loaf of bread turned upside-down on a table'. **1890** *N & Q* 7th ser. IX 486 [Fareham, Hants.] If you turn a loaf of bread the wrong way, you will turn someone out of the house. **1912** *Folklore* 354. 'Don't turn the loaf upside down, or you'll drown the sailors,' was told me by a Gravesender born at Devonport. **1956** Woman, *c.*65 [Southsea, Hants.] My mother used to say it is very unlucky to put a loaf upside down on the table.

BREAD: loaves joined

1883 BURNE *Shropshire* 276. If four loaves adhere together on being taken out of the oven, it is a sign of a wedding; if five, of a funeral. **1923** [Martock, Som.] If the baker has brought two loaves joined together, 'tis to be hoped Mother won't have twins this time.

BREAD: upper crust

*c.*1460 J. RUSSELL *Book of Nurture* 342. Kutt þe vpper crust [of the loaf] for youre souerayne. **1861** *N & Q* 2nd ser. XII 491. Cut the topside of the loaf before you cut the bottom; you will rise in the world. **1889** *Folklore* 198 [N. Scotland] To break off 'the croon (crown, i.e. top) o' the quarter', when first beginning to eat bread, was set down as a breach of good manners. One must begin with the broad end.

BREAD AND BUTTER on plate

1923 [Bridgwater, Som.] If bread and butter and cake are taken on your plate together it's a sign of matrimony. **1954** Girl, 15 [Tunstall, Staffs.] If a woman eating bread and butter unthinkingly takes a second piece before she has finished the first it means that she is going to get married.

Cf. LAST FOOD/DRINK: bread etc. on plate.

BRIDE cries on wedding day

1923 [Bridgwater, Som.] It is very unlucky for the bride to cry on her wedding day.

BRIDE crosses running water

1898 BLAKEBOROUGH *Yorkshire Customs* 102–3. Had they [the bridal party] to pass over a stream, it was usual for both to throw something over their shoulder into the stream, saying as they did so, 'Bad luck cleave to you,' being very careful not to set eyes on the object again.

BRIDE feeds cat

1909 M. TREVELYAN *Folk-Lore of Wales* 80. Girls are told to feed the cats well, so that the sun may shine on their wedding-day. **1923** [Somerset] A bride should feed the cat herself, before she goes to church, to bring her happiness in wedded life.

BRIDE lifted over threshold

ante **50** BC CATULLUS *Poems* (tr. Michie, 111) Step high, then, for good luck . . Over the new threshold. **1546** P. VERGIL *De Rerum Inventoribus* I iv (tr. Langley) In Rome . . neither might the bride step ouer the thresholde, but must be borne ouer, to declare that she loseth her Uirginitie vnwillyngly. **1815** SCOTT *Guy Mannering* Note 5. The threshold of a habitation was in some sort a sacred limit, and the subject of much superstition. A bride, even to this day, is always lifted over it, a rule derived apparently from the Romans. **1834** DALYELL *Darker Superstitions of Scotland* 292. This ceremony of carrying the bride over the threshold . . seems to involve that superstition dreading the abstraction of some essential virtue by contact with the earth. **1879** J. NAPIER *West of Scotland* 51. In some parts of Scotland, at the beginning of the century, the young wife was lifted over the threshold, or first step of the door, lest any witchcraft . . should be cast upon her. **1954** Girl, 14 [Stoke-on-Trent, Staffs.] A bride should be carried over the steps of her new home. **1980** *Mirror* 8 May 24. I am to be married in August but my boyfriend is refusing to conform to tradition unless I can discover how the custom of carrying the bride over the threshold originated.

Cf. PETTING STONE, bride steps or leaps over; THRESHOLD.

BRIDE married after sunset

*c.*1816 Wilkie MS (HENDERSON *Northern Counties* 1866, 21) A wedding after sunset entails on the bride a joyless life, the loss of children, or an early grave.

Cf. SUN, rising and declining.

BRIDE not to be seen by bridegroom

1819 SCOTT *Montrose* XXIII. It had been settled that, according to the custom of the country, the bride and bridegroom should not again meet until they were before the altar. **1879** J. NAPIER *West of Scotland* 46–7. Sixty years ago when a young woman became a bride, she in a great measure secluded herself from society, and . . on no account would she show herself at church until after her marriage, as that was considered very unlucky. **1896** *N & Q* 8th ser. IX 5. A short time since I was at a wedding in Lincolnshire. On the important morning the bridegroom had an interview with his mother-in-law to be in the garden of her house, it not being considered right that he should come indoors until after the marriage ceremony. **1929** H. V. MORTON *In Search of Scotland* VI. 'It's an awfu' anxious business,' explains the head porter. 'They mustna see each ither until they meet at the wedding. It's awfu' bad luck.' **1952** Girl, 14 [Aberdeen] If the bridegroom sees his bride on the morning of the wedding it means bad luck. **1982** Woman, *c.*50 [Stockton-on-Tees, Co. Durham] Prospective groom must leave the prospective bride before 12 o'clock on the eve of the wedding and he mustn't see her any more before they're at the altar; and then he mustn't look back over his shoulder to watch her coming up the aisle. **1983** Girl, 14 [Maldon, Essex] If the groom sees the bride before the wedding it is unlucky.

BRIDE, sun shines on

1601 SHAKESPEARE *Twelfe Night* IV iii. Plight me the full assurance of your faith . . & heavens so shine, That they may fairely note this acte of mine. **1648** HERRICK *Hesperides* 129 'Nuptiall Song' st. 5. While that others doe divine; Blest is the Bride, on whom the Sun doth shine. **1678** RAY *Proverbs* 348. Happy is the bride the Sun shines on, and the corse the Rain rains on. **1777** BRAND *Antiquities* 53. Happy (says the old Proverb) is the Bride the Sun shines on, and the Corpse the Rain rains on. **1818** *Edinburgh Magazine* Nov. 412 [Angus] I have repeatedly heard . . 'Rain to the corpse Carried to its long hame. A bonnie blue sky To welcome the bride, As she gangs to the kirk, Wi' the sun on her side.' **1847** R. CHAMBERS *Popular Rhymes of Scotland* 123. If the day be foul That the bride gangs hame, Alack and alace But she lived her lane! If the day be fair That the bride gangs hame, Baith pleasure and peace Afore her are gane! **1873** KILVERT *Diary* 1 Jan. The four old bells rang out merrily, and 'Blessed is the bride whom the sun shines on.' 'I have had a great deal of sunshine today,' she said. 'I hope it is a good omen,' I said. 'I hope so,' she said, sweetly and seriously. **1883** BURNE *Shropshire* 296. Bridal and burial are linked together in the sweet old adage so often in the mouths of the poor: 'Happy is the bride that the sun shines on, And happy is the corpse that the rain rains upon.' **1911** J. C. DAVIES *Welsh Folk-Lore* 36. It is considered unlucky to marry on a wet day. **1923** [Castle Cary, Som.] If it rains when a girl is going to get married, she will have so many whops as she has drops. **1965** S. TURNER *Honestly, the Country!* 126. Happy the bride the sun shines on. **1987** Woman, *c*.40 [Midhurst, Sussex] Well, I always hope the sun will shine for a bride—but just so that she has a nice day.

Cf. CORPSE, rain rains on.

BRIDE: threshold washed

1849 *Athenaeum* 8 Sept. 911 [Lincs.] When a bride leaves the house to be married they wash the flags at the entrance of the house—and the first single lady who enters afterwards will be the next married. **1861** *N & Q* 2nd ser. XII 490 [Yorks.] After the happy couple had driven away .. the cook came out with a kettle of hot water, which she poured on the stone in front of the house door, as an auspice that there would soon be another wedding from the same house. It is called keeping the threshold warm for another bride. **1870** *N & Q* 4th ser. V 172. At a wedding the other day in Richmondshire—the wedding of the squire's daughter—hot water was poured over the door-steps of the hall-door as the bride and bridegroom drove away. **1895** S. O. ADDY *Household Tales* 121. In Derbyshire it is customary to pour a kettleful of boiling water over the

doorstep just as the bride leaves the house on her way to church. It is said that before the water dries up another wedding will be arranged in the house. In some cases the water is poured over the doorstep 'after the bride and groom have entered', it being said that the next girl who enters will become a bride, provided that her dress is wetted. This generally happens to be the first bridesmaid. **1898** BLAKEBOROUGH *Yorkshire Customs* 103. Before the bride and bridegroom left for their own home, it was common for a kettleful of boiling water to be poured on the front step, upon which the bride stepped, being careful to wet both her shoes. The due observance of this custom ensured another happy marriage being arranged amongst the company there assembled. **1901** P. H. DITCHFIELD *Old English Customs* 197. At Holderness the young folks pour hot water on the door-step after a wedding, in order that other marriages might flow. **1909** *Folklore* 222. After a wedding at Honor Oak, Surrey, in 1905, boiling water was poured over the doorstep of the bridegroom's house, 'to warm the threshold for the next wedding'. This was done by the bridegroom's mother, who was born in Camberwell. **1923** [Somerset] When a bride and bridegroom leave the house for their honeymoon, if the bridesmaids immediately pour a kettle of hot water over the front doorstep, there will be another wedding in the company within a year.

Cf. CORPSE defiles: threshold washed.

BRIDE'S BOUQUET

1923 [Martock, Som.] Catch sprigs from bride's bouquet and marry first. **1963** M. LAWRENCE *Guide to Wedding Etiquette* 143. The custom of the bride turning as she leaves the reception and throwing back her bouquet—preferably from a turn in the staircase—is a rather charming American tradition that is not very widely adopted here as yet .. If, however, her going is noticed, or she feels she would like to adopt the idea of throwing back her bouquet (with the superstition that the girl who catches it will be the next bride) there is no reason why she shouldn't do so. **1983** Girl, 14 [Maldon, Essex] When the bride at the wedding throws her bouquet the one who catches it is the next one to marry.

BRIDE'S CLOTHES: garter

1648 HERRICK *Hesperides* 130 'Nuptiall Song' st. 8. Let the Young-men and the Bride-maids share Your Garters. **1698** MISSON *Voyageur en Angleterre* (1719, 352) When Bed-time is come, the Bride-men pull off the Bride's Garters, which she had before unty'd, that they might hang down, and so prevent a curious Hand coming too near her Knee. This done, and the Garters being fasten'd to the Hats of the Gallants, the Bride-maids carry the Bride into the Bride-chamber, where they undress her, and lay her in Bed. **1760** *Hymen* 173. A glass goes round before they go to bed, and, when the hour is come, the bridemen take off the bride's garters, which she had before untied for that purpose, and put them to their hats. *c.*1820 (BLAKEBOROUGH *Yorkshire Customs* 100–1) Lady ——, stepping from her bridal coach, inquired who had won the race .. Her ladyship stepped half over the threshold .. raised her silken gown [and] turning to the young fellow [said] 'Take it off, Tom, and give it to your sweetheart, and may it bring luck to both of you.' *c.*1828 Calvert MS, Pickering, Yorks. (G. HOME *Evolution of an English Town* 218–20). The youths of the company would race from the church porch to the bride's house, and the first who arrived claimed the right of removing the garter from her left leg .. He would afterwards tie it round his own sweetheart's leg as a love charm against unfaithfulness. **1849** BRAND *Antiquities* II 127–9. **1987** Woman, 58 [Northampton] The bride was posing for her photograph outside the church, and the younger onlookers started shouting 'Hitch it up a bit—let's see the garter.'

Cf. GARTER comes untied.

BRIDE'S CLOTHES: shoe, gold coin in

1961 *Malton Gazette* 10 Feb. 8 [The bridegroom's father] told me that Miss King asked for a sovereign as there were none in her family. 'I took it with me .. and gave it to her, but she only put it inside her shoe. I told her it should be placed inside the stocking, so she went

and changed it.' **1978** *English Dance & Song* 105 [Darlington, Co. Durham] When she got married she 'walked on gold' to ensure prosperity, by taping a half sovereign to the instep of her shoe.

Cf. SILVER protects: in shoe.

BRIDE'S CLOTHES: shoe, throwing

1901 P. H. DITCHFIELD *Old English Customs* 194. In Kent the shoe of the bride is thrown by the principal bridesmaid, and the others run after it. It is supposed that she who gets it will be married first. It is then thrown amongst the men, and he who is hit will be first wedded.

BRIDE'S CLOTHES: 'something blue'

*c.*1390 CHAUCER Squire's Tale ll. 643–5. By hire beddes heed she made a mewe, And covered it with veluettes blewe, In signe of trouthe that is in wommen sene. **1601** JONSON *Cynthia's Revels* v ii. Steal into his hat the colour, whose blueness doth expresse truenesse. **1609** N. FIELD *Woman Is a Weathercock* I i. Well, since I'm distain'd, off garters blew, Which signifies Sir Abram's love was true. **1842** R. CHAMBERS *Popular Rhymes of Scotland* 35. Her seniors, all .. recommended blue as the lucky colour [for her wedding dress]. **1988** [St Albans, Herts.] 'This is my daughter's wedding dress,' she said, and added with a little giggle, 'And the blue garter of course.'

Also see BRIDE'S CLOTHES: 'Something old, something new' rhyme.

BRIDE'S CLOTHES: 'something borrowed'

1866 HENDERSON *Northern Counties* 35. The bride .. should wear something borrowed—for what reason I am not informed. **1883** BURNE *Shropshire* 289. A peasant bride about to dress for her wedding, first strips herself of every article of clothing, and begins absolutely *de novo* to attire herself in new and unwashed garments, rejecting even pins that have ever been used before. But, nevertheless, it is widely accounted 'lucky' to wear something on the wedding day which has already been worn by a happy bride at her wedding, and ladies consider it rather a compliment to be asked to lend their wedding-veils to their friends for this purpose. **1905** *Folklore* 66 [Mon.] The bride should always borrow something, a veil or lace, etc., to be married in. **1981** *The Lady* 23 July 175. Princess Elizabeth's . . veil . . was worn with a diamond tiara lent to her by her mother, then Queen Elizabeth. As the Lady Elizabeth Bowes-Lyon, she had borrowed for her wedding in 1923 to the Duke of York, the veil of old point de Flandres lace that was Queen Mary's, thus following closely the old adage of 'something borrowed'.

Cf. BORROWING AND LENDING.

BRIDE'S CLOTHES: 'something old'

1917 *Folklore* 314 [Clifton, Bristol] The night before the wedding, the bride was dressed by the bridesmaids in her very oldest night attire. This is known to have been done at the wedding of a doctor's daughter, *c.*1872. **1948** E. & M. A. RADFORD *Superstitions* 46. Lucky is the bride who marries in old shoes.

Cf. BABY protected by 'something old'.

BRIDE'S CLOTHES: 'Something old, something new' rhyme

1883 BURNE *Shropshire* 290. The dictum of some Lancashire friends . . is, 'Something old, something new, Something borrowed, and something blue.' When the wedding gown is of the orthodox white, the obligation to wear 'blue' is carried out by making the garters of that colour. **1957** *Folklore* 416. 'Something old, something new, something borrowed and something blue' is almost always worn, even by the most sophisticated brides. **1987** Woman, *c.*40 [Midhurst, Sussex] That rhyme, 'Something old, something new, something borrowed, something blue,' that's *always* observed.

BRIDE'S CLOTHES: stocking, throwing

1604 Letter from Sir Dudley Carleton (E. SAWYER *Memorials* II 43) We had the Marriage of Sir Philip Herbert and the Lady Susan performed at Whitehall . . No Ceremony was omitted of Bride-Cakes, Points, Garters, and Gloves . . and at Night there was . . casting off the Bride's left Hose, with many other pretty Sorceries. **1656** R. FLETCHER *Poems and Fancies* 230. Clarinda lay . . Whiles at her head each twitt'ring Girle The fatal stocking quick did whirle To know the

lucky hap. **1698** MISSON *Voyageur en Angleterre* (1719, 352–3) The Bride-men take the Bride's Stockings, and the Bride-maids the Bridegroom's. Both sit down at the Bed Feet, and fling the Stockings over their Heads, endeavouring to direct them so that they may fall upon the marry'd couple. If the Man's Stockings, thrown by the Maids, fall upon the Bridegroom's Head, it is a Sign she will quickly be marry'd herself; and the same Prognostick holds good of the Woman's Stockings, thrown by the Man. **1711** *West Country Clothier Undone by a Peacock* 65. The sack posset must be eaten and the stocking flung, to see who can first hit the bridegroom on the nose. **1721** A. RAMSAY *Poems* 116. The Bride was now laid in her Bed, Her left leg Ho was flung; And Geordy Gib was fidgen glad, Because it hit Jean Gun. **1733** *Palace Miscellany* 49 'Progress of Matrimony'. Then come all the younger Folk in, With Ceremony throw the Stocking; Backward, o'er head, in Turn they toss'd it. 'Till in Sack-Posset they had lost it. Th' Intent of flinging thus the Hose, Is to hit him or her o' th' Nose: Who hits the Mark, thus, o'er left Shoulder, Must married be, e're twelve Months older. **1823** W. GRANT STEWART *Highlanders of Scotland* 277–8. The devoted bride . . stripped nearly to the state of nature, is placed in bed in presence of the whole company. Her left stocking is then flung, and falls upon some individual, whose turn to the Hymeneal altar will be next. **1824** MACTAGGART *Gallovidian Encyclopedia* 447. Throwing the Hoshen—At weddings, when the time of bedding comes on, the young fowk are surrounded by the people at the wedding, to witness the ceremony; one part of which is, that the bride takes the stocking off her left leg, and flings it at random amongst the crowd, and whoever it happens to hit will be the first of them who will get married. **1824** W. CARR *Craven Dialect* 113. The young guests . . instantly repaired to the bed room, where the bride and bridegroom sat up in bed, in full dress, exclusive of their shoes and stockings. One of the bridesmaids repeated an epithalamium. Afterwards, she took the bridegroom's stocking, and standing at the bottom of the bed, and with her back towards it, threw the stocking with her left hand over the right shoulder, aiming at the face of the bridegroom. This was done first by all the females in rotation; and afterwards the young men took the bride's stocking, and .. threw it in her face .. The best marksman was to be married first. 1929 *Folklore* 281. In Cumberland, until mid-Victorian times, the bride, after being conducted to bed by her bridesmaids, slipped off her stockings and flung one with her right hand over her left shoulder; the one hit by the stocking would be the next married. My grandmother .. was so hit by her cousin, a bride of seventy years ago, simultaneously with a cousin of the bridegroom, and the two girls .. were married on the same day in 1863.

BRIDE'S CLOTHES: wedding dress, bride tries on completed
1873 HARLAND & WILKINSON *Lancashire Legends* 222. No one ought to try on her wedding-dress before the day of the marriage .. if she does she will never live happily with her husband. 1953 Girl, 14 [Aberdeen] If the bride tries on a completed wedding dress it is unlucky. 1957 *Folklore* 416 [The bride] must not see herself in her complete bridal array until she is dressed for the ceremony; hence, when the dress is fitted, it must be tried on in sections. If it is bought ready-made, the belt, or some .. part must be left off during the fitting .. It is safest to leave a few stitches to be added .. and thus guard against any danger of the finished dress being worn too soon. 1983 *Mirror* 4 July 20. My late mother was a Court dressmaker more than a hundred years ago and she told me that it was unlucky to try on a finished wedding dress. So two inches of seam was left until the last fitting, when the hair was sewn in for luck.
    Cf. MIRROR, looking in: bride arrayed for wedding.

BRIDE'S CLOTHES: wedding dress by candlelight
1910 *Folklore* 226 [Pontefract, Yorks.] It is unlucky to see the bridal dress by candle light.

Cf. MIRROR, looking in: by candle-light/after dark.

BRIDE'S CLOTHES: wedding dress, colour of
1768 GOLDSMITH *Good-Natured Man* IV. I wish you could take the white and silver to be married in. It's the worst luck in the world in anything but white. 1859 ELIOT *Adam Bede* LV. [refers to 1801] She [a Methodist] was not in black this morning; for her aunt Poyser would by no means allow such a risk of incurring bad luck, and had herself made a present of the wedding dress, made all of grey, though in the usual Quaker form, for on this point Dinah could not give way. 1957 *Folklore* 416. White, silver, blue, pink, or gold are commonly considered the most fortunate shades. Green is generally avoided and so .. is black. 1982 Woman, 20 [Sutton Coldfield, Warwicks.] Married in white, you have chosen all right; Married in green, ashamed to be seen; Married in grey, you will go far away; Married in red, you will wish yourself dead; Married in blue, you will always be true; Married in yellow, ashamed of your fellow; Married in black, you will wish yourself back; Married in pink, of you he'll think.
    Also see GREEN unlucky.

BRIDE'S CLOTHES: wedding dress, hair sewn into
1898 *Weekly Scotsman Christmas Number* 6. A hair pulled out of your [the dressmaker's] head and sewed into a bride's dress will bring your own husband along pretty soon. 1929 *N & Q* CLVI 319. The girl, whose wedding-dress was being made by a friend, was having sewn into it, for luck, besides the 'something blue', three hairs.

BRIDE'S CLOTHES: wedding dress not to be seen by bridegroom
1952 Girl, 14 [Aberdeen] If the bridegroom sees his bride in her wedding dress it is unlucky. 1982 Woman, *c.*50 [Stockton-on-Tees, Co. Durham] The groom mustn't see the wedding dress before he sees the bride in it.
    Cf. BRIDE'S CLOTHES: wedding dress, bride tries on completed.

BRIDESMAID too many times

1834 DALYELL *Darker Superstitions of Scotland* 292. It is yet held ominous for any damsel to officiate frequently as bridesmaid .. Superstition assigns perpetual celibacy as her lot. **1898** *Weekly Scotsman Christmas Number* 7. Three times a bridesmaid, never a bride. **1935** Girl, 12 [Poole, Dorset] Three times a bridesmaid, never a bride. **1953** Girl, 13 [Ipswich, Suffolk] If you are a bridesmaid more than three times you will never get married.

bride: also see WEDDING.

BROOM: buying in May or at Christmas

1871 *N & Q* 4th ser. VIII 47. In Carrickon-Suir there is a curious superstition that it is unlucky to buy brooms in May .. 'Brooms bought in May, Sweep the family away.' **1912** LEATHER *Herefordshire* 18–19. It is unlucky to make a besom in 'the Christmas' (that is, from Dec. to Jan. 6th), or in May. **1923** [Rowbarton, Som.] 'Never buy a broom in May, Or you'll brush one of the family away.' **1933** *Sussex County Mag.* 210. A popular saying was: 'Buy a broom in May, Sweep your friend away.' **1949** *Mirror* 3 Feb. 2. Said Mr Cyril Foster, proprietor of the village store in Moorswater [Cornwall]: 'For the whole month we never sell a single brush. Women here will consider it is as good as murder to buy one.' **1953** Girl, 13 [Knighton, Radnor.] My great great grandmother thought it unlucky to buy a broom in the twelve days of Christmas. She bought one once and made up her mind that she would not live to see another Christmas Day; but she lived many years after that. **1954** *Trans. Devon. Ass.* 297. It is a well-known saying in the West-country: 'Buy a brush in May, Sweep a friend away' .. The local representative of Kleen-e-ze for the Bovey Tracey and Newton Abbot area assures me that May is always his worst month. **1974** *Mirror* 15 May 24. My family are demanding to know why I will not buy brushes and brooms during the month of May. My grandmother [said] it was unlucky, and nothing would induce me to buy them even now, and she has been dead for thirty-four years. **1982** Student, 20

[Cleveland, Yorks.] It is now thought in some places that it is unlucky to purchase brooms or brushes in May. Apparently buying a toothbrush can also fall into this category!
Cf. BROOM (plant) in house in May.

BROOM: losing at sea

1880 W. JONES *Credulities* 117. It is considered unlucky to lose .. a mop at sea. **1900** S. HEWETT *Nummits* 58 [Devon] It is unlucky .. to lose a mop or a broom at sea.

BROOM ominous

1830 FORBY *East Anglia* 414. If you set the broom in a corner, you will surely have strangers come to the house. **1912** LEATHER *Herefordshire* 86. It is said that if the handle come off the broom when sweeping, the servant will not get her wages. **1923** [Bridgwater, Som.] You must never rest the sweeping brush on the bristles as it's very unlucky. If you stick the brush on its handle it's very lucky.

BROOM on table

1883 BURNE *Shropshire* 280. It is unlucky .. to sweep a table with a broom. **1923** [Trowbridge, Wilts.] It is an ill omen to put a sweeping brush on a table.

BROOM protects house

1873 HARLAND & WILKINSON *Lancashire Legends* 235. Persons are advised to lay a broom across the doorway when any suspected person is coming in .. The witch will make excuse and pass along the road.

BROOM thrown for luck

1824 MACTAGGART *Gallovidian Encyclopedia* 210. A broom or cow [besom] is thrown after curlers [curling players], when they leave a house; this is shaning them good luck [breaking the spell of witchcraft]. **1881** W. GREGOR *North-East of Scotland* 188. When an animal was led away to market the besom was thrown on it to ward off all harm from witches, the 'ill-ee', or 'fore-speaking'. **1885** *Folklore* 308 [Rosehearty, Aberdeen.] When the men were going to the herring fishing for the first time, one of the women of the house used to throw the besom after them. The same thing was done, when a new net was taken out of the house. **1886** *Folklore* 16 [Banff.] A woman .. threw the besom after him [unsuccessful fisherman]. That night a good fishing was made. **1939** *Folklore* 345 [NE coast of Scotland] A besom was thrown after a new net when it first left the house and also after the men starting out on an expedition; it was sometimes taken out to sea in the boat.

Cf. SHOES, old: thrown etc. for luck.

BROOM (plant) in house in May
1868 *N & Q* 4th ser. I 550. Bring broom into the house in May, It will sure sweep one of the family away. **1878** *Folk-Lore Record* 52 [Fittleworth, Sussex] I should be very glad if you would throw away that piece of yellow broom; for they do say that death comes with it if it is brought into the house in blossom during the month of May. **1956** *Scottish Field* Oct. 10. I took the broom home .. but my landlady saw me coming and put her head out of the window to tell me that I mustn't bring it into the house as broom is unlucky. **1983** Woman, 81 [Liss, Hants.] My mother would never have broom indoors. It would sweep one of the family away.

Cf. BROOM: buying in May or at Christmas.

BROOM (plant): sweeping with in May
1850 *N & Q* 1st ser. II 5 [Suffolk] If you sweep the house with blossomed broom in May, Y're sure to sweep the head of the house away. **1878** *Folk-Lore Record* 52 [Fittleworth, Sussex] The old gentleman .. strictly forbade green brooms being used in his house during May, and .. used to quote the adage 'If you sweep the house with broom in May You'll sweep the head of that house away.' **1923** [Trowbridge, Wilts.] Sweep the house with blossomed broom in May, You'll sweep the head of the house away. **1938** *Sussex County Mag.* 309. 'If you sweep the house with a broom in May, You sweep the head of the house away' .. only attaches to brooms made of broom. This version from a Sussex aunt who reached the long age of 87.

BROOM (plant), whipping with
1882 *N & Q* 6th ser. VI 326 [Felday,

Surrey] If a child be whipped with a branch of green broom he will never grow any more. **1883** BURNE *Shropshire* 248. I am told of a boy .. born at Wrenthall .. whose stunted growth is attributed to his having been beaten with 'brum' in early childhood.

Cf. ELDER malevolent.

BUCKET, jumping over
1876 *N & Q* 5th ser. VI 24 [Cumb.] After a christening, the mother .. would give a tea to all her neighbours that were wives .. When all were ready to depart, a pail or milk-pail was placed .. on the door sill. Over this each wife had to jump, that being the only way in which they were allowed to pass out of the house .. If they cleared the pail, they were themselves clear; but those who stumbled, or put their foot in the pail .. were considered .. to be in that interesting state out of which their entertainer had just emerged. **1929** *Folklore* 279 [Cumb.] Before the women left at the end of the [christening] party, an empty bucket was placed in the room doorway, and in it a lighted candle, over which each woman had to jump as she left the room. Should the draught of her petticoats waft the candle out, it was taken as an omen that she would be the next to require the midwife. **1982** Woman, 20 [Cleveland, Yorks.] Jump over a bucket to bring on labour.

BUCKET: losing at sea
1880 W. JONES *Credulities* 117. It is considered unlucky to lose a water-bucket .. at sea. **1909** M. TREVELYAN *Folk-Lore of Wales* 2. When a sailor .. lets a pail fall overboard, he feels 'uncomfortable'. **1936** E. H. RUDKIN *Lincolnshire* 18. A bucket lost overboard means ill luck.

BUCKET upturned
1957 *Kent Messenger* 23 Aug. 11. Ten frogmen went out to find a valuable trawl .. but they unwittingly broke a fisherman's superstition—and they had no luck all day. One of them sat for hours on an upturned bucket.

Cf. BOWL overturned.

BUILDING left unfinished

1974 *Mirror* 10 June 24. Have you any record of a superstition in the building trade which causes them to always leave a defect, unseen, because only God can make anything perfect? Ibid. 28 June 24. Years ago I was in charge of re-plastering Bush House, in the Strand, and noticed that a cap on a column was unfinished. I thought I had discovered something important, but I was told that this was deliberate.

BUMBLE BEE, first: killed

1880 *N & Q* 6th ser. II 224. Among the fishermen of the Isle of Man .. To catch the first 'bumble-bee' seen in the spring and carry it out 'to the fishing' is considered a sure talisman for good luck. 1952 Man, *c.*65 [Dundee, Angus] Working with my father on his croft fifty years ago my father said 'You catch that bee—that's the first of spring—and you keep it and you'll never be broke,' and to this day I have what is left of it in my purse.

BUMBLE BEE in house = death

*c.*1050 Cotton Tib. A. iii (COCKAYNE *Leechdoms* III 169) If a man .. dreams he sees bees fly into his house, that shall be the destruction of the house. 1850 *N & Q* 1st ser. II 165 [Northants.] The entrance of [a humble bee] into a cottage is deemed a certain sign of death. 1923 [Somerset] If a bumble bee enters the house someone in the house will never leave it alive.

BUMBLE BEE in house = stranger

1868 *N & Q* 4th ser. II 221 [Yaxley, Suffolk] A servant was standing in a kitchen with the windows open when in flew a humble-bee. 'O see!' she said, 'a stranger is coming! Has it a red tail or a white? Red for a man and white for a woman.' 1879 JEFFERIES *Wild Life in a Southern County* x. There is a superstition that if a humble-bee buzzes in at the window of the sitting-room it is a sure sign of a coming visitor. 1889 *Dorset Field Club* 29. If a 'dumble-dore' comes inside the house it denotes the arrival of a stranger. You must not .. drive it out, or it will bring you ill luck. 1935 *I Walked by Night* (ed. L. Rider Haggard, 18) [Norfolk] If a large Humble

bee flew in the door that was a Stranger comen. 1956 Woman, 19 [Langham, Rutland] If a bumble bee comes into the house you are sure to have a visitor. 1962 Woman, *c.*70 [Liss, Hants.] I'm sure I'm going to have a stranger come to see me soon, there's been a great big bumblebee in and out of the house these past two days.

BURIAL: first in churchyard

1866 HENDERSON *Northern Counties* 89 [Aberdeen] There was great difficulty in bringing the new churchyard into use. No-one would be the first to bury his dead there, for it was believed that the first corpse laid there was a teind [tithe] to the Evil One. 1885 *Folklore* 281. It was thought unlucky to be buried first in a churchyard. At Loudon, in Ayrshire, when first the burying-place round the church was opened, no one would be buried there. At last a funeral, passing it as usual, was stopped by the villagers and the body forcibly taken and buried. After that no one had any objection to be buried there.

BURIAL: last person buried

late 18th c. J. RAMSAY (*Scotland in the Eighteenth Century* II 433) In some Highland countries, the vulgar believed that the ghost of the person last buried watched the churchyard. 1868 *Belfast News Letter* 24 Jan. 3. A belief still prevails among the people of the rural districts, that when two funeral processions reach a graveyard together, the last corpse in 'must watch the other till morning'. 1884 *N & Q* 6th ser. X 326 [Isle of Islay, Argyll.] In the parish of Oe it is believed that the spirit of the last buried watches over the kirkyard till relieved by another interred. 1899 *Newcastle Weekly Chronicle* 4 Feb. 7 [Jesmond] The spirit of the last person buried has to watch the churchyard until relieved by another, hence enquiries after sick persons are often rudely resented. 1923 *Folklore* 337 [Connaught, Eire] Two funerals on the same day .. lead to quarrels, as the spirit of the person last buried must sit and watch the place until the next burial releases it from its lonely vigil.

BURIAL of woman

*c.*1940 [Great Paxton, Hunts.] If church-yard opens for a she, It will open for three.

BURIAL on north side of churchyard

1551 J. HAMILTON *Catechisme* pt. I 22–3 [Scotland] Syclik supersticion is amang thame, that will nocht berisch or erde the bodis of thair freindis on the North part of the kirk yard. 1594 T. MORISON *Papatus* 157. In Popish burying-grounds, those who were reputed good Christians lay towards the south and east; others, who had suffered capital punishment, laid violent hands on them-selves, or the like, were buried towards the north: a custom that had formerly been of frequent use in Scotland. 1657 P. SAMWAIES *Wise and Faithful Steward* 27. He requested to be interred in the open Church yard, on the North-side (to crosse the received superstition, as he thought, of the constant choice of the South-side). 1683 Ashton-under-Lyne church register, 11 June (P. LASLETT *World We Have Lost* 145) Roger Peake of Treehouse Bank, who hanged himself in his own barn the 9th day and was stolen into the churchyard and buried on the north side about one of the clock in the morning. 1789 WHITE *Antiquities of Selborne* IV. The church-yard is very scanty; and especially as all wish to be buried on the south-side .. At the east end are a few graves; yet none till very lately on the north-side; but, as two or three families of best repute have begun to bury in that quarter, prejudice may wear out by degrees. 1856 *Gents Mag.* pt. I 38 [Worcs.] The custom of burying exclusively on the south side of church-yards prevails very generally in the rural districts of this county, except where the smallness of the ground .. rendered it compulsory to use the north side, which .. was formerly reserved for suicides and strangers. 1865 R. HUNT *West of England* 2nd ser. 164–5. I have sought to dis-cover .. the origin of this prejudice [and] have been answered, 'Oh, we like to bury a corpse where the sun will shine on the grave,' and 'The northern grave-yard is in the shadow, and cold.' 1871 KILVERT *Diary* 30 Sept. It was surmised that she would be buried as a suicide

without any service on the 'backside of the Church', but she was buried by Mr Venables with the usual ceremony. 1896 HOUSMAN *Shropshire Lad* 'Hughley Steeple'. North, for a soon-told number, Chill graves the sexton delves, And steeple-shadowed slumber The slayers of themselves. 1911 *Folklore* 320. The last time I was in Hampshire, I was told by a girl from Fordingbridge that no one would be buried in the north-east of a churchyard, as it was 'Hell Corner'.

Cf. NORTH door of church.

BURIAL, symbolic: counteracts Whit-suntide birth

1862 M. LEADBEATER *Leadbeater Papers* I 403 [Ballitore, Co. Kildare, 1821] On Whit-Sunday a child was born to Pat Mitchell, a labourer. It is said that the child born on that day is fated to kill or be killed. To avert this doom a little grave was made, and the infant laid therein, with clay lightly sprinkled on it and sods supported by twigs covering the whole. Thus was the child buried, and at its resurrection deemed to be free from the malediction. 1887 'SPERANZA' WILDE *Superstitions of Ireland* I 270. A child born at Whitsuntide will have an evil temper, and may commit a murder. To turn away ill-luck from a child born at that time, a grave must be dug and the infant laid in it for a few minutes. After this process the evil spell is broken, and the child is safe. 1904 *Folklore* 347 [Ireland] Children or animals born on Whit-Monday are evil-tempered and likely to take some man's life. It was customary in Louth to bury a Whit-Monday foal or calf, but this method of breaking the charm is now almost forgotten, though such animals are still distrusted .. In Cavan [Co. Leitrim] when a cow calved on Whit-Monday a hole was dug right through a 'ditch' (i.e. a bank), and the calf was passed along the tunnel thus made.

Cf. MAY, born in.

BURIAL, symbolic: cure

11th c. MS Pseudo-Theodore Penitential (THORPE *Ancient Laws* XXVII § 16 293) If anyone for the health of their little boy passes him through an opening in the earth, and closes it up with branches after him, he shall do penance. **1590** Witchcraft trial (R. PITCAIRN *Criminal Trials in Scotland* II pt. 2 202–4) The Witch .. declarit, that thair wes na remeid for yow to recover your health, without the principall man of your blude sould suffer death for yow [and] this sould be George Munro, your brother .. The said Wich, with .. hir complices .. maid ane graif of your lenth .. and yow .. wes laid in the said graif; and the grene eird [earth] wes laid abone [on top]. Your foster-mother .. inquyrit at the said Witch, 'Quhilk wes hir schois [choice]?' Quha ansuerit .. Mr Hector wes hir schois to leif, and your brother George to die for yow' .. Ye gat your health, be the dewelisch moyan foirsaid [and] ar indytit, for the crewall .. slauchter of the said .. George Munro .. be the Inchantmentis and Witchecraftis vsit vboune yow. late **18th c.** J. RAMSAY (*Scotland in the Eighteenth Century* II 451) In Breadalbane [Perth.] when a person is seized with a lingering fever, it is usual to lay him for a few minutes under clods of earth. The cure must be repeated thrice before or after sunset. **1829** BROCKETT *North Country Words. Kinkcough, Kink-haust*, the hooping-cough .. The ignorant .. have various fooleries, for curing or alleviating this epidemic disorder—such as .. dipping the persons affected nine times in an open grave. **1873** HARLAND & WILKINSON *Lancashire Legends* 227 [Whooping cough] is frequently sought to be cured by digging a hole into the earth and causing the patient to lie down and breathe into it. **1883** BURNE *Shropshire* 202. Sufferers from consumption will infallibly be cured if they get up before sunrise, cut a sod from the turf, replace it, and 'for nine mornings running' visit the spot, remove the sod, and breathe nine times into the hole. **1909** M. TREVELYAN *Folk-Lore of Wales* 45. It was customary for persons suffering from rheumatism to be buried in earth in the churchyard. The patient was stripped naked [and] was buried in a standing position for two hours, with only his head above the ground .. the process was to be repeated .. nine times. **1966** C. WOODFORD *Sip from Any Goblet* 23 [*c.*1847] They dug a large hole and placed the child's head

therein, a turf being laid over it and left until the child coughed.

BURIAL CAKE

*c.*1890 [Belford, Northumb.] Burial cakes .. were a sort of yellow bread, but quite sweet and spicy. She says a piece had to be taken in your mouth when you looked at a 'corp' or evil would come of it. The cake was always stood close by the dead person's head.

Cf. BREAD cures and protects.

BURN OR SCALD, charm for

1568 Sandwich Corporation Records (BOYS *History of Sandwich* 690) Sayeth that she can charme for fyer and skalding, in forme as oulde women do, sayeng 'Owt fyer in frost, in the name of the Father, the Sonne, and the Holly Ghost.' **1664** PEPYS *Diary* 31 Dec. Charme, for .. A Burning. There came three Angells out of the East; The one brought fire, the other brought frost—Out fire; in frost. In the name of the Father and Son and Holy Ghost. Amen. **1804** MS charmer's book (LEATHER *Herefordshire* 73) The Virgin Mary burnt her child with a spark of fire: out fire in frost, in the name, etc. Amen. **1832** *Light from the West* I no. 4 84–5 [Cornwall] These wise persons .. must be Rhymers as well as Charmers; and to shew what charming rhymes they can make, take the following specimen: '*For a Scald, or Burn!* There were three angels came from the North-west, One brought Fire, and the other brought Frost, Out Fire, in Frost, in the name of Father, Son, and Holy Ghost!' Repeat this, three times! Pray! what is the authority for such a story? **1842** R. CHAMBERS *Popular Rhymes of Scotland* 37. 'Here come I to cure a burnt sore; If the dead knew what the living endure, The burnt sore would burn no more.' The operator [then] blows three times upon the burnt place. **1868** *N & Q* 4th ser. II 554. She said her child was scalded .. I charmed it in the road. I charmed it by saying to myself, 'There was two angels come from the north, one of them being fire and the other frost; in frost, out fire,' &c. I repeat this three times; this is good for a scald. I can't say it is good for anything else. **1946** UTTLEY *Country*

Things 119. I heard an old woman say this rhyme for a burn as she spread the soap [on the burn]: 'There came two angels from the North, One was Fire, and t'other 'un Frost. Out Fire, in Frost. In Name of Father, Son, and Holy Ghost. Amen.' **1972** *Lore and Language* July 7 [Coalisland, Co. Tyrone] To prevent a burn blistering hold the burn as near to the fire as you can and say nine times slowly: 'Jesus was burnt on a gridiron.'

Cf. NETTLE STING, charm for.

BUS TICKETS

1952 Woman, *c*.40. In Hull as a school-girl the rhyme 'One for sorrow, Two for joy', going up to seven, was always applied to the numbers on tram tickets. The number was added up and divided by seven and the rhyme applied to the figure remaining. **1954** Girl, 13 [Pontypool, Mon.] If on getting on a bus I find that the number of the issue of the ticket adds up to 21 then I always keep that ticket as a kind of charm. **1954** Boy, 12 [Southwark, London] If the last number of the ticket is a seven you are going to have a lucky day.

'BUSH', burning

1877–8 KILVERT *Diary* 31 Dec. [Bredwardine, Herefords.] After I had gone to bed I saw . . a bright blaze sprung up in the fields . . they were keeping up the old custom of Burning the Bush on New Year's Day in the morning. **1912** LEATHER *Herefordshire* 91. The 'Bush' is a globe made of hawthorn, which is hung up in the kitchen of the farmhouse, with the mistletoe, after the bush-burning ceremony each New Year's morning; it hangs there till the day comes round again, when it is taken out to be burnt, and a new one is made. **1932** WOMEN'S INSTITUTE *Worcestershire Book* 32 [Knighton-upon-Teme] On New Year's morning before it is light, you bake a piece of Blackthorn plaited like a Crown, and burn it in the field, then scatter the ashes over the ridges of the first sown, or last sown wheat.

Cf. MISTLETOE.

BUTTER, charm for

1624 Witchcraft trial, Orkney (*Ab-botsford Club Misc.* I 144) Being demandit . . how ye tuik the proffeit of the kyne and gaue it to vtheris, ye ansuerit, it was to tak thrie hairis of the kowis taill, thrie of her memberis, and thrie of hir papis, and gang thryse woderwardis about the kow, and straik hir in the left syd, and cast the hair in the kirne, and say thryse, 'Cum butter, cum.' **1656** ADY *Candle in the Dark* 59. 'Come Butter come, come Butter come, Peter stands at the Gate, waiting for a buttered Cake, come Butter come.' This, said the old Woman, being said three times, will make your Butter come, for it was taught my Mother by a learned Church-man in Queen Marie's days. **1854** A. E. BAKER *Northamptonshire Words* I 138. Churn, butter, churn, In a cow's horn; I never see'd such butter, Sin' I was born. Peter's standing at the gate Waiting for a butter'd cake, Come, butter, come! **1877** E. PEACOCK *Lincolnshire Glossary* 66–7. Churn, butter, dash, Cow's gone to th' marsh, Peter stands at th' toll-gate, Beggin' butter for his cake; Come, butter, come. **1937** ST J. GOGARTY *Sackville Street* 116 [Co. Tipperary] Gasping, she sang: 'Come, butter! Come, butter! Come, butter, Come! Every lump As big as My bum!'

BUTTER, stranger helps to churn

1865 *Gents Mag.* pt. 2 700 [Ireland] When a stranger comes into a farm-house whilst a churning takes place, if a hand be not given to the well-plied dash by this visitant, it is supposed the butter will be abstracted . . Even the upper classes will not refuse a share in this labour . . to prevent ill-luck. **1911** *Folklore* 203 [Co. Clare] It is unlucky . . to go out of a house where they are churning without 'putting your hand to the churn'. **1972** *Lore and Language* July 7 [Coalisland, Co. Tyrone] If someone goes into the house where someone is churning she must give a 'brash' before going out. (A 'brash' is a few up and down strokes with the churn stick.) No-one must ever leave the house . . without saying: 'Good luck to your work,' otherwise the milk won't turn.

Cf. CHRISTMAS PUDDING, stirring; FISHING LINE, baiting.

BUTTER will not come = someone in love
1891 HARDY *Tess of the D'Urbervilles* XXI.
The butter would not come . . 'Perhaps
somebody in the house is in love . . I've
heard tell in my younger days that that
will cause it.'

BUTTERFLIES, three
*c.*1816 Wilkie MS (HENDERSON *Northern
Counties* 1866, 33) The appearance of a
trio of butterflies flying together [is held
to presage death]. **1851** *N & Q* 1st ser.
III 4 [Northants.] Omens of death and
misfortune are . . drawn from . . the
sight of a trio of butterflies. **1893** *N & Q*
8th ser. IV 165–6. A correspondent
informs me that it is considered an omen
of misfortune in Northamptonshire if
three butterflies are seen together.

BUTTERFLY, first: colour of
1878 DYER *English Folk-Lore* 133. In
Gloucestershire there is a superstition
that if the first butterfly you see in the
opening year is white, you will eat white
bread during the remainder of the year,
which is another way of saying you will
have good luck; if, however, the first is
brown . . you will eat brown bread—that
is, be unlucky. **1890** *Hospital* Nursing
Suppl. 12 July LXV. A white butterfly
settles on the wild parsley growing near:
it is the first I have seen this year, so I
shall eat white bread till spring comes
round again, which does not seem such
an advantage as in olden days. Of course
everybody knows that a brown butterfly
means brown bread.

BUTTERFLY, first: killed
1827 HONE *Table Book* I 678 [Devon]
'Tis a butterfly, miss, the furst hee'th a
zeed for the year; and they zay that a
body will have cruel bad luck if a dit'en
kill a furst a zeeth. **1874** KILVERT *Diary* 4
June. As we drove home up Huntsman's
Hill from Chippenham Station [Wilts.]
we overheard the following conversation between two boys. 'Was that
the first butterfly thee'st seed this year?'
'Ees.' 'Why didn'st kill him then?' 'What
for?' ''Cause theeds't had good luck,
mon.' 'Don't tell I.' 'I know thee woulds't
then have good luck too.' **1904** E. V.
LUCAS *Sussex* 76. The first butterfly you
see, Cut off his head across your knee,

Bury the head under a stone And a lot
of money will be your own. **1922**
[Taunton, Som.] The first butterfly you
see of the year, wish. If you can catch it
you will have luck. **1944** QUILLER-COUCH
Shorter Stories 'Psyche'. One Saturday
afternoon the mason came over to look
at the ground . . It was bright weather,
and while the two men talked a white
butterfly floated past them—the first of
the year. Immediately the mason broke
off his sentence and began to chase the
butterfly round the garden: for in the
West country there is a superstition that
if a body neglect to kill the first butterfly
he may see . . he will have ill luck
throughout the year.

BUTTON, four-holed
1899 *Newcastle Weekly Chronicle* 4 Feb.
7 [Jesmond] It is . . lucky to find a
button. **1954** Girl, 15 [Forfar, Angus]
If a button with four holes is dug up,
you will soon hear good tidings. **1970**
Woman, 23 [Liss, Hants.] To find a
four-hole button is lucky. **1984** Woman,
37 [Harrow, Middx.] I'd pick up a button
off the street for luck, but only if it had
four holes in it.
  Cf. CLOVER, four-leaved.

BUTTONS OR FRUIT STONES: divination
1695 SANSON *Present State of Persia* (tr.
Savage) 24–5. The Great Astrologer . .
is always very near the King, to acquaint
him with his good or bad Fortune . . He
casts his Hand at random upon his
Beads, and counts from thence by way
of Even and Odd; so that he rules his
Predictions, as the Soldiers are wont to
do theirs by their Buttons. **1823** MOOR
Suffolk Words 377–8. We have a curious
old *sortes fibularae* . . by which the destiny of school-boys is fore-shadowed. On
a first appearance with a new coat or
waistcoat, a comrade predicts your fate
by your buttons, thus: sowja, sailor,
tinker, tailor, gentleman, apothecary,
plow-boy, thief—beginning at top, and
touching a button . . at each epithet.
That which applies to the lower button
is your promised or threatened avocation in life . . Young ladies gather similar
results as to the station and character
of their future husbands; by taking hold,
in lack of buttons, of a bead of their own

or school-fellow's necklace, touching and passing one onward to the end. **1849** HALLIWELL *Popular Rhymes* 222. In counting the buttons of the waistcoat upwards, the last found corresponding to one of the following names indicates the destiny of the wearer: 'My belief— A captain, a colonel, a cow-boy, a thief.' **1858** DENHAM *North of England* (1895, 46) Button Rhyme. A Tinkler, a Tailor, A Soldier, or a Sailor: A rich man, a poor man, A priest, or a parson, A ploughman, or a thief. **1873** *N & Q* 4th ser. XII 396 [Notts.] These good folk . . make plum-jam tarts for single young women and men to eat at wedding parties. The first tart a person eats . . is particularly noticed, for according to the number of plum-stones found, so will be years before the person gets married! **1900** *N & Q* 9th ser. VI 456. When I was a schoolboy in Herefordshire, 1873–4, we used to cast each other's horoscope by means of plum, or cherry, or damson stones, left on our plates at dinner, 'Tinker, tailor' being repeated. A variation was 'This year, next year, some time, never'. This usually referred to marriage or some other desirable event in life. **1904** R. FORD *Children's Rhymes* 20–1. Touching . . the various buttons on the child's dress . . 'A laird, a lord, A rich man, a thief, A tailor, a drummer, A stealer o' beef'. **1908** FORSTER *Room with a View* XIII. Freddy played at 'This year, next year, now, never', with his plum-stones. **1923** [Martock, Som.] I counted they stones out o' plum pie and said to 'em 'He loves, He don't, He'll marry me, He won't, He would if he could, But he can't', and then 'This year, next year, sometime, never'. **1953** Girl, 8 [Manchester] Count the buttons you are wearing and say 'Lady, baby, gypsy, queen, elephant, monkey, tangerine'. **1954** Girl, 11 [Perth] You count all the buttons that you have on, saying 'Tinker, tailor, soldier, sailor, rich man, poor man, beggar man, thief, ploughboy, cowboy, doctor, dentist'. **1988** Girl, 13 [Liss, Hants.] When you're eating those shrivelled-up things—prunes —you go round the stones saying 'Tinker, tailor, soldier, sailor, rich man, poor man, beggarman, thief', and that is who you're going to marry.

Cf. NAILS, specks on finger nails: divination.

C

CABBAGE STALK: divination

1787 BURNS *Poems* 157–8 n. The first ceremony of Halloween is, pulling each a *Stock* or plant of kail. They must go out, hand in hand, with eyes shut, and pull the first they meet with: its being big or little, straight or crooked, is prophetic of the size and shape of the grand object of all their Spells—the husband or wife. If any *yird*, or earth, stick to the root, that is *tocher*, or fortune; and the taste of the *custoc*, that is, the heart of the stem, is indicative of the natural temper and disposition. Lastly, the stems, or, to give them their ordinary appellation, the *runts*, are placed somewhere above the head of the door; and the Christian names of people whom chance brings into the house, are, according to the priority of placing the *runts*, the names in question. 1817 HOGG *Dramatic Tales* II i. 'All-Hallow-Eve.' [*Enter Shepherds and Maids, laughing—the former carrying long stalks of Colwort*] . . FIRST SHEP. By my life, but mine is a strapper! SECOND SHEP. See what a crooked carling I have got! 1865 *Gents Mag.* pt. 2 701 [All Hallows Eve, among the Irish peasantry] Cabbages were torn up from the root by boys and girls blindfolded, about the hour of midnight. Their heads and stalks were supposed to indicate the physical and mental peculiarities, tidiness, slovenliness, &c., of a future husband or wife. 1882 *People's Friend* 1 Nov. 693 [Hallowe'en] Lads are . . casting an eye to the kailyards . . lasses are wondering what kind of stock they will get, straight and comely, or bowed and crooked. 1893 *Folklore* 361–2 [Co. Leix] Hallow Eve . . You go into the garden blindfolded, and each pull up a cabbage. If the cabbage was well grown the girl was to have a handsome husband, but woe betide the unlucky damsel who got one with a crooked stalk; her husband would be a stingy old man. 1912 LEATHER *Herefordshire* 64. If a girl go into the garden [at Hallowe'en] and cut a cabbage, as the clock strikes twelve, the wraith of her future husband will then appear. 1952 Girl, 14 [Helensburgh, Dunbarton.] At Hallowe'en a spinster has to creep into a bachelor's garden, seize a cabbage or brussels-sprout, and if it has any peculiarities, i.e. a club root, those will be the peculiarities of her future husband, i.e. a club foot.

CALENDAR showing future date

1934 *Folklore* 162 [Birmingham] Calendars received about Christmas time should not be hung on the wall till the new year, as it is unlucky to do so. 1946 Girl, 12 [Abertillery, Monmouth.] It is bad luck to turn the calendar forward before the day has arrived. 1956 Woman, c.50 [Scarborough, Yorks.] My mother will hardly look at a calendar if it comes among her Christmas cards. It is hastily pushed back into its envelope and put away in a drawer until its appointed day. 1983 Woman, 81. When I was a girl in London it was considered unlucky to turn a calendar in advance of the day or month.

CANDLE alone in room

1855 *N & Q* 1st ser. XII 488. A capital penalty is attached to leaving a lighted candle or lamp in a room by itself, and allowing it to burn out in utter forgetfulness. 1924 *Folklore* 350 [Westleton, Suffolk] If a lighted candle is accidentally shut up in a pantry, it is a sure sign of a death in the family soon.

CANDLE burns blue

1594 SHAKESPEARE *Richard the Third* v iii. *Enter the Ghost of Buckingham* . . The Lights burne blew. It is now dead midnight. 1620 MELTON *Astrologaster* 46. If a Candle burne blew, it is a signe there is a spirit in the house, or not farre from it. 1726 DEFOE *History of the Devil* pt. 2 x. That old chimney-corner story, 'the candles burn blue when spirits are in the room' . . put me upon inquiry . . which . . amounts to no more than this:

that upon any extraordinary emission of sulphurous or of nitrous particles, either in a close room, or in any not very open space, if the quantity be great, a candle or lamp .. will seem to be, or to burn blue. 1787 GROSE *Provincial Glossary* Superstitions 10. If, during the time of an apparition, there is a lighted candle in the room, it will burn extremely blue: this is so universally acknowledged, that many eminent philosophers have busied themselves in accounting for it, without once doubting the truth of it. 1824 W. CARR *Dialect of Craven* 99. The watching of the pig-tail [farthing candle] was observed on the Eve of St Mark .. A party of males or females, but never a mixed company, place on the floor a lighted pig-tail. This, however, must be .. stolen .. When it begins to burn blue, the person whom they are respectively to marry, will make his appearance. 1827 T. F. FORSTER *Pocket Encyclopaedia* 36. When [candles] burned blue, it was accounted ill luck, or else that some ghostly apparition was announced. 1899 W. DICKINSON *Dialect of Cumberland. Deeth lowe.* A ragged piece of wick, which glows in the candle flame with a blue flare. It is always considered to be a presage of death unless the flame be extinguished by immersion of the candle in running water.

CANDLE, failing to blow out

1855 *Gents Mag.* pt. 2 386 [Shrops./ Worcs.] Omens of death, adhere to the popular belief .. more than any other relic of superstition .. Among them is prominently the issuing of a light from a candle after it has been blown out. 1957 Girl, 12 [Langholm, Dumfries.] If you blow out all the candles on your birthday cake with one breath it brings you luck. 1960 D. H. HUNT *My Grandmothers and I* 20 [refers to c.1916] Aren't the candles pretty? You must blow them out together. When you cut the cake, you have a wish .. you mustn't tell it or it won't come true.

Cf. FIRE, behaviour of: fails to go out.

CANDLE, funeral: cures and protects

c.1816 Wilkie MS (HENDERSON *Northern Counties* 1866, 36–7) In the Scottish Lowlands .. when a body has been washed and laid out, one of the oldest women present must light a candle, and wave it three times around the corpse .. The candle for 'saining' [blessing the corpse] should be procured from a suspected witch or wizard, a seer .. or from a person with .. flat feet, 'ringlet-eyed' .. or 'lang-lipit' .. for all these persons are unlucky, or, in this affair, unlucky really means fortunate in the extreme .. The saining [blessing] candle must be kept burning through the night. 1868 *N & Q* 4th ser. I 51 [Dublin] A woman .. had rung the bell; and .. said 'Please, sir, will you give me a candle?' .. One of the servants called out to me, 'Please shut the door, sir! What does she mean coming here with her popish superstition.' .. The woman went away, evidently much annoyed .. for she .. knew that death had just taken place in the house. 1887 'SPERANZA' WILDE *Superstitions of Ireland* I 153. The ends of candles used at wakes are of great efficacy in curing burns. 1888 *Folklore* 263 [Achterneed, Ross.] When a death takes place .. lights are burned not only beside [the body], but in every apartment of the house during the whole of each night till it is buried.

CANDLE, holy: cures and protects

1486 SPRENGER & KRAMER *Malleus Maleficarum* (tr. Summers, 89, 91) That detestable race [witches] cannot injure with their witchcraft .. those who [by] the carrying of blessed candles on the Day of the Purification of Our Lady .. thus fortify themselves .. so that the powers of devils are diminished .. In the case of a Blessed Candle, although it is more appropriate to light it, the wax of it may with advantage be sprinkled about dwelling-houses. 1584 SCOT *Discoverie of Witchcraft* XII xx. Such as observe dulie the rites and ceremonies of holie church .. by the lawfull use of candles hallowed on Candelmas daie .. are preserved from witchcraft. c.1740 *Aristotle's Midwife* 107. To assist in the Cutting of the Teeth .. the Nurse must .. let the Child have a Virgin's Wax-candle to chew upon. 1795 *Gents Mag.* pt. 1 201–3 [Ireland] On Candlemas day .. candles are blessed by the priests in high mass; after which they are dispersed .. in the cure of wounds, aches, and diseases. 1812 J. BRADY *Clavis Calendaria* I 189. Some ignorant and timid persons .. still light candles as a charm against thunder and lightning, in the efficacy of which belief was formerly almost universally prevalent, 'provided that the Priest had given them his benediction on the day of Purification'.

CANDLE, lighting third

1870 KILVERT *Diary* 26 July [Tullimaar, Cornwall] Three candles were burning on the kitchen table and the cook said that the person who was nearest to the shortest candle would be married first. Some people put it, 'Will die first'. It seems to be an old saying about three lighted candles together, but it was quite new to me. 1893 *Westminster Gazette* 3 Nov. 2. On this Sunday of October, 1882, while I worked away at the draft Constitution of the National League .. the sick man [Parnell] lay with his face to the wall .. I wrote at a table by his bedside on which four candles stood lighted. Hours passed by, and .. I did not heed the fact that one of the candles [had] spluttered itself out. A stir from the patient aroused me, and .. with astonishment I saw that Mr Parnell .. was furiously blowing out one of the remaining candles .. 'Don't you know that nothing is more unlucky than to have three candles burning?' .. said he .. Afterwards I learnt that three candles are lit at wakes in Ireland around a corpse. 1906 *N & Q* 10th ser. VI 509. A few months since an Irish girl hastily blew out a candle placed near two others on her toilet table, saying 'Three bring death.' 1930 T. F. POWYS *Kindness in a Corner* XXXII. Without thinking what she was doing, she lit three candles. Her husband hastily blew one of them out. 'Do thee know what 'ee have done? .. 'Tis three lighted candles that be put beside a coffin. 'Twill be cold death for we within a year.' 1948 E. & M. A. RADFORD *Superstitions* 58. Stage candle superstition demands that on no account must three candles be alight at the same time in a theatre dressing room.

Cf. CIGARETTE, lighting third.

CANDLE lit from fire

c.1835 JOHN BELL MS add. to *Gammer Gurton's Garland* [Newcastle Univ. Lib.] They've little wit within their pow That light a candle at a low. 1933 *Folklore* 197 [Navenby, Lincs.] If you light a candle from the flame of a fire you will end your days in the workhouse.

Cf. FIRE not allowed out of house.

CANDLE, pricking: spell

1866 HENDERSON *Northern Counties* 139. Buckinghamshire damsels desirous to see their lovers would stick two pins across through the candle .. taking care that the pins passed through the wick. While doing this they recited .. 'It's not this candle alone I stick, But A.B.'s heart I mean to prick; Whether he be asleep or awake, I'd have him come to me and speak.' 1936 E. H. RUDKIN *Lincolnshire* 23 [Hallowe'en] Get a candle, set it up, and light it, and stick pins in it—every pin has to have a 'ditty' said (this 'ditty' is forgotten, unfortunately, but each pin seems to stand for a separate man known to the charm worker). The candle burns down first to one pin then to another; when it gets to the right man the door will open and he will appear.

Cf. BLADE-BONE: spell; SALT, burning: in spell.

CANDLE, reviving flame of

1755 *Connoisseur* 13 Mar. Poor cousin Nancy was ready to cry one time, when she snuffed [the candle] out and could not blow it in again; though her sister did it at a whiff, and consequently triumphed in her superior virtue.

CANDLE, signs in: letter

1708 *British Apollo* 7 Apr. The reason .. is as Wise an one as that of Letters .. in a Candle. 1755 *Connoisseur* 13 Mar. My aunt one night observed, with great pleasure, a letter in the candle, and the very next day one came from her son in London. 1777 BRAND *Antiquities* 94. The fungous Parcells (so Browne calls them) about the Wicks of Candles, are commonly thought to foretell Strangers: With us [in Northumberland] they are called Letters at the Candle. 1823 MOOR *Suffolk Words* 426. A coming letter is foretold by a projecting spark on the snaste [snuff]. **1830** M. R. MITFORD *Our Village* IV 299. Who looks in the candles for expected letters? **1855** *Gents Mag.* pt. 2 385 [Shrops./Worcs.] A bright speck in the candle is a sure indication that a letter is coming to the individual to whom it points. **1880** HARDY *Trumpet Major* XII. Ah, I now call to mind that there *was* a letter in the candle . . a large red one. **1899** J. SHAW *Schoolmaster* 34 [Tynron, Dumfries.] The bright speck often seen on a candle declares, if it falls, a letter is posted to you; but if it sticks to the side of the candle . . it is only on the way to be posted. **1923** [Rowbarton, Som.] If a spark flies off the candle, it's a letter gone to post for you.

Cf. FIRE, behaviour of: sends out sparks.

CANDLE, signs in: ring or sweetheart

1766 GOLDSMITH *Vicar of Wakefield* X. The girls themselves had their omens . . they saw rings in the candle. **1946** UTTLEY *Country Things* XI. A brightly glowing tip to the wick was a sweetheart in the candle.

CANDLE, signs in: stranger

1646 BROWNE *Vulgar Errors* V xxiv. Of lower consideration is the common fore-telling of strangers, from the fungous parcels about the wicks of candles. **1711** *Spectator* 8 Mar. After having looked upon me a little while, 'My dear' (says she turning to her husband) 'you may now see the stranger that was in the candle last night.' *c.*1850 J. HUNTER MS note in Brand's *Antiquities* II 502. Strangers—Letters—Coffins—I do not remember to have heard of anything else indicated by the phases of a Candle. **1923** [Bradford-on-Tone, Som.] If there is a lump of soot on the wick of a candle it means you will soon meet a stranger.

Cf. FIRE, behaviour of: 'stranger' on grate.

CANDLE, signs in: winding sheet

1708 *British Apollo* 7 Apr. The reason . . is as Wise an one as that of . . Winding Sheets, &c. in a Candle. **1755** *Connoisseur* 13 Mar. The squire of the parish came one night to pay them a visit, when the tallow winding-sheet pointed towards him, and he broke his

neck soon after in a fox chase. **1825** JAMIESON *Scottish Dict.* Suppl. *Dede-spale.* That part of the grease of a candle, which, from its not being melted, falls over the edge in a semicircular form; denominated from its resemblance to the shavings of wood. This, by the vulgar, is viewed as a prognostic that the person to whom it is turned will soon die. **1853** GASKELL *Cranford* IX. Miss Jenkyns . . would never allow a servant to call the little rolls of tallow that formed themselves round candles 'winding-sheets', but insisted on their being spoken of as 'roley-poleys!' **1861** DICKENS *Great Expectations* XLVIII. The pair of coarse fat office candles that dimly lighted Mr Jaggers [the lawyer] as he wrote in a corner, were decorated with dirty winding-sheets, as if in remembrance of a host of hanged clients. **1864** R. CHAMBERS *Book of Days* II 53 [Suffolk] A winding-sheet is produced from a candle, if, after it has guttered, the strip, which has run down instead of being absorbed into the general tallow, remains unmelted; if . . it curls over away from the flame, it is a presage of death to the person in whose direction it points. **1928** HARDY *Winter Words* 'Standing by the Mantlepiece'. This candle-wax is shaping to a shroud To-night . . By touching it the claimant is avowed, And hence I press it with my finger—so.

CARDS, lucky at

1738 SWIFT *Polite Conversation* III 213. Well, Miss, you'll have a sad Husband, you have such good Luck at Cards. **1755** *Connoisseur* 13 Mar. She is . . sure of a good one [husband] because she generally has ill-luck at cards. **1865** T. W. ROBERTSON *Society* II ii. I'm always lucky at cards!—Yes, I know an old proverb about that . . Lucky at play, unlucky in ——. **1945** N. COLLINS *London Belongs to Me* LX. 'Lucky at cards, unlucky in love,' Mrs Vizzard remarked absently.

CARDS, unlucky

1784 COWPER *Task* IV ll. 221–2. Ensanguin'd hearts, clubs typical of strife, And spades, the emblem of untimely graves. **1829** BROCKETT *North Country*

Words 155. *Hob Collingwood*, a name given to the four of hearts at whist; considered by old ladies an unlucky card. **1855** *Gents Mag.* pt. 2 385 [Shrops./Worcs.] To have a long succession of black cards (spades or clubs) dealt to a person .. is prophetic of death to himself or some member of the family. **1862** *N & Q* 3rd ser. I 223 [Totnes, Devon] The other night, in my deal, I turned up the four of clubs. 'Oh!' said one of my opponents, 'that's an unlucky card, you won't win this game.' **1873** *N & Q* 4th ser. XII 44. Far distant be the day when the dealer at whist who turns up the two of spades or of clubs, may not be consoled by the saying, 'There is luck under the black deuce.' **1879** *N & Q* 5th ser. XII 426. There was never a good hand at cards if the four of clubs was in it .. it's the Devil's four-post bedstead. **1962** Schoolchild, 12 [Cumnock, Ayr.] The Queen of Spades is bad luck. **1969** *Times* 9 Aug. 6. Peter Lumley, director of one of London's leading model agencies, has sent a dozen packs of cards—all but the Ace of Spades bearing pictures of his agency's models—to the matrons of .. London .. hospitals for their male patients. **1989** Woman, 60 [South Shields, Co. Durham] The Ace of Spades means death— I've known that since a child.

CAROL out of season

1887 *Folk-Lore Record* 220 [Cornwall] It is unlucky to sing carols before Christmas. **1909** *N & Q* 10th ser. XII 66 [nr. Exeter, Devon] It is unlucky to sing Christmas carols at any time save during that festive season. **1923** [Taunton, Som.] It is unlucky to sing Christmas carols except at Christmas time. **1984** Woman, 56 [South Shields, Co. Durham] We used to think it was very unlucky to sing a Christmas carol at any time other than Christmas. Even now if I catch myself doing it, I stop immediately.

CAROL SINGERS

1832 *Gents Mag.* pt. 2 491 [Lincs.] Our ears are saluted with the dissonant screaming of Christmas Carols, which the miserable creatures sing who travel from house to house with the vessel cup .. a small chest, which incloses an image, intended to represent the sacred person of our Saviour Jesus Christ .. It is reputed unlucky to dismiss the singer without a present. **1851** DENHAM *North of England* (1895, 25) To send a 'Vessel-Cup Singer' away from your doors unrequited (at least the first that comes), is to forfeit the good luck of all the approaching year. **1855** F. K. ROBINSON *Yorkshire Words* 29. It is unlucky not to reward the first set of those itinerants [carol singers] who call at your door, and we have known old fashioned folks who looked upon their crossing the threshold as a species of consecration! **1886** M. LINSKILL *Haven under the Hill* IX [Whitby, Yorks.] You remember what I said when I'd refused to let Nan Skaife sing when she came wi' the Vessel Cups? She was the first to come, an' I ought to ha' let her sing; but I couldn't, knowin' the sort o' woman she was. An' I'll never forget her word. 'You'll repent afore next Kessenmas, missis,' she said. **1923** [West Malling, Kent] The first carollers calling on Christmas Eve must never be turned away empty or bad luck will follow.

Cf. FIRST-FOOT at New Year/Christmas.

CAT = witch

1570 W. BALDWIN *Beware Cat* (1584, *Coll. Anglo-Poet*, ed. Corser, I 114) Touching this Grimmalkin: I take rather to be an Hagat or a Witch then a Cat. For witches haue gone often in that likenes. **1673** *Depositions, York Castle* 2 Apr. (1861, 191) She .. saith that the said Ann hath been severall times in the shape of a catt. **1757** MS diary (P. S. JEFFREY *Whitby Lore* 140) On Friday night, September ye 9th, Robert George Tinbull, of Marske, was spelled on ye bridge ower an hour by Hester Dale, the old witch of Marrick. His horse would not move until Tom Wilson came along with a wicken [rowan] staff. Then they both saw Aister run ower the road as a black cat. They both ken'd it was her, for she hath meant him harm for a good spell. **1793** R. WARNER *Topographical Remarks* I 243–4 [speaking of Mary Dore, parochial witch of Beaulieu, Hants.] Her spells were chiefly used for the purpose of self-extrication in situations of danger; and I have conversed with a rustic whose father had seen the old lady convert herself more than once, into the form of [a] cat, when likely to be apprehended in wood-stealing, to which she was somewhat addicted. **1830** SCOTT *Demonology* 337. A certain carpenter .. was so infested with cats, which, as his servant-maid reported, 'spoke among themselves', that .. betwixt his Highland arms of knife, dirk, and broadsword, and his professional weapon of an axe, he made such a dispersion that they were quiet for the night. In consequences of his blows, two witches were said to have died. **1851** H. COLERIDGE *Essays* I 40–1. Why should Bridget's cat be worried? Why, to be sure, she's black, an imp of darkness, the witch's own familiar: nay, perhaps, the witch herself in disguise.

CAT, behaviour of: forehead on ground
1959 Woman, 74 [London] If a cat lies curled up with the flat part of its head (between its ears) on the ground, it is going to rain: 'Cat on its brain, It's going to rain.'

CAT, behaviour of: rushes about
1710 SWIFT 'Description of a City Shower' ll. 3–4 (1938, I 136) While Rain depends, the pensive Cat gives o'er Her Frolicks, and pursues her Tail no more. **1773** *Poetical Description of Beasts* 46. Against the times of snow or hail, Or boist'rous windy storms; She frisks about and wags her tail, And many tricks performs. **1849** BRAND *Antiquities* III 188. Sailors, I am informed on the authority of a naval officer, have a great dislike to see the cat, on board ship, unusually playful and frolicsome: such an event, they consider, prognosticates a storm: and they have a saying on these occasions, that 'the cat has a gale of wind in her tail.' **1864** *N & Q* 3rd ser. V 236 [Sheringham, Norfolk] The old women are apt to feel uncomfortable if a cat should begin to play with their gowns or aprons, for that is a sign of a gale. **1922** [Somerset] Sailors do not like cats, and say that when a cat is frisky she has a gale of wind in her tail. **1954** Girl, 13 [Garndiffaith, Monmouth.] My aunt and mother can

always tell if it's going to rain for the cats go absolutely mad.

CAT, behaviour of: sits with back to fire
1755 *Connoisseur* 13 Mar. If the cat turned her tail to the fire, we were to have a hard frost. *c.***1780** T. PARK MS note in Brand's *Antiquities* 92. Cats sitting with their Tails to the Fire .. are said to foretel change of weather. **1825** JAMIESON *Scottish Dict.* Suppl. I 190. Her sitting with her back to the fire betokens frosty or chilly weather. **1909** *N & Q* 10th ser. XII 66. It is unlucky for a cat to sit with its tail towards the fireplace. **1923** [Somerset] If a cat sits with his back to the fire, it's a sign of cold or rough weather. **1954** Girl, 14 [Tunstall, Staffs.] My mother always says if the cat sits with her back to the fire it is going to rain and nearly always this is true.

CAT, behaviour of: washes = rain
1507 *Gospelles of Dystaues* pt. 2 XXII. Whan ye se a cat syt in a wyndowe in the sonne, & that she lycke her ars, and that one of her fete be aboue her ere ye nede not doubte but y^t shall rayne that daye. **1607** TOPSELL *Foure-footed Beastes* 105. It is a neate and cleanely creature, oftimes licking hir own body to keepe it smooth and faire .. and washing hir face with her fore feet: but some obserue, that if she put her feete beyond the crowne of her head, that it is a presage of raine. **1648** HERRICK *Hesperides* 155 'His age'. True Calenders, as Pusses eare Wash't o're, to tell what change is neare. **1658** T. WILLSFORD *Nature's Secrets* 131. Cats .. licking their feet, and trimming the hair of their heads, and mustachios, presages rainy weather. **1773** *Poetical Description of Beasts* 46. Pussey a prophet too appears, Against a rainy shower; She with her paws still cleans her ears, And then her face does scour. **1825** *Time's Telescope* 170 ['Signs of Rain,' 'by the late Dr Jenner'] Puss on the hearth, with velvet paws, Sits, wiping o'er her whiskered jaws. **1877** *N & Q* 5th ser. VII 54 [Derbys.] When I observe 'my puss' washing her face I watch if she goes over the ear, and if so, from force of habit acquired when a child, remark, 'We shall have rain; the cat goes over her ear.' **1896** BARRIE *Sentimental*

Tommy 197. About ten o'clock Ballingall's cat was observed washing its face, a deliberate attempt to bring on rain. It was immediately put to death. **1922** [Somerset] A cat washing vigorously behind its ears is a sign of heavy rain, and the wind will blow from the way she is facing. **1984** Woman, 56 [South Shields, Co. Durham] If a cat washes behind its ears, it's going to be stormy.

CAT, behaviour of: washes behind ear = stranger

1755 *Connoisseur* 13 Mar. They wondered what stranger they should see, because puss washed her face over the left ear. **1922** [Somerset] When a cat sit on the mat and clean her face, if she put her paw around her right ear a gentleman is going to enter the house, and if over her left a lady. **1955** Girl, 11 [Swansea, Glam.] If our cat washes herself in the evening my mother says that we shall have visitors.

CAT, black: cures

1602 (G. HOME *Evolution of an English Town* 159) To cure an ill caste by any Witch putt upon any childe . . Take a childe so ill held & strike y^t seven times on ye face & like upon ye navel with ye heart of a blacke cat then roast ye heart and give of y^t to eat seven nights at bed meale & y^t shalle be well butt ye cat must be seven years olde & ye seventh dropped at birth . . Blood from such an heart laid to any witches dorepost or thrown over nighte upon her doresterp will cause a sore & great paine in her belly. **1607** TOPSELL *Foure-footed Beastes* 106–7. For the paine and blindnesse in the eye . . Take the head of a blacke Cat, which hath not a spot of another colour in it, and burne it to pouder . . then take this poulder and through a quill blow it thrice a day into thy eie . . A neezing poulder made of the gall of a black cat . . and the waight of a groate thereof taken . . helpeth the conuulsion and wrynesse of the mouth. **1678** W. SALMON *London Dispensatory* 205. The Head of a black Cat (I suppose another may do) burnt to ashes, and they thrice a day blown into the Eyes, are a Remedy for all Diseases of the Eyes. *Ibid.* 206. The Skin worn upon the Stomach takes away

the pain thereof . . so also on the Joynts. **1678** *Yea and Nay Almanack* C7^v. A good Medicine for the Eyes. In the morning as soon as you rise, instead of . . a Cat's tail, rub your eyes with . . Gold. **1684** H. WOOLLEY *Queen-like Closet* Suppl. 35. For the Shingles. Take a Cat, and cut off her Ears, or her Tail, and mix the Bloud thereof with a little new-Milk, and anoint the grieved place with it Morning and Evening for three days. **1712** D. TURNER *Diseases of Skin* (1726, 81–2) I told her Mistress it was the Shingles . . she said . . she had a Remedy which she doubted not would cure her . . The Experiment, as I after understood, was made with the Blood of a black Cat (for it must be of no other Colour) which was smeared on the Parts . . It was taken from the Cat's Tail, being cut off for this Purpose. **1791** WOODFORDE *Diary* 11 Mar. The Stiony on my right Eye-lid still swelled and inflamed very much. As it is commonly said that the Eye-lid being rubbed by the tail of a black Cat would do it much good if not entirely cure it, and having a black Cat, a little before dinner I made a trial of it, and very soon after dinner I found my Eye-lid much abated of the swelling and almost free from Pain. **1850** *N & Q* 1st ser. II 37 [Northants.] It is customary for the sufferer, on the first night of the new moon, to procure the tail of a black cat, and after pulling from it one hair, rub the tip nine times over [the sty]. **1866** HENDERSON *Northern Counties* 117–18. The remedy for erysipelas, lately practised in the parish of Lochcarron, in the North-west Highlands . . consists in cutting off one half of the ear of a cat, and letting the blood drop on the part affected. **1883** *Folklore* 331. Brush the sty seven times with the tail of a black cat, and the sty will be gone by the next morning. **1887** 'SPERANZA' WILDE *Superstitions of Ireland* II 92. Nine hairs from the tail of a black cat, chopped up and soaked in water, which is then swallowed, and the [whooping] cough will be relieved. **1893** *Folklore* 350 [Valentia Isl., Co. Kerry] To arrest erysipelas, the name of the patient must be written round the part affected in the blood of a black cat, a cat that has not a single white hair. **1942** *N & Q*

CLXXVII 23. I suffered from styes as a
child and one day, when I was out with
my mother, a gipsy woman approached
us and, in a somewhat hesitant manner,
said that if my eye-lids were stroked with
a cat's tail the styes would disappear
.. The experiment was tried with the
result—strange as it may seem—that the
styes vanished and have not recurred.

CAT, black: lucky to possess

1866 HENDERSON *Northern Counties* 171.
At Scarborough, a few years back, sailors' wives liked to keep black cats in
their homes, to ensure the safety of their
husbands at sea. This gave black cats
such a value that no one else could keep
them; they were always stolen. 1907
N & Q 10th ser. VIII 227. Football teams
are sometimes in the habit of taking a
black cat on to the field with them, in
the hope that it will bring good luck.
1922 [Somerset] Although a perfectly
black cat was considered rather a creature of the devil, its owner was looked
upon as having a lucky talisman. 1983
Student, 21 [Yorks.] One lady told me
she was not superstitious at all but when
showing me her postcards said 'I always
keep my views with a black cat on.'
Many seaside postcards do, in fact, include a picture of a black cat.

CAT, black: lucky to touch

1953 Boy, 12 [Aberystwyth, Cardigan.]
If you see a black cat stroke it and wish.
1961 *Weekend* 8 Nov. 2. A friend asked
me to cut a piece of fur from my black
cat—to bring her luck at Bingo.
Cf. WHITE CAT.

CAT, black: meeting

1620 MELTON *Astrologaster* 46. It is a
very unfortunate thing for a man to
meete early in a morning .. a blacke
Cat. 1797 MS diary (P. S. JEFFREY *Whitby
Lore* 140) Saw three black cats last night
so did not go to market to-day fearing
some evil. 1882 *Gents Mag.* 363 [Shet-
land] It is a good omen if a cat runs
before a fisherman on his way to the
fishing; a bad omen if she crosses his
path. 1885 *Folklore* 309 [Aberdeen./
Banff.] If the catch of fish .. is poor ..
the usual saying is, 'We've met the cat
i' the mornin'.' This is a common saying

.. when any undertaking has gone
amiss. 1890 *Young Ladies' Journal* XXXV
4. Many a woman dislikes [to] encounter
a black cat. 1898 BLAKEBOROUGH *Yorkshire Customs* 157. A few months before
she was married, she and her sweetheart
were walking to Feetham Holme .. a
black cat sprang across their path, which
was a most unlucky omen. 1909 *N & Q*
10th ser. XII 484 [Stromness, Orkney]
It is unlucky to have a black cat cross
your path, unless you spit. 1922 [Som-
erset] It is unlucky to meet a cat on your
wedding morning; and if a sailor meets
a black cat when on his way to join his
ship he will turn back. 1952 Boy, 12
[Manchester] If a black cat crosses in
front of a car from left to right, you
will have a puncture. 1962 Boy, 13
[Cumnock, Ayr.] If a black cat crosses a
miner's path he would turn back and
not go down the pit that day. 1971
Farmers Weekly 16 Apr. 71 [Cornwall]
It is said to be lucky to see a black cat
on the way to church [to be married].
1983 Girl, 13 [Maldon, Essex] I think
that if a black cat crosses the road it
gives you good luck.

CAT, black: seeing back of

1922 [Somerset] If a black cat comes to
meet you it is good luck, but if it only
comes half way, and walks away from
you it is bad. 1923 [Somerset] If a black
cat on board ship walks away from a
sailor he won't sail. 1957 Boy, 12
[Ongar, Essex] The front of a black
cat is lucky, the back unlucky. 1985
Woman, *c.*65 [Co. Cork] If the cat sits
with its back to you, it's bad luck.

CAT, black: visit from

1882 *People's Friend* 8 Nov. 712. The
visit of a black cat is lucky, curious to
say, considering the intimate terms in
which those sable gentry were supposed
to stand with the witches. 1913 E. M.
WRIGHT *Rustic Speech* 218. It is very
unlucky to drive away a black cat .. An
Oxford landlady told us quite recently
that she had driven away a black cat
from her door .. some years previously,
and since then she had 'buried twenty-
three relations'! 1923 [Taunton, Som.]
If a black cat wishes to enter your house
by all means let him in, and good

fortune will follow. **1982** Woman, *c.*50 [Middlesbrough, Teesside] Never chase a black cat away.

CAT, buying

1889 *Dorset Field Club* 25. A cat that is bought is never good for much. **1923** [Castle Cary, Som.] To have a cat given you, especially a black one, is good luck.

CAT disliked

1887 'SPERANZA' WILDE *Superstitions of Ireland* II 10. On entering a house the usual salutation is, 'God save all here, except the cat.' **1919** *Folklore* 239 [Co. Tipperary] The cat is a demoniac creature; on entering a house it usual to say, 'God save all, barring the cat!'

CAT: drowning at sea

1590 Witchcraft trial (R. PITCAIRN *Criminal Trials of Scotland* I pt. 2 237) The said Agnes Sampsoune . . baptesit ane catt . . in maner following . . thay patt the catt thryis throw the linkis of the cruik, and passit itt thryis vnder the chimnay. Thairefter . . thay . . caist the catt in the see . . Efter quhilk, be thair insorcerie and inchantment, the boit perischit betuix Leith and Kinghorne; quhilk thing the Devill did. **1755** FIELDING *Voyage to Lisbon* 89. The kitten at last recovered . . to the great disappointment of some of the sailors, who asserted that the drowning a cat was the very surest way of raising a favourable wind. **1787** GROSE *Provincial Glossary* Superstitions 66. Drowning a cat at sea, is extremely unlucky. **1789** J. ANDREWS *Anecdotes* 225. Superstition and profaneness . . are too often found united in the sailor; and the man who dreads the stormy effects of drowning a cat . . will . . wantonly defy his Creator by the most daring execrations. **1813** BRAND *Antiquities* II 551–2. The common Sailors account it very unlucky . . to throw a Cat over-board, or drown one at Sea. **1830** MARRYAT *King's Own* VI. I'll leave you to guess whether the sailors didn't declare that he got his death all along of murdering the cat. **1854** *N & Q* 1st ser. X 26. An infallible recipe for raising a storm is to throw a cat overboard. **1900** S. HEWETT *Nummits* 59 [Devon] Fisher men consider it most unlucky to

throw a cat overboard, or to drown one at sea.

Cf. CAT, killing.

CAT endangers health by sucking breath

1607 TOPSELL *Foure-footed Beastes* 106. It is most certaine that the breath and Sauour of cats . . destroy the lungs, and . . they which keepe their cats with them in their beds haue the aire corrupted and fall into feuer hectickes and consumptions. **1708** *British Apollo* 24 Nov. *Q.* Can a Cat kill a Person, when asleep, by sucking his Breath? *A.* This we take to be the Curious Notion of some Eminent Old Woman, endeavouring to Prove the Cat an Air Pump. **1791** *Annual Register* 25 Jan. 4. A child of eighteen months was found dead near Plymouth; and it appeared, on the coroner's inquest, that the child died in consequence of a cat sucking its breath, occasioning a strangulation. **1825** JAMIESON *Scottish Dict.* Suppl. I 190. It is reckoned highly improper to leave a cat alone with an infant; as it is believed, that it has the power of taking away the life of the child by sucking out its breath . . Some say that in this manner it sucks the blood of the child. **1864** R. CHAMBERS *Book of Days* II 39 [Suffolk] Cats suck the breath of infants and so kill them. This extremely unphilosophical notion of cats preferring exhausted to pure air, is frequently a cause of great annoyance to poor pussy. **1867** HARLAND & WILKINSON *Lancashire Folk-Lore* 219–20. If a cat sleeps in a child's cradle it is supposed to inhale the child's life. **1922** [Somerset] Old women believe that cats suck children's breath and kill them. **1987** Woman, 32 [London] Be sure to shut the door of the baby's room when she's asleep. I don't want the cat to jump into her cot. I don't think he'd do her any harm, but better be on the safe side.

CAT endangers health if reared with baby

1861 *N & Q* 2nd ser. XII 500. It is very unlucky (said an old nurse) to rear a kitten and a baby together. **1883** BURNE *Shropshire* 212. If a baby and a kitten are born on the same day the child will not grow, says an old Pulverbatch dame. **1900** S. HEWETT *Nummits* 54 [Devon] It is unlucky .. to have a kitten and a baby in a house together. The kitten should be sent away in order to secure good health to the baby. **1922** [Somerset] If a cat and a baby are born the same day, one will thrive and the other will die. **1955** [Staindrop, Co. Durham] My mother came to help me with our new daughter, and seeing the kitten we had also just acquired, said, 'When did you get that? I don't like having a cat around with a new baby.'

CAT endangers health of unborn child

1988 Woman [Bermondsey, SE London] I'm sixty-four. Had seven children, two dead. One went under a bus, two and a half he was. The other was born dead. Cat went over me.

CAT, killing

1922 [Somerset] It is unlucky to kill a cat or kitten. Many people prefer to pay someone else to do it. It is very unlucky for a farmer to drown a cat, it foretells bad luck with his cattle.

Cf. CAT: drowning at sea.

CAT: nine lives

1546 HEYWOOD *Proverbs* II IV G2ᵛ. No wyfe, a woman hath nyne lyues like a cat. **1570** W. BALDWIN *Beware Cat* (1584, *Coll. Anglo-Poet.*, ed. Corser, I 114) A Cat hath nine liues, that is to say, a witch may take on her a Cats body nine times. *c.***1595** SHAKESPEARE *Romeo and Juliet* III i. Good King of Cats, nothing but one of your nine lives. **1727** GAY *Fables* XXIII. 'Old Woman and Her Cats'. Boys against our lives combine, Because, 'tis said, your cats have nine. **1788** GROSE *Dictionary*. Cat's Foot. Cats, according to vulgar naturalists, have nine lives, that is, one less than a woman. **1894** BLACKMORE *Perlycross* ii. If a cat has nine lives, sir; a lie has ninety-nine. **1966** B. LLOYD-JONES *Animals Came in One by One* 87. One cat took me three and a half weeks to coax from the [bombed] ruins of his home .. I caught him .. A week later he was sleek, gentle and loving again. One life gone, eight to go.

CAT on table

1922 [Somerset] It is unlucky to have a cat jump on your table.

CAT, shutting up

1957 *Folklore* 425. The oven was cold, and the cat was kept in it till the lots for the cavills, or seams [of coal], were drawn .. It is, or was until recently, so common that miners in Co. Durham seem amazed when any one confesses ignorance of it.

CAT, shutting up: raises wind

1831 DARWIN *Diary of HMS Beagle* 20 Dec. [waiting for a favourable wind] The sailors declare there is somebody on shore keeping a black cat under a tub, which it stands to reason must keep us in harbour. **1883** *Folklore* 330 [Castletown, Co. Limerick] She laughingly threatened to put the cat under the pot to bring bad weather and force me to stay. She assured me it was a common practice among the sailors' wives. **1895** J. HARDY *Denham Tracts* II 365. Seventy years or so ago it was a common practice among the Hauxley fishermen, when shipwrecks had been scarce, to shut up the cat in a cupboard.

'CAT' taboo word

1809 A. EDMONSTON *Zetland Islands* II 74. Certain names must not be mentioned while they are setting their lines, especially .. the cat; and many others equally unmeaning. **1883** J. R. TUDOR *Orkneys and Shetland* 166 [Shetland] When setting their lines they avoided, and do still, mentioning certain objects, except by certain special words. Thus .. a cat [is called] *kirser, fitting, vengla,* or *foodin.* **1885** *Folklore* 182 [St Combs, Aberdeen.] The word 'cat' lies under the ban [of being uttered]. A man told me that .. when a boy he went to the door of a .. fisherman's house and called out 'Cat' .. The fisherman was engaged in some work by the side of the fire. No sooner did he hear the word, than he seized the tongs, and threw it at the head of the offender. It was caught on the corner of the 'bun-bed' [box-bed], and fell, 'An gehn it hidna deen that, I hidna been here the nicht,' said the man.

CAT OR DOG, disease transferred to

1590 Witchcraft trial (R. PITCAIRN *Criminal Trials in Scotland* II pt. 2 234) For cureing of .. Robert Kerse of Dalkeyth, quha wes havelie tormentit with wichcraft and diseis .. quhilk seiknes sche [Wise Wife of Keith] tuik vpoun hir selff .. with grit groining and torment quhill the morne: one quhilk tyme, thair wes ane gritt dyn hard in the hous; quhilk seiknes sche caist of hir selff .. to the effect ane catt or dog mycht haif gottin the samin. **1663** BUTLER *Hudibras* II iii ll. 288–9. Fright Agues into Dogs, and scare With Rimes, the Tooth-ach and Catarrh.' *ante*1672 BROWNE Commonplace book (*Works*, ed. Keynes, 1964, III 301) Since you are so unsatisfied with the many rationall medicines which you .. have tried for the gout, you have leasure enough to make triall of these empericall medicines .. Trie the way of transplantation .. Give pultesses taken from the part unto doggs, & lett a whelpe lye in the bed with you. **1721** J. KELLY *Scotish Proverbs* 80–1. *Cast the cat o'er him*. It is believed that when a Man is raving in a Fever, the Cat cast over him will cure him; apply'd to them whom we hear telling extravagant Things, as they were raving. **1750** W. ELLIS *Country Housewife's Companion* 298. It is said, that a Gentlewoman having a swelled tumid Hand, put her Finger into a Cat's Ear, and within two Hours she was delivered of her Pain; but the Cat was so pained that two Men could hardly hold her. **1849** BRAND *Antiquities* III 289 [Gloucester] If a child has the hooping-cough, cut off some of the hair of its head, roll it up in butter, and throw it to a dog, upon whose swallowing it all symptoms of coughing in the child will at once cease, and manifest themselves in the dog. **1881** W. GREGOR *North-East of Scotland* 124. If a cow or other domestic animal was seized with disease, one .. cure was to twist a rope of straw the contrary way, join the two ends, and put the .. animal through .. along with a cat. The disease was transferred to the cat, and the animal's life was saved by the cat dying. **1883** BURNE *Shropshire* 202–3 [Clungunford] For whooping-cough .. cut a lock of hair from the crown of the sick child's head, put it between bread and butter, and give it to a dog. If the dog ate it he would die, but the child would recover.

1888 *Christian Leader* 21 June 392 [Hebrides] Within the last fortnight .. a certificated midwife [advised] 'If the baby is ill and not thriving, take a cat by the four feet, swing it round and round the infant several times, then throw it out of the hole in the roof for letting out the smoke; if it is a black cat, or if the house has a chimney, then throw the cat out of the window; if the cat dies the child will live, because the witches or brownies have left the child and gone into the cat. If the cat does not die then the child will.' **1892** *N & Q* 8th ser. I 106. All my family being laid up with the influenza, our help .. proposed .. to cut off some hair from the hollow of the neck, put it in milk, and give it to an animal to drink. The disease would then be transferred to the animal, and the patient would recover, while the animal would die. She had been for several days trying to entice a neighbour's dog, as she would not harm our own family pets. **1923** [Somerset] To get a bad place well, let a cat lick it.

CAT OR DOG passes over corpse

1771 PENNANT *Tour in Scotland* 92. It is reckoned so ominous, for a dog or cat to pass over [the corpse] that the poor animal is killed without mercy. **1786** R. GOUGH *Sepulchral Monuments* II pt. I 205 [Orkney] I know not for what reason they lock up all the cats of the house .. as soon as any person dies. **1799** *Stat. Acc. of Scotland* XXI 147 n. [Monquhitter, Aberdeen.] If a cat was permitted to leap over a corpse, it portended misfortune. The meaning of this was to prevent that carnivorous animal from coming near the body of the deceased, lest, when the watchers were asleep, it should endeavour to prey upon it. **1814** J. TRAIN *Mountain Muse* [Scottish Highlands] Now he's beyond the reach of pain .. And Gib [the cat] Imprison'd is, lest any thing Should make him o'er his master spring. **1825** JAMIESON *Scottish Dict.* Suppl. I 193. In Angus it has been supposed, that a cat, if it has passed over a corpse, has the power of causing blindness to the person whom it first leaps over afterwards. **1852** DICKENS *Bleak House* XI. As they left the room where the corpse lay the young surgeon said 'Don't leave the cat there .. that won't do!' **1866** HENDERSON *Northern Counties* 43 [Northumb.] Just as a funeral was about to leave the house, the cat jumped over the coffin, and no one would move till the cat was destroyed. **1888** *Folklore* 263 [Achterneed, Ross.] It is accounted very unlucky for a cat to pass between one and a dead body. Cats are, therefore, shut out of the apartment in which the body lies. Some do not allow a cat to remain in the apartment in which one lies dying. **1909** *N & Q* 10th ser. XII 484 [Stromness, Orkney] It is unlucky for a dog to cross the path of a funeral party: the relatives of the deceased will never prosper till the dog has been killed. **1962** Priest, 44 [Workington, Cumb.] They always say to me 'Come in, Father, come in. Don't let the cat in.' They think the cat might get on the corpse and maul it.

CATERPILLAR, hairy: cures

1851 *N & Q* 1st ser. III 516 [Lancs.] Hooping-cough may be cured by tying a hairy caterpillar in a small bag round the child's neck, and as the caterpillar dies the cough goes. **1855** F. K. ROBINSON *Yorkshire Words. Kincough* .. it is the practice to put a live hairyworm into a small bag, which is hung round the neck of the patient, and as it decomposes, the cough will decrease. **1878** *Folk-Lore Record* 39 [Fittleworth, Sussex] Our coachman's daughter was advised to cure her ague by putting a caterpillar into a box and carrying it in her pocket [and] as the caterpillar wasted away, her ague-fits would decrease. **1883** BURNE *Shropshire* 194. A 'miller', or hairy caterpillar, enclosed in the shell of a hazelnut [is] then sewn up in a cotton band and tied round the sufferer's neck. If the [whooping] cough does not disappear .. the 'miller' must be .. replaced by a living spider. **1903** *Globe* 6 Aug. 7. In Cornwall .. many of the villagers firmly believe that the way to cure whooping-cough is to tie a hairy caterpillar in a muslin bag to the chest of the patient. When the caterpillar dies, the cough is supposed to leave the sufferer. **1951** *Trans. Devon. Ass.* 75. Woolly caterpillars .. have been used in this way [in bag round neck, to cure whooping cough].

CATERPILLAR, hairy: lucky

1883 BURNE *Shropshire* 239. It is lucky .. if a Tom Tailor [hairy caterpillar] creeps upon you. **1957** Girl, 13 [Langholm, Dumfries.] If you throw a black hairy caterpillar over your shoulder you have good luck.

CATTLE: burning entrails gives power over witch

*c.*20 BC VIRGIL *Aeneid* VI (tr. Dryden, ll. 352–68) Invoking Hecate hither to repair .. Sev'n brawny Bulls with his own Hand he [Aeneas] kills: Then on the broiling Entrails Oyl he pours; Which, ointed thus, the raging Flame devours. Late, the Nocturnal Sacrifice begun; Nor ended, 'till the next returning Sun .. E're Hecate came. **1486** SPRENGER & KRAMER *Malleus Maleficarum* (tr. Summers, 162) When an animal has been killed by witchcraft, and they wish to find out the witch, or to make certain whether its death was natural or due to witchcraft, they go to the place where dead animals are skinned, and drag its intestines along the ground up to their house; not into the house by the main door, but over the threshold of the back entrance into the kitchen; and then they make a fire and put the intestines over it on a hurdle. Then .. just as the intestines get hot and burn, so are the intestines of the witch afflicted with burning pains. **1584** SCOT *Discoverie of Witchcraft* XII XXI. When anie of your cattell are killed with witchcraft, hast you to the place where the carcase lieth, and traile the bowels of the beast unto your house, and drawe them not in at the doore, but under the threshold of the house into the kitchen; and there make a fier, and set over the same a gridiron, and thereupon laie the inwards or bowels; and as they wax hot, so shall the witches entrailes be molested with extreame heate and paine. But then must you make fast your doores, least the witch come and fetch awaie a cole of your fier: for then ceaseth hir torments. **1612** J. COTTA *Short Discoverie* 54. Neither can I beleeue (I speake it with reuerence vnto grauer iudgements) that the forced coming of men or women to the burning of bewitched cattell [is] any trial of a witch. **1901** J. RHYS *Celtic*

Folklore I 305 [Isle of Man] If you want to know to whom you are indebted for the loss of the beast, you have simply to burn its carcase in the open air and watch who comes first to the spot or who first passes by: that is the criminal to be charged with the death of the animal, and he cannot help coming there—such is the effect of the fire.

Cf. EXCREMENT, burning human.

CATTLE: carcass hung in chimney to protect livestock

late **18th c.** J. RAMSAY (*Scotland in the Eighteenth Century*, II 446–7) There is a disease called the *black spauld*, which sometimes rages like a pestilence among black cattle, the systems of which are a mortification in the legs and a corruption of the mass of blood .. It is remarkable that the leg affected is cut off, and hung up in some part of the house or byre, where it remains suspended, notwithstanding the seeming danger of infection. There is hardly a house in Mull where these may not be seen. **1808** JAMIESON *Scottish Dict*. Quarter-ill. A disease among cattle, affecting them only in one limb or quarter. A very gross superstition is observed by some people in Angus, as an antidote against this ill. A piece is cut out of the thigh of one of the cattle that has died of it. This they hang up within the chimney .. It is believed that as long as it hangs there, it will prevent the disease from approaching the place. It is therefore carefully preserved; and in case of the family removing, transported to the new farm, as one of their valuable effects. It is handed down from one generation to another. **1879** HENDERSON *Northern Counties* 167 [Co. Durham] The good wife told me that they had experienced great difficulty that year in rearing their calves; the poor little creatures all died off, so they had taken the leg and thigh of one of the dead calves, and hung it in the chimney by a rope, since when they had not lost another calf.

CATTLE: carcass hung in thorn tree to protect livestock

1868 *N & Q* 4th ser. II 557 [Danby-in-Cleveland, Yorks.] A lamb that is dropped dead, or that dies while still very young, is customarily hung up in a tree—properly in a thorn, though any fruit- or berry-bearing tree will do. In the last case under my notice the tree was a rowan-tree. **1879** HENDERSON *Northern Counties* 167 n. I have often observed in the Weald of Sussex dead horses or calves hung up by the four legs to the horizontal branch of a tree .. I never could ascertain the reason .. further than that it was thought lucky for the cattle. **1935** *I Walked by Night* (ed. L. Rider Haggard, 18) [Norfolk] Wen Cows calved, the after berth had to be hung on a White thorn bush, as it was said to prevent Milk fever and other ills.

CATTLE: one sacrificed to protect rest of herd

1643 Witchcraft trial, Orkney (DALYELL *Darker Superstitions of Scotland* 185) Many cattle having died .. the surviving animals were drove past a tub of water containing two enchanted stones, and each was sprinkled .. One, however, being unable to walk 'was by force drawin out at the byre dure; and the said Johnne .. smelling the nois thereof said it wald not leive, caused ane hoill to be maid in Maw Greane, quhilk was put quick [alive] in the hole and maid all the rest of the cattell theireftir to go over that place: and in that devillische maner, be charmeing', they were cured. **1784** *Gents Mag*. pt. 1 350 [Suffolk] I met my labourer carrying an abortive calf .. 'To bury it in the gateway of the close, for the other three cows to pass over, else they would all cast their calves.' **1824** F. HITCHINS *History of Cornwall* I 106. An ignorant old farmer in Cornwall, who is still alive, and well known to the writer .. met with some severe losses in his cattle, about the year 1800 .. All remedies failing, he thought it necessary to have recourse to some extraordinary measure. Accordingly, on consulting with some of his neighbours .. they recalled .. a tale which tradition had handed down from remote antiquity, that the calamity would not cease, until he had actually burned alive the finest calf which he had upon his farm; but that when this sacrifice was made, the murrain would afflict his cattle no more. **1866** HENDERSON *North-*

ern *Counties* 117 [Moray.] Not fifteen years ago, a herd of cattle .. being attacked with murrain, one of them was sacrificed by burying alive, as a propitiatory offering for the rest. **1891** J. C. ATKINSON *Moorland Parish* 62 [Danby, Yorks.] If one of the cows in a dairy .. produces a calf prematurely .. the remainder of the cows are only too likely to follow suit .. The folklore-prescribed preventative .. used to be to remove the threshold of the cow-house .. dig a deep hole .. deep enough, indeed, to admit of the abortive calf being buried in it, on its back, with its four legs all stretching .. upwards in the rigidity of death, and then to cover all up as before. **1905** *Folklore* 337. A cowman (a Suffolk man), lately said to me that the only cure for cows when there was an epidemic of abortion was to bury one of the premature calves in a gateway through which the herd passed daily. **1909** M. TREVELYAN *Folk-Lore of Wales* 23. I have heard my grandfather and father say that in times gone by the people would throw a calf in the fire [May fire, or Midsummer Eve] when there was any disease among the herds.

CAUL, possession of: lucky

ante **1500** 'Piers of Fullham' (HAZLITT *Remains of Early Eng. Poetry* II 14) He vnware hath lost his galle [caul] .. Whiche, as clerkys determyne, Is right a perfyte medicyne, Both on ffreshe water and on see, That folke shall not drowned be. **1507** *Gospelles of Dystaues* pt. 6 XII. I tell you for a trouthe that yf ony man bere vpon hym in some batayll the lytell skynne that he bryngeth out of his moders wombe, knowe that he may not be hurte nor wounded in his body. **1540** PALSGRAVE *Acolastus* 80. May not men .. thinke, that I was borne in a good howre, or that I was borne with a syly hoffe on myn heed. **1616** A. ROBERTS *Treatise of Witchcraft* 65–6. That naturall couer wherewith some children are borne, and is called by our women, the sillie how, Midwiues were wont to sell to credulous Aduocates and Lawyers, as an especiall meanes to furnish them with eloquence and perswasiue speech, and to stoppe the mouthes of all, who should make an opposition against

them. **1646** BROWNE *Vulgar Errors* V XXI. Great conceits are raised of the involution or membranous covering, commonly called the silly how, that sometimes is found about the heads of children upon their birth, and is therefore preserved with great care, not onely as medicall in diseases, but effectual in success, concerning the Infant and others. **1691** *Athenian Mercury* III no. 25. Quest. What are we to think of such as are born with Cawls about their Heads? Answ. Some wou'd perswade us that they are not so subject to the Miseries & Calamities of Humanity as other persons .. Some have had the vanity to believe, that such as have come with this Coif into the World, were to expect all good fortune, even so far as to become invulnerable, provided they be always careful to carry it about 'em .. This Opinion was so strongly rooted in the Primitive Ages Persuasion that St Chrysostom in several of his Homilies speaks against such as made use thereof to gain Esteem, particularly one Praetus, a Clergyman, being desirous to be fortunate, bought such a Coif of a Midwife, which was very highly censur'd, as Balsamon affirms in his Commentaries upon the Canons of the Apostles. **1708** *British Apollo* 3 Nov. I ever have been told, that being born with a Cawl was a Token of good luck, hitherto I have seen none, I'm 22 and see no Husband come, no not one Wooer. **1738** SWIFT *Polite Conversation* I 82. I believe you were born with a Cawl on your Head; you are such a Favourite among the Ladies. **1779** *Morning Post* 21 Aug. 3. To the Gentlemen of the Navy, and others going long voyages to sea. To be disposed of, a CHILD'S CAUL. Enquire at the Bartlet Buildings Coffee-house, in Holborn. NB To avoid unnecessary trouble the price is Twenty Guineas. **1787** GROSE *Provincial Glossary* Superstitions 60. It is deemed lucky to be born with a caul, or membrane, over the face .. This caul is esteemed an infallible preservative against drowning; and, under that idea, is frequently advertised for sale in our public papers, and purchased by seamen. *c.***1816** Wilkie MS (HENDERSON *Northern Counties* 1866, 13) Children born with a hallihoo (holy or fortunate hood) are deemed lucky, but the caul must be preserved carefully; for should it be lost .. the child will pine away. **1822** *John Bull* 20 Jan. 462–3. Will your readers believe that, on the walls of the Exchange of the first city in the world [London] the resort of the most intelligent merchants and traders of this great empire, bills, advertising for sale CHILDREN'S CAULS, as an infallible preservative from 'drowning, &c.' are still impudently exhibited. **1879** J. NAPIER *West of Scotland* 32. The carrying of a caul on board ship was believed to prevent shipwreck, and masters of vessels paid a high price for them. **1899** *N & Q* 9th ser. III 27 [Liphook, Hants.] So potent was the influence of the caul that when his mother tried to bathe him he sat on the surface of the water, and if forced down, came up again like a cork. **1919** *Morning Post* 9 June 3. Soon after the submarines got to work I was in the neighbourhood of the [London] docks and seeing in a shop a child's caul for sale I inquired the price. 'Three guineas,' said the man. I told him I had one for which I gave 1s. 6d. 'Yes, that was before the war .. the submarine has made life at sea so dangerous.' **1980** Sea captain's wife, 59 [South Shields, Co. Durham] Anybody that makes their living on small boats—pilot cutters, tugs—if they had a baby boy, they'd save the caul, because he'd follow in his father's footsteps, and would need it.

CAUL, state of health indicated by

1787 GROSE *Provincial Glossary* Superstitions 61. A person possessed of a caul may know the state of health of the party who was born with it: if alive and well, it is firm and crisp; if dead or sick, relaxed and flaccid. **1897** *N & Q* 8th ser. XI 144 [Lincs.] He was born with a silly-hood, a sort of veil over his head. And if they don't take care of it, the child will grow up a wanderer. They stretch it out, real thin it is, like tissue paper, and they put it on paper. And they always know by it if the person is ill .. it'll go damp always if he ails anything. **1899** *N & Q* 9th ser. III 175 [Worksop, Notts.] The nurse said that .. the boy who kept his veil would never

be drowned. When he was ill, the veil became damp and flabby. While he was well it was dry, and 'snerept up'. **1953** Unpublished letter to *Woman* [Pellon, Yorks.] My mother had sixteen children. Four of the children was born with what we called veils over the face. It was like skin. It would be taken off the face, hung up to dry, then it would be put away careful. Because it was said whatever happen to the veil would happen to the child.

CAVE cures whooping cough

1817 G. YOUNG *History of Whitby* II 883. Another aerial being .. had his dwelling in Hob-hole, near Runswick .. His powers were exercised in curing young children of the hooping-cough .. One of its parents carried it into the cave, and with loud voice thus invoked the demigod of the place: 'Hob-hole Hob! my bairn's got kink-cough: take't off; take't off!'

Cf. RAILWAY TUNNEL cures whooping-cough.

CHAIN-LETTER

1922 R. LYND *Solomon* 75–6. When the world was more pious, post cards containing chain prayers used to be popular .. The post card .. now going the rounds .. does not pretend to any religious sanction. It simply .. runs .. 'Good Luck! Copy this out and send it to nine people .. Do not break the chain, as whoever does will have bad luck. Do it within twenty-four hours and count nine days and you will have great good luck.' **1928** A. R. WRIGHT *English Folklore* 68. 'Chains of luck' .. for a number of years, right up to 1928, have worried nervous women. You are requested to send a copy of the message to nine people, and then comes the threat of 'luck'. 'Whoever does this will have great joy and happiness, but to those who neglect this will come misfortune. Do not break the chain. It was started on a Flanders battlefield.' **1958** *Daily Express* 10 Mar. 7 [Swiss Cottage, London] A priest warned his congregation last night: 'Throw these letters away. Ignore their threats.' Afterwards he said: 'Some of my congregation are becoming obsessed by the letters.' **1979** *Home* *and Country* Mar. 143 [Eckington W.I., Derbys.] The very sad photograph of a young couple in our local paper, who have received a chain letter and are now spending days and nights worrying about what their fate might be because they broke the link by destroying the letter. 1987 *The Messenger* [Haslemere, Surrey] 20 May 13. Some local residents have been disturbed by an unusual chain letter which is in circulation . . The letter is claimed to have been written by a Venezuelan missionary, Saul Anthony De Croff. Those who receive it are ordered to send it on to 12 friends within 96 hours, otherwise a terrible tragedy will strike them . . Dom Fairchild failed to send it on, and nine days after receiving the letter, his wife died.

CHAIR, empty

1899 *Newcastle Weekly Chronicle* 4 Feb. 7 [Jesmond] It is unlucky to sit next an empty chair.

CHAIR falls over

1738 SWIFT *Polite Conversation* I 55 As *Miss* rises, the chair falls behind her. MISS. Well; I shan't be Lady-Mayoress this Year. NEVEROUT. No, Miss; 'tis worse than that; you won't be marry'd this Year. 1879 J. NAPIER *West of Scotland* 138. If a person in rising from table overturned his chair, this shewed that he had been speaking untruths. 1887 'SPERANZA' WILDE *Superstitions of Ireland* II 103. If a chair fall as a person rises, it is an unlucky omen. 1932 C. IGGLESDEN *Those Superstitions* 235. If a nurse knocks over a chair it is a sign that a new patient will be soon arriving. 1958 *Daily Herald* 31 July 4. If the chair over which the bedclothes are folded falls over, an emergency case will come into the ward. I have never seen the chair fall without hearing the ward phone ring for an emergency.

CHAIR passed over table

1955 MRS R. HENREY *Bloomsbury Fair* 97 [Bloomsbury, London] When a chair was passed over a table it foretold a row.

CHAIR put back in place

1933 *Folklore* 196 [Hemswell, Lincs.] When having a meal with an ac-

quaintance, do not push your chair under the table when you get up, or you will not come there again for a meal. 1963 Man, 75 [Halifax, Yorks.] When out to tea, don't put the chair you have used back to where it belongs. If you do, you won't be asked to go there again.

Cf. TABLE-NAPKIN, folding.

CHAIR, sitting in someone else's

1923 [Trowbridge, Wilts.] To sit down in a chair immediately after someone else has risen from it is an evil omen. The second person will follow the first as quickly to the grave. 1972 *Lore and Language* July 7 [Coalisland, Co. Tyrone] If someone leaves the room you shouldn't sit in his chair if you know he'll be back; otherwise it may be thought you want his death and he will be within his rights in asking you: 'Would you be in my grave as quick?'

CHAIR turned or changed for luck

1728 SWIFT 'Journal of a Modern Lady.' ll. 240–1 (*Works*, 1937, I 452) This odious chair, how came I stuck in't? I think I never had good luck in't. 1753 *Adventurer* 6 Mar. Mrs Overall . . having lost three rubbers at whist running . . notwithstanding she had changed chairs . . grew out of all patience; and taking up the devil's books, as she called them, flung them into the fire. 1832 *Gents Mag.* pt. 2 493 [Lincs.] I have seen many young ladies, and some old ones, turn their chairs three times round . . as a charm to ensure good luck at cards. 1883 BURNE *Shropshire* 272. Children, playing . . at cards on Christmas evenings, when they lose, jump up and hastily turn the chair on which they have been sitting, saying they will 'turn the luck'. 1900 S. HEWETT *Nummits* 59 [Devon] When unfortunate at cards you should rise from your chair, twist it round on one of its legs four times. This action is supposed to change the luck. 1925 *N & Q* CXLVIII 153. 'Turn your chair and turn your luck.' This is quite a common expression in Somerset. 1932 C. IGGLESDEN *Those Superstitions* 190–1. There is the habit of turning your chair for luck when cards are going against you—another ridiculous superstition that has no meaning.

CHAIR turned round = quarrel

1831 HONE *Year Book* 29 Feb. When talking thoughtlessly with a good woman, I carelessly turned a chair round two or three times; she was offended, and said it was a sign we should quarrel: and so it proved, for she never spoke friendly to me afterwards. 1925 *N & Q* CXLVIII 153. In some parts of the country to turn a chair round two or three times is considered unlucky, and a means of bringing about quarrels between parties.

CHAMBER POT

1879 NAPIER *West of Scotland* 47. The evening before the marriage .. the best maid .. carried with her a certain domestic utensil filled with salt, which was the first article of the bride's furnishing taken into the house. A portion of the salt was sprinkled over the floor as a protection against an evil eye. 1934 *Folklore* 343 [Scottish Borders] As a wedding present the pot is important among shepherd families about Hawick and Galashiels and the filling with salt is imperative .. [At] a wedding party of recent date the pot, duly filled with salt, was placed on the floor and jumped over three times by both bride and bridegroom.
Cf. BUCKET, jumping over.

CHAMPAGNE CORK

1954 Girl, 15 [Forfar, Angus] I know of a footballer who earned the name of 'Corky' because he always carries a champagne cork in his pocket when playing. 1956 *Evening Standard* 21 Nov. 4. To the two opening nights she [Terence Rattigan's mother] took a mascot—a champagne cork. The cork was popped on the first night of *French Without Tears* and she has taken it to every first night since then. 1984 [Nottingham] She took the champagne cork, cut a slit in it, and asked for a coin. This she put into the slit, and then placed the cork on the mantelpiece. She said it was lucky to keep it until one had the next bottle of champagne. 1988 Woman, 50 [London] For a birth, or a wedding, or a twenty-first birthday, you must slit the cork of the first bottle of champagne you open, and push a coin in the slit, and

you're supposed to keep that cork all the rest of your life.

CHARMS in food

1778 W. HUTCHINSON *View of Northumberland* II app. 14. The syllabub, prepared for the May Feast .. is made of warm milk from the cow, sweet cake, and wine; and a kind of divination is practised, by fishing with a ladle for a wedding ring, which is dropt into it for the purpose of prognosticating who shall be first married. 1823 W. GRANT STEWART *Highlanders of Scotland* 255. Peculiar to this night [Fasten's Eve, i.e. Shrove Tuesday] is the matrimonial brose .. Before the bree [broth] is put in the bicker or plate, a ring is mixed with the meal, which it will be the aim of every partaker to get. 1850 *N & Q* 1st ser. II 117 [Burnley, Lancs.] The following practice is very prevalent at marriages in these districts .. Make a common flat cake of flour, water, currants, &c. and put therein a wedding ring and a sixpence. When the company is about to retire on the wedding-day, the cake must be broken and distributed amongst the unmarried females. She who gets the ring in her portion of the cake will shortly be married, and the one who gets the sixpence will die an old maid. 1850 DENHAM *Isle of Man* (1892, 200–1) On Shrove Tuesday it is customary to have .. pancakes. Into the latter are thrown a ring and a piece of silver money, with which the candidates for matrimony try their fortune. It is quite a Manx merry-making. 1863 H. CULLWICK *Diary* (1984, 145) Christmas Eve. After supper was over the Master had the hot mince pie up wi' a ring & sixpence in it—they had good fun over it, 'cause Mr Grant got the ring & a young lady sixpence. 1866 *N & Q* 3rd ser. IX 480. I remember as a boy having a ring in my share of a Michaelmas apple-pie in Ireland, and being then of the mature age of thirteen and a half, I was informed that I would be married within a twelvemonth; but I was not. 1896 *Trans. Buchan Field Club* IV 225 [Shrove Tuesday] Into the huge dish of brose there were skilfully put certain articles of virtue, a ring, a sixpenny piece, a bawbee, a button, each of them sure to indicate the future in regard to marriage. **1899** *Newcastle Weekly Chronicle* 11 Feb. 7 [Jesmond, Northumb., Shrove Tuesday] A button, a ring, and a sixpence, are put in a pancake, which is cut into sections and distributed; and the finder will be unmarried, married, or rich, according to the article found. **1923** [Taunton, Som.] If you get a wedding ring in the Christmas pudding you will be married before the year is out. If the thimble, old maid; if the button, a bachelor. **1939** M. E. L. COX *Practical Cookery* 163. If money or charms are to be put in the pudding, these should be washed and boiled for at least 5 minutes in a pan of water, to sterilize them. If there are children in the party, it is safer to wrap the money and charms in separate wisps of paper. **1966** J. DUNCAN *My Friend My Father* 3–4 [N. Scotland] In our house somebody's birthday was always coming along and a dumpling would be made .. mixed .. in the big basin .. the suet .. the raisins .. the brown spice. Then .. from the top shelf of the dresser .. the 'dumpling things'— the tiny silver thimble, which if you found it in your helping .. meant that you would be an old maid .. the pearl bachelor's button and the silver three-penny piece .. Aunt Kate .. had a way of getting the ring that meant you were to be married soon. **1986** Woman, 35 [Malvern, Worcs.] We still use my mother-in-law's charms in our Christmas pudding. The silver ring means you'll get married within the year; the bachelor's button—a plain bone button—means you won't get married; and the sixpence means you'll be rich. We think the bought charms are cissy.

CHILDERMAS DAY/HOLY INNOCENTS' DAY (28 Dec.)

1600 A. MUNDAY *Sir John Oldcastle* D2. Friday quoth a, a dismall day, Child-ermasse day this yeare was friday. **1602** R. CAREW *Cornwall* 32. [As] ominous to the fishermen, as the beginning a voyage on the day when Childermas day fell, doth to the Mariner. **1620** MELTON *Astrologaster* 46. It is not good to put on a new sute, pare one's nailes, or begin anything on a Childermas day. **1688** R. HOLME *Academy of Armory* III 131. Innocence-Day on what Day of the Week soever it lights upon, that Day of the Week is by Astronomers taken to be a Cross Day all that Year through. **1711** *Spectator* 8 Mar. A little boy at the lower end of the table told her, that he was to go into join-hand on Thursday. 'Thursday?' (says she) 'No, child, if it please God, you shall not begin upon Childermas-day; tell your writing-master that Friday will be soon enough.' **1817** G. YOUNG *History of Whitby* II 880. Some years ago, when a ship was going to sail from Whitby on childermas day, one of the crew, at the persuasion of his wife, left the vessel. **1855** *N & Q* 1st ser. XII 201. I visited one of the lead mines in Allendale, and I found that, rather than work [on Innocents' Day] they would sacrifice their employment. Ibid. 507 [Cornwall] Our housewives strictly refrain from scrubbing and cleaning on this day, on what account I cannot discover. **1873** *N & Q* 4th ser. XII 185 [Limerick, Eire] The Irish have 'a cross day of the year' [28 Dec.] .. On that day the .. housewife will not warp thread .. and the Irish say that anything begun on that day must have an unlucky ending. **1883** BURNE *Shropshire* 408–9 [Cross Day] The ancient sages of Pul-verbatch applied this name [Cross Day] not only to Innocents' Day itself, but throughout the year to the day of the week on which it had last fallen, which was counted an unlucky day for the beginning of any work or other un-dertaking. 'It must have been begun on Cross Day' was a proverbial saying applied to any unfortunate enterprise. **1891–3** *Proceedings Royal Irish Acad.* 3rd ser. II 820 [Aran Islands] Some days are considered here unlucky upon which to begin any work of importance .. even to bury the dead .. one of those days [is] the feast of the Holy Innocents .. No person will be buried on that day in any week throughout the following year. **1923** [Somerset] If you begin a new piece of work on Childermas Day it will never be finished. **1985** Woman, *c.*65 [Gorran Haven, Cornwall] Wash on In-nocents' Day, Wash one of your relatives away.

CHILDREN, dreaming of

1847 C. BRONTË *Jane Eyre* XXI. When I was a little girl, only six years old, I one night heard Bessie Leaven say that . . to dream of children was a sure sign of trouble, either to one's self or one's kin. The saying might have worn out of my memory, had not a circumstance immediately followed which served indelibly to fix it there. The next day Bessie was sent for home to the deathbed of her little sister. **1988** Woman, 60. In County Durham we used to say if you dreamed of a baby you would hear of a death.

Cf. DREAMS by contraries.

CHILDREN on ship

1787 GROSE *Provincial Glossary* Superstitions 63. Children are deemed lucky to a ship; their innocence being, by the sailors, supposed a protection. **1900** S. HEWETT *Nummits* 58 [Devon] Children bring good luck to a ship. **1909** M. TREVELYAN *Folk-Lore of Wales* 4. A child of either sex [on board] indicated successful voyages.

CHIME CHILD

1849 DICKENS *David Copperfield* I. I was born . . on a Friday, at twelve o'clock at night . . It was declared by the nurse . . that I was destined to be unlucky in life; and . . that I was privileged to see ghosts and spirits; both these gifts inevitably attaching . . to all unlucky infants of either gender, born towards the small hours on a Friday night. **1853** *N & Q* 1st ser. VII 152 [Somerset] A child born in the chime-hours will have the power to see spirits. **1896** *N & Q* 8th ser. X 92 [Lincs.] Persons born on Good Friday night cannot be frightened. **1916** *N & Q* 12th ser. I 329. A recent experiment in clairvoyance that chanced to be successful evoked the comment from an observer in a Norfolk village that the experimentalist must have been 'born in the chime hours'. **1968** R. TONGUE *Chime Child* 1–3. Chime children . . must be born between midnight on a Friday and cock-crow on a Saturday, as I am told I was . . they see the dead and fairies . . have immunity from all ill-wishing . . love and control all animals [and] have

a knowledge of herbs and a way of healing others.

CHIMNEY brings luck

1965 *News of the World* 10 Oct. 6. He holds [his football coupon] up the chimney for a few minutes to bring him luck.

CHIMNEY SWEEP, meeting: and actions to avert evil

1887 *Brighton Gazette* 1 Sept. 4 [leaving London on the Brighton coach] Now, as custom is, off went our bonnets . . to a chimney sweep, sitting cross-legged, tailor-wise, on the rough plank of a shabby pony cart. It is said to bring luck, this bowing to a black man. **1893** *Folklore* 362 [Dublin] You must always bow when you meet a sweep, or even see one in the distance. If you don't, you will never have any luck. **1899** *N & Q* 9th ser. III 188. What is the origin of the custom among coaching men (amateur and professional), when driving four-in-hand or tandem, of lifting their hat to a chimney-sweep if they happen to meet one on the road? **1914** *Folklore* 382. Sitting in front of two women . . on an omnibus yesterday I heard one remark in excitement to the other, 'Look, there is a sweep!' and the other replied, 'Yes, and there are two more! We *are* in luck!' Then each speaker bade the sweeps goodmorning. **1925** *N & Q* CXLVIII 425. To meet a sweep as the first human being one 'claps eyes on' was always considered to be a lucky omen by the old Yorkshire racehorse trainers of the last generation. **1950** *N & Q* CXCV 168. Not by mere chance was a sooty chimney-sweeper sauntering in front of Kensington Palace on the wedding morning of Prince Philip and Princess Elizabeth, thereby affording the excited bridegroom an opportunity to dash out from the royal apartments to wring his grubby hand for 'sweeps' luck'. **1952** E. HULTON *When I Was a Child* 47. Mama was of the superstitious type . . if she saw a chimney-sweep in the street, she thought it was essential to call out, 'Good-morning sweep! Good-morning sweep!! Good-morning sweep!!!' and to turn round three times. **1953** Woman, 50 [Nutfield, Surrey] It is lucky to curtsey on seeing a sweep. **1954** Girl, 13 [Stoke-on-Trent, Staffs.] If you see a chimney sweeper you touch your collar till you see a horse, a dog, and a cat. **1954** Girl, 14 [Stoke-on-Trent, Staffs.] If you see the back of a chimney sweep on your wedding day you will have bad luck. **1958** *Scarborough Evening News* 31 Mar. 4. The bride [received] a good-luck kiss from .. the family's sweep. **1959** *Yorkshire Post* 8 Oct. 8. Once on the way to a point-to-point meeting he saw a sweep throw him a kiss. His mount won. **1983** *Daily Telegraph* 26 Aug. 7. A chimney sweep, Mr Cyril Buckland, is finding that kissing brides at weekend weddings is more profitable than sweeping chimneys .. His charge for a 20-minute chimney sweeping is £4, but a five-minute 'good luck' attendance at a wedding is £5.

Cf. BLACK MAN.

CHIMNEY SWEEP'S BRUSH
1985 Sweep, 55 [Liss, Hants.] Would you like to check the brush out top? It's good luck, or so they say.

CHRISTENING as protection for baby
1486 SPRENGER & KRAMER *Malleus Maleficarum* (tr. Summers, 100–1) One of the captive witches .. replied .. 'We set our snares chiefly for unbaptized children .. with our spells we kill them in their cradles or even when they are sleeping by their parents' side, in such a way that they afterwards are thought to have been overlain or to have died some other natural death. Then we secretly take them from their graves, and cook them in a cauldron [and] make an unguent which is of virtue to help us in our arts and pleasures.' **1685** EVELYN *Diary* (1906, III 177) The Bishop added a great miracle happening in Winchester .. of a poor miserably sick and decrepit child (as I remember long kept unbaptized) who, immediately on his baptism, recovered. **1819** *Gents Mag.* pt. I 110 [Herefords.] They consider the earliest possible baptism of a child newly-born, as essential to its future health. **1830** FORBY *East Anglia* 406–7. It is generally believed by East Anglian nurses that a child never thrives well till it is named; and this is one cause of the

earnest desire, frequently expressed, to have children privately baptized. If the child is sick, it is even supposed to promote the cure. **1851** *N & Q* 1st ser. III 516 [Lancs.] A strong hope is sometimes entertained that a very cross child will 'be better' after it has been christened. **1866** HENDERSON *Northern Counties* 7. The infant child of a chimney-sweeper at Thorne .. appeared to be pining away. A neighbour looked in, and enquired if the child had been baptised. On an answer .. in the negative, she gravely said, 'I would try having it christened.' **1883** BURNE *Shropshire* 192. If an unchristened baby should be seized with convulsions, 'the only remeddy is to baptize 'em.' **1962** *Daily Express* 15 Nov. 20 [headline] Vicar says bar baptism of 'good luck' babies.

Cf. CONFIRMATION good for rheumatism; GODPARENTS, healing powers of.

CHRISTENING, baby cries during
1787 GROSE *Provincial Glossary* Superstitions 51. A child, who does not cry when sprinkled in baptism, will not live. **1831** HONE *Year Book* 29 Feb. If they do not cry during the ceremony .. they will not live long. **1852** *N & Q* 1st ser. VI 601. I have often heard that it was lucky for infants to cry at the time when they were baptized, but have only lately been informed of the reason, which is, that if they are quiet and good then, it seems to show that they are too good to live. **1853** *N & Q* 1st ser. VII 96–7. I am inclined to suspect that the idea of its being lucky for a child to cry at baptism arose from the custom of exorcism, which was retained in the Anglican Church in the First Prayer-Book of King Edward VI, and is still commonly observed in the baptismal services of the Church of Rome. When the devil was going out of the possessed person, he was supposed to do so with reluctance: 'The spirit cried, and rent him sore, and came out of him: and he was as one dead' (St Mark ix 26). The tears and struggles of the infant would therefore be a convincing proof that the evil one had departed. In Ireland (as every clergyman knows) nurses will decide the matter by pinching the baby, rather than allow him to remain silent

and unlachrymose. **1878** *Folk-Lore Record* 11. I was lately present at a Christening in Sussex, when [the] grandmother of the child whispered in a voice of anxiety, 'The child never cried; why did not the nurse rouse it up?' **1923** [Martock, Som.] A baby's cry at christening is because the Holy Water is driving out the Devil. **1969** E. PORTER *Cambridgeshire* 16. She felt uneasy because her first grandchild, born that year (1959) did not cry; she was afraid this meant he was not going to live long.

CHRISTENING boys before girls

*c.*1050 LEOFRIC *Missal* (1883, 238) The priest receives them from their parents, and they are baptized first males, then females. **1795** *Stat. Acc. of Scotland* XV 311 [Orkney] Within these last seven years, the minister has been twice interrupted in administering baptism to a female child, before the male child .. When the service was over, he was gravely told, that .. the female child .. would, on her coming to the years of discretion, most certainly have a strong beard, and the boy .. none. *c.*1816 Wilkie MS (HENDERSON *Northern Counties* 1866, 9) If a boy and girl are brought together to the font, care must be taken that the former be christened first; else he is condemned to bear through life a smooth and beardless face, and still worse, the young lady will .. be endowed with the ornament he lacks. This belief holds its ground in Durham, and extends as far north as the Orkney Islands. **1909** *N & Q* 10th ser. XII 66 [nr. Exeter, Devon] It is unlucky for boys to be baptized before girls.

CHRISTENING postponed

1793 *Stat. Acc. of Scotland* VII 560–1 [Kirkwall and St Ola] The inhabitants would consider it as an unhappy omen, were they, by any means, disappointed in getting .. their children baptised on the very day which they had previously fixed in their mind for that purpose.

CHRISTENING: unchristened baby dangerous

1887 'SPERANZA' WILDE *Superstitions of Ireland* II 101. It is not safe to take an unbaptized child in your arms without making the sign of the cross over it. **1923** [Somerset] If you take an unchristened child into anyone's house, you take in bad luck with it. **1958** *John Bull* 19 July 4. In the north it is considered very unlucky for either mother or child to enter anybody else's house until the baby has been christened and the mother has been churched. **1968** *Observer* Suppl. 24 Nov. 10. Woman, 68 [Staithes, Yorks.] Our mothers wouldn't let us go out of the house till the children were christened.

Cf. CHURCHING after childbirth.

CHRISTENING CAKE: divination

1817 G. YOUNG *History of Whitby* II 883. At the birth of a first child, the first slice of the gingerbread .. is cut into small pieces, to be used by the unmarried as dreaming-bread. **1872** *N & Q* 4th ser. IX 130 [Fife] It was customary .. to pin a bit of shortbread on the child's frock before being taken to church, and to remain during the ceremony. This piece was eagerly coveted by young maidens as a dreaming piece, certain to ensure happy dreams of their lovers. *c.*1890 [Belford, Northumb.] The birth cakes as now made are just ordinary currant ones. The only thing that remains is the sleeping on it; if the baby is a boy pins are given to girls, and if it is a girl, then they are given to the young men, and if they do not speak a word 'from food to food', that is supper to breakfast, they will dream of the person they will marry.

Cf. WEDDING CAKE: divination.

CHRISTENING CLOTHES, baby must sleep first night in

1866 HENDERSON *Northern Counties* 8. It is the custom .. to make the chrisom child sleep the first night in the cap he wore at baptism. **1893** *N & Q* 8th ser. IV 429 [Dumfries.] Its mother wished, on its return home, to take off its robe, as being too gorgeous for common uses. The nurse, however, insisted that it must sleep in the robe in which it was baptized. **1915** *Folklore* 213. A Speyside woman told me it must be put back to bed wearing the clothes in which it had been baptized, and, having thus taken its first post-baptismal sleep, it would be much better in health afterwards.

CHRISTENING ROBE, buying

1964 *Yorkshire Post* 10 Apr. 7. I had
been married four years and was hoping
so much for a child. I saw the robe in a
lace shop, but I was too superstitious to
buy it.

CHRISTENING SHEET, burning

1882 *N & Q* 6th ser. V 159. Unless it
[christening sheet] is burned within a
year of the child's birth the child will
never be able to keep a secret.

CHRISTMAS, born at

c.1525 MS Harl. 2252 (BRAND *Antiquities*
1849, I 478–80) Yef that day that Cryste
was borne Falle uppon a Sunday . .
Whate chylde that day borne be, A grete
lorde he shalle ge . . Yf Crystemas day
on Monday be . . They that be borne
that day, I wene, They shalle be stronge
eche on and kene . . Yf Crystmas day on
Tuysday be . . Alle that be borne there
in may se, They shalbe stronge and
covethowse . . Yf Crystmas day, the
sothe to say, Fall uppon a Wodnysday
. . Whate chylde that day borne ys, He
shalbe dowghte and lyghte i-wysse . . Yf
Crystemas day on Thursday be . . What
chylde that day borne bee, He shalle
have happe ryghte well to the, Of dedes
he shalbe good and stabylle; Of speche
and tonge wyse and reasonabylle . . Yf
Crystmas day on the Fryday be . . The
chylde that ys borne that day, Shall
longe lyve and lecherowus be aye . .
Yf Crystmas on the Saterday falle . .
chyldren that be borne that day, Within
halfe a yere they shall dye, par fay.
1787 GROSE *Provincial Glossary* Superstitions 11. Some persons . . particularly those born on a Christmas eve
. . cannot see spirits. 1838 A. E. BRAY
Devonshire II 304. Having had the good
fortune to be born on Christmas-day,
my old nurse used to tell me . . 'I could
never see a ghostie as long as I lived,'
all persons so born being ghost-free to
the end of their days. 1851 DENHAM
North of England (1895, 77) Those born
on X'tmas Day cannot see spirits; which
is an incontrovertible fact. 1854 *N & Q*
1st ser. IX 197. Last Christmas having
fallen on the Sunday, I am reminded of
the following lines: 'What child that day
born may be, A great lord he shall

live to be.' 1878 *Folk-Lore Record* 9
[Fittleworth, Sussex] If you were born
on Christmas Day, you will neither be
drowned nor hanged. 1957 *Folklore*
413. A child born . . on Christmas Eve
or Day is commonly expected to be lucky
in life.

Cf. BIRTH, day of: divination rhyme.

CHRISTMAS, first to open door at

1878 *Folk-Lore Record* 9 [Fittleworth,
Sussex] It is lucky to be the first to open
the house-door [at] Christmas . . saying
'Welcome, Old Father Christmas.' 1933
Sussex County Mag. 54 [from nona-
genarian] On Christmas morning, the
first to come downstairs was expected
to take a broom, set wide the front door,
and sweep 'trouble' from the threshold.

Cf. NEW YEAR and house/home: bringing in the New Year.

CHRISTMAS, working at

1621 W. BRADFORD *History of Plimoth
Plantation* (1896, 159) One yᵉ day called
Christmas-day, yᵉ Gou:r caled them out
to worke, (as was used) But yᵉ most of
this new-company excused them selues,
and said it wente against their con-
sciences to work on yᵗ day. So yᵉ Gou:r
tould them that . . he would spare them
. . But when they came home at noon,
from their worke, he found them in yᵉ
streete at play openly; some pitching yᵉ
barr, & some at stoole-ball . . so he tooke
away their ymplements, and tould them,
that was against his conscience, that
they should play, and others worke.
1793 Correspondent [Brampton,
Cumb.] (J. HUNTER MS note in Brand's
Antiquities I 360] Nothing but unavoidable work, such as tending cattle,
is ever thought of all Christmas time . .
If any one was found by the Fidler and
his men at work on the Twelfth day he
is mounted on a stang (a pole), carried
to the ale-house, and pays a quart of
ale. Women are carried in a swill (barrel)
and pay the same. 1883 BURNE *Shropshire* 403. The horses might not go to
plough during the whole twelve days [of
Christmas]; nor might any spinning be
done; and the distaff, set aside, was
not uncommonly dressed with flowers.
1966 *English Dance and Song* 20 [Ludlow,
Shrops., 1959] Oh man, oh man, why

dost thou plough So hard upon Our Lord's birthday? The Farmer answered him with great speed, For to plough this day I have got need. Now his arms did quaver .. he could not plough, For the ground did open and lose him in .. His wife and children's out of place, His beasts and cattle they .. die away, For ploughing on Old Christmas Day.

Cf. NEW YEAR, working at.

CHRISTMAS CAKE, cutting and eating

1832 *Gents Mag.* pt. 2 491 [Lincs.] Christmas Eve is the time of gaiety and good cheer .. the hospitable board .. is amply replenished with .. yule-cake cut in slices, toasted and soaked in spicy ale .. A portion of the yule-cake must be necessarily reserved for Christmas Day; otherwise .. the succeeding year will be unlucky. A similar fatality hangs over the plum-cake provided for this occasion, unless a portion of it be kept till New Year's day. **1851** DENHAM *North of England* (1895, 25) Every family, that can possibly afford it .. have a Yule Cheese and Yule Cake provided against Christmas Eve; and it is considered very unlucky to cut either of them before that festival of all festivals! **1855** F. K. ROBINSON *Yorkshire Words. Yule-cake* .. is not to be cut before Christmas-eve on any account.

CHRISTMAS CANDLE

1817 G. YOUNG *History of Whitby* II 879 [Christmas Eve] The yule candle, a tall mould-candle, is lighted and set on the table. It would be unlucky to light [it] before the time .. The candle must not be snuffed, and no one must move from the table, till supper be ended. **1855** F. K. ROBINSON *Whitby Glossary* 29. Christmas eve at length arrives .. the candles are not to be snuffed the evening through, for that would be an unlucky perpetration .. Our host is reminded to save a bit of the yule candle for luck. **1862** C. C. ROBINSON *Dialect of Leeds* 265–6. The first thing to be done on the eve is to light the candle—a large mould, decked with evergreens—which is done by igniting a long piece of paper that will burn some time, for it is considered unlucky if the wick is not so as it will

continue to burn after the spell [spill] has been withdrawn. Then the good housewife sees to the snuffers being carefully put away, for the luck is lost once for all if the candle is snuffed either on that or any other night while it lasts. The length of snuff, or burnt wick, must be preserved intact till the whole of the candle is consumed; and for this reason the light is never *blown* out, for, with a strong breath, the ghost of wick would go with it; so when bed-time arrives, the wick is carefully pressed between the tongs, when of course the flame dies out, and the tongs being cautiously opened again, all is as it should be. **1883** *N & Q* 6th ser. VII 24. In the neighbourhood of Harrogate .. at Christmas, 1882 .. we had yule-candles, a gigantic pair, one red, one blue, presented by our attached grocer—for yule-candles must be given, and not bought. **1895** S. O. ADDY *Household Tales* 105. A candle or lamp should be left burning all night on Christmas Eve. Unless this is done there will be a death in the house. It was usual for the grocers in Yorkshire to present their customers with candles at Christmas. They were made for the purpose, and were burnt on Christmas Eve. Usually one very large candle was given; sometimes two smaller ones.

CHRISTMAS DECORATIONS (evergreens): bringing in before Christmas/New Year

1873 *N & Q* 4th ser. XII 467. I was told, in Rutlandshire, the other day, that it is very unlucky to bring holly into a house before Christmas eve. **1912** LEATHER *Herefordshire* 20. It is very unlucky to bring holly into the house before Christmas. Ibid. 92. Mistletoe is never brought into the house before New Year's Day; to do so would be most unlucky. **1960** Man, 45. My missus won't have a bit of holly in the house before Christmas morning, and I shouldn't think there's anyone in Harwood Dale [Yorks.] who would. **1985** R. VICKERY *Unlucky Plants* 35 [Boundary, Staffs.] Holly and ivy must not be taken into the house until Christmas Eve.

Cf. MAY BOUGHS AND FLOWERS.

CHRISTMAS DECORATIONS (evergreens), burning

ante 1072 *Exeter Book* (ed. G. P. Krapp *et al.*, maxim 2, ll. 79–80) Holly must be burned, a dead man's legacy divided. Good fame is ever best. 1648 HERRICK *Hesperides* 146 'New-yeares gift'. A jolly Verse crown'd with Yvie, and with Holly; That tels of .. cracking Laurell, which fore-sounds, A Plentious harvest to your grounds. 1719–20 *Hist. MSS Commission Reports* MSS of Duke of Portland VII 269 [Christ Church, Oxford] It has been usual for our choristers to burn the day before Candlemas the greens which are put up in the hall at Christmas. They did so on Monday at noon. 1853 *N & Q* 1st ser. VII 152 [London etc.] All your *Christmas* should be burnt on Twelfth-day morning. 1866 HENDERSON *Northern Counties* 88. It is thought sinful to burn evergreens which have been used for decorations .. Many, they say, have been struck dead for so doing. 1883 BURNE *Shropshire* 245. The cottagers [of Little Wenlock] never allowed the evergreens to be thrown out of doors, as, if so, a death would certainly happen in the house before next Christmas. They were therefore burnt on Candlemas Eve [1 Feb.] but at Shrewsbury, Ruyton, Ford, Worthen, and in South-east Montgomeryshire it is considered exceedingly unlucky to burn them, a thing not to be done on any account. 1909 M. TREVELYAN *Folk-Lore of Wales* 30. The morning after Twelfth Night all the Christmas holly and mistletoe is burnt. It is unlucky .. to destroy it in any other way. 1928 HARDY *Winter Words* 'Burning the Holly'. We were burning the holly On Twelfth Night; the holly, As people do: the holly, Ivy, and mistletoe. 1956 *Farmer and Stock-Breeder* 7 Feb. 51. My grandfather [said] if holly ever went on the fire there would be a death in the house during the twelve months that followed. 1960 [Scarborough, Yorks.] Of course you mustn't throw holly out, you must burn it. 1962 Girl, 12 [Cumnock, Ayr.] It is bad luck to burn holly. Put it in the bucket. 1988 Woman, 61 [Redhill, Surrey] We used to burn the holly in the grate on Twelfth Night, with *great* excitement. I thought everybody did.

Cf. MISTLETOE, kissing under.

CHRISTMAS DECORATIONS (evergreens): burning on Shrove Tuesday

1902 *N & Q* 9th ser. IX 86. It is proper to take down Christmas decorations at Candlemas, but they ought to be kept till Shrove Tuesday, and then burnt in the fire over which the pancakes are fried. I have this from a Welsh cousin. 1947 *Folklore* 239 [Isle of Man] 'Hibbyn as hollin' (ivy and holly)—were kept up on the walls until Shrove Tuesday and then used for frying the pancakes .. This custom .. is still occasionally done even in Peel and Douglas.

CHRISTMAS DECORATIONS (evergreens) fed to cattle

1883 BURNE *Shropshire* 245. At Worthen, in the beginning of this century, the evergreens were .. carefully carried to the cows' 'Boosey' to be eaten by them .. And at Edgmond, in much later years, it was customary to burn the holly, but to give the ivy to the milking cows. 1938 *Folklore* 233 [Shrops.] Farmers used to give their cattle ivy to eat on Candlemas Day, though formerly this was the remains of the Christmas decorations.

Cf. MISTLETOE brings luck to farm.

CHRISTMAS DECORATIONS (evergreens) from church

1879 *N & Q* 5th ser. XI 206 [Worcs./ Herefords.] The holly and ivy that have adorned churches at Christmas time are much esteemed and cherished. If a small branch of holly with the berries upon it is taken home and hung up in the house, it is considered sure to bring a lucky year.

CHRISTMAS DECORATIONS (evergreens etc.), taking down

1648 HERRICK *Hesperides* 361 'Ceremony upon Candlemas Eve'. Down with the Holly, Ivie, all, Wherewith ye drest the Christmas Hall: That so the superstitious find No one least Branch there left behind: For look how many leaves there be Neglected there .. So many Goblins you shall see. 1811 *Gents Mag.* pt. 1 423 [Yorks.] From the journal of a deceased friend. 'The windows and pews of the Church (and also the windows of houses) are adorned with branches of holly, which remain till Good Friday.' **1863** *English Church Kalendar* 94. Saturday 31 January. Vigil of the Purification of Blessed Virgin Mary [normally 1 Feb.]. The Christmas Decorations should be removed. **1864** R. CHAMBERS *Book of Days* II 53 [Suffolk] If every remnant of Christmas decoration is not cleared out of church before Candlemas-day there will be a death that year in the family occupying the pew where a leaf or berry is left. An old lady whom I knew . . used to send her servant on Candlemas-eve to see that her own seat at anyrate was thoroughly freed from danger. **1897** *N & Q* 8th ser. XII 96. Recently I was told it was unlucky to allow the Christmas decorations to remain up after Twelfth-cake Day. Is this a common belief? **1899** *Newcastle Weekly Chronicle* 4 Feb. 7 [Jesmond] Christmas decorations both in house and church must be removed before Candlemas; otherwise there will be a death in the family or occupants of the pew. **1923** [Rowbarton, Som.] If you keep up Christmas decorations after the Twelfth Night it's bad luck all the year. **1982** Teenage girl [Yorks.] If by any chance we leave a piece of holly or other evergreen in the house after Twelfth Night we keep it in a box (in the house) until the following Christmas and then dispose of it (not before). **1986** *Woman*, 63 [Chichester, Sussex] I really worry if I haven't cleared away every trace of Christmas by Twelfth Day—decorations, cards, everything.

Christmas decorations: also see index: greenery; New Year/Christmas.

CHRISTMAS LOG: stirring fire during supper
1817 G. YOUNG *History of Whitby* II 879 [Christmas Eve] It would be unlucky to stir [the yule log] during the supper. **1923** [Somerset] You must not stir the fire during supper on Christmas Eve if you wish to be lucky.

CHRISTMAS LOG/ASHEN FAGGOT: piece kept for luck/protection
1648 HERRICK *Hesperides* 337–8 'Ceremonies for Candlemasse Day'. Kindle the Christmas Brand and then Till Sunneset, let it burne; Which quencht, then lay it up agen, Till Christmas next returne. Part must be kept wherewith to teend The Christmas Log next yeare; And where 'tis safely kept, the Fiend, Can do no mischiefe (there). **1790** *Gents Mag.* 719 [Ripon, Yorks.] Yule-clogs . . used on Christmas-eve; but, should it be so large as not to be all burnt that night . . the remains are kept till Old Christmas-eve. **1817** G. YOUNG *History of Whitby* II 879. Sometimes a piece of the clog is saved, and put below the bed, to remain till next Christmas; when it is burnt with the new clog: it secures the house from fire. **1879** *N & Q* 5th ser. XI 375 [Derbys.] I have seen the last bit of the yule log taken from the fire and hung the next day close to the ceiling in the kitchen, to be for the purpose of lighting the next year's Christmas Eve fire . . It is . . lucky to do this, besides its usefulness as 'a charm against fire'. **1910** *N & Q* 11th ser. I 357. If the last fragment of the [ashen] faggot, partly burnt, was placed in the stall, it would keep the cows from all harm or disaster. This is known to have been done within comparatively recent years in Somerset. **1910** *Cornish and Devon Post* 22 Jan. 5 [Boy, 14, Boyton, Cornwall] Christmas Eve we brought in the Yule Log . . It is the old custom to keep a small fragment of last year's log to light that of next year. If this was not done, the old folk thought that their house would catch fire. Of course, I do not believe in this . . but one year . . the fragment was accidentally burnt. Rather strangely, our chimney caught fire the same year. **1923** [Somerset] The Devonshire farmers believe that when you have burnt your ash faggot on Christmas Eve, if you take some of the ends and ashes and put them on the cowstall walls you will be free from ill luck with your cattle.

CHRISTMAS PUDDING, stirring
1861 *N & Q* 2nd ser. XII 491. Stirring the Christmas pudding. Every one in the house should do this 'for luck'. **1883** BURNE *Shropshire* 277. Every young woman in each household should help

to stir the Christmas pudding if she has any wish to be married during the ensuing twelve months. **1905** K. BURRILL *Amateur Cook* 274. Every one in the house must stir the Christmas pudding— stir it three times round, wishing hard all the time, and you must see the bottom of the basin. **1910** *N & Q* 11th ser. II 504 [Derbys.] In the making of the puddings there was more stirring than in any other of the many mixings .. All had to stir .. If there was a baby, its hand was guided. **1940** E. GOUDGE *City of Bells* 160. The flaming plum-pudding, that they had stirred laboriously in its earlier stages, was alight with the wishes they had wished as the spoon went round. **1978** D. NOEL *Five to Seven* 48. Everyone stirred the enormous bowl of Christmas pudding mixture, making a wish for each month in the year.

Cf. BUTTER, stranger helps to churn.

CHURCH, dust from

AD **731** BEDE *Historia Ecclesiastica* III XI (tr. Sherley-Price) The bones [of King Oswald] were washed and .. placed in the church [Bardney Abbey, Lincs.]. Some while later, when Queen Osthryd was staying in the monastery .. Ethelhild, abbess of a neighbouring house, visited her .. This lady is still living .. The queen informed her how the dust from the pavement, on which the water that had washed the bones had been spilt, had already healed many sick people. The abbess then asked for some [which] she put into a little casket and took away with her. [A man was later cured of demonic possession with it.] **1866** HENDERSON *Northern Counties* 124-5. The poor fellow had walked by night from Teignmouth to Exeter [Devon], had flung stones against the figures on the west front of the cathedral [and] had succeeded .. in bringing down the arm of one of them .. Part of this relic had been pulverised, mixed with lard, and applied to the sore. **1873** *N & Q* 4th ser. XII 385. In Clynnog Church (Diocese Bangor, North Wales), there is a chapel dedicated to St Beuno, the founder, to which attaches this peculiar belief that the powdered scrapings of the stone columns that support the

chapel are efficacious as a sovereign cure for sore eyes. For this purpose people resort to the building, coming even from long distances; and although the edifice has been recently restored, and consequently little or no whitewash left, yet such is the strong belief of these poor country people, that they still scrape on to obtain a scanty supply of the precious dust .. A pinch of it is added to a bottle of spring water. **1954** *Trans. Devon. Ass.* 299 [Plymouth] Sprinkle 'gratings' of figures of saints, found in church, at the entrance of pigs' houses or 'shippens' to ensure against disease or fever.

Cf. COMMUNION table/altar.

CHURCH, illness in

1858 DENHAM *North of England* (1895, 72) Folks never catch Cold at Church. This is a saying very common in the mouths of old people. **1883** *Folklore* 364 [NE Scotland] If one is seized by any illness when in church, it is the death illness.

CHURCH, lead from

1838 A. E. BRAY *Devonshire* II 291 [Tavistock] Mr Bray received, as clergyman of the place, the following letter .. 'Rev. Sir, I should take it as a great favour if your Honour would .. let me have the key of the churchyard to-night, to go in at twelve o'clock, to cut off three bits of lead about the size of a half farthing; each from three different shuts (spouts), for the cure of fits. **1851** *N & Q* 1st ser. III 259. An inhabitant of this parish told me that his father went into Lydford Church (Cornwall), at twelve o'clock at night, and cut off some lead from every diamond pane in the windows; with which he made a heart, to be worn by his wife afflicted with 'breastills', i.e. sore breasts.

Cf. LEAD shapes in water: divination of cause of sickness.

'CHURCH' taboo word

1883 J. R. TUDOR *Orkneys and Shetland* 166 [Shetland] When setting the lines they avoided, and do still, mentioning certain objects, except by certain special words. Thus .. a church [is called] *büanhoas*, or *banehoos*. **1965** P. F. ANSON *Fisher Folk-Lore* 102 [NE Scotland] The word 'kirk' could never be used, and this presented difficulties, because churches often served as landmarks at sea. All one could do was to refer to them as a 'bell-hoose'.

CHURCH BELL cures

c. AD 950 MS Reg. 12 D. xvii (COCKAYNE *Leechdoms* II 137) A drink for a fiend-sick man, to be drunk out of a church bell. 1584 SCOT *Discoverie of Witchcraft* XI xv. Women with child run to church, and tie their girdles or shoe-lachets about a bell, and strike upon the same thrice, thinking that the sound thereof hasteth their good delivery. 1882 *N & Q* 6th ser. V 375 [Shiplake, Oxon.] An old village acquaintance .. was troubled with this complaint [shingles]. 'The doctor's stuff,' she said, 'in course it did me no good, but I got one of the bell-ringers to scrape me some of the coomb [grease] off the church bells; and I rubbed it in, and I be cured.' 1883 BURNE *Shropshire* 191. At Oswestry, grease (called *bletch*) from the church bells is an approved remedy for ring-worm. 'There is no doubt, sir,' said the church-cleaner, 'that it is very good for the purpose.' 1907 *N & Q* 10th ser. VII 206 [Egham, Surrey] Our parish clerk informs me that up to a few years ago he had applications for 'bell-comb', the grease from the church bells, which was used as an ointment in cases of ring-worm and shingles. 1933 *Folklore* 309 [Herefords.] One of the ringers does quite a good trade with oil from the bells [for shingles] .. Coming from church bells it is supposed to possess magical healing powers. 1978 *Sussex Express* 30 June 4. I am told that Sussex folk believe that verdigris from church bells will cure the shingles.

CHURCH BELL drives away devils and storms

1483 CAXTON *Golden Legend* 22ᵛ. The euyll spyrites that ben in the region of thayer, doubte moche whan they here the trompes of god whiche ben the belles rongen .. And this is the cause why the belles be rongen whan it thondreth, and whan grete tempestes and outrages of wether happen, to thende that the fendes and wicked spyrites shold be abasshed

and flee. 1563 J. PILKINGTON *Burnynge of Paules Church* sig. 3. Some witch-craftes, as .. ringinge the halowed belle in greate tempestes or lightninges. 1584 SCOT *Discoverie of Witchcraft* I I. A clap of thunder, or a gale of wind is no sooner heard, but .. they run to ring bels .. as though spirits could be fraied awaie with such externall toies. 1587 G. GIFFORD *Discourse of the Subtill Practises of Devilles* v D3ᵛ. Had they not hallowed belles to ring in great tempestes, that the Devill might be driuen awaie, as not able to come within the sound of them? 1627 BACON *Sylva Sylvarum* § 127. It is beleeved by some, that Great Ringing of Bells in populous Cities, hath chased away Thunder. 1696 AUBREY *Miscellanies* (1890, 141) When it thundered and lightened, they did ring St Aldhelm's bell, at Malmsbury Abbey. The curious do say, that the ringing of bells exceedingly disturbs spirits. 1911 *Folklore* 313. When I was Vicar of Upton Grey [Hants.] I noted .. that, when the time came for the tolling of the Passing Bell, instead of the sexton tolling only the big Tenor Bell .. he tolled all the bells .. When I enquired the reason, I got this delightful reply, 'You know, Sir, devils can't abide o' bells. And there's some devils as are feared of some bells, and there's other devils as are feared of other bells, and so we tolls them all to fear them all.' 1923 [Martock, Som.] He's sure to be a forchinit kid for bells struck out just as he wur borned.

CHURCH BELL foretells length of incumbency

1875 *N & Q* 5th ser. IV 184. The churchwarden .. said to him [the new rector] as he went into the church to toll the bell, or 'ring himself in'—'If you want to stay with us, you must knoll for as many years; you'll stay one year for every knoll.' The rector said that he would keep on ringing for some minutes .. After a brief interval, we heard the bell give out one 'tang', and one only. Finally, the new rector appeared, and explained that, in the act of pulling the bell, the bell-rope had unexpectedly given way. The churchwarden shook his head, and said it was 'a bad job'. 1881 *N & Q* 6th ser. IV 307 [Ballaugh

Rectory, Isle of Man] There is an old saying that the number of strokes a new incumbent gives the bell at his induction will indicate the number of years he will remain in the parish.

CHURCH BELL omen of death

1883 BURNE *Shropshire* 296. The church bell tolling with a heavy sound [is a death-token]. 1886 *N & Q* 7th ser. II 66 [Kent] SEXTON: Leave the tenor 'up'; I may want it during the week. RINGER: Aye, that you will; for the tenor 'hummed' so much tonight in the ringing that it will be sure to be wanted before next Sunday. (The tenor is the tolling bell.) That night there was a death in the Union. Ibid. 158 [Foxhill, Lincs.] The tenor bell which was rung for five minutes before the services .. was always said by the people to ring louder before a death. 1889 *N & Q* 7th ser. VIII 78 [W. Somerset] There is a .. superstition that if at its tolling the death bell sounds heavy, or not clear, there will be occasion for it to ring again within a short time. 1894 HARDY *Life's Little Ironies* 250. The bell that was ringing for church went very heavy all of a sudden; the sexton, who told me o't, said he'd not known the bell go so heavy in his hand for years—and he feared it meant a death in the parish.

CHURCH DOOR/GATE rattles/clicks

1926 *Folklore* 174 [Cardigans.] At Llandyssyl, it is said that the minister has often been warned, by hearing the lychgate .. click at night as if someone were opening it, when there is no one there, that he will shortly be sent for to a dying man. 1946 *Sussex N & Q* 59. If the church door rattles unduly at night .. it will soon be opening to admit a corpse.

CHURCH HASSOCK

1932 C. IGGLESDEN *Those Superstitions* 230. You should never turn the hassock, even if you find it upside down, unless you are willing to face a sequence of twenty unlucky Sundays.

CHURCH PORCH, watching in

1608 Nottingham Archdeaconry Papers (*Trans. Thoroton Soc.* XXX 112) Katherine Foxegale, of Walesbie, presented 26 July at East Retford .. 'for watchinge upon Saint Markes even at nighte laste in the Church porche to presage by divelishe demonstracion the deathe of somme neighbours within this yeere.' 1634 MS Lansdowne 207 (R. CHAMBERS *Book of Days* I 549) [Burton, Lincs.] They repaired to the church porch [on St Mark's Eve, 24 Apr.] and there seated themselves, continuing there till near twelve of the clock. About which time .. they resolved to depart, but were held fast by a kind of insensible violence, not being able to move a foot. About midnight .. appears, coming towards the church porch, the minister of the place, with a book in his hand, and after him one in a winding-sheet, whom they knew to resemble one of their neighbours. The church doors immediately fly open, and through pass the apparitions, and then the doors clap to again. Then they seem to hear a muttering, as if it were the burial service, with a rattling of bones and noise of earth, as in the filling up of a grave. Suddenly a still silence, and immediately after the apparition of the curate again, with another of their neighbours following in a winding-sheet, and so a third, fourth, and fifth. 1813 BRAND *Antiquities* I 166. It is customary in Yorkshire, as a clergyman of that county informed me, for the common people to sit and watch in the church porch on St Mark's Eve, from eleven o'clock at night till one in the morning. The third year (for this must be done thrice), they are supposed to see the ghosts of all those who are to die the next year, pass by into the church. When any one sickens that is thought to have been seen in this manner, it is presently whispered about that he will not recover, for that such, or such an one, who has watched St Mark's Eve, says so. 1866 HENDERSON *Northern Counties* 34–5. I have heard .. of an old woman at Scarborough, who kept St Mark's vigil in the porch of St Mary's in that town about eighty years ago. Figure after figure glided into the church, turning round to her as they went in .. At last a figure turned and gazed at her; she knew herself .. and fell senseless .. She did not long survive the shock. An old man who recently died at Fishlake

.. was in the habit of keeping these vigils, and was in consequence an object of some dread to his neighbours. The old sexton did so too, in order, it was said, to count the gains of the coming year.

CHURCH ROOF, water from

1838 W. HOWITT *Rural Life of England* I 320. He drank the water which dropped from the church-roof in rainy weather, in the hope that it would do him good. 1855 F. K. ROBINSON *Yorkshire Words*. *Church-lead-water*, the rain which runs off the leads or roof of the church, said to be restorative when sprinkled upon the sick, especially that from the chancel where the altar is situated. 1932 J. M. E. SAXBY *Shetland Lore* 183. The children were laid [i.e. buried] nearer the church than the others, so that the rain-water from the sacred roof might fall on their grass.

Cf. WATER, holy.

CHURCH TOWER

1900 S. BARING-GOULD *Book of Dartmoor* 126 [Lydford, Devon] This Peter remained clerk for fifty years. He obtained a subsidiary revenue by carrying children afflicted with 'the thrush' up the tower, and holding them over the battlements at each pinnacle, whilst he recited the Lord's Prayer. For this he received a small gratuity.

CHURCHING after childbirth

*c.*580 BC Leviticus 12: 2–7. If a woman have .. born a .. child: she shall be unclean .. She shall touch no hallowed thing, nor come into the sanctuary, until the days of her purifying be fulfilled .. when .. she shall bring .. a young pigeon, for a sin offering, unto the door of the tabernacle of the congregation, unto the priest: Who shall offer it before the Lord, and make an atonement for her; and she shall be cleansed. 1776 PENNANT *Tour in Scotland* 45–6. The mother never sets about any work till she has been kirked. In the church of Scotland there is no ceremony on the occasion: but the woman, attended by some of her neighbours, goes into the church, sometimes in service time, but oftener when it is empty, goes out again, surrounds it [probably sunwise], re-

freshes herself at some public house, and then returns home. Before this ceremony she is looked on as unclean, never is permitted to eat with the family; nor will any one eat of the victuals she has dressed. 1799 *Stat. Acc. of Scotland* XXI 147 n. [Monquhitter, Aberdeen.] It was most unhappy for a woman, after bringing forth a child, to offer a visit, and for her neighbours to receive it, 'till she had been duly churched. 1808 JAMIESON *Scottish Dict. Kirk*. She, who has been in childbed, it is believed, cannot with propriety, before she be kirkit, enter into the house of her nearest neighbour or most intimate friend. Her unhallowed foot would expose the tenement to some mischance. Some carry this so far, that they would not taste any food that she has dressed. 1851 DENHAM *North of England* (1895, 23) Neither must a mother enter the house of either friend, relative, or neighbour till she has been churched. If she is so uncanny, it betokens ill-luck to the party so visited. 1875 W. D. PARISH *Sussex Dialect* 77. It is considered most unlucky for a woman after giving birth to a child to cross the high-road, or to pay a visit before she has been to church to return thanks. 1879 J. NAPIER *West of Scotland* 33. Few mothers would enter any house until they had been to the house of God. 1939 *Folklore* 185 [East Anglia] The mother must not enter a neighbour's house before the churching has taken place, or the neighbour will become pregnant within a year, and a baby is sometimes taken on its first outing to a house where a child is desired. This custom is known as 'shaking feathers', and the hostess will become a mother within a year. 1957 M. YOUNG & P. WILLMOTT *East London* 40. It's superstition really. It's supposed to be unlucky if you go out before you're churched.

Cf. BIRTH, contact with; MENSTRUATING WOMAN defiles.

CHURCHING after childbirth: divination

1579 LUPTON *Thousand Notable Things* I § 49. If a Man be the first that a Woman meetes after she comes out of the Church, when she is newlye Churched, it sygnifies that her next chylde wyll be a boye. If she meete a Woman, then a wench is lyke to be her next chyld. This was credibly repeated to me to be true. But prayse it as it proues.

Cf. FUNERAL: divination.

CHURCHING after childbirth: woman must not cross road

1854 *N & Q* 1st ser. II 446 [Hants.] A woman in this village, when going to church, for the first time after the birth of her child, keeps to the same side of the road, and no persuasions or threats would induce her to cross it. She wears also upon that occasion a pair of new boots or shoes. 1873 *N & Q* 4th ser. XI 341. My grandmother used to say, that if a woman after childbirth crossed a cart or wheel rut before she was churched, a man might shoot her, and he could not be punished for it.

CHURCHING after funeral

1808 JAMIESON *Scottish Dict. Kirk.* A family is said to be kirkit, the first time they go to church after there has been a funeral in it. Till then, it is deemed inauspicious for any of them to work at their ordinary employment.

CHURCHING after marriage

1808 JAMIESON *Scottish Dict. Kirk.* A bride is said to be kirkit, the first time she goes to church after she has been married; on which occasion she is usually attended by some of the marriage-company. She still retains the name of bride, among the vulgar, till she has been at church.

CHURCHYARD, grass etc. from

*c.*1816 Wilkie MS (HENDERSON *Northern Counties* 1866, 156) The younger apprentice was at last restored to health by eating butter made from the milk of cows fed in kirk-yards, a sovereign remedy for consumption brought on through being witch-ridden. 1848 *Maidstone Gazette* 12 Sept. 2. So strong a hold has the genius of superstition among the peasantry of South Wales that a woman recently bitten by a mad donkey was sent to the churchyard of St Edrin's [Carmarthen] to eat the grass, which, it is believed, has the peculiar property of being an antidote to hydrophobia. 1887 'SPERANZA' WILDE *Su-*

perstitions of Ireland II 98. Nettles gathered in a churchyard and boiled down for a drink, have the power to cure dropsy.

CIGARETTE, lighting third

1916 *N & Q* 12th ser. I 208. What is the origin of the extremely common superstition against lighting three cigarettes with one match? Hundreds of times I have seen two cigarettes lit up, and then the match solemnly blown out lest it should light the third; but if there are four cigarettes to light there is no objection! [Signed] Private Bradstow. Ibid. 276. During the Boer War it happened that three pals were taking a light from the same match, and the third had no sooner done so than he was picked off by the enemy. If the tale is correct, this happened two or three times afterwards, and doubtless such a coincidence would make no small impression, and would cause a local taboo on economy in matches .. This is how a friend of mine, who is an officer, accounted for this universal practice. 1922 LYND *Solomon* 162. Two men, equal in brain and courage, will behave quite differently when it comes to .. lighting a cigarette from a match from which two cigarettes have already been lit. 1969 G. COPPARD *With a Machine Gun to Cambrai: the tale of a young Tommy in Kitchener's army* 20. No matches were used in darkness. A simple lighter which sparked off a thick corded wick into a smouldering glow was a popular substitute for matches. The origin of the unlucky third light from one match probably started in the South African War, but soldiers in all wars are superstitious and will not go out of their way to offend the gods. 1983 Girl, 13 [Maldon, Essex] Never offer anyone a match three times.

Cf. CANDLE, lighting third.

CIGARETTE PACKET, stepping on

1952 Girl, 14 [London] If you see an empty cigarette packet with a picture of a black cat on it you put one foot on it and say 'Black cat, black cat, Bring me luck, If you don't I'll tear you up.' 1953 Girl, 12 [Aberystwyth, Cardigan.] If we see a sailor on a cigarette carton we step on it and say 'Sailor, sailor, bring me luck, Find a shilling in the muck.' If we don't find any money we come back and tear it up. **1986** Woman, 56 [South Shields, Co. Durham] When I was a child we used to put a foot on a Woodbine packet and say 'Willie, Willie Woodbine, bring me luck, If you don't I'll tear you up.' But I can't remember whether it ever did, or whether I ever carried out the threat.

Cf. CAT, black: lucky to possess; SAILOR, touching: lucky.

CINDERS: divination

1727 GAY *Fables* XXXVII Last night (I vow to heav'n 'tis true!) Bounce from the fire a coffin flew. **1755** *Connoisseur* 13 Mar. I need not mention to you the common incidents, which were accounted by them no less prophetic. If a cinder popped from the fire they were in haste to examine whether it was a purse or a coffin. **1830** M. R. MITFORD *Our Village* IV 299. Who is in or out of spirits according as the concave cinder which does him the honour to jump from the fire on his foot be long or round—a coffin or a purse? **1864** R. CHAMBERS *Book of Days* II 53 [Suffolk] Coffins out of the fire are hollow oblong cinders spirted from it, and are a sign of a coming death .. If the cinder .. is oval, it is a cradle, and predicts the advent of a baby; while, if it is round, it is a purse, and means prosperity. **1882** *People's Friend* 8 Nov. 711. When a morsel of coal leaps from the fire on to the hearth rug it is a coffin if it does not crack—a purse if it does. **1923** [Rowbarton, Som.] If a coal hops out of the fire examine it. If it is purse-shaped you will have money soon; if heart-shaped, a lover; if a coffin, there will shortly be a death in the family. **1984** Woman, 56 [South Shields, Co. Durham] I used to love picking up the cinders that flew out of the fire onto the hearth. My mother would say, 'Oh, that's a purse,' and it really did look like a tiny clasped purse. That meant money was coming our way. The small round hollow ones were 'cradles' and meant we'd hear of a new baby.

CLERGYMAN, meeting

1159 JOHN OF SALISBURY *Policraticus* (*Frivolities of Courtiers*, ed. J. B. Pike, 50) They tell us it is ominous to meet a priest or monk. late **12th c.** BARTHOLOMEW OF EXETER *Penitential* (*Rel. Ant.*, I 286) He who believes that anything comes out favourably or unfavourably because of .. meeting a priest, shall do penance for 7 days. *c.***1225** *Vices and Virtues* 29. When some evil or misfortune come to you .. do not believe as some people who have never properly believed and say that they met an evil foot, a priest or monk. **1496** H. PARKER *Dives & pauper* 1st com. I. What sayste thou of them that wyll haue no men of holy chirche and namely men of relygyon with them on huntynge for theyr beleue is .. that they sholde spede the worse bycause of theyr companye. **1583** *Schoolemaster* IV VIII. It was counted ill lucke to meete with a Priest, if a man were going foorth to warre, or to turnament. **1652** GAULE *Mag-astro-mances* 312. Meeting of Monks is commonly accounted as an ill omen, and so much the rather if it be early in the morning. **1728** SWIFT 'Journal of a Modern Lady'. ll. 238–9. This morning, when the parson came, I said I should not win a game. **1868** *N & Q* 4th ser. II 67. I was, a few years since, the clergyman of a parish within ten miles of Birmingham, much frequented on holiday by a low class of mechanics, and I invariably noticed that, whenever I passed, some one or more of them spit aside; giving me the idea that they belonged to some sect or society which enjoined the rule to spit whenever a clergyman passed, or perhaps any known churchman. **1875** *N & Q* 5th ser. III 204 [Flamborough, Yorks.] It was considered a most unlucky thing for a clergyman to enter a cottage when the 'gude man' was baiting his lines. **1954** Girl, 13 [Ferryden, Angus] If a fisherman meets a minister it will be a very unlucky day for him. **1959** Clergyman, *c.*55. In Tunstall *c.*1930 the majority of young women in the Potteries made a point of touching cold iron (a lamp-post or a drain pipe) when they met a minister of religion in the street.

CLERGYMAN on ship

1854 *N & Q* 1st ser. X 26. A clergyman
.. on board a ship is said to bring
bad weather. 1898 *Weekly Scotsman
Christmas Number* 6 [Fogo, Berwick.]
While the steamer was labouring under
the fury of a tempest .. I heard a sailor
say, 'What can you expect with so many
ministers aboard? If they have the better
of the devil on land, he has the better of
them at sea.' 1913 M. ROBERTS *Salt of
the Sea* 124. It is well known to all who
follow the sea that gentlemen of that
kind are unlucky to have on board. For
Davy Jones is the very devil, and if he
gets a chance to drown a minister he
does it at once. 1960 *Woman* 3 Sept.
5. The wife of a boatman at St Ives
[Cornwall] says older sailors are still
upset if a dog-collared tourist wants a
trip. 'If it's for fishing, they're convinced
that the parson's presence will mean a
small catch.' 1963 *Scottish Daily Mail*
4 Sept. 8. A sailor I once served with
would do anything rather than meet the
ship's chaplain once we were at sea.
  Cf. 'MINISTER' taboo word.

CLERGYMAN'S WIFE gives luck in horses

1621 JONSON *Gypsies Metamorphosed*
l. 842. You'll have good luck to horse-
flesh, o' my life, You ploughed so late
with the vicar's wife. 1640 GLAPTHORNE
Wit in Constable II 183. If he be a parson
And I his wife, I sure shall make my
friends Lucky to horse-flesh. 1678 RAY
Proverbs 86. He that would have good
luck in horses, must kiss the Parson's
wife. 1738 SWIFT *Polite Conversation* II
132. I have had devilish bad Luck in
Horse-flesh of late .. Why then, Sir John,
you must kiss a Parson's Wife.

CLERGYMEN: divination

1950 Woman, *c.*50 [Forfar, Angus] If
you counted all the ministers you saw
up to 100 the next man you spoke to
would be your future husband. We used
to haunt the Lour Road, where most
ministers lived.

CLOCK facing fire

1895 S. O. ADDY *Household Tales* 96. It is
unlucky for a clock to stand opposite
the fire. 1982 Woman, 20 [Cleveland,
Yorks.] It is thought that a fire will go

out if .. a clock is facing towards the
fire place.
  Cf. SUN puts out fire.

CLOCK falls down in presence of un-churched woman

1861 C. C. ROBINSON *Dialect of Leeds* 297.
There is a superstition called 'Clock-
falling', which is, that if a woman enter
a house after child-bearing, and before
being churched, the house-clock will
immediately fall on its face. But a woman
would never think of doing so, under
any circumstances.
  Cf. CHURCHING after childbirth.

CLOCK is stopped at death

1825 *Newcastle Mag.* Sept. 393. At a
northern latewake .. the clock is
shrouded and stopped, to signify that
time has become a blank [with the
deceased]. *c.*1828 Calvert MS, Pickering, Yorks. (G. HOME *Evolution of an
English Town* 215) It be the custom as
soon as death doth enter the chamber
for one present to .. on the instant stop
the clock. 1855 *N & Q* 1st ser. XI 215.
I knew an intelligent, well-informed gentleman in Scotland, who .. ordered that
as soon as he expired the house clock
was to be stopped. 1862 *N & Q* 3rd ser.
II 483 [Aberdeen.] [A] custom is to stop
the clock at the moment of death, and
not to set it going again until the body
is carried out of the house for burial.

CLOCK stops at moment of death

1820 Memorandum from Mr Vulliamy,
the King's Clockmaker (*N & Q* 3rd ser.
VI 519) On Sunday morning, the 29th
Jan. 1820, Sir Thomas Tyrwhitt, Black
Rod, called at Mr Vulliamy's .. and
said, the Lords were summoned for one
o'clock, and he desired some one might
be sent immediately to wind up the clock
in the House, for it stood still .. We found
the clock .. had stopped the preceding
evening, without any apparent cause,
at a quarter before eleven o'clock, being
nearly the hour at which HM King
George the Third had expired. 1864
N & Q 3rd ser. VI 27. A relative, describing to me the death of a parent,
said the clock stopped just at the time
of his decease: adding, the nurses said
it was a usual occurrence. 1875 H. C.

WORK 'Grandfather's Clock'. It stopp'd short—never to go again—When the old man died. 1883 BURNE *Shropshire* 281. An old man from Welshampton died in the Shrewsbury Infirmary. His daughter says that during his illness the clock stopped every night at a certain hour, which in the end proved to be that of her father's death. 1905 *N & Q* 10th ser. III 124. On the day of Queen Victoria's funeral he photographed Balmoral .. showing the clock in the tower with the hands pointing to the hour at which on 22 January she had passed away, now four years ago .. Five months later [he] had some conversation with constable Reed, an old residenter, who .. declared that .. the clock had not been stopped by any human hand. The clock was still going at ten o'clock on the evening before the funeral. The photograph was taken at twelve noon on the day of the funeral; but the hands pointed to 6.25—the exact hour of the Queen's death. It was the snow that did it. A crescent-shaped wreath .. had gathered on the lower part of the dial, arresting the hour hand at VI and the minute hand at V. 1905 *N & Q* 10th ser. III 175. At Normanton Park, Rutlandshire .. is a grandfather clock, to which is attached a brass plate, stating that it had been the private property of his Majesty William IV, and stood in the sovereign's private room in the House of Lords, and was kept in order and regularly wound by the king's own clockmaker .. The clock stopped at the exact moment his Majesty expired, and so remained. 1925 *N & Q* CXLIX 157. There is a legend about the old clock in Castle Rushen, Castletown, Isle of Man, which tradition states was presented to the island by Queen Elizabeth. The story is that the clock stopped suddenly (although wound up) at the moment the queen expired and remained inactive until after the interment of her majesty, when, 'of its own accord', it resumed its ordinary avocation. 1973 *Daily Telegraph* 12 Feb. 14. Since the seventeenth century, when the [astronomical] clock mysteriously stopped at the very moment James I's wife, Anne, died [at Hampton Court] the superstition has grown that 'it stops whenever anyone long resident in the palace should die there.'

CLOCK stops: warning of death

1923 [Cosham, Hants.] A grandfather clock which stops without need of winding foretells death. 1941 F. THOMPSON *Over to Candleford* XXIII. The morning after a death in the hamlet would see them with serious faces discussing the signs which were supposed to have foretold it .. the unexplained stopping of a clock. 1953 Woman, 50. In my mother's home in Suffolk it was considered extremely unlucky if the old Dutch clock stopped. It was supposed to have done so when my grandfather and my maiden aunt died. 1961 *Yorkshire Post* 4 Oct. 14.The clock, which stopped before his mother and father died, stopped again just before his son, aged nine, was burned to death in a haystack fire.

CLOCK strikes during hymn

1870 *N & Q* 4th ser. V 596. In the village in Sussex in which I live it is generally believed, at least by the female portion of the community, that if the church clock strikes twelve while a hymn is being sung in the morning service a death will follow in the week. 1874 *N & Q* 5th ser. I 204. There is a tradition in the parish of Veryan, Cornwall, to the effect that when the church clock strikes during the singing of the hymn before the morning sermon, or before the collect against perils at evening prayer, there will be a death in the parish before the next Sunday. 1889 *N & Q* 7th ser. VII 488 [Somerset] If the church clock strikes whilst a hymn is being sung, the belief is that some parishioner will die within the week. So strong is this belief that the striking mechanism of the clock is always stopped during services in which hymns are sung.

CLOCK strikes during marriage ceremony

1858 DENHAM *North of England* (1895, 51) It is looked upon as decidedly unlucky for a Bridal party to be making their vows .. during the striking of the Church clock. It portends the death of the bride or bridegroom before the expiration of the year. 1890 *N & Q* 7th ser. X 465. I have just been told by a native of Sheffield that it is very unlucky indeed to be married while the church clock is striking. The death of bride or bridegroom, separation, divorce, or some similar calamity is indicated. 1910 *Folklore* 226 [Pontefract, Yorks.] A bride is fortunate in her choice if the clock chimes just before she enters the church, but will be unhappy if it strikes while she is inside. Local brides will wait outside the church until the chimes have sounded. 1923 *N & Q* 13th ser. I 172 [Worcs.] I have several times been asked .. to arrange a wedding at five minutes past the hour—'so that we may not be in church when the clock strikes.'

CLOCK strikes, speaking while

1900 S. HEWETT *Nummits* 54 [Devon] It is unlucky .. to speak while the clock is striking.

CLOCK strikes while church bells are ringing

1909 M. TREVELYAN *Folk-Lore of Wales* 33. If the town clock strikes while the church bells are ringing there will soon be a fire in the parish. Ibid. 283. If the town or church clock strikes while the passing bell or a funeral knell is tolling there will soon be a death in the parish.

CLOCK strikes wrong time

1751 Journal of Walter Gale 14 Jan. (*Sussex Archeolog. Coll.* IX 191) My sister was still extremely ill. I told them in discourse, that on Thursday night the town clock was heard to strike 3 in the afternoon twice .. this I look to be [a] sure presage of my sister's death. 1892 *N & Q* 8th ser. II 86. There is, it seems, a superstition that when 'Big Ben' .. strikes irregularly at midnight evil will befall the Royal House within three months. At 12 o'clock on the night of November 14, the members of a political club within a stone's throw of the Houses of Parliament were astonished to hear the quarter chimes sounding simultaneously with the hour strokes, and to note that Big Ben struck thirteen times .. The day being a critical one in the illness of Prince George, his name was, happily incorrectly, associated with

the evil omen. Two months after, to the very day, his elder brother died. 1942 A. L. ROWSE *Cornish Childhood* II. One morning about eight o'clock, some months after he had gone away .. the clock suddenly struck 'one' out loud .. Three weeks later they got the news that Cheelie had been killed on that day, about that time. They ever afterwards took it as a 'token', a signal of his death. 1954 *Tit-Bits* 6 Nov. 6. My grandfather died—away from home. At two o'clock (the time of his death) the clock at his home chimed thirteen. Since that day every hour has thirteen chimes. The clock has been sent to the makers but while there chimed perfectly.

CLOCKS: two strike together

1909 M. TREVELYAN *Folk-Lore of Wales* 283. If two clocks strike exactly at the same moment, a married couple will die in the village.

CLOTHES, clean/new

1775 L. SHAW *History of Moray* 242–3. The Scots Highlanders .. put on clean clothes on the Sabbath day, as others do. 1878 *N & Q* 5th ser. X 24 [Dorset] Yer clothes .. they do wear twice so long if you put 'em on fust time a Sunday. 1962 Girl, 12 [Cumnock, Ayr.] It is bad luck to put on new clothes on Friday. 1985 Woman, 78. When I was a child, in Oxford, we *never* put clean clothes on on a Friday, we *always* put them on on a Sunday—and I've done that all my life.

CLOTHES: first time worn

1869 EWING 'Christmas Crackers' (*The Brownies*, 1894–6, 179) [The young lady finds she is a bride, and wearing the family wedding-dress.] The old lady .. was .. blessing her, and wishing her, in the words of the old formula—'Health to wear it, Strength to tear it, And money to buy another.' 1913 E. M. WRIGHT *Rustic Speech* 224. Making a first appearance in new clothes .. my grandmother always wished the possessor: 'Health to wear it, Strength to tear it, And money to buy another,' a formula still repeated in Northumberland.

CLOTHES inside out

1340 HIGDEN MS Speculum Curatorum (OWST, in *Studies*, ed. J. Conway Davies, 1957, 288) Examples chosen to illustrate the idolatrous cult of times and seasons comprise .. putting on one's clothes inside out. **1507** *Gospelles of Dystaues* pt. 4 XVII. Who that wyll be vyctoryous in warre and batayll, or happy and fortunate in marchaundyse, let hym put on his sherte in the mornynge the contrary wyse. **1584** SCOT *Discoverie of Witchcraft* XI xv. He that receiveth a mischance, wil consider whether he .. put not on his shirt the wrong side outwards. **1648** R. CORBET *Poetica Stromata* 55 'Iter Boreale'. Turne your Cloakes Quoth hee, for Puck is busy in these Oakes: If ever wee at Bosworth will be found Then turne your Cloakes, for this is Fayry-ground. **1659** HOWELL *Proverbs* 18. Wear the inside of thy stockins outward to scare the witches. **1695** CONGREVE *Love for Love* II i. Pray Heaven send your worship good luck! .. for you have put on one stocking with the wrong side outward. **1755** *Connoisseur* 13 Mar. The same young lady one morning came down to breakfast with her cap the wrong side out; which her mother observing, charged her not to alter it all the day for fear she should turn luck. **1838** A. E. BRAY *Devonshire* I 183. This turning of jackets, petticoats, &c., being found so good as a remedy .. our good old towns-folk practise this .. ere they venture on a walk after sun-down, near any suspected place, as a certain preventive against being led astray by a pixy. **1855** F. K. ROBINSON *Yorkshire Words. Smock-turning*, the practice of the wives and sweethearts of sailors and fishermen putting on their shirts inside out for success and a fair wind. **1886** *Folklore* 15 [Portessie, Banff.] When the herring fishing was going on in a poor way .. the fisherman .. would say, 'Wife, for God's sake, turn your sark!' **1890** *Cork Constitution* 24 Jan. 3. He said .. that he was led away by a will o' the wisp and never knew where he was until he was at Gurtnascreena .. He turned his vest inside out for fear he would be led astray again. **1898** BLAKEBOROUGH *Yorkshire Customs* 152. To this day there are fisher lassies who wear their chemises wrong side out when their sailor lads are away at sea and stormy weather threatens. **1955** [Redhill, Surrey] Our office-cleaner has just arrived with her frock on inside out, having accidentally dressed so this morning and being superstitious of changing it. **1988** Woman, 44 [Liphook, Hants.] If you put something on the wrong way out you're supposed to keep it that way. It's in the back of your mind that something dreadful will happen if you don't.

CLOTHES: mending while wearing

1850 *N & Q* 1st ser. II 4 [Suffolk] If you have your clothes mended upon your back, you will be ill spoken of. **1871** *N & Q* 4th ser. VIII 322 [East Anglia] If a button, tape, &c. be sewn on a garment while it is worn on the person, it is unlucky. **1922** JOYCE *Ulysses* (1960, 910–11) When I was biting off the thread of the button I sewed on to the bottom of her jacket she couldnt hide much from me I tell you only I oughtnt to have stitched it and it on her it brings a parting. **1923** [Martock, Som.] You be a fool not to teake off to mend, when you know 'To mend your clothes on your back, You'll have to wear black, And *that* you'll lack.' **1932** C. IGGLESDEN *Those Superstitions* 174. A bit of doggerel heard in many a homestead: 'If you mend your clothes on your back You will live much money to lack.' **1953** Girl, 15 [Ipswich, Suffolk] If you mend any clothing *on* you, someone is telling lies about you. **1972** Woman, 62 [Scarborough, Yorks.] When you mend something while still wearing it (e.g. a hole in a stocking, or a button) you are 'stitching sorrow to your back'. **1987** Woman, *c.*45 [Petersfield, Hants.] You shouldn't mend your clothes while you're wearing them—say you turned up the hem of your dress to put a few stitches in it—it's unlucky. It is something to do with sewing a shroud.

CLOTHES of the dead

1864 R. CHAMBERS *Book of Days* II 322 [Suffolk] When a person dies, and his or her clothes are given away to the poor, it is frequently remarked: 'Ah, they may look very well, but they won't wear;

they belong to the dead.' **1912** LEATHER *Herefordshire* 89. The poor will not say 'thank you' for clothes which belonged to anyone that has died. They believe that they will soon become rotten. **1925** *Folklore* 257 [Norfolk] A woman told me she had been left some house-linen by a lady but it rotted away 'as they fretted' for their former owner. **1930** *Folklore* 256. There arose a belief among the men that it was unlucky to wear dead men's boots or clothing [British Army, 1914–18.] All sorts of devices were used to get new clothing and footwear. **1986** Woman, 47 [Fringford, Oxon.] Don't accept dead people's clothes, because 'As the body rots, the clothes rot.'

CLOTHES, tacking thread/pins left in

1868 *N & Q* 4th ser. II 221 [East Anglia] A coat was sent home from the tailor's, out of which he had not taken the basting-stitches. 'Ah!' some one exclaimed, 'that coat is not paid for . . And here's a pin left in, and that means the same.'

Cf. SHOES, new: squeaking.

CLOVER as protection

1580 LYLY *Euphues and his England* (*Works*, 1902, II 142) For as salfe being is it in the companie of a trustie mate, as sleeping in the grass Trifole, where there is no serpent so venemous that dare venture.

CLOVER, four-leaved: lucky to find

1507 *Gospelles of Dystaues* pt. 2 xv. He that fyndeth the trayfle with foure leues, and kepe it in reuerence knowe for also true as the gospell yᵗ he shall be ryche all his lyfe. **1584** SCOT *Discoverie of Witchcraft* XI XIII. The object . . whereon men divine, must be sudden and unlooked for: which regard, children and some old fooles have to the gathering . . foure leaved grasse. **1620** MELTON *Astrologaster* 46. If a man walking in the fields, finde any four-leaued grasse, he shall in a small while after finde some good thing. **1648** HERRICK *Hesperides* 'Nuptiall Song' st. 5. Passe the . . lucky-foure-leav'd grasse. **1839** S. LOVER *Songs* 17 [Ireland] I'll seek a four-leaved shamrock in all the fairy dells, And if I find the charmed leaves, oh, how I'll weave

my spells! **1860** *N & Q* 2nd ser. IX 381 [Inverness.] Some few years ago . . walking through a field I observed a herd-boy diligently searching for something . . He was . . looking for four-bladed clovers . . when discovered he did not pull them, but put a stone . . to show where they lay. **1887** 'SPERANZA' WILDE *Superstitions of Ireland* II 103. The fortunate possessor of the four-leaved shamrock will have luck in gambling, luck in racing, and witchcraft will have no power over him. But he must always carry it about his person, and never give it away, or even show it to another. **1923** [Taunton, Som.] If you find a four-leaf clover you will meet your true lover. **1935** *I Walked by Night* (ed. L. Rider Haggard, 19) [Norfolk] Evry one know that maids look for four leaf clover to bring them fortune—they used to say they onley grow where a mare have dropped her first foal. **1936** *Sussex County Mag.* 824. Four-leaved clovers in Sussex: 'The first [leaflet] is for fame, the second for wealth, the third a faithful lover and the fourth, glorious health.' **1972** C. KETTERIDGE & S. MAYS *Five Miles from Bunkum* 139 [Ashdon, Essex] Every village child knew one old rhyme, believed every word of it, and would search great areas of meadowland in the hope of discovery . . 'If you find a four-leaved clover, All your trouble will be over.' **1983** Girl, 13 [Maldon, Essex] My mother found a four-leaved clover and put it in the middle of a big dictionary where it would dry. It brought us good luck.

CLOVER, four-leaved: opens eyes to fairy deceptions

1835 S. OLIVER *Rambles in Northumberland* 106. Many years ago . . a girl who lived near Nether Witton, returning home from milking, with a pail upon her head, saw many fairies gamboling in the fields, but which were invisible to her companions . . On reaching home . . the cause [was] at length discovered in her *weise* [head pad] which was found to be of four-leaved clover: persons having about them a bunch, or even a single blade, of four-leaved clover being supposed to possess the power of seeing fairies. **1860** *N & Q* 2nd ser. IX 381

[Inverness.] A woman returning from the field with a sheetful of clover .. stands amid the rustic crowd to witness the performance of sleight-of-hand tricks .. by a mountebank .. She began to cry out that the poor player was deceiving the people—playing witchcraft upon them, that the immense poles he was balancing were but straws .. The power given to the woman was .. ascribed to .. her having a four-bladed clover amid the heap on her back. 1865 R. HUNT *West of England* 1st ser. 101. Before rising from the milking stool, the maid plucked up a handful of grass and clover to put in the head of her hat, that she might carry the bucket the steadier. She had no sooner placed the hat on her head, than she saw hundreds and thousands of Small People swarming .. about the cow, and dipping their hands into the milk. 1879 J. NAPIER *West of Scotland* 133. A certain man came to the village to exhibit the strength of a wonderful cock, which could draw, when attached to its leg by a rope, a large log of wood .. One of the spectators present on one occasion had in his possession a four-leaved clover, and while others saw, as they supposed, a log of wood drawn through the yard, this person saw only a straw attached to the cock's leg by a small thread.

CLOVER, two-leaved: divination

1854 *N & Q* 1st ser. X 321 [Cambs.] A Clover, a Clover of two, Put it in your right shoe; The first young man you meet, In field, street, or lane, You'll have him or one of his name [applicable to either sex].

COAL carried for luck

1873 *Chambers' Journal* 810 [Scotland] We have lately learned that success is to be retrieved .. by simply pocketing a bit of coal. 1879 *Daily News* 17 Feb. 2 [Bow Street police court, London] He [the supposed burglar] also had a piece of coal in his pocket .. Witness [a policeman] said that burglars usually carried a piece of coal in their pockets 'for luck'. 1899 *Daily Mail* 11 May 4. It appears, judging by the remarks made in a case at the Mansion House Police-Court, that burglars almost invariably

carry a small piece of coal with them when they start out on an expedition .. They choose another piece of coal when their old treasure has lost its charm, and they are unfortunate enough to fall into the hands of the police. 1954 PHILIP GIBBS Letter to *Times* 7 Aug. 5. Early in the First World War I had to spend a night in .. Ypres, which was, as usual, under heavy bombardment. Before I went up an Irish officer fumbled in the breast pocket of his tunic and produced a small piece of coal .. 'If you take that with you,' he told me, 'you will come through safely.' 1954 Girl, 11 [Blaenavon, Monmouth.] When my auntie and uncle has to do examinations or driving tests they always carry a piece of coal wrapped up in paper. 1982 Woman, c.50 [Stockton-on-Tees] A sailor carries a piece of coal wherever he goes—they're very superstitious, are sailors.

Cf. FIRST-FOOT at New Year/Christmas: ritual of gifts.

COAL, dreaming of

1882 *N & Q* 6th ser. VI 524 [Cardiff, Glam.] I remember being told as a child that 'to dream of coals was a sign of riches.'

COAL, finding

1929 *N & Q* CLVI 319. One must pick up any bit of coal one finds in one's path, as it would bring luck. 1953 Girl, 12 [Aberystwyth, Cardigan.] If a piece of coal is dropped in the road by the coalman, the first person who comes along is supposed to pick it up and spit on it and throw it over their left shoulder and wish. 1970 *Trans. Devon. Ass. 271*. If you find a lump of coal in the road, throw it over your left shoulder.

COAL in Christmas stocking

1936 E. H. RUDKIN *Lincolnshire* 22. Coal should always be put in the Christmas stocking. Take the coal, spit on it and burn it and wish while it burns and you will get your wish.

'COAL' magic

1650 T. HILL *Natural and Artificial Conclusions* CXLVI. This Cole .. onely to be found upon Midsummer-Eve .. just at noon, under every root of Plantine and of Mugwort .. whosoever weareth or beareth the same about with them, shall be freed from the Plague, Fever, Ague, and sundry other diseases. **1675** *Practice of Paul Barbette* 7. Against the Falling-Sickness .. some ascribe much, to coals pulled out (on St John Baptist's Eve) from under the roots of Mugwort: But those authors are deceived, for they are not coals, but very old acid roots, consisting of much volatile Salt; and are almost always to be found under Mugwort: So that it is only a certain Superstition, that those old dead roots ought to be pulled up on the Eve of St John Baptist about 12 at night. **1696** AUBREY *Miscellanies* (1890, 131) The last summer, on the day of St John the Baptist, 1694, I accidentally was walking in the pasture behind Montague house, it was 12 o'clock. I saw there about two or three and twenty young women, most of them well habited, on their knees very busy, as if they had been weeding .. they were looking for a coal under the root of a plantain, to put under their head that night, and they should dream who would be their husbands. **1923** [Somerset] On Midsummer Day between 10 and 12 take a live coal from the fire and bury it in the garden without speaking to anyone, and you'll be lucky all the year.

Cf. MUGWORT.

COAL, turning over

1846 *Athenaeum* 1299. Persons with the power of an evil eye go through certain forms before they can effect their object; and it is supposed that during these forms the evil they wish is seen by them .. before it takes effect upon their victim. One of the simplest of these forms is looking steadfastly into the fire; so that a person seen sitting musing with his eyes fixed upon the fire is looked upon with great suspicion. But if he smokes, and in lighting the pipe puts the head into the fire and takes a draw while it is there, it is an undeniable sign that there is evil brewing. Now, if any person observe this, and (it being a common custom in the country to have a large piece of coal on the fire) the tongs be taken privately, and this coal be turned right over, with the exorcism

uttered .. 'Lord be wi' us' .. it thwarts for the time all evil intentions. Or if an individual who is suspected of having wished evil, or cast an 'ill e'e', upon anything, enter the house upon which the evil is, and the *coal be turned upon him*, as it is termed, that person feels as if the coal was placed upon his heart, and has often been seen to put his hand to his breast, exclaiming 'Oh!' Nay, more, he is unable to move so long as the coal is held down with the tongs—and has no more power over that house. **1883** BURNE *Shropshire* 275. It is very unlucky to turn a coal over when poking the fire, for 'then you turn sorrow to your heart.' On the Welsh Border it portends poverty. **1932** WOMEN'S INSTITUTE *Worcestershire Book* 34 [Cotheridge] Never turn coal on the fire. **1978** A. WRIGHT *Holderness* 18 [nr. Hull, Yorks.] The refusal to turn a coal right over in the hearth. By turning the coal over, a sailor's wife feared she was turning her husband's ship over at sea.

Cf. FIRE, poking: as defensive measure.

COCK crows = ill omen

c. AD **65** PETRONIUS ARBITER *Satyricon* LXXIV (tr. Mitchell, 136) A cock crowed .. 'It's not for nothing that yonder trumpeter has given the signal; it means either a house on fire, or else some neighbour giving up the ghost. Save us all!' *c.* AD **390** ST JOHN CHRYSOSTOM *Homilies on Ephesians* XII (1879, 242) You may see a man .. spending much zeal in the pursuit of riches, and yet supposing the whole is undone by the crowing of a single cock. **1688** AUBREY *Remaines* (1881, 196) So at the same instant, that Mr Ashton was goeing out of the house, when he was goeing to France, the Cock happened to crow: at which his wife was much troubled, and her mind gave her, that it boded ill luck. He was taken at sea & after tryed and executed. **1887** 'SPERANZA' WILDE *Superstitions of Ireland* II 64. It is unlucky .. for a cock to meet a person in the doorway and crow before him—then the journey should be put off. **1953** Unpublished letter to *Woman* [Prescot, Lancs.] A mother who hears a cock crowing on the day her baby is born is in for a spell of bad luck, consequently

all cocks in ear-range are slaughtered ..
it is associated with the denial mentioned
in Scripture.

COCK crows on doorstep = stranger

1850 *N & Q* 1st ser. II 164. When the
cock struts up to the door and sounds
his clarion .. the housewife is warned
that she may soon expect a stranger.
1855 *N & Q* 1st ser. XII 37 [Cornwall]
The inhospitable housewife who drives
off the cock that crows on the door-step,
thereby warning her of the approach of
strangers [is] only a fresh illustration of
the very old fallacy that the way to avert
the prediction is to silence the prophet.

COCK crows unseasonably

1594 T. MORESIN *Papatus* 21 [among ill
omens] The unseasonable crowing of
the barnyard cock. **1652** GAULE *Mag-
astro-mances* 181 [among 'superstitious
ominations'] The cocks crowing unseasonably. **1865** R. HUNT *West of England* 2nd ser. 166. If a cock crows at
midnight, the angel of death is passing
over the house; and if he delays to strike,
the delay is only for a short season.
1868 *N & Q* 4th ser. I 10. A worthy
laundress neighbour is in sore distress—
the cock has crowed on two or three
nights at nine o'clock! It is the sure sign
of an early death in her family, and
that will be the dying hour. The event
happened exactly as fore-crowed when
she lost her last daughter. **1891** HARDY
Tess of the D'Urbervilles XXXIII. It was
interrupted by the crowing of a cock ..
'Oh?' said Mrs Crick. 'An afternoon
crow?' Two men were standing by the
yard gate .. 'That's bad,' one murmured
to the other. **1922** R. KEARTON *At Home
with Wild Nature* 63–4. A visit was
straightway made to the fowlhouse to
study the omens. If the .. bird's legs
were warm his nocturnal music was a
sign of good luck .. but if they were
cold, alas! the prophet prophesied no
more. **1932** J. M. E. SAXBY *Shetland Lore*
183. If a cock crowed after dark you
had to run and feel his feet. If they were
warm, good news was coming to you.
If they were cold, it was a death. **1953**
Folklore 293 [Essex] If a cock crows at
midnight it means that there will be a
death in the family.

COCK AND HEN on St Valentine's morning

1872 *N & Q* 4th ser. IX 135 [Derbys.]
In the early morn of St Valentine young
women would look through the keyhole
of the house door. If they saw only a
single object, or person, they would go
alone all that year. If they saw two or
more .. they would be sure to have a
sweetheart .. but if .. they saw a cock
and a hen, they might be quite certain
of being married before the year was
out. **1882** *People's Friend* 8 Nov. 712.
On St Valentine's morning .. if they
shoud be fortunate enough to see a cock
and a hen sitting together, it is a sure
omen of a marriage in the household
during the year.

COFFIN, parts of

1787 GROSE *Provincial Glossary* Superstitions 55. A ring made of the hinge
of a coffin is supposed to have the virtue
of preventing the cramp. **1794** *Gents
Mag.* 889. In Devonshire .. the ring [to
cure fits] must be made of three nails or
screws which have been used to fasten
a coffin, and must be dug out of the
churchyard. **1831** HONE *Year Book* 29
Feb. Some persons carry in their pockets
a piece of coffin, to keep away the cramp.
1846 BROCKETT *North Country Words.
Cramp-ring,* a ring made out of the
handles of decayed coffins, and supposed
to be a charm against the cramp. **1855**
F. K. ROBINSON *Yorkshire Words. Coffin
lead rings,* finger rings made of a piece
of a leaden coffin obtained from a
churchyard and worn as a cure for the
cramp. **1883** BURNE *Shropshire* 193.
The talisman against rheumatism ..
consisted of a ring made of three nails
taken from three coffins out of three
several churchyards. **1891** J. C. AT-
KINSON *Moorland Parish* 247–8. John
wore a ring, made out of an old coffin-
tyre he met with in digging graves in
the well-worked churchyard [at Danby,
Yorks.] This ring was good against 'falling fits'. **1909** M. TREVELYAN *Folk-Lore
of Wales* 226–7. Epilepsy was overcome
by a curious charm. When a grave was
re-opened, people stripped a piece of
metal from an old coffin. It was cut in
circular shape, a hole was bored in it,
and the amulet was worn suspended

from a ribbon round the neck. 1923
Folklore 90 [Skye, Hebrides] A charm
for toothache was to take a nail from a
coffin in the churchyard and hold it to
the aching tooth.

COFFIN, sound of earth on

*c.*1816 Wilkie MS (HENDERSON *Northern
Counties* 1866, 27–8) If the sound of the
'mools' falling on the coffin be heard by
any person at a considerable distance
from the spot, it presages a death in that
person's family.

COFFIN LID undone

1866 HENDERSON *Northern Counties* 43.
An old Yorkshire woman . . ordered two
holes to be made in its lid, that, when
the devil came in at one hole to catch
her, she might slip out at the other.
1880 *N & Q* 6th ser. I 173 [Waterville,
Co. Kerry] At the funeral of one of my
parishioners . . as soon as the coffin was
lowered into the grave, the nails . . were
all drawn out by the direction of the
relatives, one of whom . . produced a
claw-hammer . . for the purpose . . So
that at the resurrection day the poor
tenant of 'the narrow house' might find
nothing to prevent his coming forth.

Cf. DEATH: opening locks/doors and
windows frees spirit; KNOTS in shroud.

COFFIN SUPPORTS turned over

1879 *Folk-Lore Record* 214. The coffin
[is placed] on a table, tables, or chairs
at the door of the house before the
procession moves. After the coffin is
taken off for interment the chairs or
tables are placed upside down, and allowed to remain so for a considerable
time. This formula was observed by the
Rev. John Stevenson, of Glamis, at the
funeral of one of the Earls of Aberdeen,
and it is remarkable that such a custom
should be observed in a family which
might be supposed to be above such
superstition. 1883 J. R. TUDOR *Orkneys
and Shetland* 174 [Shetland] As soon as
ever the procession moves off, the chairs,
or whatever else the coffin has been laid
on, are carefully upset, as otherwise
there will be another death in the house
within a week. 1959 *Journal of School
of Scottish Studies* 197. There have been
fairly recent instances of the chairs and

tables supporting the coffin before it was
borne away, being turned over in case
the dead should return.

COIN, date of birth on

1953 *Reveille* 2 Oct. 2 [St Anne's-on-Sea,
Lancs.] There are . . women who believe
that taking a coin stamped with their
birthday year will bring them luck [at
whist drives]. After each drive it is put
away in a charm box ready for the next
time. 1957 HOGGART *Uses of Literacy* 18.
At whist-drives some women always
carry a coin issued in the year of their
birth.

COIN for luck in fishing

1923 P. S. JEFFREY *Whitby Lore* 141–2.
Some of the fishermen, when the nets
are being paid out, cut a slice in one of
the pieces of cork attached to them
and insert a coin, by way of informing
Neptune that they are prepared to pay
for the fish they catch—indeed there is
hardly a 'pole cork' round our shores
that has not a coin of some kind pushed
into a slit made for it . . Wherever a new
fishing boat is launched, a coin of some
sort is put and kept permanently under
the mast for good luck. 1925 E. LOVETT
Magic in London 54. An old Brixham
fisherman . . told me that . . his skipper
. . made a slit . . in the beam of the trawl
and pushed a half sovereign into it (this
was about thirty years ago). That night
they had such a big catch that it . . filled
the boat. Ibid. 55. In . . 1913 . . I made
. . extensive . . enquiries as to the custom
of placing money under the mast . . to
bring luck in fishing, and I received
letters from harbour masters confirming
this custom.

COIN with hole

1831 HONE *Year Book* 29 Feb. To always
have money in your pocket . . keep in
your purse . . a coin with a hole in it;
at every new moon take it out and spit
upon it, return it to your pocket, and
wish yourself good luck. 1861 C. C.
ROBINSON *Dialect of Leeds* 300. Those
coins are 'lucky' which . . have holes in
them . . and being of silver, are generally
suspended to the watch chain, and it is
no uncommon sight to see a man with
half-a-dozen of these coins preserved

after this fashion, and dangling from his fob. **1883** BURNE *Shropshire* 272. The well-known luckiness of a sixpence with a hole in it. **1899** *St Neots Advertiser* 25 Mar. 3. Mr Hooley [the financier] believed in the luck-bringing qualities of threepenny bits with holes pierced in them. He gave his bankers a standing order to collect them for him, and used to give some to his friends, always carrying about a lot of loose ones in his pocket. **1925** E. LOVETT *Magic of London* 13 [The soldier] showed me an old farthing with a hole through it . . 'I reckon that thing saved my life.' **1953** Boy, 12 [Croydon, Surrey] What things are lucky? Coins with holes in them.

Cf. STONE with hole.

COMET = death or disaster

c. AD **120** TACITUS *Annals* XIV XXII. A comet blazed—a phenomenon which, according to the persuasion of the vulgar, portended change to kingdoms. *ante* AD **725** BEDE *De Natura Rerum* XXIV. Comets are long-haired stars with flames, appearing suddenly, and presaging a change in sovereignty, or plague, or war, or winds, or floods. **1011** BYRHTFERTH *Manual* (EETS 117: I 133) There is a star called comet. When it appears, it betokens famine or pestilence or war or the destruction of the earth or fearful storms. **1066** *Anglo-Saxon Chronicle* (tr. Whitelock, 140) In this year Harold came from York to Westminster at the Easter . . Then all over England there was seen a sign in the skies such as had never been seen before [Halley's comet]. Some said it was the star 'comet' which some called the long-haired star. **1549** *Complaynt of Scotlande* VI (1872, 58) Ane sterne . . callit ane comeit; quhen it is sene, ther occurris haistyly efter it sum grit myscheif. **1583** HENRY HOWARD *Poyson of Supposed Prophecies* sig. V4. When dyuers vppon greater scrupulosity then cause, went about to disswade her majestye [Queen Elizabeth] . . from looking on the Comet which appeared last: with a courage aunswerable to the greatnesse of her state, shee caused the windowe to be sette open, and cast out thys worde *Iacta est alia* the dyce are throwne, affirming that her stedfast hope . . was

too firmly planted in the prouidence of God, to be . . affrighted with those beames. **1667** MILTON *Paradise Lost* II 708. Like a comet burn'd That fires the length Ophiuchus huge In the Arctic sky, and from his horrid hair Shakes pestilence and war. **1697** J. CASE *Angelical Guide* 78. I saw myself, with many others, a strange Comet but two days before the Duke of Monmouth was taken in the West, and a Blazing Star over all Europe before the death of King Charles II. **1713** HALLEY 'Ode' prefixing Newton's *Principia.* Now we know The sharply-veering ways of Comets, once A source of dread, nor longer need we quail Beneath appearances of bearded stars. **1722** DEFOE *Journal of Plague Year* (1909, 30) A blazing star or comet appeared for several months before the plague . . so very near the houses that it was plain [it] imported something peculiar to the city alone. **1761** JOHNSON *Idler* no. 11 62. Those that laugh at the portentous glare of a Comet . . will yet talk of times and situations proper for intellectual performances. **1882** HARDY *Two on a Tower* XIII. 'And what do this comet mean?' asked Haymoss. 'That some great tumult is going to happen, or that we shall die of famine?' **1910** *N & Q* 11th ser. I 448. The beloved ruler of the United Kingdom has been suddenly called away [death of Edward VII] and Halley's Comet has reappeared.

Cf. STAR, falling/shooting = death or disaster.

COMMUNION chalice/wine

*c.***1000** MS Harl. 585 (COCKAYNE *Leechdoms* III 11–13) This is the holy drink against one full of elfin tricks and for all temptations of the devil. Write upon the housel dish several texts . . Take [herbs] and . . a sextarius full of hallowed wine [etc.] . . Bless the man earnestly in the name of the Lord Almighty . . Then use it. **1584** SCOT *Discoverie of Witchcraft* XII XVII. A charme for the choine cough. Take three sips of a chalice, when the preest hath said masse, and swallow it downe with good devotion. **1775** J. COLLIER *Musical Travels* app. 14. He had . . heard [the parson] refuse to bottle up the remains of the consecrated wine as a remedy for the hooping-cough. **1807**

SOUTHEY *Letters from England* L. At this day the rinsings of the cup are eagerly sought after by the sick, notwithstanding the prohibition of the church. 1851 *N & Q* 1st ser. III 220. In one of the principal towns of Yorkshire, half a century ago, it was the practice for persons in a respectable class of life to take their children, when afflicted with the hooping cough, to a neighbouring convent, where the priest allowed them to drink a small quantity of holy water out of a silver chalice. Ibid. 368. In Ireland a weakly child is frequently brought to the altar rails, and the priest officiating at mass requested to allow it to drink from the chalice .. the wine and water with which the chalice is rinsed .. I have heard it seriously recommended in a case of hooping cough. 1882 *N & Q* 6th ser. VI 387. It is still quite a common practice at the present day for parents of all ranks and persuasions, including Jews, to take children sick with whooping cough to Catholic churches, that they may be allowed to drink out of the chalice after mass. 1913 E. M. WRIGHT *Rustic Speech* 236. In October, 1910, a young friend of mine, then in lodgings in Liverpool, had the misfortune to burn her hand. Her landlady—who .. as charwoman in the neighbouring church .. received gifts of old church linen—offered to bind up the wound with a piece of an old chalice veil; and she subsequently attributed the quick healing .. to .. her 'holy linen'.

COMMUNION plate

c. AD 950 MS Reg. 12 D. xvii (COCKAYNE *Leechdoms* II 137) [for fever] A man shall write this upon the sacramental paten .. and sing over it .. In the beginning, etc. (John i 1). Then wash the writing with holy water off the dish into the drink, then sing the Credo, and the Paternoster .. And let each of the two men [the leech and the sick] then sip thrice the water so prepared. 1852 *N & Q* 1st ser. VI 480 [Norfolk] The rector of a neighbouring parish was solicited (in vain of course) for the loan of the church plate, to lay on the stomach of a child, which was much swelled from mesenteric disease, this being held to be a sovereign remedy in such cases.

COMMUNION table/altar

*c.*1040 MS Harl. 55 (COCKAYNE *Leechdoms* II 335) Pound all the worts .. set them under the altar, sing nine masses over them .. This salve is good for every temptation of the fiend .. and for typhus fever. 1570 NAOGEORGUS *Popish Kingdome* (tr. Googe, IV 45) In that same houre that Christ himselfe was borne .. There are .. that mindfully the money still do watch, That first to aultar commes, which then they priuily do snatch .. Whereby they thinke throughout the yeare to haue good lucke in play, And not to lose: then straight at game till daylight do they striue, To make some present proofe how well their hallowede pence wil thriue. 1838 A. E. BRAY *Devonshire* II 291 [Tavistock] Going into the church at night whilst the chimes are playing twelve o'clock, in order to creep three times under the communion table to be cured of fits, is still held in repute. 1851 *N & Q* 1st ser. III 259. For fits. Go into a church at midnight and walk three times round the communion table. This was done in this parish [Launceston, Cornwall] a few years since. 1871 *N & Q* 4th ser. VIII 505. An old woman of my acquaintance, who acted as the beadle or 'bobber' of a church, once brought to the bed of a dying person some of the sweepings from the floor of the altar, to ease .. a very lingering death. 1883 BURNE *Shropshire* 247. When I was a young man I was fond of cock-fighting [but] he bewitched my cocks .. and I lost every year. The fourth year .. I broke the spell. I swept the dust off the communion-table .. and sprinkled the dust round the cock-pit.

CONFIRMATION good for rheumatism

1830 FORBY *East Anglia* 406–7. At one of the Confirmations of the present Venerable Bishop of Norwich, an old woman was observed eagerly pressing forwards .. A standerby .. inquired if she was going to be confirmed: and being answered in the affirmative expressed his surprise that she should have deferred it to such an advanced age. The old woman replied with some asperity, 'that it was not so; that she had already been bishopped seven times, and intended to be again: it was so good for her rheumatism.' **1887** N & Q 7th ser. IV 534. My grandmother . . used often to tell me that in her young days there was an old Brighton woman who said, 'Please as how I gets confarmed as often as ever I can, coz as how I heers 'tis good for the rheumatiz.' **1922** J. A. PENNY *More* . . *Horncastle* 38 [Lincs.] 'Have you been confirmed?' he said . . 'The Bishop wants older people to come forward as well as the young.' 'Does he want to cure our rheumatics?' says I, for I've heard Bishops can, same as Spa water.

CONVERSATION, lull in

AD 77 PLINY *Natural History* XXVIII V (1856, V 285) It has been remarked . . that there is never a dead silence on a sudden among the guests at table, except when there is an even number present; when this happens, too, it is a sign that the good name and repute of every individual present is in peril. **1909** M. TREVELYAN *Folk-Lore of Wales* 328. When people talking became suddenly silent, they said, 'The parson is passing; no luck today.' **1923** [West Malling, Kent] A sudden lull in the buzz of conversation denotes that an angel is passing over the company. It usually happens at twenty minutes to or past the hour. **1940** DYLAN THOMAS *Portrait of the Artist* 243. 'A host of angels must be passing by,' said Mr O'Brien. 'What a silence there is!' **1952** Woman, 24 [Bath, Som.] I still remember the impression it made on me when, in a senior form at school, we all fell silent for no apparent reason, and a girl looked at her watch and said that such a silence at twenty past or twenty to the hour, meant that an angel was passing over the house. **1973** *Sunday Express* 23 Sept. 13. Then, in one of those silences which are said to occur at twenty past the hour, the words of a chap sitting opposite me went ringing round the table. 'In my opinion,' said he, 'women in business are an absolute dead loss.'

COOKING: two together

1883 BURNE *Shropshire* 275. Two persons . . will inevitably quarrel . . if [they both] stir a boiling pot [and] if there be a pot boiling on the fire, and a stranger should come in and lift the lid, there will be a fight. Ibid. 276. An old woman at Moreton Say . . is in the habit of occasionally letting her neighbour make use of her brick-oven, both baking on the same day . . but on no account will the old dame allow the two bakers each to put in her own 'batch'. Either she or her friend may put in both batches, but whichever begins to do it must put in every loaf herself.

CORAL

AD 77 PLINY *Natural History* XXXII XI (1857, VI 12) Branches of coral, hung at the neck of infants, are thought to act as a preservative against danger. *c.* **1240** BARTHOLOMAEUS *De Proprietatibus Rerum* (tr. Trevisa, VI 32) Corallo . . Wytches tell y^t this stone wythstondyth lyghtnynge . . [The red coral] helpyth ayenst the fallynge euyll: & ayenst the fendes gyle & scorne, and ayenst dyuers woundes doyng. **1584** SCOT *Discoverie of Witchcraft* XIII VI. The corrall preserveth such as beare it from fascination or bewitching, and in this respect they are hanged about children's necks. But from whence that superstition is derived, and who invented the lie, I know not: but I see how readie the people are to give credit thereunto, by the multitude of corrals that waie emploied. **1650** BROWNE *Vulgar Errors* V XII. Though Corall doth properly preserve and fasten the Teeth in men, yet it is used in children to make an easier passage for them: and for that intent is worn about their necks. But whether this custome were not superstitiously founded, as presumed an amulet or defensative against fascination, is not beyond all doubt. **1653** H. PLATT *Jewel House* 232. Coral . . is . . good to be hanged about children's necks, as well to rub their gums, as to preserve them from the falling sickness. **1658** L. LEMNIUS *Secret Miracles of Nature* 391. Corall bound to the neck takes off turbulent dreams, and allays the nightly fears of Children. **1661** WEBSTER *Cure for a Cuckold* I I. NURSE. I fear shortly it will breed teeth, you must provide him therefore a Corral, with a Whistle and a Chain. *c.* **1740** *Aristotle's Midwife* 52–3.

If .. the Waters break away too long before the Birth .. there are many .. Things .. Physicians affirm are good .. among which [is] a Piece of red Coral hung near [the Privities]. **1879** J. NAPIER *West of Scotland* 36. Coral beads .. hung round the necks of babies .. are still used in country districts to protect them from an evil eye. Coral bells are used at present .. to frighten away evil spirits. **1948** *Dental Magazine* Feb. 3. My own children were presented [with coral necklaces] by a doting aunt .. although she did not know of the belief in such things as teething amulets.

CORK cures cramp

1850 MRS LOUDON *Ladies' Companion* 4 May 304. A subscriber who suffers from cramp, advises a cork to be put under the pillow at night, and carried in the pocket during the day, as a cure. What connexion there can possibly be between the *cork* and the *cramp*, I cannot imagine; but I give my correspondent's receipt for the benefit of those who may like to try it. Faith has a wonderful effect in matters of this kind. **1870** *N & Q* 4th ser. V 380. It is believed pretty generally in some parts of Lincolnshire that cork has the power of keeping off cramp. It is placed between the bed and the mattress, or even between the sheets; or cork garters are made by sewing together a series of thin discs of cork between two silk ribbons. **1951** *Folklore* 268. A St John's Ambulance nursing sister who was recently called to 'lay out' an old woman aged 100 told me she had corks round her toes to 'keep away the cramp'. **1957** *Sunday Post* 6 Jan. 6 [North Shields, Northumb.] I keep a cork under my pillow and, when the pain comes, I press it tightly from one hand to the other.

CORN DOLLY hung up in house

1688 AUBREY *Remaines* (1881, 172) The Irish doe keepe some of the last yeares Wheat or Barley, to hang up in their Houses, as a Lar [household god] .. Some used to hang these idols in their chimneys. **1797** *Stat. Acc. of Scotland* XIX 550–1 [Longforgan, Perth.] It was, till very lately, the custom to give what was called a Maiden Feast, upon the finishing of the harvest; and to prepare for which, the last handful of corn reaped in the field was called the Maiden. This was generally contrived to fall into the hands of one of the finest girls in the field, was dressed up in ribands, and brought home in triumph, with the music of fiddles or bagpipes .. The evening was spent in joviality and dancing, while the fortunate lass who took the Maiden was the queen of the feast; after which, this handful of corn was dressed out, generally in the form of a cross, and hung up, with the date of the year, in some conspicuous part of the house. This custom is now entirely done away, and in its room to each shearer is given 6d and a loaf of bread. **1813** BRAND *Antiquities* I 442–3 n. At Werington in Devonshire, the clergyman of the parish informed me that when a farmer finishes his reaping, a small quantity of the ears of the last corn are twisted or tied together into a curious kind of figure, which is brought home with great acclamations, hung up over the table, and kept till the next year. The owner would think it extremely unlucky to part with this, which is called 'a Knack'. **1899** *Newcastle Weekly Chronicle* 11 Feb. 7 [Jesmond] When reaping is completed a few stalks of corn are made into a cross, decorated and hung in the farm kitchen—it is called the 'kern baby'. If there is no 'kern baby', the next harvest will be bad; it must be removed before Christmas. **1912** LEATHER *Herefordshire* 104. As for the mare, or last sheaf, it was carefully plaited in a variety of ways, and hung up in a farm-house kitchen .. to be kept till next harvest for luck. **1938** *Folklore* 235 [Shrops.] One fairly frequently sees little affairs made of wheat hanging from the beams of farm houses, and although nowadays they are made from the first corn cut, as being easier to plait, and they are hung up 'for luck', strange to say, I have never been able to find anyone to give them a name. **1951** *Folklore* 328 [Maidstone, Kent] Straw 'harvest babies' are still made by an old man, or were. He is now too ill to do them. They used to be hung up by the hearth until the next harvest. **1952** *Sunday Times* 21 Sept. 2 [Worcs.] Mr William T. Dipper .. learned

from his father over sixty years ago
how to plait straw into these attractive
pendent shapes .. His 'corn dollies' have
attracted interest from museums and
housewives looking for winter 'flower'
decorations. **1959** *Journal of School of
Scottish Studies* III 197. The Harvest
Maiden or Clyack last Sheaf is still cut
and brought home .. As recently as
1954 I saw a Clyack Sheaf on the wall
of a house in Laggan, Badenoch. **1984**
Woman, 56 [Colchester, Essex] I had
never come across corn dollies until I
moved here. People make them for a
hobby, and learn how to at evening
classes. All the gift shops sell them. I
always have one hung up in my kitchen
for luck.

CORNER HOUSE unlucky

1848 DICKENS *Dombey and Son* LI. Mr
Towlinson .. frequently begs to know
whether he didn't say that no good
would ever come of living in a corner
house. **1875** *N & Q* 5th ser. IV 216
[Herefords.] I once resided next to a
corner house, and was frequently congratulated on having escaped that un-
enviable position. **1947** Woman, 50
[South Shields, Co. Durham] I know
corner houses are supposed to be
unlucky, but we haven't done too badly
in this one.

CORPSE carried feet first

1658 BROWNE *Urn Burial* IV. They [the
ancients] carried them out of the world
with their feet forward, not inconsonant
unto reason, as contrary unto the native
posture of man, and his production first
into it. **1923** [Trowbridge, Wilts.] A
coffin must always be carried out of a
house 'feet first'. If carried the reverse
way the ghost of the dead man would
return. **1955** Woman, 53 [Oxted, Sur-
rey] The sisters in the hospital here say
that a patient must be taken in and out
of the operating theatre with their head
first, otherwise it is bad luck.

CORPSE defiles: makes earth barren

1849 *Norfolk Archaeology* II 44. If a dead
body be carried across a field, that field
will become barren, no matter how
fruitful previously.

Cf. MURDER: earth remains barren.

CORPSE defiles ship

c. AD 110 PLUTARCH *Lives* (tr. North,
1928, VII 303) When he [Cato] was
ready to embark, to pass over the sea
again unto Brundusium, some of his
friends persuaded him, that it was better
to put the ashes of his brother Caepio's
bones into another ship. But he
answered them, That he would rather
lose his own life, than to leave his
brother's relics .. and it is reported that
he passed over in great danger, where
other ships arrived very safely. **1608**
SHAKESPEARE *Pericles* III i. FIRST SAILOR.
The sea workes hie, The Wind is lowd,
and will not lie till the Ship Be cleard of
the dead. PERICLES. That's your superstition. **1639** FULLER *Holy Warre* IV
XXVII. A ship cannot abide to be made
a bier of. **1688** AUBREY *Remaines* (1881,
67) A dead body on shipboarde .. they
hold to be very unlucky, and if a storme
arises they will throw it into yᵉ sea; as
they did that rare Mummie that Sir Peter
Wych brought from Egypt. **1777** BRAND
Antiquities 98. Sailors .. have various
puerile Apprehensions concerning ..
carrying a Corpse .. all of which are
Vestiges of the old Woman in human
Nature. **1854** *N & Q* 1st ser. X 26. A
corpse .. on board a ship is said to
bring bad weather. **1885** *Folklore* 55. A
Rosehearty [Aberdeen.] fisherman told
me that he was once fishing for lobsters
.. and that he came upon a human body
floating. It was carefully lifted into the
boat and brought ashore. The owner of
the boat .. was not at sea, and when he
learned what had been done he was in
distress and in a passion. He filled his
boat with water, and for three successive
days .. he rubbed, and scrubbed it. **1900**
N & Q 9th ser. VI 246–7. About 1827–
9 my father, then a young surgeon,
made two voyages in a whaling ship
from Hull to Greenland .. On one occasion he and a companion were landed
on a small island, where .. they found
the skeleton of an Esquimaux .. They
carefully packed up the bones and carried them to the shore. But when the
boat arrived to take them off, the sailors,
seeing the bones, absolutely refused to
receive them on board, and to my
father's chagrin .. he had to leave the
specimen behind.

CORPSE defiles: threshold washed

1961 [Scarborough, Yorks.] He had seen a coffin brought out of a house, and as soon as the funeral party had gone a woman came out and washed the front door step.

Cf. BRIDE: threshold washed.

CORPSE, eyes of

*c.*1828 Calvert MS, Pickering, Yorks. (G. HOME *Evolution of an English Town* 215) It be a good sign if the eyes [of the corpse] do shut of themselves, if not then but a few years sen it was held to be the work of some evil spirits in some cases owing to a misspent life. **1923** [Martock, Som.] A corpse whose eyes remain open is 'waiting for the next'. **1978** N. MAYES *Nature Notebook* 88 [Cornwall] It was said that if the eyes of the dead remained open, they were searching for the next person to die.

CORPSE, rain rains on

1607 *Puritan Widow* I A3ᵛ. If, Blessed bee the coarse the raine raynes vpon, he had it, powring downe. **1774** BOSWELL (*For the Defence*, 1960, 302) Edinburgh, 30 Aug. A woman who was executed .. told .. to a minister .. 'If ye see some clear draps o' rain faw on me after I'm custen owr [thrown over], I'm happy. **1777** BRAND *Antiquities* 53. If Rain fell during the Funeral Procession, it was vulgarly considered as a Presage of the Happiness of the Deceased in the other World. **1859** ELIOT *Adam Bede* II XVIII. 'It 'ud ha' been better luck if they'd ha' buried him i' the forenoon when the rain was fallin'.' **1952** A. HARE *Years with Mother* 171 [Alderley Edge, Cheshire, 1862] It poured with rain. The crowds of poor people present, however, liked this, for 'blessed', they said, 'is the corpse that the rain falls on.' **1964** Woman, 36 [Liss, Hants.] It was pouring with rain—and d'you know what Harry Lemon's wife said to me? 'Well, she's happy. Happy the corpse the rain rains on.'

Cf. BRIDE, sun shines on.

CORPSE remains supple

1672 BROWNE *Vulgar Errors* V XXII. § 9. If a Child dieth, and the neck becometh not stiff, but for many howers remaineth Lythe and Flaccid, some other in the same house will dye not long after. **1854** *N & Q* 1st ser. X 88 [West Tofts, Norfolk] Having had three deaths in my parish lately, I was gravely informed at the last funeral that it was not to wondered at, as the first two corpses were quite limp till the time of their burial. **1870** *N & Q* 4th ser. VI 130 [North Kelsey, Lincs.] I was told by an old woman the other day that if a corpse remained warm and 'limmack' (i.e. flexible) longer than usual, it was a sign there would soon be another death in the house or family. **1923** [Wellington, Som.] If a corpse is limp when put into the coffin there will shortly be another death in the family.

CORPSE: speaking of the dead

6th c. BC CHILON De mortuis nil nisi bonum. **1607** MIDDLETON *Your Five Gallants* II D3. TAYLBY. Agen? pax [pox] of these dice! BUNGLER. 'Tis ill to curse the dead sir. TAYLBY. Mew, where should I wish the pox but among bones? **1609** S. HARWARD MS Trinity Coll. Camb. 81ᵛ. Speake not evill of the dead. **1825** JAMIESON *Scottish Dict.* Suppl. II 301. *De mortuis nil nisi bonum,* is an adage which may at first view be ascribed to the humanity of the living. But .. it seems very questionable whether it may not justly be traced to superstitious fear. In our own time, when men speak of the dead, especially if anything is said to their dispraise, it is common to qualify it by some phrase, apparently expressive of sympathy or regard,—as, 'poor man!' 'honest man!' .. while what is said often directly contradicts the mollifying qualification. Some good Protestants are accustomed to say, 'Rest his soul!' .. The ancient Romans, in speaking of the dead, seem to have been afraid, not merely of causing disquietude to them, but of being themselves troubled with their unwelcome visits, if they should say anything to provoke them. **1902** *Spectator* 1 Nov. The dislike to speake ill of those lately dead has been proverbial for ages. **1945** F. THOMPSON *Lark Rise* XIV. 'Never speak ill of the dead' was one of their maxims. **1959** J. CAREY *Captive & Free* XLVII. 'Nothing but good about the dead.' What a lie. Of a piece with all this English softness, sentiment, slop.

CORPSE, tears falling on

1799 Stat. Acc. of Scotland XXI 147 n. [Monquhitter, Aberdeen.] It disturbed the ghost of the dead, and was fatal to the living, if a tear was allowed to fall on a winding-sheet. **1885** Folklore 281. In the Highlands of Scotland .. it was thought wrong to weep [at a funeral] lest the tears should hurt the dead. **1909** M. TREVELYAN Folk-Lore of Wales 283. If you allow your tears to fall on the dead, they will have no rest. **1910** Folklore 90 [Argyll.] Never let your tears drop on a corpse, or harm will befall you.
Cf. DEATH: 'wishing' or 'crying back'.

CORPSE, touching

1787 GROSE Provincial Glossary Superstitions 57. Touching a dead body, prevents dreaming of it. c.**1816** Wilkie MS (HENDERSON Northern Counties 1866, 38) It is imperative that every watcher at a lykewake should touch the corpse .. to keep him from dreaming of the dead. **1858** DENHAM North of England (1895, 59) It was done to prevent the unhouseled spirit troubling you .. But we moderns, having, in part at least renounced our belief in Ghosts, say that it is to prevent our dreaming of seeing the dead body. **1920** Folklore 154 [Cumberland coroner] The deceased was a yeoman and the jury were mostly farmers [and] I observed that nearly every one took the deceased's chin between his thumb and forefinger .. One man told me that if one touched a dead body, the idea of it did not haunt one. **1959** Journal of School of Scottish Studies 197. The corpse is touched to prevent dreams about the dead. **1972** MOLLY WEIR Best Foot Forward 46 [Glasgow] Adults lifted us children up to place a hand on the brow of the corpse, because this was said to prevent nightmares afterwards.

CORPSE, unburied: miner

1856 Gents Mag. pt. 1 39 [Dudley, Worcs.] The colliers, in the event of a fatal accident to one of their number, all in the same pit immediately cease from working until the body is buried. **1899** Newcastle Weekly Chronicle 11 Feb.

7. Durham miners decline to work while there is a dead body in the mine.

CORPSE, unburied: on New Year's Day

1821 GALT Annals of the Parish IV. She was removed from mine to Abraham's bosom on Christmas day, and buried on Hogmanae, for it was thought uncanny [unlucky] to have a dead corpse in the house on the new-year's day.

CORPSE, unburied: over Saturday/Sunday

1904 N & Q 10th ser. I 127 [Sussex] A villager .. presaged another death within the month, because the corpse would of necessity lie unburied 'over a Sunday'. **1932** WOMEN'S INSTITUTE Worcestershire Book 35 [Broadway] If a dead body lies over Sunday there will be another death the following Sunday. **1959** Trans. Devon. Ass. 203 [Northlew, c.1915] There was a saying in the village that if a body lay unburied over the week-end there would be another death during the following week. **1963** Woman, c.65 [Liss, Hants.] She's just told me the funeral's not to be till Monday—but it's very unlucky to leave someone unburied over Sunday, it means there will be another death within the month. **1986** Woman, 47 [Fringford, Oxon.] If you leave the body unburied over Saturday there will be another death within the week.

CORPSE'S HAND cures

AD **77** PLINY Natural History XXVIII XI (1856, V 292) Scrofula .. and throat diseases .. may be cured by the contact of the hand of a person who has been carried off by an early death: indeed .. some .. assert that any dead body will produce the same effect, provided it is of the same sex as the patient, and that the part affected is touched with the back of the left hand. **1584** SCOT Discoverie of Witchcraft XII XIV. To heale the Kings or Queenes evill, or any other sorenesse in the throte .. touch the place with the hand of one that died an untimelie death. **1650** BROWNE Vulgar Errors V XXII. For Warts we .. commit any maculated part unto the touch of the dead. **1688** AUBREY Remaines (1881, 198) Mdm. The wenne that grew in yͤ man's cheeke at Stowell, in Somerset, as big as an egge, was cured by stroking it with his dead kinswomans hand; and Mr Davy Mell (Musitian), had a child w^h a hunch back cured in the like manner. 1708 *British Apollo* Supernumerary no. 8, for Nov. A Woman that had a Wen in her Neck of a Considerable Size .. made Tryal of [a hand] of one that was hang'd, after which it abated gradually, and is now sunk to less than half its Primitive Bigness. 1787 GROSE *Provincial Glossary* Superstitions 56. A dead man's hand is supposed to have the quality of dispelling tumours, such as wens, or swelled glands, by stroking with it, nine times, the place affected. It seems as if the hand of a person dying a violent death was deemed particularly efficacious; as it very frequently happens, that nurses bring children to be stroked with the hands of executed criminals, even whilst they are hanging on the gallows. 1850 *N & Q* 1st ser. II 36. On execution days at Northampton, numbers of sufferers used to congregate round the gallows, in order to receive the 'dead-stroke', as it is termed. At the last execution .. a very few only were operated upon, not so much in consequence of decrease in faith, as from the higher fee demanded by the hangman. 1859 *N & Q* 2nd ser. VIII 489 [Cornwall] If a person with a sore be taken secretly to a corpse, the dead hand passed over the sore place, and the bandage afterwards dropped upon the coffin during the reading of the burial service, a perfect cure will be the result. 1887 'SPERANZA' WILDE *Superstitions of Ireland* I 152–3. A dead hand is esteemed a certain cure for most diseases, and many a time sick people have been brought to a house where a corpse lay that the hand of the dead might be laid on them. 1945 *Folklore* 270 [Suffolk] The touch of a dead man's hand will cure warts. This has been tried well within living memory.

CORPSE'S HAND gives power over butter

1616 Witchcraft trial, Shetland (DALYELL *Darker Superstitions of Scotland* 264) She wald gif her sum thing gif she wald heild [hide] it, that wald do hir guid: and oppnit hir pwrs and tuik ane bone furth therof, quhilk wes the bone of ane manes finger .. and bad hir steir hir milk with it and she wald get hir profeit. 1882 *Folk-Lore Record* 81 [Co. Wexford] A person taking a dead hand from a graveyard is supposed to have the power of taking butter from any person he pleases so long as the hand is retained in the house. 1887 'SPERANZA' WILDE *Superstitions of Ireland* I 152. Many strange spells are effected by the means of a dead man's hand—chiefly to produce butter in the churn. The milk is stirred round nine times with the dead hand, the operator crying aloud all the time 'Gather! gather! gather!'

CORPSE'S HAND holding candle

1440 Coroner's Court, Maidstone, Kent (*Bull. Inst. Hist. Research* XXXVI 86–7) I shalle telle the what strenghe þat arme hathe, and what power it hathe .. take when þu wolt the arme of adede manne þat hathe leyen in the erthe ix daies and ix nyghtes, and putte in the dede hande a brennynge candele, and go to aplace wheþer þu wilt, and thoughe ther be þerin an C pepille, thei þat slepe shalle slepe, and thei þat wake shulle not meve what ever þu do. 1686–7 AUBREY *Remaines* (1881, 103) A story .. was generally believed when I was a Schooleboy (before the civill Warres) that Thieves when they broke open a house, would putt a Candle into a Dead man's hand, and then the people in the Chamber would not awake. 1831 *Observer* 16 Jan. 4. On the night of the 3d inst. some Irish thieves attempted to commit a robbery on the estate of Mr Napper, of Lough-screw, county Meath [Eire]. They entered the house armed with a dead man's hand, with a lighted candle in it, believing .. that a candle placed in a dead man's hand will not be seen by any but those by whom it is used; and that .. it will prevent those who may be asleep from awaking! 1866 HENDERSON *Northern Counties* 202–3 [Stainmore, c.1795] The traveller .. pulled out of his pocket a dead man's hand, fitted a candle to it, lighted the candle, and passed hand and candle several times before the servant-girl's face, saying .. 'Let those who are asleep be asleep, and let those who are awake be awake.' 1870 *N & Q* 4th ser. VI 211 [Walton-le-Dale, Lancs., c.1820] A dead man's hand had been .. considered part of the stock-in-trade of a Lancashire burglar, just as a crow-bar and 'jemmy' are now. It was supposed that a lighted candle placed on the hand could neither go out nor burn out, and that whilst it was lit the inmates could never awake. **1887** 'SPERANZA' WILDE *Superstitions of Ireland* I 152. If a candle is placed in a dead hand, neither wind nor water can extinguish it. And if carried into a house the inmates will sleep the sleep of the dead as long as it remains under the roof, and no power on earth can wake them while the dead hand holds the candle.

CORPSE'S LINEN cures

1887 'SPERANZA' WILDE *Superstitions of Ireland* I 153-4. The corner of a sheet that has wrapped a corpse is a cure for headache if tied round the head .. A piece of the linen wrap taken from a corpse will cure the swelling of a limb if tied round the part affected.

CORPSE'S LINEN lucky

1813 BRAND *Antiquities* II 144. Laying out the corpse is an office always performed by women, who claim the linen, &c. about the person of the deceased at the time of performing the ceremony. It would be thought very unlucky for the friends of the person departed, were they to keep back any portion of what is thus found. These women give this away in their turn by small divisions; and they who can obtain any part of it, think it an omen or presage of future fortune to them or theirs.

CORPSE'S WASHING WATER cures

1883 W. G. BLACK *Folk-Medicine* 99. There is, at the time I write, in a poorhouse in Glasgow, a man to whom the water with which a corpse had been washed was administered with a view to curing him of fits.

COUNTING cures warts

1855 *N & Q* 1st ser. XII 37 [Cornwall] Some mysterious vagrant desires them to be carefully counted, and marking the number on the inside of his hat, leaves the neighbourhood—when the warts also disappear. **1866** HENDERSON *Northern Counties* 109-10. I know .. a curious case .. substantiated by the master and boys of Marlborough Grammar School .. A boy had his hands covered with warts .. most unpleasantly. As the lad passed the window of an old woman in the town who dabbled a little in charms .. she .. called to him to count his warts. He did so, and told her the exact number. 'By such a day,' she said, 'they shall be gone' .. By the day indicated .. every one of the warts .. was gone. **1870** *N & Q* 4th ser. VI 130 [Eaton, Norfolk] My daughter Phoebe had got a terrible lot o' warts on both of her hands, so I said to her: 'Why don't you go to Joe Dains and get rid of 'em?' So she went; and he asked her to count 'em, which she did, telling him the number. 'That'll do, young 'ooman,' ses he; 'I know enow.' A few weeks after that she met him again, quite accidental; and he then asked her how was her warts, and when she looked there wasn't one. **1983** [Colchester, Essex] Her teenage son had a lot of warts on his hands. Nothing seemed to cure them, until an old man told her to count them, and tell him the number but otherwise tell no one. The warts began to disappear from that day and finally altogether.

COUNTING dangerous/unlucky

10th c. BC II Samuel 24: 10. David's heart smote him after that he had numbered the people. And David said unto the Lord, I have sinned greatly in that I have done. *ante* **50** BC CATULLUS *Poems* (tr. Michie, v) Kiss me .. until .. we've lost track of the amount And nobody can work us ill with the evil eye by keeping count. **1773** BYROM *Misc. Poems* I 72. He knew a wise old Saying, which maintain'd That 'twas bad Luck to count what one had gain'd. late **18th c.** J. RAMSAY (*Scotland in the Eighteenth Century* II 449) In Morven [Argyll.] it is reckoned unlucky to number the people or cattle belonging to any family, but more particularly upon Friday .. And fishermen do not care to confess the number of salmon or other fish which they have taken at a draught or in a day, imagining that this discovery would spoil their luck. **1863** R. CHAMBERS *Book* *of Days* I 678 [Suffolk] It is unlucky to count lambs before a certain time; if you do, they will be sure not to thrive. Ibid. II 322–3 [West Country] A gentleman .. when out with professional fishermen, has been prevented by them from counting the fish caught till the day's sport was over. 1878 A. MACGREGOR *Brahan Seer* 128. 'Superstitions of Highlanders'. It is unfortunate if a stranger counts the number of your sheep, cattle, or children. It is quite common if one asks .. to add .. 'Bless them' to the question. Ibid. 130. If, when fishing, you count what you have taken, you will catch no more. 1881 W. GREGOR *North-East of Scotland* 200. On no account must the boats be counted when at sea, neither must any gathering .. Nothing aroused the indignation of a company of fisherwomen .. more than to point towards them .. and begin to number them aloud: 'Ane, twa, three, Faht a fishers I see' [etc.].' 1895 S. O. ADDY *Household Tales* 101 [Yorks.] It is unlucky to count your teeth. 1932 J. M. E. SAXBY *Shetland Lore* 184. It is unlucky to count your possessions, be they fish, or bairns, or money, or clothing. 1943 *Folklore* 390. A Suffolk shepherd will seldom willingly tell even his master the number of lambs born until the lambing-season is over for fear of bad luck. 1986 Woman, *c.*40 [Scone, Perth.] In Scotland, you should never count how many are seated round the fire—but I don't know why.

COUNTING/MEASURING ancient stones

ante 1581 SIDNEY *Seven Wonders of England* (ed. Ringle, 149) Neere Wilton sweete, huge heapes of stones are found, But so confusde that neither any eye can count them just. *c.*1690 C. FIENNES Journal (*Journeys*, ed. Morris, 15–16) To Stoneage [Stonehenge] that stands on Salsebury plaine .. to increase the wonder the story is that none can count them twice alike, they stand confused .. but I have told them often and bring their number to 91. Ibid. 201. A mile from Peroth [Penrith, Cumb.] in a low bottom .. stands Great Mag and her Sisters .. they affirme they cannot be counted twice alike as is the story of Stonidge, but the number of these [stones] are not above 30. 1724 DEFOE *Tour Through England and Wales* I III 41–2. Stone-Henge [Wilts.]. The common Opinion that no Man could ever Count them, that a Baker carry'd a Basket of Bread, and laid a Loaf upon every Stone, and yet could never make out the same Number twice. 1750 J. WOOD *Choir Gaure* 23 [Stanton Drew, Som.] Those that do know it [group of standing stones] tell us that no one was ever able to reckon the number of Stones .. or to take a Draught of them, though several have attempted to do both, and proceeded till they were either struck dead on the spot, or with such an Illness as soon carried them off. 1847 G. SOANE *New Curiosities of Literature* I 293. One of the most popular superstitions connected with figures was a belief in the impossibility, or in the danger, of counting certain objects—druidical monuments for the most part. 1908 *N & Q* 10th ser. X 137. When, visiting the Standing Stones at Callernish [Lewis, Hebrides] he asked a peasant boy how many stones there were in the monument, but was told that no one knew, for it was unlucky to count them. The lad looked as if he expected the ground to open when my friend replied that he had just counted them, and knew the exact number. 1946 *Folklore* 38–9 [Medway, Kent] Up to the last generation there was a widespread belief that the monuments could not be measured, nor the stones which composed them counted. Hence the name of 'The Countless Stones' for the destroyed Lower Kits Coty.

counting/measuring: cf. POINTING AT; MEASURING; WEIGHING.

COW cures consumption

1806 MRS THRALE *Diary* 11 May (ed. Balderston, II 1074) We had much Talk in our Chymical Lectures [given by a Doctor Archer in Bath] concerning Oxygen, & much Talk concerning the Analogy between our Animal and Vegetable Kingdoms; more Talk still about Doctor Beddowes the great Bristol Philosopher, who tries to cure Phtisis by the Breath of Cattle, wth which Creatures he shuts his Consumptive Patients *up*. Well says M[rs] Falconer humourously—Here's a

World of Bustle with their *Oxygen* and their *Cow* again;—yet People dye just the same for ought I can find as ever they did,—& perhaps a little more. **1851** *N & Q* 1st ser. III 368. For pulmonary complaints . . sleeping in a room over a cowhouse. **1954** Man, *c*.40. My grandfather was a butcher in Pembroke. He told me a gruesome cure for TB. After a beast has been slaughtered, while it is still steaming thrust your head into the carcass, draw the folds of flesh around your neck and inhale. **1986** Woman, 47 [Fringford, Oxon.] People who live in the smell of a cowyard never get TB.

Cf. SHEEP, flock of: cures.

COW trespasses

1850 *N & Q* 1st ser. I 258. About the middle of March, 1843, some cattle were driven close to my house; and . . *three* got into our little bit of garden . . When our school-drudge came in the afternoon . . she . . said it was a bad sign—and that we should hear of *three* deaths within the next six months. Alas! in April, we heard of dear J——'s murder; a fortnight after, A—— died; and tomorrow, August 10th, I am to attend the funeral of my excellent son-in-law. **1895** S. O. ADDY *Household Tales* 97. When a man's cow gets into his neighbour's pasture she is said to be 'unlucky'. **1923** [Chard, Som.] If a cow wanders from the field into your garden it is a sign of death in the family.

COW'S DUNG

1691 R. KIRK *Secret Commonwealth* (1815, 5) [Aberfoyle, Perth.] The Method they take to recover their Milk is a bitter chyding of the suspected Inchanters . . But a little of the Mother's Dung stroakit on the Calves Mouth before it suck any, does prevent this theft. **1795** *Stat. Acc. of Scotland* XVI 122 [Killearn, Stirling.] Cow dung is forced into the mouth of the calf immediately after it is calved . . the vulgar believe that witches and fairies can have no power ever after to injure the calf.

CRADLE, buying

1898 BLAKEBOROUGH *Yorkshire Customs* 114–15. In such fear was this forestalling of the cradle held, that one

was rarely purchased until absolutely needed. A cradle should always be paid for before it crosses the threshold. It is said that the child who sleeps in an unpaid-for cradle will end its days lacking the means to pay for its own coffin. **1912** LEATHER *Herefordshire* 113. It is unlucky to buy a new cradle, and bring it into the house before the birth of the child.

Cf. PRAM, buying.

CRADLE, rocking empty

c.**1816** Wilkie MS (HENDERSON *Northern Counties*, 1866, 10) [There is] a caution against rocking a cradle when it is 'toom', or empty. **1858** DENHAM *North of England* (1895, 49) To rock an empty cradle is considered ominous of a coming occupant. **1864** R. CHAMBERS *Book of Days* II 39 [Suffolk] If you rock an empty cradle, you will rock a new baby into it . . It is quite curious to see the face of alarm with which a poor woman, with her tenth baby in her arms, will dash across the room to prevent the 'baby-but-one' from engaging in such a dangerous amusement. **1878** *Folk-Lore Record* 11 [West Sussex] 'If you rock the cradle empty Then you shall have babies plenty.' A schoolmistress in the adjoining parish was always rating her scholars if they touched her cradle, and exclaiming, 'There, leave that alone, can't ye! I have children enough already!' **1923** [Somerset] Rocking the cradle brings a large family. **1932** C. IGGLESDEN *Those Superstitions* 143. During the War I entered a cottage for the purpose of visiting the young wife of a soldier at the front. With a baby in her arms the mother was standing by the fireplace, while at my side was the cradle. Thoughtlessly I placed my hand upon it, when a terrified scream came from the young woman. 'Oh! sir, please don't rock an empty cradle. If you do it will be filled with another baby before the year is out.' **1953** Girl, 15 [Knighton, Radnor.] If you rock a cradle empty, You shall have babes in plenty.

Cf. PRAM, pushing.

CRAMP, verbal charm for

1664 PEPYS *Diary* 31 Dec. Charme, for . . A Cramp. Cramp be thou faintless, As our Lady was sinless, When she bare Jesus. **1846** *Athenaeum* 3 Oct. 1018 [Devon/Cornwall] Cramp — be thou painless! As Our Lady was sinless When she bare Jesus.

CRAMP BONE

1579 LUPTON *Thousand Notable Things* I § 87. The lytle bone in the knee ioynt of the hinder legge of an Hare, doth presently helpe the crampe if you touch the grieued place therwith. Often proued. **1823** E. MOOR *Suffolk Words. Cramp-bone.* The *Patella* of a sheep or lamb .. It is carried in the pocket— the nearer the skin the better, of the credulous person, or laid under the pillow at night. **1870** *N & Q* 4th ser. VI 394–5. It is common in some parts of England to wear the fin bone of a haddock as a preservative from cramp. **1895** F. T. ELWORTHY *Evil Eye* 437 [West Country] The carrying of the knucklebone of a sheep, called commonly a 'cramp-bone' .. is still a daily practice. I have known persons, well to do, and by no means generally ignorant, who always had one about them. It must never have touched the ground or its virtue is lost. **1914** *Folklore* 367 [Kent] A knucklebone of mutton carried in the pocket cures or prevents cramp. **1968** A. FRANCIS *Guinea a Box* 24 [Curbridge, Oxon., 1920s] Patellas of sheep or lambs were placed by the credulous under pillows to dispel muscular pains.

CRICKET as omen

*c.*1614 WEBSTER *Duchess of Malfi* II ii. How superstitiously we mind our evils! The .. singing of a Criket [is] of powre To daunt whole man in us. **1620** MELTON *Astrologaster* 46. It is a signe of death to some in that house, where Crickets have bin many yeeres, if on a sudden they forsake the Chimney Corner. **1650** N. HOMES *Daemonologie* 59. The same they conclude [i.e. death] of a Cricket crying in an house, where was wont to be none. **1652** GAULE *Mag-astro-mances* 181 [Among] superstitious ominations .. the crickets chirping behind the chimney stock; or creeping upon the foot-pace. **1691** *Athenian Mercury* 18 July. Upon some par-

ticular Cases God Almighty may make use of .. Crickets, &c., to warn us of our approaching End, as I knew a Family never without one Cricket before some one dy'd out of it. **1782** COWPER *Poems* 339. 'The Cricket'. Little inmate, full of mirth, Chirping on my kitchen hearth, Wheresoe'er be thine abode, Always harbinger of good. **1830** FORBY *East Anglia* 414. Crickets betoken good luck to the house they inhabit, and if they quit it suddenly, it is a very bad omen. **1846** DICKENS *Cricket on the Hearth* I. 'It's merrier than ever, to-night, I think.' 'And it's sure to bring us good fortune, John! It always has done so. To have a Cricket on the Hearth, is the luckiest thing in all the world!' **1866** MOORE *Life of Byron* 11 n. [Newstead Abbey, 1798] On the day of their patron's death, these crickets all left the house simultaneously, and in such numbers, that it was impossible to cross the hall without treading on them. **1883** BURNE *Shropshire* 238. The cricket on the hearth appears somewhat in the light of a domestic familiar, or household bogy, sometimes regarded as a 'lucky' inmate and sometimes as quite the reverse. **1908** *Folklore* 318 [Eire] The coming of a cricket to a house is a sign of death, but the evil may be averted and the insect driven away by saying to it, 'Cricket, cricket, if you come for good luck, stay; but if you come for bad luck, go.' This belief was obtained from a policeman in Tipperary. **1910** *Folklore* 225 [Yorks.] In Craven it is lucky to hear a cricket whistling. **1918** *Folklore* 310. On the north coast of Mayo east from Portacloy [Eire] the crickets usually foretell death, 'for they are hundreds of years old and very cunning and understand all that they hear.' **1922** [Creech St Michael, Som.] If a cricket keeps chirping it is a sign of death. **1952** A. HARE *Years with Mother* 301. Our parting was very near. Lea .. called me downstairs to hear the extraordinary sound that was going on .. It was as if hundreds of thousands of crickets were all chirping together. They appeared everywhere in swarms on the hearths downstairs. The noise .. was quite deafening; but they only came out that night, they never were heard before, and the next day they had totally disappeared.

Cf. RATS AND MICE, influx of: ominous.

CRICKET, harming

1787 GROSE *Provincial Glossary* Superstitions 64. It is held extremely unlucky to kill a cricket .. perhaps from the idea of its being a breach of hospitality. **1823** *Time's Telescope* xxxiii–iv. A popular prejudice .. frequently prevents any attempts at their destruction; many people imagining that their presence is attended with good luck, and that to kill or drive them away will surely bring some unfortunate occurrence on the family. **1851** *N & Q* 1st ser. III 516 [Lancs.] Crickets are lucky about a house, and will do no harm to those who use them well; but .. they eat holes in the worsted stockings of such members of the family as kill them. I was assured of this on the experience of a respectable farmer's family. **1882** *People's Friend* 8 Nov. 711. Unlucky is the person who kills a cricket. **1889** H. J. BARKER *Original English* 53. Never kill crickets, for I tell yer I once killed a cricket while my mother was a mangling and I was a rocking the baby .. and then my mother began crying, saying baby would never have no luck. **1922** [Martock, Som.] Leave the cheerful cricket alone. Clear out and kill it, and your household will not thrive.

CRIPPLE, meeting

AD **77** PLINY *Natural History* XXVIII VII (1856, V 289) [There are] evil presages attendant upon meeting a person who is lame in the right leg. *c.* AD **388** ST JOHN CHRYSOSTOM *Baptismal Instructions* (ed. Harkins, 189) Often a man leaves his own house and sees a man who .. is lame, and counts it an omen. *c.***1180** PETER OF BLOIS (*Petri Blesensis Bathoniensis Archdiaconi, Opera Omnia*, ed. Giles, I 191) The error of those who hate to encounter .. a cripple. **1526** ERASMUS *Familiar Colloquies* (tr. Bailey, 397) Human Constitutions require that no .. lame [person] be admitted to any sacred Function. **1652** GAULE *Mag-astro-mances* 181. To bode good or bad luck .. to meet one fasting that is lame. **1721** KELLY *Scotish Proverbs* 311. *Take a Care*

of that Man whom God has set a Mark on .. The Scots generally have an Aversion to any that have any natural Defect or re-Dundancy. **1887** 'SPERANZA' WILDE *Superstitions of Ireland* II 64. It is unlucky to meet .. a lame woman when going a journey. **1889** *Folklore* 45. Until within recent years no Cockenzie [E. Lothian] fisherman would have ventured out to sea had .. a lame man crossed his path on his way to the beach. **1898** BLAKEBOROUGH *Yorkshire Customs* 102. It is a bad omen .. should a cripple cross the path [of the bridal party].

CROCKERY, breaking

1864 R. CHAMBERS *Book of Days* II 105 [Suffolk] I once had a servant who was very much given to breaking glass and crockery .. 'Let her buy something,' said the cook, 'and that will change the luck.'

CROOKED

1888 *Yorkshire Folk-Lore Record* 195. Crooked things are lucky things.

CROOKED COIN

1570 FOX *Book of Martyrs* 216–18 (1888, 812) A shilling .. of Phillip and Mary shee tooke forth, which her father had bowed and sent her when she was first sent to prison .. which she had kept and now sent him to doo him to understand that shee neuer lacked money while she was in prison. *c.***1797** H. MORE *Tawney Rachel* 9. She .. would bring down a bright queen Ann's sixpence very crooked .. 'It cured me of a very bad ague last spring, by only laying it nine nights under my pillow without speaking a word.' **1854** *N & Q* 1st ser. X 505 [West Country] A crooked sixpence is usually selected by careful grand-mothers, aunts, and uncles, to bestow as the 'handselling' of a new purse. **1858** DENHAM *North of England* (1895, 72) A crooked sixpence worn .. in the left side pocket is .. indicative of good luck to the wearer. I know a lady who I have seen turn not less than half a dozen out of her purse at one time. **1866** HENDERSON *Northern Counties* 146. The witch is driven away by .. popping in [the churn] a crooked sixpence. **1873** HARLAND & WILKINSON *Lancashire Legends* 227. A coin that's crook Brings more to t'rook [heap]. **1899** J. SHAW *School-master* 30 [Tynron, Dumfries.] Crooked sixpences are worn at the watch chain, so you shall have silver when you first see the new moon. **1923** [Trowbridge, Wilts.] It is lucky to be paid or to receive as a gift a 'crooked sixpence'. It should be kept in your purse and will bring you good fortune. **1952** Girl, 14 [Aberdeen] If a person has a crooked penny it is supposed to be lucky. **1987** [Waterlooville, Hants.] Man, 50, pulling a handful of change out of his pocket: 'See those? [two crooked coins] I've had them years. I'll never spend them.'

Cf. MONEY, having: in purse etc.

CROOKED FURROW

1857 *N & Q* 2nd ser. IV 487 [Lanark.] Attached to the houses are long .. crofts of ground, in ploughing which it is all done in curved and crooked rigs or ridges .. under the belief that the Evil One will be unable to follow out with his eye .. the growing crop, and thus prevent it being blasted. **1895** J. HARDY *Denham Tracts* 146. On Tweedside (North Durham), in some old pasture fields, there still remain the twisted ridges .. cast up by the plough .. The story is that it was a precaution against .. the fairies, who took a malicious pleasure in shooting their fatal bolts at the patient beasts of burden who tore up their grassy hillocks .. They aimed their arrows along the furrows .. but .. were baffled by their being drawn crooked.

CROOKED HORSESHOE NAIL

1586 CAMDEN *Britannia* (tr. Gibson, II 378) [Limerick, Eire, *c.*1566] If the infant is sick .. they hang .. about the child's neck .. a crooked nail out of a horse's hoof.

CROOKED PIN

1695 CONGREVE *Love for Love* III iv. Cheer up, look about thee .. [*Aside*] Now is he poring upon the Ground for a crooked Pin. **1865** *Gents Mag.* pt. 2 700 [Ireland] It is regarded as .. lucky .. to find a crooked pin. **1878** *Folk-Lore Record* 33 [Fittleworth, Sussex] A yellow, crooked pin must on no account be picked up, or the tidy person who removes it from the floor will die an old maid. **1887**

'SPERANZA' WILDE *Superstitions of Ireland* II 105. If you want a person to win at cards, stick a crooked pin in his coat. **1898** *Aberdeen Weekly Free Press* 29 Oct. 3. I have seen a trawl fisherman throw a crooked pin overboard to bring good luck when the fishing was poor. **1908** *Folklore* 344 [New Galloway, Kirkcudbright., *c.*1874] Her husband came up the road .. with me, when suddenly he turned abruptly and began walking homewards. I .. expostulated [and] at length he did turn in the direction we had started, reached the spot where we halted, stooped down, and pointing to a minute object on the road said, 'D'ye think I wad gang ony furder that road the day?' It was a bent pin that caused him to pause. **1957** Schoolboy, 12 [Westerkirk, Dumfries.] If you find a bent pin it is supposed to bring you luck.

Cf. PIN, finding.

CROOKED STICK

1883 BURNE *Shropshire* 253 n. [Hanwood, *c.*1805] At Christmas, my excellent mother always made pigs' puddings, which were boiled in a small furnace, in the flue of which my mother always placed a crooked stick to prevent the puddings breaking in the boiling. If any did break, it was because the stick was not crooked enough.

CROSS cures

AD 731 BEDE *Historia Ecclesiastica* III 11 (tr. Sherley-Price) When King Oswald was about to give battle to the heathen [AD 634], he set up the sign of the holy cross .. Even to this day many folk take splinters of wood from this cross, which they put into water, and when any sick men or beasts drink of it or are sprinkled with it, they are at once restored to health .. A few years ago, one of the brothers of the church of Hexham .. fractured an arm .. A bit of old moss that grew on the cross .. he thrust next his breast .. Waking up in the middle of the night .. he found that his arm was whole and sound as if he had never suffered such great pain. *c.*1040 MS Harl. 55 (COCKAYNE *Leechdoms* II 345) Against elf disease .. take .. moss or lichen from the hallowed sign of Christ. **1584** SCOT *Discoverie of Witchcraft* XII

XVIII. Charm for ague. Wear about your necke, a peece of a naile taken from a crosse, and wrapped in wooll. **1911** *Folklore* 56 [Co. Clare] The mud and water in the socket of the cross at Kilvoydan .. cure warts. **1953** Boy, 11 [Presteigne, Radnor.] Carve a piece of wood into a shape of a cross, and put X for each wart. Then bury it deep in the ground. **1956** *Belfast Weekly Telegraph* 13 Jan. 8 [Kilkeel, Co. Down] On the town side of the ruined church stands the 'wart well'. This is an old stone cross, obviously belonging to the pre-Reformation building which was later superseded .. At the foot of the cross is a holy water stoup, the bottom of which is full of pins, some almost rusted away, others of far more recent origin .. the idea being that any sufferer from warts who drops a pin into the water and walks three times round the cross .. will find the warts have disappeared within a few weeks.

CROSS, making sign of: cures and protects

*c.***1050** MS Junius 85 (COCKAYNE *Leechdoms* I 393) For a stitch. Write a cross of Christ, and sing over the place this thrice .. 'The soldier .. pierced the Lord with a spear. The blood did not flow and the pain diminished.' **1618** W. PERKINS *Works* III 634. The crossing of the body .. that we may be blessed from the deuill .. wherein the crosse carrieth the very nature of a Charme, and the vse of it in this manner, a practice of Inchantment. **1835** COLERIDGE *Table Talk* II 59. June 10, 1832. Charm for Cramp. When I was a little boy at the Blue-coat School, there was a charm for one's foot when asleep; and I believe it had been in the school since its foundation, in the time of Edward the Sixth. The march of intellect has probably now exploded it. It ran thus: 'Foot! foot! foot! is fast asleep! Thumb! thumb! thumb! in spittle we steep: Crosses three we make to ease us, Two for the thieves, and one for Christ Jesus!' And the same charm served for a cramp in the leg, with the following substitution: 'The devil is tying a knot in my leg! Mark, Luke, and John, unloose it, I beg! Crosses three, &c.' And really, upon getting out of bed .. pressing the sole of the foot on the cold floor, and

then repeating this charm with the acts configurative thereupon prescribed, I can safely affirm that I do not remember an instance in which the cramp did not go away in a few seconds. **1855** F. K. ROBINSON *Yorkshire Words. Shoe-cross,* a cross made with your wet finger upon the shoe-toe, to cure the cramp or thrill in the foot. **1865** R. HUNT *West of England* 2nd ser. 240. To Cure the Hiccough. Wet the forefinger of the right hand with spittle, and cross the front of the left shoe or boot three times, repeating the Lord's Prayer backwards. **1869** *N & Q* 4th ser. IV 506. On the Chilterns in the neighbourhood of Tring the superstition still exists that if you wet your finger and sign a cross on your foot it immediately cures 'pins and needles'. **1881** W. GREGOR *North-East of Scotland* 181. Before commencing work on the harvest field, each reaper cast a cross on the ground with the sickle 'to keep the wrist from being sprained'. **1887** 'SPERANZA' WILDE *Superstitions of Ireland* II 94. Rub the part affected [with stitch] with unsalted butter, and make the sign of the cross seven times over the place. **1932** WOMEN'S INSTITUTE *Worcestershire Book* 37. To put crosses on one's shoes is supposed to cure the stitch after running. **1934** *N & Q* CLXVI 121–2. This custom of wetting one's forefinger and making a cross on the toe of one's boot, is an old one in NW Durham and S. Northumberland. I have known of it for sixty years. It is fast becoming obsolete, only old persons (generally women) now do it. It was always more common in the winter months, and was considered 'a charm' against frostbite. There was a rhyme .. 'Christ-cross, Keep away the frost bite every day.'

CROSS, making sign of: on bread

1252 *Mandate of Henry III* (Close Rolls, 249) A mandate to the counties of Essex and Hereford proclaims that bakers throughout the region, are forbidden to mark the bread they sell, with the sign of the Cross. **1549** *Common Prayer* 133ᵛ. It is mete that the breade prepared for the Communion, bee made through all this realme, after one sort and fashion: that is to saie, unleauened, and rounde, as it was afore, but without any maner of print. **1648** HERRICK *Hesperides* 383 'Charmes'. Maidens when ye Leavens lay, Crosse your Dow, and your dispatch, Will be better for your Batch. *ante* **1738** W. KENNETT Note in Aubrey's *Remaines* (1881, 51) In Kent & many other parts the women when they have kneaded their dough into a loaf cut ye form of a cross on the top of it. **1771** PENNANT *Tour in Scotland* 94. Before women bake their bannocks, or oatmeal cakes, they make a cross on the last [i.e. the meal]. **1813** BRAND *Antiquities* I 131 n. The country-people in the North of England make, with a knife, many little cross-marks on their cakes, before they put them into the oven. I have no doubt but this .. is a remain of Popery. **1828** W. CARR *Craven Dialect* 131 [Yorks.] The person .. never fails .. to make a cross with the finger on the surface of the dough. This is called crossing the witches out .. If this should be neglected, the servants or matrons are convinced that some evil influence would cause the cakes to stick to the back-board, or, in some other way render the operation difficult. **1852** DENHAM *North of England* (1895, 45) This .. ceremony is performed by all good housekeepers the moment they lay the leaven-trough, containing the .. dough, down upon the hearth-stone to rise .. by making the sign of the + thereon .. This .. prevents Witches exercising any of their devilish arts in connexion therewith. My housekeeper performs this duty as regularly as the baking-day comes. **1908** *N & Q* 10th ser. IX 346 [Derbys.] Each loaf of bread, each cake and 'fatty' cake, every pastry and pie, were cross marked before going into the side oven, the cross being, as one and all said, 'to keep the devil out'. **1923** *Folklore* 325 [Northleigh, Oxon.] If dough (made into a loaf) was placed before the fire to make it rise, a cross was made on it to keep the Devil from sitting upon it. **1963** Man, 78 [Halifax, Yorks.] When a Yorkshire woman bakes bread she places the dough in front of the fire to rise and then cuts it with a knife, making a large cross in it. This is commonly believed to be the sign of the Cross.

Cf. GOOD FRIDAY, bread made on.

CROSS, making sign of: on other food

1811 *Gents Mag.* pt. 1 423 [Yorks.] From the journal of a deceased friend. 'Every rustic dame produces a cheese preserved for the sacred festival [Christmas] upon which, before any part of it is tasted .. she, with a sharp knife, makes rude incisions to represent the cross.' **1850** *N & Q* 1st ser. II 164 [Northants.] Each egg is always marked with a little black cross, ostensibly for the purpose of distinguishing from the others, but also supposed to be instrumental in producing good chickens, and preventing any attack from the weasel. **1888** S. O. ADDY *Sheffield Glossary* xxii. When ale is brewed, the farmer's wife makes a cross upon the yeast which floats on the top of the wort in the brewing vat. She also throws a few red-hot cinders into the vat. The process is called 'crossing the old witch out'. **1925** W. JOHNSON *Talks with Shepherds* 220. When the old man had dressed a sheep, he followed the age-long custom of cutting a fancy pattern .. in the rind of the carcase, while it was still warm .. In Durham .. a cross was incised on the body. **1963** Girl, 14 [boarding school, Wilts.] When we cut a birthday cake, the custom is to make a cross in the middle. When you make the second part of the cross you plunge the knife right in and scream—to let the devil out—and then have a wish. **1980** Woman, 59 [South Shields, Co. Durham] I make a covered lid on my mince pies at Christmas, and I always make a proper cross on them—they were given to the poor, you know. **1985** Woman, *c.*50. At boarding school in the south of England in the forties, whenever we opened a new jar of jam or marmalade, before taking any, we used to make a cross in the top of the jam with a knife. I still do it to this day.

Cf. IRON, food pricked with.

CROSS, witch unable to pass

1711 *Spectator* 14 July. This very old woman had the reputation of a witch .. If she chanced to stumble, they always found sticks or straws that lay in the figure of a cross before her. **1727** GAY *Fables* I xxiii. 'Old Woman and Her Cats'. Straws laid across, my pace retard. **1753** *The World* 23 Aug. A lady of my acquaintance, who has often been bewitched, assures me of her having detected multitudes of these hags by laying two straws one across the other in the path where they are to tread. It is wonderful, she says, to see how a witch is puzzled at these straws; for that after having made many fruitless attempts to step over them, she either stands stock still, or turns back. **1755** *Connoisseur* 13 Mar. A witch .. had threatened to do the family a mischief because my young cousins laid two straws across to see if the old hag could walk over them. **1776** PENNANT *Tour in Scotland* 49. The old highlanders were so remarkable for their hospitality that their doors were always left open, as if it were to invite the hungry travellers to walk in .. But if two crossed sticks were seen at the door, it was a sign that the family were at dinner, and did not desire more guests. *c.*1797 H. MORE *Tawney Rachel* 12. She walked away .. paying great attention as she went not to walk over any straws which lay across. *c.*1816 Wilkie MS (HENDERSON *Northern Counties* 1866, 220) A deep cut is now invariably made in the iron of the crook hook in the chimney for pots in the form of a cross, and is called the witches' mark, because it warns witches from the fire. **1868** *N & Q* I 431 [Plumpton, Lancs.] On the place where she sat two forks had been previously laid crosswise, so that Madge [a witch] could not stir. **1913** *Folklore* 83 [Long Hanborough, Oxon.] An old lady told me that, many years before, she was in a low, depressed state of mind, and her brother said solemnly, 'Jane, you're bewitched .. I will put a cross over your door' .. He then placed two straws in the shape of a cross over the doorway. **1916** *Folklore* 415. He was cycling lately in the neighbourhood of Hay, on the Welsh border, when he was stopped by some ladies in a motor car, which was standing by the roadside. They pointed out to him a spot on the road a little way back, where someone had been hedging, and two sticks crossed lay on the road. One of the ladies asked him to throw the sticks over the hedge, to 'turn the bad luck'. She had been afraid to proceed, for fear of some mishap, until this was done for

her by some passer-by. **1923** [Trowbridge, Wilts.] If you are in fear of suspicious characters who are about your neighbourhood you must guard all the doorways and windows with little bits of twig placed in the shape of crosses. **1926** *Folklore* 77 [Shelton, Beds.] Put two crossed straws before a pig-stye, so that you ensure its safety from any harm.

Cf. STRAW magic.

CROSSED FINGERS

1912 LEATHER *Herefordshire* 88. The ill-luck supposed to follow a passage beneath a ladder may be averted by crossing the fingers and thumbs. **1949** A. WILSON *Wrong Set* 162. If only meanwhile he could just sit here in the cool, with his fingers crossed against all dangers. **1952** Girl, 15 [Aberdeen] If a person hopes for a holiday she says 'Crosses on', which means to keep one's fingers crossed. **1959** *Journal of School of Scottish Studies* III 199. We need only consider how often in our daily lives we use such expressions as .. 'Keep fingers crossed'. **1967** M. WOODRUFF *Woody* 109. There have been times when I have sat in the theatre with my fingers crossed because certain music is being played .. if I listen to that music bad luck will follow—as sure as oats. **1987** Woman, 58 [Cheltenham, Glos.] If I don't want something to happen—like catching 'flu—I say 'Oh, I hope I don't get it. Fingers crossed!' and I do it, I cross my fingers.

Cf. THUMB, holding.

CROSSING LEGS for luck

1671 *Westminster Drollery* 64. Run to Loves Lottery, run Maids, and rejoice, Whilst seeking your chance, you meet your own Choice, And boast that your luck you helpt with design, By praying cross-legg'd to S. Valentine. **1688** AUBREY *Remaines* (1881, 199) When one has ill luck at Cards, 'tis common to say, that some-body sits with his legges acrosse, and brings him ill luck. **1753** *Adventurer* 6 Mar. Mrs Overall .. having lost three rubbers at whist running, notwithstanding she had .. ordered Jemmy the foot-boy to sit cross-legged for good luck, grew out of all patience;

and taking up the devil's books, as she called them, flung them into the fire. *c.*1780 T. PARK MS note in Brand's *Antiquities* 95. To sit cross-legg'd I always understood was intended to produce good or fortunate consequences. Hence, it was employ'd as a charm at school by one boy who wish'd well for another, in order to deprecate some punishment which both might tremble to have incurred the expectation of. At a card table, I have also caught some superstitious players sitting cross-legged with a view of bringing good luck. 1787 GROSE *Provincial Glossary* Superstitions 60. It is customary for women to offer to sit cross-legged, to procure luck at cards for their friends. 1895 J. HARDY *Denham Tracts* II 299 [Northumb.] To obtain a clock at a raffle, sit cross-legged and you will be sure to get it. 1953 *Woman,* 25 [Bath, Som.] When I was at school here, one of the teachers was having difficulties with collapsible desks in the examination room. She asked a girl why she was sitting with her knees bumped under the flap, and the girl said she did not think she would pass the exam unless she sat with her legs crossed. 1955 MRS R. HENREY *Bloomsbury Fair* 98 [Bloomsbury, London] If you have just finished a hat or a dress and the customer comes in to fit it, keep your legs crossed and there will be no complaints.

CROSSING LEGS hinders birth

c. AD 8 OVID *Metamorphoses* IX ll. 290–301 (tr. Miller) When the natal hour of toil-bearing Hercules was near . . seven nights and days I [Alcmene] was in torture . . There cruel Juno sat . . listening to my groans, with her right knee crossed over her left, and with her fingers interlocked; and so she stayed the birth . . and prevented my deliverance. AD 77 PLINY *Natural History* XXVIII XVII (1856, V 298) To sit by a pregnant woman, or by a person to whom any remedy is being administered, with the fingers of one hand inserted between those of another, acts as a magic spell; a discovery that was made, it is said, when Alcmena was delivered of Hercules. If the fingers are thus joined, clasping one or both knees, or if the ham of one leg

is first put upon the knee of the other, and then changed about, the omen is of still worse signification. Hence it is, that in councils held by generals and persons in authority, our ancestors forbade these postures, as being an impediment to all business. 1659 *London Chaunticleres* 35. And for th' women beg, That when they travell [travail], you'd not sit crosse-leg. 1690 BROWNE *Letter to a Friend* (1852, III 67) If it could be made out, that such who have easy nativities have commonly hard deaths, and contrarily; his departure was so easy, that we might suspect his birth was of another nature, and that some Juno sat cross-legged at his nativity.

Cf. KNOTS hinder birth.

CROWN (five-shilling piece)

1954 *Times* 22 Oct. 9. At one time superstition forbade innkeepers to accept these coins [crowns] on pain of bad luck attacking their businesses. Ibid. 23 Oct. 7. It was almost impossible to change a crown in a public house before the war because superstition had it that the barmaid who accepted it would be the first person to lose her job. 1958 *Sunday Times* 5 Jan. 4. There was a superstition that a five-shilling piece taken at a theatre box-office meant that the show would close down, or that some bad luck would befall a member of the cast. 1963 *Daily Telegraph* 28 Sept. 8. When buying a drink at my club recently I tendered a five-shilling piece in payment and was surprised at the reaction of the barmaid. Not only did she refuse to touch it but she begged me never to do such a thing again. Ibid. 2 Oct. 14. I have been a barmaid for a good few years, and still am. It is a superstition that to be handed a five-shilling piece over the counter means that some one will leave or get the 'sack'.

CROWS, two or more

1692 L'ESTRANGE *Æsop* 15. If you see Two Crows . . you'll have good Luck after it, but if you should Chance to spye One Crow Single, 'tis a Bad Omen, and some Ill will betide you. *c.*1815 CLARE *Autobiography* (*Prose,* 1951, 33) [Helpston, Northants.] I remember the morning we saw two crows as soon as we got into the fields & harpd on good luck & success. **1861** C. C. ROBINSON *Dialect of Leeds* 300. When one crow is seen, it is a sign of bad luck; two, of good luck; three, of death; and four, of a wedding. **1963** Woman, *c*.40 [Ayr] One crow sorrow, two crows joy, Three crows a letter, four crows a boy. Five crows silver, six crows gold, Seven crows a secret never to be told. **1985** *Mirror* 21 May 27. In all my 70 years I have always said, 'One crow's sorrow, two crows' joy.'

Cf. MAGPIE: divination rhyme.

CROWS OR RAVENS ominous

c. AD 35 PHAEDRUS *Fables* III XVIII (tr. Perry, 289) By the will of the Fates . . your respective lots have been assigned . . to the raven prophecy, unfavourable omens to the crow. AD 77 PLINY *Natural History* X XIV (1855, II 491) The crow . . is a bird with a very ill-omened garrulity. *ante* AD 633 *Gregory the Great*, ed. B. Colgrave, 97–9. A crow set up a hoarse croaking from an unpropitious quarter of the sky. Thereupon the whole of the royal company . . turned towards it, halting in amazement as if they believed that the 'new song' in the church was not to be 'praise unto our God', but something false and useless. Then the reverend bishop said to one of his youths, 'Shoot the bird down quickly with an arrow.' Then [after the baptism] he gave the recent converts . . a very good reason for this event . . he said, 'if that senseless bird was unable to avoid death, still less could it foretell the future to men who have been reborn and baptized into the image of God.' late **12th c.** BARTHOLOMEW OF EXETER *Penitential* (*Rel. Ant.* I 286) He who believes that anything comes out favourably or unfavourably because of the croaking of a young crow or raven . . shall do penance for 7 days. *c*.**1380** CHAUCER *Parliament of Fowls* l. 363. The crowe with vois of care. **1599** SHAKESPEARE *Julius Caesar* v i. Crowes, and Kites Fly ore our heads . . their shadowes seeme A Canopy most fatall, under which Our Army lies, ready to give up the Ghost. **1652** GAULE *Mag-astro-mances* 181. To bode good or bad luck . . from . . a crow lighting on the right hand, or on the left. **1668** w.

RAMESEY *Elminthologia* 271. If a Crow fly but over the House and Croak thrice, how do they fear, they, or some one else in the Family shall die? **1761** JOHNSON *Idler* no. 11 62. Those that . . hear a Crow with equal tranquillity from the right or left . . will yet talk of times and situations proper for intellectual performances. **1841** M'CRIE *Scotch Church History* I 118. The commissioners of the church having met at St Andrews [in 1586] to protest against the inauguration of Adamson as archbishop, one came in and told them that 'there was a corbie crouping' on the roof of the church. 'That's a bad omen,' said David Ferguson, minister of Dunfermline; 'for inauguration is from *avium garritu*; the raven is *omnimodo* a black bird, and therefore ominous; and if we read rightly what it speaks, it will be found to be Corrupt! corrupt! corrupt!' **1877** JEFFERIES *Gamekeeper at Home* VI [nr. Swindon, Wilts.] I have heard the women working in the fields remark that such and such a farmer then lying ill would not recover, for a crow had been seen to fly over his house but just above the roof-tree. **1878** *Folk-Lore Record* 52 [Fittleworth, Sussex] He had a perfect faith that the thrice-repeated caws of a carrion crow are a token of death. **1883** BURNE *Shropshire* 224. I am told that there are people in South Shropshire who will actually turn back after having set out on a journey if a crow should fly across the road in front of them. **1911** LAWRENCE *White Peacock* pt. I VII. You should have heard old Mrs Wagstaffe . . She declares an old crow croaked in their apple tree every day for a week before Jerry got drowned. **1952** Man, *c*.30. When I was a boy in Worcester, if we caught sight of a solitary crow we could nullify our bad luck by saying 'Break'. **1959** *Trans. Devon. Ass.* 202 [North Bovey] When the old crow sits on the bough and croaks, that means someone is going to die, and whichever way he flies off shows the way the funeral will go. **1984** Woman, 22 [Colwyn Bay, Denbigh.] My mother was driving to the hospital because her father was dying and a crow flew across the road, and she looked at her watch and it was five past, and he had died at that exact time. Since then I've always had a weird feeling about crows. But it's all right if two people see a crow, because 'Seen by two, Will never come true.' **1984** Woman, 37 [Harrow, Middx.] If a crow settles on your house, watch out, there's death about. **1987** Man, 29 [Birmingham] Crows on the garden fence—that's pretty devastating, it means a death in the family.

Cf. RAVEN ominous.

CUCKOO: divination of years till death

14th c. MS Arundel 506 (WRIGHT *Latin Stories* 42) Whoever .. heard the cuckoo and observed its successive notes, could, from its song, anticipate the number of years he had to live. **1638** COWLEY *Love's Riddle* v i. Are you ready? The fatall Cuckow on yon spreading tree Hath sounded out your dying knell already. **1748** S. WERENFELS *Dissertation upon Superstition* 6. If [the superstitious man] has a Desire to know how many Years he is to live, he will enquire of the Cuckow. **1846** *Athenaeum* 22 Aug. 982. Children in Yorkshire were formerly (and may be still) accustomed to sing around a cherry-tree the following invocation: 'Cuckoo, Cherry-tree, Come down and tell me How many years I have to live!' Each child then shakes the tree, and the number of cherries which fell betokened the years of its future life. **1866** HENDERSON *Northern Counties* 72. In many places children say: 'Cuckoo, cherry tree, Good bird, tell me How many years before I dee?' **1873** HARLAND & WILKINSON *Lancashire Legends* 218. Cuckoo! cuckoo! cherry tree, Pretty bird, come tell to me, How many years! Before you fly, How many years before I die?

CUCKOO: divination of years till marriage

1852 S. WILKIN Note in Browne's *Vulgar Errors* II 80. It is a .. common popular divination, for those who are unmarried to count the number of years yet allotted to them of single blessedness, by the number of the cuckoo's notes which they count when first they hear it in the spring. **1886** SWAINSON *British Birds* 115. In several counties children say, on hearing the cuckoo, 'Cuckoo, cherry tree, Good bird, tell me How many years

I shall be Before I get married?' The number of times the cuckoo calls usually is accepted as the number of years. **1923** [Somerset] An unmarried girl, if she listens carefully, can find out how many years must pass before she weds, as the number of calls denotes the number of years.

CUCKOO, first: divination with hair

1579 LUPTON *Thousand Notable Things* X § 80. When you first see the Cuckoo, marke well where your right foote doth stande: for you shall fynde there an heair. Which if it be black, it sygnifyes that you shall haue very euyll lucke all that yeare after. If it be whyte, then very good lucke: But if it be graye then indyfferent. **1685** *Mother Bunch's Closet* (1885, 6) I have not heard [the cuckoo] sing this year before now .. Put off thy right foot shoe and stocking, and let me look between thy great toes. Now, daughter, see, this hair .. look well at it, and what colour it is .. The very same colour will thy husband's hair be. **1714** GAY *Shepherd's Week* 32. When first the Year, I heard the Cuckow sing, And call with welcome Note the budding Spring, I straitway set a running .. 'Till spent for lack of Breath, quite weary grown, Upon a rising Bank I sat adown, Then doff'd my Shoe, and by my Troth, I swear, Therein I spy'd this yellow frizled Hair, As like to Lubberkin's in Curl and Hue, As if upon his comely Pate it grew. **1775** *Poor Robin's Almanack* June B2. Upon the 9th of April I heard it [the cuckoo] myself with great joy and immediately (being now a widower) I pluck'd off my shoe to see what colour'd hair my next wife would have, and found two *red* ones, which gave me great satisfaction, according to an ancient receipt, approved by many experiments. **1833** W. CARLETON *Irish Peasantry* 2nd ser. II 342–3. When the cuckoo uttered her first note .. with what trembling anxiety did I, an urchin of some eight or nine years, look under my right foot, for the white hair, whose charm was such, that, by keeping it about me, the first female name I should hear was destined, I believed in my soul, to be that of my future wife. **1882** *Folk-Lore Record* 82 [Co. Wexford] When

you hear the cuckoo for the first time ..
on taking off your left shoe you will find
a hair of precisely the same colour as
the hair of the person you will be married
to. 1957 *Yorkshire Post* 11 May 6. On
hearing the first clear [cuckoo's] call this
year .. I took off my left shoe to look for
a hair, the forerunner (so I've been told)
of the hair of my future husband.

**CUCKOO, first: heard before swallow
arrives**
1915 *N & Q* 11th ser. XII 250. If you
hear the cuckoo before you see the
swallow, All the year will be misery and
sorrow.

**CUCKOO, first: hearer will do same thing
all year**
1856 *N & Q* 2nd ser. I 386 [Taunton,
Som.] He told me he had heard the
cuckoo for the first time this year, and
that if he ran round in a circle as soon
as he heard it, he would not be idle
during the year. 1875 *N & Q* 5th ser.
III 424 [Somerset] When boys first hear
the cuckoo they run away as fast as
they can to prevent their being lazy
all the year round. 1877 JEFFERIES
Gamekeeper at Home IV [nr. Swindon,
Wilts.] There was a superstition that
where or in whatever condition you
happened to be when you heard the
cuckoo the first time in the spring, so you
would remain for the next twelvemonth;
for which reason it was a misfortune to
hear her first in bed, since it might mean
a long illness. This, by the by, may have
been a pleasant fable invented to get
milkmaids up early of a morning. 1923
[Martock, Som.] If you be a bed when
you mid first hear the cuckoo, git up
and rin for all you be worth, never mind
about your clothes, and that mid alter
the blackness o' your luck. 1953 Boy,
14 [Yardro, Radnor.] When you hear
the cuckoo for the first time, whatever
job you are doing you will be doing that
job for twelve months afterwards.
    Cf. NEW YEAR activities set precedent.

**CUCKOO, first: hearing on an empty
stomach**
1878 A. MACGREGOR *Brahan Seer* 128
'Superstitions of Highlanders'. It is unlucky to hear the cuckoo .. before break-

fast. 1889 *Folklore* 43 [Advie, Moray.]
It is unlucky to hear the cuckoo for the
first time .. before partaking of food. It
is indicative of misfortune of some kind
or other during the year. 1959 *Journal
of School of Scottish Studies* 198. The
belief that it is unlucky to hear the
cuckoo on an empty stomach is .. commonly met with in this country still.

CUCKOO, first: money in pocket
1763 *Poor Robin's Almanack* Apr. And
now take this Advice from me, Let
Money in your Pockets be When first
you do the Cuckow hear, If you'd have
Money all the Year. 1813 BRAND *Antiquities* II 115 n. It is vulgarly accounted
to be an unlucky omen if you have no
money in your pocket when you hear
the Cuckow for the first time in a season.
1852 *N & Q* 1st ser. VI 311 [Hull,
Yorks.] If when you hear the cuckoo
you turn a penny over in your pocket,
you will never be without one until
you hear him again. 1953 Boy, 14
[Presteigne, Radnor.] If you hear a
cuckoo and have money in your pocket
they say you will have money all the
year round. 1957 UTTLEY *Year in the
Country* v [Cromford, Derbys., c.1900]
We used to listen for days, with ears
pricked for that shout through the
woods. Then we .. made our wishes, and
purses were turned over in voluminous
skirts, and coppers were jingled in men's
pockets, and a sixpence was borrowed
very quickly, to bring good luck. 1984
Woman, 44 [Ruthin, Denbigh.] When
you hear the cuckoo for the first time,
if you have money in your pocket you'll
be rich, if not you'll be poor.
    Cf. NEW MOON and money.

CUCKOO, first: on Easter morning
1870 KILVERT *Diary* 17 Apr. It is very
well to hear the cuckoo for the first time
on Easter Sunday morning.

CUCKOO, first: on left
1838 A. E. BRAY *Devonshire* I 326. The
cuckoo is still an ominous bird; since to
hear him for the first time on the left
hand—as I did this year—is considered
a marvellous sign of ill luck. 1855
N & Q 1st ser. XII 38. If .. the sounds
proceed from the right, it signifies that

you will be prosperous; or, to use the language of my informant, a country lad, 'You will go vore in the world': if from the left, ill-luck is before you. **1887** 'SPERANZA' WILDE *Superstitions of Ireland* II 63. If you hear the cuckoo on your right hand you will have luck all the year after. **1923** [Somerset] Lucky to hear the first cuckoo from your right, unlucky from your left. **1932** C. IGGLESDEN *Those Superstitions* 83. If, when you first hear the cuckoo, the sound comes from the right, you will be prosperous; if from the left, ill luck is before you.

CUCKOO, first: where standing, when heard: divination

1909 M. TREVELYAN *Folk-Lore of Wales* 282. If when you hear the cuckoo for the first time you are standing on grass or any green leaves, you will certainly live to hear the bird next season; but if you are standing on a roadway, or the earth, or even upon stone, you will not live to hear the cuckoo when it comes next. **1982** Woman, c.50 [Stockton-on-Tees] Try not to be standing on hard ground when you hear the first cuckoo of spring.

CUTLERY, dropping

1914 *N & Q* 11th ser. X 146. New to me is this fancy. A servant dropped a spoon, and as she made no attempt to pick it up, her mistress told her to do it. Without speaking, the girl left the kitchen, but soon returned with another maid who performed the duty. The one who dropped the spoon explained .. if she herself had picked it up she would have met with some dire misfortune. **1987** Man, 31 [London] I dropped a carving knife the other day—all greasy, it was. But I left it there till my wife could come and pick it up. I don't know why I do it, except that my mother's always done it.

CUTLERY falls = visitor

1883 BURNE *Shropshire* 279. The knife and fork (= the right hand and the left) correspond to man and woman. If the former falls or is dropped, a man is coming to the house; if the latter, a woman is coming. **1923** [Martock, Som.] To drop a knife means a gentleman visitor, a fork a lady, and a spoon a child. **1932** C. IGGLESDEN *Those Superstitions* 173. Here is [a] maid's rhyme, commonly known in the servants' hall: 'Knife falls Gentleman calls; Fork falls Lady calls; Spoon falls Baby calls.' c.**1948** Girl, 11 [Peterborough, Northants.] Drop a spoon and your love will come soon. **1953** Girl, 15 [Presteigne, Radnor.] If you drop a fork a lady is coming to your house. If you drop a knife a man is coming. If you drop a carving knife—a policeman.

Cf. KNIFE falls.

D

DAFFODIL, head of

1648 HERRICK *Hesperides* 40 'Divination by a Daffadill'. When a Daffadil I see, Hanging down his head t'wards me; Guesse I may, what I must be: First, I shall decline my head; Secondly, I shall be dead; Lastly, safely buried. **1923** [Trowbridge, Wilts.] When you see the first daffodil of the year, and its hanging head is turned towards you, there will be nothing but ill luck for you for the rest of the twelve months.

DAFFODIL in house

1877 *N & Q* 5th ser. VIII 181–2 [Christow, Devon] When he got to the farmhouse he laid [the daffodil] on the table. Soon after a servant came into the room and saw the flower, and at once exclaimed, 'Who brought in this daffodil? Did you, Mr G——? We shall have no ducks this year!' **1911** J. CLAGUE *Manx Reminiscences* 177. Daffodils were not to be brought into the house as long as the geese were hatching. They were thought not to bring good luck. **1912** LEATHER *Herefordshire* 17. If daffodils be brought in when hens are sitting, they say there will be no chickens.

Cf. PRIMROSES etc.: first of the year.

DAISY: divination

1831 HONE *Year Book* 8 Oct. [Dorset] In my childhood . . I recollect some of my female friends, while gathering flowers in a meadow, would stop, and, plucking a large daisy, pull off the petals one by one, repeating . . 'Rich man, poor man, farmer, ploughman, thief', fancying that the one which came to be named at plucking the last petal would be her husband. **1909** M. TREVELYAN *Folk-Lore of Wales* 97. Gathering a daisy, she commences plucking the petals off, saying with each one, 'Does he love me?—much—a little—devotedly—not at all?' And the last petal settles the question. **1932** C. IGGLESDEN *Those Superstitions* 64. Petals of flowers have a superstitious meaning in the eyes of the maidens, who will pluck them one by one and breathlessly say: 'He loves me—he loves me not.' **1986** *Woman*, 45 [Tredegar, Monmouth.] When we were little, we used to pick off the daisy-petals and say, 'Loves me, loves me not.'

DALMATIAN DOG

1923 [Taunton, Som.] To meet a plumpudding dog—the spotted carriage dog—in the street is lucky. Wish, and your wish will be fulfilled. **1953** Boy, 15 [Oxford] The sight of a spotted dog is supposed to bring luck in, for instance, exams, if one crosses one's fingers.

DANDELION OR HAWKWEED SEEDS: divination

1830 FORBY *East Anglia* 423–4. The flower-stalk must be plucked carefully, so as not to injure the globe of seeds, and you are then to blow off the seeds . . So many puffs . . to blow every seed clean off, so many years it will be before you are married. **1854** W. B. SCOTT *Poems* 55. Will he come? I pluck the flower-leaves off, And at each, cry, yes, no, yes—I blow the down from the dry hawkweed, Once, twice, hah! it flies amiss! **1884** R. FOLKARD *Plant Lore* 309. These downy seed-balls, which children blow off to find out the hour of the day, serve for other oracular purposes. Are you separated from . . your love?—carefully pluck one of the feathery heads, charge each of the little feathers . . with a tender thought; turn towards the spot where the loved one dwells; blow, and the seed-ball will convey your message . . Blow again; and if there be left upon the stalk a single aigrette, it is proof you are not forgotten. **1899** *Newcastle Weekly Chronicle* 11 Feb. 7 [Jesmond] The downy heads of dandelion, hawkweed, and goatsbeard are blown, and the words, 'Love me, love me not,' repeated, and prognostications drawn from the number of seeds left. **1980** *Woman*, 69 [Sheffield, Yorks.] Dandelion clocks were plucked by girls getting to the sentimental age. They would blow on it, watch the seeds blow away and say 'Does he love me? Yes, No, Yes, No' and so on till they had blown every seed away.

DEATH: dying creature

1632 M. PARKER 'Nightingale' st. 59. And if in any's hand she [the swallow] chance to dye, 'Tis counted ominous, I know not why. **1654** GAYTON *Notes upon Don Quixote* 226–7. Woe is me that she died in my Armes! . . No body ever died in my armes before but your Lordships gibb'd Cat . . and I kept my bed a month upon it, and what will follow after this who can tell? **1863** R. CHAMBERS *Book of Days* I 678 [Suffolk] I said one day to a boy in our parish school, 'Your hand shakes so that you can't hold the pen steady. Have you been running hard, or anything of that sort?' 'No,' replied the lad, 'it always shakes; I once had a robin die in my hand; and they say that if a robin dies in your hand, it will always shake.' **1884** *N & Q* 6th ser. X 186 [Lincs.] It's very unlucky to hold anything while it is dying.

DEATH, opening locks/doors and windows eases

1815 SCOTT *Guy Mannering* II v. And wha ever heard of a door being barred when a man was in the dead-thraw?— how d'ye think the spirit was to get awa through bolts and bars like these? *c.*1816 Wilkie MS (HENDERSON *Northern Counties* 1866, 36) All the windows in the house are opened, in order to give the soul free egress. **1838** A. E. BRAY *Devonshire* II 293–4. A very old custom prevails amongst the poor, that of unlocking their boxes in the house where a friend is dying: they consider it makes the sick person die easy. **1846** *Athenaeum* 17 Oct. 1068. There is a curious superstition in Devonshire, that the departure of life is delayed whilst any lock is closed in the dwelling or any bolt shot. It is a practice, therefore, when a dying person is at the last extremity, to open every door in the house. **1850** *N & Q* 1st ser. I 467. The practice of opening doors and boxes when a person dies, is founded on the idea that the ministers of purgatorial pains took the

soul as it escaped from the body and . . crammed it into the hinges and hinge openings. **1863** *Times* 4 Sept. 10 [Taunton, Som.] A jury of matrons was, as it were, empanelled, and to prevent the child 'dying hard' all the doors in the house, all the drawers, all the boxes, all the cupboards were thrown wide open, the keys taken out, and the body of the child placed under a beam, whereby a sure, certain, and easy passage into eternity could be secured. **1873** *N & Q* 4th ser. XII 468 [Glos.] Sometimes the strange precaution . . is adopted, when the sick man is in extremis, of drawing aside the curtains of the bed . . It is usual to open the curtains and the door . . that the soul of the person may pass forth. **1878** *Folk-Lore Record* 60 [Fittleworth, Sussex] She . . said, that, as the poor gentleman's death struggles did not cease after she had left a passage for the spirit to go out by opening the door and window, she thought it might be the cabinets being locked that hindered it. **1932** WOMEN'S INSTITUTE *Worcestershire Book* 36 [Mamble-cum-Bayton] The door of a dying man's room must be kept open so that the departure of the soul should not be hindered.

Cf. BIRTH: opening locks.

DEATH: opening locks/doors and windows frees spirit

1814 J. TRAIN *Mountain Muse* 28. Superstition . . display'd In every small arrangement [for the wake] The chest unlock'd, to ward the power of spells. **1850** *N & Q* 1st ser. II 259 [Sheffield, Yorks.] A few days ago the body of a gentleman . . was conveyed to the hearse, and while being placed in it, the door of the house . . was closed before the friends came out to take their places in the coaches. An old lady . . immediately exclaimed, 'God bless me! they have closed the door upon the corpse: there will be another death in that house before many days are over.' **1860** *N & Q* 2nd ser. IX 381 [Berks.] She . . refused to shut the house door when the body was placed in the hearse, under the idea that she would be shutting out her old mistress. **1867** *Trans. Devon. Ass.* 40–1. When the funeral procession leaves the house, all the doors are carefully set open . . the superstition running 'Shut one corpse out, three corpses in.' **1878** *Folk-Lore Record* 58 [Fittleworth, Sussex] One [of the inmates of the almshouses] exclaimed, 'Hang that good-for-nothing woman! her locking this door before the old girl is buried will bring death among us pretty soon again.' **1891** *Church Times* 23 Jan. 78. Yesterday, at Willey, in Warwickshire, I buried a little boy three years old. It was snowing hard, yet the parents (of the labouring class) would have both front and back doors of their cottage wide open all the time of the funeral. **1923** [Martock, Som.] When a funeral leaves a house you must not shut the front door until it returns or the door will quickly be again opened for another corpse. **1936** *N & Q* CLXX 231 [Warwicks.] Immediately a death occurs, one house door, usually the front one, is opened and left ajar, night and day, for several days, until after the funeral. The belief is that deceased's spirit, having left the body, is wandering round precincts of the dwelling, and would otherwise be unable to enter the house at will if all doors and windows were kept shut. The last instance of this usage happened recently, in Shakespeare Street, Stratford-on-Avon. **1948** S. M. LEHRMAN *Jewish Customs* (1964, 174) Upon death . . the windows are opened for obvious reasons, but mystics assure us that this was in order to facilitate the exit of the Angel of Death.

DEATH: standing in front of the dying

1880 *Folk-Lore Record* 136 [from MS diary, entry dated Sompting, Sussex, 11 Aug. 1820] Whilst the woman was dying I was standing at the foot of the bed, when a woman desired me to remove, saying, 'You should never stand at the foot of a bed when a person is dying.' The reason, I ascertained, was because it would stop the spirit in its departure to the unknown world. **1885** *Folklore* 281 [Scotland] People should not lean over a dying person, that the spirit might take flight without obstruction. **1923** [Trowbridge, Wilts.] People do not die easy if anyone stands in front of them during the last ten minutes.

DEATH: 'wishing' or 'crying back'

*c.*1828 Calvert MS, Pickering, Yorks. (G. HOME *Evolution of an English Town* 214) A body cannot get their time over with ease to themselves if there be one in the room who will not give them up. It will be better for all such who cannot bring themselves to part with those they love to withdraw from the room so that death may enter and claim his rights. **1848** MRS GASKELL *Mary Barton* VII. We mun get him away from his mother. He cannot die while she's wishing him . . There's none can die in the arms of those who are wishing them sore to stay on earth. **1870** *N & Q* 4th ser. VI 385 [Fife] If the beloved one is withheld from dying by being 'cried back', as the prayers for their recovery are called, the person so called back will be deprived of one or more faculties, as a punishment to the parent or other relative who would not acquiesce in the Divine will.

DEATH-WATCH BEETLE

1672 BROWNE *Vulgar Errors* II VII. Few ears have escaped the noise of the Deadwatch, that is, the little clicking sound heard often in many rooms, somewhat resembling that of a Watch; and this is conceived to be of an evil omen or prediction of some person's death . . this noise is made by a little sheath-winged gray Insect, found often in Wainscot, Benches, and Wood-work in the Summer. We have taken many thereof, and kept them in thin boxes, wherein I have heard and seen them work and knack with a little *proboscis* or trunk against the side of the box, like [a] Woodpecker against a Tree. **1691** R. BAXTER *Worlds of Spirits* 203. I have had many discreet Friends that have been affrighted with the Noise called a Death-Watch, whereas I have since, near three Years ago, oft found by trial, that it is a Noise made upon Paper, by a little, nimble, running Worm, just like a Louse, but whiter and quicker: And it is most usually behind a Paper pasted to a Wall, especially to Wainscot; and is rarely, if ever heard, but in the Heat of Summer. **1691** *Athenian Mercury* 18 July. Quest. I have been for some time since accompanied in my Chamber with the Noise of what the common People call a Death-watch .. I would gladly know .. whether the Presage of Death grounded thereon has any other Basis than Superstition. Answ. .. There was such a Noise as this heard in a plain Wall, where there was a little hole eaten with a Worm; we us'd what Endeavours we could to get the little Disturber out of its hole, and after some time, with a little Care, and a Paper Trap, we took it, and it was only a small sort of a Spider. **1708** *Aristotle's New Book of Problems* 131. Q. What is the Cause of that clinking Noise in Rooms like the going of a Watch, commonly call'd the Death-watch, so frightful to many, and so ominous? A. This Experience has shewn us to be no more than an old Spider in a Wall. **1735** SWIFT *Miscellanies* V 73. Chambermaids christen this Worm a Death-Watch: Because like a Watch, it always cries *Click*: Then Woe be to those in the House who are sick: For, sure as a Gun they will give up the Ghost. *c.*1828 Calvert MS, Pickering, Yorks. (G. HOME *Evolution of an English Town* 215) If there be a death watch heard, then the ailing one need not longer hold on to hope, for it be for that time gone from that house and will not enter again until a corpse be hugged out. **1879** JEFFERIES *Wild Life in a Southern County* x. Somewhere within doors, in the huge beams or wood-work, the death-tick is sure to be heard in the silence of the night: even now the old folk listen with a lingering dread. **1882** *N & Q* 6th ser. VI 386. In the evening they were .. singing after dinner, when above the sound of the .. voices made itself heard the death-tick .. It had never before been heard in that house; but the head of the family was a scientific man, and it was not in the mind of any of them .. to allude to the popular superstition. Nevertheless, the next day brought the news that the lady of the house had died that evening [in London, where she had gone for an operation]. **1941** F. THOMPSON *Over to Candleford* XXIII. The morning after a death in a hamlet would see them with serious faces discussing the signs which were supposed to have foretold it: the ticking of a death-watch spider.

DESTINATION, unlucky to be asked one's

1809 A. EDMONSTON *Zetland Islands* II 73–4. If a man .. be asked where he is going, he need not go to the fishing that day. **1881** W. GREGOR *North-East of Scotland* 199. A fisherman, on proceeding to sea, if asked where he was going, would have put out with the thought that .. some disaster would befall him .. Sometimes such an answer was given as, 'Deel [devil] cut oot yer ill tongue.' **1886** *Folklore* 12–13 [Portessie, Banff.] There were some that, if they had met one who asked them on their way to sea where they were going, would have struck the one so asking 'to draw blood', and thus turn away the ill luck that was believed to follow such a question. **1887** 'SPERANZA' WILDE *Superstitions of Ireland* II 64. It is very unlucky to ask a man on his way to fish where he is going. And many would turn back, knowing that it was an evil spell. **1930** P. F. ANSON *East Coast of Scotland* 38 [Buckie] If anyone met [the fisherman] and asked where he was going, that was quite enough to make the man turn back home and not go to sea that day. **1987** [Bristol: guests at wedding] 'Where are they going for their honeymoon?' 'Nobody knows.'

'DEVIL' taboo word

1663 PEPYS *Diary* 21 May. Being at supper, my wife did say something that caused me to oppose her in; she used the word 'Devil', which vexed me. **1678** RAY *Proverbs* 125. Talk of the Devil, and he'll either come or send. **1800** W. BINGLEY *Tour Round North Wales* II 226 [242] In the churches, when the name of the Devil occurred, an universal spitting used formerly to seize the congregation, as if in contempt of that evil spirit. **1838** A. E. BRAY *Devonshire* I 184. A strange, squint-eyed, little, ugly, old fellow, who had a look .. very like a certain dark personage, who ought not at all times to be called by his proper name. **1871** *N & Q* 4th ser. VIII 547. There is an old woman now living in Wales .. who was much vexed at my saying .. Devil's Bridge, requesting me to wipe my tongue and spit for mentioning such a dreadful name .. I ought to have called it *pont y gwr drwg* = the bridge of the wicked man or the evil one. Her fear was lest something evil might follow if his Satanic majesty's name should be mentioned. **1883** J. R. TUDOR *Orkneys and Shetland* 166 [Shetland] When setting their lines they avoided, and do still, mentioning certain objects, except by certain special words. Thus .. the devil [is called] *da Auld Chield, da Sorrow, da ill-healt* (health), or *da black tief.* **1895** J. HARDY *Denham Tracts* II 276. My son Harry, I daurena ca'ye Harry at neet, for fear the deil should come. **1911** *N & Q* 11th ser. III 148 [MS note, by member of congregation] Habit to spit and stamp the feet in the Litany—when we pray to beat down Satan under our feet .. It was the custom of the .. Rector of Llanmerewig, Montgomeryshire 1794–1827. **1932** J. M. E. SAXBY *Shetland Lore* 180. Neither on land or sea was it wise to speak of the devil's recognised names. You referred to him as the fiandiu, the shooskie, the fule tief, the auld sheeld, him with the cloven foot, and muckle maister. **1936** [South Shields, Co. Durham] The first thing my German correspondent did when we showed her to her bedroom, was to pin a picture of Adolf Hitler over her bed. When my mother saw it, she said, nodding in the direction of the picture, 'Old Nick!' 'Who is old Nick?' asked Ursula. My mother pointed downwards, and whispered, 'the Devil'. **1979** *Radio Times* 27 Oct. 66. Talk of the Devil .. and he's bound to appear, they say.

DIAMOND

1646 BROWNE *Vulgar Errors* II v. That a Diamond laid under the pillow, will betray the incontinency of a wife .. we are yet .. to believe.

DIMPLES

1958 Woman, 48 [Scarborough, Yorks.] Dimple in your chin, Your living's brought in; Dimple in your cheek, Your living's to seek.

DIRT lucky

1587 HOLINSHED *Chronicles* (1808, VI 251–2) In these daies [1323] the ladie Alice Kettle .. was charged to haue nightlie conference with a spirit .. to whome she sacrificed on the high waie

nine red cocks, and nine peacocks eies. Also that she swept the streets of Kilkennie [Eire] betweene compleine and twilight, raking all the filth towards the doores of hir sonne .. murmuring & muttering secretlie with her selfe these words: 'To the house of William my sonne, Hie all the wealth of Kilkennie towne.' *c.***1595** SHAKESPEARE *Midsommer Nights Dreame* v i PUCK. Not a Mouse Shall disturbe this hallowed house. I am sent with broome before, To sweep the dust behind the doore. **1866** HENDERSON *Northern Counties* 87. To sweep the dust out of your house by the front door is to sweep away the good fortune of your family: it must be swept inwards, and carried out .. then no harm will follow. **1875** W. D. PARISH *Sussex Dialect. January-butter.* Mud. It is considered lucky to bring mud into the house in January. **1881** W. GREGOR *North-East of Scotland* 53. It was accounted unlucky to get possession of a clean house. 'Dirt's luck,' says the proverb. If one, who was removing from a house, was jealous of the successor, and wished to carry off the good fortune of the house, the out-going tenant swept it clean on leaving it. **1895** S. O. ADDY *Household Tales* 98. In the East Riding they say that if men sweep dust out of a house ill-luck will follow; women sweep dust up in the house for luck. If you sweep dirt out of a house you will sweep all the money out. When you sweep a house do not sweep the dust out at the door, or the good luck of the house will go with the dust. **1909** M. TREVELYAN *Folk-Lore of Wales* 329. You should never tread upon the sweepings on the floor. **1923** [Nynehead, Som.] If you sweep the dirt out over the threshold, you will sweep one of the family away. **1932** C. IGGLESDEN *Those Superstitions* 173. In country houses it was considered bad form for a housemaid to sweep out a bedroom until the guest had departed at least an hour. Otherwise she would be deliberately bringing bad luck to a friend of the family. **1949** *Mirror* 3 Feb. 2 [Sennen Cove, Cornwall] If a housewife does not polish her floor with her back to the door she will bring bad luck upon her shoulders. **1952** Girl, 14 [Aberdeen] If dust is swept out of a shop door it is said to sweep away trade. **1966** *Woman's Realm* 8 Jan. 4. When my mother moved, she cleaned the house from top to bottom but left the open fireplace dirty and grey, the previous day's ashes untouched. 'It's not lucky to move into a clean house,' she told me.

Cf. NEW YEAR and house/home: nothing to be taken out.

DISHES, three: divination

late **12th c.** BARTHOLOMEW OF EXETER Penitential (*Rel. Ant.*, I 286) He who practises fortune telling from the funeral of any dead person or from his body or clothes, so that the dead do not take vengeance or another person die in that house, or to acquire any benefit .. through this [shall do penance for 40 days]. **1787** BURNS *Poems* 171–2 [note to 'Halloween'] Take three dishes, put clean water in one, foul water in another, and leave the third empty: blind-fold a person, and lead him to the hearth where the dishes are ranged; he (or she) dips the left hand: if by chance in the clean water, the future husband or wife will come to the bar of Matrimony a maid; if in the foul, a widow; if in the empty dish, it foretells, with equal certainty, no marriage at all. It is repeated three times, and every time the arrangement of the dishes is altered. *c.***1816** Wilkie MS (HENDERSON *Northern Counties* 1866, 36–7) In the Scottish Lowlands .. one of the oldest women present [at the funeral] must light a candle, and wave it three times around the corpse. Then she must measure three handfuls of common salt into an earthenware plate, and lay it on the breast. Lastly, she arranges three 'toom' or empty dishes on the hearth, as near as possible to the fire; and all the attendants going out of the room return into it backwards, repeating this 'rhyme of saining' [blessing]: 'Thrice the torchie, thrice the saltie, Thrice the dishies toom for 'loffie' [praise]. These three times three ye must wave round The corpse, until it sleep sound. Sleep sound and wake nane, Till to heaven the soul's gane. If ye want that soul to dee Fetch the torch frae th' Elleree; Gin ye want that soul to live, Between the dishes place a sieve, An it sall have a fair, fair

shrive.' This rite is called Dishaloof. Sometimes, as is named in the verses, a sieve is placed between the dishes, and she who is so fortunate as to place her hand in it, is held to do most for the soul. If all miss .. it augers ill for the departed .. In some of the western counties .. the dishes are set upon a table .. close to the deathbed; and .. while the attendants sit with their hands in the dishes they 'spae', or tell fortunes, sing songs, or repeat rhymes, in the middle of which the corpse, it is averred, has been known to rise frowning, and place its cold hand in one of the dishes, thus presaging death to her whose hand was in that dish already. **1848** A. SOMERVILLE *Autobiography of a Working Man* 86. Hallowe'en I knew about, for we had .. put three basins on the table, one with clear water in it, one with muddy water, and one with none, and the young women and men had gone blindfold to choose a basin—the maiden who got the basin with none being destined to live without a husband, she who got the muddy water being destined to marry a widower, and she who got the clear water .. a lover who had loved no other. **1862** *N & Q* 3rd ser. II 62 [Devon] On Midsummer Eve at midnight an empty room in the house is selected [and] round .. this room on the floor, various objects are placed—a turf, a basin of water, a ring, and some others. Having been led into this room blindfold .. you walk at hazard, or creep on all fours. If you go to the turf, you will die before the year is out; if to the basin of water, you will be drowned; if to the ring, you will be married, and so on. **1865** *Gents Mag.* 702 [Ireland, All-Hallows Eve] They place three plates before a person blindfolded .. One .. contains water, another earth, and the third meal. If the person put his hand in the water, it indicates that he shall live longer than a year; if in the earth .. he will die before the close of a year; if in the meal, it betokens the attainment of wealth. **1911** J. C. DAVIES *Welsh Folk-Lore* 12. In Cardiganshire only about twelve years ago—three dishes were placed on a table, one filled with clean water, the other with dirty water, and the third empty. Then the young man or young woman .. advanced to the table blindfolded and put their hand in the dish; and the one who placed his hands in the clean water was to marry a maiden; if into the foul water, a widow; but if into the empty basin, he was doomed to remain single all his life. **1923** *Folklore* 155 [Glos., *c.*1890] Hallowe'en .. Three plates were set out at one end of the room, one containing gold, another a ring, the third a thimble. The children walked up to them blindfolded and took the contents of the first plate they touched, which signified respectively a rich marriage, an early marriage .. and no marriage.

DOG: evil transferred to at New Year

late **18th c.** J. RAMSAY (*Scotland in the Eighteenth Century* II 439) On the morning of New Year's Day it is usual, in some parts of Breadalbane, to take a dog to the door, give him a bit of bread, and drive him out, pronouncing these words: 'Get away you dog! Whatever death of men, or loss of cattle, would happen in this house to the end of the present year, may it all light on your head!'
Cf. CAT OR DOG, disease transferred to.

DOG, followed by

*c.*1700 (W. PAUL *Aberdeenshire* 18–19) Alex. Thomson, minister of Peterculter .. is guilty of superstitious observances .. saying that he knew some evil would befall him that day he fell and hurt his leg, for .. his dog would not follow him. **1755** *Connoisseur* 13 Mar. To be followed by a strange dog, I found [was] very unlucky. **1923** [Somerset] It is lucky for a dog to follow you.

DOG, hair of

1546 HEYWOOD *Proverbs* I xi E4. I praie the leat me and my felowe haue A heare of the dog that bote vs last nyght. **1666** TORRIANO *Italian Proverbs* 226 n. 164. The tradition goes, that the hair of the same dog cures the wound. **1738** SWIFT *Polite Conversation* II 166–7. Your Ale is terrible strong and heady .. and will soon make one drunk and sick; what do you do then? Our way is, to take a Hair of the same Dog next morning. **1873** HARLAND & WILKINSON *Lancashire*

Legends 225. When a child is bitten by a dog, the bite is said to be effectually cured by binding a few hairs from the dog over the wound .. During **1872** an assault case was heard before two of our magistrates, which arose from the owner of the dog refusing to give some of its hairs to the mother of the child that had been bitten. **1988** Woman, 32 [London] Best cure for a hang-over? People always say a hair of the dog that bit you. But I think a good breakfast is the best cure—if you can force yourself to eat it.

DOG howling

1507 *Gospelles of Dystaues* pt. 3 ix. Whan one hereth dogges houle and crye he ought for to stoppe his eres, for they brynge euyell tydynges. *c.***1592** SHAKESPEARE *3 Henry the Sixth* v vi. At thy birth, an evill signe .. Dogs howl'd. **1651** A. ROSS *Arcana Microcosmi* 218–19. That dogs .. by their howling portend death and calamities, is plain by historie and experience. **1732** D. CAMPBELL *Memoirs* 76. I have some little Faith in the Howling of a Dog, when it does not proceed from Hunger, Blows, or Confinement. As odd and unaccountable as it may seem, those Animals scent Death. **1816** COLERIDGE 'Christabel' ll. 7–13. A mastiff bitch .. howls .. Some say, she sees my lady's shroud. **1844** DICKENS *Martin Chuzzlewit* xix. The howling of a dog before the house, filled him with a terror he could not disguise. **1863** H. CULLWICK *Diary* 24 Feb. Got a letter to say my Aunt Ellen was dead. I expected it quite, for a dog came in yesterday morning and howl'd piteously. **1873** EWING *Flat Iron for a Farthing* (1894–6, 235) Sweep .. added omen to superstition by sitting under the window .. and howling like a Banshee .. For some days Sweep and I were absent, fishing. When I returned, I found on my mantlepiece a black-edged letter. **1935** *I Walked by Night* (ed. L. Rider Haggard, 17) [Norfolk] Wen a dog howled it was shure sign of death, or some disaster to come to those that herd it. **1971** *Trans. Devon. Ass.* 268 [Stockleigh Pomeroy] If a dog howled in a sobbing, mournful way during the night, it was a death sign for its owners or a near relation.

Mr Brown says he has known this to happen.

DOG-ROSE

1838 GASKELL (*Letters*, ed. Chapple & Pollard, 31) [Cheshire/Lancs.] The dog-rose, that pretty libertine of the hedges .. is unlucky. Never form any plan while sitting near one, for it will never answer.
Cf. ROSE GALL cures.

DONKEY cures

1758 *Food for the Mind* (1787, 29) What being's most despis'd by man, And does him all the good he can; Who bore the greatest Prince on earth, That gave to righteousness new birth; Who does sometimes o'er death prevail, And health restore when doctors fail. **1932** WOMEN'S INSTITUTE *Worcestershire Book* 37 [Lenches] To place a child on the dark cross on the donkey's back is sure to do him good.

DONKEY cures: by transference

1646 BROWNE *Vulgar Errors* I VII. What wise man would rely upon that Antidote .. against the sting of a Scorpion: that is, to sit upon an Asse with ones face towards his taile; for so the paine .. leaveth the man, and passeth into the beast. **1852** *N & Q* 1st ser. VI 600. The Irish, when any one has been attacked with scarlet fever, are accustomed to cut off some of the hair of the sick man, which they put down the throat of an ass. By this means the disease is supposed to be charmed away from the patient, and to attack the ass instead.

DONKEY cures: hair from 'cross'

1853 *N & Q* 1st ser. VII 105. A certain number of hairs taken from the black cross on the shoulders of a donkey, and put into a small bag made of black silk, and worn round a child's neck afflicted with [whooping cough] is a never-failing remedy. **1885** *N & Q* 6th ser. XII 205. In Kent and Essex .. measles will be cured by giving to the sufferer some hair from the node where the stripes of an ass cross, sprinkled on bread-and-butter. [This] in the year 1885! **1892** *Dorset Field Club* 52. Bronchitis or Whooping Cough. Take nine hairs from the 'cross' or back of a white she-ass; sew them in a silken bag, and wear them round the neck. **1912** LEATHER *Herefordshire* 81. At Staunton-on-Wye a necklace of hair from the donkey's cross was worn during the whole period of teething. **1959** *Trans. Devon. Ass.* 199 [farmer's wife, Ford] You take a little bit of hair from the sign of the cross on his [the donkey's] shoulder, and you make it into a small pad. A boy has to wear the pad in his breast pocket, and a maiden puts it round her neck.

DONKEY cures: passing under

1823 SOUTHEY *Letters* (ed. Warter, III 384) 25 March. To-day I have heard of a remedy for the hooping cough, practised at this time in this town [Keswick, Cumb.]: it is to pass the child three times under the belly of an ass! **1827** CONSTABLE Letter 26 Aug., Hampstead (C. R. LESLIE *Life of Constable* 61) My pretty infant soon after you saw him was seized with whooping-cough. I find medical men know little of this terrible disorder, and can afford it no relief, consequently it is in the hands of quacks. I have been advised to put him *three times over and three times under a donkey*, as a certain cure. **1855** *N & Q* 1st ser. XII 260. The last time .. I saw the 'operation' for rickets performed by passing a child over the back and under the body of a donkey, was in Hoxton market-place, in May, 1845 .. The mother of the child took the patient in her arms, and began with the odd number 1, whilst the proprietor of the donkey repeated the even number; and thus the poor creature was passed over and under, no other word except the numbers being spoken by either individual. **1862** *N & Q* 3rd ser. I 503 [Honiton, Devon, 1847] A girl .. in the last stages of consumption, had been taken out and .. passed three times under the belly and three times over the back of a donkey .. this operation had to be performed at some place where four roads meet, and .. when the moon was at the full. **1865** R. HUNT *West of England* 2nd ser. 218 [Cornwall] A female donkey of three years old was taken, and the child was drawn naked nine times over its back and under its belly. Then three teaspoonfuls of milk were drawn from the teats of the animal, and three hairs cut from the back and three hairs cut from the belly were placed in it, this was to stand for three hours to acquire the proper virtue, and then the child drank it in three doses. This ceremony [to cure whooping cough] was repeated three mornings running. 1887 *N & Q* 7th ser. IV 5 [Glasgow] The mothers .. took up a position one on each side of the animal. One woman then took one of the children and passed it below the ass's belly to the other woman, the child's face being towards the ground. The woman on the other side caught hold of the child, and, giving it a gentle somersault, handed it back to the other woman over the ass, the child's face being turned towards the sky. The process having been repeated three times, the child was taken away to the house .. At the close of each ceremony [to cure whooping cough] each mother must carry her child to the head of the animal, and allow it to eat something, such as bread or biscuits, out of the child's lap. 1908 *Down Recorder* 26 Sept. 3. In the enlightened county-town of Down [N. Ireland] the practice is still followed of putting a child under a donkey either as a preventive in the case of measles and whooping-cough or as a means of moderating the violence of whooping-cough. 1932 C. IGGLESDEN *Those Superstitions* 175. I remember being taken into the fields in search of a donkey, so that I might pass under that animal nine times. This was the method of curing whooping-cough. We found a donkey, the nurse bribed a boy to keep it still, and I was rolled under it nine times. 1959 *Trans. Devon. Ass.* 199 [farmer's wife, Ford] Pass the child who had scarlet fever .. three times over the donkey's back and under the belly.

DONKEY lucky

1904 *Folklore* 338 [Cavan, Co. Leitrim] A donkey is a lucky animal owing to the cross on its back. 1953 Unpublished letter to *Woman*. For an expectant woman to meet in her travels a donkey, it is an omen that the baby .. will be very pious and learned .. My grandmother used to recall [that] when a

farmer's wife was expecting her first baby .. her husband journeyed seven miles to a local wild beast show and paid a man to bring the donkey for his wife to see. 1970 Woman, 27. My mother's grandfather, who lived in Cambridge, always took off his hat to a donkey.

DONKEY with cows

1799 COLERIDGE *Notebooks* (ed. Coburn) Nov. All about Sockburn, & indeed generally in Yorkshire, N. Riding, & in Durham Asses are counted so lucky, that they are almost universally found among Cows in Dairy Farms—& if a man should happen to have a Horse of great value, he immediately purchases an Ass—for luck!—The ass runs both with the Horse & with the Cows—especially with the Cows, as in calving &c they are more subject to accidents. 1900 *N & Q* 9th ser. V 360. A few weeks ago a strange donkey strayed into my orchard. On making inquiries I found it had been bought that day by a neighbouring farmer, and I was told that it was considered beneficial to the milch kine to have a donkey with them. This is in Worcestershire. Ibid. 522. Most of the large dairy farmers in the south of England have a donkey or a goat to graze with the herd. The practice is avowedly pursued with the view of checking the tendency of cows to drop their calves prematurely. 1972 F. ARCHER *Lad of Evesham Vale* 18. In a field full of milking cows and in-calf heifers, Farmer Dunn kept a donkey. It was always supposed that by keeping a donkey among the milkers they would never 'slip a calf'—the term used by local stockmen for an abortion. 1973 *Farmers Weekly* 5 Oct. 117 [Semington, Wilts.] An old farming tale says you get no brucellosis problems if you have a donkey running with your herd. And 'Jenny' has certainly proved that true. We have not had one abortion in the five years he has been with us.

Cf. GOAT on farm.

DOOR, back

1864 R. CHAMBERS *Book of Days* II 322 [Suffolk] It is unlucky to enter a house, which you are going to occupy, by the back-door. 1883 BURNE *Shropshire* 294.

It is unlucky [after a wedding] to re-enter the house by the back door. In the case of a servant married from her mistress's house, I have known the wedding-party on their return from church drive up to the hall-door in the most matter-of-course fashion. **1891–3** *Proceedings Royal Irish Acad.* 3rd ser. II 818 [Aran Islands, Co. Galway] The corpse is carried out through the back door. **1907** *Folklore* 81 [W. Ireland] At this first home-coming [after the wedding] the entrance is always by the back door of the cabin, it being deemed unlucky to go in at the front, through which the dead are always carried out. **1912** LEATHER *Herefordshire* 114. It is very unlucky for the bride and bridegroom to leave the bride's home by the back door after the wedding. This was done near Hereford recently, by a couple wishing to escape showers of rice; the old people present shook their heads, and thought it a very bad omen. **1923** [Taunton, Som.] It is considered very unlucky when moving into a new house to enter by the back door.

DOOR: bride's left open
1910 *Folklore* 226 [Pontefract, Yorks.] The door of the bride's home must not be closed while she is at church.

DOOR, changing
1882 *Folk-Lore Record* 81 [Wexford, Eire] Another plan of averting . . misfortune is to change the doors of the house, viz., to block up an existing door and open another in its place. **1926** *Folklore* 369 [Norfolk] A village woman, speaking of ghosts, said, 'You can keep 'em out if you unhangs the door and puts it on the other way round.'

Cf. CLOTHES inside out.

DOOR, front
1883 BURNE *Shropshire* 304. A few years ago, a butler in the service of a family in North Shropshire died in his mistress's house, and on the day of the funeral the servants specially begged leave for the body to be carried out through the front door, as otherwise there would certainly be another death in the house within a short time. **1923** [Wellington, Som.] It is lucky for a baby to go out of the front door for the first time.

DOOR, leaving by same
1852 *N & Q* 1st ser. VI 311 [Hull, Yorks.] Be sure when you go to get married that you don't go in at one door and out at another, or you will always be unlucky. **1961** [Scarborough, Yorks.] I'll let you out by the front door . . unless you are superstitious and won't go out except by the same door as you came in. **1985** Woman, *c.*35 [Gorran Haven, Cornwall] [on being shown to the front door after her visit] If you don't mind, I'll use the back door. I always like to go out by the same door as I came in by.

Cf. NEW YEAR and house/home: bringing in the new year and expelling the old.

DOORS AND WINDOWS opened in thunderstorm
1873 KILVERT *Diary* 23 July. At 2 a.m. began the great lightning storm . . There were lights in the houses all over the village and the cottage doors and windows were opened wide to let the lightning out easily if it should come in. **1964** Girl, 16 [London E.18] If there is a storm, there must be a window open at the back and the front of the house so that the lightning can pass right through. (My mother comes from Durham and was brought up to believe superstitions.) **1984** Woman, 56 [South Shields, Co. Durham] My mother always opened the windows during a thunderstorm. She said it was to prevent the build-up of hot air in the room, which might draw the lightning to strike the house.

DOORSTEP PATTERNS keep Devil out
*c.***1887** [Northumb.] I watched a young girl doing the kitchen hearth and doorstep with a definite pattern. My mother to my disappointment desired her to wash it all out, telling me it was used in very poor remote places in Northumberland. **1910** M. B. MIREHOUSE *South Pembrokeshire* 75. An old custom . . gradually falling into disuse, is the chalking of patterns on the doorstep . . The patterns run round the edge of the stone

only, and are often quite elaborate, the one thing necessary being that they must absolutely join, leaving no end or space, and also join the doorposts on either side, otherwise 'The Devil will creep in!' 1935 *Folklore* 78. An old lady in Galloway said her granny explained the tracing by the couplet 'Tangled threid and rowan seed Gar the witches lose (or lowse) their speed.' Ibid. 80. A Sussex woman .. speaks of tracings on thresholds of houses .. 'to keep away the evil spirits'. Ibid. 170–1 [Wye Valley, Derbys.] The only thing I have seen in the way of doorstep trimmings is a line of white carried round not only the doorstep but the whole kitchen floor, close to the wall, to keep out the Devil. 1937 *Folklore* 268. This summer, 1937, on the doorstep of a Dumfriesshire cottage .. a friend pointed out to me a pattern traced to cover the whole surface of the entrance stone. It represented a thread drawn from side to side, distinctly witch-baffling. 1938 *Folklore* 237 [Shrops.] When I was a child, one of our maids used to decorate the back doorstep with a border of loops [which] had to be done straight round in an unbroken chain. It would have been 'unlucky' to do the top of the step and then break off and do the bottom of it before the sides .. These patterns were said to keep the Devil away. 1951 *Trans. Devon. Ass.* 77. I remember, as a child [in Belstone] certain old women who used to trace out the thresholds of cottages with an elaborate chalk pattern, I was told, to keep out the devil.
Cf. CROOKED.

DOVE sign of peace to departing soul
1774 BOSWELL (*For the Defence*, 1960, 302) Edinburgh 30 August .. I asked Ritchie what was the meaning of pigeons flying when people were executed. He said he thought the notions which some people entertained of that signifying good to the persons executed were *fab-lish*. *c.*1828 Calvert MS, Pickering, Yorks. (G. HOME *Evolution of an English Town* 215) It be a good sign of peace to a parting soul if there do come near to the window a white dove. 1866 HENDERSON *Northern Counties* 34. I am permitted to mention that the death of

a clergyman of some eminence in Hull recently, was preceded by the flight of a pure white pigeon around the house, and its resting again and again on his window-sill. 1881 W. GREGOR *North-East of Scotland* 142. A dove flying round and round a person was looked upon as an omen of death not far distant, and at the same time a sure proof that the one so soon to die was going to everlasting happiness.
Cf. PIGEON settles = death omen; WHITE BIRD.

DREAM, telling: before breakfast
*c.*1875 LEAN *Collectanea* II pt. 1 191 [information from a fortune-teller] Ill Luck—To tell a dream before you have broken your fast in the morning. 1882 *People's Friend* 8 Nov. 711. A dream to come true must be told before breakfast. 1950 Woman, *c.*45 [Forfar, Angus] Never tell a dream till ye've broken yer fast.

DREAM, telling: Friday night's
1615 SIR T. OVERBURY *Characters* 'Milk-maid'. A Frydayes dreame is all her superstition: that shee conceales for feare of anger. 1733 *Palace Miscellany* 'Progress of Matrimony' 32. This is the Man!—The Man for me! The Sage describ'd him to a T—I fasted *Friday*, had my Dream, And dreamt of none but perfect him. 1831 HONE *Year Book* 29 Feb. It is a common saying, and popular belief, that, 'Friday nights' dreams on the Saturday told Are sure to come true be it never so old.' 1888 *Dorset County Chronicle* 31 May 12. All dreams that are dreamt on a Friday night and re-peated on Saturday morning are sup-posed to be trustworthy, for 'A Friday night's dream on a Saturday told Is sure to come true if it's ever so old.' 1909 *N & Q* 10th ser. XII 484 [Stromness, Orkney] It is unlucky to tell Friday's dream on Saturday. 1964 Girl, 15 [Tisbury, Wilts.] You're not allowed to tell a dream on a Saturday—but you can if it's a good one, because they come true.

DREAM unseasonable
1883 BURNE *Shropshire* 264. To dream

of things out of season Is trouble without reason.

DREAMS by contraries

c. AD 150 APULEIUS *Golden Ass* (tr. Graves, VI) Even night-dreams often go by contraries. For instance, that one is weeping or being beaten or even having one's throat cut, is good luck and usually means a prosperous change. c.1050 MS Cotton Tib. A. iii (COCKAYNE *Leechdoms* III 209) To weep in dreams betokens bliss. c.1400 *Tale of Beryn* prol. 108. Comynly of these swevenys [dreams] the contrary man shul fynde. 1496 H. PARKER *Dives & Pauper* 1st com. XLV. Moche people hadde leuer for to dreme of the fende than of god or of his moder Marye for as they saye whan they dreme of the fende they fare well in the daye followynge but whan . . of god or of our lady they fare euyll afterwarde. 1548 LYLY *Sappho & Phao* IV III. I dreamed last night, but I hope dreams are contrary, that . . all my hair blazed on a bright flame. 1639 CLARKE *Paroemiologia Anglo-Latina* 236. After the dream of a wedding comes a corpse. 1766 GOLD-SMITH *Vicar of Wakefield* X. My wife had the most lucky dreams in the world . . It was one night a coffin and cross-bones, the sign of an approaching wedding: at another time she imagined her daughter's pockets filled with farthings, a certain sign of their being shortly stuffed with gold. 1819 KEATS To Fanny Brawne, 15 July (*Letters*, ed. Forman, 359) I took your letter last night to bed with me. In the morning I found your name on the sealing wax obliterated. I was startled at the bad omen till I recollected that it must have happened in my dreams, and they you know fall out by contraries. 1883 BURNE *Shropshire* 263. 'Dreams go by contraries' is a received axiom. Thus we have the sayings, 'To dream of the dead, good news of the living;' 'Dream of a funeral, hear of a wedding; dream of a death, hear of a birth,' and vice versa. On this principle, to dream of finding money is considered unlucky. 1972 *Lore and Language* July 6 [Coalisland, Co. Tyrone] Dream of a wedding you'll hear of a wake.

DRINK, spilling

1584 SCOT *Discoverie of Witchcraft* XI xv. Amongst us there be manie women, and effeminat men . . that make great divinations upon the shedding of . . wine. 1603 W. PERKINS *Works* 39. It is good lucke to have drinke spilled on him. 1608 J. HALL *Characters* 88. If the salt fall toward him, hee . . is not quiet till one of the waiters haue powred wine on his lappe. 1620 MELTON *Astrologaster* 46. If the Beere fall next a man, it is a sign of good luck. 1652 GAULE *Mag-astro-mances* 181. To bode good or bad luck . . from . . the spilling of the wine.

Cf. WASSAILING fruit trees.

DRINKING: two from one cup

1980 Woman, 69 [Sheffield, Yorks.] It was thought unlucky for two people to drink from one cup. But actually it was not hygienic. 1988 Woman, 58 [Cheltenham, Glos.] Two people must not drink out of the same cup (unless they are married). If they do, their destinies will be linked.

DROPPING THINGS

1954 Girl, 12 [Swansea, Glam.] If an umbrella or glove is dropped the owner must not pick it up or she will experience a disappointment. But the picker-up will have a pleasant surprise, as long as the owner does not say thank you. 1959 Woman, 56 [Nutfield, Surrey] If you drop something and it is picked up for you, say 'I won't say "Thank you" then I'll have a surprise.'

Also see index: falling/dropping/spilling.

DROWNING STRANGER, unlucky to save

1601 SHAKESPEARE *Twelfe Night* II i. Before you tooke me from the breach of the sea, was my sister drown'd . . If you will not murther me for my love, let mee be your servant. 1822 SCOTT *Pirate* I VII. 'Are you mad . . you that have lived sae lang in Zetland, to risk the saving of a drowning man? Wot ye not, if you bring him to life again, he will be sure to do you some capital injury?' 1851 MAYHEW *London Labour* 376. The Wreckers . . who sometimes became possessed of rich silks, velvets, laces, &c. (not unfrequently murdering all the mariners cast on shore, and there was a convenient superstition among the wreckers, that it was unlucky to offer help to a drowning man) disposed of much of their plunder to the hawkers. **1876** S. BARING-GOULD *Vicar of Morwenstow* 106 [Cornwall] The cruel and covetous natives .. held as an axiom and an injunction to be strictly obeyed: 'Save a stranger from the sea, And he'll turn your enemy.' **1885** *Folklore* 184 [Peterhead, Aberdeen.] The reluctance to save one drowning .. arises from the notion that the one who saves another .. will in no long time be drowned. The sea takes the saver of life instead of the saved, as it 'maun hae its nummer', according to the saying. **1923** [Trowbridge, Wilts.] Save a stranger from the sea, He shall be thy enemy.

DUCK OR GOOSE: bill in patient's mouth
1604 *Depositions, York Castle* 23 July (1861, 127 n.) Office against Katharine Thompson and Anne Nevelson, pretended to be common charmers of sick folkes .. that they use to bring white ducks or drakes, and to sett the bill thereof to the mouth of the sick person, and mumble upp their charmes in such a strange manner as is damnible and horrible. **1853** *N & Q* 1st ser. VIII 265 [Devon] Capture the nearest duck .. and place its mouth, wide open, within the mouth of the sufferer. The cold breath of the duck will be inhaled by the child, and the disease [thrush] will gradually .. take its departure. **1881** *N & Q* 6th ser. III 163 [Ireland] A goose .. was brought to the little patient's side, and the bird's head was thrust into the child's open mouth, and held there for about five .. minutes, for nine successive mornings. By that time the inflammation [of the mouth] had disappeared. **1903** *Devon Evening Express* 27 Jan. 3. Cure for 'thrush' .. Catch a duckling, place its mouth wide open within that of the affected child, and as the sufferer inhales the duck's breath the complaint will disappear.

Cf. FROG, live: in patient's mouth.

DUMB CAKE: divination
1685 G. SINCLAIR *Satans Invisible World Discovered* 215 [Highlands] Whether there be any Magie in the practise of some young Women too curious, who upon Allhallow even goe to bed without speaking to any, having first eaten a cake made of soot, and dreaming, see in their sleep, the man that shall be their husband, I shall not determine. But it looks like a very bad practise. **1685** *Mother Bunch's Closet* (1885, 18) *Dutch Cake*. Three, or four, or more of you are to make a cake of half flour and half salt .. and some of every one of your own water, make this cake broad and thin, then every one of you either make a mark that you know or set the two first letters of your name on it with a pin or bodkin, but leave such a distance that it may be cut; then set it before the fire to bake, but all this while speak not a word. Turn it every one of you once, then let it bake a little more and then throw on every one a little salt and she that turn'd it first let her turn it again, then the person to be her husband will cut out her name and break it in two and give her one half, and so the next, and the next, till the last. *ante* **1728** W. KENNETT Note in Aubrey's *Remaines* (1881, 65) The maids in Oxfordshire have a way of foreseeing their sweethearts by making a *dumb cake*; that is, on some Fryday-night, several Maids and Batchelors bring every one a little flower, and every one a littel salt, and every one blows an egge, and every one helps to make it into past, then every one makes ye cake and lays it on the gridiron, and every one turns it, and when bakt enough every one breaks a piece, and eats one part and laies the other part under their pillow to dream of ye person they shall marry. But all this to be done in serious silence w'hout one word or one smile, or els the cake looses the name and the vertue. **1755** *Connoisseur* 20 Feb. [Midsummer Eve] I and my two sisters tried the Dumb-Cake together .. two must make it, two bake it, two break it, and the third put it under each of their pillows, (but you must not speak a word all the time,) and then you will dream of the man you are to have. **1823** W. GRANT STEWART *Highlanders of Scotland* 257 [Fasten's Eve, i.e. Shrove Tuesday] 'Dreaming bannocks', with which a little soot is

mixed .. In baking these bannocks the baker must be as mute as a stone .. One is given to each person, who .. sleeping with his head on his bannock .. will be gratified with a sight of his future beloved. **1830** FORBY *East Anglia* 408 [St Mark's Eve] Girls bake the dumb-cake; which is made of the following ingredients: An egg-shell-full of salt, An egg-shell-full of wheat meal, An egg-shell-full of barley-meal .. The maker of the cake must be quite alone, must be fasting, and not a word must be spoken. At twelve o'clock exactly the sweetheart will come in and turn the cake. The door must be left open, for a reason pretty obvious. **1832** *Gents Mag.* pt. 2 493 [Scopwick, Lincs.] Three .. pure unspotted virgins .. search for a virgin egg, and having found one, they take flour, salt, water .. to form a cake; which they unitedly mix with the same spoon, unitedly place in the oven, and when baked .. it is then divided into three equal portions, and each taking one, they proceed .. to occupy the same bed; and placing each part under their pillows, they disrobe themselves and walk backwards into bed. Should the parties laugh, or utter a single syllable during the whole process, the charm is broken. This cake is intended to produce pleasant dreams, in which the future husband of each damsel will manifest himself. **1898** BLAKEBOROUGH *Yorkshire Customs* 73–5 [St Agnes's Eve] The making of the dumb-cake .. differs only in one particular throughout the riding. Some hold that those engaged in its preparation must stand on something upon which they have never stood before [long description follows].

E

EAGLE-STONE (ÆTITES) eases childbirth

AD 77 PLINY *Natural History* X IV (1856, II 480) Eagles employ in the construction of their aerie the stone aëtites .. employed also for many remedial purposes, and .. proof against the action of fire .. It has no medical properties, however, except immediately after it has been taken from the nest. *c.*1240 BARTHOLOMAEUS *De Proprietatibus Rerum* (tr. Trevisa, VI 39) Echites .. is a stone wyth red colour .. And it is dowble .. male & female. And alwaye two ben founde in the Egles neste. And the Egle maye not brede wythout thyse stones .. And thise stones bounde to a woman yᵗ traueleth of chylde maketh her soone to beere chylde. This stone Echites conteyneth & bredith a nother stone wythin: lyke as it were a woman wyth chylde. 1579 LUPTON *Thousand Notable Things* II § 52. Ætites, called the Eagles stone .. If a woman haue a painefull trauayle in the byrth of her chylde, this Stone tyed to her thygh, bringes an easie & lyght birth: but you must take it away quicklie after the byrth. 1658 LEMNIUS *Secret Miracles of Nature* 270. The Jewel called Ætites .. makes women that are slippery able to conceive, being bound to .. the left arm .. all the time the woman is great with child, it strengthens the child, and there is no fear of abortion, or miscarrying. On the contrary, being applyed to the thigh of one that is in labour, it makes a speedy and easy delivery. 1662 J. BARGRAVE *Catalogue of Dr Bargrave's Museum* (1867, 125–6) Item, Aëtites .. or the eagle stone .. It is so useful that my wife can seldom keep it at home, and therefore she hath sewed the strings to the knitt purse in which the stone is, for the convenience of the tying of it to the patient on occasion, and hath a box to put the purse and stone in. It were fitt that either the Dean's (Canterbury) or vice-dean's wife (if they be marryed men) should have this stone in their custody for the public good. 1669 BROWNE *Vulgar Errors* II v 9. Whether the Ætites or Eagle-stone hath that eminent property to promote delivery or restrain abortion, respectively applied to lower or upward parts of the body, we shall not discourage common practice by our question; but whether .. taken out of Eagles' nests, co-operating in Women into such effects, as they are conceived toward the young Eagles: or whether the single signature of one stone included in the matrix and belly of another, were not sufficient at first, to derive this virtue of the pregnant Stone, upon others in impregnation, may yet be farther considered. *c.*1740 *Aristotle's Midwife* 52. The Stone Ætites held to the Privities, is of extraordinary Virtue, and instantly draws away both Child and After burden, but great Care must be taken to remove it presently, or it will draw forth the Womb and all. 1782 PENNANT *Journey from Chester to London* 264. The Gems [for the shrine of St Alban] were taken from the Treasury, one excepted, which being of singular use to parturient women, was left out .. the famous Ætites or Eagle Stone, in most superstitious repute from the Days of Pliny. 1881 *N & Q* 6th ser. III 327 [Norfolk] Among the relics .. of my family is a dark-coloured, heart-shaped stone, an inch and an eighth long .. pierced in its upper edge with a hole for suspension by a thin cord. The tradition that has descended with this stone relates that, worn by women before childbirth, it confers exemption from those accidents to which the daughters of Eve are liable .. In .. family letters .. 'the eagle stone' .. is constantly spoken of throughout the last century .. Reliance upon its merits did not pass away until the early part of this century.

EAR, ringing in: divination

1865 *N & Q* 3rd ser. VIII 494 [Combe, Oxon.] A young lady, a parishioner of mine, said suddenly, in my hearing, to another lady present, 'Give me a number!' The lady she addressed .. did not notice the request at once; she was almost immediately told that it was too late. The young lady .. had a 'singing' in her ears; when this occurs .. one should ask at once for a number, and at once get it; one should then count the letters of the alphabet till one comes to the number given: the corresponding letter will be the initial letter .. of the person one is destined to marry. **1959** Woman, 56 [Nutfield, Surrey] A ringing in your ears is 'News Bells'. Ask someone for a letter of the alphabet and from that you will find the name of the young man who is thinking of you. **1984** Woman, 37 [Harrow, Middx.] If you get a ringing in your ear you quickly ask someone for a number and go through the alphabet up to that number and you know who's talking about you.

EAR, ringing in: ill omen

1732 DEFOE *Memoirs of Mr Campbell* 61. Others .. by having caught Cold, feel a certain Noise in their Heads, which seems to them like the Sound of distant Bells, fancy themselves warned of some great Misfortune. **1808** SCOTT *Marmion* III st. 3. 'Is it not strange that, as ye sung, Seem'd in mine ear a death-peal rung .. Say, what may this portend?' .. 'The death of a dear friend.' *Note.* Among other omens to which faithful credit is given among the Scottish peasantry, is what is called the 'dead-bell', explained by my friend James Hogg, to be that tinkling in the ears which the country people regard as the secret intelligence of some friend's decease. **1874** HARDY *Madding Crowd* VIII. 'What a night of horrors!' murmured Joseph Poorgrass .. 'I've had the news-bell ringing in my left ear quite bad enough for a murder.' **1937** J. NICOLSON *Restin' Chair Yarns* 82. 'I fear I'm goin' ta hear some ill-news, da dead bell is strucken me deaf.' In the right ear it meant a relation. The left betokened some 'fremd [strange] boddy'.

EAR OR CHEEK tingles = someone talking about you

AD **77** PLINY *Natural History* XXVIII v (1856, V 284) It is a notion universally received, that absent persons have warning that others are speaking of

them, by the tingling of the ears. *c.*1374 CHAUCER *Troilus* II ll. 1021–2. And we shal speek of the somwhat, I trowe, Whan thow art gon, to don thyn eris glowe! **1507** *Gospelles of Dystaues* pt. 2 viii. Whan the eres of one dothe brenne or ytche, knowe and it be the ryght ere it is a good token, and yf it be the lefte ere it is an euyll synge. **1584** SCOT *Discoverie of Witchcraft* XII XVI. By the tingling of the eare, men heretofore could tell what was spoken of them. **1603** W. PERKINS *Works* 39. It is vnluckie for one .. to burne on the right ear .. it is contrarily good lucke .. for the left eare to burne. **1646** BROWNE *Vulgar Errors* V XXI. When our cheeke burneth or eare tingleth, wee usually say that some body is talking of us. **1738** SWIFT *Polite Conversation* I 70. Miss, didn't your Left Ear burn last Night? .. Because I was then in some Company where you were extoll'd to the Skies. **1748** S. WERENFELS *Dissertation upon Superstition* 6. When his right Ear tingles he will be chearful, but if his left he will be sad. **1787** GROSE *Provincial Glossary* Superstitions 59–60. When a person's cheek, or ear, burns, it is a sign that some one is then talking of him or her. If it is the right cheek, or ear, the discourse is to their advantage; if the left, to their disadvantage. **1813** BRAND *Antiquities* II 494. Mr Douce's MS Notes say: 'Right Lug, left Lug, whilk Lug lows?' If the left Ear, they talk harm; if the right, good. **1852** DENHAM *North of England* (1895, 36) My left cheek, my right cheek, My left cheek burns: If it be my enemy, turn cheek turn; But if it be my true-love, Burn cheek burn. Note: Always begin the rhyme with the ear, or cheek that burns. **1887** *Folk-Lore Record* 219 [Cornwall] Right cheek burning, some one praising you; left one, abusing (a knot tied in the apron-string will cause the slanderer to bite his or her tongue); but left or right are both good at night. **1890** *N & Q* 7th ser. X 7 [Hants.] If your ears burn, the sign is: 'Left for love, and right for spite: Left or right, good at night.' In the case of the right ear I have been advised to pinch it, and the person who is speaking spitefully of me will immediately bite his or her tongue. Ibid. 137. In Wiltshire the old form was to cross the ear with the right or left forefinger and to say: 'If you're speaking well of me I wish you to go on, But if you're speaking ill of me I wish you'll bite your tongue.' **1953** Girl, 15 [Loughton, Essex] Left ear your lover, Right ear your mother. **1988** Woman, 60 [Liss, Hants.] When my ear itches I ask myself 'Is it the right or the left?' and think 'Oh good, they're saying nice things about me,' if it's the right.

EARTH, hole in: divination

1887 HARDY *Woodlanders* xx. I wish we had .. contented ourselves with the hole-digging tomorrow [Midsummer Day] at twelve, and hearing our husbands' trades. **1899** J. SHAW *Schoolmaster* 32 [Tynron, Dumfries.] Should a girl scoop a hole where three or more roads meet and apply her ear to it, she may hear a whisper telling her the trade of her future lover. **1941** M. MACLEOD BANKS *British Calendar Customs: Scotland* III 130 [Aberdour, Aberdeen.; Hallowe'en] Let a young woman go over 'bere rigs' [barley-field ridges], lay her head in the furrow between the third and fourth rig, and listen to whatever sound she may hear. That sound will indicate what trade or occupation her future husband will follow, e.g. knocking will indicate .. a carpenter, the sound of cartwheels, the occupation of farmer.

EASTER: new clothes

1596 LODGE *Wits Miserie* 14. The farmer that was contented in times past with his Russet Frocke & Mockado sleeues, now sels a Cow against Easter to buy him silken geere for his credit. **1597** SHAKESPEARE *Romeo and Juliet* III i. Did'st thou not fall out with a Tailor for wearing his new Doublet before Easter? **1662** PEPYS *Diary* 9 Feb. *Lordsday.* Was all day in my chamber—talking with my wife about her laying out of 20l [£20]: which I had long since promised her to lay out in clothes against Easter for herself. **1735** POOR ROBIN *Almanack* Apr. Now Easter holidays draw near For maids their best new gowns to wear. **1830** FORBY *East Anglia* 414. Every person must have some part at least of his dress new on Easter Sunday, or he will have no good fortune that year. **1857** *N & Q*

2nd ser. IV 432 [Norwich] Rustics returning from Tombland fair .. carry new hats, not on their heads, but in boxes, &c. They are worn for the first time on Easter Day; and by so doing, the bearer is secured from any bird's dropping its 'card' upon him during the ensuing year. Indeed, it is very unlucky not to wear some new .. clothing on Easter Day. **1880** W. SIKES *British Goblins* 269. A servant of mine, born in Hampshire, used always to say, 'If you don't have on something new Easter Sunday the dogs will spit at you.' **1950** *Sunday Times* 9 Apr. 5. In 1867 on Easter Day in the City of Cork I had a new pair of drawers which my nurse told me she had kept for me to wear on Easter Day to prevent the crows from picking my eyes out. **1952** In Grimsby [Lincs.] about 1920 new clothes had to be worn for Easter Sunday or else the birds would dirty you. **1957** Boy, 12 [Canonbie, Dumfries.] On Easter Monday if you do not have on something new it is supposed to be bad luck for you. **1970** *Bath Chronicle* 13 Mar. 1 [advertisement] Only 2 weeks to Easter—It's lucky to wear something new!

EASTER: sun dancing, or Lamb seen in sun

1646 SUCKLING *Fragmenta Aurea* 37 'A Ballade Upon a Wedding'. But oh! she dances such a way! No Sun upon an Easter day Is half so fine a sight. **1691** *Athenian Mercury* 16 May. Quest. Why doth the Sun, at his rising in the Firmament play more on Easter-day than Whitsunday? Answ. That the matter of Fact is an old, weak, superstitious Error, and the Sun neither plays nor works on Easter-day more than any other .. In some parts of England they call it—The Lamb playing, which they look for as soon as the Sun rises, in some clear Spring or River, and is nothing but the pretty Reflection it makes from the Water. **1725** BOURNE *Antiquitates Vulgares* 188. It is a common Custom among the Vulgar and uneducated Part of the World, to rise before the Sun on Easter-day, and walk into the Fields: The Reason of which, is to see the Sun Dance. **1826** HONE *Every-Day Book* I 5 Apr. In the middle districts of Ireland, great preparations are made for the finishing of Lent .. they .. rise about four o'clock to see the sun dance in honour of the resurrection. This ignorant custom is not confined to the humble labourer and his family, but is scrupulously observed by many highly respectable and wealthy families, different members of whom I have heard assert positively that they had seen the sun dance on Easter morning. **1864** *N & Q* 3rd ser. V 394 [Devon] I called last week upon an old parishioner, who had been absent from church on Easter-day. Sickness in her family had kept her at home, but, she said, she had looked out at her window, and seen the sun dancing beautifully .. 'Dancing for joy, to be sure, at Our Saviour's resurrection on Easter morning.' **1866** HENDERSON *Northern Counties* 63. Devonshire maidens get up to see the sun rise on Easter morning, as do their northern sisters, though what they look for is the Lamb and flag in the centre of the sun's disc. **1870** KILVERT *Diary* 14 Oct. To this pool the people used to come [in the 18th c.] on Easter morning to see the sun dance and play in the water and the angels who were at the Resurrection playing backwards and forwards before the sun. **1875** W. D. PARISH *Sussex Dialect. Holy-Sunday.* Easter-Day. There is a tradition that the sun always dances on the morning of Holy-Sunday, but nobody has ever seen it because the devil is so cunning that he always puts a hill in the way to hide it. **1883** BURNE *Shropshire* 335. She had heard of the thing but did not believe it true, ''till,' she said, 'on Easter morning last, I got up early, and then I saw the sun dance, and dance, and dance, three times, and I called to my husband.' **1929** *N & Q* CLVI 116. Irish children still get up to see the sun dance .. on Easter Sunday.

EEL-SKIN GARTERS prevent cramp/ rheumatism

1684 H. WOOLLEY *Queen-like Closet* Suppl. 38. For the Cramp in the Legs .. Eelskins are .. good to tie about the thighs; but first they must be made gentle and easie. **1813** BRAND *Antiquities* II 618. I remember it was a custom in the North of England for Boys that swam, to wear an Eel's Skin about their naked Leg to prevent the Cramp. **1866** HENDERSON *Northern Counties* 17. In my own day .. no boy would commit himself to the Wear without .. the precaution of an eel-skin tied round his left leg to save him from cramp. **1910** *Folklore* 227. Two well-known residents in Castleford [Yorks.] wear garters made of eelskins to prevent attacks of rheumatism. **1912** LEATHER *Herefordshire* 78. An eelskin garter worn below the knee will prevent cramp. **1969** E. PORTER *Cambridgeshire* 86. Only eels caught in the spring provided suitable skins. After the heads and tails had been cut off the skins were removed in one piece and hung up to dry in the sun .. Then two ends of each were tied and the skins well greased with fat and rubbed with a round piece of wood until they were pliable again, when the .. skins [were] re-stiffened by the insertion of a 'stuffing' of finely chopped thyme and lavender leaves. The skins were next inserted in linen bags which were buried in the peat for the rest of the summer between layers of freshly gathered marsh mint .. In the autumn the skins were dug up and a final polish was given to them, after the removal of the [herbs]. The garters, called 'yorks', were tied just above the knees .. as a cure and preventive of rheumatism.

Cf. SNAKE SLOUGH/SKIN preserves health.

EEL-SKIN JACKET bullet-proof

1810 R. H. CROMEK *Nithsdale Song* 281 [Dumfries.] Jackets, woven of water snake skins .. were much in vogue among the crusading servants of Satan; and are yet remembered by the name of *warlock feckets* .. The brave persecutor Claverhouse in a lead proof jacket .. rode through the hail of bullets unhurt .. but at length .. his charmed *fecket* could not resist a 'silver sixpence' from the mouth of a Cameronian's fusee.

Cf. SILVER BULLET.

EGG: double yolk

*c.*1816 Wilkie MS (HENDERSON *Northern Counties* 30) Presages of death on the Border are very numerous .. hens .. laying eggs with double yolks. **1923**

[Somerset] To break a double-yolked egg means a wedding.

EGG, first: lucky/curative

1850 *N & Q* 1st ser. II 164 [Northants.] The first egg laid by a pullet is usually secured by the shepherd, in order to present to his sweetheart—the luckiest gift, it is believed, he can give her. 1883 BURNE *Shropshire* 179. Take the first egg laid by a white pullet, and lay it under your pillow: you will dream of your future partner. 1893 *Folklore* 350 [Valentia Isl., Co. Kerry] The first egg laid by a little black hen, eaten the very first thing in the morning, will keep you from fever for the year. 1923 [Somerset] The one who eats the first egg laid by a brown pullet may have a wish and that wish is supposed to come true. If on Easter Day it is very lucky, for then you could have three wishes and the eggshell would always bring you luck afterwards if you kept it in the house.

EGG, last: unlucky

1748 S. WERENFELS *Dissertation upon Superstition* 7. He will often be in Fear, too, lest a Cockatrice should happen to be hatch'd from his Cock's Egg, and kill him with its baneful Aspect. 1883 BURNE *Shropshire* 229. The small yolkless eggs which hens sometimes lay are called 'cock's eggs' .. in the firm persuasion that the name states a fact. They are very unlucky, and must never be brought into a house. The old .. practice is to 'chuck 'em o'er the barn' to prevent misfortune. 1893 E. C. GURDON *County Folk-Lore: Suffolk* 9. Them there little eggs is cock's eggs, an' if you was to hatch 'em, a cockytrice would come out. Tha's a sort o' sarpent. 1898 BLAKEBOROUGH *Yorkshire Customs* 149. You must not eat a 'cock's egg', i.e. a small egg, the last one a hen lays before sitting. When such are found, the contents are blown from the shell and burnt .. The devil is said to superintend the laying of this last egg. 1953 Girl, 14 [Stowe, Radnor.] When a hen lays her last egg she sometimes lays a very small round one. Do not bring it into the house because it is bad luck. They say that if you do someone will die in the family, so as soon as you see it throw it over your left shoul-

der. 1961 *Mirror* 14 Dec. 19. Around this district [Barmby-on-the-Marsh, Yorks.] when a chicken lays an especially small egg it is the custom to throw that egg over the house for luck.

EGG opened at small end

1650 BROWNE *Vulgar Errors* III XXVII. Why we open them [eggs] at that part [the larger end]? 1832 *Gents Mag.* pt. I 591 [Scopwick, Lincs.] It is esteemed unlucky .. to break the small end of an egg. 1923 [Taunton, Som.] Never crack an egg at the small end, it will cause you keen disappointment.

'EGG' taboo word

1875 *N & Q* 5th ser. III 204 [Flamborough, Yorks.] The fishermen .. had a great fear if .. eggs were spoken of. 1923 P. S. JEFFREY *Whitby Lore* 138 [Staithes, Yorks., 1885] An egg is deemed so unlucky that the fishermen will not even use the word, but call the produce of the fowl a 'roundabout'.

EGGS after sunset

1853 *N & Q* 1st ser. VII 7 [Notts.] A person in want of some eggs called at a farm-house in East Markham, and inquired of the good woman of the house whether she had any eggs to sell, to which she replied that she had a few scores to dispose of. 'Then I'll take them home with me in the cart,' was his answer; to which she somewhat indignantly replied, 'That you'll not; don't you know the sun has gone down? You're welcome to the eggs at a proper hour of the day; but I would not let them go out of the house after the sun is set on any consideration whatsoever!' 1882 *People's Friend* 8 Nov. 712 [Scotland] Nothing is more unlucky than to meddle with eggs after dark. They ought not to be gathered then, but each day at noon; neither should they be sold or set under the hen after nightfall. 1923 P. S. JEFFREY *Whitby Lore* 138 n. In some remote villages it is still considered unlucky to buy eggs after sunset, and any enquiry for eggs at this advanced hour is resented as bringing ill-fortune to the house. 1932 C. IGGLESDEN *Those Superstitions* 83. Duck's eggs should never be brought into a house after sunset if they are to be set, or they will never hatch. **1982** *Woman*, 20 [Cleveland, Yorks.] In the country, it is considered bad luck to bring eggs into the house after dark.

EGGS: breaking accidentally

1932 C. IGGLESDEN *Those Superstitions* 172. Slowly and solemnly she [the maid-servant] recited .. 'Break an egg, Break your leg; Break three, Woe to thee; Break two, Your love's true' .. 'You may be sure that if I break one, I take good care to break another one as well.'

EGGS carried over running water

1853 *N & Q* 1st ser. VIII 382 [Lincs.] If eggs are brought over running water they will have no chicks in them.

EGGS dangerous to horses

1586 CAMDEN *Britannia* (tr. Gibson, II 380) [Limerick, Eire, *c.*1566] When the owner of a horse eats eggs, he must be very careful to eat an even number, otherwise they indanger the horses. Jockies are not allowed to eat eggs; and, whatever horseman does it, he must wash his hands immediately after.

EGGS on board ship

1885 *Folklore* 55 [Rosehearty, Aberdeen.] Eggs are [supposed to cause contrary winds], and there are fishermen that would not allow a single one on board.

EGGS, setting: at waxing moon or flowing tide

AD 77 PLINY *Natural History* XVIII LXXV (1856, IV 111) Put eggs under a hen at a new moon. **1886** *Folklore* 9 [Buckie, Banff.] Hens should be set when the tide is 'flouwin'. The chickens are stronger, and thrive better. **1889** *Dorset Field Club* 33. Many [country people] .. are careful to set .. during the increase of the moon. **1923** [Somerset] Farmers' wives believe that if they set their broody hens during the time of the new moon, more eggs will be hatched. **1935** *I Walked by Night* (ed. L. Rider Haggard, 20) [Norfolk] The Old People worked verry much by the moon .. Wen it was risen and in the second quarter they said that .. eggs

set then were shure not to go bad under the hens.

Cf. MOON affects birth/health.

EGGS, setting: Friday and Sunday

1507 *Gospelles of Dystaues* pt. 5 XIII. One ought neuer to sette the hennes on broude vpon a fryday, for lyghtly the checkens that cometh of them is de-uoured by wylde beestes. **1882** *People's Friend* 8 Nov. 712. They must not be gathered at all on a Sunday, and no hen must be set on that day.

EGGS, setting: odd number

AD 77 PLINY *Natural History* X LXXV (1856, II 535) An uneven number .. ought to be placed. **1688** AUBREY *Remaines* (1881, 194) Our House-wives, in setting of their egges under the Hen, do lay an odd number. **1790** WHITE *Journal* 20 Apr. Set the old Bantam speckled Hen with eleven eggs. My cook-maid desired there might be an odd egg for good luck. **1850** *N & Q* 1st ser. II 164 [Northants.] In .. setting a hen, care is taken that the nest be composed of an odd number of eggs. **1882** *People's Friend* 8 Nov. 712 [Scotland] Thirteen—*mirabile dictu*—is the lucky number [of eggs] to set. Eleven is the next best; but .. twelve .. will come to no good. **1915** *Folklore* 97. It is curious that in the Shipston-on-Stour [Warwicks.] district, in which thirteen is in most things regarded as an unlucky number, thirteen should be considered, and from time immemorial has been considered, the most lucky number .. for the eggs to be placed under a sitting hen. **1933** *Folklore* 197 [Gunthorpe, Lincs.] It's a strange queer thing, but a eäven number o' eggs niver hetches nowt but stags [cockerels].

Cf. ODD NUMBER lucky.

EGGS: two laid

1882 *People's Friend* 13 Sept. 580 [Scotland] One would think it would be a lucky man's hen that would lay two eggs in one day—not so .. he may look out for very bad luck. **1909** M. TREVELYAN *Folk-Lore of Wales* 328. If a goose lays .. two eggs in a day, it means misfortune to the owner.

EGGS (whites of): shapes in water: divination

1684 I. MATHER *Illustrious Providences* 288. The foolish Sorcery of those Women that put the white of an Egg into a Glass of Water, that so they may be able to divine of what Occupation their future Husbands shall be. It were much better to remain ignorant than thus to consult with the Devil. 1688 AUBREY *Remaines* (1881, 133) 'Tis *Midsommer-night*, or Midsommer-eve (S^t Jo: Baptist) is counted or called the *Witches night*. q. M^ris Fincher, &c., of the breaking of Hen-egges this night, in which they may see what their fortune will be. *c.*1800 S. SIBBALD (*Memoirs*, ed. Hett, 106) 'On a Midsummer day,' she said, 'if you break an egg into a bowl of water in the eye of the sun and allow it to stand there some minutes the white by floating on the surface will indicate the profession of your intended.' So Betsey, two young ladies and myself, had each an egg given us to try, but somehow or other, there was little or no difference in the appearance of any of them. 1832 J. CRABB *Gipsies Advocate* 40–1. A gipsy fortune-teller . . ordered a large glass of spring-water, into which she poured the white of a newly-laid egg. After shaking the mixture for some time, she so far succeeded as to induce the credulous observer to declare that he saw most distinctly the image of the ship in which he was to hoist his flag, the church in which he was to be married, and his bride going with him into the church. 1835 H. MILLER *Scenes of North Scotland* 117 [Ross. Cromarty] 'Ah,' said a young girl whom I overheard . . regretting the loss of a deceased companion. 'Ah, I knew when she was first taken ill that there was little to hope. Last Halloween she and I went to Mrs —— to break our eggs. Betsie's was first cast, and there rose under her hand an ugly scull. Mrs —— said nothing, but reversed the glass, while poor Betsie laid her hand on it the second time, and then there rose a coffin. Mrs —— called it a boat, and I said I saw the oars; but Mrs —— well knew what it meant, and so did I.' 1866 HENDERSON *Northern Counties* 81. Perforate with a pin the small end of the egg, and let three drops

of the white fall into a basin of water. They will diffuse . . into fantastic shapes . . From these the initiated will augur the fortunes of the egg-dropper. 1905 *N & Q* 10th ser. IV 27. In the West Country on Midsummer Day, exactly at noon, maidens have been wont, for generations, to take a glass and half fill it with water. Into this is thrown the white of an egg . . The receptacle is then left to stand for five minutes upon a window sill exposed to the sun's rays. The form the contents are then supposed to assume, as they float upon the water, is believed to indicate the trade of a possible prospective husband . . On Midsummer Day just past, in one hospital here [Exeter] I heard a large wardful of women sorely lamenting that they had not been able to procure eggs that morning for the purpose of reading their fortunes. 1942 A. L. ROWSE *Cornish Childhood* 78 [refers to *c.*1910] Merry-making among the girls in the kitchen; putting the white of an egg in a glass of water to stand outside on Midsummer's Day to see the shape of your future husband; Budd declaring that hers would be a sailor—she could see the rigging. 1956 Woman, *c.*65. On Midsummer's Day at noon you put a glass of water on the wall and break an egg into it and it will foretell what your husband is to be. And believe it or not, I did, and I distinctly saw a desk. My husband is a school teacher.

Cf. LEAD shapes in water: divination of future spouse.

EGGSHELL, piercing or crushing

AD 77 PLINY *Natural History* XXVIII v (1856, V 282) There is no one . . who does not dread being spell-bound by means of evil imprecations; and hence the practice, after eating eggs or snails, of immediately breaking the shells, or piercing them with the spoon. 1584 SCOT *Discoverie of Witchcraft* I IV. Witches, as some affirme . . can go in and out at awger holes, & saile in an egge shell, a cockle or muscle shell, through and under the tempestuous seas. 1601 HOLLAND editorial note in Pliny's *Natural History* XXVIII v. Because afterwards no witches might pricke them [eggshells] with a needle in the name and behalfe of those whom they would hurt and mischeefe, according to the practice of pricking the images of any person in wax; used in the witchcraft of these daies. **1688** AUBREY *Remaines* (1881, 193) This custome of breaking the bottom of the Egge-shell is (yet) commonly used in the countrey. **1799** S. SIBBALD (*Memoirs*, ed. Hett, 78) He was a very passionate and superstitious man, and would before he left the breakfast room, wheel himself round the table and crush to atoms every egg shell on it. **1832** *Gents Mag.* pt. 2 494 [Scopwick, Lincs.] Some people, after eating boiled eggs, will break the shells to prevent the witches from converting them into boats. **1839** C. BARON-WILSON *Harriot, Duchess of St Albans* II 134 [Ireland] After eating an egg, she always made an aperture at both ends of the shell, so that the witches might not find shelter there, otherwise they were permitted to haunt with an incubus the luckless wight who had eaten the contents. **1853** *N & Q* 1st ser. VII 152 [Somerset] Always poke a hole through your egg-shell before you throw it away. If you don't the fairies will put to sea to wreck the ships. **1887** 'SPERANZA' WILDE *Superstitions of Ireland* II 102. People ought to remember that egg-shells are favourite retreats of the fairies, therefore the judicious eater should always break the shell after use, to prevent the fairy sprite from taking up his lodgment therein. **1942** *Folklore* 105 [East Anglia] Even now the custom of breaking a hole in the bottom of the shell of the breakfast egg is quite widely spread .. people do it without any conscious intention of carrying out a serious protective rite. **1984** Woman, 86. I can still hear my father telling us—about 1903, in Tonbridge [Kent]—'You must sink the witch boats—you must make a cross with your spoon in the bottom of the egg shell, or the witches will knock holes in the sailing boats.' I still do it, and my great-grandchildren do the same, of course.

Cf. FOOD: giving away potentially dangerous.

EGGSHELLS, burning

1853 *N & Q* 1st ser. VIII 382 [Lincs.] Never burn egg-shells; if you do, the hens cease to lay. **1895** S. O. ADDY *Household Tales* 66. If you burn egg-shells the hens will not lay. **1932** C. IGGLESDEN *Those Superstitions* 82 [Rye, Sussex] Two gentlemen .. came in for breakfast. When they'd finished what do you think they did? Threw the shells in the fire. They wanted their plates for jam .. The next morning there wasn't a single egg laid .. Now, I'd like to ask you, didn't that prove that the superstition is right—never throw an eggshell in the fire? **1942** *Folklore* 105 [East Anglia] Shells left after a meal must on no account be burnt, as it would lead to burn-like injuries in the egg-laying apparatus of the unfortunate producer.

EGGSHELLS protect chickens

1586 CAMDEN *Britannia* (tr. Gibson, II 380) [Limerick, Eire, *c.*1566) To prevent the kites stealing their chickens, they hang up the egg-shells in which the chickens were hatched .. somewhere in the roof of the house. **1916** *Folklore* 256 [N. Ireland] They [Catholics] are very superstitious. There was a neighbour of me father's now who would always put the eggshells on top of the coop when the chickens were hatched. He would keep them there or the chickens would die.

Cf. CAUL, possession of: lucky.

ELBOW itches

1584 SCOT *Discoverie of Witchcraft* XI XIII. The tingling in .. the elbow .. to be observed in this art [of prognostication]. *c.*1597 SHAKESPEARE 1 *Henry the Fourth* v i. Fickle Changelings, and poore Discontents, Which gape, and rub the Elbow at the newes Of hurly burly Innovation. **1659** HOWELL *Proverbs* 12. My Elbow itches, I must change my bedfellow. **1738** SWIFT *Polite Conversation* III 195. Well, my Elbow itches; I shall change Bed-fellows. **1800** BURNS 'To Colonel De Peyster'. Thy damn'd auld elbow yeuks wi' joy And hellish pleasure, Already in thy fancy's eye Thy sicker treasure! **1855** *N & Q* 1st ser. XII 38 [Cornwall] If the elbow [itches] you will walk over strange ground. **1883** BURNE *Shropshire* 270. If your elbow itches, you will have a strange bedfellow. **1904** *Folklore* 462 [Abbeyleix, Co. Leix]

If the inside of your elbow itches it is a sure sign that someone will be coming to the house; or the outside of your elbow, that someone will soon be leaving. **1923** [Chard, Som.] If your right elbow itches it is a sign of good luck, if the left one itches it is bad luck—to prevent it knock the right one against something.

ELBOW, knocking

1958 Woman, *c.*30 [Heydon, Norfolk] If you knock your elbow, don't forget to knock the other. It breaks the spell of bad luck. **1984** Girl, 7 [Liss, Hants.] If you hit your elbow on anythink, you hit the other for luck. **1987** Man, 31 [London] My mother believes that if you knock one part of your body you've got to knock the corresponding part on the other side, against the same thing that you knocked the first part. She's got me doing it, now.

ELDER

10th c. Canon enacted under King Edgar (THORPE *Ancient Laws of England* 396) We enjoin that every priest .. totally extinguish every heathenism; and forbid .. the vain practices which are carried on .. with elders, and also with various other trees.

ELDER, burning

1830 FORBY *East Anglia* 414. It is very unlucky to burn green elder. **1853** *N & Q* 1st ser. VII 177. I was visiting a poor parishioner the other day, when the following question was put to me. 'Pray, sir, can you tell me whether there is any doubt of what kind of wood our Lord's cross was made? I have always heard that it was made of elder, and we look carefully into the faggots before we burn them, for fear that there should be any of this wood in them.' **1883** BURNE *Shropshire* 243–4. It is considered dangerous, or even wrong, to burn boughs of Elder wood. In North Staffordshire they say that 'if you do, you'll bring the Old Lad on the top of the chimney.' **1899** *Eng. Dialect Dict.* II 245 [Notts.] Folks say it's not lucky to burn eldern. My missis wouldn't like the eldern brought into the house, thank you. **1912** *Folklore* 356. I told our gardener

at Basford [Notts.] to burn an old elder tree which had been blown down, but he refused, giving as his reason that it was 'wicked wood'. **1920** C. CONGREVE *The Castle* 41 'Wood Fires'. Make a fire of elder-tree Death within your house you'll see. **1963** N. GOODLAND *Old Stan's Diary* v [nr. Romsey, Hants.] That old elder. When you comes to he, don't thee burn him, because 'tis bad luck .. My old Dad never burned no witch-wood, so no more don't I! 'Tis said, if you buries 'em side by side, a steel bar will rot and be gone before the witch-wood will. **1982** Woman, 20 [Cleveland, Yorks.] A fire will go out if elder wood is put on to it.

ELDER, cutting

1970 *Seaford Naturalist* XX 10 [Sussex] It is supposed to be unlucky to cut down an Elder tree and should one need pruning an apology is necessary when cutting. **1985** R. VICKERY *Unlucky Plants* 61 [Whitwick, Leics.] If you chop an elder tree .. you should bow three times and say: 'Old Woman, Old Woman, Give me some of your wood And when I am dead I'll give you some of mine.'

ELDER malevolent

1813 BRAND *Antiquities* II 588. There is a vulgar prejudice that 'if boys be beaten with an elder stick, it hinders their growth.' **1875** *Birmingham Archaeol. Soc. Trans.* 24 Nov. 15. Hawthorn bloom and elder flowers, Will fill a house with evil powers. **1889** *Lincolnshire N & Q* I 56. We chanced to visit a house to enquire after a sick baby, and were told that it was quite well again: 'You see, Sir, one of the rockers of the cradle were made of iller, and in course the old woman did not like that, and she would not let the wean alone till we took it off.' **1904** *Daily Chronicle* 16 Dec. 5. A few days ago a gamekeeper .. tripped up on an elder-bush, a spike of which entered his hand. It is a popular superstition that a wound from the elder is fatal, and it proved so in this case. **1938** *Folklore* 232 [Shrops.] Farmers will not use elder sticks to drive cattle to market, and their wives will not use the wood to make skewers for dressing poultry. **1961** E. SALISBURY *Weeds and*

Aliens 267. An Elder bush can quickly create a sunshade over the adjacent shrubs, which it weakens or even kills .. The rural belief that it poisons neighbouring growth is based on this effect but is linked also with the superstition that Judas Iscariot hanged himself on an Elder tree, which was therefore held to be accursed and lethal to the plants around. **1985** R. VICKERY *Unlucky Plants* 60 In Wootton [Oxon., 1950s] they say that the elder is a witch tree. You should not mend a wattle hedge with it, as it will give the witches power. Ibid. 63 [Kill Village, Co. Kildare] My own people .. would not .. allow an elder stick in the house, and it would be an unforgivable act to strike a child or even an animal with one .. I have heard the old people say it was unhealthy to have an elder tree growing near the house as it was often noted the inhabitants seemed more prone to TB or 'Consumption' as it was known in Ireland in the old days.

Cf. WILLOW STICK.

ELDER protects against and cures disease

AD 77 PLINY *Natural History* XXIV xxxvi (1856, V 24) For its [shingles] cure the patient is scourged with a branch of elder. *c.* AD 950 MS Reg. 12 D. xvii (COCKAYNE *Leechdoms* II 105) For fellons [whitlows] take, to begin, a hazel or an elder stick or spoon, write thy name thereon, cut three scores on the place, fill the name with the blood, throw it over thy shoulder or between thy thighs into running water. **1507** *Gospelles of Dystaues* pt. 2 XVII. Who someuer rubbeth a warte vpon saynt Johans euen with an eldren lefe, and after put the lefe depe in the erthe as it may rotte, ye warte shall drye vpanone. **1631** BLOCHWICH *Anatomie of the Elder* (1655, 53) [against epilepsy] Pluck a twig of the Elder, and cut the cane that is betwixt two of its knees, or knots, in nine pieces; and these pieces being bound in a piece of linnen .. so hung about the neck, that they touch the spoon of the heart .. till the thred break of itself .. The Amulet is not at all to be touched with bare hands, but it ought to be taken hold on by some instrument, and buried in a place that no body may touch

it. **1870** KILVERT *Diary* 18 Oct. [Clyro, Brecon.] Old James Jones .. told me how he had once cured his deafness for a while by .. sticking into his ear an 'ellern' twig, and wearing it there night and day. **1878** *Folk-Lore Record* 39 [Fittleworth, Sussex] My old dame Mrs Cooper's infallible cure [for rheumatism] is 'find an elder stick with three, five or seven knots upon it; carry it in your pocket.' **1887** 'SPERANZA' WILDE *Superstitions of Ireland* II 95 [for epilepsy] Take nine pieces of young elder twig; run a thread of silk of three strands through the pieces, each piece being an inch long. Tie this round the patient's neck next the skin. Should the thread break and the amulet fall, it must be buried deep in the earth and another amulet made like the first, for if once it touches the ground the charm is lost. **1969** E. PORTER *Cambridgeshire* 88. Women's Institute members of Chrishall recorded in 1958 that the chewing of an elder twig was thought to relieve toothache.

Cf. WARTS cured with elder wood.

ELDER protects against evil

1656 W. COLES *Art of Simpling* 66–7. The common people formerly gathered the Leaves of Elder upon the last day of Aprill, which to disappoint the Charmes of Witches, they had affixed to their Doores and Windowes. **1790** GROSE *Provincial Glossary* Superstitions 43 [Scotland] The elder is supposed to have the virtue of protecting persons, bearing a branch of it, from the charms of witches and wizards. **1829** BROCKETT *North Country Words. Bur-tree*, the common elder .. A branch of this tree is supposed to possess great virtue in guarding the wearer against the charm of witchcraft and other familiar agency. I remember, when a boy, during a school vacation in the country, at the suggestion of my young companions, carrying it in my button-hole .. when under the necessity of passing the residence of a poor decrepit old woman, who, though the most harmless creature alive, was strongly suspected of holding occasional converse with an evil spirit. **1891** A. W. MOORE *Isle of Man* 152. Even at the present time an elder-tree may be observed growing by almost every old cottage in the Island. Its leaves .. were picked on May-eve, and affixed to doors and windows to protect the house from witchcraft. **1895** J. HARDY *Denham Tracts* 325 [Northumb.] An old man told me that his aunt used to keep a piece of bour tree .. constantly in her kist to prevent her clothes from malign influence. **1985** R. VICKERY *Unlucky Plants* 62 [Dyfed] Mother used elder leaves to make a pattern on the floor-bricks. Painting around them with red paint. Marking the cross with elder leaves. This .. going back to her grandmother's time .. The old Welsh people .. must have believed that there was 'magic and special protection' in having elder nearby.

ELDER protects against lightning

1864 R. CHAMBERS *Book of Days* II 322 [Suffolk] Speaking to some little children one day about the danger of taking shelter under trees during a thunderstorm, one of them said .. 'You will be quite safe under an eldern-tree, because the cross was made of that, and so the lightning never strikes it.' **1907** *N & Q* 10th ser. VIII 315. I remember being told, 'when that I was and a little tiny boy', that an elder tree was always safe shelter in a thunderstorm; the Cross of Calvary was made of elder, and .. it was exempted from being struck by lightning.

ELDER protects against saddle sores

1656 W. COLES *Art of Simpling* 68. It hath beene credibly reported to me, from severall hands, that if a man take an Elder stick, and cut it on both sides, so that he preserve the joynt, and put it in his Pocket when he rides a journey, he shall never gall. **1656** R. FLECKNOE *Diarium* 65. How Alder-stick in pocket carried, By Horseman who on high-way feared His breech should nere be gall'd or wearied .. It had, he said, such vertuous force, Where Vertue of't from Judas came, Who hang'd himself upon the same. **1688** AUBREY *Remaines* (1881, 178) Elder stick, wch our Wilts, &c butchers & grasiers &c. doe carrie in their pockets to preserve them from galling. **1692** *Athenian Mercury* 19 July. A Friend of mine being lately upon the Road a

Horseback, was extreamly incommoded by loss of Leather; which coming to the knowledge of one of his Fellow Travellers, he overperswaded him to put two Eldersticks in his Pocket, which not only eas'd him of his pain, but secur'd the remaining portion of his Posteriors .. throughout the rest of his Journey. **1829** BROCKETT *North Country Words*. *Losing-leather*, an injury in a *tender* part, to which inexperienced riders are subject .. It is a rustic idea .. that a sprig of elder, in which there is a joint, worn in one of the lower pockets, will operate as a charm against this *galling* inconvenience.

ELEPHANT lucky

1953 *Folklore* 294 [Westmorland] Elephants are lucky. **1957** *Folklore* 418. I was once at a marriage in Morecambe [Lancs.] when the bridegroom did meet such a beast as he drove to church, and afterwards received numerous congratulations on his singular good fortune. **1974** D. SCANNELL *Mother Knew Best* 53. Everyone knew that an elephant's hair bracelet was lucky.

ELEPHANT ORNAMENT etc. must face door

1957 *Woman's Own* 4 Apr. 7. I have two small black ebony elephants which I kept on the mantlepiece, but they did not bring any luck. Then a friend told me that elephants should always face the door. I moved them the next day and our happiness, health and luck really seem to have changed for the better. **1969** *Folklore* 308. If you own a drawing or a carving of an elephant, it must always be so placed in the room that its head is facing the door. **1970** *Folklore* 144. It is a superstition in my family [East London/Essex] that any ornament that has a face should be so placed that it is facing the door by which one normally enters the room .. It was suggested that the death of my father in 1967 was affected (or portended) by an ornament being accidentally turned round some weeks earlier. **1984** Woman, 72 [Hawkhurst, Kent] I know people who have elephants in the room always face them to the door, as they get wild if they do not know what is going on.

Cf. FIRST ANIMALS in spring: facing observer.

ELF-SHOT

10th c. MS Reg. D. xvii (COCKAYNE *Leech-doms* II 291) If a horse is elf shot, then take the knife of which the haft is horn of a fallow ox, and on which are three brass nails, then write upon the horses forehead Christs mark, and on each of the limbs which thou may feel at: then take the left ear, prick a hole in it in silence; this thou shalt do; then take a yerd [stick], strike the horse on the back, then it will be hole. And write upon the horn of the knife these words, 'Benedicite omnia opera domini, dominum.' Be the elf what it may, this is mighty for him to amends. 1669 BROWNE *Vulgar Errors* II v § 10. Terrible apprehensions and answerable unto their names, are raised of .. Elves spurs .. which .. are no more then .. Belemnites .. the Dart-stone. 1721 A. RAMSAY *Poems* 224 n. *Elf-shot*, Bewitch'd, shot by Fairies. Country people tell odd Tales of this distemper amongst Cows. When Elf-shot, the Cow falls down suddenly dead, no part of the skin is pierced, but often, a little triangular flat stone is found near the Beast, as they report, which is called the Elf's Arrow. 1749 W. COLLINS 'Ode on the Popular Superstition of the Highlands of Scotland' (*Trans. Royal Soc. Edinburgh*, I pt. 2 68) Every herd, by sad experience, knows How, wing'd with fate, their elf-shot arrows fly; When the sick ewe her summer food foregoes, Or, stretch'd on earth, the heart-smit heifers lie. 1771 PENNANT *Tour in Scotland* 94–5. *Elf-shots*, i.e. the stone arrow heads of the old inhabitants of this island, are supposed to be weapons shot by Fairies at cattle, to which are attributed any disorders they have: in order to effect a cure, the cow is to be touched by an elf-shot, or made to drink the water in which one has been dropped. 1783 C. VALLENCY *De Rebus Hibernicis* IV no. 13 [Description of Pl. XI] An arrow head [of hard black stone] .. these are found of the size of one third of this; the peasants call them Elf arrows, and frequently set them in silver .. and wear them about the neck

as an amulet against being *aithadh* or elf-shot. *c.*1816 Wilkie MS (HENDERSON *Northern Counties* 1866, 149) A few years ago a ploughman in Ettrick Forest .. obtained an elf-stone thus. While ploughing .. he heard a whizzing sound .. and looking up perceived a stone aimed at one of his horses .. It fell by the animal's side .. He picked up the stone, but found the angles so sharp that they cut his hand. 1855 F. K. ROBINSON *Whitby Glossary. Awfshots.* Fairies are said to shoot at cattle, with small arrows headed with flint; hence those numbers found in the ploughed soil are accounted for, which belong to the prehistoric period of our island chronology. 1881 W. GREGOR *North-East of Scotland* 184. Flint arrows and spear-heads went by the name of 'faery dairts' .. and were coveted as the sure bringers of success, provided they were not allowed to fall to the ground. When an animal died suddenly the canny woman of the district was sent for to search for the 'faery dairt', and in due course she found one. 1905 *Folklore* 336. When cattle sickened it used to be the custom .. until quite recently—to call in a man .. to conjure out the evil spirit. The grandfather of a man .. now living in Caithness was celebrated for his wonderful cures, and declared that he had often seen the 'fairy darts' sticking in the sick oxen when called in to doctor them. 1910 W. RAYMOND *English Country Life* XII [Somerset] The fairy-bolt was but a little flint arrowhead .. 'It used to be lucky, so I've a-been told, to find a fairy-bolt.' 1970 *Woman*, 32. When I was a child and lived in Clifton, we used to pick up elf-bolts on the shore of the Avon, at the foot of the Gorge. They were arrow-head flints.

ENGAGED COUPLE as godparents

*c.*1800 Correspondent (J. HUNTER MS note in Brand's *Antiquities* 1813, II 16) Some vestige of this idea that Co-sponsors, God-sibs, were prohibited from marrying together may be traced perhaps in the notion which still subsists .. that it is ominous for a couple attached to each other, or engaged, to stand together as sponsor for the same child: if they do it is apprended something will happen to prevent their marrying together. 1887 *Folk-Lore Record* 211 [Cornwall] I remember once hearing in Penzance a couple refusing [to become godfather and godmother of the same child] saying it was unlucky. 'First at the font, never at the altar.' 1888 *N & Q* 7th ser. V 46 [Worcs.] At the conclusion of the [christening] service the parish clerk said to the officiating clergyman, 'I wonder Mr Brown and Miss Smith stood to that child .. while they're engaged they ought not to be godfather and godmother to the same child; for it's a sure sign that their engagement will never end in marriage.' Ibid. 133. In Lancashire this bit of folklore is tersely rendered, 'Those who meet at the font will never meet at the altar.' 1913 E. M. WRIGHT *Rustic Speech* v. I once happened to mention at a dinner-party the superstition that it is a sure presage of a parting for an engaged couple to stand as fellow sponsors at a baptism. My neighbour .. a clergyman, immediately explained the reason .. in pre-Reformation days god-parents were not allowed to marry each other.

ENGAGED COUPLE photographed together

1926 *Folklore* 366 [London] It is unlucky .. for an engaged couple to be photographed together. 1932 C. IGGLESDEN *Those Superstitions* 149–50. According to a Brighton [Sussex] beach photographer the objection of an engaged couple to having their portraits taken together has again come into vogue. It is a very old superstition, dating back to the earliest days of photography .. The superstition is that if the couple are photographed together the engagement will be broken off. 1960 Woman, 57 [Nutfield, Surrey] It is considered unlucky for a couple to have their photograph taken together before marriage.

ENGAGED COUPLE walk together at wedding

1885 *N & Q* 6th ser. XII 144. At a recent wedding on the return from church the bridesmaid .. walked with the 'best man', to whom she was engaged to be married. This was noticed by the villagers, who pronounced it to be bad luck; for they said, 'as they have walked

back from church together before they are married, they will never walk back from church .. as man and wife.'

ENGAGEMENT RING

1890 *N & Q* 7th ser. IX 486 [Fareham, Hants.] Never allow any one else to put on your engagement ring; trouble will follow the rash act. 1955 *Woman's Illustrated* 12 Feb. 5. When a Scots girl gets her engagement ring, it's considered 'lucky' and she gives all her friends the opportunity of wishing on it. The friends put the ring on their engagement finger—but no further than the knuckle!—turn the ring three times towards their heart while they wish .. When the ring is returned, neither of the girls must say 'thank you'. Instead, one wishes the other good luck, and the other says, 'I hope your wish comes true.' 1983 Girl, 14 [Maldon, Essex] If people wear a ring on their ring finger before they get engaged then it is supposed to be unlucky.

EXCREMENT

ante 1628 *Carmichaell MS Proverbs* no. 1173 (ed. M. L. Anderson) Muk is luk, dame dryte there ben. 1662 *Rump Songs* II 3. There's another Proverb .. That of all kind of Lucks, Shitten Luck is the best. 1788 GROSE *Dictionary. Luck or Good Luck.* To tread in a sirreverence, to be bewrayed [dirtied]: an allusion to the proverb, Sh-tt-n luck is good luck. 1894 NORTHALL *Folk-phrases* 22. Sh----n luck is good luck. Said by one who treads accidentally into excrement, or is befouled by mischance. This .. probably owes its existence to an ancient term for ordure—*gold* or *gold* dust. 1898 BLAKEBOROUGH *Yorkshire Customs* 93. If a [wedding] guest stepped in any kind of filth on his .. way to the house, on no account would it be wiped off, it being considered very unlucky to do so. 1910 *N & Q* 11th ser. I 296–7. It was .. a common belief among [burglars] that *exonerando alvum* [by defecating] on the scene of their depredations they secured immunity from .. discovery. I remember .. the old parish clerk of Woodford Church, Essex .. telling me that some fellows who broke into the sacred building left behind this objectionable evidence of their presence [c.1860–70]. **1923** [Somerset] If a dog makes a mess in your doorway you will be very lucky. **1930** N & Q CLVIII 403. In Great Britain horse-dung is placed in front of house-doors or inside houses, in order not only to avert the evil eye but also to bring good luck. **1952** Girl, 11 [Swansea, Glam.] To step on manure means good luck. **1956** Woman, 20 [Brierley Hill, Staffs.] Good luck to tread in dog's faeces without realizing it until afterwards. **1985** Man, c.55. When I was an evacuee on a farm in Nottinghamshire, they always said it was lucky if you stood in a cow-pat. **1985** Woman, 55 [Colchester, Essex] Well, they say 'Where there's muck there's luck,' don't they.

Cf. DIRT lucky.

EXCREMENT, baby's first

AD **77** PLINY Natural History XXVIII XIII (1856, V 295) In the case of women afflicted with sterility, they recommend the application of a pessary, made of the first excrement that is voided by an infant at the moment of its birth.

Cf. BABY'S NAPPY: first.

EXCREMENT: birds' droppings

1878 N & Q 5th ser. X 287. Sitting on the box of a coach the other day .. a youth who sat by me called my attention to certain droppings on his knee, just inflicted on him by a passing bird. 'It's a pity this isn't Easter Day,' said he; 'for we say in Cleveland [Yorks.] that if a bird drops on you on Easter Day you'll be lucky all the year after.' **1911** LAWRENCE White Peacock pt. 3 1. 'Look here, a bird has given me luck'—he showed me a white smear on his shoulder. **1923** [Somerset] Bird droppings on your clothes or person bring luck. **1953** Boy, 12 [Croydon, Surrey] What things are lucky? If a bird dirts on you. **1964** Man, 80 [Halifax, Yorks.] I was going to wipe bird droppings from a friend's car, when the lady owner stopped me. She said it was good luck to have such a thing. **1988** Woman, 66 [Ockham, Surrey] You've got a bird mess on your car! That's lucky, isn't it?

EXCREMENT, burning human

1612 J. COTTA Short Discoverie 54. Nei-

ther can I beleeue .. that the forced coming of men or women .. to the burning of the dung or vrine of such as are bewitched [is] any trial of a witch. **1658** SIR K. DIGBY Late Discourse 125–9. Their little child .. had a Burning fever .. They could not conjecture any cause .. I told them that .. I observed one particulariry .. that their child .. let fall his excrements on the ground and his nurse presently took the Fire-shovel, and covered it with embers, and then threw all into the fire, the mother began to make her excuses .. I replyd, that twas not for this consideration .. but I was curious to know the reason of her child's distemper. I caused [the excrement] to be put in a bason of cold water .. every time that the child gave occasion. He began to amend the very same hour. Ibid. 126–8. If it happens that there be a Farmer who .. keeps more neatly the approches to his house than his neighbours do, the boyes use to come thither in the night-time .. to discharge their bellies there, because that in such Villages there is not much commodity of easements .. but they who are acquainted with this trick .. make red-hot a .. fire-shovel, and then thrust it into the excrements all hot. In the mean time the boy which made the ordure feels a kind of pain and collick in his bowels .. and he is hardly quit of it till he suffer a kind of fever .. which is the cause that he returns thither no more: And these women to be freed from the like affronts do passe among the Ignorant for Sorceresses, and Witches, being they can torment people in that fashion. **1684** I. MATHER Illustrious Providences 269. How persons that shall unbewitch others .. by casting Excrements into the fire .. can wholly clear themselves from being white Witches, I am not able to understand. **1895** F. T. ELWORTHY Evil Eye 74 [Somerset] An old midwife .. said: ''Tis a very bad thing to throw a child's stooling on the fire, 'cause it do give the child such constipation and do hurt it so in his inside.'

Cf. CATTLE: burning entrails gives power over witch.

EXHUMATION

1616 Epitaph on Shakespeare's tombstone [Stratford-on-Avon Church, War-wicks.] Good frend for Jesvs sake forbeare, To digg the dust encloased heare Blese be ye man yt spares thes stones. And curst be he yt moves my bones. **1697** W. TURNER *Remarkable Providences* 77. Thomas Fludd, of Kent, Esq; told me, That it is an old Observation which was pressed earnestly to King James I, that he should not remove the Queen of Scots Body from Northamptonshire, where she was Beheaded, and Interred: For that it always bodes ill to the Family, when Bodies are remov'd from their Graves. For some of the Family will die shortly after, as did Prince Henry, and, I think, Queen Anne. **1850** *N & Q* 1st ser. II 4 [Leics./Northants.] There is a superstitious idea that the removal or exhumation of a body after interment bodes death or some terrible calamity to the surviving members of the deceased's family. **1911** *Folklore* 56 [Co. Clare] There is a strong feeling against removing a body from the place of its first burial to one in another parish [and] that sickness and death would come into the other parish with the remains.

Cf. SKULL unlucky to move.

EYE itches

*c.*275 BC THEOCRITUS *Idylls* III (tr. Creech, 1684) My right Eye itches now, and shall I see My Love? **1604** SHAKESPEARE *Othello* IV iii. Mine eyes do itch: Doth that boade weeping? **1650** N. HOMES *Daemonologie* 61. If their right eye itcheth, it betokens sorrowful weeping; if the left .. joyfull laughter. **1652** GAULE *Mag-astro-mances* 181. To bode good or bad luck .. from .. the itching of the eye. **1738** SWIFT *Polite Conversation* III 196. My Right Eye itches; I shall cry. **1755** *Connoisseur* 13 Mar. If your right eye itches, you will cry; if your left you will laugh; but left or right is good at night. **1787** GROSE *Provincial Glossary* Superstitions 60. When the right eye itches, the party affected will shortly cry; if the left, they will laugh. **1831** HONE *Year Book* 29 Feb. When your right eye itches, it is a sign of good luck; or your left eye, of bad luck; but 'Left or right Brings good at night.' **1883** BURNE *Shropshire* 270. The right eye itching is

a sign of coming laughter; the left eye, of tears. **1923** [Somerset] If your left eye itches you will cry, if your right itches you will laugh. **1972** *Lore and Language* July 7 [Coalisland, Tyrone] If your left eye is itchy you'll cry.

EYEBROWS

1579 LUPTON *Thousand Notable Things* VI § 99. They whose heaire of the eye browes doo touch or meete together, of all other are the worst. They doo shewe that he or she is a wicked personne, and an intyser of seruauntes, and geuen to unlawfull and naughty artes: which Johannes Indagnies sayth, hee hath obserued in olde Women being Wytches, which were ledde to be burned, whose eye browes were such. *c.*1598 SHAKESPEARE *Much Adoe about Nothing* II v. Infaith honest as the skin betweene his browes. **1825** JAMIESON *Scottish Dict.* Suppl. [Lothian/Yorks.] *Lucken-brow'd.* Having the eye-brows close on each other. It is reckoned a good omen, if one meet a person of this appearance as the first foot, or first in the morning. **1853** *N & Q* 1st ser. VII 152. It's a good thing to have meeting eyebrows. You'll never know trouble. **1857** KINGSLEY *Two Years Ago* IX. Tom .. began scrutinizing Mrs Harvey's face. It had been handsome .. but the eyebrows, crushed together downwards above her nose .. indicated .. a character self-conscious, furtive, capable of great inconsistencies, possibly of great deceits. **1873** Harland & Wilkinson *Lancashire Legends* 225. When the hair of the eyebrows meets over the bridge of the nose .. the person .. will certainly be hanged. **1878** *N & Q* 5th ser. X 288. A friend .. heard quoted: 'Trust not the man whose eyebrows meet, For in his heart you'll find deceit.' **1895** J. HARDY *Denham Tracts* 325 [Northumb.] Those who have the eyebrows met are witches and warlocks. Ibid. 340. On New Year's day .. to meet as first-foot a person with the eyebrows met was considered a bad encounter. **1899** J. SHAW *Schoolmaster* 32 [Tynron, Dumfries.] The hair of the eyebrows meeting above the nose signifies unsteadiness and love of change. **1909** M. TREVELYAN *Folk-Lore of Wales* 209. Witches .. their eyebrows meet over

their noses. **1964** E. O'BRIEN *Girls in
their Married Bliss* 1 [Eire] He was a big,
rough fellow with oily hair and his
eyebrows met. So I said to him, 'Beware
of the one whose eyebrows meet, because in his heart there lies deceit.' And
sweet Jesus, next time we met he'd had
them plucked over his broken nose. He's
so thick he didn't understand that the
fact they met was the significant thing.
1985 *Woman*, 56 [South Shields, Co.
Durham] I was told by my mother never
to trust people whose eyebrows met,
they were very bad-tempered, she said.

EYELASH, wishing on

1858 M. E. HAWEIS [aged 9] *Letter* 18
Jan. (B. HOWE *Arbiter of Elegance* 19) Did
you know we had a dolls-house? I had
been wishing to my eyelashes and was
always curtseying to the moon, for
years. **1883** BURNE *Shropshire* 268. If an
eyelash comes out, put it on the back of
the hand, wish, and throw it over the
shoulder. If it leaves the hand the wish
will come true. **1887** *Folk-Lore Record*
214 [Cornwall] When an eyelash falls
out its owner puts it on the tip of her
nose, wishes and blows at it; should she
blow it off, she will have her wish. **1895**
S. O. ADDY *Household Tales* 85–6. If you
find an eyelash on your cheek take it
and put it upon the back of the hand.
Then shut your eyes, blow three times,
and guess at which blow it went off.
Then wish something, but do not speak
to anybody until you can answer 'Yes' to
the question. **1953** Girl, 15 [Loughton,
Essex] If you lose an eyelash, put in on
your finger, wish, and blow. If it doesn't
blow off, your wish will not come true.

EYES, peculiar

AD **77** PLINY *Natural History* VII II (1855,
II 127–8) Some persons of this description [enchanters] have two pupils
in each eye .. These persons will not
sink in water, even though weighed
down by their garments .. Cicero also
.. makes the remark, that the glances
of all women who have a double pupil
is noxious. *c.* AD **388** ST JOHN CHRYSOSTOM
Baptismal Instructions (ed. Harkins, 189)
Often a man leaves his own house and
sees a man who has one eye .. and
counts it an omen. This is the pomp of

the devil. *c.***1350** HIGDEN *Polychronicon*
(MS Harl. 2261, tr. Trevisa: Rolls II
189) In Triballis and in Illyricis beeþ
men þat sleeþ [slayeth] wiþ hir siȝt
[sight] what þey beholdeþ and lokeþ on
longe, nameliche and þey be greued and
wroþ while þey lokeþ so .. and þese
hauen in eueriche yȝe [eye] tweie
blakkes. **1530** PALSGRAVE *L'éclair-
cissement de la langue francoyse* (ed. F.
Génin, 1852, 782) He that winks with
one eye and looks with the other, I will
not trust him and he were my brother.
1579 LUPTON *Thousand Notable Things* VI
§ 22. Women that haue double apples
in theyr eyes, or strayles: do euery
where hurt with their looking (Which
is called of some ouerlooking). **1584**
SCOT *Discoverie of Witchcraft* XVI IX.
Manie writers agree with Virgil and
Theocritus in the effect of witching eies,
affirming that in Scythia, there are
women called Bithiae, having two balles
or rather blacks in the apple of their eies
.. These (forsooth) with their angrie
lookes doo bewitch and hurt not only
yoong lambs, but yoong children. **1621**
JONSON *Gypsies Metamorphosed* ll. 1329–
30. From a Gypsie in the morninge, Or
a paire of squint-eies torninge. **1688**
AUBREY *Remaines* (1881, 177) [double
pupil = evil eye] This is observed by the
Scotts to this day. **1721** KELLY *Scotish
Proverbs* 169. He that looks with one
Eye, and winks with another, I will not
believe him, though he was my Brother.
If the Man naturally squint, my Coun-
trymen have an Aversion to him, and
all who have any Thing disagreeable, if
he wink, or nod, they look upon him to
be a false Man. *c.***1816** Wilkie MS
(HENDERSON *Northern Counties* 1866, 37)
A person .. 'ringlet-eyed', that is with
a great portion of white in the eye [is]
unlucky. **1829** BROCKETT *North Country
Words. Wall-eyed.* Persons are said to be
wall-eyed, when the white of the eye is
very large, and to one side. On the
borders, 'sic folks' are considered
unlucky. **1831** HONE *Year Book* 29
Feb. To prevent ill luck from meeting a
squint-eyed person, you must spit three
times. **1836** MARRYAT *Midshipman Easy*
XVIII. I don't much like the look of the
padrone—he squints. **1836** A. E. BRAY
Devonshire I 176. The wicked and thiev-

ish elves, who are all said to be squint-eyed, are dispatched on the dreadful errand of changing children in the cradle. 1855 *Gents Mag.* pt. 2 384–5 [Shrops./Worcs.] It is considered un-lucky to meet a squinting woman, unless you talk to her, which breaks the charm. 1861 *N & Q* 2nd ser. XII 491. It is lucky for a man to meet a squinting woman, unlucky to meet a squinting man, and vice versa for the other sex. This is another of the inexplicable sayings so common in England. 1864 R. CHAMBERS *Book of Days* II 735. It was regarded as a sign of very bad luck if a squinting person entered the hall when the [yule] log was burning. 1882 *N & Q* 6th ser. VI 357. I had it from my father that to meet a squinting woman was reckoned of bad omen in Yorkshire . . The spell might be broken by spitting back over the left shoulder. 1909 *N & Q* 10th ser. XII 483 [Stromness, Orkney] Fishermen count it unlucky to meet a squint-eyed person. 1909 M. TREVELYAN *Folk-Lore of Wales* 209. In Wales it is commonly said that if you look steadily into the eyes of a witch you will see yourself 'upside down', and these women have two pu-pils in their eyes. 1914 *Folklore* 366 [Cambs.] If a cross-eyed person looks at you you will have ill-luck all day, for such people can see right through you and know your thoughts. 1939 *N & Q* CLXXVI 298. I recently heard a bit of modern folklore which was new to me. If you meet a cross-eyed woman, you should turn your head away, and care-fully not look at her. She is very unlucky

to meet. If, on the other hand, you encounter a cross-eyed man, you should turn towards him and fix your eyes steadily and long upon him . . he will bring you great luck. My informant is a Cambridgeshire woman. 1953 Girl, 15 [Oxford] When somebody who is boss-eyed goes by you spit on the ground. 1956 Woman, 49 [Scarborough, Yorks.] My grandmother always said she would never have strained the tendon in her ankle if she had spat over her little finger that time she met the cross-eyed man. 1957 *Folklore* 424 [Co. Durham] A miner . . would return home if he met a cock-eyed (squinting) woman. 1960 *Folklore* 37. I was told that in the Had-leigh [Essex] of 1880 there were still old men who regarded 'trough-eyed' persons 'those with one eye set lower than the other' as witches, and ex-pressed contempt for all opinion to the contrary. 1968 *Observer* Suppl. 24 Nov. 10 [trawler skipper, Staithes, Yorks.] I never like to meet a strange woman first thing on a morning when I'm going fishing . . I don't like to meet a cross-eyed woman. 1979 D. MORRIS *Gestures* 143–4 [Glam.] My nurse told me to 'make horns' to keep off the evil eye . . When the woman reached us I saw that she had dreadful cross-eyes. 1988 Woman, 60 [South Shields, Co. Durham, 1941] Auntie B. brought her husband-to-be to meet my mother. One of his eyes winked involuntarily all the time. After they'd gone, my mother said 'Well, I don't give much for that marriage—not with that winking eye.'

F

'FAIRY' taboo word

1585 A. MONTGOMERIE 'Flyting' in James I *Essayes on Poesie* (ed. Arber, 1869, 68) Vpon Alhallow eue, Quhen our gude nichtbors rydis. **1691** R. KIRK *Secret Commonwealth* (1815, 1) Fairies, they call .. the Good People, it would seem, to prevent the Dint of their ill Atempts, (for the Irish use to bless all they fear Harme of). **1868** *N & Q* 4th ser. II 197. The belief in fairies is not yet extinct. In the writer's native parish, in the Lowlands of Scotland .. 'fairy' was never used—the term was 'good neighbour' .. 'Call us good neighbours, good neighbours we'll be; Call us fairies, fairies we'll be' .. 'fairy' meaning a malicious imp. Ibid. 366 [Ireland] The peasants .. avoid mentioning the word 'fairy', and use instead the complimentary term 'good people', generally accompanying it with a pious 'God save us!' and the sign of the Cross.

FAIRY LOAF

1669 BROWNE *Vulgar Errors* II v 10. Terrible apprehensions .. are raised of Fairy stones .. which are no more than Echinomitrites .. Common opinion commendeth them for the Stone; but are most practically used against Films in Horses eyes. **1877** BREWER *Dict. Phrase and Fable* 284. *Fairy loaves* .. fossil sea-urchins (echini), said to be made by the fairies. **1956** G. E. EVANS *Ask the Fellows* xxiv [Blaxhall, Suffolk] The people of this district call the fossils [echinites] Fairy Loaves. They are, in fact, shaped like daintily marked cottage loaves .. One old man .. said as he fingered the Fairy Loaf on his mantle-piece: 'They say that while you have one of these in the house you'll niver want for bread. Neither have I!' Some housewives used to polish these fossils with blacklead and place them on the hob.

FAIRY RINGS

1610 SHAKESPEARE *Tempest* v i. You demy-Puppets, that By Moone-shine doe the greene sowre Ringlets make, Whereof the Ewe not bites. **1668** W. RAMESEY *Elminthologia* 72. Many [witches] were carryed away [by the Devil] to Banquets and meetings, whence perhaps, those green Circles and Rings that are frequently found in Plains, may by their Sports and Dances be occasioned. **1777** BRAND *Antiquities* 107. Fairies .. are always clad in Green, and frequent the Woods and Fields .. They dance in Moon-Light when Mortals are asleep, and not capable of seeing them, as may be observed on the following Morn; their dancing-Places being very distinguishable; For as they dance Hand in Hand, and so make a Circle in their Dance, so next Day there will be seen Rings and Circles on the Grass. **1802** SCOTT *Minstrelsy of Scottish Border* II 214. The fairies of Scotland .. inhabit the interior of green hills, chiefly those of a conical form .. on which they lead their dances by moon-light; impressing upon the surface the mark of circles, which sometimes appear yellow and blasted, sometimes of a deep green hue; and within which it is dangerous to sleep, or to be found after sunset. **1823** MOOR *Suffolk Words. Farrisee Rings.* The green circles seen in grass lands; in and round which it has been fancied the fairies, or farisees, dance by moonlight .. Sheep and cattle avoid it. **1854** A. E. BAKER *Glossary of Northants. Fairy-rings.* Circles of dark green grass, occasionally seen on old pasture land; round which, according to vulgar belief, the 'Elf quene with hire jolly compagnie Danced full oft in many a grene mede.' Various are the conjectures as to the cause of these verdant circles .. but they are more correctly attributable to a small esculent fungus, called the *fairy-ringed* fungus, *Agaricus orcades*. **1870** KILVERT *Diary* 14 Oct. [refers to early 19th c.] Boys would wear their hats the wrong way lest they should be enticed into the fairy rings and made to dance. **1876** S. BARING-

GOULD *Vicar of Morwenstow* 126 [Cornwall] Mr Hawker had a curious superstition about fairy-rings. There was one on the cliff. Some years ago he was visited by Lady - -, who drove ove from Bude. As he walked with her .. they came to the ring in the grass, and she was about to step into it when he arrested her abruptly, and said .. 'It will bring ill-luck.' 'Oh, nonsense .. the circle is made by toadstools. See, here is one: I will pick it.' 'If you do, there will shortly be a death in your house.' She neglected the warning, and .. within a week a little daughter died.

FEATHER stuck in ground

1883 BURNE *Shropshire* 226 [Church Stretton] You should never pass a black feather lying on the ground, without picking it up and sticking it upright in the soil. **1909** M. TREVELYAN *Folk-Lore of Wales* 325. It is lucky to find a crow's feather stuck in the ground before your feet. **1960** Boy, 11 [Selborne, Hants.] If you see a feather and walk straight past it you will have bad luck. You have to stick it up in the ground, then it will bring you good luck.

FENDER upturned for luck

1933 *Newcastle Weekly Chronicle* 30 Dec. 7 [caption to picture] Cavilling Day [when coal seams are drawn for] at Marley Hill Colliery. In accordance with old custom, a miner's wife is seen here with her youngest child sitting on an upturned fender, to ensure good luck for her husband.

FERN, harming

1862 *N & Q* 3rd ser. II 342 [Black Country, Staffs.] The natives .. look upon [ferns] with a superstitious feeling, think it bad luck to gather them (even for fuel) or to touch them, and call them by the singular name of 'the Devil's Bushes'. **1978** N. MAYES *Nature Notebook* 125. It was once a widespread belief that to cut or burn ferns would bring rain.

FERN protects

1909 M. TREVELYAN *Folk-Lore of Wales* 89. It was formerly customary for waggoners to place a bunch of fern over the horse's ears or on the horse-collar, to 'keep the devil away' and to 'baffle witches'.

FERN LEAF in shoe: spell

1507 *Gospelles of Dystaues* pt. 4 XXIII. Yf ony woman wyll that her husbande, or her paramoure loue her well, she ought to put in his shoo a lefe of brekens that had ben gadred on saynt Johans euen whyles that they rynge none, so that it be in the left shoo, and without faute he shall loue her meruaylously.

FERN SEED makes invisible

1596 SHAKESPEARE *1 Henry the Fourth* II i. We have the receit of Fernseede, we walke invisible. **1625** T. JACKSON *Originall of Vnbeliefe* XIX 179–80. The Angell did foretell John Baptist should be borne at that very instant, in which the Ferneseede, at other times invisible, did fall; intimating .. that this Saint of God had some extraordinary vertue from the circumstance of his birth .. All the hidden vertues of the .. seed, invisible save only to the superstitious, I now remember not. **1681** MARVELL 'Daphnis and Chloe' ll. 81–4. The witch that midnight wakes For the fern, whose magic weed In one minute casts the seed, And invisible him makes. **1813** BRAND *Antiquities* I 251 n. A respectable countryman at Heston, in Middlesex, informed me in June 1793, that, when he was a young man, he was often present at the ceremony of catching the Fernseed at midnight on the Eve of St John Baptist. The attempt, he said, was often unsuccessful, for the seed was to fall into the plate of its own accord, and that too without shaking the plant. *Ibid.* The ancients, who often paid more attention to received opinions than to the evidence of their senses, believed that fern bore no seed. Our ancestors imagined that this plant produced seed which was invisible. Hence, from an extraordinary mode of reasoning, founded on the fantastic doctrine of signatures, they concluded that they who possessed the secret of wearing this seed about them would become invisible. **1865** *Gents Mag.* 702 [Ireland] Whoever can find fern-seeds will be able to render himself invisible whenever he chooses. **1887** O. J. BURKE *South Isles of Aran* 99–100. After a fruitless search [for a foal that had strayed] he returned [and] was amazed .. that neither wife nor children welcomed him home. At length .. he said, 'I have not found the foal' .. They all sprang to their feet, and his wife called him by name to give over that nonsense, and to come out from his hiding-place .. Then he remembered that he had, on the previous night, crossed a meadow loaded with ferns, and that some of the seeds must have got into his shoes, and that he was therefore invisible.

FERN STALK

c.1816 Wilkie MS (HENDERSON *Northern Counties* 1866, 190) The bracken also they [witches] detest, because it bears on its root the letter C, the initial of the holy name Christ, which may plainly be seen on cutting the root horizontally. 1830 FORBY *East Anglia* 414–15. If a brake is cut across, the veins are supposed to shew the initial of the name of the future husband or wife. 1853 *N & Q* 1st ser. VII 152 [Croydon, Surrey] Cut a fern-root slantwise, and you'll see a picture of an oak-tree: the more perfect, the luckier chance for you. 1865 *Gents Mag.* 703 [Ireland] If the root of fern be cut transversely, the initial letter of a chief's name will be found, and to him it is thought the land on which this plant grew formerly belonged. 1979 *Sunday Express* 17 June 4 [Scotland] My mind went back over some 70 years to a childish game we used to play called 'Holy Bracken'. Selecting a fat, juicy specimen, I used my pocket knife to sever it close to the ground and .. there it was: a perfect example of the most famous initials in the world—JC .. It is considered very lucky to find a good example.

FERRET cures whooping cough

1866 HENDERSON *Northern Counties* 112–13 [Byer's Green, Co. Durham] A boy came into my kitchen the other day with a basin .. of new milk, saying his mother hoped I would let my son's white ferret drink half of it, and then he would take the other half home to the bairn to cure its cough. 1867 *Gents Mag.* pt. I 729 [Suffolk] For the Hooping cough .. let the patient drink some milk which a

ferret has lapped. 1893 *Folklore* 351 [Co. Kerry] For Whooping-cough. Milk to be poured into a saucer, a ferret to drink some of it, and the rest to be given to the patient. 1924 *Folklore* 356 [Westleton, Suffolk] For whooping cough, people used to say that ferrets must drink out of a saucer of milk, and the patient must drink the milk afterwards.

FEVER cured by transference

1787 *Gents Mag.* pt. 2 719 n. It is usual in this neighbourhood [Exeter], with those who are affected by an ague, to visit at dead of night the nearest cross-road, five different times, and there bury a new-laid egg .. and they are persuaded that, with the egg, they shall bury their ague. 1867 *Gents Mag.* pt. I 732 [Suffolk] Take a handful of salt and bury it in the ground, and as the salt dissolves, you will recover. 1871 *N & Q* 4th ser. VIII 133. The remedy .. held in great repute by .. villagers of Leverington, Co. Cambridge, at the beginning of the present century .. consisted in the invalid having to put on two under-linen garments instead of the usual quantity; then for the nearest relative or friend to tear off (daily) a piece of the one nearest the person of the sufferer, until that garment was completely destroyed.

FEVER, verbal charm for

1804 MS charmer's book (LEATHER *Herefordshire* 73) When Jesus saw the cross whereon he was to be crucified he trembled and shook and the Jews asked him, 'Art thou afraid or hast thou the ague?' Jesus answered and said 'I am not afraid neither have I the evil ague, whoever wears this about them shall not be afraid nor have that evil ague.' 1827 HONE *Every-Day Book* II 19 Nov. This charm for the ague, on St Agnes' Eve, is customary to be said up the chimney, by the eldest female in the family—'Tremble and go! First day shiver and burn: Tremble and quake! Second day shiver and learn: Tremble and die! Third day never return.' 1860 *N & Q* 2nd ser. X 184 [Edgbaston, Warwicks.] The first was given to a young woman at Stourport about sixty years ago. 'Ague, farewell, Till we meet in

Hell.' The other is similar: 'Good dear Devil, Shake not Nell here; But when you get her to Hell, Shake her well there.' **1875** W. D. PARISH *Sussex Dialect. Ague.* In some places it is believed that it may be cured by the following charm, which, to be efficacious, must be written on a three-cornered piece of paper and worn round the neck till it drops off— 'Ague, ague, I thee defy, Three days shiver, Three days shake, Make me well for Jesus' sake!' **1964** *West Sussex Gazette* 13 Feb. 6. My granny said as she'd seed a old man tied to that tree by a rope as he'd got the other end round his waist an' he ran round an' round the tree till the rope was tight, an' then he went the other way till 'twas loose again, an' he called out three times: 'Ague, ague, I do de defy, Make me well for Jesu's sake.' An' Granny said as he was better after.

FINGERS, cracking joints of

1755 *Connoisseur* 13 Mar. But the other will have the advantage of her in the number of children, as was plainly proved by snapping their finger-joints. *c.***1840** 'Women's Sayings' (J. ASHTON *Modern Street Ballads* 28) If a girl snaps one finger, She'll have a child it deems, And if she snaps two, She's sure to have twins. **1887** *Yorkshire Folklore Journal* pt. 6 85. Perhaps the commonest [divination] and yet least-believed, is that the cracks caused by pulling each of the ten fingers indicate the number of sweethearts. **1953** Woman, 50 [Eastbourne, Sussex, *c.*1915] We pulled each finger and the number of joints that cracked meant one had that number of sweethearts. **1959** OPIE *Lore and Language of Schoolchildren* 328. If a girl's fingers crack when they are pulled it reveals that she has a boy friend, and classmates will pull a child's finger to discover what she herself is unwilling to divulge.

FINGERS: divination

1686-7 AUBREY *Remaines* (1881, 25) To divine whether such a one will returne this night or no, is by the sheath of a knife, wch one holds at ye great end with his two fore fingers, & sayes *he comes,* then slips downe his upper finger under

his lower, & then the lower under that & sayes, *he comes not,* and *sic deinceps* till he is come to the bottome of his sheath, wch gives the Answer. **1849** J. O. HALLIWELL *Popular Rhymes* 111. 'It's time, I believe, For us to get leave: The little dog says It isn't, it is; it 'tisnt, it is, &c.' Said by a schoolboy, who places his book between his knees. His two forefingers are then placed together, and the breadth of each is measured alternately along the length of the book. The time to get leave (to be dismissed) is supposed to have arrived or not according as one finger or the other fills up the last space.

FINGERS: power for good/evil

15th c. MS Camb. Univ. Lib. Ff. v. 48 f. 82^v. Ilke a fyngir has a name, als men thaire fyngers calle, The lest fyngir hat lityl man . . The next fyngir hat leche man, for quen a leches dos oȝt, With that fynger he tastes all thyng howe that hit is wroȝt. **1646** BROWNE *Vulgar Errors* IV iv. An opinion there is, which magnifies the condition of the fourth finger of the left hand; presuming therein a cordiall relation, that a . . nerve, veine, or arterie, is conferred thereto from the heart, and therefore that especially hath the honour to beare our rings. Which was not only the Christian practise in Nuptiall contracts, but observed by the heathens . . as . . Lemnius hath confirmed . . adding moreover that rings hereon peculiarly affect the heart; that in . . swoundings he used the frication of this finger . . that the ancient Physicians mixed up their Medicines herewith. **1849** BRAND *Antiquities* III 177–8. The fore-finger of the right hand is considered by the vulgar to be venomous; and consequently is *never* used in applying anything to a wound or bruise. **1853** *N & Q* 1st ser. VII 152 [Somerset] The ring-finger, stroked along any sore or wound, will soon heal it. All the other fingers are poisonous, especially the fore-finger. **1988** Woman, 58 [Cheltenham, Glos.] My old governess caught me using my index finger to put on some wintergreen ointment, and she said 'Darling, you must never use that finger, it's poisonous.' She came from Bawtry, in Yorkshire.

Cf. POINTING AT.

FIRE, behaviour of: blazes suddenly

1850 *N & Q* 1st ser. II 512 [Devon] If the fire blazes up brightly when the crock is hung up, it is a sign there is a stranger coming. 1878 *Folk-Lore Record* 57 [Fittleworth, Sussex] Its sudden blazing up is a sign of some stranger being near. 1922 UDAL *Dorsetshire* 277–8. If a wood fire, smouldering on the hearth, suddenly bursts out into a flame without any person's intervention it is considered a sure sign that a stranger will arrive very shortly. 1932 C. IGGLESDEN *Those Superstitions* 174. A saying about a fire: 'When it burns without blowing You'll have company without knowing.'

FIRE, behaviour of: blue flames in

late 18th c. J. RAMSAY (*Scotland in the Eighteenth Century* II 434) The various configurations in the fire are .. supposed to be a species of spirits. They are called *Corracha cagalt*, i.e. the spectres or spirits of the hearth. The bluish appearances excited by stirring the embers are reckoned the signs of their existence. In the winter nights, it is still usual to frighten children with them; and when such appearances abound they are supposed to forebode bad weather.

Cf. CANDLE burns blue.

FIRE, behaviour of: burns badly

c.1855 *Fortune-Teller* 17. For a fire to burn black and gloomy, is a certain sign of dissension .. from a distant quarter. 1883 BURNE *Shropshire* 274–5. A Welsh Border lady says, 'If a wife lights the fire and it burns down, her husband is in a bad temper.' 1912 LEATHER *Herefordshire* 87. If a servant be trying to light a fire and it will not burn, she will frequently say 'Oh dear, my young man's in a temper!' 1923 [Martock, Som.] The fire's smokey coz you be bad tempered.

FIRE, behaviour of: burns hollow

1932 *Folklore* 338 [Ayr] If the fire burns hollow, it is a sure omen of death. The informant remembered the attendant on a sick person bursting into tears and despairing of the patient's life .. this was in 1922. 1939 *N & Q* CLXXVI 173.

Whenever the fire in my sitting-room burns with a large cavity my maid promptly pokes it down, because she says that a hollow fire foretells parting.

FIRE, behaviour of: burns on one side

1861 *N & Q* 2nd ser. XII 491. The fire burning on one side of the grate [is] a sign of a wedding. 1875 *N & Q* 5th ser. III 247. The fire .. obstinately refused to burn on the right hand side of the grate .. 'You know,' he [said] 'that it is commonly thought to portend a removal.' Ibid. 299. My little boy's nurse, who is a Suffolk woman, told my wife that a fire burning on one side of the grate was a sign that the master of the house was a bad husband. 1883 BURNE *Shropshire* 275. If a fire burns only on one side, it is a sign of parting; or at Ruyton and Baschurch, of a stranger coming. I have known of an Irish lady seizing the tongs and spreading the burning coals about the grate, because there would certainly be a death in the family if the fire were allowed to burn on one side. 1896 *N & Q* 8th ser. IX 225 [Romford, Essex] I was lately told by a tradesman that his wife had that morning been complaining that all the fires in the house burnt only on one side of the grate, which she considered a sure sign that a death would shortly occur in the family. 1932 WOMEN'S INSTITUTE *Worcestershire Book* 37 [The Lenches] If a fire burns on one side only there will be a quarrel in the house. 1953 Girl, 15 [Ipswich, Suffolk] If the fire burns to the side of the grate there will be a removal.

FIRE, behaviour of: fails to go out

1884 *N & Q* 6th ser. IX 137 [Shrops./Staffs.] Servant-maid: 'If you find the fire still burning from overnight .. when you come in to light it of a morning .. it's a certain sign as you'll hear tell of an illness that day.' 1890 *N & Q* 7th ser. IX 466. A short time ago our servant-maid .. found a piece of live coal among the ashes, 'though the grate was quite cold'. This, she told [us] was a sure sign of death. 1923 [Trowbridge, Wilts.] It is an unlucky omen for a fire which has been left overnight to be found still alight in the morning. 1953 Woman,

66 [Patrington, Yorks.] A saying was that if there was a red cinder in the grate in the morning it was a sure sign that someone in the family would die. **1982** Woman, 20. In Lincolnshire, it is believed that it is a sign of imminent death if a fire which has been neglected stays on for a long time.

Cf. CANDLE, failing to blow out.

FIRE, behaviour of: sends out sparks
1923 [Trowbridge, Wilts.] A large spark flying up the chimney denotes the coming of 'hasty news'. **1956** Woman, *c.*70 [Suffolk] Count the sparks coming from a fire. Each one means a letter to be received.

Cf. CANDLE, signs in: 'letter'.

FIRE, behaviour of: spits and roars
1668 W. RAMESEY *Elminthologia* 271. If the . . fire [fall towards them] then they expect anger. *c.*1855 *Fortune-Teller* 17. For a fire . . to spit and roar . . a sign of heavy displeasure from a superior. **1883** BURNE *Shropshire* 275. A spark [means] that he towards whom it flies is about to quarrel with some one. **1909** *N & Q* 10th ser. XII 484 [Stromness, Orkney] It is unlucky for the fire to send out sparks in front of you: you will receive a scolding from some one. **1923** [West Malling, Kent] If the fire crackles and spits into the room the person towards whom it spits must spit back. It signifies that someone is talking ill and this must be counteracted. **1932** C. IGGLESDEN *Those Superstitions* 174. The housemaid . . believes that if a fire roars it is a sign of a row in the house. *c.*1953 [Suffolk, 1890s] Sparks flying towards you from the fire meant someone had a spite against you.

FIRE, behaviour of: 'stranger' on grate
1755 *Connoisseur* 13 Mar. They were aware of my coming long before I arrived, because they had seen a stranger on the grate. **1777** BRAND *Antiquities* 94. The present northern Notion of foretelling Strangers from the black filmy Appendages . . on the Bars of our Fire Grates. **1784** COWPER *Task* IV ll. 296–300. The sooty films that play upon the bars Pendulous, and foreboding in the view Of superstition,

prophesying still, Though still deceived, some stranger's near approach. **1861** C. C. ROBINSON *Dialect of Leeds. Stranger.* A name given to the soot-flakes which peel off, and flutter on the bars of fire-grates. The appearance of one of these is regarded as a sure sign of the approaching visit of some one who has been long absent . . If the particle is drawn into the fire the stranger comes to a certainty, but if it drops on the hearthstone he or she will stay away, having (we presume) changed their minds. **1873** HARLAND & WILKINSON *Lancashire Legends* 239. A flake of soot on the first bar of the fire-grate betokens a boy visitor; on the second a man; on the third, a woman; and on the fourth a girl. If the hands are clapped before the flake, it will fly off at the end of as many strokes as there will be days before the visitor arrives. **1910** *N & Q* 11th ser. I 415. 'If the stranger on the bar goes in the fire, Your friend will come nigher; If the stranger goes in the ash, Your friend will come none the less; If the stranger goes up the chimney, Your friend will come, but you'll not see him' . . The rule is to wait and see . . but you may 'waft' it with your hands, and say: 'Stranger mine, come to me; If not mine, flee a-wee!' A little stranger is a child . . medium . . a lady; and a big one, a man. Two together . . a married couple, or . . a wedding in the family if both fly away together. **1923** [Castle Cary, Som.] Fan the flake of soot with your hand till it falls off, repeating the days commencing the same day, and finishing on the day it comes off. A stranger is coming on that day. **1983** Woman, 63 [Colchester, Essex] A trail of sparks burning on the grate—mother'd say, 'There's a stranger on the bar.'

Cf. CANDLE, signs in: stranger.

FIRE blackens chalk mark: cure for ague
1849 *Athenaeum* 11 Aug. 814 [Hants.] Let the patient make three crosses with white chalk on the back of the kitchen chimney—a large one in the middle and a smaller one on each side (as in the Crucifixion) and as the smoke from the fire obliterates them, so will the ague disappear. **1864** *N & Q* 3rd ser. V 237 [Aylesbury, Bucks.] A remedy for ague

.. was to take a black kettle, and draw a line on it with a piece of chalk, and put it on the fire. As the line becomes black like the rest of the kettle, the ague should disappear. 'But lor, Sir!' as my good informant said .. 'I don't know as that do do any good.' **1898** BLAKEBOROUGH *Yorkshire Customs* 136. Master Sadler, of Bedale, in the year 1773, undertook the cure of ague in quite a simple way. After the patient had answered a few searching questions touching his past life .. his name was chalked at the back of the hob, an incantation pronounced, and he went home whole.

FIRE: divination: sparks from burning brand

*c.*1816 Wilkie MS (HENDERSON *Northern Counties* 1866, 75) Another fiery ordeal consists in whirling before the face a lighted brand, singing .. 'Dingle, dingle, dowsie, the cat's in the well; The dog's awa' to Berwick, to buy a new bell.' They then observe the last sparks .. many round spots mean money, a quick extinction loss of property, and so on. **1883** BURNE *Shropshire* 530 [Pulverbatch] Children wave a burning stick in the air, saying, 'A girdle o' gold, a saddle o' silk, A horse for me as white as milk!' An evident relic of divinations or incantations practised with bonfires.

FIRE: divination: stones in bonfire

1794 *Stat. Acc. of Scotland* XI 621–2 [Callander, Perth.] On All-Saints Even, they set up bonfires in every village. When the bonfire is consumed, the ashes are carefully collected in the form of a circle. There is a stone put in, near the circumference, for every person of the several families interested in the bonfire; and whatever stone is moved out of its place, or injured before next morning, the person represented by that stone is devoted, or *fey*; and is supposed not to live twelve months from that day. **1806** R. C. HOARE *Itinerary through Wales* II 315. The autumnal fire is still kindled in North Wales, being on the eve of the 1st day of November, and is attended by many ceremonies; such as running through the fire and smoke, each casting a stone into the fire .. On the following morning the stones are searched for in the fire, and if any be missing, they betide ill to those who threw them in. **1813** BRAND *Antiquities* I 308 n. In North Wales there is a custom upon All Saints' Eve of making a great fire called Coel Coeth, when every family about an hour in the night makes a great bonfire in the most conspicuous place near the house, and when the fire is almost extinguished every one throws a white stone into the ashes, having first marked it; then having said their prayers turning round the fire, they go to bed. In the morning .. they come to search out the stones, and if any one of them is found wanting they have a notion that the person who threw it in will die before he sees another All Saints' Eve.

Cf. ASHES, footprint in.

FIRE extinguished in presence of corpse

1771 PENNANT *Tour in Scotland* 92. All fire is extinguished where a corpse is kept.

FIRE, newcomer gives priority to

1818 *Edinburgh Magazine* Nov. 413 [Angus] The same woman who received the bride at the door, now leads her across the floor to the fire-side, lifts the tongs, and puts them into the hands of their new mistress. **1883** BURNE *Shropshire* 274. Arrived at her 'new place', the maid's first care, if she would have 'luck' there, must be to light a fire, or to poke or mend a fire. Ibid. 317. An old man, who upwards of forty years ago was in the habit of coming to let the New Year into a farmhouse at Longnor, always entered without knocking or speaking, and silently stirred the fire before he offered any greeting to the family.

FIRE not allowed out of house, especially at certain times

7th c. MS Trinity Coll. Dublin H. 3. 18 (o'CURRY *Ancient Irish* III 485–6) Every item of these [shall the householder have] without borrowing; a grinding stone, a bill-hook, a hatchet .. a spear for killing cattle, an ever-living fire, a candle upon a candelabrum. late 12th c. BARTHOLOMEW OF EXETER *Penitential* (*Rel. Ant.* I 286) Whosoever .. shall

forbid the carrying away of fire or aught
else from his house, lest the young of
his beasts perish [shall do penance].
1486 SPRENGER & KRAMER *Malleus Maleficarum* (tr. Summers, 163) When they
perform this experiment [to discover a
witch] they take great care that the door
is securely locked; because the witch is
compelled by her pains to try to enter
the house, and if she can take a coal
from the fire, all her pains will disappear.
1586 CAMDEN *Britannia* (tr. Gibson, II
380) [Limerick, Eire, c.1566] They take
any one for a witch that comes to fetch
fire on May-day, and therefore refuse to
give any, unless the party asking it be
sick; and then it is with an imprecation;
believing, that all their butter will be
stolen the following summer by this
woman. If they never lend fire to their
neighbours, they imagine it adds to their
horses length of life and health. **1612**
HOSPINIAN *De Origine Fest. Christ.* 32. In
Rome .. at New Year .. no one would
allow a neighbour to take fire out of his
house, nor anything made of iron, nor
lend anything. **1647** HERRICK *Noble
Numbers* 32 'New-Yeeres Gift'. Cast Holy
Water all about, And have a care no fire
gos out. **1744** WALDRON *Isle of Man* 14.
Not a Family in the whole Island, to this
day, of the Natives but keeps a small
Quantity [of fire] continually burning,
no one daring to depend on his Neighbour's Vigilance in a Thing which he
imagines is of so much consequence:
every one confidently believing, that if
it should ever happen that no Fire were
to be found throughout, most terrible
Revolutions and Mischiefs would immediately ensue. **1811** *Gents Mag.* pt. 1
424 [Yorks.] From the journal of a
deceased friend. 'Those who have not
the common materials of making a fire,
generally sit without one, on New Year's
Day; for none of their neighbours, although hospitable at other times, will
suffer them to light a candle at their
fires. If they do, they say that some one
of the family will die within the year.'
1821 T. D. FOSBROKE *Ariconensia* 59
[Ross-on-Wye, Herefords.] Old Christmas Day. No person must borrow fire,
but purchase it, with some trifle or other,
for instance, a pin. The restriction ..
lasts during the twelve days. **1851**

N & Q 1st ser. III 56 [Lancs.] If any party
allow another a live coal, or even a
lighted candle [on New Year's Eve] the
bad luck is extended to the other party
for commiserating with the former in
his misfortunes. **1852** W. R. WILDE *Irish
Superstitions* 55. On no account would
fire or water—but, above all things, a
coal of fire, even the kindling of a pipe—
be given .. out of a house during the
entire of May Day. **1862** *N & Q* 3rd ser.
II 484 [Pendle, Lancs.] An unlucky old
woman .. having allowed her fire to go
out on New Year's Eve, had to wait until
one o'clock on the following day before
any neighbour would supply her with a
light. **1870** *Bradford Times* 1 Jan. 8.
West Riding Police Court .. He had gone
into the house at Christmas and asked
for a light to his candle. It being a
common superstition that to allow anyone to take out a light at Christmas
is unlucky, the woman of the house
objected, but offered the man a few
matches. He then created a disturbance,
and on the husband attempting to eject
him he broke the window. **1877** *N & Q*
5th ser. VII 86. I have just heard of a
London woman going to take a light
from the fire of an Irish neighbour, in
whose room lay a sick child, and who
was sternly and peremptorily repulsed,
under the idea that to take a portion of
the light away would take from the life
of the child. **1883** BURNE *Shropshire* 401.
A fall of snow from the hill-side .. which
in 1772 buried a cottage at the foot of
the Longmynd and caused some loss of
life .. was ascribed, according to the
yet-remembered tradition, to fire having
been given out of the house during the
tabooed season .. Many people would
rather see their neighbours 'starve' than
give them a live coal till after Old Twelfth
Day. **1885** *Folklore* 309 [Macduff,
Banff.] It is accounted unlucky to give
fire out of the house, so much so that
one would not enter a house, and light
his pipe at the fire, and walk out. Luck
would leave the house. **1887** 'SPERANZA'
WILDE *Superstitions of Ireland* I 225–6. It
is unlucky and a bad omen to carry fire
out of a house where any one is ill. Ibid.
II 102. It is unlucky to give a coal of fire
out of the house before the child is
baptized. **1910** *Folklore* 224. At Con-

iston [Lancs.] it is believed that no light should be taken outside the house from Christmas Eve to the New Year, and that, for the same period, the ash-pit under the kitchen fire must not be emptied lest a death should follow speedily. **1930** P. F. ANSON *East Coast of Scotland* 42. On New Year's Day no fire was ever allowed to be taken out of a house.

FIRE not to die out on certain days

*c.***1816** Wilkie MS (HENDERSON *Northern Counties* 1866, 54) New Year's Eve is one of the nights on which it is deemed highly unlucky .. to let the fire out, the others being All Hallowe'en, Beltane or Midsummer Eve, and Christmas Eve .. No one is willing on the following morning to give his neighbour a light, lest he should thus give away all his good luck for the season. **1887** 'SPERANZA' WILDE *Superstitions of Ireland* I 201. If the fire goes out on May morning it is considered very unlucky, and it cannot be re-kindled except by a lighted sod brought from the priest's house. And the ashes of this blessed turf are afterwards sprinkled on the floor and the threshold of the house. **1964** *Yorkshire Post* 31 Dec. 4. It is .. considered bad luck to let your fire die out on New Year's Eve and some folk even go to the extent of leaving their ashes in the grates until Jan. 2.

Cf. CHRISTMAS LOG/ASHEN FAGGOT: piece kept for luck/protection.

FIRE, poking: as defensive measure

1912 LEATHER *Herefordshire* 86. If you go to see a neighbour and find that she is poking the fire as you enter, it is a sign that you are not welcome. She may pretend to be glad to see you, 'but that's no difference.' **1923** [Trowbridge, Wilts.] While you have an iron poker in your fire a witch cannot harm you.

Cf. IRON deters evil.

FIRE, poking: divination

1738 SWIFT *Polite Conversation* I 16. Good Miss, stir the Fire, that the Tea-Kettle may boil. —— You have done it very well; now it burns purely. Well, Miss, you'll have a chearful Husband. **1755** *Connoisseur* 13 Mar. The youngest Miss will let nobody use the poker but herself; because, when she stirs the fire

it always burns bright, which is a sign that she will have a brisk husband. **1851** *N & Q* 1st ser. III 55 [Lancs.] A young person frequently stirs the fire with the poker to test the humour of a lover. If the fire blaze brightly, the lover is good-humoured; and vice versa. **1862** *N & Q* 3rd ser. II 484 [Lancs.] My maid, who comes from the weird neighbourhood of Pendle, informs me that she has often heard girls say, on poking the fire, 'My sweetheart's coming,' if it burnt brightly. **1895** S. O. ADDY *Household Tales* 97 [Yorks.] If one stirs up the fire and it burns brightly another may say, 'Your spark's bright to-night,' meaning that your lover is in a good humour.

FIRE, poking someone else's

1880 *N & Q* 4th ser. I 55. You must be a seven years' friend of the house before you dare stir the fire. **1923** [West Malling, Kent] It is unlucky for a visitor to replenish or stir the fire unless he has known his host for seven years. **1938** *N & Q* CLXXIV 103. One is still admonished that one should not ask any one to poke one's fire whom one has not known for seven years. Ibid. 142 [*c.*1870] You mustn't poke your neighbour's fire until you have known him seven years or been drunk with him three times.

FIRE protects cattle and crops/brings luck

1496 H. PARKER *Dives & Pauper* 1st com. xxxiv. All that .. use nyce obseruaunces .. in the newe yere as .. ledynge of the ploughe aboute the fyre .. that they sholde fare the better all the yere folowynge. **1546** P. VERGIL *De Rerum Inventoribus* V vii (tr. Langley) Oure Midsomer bonefyres may seme to haue comme of the sacrifices of Ceres goddese of corne, that menne did solemnise with fyres, trusting therby to haue more plenty and abundance of corne. **1775** L. SHAW *History of Moray* 241. On that day [1 May] several herds met together; Every one had two eggs, and a bannock .. They raised a pile of dry wood .. on a hillock, and striking Fire with a flint they kindled the pile; Then they made the Deas-Soil thrice round the Fire; after which they roasted their eggs, and eat them with a part of the bread. The rest of the bread they brought home, to be eaten by the family .. On Mid-Summer Eve, they kindle Fires near their Corn Fields, and walk round them with burning torches. The like [at Hallow Eve] as a thanksgiving for the safe in-gathering of the produce of the fields. 1821 T. D. FOSBROKE *Ariconensia* 60 [Ross-on-Wye, Herefords.] On Twelfth Day .. they make twelve Fires of straw, one large one to burn the old witch. They sing, drink and dance around it. Without this festival, they think that they should have no crop. 1825 T. C. CROKER *Fairy Legends of S. Ireland* I 308. 'Mi na Beal-tine'. The ceremony practised on May-eve, of making the cows leap over lighted straw or faggots .. is now vulgarly used in order to save the milk from being pilfered by 'the good people'. 1887 F. T. HAVERGAL *Herefordshire Words* 48. At Eardisland as late as ten years ago .. on the first of January .. the labouring men and boys .. having tied some bundles of straw together on a high pole, set the straw on fire .. A man then .. runs over twelve lands of growing wheat .. and stops on the thirteenth .. Should the straw cease burning before the man .. reaches the thirteenth ridge of land it would be considered a bad omen for the crops. 1893 *Folklore* 351 [Co. Kerry] Fires were (and are still in a less degree) lighted all over the country on St John's Eve, especially little fires across the road; if you drove through them, it brought you luck for the year. Cattle were also driven through the fires. Ibid. 359 [Beal-adangan, Co. Galway] Part of the ashes, from the bonfire on the 24th June, is thrown into the sown fields to make their produce abundant.

Cf. WASSAILING cornfields and cattle.

FIRE protects child

late 12th c. BARTHOLOMEW OF EXETER *Penitential* (*Rel. Ant.*, I 286) Fire brought into the house to prevent a foetus from dying. 1594 MORESIN *Papatus* 72 [NE Scotland] They take .. on their return from church the newly-baptised infant, and vibrate it three or four times gently over a flame, saying, and repeating it thrice, 'Let the flame consume thee now or never.' 1768 A. ROSS *Fortunate Shepherdess* 6. A burning coal with the hett

tangs was ta'en, Frae out the ingle mids, well brunt an' clean, An' thro' the corsy-belly [infant's first shirt] letten fa', For fear the wean should be ta'en awa'. 1776 PENNANT *Tour in Scotland* 46. After baptism, the father .. placed a basket, filled with bread and cheese, on the pot-hook that impended over the fire in the middle of the room .. and the child is thrice handed across the fire, with the design to frustrate all attempts of evil spirits. 1793 *Stat. Acc. of Scotland* V 83 [Logierait, Perth.] When a child was baptised privately, it was not long since customary, to put the child upon a clean basket, having a cloth previously spread over it, with bread and cheese put into the cloth; and thus to move the basket three times successively round the iron crook, which hangs over the fire .. This might be anciently intended to counteract the malignant arts, which witches and evil spirits were imagined to practise against newborn infants. 1883 *N & Q* 6th ser. VII 357. In the west of Co. Cork, some sixty years ago, it was customary, when a woman with a child in her arms was leaving a cottage at night .. for her to say, 'Wait until I put the fire in the bosom of my child'; and taking a portion of turf from the fire, she would quench it in water and place it in the bosom of the child's dress. The fairies were thus deprived of all power over the child, and the mother went home with a full sense of security.

FIRE protects fishing line

1885 *Folklore* 181 [St Combs, Aberdeen.] If, in making ready a line, one with an 'unlucky fit' did find his way into the house, the end of the line was drawn through the fire .. If one reputed as carrying bad luck was met when going to the boat, the fisherman lighted a match .. and threw it after the misfortune-bearer.

FIRE, spitting into

1879 J. NAPIER *West of Scotland* 37. I remember being taught that it was unlucky to spit into the fire. 1886 *Folklore* 12 [Banff.] It is a custom to spit in the fire when the 'girdle' is taken off the fire when the baking of the bread, oaten cakes, is finished. 1982 Woman,

20 [Cleveland, Yorks.] Seven years' bad luck is indicated by spitting onto the hearth stone.

'FIRE' taboo word

1808 JAMIESON *Scottish Dict. Ingle*. Some silly superstition is connected with the use of this term in relation to a kiln. For the fire kindled in it is always called *the ingle*, in the southern parts of Scotland at least. The miller is offended, if it be called *the fire*. 1895 *Folklore* 170 [Isle of Lewis, *c*.1860] The fire taken to the kiln was called augel. Evil be to him who called it fire or who named fire in the kiln. It was considered the next thing to setting it on fire. 1899 *Folklore* 265 [Outer Hebrides] The fire of a kiln is spoken of as *aingeal*, not by the more obvious name of *teine*. The fire . . is a dangerous thing and should not be talked of except by a euphemism. One man said he always blessed the kiln before leaving it, but should feel even then no security if he called the fire *teine*.

FIRE, two people making

1883 BURNE *Shropshire* 275. It is very unlucky for two persons to kindle a fire, as they will inevitably quarrel. 1981 *Woman*, 20 [S. England] Two women laying a fire was the sign of a quarrel— probably explained by the fact that two women working together get in each other's way, and will in all likelihood quarrel.

FIRE HOOK OR CROOK, vibrating

1787 GROSE *Provincial Glossary* Superstitions 71. When a maid takes the pot off the fire, she sets it down in great haste, and with her hands stops the pot-hooks from vibrating; believing that our lady greeteth (that is, weepeth) all the time the pot-hooks are in motion. *c*.1816 Wilkie MS (HENDERSON *Northern Counties* 1866, 219–20) It is deemed wrong and foolish ever to wag the crook [iron hook in the chimney to hold pots] . . Mr Wilkie . . has seen a visitor . . leave the house, because one of the boys of the family idly swung the crook: she was so horrified at this 'invokerie' that she declared 'she wad na abide in the house where it was practised.'

FIRE TONGS fall

1899 J. SHAW *Schoolmaster* 32 [Tynron, Dumfries.] The tongs falling head foremost into the ash-pit is a sign that a stranger is coming.

FIRE TONGS on table

1923 [Trowbridge, Wilts.] It is held to be unlucky if the firetongs are placed upon the table. It is to be imagined that would be the case in any well-conducted household.

FIRE TONGS, treading on

1809 A. EDMONSTON *Zetland Islands* II 73–4. If a man tread on the tongs in the morning . . he need not go to the fishing that day.

FIRE TONGS turned for luck

1913 E. M. WRIGHT *Rustic Speech* 226 [Northumb.] If a person is setting out on a journey, one of the family sometimes turns the fire-tongs for luck.

FIREWOOD: faggot band

1830 FORBY *East Anglia* 415. You must never burn the withes (or bands) of the faggots. 1933 *Sussex County Mag.* 210. When bread was baked by the Sussex cottage wife . . the 'withe' or band of the faggot used to heat the brick oven must not be burnt or the oven would not get hot.

FIRST ANIMALS in spring: facing observer

1826 R. CHAMBERS *Popular Rhymes of Scotland* 284 n. In the Highlands, it is reckoned lucky to see a foal, calf, or lamb, for the first time, with the head towards the observer. 1832 *Gents Mag.* pt. 2 493 [Lincs.] If the tail of the first lamb you see in the spring be towards you, it denotes misfortune; if otherwise, good luck throughout the year. 1852 *N & Q* 1st ser. V 293. It is . . considered lucky if you see the *head* of the first lamb in spring . . his *tail* is the certain harbinger of misfortune. 1888 *Bye-Gones* 125–6 [Shrops.] It used to be— and I believe . . is still—considered unlucky, if when you saw the first lamb or calf of the season its hinder part were towards you. It was supposed to be a sign that your progress would be reversewards for the whole of the following year . . I remember . . my mother, when the first calf appeared, sending the servant girl to turn its head towards the kit door before she went to see it herself. **1923** [Somerset] A shepherd seeing the first lamb in spring notes whether head or tail is turned towards him. If the former, food will be plentiful during the year and vice versa. **1981** Woman, 63 [Coreley, Shrops.] It was supposed to be dreadfully bad luck to see your first lamb with its back facing to you.

FIRST ANIMALS/BIRDS in spring: divination

1824 MACTAGGART *Gallovidian Encyclopedia* 211. 'Sit and see, the swallow flee, Gang and hear the gowk yell, See the foal afore its minnies e'e, And luck that year will fa' thysell.' Which means, when we are sitting, the first time we see the swallow flying; walking, when we first hear the cuckoo; and the first foal we meet with, if it be before the eyes of its mother, that will be a fortunate year. **1883** BURNE *Shropshire* 215. If you see the cuckoo sitting, The swallow flitting, And a filly foal lying still, You all the year shall have your will. **1899** J. SHAW *Schoolmaster* 31 [Tynron, Dumfries.] Gang and see the swallow flee, Sit and hear the gowk, The foal before its minnie's e'e, And all that year ye've luck.

FIRST DAY of month/moon/year, born on

*c.*1850 *True Fortune Teller* 16. To be born the first day of the new moon, is very fortunate . . they shall have long life and increase of riches. **1923** [Chard, Som.] A child born on New Year's Day is supposed to be very lucky. **1957** Boy, 12 [Somerset] Lucky to have a birthday on the first of the month.

FIRST FRUITS AND FLOWERS

AD **77** PLINY *Natural History* XXVIII v (1856, v 283) Why is it that, when gathering the earliest fruit, apples or pears, as the case may be, we make a point of saying—'This fruit is old, may other fruit be sent us that is new'? **1838** A. E. BRAY *Devonshire* II 295. When the poor get a loaf from the flour of *new* corn, the first who gets it gives a mouthful . . to . . her neighbour, and they fill their

mouths as full as they can in order not to want bread before the harvest comes round again. **1873** *N & Q* 4th ser. XII 44 [Birmingham] Early this spring a farmer in this county, when walking round his fields, saw the first daisy of the year. He immediately went down on his face and bit it off, carefully preserving his mouthful. **1883** W. G. BLACK *Folk-Medicine* 202. To bite the first seen fern that appears in spring off by the ground is said, in Cornwall . . to cure toothache, and prevent its return during the remainder of the year. **1889** *Dorset Field Club* 45. On first eating anything made of new wheat . . fill your mouth full, and you will not want . . during the year. **1911** J. C. DAVIES *Folk-Lore of West and Mid Wales* 218. Wish whenever you get the first taste of the season of any kind of food. **1923** [Taunton, Som.] Wish when you taste the first fruit of the season, and your wish will come true. **1946** UTTLEY *Country Things* 135. Many things discovered for the first time in the year had the property of bestowing a wish . . the first snowdrop we saw . . the first primrose . . the first strawberry we ate. **1953** *Folklore* 295 [Westmorland/ Essex] Wish when eating something for the first time. **1987** Woman, *c.*65 [Isle of Wight] Mm, first plums this year— should wish, I suppose.

FIRST FURROW

*c.*1050 MS Cotton Calig. A. vii (COCKAYNE *Leechdoms* I 405) Let one drive forward the plough and cut the first furrow . . Then take meal of every kind and let one bake a broad loaf, as big as will lie within his two hands, and knead it with milk and with holy water, and lay it under the first furrow. **1881** W. GREGOR *North-East of Scotland* 181. When the plough was 'strykit', i.e., put into the ground for the first time in autumn or spring, to prepare the soil for the seed, bread and cheese, with ale or whisky, were carried to the field, and partaken of by the household. A piece of bread with cheese was put into the plough, and another piece was cast into the field 'to feed the craws'. **1944–5** *Sussex N & Q* 60 [South Harting, Sussex, 1924] An old ploughman was starting his day's work and I saw him drop into his first furrow a portion of his 'levenses'—to be exact a small 'plum heavy' .. The only explanation he could offer was that this action brought luck to the land.

Cf. WASSAILING cornfields.

FIRST PATIENT

1883 w. g. black *Folk-Medicine* 124. A doctor's first patient, people say, is always cured.

FIRST PLOUGH in spring: coming towards one

1879 j. napier *West of Scotland* 136. The first plough in the season .. was lucky if it were seen coming towards the observer, and he or she, in whatever undertaking then engaged, might be certain of success in it; but if seen going from the observer, the omen was reversed. **1899** j. shaw *Schoolmaster* 30 [Tynron, Dumfries.] If you see the plough coming towards you for the first time of the new year, it augers well, but if you observe it going away, it is unlucky.

Cf. FIRST ANIMALS.

FIRST VISIT

1960 [Liverpool] Today I saw a middle-aged woman on her first visit to a new pub spit on her hand and hit the table saying 'Spit on it for a wish!' **1988** Woman, 70. You know the Scottish belief, don't you—that when a person first sets foot in your house they can have a wish. That's from my childhood in Edinburgh. My mother always said it helped to break the ice, if a visitor was shy.

FIRST-BORN

1750 heath *History of Scilly Islands* 128–9. Some few here imagine, (but mostly old Women) that Women with Child, and the First-born, are exempted from the Power of Witchcraft. **1838** a. e. bray *Devonshire* II 300. It is said that no witch, ghost, or pixy can injure the first-born child.

FIRST-FOOT: animal or person first encountered

1303 mannyng *Handlyng Synne* (EETS 119 ll. 363–8) Also yf metyng on þe morwe when þou shalt go to bye or to

borwe; ȝyf þan þy erende spede ne sette, þan wylt þou curse hym þat þou mette. Hyt ys þe tycement of þe deuyl To curse hem þat þoght þe no euyl. *c.*1450 p. idley *Instructions to his Son* (1935, ll. 356–62) Also if oon meete som man on the morowe Goyng to the place wher he hadd hight, Whethir it be to bye, to begge, or to borowe, If he can not spede his erant aright, Than woll he sey, 'I wyte it the foule wight!' And curse hym þat first þat day he mett, Wenyng his metyng were cause of his lett. **1584** scot *Discoverie of Witchcraft* XI xv. He that receiveth a mischance, wil consider whether he met not a cat .. when he went first out of his doores in the morning. **1586** camden *Britannia* (tr. Gibson, II 379) When they [the wild Irish] are upon the road, for robbing, or any other design, they take particular notice who they first meet in the morning, that they may avoid or meet him again, as their luck answers that day. **1776** pennant *Tour in Scotland* 47. They consider the looks of the first person they see. If he has a good countenance, is decently clad, and has a fair reputation, they rejoice in the omen. If the contrary, they proceed with fears, or return home, and begin their journey a second time. **1818** *Edinburgh Magazine* Nov. 412 [Angus] Great attention is paid to the first foot, that is, the first person who happens to meet them [the bride and her escorts, on their way to the church] and if such person does not voluntarily offer to go back with them, they are generally compelled to do so [i.e. they must turn, and accompany the bride to church]. **1842** j. calder *John o' Groats* 224. No one would go on a journey, begin a job, or even run a message without observing who was first-foot—that is, the first individual or animal one met. **1879** j. napier *West of Scotland* 32. The first person .. met [on way to christening] should be lucky .. Forecasts were made from such facts as the following .. Was this person male or female, deformed, disfigured, plain-soled, etc. **1881** w. gregor *North-East of Scotland* 130. In setting out on a journey, to meet a horse as the 'first fit' was accounted a good omen of the success of the journey. **1885** *Folklore*

181. 'The first fit' is always a matter of much weight. In St Combs [Aberdeen.] it used to be the custom to bolt the door when the lines were being baited, in case one with an unlucky foot should enter. **1886** *Folklore* 13 [Banff.] To meet the cat in the morning as the 'first fit' was the sure forerunner of disaster that day. A. R——, of Crovie, did not leave his bed in the morning without calling out 'Hish, hish, hish', to drive away the house cat, lest it might be lying near, and thus be his 'first fit'.

FIRST-FOOT at New Year/Christmas: dark male usually preferred

1805 J. NICHOL *Poems* I 33 n. It is supposed that the welfare and prosperity of every family, especially the fair part of it, depend very much upon the character of the person who is first admitted into the house, on the beginning of the new year. Hence every suspected person is carefully excluded; and the lasses generally engage, beforehand, some favoured youth, who willingly comes, happy in being honoured with that signal mark of female distinction. **1817** G. YOUNG *History of Whitby* II 879 [Christmas Day] No person (boys excepted) must presume to go out of doors till the threshold has been consecrated by the entrance of a male. **1845** J. TRAIN *Isle of Man* II 115. A person of dark complexion always enters first, as a light-haired male or female is deemed unlucky to be a first-foot or quaaltagh on New Year's morning. **1851** *N & Q* 1st ser. III 56 [Lancs.] A red-haired person is supposed to bring in ill-luck if he be the first to enter a house on New Year's Day. Black-haired persons are rewarded with liquor and small gratuities for 'taking in the new year' to the principal houses in their respective neighbourhoods. **1855** *N & Q* 1st ser. XI 105. There is an ancient custom in Yorkshire .. of having a boy to enter your house *early* on Christmas and New Year's Day; and this boy is called a *lucky bird* .. can you inform me why a black-hair'd boy is generally preferred? **1861** C. C. ROBINSON *Dialect of Leeds* 266. The first-comer, or 'lucky-bird' .. receives bread and cheese and always money. The later comers may or may

not have money given them, but he has this privilege. **1872** H. CULLWICK *Diary* [Shifnal, Shrops.] New Year's Day. Mr Smith the grocer came in the house first this morning—not lucky, for he's got reddish hair. **1883** BURNE *Shropshire* 314 n. A Lilleshall girl said that a light-haired man was the luck-bringer. **1905** G. HOME *Evolution of an English Town* 259 [Pickering, Yorks.] In the villages the custom of 'lucky birds' still survives. The boy who first reaches any house on Christmas morning is called a 'lucky bird', and unless great misfortune is courted some small coin must be given to that boy. **1906** *N & Q* 10th ser. V 94–5 [Bristol and 'some parts of the West'] On the stroke of twelve a light-haired man should enter the house, and, proceeding to each room, wish the inmates a happy new year. Only a light-haired man must do this. **1957** [Yorks., from childhood] 'I'm your lucky bird, Chuck, chuck, chuck. If you don't let me in I'll bring you bad luck.' **1975** Woman, 64 [Sheffield, Yorks.] The first person to enter a house as the New Year came in had to be a male with dark hair. We used to make arrangements for a dark-haired male to come and knock on the door after midnight on New Year's Eve. **1986** Man, 35. In my childhood in Paisley [Renfrew.] we always said the first-foot must be tall, dark, not have flat feet nor his eyebrows meeting in the middle of his brow.

FIRST-FOOT at New Year/Christmas: female unlucky

1804 DUNCOMB *Herefordshire* I 210. On Christmas Day it is deemed an omen of ill fortune .. when a female first enters the house in the morning. **1821** T. D. FOSBROKE *Ariconensia* 58 [Ross-on-Wye, Herefords.] On the first day of the year, it is deemed very unfortunate, for a woman to enter the house first; and therefore an enquiry is mostly made, whether a male has previously been there. **1825** JAMIESON *Scottish Dict.* I 408. The First Fit is of great importance on the morning of the new year. That of a female, is deemed unlucky; there is no objection, however, to that of a man. As women are most apt to attend to these things, the reason of the preference may be, that the approach of a male seems to give a fairer promise of a sweetheart. 1855 *Gents Mag.* pt. 2 384–5 [Shrops./Worcs.] Considered unlucky .. to have a female come into your house the first thing on New Year's morning .. Young lads make 'a good thing of it' by selling their services .. to enter the houses first that morning. 1866 HENDERSON *Northern Counties* 56 n. [W. Riding, Yorks.] Doors are there chained up to prevent females from entering. 1870 KILVERT *Diary* 20 Oct. [Clyro, Brecon.] Hannah Whitney, aged about ninety, told me of the death of her mother who was seized suddenly with putrid fever one New Year's Day. She had risen quite well early in the morning, and was sitting sewing with Hannah, when two girls from a neighbour's house came to the door to ask for horseradish. It was before noon, and the sight of the girls gave her a turn. It was very unlucky .. 'Name of goodness,' she screamed, 'what ails the girls to come about to folk's houses on New Year's Day in the morning? Sure as fate something will happen before twelve months are out.' 1872 H. CULLWICK *Diary* 31 Dec. [London] The churches were open for service & I went into St Clement's, till just before 12. I wouldn't be the first to come in the house in the New Year, as it's bad luck for a woman to be the first. 1875 *N & Q* 5th ser. III 6 [Worcs./Herefords.] At some of the farm-houses, should washing-day chance to fall on the first day of the year, it is either put off, or to make sure, before the women can come, the waggoner's lad is called up early, that he may be let out and let in again. 1959 *Trans. Devon. Ass.* 202. I knew a woman in her fifties who always arranged for a young man, preferably dark .. to call at her house immediately after midnight on New Year's Day .. She told me it would be very unlucky were the first caller in a new year to be female .. She had .. been bred and born in Totnes.

Cf. WOMAN, meeting.

FIRST-FOOT at New Year/Christmas: ritual of gifts

1861 C. C. ROBINSON *Dialect of Leeds* 266. If the duty of 'letting Christmas in' has not fallen to the lot of some other individual, by pre-arrangement, which is generally the case, the lad is admitted, who brings along with him a twig or leaf of evergreen and leaves it behind him, as he is the first-comer, or 'lucky-bird' .. A 'lucky-bird' with red hair, might, by force of circumstance, be allowed to enter, but a girl, or woman, never; and, chiefly for this reason, the door is kept secured till Christmas has been duly 'let in'. 1866 HENDERSON *Northern Counties* 56 [New Year] At Stamfordham [Northumb.] .. the first-foot must be a bachelor. He generally brings in a shovelful of coals, but, unfortunately, whisky is coming into fashion as his offering. 1878 *Holderness* 69 [E. Yorks.] The 'lucky-bod' [lucky-bird] .. brings in a 'clog' or 'chump' of wood, and every 'new year's gifter' does the same. 1885 *Folklore* 282. A relative, who spent the new-years of 1872, 1873, and 1874 at Croxdale, county Durham, tells me that he was employed on each occasion to act as the 'first foot' .. The first foot must always be a man, and .. must bring in with him a piece of coal, a piece of iron, and a bottle of whiskey .. He gives every one in the house a glass of the whiskey and every woman a kiss besides .. [He] was sent out of the house late on new-year's eve, to return just after midnight and go through this ceremony. 1901 E. GUTCH *County Folk-Lore II: Yorkshire* 230–1 n. Here and there in the North Riding people not only require the visitor to be dark-haired, but exact that he shall carry something dark in his hand, e.g. a piece of coal or a dark green sprig, 'never variegated holly'. 1940 F. KITCHEN *Brother to the Ox* XV [Worksop, Notts., 1930] I begin the new year by taking a log of wood into the farm-house kitchen. This is my duty at about five-thirty every New Year's morning, and it is supposed to bring good luck to the farm during the coming year. Fortunately I am the darkest-haired person on the farm, and, for the charm to be successful, it is essential that the person who lets in the new year shall have dark hair. 1954 Boy, 14 [Forfar, Angus] You are not supposed to go into the house empty-handed. Some of the gifts are a herring or a piece of coal. 1957 Girl, 12 [Canonbie, Dumfries.] If somebody who is fair-haired comes to your door first-footing, carrying a piece of coal, it will bring you a very happy new year. **1968** *Observer* Suppl. 24 Nov. 10 [Trawler skipper, Staithes, Yorks.] At New Year the first-footer had to go out and bring in a piece of coal—it was black for good luck. **1969** A. BARTON *Penny World* 145 [Jarrow, Co. Durham, 1925] That was the time for bringing in—beginning .. at midnight, when the dark-haired first-foot would give his ritual knock and enter with gifts of coal and bread and salt. **1970** J. MCPHEE *Crofter and Laird* 9 [Colonsay, Hebrides] If the first-footing is done by a fair-haired person, that is all right as long as a lump of coal or some other dark object is thrown across the threshold first. **1978** A. WRIGHT *Holderness* 6 [E. Yorks.] Outside each back door a piece of coal or a bundle of sticks, a silver coin, a sprig of evergreen and a piece of bread were placed. As midnight struck .. the Lucky Bod came to call .. He carried the coal, the coin, the evergreen and the bread inside, and wished everyone a Happy New Year. The explanation given for this locally is that the bringing in of the coal would guarantee the household warmth for the year, the silver—wealth, the evergreen—good luck, and the bread—food. Nothing which the Lucky Bod brought in was to be taken out of the house again, although the coin could be spent after a year had passed. **1982** *Woman*, *c.*55 [Tyneside] On New Year's Eve, the lady of the house puts out on the front doorstep a piece of coal, a piece of silver, and a piece of bread, and the first-footer, which is a dark gentleman, brings those in with him and presents them to the lady of the house. The silver coin that she never wants for money, the coal that she never needs a fire, and the bread that she never goes hungry.

Cf. NEW YEAR and house/home.

FIRST-FOOT on occasion of wedding

1885 *Folklore* 311 [Macduff, Banff.] When the bridegroom goes to meet the bride to have the marriage celebrated, he has to give money to the first one he meets, no matter of what rank. When the marriage-party is going to the new home after the celebration .. it is the bride that gives the money to the 'first fit'. My informant told me he did this himself. **1900** S. HEWETT *Nummits* 23 [Devon] The bride .. should .. carry a small packet of bread and cheese in her pocket to give to the first woman or girl she meets after leaving the church.

FIRST-FOOT on way to christening

1813 BRAND *Antiquities* II 15. It is customary [in Northumberland] for the Midwife, &c., to provide two slices, one of bread and the other of cheese, which are presented to the first person they meet in the procession to Church at a Christening. The person who receives this homely present must give the Child in return three different things, wishing it at the same time health and beauty. The gentleman who informed me of this, happening once to fall in the way of such a party, and to receive the above present, was at a loss how to make the triple return, till he bethought himself of laying upon the Child which was held out to him, a Shilling, a Halfpenny, and a Pinch of Snuff. **1821** T. D. FOSBROKE *Ariconensia* 57–8. In the north of England it is customary, when a child is taken to church to be christened, to engage a little boy to meet the infant, upon leaving the house, because it is deemed an unlucky omen to encounter a female first, for which service the boy receives a small present of a cake and Cheese, wrapped in paper. **1852** DENHAM *North of England* (1895, 43) A few families still adopt the practice of taking a slice of the Christening Cake along with them .. and making an offering of it to the first person they meet. Should this be a man, they say that the next child born in the village will be a male! if a woman, it will be a female! **1857** *N & Q* 2nd ser. III 59 [Glasgow] The custom .. of persons when carrying infants to church for baptism, taking .. bread and cheese to be given to the first individual met, is not yet gone into disuse. One Sunday forenoon, about two years ago .. I saw the practice carried out .. A silver coin was given in return for the eatables. I was told that .. copper in such transactions was .. to be avoided. **1879** J. NAPIER *West of Scotland* 32. When the baby was being carried to church .. the woman appointed to this post .. took with her a parcel of bread and cheese, which she gave to the first person she met .. If the party accepted the gift willingly .. this was a good sign .. but should this person refuse the gift .. this was tantamount to wishing evil to the child, and should any serious calamity befall the child, even years after, it was connected with this circumstance. 1887 *Folk-Lore Record* 209 [Cornwall] I well recollect seeing the old nurse wrap in a pure white sheet of paper what she called the 'cheeld's fuggan' [*fuggan*, a flat cake]. It happened that .. no one was met until near home .. when a tipsy village carpenter rambled round a corner .. and received the cake. Regrets were expressed that the 'cheeld's fuggan' should have fallen to the lot of this notoriously evil liver. 1943 *Folklore* 308 [Dundee, Angus] When a woman is carrying a child to church to the christening she takes a bag of cake etc., and gives it to the first person she meets of the opposite sex to the child. The receiver gives back a luck coin. Great good-luck is given and received. 1956 *Sunday Post* 2 Dec. 6 [Thornton, Fife] When a child is christened in our village, it's the custom for the godmother to give the first person she meets outside the church a piece of the christening cake. 1978 T. CALLAGHAN *Lang Way to the Panshop* 24 [Newcastle upon Tyne, 1930s] When we came out of Sunday school we always did the christening rounds .. It was the custom .. to hand out to some passing individual the 'christening', which was a small package usually containing a portion of cake, and a scone with a silver threepence or sixpence, wrapped up in a small piece of tissue-paper inside it. In practice, the couple gave it to the first kiddy they met near the church, and as my brother and I patrolled all the local churches, our chances were always high.

Cf. BABY, gifts to: on first visit.

FIRST-FOOT when making fishing line
1886 *Folklore* 12 [Banff.] In Portessie, Buckie, and other villages, the first one that enters the house when a 'greatlin'—a great line .. for catching cod,

ling, skate, and the larger kinds of fish— is being made, has to pay for a mutchkin of whiskey, which is drunk in the house after the line is finished .. The first glassful is poured over the line.

first-foot: also see FOOT = lucky/unlucky person.

FISH, live

1852 H. MILLER *My Schools and Schoolmasters* 106. I saw him administer to an ailing cow a little live trout, simply because the tradition of the district [Loch Shin, Sutherland] assured him that [this] was the only specific in the case. 1866 HENDERSON *Northern Counties* 110 [Stamfordham, Northumb.] Several cures for whooping-cough are practised in this village .. such as putting a trout's head into the mouth of the sufferer and .. letting the trout breathe into the child's mouth. Ibid. 122 [Stainsby Beck, N. Yorks.] A peasant came along the stream in search of a 'wick' [live] trout, to lay on the stomach of one of his children who was much troubled with worms. 1878 *N & Q* 5th ser. IX 64–5. An old fisherman, formerly well known at the Forge, Keswick, once caught a fish, which he put into the mouth of a child suffering from whooping cough. He then replaced the fish in the Greta. He affirmed that the fish, after being placed in the mouth of the child and returned to the river, gave the complaint to the rest of its kind, as was evident from the fact that they came to the top to cough. 1879 *Folk-Lore Record* 205 [Weardale, Co. Durham] To cure worms, a trout is to be obtained and placed alive upon the bowels of the patient, and bound with a bandage, and kept there all night. The writer remembers this being done to a boy about seven years old about the year 1830. 1883 BURNE *Shropshire* 204. Drinking beer in which a live fish has been drowned [is] said to have been .. prescribed [for whooping-cough]. 1922 R. KEARTON *At Home with Wild Nature* 59. In the West of England a drink of cow's milk, in which a live trout had been made to swim, used to be regarded as an infallible cure for whooping cough. 1932 WOMEN'S INSTITUTE *Worcestershire Book* 37 [Mamble-cum-Bayton] An old

Bayton woman had this remedy for whooping cough: Take a pie dish full of cider to the River Rea and catch a decent sized trout and drown him in the cider, take it back carefully. Fry the trout and make the patient eat the fish and drink the cider.

FISHING: first catch
1886 *Folklore* 14. 'W.W.' of Crovie [Banff.], had gone to the West Highlands to prosecute the cod and ling fishing. The first time the boat went to the fishing-ground the first fish that came up on the line was a ling. The skipper at once ordered it to be thrown overboard, as being unlucky to have a ling for the first fish caught. [The ling is considered inferior to the cod.]
Cf. SALMON unlucky first catch.

FISHING: fish scales not to be cleaned off
1885 *Folklore* 308 [Aberdeen.] During the herring fishing the scales of the fish must not be washed off the boat, neither must they be cleaned off the fishermen's sea-boots. If this is done good luck flees away.
Cf. FOOD: giving away potentially dangerous.

FISHING HOOK: first baited
1886 *Folklore* 12 [Banff.] The first hook baited is spit upon, and then laid in the scull.

FISHING LINE, baiting
1939 *Folklore* 345 [NE coast of Scotland] If any one came in while the line was being baited, the person at work got up while the other took his place and put bait on a few of the hooks. On laying down the line he expressed a wish for the success of the fishing. He was thus associated with the success of the fishing and could not impart an evil influence.
Cf. BUTTER, stranger helps to churn; CHRISTMAS PUDDING, stirring.

FISHING LINE etc., walking over
late 18th c. J. RAMSAY (*Scotland in the Eighteenth Century* II 456) If the sportsman saw any person stepping over his gun or fishing-rod, he presumed but little on that day's diversion. 1875 *N & Q* 5th ser. III 204 [Flamborough,

Yorks.] It is still considered very unlucky for a woman to walk over the nets or any of the fishing tackle. 1878 A. MACGREGOR *Brahan Seer* 129 'Superstitions of Highlanders'. It is unlucky if a stranger walks across a parcel of fishing-rods . . over ropes, oars, or sailing gear, when a ship is about to go to sea. Means are used to get the stranger to retrace his steps. 1889 *Folklore* 44 [Advie, Moray.] It is unlucky to tread on the line. 1939 *Folklore* 344 [Fishermen in NE and W. of Scotland, and Isle of Lewis] No one was permitted to step over a line; both men and women must lift the line and pass under or go round, the owner alone was free to pass over.

FISHING LINE, making
1886 *Folklore* 12 [Crovie, Banff.] When a new line was to be made by a few neighbours, it had to be begun . . and finished without any interruption.

FLOWERS in pairs: divination
1827 HONE *Table Book* I 856–7. There is a love custom still observed in the village of Sutton Bangor, Wilts. Two flowers that have not blossomed are paired, and put by themselves—as many pairs as there are sweethearts in the neighbourhood, and tall and short as the respective sweethearts are. The initials of their names are attached to the stamens, and they are ranged in order in a hayloft or stable, in perfect secrecy, except to those who manage and watch their ominous growth. If, after ten days, any flower twines the other, it is settled as a match; if any flower turns a contrary way, it indicates a want of affection; if any flower blossoms, it denotes early offspring; if any flower dies suddenly, it is a token of the party's death; if any flower wears a downcast appearance, sickness is indicated. True it is that flowers, from their very nature, assume all these positions; and in the situation described, their influence upon villagers is considerable.
Cf. ORPINE: divination.

FLOWERS, picking up
c.1915 [Eastbourne, Sussex] Don't pick up flowers you find lying in the road-

way—'Pick up flowers, pick up sickness.'
1947 Girl, 11 [Aldeburgh, Suffolk] If
you see a flower someone has picked
and then dropped never pick it up as it
will mean a death in the family. **1979**
R. GAMBLE *Chelsea Child* 94 [refers to
1920s] It was not a rare occurrence,
particularly near the stall at the top of
our street or in the Fulham market, to
see a cut flower lying on the ground,
and if one of the younger children went
to touch it, the rest of us dragged him
back gasping 'pick up a flower, pick up a
fever!' **1983** Woman, *c.*20 [Colchester,
Essex] Pick up a flower, pick up sorrow.

FLOWERS: red and white together
1896 *'Sunlight' Almanac* 333. 'Dreams
and their Significations'. *Flowers*. If only
red and white they are omens of death.
1953 My niece, nursing at St Mary's
Hospital, Paddington, said that if a patient were given a bunch of red and
white flowers mixed together, it was
regarded as a sign of death, and the two
colours were served up to the patient
separately. **1954** Girl, 12 [Forfar,
Angus] My friend's aunt put red and
white flowers together and the next day
she was killed on her cycle. **1955** *Sunday
Times* 6 Mar. 2. I knew red and white
flowers were regarded as unlucky—my
mother always used to add another
colour to a bowl. **1963** *Daily Telegraph*
6 Nov. 14. When I was ordering flowers
for a hospital patient the salesgirl was
quite horrified when I suggested the
inclusion of red and white dahlias: one
or other of the colours was all right, but
not both. **1978** *Folklore* 158 [Dorset] My
grandmother had never allowed vases of
white and red flowers in her house as
she believed that these would bring
death. **1986** Clergyman's widow, *c.*80.
In the Furness area of Cumbria there
was a strong feeling about mixing red
and white flowers. A bride has often
asked me to see that red and white are
not used in church on her wedding day.
    Cf. RED FLOWERS unlucky.

FLOWERS: taking home from hospital
1955 Nursing aide, 53 [Oxted, Surrey]
If patients take home flowers that have
been brought in to them, they'll soon
be back again—once more as patients.

1984 [London] My daughter had some
beautiful flowers sent her, and I suggested she should take them home with
her when she left hospital the next
day. But another visitor said no, on no
account—it would be very bad luck.

FLY in drink
1855 *N & Q* 1st ser. XII 488 [Greenock,
Renfrew.] Amongst our deep sea fishermen .. if a fly falls into the glass from
which any one has been drinking, or is
about to drink, it is considered a sure
and true omen of good luck to the
drinker. **1898** *Aberdeen Weekly Free
Press* 29 Oct. 3 [Greenock fishermen] If
a fly fell into the glass when one of the
men was about to drink it was an omen
of good luck to him for the day. **1923**
[Wellington, Som.] If a fly falls into your
cup of tea it brings good luck.

FLY, last
1948 Woman, *c.*20 [Millom, Cumb.]
The last fly of winter has a special magic
value. **1960** *Folklore* 255 [Hartlepool,
Co. Durham] Is there anywhere else in
England where it is thought to be the
height of good luck to have an ordinary
house-fly hovering around the house
between Christmas and New Year?
1960 [Oban, Argyll.] In December she
had a fly in her kitchen. It was annoying
her and landing on everything. But she
would not kill it. A solitary fly at that
time of year was, she said, a stranger
come to help her and she could not kill
it as this would bring bad luck. **1970**
Sussex Express 9 Jan. 10. We had a
perky 'lucky Christmas fly' in the kitchen
on both Christmas and Boxing Days, but
yesterday I found it dead on the window
ledge. Bad luck for the fly, but the cottage
has had its blessing. **1987** Woman, 59
[NE England] My father always called
the odd fly still hovering around in the
winter 'Poppy', and seemed to regard it
with affection. It was never pursued and
killed.

FOOD, dropping
AD **77** PLINY *Natural History* XXVIII v
(1856, V 285) When food fell from the
hand of a guest .. auguries .. have been
derived from the words or thoughts of a
person at the moment such an accident

befalls him. **9th** or **10th c.** Solomon and Saturn II (*Anglo-Saxon Poetic Records* VI, ed. E. van Kirk Dobbie 45 ll. 403–5) When a morsel slips away from a wise man he .. bends down after it, blesses and flavours it and eats it himself. **1787** GROSE *Provincial Glossary* Superstitions 62. If, in eating, you miss your mouth, and the victuals fall, it is very unlucky, and denotes approaching sickness. **1923** [Ruishton, Som.] It is unlucky to drop food from your fork on the way to your mouth.

FOOD: giving away potentially dangerous
1886 *Folklore* 15 [Nairn] Some will not give away a 'fry o' herrin'', that is, a few herrings as a dish. The luck of the fishing goes with them. **1895** S. O. ADDY *Household Tales* 99. When a pig is killed, and fry is sent to a neighbour, the dish must not be washed out, or the pig will not take the salt. **1940** F. KITCHEN *Brother to the Ox* II [Yorks.] All the neighbours had pig's fry for dinner .. and a number of children could be seen trotting backwards and forwards carrying pig's fry trapped between two plates. There was one condition to be observed about these plates. They must be returned unwashed, else it would wash away the luck from the pig .. and once when a young girl washed the plates, she not knowing any different, there was no end of a to-do. *c.*1940 [Great Paxton, Hunts.] 'Beastins' is a jug of the first milk after a cow calves, given to friends for making a custard pudding. Bad luck to the cow if the recipient washes the jug before returning it. In the same way, if a cottager kills a pig and a plate of 'fry' is given to special friends the plate must be returned unwashed. **1966** *Farmers Weekly* 18 Nov. 90 [Sleaford, Lincs.] I am now 70 but as a small girl I had the job of delivering [pig's fry] each time my father killed a pig and always with the same request: 'Mother says please don't wash the plate.'

FOOD left out overnight
*c.***600** BC Deuteronomy 16: 2–4. Thou shalt therefore sacrifice .. unto the Lord thy God, of the flock and the herd .. And there shall be no leavened bread ..

neither shall there any thing of the flesh, which thou sacrificedst the first day at even, remain all night until the morning. **1486** SPRENGER & KRAMER *Malleus Maleficarum* (tr. Summers, 193) There was an erroneous belief that when devils came in the night (or the Good People as old women call them, though they are witches, or devils in their forms) they must eat up everything, that afterwards they may bring greater abundance of stores. **1686–7** AUBREY *Remaines* (1881, 29) They were wont to please the Fairies, that they might doe them no shrewd turnes, by sweeping clean the Hearth and setting by it a dish of fair w^r [water] halfe sadd .. bread, wheron was set a messe of milke sopt with white bread. **1923** [Trowbridge, Wilts.] To leave the remains of supper on the table all night is a very unlucky thing to do.

FOOD left unfinished
1955 P. WILDEBLOOD *Against the Law* 172. We sat in the Reception drinking tea and eating porridge. It was part of the prison lore that a man who left his plate of porridge would return some day to finish it.

FOOT = lucky/unlucky person
1486 SPRENGER & KRAMER *Malleus Maleficarum* (tr. Summers, 215) [After the trial] the witch .. should be lifted from the ground by the officers, and carried out in a basket or on a plank of wood so that she cannot again touch the ground .. We know from experience and the confessions of witches that when they are taken in this manner they more often lose the power of keeping silence under examination: indeed many who have been about to be burned have asked that they might be allowed at least to touch the ground with one foot; and when .. asked why .. they have answered that if they had touched the ground they would have liberated themselves, striking many other people dead with lightning. **1685** G. SINCLAIR *Satans Invisible World Discovered* 214 [Highlands] I will not speak of ridiculous Friets, such as our meeting with a Lucky or unlucky foot, when we are going about important business. **1795** *Stat. Acc. of Scotland* XIV 541 [Forglen, Banff.]

There are *happy* and *unhappy feet*. Thus, they wish bridegrooms and brides *a happy foot*; and to prevent any bad effect, they salute those they meet on the road with a kiss. It is hard, however, if any misfortune happens when you are passing, that you should be blamed, when neither you nor your feet ever thought of the matter. Ibid. XV 258 [Monzie, Perth.] The people are .. not entirely free of superstition. *Lucky and unlucky days*, and *feet*, are still attended to, especially about the end and beginning of the year. **1868** QUEEN VICTORIA *Journal of our Life in the Highlands* [Balmoral, 18 Sept. 1858] The sport was successful, and every one was delighted—Macdonald and the keepers in particular; the former saying, 'that it was her Majesty's coming out that had brought the good luck.' I was supposed to have 'a lucky foot', of which the Highlanders 'think a great deal'. **1881** W. GREGOR *North-East of Scotland* 198. It was the custom in each village for an aged experienced man to get up in the morning, and examine the sky, and .. prognosticate the weather for the day. If the weather promised to be good, he went the round of the village to awaken the inmates. In doing this great attention was paid to the 'first fit'. In every village there were more than one to whom was attached the stigma of having an 'ill fit'. Such were dreaded, and shunned, if possible, in setting out on any business .. A man [so] reputed was met with an oath and the words 'Keep aff o' ma boat, ye hiv an ill fit.' **1885** *Folklore* 308 [Macduff, Banff.] If a fisherman meets one that has the reputation of having 'an ill fit', he makes some excuse for turning and walking a few steps with him or her to turn away the ill luck.

FOOT, bare

1180 NIGEL DE LONGCHAMPS *Mirror for Fools* (tr. Mozley, 96–7) A barefoot woman spinning wool black-hued With distaff fashioned from the yew-tree's wood .. may they [his enemies] perceive As they go walking. *c.*1700 (W. PAUL *Aberdeenshire* 18–19) Alex. Thomson, minister of Peterculter .. is guilty of superstitious observances .. saying that he knew some evil would befall that day

that he fell and hurt his leg, for .. he met a barefooted child. **1726** J. KELLY *Proverbs* Intro. It's no Sonsie [lucky] to meet a bare Foot in the Morning. **1775** L. SHAW *History of Moray* pt. 5 232. Upon an expedition, they much regarded Omens .. If a woman barefoot crossed the road before them, they seized her, and fetched blood from her forehead. **1818** *Edinburgh Magazine* Nov. 412 [Angus] A bare-footed woman [is] almost as bad as a witch [when met by a bride on her way to church]. **1820** WASHINGTON IRVING *Sketch Book* II 67 n. The yule clog is still burnt in many farmhouses and kitchens in England, particularly in the north .. If a squinting person come to the house while it is burning, or a person barefooted, it is considered an ill omen. **1864** R. CHAMBERS *Book of Days* II 735. An evil omen was exhibited in the arrival of a barefooted person [when the yule log was burning]. **1869** *N & Q* 4th ser. II 505 [Dublin serving-woman.] It is unlucky to meet .. a barefooted woman early in the morning. Should you meet a woman with bare feet and red hair, turn back in haste, lest some evil thing come upon you.

FOOT, flat

1627 R. BERNARD *Guide to Grand-Jury Men* XIV 183. Dismayed at signes, as .. when they meet with a splay-footed woman. **1825** JAMIESON *Scottish Dict.* Suppl. [Roxburgh.] *Platch*, a plain-soled foot. If you are going on a journey, on Monday morning, and meet a man who has platches .. it is an evil omen .. The only way to prevent the bad effect .. is to return to your own abode, to enter it with the right foot foremost, and to eat and drink. Then you may safely set out again on your journey; the spell being dissolved. **1864** R. CHAMBERS *Book of Days* II 735. An evil omen was exhibited in the arrival of a .. flat-footed woman [when the yule log was burning]. **1879** HENDERSON *Northern Counties* 74. In some districts .. special weight is attached to .. a high-arched instep, a foot that 'water runs under'. A flat-footed person would bring great ill-luck for the coming year. Ibid. 87. It is unlucky on a Monday morning to meet a man with 'schloof', or flat feet. **1880** W. JONES *Credulities* 117. A flat foot in the sand is considered unlucky [by fishermen]. **1892** *Folklore* 79 [Isle of Man] All are agreed that he [the first-foot] must not be *spaagagh* or splay-footed. **1909** *N & Q* 10th ser. XII 483 [Stromness, Orkney] Fishermen count it unlucky to meet a flat-footed person when leaving for the fishing. **1930** P. F. ANSON *Fisher Folk on East Coast of Scotland* 38. It was .. unlucky to meet .. anyone who was flat-footed. **1941** *Folklore* 269 [Isle of Man] The first-foot .. was required to be a dark man of good presence, with insteps high enough to allow a mouse to run under.

FOOT: sole itches

1755 *Connoisseur* 13 Mar. If your foot itches, you will tread strange ground. **1861** C. C. ROBINSON *Dialect of Leeds* 300. When the sole of the foot tickles, you are about to go over strange ground. **1912** LEATHER *Herefordshire* 88. Irritation of the soles of the feet is said to mean that their owner will soon tread strange ground. **1946** UTTLEY *Country Things* 136. I went to the Post Office in the Buckinghamshire town and waited for stamps while the young women behind the counter chattered to one another. 'The sole of my foot is tickling,' said one, 'What does it mean?' 'You will soon walk on foreign soil,' said the other. **1953** Girl, 15 [Loughton, Essex] If your foot itches, you are going to tread on strange soil.

foot: also see FIRST-FOOT.

FRIDAY an unlucky day

1390 CHAUCER Nun's Priest's Tale l. 3341. And on a Friday fil al this meschaunce. **1656** R. FLECKNOE *Diarium* 38. Now Friday came, you old wives say, Of all the week's the unluckiest day. **1727** GAY *Fables* XXXVII. Friday, too! the day I dread! **1795** T. WILKINSON *Wandering Patentee* II 263. A bad benefit [which] she expected .. to rise, not to fall off .. But this said benefit, be it known to all men, was on a Friday, though not a *good* Friday. **1831** HONE *Year Book* 29 Feb. There are still a few respectable tradesmen and merchants who will not transact business, or be bled, or take physic, on a Friday, because it is an unlucky day. **1867** *Gents Mag.* pt. 1 740 [Suffolk] In our rural parishes .. Friday is considered unlucky, as being the day, I suppose, on which our Blessed Saviour suffered on the Cross. **1869** *N & Q* 4th ser. IV 130 [Scarborough, Yorks.] One of the assistants at the bathing-machines assured me that most accidents happened on Fridays, especially Good Fridays.

FRIDAY, beginning anything on

1804 C. SMITH *Conversations on Poetry* I 62. I knew another poor woman, who lost half her time in waiting for lucky days, and made it a rule never to begin any work [or] write a letter on business .. on a Friday—so her business was never done, and her fortune suffered accordingly. **1830** FORBY *East Anglia* 414. Never begin any piece of work on a Friday. **1883** BURNE *Shropshire* 260. I knew an old lady who, if she had nearly completed a piece of needlework on a Thursday, would put it aside unfinished, and set a few stitches in her next undertaking, that she might not be obliged either to begin the new task on Friday or to remain idle for a day. **1885** *Folklore* 180 [Aberdeen.] Fishermen would have great misgivings about laying the keel of a new boat on Friday, as well as launching one on that day. **1909** *N & Q* 10th ser. XII 484 [Stromness, Orkney] It is unlucky to start a new piece of work on Friday: 'A crow would not carry a straw to its nest on Friday.' **1924** J. A. EGGAR *Remembrances* 148 [Binstead, Hants.] My father would never begin harvest on a Friday. **1933** A. G. STREET *Country Days* 42. My father once decided to start harvest on a Friday, and the men went out on the Thursday evening, and, unpaid, cut along one side of the first field with their scythes, in order to dodge the malign fate which a Friday start would begin. **1953** Girl, 15 [Knighton, Radnor.] They say if you start anything on a Friday it will come to no good. **1968** L. BECKWITH *A Rope—in Case* 156 [Bruach, Hebrides] Never cast on knittin' on Fridays or you'll not finish it.

FRIDAY, beginning journey on

1804 C. SMITH *Conversations on Poetry* I
62. I knew another poor woman, who
. . made it a rule never to . . set out on
a journey on a Friday. 1855 *Gents Mag.*
pt. 2 384–5 [Shrops./Worcs.] Considered unlucky . . to go a journey on a
Friday. 1865 SURTEES *Mr Facey
Romford's Hounds* LX. Friday is generally
considered an unlucky day; at all events
a day that people do not generally choose
for their pleasure expeditions. 1890 MRS
HENRY WOOD *Johnny Ludlow* 4th ser. 343
[Worcs.] We took the train at Evesham.
It was Friday . . Some people do not care
to begin a journey on a Friday, thinking
it bodes ill-luck: I might have thought
the same had I foreseen what was to
happen before we got home again. 1946
UTTLEY *Country Things* 128 [Cromford,
Derbys., *c.*1900] Many people refused to
start a journey on Friday, but Friday
was market-day, and we took no notice
of this.

FRIDAY, beginning voyage on

1823 *Gents Mag.* pt. I 17 [Ipswich,
Suffolk] Sailors are many of them very
superstitious . . A voyage begun [on a
Friday] is sure to be an unfortunate one.
1838 *Wilson's Tales of Borders* IV 142.
Never say 'die' . . we'll weather many a
Friday's sailing yet. 1857 *N & Q* 2nd
ser. IV 432 [Norfolk] Notwithstanding
the prejudice against sailing on a Friday
. . most of the pleasure-boats . . make
their first voyage for the season on Good
Friday. 1885 *Folklore* 180 [Aberdeen.]
Sailors do not like to sail on Friday.
1890 MRS HENRY WOOD *Johnny Ludlow*
4th ser. 232. Sailors are more foolish on
this point than you can imagine: and I
believe . . that ships, sailing on a Friday,
have come to grief through their crew
losing heart. No matter what impediment is met with—bad weather,
accidents, what not—the men say at
once it's of no use, we sailed on a Friday.
1924 *Folklore* 347 [Westleton, Suffolk]
The fishermen say: 'A Friday's sail,
Always fail.'

FRIDAY, born on

1846 DENHAM *Proverbs* 11 n. A child
born on a Friday is doomed to misfortune. 1870 *N & Q* 4th ser. VI 211

[Walton-le-Dale, Lancs., *c.*1820] It was
accounted unlucky for a child to be born
on a Friday, unless it happened to be
Good Friday, when the untowardness of
the event was counterbalanced by the
sanctity of the day. 1967 S. MARSHALL
Fenland Chronicle pt. I XIII. The old song
says: 'Never be born on a Friday, Choose
some other day if you can.'
   Also see BIRTH, day of: divination
rhyme.

FRIDAY butter and eggs

1923 [Trowbridge, Wilts.] Harm will
come to the child if you put Friday
churned butter, or Friday laid eggs into
its christening cake.

FRIDAY, courting on

1851 *N & Q* 1st ser. III 516 [Lancs.] A
man must never 'go a courting' on a
Friday. If an unlucky fellow is caught
. . he is followed home by a band of
musicians playing on pokers, tongs,
pan-lids, &c. 1890 T. C. SMITH & J. SHORTT
History of Ribchester 75 [Lancs.] No
'chap' might meet his 'woman' on a
Friday evening. That was 'jinglin neet'.
If he did, he would be sure to set all the
old frying pans and kettles in motion, as
if a thousand bees were aswarm. 1901
P. H. DITCHFIELD *Old English Customs* 199
[Lancs.] Friday evening is not considered
a correct or suitable time for courtship.
The first person spying a couple so
engaged enters the house, seizes the
frying-pan, and beats on it a tattoo. This
arouses the neighbours, who give a
warm reception to the offending couple
if they do not withdraw hurriedly. 1957
Man, *c.*80 [Burford, Oxon.] Never court
on a Friday or you'll never meet again.

FRIDAY, getting married on

1795 *Stat. Acc. of Scotland* XIV 541 n.
[Forglen, Banff.] Few would choose to
be married here on Friday, though it is
the ordinary day in other quarters. 1829
BROCKETT *North Country Words* I 178.
This day is viewed as one of ill omen,
on which no new work or enterprise
must be begun. Marriages, I believe,
seldom happen on it, from this cause.
1870 *N & Q* 4th ser. V 74. The
Registrar-General of England, in his last
report, says . . 'Women will not wed on

a Friday so willingly as on other days of the week.' **1879** HENDERSON *Northern Counties* 33. As to Friday, a couple married on that day are doomed to a cat-and-dog life. **1923** [Bridgwater, Som.] It is very unlucky to be married on a Friday.

FRIDAY, getting up after illness on
1923 [Taunton, Som.] If you have been ill, don't get up for the first time on Friday.

FRIDAY, hearing news on
1883 BURNE *Shropshire* 260. If you hear anything new on a Friday, it gives you another wrinkle on your face, and adds a year to your age.

FRIDAY, moving to new home on
1900 *Scotsman* 6 Sept. 7. A few days ago Mr H. MacPherson, Inspector of Poor, visited Aharacle in order to superintend the removal of the ten selected female paupers to the new cottages. They all occupied houses which were in a wretched state of disrepair, yet each of them resolutely .. refused to 'flit' .. The aged dames were invincibly proof against all argument .. threats .. and .. warrants .. At length it was elicited that the disinclination to remove was based simply on superstition. The day of the week happened to be Friday. **1900** *N & Q* 9th ser. VI 273 [Worksop, Notts.] A Friday flit: Never sit! **1972** *Lore and Language* July 7 [Coalisland, Co. Tyrone] Friday's flit's a short sit, Saturday's flit is a shorter sit. **1982** *Woman,* c.55 [Stockton-on-Tees, Co. Durham] Don't move house on a Friday or you won't stay there very long.

FRIDAY, moving to new job on
c.**1797** H. MORE *Tawney Rachel* 7. Sally had so many unlucky days in her calendar, that a large portion of her time became of little use, because on these days she did not dare set about any new work. And she would have refused the best offer if made to her on a Friday. **1900** *N & Q* 9th ser. VI 454. My wife recently wanted a fresh servant, and advertised for one in a local newspaper. A girl, a native of Devonshire, applied .. and .. was engaged and asked to come on a given date .. a Friday, but the girl positively refused to enter on a new situation on a Friday .. she would 'rather give up the place'. **1923** [Castle Cary, Som.] Servants who go into their situations on Friday, never go to stay. **1953** Girl, 13 [Whitton, Radnor.] It is unlucky to start a new job on a Friday. Maybe this is because Jesus Christ was crucified on a Friday.

FRIDAY THE THIRTEENTH
1913 *N & Q* 11th ser. VIII 434. I have met a 'coach' of fine mental capacities .. who dreaded the evil luck of Friday the 13th. **1960** *Yorkshire Post* 21 May 18. A note left by a window cleaner who was found dead in a gas-filled room at his home said: 'It just needed to rain today—Friday the 13th—for me to make up my mind.' **1967** *Times* 28 Aug. 6. When she telephoned [to Caxton Hall, for a wedding] to inquire what day would not be unduly crowded, she was assured that Friday the 13th was guaranteed to find the market sluggish. **1983** Girl, 12 [Maldon, Essex] Friday the thirteenth is very unlucky because every Friday the thirteenth one person in my family always hurts their self. **1984** *Woman,* c.50 [St Neots, Hunts.] You don't think I'm going to reply to a business letter written on Friday the Thirteenth do you?

Cf. FRIDAY an unlucky day; THIRTEEN unlucky number.

FROG, live: in bag up chimney
1867 *Gents Mag.* pt. 1 738 [Monks Eleigh, Suffolk] An old man and his sister told me, that they once knew of a frog being hung up in a chimney in a bladder, as a cure for some complaint .. The scratchings and noise made by the poor frog were awful, they said; but the man recovered.

FROG, live: in patient's mouth
1696 AUBREY *Miscellanies* (1890, 137–8) To cure a Thrush. Take a living frog, and hold it in a cloth, that it does not go down into the child's mouth; and put the head into the child's mouth 'till it is dead; and then take another frog, and do the same. **1851** *N & Q* 1st ser.

III 258. In Cheshire .. hooping cough may be cured by holding a toad for a few moments with its head within the mouth of the person affected. I heard only the other day of a cure by this somewhat disagreeable process; the toad was said to have caught the disease, which in this instance proved fatal to it in a few hours. 1872 *N & Q* 4th ser. IX 401 [Yorks.] [for a sore mouth] Obtain a live frog and put it into the child's mouth and pull it out by the legs. 1883 F. BUCKLAND editorial note to White's *Selborne* 304. In my own experience a woman gave her child a half-grown frog to suck, as she had been told it would cure the thrush round the child's mouth. 1895 J. HARDY *Denham Tracts* 294. This distemper [thrush] is .. called in North Northumberland 'the frog in the mouth'. 1912 LEATHER *Herefordshire* 82. A Pembridge woman used to think that she cured her baby of thrush by holding the head of a live frog in its mouth. 'Not to touch, mind,' she said, 'but to get the breath. I mind one time as I done it, the frog drawed a breath and puffed hisself out ever so, and the youngster was well the day after.' 1959 *Folklore* 414 [Ongar, Essex] Thrush in a child can be cured by holding a frog inside the child's mouth.

Cf. DUCK OR GOOSE: bill in patient's mouth.

FROG, live: swallowed

1857 *N & Q* 2nd ser. IV 145. More than forty years ago I recollect seeing one of my father's reapers .. swallow several live frogs .. to cure herself of some stomach complaint (water-brush, I believe) .. She said, 'there was naething better than a paddy for reddin' ane's puddins' .. Mary is still alive, nearly fourscore years of age, in the village of Auchencrow [Berwick.]. 1913 E. M. WRIGHT *Rustic Speech* 242. My old nurse remembers when she was a young nursemaid, seeing her master, who was consumptive, swallow baby frogs before breakfast by way of a cure .. The treatment proved successful, for these reminiscences had been called forth by a newspaper notice of the gentleman's death in 1910 at the age of eighty-eight!

FROGS, nine: in soup

1898 BLAKEBOROUGH *Yorkshire Customs* 145. For whooping-cough I was assured that nothing was better than to walk along a road until you found nine frogs; these had to be carried home and made into soup. The patient on no account must see the frogs, or be told of what the soup was composed—a most wise precaution—but on his or her finishing the whole nine, soup and all, they would be found to be quite recovered.

FROG'S EYES

1874 *Journal of Anthropological Inst.* III 271 [Banff.] Catch a live frog, and lick the frog's eyes with the tongue. The person who does so has only to lick .. any diseased eye, and a cure is effected.

Cf. LIZARD cures.

frog: also see TOAD OR FROG.

FUNERAL: divination

1858 DENHAM *North of England* (1895, 49) If the first person at a funeral procession meets .. is a male, a female is sure to be the next who dies in the village .. if a female, then it will be a male. 1879 J. NAPIER *West of Scotland* 51. To meet a funeral either in going to or coming from marriage was very unlucky. If the funeral was that of a female, the young wife would not live long; if a male, the bridegroom would die soon. 1923 [Castle Cary, Som.] When burying a corpse, whichever sex you meet first on the route, will be the same sex to follow. 1933 *Folklore* 191 [Trentside, Lincs.] Should a funeral party be proceeding to the place of burial, the sex of the first person to meet the procession will determine whether the next to die will be a man or a woman .. a man indicates that a man will be the next victim; meet a woman and it will be a woman.

FUNERAL, meeting: and actions to avert evil

1787 GROSE *Provincial Glossary* Superstitions 62. If you meet a funeral procession, or one passes by you, always take off your hat: this keeps all evil spirits attending the body in good humour. *c.*1816 Wilkie MS (HENDERSON *Northern*

Counties 1866, 27) He who meets a Border funeral is certain soon to die, unless he bares his head, turns, and accompanies the procession some distance .. This done .. he may .. go on his way without fear. 1887 'SPERANZA' WILDE Superstitions of Ireland I 154. Any one meeting a funeral must turn back and walk at least four steps with the mourners. 1952 Girl, 14 [Aberdeen] If one sees a hearse in the street and spits, it is supposed to be lucky. 1953 Girl, 15 [Loughton, Essex] If you see a funeral, cross your fingers till you see a four-legged animal. 1973 Woman, 46 [Liss, Hants.] People don't seem to have the same attitude to death .. In the old days when a funeral passed, the men all took off their hats. You don't see that any more.

FUNERAL, meeting: unlucky for bridal party

c.1855 Fortune-Teller 17. To meet a funeral [on the way to the church to be married], shows you will have to encounter a life of domestic jars, and a very indifferent partner. 1883 BURNE Shropshire 296. It is accounted very unlucky for a wedding to meet a funeral. In fact, meeting a funeral is no good omen at any time. 1898 BLAKEBOROUGH Yorkshire Customs 102. It is a bad omen should the bridal party meet a coffin. 1954 Girl, 15 [Forfar, Angus] If a bride going to church passes a funeral procession, that's an unlucky happening.

FUNERAL: room rearranged

1978 Sussex Express 30 June 4 [Yorks.] A practice still maintained is that during the absence of the funeral party somebody will change the furniture in the bedroom of the deceased so that if the ghost returns it will not recognise the place and will leave the family in peace.

FUNERAL: route changed

1899 Newcastle Weekly Chronicle 4 Feb. 7 [Jesmond] Where possible, the mourners return by a road different from that along which the body was carried; they fear the ghost might follow them home.
Cf. WEDDING: route changed.

FUNERAL seen through window or doorway

1823 W. GRANT STEWART Highlanders of Scotland 293 n. It is considered very imprudent to look at a passing funeral from the door of the house, or from a window having a stone lintel. 1888 Folklore 263 [Acterneed, Ross.] It is unlucky to look at a funeral procession through a window, or to stand in the door to do so. One must go right outside. 1972 Lore and Language July 7 [Coalisland, Co. Tyrone] Never look at a hearse through a window. 1973 Woman, 46 [Liss, Hants.] Mum was always very particular to draw the curtains when a funeral cortege was passing even if she peeped round the side of them to see who it was. 1987 Woman, c.60 [Co. Antrim] My mother would never let us look at a funeral through the window—she always took us out into the street to see it go by.
Cf. NEW MOON seen through glass or tree.

FUNERAL: sun shines on mourner's face

c.1816 Wilkie MS (HENDERSON Northern Counties 1866, 27) If, at a funeral, the sun shines brightly on the face of one among the attendants, it marks him for the next to be laid in that churchyard.

FUNERAL FEES

1887 F. T. HAVERGAL Herefordshire Words 46. If the parish clerk is asked at a church-yard for change by the undertaker or other person in paying the funeral fees, it is believed that there will be a second death in the family of the deceased within a year.

G

GABRIEL'S HOUNDS/SEVEN WHISTLERS

1590 SPENSER *Faerie Queene* II XII 36. The Whistler shrill, that who so heares, doth dy. *c.***1700** KENNETT MS Lands. 1033 (*Cath. Angl.* 147 n.) At Wednesbury in Staffordshire, the colliers going to their pits early in the morning hear the noise of a pack of hounds in the air, to which they give the name of Gabriel's Hounds, though the more sober and judicious take them only to be wild geese making this noise in their flight. **1807** WORDSWORTH *Misc. Sonnets* II XXIX. He the seven birds hath seen, that never part, Seen the Seven Whistlers in their nightly rounds, And counted them: and oftentimes will start—For overhead are sweeping Gabriel's Hounds Doomed, with their impious Lord, the flying Hart To chase for ever, on aerial grounds! **1856** *Gents Mag.* pt. I 38. Not many years ago at Suckley .. the country people used to talk .. about 'The Seven Whistlers', and that they oftentimes at night heard six out of these .. pass over their heads .. When the seven should whistle together there would be an end of the world .. Leicestershire colliers .. when they hear 'the whistlers' will not venture below ground, thinking that death to some one is foreboded. **1860** F. BUCKLAND *Curiosities of Natural History* 2nd ser. 286–7 [Folkstone, Kent] The 'Seven Whistlers' .. 'I never thinks any good of them,' said old Smith; 'there's always an accident when they comes. I heard 'em once one dark night last winter. They come over our heads .. singing 'ewe-ewe', and the men in the boat wanted to go back .. Before morning, a boat was upset, and seven poor fellows drowned. I know what makes the noise, sir; it's them long-bill'd curlews; but I never likes to hear them.' **1866** HENDERSON *Northern Counties* 98. When a child was burned to death in Sheffield, a few years ago, the neighbours immediately called to mind how the Gabriel hounds had passed above the house

not long before. **1880** *Gents Mag.* 493 [Lancs.] These spectre hounds are locally termed 'Gabriel Ratchets', and are supposed to foretell death or misfortune to all who hear their sound.

GALLOWS, chips of: cure

1650 BROWNE *Vulgar Errors* V XII § 9. For amulets against Agues we use the chips of Gallowes and places of Execution. **1787** GROSE *Provincial Glossary* Superstitions 57. The chips or cuttings of a gibbet or gallows, on which one or more persons have been executed or exposed, if worn next the skin, or round the neck, in a bag, will cure the ague, or prevent it. **1823** R. SURTEES *History of Durham* III 281 & n. [Ferryhill] The gibbet .. was .. called Andrew Mill's stob [and] was in a fair way of being pulled down piecemeal, under the effects of a belief in its efficacy as a charm against ague or tooth-ache. **1866** HENDERSON *Northern Counties* 113. The inhabitants of Stamfordham [Northumb.] walk to Winter's Gibbet .. for a splinter of the wood to cure the toothache. **1880** L. J. JENNINGS *Rambles among the Hills* 202 [Ditchling, Sussex] A Jew pedlar once .. murdered an innkeeper, his wife, and their servant, and was .. hanged upon a scaffold hard by. A piece of the gibbet .. was long considered a certain cure for toothache. **1899** H. S. COWPER *Hawkshead* 317 [Lancs.] George Milligan .. assures us that even in his time people .. used to repair there [to the rotting stump of the gibbet] to obtain a stopping from the wood of the gallows tree. This placed in the tooth was considered, he said, 'a terrble suer thing for toothwork'.

GARLIC protects from evil

1865 *Gents Mag.* pt. 2 700 [Ireland] Cloves of wild garlic are planted on thatch over the door, for good luck. **1948** E. & M. A. RADFORD *Superstitions* 130 [Scotland] Garlic, hung about the house on All Hallows Eve, will keep away evil spirits.

Cf. ONION protects and cures.

GARTER comes untied

1507 *Gospelles of Dystaues* pt. I xxv. Nowe ye for as true as the gospell that y^f the hose of a woman or of a mayden unbyndeth in the strete & that she lese it, it is sygne & fayleth neuer that her husbande or her loue gothe elles where. **1620** MELTON *Astrologaster* 46. It is naught [unlucky] for a man or woman to lose their hose Garter. **1865** R. HUNT *West of England* 2nd ser. 240. If an unmarried woman's garter loosens when she is walking, her sweetheart is thinking of her. **1895** S. O. ADDY *Household Tales* 98 [Yorks.] If a woman loses her garter in the street her lover will be unfaithful to her. **1899** *Newcastle Weekly Chronicle* 4 Feb. 7 [Jesmond] If your garter fall off, your lover is thinking of you. **1910** *Folklore* 89 [Argyll.] If a girl's stocking wrinkles and refuses to remain 'pulled up', her lover is thinking of her.

Cf. APRON comes untied.

GATE: divination

1883 BURNE *Shropshire* 177. A bachelor was told, if he would notch three notches in a gate that had five bars on it, for nine nights, he would see his sweetheart the last night.

GLASS, breaking

1893 *N & Q* 8th ser. IV 244 [Dublin] A group of persons stood discussing the state of a sick friend, when one of the number accidentally knocked down a glass, and shattered it into fragments, '—— is dead,' said one. 'It is a death notice,' said another. Such it turned out; the person had died in the same hour. **1899** *N & Q* 9th ser. IV 6. Thrice within the two or three months before my father's death the glass of his framed photograph was found broken, and without any ostensible cause. **1910** *Folklore* 89 [Argyll.] If a glass is accidentally broken during a marriage feast, it foretells misfortune to the bridal pair. **1923** [Wellington, Som.] Break the glass of a grandfather clock and you will hear of a friend's death. **1925** R.

BACON *Naval Scrap-Book* 186 [refers to 1893] A wine glass that was standing on the table broke through the stem without warning or anyone touching it. Someone, I forget now who, remarked: 'That should mean a big naval disaster.' Allowing for the difference in time owing to longitude, the glass broke just about the time that the *Victoria* was rammed. **1937** *Folklore* 56 [Mon.] The breaking of glass used to be regarded as a death omen. One man told me that one night a glass sugar basin in the middle of the table broke in two. Next morning he heard that his mother had died. **1953** Boy, 14 [Presteigne, Radnor.] When you break a window or a glass you get seven years' bad luck. But I don't think it's right because I have not heard of anybody having it yet. **1961** Woman, *c*.30 [Leeds, Yorks.] It's a strange thing, but in our family if the rim of a glass breaks all round so that you can lift it straight off, it's supposed to foretell a death. **1978** Woman, 67 [Sheffield, Yorks.] If a collier on his way to work saw a broken bottle he would go home and not work that day.

Cf. MIRROR, breaking.

GLASS, ringing

1909 *N & Q* 10th ser. XII 310. Can any one tell me the particulars of the legend which connects the ringing, or singing, of a glass (tumbler or wineglass), after it has been accidentally struck, with the drowning of a sailor? **1910** *Folklore* 224 [Somerset] If you strike any glass vessel and stop it ringing, a sailor is saved from drowning. **1923** [West Malling, Kent] If a glass is accidentally knocked so that it rings it must be touched again and the 'ring' stopped. If it rings to the end it signifies a death at sea. **1932** C. IGGLESDEN *Those Superstitions* 26. Have you ever noticed the effect upon a dinner-party should anyone hit a glass and make it ring? Nothing less than an interruption in conversation—a momentary silence—relieved only when the culprit placed a finger on the rim 'to save a sailor from drowning'. **1970** Naval officer's wife, *c*.35. I know this superstition well. We always say 'Save the sailor, and drown a marine.'

Cf. GLASS, breaking.

GLASS, things seen through

1883 BURNE *Shropshire* 282. Mr Hubert
Smith, Town Clerk of Bridgnorth, was
present in court .. when a witness
who had seen the prisoner through a
window, under suspicious circumstances, refused to take the oath, saying,
'I canna swear through glass.'
  Cf. FUNERAL seen through window or
doorway; NEW MOON seen through glass.

GLOVE, dropping

1925 *Folklore* 252 [Northumb.] It is not
lucky to pick up an old glove you find
on the road. 1925 D. R. PHILLIPS *Vale of
Neath* 597. Ill Omens .. still exercise
their power .. the fall of a pair of
gloves in the street. 1936 E. H. RUDKIN
Lincolnshire 18. Anyone dropping a
glove and picking it up will have a
disappointment—if someone else picks
it up then the owner will have a surprise.
1984 Woman, 37 [Harrow, Middx.] If
you drop your gloves they must be
picked up by someone else, and you
mustn't say 'Thank you' when they are
returned.

GLOVES as present

1862 *Welcome Guest* 17 May 304. Certainly it would not be unlucky for you
to give your brother a pair of black
kid gloves. Notions about 'luck' are
all exploded. 1953 Girl, 14 [Hollesley,
Suffolk] If you give a pair of gloves as a
present to a friend of the opposite sex
the friendship will be broken. 1969
Woman, 43 [Liss, Hants.] If you are
given a pair of gloves you must pay
something for them, no matter how
little, just as you do for a knife or a
brooch or a packet of pins. 1984
Woman, 37 [Harrow, Middx.] I'd never
give gloves to a friend. It means you will
quarrel.

GOAT at mast

1703 M. MARTIN *Western Isles of Scotland*
109. It was an ancient Custom among
the Islanders to hang a He Goat to the
Boats Mast, hoping thereby to procure
a favourable Wind.

GOAT killed at Christmas

late 18th c. J. RAMSAY (*Scotland in the
Eighteenth Century* II 447) On the western coast and in the Isles, it is reckoned
lucky to kill a goat at Christmas.

GOAT on farm

c.1840 *Riddle-Book* 12. Some may think
it all a fable, When I say that in the
stable I'm a doctor, and my scent Does
many maladies prevent. 1858 DENHAM
North of England (1895, 75) One of these
animals kept about an Inn or Farmstead,
is not only conducive to the health of
the other .. animals, but also brings
good luck to the owner. 1866 *Manchester Courier* 29 Jan. 4. It is very
remarkable that .. we hear very little of
the cattle plague in Wales or yet in
Ireland, both places notorious for breeding and keeping goats on the farms. The
old farmers looked upon the goat as the
doctor among the cattle. 1872 ELIOT
Middlemarch IV xxxix. There was an
aged goat (kept doubtless on superstitious grounds) lying against the
open back-kitchen door. 1910 *N & Q*
11th ser. II 534 [Northleach, Glos.] It
must be a 'Billy' goat, and the more it
stinks the better .. Since I introduced a
he-goat among my shorthorns, abortion
has ceased. Previously it was very
troublesome. 1915 *Folklore* 213 [Don-
caster, Yorks.] A large farmer here ..
told me it was considered good for cattle
and sheep to have a goat with them,
and that the smell keeps off diseases ..
It appears to be a convention, at least
from 13th century, to represent pastoral
scenes with sheep feeding on the ground,
and a goat on his hind legs craning up
to browse on a tree. 1938 *Folklore* 232
[Shrops.] It is said to be lucky to let a
goat run with the cows—it is said to
prevent the cows casting their calves.
1973 *Farmers Weekly* 9 Nov. 93 [Glos.]
As a small boy I saw a goat running
with the herd on several farms in the
county and was told that as long as the
animal was with the cows they would
be safe from foot-and-mouth disease.
  Cf. DONKEY with cows.

GODPARENTS, healing powers of

1883 BURNE *Shropshire* 192. Faith in the
healing virtues of baptism must be very
strong where (as at Pulverbatch and
Wenlock respectively) the godmother's
stay-lace or the godfather's garter is

worn round the neck as a cure for whooping-cough.

Cf. CHRISTENING as protection for baby.

GOLD cures

1387 CHAUCER *Tales*, Prol. ll. 443–4. For gold in phisik is a cordial, Therefore he [the doctor of physic] lovede gold in special. **1646** BROWNE *Vulgar Errors* II v. That Gold inwardly taken .. is a special cordiall of great efficacy .. is by no man determined beyond dispute. **1616** SIR T. OVERBURY *Characters* (1630, M3) Hee hoordes vp faire gold, and pretends 'tis to seethe in his Wiues broth for a consumption. **1665** J. ALLIN Letter 22 Sept. (*Archaeologia* XXXVI 15) Plague 7,165 [victims] Much rageing now in the city .. Freind get a piece of angell gold, if you can of Eliz. coine (y^t is ye best), wch is phylosophicall gold, and keepe it allways in yor mouth when you walke out or any sicke persons come to you. **1688** AUBREY *Remaines* (1881, 206) Some doe use pure gold bound to old ulcers or fistulas, as a secret; and w^h good successe: gold attracts mercury; and I have a conceite, that the curing of ye Kings evil by gold was first derived from hence: but the old gold was very pure; and printed w^h St Mich: the Arch-Angel, & to be stamped according to some Rule Astrological. **1863** R. CHAMBERS *Book of Days* I 220–1. The peasantry, both in England and Ireland .. fancy any growth like a wart on the skin may be removed by rubbing a wedding ring upon them. **1879** *Northern Counties* 167. She borrowed a half-sovereign of her neighbour, and .. proceeded to rub the child on the chest with the gold. The eruption went in and the child has never since been afflicted. **1960** Girl, 11 [London] Well, this one is true, because my grandmother used to do it to my mother. She had a lot of warts, my mother, and my grandmother used to tape her wedding ring on them and they used to go. **1961** Girl, 11 [Swansea, Glam.] Stick a pin in the wart and then rub it with gold.

GOLD cures sore eyes

*c.*1050 MS Cotton Vitell. C. iii (COCKAYNE *Leechdoms* I 113) Go to the .. wort proserpinica, and scratch it round about with a golden ring, and say that thou wilt take it for leechdom of eyes, and after three days go again thereto .. and take it, and hang it about the man's swere [neck]; it will profit well. *c.*1614 WEBSTER *Duchess of Malfi* I i. One of your eyes is blood-shot, use my Ring to't, They say 'tis very soveraigne, 'twas my wedding Ring. *c.*1616 FLETCHER *Mad Lover* v iv. FOOL. I have a sty here, Chilax. CHILAX. I have no gold to cure it, not a penny. **1678** *Yea and Nay Almanack* C7^v. Rub your eyes with a hundred broad pieces of your own Gold .. it will not only do thy eyes good but thy purse also. **1823** MOOR *Suffolk Words. Sty* .. We fancy that the application of gold, especially of a gold ring, and more especially of a wedding-ring, is a cure. **1829** BROCKETT *North Country Words. Sty* .. Great relief .. is supposed to be effected by the application of a wedding ring, nine times repeated. **1874** *N & Q* 5th ser. II 184 [Tiverton, Devon.] To cure a sty in the eye, rub the part three times all one way with a wedding ring. **1895** J. HARDY *Denham Tracts* 298. At Wooler [Northumb.] to cure the stye a gold ring is applied nine times. **1953** Girl, 15 [Suffolk] Many people would not buy ointment if they have a sty, but would rub a wedding ring across it. **1969** M. HARRIS *A Kind of Magic* 114 [Ducklington, Oxon., *c.*1925] A small piece of real silk was carefully hoarded away by most families to be used if anyone had a stye on the eye: first the silk had to be drawn through a gold wedding ring and then the stye was stroked with the silk twelve times night and morning. **1975** Woman, 35 [Liss, Hants.] When I have a sty, I always rub it with a gold ring and it goes. But it doesn't work with everyone. **1983** *Folklore* 187. In the Swansea area .. it was commonly believed (perhaps still is believed today) that twisting a wedding ring on the eyelid would cure the eye ailment.

GOLD: eyes rubbed with for luck

1841 T. MILLER *Gideon Giles* 189 [Lincs.] 'Locky-daisy me!' exclaimed Mrs Cawthry taking up the sovereign, and turning it all ways, 'and good gowd too! I'll hev a lucky rub at any rate'; and she rubbed both her eyes with the sovereign, then handed it to her gossip, who did the same, saying .. 'I've never rubbed my eyes before for above seven years, the last time I did .. I fun sixpence .. so you see that proves it's lucky.'

'GOLD AND SILVER WATER'

1866 HENDERSON *Northern Counties* 131. At Lockerby, in Dumfriesshire, is still preserved a piece of silver called the Lockerby Penny, which is thus used against madness in cattle. It is put in a cleft stick, and a well is stirred round with it, after which the water is bottled off and given to any animal so affected. Ibid. 151. In the North-west of Scotland, according to Dr Mitchell, the 'gold and silver water' is the accredited cure for a child suffering from the evil eye. A shilling and a sovereign are put into water, which is then sprinkled over the patient in the name of the Trinity. **1885** *Folklore* 311 [Banff.] The belief in 'forespeaking' [bewitching] a child has not yet died out. The cure for it is a drank off a shilling. My informant said that .. he happened to enter a house in which a child had suddenly become sick .. The cry was raised that it was 'forespoken'. One of the women .. drew out a shilling from her pocket, put it into a dish, poured a little water over it, and then held the water to the child's lips. The sickness soon passed off. **1888** *Christian Leader* 21 June 392. Within the last fortnight .. a certificated midwife, in an island on the west coast of Scotland [advised] 'Take a piece of gold and put it into a dish, pour water on to the gold, then sprinkle the water over the children that are sick, and immediately they will begin to recover.' **1905** *Folklore* 335 [Beauly, Inverness.] Water had to be fetched in a bucket made entirely of wood, from a brook .. over which the living and the dead had crossed (this was a brook running under a road leading to the local church-yard). In this water silver had to be placed (a threepenny-piece usually). Then the water was .. sprinkled over the sick cow. Ibid. When cattle sickened .. to conjure out the evil spirit .. he administered a 'drink of silver' (water with a piece of silver money in it) .. still believed to be very effective in many parts of Caithness. **1923** *Folklore* 91 [Skye] To cure a cow of any ailment the best way is to take a piece of silver money or a silver ornament, pouring water over it while saying an incantation .. and giving it to the cow to drink. **1951** *Folklore* 326 [Duthil, Inverness., *c.*1910] A sister of the farmer .. sprinkled some water on the prostrate form of the foal .. Some minutes later the foal suddenly staggered to its feet, apparently quite recovered. 'Do you know what that was,' said Farmer Cameron, 'There was a silver coin in the coggie [bucket] and the water came from a burn over which the living and dead cross.' He explained that such water was a certain cure for ailments of horses and cattle.

Cf. SILVER protects.

GOLD EAR-RINGS good for eyes

1878 A. MACGREGOR *Brahan Seer* 131 'Superstitions of Highlanders'. Healing sore eyes by putting gold rings in the ears, by rubbing them with jewels of pure gold, and by repeating certain rhymes. **1924** *N & Q* CXLVII 341. In Somerset, years ago, it was quite a common thing for young children to have their ears pierced and gold wire inserted as a cure for sore eyes. **1927** G. STURT *Small Boy in the Sixties* 128 [Farnham, Surrey] I am surprised, now, at the number of men I seem to have seen said to have been sailors, and certainly wearing ear-rings, to strengthen their eyes it was alleged. **1945** *Folklore* 269 [Walberswick, Suffolk, fishermen] The habit of wearing gold earrings, still not unknown, is supposed to help the sight.

GOLD EAR-RINGS prevent drowning

1919 *Morning Post* 9 June 3. Nearly all fishermen on the East Coast, especially in Norfolk, believe that by wearing gold earrings they enjoy immunity from drowning. The origin of this superstition is lost in antiquity. **1953** *Sunday Express* 30 Aug. 9. No one has been able to tell me I am breaking [Admiralty] regulations .. sailors have worn earrings since the days of Elizabeth I. The legend is that a man who wears one will never go down with a ship.

GOOD FRIDAY beneficial

1813 BRAND *Antiquities* II 202. A clergyman in Devonshire informed me that . . bees are never removed but on a Good Friday. 1838 A. E. BRAY *Devonshire* II 286. Good Friday . . To wean children on this day is deemed very lucky. Many people then begin to till their gardens, as they believe . . that all things put in the earth on a good Friday will grow *goody*, and return to them with great increase. 1851 *N & Q* 1st ser. III 516 [Lancs.] Good Friday is the best day of all the year to begin weaning children. 1867 *N & Q* 3rd ser. XI 233 [Glos.] I used to suffer very much from toothache many years ago, till a neighbour told me how to cure it. I got up on Good Friday before the sun rose, and cut all the nails on my hands and my feet, and wrapped it all up in a bit of writing paper, and put it in my pocket. 1883 BURNE *Shropshire* 334. Sewing done on Good Friday will never come undone. 1898 C. M. YONGE *John Keble's Parishes* 175 [Otterbourne, Hants.] If possible, a baby was short-coated on Good Friday, to ensure not catching cold.

GOOD FRIDAY, born on

1880 W. SIKES *British Goblins* 267 [Wales] The birth of a child on that day [Good Friday] is to be deprecated as a most unfortunate circumstance.

GOOD FRIDAY, bread made on: cures

*c.*1001 ÆLFRIC *Letter to Bishop Wulfsige* (*Hirtenbriefe Ælfrics*, ed. Fehr, 29) Some priests keep the sacrament which was consecrated on Easter Day the whole year long for sick men. 1807 SOUTHEY *Letters from England* xx. For Good Friday, hot buns marked with a cross for breakfast . . These buns will keep for ever without becoming mouldy, by virtue of the holy sign impressed upon them . . In the province of Herefordshire a pious woman annually makes two upon this day, the crumbs of which are a sovereign remedy for diarrhoea. 1809 *Gents Mag.* 316. Yesterday being Good Friday, the antient dames of this place [Birmingham] were especially careful to lay up a sufficient stock of Cross Buns (which will keep without growing mouldy!), as a panacea for all disorders during the succeeding twelve-month. 1846 *Athenaeum* 1142 [Herstmonceux, Sussex] Some time since, when visiting at a cottage [he] noted something carefully tied up in a bag hanging from the clock, and . . was told that it was 'Good Friday's bread', which, when grated, was good for the disorders of the stomach that children are subject to. 1847 *Athenaeum* 95 [Staffs.] My father tasted some bread . . baked on Good Friday. It was . . twenty-one years old—and was perfectly sweet, but (as you may suppose) as hard as a stone. The cause of its keeping so long appears to be the length of time it remains, while being baked, in a moderately heated oven—often for two days and a night. 1863 *N & Q* 3rd ser. III 262 [Warwicks.] I took him a piece of Good Friday bread, and grated some of it in a little brandy. The child took it, and it cured him [of a bowel-complaint]. The piece I have now has been baked seven or eight years . . I always keep it wrapped in paper in a box upstairs. 1874 KILVERT *Diary* 10 Feb. [Clyro, Radnor.] Speaking of the custom of keeping the Good Friday holy bread (the bread or buns baked on Good Friday) for a year, and then grating it up for giving to sick people, Charles Awdry suggested that this superstition may be a relic of the ancient Catholic usage of 'the Reservation of the Sacrament'. Good Friday bread is said never to grow mouldy. 1908 *N & Q* 10th ser. IX 345 [Derbys.] Though my mother did not believe in it, she always put one of the hot cross buns she made aside on a cupboard shelf to keep till the following Good Friday, for 'good luck', just as all the other women did who baked their own bread. Some 'goodies' in the villages grated, I know, a bit from an old Good Friday bun to administer to children during their common ailments.

GOOD FRIDAY, bread made on: protects

1826 HONE *Every-Day Book* I 31 Mar. In the houses of some ignorant people, a Good Friday bun is still kept 'for luck', and sometimes there hangs from the ceiling a hard biscuit-like cake of open *cross*-work .. to remain there till displaced on the next Good Friday by one of similar make; and of this the editor .. has heard affirmed, that it preserves the house from fire. **1870** *N & Q* 4th ser. V 595 [E. Yorks.] A hot-cross-bun used to be kept from one Good Friday to the next, as it was reputed not to turn mouldy, and to protect the house from fire. **1879** HENDERSON *Northern Counties* 82. The Sunderland [Co. Durham] wives see that their husbands take some [bread baked on Good Friday] to sea with them to avert shipwrecks.

GOOD FRIDAY, egg laid on

1921 *N & Q* 12th ser. IX 489. A lady told one of my nearest relations that if an egg, laid on Good Friday, is kept without being disturbed, it will generally be perfectly fresh at the time when the Christmas pudding is made. **1922** R. KEARTON *At Home with Wild Nature* 65. A superstition still rife in many parts of the country is that eggs laid on Good Friday never become stale. **1923** [Somerset] It is a very old belief that with the eggs laid on Good Friday any fire can be extinguished, simply by throwing the said egg into the heart of it.

GOOD FRIDAY, ploughing on

1859 ELIOT *Adam Bede* XVIII [refers to 1799] Had not Michael Holdsworth had a pair of oxen 'sweltered' [killed] while he was ploughing on Good Friday? **1866** HENDERSON *Northern Counties* 61–2. I learn from a clergyman familiar with the North Riding of Yorkshire, that great care is there taken not to disturb the earth in any way; it were impious to use spade, plough, or harrow .. A villager .. shocked his neighbours by planting potatoes on Good Friday, but they never came up. **1976** *Trans. Devon. Ass.* 188 [Peck Pitt pool] A ploughman with his two horses and his plough— because he *would* plough the land on Good Friday—disappeared into the Pool and was never seen again.

GOOD FRIDAY, prayer said on

1933 A. WHITE *Frost in May* XIII. After their lunch of salt fish and bread and water, the children returned to the chapel to watch there in spirit with Christ on the cross until three o'clock. There is a tradition that any prayer made as the clock strikes three on Good Friday will be granted.

GOOD FRIDAY, washing on

1838 A. E. BRAY *Devonshire* II 286. Washing clothes on a Good Friday is with us considered a great sin; and productive of the worst luck. Whoever does so is sure to wash away one of the family, who will die before the year is out. **1855** F. K. ROBINSON *Yorkshire Words* 74 [Whitby] If clothes are hung out to dry on that day [Good Friday] it is believed they will be taken down spotted with blood. **1866** HENDERSON *Northern Counties* 62. Once, when I was hanging out my clothes, a young woman passed by (a Methodist); and she reproved me, and told me this story. While our Lord Jesus was being led to Calvary .. a woman who was washing .. 'blirted' the thing she was washing in His face; on which He said, 'Cursed be every one who hereafter shall wash on this day!' And never again .. have I washed on Good Friday. Now it is said, in Cleveland [Yorks.] that clothes washed and hung out to dry on Good Friday will become spotted with blood. **1932** WOMEN'S INSTITUTE *Worcestershire Book* 34 [Malvern] If you leave your soapsuds in your boiler over Good Friday there will be a death in the house. **1940** *Folklore* 298 [Weobley, Herefords., 1925] My mother always told me not to pour anything down the sink till after three o'clock on Good Friday .. because the gutters of Jerusalem was running with our Lord's blood up till three o'clock.

Cf. NEW YEAR, working at.

GOOD FRIDAY, working on

1849 *Norfolk Archaeology* II 296 [Irstead] Good Friday. If work be done on that day, it will be so unlucky that it will all have to be done over again.

GOOSE eaten on Michaelmas Day

1708 *British Apollo* 22 Oct. Pray tell me whence The custom'd proverb did commence, That who eats Goose on Michael's Day, Shan't money lack his debts to pay. **1790** GROSE *Provincial*

Glossary Superstitions 53. Whosoever does not eat goose at Michaelmas, runs a risk of wanting money all that year. **1812** J. BRADY *Clavis Calendaria* II 179–80. Michaelmas Day is one of the regular periods of settling rents .. but it is no longer peculiar for that hospitality which we are taught .. formerly existed, when the landlords used to entertain their tenants .. upon Geese, then only kept by persons of opulence .. As Geese are .. in their greatest perfection in the autumnal season, there are but few families who .. neglect the antient custom of making the Bird a part of their repast on the Festival of St Michael. There is a current, but erroneous tale, assigning to Queen Elizabeth the introduction of this custom: Being on her way to Tilbury Fort, on the 29th September, 1588, she is alleged to have .. partaken of a Goose .. After dinner, she drank .. to the destruction of the Spanish Armada, soon after which she received the joyful tidings that her wishes had been fulfilled [and] commemorated the day annually by having a Goose for dinner .. But the custom is of much older date. **1813** JANE AUSTEN Letter 11–12 Oct. (ed. Chapman) [Godmersham Park, Kent] I dined upon Goose yesterday [Old Michaelmas Day] which I hope will secure a good Sale of my 2^d Edition. **1839** C. BARON-WILSON *Harriot, Duchess of St Albans* I 163–4. She regretted bitterly that, on her first metropolitan 29th of September, she should not be able to purchase a goose, for the sake of tasting a small portion to bring good luck. **1923** [Ruishton, Som.] If you dine on goose on Michaelmas Day you will not be short of money for a year. **1944** S. G. KENDALL *West Country Yeoman* 173. One of our dishes especially at harvest home, which was usually near Michaelmas Day, was a Michaelmas roast goose, when sometimes we thought of the couplet—'He who eats goose on Michaelmas day Will never lack money his debts to pay.'

Cf. PANCAKES eaten on Shrove Tuesday.

GOOSEBERRY BUSH, babies found under
1903 *N & Q* 9th ser. XII 413. In Lincolnshire .. children of inquiring mind are commonly told, when a baby arrives, that the doctor dug it up with a golden spade under a gooseberry bush. **1941** F. THOMPSON *Over to Candleford* xxv. If the younger children of the family asked where it had come from, they were told from under a gooseberry bush. **1971** F. ARCHER *Secrets of Bredon Hill* 114. She still believed that babies were found under gooseberry bushes.

Cf. PARSLEY BED, babies found in.

GOOSEBERRY THORN
1850 *N & Q* 1st ser. I 349 [Kilkenny, Eire] A wedding-ring is procured, and the wart touched or pricked with a gooseberry thorn through the ring. **1862** *N & Q* 3rd ser. I 446 [Co. Wexford] A 'stye on the eye' .. was supposed never to get well unless it was pricked with a thorn from a goose-berry bush, and I have known the peasantry to go two or three miles for a thorn of that fruit tree. **1887** 'SPERANZA' WILDE *Superstitions of Ireland* II 93. Point a gooseberry-thorn at it nine times, saying, 'Away, away, away!' and the stye will vanish presently and disappear. **1893** *Folklore* 356 [Co. Derry] Take ten gooseberry jags, throw the tenth away, an' point the nine at the sty, an' throw them away, an' this will cure it.

GORSE in house
1893 *Dorset Field Club* 186. If the yaller vuz be a-cärd in A-thin a year there's nar a doubt A coffin 'ill be a-cärd out. **1923** [Castle Cary, Som.] To carry furze flower into the house—carrying death for one of the family.

GRASS: divination
1870 HERACLITUS GREY *Playing Trades* 117–18. Here they had gathered flowers, and played at Tinker, tailor, soldier, sailor, with long grasses. **1946** UTTLEY *Country Things* 133 [Cromford, Derbys., c.1900] The wild rye-grass, called tinker-tailor grass, was picked .. and we touched the seeds, saying 'Tinker, tailor, soldier, sailor, rich man, poor man, beggar man, thief.' **1969** M. HARRIS *A Kind of Magic* 42 [Ducklington, Oxon., c.1925] Grass with little seeds growing alternately up the stalk. With this we tried to find out what sort of

man we were going to marry. As our fingers moved up the stalk touching each seed we would chant—'Tinker, Tailor, Soldier, Sailor, Rich man, poor man, beggar-man, thief.'

GRAVE cures

c.1000 MS Harl. 585 (COCKAYNE *Leech-doms* III 67) Let the woman who cannot bring her child to maturity go to the barrow of a deceased man, and step thrice over the barrow, and then thrice say these words: 'May this be my boot [remedy] Of the loathsome late birth. May this be my boot Of the heavy swart birth. May this be my boot Of the loathsome lame birth.' 1865 *N & Q* 3rd ser. VIII 332 [Dublin] The person affected was to proceed, at an early hour in the morning, to some graveyard, and procure a sharp pointed piece of wood, a skewer, and with the aching tooth push it into a newly covered grave, and the pain would cease. 1867 *Trans. Devon. Ass.* 39. To cure a friend of Boils. Go into a churchyard on a dark night, and to the grave of a person who has been interred the day previous; walk six times round the grave, and crawl across it three times. If the sufferer from boils is a man, this ceremony must be performed by a woman, and the contrary. 1874 *N & Q* 5th ser. I 204 [Devon] At the close of the [suicide's] funeral .. a woman advanced and threw a new white pocket-handkerchief on the coffin .. The belief is that as, in the grave of the suicide, the handkerchief decays, so will any disease .. which the depositor may have. 1887 'SPERANZA' WILDE *Superstitions of Ireland* II 90. Go to a graveyard; kneel upon any grave; say three paters and three aves for the soul of the dead lying beneath. Then take a handful of grass from the grave, chew it well, casting forth each bite without swallowing any portion. After this process the sufferer, were he to live a hundred years, will never have toothache any more.

Cf. CHURCHYARD, grass etc. from.

GRAVE cures incontinence

1878 *Folk-Lore Record* 49 [Fittleworth, Sussex] Upon the day appointed for the funeral of a person not of the same sex as the child, while the first part of the burial service is being read within the church, the child is to be taken to the open grave and is there to do that which constituted the original offence [i.e. to urinate, this being a cure for incontinence]. 1898 BLAKEBOROUGH *Yorkshire Customs* 145–6. Those who suffer from a weak bladder .. simply had to stand astride at the head of an open grave, after the coffin had been lowered, but before being filled in, and then walk backwards to the foot of the same. 1933 *Folklore* 204 [Willoughton, Lincs.] [To cure] bed-wetting .. A girl-child should be taken to the grave of a boy on which she should pass water. A boy-child should be taken to the grave of a girl in the same way.

GRAVE, earth/dew from: cures

AD 731 BEDE *Historia Ecclesiastica* III IX (tr. Sherley-Price) Many people took away the very dust from the place where [St Oswald's] body fell, and put it in water, from which sick folk who drank it received great benefit. 1824 *Trans. Coll. Physicians in Ireland* IV 211 [Kinsale, Co. Cork] It appears that two much-respected and popular clergymen .. having died, she was told by some old women, that if she would drink daily, during a certain period of time, a portion of water imbued with clay, taken from the graves of these clergymen, she would be secured for ever against both disease and sin. 1850 *N & Q* 1st ser. II 474–5 [Launceston, Cornwall] A swelling in the neck may be cured by the patient's going before sunrise, on the lst of May, to the grave of the last young man who has been buried in the church-yard, and applying the dew, gathered by passing the hand three times from the head to the foot of the grave to the part affected by the ailment.

GRAVE, meeting/parting at

1881 G. L. BANKS *Glory* 3, 48 [Wilts.] The first meeting of Jesse W. and Rosanna B. boded evil for one or both .. 'They met by a graveside. My zakes, did iver anybody hear anything so unlucky!' 1890 MRS HENRY WOOD *Johnny Ludlow* 4th ser. 10 [Worcs.] To be in love with a charming young lady, and to have her all to yourself in a solitary graveyard under the light of the moon, presents an irresistible temptation for taking a kiss, especially if the kiss is to be a farewell kiss for days and for years .. But sundry superstitious gossips, hearing of this afterwards, assured Ellen that it must be unlucky to say farewell amidst graves.

Cf. MOURNING CLOTHES unlucky to lovers.

GRAVE open on Sunday

1864 R. CHAMBERS *Book of Days* II 52–3 [Suffolk] A woman coming down from church, and observing an open grave, remarked: 'Ah, there will be somebody else wanting a grave before the week is out!' .. Strangely enough .. her words came true, and the grave was dug for *her*. **1909** *N & Q* 10th ser. XII 66 [nr. Exeter, Devon] It is unlucky for a grave to be left open on a Sunday, because in that case one of the same family will die within the year. **1965** Woman, *c*.80 [East Drayton, Notts.] An old superstition, which was proved in 1891, was that if the churchyard is opened on a Sunday for a man to be buried, there will be three deaths soon afterwards, all of them men.

Cf. CORPSE unburied: over Sunday/ Saturday.

GRAVE, picking leaves/flowers from

1909 M. TREVELYAN *Folk-Lore of Wales* 283. It is considered very unlucky to pluck a flower that is growing on a grave. **1923** *Folklore* 236 [Iniskea, Co. Connaught] It is unlucky .. to pluck a leaf from a grave. **1957** UTTLEY *Year in the Country* II. It is a superstition that nobody must ever gather a flower which grows on a grave.

GRAVE, possession falls into

1891 *Church Times* 23 Jan. 78. In Yorkshire, during a burial, if anything, say a hat or handkerchief, happens to fall into the grave it is left there, otherwise the person owning it would die.

GRAVE, pregnant woman treads on

1826 *Dumfries Monthly Mag.* Sept. 253 [Annandale] If a woman, while pregnant, happen to enter a churchyard, and inadvertently wipe her feet upon a

grave, the child which she bears will be club-footed, or kirk-wiped. **1887** 'SPERANZA' WILDE *Superstitions of Ireland* II 104. A married woman should not walk upon graves, or her child will have a club-foot. If by accident she treads on a grave she must instantly kneel down, say a prayer, and make the sign of the cross on the sole of her shoe three times over. Ibid. 106. The cause of a club-foot is this—The mother stood on a cross in a churchyard before her child was born—so evil came. **1909** M. TREVELYAN *Folk-Lore of Wales* 266. A woman who is about to become a mother .. must not walk or step over a grave. If she does so, her child will die.

GRAVE, treading on

c.**319** BC THEOPHRASTUS *Characters* (tr. Jebb, ed. Sandys, 143) 'The Superstitious Man'. He will not tread upon a tombstone. **1798** COLERIDGE 'The Three Graves'. IV st. 1. To see a man tread over graves I hold it no good mark; 'Tis wicked in the sun and moon, And bad luck in the dark! **1874** *Journal of Anthropological Inst.*III 267 [Banff.] Passing over a hidden grave produced a rash. **1923** *Folklore* 337 [Connaught, Eire] It is unlucky to stand on the grave. **1989** Woman, 60 [Liss, Hants.] I'm not really happy about walking on the tombstones set into the floor in churches.

GRAVE: treading on grave of stillborn/ unchristened child

1813 BRAND *Antiquities* II 8 n. In the North of England it is thought very unlucky to go over [the graves of unbaptized children]. It is vulgarly called going over 'unchristened ground'. *c*.**1816** Wilkie MS (HENDERSON *Northern Counties* 1866, 4) He who steps on the grave of a stillborn or unbaptised child .. subjects himself to the fatal disease of .. grave-scab.

GREEN unlucky

1793 *Gents Mag.* 300. Passing .. between Bradford in Yorkshire to Kendal, we saw a number of country people .. following a new-married couple: the whole bedizened with ribbands—the bride most glaringly so—large true-blue bows .. reached the waist; white, red, and every other colour .. about her gown and hat, except forsaken green, which I was glad to perceive was not worn by one of the throng. 1806 P. GRAHAM *Sketches of Perthshire* 107. The Daoine Shi', or men of peace .. are believed to be a peevish repining race of beings .. The men of peace are believed to be always dressed in green; and are supposed to take offence, when any of mortal race presume to wear their favourite colour. 1810 SCOTT *Lady of the Lake* Note to canto IV st. 13. An aged gentleman .. when his horse fell in a fox-chase .. accounted for it at once by observing, that the whipcord attached to his lash was of this unlucky colour. 1826 R. CHAMBERS *Popular Rhymes of Scotland* 286. In Morayshire, there is a saying—'Green, Is love deen.' That is *done* or abandoned; and it is well known, that to dream of any thing green is accounted unlucky. Ibid. 1842 edn., 35. 'They that marry in green, Their sorrow is soon seen.' To this day, in the north of Scotland, no young woman would wear such attire on her wedding day. 1866 HENDERSON *Northern Counties* 21. Green .. must on no account be worn .. at a wedding .. In fact, nothing green must make its appearance .. kale and all other green vegetables are excluded from the wedding-dinner. Ibid. 1879 edn., 35. Those dressed in blue Have lovers true; In green and white, Forsaken quite. 1883 BURNE *Shropshire* 289 n. A lady about to put on mourning said to me, 'I knew how it would be when I bought that green dress this summer. I never bought a green dress that I did not have to get a black one directly afterwards.' 1908 MRS MOLESWORTH *Fairies—Of Sorts* 'Those Green Ribbons' pt. 3. Green's the fairies' colour, you know, and it's never lucky to put green on a baby, the country people say. 1916 *Folklore* 307 [Beesands, Devon] In 1910 I said to a fisherman's daughter, who had been telling me about the piskies, 'What colour are piskies?' 'Why, they'm like you, in that green dress!' She said a green dress was an object of much criticism in the village. I was told that 'if you wear green, you will soon after wear mourning.' 1922 LYND *Solomon* 162–3. Parnell was em-

inent for moral courage, but he believed that green was an unlucky colour, and was horror-stricken .. when he was presented with a green smoking-cap by a too patriotic lady. 1960 *Daily Express* 15 Sept. 2. The Lotus .. car which was rushed over for Mr [Donald] Campbell to get the feel of speed on the treacherous salt flats is to be sent back—because it is green .. Mr Campbell is superstitious about green. 1982 Woman, *c.*50 [Middlesbrough, Teeside] Never wear green—'After green comes black.'

GREENERY, burning

1889 *Dorset Field Club* 39–40. When a plant is pruned .. take care that .. cuttings are never put in the fire, but are thrown away; otherwise the plant will never thrive. 1909 *Folklore* 489 [Kirton, Lincs.] I have always heard that a body should not burn anything while it is green. 1926 *Folklore* 297 [Herefords.] Burn green, Sorrow soon seen. 1954 Girl, 15 [Forfar, Angus] For general luck in a garden, anything green or still blooming should never be burned. 1957 Boy, 11 [Beccles, Suffolk] Old people expect bad luck after burning fir-tree branches. 1958 Woman, *c.*30 [Heydon, Norfolk] To burn evergreens on the fire is bad luck.

Cf. CHRISTMAS DECORATIONS (evergreens), burning.

GREENERY, circle of: cures

1774 L. SHAW (PENNANT *Tour in Scotland* I app. 2 291) At the full moon in March they cut withes of the mistletoe .. make circles .. keep them all year, and pretend to cure hecticks and other troubles by them. 1775 L. SHAW *History of Moray* 232. In the increase of the March Moon, the Highlanders cut withes of the woodbind that clings about the Oak. These they twist into a .. circle, and carefully preserve it till the next March. And when children are troubled with hectick fevers, or when any one is consumptive, they make them pass through this circle thrice, by putting it over their heads and conveying it down about their bodies .. This I have often seen.

GROANING CHEESE, child passed through

1787 GROSE *Provincial Glossary* Superstitions 59. In the North, children are drawn through a hole cut in the groaning cheese, on the day they are christened. 1813 BRAND *Antiquities* II 6. It is customary at Oxford to cut the Cheese (called in the North of England, in allusion to the Mother's complaints at her delivery, 'the Groaning Cheese') in the middle when the Child is born, and so by degrees form it into a large kind of Ring, through which the Child must be passed on the Day of the Christening.

GROANING CHEESE OR CAKE: divination

1787 GROSE *Provincial Glossary* Superstitions 54. The same [divination by sleeping on] is practised in the North with a piece of the groaning cheese. 1813 BRAND *Antiquities* II 6 n. The first Cut of the sick Wife's Cheese . . is to be divided into little pieces, and tossed in the Midwife's Smock, to cause young Women to dream of their Lovers. 1829 BROCKETT *North Country Words* 141. *Groaning-Cheese*, or the *Sick Wife's Cheese*, a large Cheshire cheese provided on the same occasion as the [groaning] cake. I understand a slice of the first cut laid under the pillow, enables young damsels to dream of their lovers, particularly if previously tossed in a certain nameless part of the midwife's apparel. In all cases it must be pierced with three pins, taken from the child's pincushion. 1849 BRAND *Antiquities* II 71 n. In some parts of the north of England, at the birth of a child, the first slice of the Groaning Cake is cut into small pieces, and well shaken in the smock of the howdie wife: or should a man attend on the occasion, it undergoes the same process in the shirt of the accoucheur. 1866 HENDERSON *Northern Counties* 3. Most important of all is the 'shootin' or groaning cheese, from which the happy father must cut a 'whang-o'luck' for the lassies . . taking care not to cut his own finger while so doing, since in that case the child would die before reaching manhood . . The girls put these bits of cheese under their pillows, and ascribe to them the virtues of bridecake similarly treated.

GUINEA FOWL

1899 *Newcastle Weekly Chronicle* 11 Feb. 7 [Jesmond] Guinea fowl, by uttering their monotonous 'cognac, cognac', are said to bring sunshine and good luck to a farm.

H

HAIR: combing after sunset

1885 *Folklore* 309 [Rosehearty, Aberdeen.] If a woman has any relations or friends at sea she must on no account comb and dress her hair after nightfall. Such an act brings disaster upon them. **1930** P. F. ANSON *East Coast of Scotland* 40. No fisherman's wife would venture to comb her hair after sunset if her 'guid man' was at sea.

HAIR: disposing of combings/cuttings

1856 *N & Q* 2nd ser. I 386 [Greenock, Renfrew.] I have often noticed the careful anxiety of countrywomen in .. sweeping up the place where hair had fallen or been cut, and scrupulously burning the sweeping in the fire .. If left about, the birds would build their nests with the hair; a fatal thing for him or her from whose head it had fallen; and .. if a 'pyet' [magpie] got hold of it for any such purpose .. the person's death, within 'year and day' was sure. **1866** *N & Q* 3rd ser. X 146 [Dublin] It is held by the lower orders .. that human hair should never be burned, but should be *buried*, it being stated in explanation that at the resurrection the former owner of the hair will come to seek for it. **1878** *Folk-Lore Record* 44 [Fittleworth, Sussex] 'I knew how it would be,' exclaimed a servant to me one day, 'when I saw that bird fly off with a bit of my hair in its beak that blew out of the window this morning when I was dressing; I knew I should have a clapping headache, and so I have.' **1879** J. NAPIER *West of Scotland* 39. I have seen the door locked during hair-cutting, and the floor swept afterwards, and the sweepings burned, lest perchance any hair might .. be picked up by an enemy. **1888** *Dorset County Chronicle* 31 May 12. The superstitious are very careful .. not to throw [the hair] carelessly away, for if a magpie find it, and use it for the lining of its nest, the death of the person from whose head it has fallen is inevitable within the space of one short year. **1908**

Folklore 319 [Co. Cavan & Co. Leitrim] It is most unlucky to burn any of your hair, as on the Last Day you will have to collect it so as to appear with the whole of it as God created you. **1909** M. TREVELYAN *Folk-Lore of Wales* 209. Never throw the combings of your hair into the roadway. If you do you will get into the power of witchcraft. **1911** FRAZER *Golden Bough* 280–1. In the village of Drumconrath, near Abbeyleix, in Ireland, there used to be some old women who, having ascertained from Scripture that the hairs of their heads were all numbered by the Almighty, expected to have to account for them at the day of judgement. In order to be able to do so they stuffed the severed hair away in the thatch of their cottages. **1972** *Lore and Language* July 7 [Coalisland, Co. Tyrone] When you comb your hair never throw away the loose hair. If a bird uses it in making a nest you'll never lack a headache.

HAIR: double crown

1909 M. TREVELYAN *Folk-Lore of Wales* 265. A child with two crowns to its head will be lucky in money matters. **1950** [Forfar, Angus] Peter has a double croon on eez napper. He'll never droon. **1954** Boy, 13 [Liverpool] If you have a double crown you won't die in the country in which you were born. **1955** J. LEHMANN *Whispering Gallery* 334. When I was very young, someone brushing my hair told me I had a double crown, and that it meant I should eat my bread in two countries.

HAIR falling out

*c.*1816 Wilkie MS (HENDERSON *Northern Counties* 1866, 83) Sudden loss of hair is a prognostic of the loss of children, health, or property. **1948** J. C. RODGER *Lang Strang* 18 [Forfar, Angus, 1880] There's nae luck follows the dame That laives her hair in the reddin' caimb [comb].

Cf. TEETH, dreaming about.

HAIR, keeping

1895 S. O. ADDY *Household Tales* 93 [Yorks.] Parents should not keep locks of their children's hair if they wish them to live. **1926** *Folklore* 367 [Cheshire] It is unlucky to keep your own hair (combings),—*terrible*! My grandmother said to my mother .. 'Don't you ever keep your own hair.' But she did, and she died when she was forty.

HAIR, long

1961 *Weekend* 1 Nov. 2 [Newport, Monmouth.] When I was at school, I envied three classmates whose hair was so long they could sit on it, but my grandmother quoted: 'With hair below the knee Ne'er a bride will she be.' That was 25 years ago and, although their hair is now short, those three girls are still spinsters.

HAIR, strand of: divination

1881 W. GREGOR *North-East Scotland* 26. Take a hair of the head and pull it tightly between the nails of the first finger and thumb. If it curls, the owner is proud; and the amount of curl it takes is the measure of pride. **1883** BURNE *Shropshire* 268. Children draw a single hair between the finger and thumb, and say, if it curls up when released, that it is a sign of pride. **1895** S. O. ADDY *Household Tales* 86–7.To find out whether you will be rich or poor, take a single hair from your head and draw it between your wetted first finger and thumb. If it curls you will be rich, if not you will be poor. **1935** Girl, 12 [Parkstone, Dorset] Pull a hair out of a girl's head and pull it between your finger and thumb. If it curls up she is flirtatious. **1957** Woman, 18 [Glasgow] Pull a hair and the number of kinks found equals the number of husbands.

HAIR thrown into fire: divination of future husband

1849 HALLIWELL *Popular Rhymes* 215. Two young unmarried girls must sit together in a room by themselves, from twelve o'clock at night till one o'clock the next morning, without speaking a word. During this time each of them must take as many hairs from her head as she is years old, and, having put them into a linen cloth with some of the herb true-love [herb paris] as soon as the clock strikes one, she must burn every hair separately, saying—'I offer this my sacrifice To him most precious in my eyes; I charge thee now come forth to me, That I this minute may thee see.' Upon which her first husband will appear, and walk round the room, and then vanish. **1888** *Dorset County Chronicle* 31 May 12. [To] discover who is fated to be their future partner .. two girls sit together in a room from twelve till one o'clock in the morning unknown to any one. They then take as many hairs from their heads as they are years old .. Immediately on the clock striking one they put each hair separately on the fire saying: 'I offer this my sacrifice To him most precious in my eyes, I charge thee now come forth to me That I this minute may thee see' .. The spirit of her future husband will appear .. each seeing her own and not her friend's fiancé.

HAIR thrown into fire: divination of life or death

1851 *N & Q* 1st ser. III 55 [Lancs.] If a person's hair, when thrown into the fire, burns brightly, it is a sure sign that the individual will live long. The brighter the flame the longer life, and vice versa. **1861** C. C. ROBINSON *Dialect of Leeds* 300. If a person's hair, when thrown into the fire, blazes instantly, he or she will live long; but if it smudges away, or for any length of time, they will die soon: the sooner it blazes, the longer the life. **1912** LEATHER *Herefordshire* 88. In burning hair, they say, if it smoulders, the owner's life will be short, but if it blazes brightly it will be long. **1936** E. H. RUDKIN *Lincolnshire* 21. Burn your hair-cuttings, and if they singe you will have yet another year to live. **1970** J. MCPHEE *Crofter and Laird* 150 [Colonsay, Hebrides] When a young woman combed her hair at night, she put every loose strand in the fire. If the hair did not burn, it meant that she would one day drown.

HAIR, woman's

1586 CAMDEN *Britannia* (tr. Gibson, II 378) [Limerick, *c.*1566] Both nurses and sucklings wear always a girdle of

women's hair about them. It is, moreover, observed, that they present their
lovers with bracelets of hair. 1755
Connoisseur 20 Feb. If .. the mistress
gives the dear man her hair wove in a
true lover's knot .. she thinks herself
assured of his inviolable fidelity. 1982
Times 25 Oct. 11. I recall that as a boy
in Belfast I was suffering from whooping
cough. As I whooped my way along the
street, a woman who had been observing
me from her doorway produced a pair
of scissors and snipped off a length of
her long black hair. She then wrapped
this around my neck. Whether or not it
was the shock of a possibly bizarre
form of strangulation, I certainly stopped
coughing.

hair: also see NAILS AND HAIR.

HAIRPIN falls out

1883 BURNE *Shropshire* 270. A hair-pin
falling out of the hair is a sign, say the
maids, that 'some one' wants to speak
to you. 1923 [Taunton, Som.] If a lady
accidentally drops a hair pin, it is a sure
sign that someone is thinking about
her—probably writing a letter to her.
1956 Woman, 46 [Scarborough,
Yorks.] There aren't so many of us
wearing hairpins these days, but if we
do, and one falls out, we know someone
is thinking of us.

HAND above grave

1893 W. GIBSON *Reminiscences of Dollar*
155-6. A curious legend is told about
the old churchyard of Tillicoultry [Clack-
mannan.] A wicked laird quarrelled with
one of the monks of Cambuskenneth,
and .. knocked the holy father down.
Dying shortly after this, it was discovered .. after the funeral, that the
wicked clenched fist that had dealt the
sacrilegious blow was projecting out of
the grave, and it was looked upon as a
punishment sent upon him from heaven
.. This legend gave rise to the old Scotch
saying, when any one had given a blow,
'Your hand'll wag abune the grave for
this yet.' 1984 Woman, 56 [South
Shields, Co. Durham] The hand that
strikes a parent will wag above its
owner's grave, and a puppy dog will
wee on it.

HAND itches = money

1599 SHAKESPEARE *Julius Caesar* IV iii.
Let me tell you Cassius, you your selfe
Are much condemn'd to have an itching
Palme, To sell, and Mart your Offices
for Gold to Undeservers. 1620 MELTON
Astrologaster 46. When the palme of the
right hand itcheth, it is a shrewd sign
he shall receive money. 1755 *Connoisseur* 13 May. If your right hand
itches, you will pay away money; if
your left you will receive some. 1850
N & Q lst ser. I 451 [Midlands] The
itching of the right hand palm is said to
portend the reception of a gift; which is
rendered more certain if the advice in
this distich be followed: 'Rub it 'gainst
wood, 'Tis sure to come good.' 1883
BURNE *Shropshire* 241. When the palm
of your hand itches, rub it against oak,
as it is a sign of money coming. 1885
Folklore 91. Palm, you will have money;
back, you will give money .. 'Rub it on
wood, Sure to be good. Rub it on brass,
Sure to come to pass. Rub it on brick,
Sure to be quick.' 1965 Woman, c.50
[Scarborough, Yorks.] My hand keeps
on itching. Do you think my pool's
going to come up? Left to receive, and
right to relieve, you know, and you've
got to rub it on wood. 1987 Man,
50 [Waterlooville, Hants.] Scratch on
wood, Sure to come good. Scratch on
arse, Sure to come farst.
    Cf. WOOD, touching.

HAND, lucky

1957 [Scarborough, Yorks.] 'I won at
two whist drives last week,' said Mrs
Simpson in the bus this morning, 'Won
£4.' So I carefully rubbed her hand. 'Oh
yes, they're all wanting to rub me now,'
she said.

HAND, yellow spots on

1612 WEBSTER *White Devil* v iv. When
yellow spots doe on your handes appeare, Bee certaine then you of a
Course [corpse] shall heare. Out upon't,
how 'tis speckled! h'as handled a toad
sure. 1620 MELTON *Astrologaster* 45.
That to haue yellow speckles on the
nails of ones hand [is] a great sign of
death.

HANDKERCHIEF, dropping

1982 Woman, 21 [Yorks.] The incredible story of my grandmother dropping her handkerchief while on her way to work and kicking it all the way to her destination until she could persuade somebody to pick it up for her, firm in her belief that it would be extremely unlucky to pick it up herself.

HANDKERCHIEF, folded

1954 Boy, 13 [Forfar, Angus] Amongst traditions I have heard from my grandfather, if you don't want to have bad luck never take a clean handkerchief and put it in your pocket without unfolding it. **1954** *Daily Express* 13 Aug. 4. Her mother always stressed that it was unlucky to carry a newly ironed and folded handkerchief.

HANDKERCHIEF means tears

*c.***1614** W. DRUMMOND *Poems* (1913, I 62) Ah Napkin, ominous Present of my Deare. Gift miserable, which doth now remaine The only Guerdon of my helplesse Paine. **1984** Woman, 55. I always hesitate over borrowing a handkerchief because in our family, in South Shields, it meant 'borrowing tears'.

HANDSEL (first sale of day)

*c.***1225** *Vices and Virtues* 29. Or they persist in some other error and say that he did not have a good hansel who sold him that. *c.***1340** BROMYARD *Summa Predicantium* (OWST, in *Studies*, ed. J. Conway Davies, 1957, 292) A rebuke to those who believe .. in handsels in trade, the lucky gifts 'to which salesmen pay heed, who wish to purchase nothing at the beginning of the morning until they have sold something, or received such a gift, believing it will bring them greater profit.' *c.***1450** P. IDLEY *Instructions to his Son* (1935, ll. 367–9) Som man if he can not lightly wynne, They haue badd hansell, thus they sey; And þan they curse and warrie al the day. **1607** MIDDLETON *Your Five Gallants* IV G4. Surely a marchant's wife gives lucky handsell. **1614** JONSON *Bartholmew Fayre* II ii. VRSLA [a stall-holder]. Bring him a sixe penny bottle of Ale; they say, a fooles handsell is lucky. **1632** R. BROME *Court Beggars* V ii. MENDICANT. My purse? (I mist it at my Lady Strangeloves.) CITIZEN. This Picture-

drawer [pick-pocket] drew it, and has drawne more of the Kings-pictures [bank notes] then all the Limners in the Towne .. MEND. I doe not like Thieves handsell though, This may presage some greater losse at hand. **1659** *London Chaunticleres* 12. WELCOM [the publican]. To see what lucky handsell will procure, no sooner the cup out of my mouth, but another call'd for. **1686–7** AUBREY *Remaines* (1881, 80, 120) 'Tis a common use in London, and now perhaps over great part of England, for Apple-woemen, Oyster-woemen, &c., & some Butchers, to spitt on the money wch they first recieve in the morning, wch they call good handsell .. Theeves' handsell ever unlucky.—Proverb. **1698** MISSON *Voyageur en Angleterre* (1719, 130) A Woman that goes much to market told me t'other Day, that the Butcher Women of London, those that sell Fowls, Butter, Eggs, &c. and in general most Tradespeople, have a particular Esteem for what they call Handsell; that is to say, the first Money they receive in a Morning; they kiss it, spit upon it, and put it in a Pocket by itself. **1783** G. LEMON *English Etymology. Hand-sell.* The first money received at market, which many superstitious people will spit on; either to render it tenacious, that it may remain with them, and not vanish away like a fairy gift; or else to render it propitious, and lucky, that it draw more money to it. **1829** J. HUNTER *Hallamshire Glossary* [*Yorks.*] *Handsel*, the first purchaser in a shop newly opened *handsels* it; as the first purchaser of the day does a market. **1867** H. CULLWICK *Diary* (1984, 65) The old gentleman .. put 1/2 a crown in my hand .. His was my handsell & of course I hoped to see a good many more come & go before the end o' the season, & so I spit on the 1/2 crown for luck, same as you see the hawkers do with their'n. **1869** *N&Q* 4th ser. IV 132 [Scarborough, Yorks.] Some boys and myself bought some variegated stones of an old woman aged eighty-four. She spat upon our money, and wished for good sale during the day. **1880** W. JONES *Credulities* 479 [London] In the street market-places, amongst the stall-keepers, it is reckoned to be nothing else than ruinous to turn away a 'first bid' for an article.

It brings bad luck on the day's selling, and it is better to get the 'hansel' (as the first sale is called) over, even at a loss .. There are to be found mean folks who are known as hansel-hunters .. who are early in the field, and alert to take full advantage of the poor vendor's superstition. **1900** *N & Q* 9th ser. VI 273–4. The van and tent dwellers whom we call gipsies .. wheedle you into buying almost before you know it ‿ 'Pray gi'me hansel, good lady. You speak fairly [kindly], an' it'll bring me luck for the day.' **1909** M. TREVELYAN *Folk-Lore of Wales* 329. At market, do not let the first customer go; sell under value rather than lose him .. It is customary for people in the markets in Wales either to spit on the first money they take in the morning, or to throw the coin on the ground and tread on it. **1916** JOYCE *Portrait of the Artist* 213. A hand was laid on his arm and a young voice cried: 'Ah, gentleman, your own girl, sir! The first handsel today, gentleman. Buy that lovely bunch. Will you, gentleman?' **1926** *Folklore* 173–4 [Aberystwyth, Cardigan.] Our house is the first in the row, and the first to which our fishmongers come on their morning round with the cart .. They are very unwilling to pass on without selling us something, for they think that to sell fish to us brings them luck for the whole day. **1957** *Woman*, 47. After some bargaining I bought an agate brooch in Altrincham market today. When I handed the stallholder the money he spat on it heartily, and adjured his wife not to row him afterwards for selling the brooch so cheap, because it was, after all, 'the first sale'. **1957** Man, *c.*35 [Brentwood, Essex] Usherettes in a theatre spit on the first tip they receive to give the play a long run.

HANDSEL MONDAY

1881 *Folk-Lore Record* 107 [Ireland] Hansel Monday. The first Monday in the year, when formerly a present or hansel was given by a master or mistress to the servants, and by fathers or mothers to children .. Anything that comes into your possession that day indicates luck, such as a child, calf, lambs, or money. If you receive on Hansel Monday you will sure to be lucky the rest of the year. **1881** W. GREGOR *North-East of Scotland* 164. In parts of Buchan it was deemed unlucky to spend money in any form on 'Hansel Monandy' .. If money was spent, or anything given away, the luck of the year fled with the money or the gift. **1887** 'SPERANZA' WILDE *Superstitions of Ireland* II 116. Never pay away money on the first Monday of the year, or you will lose your luck in gaining money all the year after. **1952** Girl, 14 [Aberdeen] When Hansel Monday comes give one another money, and keep it till next Hansel Monday, and it brings good luck throughout the year.

Cf. MONDAY, giving/receiving on; NEW YEAR and money.

HANDSELLING new clothes

1866 HENDERSON *Northern Counties* 88. No one .. will put on a new coat or dress without placing some money .. in the right-hand pocket .. This ensures the pocket being always full; but if .. it is put in the left-hand pocket, you will never have a penny so long as you wear the coat. **1881** W. GREGOR *North-East of Scotland* 31. When one put on a piece of new dress, a coin of the realm, called 'handsel', had to be put into one of the pockets. **1901** *Eng. Dialect Dict. Handsel* [Northumb.] 'A hansel penny' is usually put into the pocket of any garment to hansel it and the formula repeated, 'Health to wear, strength to tear, an money to buy another.' **1913** E. M. WRIGHT *Rustic Speech* 225. In the North-country dialects *handsel* is .. a gift conferred at a particular season, or on commencement of a new undertaking, to confer luck. The gift of a coin, for instance, to the wearer of a new suit of clothes makes the suit lucky. **1952** Girl, 13 [Kirkcaldy, Fife] When a person has a new suit friends and relations put money in the pockets to 'hansel' it.

HANDSELLING new purse

1923 [Chard, Som.] To give an empty purse to anyone is very unlucky. To prevent the ill-luc give or put a coin in it. **1936** E. H. R KIN *Lincolnshire* 21. If anyone gives you a purse, let them put a halfpenny in it and you will never want for money. **1952** Girl, 14

[Aberdeen] When someone has a new handbag, anyone that notices is supposed to 'handsel' it, that is to put a piece of money in it. **1984** Woman, 37 [Harrow, Middx.] You should never give a purse without money in it.

Cf. MONEY, having: in purse etc.

HANGMAN'S ROPE cures/protects

AD 77 PLINY *Natural History* XXVIII XII (1856, V 294) Binding the temples with a halter with which a man has been hanged [will alleviate headache]. **1584** SCOT *Discoverie of Witchcraft* XII XIV. *A charme for the headach.* Tie a halter about your head, wherewith one hath beene hanged. **1688** AUBREY *Remaines* (1881, 198) This [as in Pliny] is oftentimes donne at London: many have great faith in it: y[t] hangman getts mony for pieces of the halters for this purpose. **1752** *Life of Nicholas Mooney* (BRAND *Antiquities* 1813, II 538) A young woman came fifteen miles for the sake of the rope from Mooney's neck, which was given to her; it being by many apprehended that the halter of an executed person will charm away the ague, and perform many other cures. **1813** BRAND *Antiquities* II 583. I remember once to have seen, at Newcastle-upon-Tyne, after a person executed had been cut down, men climb up upon the gallows and contend for that part of the rope which remained, and which they wished to preserve for some lucky purpose or other. I have lately made the important discovery that it is reckoned a cure for the headache. **1867** *Trans. Devon. Ass.* 39. A portion of a rope with which a suicide has hanged himself is a wondrous charm against all accidents, when worn around the person. **1933** *Folklore* 202 [Willoughton, Lincs.] Fits can be cured by procuring a strand from a rope with which a man has hung himself, and wearing it always round the neck. **1944** O. SITWELL *Left Hand, Right Hand!* 121 [in his mother's room] I did not understand one thing, a loop of thick rope, a foot or two long, twisted in a knot round the head of the bed . . Eventually, after many implorings, I was told what it was. 'It's a bit of a hangman's rope, darling. Nothing's so lucky!'

Cf. GALLOWS.

HANGMAN'S ROPE lucky to card players

1868 *N & Q* 4th ser. I 193. It is held by certain gamesters that a bit of a hangman's rope is a charm for success at cards. It cost eight pounds—they're very difficult to get now.'

HARE = witch

1184 GIRALDUS CAMBRENSIS *Topographica Hibernica* II XIX. It has been a frequent complaint, from old times, as well as in the present, that certain hags in Wales, as well as in Ireland and Scotland, changed themselves into the shape of hares, that, sucking teats under this counterfeit form, they might stealthily rob other people's milk. *c.*1350 HIGDEN *Polychronicon* (MS Harl. 2261, tr. Trevisa: Rolls I 359) Hit is seide amonge commune peple, olde women of that londe [Ireland], and of Wales, to chaunge theyme in to the forme of an hare. **1586** CAMDEN *Britannia* (tr. Gibson, II 380) [Limerick, Eire] On Mayday . . if they [the 'wild Irish'] can find a hare among the herd, they endeavour to kill her, out of a notion, that it is some old witch that has a design upon their butter. **1673** *Depositions*, *York Castle* 2 Apr. (1861, 191) She . . saith that the said Ann hath been severall times in the shape of . . a hare. **1711** *Spectator* 14 July. If a hare makes an unexpected escape from the hounds, the huntsman curses Moll White [the 'witch']. **1827** CLARE *Shepherd's Calendar* Jan. ll. 194–6. Witches . . when met with unawares . . turn at once to cats as hares. **1830** SCOTT *Demonology* 288 [trial of Isobel Gowdie, Auldearn, Nairn., 1662] Isobel only escaped by getting into another house, and gaining time to say the disenchanting rhyme: 'Hare, hare, God send thee care! I am in a hare's likeness now; But I shall be woman even now—Hare, hare, God send thee care!' **1838** A. E. BRAY *Devonshire* II 277. An old witch . . would assume the shape of a hare . . often seen, but never caught . . a sportsman . . began to suspect . . 'that the devil was in the dance.' **1866** HENDERSON *Northern Counties* 165. The hare . . into which the witch of modern days transforms herself when in extremity. **1887** 'SPERANZA' WILDE *Superstitions of Ireland* I

201. Hares found on May morning are supposed to be witches, and should be stoned. 1901 J. RHYS *Celtic Folklore* I 309. The break of this day [May Day] is .. the signal for setting the ling or the gorse on fire, which is done in order to burn out the witches wont to take the form of the hare. 1909 M. TREVELYAN *Folk-Lore of Wales* 212. When a hare is very difficult to skin, the women say: 'This one was a bad old witch;' or when a hare is slow in being cooked, they say: 'This old witch has many sins to answer for.'

HARE, eating: taboo

*c.*600 BC Deuteronomy 14: 7–8. Ye shall not eat .. the hare and the coney .. they are unclean unto you. *c.*50 BC CAESAR *Gallic War* V XII (tr. Brodie) [The Britons] do not regard it lawful to eat the hare. 1507 *Gospelles of Dystaues* pt. 3 II. For to kepe them that they fall not in to the palsye, they must absteyne them from etynge .. the fleshe of heres. 1738 SWIFT *Polite Conversation* II 143. Madam, will your Ladyship have any of this Hare? No, Madam, they say, 'tis melancholy Meat. 1777 BRAND *Antiquities* 92. The antient Britons made Use of the Hare for the Purposes of Divination. They were never killed for the Table. 'Tis perhaps from hence that they have been accounted ominous by the Vulgar. 1893 *Folklore* 352. Country people in Kerry don't eat hares; the souls of their grandmothers are supposed to have entered into them. 1926 *Folklore* 370–1. No Norfolk labourer will take a hare as a gift, although they are very fond of rabbits.

HARE, killing

1972 EVANS & THOMSON *Leaping Hare* 99 [Lissduff, Co. Offaly] They say it's unlucky to make a practice of killing hares. Something always turns up. Something happens. They say about poachers—that if something happened to one, they'd say: 'He can't have better luck! He's always going about killing and catching hares.'

HARE portends fire

1851 *N & Q* 1st ser. III 3 [Northants.] The running of [a hare] along the street or mainway of a village, portends fire to some house in the immediate vicinity. 1866 *Cambridge Chronicle* 10 Nov. 6. On Saturday last, a foolish hare ventured from broad fields and open pastures, to visit the city of Ely .. she was hotly pursued .. and when near the Bell Inn, she [was] laid by the heels by a stout walking stick. The fact being generally known, great consternation prevailed; many persons being certain that Ely was to be visited by a fire. 1884 *Northampton Daily Chronicle* 9 Oct. 4. At Rushden on the day of the fire .. a hare was seen to run along one of the streets a few hours previous to the fire, and some who saw it expressed the hope that should the omen prove true, the fire would not occur at a factory or any other public works. 1909 *N & Q* 10th ser. XI 413 [Peterborough, Northants.] If in the Minster Close a hare Should for herself have made a lair, Be sure before a week is down A fire will rage within the town. 1909 *N & Q* 10th ser. XI 458. In April 1908, one of the masters' houses at Harrow was burnt down. A hare was said to have run through the town that morning; and there was a similar tradition about a similar fire there in the thirties. 1972 EVANS & THOMSON *Leaping Hare* 126 [St Olaves, Suffolk] I've heard about the hare running and a fire coming afterwards. In fact, an old character out this way used to reckon that they were bad luck to have run through your garden because you'd probably have your house on fire before the end of the year.

HARE OR RABBIT, meeting

1159 JOHN OF SALISBURY *Policraticus* (*Frivolities of Courtiers*, ed. J. B. Pike, 49) You may ascertain the outcome of your journeys from beasts .. You are to avoid the hare; that is if it escape, for undoubtedly its fitting place is the table, not the road. 1180 NIGEL DE LONGCHAMPS *Mirror for Fools* (tr. Mozley, 96) May running hare And limping she-goat their own omens bear, In morning met. late 13th c. MS Digby 86 (*Proceedings Leeds Phil. Soc.* III 350) [Shrops.] 'The Names of the Hare in English' l. 19. þe euelelmet [The one it's bad luck to meet]. 1507 *Gospelles of Dystaues* pt. 2 III. I saye to you as a gospell that whan one goothe on his waye and yf he encountre a haare it is an euyll sygne. And for to eschewe all daungers he ought for to retorne thryes from whens he was departed, and after goo on his waye withouten peryll. **1584** SCOT *Discoverie of Witchcraft* XI xv. He that receiveth a mischance, wil consider whether he met not a .. hare, when he first went out of his doores in the morning. **1587** GIFFORD *Subtill Practises of Devilles* C2. Another goeth abrode early in the morning, & a hare crosseth his way: a very unlucky signe he taketh it to be, and looketh not to speede well that day. **1603** W. PERKINS *Works* 39. It is vnluckie for one .. to haue an hare crosse him. *c.***1614** WEBSTER *Duchess of Malfi* II ii. How superstitiously we mind our evils! .. The .. crossing of a Hare .. of powre To daunt whole man in us. **1639** DELONEY *Gentle Craft* pt. 2 F3. These shoomakers have vs by the eares .. sblood they be as unluckie to be met, as a Hare on a iorney. **1691** *History of Athenian Society* pt. 2 16. I cannot but wonder to find Tycho Brahe, running back to his House .. if an Hare cross'd the Path he was going. **1818** *Edinburgh Magazine* Nov. 412 [Angus] Should a hare cross the road before the bride, it is ominous. **1822** SCOTT *The Pirate* II 277–8. Neither Clawson's boat, nor Peter Grot's, are out to the haaf this morning, for a rabbit ran across them as they were going on board, and they came back like wise men. **1857** *N & Q* 2nd ser. IV 25. There are fishermen in Forfarshire who, on a hare crossing their path while on their way to their boats, will not put to sea that day. **1864** *N & Q* 3rd ser. V 353 [SE Ireland] It is considered particularly unfortunate for a farmer or his wife if they should, on a May morning, meet a hare, as that animal is [then] said to take away the milk from the cows. **1875** *Monthly Packet* 517–18. It is still bad luck to meet a hare, yet if you are unfortunate enough to do so, you can easily set matters right by spitting over your left shoulder, and saying, 'Hare before, Trouble behind: Change ye, Cross, and free me,' or else by the still more simple charm which consists in touching each shoulder with your fore-

finger, and saying, 'Hare, hare, God send thee care.' I have never heard of more than these two lines being used, and indeed I do not think that the old man who told me of them knew any more. **1878** *Folk-Lore Record* 56 [Fittleworth, Sussex] I have met with even educated persons who, if a hare were the first animal that crossed their path upon their leaving home, would turn back, regarding it as a warning. **1883** BURNE *Shropshire* 212. It is lucky to meet a hare (Waters' Upton and Cold Hatton), but unlucky to see it run across the path. Should it cross the path of a wayfarer from right to left, his journey will be disastrous; if it scuds along the way before him, the issue of his affairs will be doubtful for some time; but if it crosses from left to right it is a lucky token (Condover). **1898** *Weekly Scotsman* Christmas Number 6 [Fogo, Berwick.] Who among fishermen of the older generation would not consider it a plain intimation of a very meagre catch .. were he to see a hare limping across his path to the shore? **1953** Boy, 15. The inhabitants of the Isle of Portland [Dorset] have one very big superstition in which all Portlanders believe. The rabbit is the omen of the very worst luck. Should a quarryman see a rabbit on his way to work, he will immediately turn about and go home, refusing to work that day. **1972** EVANS & THOMSON *Leaping Hare* 215 [Norfolk] I was driving out with a man the other day when a hare crossed the road: 'Had that been my old father driving he'd have turned back and gone straight home,' said the car driver. He didn't. But I noticed that he drove with special care the rest of the way.

HARE OR RABBIT on ship

1854 *N & Q* 1st ser. X 26. A dead hare on board a ship is said to bring bad weather. **1919** *Morning Post* 9 June 3 [Isle of Thanet] Two families .. had a deadly quarrel. One night, when the smack of one family was not at sea, members of the other family nailed a rabbit skin so thoroughly to the mast that it took the owner a couple of days to get every bit of material free. It would have been very unlucky to go to sea with even a fragment of rabbit's hair anywhere on the boat. **1930** P. F. ANSON *East Coast of Scotland* 38. Stories are told all along the coast of mischievous boys getting hold of rabbit skins, filling them with rubbish and placing [them] in the sterns of boats, in order to stop the men from going to sea. **1939** *Folklore* 346. Hares were dreaded in Cullen and in Portknockie [Banff.]; if a fisherman from these places found a hare on his net he would burn it rather than go to sea with it.

'HARE' OR 'RABBIT': saying at change of month

1920 *Folklore* 319. According to several correspondents in the *Westminster Gazette* (spring of 1919) the following belief is common in many parts of Great Britain, with local variants: To secure good luck of some kind, usually a present, one should say 'Rabbits' three times just before going to sleep on the last day of the month, and then 'Hares' three times on waking the next morning. **1922** LYND *Solomon* 49. 'Coming on to midnight, gentlemen,' he said; 'I hope everybody here will remember to say "Rabbit, rabbit, rabbit" first thing in the morning.' **1953** Girl, 14 [Llangunllo, Radnor.] On the first day of the month when you wake up in the morning shout 'White Rabbit' and when you go to bed at night shout 'Black Rabbit' and you will have good luck. **1959** *Yorkshire Post* 22 Oct. 6. My childhood was spent in Teesdale .. and one of my earliest memories is that of proclaiming 'Rabbits' triumphantly, before anyone else got in first, on the first of the month. It was supposed to assure one of good fortune for the rest of the month. **1964** [Suffolk, *c*.1915] On the last night of the month we said 'Hares' and 'Rabbits' the next morning, and wished if we had not spoken between. **1972** EVANS & THOMSON *Leaping Hare* 113. A Suffolk farmer [born 1891] recalled a saying that used to be repeated at the end of the month: 'Let the owd hare set.' **1982** Woman, *c*.50 [Stockton-on-Tees, Co. Durham] The first words you say for a lucky month are 'White Rabbits'. If you can remember to say that twelve times a year, you'll have a very lucky year.

1984 Woman, 47 [Chichester, Sussex] If you say 'Black cats' on the last night of the month and 'White rabbits' next morning, you will get a present before the month is out.

Cf. NEW MOON, bowing etc. to.

'HARE' OR 'RABBIT' taboo word

late **13th c.** MS Digby 86 (*Proceedings Leeds Phil. Soc.* III 351) [Shrops.] 'The Names of the Hare in English.' þe der þat nomon nedar nemnen [The animal that no one dare name]. **1602** R. CAREW *Cornwall* 31–2. We will launch out into the deepe, and see what luck of fish God there shall send vs, which (so you talke not of Hares or such vncouth things, for that proues ominous to the fisherman ..) may succeed very profitable. **1875** *N & Q* 5th ser. III 204 [Flamborough, Yorks.] The fishermen .. had a great fear if rabbits .. were spoken of. **1881** W. GREGOR *North-East of Scotland* 129. To say to a fisherwoman that there was a hare's foot in her creel, or to say to a fisherman that there was a hare in his boat, aroused strong ire, and called forth strong words. The word 'hare' was not pronounced at sea. **1886** *Folklore* 14 [Buckie, Banff.] Rabbit [is a] word of ill-omen [to the fisherfolk]. **1896** *N & Q* 8th ser. X 393 [Cornwall] If a pilchard-driver were going out for the night's work, and anybody aboard should drop the dreaded word [rabbit] the crew would .. make for harbour as fast as they could, 'for fear of what might happen to them'. **1916** *N & Q* 12th ser. I 66. Some newly joined 'subs' had talked at mess of how many rabbits they had shot the last day they were out .. A lieutenant observed that, had he been there to hear it, he would rather have taken his baggage off the ship and gone ashore. **1919** *Morning Post* 9 June 3. During a visit to the Isle of Thanet I [Edward Lovett] led the conversation up to the subject of rabbits. To my amusement, but not astonishment, the man would not repeat the word 'rabbits'. He referred to them as 'those hairy things' .. He told me that a new hand on one of the boats was one night at a drinking party when another man, out of pure mischief, started a conversation on rabbits. The new hand was so frightened that he got up, and went out, even forgetting to drink his own beer. **1953** Boy, 15 [Isle of Portland, Dorset] So powerful is the animal supposed to be [as an ill omen] that people will not even say the word. They refer to it as a 'Wilfred' or 'One of them furry things'. But if one person is very angry with another and really wishes them bad luck he will say 'Rabbits to you'. **1963** *Daily Express* 20 Nov. 10. On the Isle of Portland, near Weymouth, there is a superstitious fear of even the word 'rabbit'. The local paper makes a solemn check to keep the word out of its Portland edition. **1965** P. F. ANSON *Fisher Folk-Lore* 131 n. Rabbit Island .. was usually called 'Gentlemen's Island' by the Buckie [Banff.] fishermen to avoid using the unlucky word. **1981** Man, 60 [Norfolk] You don't talk about rabbits on board ship.

hare or rabbit: cf. PIG.

HARE-LIP

1507 *Gospelles of Dystaues* pt. I VIII. Ye sholde not gyve to yonge maydens to ete the heed of a hare .. and in especyall to them that be with chylde, for certaynly theyr chyldren might haue clouen lyppes. **1579** LUPTON *Thousand Notable Things* IV § 15. If a Woman with chylde haue her smocke, that she weares, slyt at the neather ende or skyrt thereof .. the .. chylde .. shal be safe from hauing a cloven or hare lyppe. Yea, though she chaunce to meete suddenly a Hare, or though a hare doth leape ouer her, or suddenly touch her. Which happens to many Chyldren by such meanes. **1650** N. HOMES *Daemonologie* 60. If an Hare .. crosse the way where one is going, it is (they say) a signe of very ill luck. In so much as some in company with a Woman great with Childe, have upon the crossing of such creatures, cut or torne some of the clothes off that Woman with Childe, to prevent (as they imagined) the ill luck that might befal her. I know I tell you that which is most true: And I hope in such a subject as this touching these superstitions, I shall not offend in acquainting you with these particulars. **1881** W. GREGOR *North-East of Scotland* 129. Harelip was produced

by a woman *enceinte* putting her foot into a hare's lair. If the woman noticed she had done so, she immediately took two stones and put them into the lair. The evil effects were averted. **1883** BURNE *Shropshire* 212–13. If a hare crosses the path of a woman with child, she must instantly stoop down and tear her shift, or her child will have a hare-lip—an 'ar-shotten' lip, as it is called in the Clun Forest neighbourhood, where instances have been known of women actually dismounting from horseback to take the prescribed precaution. **1959** LADY DIANA COOPER *Light of Common Day* 95 [refers to 1929] A sitting hare would not get out of the way of our car: this, to one who had read Mary Webb's 'Precious Bane', augured a hare-lip for my baby. **1972** EVANS & THOMSON *Leaping Hare* 220 [Co. Antrim] A hare .. run across the way they were going .. He whipped out his knife and lifted up her clothes and he split her shift from the shoulders down .. If he hadn't done that, the child would be born with a 'hare-scaart'.

HARE'S OR RABBIT'S FOOT cures

AD **77** PLINY *Natural History* XXVIII LXII (1856, V 352) Gout .. may be allayed by the patient always carrying about him a hare's foot. **1584** SCOT *Discoverie of Witchcraft* XIII x. The bone in a hares foot mitigateth the crampe, as none other bone nor part else of the hare doth. **1608** WITHALS *Dictionarie* 215. The bone of a haires foote closed in a Ring, Will driue awaye the cramp when as it doth wring. **1664–5** PEPYS *Diary* 20 Jan. So homeward, in my way buying a hare and taking it home, which arose upon my discourse to-day with Mr Batten, in Westminster Hall, who showed me my mistake that my hare's foote hath not the joynt to it; and assures me he never had his cholique since he carried it about him. **1850** *N & Q* 1st ser. II 37 [Northants.] The right forefoot of a hare, worn constantly in the pocket is considered a fine amulet against the 'rheumatiz'. **1899** *Newcastle Weekly Chronicle* 4 Feb. 7 [Jesmond] A hare's foot with a joint carried about the person wards off rheumatism.

Cf. CRAMP BONE; MOLE'S FEET cure.

HARE'S OR RABBIT'S FOOT protects/is lucky

1827 HONE *Table Book* I 675 [Wither-slack, Lancs.] My mother .. carries a hare's foot in her pocket, to guard against all attacks in that quarter [witch-craft] by day. **1932** C. IGGLESDEN *Those Superstitions* 146. At its birth the infant should be brushed with a rabbit's foot, and I am told that hundreds of mothers even today place it in the perambulator when a child is taken out by its nurse .. Adults believe in the rabbit's foot as a charm, and it is astonishing to find it a common custom, not only among the ignorant but the cultured classes. **1953** *Reveille* 2 Oct. 2 [St Anne's-on-Sea, Lancs.] There are the rabbits' feet pro-duced from the handbags at the be-ginning of play [whist drives] and placed on the table. **1969** C. WOODFORD *Sussex Ways* 60. Another charm of good luck was a rabbit's foot .. used at birth to brush the baby's face and so ward off evil spirits, or to lay beneath its pillow to prevent an accident happening. **1972** EVANS & THOMSON *Leaping Hare* 234 [Suffolk] Just before I went off into the Navy at the outbreak of war .. he say: 'Boy, got you hare's foot?' **1981** *Sunday People* 10 May 29 [Sheringham, Norfolk] I always carried a rabbit's foot for luck until someone said: 'Well, the rabbit wasn't lucky, was he?' **1982** Woman, *c*.50 [Stockton-on-Tees, Co. Durham] Always carry a rabbit's foot for luck—that's very lucky. A sailor carries a rabbit's foot wherever he goes—they're very superstitious, are sailors. **1982** Woman, 20 [Sheffield, Yorks.] Actors will put on make-up with a rabbit's foot, kiss it for luck or rub it on their face and hands the night a play opens.

HAT worn in church

1923 [Somerset] If females don't wear hats in church it is unlucky. **1954** Girl, 11 [Perth] It is supposed to be bad luck if you take your hat off in church.

HAY, load of

1932 C. IGGLESDEN *Those Superstitions* 106. There is an antidote to the calamity of meeting a load of hay—if you turn when it has passed and spit at it all will be well .. In Wales we find the superstition is reversed, and a load of hay brings good luck. **1952** Farmer's daughter, *c*.25 [Dunvant, Glam.] It is unlucky to see a hay-wain disappear, round a bend or over the crest of a hill, and you must look away at that point. **1953** Girl, 15 [Loughton, Essex] If you see a hay cart and wish, your wish will come true, provided you don't see the back of it. **1954** A woman from Llanelly [Mon.] says she spits and touches leather if she sees the back of a loaded hay-wain, to ward off ill-luck. **1979** D. MORRIS *Gestures* 144. A girl, from Swansea, said she [made 'horns' with index and little finger] when a hay lorry went past in the street. **1983** Woman, 52 [South Petherton, Som.] I hate following a load of hay in my car. I'm constantly looking for one coming in the other direction. I think they cancel each other out.

HAY RICK

1953 R. DUNCAN *Where I Live* 123 [Devon] When I first settled in the coun-try I heard that it was the custom that each new rick of hay should be slept on by a young man and a girl, in order to ensure that the hay would prove sweet, and the fiancée pregnant.

HEARSE comes to house

1755 *Connoisseur* 13 Mar. They had a dairymaid who died the very week after a hearse had stopped at the door on its way to church. **1923** [Ruishton, Som.] If the hearse returns to the house after a funeral it is a menace to someone in the house.

HEARSE turns back

1893 *Northampton Mercury* 1 Sept. 6. At the funeral of Mr J. Sarrington it was noted that the hearse, after the coffin was placed in it, had to be turned round to proceed on its journey, a sure sign, gossip said, of another early death in the family. The demise of Mr W. B. Sarrington has given the superstition another lease of life. **1939** *Folklore* 72–3 [Norfolk] A coffin ought not to be turned round during the journey to the church, otherwise the head of the bereaved family will die within a year .. The relatives of the dead woman .. discovered that if the hearse went by the

main road from the hospital to the house
and then to the chapel, it would be
necessary to turn the hearse round ..
when it reached the house. They therefore insisted that the hearse should go
.. by a secondary road.

Cf. WEDDING CARRIAGE turns back.

HEART stuck with pins etc. and burned to detect witch

1793 Correspondent [Brampton,
Cumb.] (J. HUNTER MS note in Brand's
Antiquities II 372) I have seen the heart
taken out of a horse (bewitched to be
cured) a large fire made and the heart
thrown into it, when the wizard (for in
this instance it was a man) came
forward, and was nearly killed by the
Miller and his wife, whose the horse
was. **1856** *N & Q* 2nd ser. I 415 [Lincs.]
His next-door neighbour .. had two
young horses making up for Lincoln
April fair [and found] them both dead
the very morning he was about to set
out with them .. So he went to a person
learned in forbidden lore, who told him
that if he cut out the heart of one of the
dead animals, stuck it full of pins, and
boiled it in a pot, the man who had the
evil eye would present himself at the
door, and knock loudly for admittance;
but was on no account to be let in, for
if he once crossed the threshold the
charm would fail .. The result was that
the wizard was so badly scalded, that he
could not work for several months.
1866 HENDERSON *Northern Counties* 182
[Stokesley, Teesside, c.1830] The farmer
was directed to take the heart of one of
the dead beasts [cattle] and stick in it
nine new nails, nine new pins, and
as many new needles. The heart thus
prepared was to be burnt on a fire made
.. with witchwood (rowan) a little before
midnight, at which hour a certain verse
of the Bible was to be read over the
flames .. The doors [were] secured .. He
read the appointed verse, and at the
same moment a rushing and clattering
was heard down the paved causey ..
Next began a terrible knocking and
hammering, first at the front door, then
at the back .. but as the embers of the
heart wasted in the fire .. the noise
ceased. Ibid. 186-7. At Durham, about
four years ago .. a poor woman was

brought before the bench of magistrates
on the charge of stealing a fowl .. [Her]
child had long been ailing [and] the
witch solemnly charged her to steal a
hen, take out the heart, stick it full of
pins, and roast it at midnight over a
slow fire. Ibid. 187. [They] had lost two
horses during the last year and therefore
consulted 'Black Willie' at Hartlepool
[Co. Durham], who assured them that
they had been bewitched. Acting on
his advice, they adopted the following
means for discovering the witch. Having
procured a pigeon, and tied its wings,
every aperture to the house, even to the
key-holes, was carefully stopped, and
pins were run into the pigeon whilst
alive by each member of the family, so
as to pierce the poor bird's heart. The
pigeon was then roasted, and a watch
kept at the window during the operation,
for the first person who passed the door
would, of course, be the guilty party.
1885 *Folklore* 378 [Staithes, Yorks.]
Until quite recently—and I am informed
that by some of the older habitants the
custom is still secretly maintained—it
was customary when a smack or coble
had had a protracted run of ill-fortune,
for the wives of the crew and owners of
the boat to assemble at midnight, and,
in deep silence, to slay a pigeon, whose
heart they extracted, stuck full of pins,
and burned over a charcoal fire .. The
unconscious witch would come to the
door, dragged thither unwittingly by
the irresistible potency of the charm,
and the conspirators would then make
her some propitiatory present. **1889** *Dorset Field Club* 23-4. A few years ago ..
at Hawkchurch .. an obstruction was
found in one of the chimneys, which ..
was .. a bullock's heart, into which was
stuck .. prickles of the white thorn.
1900 S. HEWETT *Nummits* 74 [Devon]
To destroy the power of a witch. Take
three small-necked stone jars: place in
each the liver of a frog stuck full of new
pins, and the heart of a toad stuck full
of thorns from the holy thorn bush. Cork
and seal each jar. Bury in three different
churchyard paths seven inches from the
surface and seven feet from the porch.
While in the act of burying each jar
repeat the Lord's prayer backwards.
1925 E. LOVETT *Magic in Modern London*

67 [NE London, c.1902] A cowkeeper
.. originally from Devonshire, had the
misfortune to incur the intense wrath of
a man of very vindictive temper. He
threatened to bewitch the poor man's
cows, and two of them died. The cowkeeper thereupon took the heart of one
of the dead animals, stuck it all over
with pins and nails and hung it up in
the chimney of his house. **1946** M.
SUMMERS *Witchcraft and Black Magic*
189–90. In the Somerset County Museum at Taunton .. may be seen shrivelled hearts of pigs, studded with pins,
which were discovered hidden away in
old cottages. This was .. to rack the old
witch who had killed the animals with
pains and cramps in every joint of her
body. **1951** Woman, c.70. My eldest
brother, a delicate baby, was declared
by his north country nurse to have been
bewitched, so, my mother consenting,
she got a calf's heart, stuck it full of pins
and roasted it in front of the fire.

Cf. CATTLE: burning entrails gives
power over witch; EXCREMENT, burning
human.

HEART stuck with pins: lover's spell

1861 C. C. ROBINSON *Dialect of Leeds* 302.
[to dream about future husband] Kill a
pigeon, take out its heart, and stick that
full of pins, and put it under the pillow,
going backwards-way to bed. **1904**
N & Q 10th ser. II 273 [Lincs., 1837]
The sexton of St Mary's .. watched her
rake up the earth with her foot, and after
depositing something in the ground,
carefully cover it up .. He opened the
place, and found a hare's heart, in which
385 pins were stuck, buried. It is an old
superstition in this county, that if a
person .. shall bury a hare's heart stuck
full of pins, near a newly-made grave ..
as the heart decays .. the health of the
faithless swain will decline, and that he
will die when it is mouldered into dust.
1915 J. A. PENNY *Horncastle* 66 [Lincs.]
A horrible Love Charm .. a girl tearing
the heart out of a pigeon to kill it, to
compel the man she loves to marry her
against his will.

HEART stuck with pins: witch's spell

1584 SCOT *Discoverie of Witchcraft* XII
XVI. The witch told them that there was
great cause of their suspicion: for the
same (said she) is the verie partie that
wrought the maidens destruction, by
making a hart of wax, and pricking the
same with pins and needels.

Cf. IMAGE/PICTURE used to injure or
kill.

HEATHER, white

1862 (G. BATTISCOMBE *Queen Alexandra*
36) The Queen's heart warmed towards
this exquisite creature who was to be
her son's wife. She spoke kindly to her
and presented her with a sprig of white
heather picked by the Prince at
Balmoral, saying she hoped it would
bring her luck. **1900** S. BARING-GOULD
Book of Dartmoor 162 [Devon] To him
who wanders over the moor .. some day
comes the proud felicity of lighting on
the white heather—and that found ensures happiness. **1911** J. C. DAVIES *West
and Mid-Wales* 215. To bring heather
into the house is a sign of death: white
heather, however, is considered extremely lucky. **1923** [Bridgwater, Som.]
It is very lucky to keep a piece of white
heather. **1932** C. J. S. THOMPSON *Hand of
Destiny* 287. That a sprig of white
heather will bring good luck to the
wearer, is still an article of faith with
some of our leading politicians who are
frequently seen with it in their button-
holes. **1960** *Woman* 3 Sept. 5. Some
apple trees she [the Queen Mother] planted years ago are ringed by white
heather. For there's an old Highland
tradition that what grows in a lucky
heather circle will be particularly fruitful. **1984** Woman, 55. I chose white
heather for my head-dress when I was
married in 1953. In the North, the white
variety was considered lucky, because it
was rare I suppose.

HEMP SEED: divination

1685 *Mother Bunch's Closet* (1885, 18)
Carry the seed in your apron, and with
your right hand throw it over your
left shoulder, saying thus: 'Hemp-seed I
sow, hemp-seed I sow, And he that must
be my true love, Come after me and
mow.' And at the ninth time expect to
see the figure of him you are to wed, or
else hear a bell. **1688** AUBREY *Remaines*
(1881, 95) 'Hempe-seed I sow, And

Hempe-seed I mowe, And he that is my sweetheart come follow me, I trow.' Mdm. green Hemp leaves will make one to be in the same condition with Dotroa [Datura, the Thornapple—which is intoxicating]. 1714 GAY *Shepherd's Week* 33. At Eve last Midsummer no Sleep I sought, But to the Field a Bag of Hemp-seed brought, I scatter'd round the Seed on ev'ry side, And three times in a trembling Accent cry'd. This Hempseed with my Virgin Hands I sow, Who shall my True-love be, the Crop shall mow. 1755 *Connoisseur* 20 Feb. [Midsummer Eve] Exactly at twelve o'clock, I sowed Hempseed in our back yard, and said to myself, 'Hempseed I sow, Hempseed I hoe, and he that is my true-love come after me and mow.' Will you believe me? I looked back and saw him behind me, as plain as eyes could see him. 1787 BURNS *Poems* 165 [note to 'Halloween'] Steal out unperceived, and sow a handful of hemp-seed, harrowing it with any thing you can conveniently draw after you. Repeat, now and then—'Hemp-seed I saw, hemp-seed I saw thee; and him (or her) that is to be my true-love, come after me and pou thee.' Look over your left shoulder, and you will see the appearance of the person invoked, in the attitude of pulling hemp. Some traditions say, 'Come after me and shaw thee,' that is, show thyself; in which case it simply appears. Others omit the harrowing, and say, 'Come after me and harrow thee.' 1830 FORBY *East Anglia* 408. Precisely at midnight the husband-seeker must go alone into the garden, taking with her some hemp-seed, which she is to sow, repeating . . 'Hemp-seed I sow; Hemp-seed, grow; He that is my true love Come after me, and mow.' 1831 HONE *Year Book* 8 Oct. [Dorset] A maiden will walk through the garden at midsummer, with a rake on her left shoulder, and throw hemp-seed over her right, saying, at the same time, 'Hemp-seed I set, hemp-seed I sow, The man that is my true-love come after me and mow.' It is said by many who have never tried it, and some who have, without effect, that the future husband of the hemp-sowing girl will appear behind her with a scythe, and look as substantial as a brass image of Saturn

on an old time-piece. 1880 W. SIKES *British Goblins* 304 [Wales] Go into the garden at midnight, in the season when 'black seed' was sown, and sow leeks, with two garden rakes. One rake was left on the ground while the young woman worked away with the other, humming to herself the while, 'Y sawl sydd i gydfydio, Doed i gydgribinio!' Or in English: 'He that would a life partner be, Let him also rake with me.' 1923 *Folklore* 324 [Northleigh, Oxon.] She . . went to the churchyard one Christmas Eve at midnight, carrying some hemp-seed, and while throwing it over her left shoulder said: 'I sow hempseed, Hempseed I sow, He that is to be my husband, Come after me and mow, Not in his best or Sunday array, But in the clothes he wears every day!' . . some people said she saw a coffin, but whatever she saw . . it is certain she died soon afterwards, and the people in the village . . forbade their daughters to try this charm any more.

HEN cackles

1852 *N & Q* 1st ser. VI 602 [Yorks.] When a newly married couple first enter their house, a person brings in a hen and makes it cackle, to bring good luck to the new married people. 1873 *Chambers's Journal* 810 [Scotland] If a hen cackles in her [the bride's] new home as she crosses its threshold, she will be a happy mother as well as a contented wife. 1923 [Somerset] If a bride hears hens cackle on her wedding eve it means a happy life and a long family.

HEN crows

1708 *British Apollo* 17 Sept. When my Hens do crow, Tell me if it be ominous or no? 1755 *Connoisseur* 13 Mar. The youngest miss declared that she had heard the hen crow that morning, which was another fatal prognostic. *c.*1816 Wilkie MS (HENDERSON *Northern Counties* 1866, 28) A crowing hen is counted on the Borders a forerunner of death . . An old woman in the parish of East Kilbride heard one of her hens crow loudly . . before her house . . and accordingly her husband soon died. 1838 C. WATERTON *Natural History* 136. An old woman has made me a present of a barn-door hen.

'Take it, sir,' said she, 'and welcome; for, if it stays here any longer, we shall be obliged to kill it. When we get up .. in the morning it crows like a cock [and] when hens turn cocks people say that they are known to be very unlucky.' **1873** *N & Q* 4th ser. XI 353. Only a year ago a sailor friend of mine .. killed a very goodly hen .. because she had suddenly 'crowed three times right on end', and he was told that such a hen would bring all the roost to trouble. **1887** 'SPERANZA' WILDE *Superstitions of Ireland* II 107. A hen that crows is very unlucky and should be killed; very often the hen is stoned, for it is believed that she is bewitched by the fairies. **1923** [Somerset] To hear a hen crow is very unlucky—it's a sign of sickness and death. Her head must be chopped off at once. **1938** *Folklore* 232 [Shrops.] I once possessed a crowing hen and the cowman begged me to have her killed. She was a good layer and I hesitated. However, after three misfortunes I told the man he might kill her. To which he replied, 'yer needn't trouble now. Er's done 'er work.'

Also see WHISTLING WOMAN AND CROWING HEN.

HERON bird of ill omen

1593 NASHE *Christs Teares over Jerusalem* 90. The vulgar meniality conclude, therefore it [the plague] is like to encrease, because a Hearneshaw (a whole afternoone together) sate on the top of S. Peters Church in Cornehill. **1932** C. IGGLESDEN *Those Superstitions* 79. In the marshlands of England the heron was never shot for fear of ill luck. **1949** S. P. B. MAIS *Who Dies?* 240 [Wales] As we drew up at the door of the hotel at Maes-yr-Afon I saw a heron fly slowly over the house, that bird of ill omen to travellers. **1960** K. STEWART *Croft in the Hills* 164 [Loch Ness, Inverness.] There are intangible legacies from the past. A neighbour of ours, young and active and full of fun, will still look anxiously at a heron, bird of ill-omen, flapping his way from the hill, lest he should pass too near her place.

HERRING MEMBRANE: divination

1824 J. MACTAGGART *Gallovidian En-*

cyclopedia 430. *Herring Soam*, the fat of herrings. Young girls throw this against a wall, and if it adheres to it in an upright manner, then the husband they will get will also be so; if crooked, he will be crooked. **1873** *N & Q* 4th ser. XI 274 [Belfast, *c.*1850] I take it for granted that everyone knows, that in a herring, a small, silvery-coloured, glutinous membrane, of perhaps an inch and a half in length, lies along the under side of the backbone of the fish .. I recollect seeing .. the woman servants in my father's kitchen divining by means of this little membrane, and ascertaining thereby the characters .. of their future husbands. The mode of operation .. consisted merely in throwing the little object .. against a whitewashed wall, where .. it adhered, and it depended on the way in which it rested, if it stretched out quite straight, curved, crooked, very crooked, or all in a little heap, whether the future husband would be tall and handsome, or small and ugly .. Each person had to throw for herself, and .. could only use the membrane of the herring which she had herself eaten. **1923** [Trowbridge, Wilts.] If the white air bladder of a fish be thrown against the ceiling and sticks there the thrower will soon have new clothes. If it fails to stick he will have to go without them.

Cf. CABBAGE STALK: divination.

HERRINGS dislike quarrels

1853 H. MILLER *Scenes of North Scotland* 284 [Ross./Cromarty] Tradition affirms that herrings have a strong antipathy to human blood, especially when spilt in a quarrel. On the last day of the fishing, the nets belonging to two boats became entangled .. A quarrel was the consequence .. and blood was spilt .. in the sea; the affronted herrings took their departure.

Cf. BEES dislike bad behaviour.

HICCUP, cures for

AD 77 PLINY *Natural History* XXVIII LXXXI (1856, V 366) When a horse-shoe becomes detached from the hoof .. if a person takes it up and puts it by, it will act as a remedy for hiccup the moment he calls to mind the spot where he has placed it. **1040** MS Harl. 55 (COCKAYNE

Leechdoms II 295) If a man have sudden ailments [hiccups] make three marks of Christ, one on the tongue, the second on the head, the third on the breast, soon he will be well. *c.*1550 J. BALE *Comedye Concernynge Three Lawes* B5ᵛ. Thre syppes are for the hyckock, And vi more for the chyckock. 1584 SCOT *Discoverie of Witchcraft* XI xv. Some will hold fast their left thombe in their right hand when they hickot; or else will hold their chinne with their right hand whiles a gospell is soong. 1823 MOOR *Suffolk Words* 167. The following charm, thrice repeated, holding the breath, is, or used to be, with us, a cure for this diaphragmatic convulsion: 'Hiccup—sniccup—look up—right up—Three drops in a cup—is good for the hiccup.' 1842 R. CHAMBERS *Popular Rhymes of Scotland* 59. An address to the hiccup: 'Hiccup, hiccup, gang away, Come again another day; Hiccup, hiccup, when I bake, I'll gie to you a butter cake!' 1881 W. GREGOR *North-East of Scotland* 49. Charm repeated as a cure: 'My love's ane, The hiccup's twa, Gehn my love likes me, The hiccup'll gang awa'.' 1962 *Woman*, 18 [Southport, Lancs.] Verse said when anyone had hiccups: 'Hiccups I have thee, Take a bite of thee, And run away with thee.'

Cf. THUMB, holding.

HOLE in stone: passing through

1754 BORLASE *Antiquities of Cornwall* 169 [Parish of Maddern] When I was last at this Monument, in the year 1749, a very intelligent farmer of the neighbourhood assur'd me, that he had known many persons who had crept through this holed Stone for pains in their back and limbs, and that fancyful parents, at certain times of the year, do customarily draw their young Children thro', in order to cure them of the Rickets. He shew'd me also two pins, carefully lay'd a-cross each other, on the top-edge of the holed Stone. 1865 R. HUNT *West of England* 1st ser. 191. Beyond the village of Lanyon [nr. Penzance, Cornwall] stands the Mên-an-tol, or the 'holed stone' . . If scrofulous children are passed *naked* through the Mên-an-tol three times, and then drawn on the grass three times *against the sun*, it is felt by the faithful that much has been done towards insuring a speedy cure. Even men and women who have been afflicted with spinal diseases, or who have suffered from scrofulous taint, have been drawn through this magic stone, which all declare still retains its ancient virtues. If two brass pins are carefully laid across each other on the top edge of this stone, any question put to the rock will be answered, by the pins acquiring, through some unknown agency, a peculiar motion. Ibid. 215–16. *Rickets, or a crick in the back.* The holed stone—Mên-an-tol—in Lanyon, is commonly called by the peasantry the crick-stone. Through this the sufferer was drawn nine times against the sun—or, if a man, he was to crawl through the hole nine times. 1918 *Folklore* 86. In the Brahan Wood [nr. Dingwall, Ross.] two . . boulders lean against each other, meeting at the top. A few years ago an old woman . . died near this town. When she was a child she had a fit . . which her parents supposed to be epileptic. They lighted a fire at the top of the leaning stones, and passed the child through the opening below. 1950 H. GRAHAM *Eternal Eve* 12. Aberdeenshire women still crawl through the hole in the Devil's Needle 'for luck', but the original custom was applied only to barren women and was a simple fertility rite. 1963 *Daily Telegraph* 8 Aug. 15. These strange old stones, standing for thousands of years at Madron in Cornwall . . If a child was passed through the hole in the central stone, it was believed that the child would be cured of wryneck or rickets—it depended on the number of times that the child was passed through. Old customs die hard, for a St Ives resident said that in his young days he had seen a child being hurriedly dressed after such a ceremony. 1970 J. HILLABY *Journey through Britain* 27 [Cornwall] Mên-an-tol, a stone that resembles a cartwheel standing upright on its rim . . Children used to be pushed through the hole to be cured of rickets and arthritis, and, just to be on the safe side, for I felt a bit stiff, I crawled through myself.

HOLLY cures chilblains

1932 C. IGGLESDEN *Those Superstitions*

52. To thrash chilblains with holly is an old-fashioned cure, but in some places it is only efficacious if the feet are crossed during the painful operation. **1935** Woman, 43. At the Dame School in Brentwood, Essex, where my husband was sent home from India as a little boy, *c.*1887, the boys who had chilblains were sent barefoot out in the snow, and had to thrash their feet with holly. **1955** Girl, 12 [Swansea, Glam.] Prick your chilblains with holly and walk through the snow to cure them. **1969** R. WHITLOCK *Family and Village* 40 [Pitton, Wilts., 1870s] Chilblains .. Improvin' they be. I bin rubbin' em well wi' hollyberry ashes, and do do em a power of good.

HOLLY, harming

15th c. MS Eng. poet. e. I (R. L. GREENE *Carols* 1977, 83) Whosoeuer ageynst Holly do crye, In a lepe shall he hang full hye .. Whosoeuer ageynst Holly do syng, He maye wepe and handys wryng. **1917** KIPLING *Diversity of Creatures* 46. By noon a length of unclean jungle had turned itself into a cattle-proof barrier, tufted here and there with little plumes of the sacred holly which no woodman touches without orders. **1956** G. E. EVANS *Ask the Fellows* XXIV [Blaxhall, Suffolk] There is a field with a holly-tree standing somewhere near the centre. The field would be much easier to farm if the tree were removed: but the farmer will not have it touched as he believes that cutting down a holly-tree is always followed by bad luck. **1963** Man, *c.*40 [East Meon, Hants.] We had some holly trees which had to be cut down by the Council last winter, and we couldn't get anyone who would. Then they went and got a German who would do it, and you know this man who did it he went and lost three fingers soon afterwards. **1975** Man, 57 [Liss, Hants.] It is now believed that holly is a protected tree. When they do cut down a holly they do so furtively, in case the Forestry Commission or someone should catch them at it. When Graham Clark cut down Mr Coombe's tree he covered over the stump so no one could see what he had done. **1987** [Reigate, Surrey] When the people moved into the house on the corner,

they had the big holly tree cut down. The trunk lay in the lane for a long time all covered over with debris, because the holly was a protected tree and they didn't want anybody to see it, they said.

HOLLY indicates dominant partner

1871 *N & Q* 4th ser. VIII 507 [Derbys.] It depends upon the kind of holly that comes into a house at Christmas which shall be master during the coming year, the wife or the husband. If the holly is smooth, the wife will be the master; if the holly is prickly, the husband will be the master. **1881** *N & Q* 6th ser. IV 509. In Derbyshire it was considered bad luck not to have holly .. in the house at Christmas. Part of the holly should be of the smooth kind, and part prickly; and if this was so affairs in the household would go on through the coming year in an even, prosperous way. Both kinds should, however, come in together. Should the prickly be first .. then the master would absolutely rule throughout the year; should the smooth .. then the wife would be mistress and master too. I have known of women who have made quite sure about the holly by gathering it on the previous day, and bringing it in the next morning as soon as it was fairly light.

HOLLY prevents fever

1969 E. PORTER *Cambridgeshire* 71. Old fenmen [claimed] that scratching the legs with a holly branch was excellent for preventing an attack of ague.

HOLLY protects

1688 AUBREY *Remaines* (1881, 189) *Holly-tree.* They use to be planted near houses: and in churchyards, e.g. within Westminster abbey cloister, &c. **1778** CHATTERTON *Miscellanies* (ed. Southey, III 84) Against the foul fiends .. the holy bush and church-yard yew were certain antidotes. **1906** *N & Q* 10th ser. V 167. Can anyone illustrate from his own local experience the belief that a holly tree protects from lightning in a storm? **1969** E. PORTER *Cambridgeshire* 62. It was a Fenland tradition that the Scots who were taken prisoners at Dunbar and brought south .. used to stick sprigs of holly round the huts in which they lived in order to protect themselves from witches .. A young man .. faced with a long walk home .. would cut a holly stick from a hedge .. secure in the knowledge that no witch would dare to accost him. Coachmen did not like to drive at night unless they had a whip of which the handle was made of holly wood. **1971** *Trans. Devon. Ass.* 268 [Stockleigh Pomeroy] Lightning never struck anyone if you were under a holly tree. Lightning never struck a holly tree.

HOLLY, sweeping chimney with
1957 UTTLEY *Year in the Country* VI. Never must holly be used for sweeping a chimney.

HOLLY AND IVY = male and female
15th c. MS Harl. 5396 (R. L. GREENE *Carols* 1977, 82) Nay, Iuy, nay, hyt shal not be, iwys; Let Holy hafe the maystry [mastery], as the maner ys. **1661** M. STEVENSON *Twelve Moneths* 50. Great is the contention of Holly and Ivy, whether Master or Dame weares the breeches. **1779** *Gents Mag.* 137 [E. Kent, Tuesday before Shrove Tuesday] In a little obscure village .. I found an odd kind of sport going forward: the girls, from eighteen to five or six years old .. were burning an uncouth effigy which they called an Holly Boy .. which .. they had stolen from the boys, who, in another part of the village were .. burning what they called an Ivy Girl, which they had stolen from the girls; all this ceremony was accompanied with loud huzzas, noise, and acclamations. **1883** BURNE *Shropshire* 245. There must have been some sort of mythical rivalry between Holly and Ivy, to judge from the following rhyme, which is current in most parts of North Shropshire. "Olly an' Ivvy wun runnin' a race, 'Olly gid Ivvy a smack o' the face; Ivvy run home to tell 'er mother, 'Olly run a'ter 'er an' gid 'er another!'

HOLLY-WOOD CUP
1851 *N & Q* 1st ser. IV 227. It is said by the inhabitants of the forest of Bere, East Hants., that new milk drank out of a cup made of the wood of the variegated holly is a cure for the hooping cough.
Cf. IVY-WOOD CUP.

HOPS kept for luck
1920 G. BOURNE *William Smith* 228 [Farnborough, Hants.] It seems the bunch of hops in 'the other room', over the mirror on the chimney mantel, had been renewed there every year as long even as Ann could remember: her father liked to have them, 'for luck', he was wont to say. **1951** *Folklore* 328 [Maidstone, Kent] During the hop picking season, a wreath of hops was brought as a present to my sister by an old man, presumably to be kept [by the hearth until the next season], as dried hops are still put on mantelshelves as decorations. **1972** C. KETTERIDGE & S. MAYS *Five Miles from Bunkum* 139 [Ashdon, Essex] If hung in the room where the family ate meals, a spray of hops in flower, would ensure the household's prosperity.
Cf. CORN DOLLY.

HORSE/HORSEMAN lucky to meet
1818 *Edinburgh Magazine* Nov. 412 [Angus] A man on horseback is reckoned very lucky [as first foot to the bride on her way to church]. **1881** W. GREGOR *North-East of Scotland* 130. The meeting of a horse by a bridal party as the 'first fit' was looked upon as a sure proof of a happy marriage. **1886** *Folklore* 13. It is a notion among some that if you see below one having an 'ill fit', no harm will follow. One morning a Spey salmon-fisher said to his companion .. that he had met a certain man well known as having an 'ill fit'. 'We'll hae naething the day, than.' 'Oh, bit he wiz ridin, an I saw through aneth [below] the horse-belly,' was the answer.
Cf. FIRST-FOOT: animal or person first encountered.

HORSE'S HAIR cures
1873 *N & Q* 4th ser. XI 500 [Glos.] A young woman, with a large wen on her neck .. declares that she got rid of her encumbrance by wearing round her neck .. a plaited braid, made from the tail-hair of a grey stallion. **1912** LEATHER *Herefordshire* 84. A woman at King's Pyon .. cured her wen thus: 'You get somebody to give you nine hairs from a stallion's tail; you must not say 'thank you', nor pay. Fasten them in a little

bag in a little plait and wear it round your neck till the bag wears out.'

HORSE'S (OR DONKEY'S) HOOF

1586 CAMDEN *Britannia* (tr. Gibson, II 380) [Limerick, Eire] When a horse dies, the master hangs up the feet and legs in the house, and looks upon the very hooves as sacred. **1621** BURTON *Anatomy of Melancholy* pt. 2 sect. 5 mem. 1 sub. 5. Amulets . . A ring made of the hooffe of an Asses right forefoot carried about. *c.***1740** *Aristotle's Midwife* 52–3. If it happens . . that the Waters break away too long before the Birth . . there are many . . Things . . Physicians affirm are good in this Case: among which [is] an Ass's or Horse's-hoof, hung near the Privities.

HORSE'S TOOTH

1887 'SPERANZA' WILDE *Superstitions of Ireland* II 100. If, by accident, you find the back tooth of a horse, carry it about with you as long as you live, and you will never want money; but it must be found by chance.

HORSESHOE at threshold

1584 SCOT *Discoverie of Witchcraft* XII XVIII. To prevent and cure all mischeefes wrought by these charmes & witchcrafts . . naile a horse shoo at the inside of the outmost threshold of your house, and so you shall be sure no witch shall have power to enter . . You shall find that rule observed in manie countrie houses. **1668** W. RAMESEY *Elminthologia* 73, 76. It is no easy matter to discover who is a Witch . . nailing of Horse-shoos on their Thresholds and Dores [it was thought the witch could not then get out] is fallacious. **1684** I. MATHER *Illustrious Providences* 269. How persons that shall unbewitch others by . . nailing of Horse-shoes at Mens doors, can wholly clear themselves from being white Witches, I am not able to understand. **1686–7** AUBREY *Remaines* (1881, 27) A Horse-Shoe nailed on the threshold of ye dore is yet in fashion: and no where more than in London: it ought (Mr Lilly sayes) to be a Horse-shoe that one finds by chance on the Roade. The end of it is to prevent the power of Witches, that come into your house.

1698 MISSON *Voyageur en Angleterre* (1719, 129–30) Having often observed a Horseshoe nail'd to the Threshold of a Door, (among the meaner Sort of People) I ask'd several what was the Reason of it: They gave me several different Answers; but the most general was, That they were put there to keep out Witches. 'Tis true, they laugh when they say this, but yet they do not laugh at it altogether; for they believe there . . may be some secret Virtue conceal'd in it. **1753** *The World* 23 Aug. To secure yourself within doors against the enchantment of witches, especially if you are a person of fashion, and have never been taught the Lord's Prayer, the only method I know of is, to nail a horseshoe upon the threshold. This I can affirm to be of the greatest efficacy; insomuch that I have taken notice of many a little cottage in the country, with a horseshoe at its door, where gaming, extravagance, routs, adultery, jacobitism, and the catalogue of witchcrafts have been totally unknown. **1813** BRAND *Antiquities* II 379 n. In Monmouth street [London] many Horse-shoes nailed to the Thresholds are still to be seen (1797). The Editor of this Work April 26th, 1813, counted no less than seventeen Horse-shoes in Monmouth-Street nailed against the Steps of Doors. **1828** MITFORD *Our Village* III 295. Isaac, certainly the most superstitious personage in the parish . . was fain to nail a horse-shoe on his door for the defence of his property [against the curses of his aged female neighbour]. **1839** C. BARON-WILSON *Harriot, Duchess of St Albans* II 128–9. The steps at Holly Lodge . . are composed of beautiful blocks of white marble . . but the highest step is disfigured by two rusty, old, broken horseshoes fastened to it, which she and Mr Coutts (who was likewise superstitious) had found in the road, and they had caused these hideous bits of rusty iron to be nailed on the threshold to avert evil and bring good luck. **1846** BROCKETT *North Country Words* II. Old horse-shoe. If found by one of the family, and nailed against the door, it is still believed to be a preservative against witchcraft and bogles. **1855** *N & Q* 1st ser. XI 498 [Cornwall] The house and all it contains are protected by the nailing of a horse-shoe over the centre of the door-way. There are few farm-houses without it. 1867 *Gents Mag.* pt. 1 318 [Whatfield, Suffolk] One case was that of a poor girl, who had been ill for a long time, and .. of an aged female, who came every day to enquire after her. It occurred to one of the family that the old lady must needs be a witch, and .. that a horse-shoe should be affixed to the sill of the outer door, in order to prevent her from entering .. The precaution succeeded; the old woman was never able to cross the threshold .. and the young woman rapidly regained her health. 1886 *Folklore* 226 [Cornwall] 1st of May you must take down all the horse-shoes (that are nailed over doors to keep out witches, &c.) and turn them, not letting them touch the ground. 1888 S. O. ADDY *Sheffield Glossary* xix. If one finds a horse-shoe he should take it home and nail it to the stable door. 1913 E. M. WRIGHT *Rustic Speech* 230. The horseshoe, which people still pick up, and hang over doors and chimney-pieces 'for luck'. 1986 Woman, *c.*50 [Sunderland] It's th' first thing I did when I moved, was to put a horseshoe at my door.

HORSESHOE: how hung or placed

1671 J. BLAGRAVE *Astrological Practice* 138. To afflict the Witch, causing the evil to return back upon them .. Nail [a horseshoe] on the inside of the threshold of the door with three nailes, the heel being upwards. 1688 AUBREY *Remaines* (1881, 123) At Mr Ashmoles threshold the hollow of the horseshoe pointeth into the house. 1766 GOLDSMITH (attrib.) *Little Goody Two-Shoes* 126. Horse-shoes were nailed with the Heels upwards .. to mortify the poor Creature [a supposed witch]. 1838 A. E. BRAY *Devonshire* III 255. The old miners on the moor are rather more superstitious than those residing in towns. The horse-shoe is invariably affixed to some of the erections belonging to the mine to prevent witchcraft .. The explanation .. given is, that the devil always travels in circles, and .. is consequently interrupted when he arrives at either of the heels of the shoe, and obliged to take a retrograde

course. 1873 *Bye-Gones* 8 Oct. 220 [Wales] The other day I observed a horse-shoe nailed .. over the door of a dwelling-house on 'Sweeney Mountain' .. Considered efficacious in preventing witchcraft .. the shoe should have its heels or cogs pointing upwards. This .. is not observed in the above instance. 1891 J. C. ATKINSON *Moorland Parish* 71–2. It is but a week since I saw a lady .. in one of the most frequented streets in York .. pick up a horse-shoe .. I was quite well aware that it would be hung, as .. nearly a dozen predecessors .. fruitlessly .. with the toe upwards. 1905 *N & Q* 10th ser. III 90. Gipsies hang the shoe with its points (the heel) upward, in cup-form, 'to catch the good luck', but grooms generally hang it toe upward, in roof-form, to ward off bad luck. 1913 E. M. WRIGHT *Rustic Speech* 233. Many people today, who firmly believe that to find a horseshoe is lucky, will tell you that the luck will disappear into the ground if the shoe is hung with the ends pointing downwards; even positive ill-luck may thereby be drawn upon the house .. recently questioned two natives of Berkshire on this subject, and while one set firm faith in the importance of fastening the shoe-ends upwards, the other was quite content to see the charm 'just slung up on a nail'. 1952 Girl, 11 [Kirkcaldy, Fife.] To hang a horseshoe on the door upside down on New Year's Day will bring luck throughout the year. [She drew the horseshoe with open end upwards.] 1965 J. MOORE *Waters Under the Earth* 21. She bent down to straighten a horseshoe somewhat askew on the gate. 'That'll stop the luck from running out of it.' 1981 Female student, 20 [S. England] People in the survey knew it was lucky to have a horseshoe on the door, with the ends pointing up so the luck didn't run out—but none actually had one. 1983 Boy, 12 [Maldon, Essex] We always put a horse shoe the right side up because if you put it facing down the luck drips out.

HORSESHOE lucky to find

late 14th c. R. RYPON MS Harl. 4894 (OWST, in *Studies*, ed. J. Conway Davies, 1957, 297) In a long discourse on types of idolatry .. horseshoes .. are among the lucky finds. **1507** *Gospelles of Dy-staues* pt. 2 XVI. He y^t fyndeth a horse shoo or a pece of one, he shall haue good fortune. **1665** R. BOYLE *Occasional Reflections* VI IX. The common people of this Country have a Tradition, that 'tis a lucky thing to find a Horse-shoe. And though 'twas to make my self merry with this fond conceit of the superstitious Vulgar, I stoop'd to take this up. **1721** KELLY *Scotish Proverbs* 348. When a Fool finds a Horse Shoe, he thinks ay the like to do. Spoken when they, who have had some Fortune, think always to be as successful. *c.***1797** H. MORE *Tawney Rachel* 7. If she picked up an old horse-shoe going to church she was sure that it would be a lucky week. **1856** TIMBS *Things Not Generally Known* 145. In Sussex .. in childhood, we have more than once accounted ourselves lucky in finding a horse-shoe. **1883** BURNE *Shropshire* 164. We think in Shropshire, not only that it is lucky to find a horse-shoe, but that it is lucky to find old iron of any kind. **1898** BLAKEBOROUGH *Yorkshire Customs* 158. Any girl, whilst a maiden, who was so fortunate as to find three horse-shoes in one year, if she threw them over her left shoulder .. could never be witch-held. **1942** *Folk-lore* 97. Horse-shoes that are found by their owner have ten times the power of those acquired in other ways, while one that is bought is useless. **1954** Girl, 10 [Etton, Yorks.] If you find a horseshoe in the street it is lucky if you spit on it and throw it over your left shoulder. **1982** Woman, 21 [Yorks.] I can remember a blacksmith making and selling 'Lucky Horseshoes' at an Open Day at the Abbeydale Industrial Hamlet, Sheffield. I can remember buying one, whilst saying to my friend: 'It's only for a souvenir because it won't be lucky because I didn't find it.'

HORSESHOE on ship

1823 *Gents Mag.* pt. 1 16–17 [Ipswich] It is usual to nail a horseshoe on the foremast of vessels in the Merchant service .. It keeps Witches and Wizards from hindering the voyage, or damaging the ship. **1834** G. ROBERTS *Lyme Regis and Charmouth* 261. Our vessels, and many houses, have an old horse-shoe nailed up. **1855** *N & Q* 1st ser XI 498 [Cornwall] Scarcely a boat or vessel puts to sea without this talisman [horse-shoe]. **1919** *Morning Post* 9 June 3. Nelson had a horseshoe nailed to the mast of the *Victory*, and on the photograph, taken from the air, of the *Vindictive* blocking Zeebrugge Harbour, one can plainly see its horseshoe.

horseshoe: also see IRON.

HORSESHOE NAIL

1832 *Gents Mag.* pt. 1 591 [Scopwick, Lincs.] It is exceedingly fortunate to find .. a broken horse shoe, particularly if it be studded full of nails. **1895** J. HARDY *Denham Tracts* II 212–13. Near Wooler [Northumb.], when a horse-shoe is found, the holes clear of nails are to be counted, as these indicate how long it is before the party who picked it up is going to be married. Elsewhere the number of nails remaining indicate luck. **1955** *Times* 23 Sept. 11. It is no use hanging up a horseshoe unless it has at least one of the original nails, used when shoeing a horse, still in it. There is said to be one year's luck for each original nail. **1965** Woman, 55 [Scarborough, Yorks.] I picked up a horseshoe the other day and brought it home, and was struggling to remove two ill-clinched nails when Mrs Wrightson assured me it was very lucky to find a horseshoe nail, so I let them be. **1985** Woman, *c.*65 [Co. Cork] If there're no nails in it, it's no good. The number of nails means the number of years of good luck you're going to have. It'll never be that many, will it though?

HORSESHOE NAIL points towards one

1695 CONGREVE *Love for Love* III iv. Cheer up, look about thee .. [*Aside*] Now is he poring upon the Ground for .. an old Horse-nail, with the head towards him.
    Cf. PIN points towards one.

HOUSE, moving

1869 *N & Q* 4th ser. III 359 [Cheshire] The first time my wife entered our new home she took a Bible, some salt, and some oatmeal with her, and placed them in one of the cupboards .. She explained that the Bible was emblematic of a good foundation for our home, and the meal and salt were emblems of plenty. **1902** *Cambrian N & Q* I 39 [Tenby, Pembs.] When we changed to another house my mother always came down and placed a bar of salt on the stairs—for luck, I believe. Ibid. When we went into our present house the servant carried down some salt [and] put it in the fire-grate. Ibid. The man who carts the furniture brings a bag of salt, and before putting anything else in he flings in a few handfuls, just like sowing corn. **1904** LEAN *Collectanea* II 153. When entering a house and purchasing some of the furniture, the property of a former occupant, a Welsh gentleman told me I must purchase the salt-box .. no one attempted to bid against me [and] I was afterwards told ill luck would pursue me if I had not bought [it]. **1909** *Folklore* 217 [Co. Durham] When anyone moved into a new house, or changed houses, a child was sent into every room with a bag of salt, which he was told to sprinkle on the hearths and in every corner. I have myself been told off for the job. **1912** LEATHER *Herefordshire* 86. A box of coal and a plate of salt should be the first things taken into an empty house, before moving any furniture. At Eastnor, people leaving a house were warned that they must leave bread and salt behind them. **1923** *Folklore* 92. A newly married couple in almost all parts of Scotland, should find a dish of salt waiting them when they enter their new home. **1926** *Folklore* 174 [Aberystwyth, Cardigan.] When I was coming into my new flat a .. friend .. insisted on going in before me and carrying salt across the threshold; she also begged me not to tell her minister, as according to him it ought to have been the Bible which was carried in first. **1960** *She* Mar. 21 [Middlesbrough, Teesside] I have recently moved into a fresh house, and a friend, paying me her first visit, brought a packet of salt for luck. **1966** *Woman's Realm* 26 Feb. 6. When we moved, my sister threw salt into the fireplace of the old home 'to leave sorrow behind'. She then took into the new house a lump of coal, for luck, and some bread so that we should never want. **1981** Woman,

20 [Sheffield, Yorks.] 'Travel salt, travel sorrow.' When you move house, you should leave the salt behind and buy new for the new house. **1984** Woman, *c.*50 [Rogate, Sussex] When you move, you have to leave some salt behind in the old house—just a little bit. Funny, isn't it. **1985** Woman, 57. We always had to have a Bible first thing into a new house, in South Shields.

HOUSE, new: causes pregnancy
1957 Girl, 11 [Swansea, Glam.] New house, new baby. **1982** Woman, *c.*30. A young woman who moves house will soon get pregnant. I've heard several Derbyshire people say this.

HOUSE, new: fatal to build
1879 HENDERSON *Northern Counties* 45 [Lancs.] To build, or even to rebuild, a house, is always fatal to some member of the family—generally to the one who may chiefly have advised .. the building or alteration.

HOUSE, new: fatal to enter
1912 LEATHER *Herefordshire* 87. In the Kington district there is great reluctance to enter a new house, as the first person to live in it will probably soon die.

HOUSE, new: visitor brings present
1911 *Folklore* 203 [Co. Clare] On visiting a friend in a new house, you should give some present, however small. **1972** *Lore and Language* July 7 [Coalisland, Co. Tyrone] When visiting someone who has just moved into a new house, never go with your two hands the one length. Always take something to hansel the house. Coal is the luckiest.

HOUSELEEK protects from lightning
1562 W. BULLEIN *Defence againste Sickness* 37. Old writers do call it *Iovis barba*, Jupiter's bearde, and held an opinion supersticiously, that in what house so ever it groweth, no lightnyng or tempest can take place to doe any harme. **1637** DELONEY *Gentle Craft* pt. 1 IV. It is said, that where housleeke is planted, the place shall neuer be hurt with thunder. **1650** T. HILL *Natural and Artificial Conclusions* CXXXIX. An Ancient Author reciteth (among divers other Experiments

of Nature which he had found out) that if the herb Housleek or Syngreen do grow on the house top, the same house is never stricken with Lightning or Thunder. **1813** BRAND *Antiquities* II 611. It is still common, in many parts of England, to plant the herb houseleek upon the tops of cottage houses. **1869** *N & Q* 4th ser. IV 507 [Kent] To insure a House from Fire. Before going to a new residence, plant the day previously, a root of house-leek. **1878** *Folk-Lore Record* 13 [Fittleworth, Sussex] You will bring trouble on your house, if you cut down the house-leek .. which has sprung up on your roof. **1947** *Folklore* 278. Even still in parts of County Mayo, the people put a certain weed in the thatched roofs of their houses as a protection against fire. In my native town I discovered a house where a weed, called House-League, is put in the thatch .. for the same purpose. **1969** E. PORTER *Cambridgeshire* 69. A houseleek plant (*sempervivum tectorum*) on the roof of a house is still believed .. to provide an excellent protection against lightning. Between 1951 and 1962 three instances have been recorded of families moving from old or condemned dwellings to new Council houses and carefully taking with them houseleeks to place on the roofs of their new homes.

HUNCHBACK

1899 *The People* 11 June 2. To touch the hump of a deformed person for luck was common, and is to this day. **1914** *Observer* 6 Sept. 5. There is nothing new in the story of Lord Torrington and his friends, when leaving for the front, treating the little hunchback newsboy at the Paddington bookstall as a mascot, and rewarding him for allowing them to touch him. Years ago a hunchback used always to take his stand outside Waterloo Station on race-meeting days, and there must be many who remember paying twopence to rub his back on their way to Sandown and elsewhere. **1933** J. B. BOOTH *Pink Parade* 97. A hunchback is looked upon as a bringer of luck, and to touch the hunch is to ensure success and a long run [for a play].

HYDRANGEA near house

1957 *Folklore* 435 [Somerset] If you plant hydrangeas near your house, your daughters will not marry. **1968** *Woman*, *c.*80 [London] I must pull up that hydrangea. You know what they say, 'If you have a hydrangea by your front door your daughter won't get married.'

I

IMAGE/PICTURE used to injure or kill

*c.*35 BC HORACE *Satires* I VIII (tr. Drant)
As the flame did grow in bulke, and gan
for to increase: So did the waxen image
. . by small and small decrease. I markte
the drabbishe sorcerers and harde their
dismall spell. *c.*20 BC OVID *Heroides*
VI ll. 91–2 (tr. Showerman, 1914) She
[Medea] vows to their doom the absent,
fashions the waxen image, and into its
wretched heart drives the slender needle.
AD 972 G. BUCHANAN *History of Scotland*
(1762, I 246) From a discovery made
by a certain harlot, whose mother was
noted for a witch, [Donald] detected the
whole conspiracy. For the young girl . .
being apprehended, and brought to the
rack . . at the very first sight of it she
presently declared what was designed
against the life of the king [Duffus]. Upon
this some soldiers were sent, who found
the maid's mother, and some other gossips, roasting the king's picture, made
in wax, by a soft fire: their design was,
that as the wax did . . melt, so the king,
being dissolved into a sweat, should pine
away by degrees; and when the wax
was quite consumed . . should presently
die. When this picture . . was broken,
and the witches punished . . the king
was freed from his disease. 13th c.
'Kyng Alisaunder' (H. WEBER *Romances*
1810, I 8) Whan kyng, other eorl, cam
on him to weorre, Quyk he loked in
the steorre; Of wax made him popetis
[images] And so he leorned . . Ay to
aquelle his enemye, With charmes, and
with conjurisons. 1486 SPRENGER &
KRAMER *Malleus Maleficarum* (tr. Summers, 135) When a witch makes a
waxen image . . in order to bewitch
somebody . . and some injury is done
upon the image, such as piercing it or
hurting it in any other way, when it is
the bewitched man who is in imagination being so hurt; although the
injury is actually done to the image by
the witch . . and the devil in the same
manner invisibly injures the bewitched
man, yet it is deservedly ascribed to the
witch. 1584 H. CONSTABLE *Diana* decad.
II II. Witches which some murther doe
intend, doe make a picture, and doe
shoote at it; and in that part where they
the picture hit, the parties selfe doth
languish to his end. 1584 SCOT *Discoverie
of Witchcraft* XII XVI. Make an image in
his name, whom you would hurt or kill,
of new virgine wax; under the right arm
poke whereof place a swallowes hart,
and the liver under the left; then hang
about the necke thereof a new thred in
a new needle pricked into the member
which you would have hurt, with the
rehearsall of certeine words, which for
the avoiding of foolish superstition and
credulitie in this behalf is to be omitted.
1589 *State Papers, Dom. Eliz.* CCXXX no.
30. She desired . . that shee mighte
speake wth Birche [a 'conjuror'] . . The
cause why she desired to speake wth him
was that by his counsell & aide shee
mighte bee revenged of her enemies . .
whose pictures she said she would have
& then pricke them to the harte. 1590
Witchcraft trial (R. PITCAIRN *Criminal
Trials in Scotland* I pt. 2 192) Thow art
accusit, for the making of twa pictouris
of clay . . the ane, maid for the dis-
tructioune . . of the young Laird of
Fowlis, and the vthir for the young Ladie
Balnagoune . . Quilkis twa pictouris,
being sett on the north syd of the
chalmer . . Loskie Loncart tuik twa elf
arrow heidis . . and thow schott twa
schottis . . att the said Lady Balnagoune,
and . . thrie schottis at the said young
Laird of Fowlis. 1597 JAMES I *Daemonologie* 44. To some . . hee [the Devil]
teacheth, how to make Pictures of waxe
or clay: That by the rosting thereof, the
persones that they beare the name of,
may be continuallie melted or dryed
awaie by continuall sicknesse. 1613 T.
POTTS *Wondefull Discoverie of Witches* H3^v
[Pendle, Lancs.] There appeared vnto
this Examinate in his way, a thing like
vnto a black dog . . who bad [him] make
a Picture of Clay, like vnto . . Mistress
Towneley: and that [he] with the helpe

of his Spirit .. would kill or destroy .. Mistress Towneley .. The next morning after, this Examinate tooke Clay, and made a Picture of .. Mistress Towneley, and dried it .. by the fire: and .. began to crùmble the said Picture, every day some .. and within two daies after all was crumbled away; the said Mistress Towneley died. **1684** I. MATHER *Illustrious Providences* 185–6 [Paisley, Renfrew., 1678] One John Stuart, and his Sister Annibel Stuart, at the Assizes .. confessed .. that they had made an Image of Wax, calling it by the name of Sr. George Maxwel, sticking pins in the sides and on the breast of it. Such an Image with pins in it, was really found in the Witches Houses; and upon the removal of it, the pins being taken out, Sir George had immediate ease, and recovered his health. **1686–7** AUBREY *Remaines* (1881, 61) King Edward 6th was killed by Witch-craft by figures .. and yᵉ late D. of Buckinghams mother was killed in Ireland by a figure made with haire by her 2ᵈ husbands .. brothers nurse, who bewitched her to death because her foster-child .. should inherit yᵉ estate: and one Hammond, of Westminster, was hangd, or tryed for his life about 1641 for killing .. by a figure of wax. **1787** GROSE *Provincial Glossary* Superstitions 21–2. When a Witch wishes to destroy any one to whom she bears an ill will, she and her sister Witches make an image of wax, which, with many ceremonies, is baptized by the Devil, and named after the person meant to be injured; after which they stick thorns into it, and set it before a fire: and, as the wax melts by the heat, so the body of the person represented decays by sickness, with great torture, having the sensation of thorns stuck into his or her flesh. **1810** R. H. CROMEK *Nithsdale Song* 282 [Dumfries.] Figures were shaped in clay of those who had encroached on their [witches'] empire, which, when pierced with pins, conveyed by sympathetic feeling their maims and wounds to the person they represented. **1900** S. BARING-GOULD *Book of Dartmoor* 186 [Widecombe, c.1850] She was caught on one occasion with a doll into which she was sticking pins and needles, in the hope and with the intent thereby of producing aches and cramps in a neighbour. On another occasion she laid a train of gunpowder on her hearth, about a figure of dough, and ignited it, for the purpose of conveying an attack of fever to the person against whom she was animated with resentment. **1951** Girl, 12 [Yorks.] 'Teacher, teacher, I don't like you, If you don't mark my sums right I shall spike you.' 'Spiking' is pricking a drawing of the teacher with pins. **1953** R. DUNCAN *Where I Live* 121–2 [Devon] To see the source of this infection .. I led the doctor .. to Widow Yelston's .. cottage .. In a row sat half a dozen crudely made woollen dolls, each with the name of one of the doctor's patients .. attached to its neck, with a pin driven through a .. leg, another with a pin through its .. foot .. 'It's the first time a person under a spell has been granted benefit under the National Health,' the doctor said.

INK, drying: unlucky

1732 DEFOE *Memoirs of Mr Campbell* 62. Others have seemed .. impatient, and exclaiming against their own Want of Thought, if, thro' Haste or Forgetfulness, they have chanced to hold [a letter] before the Fire to dry. **1861** *N & Q* 2nd ser. XII 491. Drying writing by the fire [is] unlucky. **1951** Author, 32. When I was signing copies of *The Oxford Dictionary of Nursery Rhymes* the other day, in a London bookshop, I was told it is unlucky to blot an inscription in a book or autograph album with blotting paper; it must be left open to dry. **1964** *Daily Sketch* 1 June 6. If she holds a love letter in front of the fire to dry the ink her love will burn itself out.

Cf. IMAGE/PICTURE used to injure or kill.

INK, spilling: unlucky

1955 MRS R. HENREY *Bloomsbury Fair* 97 [Bloomsbury, London] Spill ink and somebody will die.

IONA STONE

1703 M. MARTIN *Western Islands of Scotland* 263 [Iona] There are many pretty variegated Stones in the shoar below the Dock, they ripen to a green colour ..

The Natives say these stones are Fortunate, but only for some particular
thing, which the Person thinks fit to
name. 1810 SCOTT (LOCKART *Life* II 320)
I hope you will set some value upon this
little trumpery brooch, because it is . .
set with Iona stones . . These green
stones, blessed of St Columba, have a
virtue, saith old Martin, to gratify each
of them a single wish of the wearer.
1960 *Times* 16 Nov. 7. The Queen
Mother . . asked to see an Iona green
stone . . The legend is that anyone who
owns one of these stones will never be
drowned.

IRON cures

AD 77 PLINY *Natural History* XXXIV XLIV,
XLV (1857, VI 210, 211) Iron is employed in medicine . . Water in which
iron has been plunged at a white heat,
is useful, as a potion, in many diseases
. . Rust itself, too, is classed among the
remedial substances . . usually obtained
. . by scraping old nails . . It has the
effect of uniting wounds . . Applied in
the form of a liniment, it is . . used for
the cure of erysipelas . . itch, whitlows . .
swellings [and] gout. 1646 *Depositions,
York Castle* 31 Dec. (1861, 8) At last
[the 'witch'] tooke six pence of her, and
wished her to goe home, for the kyne
should mende, and desired her to take
for every cow a handfull of salte and an
old sickle, and lay it underneath them,
and, if they amended not, then to come
to her againe. 1790 GROSE *Provincial
Glossary* Superstitions 40. A rusty sword
standing by the bed-side is a remedy
against the cramp. 1850 *N & Q* 1st ser.
I 293. In the south-eastern counties . .
to avert sickness from a family [they]
hang up a sickle, or iron implement, at
the bed head. 1878 *N & Q* 5th ser. IX
65 [Scotton, Lincs.] In grubbing up old
stumps of ash trees . . there were found,
in many instances, an old horse-shoe . .
The workmen seemed to be familiar with
this fact . . The shoe is so placed to
'charm' the tree, so that a twig of it
might be used in curing cattle over
which a shrewmouse had run, or which
had been 'overlooked'. If they were
stroked by one of these twigs, the disease
would be charmed away. 1883 W.
G. BLACK *Folk-Medicine* 119. In County

Wicklow . . the points of three
smoothing-irons are pointed at a painful
tooth—for then, sure enough, the pain
vanishes. 1887 'SPERANZA' WILDE *Superstitions of Ireland* II 100. An iron
ring worn on the fourth finger was
considered effective against rheumatism
by the . . peasantry from ancient times.
1901 R. RHYS *Celtic Folklore* I 296–7 [Isle
of Man] When she was a child [*c.*1870]
suffering from a swelling in the neck,
she had it charmed away by an old
woman. This charmer brought with her
no less than nine pieces of iron, consisting of old pokers, old nails, and other
odds and ends of the same metal, making
in all nine pieces. After invoking the
Father, the Son, and the Holy Ghost,
she began to rub the girl's neck with
the old irons; nor was she satisfied with
that, for she rubbed the doors, the walls,
and the furniture likewise, with the
metal. The result, I am assured, was
highly satisfactory. 1954 [Swansea,
Glam.] Put some rust on the wart. 1960
[Rothsay, Bute] To get rid of a wart they
frighten it with a red hot poker.

IRON deters evil

AD 77 PLINY *Natural History* XXXIV XLIV
(1857, VI 210) If a circle is traced with
iron, or a pointed weapon is carried
three times round them, it will preserve
both infant and adult from all noxious
influences. 1648 HERRICK *Hesperides* 336
'Another Charme for Stables'. Hang up
Hooks, and Sheers to scare Hence the
Hag, that rides the Mare . . This observ'd,
the Manes shall be Of your horses, all
knot-free. 1691 R. KIRK *Secret Commonwealth* (1815, 17) Iron hinders all
the Opperations of those that travell in
the Intrigues of these hidden Dominions.
1795 *Stat. Acc. of Scotland* XV 311
[Orkney] The existence of fairies and
witches is seriously believed by some,
who, in order to protect themselves . .
place knives in the walls of houses.
1866 HENDERSON *Northern Counties* 194.
Metallic substances are held throughout
the North to counteract the influence of
witchcraft and every kind of evil spirit.
1878 *N & Q* 5th ser. X 266. At the West
Riding Court at Bradford lately, in the
case of a husband and wife having
quarrelled, the woman stated that the

reason why she kept a coal-rake in her bedroom was that she suffered from nightmare, and had been informed that it would keep the nightmare away. **1893** *Folklore* 355 [Co. Derry, pedlar] They say, if you can get an iron hoop an' a man's coat roun' any one the wee-folk can't touch them. **1900** J. CAMPBELL *Scottish Highlands* 153. The writer remembers well that, when a school-boy, great confidence was put in a knife .. and in a nail, which another boy had, to protect us from a Fairy, which was said to have made its appearance .. near .. the road to school .. This was in Appin, Argyllshire. **1905** *Folklore* 187 [Cambs., *c.*1850] She used to live near us and would often come to see mother. Sometimes we would lay a knife or a pair of scissors just inside the door .. and she couldn't come in .. because a witch can't pass over steel. **1907** *N & Q* 10th ser. VII 157. I used to hear from my father of a woman in Hampshire who was accustomed to hang a scythe over her children's bed. When asked the reason, she replied, 'It's to keep the hags from riding the childer by nights.' **1918** *Folklore* 158-9. Twenty-five years ago an old man in one of the parishes of Anglesey invariably bore or rather wore a sickle over his neck—in the fields, and on the road, wherever he went. He was rather reticent as to the reason why he wore it, but he clearly gave his questioner to understand that it was a protection against evil spirits. For .. protection from evil spirits during the hours of the night, it was and is a custom to place two scythes archwise over the entrance-side of the wainscot bed found in many of the older cottages of Anglesey. **1923** *Folklore* 92 [Skye] To keep away witches from one's house, bury a piece of old iron near the gate. **1924** F. J. H. DARTON *Parcel of Kent* 260. Witchcraft certainly existed to my own day .. children were making the two-finger gesture against the evil eye, and their mothers burying knives under the door-step. **1928** E. LOVETT *Surrey and Sussex* 21. During the war I was talking to a man in South London, who kept a small fancy shop .. I asked him if he had ever heard of an old horse-shoe, covered with red flannel,

being hung at the head of a bedstead .. 'Oh yes! I do that, and nearly every one round here does .. That isn't superstition, for I know that it does keep away nightmare.' **1942** *Folklore* 390. In 1942 a farmer near Bungay, Suffolk, was informed by a villager that iron under the doormat was a certain protection from witches. **1968** *Observer* Suppl. 24 Nov. 18. In Essex it is still common practice to keep scissors under the doormat to ward off witches and evil spirits.

IRON, finding

late **14th c.** R. RYPON MS Harl. 4894 (OWST in *Studies*, ed. J. Conway Davies, 1957, 297) In a long discourse on types of idolatry .. iron nails are among the lucky finds. **1603** W. PERKINS *Works* 39. It is .. good lucke to finde old yron. **1617** T. COOPER *Mysterie of Witchcraft* 137. It is ordinarie to diuine of future things .. as by finding a peece of yron, signifying good lucke. **1650** N. HOMES *Daemonologie* 60. How frequent is it with people (especially of the more ignorant sort ..) to think and say .. if they finde some peices of Iron, it is prediction of good luck to the finders. late **18th c.** J. RAMSAY (*Scotland in the Eighteenth Century* II 456) It is reckoned lucky if, at the beginning of any enterprise, a person happens to find any bit of iron. **1852** *N & Q* 1st ser. V 293. I know ladies who consider it 'lucky' to find old iron; a horse shoe or a rusty nail is carefully conveyed home and hoarded up. **1866** HENDERSON *Northern Counties* 81. If you see a horseshoe, or a piece of old iron, on your path, take it up, spit on it, and throw it over your shoulder, framing your wish at the same time; keep the wish secret, and you will have it in time. **1905** *N & Q* 10th ser. III 348. A dear old lady from a country village .. picked up one or two scraps of iron (not horseshoes) as we went along, and assured me that it would have been unlucky to pass them. Ibid. 397. The correct ritual, as I know it, is to pick up the iron in the right hand, spit on it, and throw it over the left shoulder. You must on no account look to see where it falls .. I have been told that the idea is that you hit the devil who is behind you. **1909** *N & Q* 10th ser. XII 484

[Stromness, Orkney] It is unlucky to leave a pin or a horseshoe lying on the ground. 1914 *Folklore* 365 [Newmarket, Cambs.] To bring good luck, spit on a horseshoe, boot tip, or any bit of iron .. then shut your eyes and pitch it away in the air, so that you do not know where it has gone.

Cf. HORSESHOE lucky to find; PIN, finding.

IRON, food pricked with

1881 W. GREGOR *North-East of Scotland* 206. Immediately on death, a piece of iron, such as a knitting-wire or a nail, was stuck into whatever meal, butter, cheese, flesh, or whisky were in the house, to prevent death from entering them. The corruption of these articles has followed closely on the neglect of this. 1925 D. PHILLIPS *Vale of Neath* 598. They had opened a pat of butter without pricking it for luck. It was held that if this were not done, ill-luck would follow for seven years .. The whole family of seven brothers died one after another. No one could explain the cause, except an old woman who remembered that strange marks had been seen on the butter.

Cf. CROSS, making sign of: on other food.

IRON in churn

1584 SCOT *Discoverie of Witchcraft* XII XXI. There be twentie several waies to make your butter come .. as .. to thrust [into the churn] a red hot spit. 1671 J. BLAGRAVE *Astrological Practice* 138. My Father kept a Dairy at .. Shenfield near Reading, and one of my Sisters had the charge thereof, upon a time my Father desired her to make some wilde curds .. which she did endeavour to do, but could make none .. because an Old woman (suspected for a Witch) was at that time denyed whey, who went muttering away discontented .. My Fathers Brother .. called for .. an iron wedge .. and .. having heat the wedge red hot, put him into the whey, and immediately there was abundance of curds rose up .. My Unckle sent a messenger to the suspected Witches house .. where he found [her] shrunk up like a purse .. put into the fire. 1732

Letter 2 Aug. (*Morning Advertiser*, 1822, 13 Sept. 4) One master Collett, a smith by trade, of Haveningham, in the county of Suffolk, who, as 'twas customary with him, assisting the maide to churn, and not being able .. to make the butter come, threw a hot iron into the churn, under the notion of witchcraft in the case, upon which a poore labourer, then employed in carrying dung in the yard, cried out in a terrible manner, 'They have killed me, they have killed me,' still keeping his hand upon his back, intimating where the pain was, and died upon the spot. Mr Collett, with the rest of the servants present, took off the poor man's cloathes, and found, to their great surprise, the mark of the iron that was heated and thrown into the churn deeply impressed upon his back. This account I had from Mr Collett's own mouth. 1851 *N & Q* 1st ser. III 56 [Lancs.] A hot iron put into the cream during the process of churning, expels the witch from the churn. 1852 W. R. WILDE *Irish Superstitions* 57–8. Many are the means taken .. to ensure success [in churning] such as .. nailing an old ass's shoe to the bottom of the churn-dash. 1891 J. C. ATKINSON *Moorland Parish* 100 [Danby, Yorks.] Another and not ineffectual method [of protecting the churn] was— in order, I suppose, to make the place too hot to hold the witch—to take the kitchen poker, heated to an unmistakable red heat, and, inserting it at the opening or bung-hole, to turn it slowly round .. within the said utensil, nine several times. 1909 M. TREVELYAN *Folk-Lore of Wales* 210. When witches prevent butter coming, put a knife under the churn.

IRON in corner

1827 CLARE *Shepherd's Calendar* 8. On corner walls, a glittering row, Hang fire-irons—less for use than show; With horse-shoe brighten'd, as a spell, Witchcraft's evil powers to quell. 1960 Sea captain's wife, 40 [South Shields, Co. Durham] In our family, if anyone is going in for an exam, or a driving test, we put the poker in the corner of the room for luck. It must be an outside corner of the house. Even when we haven't a fireplace, we still keep a poker

specially for the purpose. **1986** Man,
28 [Pensford, Avon] My first exam
today. Had all three of our pokers in the
corner!

IRON in cradle or childbed

1648 HERRICK *Hesperides* 336 'Another'.
Let the superstitious wife Neer the childs
heart lay a knife: Point be up, and Haft
be downe .. This 'mongst other mystick
charms Keeps the sleeping child from
harms. **1691** R. KIRK *Secret Commonwealth* (1815, 6) [Scottish-Irish]
Tramontains to this Day put .. a piece
of Iron, in Womens Bed when travelling
[in labour] to save them from being ..
stollen; and .. report, that all uncouth,
unknown Wights are terrified by .. cold
Iron. late **18th c.** J. RAMSAY (*Scotland in
the Eighteenth Century* II 455–6). A sword
or other piece of iron is commonly laid
under the bolster of a lying-in woman.
1879 J. NAPIER *West of Scotland* 29. A
practice [is] common in some localities
.. of placing in the bed where lay an
expectant mother, a piece of cold iron
to scare the fairies, and prevent them
from spiriting away mother and child.
1880 W. SIKES *British Goblins* 63 [Wales]
There are special .. preventive measures
to interfere with the fairies in their quest
of infants .. You must put a knife in the
child's cradle when you leave it alone,
or you must lay a pair of tongs across
the cradle. **1887** 'SPERANZA' WILDE *Superstitions of Ireland* II 102. A piece of
iron should be sewn in the infant's
clothes, and kept there till after the
baptism. **1900** J. CAMPBELL *Scottish Highlands* 152–3. In the North of Ireland, an
iron poker, laid across the cradle, kept
away the Fairies till the child was baptized. **1909** M. TREVELYAN *Folk-Lore of
Wales* 265. If a newly-born infant cries,
three keys should be placed in the bottom
of the cradle. Ibid. 267. To insure good
luck .. a pair of tongs or a knife was
placed in the cradle the day before the
christening. **1923** *Folklore* 92 [Skye] A
piece of iron should be put in its cradle.
1951 Clergyman [Isle of Man] It used to
be the custom here that, if a stranger
called, the person in charge of the baby
would lay the tongs across the cradle in
case the visitor should be a witch.

IRON: ironing shirt-tail

1928 *Folklore* 398 [Barnton, Cheshire]
If you iron the hem of your husband's
shirt, you iron away his money.

IRON taboo on sacred occasions

*c.***1250** BC Exodus 10: 25. If thou wilt
make me an altar of stone, thou shalt
not build it of hewn stone: for if thou
lift up thy tool upon it, thou hast polluted
it. *c.***550** BC I Kings 6: 7. The house
[Solomon's Temple], when it was in
building, was built of stone made ready
before it was brought thither: so that
there was neither hammer, nor axe, nor
any tool of iron, heard in the house
while it was in building. AD **77** PLINY
Natural History XXXIV LXII (1856, V
41–2) Care is taken to gather [the herb]
without the use of iron, the right hand
being passed through the left sleeve of
the tunic, as though the gatherer were
in the act of committing a theft. Ibid.
XVI XCV (1855, III 436) Clad in a white
robe the priest [druid] ascends the tree,
and cuts the mistletoe with a golden
sickle [i.e. not iron]. *c.***1050** MS Cotton
Vitell. C. iii (COCKAYNE *Leechdoms* I 71)
This wort .. is very wholesome, and
thus thou shalt gather it, in the month
of August without [use of] iron. **1665**
R. RAPIN *De Hortorum* (tr. Gardiner,
1706, 70) No murd'ring Axes let 'em
[oaks] feel, Nor violate the Groves with
impious Steel: From rude Assaults and
Force prophane forbear, Avenging Deities inhabit there. **1691** R. KIRK *Secret
Commonwealth* (1815, 17) Sort of Seers
prognosticat many future events .. from
the shoulder-bone of a Sheep on which a
Knife never came. **1793** Correspondent
[Brampton, Cumb.] (J. HUNTER MS note
in Brand's *Antiquities* I 468) No blacksmith will drive a nail on Good Friday.
1845 J. TRAIN *Isle of Man* II 117. Good
Friday .. is, in some instances, superstitiously regarded in the Island. No
iron of any kind must be put into the
fire on that day, and even the tongs
are laid aside, lest any person should
unfortunately forget .. and stir the fire
with them; by way of substitute a stick
of rowan tree is used. **1866** HENDERSON
Northern Counties 61. A friend who
passed his boyhood in the north of
Durham informs me that no blacksmith

.. would then drive a nail on that day [Good Friday]. **1878** N & Q 5th ser. X 23 [Isle of Man] Having occasion to send a horse to be shod on the 5th of January, the smith refused, on the ground that it was very unlucky to light a fire and temper iron before Christmas had expired, saying he had never done so and never would. **1889** Folklore 46. The fishermen and seamen of Burghead .. Elginshire, on Yule Night, Old Style [prepare the old barrel, the 'Clavie', for burning]. This barrel having been sawn in two, the lower half is nailed into a long spoke of firewood, which serves for a handle. This nail must not be struck by a hammer, but driven in with a stone. **1906** N & Q 10th ser. VI 231. Crosses [of rowan] were carried on Old May Day in the Isle of Man, and placed over the doors of houses, but they must be made without the help of a knife.

Also see index: table, sacred/magical.

IRON, touching

1738 The Craftsman 4 Feb. In Queen Mary's Reign, 'Tag' was all the Play; where the lad saves himself by touching of cold Iron. **1885** E. J. GUTHRIE Scottish Customs 149. If, when at sea .. any one was heard to take the name of God in vain, the first to hear .. immediately called out 'cauld airn', when each of the boat's crew would instantly grasp fast the first piece of iron which came within reach. **1896** BARRIE Sentimental Tommy 175. Tommy faced this fearful passage, sometimes stopping to touch cold iron, but on the whole hanging back little, for Elspeth was in peril. **1906** N & Q 10th ser. VI 230 [east coast of Scotland] Once, when speaking to one of these fishermen in her kitchen, she was interrupted by the entrance of an old woman, reputed to be a witch. The fisherman's consternation was great, and he made it exceedingly emphatic by uttering the words, 'Cauld iron!' and effecting at the same time a successful dash towards an iron hook fixed in the ceiling. **1941** Folklore 237. The factory-girls of the Potteries [N. Staffs.] touch metal when they meet a clergyman—the clasps of their purses or the metal of a nearby lamp-post, grid, or railing. **1952** Girl, 11 [Swansea, Glam.]

If you go out skipping or any similar game and you want to bring back your luck you say: 'Touch wood No good; Touch iron Rely on.'

Cf. WOOD, touching.

iron: also see index: iron, magical/protective; knives/scissors.

IVY in house

15th c. MS Harl. 5396 (R. L. GREENE Carols 1977, 82) Holy stond in the hall, fayre to behold; Iuy stond without the dore; she ys ful sore a-cold. Holy and hys mery men, they dawnsyn and they syng; Iuy and hur maydenys, they wepyn and they wryng. **1884** R. FOLKARD Plant Lore 60. On All Saints' or All Hallows' Day, Roman Catholics are wont to visit the graves of departed relatives .. and place on them wreaths of Ivy .. At Christmas tide Holly .. and Ivy are hung up in churches, and are suitable also for the decoration of houses .. Ivy should only be placed in outer passages or doorways. **1946** [South Shields, Co. Durham] My father visiting my mother in the nursing home said, 'Get that ivy out of here or she'll never recover.' **1959** Woman, c.45 [Scarborough, Yorks.] A neighbour came in and said 'No wonder you're having bad luck, having that ivy plant in the house.' So I took it out and buried it and the next day Eric got a job. **1969** Woman, c.70 [London] The cook gave in her notice, just before Christmas, and I couldn't think why. Finally she said she couldn't work in a house where there was that ivy. It was for my Christmas decorations, but I threw it out.

IVY on house wall

1912 LEATHER Herefordshire 20. If ivy growing on the wall of a house die, it is thought to be a sign of the death of one of the inmates.

IVY picked off church

1923 [Somerset] Never pick an ivy leaf off the church for it indicates sickness.

Cf. GRAVE, picking leaves/flowers from.

IVY LEAF: divination

1898 Weekly Scotsman Christmas Number 7. If you pick an ivy leaf unobserved, repeat .. 'Ivy, ivy, I pluck thee, In my bosom I lay thee; The first young man who speaks to me Shall surely my true lover be.' **1948** J. C. RODGER *Lang Strang* 29 [Forfar, Angus, 1905] Ivy, ivy, I do pluck thee, Down my bosom I do put thee. The first young man that speaks to me Is my lover, sure to be, If he be handsome and pleaseth me. If his coat be brown or grey His love for me is far away. If his coat be black or blue His love for me'll aye be true. **1957** Girl, 13 [Langholm, Dumfries.] Ivy, ivy I love thee, In my bosom I'll put thee, And the first young man that speaks to me Shall be my love and marry me.

IVY LEAF in water: divination

1579 LUPTON *Thousand Notable Things* X § 87. Lay a greene Ivy leafe in a dyshe of fayre water .. on Newyeares euen at night, and .. set it in a sure or safe place, untyl Twelfe euen next after (which wyll be the fyft day of January,) and then .. marke well if the sayde leafe be fayre and greene as it was before: for then you or the party for whom you layd it into the water, wyl be whole and sound and safe from any sicknes all the next yeare following. But if you fynde any black spots theron, then you .. wyll be sicke. **1886** *Folklore* 125 [Sennen, Cornwall, c.1845; Twelfth Night] We .. drew ivy-leaves named after present or absent friends through a wedding ring, and put them into a basin of water which we left until the next morning. Those persons whose leaves had shrivelled or turned black in the night were to die before the next Twelfth-tide, and those who were so unfortunate as to

find their leaves spotted with red, by some violent death, unless a 'pellar' (wise man) could by his skill and incantations grant protection. **1912** LEATHER *Herefordshire* 65. The following Hallowe'en charm was practised recently, to satisfy a morbid desire to know if any member of the family would die during the coming year. An ivy leaf was taken for each one and placed in a bowl of water, to remain all night. The leaves were marked, so that each person knew his or her own, and it was believed that any to die soon would have a coffin marked on the leaf in the morning.

IVY-WOOD CUP

1750 W. ELLIS *Modern Husbandman* VII 179. Ivy-tree .. It grew so large at last, as to give a Turner the Opportunity to turn its Body into Drinking-cups, which he sold for Two-pence half-penny a Piece; and the more for its being deemed to yield a healthful Tincture or Vertue to the Liquor, so as to make it serviceable against the Cramp and Hooping-cough. **1853** *N & Q* 1st ser. VII 128. Drinking-cups made from the wood of the common ivy, and used by children affected with this complaint [whooping cough] for taking therefrom all they require to drink, is current in the county of Salop as an infallible remedy; and I once knew an old gentleman .. who being fond of turning as an amusement, was accustomed to supply his neighbours with them. **1912** LEATHER *Herefordshire* 82. An old man at Almeley, a woodman, firmly believed that to feed a child from a bowl made of ivy wood was a cure [for whooping cough]; he had made such bowls for the purpose.

J

JACKDAW

1042 WILLIAM OF MALMESBURY *Kings of England* II § 204 (1854, III pt. 1 196) As she was regaling, a jack-daw .. chattered .. more loudly than usual; on hearing which the woman .. grew pale .. groaning .. 'This day I shall suffer, some dreadful calamity.' While yet speaking, the messenger of her misfortunes arrived. **1873** *N & Q* 4th ser. XII 395. A stonemason of Clifton [Glos.] relating to me an accident that occurred to one of the workmen at the suspension-bridge over the Avon, at the time when the river was .. spanned by a single chain, dwelt on the fact that a solitary jackdaw had .. perched on the centre of the chain, and had .. been regarded as a precursor of ill luck. **1899** *Newcastle Weekly Chronicle* 11 Feb. 7 [Jesmond] A jackdaw falling down the chimney means sorrow. **1969** E. PORTER *Cambridgeshire* 38–9. An uncle brought round to her a tame jackdaw for her to have as a pet .. Her mother, however, flatly refused to have the bird in the house, declaring that she had always been told they brought ill luck with them.

Cf. MAGPIE.

K

KEY, dropping

1874 HARDY *Madding Crowd* XXXIII. An unlucky token came to me indoors this morning. I went to unlock the door and dropped the key, and it fell upon the stone floor and broke into two pieces. Breaking a key is a dreadful bodement. **1923** [Chard, Som.] To drop a key is the sign of a removal.

KING touches for evil

1066 WILLIAM OF MALMESBURY *Kings of England* II 222 (1854, III pt. I 209) A young woman .. had contracted a sore disorder; the glands swelling so that she became a frightful object. Admonished in a dream to have the part affected washed by the king's hands, she entered the palace. The King .. rubbed the woman's neck with his fingers dipped in water: a speedy recovery followed his healing hand. **1534** P. VERGIL *English History* VIII (tr. Ellis, 294) This goodd kinge [Edward the Confessor] was accustomed with onlie towchinge, bie the divine power of Godde, to heale the swellinge in the throte .. usuallie now termed the kings eavell. **1550** BOORDE *Introduction of Knowledge* Bi^v. The kynges of England by ye power that god hath gyuen to them, dothe make sicke men whole of a sycknes called the kynges euyll. **1580** LYLY *Euphues and his England* (*Works*, 1902, II 95) There is nothing that can cure the kings Euill, but a Prince. **1660** PEPYS *Diary* 23 June. To my lord's lodgings .. and there staid to see the king touch people for the king's evil. But he did not come at all, it rayned so; and the poor people were forced to stand all the morning in the rain in the garden. Afterwards he touched them in the banquetting-house. **1696** AUBREY *Miscellanies* (1890, 125) The curing of the King's-evil by the touch of the King, does much puzzle our philosophers: for whether our Kings were of the house of York, or Lancaster, it did the cure. **1698** MISSON *Voyageur en Angleterre* (1719,

167) When the King was weary of .. touching the Cheek or Chin, Father Peter, the Almoner, presented him with the End of the String which was round the Patient's Neck. The Virtue pass'd from the Hand to the String, from the String to the Cloaths, from the Cloaths to the Skin, and from the Skin to the Root of the Evil: After this Royal Touch, those that were really ill were put into the Hands of the Physicians; and those that came only for the Medal, had no need of other Remedies. **1838** A. E. BRAY *Devonshire* II 293. For curing the king's evil .. Queen Anne's farthing, a stale and common charm in many counties. **1887** 'SPERANZA' WILDE *Superstitions of Ireland* II 101.There is a well near the Boyne where King James washed his sword after the battle, and ever since the water has power to cure the king's evil. **1988** [W. Midlands] It is considered lucky to take a young baby to Windsor [where there is a royal residence].

KINGFISHER: 'weather vane'

1579 LUPTON *Thousand Notable Things* X § 96. A lytle Byrde called the kings fysher, being hanged up in the ayre by the neck: his nebbe or byll wyll be always dyrect or strayght against ye winde. **1592** MARLOWE *Jew of Malta* I i. How stands the wind? Into what corner peers my halcyon's bill? **1606** SHAKESPEARE *Lear* II ii. Turne their Halcion beakes With every gall, and varry of their Masters. **1646** BROWNE *Vulgar Errors* III x. That a Kingfisher hanged by the bill, sheweth in what quarter the wind is, by an occult and secret propriety, converting the breast to that point .. from whence the wind doth blow, is a received opinion, and very strange. **1807** C. SMITH *Natural History of Birds* I 88. I have seen a stuffed [kingfisher] hung up to the beam of a cottage ceiling. I imagined that the beauty of the feathers had recommended it to this sad preeminence, till .. I was assured, that it served the purpose of a weather vane. **1928** E. LOVETT *Surrey and Sussex* 26 [Arundel] The bird [kingfisher] was a stuffed specimen .. suspended .. from the beam of a room .. so that it hung horizontally. The owner assured me that the bird always pointed in one direction during fine weather, but turned .. the other way when it rained. **1973** S. POTTER & L. SARGENT *Pedigree* 294. In Britain the corpse of a Kingfisher used to play its part by being hung by a cord and spun round until, when it ceased to twirl, it came to rest with its bill pointing in the direction from which the wind was supposed to be about to blow.

KISSING for luck

1956 Girl, 11 [Gloucester] I kissed my premium bond, before I put it away. **1965** *News of the World* 17 Oct. 6. We lived in a house which had a pillar-box outside. We were surprised at the number of people—mainly men—who used to kiss their Pools envelope before posting it.

KNAPWEED: divination

1827 CLARE *Shepherd's Calendar* May 11. 157–64. They pull the little blossom threads From out the knotweed's button heads, And put the husk, with many a smile, In their white bosoms for a while—Then, if they guess aright the swain Their loves' sweet fancies try to gain, 'Tis said, that ere it lies an hour, 'Twill blossom out with a second flower. Cf. PLANTAIN: divination.

KNEE itches

1584 SCOT *Discoverie of Witchcraft* XI XIII. The tingling in .. the knee, &c: are singular notes also to be observed in this art [of prognostication]. **1855** *N & Q* 1st ser. XII 38 [Cornwall] If the knee itches, you will kneel in a strange church. **1883** BURNE *Shropshire* 270. If your knee [itches] you will kneel at a strange altar. Cf. FOOT: sole itches.

KNIFE as present

1507 *Gospelles of Dystaues* pt. 2 xx. He that gyueth a payre of knyues to his lady paramour on newe yeres daye knowe that theyr loue shall ware colde.

1611 F. DAVISON *Poetical Rapsodie* 6 'The Lots'. A paire of Kniues. Fortune doth giue this paire of kniues to you, To cut the thred of loue if't be not true. **1714** GAY *Shepherd's Week* 26. But woe is me! Such presents luckles prove, For knives, they tell me, always sever love. **1738** SWIFT *Polite Conversation* 1 30. Pray, Colonel, make me a Present of that pretty Penknife? .. Not for the World, dear Miss; it will cut Love. **1755** *Connoisseur* 20 Feb. Neither would on any account run the risk of cutting love, by giving or receiving such a present as a knife or a pair of scissars. **1787** GROSE *Provincial Glossary* Superstitions 63. It is unlucky to present a knife, scissars, razor, or any sharp or cutting instrument, to one's mistress or friend, as they are apt to cut love and friendship. To avoid the ill effects .. a pin, a farthing, or some trifling recompence, must be taken. **1858** *Worcester Herald* 10 Apr. 2. Although usually opposed to superstitious dogmas, Mr Powell demanded a penny from Miss Bright previous to delivering up the silver knife, assigning as a reason for doing so, the old saw against giving anyone a present of a knife lest it should 'sever love and acquaintance'. *c.*1871 *Jack Harkaway's Schooldays* 7. She took the knife; but quickly gave him a halfpenny. **1884** *Shreds and Patches* V 147. An old gardener near Shiffnal [Shrops.] who has a good knife given to him now and then, says 'Well, thenk ye, sur, and I'll bring ye *the* penny at dinner-time,' which he invariably does. **1890** *Young Ladies' Journal* XXXV 4. Penknives and scissors are tabooed as presents. **1912** *N & Q* 11th ser. V 91. When I was a boy (some sixty years ago) a cutler made me a present of a pocket knife; and within the past week one was given me from a Christmas tree. In both cases I was asked for a halfpenny in exchange. **1983** *Daily Telegraph* 4 Oct. 14. Hattersley had his own celebrations, at which, he says, he gave engraved Sheffield penknives as campaign mementoes 'on permanent loan' lest he violate the superstition that knives given outright cut friendships. **1984** *Times* 16 Mar. 3. At the end of the visit [to Sheffield], the Prince of Wales was presented with a cook's knife and he paid for it with a 1981 Royal Wedding crown.

Cf. PIN as present; SCISSORS as present.

KNIFE dangerous in thunderstorm

1844 DICKENS *Martin Chuzzlewit* XLIII. As a mark of her respect for the lightning, Mrs Lupin had removed her candle to the chimney-piece .. her supper spread on a round table not far off, was untasted, and the knives had been removed for fear of attraction. 1946 UTTLEY *Country Things* 132. During a thunderstorm .. Scissors, needles, scythes, all steel implements were put away, as they are lightning conductors. 1969 S. MAYS *Reuben's Corner* XIV [Essex] Never eat with a knife during thunderstorms. 1978 Man, *c*.45 [Brecon] When there was lightning my mother used to cover up the mirror .. and if there were any knives and forks on the table they'd be put away.

Cf. MIRROR covered in thunderstorm.

KNIFE edge upwards

1824 MACTAGGART *Gallovidian Encyclopedia* 210. If a knife be found lying open on the road, few will dare to lift it. 1923 [Taunton, Som.] To lay a knife on the table, and in doing so, it remains with the edge facing upwards—you will be fortunate. 1983 Woman, 81 [Liss, Hants.] I would never have a knife stand with its sharp edge up. I would always put it flat, or the fairies'd cut their feet. I'd think 'There's another poor fairy with its feet cut.'

KNIFE falls

1873 *Bye-Gones* 28 May 171. With farmers on the English side of the border—between Oswestry and Ellesmere .. it is a common remark .. when a knife falls from the table, to say, 'There's strangers coming from Wales.' 1910 *Folklore* 89 [Argyll.] If a pair of scissors, a knife, or a needle falls to the floor and sticks in an upright position, an unexpected guest will arrive ere long. 1922 UDAL *Dorsetshire* 280. If a knife should fall .. it is a sign that a stranger, a man, will come to the house during the day; if a small knife, a short man; if a large knife, a tall man. 1954 Girl, 14 [Stoke-on-Trent, Staffs.] A dropped

knife is the sign of a row, therefore tread on it. 1984 Woman, 57 [South Shields, Co. Durham] My grandmother, who was born here in 1872, used to think that a dropped knife meant death or disaster, but if you waved the knife round and round above your head three times that made it all right. I've done it myself, many times.

Cf. SCISSORS fall; SWORD falls from scabbard.

KNIFE, finding

1787 GROSE *Provincial Glossary* Superstitions 63. To find a knife or razor, denotes ill luck and disappointment to the party. 1911 J. C. DAVIES *West and Mid-Wales* 217. To find a knife on the road or in a field is .. a very bad omen. 1923 [Taunton, Som.] To find a knife foretells a disappointment.

KNIFE in mast

1884 R. M. FERGUSSON *Rambles in Far North* 169. It is quite a common practice among the Zetland fishermen, when out at the *haaf* or deep-sea fishing, to stick the blade of their knives into the mast to bring luck. 1887 'SPERANZA' WILDE *Superstitions of Ireland* II 114. To stick a penknife in the mast of a boat when sailing is most unlucky. 1932 J. M. E. SAXBY *Shetland Lore* 192. When the wind fails, should stick a knife in the mast and a breeze will come. Some men on beginning a voyage drove the point of a knife into the mast. 1980 Sea captain's wife, 59 [South Shields, Co. Durham] If you want a wind, you stick a knife in the mast.

KNIFE laid across

1646 GAULE *Select Cases of Conscience Touching Witches* 75–6. Some Marks of witches altogether unwarrantable, as proceeding from Ignorance, humor, superstition .. are .. The sticking of knifes acrosse, &c. 1711 *Spectator* 8 Mar. The Lady seeing me quitting my knife and fork, and laying them across one another upon my plate, desired me that I would humour her so far as to take them out of that figure, and place them side by side. 1727 GAY *Fables* XXXVII 7–8. To contribute to my loss, My knife and fork were laid across. 1787 GROSE *Provincial*

Glossary Superstitions 65. It is unlucky to lay one's knife and fork cross-wise: crosses and misfortunes are likely to follow. **1821** CLARE *Village Minstrel* I 159 [Northants.] The knives I keep crossing whenever laid down, Were proofs of these sorrows of mine. **1830** M. R. MITFORD *Our Village* IV 299. Superstition has fallen woefully into decay in our enlightened country .. Who .. is wretched if a knife and fork be laid across his plate? **1855** *Gents Mag.* pt. 2 384–5 [Shrops./Worcs.] Considered unlucky .. to cross knives accidentally at meal times. **1883** BURNE *Shropshire* 279. All the humbler folk say it is unlucky to cross a knife and fork, and all the gently-bred consider it a breach of good manners to do so. **1912** LEATHER *Herefordshire* 87. Crossed knives foreshadow quarrelling, or 'a row in the house'. **1923** [Highbridge. Som.] If you should accidentally cross two knives, uncross them yourself. If someone else does you will quarrel with them. **1964** Girl, 15 [Woodford, Essex] If two knives are crossed always take the underneath one away first, otherwise there will be a row. **1982** Woman, 54 [Colchester, Essex] Crossed knives mean a quarrel. To avert, knock with the handle-end of each knife in turn, three times, on the table— knife held vertically. **1985** Woman, 48 [Tredegar, Monmouth.] We always throw the knives on the floor if we see them crossed. We've done this in our family ever since my grandmother saw crossed knives on the table and a telegram arrived soon after to say her son had been wounded. That was in the First World War.

KNIFE: sharpening after sunset

1895 S. O. ADDY *Household Tales* 102 [Yorks.] It is unlucky to sharpen a knife after sunset.

KNIFE, spinning: divination

1895 S. O. ADDY *Household Tales* 82. To find out whether your husband will have light hair or dark hair, take a table-knife with a white haft and spin it round on the table. If it stops with the blade towards you your husband will be a dark-haired man; if with the haft, he will be a light-haired man. **1935** Girl,

12 [Parkstone, Dorset] At unsupervised tea, at my school, we spin a knife round on the table and ask it 'Who's going to be married first?' **1982** Woman, *c.*20 [Sutton Coldfield, Warwicks.] Sit in a circle, choose a boy's name and spin a knife and wherever the knife stops, that's the boy you love. **1987** Woman, 85 [Rogate, Hants.] When I was young, my brother (he was a master at Dulwich College at the time), showed us a game where we'd spin a knife round very fast, and while it was spinning you asked it a question, like 'Who is the most beautiful girl in the room?' It often stopped at the ugliest girl. Of course we didn't take it seriously.

KNIFE, spinning: points towards one

1895 S. O. ADDY *Household Tales* 99 [Yorks.] It is unlucky to spin a knife round on the table. **1985** Woman, 50 [Warrington, Lancs.] If a knife turns round and stops with its point towards me (say when I'm washing up and put it on the table) I always dodge to one side out of its way. **1987** Man, 48 [Hoveringham, Notts.] You should never spin a knife on a table because if you do it symbolizes the death of the person it points to.

Cf. PIN points towards one.

KNIFE, stirring with

1900 *Trans. Devon. Ass.* 66. Proverb. If you stir with a knife, You will stir up strife. **1923** [Somerset] Stir with a knife, You stir up strife. **1962** Woman, 39 [Liss, Hants.] Stir with a fork, stir up talk, Stir with a knife and you stir up strife. **1984** Man, 36 [Wooton-under-Edge, Glos.] This is not a superstition, but I'd never stir my tea with a knife, because 'Stir with a knife, Stir up strife.'

KNIFE taboo to pregnant woman

1921 *Folklore* 211. My grandmother was not allowed by her midwife to touch knives, scissors, etc. I remember hearing my grandmother say how much annoyed she was, sixty-four years ago, at having all her food cut up for her, and when later she objected, she had to have the handles of the knives and scissors tied up in flannel bags.

Cf. IRON taboo on sacred occasions.

'KNIFE' taboo word

1883 J. R. TUDOR *Orkneys and Shetland* 166 [Shetland] When setting their lines they avoided, and do still, mentioning certain objects, except by certain special words or phrases. Thus a knife is called *skunie*, or *tullie*.

KNIFE, toasting or passing bread with

1895 S. O. ADDY *Household Tales* 101 [Yorks.] If you toast on a knife You'll be poor all your life. **1923** [Taunton, Som.] If you toast with a knife, you'll never be a wife. **1923** [Bridgwater, Som.] It is very unlucky to pass a slice of bread with a knife. **1932** C. IGGLESDEN *Those Superstitions* 173. Another maid's rhyme .. 'If you toast with a knife No luck all your life.'
Cf. BREAD, cutting or pricking.

KNOCKING = death omen

1696 AUBREY *Miscellanies* (1890, 118) Three or four days before my father died, as I was in my bed about nine o'clock in the morning perfectly awake, I did hear three distinct knocks on the beds-head, as if it had been with a ruler .. Mr Hierome Banks, as he lay on his death bed, in Bell-yard, said, three days before he died, that Mr Jennings of the Inner-temple, (his great acqaintance, dead a year or two before) gave three knocks, looked in, and said, come away. He was as far from believing such things as any man. **1787** GROSE *Provincial Glossary* Superstitions 47. Three loud and distinct knocks at the bed's head of a sick person, or at the bed's head or door of any of his relations, is an Omen of his death. **1825** CLARE *Journal* 26 Jan. Ghosts .. never pay a visit without giving their (fashionable) signal of 3 raps to announce their arrival. *c*.**1850** J. HUNTER MS note in Brand's *Antiquities* II 545. Strange to say! I believe in this:—that is, I believe in one case of it, because I know it. **1866** HENDERSON *Northern Counties* 33. Three raps given by no human hand are said to give warning of death. Such were heard a few years ago, at Windy Walls, near Stamfordham .. on the outside of a window-shutter, and the same night a man belonging to the house fell accidently off a cart and was killed. **1895** J. HARDY *Denham Tracts* II 267–8. An old man who lived on Tyneside told me that three sharp taps had been applied to his window before his .. wife died .. A man .. in Wooler [Northumb.] heard three raps before his father died. His father dropped down suddenly shortly afterwards at Wooler 'High Fair'. **1908** *Folklore* 466–7 [Corringham, Lincs.] Last Wednesday night Mr B. was disturbed by a sound like someone knocking at his bedroom window .. The next morning a telegram was received which informed them that a brother of Mr B.'s had died very suddenly .. at a town on the English channel. The death took place .. some hours before the knocking was heard in Lincolnshire. After he received the telegram Mr B. expressed his conviction that the sound must have been a warning. **1923** [Taunton, Som.] If you hear distinctly a knock at the door and no one is there, it's a sign of a near friend passing away. **1963** Gardener's wife [Scarborough, Yorks.] I couldn't sleep that night, and I heard (here she rapped slowly twice on the table) on the door .. I said to my husband, 'Did you hear that?' and he said 'Aye'. So I said, 'So long as it doesn't come three times.' The next day she [their daughter] was better, but they told me it had been touch and go whether they should send for us the night I heard it. **1967** S. MARSHALL *Fenland Chronicle* pt. 2 IX. Signs when anybody were a-going to die .. like hearing footsteps, or three separate knocks on the door when nobody were there. **1986** Man, 47 [Brixton, London] My father swore blind that he heard three knocks on the wall a short time before his uncle died. It was in the middle of the night—he woke up and definitely wasn't dreaming. My father wasn't a superstitious man, he was very practical and down to earth.
Cf. TELEPHONE, ringing.

KNOTS hinder birth

AD **77** PLINY *Natural History* XXVIII VII (1856, V 292) Delivery .. will be accelerated, if the man by whom the woman has conceived, unties his girdle, and, after tying it round her, unties it, adding at the same time this formula, 'I have tied it, and I will untie it,' and then taking his departure. *c*.1450 'Willie's Lady' (CHILD *Ballads* I 87) [Willie frustrates his witch-mother's attempt to prevent the birth.] O Willie has loosed the nine witch knots That was amo that ladie's locks.

Cf. BIRTH: opening locks; CROSSING LEGS hinders birth.

KNOTS hinder conception

c.1050 MS Cotton Vitell. C. iii (COCKAYNE *Leechdoms* I 331) If to any one anything of evil has been done, (By a knot) so that he may not enjoy his lusts, then . . let him partake of [etc.]. 1588 J. HARVEY *Discoursive Probleme* 72. Plato . . appointeth them to suffer death, or . . some greeuous . . penaltie, that . . shall be conuicted, to haue prepared, or furnished themselues, by knots, inductions, incantations . . to harme, endamage, or hurt any other. 1597 JAMES I *Daemonologie* 11–12. Such kinde of Charmes as commonlie dafte wiues vses, for . . staying married folkes, to haue naturallie adoe with other, (by knitting so manie knottes vpon a poynt [a lace] at the time of their mariage). *c*.1609 MIDDLETON *Witch* 15. So sure into what House theis are Convaid, knitt with theis Charmed, and retentive Knotts, Neither the Man begetts, nor Woman Breeds; no, nor performs the least desires of wedlock. *ante* 1611 Simon Forman (ed. A. L. Rowse, 73) [in MS notebook] To tie a man not to meddle with a woman *et contra* . . In the time of matrimony take a point and tie three knots thereon. When the priest says 'Whom God hath joined together let no man separate,' then they knit the knots naming the party, saying 'Whom God hath joined together those let the Devil separate. *Sara* until these knots be undone.' And he shall never meddle with the said woman. *Probatum*. 1774 PENNANT *Tour in Scotland* 232 [Islay, Hebrides] Donald takes three threads of different hues, and ties three knots on each, three times imprecating the most cruel disappointments on the nuptial bed: but the bridegroom to avert the harm, stands at the altar with an untied shoe. 1793 *Stat. Acc. of Scotland* V 83 [Logierait, Perth.] Immediately before the celebration of the marriage ceremony, every knot about the bride and bridegroom, (garters, shoe-strings, strings of petticoats, &.) is carefully loosened. 1834 DALYELL *Darker Superstitions of Scotland* 302. If sorcerers were disposed to counteract the will of nature, they could employ the simplest, yet most efficient means. They had only to cast one or many knots, on any cord, after a special fashion. Thenceforward, the virtuous, tender and anxious couple, would be deprived of all hope of progeny. 1891–3 *Proceedings Royal Irish Acad.* 3rd ser. II 818. [Co. Galway] If anyone at a marriage repeats the benediction after the priest, and ties a knot at the mention of each of the three sacred names on a handkerchief, or a piece of string, the marriage will be childless for fifteen years, unless the knotted string is burnt in the meantime.

KNOTS in garters: divination

1696 AUBREY *Miscellanies* (1890, 131–2) *To know whom one shall marry.* You must lie in another county, and knit the left garter about the right legged stocking . . and as you rehearse these following verses, at every comma, knit a knot. 'This knot I knit, To know the thing, I know not yet, That I may see, The man (woman) that shall my husband (wife) be, How he goes, and what he wears, And what he does, all days, and years.' Accordingly in your dream you will see him: if a musician, with a lute or other instrument; if a scholar, with a book or papers. 1714 GAY *Shepherd's Week* 37. As Lubberkin once slept beneath a Tree, I twitch'd his dangling Garter from his Knee; He wist not when the hempen String I drew, Now mine I quickly doff of Inkle Blue; Together fast I tye the Garters twain, And while I knit the Knot repeat this Strain. 'Three times a True-love's Knot I tye secure, Firm be the knot, firm may his Love endure.' 1755 *Connoisseur* 20 Feb. Whenever I go to lye in a strange bed, I always tye my garter nine times round the bed-post, and knit nine knots in it, and say to myself, 'This knot I knit, this knot I tye, To see my love as he goes by, In his apparel and array, As he walks in every day.' **1842** R. CHAMBERS *Popular Rhymes of Scotland* 36 [Hallowe'en] The left leg garter is taken, and three knots are tied on it .. the person must not speak to any one, otherwise the charm will prove abortive. She repeats the following rhyme upon tying each knot: 'This knot, this knot I knit, To see the thing I ne'er saw yet—To see my love in his array, And what he walks in every day; And what his occupation be, This night I in my sleep may see. And if my love be clad in green, His love for me is well seen; And if my love is clad in grey, His love for me is far away; But if my love be clad in blue, His love for me is very true.' After all the knots are tied, she puts the garter below her pillow, and sleeps on it; and it is believed that her future husband will appear to her in a dream. **1880** W. SIKES *British Goblins* 304. In Glamorganshire this is done: A man gets possession of a girl's garters, and weaves them into a true lover's knot, saying over them some words of hope and love in Welsh. This he puts under his shirt, next his heart, till he goes to bed, when he places it under the bolster. If the test be successful the vision of his future wife appears to him in the night. **1896** *South Wales Daily News* 12 Aug. 4. Take your garter; make nine knots and one slack one; tie around bedpost; put shoes or slippers in form of T under pillow; do not utter a word to any one; go into bed backwards; undress with left hand; say 'I do this for to see Who my future wife shall be, Where she is and what she wears,' three times over when tying garter and putting shoes under pillow. **1899** *Newcastle Weekly Chronicle* 4 Feb. 7 [Jesmond] To induce favourable dreams, nine knots are tied on a garter.

KNOTS in grass: divination

*c.*1617 CAMPION *Third Book of Airs*. Thrice three times tie up this true love's knot, And murmur soft: 'She will, or she will not.' **1688** AUBREY *Remaines* (1881, 82–3) A true loves knott .. Take two blades of green Grasse folded in each other .. and then putt in your bosome or neck, while one can say 3 pater nosters; and all ye while you are folding it and wearing it you must thinke of her

that you love: and if she loves you the grass will be changed .. ye grasses will not be mutually lock't together as when folded up. **1827** CLARE 'The Rivals' ll. 33–8. When I was young, and went a-weeding wheat, We used to make them on our dinner seat: We laid two blades across and lapt them round, Thinking of those we loved; and if we found Them linked together when unlapt again, Our loves were true. **1912** LEATHER *Herefordshire* 64–5. An old woman was working in a green wheatfield near Pembridge with a girl who was hesitating between two sweethearts. She took two long leaves of the wheat, folded them nine times round the girl's waist, repeating the name of one of her admirers. The leaves were not sticking together after this, so the ceremony was gone through again with another name and other leaves, when they were found to adhere, 'So Mrs V—— told me I should have John, though Harry was all my fancy just then. And I did have John, sure enough!' **1913** *Folklore* 80 [Barnard Gate, Oxon., *c.*1840] You must gather four long blades of grass (called 'lovelaces') and hold them in your hand. Then tie them in four knots, two at each end, saying .. 'If you love me cling all round me, If you hate me fall off quite, If you neither love nor hate Come in two at last.' If the grasses form a ring, he is constant; if all the knots come undone, he hates you; if they come in two pieces, he is indifferent.

Cf. APRON comes untied; GARTER comes untied.

KNOTS in shroud/clothes of dead

1863 *Leeds Mercury* 11 May 4. In the Isle of Man a superstition exists that if the knots of the shroud are not untied when the coffin is nailed up the ghost of the deceased will wander about. A funeral recently took place, and soon after it was rumoured that the deceased's ghost had visited her former home, and it was remembered that the knots had not been untied. The vicar was applied to for leave to open the grave and allow the needful to be done, to which he of course objected .. The friends, however, were determined not to be outdone, and early on Sunday morning week the grave was opened .. the knots unloosed, and the grave made all right ere the sun rose. 1891 *N & Q* 7th ser. XII 245–6 [Ireland] The clothes of deceased relatives, after having been taken to the chapel to be blessed, or at least laid where the sprinklings of the holy-water brush may fall upon them, are taken home, and when demanded by the next of kin—or, if too well worn to be worth their having, asked for by some wandering beggar—are spread upon the ground, sprinkled again with holy water, and, after being carefully examined, lest any knots should remain in the strings, are handed to the claimant 'in the honour of God, the blessed Virgin, and the dead person's soul'. By this act and formula the naked spirits are supposed to be clothed.

Cf. COFFIN LID undone; KNOTS hinder birth.

KNOTS protect against evil

1572 R. BANNATYNE *Journal* (1806, 339) The 28 of Apryle thair was ane witche brunt in St Androis .. Efter hir handis were bound, the provest causeth lift vp hir claithis [and] thair was a white claith like a collore craig [collar] with stringis in betuene hir leggis, whairon was mony knottis vpon the stringis of the said collore craig, which was tacken from hir sore against hir will; for belyke scho thought that scho suld not have died that being vpon hir, for scho said, when it was taken from hir, 'Now I have no hoip of my self.'

KNOTS used in cures

AD 77 PLINY *Natural History* XXX xxx (1856, V 455) [For fevers.] Some enclose a caterpillar in a piece of linen with a thread passed three times round it, and tie as many knots, repeating at each knot why it is that the patient performs that operation. late 12th c. BARTHOLOMEW OF EXETER *Penitential* (*Rel. Ant.* I 285) Those who make knots or spells and various kinds of charm with magic by songs, and conceal them in grass or in a tree or at a crossroads to free their animals from harm [must do penance]. 1616 Witchcraft trial, Orkney (DALYELL *Darker Superstitions of Scotland* 118) An alleged Satanic precept was, to

make 'a wresting thread, and give it in the name of the Father, Sone, and the Holie Gaist, and say, Bone to bone, synnew to synnew, and flesche to flesche, and bluid to bluid, it wald mak ony wrest [sprain] of man or beast haill'. 1842 R. CHAMBERS *Popular Rhymes of Scotland* 37. The 'wresting thread' .. is a thread spun from black wool, on which are cast nine knots, and tied round a sprained leg or arm .. The operator .. says, but in such a tone of voice as not to be heard by the bystanders, nor even by the person operated upon: 'The Lord rade, And the foal slade; He lighted, And he righted, Set joint to joint, Bone to bone, And sinew to sinew. Heal in the Holy Ghost's name!' 1849 BRAND *Antiquities* III 288 [*Worcester Journal*, 1845] A child afflicted with the hooping-cough .. the mother pointed to its neck, on which was a string fastened, having nine knots tied in it. The poor woman stated that it was the stay-lace of the child's godmother. 1849 *Athenaeum* 911 [Manchester, Lancs., from man, 70+] First, count the warts to be removed—and then on a piece of thin twine make a corresponding number of loose knots. Touch each wart with one of the knots; and place the twine in a stagnant pool of water or any other place where it will rapidly decompose, saying at the same time these words, 'There is none to redeem it beside thee.' 1850 *N & Q* 1st ser. II 19 [N. Scotland, *c.*1800] Count most carefully the number of warts; take a corresponding number of nodules or knots from the stalks of any of the *cerealia* (wheat, oats, barley); wrap these in a cloth, and deposit the packet in the earth; all the steps of the operation being done secretly. As the nodules decay the warts will disappear. Some artists think it necessary that each wart should be touched by a separate nodule. 1854 *N & Q* 1st ser. X 221 [Orkney] A linen thread is tied about the injured part after the solemn repetition of the charm [similar to 1842]. The thread is called the 'wristing thread', from the wrist or ankle being the part to which it is most commonly applied. 1899 *Newcastle Weekly Chronicle* 4 Feb. 7 [Jesmond] Tie a knot on a straw for each wart, make into a parcel and drop it. **1923** *Folklore* 90–1 [Skye, Hebrides] A sprain was cured by taking a piece of string and tying knots in it, moistening the string with saliva as the knots are tied .. Then the healer says, 'As Jesus relieved horses in the stable, hearing them groan, so may bone go to bone, marrow to marrow, sinew to sinew.' **1929** *Folklore* 118 [Norfolk; for nose bleed] Get nine people each to tie a knot in a strand of red silk hung round the sufferer's neck. The spell acts better if the knots are tied by persons of the opposite sex. **1932** J. M. E. SAXBY *Shetland Lore* 176. Wise-women .. could cure sprains by a woollen thread spun from black wool and tied in an 'aaba k-not' for each day in the moon's age. While tying the knot the wise-women slowly whispered: 'Wir Saviour rade And the foal's fit slade, Sinnan to sinnan, bane to bane, Come do hale in Gude's name.' **1933** *Folklore* 202 [Digby, Lincs.] Take a piece of worsted and tie on it as many knots as you have warts; drop this down the lavatory. As the worsted decays the warts will disappear. **1947** *Mirror* 18 Feb. 6 [Newcastle upon Tyne, Northumb.] My wife was going round with a bit of wool tied round a wrist the other day. On asking the reason, I was told that she had slightly wrenched the wrist, and the wool was the remedy. **1957** *Girl*, 11 [Penrith, Cumb.] Get a piece of string and put as many knots in as you have warts and then go and bury them in the ground where nobody knows but yourself.

Cf. RED THREAD cures; THREAD tied round.

L

LADDER, walking under

1787 GROSE *Provincial Glossary* Superstitions 63. It is unlucky to walk under a ladder; it may prevent your being married that year. 1813 *Gents Mag.* pt. 2 431. The unluckiness of walking under a ladder .. Whence? 1831 HONE *Year Book* 29 Feb. When you pass under a ladder you must spit through it, or three times afterwards. 1855 *Gents Mag.* pt. 2 503–4. As according to the then fashion of hanging at Tyburn and elsewhere, the culprit walked under the ladder, I was considerably warned ever to walk round it. 1859 E. FITZBALL *Dramatic Author's Life* II 57–8. Macready made a sudden pause, and after a moment of irresolution and resolution, 'Mr Fitzball,' he said, 'you will no doubt think it a great weakness, but I entertain an insurmountable dislike to pass under a ladder. It is a failing, if it be a failing, which I have imbibed from childhood; excuse me, therefore, if I go round!' 1866 *N & Q* 3rd ser. IX 460. A friend of mine, who objected on principle to such superstitious nonsense, had a paint-brush dropped right on the top of his head while passing under a ladder in Cornhill. He has since been a devout believer in the ill-luck of the proceeding. 1873 HARLAND & WILKINSON *Lancashire Legends* 229. The caution that we must avoid passing under a ladder, lest we should come to be hanged, has probably descended to us from early practice in Lancaster. 1879 J. NAPIER *West of Scotland* 136. It was unlucky to walk under a ladder set up against a wall, but if passing under it could not be avoided, then, if before doing so, you wished for anything, your wish would be fulfilled. 1882 *N & Q* 6th ser. VI 357. Within the last few years I saw a gentleman, walking through the streets of Carlisle, spit over his left shoulder to avert misfortune, he having inadvertently passed under a ladder. 1883 BURNE *Shropshire* 283. 'Oh, Grace has walked under a ladder! Don't tell her, don't tell her!'

'Why not?' .. 'What, don't you know? She'll never be married now!' 1932 C. IGGLESDEN *Those Superstitions* 45. The superstition arises from the fact that when the ladder leans against the wall it forms a triangle and is thus symbolical of the Trinity. The ordinary layman of olden days would .. consider himself debarred from passing through this sacred arch. Ibid. 47 [London] A woman .. unconsciously passed under a ladder. Realising what she had done she promptly crossed two of her fingers .. 'I dare not unclasp my fingers till I see a dog,' she explained to her companion. 1943 F. THOMPSON *Candleford Green* 119. As far as Laura ever heard, one might walk under a ladder with impunity, for the absence of which inhibition she had cause to be thankful in after years, when the risk of a spattering of paint on one's clothing was a trifle compared to that of stepping off the kerb and being run over by the traffic. 1953 Boy, *c*.14 [Ipswich, Suffolk] Walking under ladders is bad luck, unless you spit directly you have passed under the ladder. 1954 Girl, 12 [South Molton, Devon] When you walk under a ladder don't speak until you see a four-legged animal. 1982 Woman, *c*.20 [Sutton Coldfield, Warwicks.] If you have to walk under it, cross your fingers. Will walk under it if not leaning against a wall. 1982 Woman, 20 [Sheffield, Yorks.] Usually the penalty is just bad luck but some say that you will be hanged .. You can stop long enough to make a wish, or cross your fingers to negate the bad luck, or make a 'fig' sign, which involves closing your fist and passing your thumb between the index and middle fingers. 1983 Woman, 52 [Wormley, Herts.] I'll go to any lengths to avoid walking under a ladder. The only time I did, I had appendicitis directly after. 1983 Girl, 13 [Maldon, Essex] I liked walking under ladders until my sister said 'You'll have a tin of paint on your head if you keep on doing that.' 1983 Girl, 16 [Colchester, Essex] One day my friends and I saw a ladder leaning up against the wall. We had just come out of Sunday School, and we all walked under the ladder to show we weren't afraid as we were Christians. You can't be superstitious if you're a Christian. **1985** Journalist, male, 57. I defy the ladder, and always make a point of walking under it.

LADYBIRD flies to lover

1714 GAY *Shepherd's Week* 36. This lady-fly I take from off the grass, Whose spotted back might scarlet red surpass. Fly, Lady-Bird, North, South, or East or West, Fly where the Man is found that I love best. He leaves my Hand, see to the West he's flown, To call my True-love from the faithless Town. **1808** JAMIESON *Scottish Dict. Landers.* In the North of Scotland .. 'Dr. Dr. Ellison, where will I be married? East, or west, or south or north? Take ye flight, and fly away.' **1818** *Edinburgh Mag.* Oct. 326–7 [Clydesdale] The beautiful little insect, the Lady Lanners of Scotland, is still a great favourite among our peasantry, though not now, in so far as I can gather, used for divining one's future helpmate .. When any of our children lights upon one of these insects, it is carefully placed upon the open palm of the hand, and the following metrical jargon is repeated .. 'Lady Lady Lanners, Lady Lady Lanners, Tak up your clowk about your head, An' flee awa to Flanners. Flee ower firth, and flee ower fell, Flee ower pule and rinnan' well, Flee ower muir, and flee ower mead, Flee ower livan, flee ower dead, Flee ower corn, an' flee ower lea, Flee ower river, flee ower sea, Flee ye east or flee ye west, Flee till him that lo'es me best.' **1842** R. CHAMBERS *Popular Rhymes of Scotland* 43 [Kincardine.] The Scottish youth are accustomed to throw it into the air, singing .. 'King, King Gollowa, Up your wings and flie awa'; Over land and over sea, Tell me where my love can be!' **1850** *N&Q* 1st ser. I 132. Bishop, Bishop Barnabee, Tell me when my wedding be: If it be to-morrow day, Take your wings and fly away! Fly to the east, fly to the west, Fly to them that I love best! **1883** BURNE *Shropshire* 237. It was a favourite game among little

girls to place a lady-bird on the back of the hand, and then toss it away, saying, 'Lady-cow, lady-cow, fly away, flee! Tell me which way my weddin's to be, Up hill, or down hill, or towards the Brown Clee!' **1912** LEATHER *Herefordshire* 64. Marygold, marygold, flitter to fly, Tell me where doth my lady-love lie?

LADYBIRD, killing

1855 *Gents Mag.* pt. 2 384–5 [Shrops./ Worcs.] Considered unlucky .. to kill a lady-cow. **1899** *Newcastle Weekly Chronicle* 11 Feb. 7 [Jesmond] It is very unlucky to kill a lady-bird. It should be set free to the rhyme: 'Lady-bird, lady-bird, fly away home Thy house is on fire, thy children all roam; Except little Nan, who sits in her pan, Weaving gold laces as fast as she can.' **1922** [Bridgwater, Som.] If you see a little insect which is commonly called God Almighty's Cow, you must not harm it as it is very unlucky. **1938** *Folklore* 33 [Essex, *c*.1880] Under no circumstances was a ladybird to be killed. If accidentally killed the corpse was buried and the grave stamped on three times while the rhyme was repeated, 'Ladybird, lady-bird, fly away home, Your house is on fire and your children are gone.'

Cf. RAINBOW, charm against.

LADYBIRD lucky

1940 Girl, 12 [South Shields, Co. Durham] It's very lucky if a ladybird lights on you. **1988** Woman, 70 [Edinburgh, 1920s] The ladybird is very, very lucky, particularly if it comes on you. I remember one coming on me before a tennis match and being overjoyed.

LANTERN on table

1887 F. T. HAVERGAL *Herefordshire Words* 46. No farmer ever puts his lantern on the table, else their cows will caste their calves. The lantern must always be put under the table. 'The reason our cow calved a month too soon was because the master put his lantern alway on the table.' The old-fashioned lanthorns, made of tin with horn plates for the sides, are falling into disuse. **1895** S. O. ADDY *Household Tales* 100 [Yorks.] It is unlucky to put a lantern on the table, and people say: 'A lantern on the table

Is death in the stable.' **1948** E. & M. A. RADFORD *Superstitions* 161. A cowman .. at a lonely farm near Ross-on-Wye [Herefords.] in 1945, bemoaning a lost calf, explained: ' .. were a'cause master put his lantern on table.'

LARK, harming

1842 R. CHAMBERS *Popular Rhymes of Scotland* 41. A list of birds whose nests it is deemed unlucky to molest: The laverock [lark] and the lintie. **1874** H. L. SAXBY *Birds* 88. Throughout the whole of Shetland, the Skylark is held .. sacred .. therefore it is seldom that either the birds or their eggs are disturbed .. When the reason .. is sought, the usual reply is, 'Weel, if ye look under a laverock's tongue, ye'll see three spots, and they say that every one is a curse upo' him that interferes wi' it.' **1884** N & Q 6th ser. IX 26. A very old lady, aged ninety-three .. said, 'No one in Shetland would eat a lark; there are three black spots on its tongue, and for every lark you eat you get three curses.' **1901** MACLAGAN *Games of Argyleshire* 206. It is not lucky to harry a lark's nest. The lark will come and say:—'Uiat, uiat, uitan, Co chreach mo neadan? [etc.]' ('Who harried my nest? .. I will chuck him over a cliff.') **1909** D. J. ROBERTSON *Orkney Book* 232. The featherless young raise feeble necks to gape for food, showing their yellow tongues with the three black spots which children here are told will appear on the tongue of that child who takes the laverock's nest.

'LAST' taboo word

1904 E. V. LUCAS *Sussex* 173 [Brighton] When the last net was overboard the master said, 'Seas all!' .. If he were to say, 'Last net,' he would expect never to see his nets again. **1953** Secretary of Folklore Society. In a flying club the pilots never talked about the 'last flight' of the day but always 'the last flight but one'.

LAST FOOD/DRINK: bite of apple

1861 C. C. ROBINSON *Dialect of Leeds* 339. The last of anything [is] supposed to ensure luck to the giver. A child begs hard for the 'last luck', or core, of an apple, and it is generally bestowed by children, from the supposition that more will come to them by so doing. Each pippin [pip] as it is arrived at, is thrown at random over the head, and a simple 'nomony' repeated, when so many apples as there have been pippins thrown, will be forthcoming, it is expected.

LAST FOOD/DRINK: bread etc. on plate

1873 HARLAND & WILKINSON *Lancashire Legends* 230. The person who takes the last piece of bread from a plate .. will either be blessed with a handsome partner, or die unmarried. **1910** *Folklore* 89 [Argyll.] The lady who takes the last piece of bread on the plate will marry a rich man. **1923** [West Malling, Kent] The person who, uninvited, takes the last slice of bread and butter from the plate will die unmarried. But the person who takes the last slice upon invitation will have a handsome spouse and an income of thousands amounting to the number of people at the table. *c.*1935 Girl, 12 [Poole, Dorset] When you offer someone the last slice of bread-and-butter, or the last cake, on the plate, you say 'Which will you have, a handsome husband or a thousand a year?' and the other person usually says 'A thousand a year, and then I'll get the handsome husband as well.' **1954** Girl, 15 [Tunstall, Staffs.] The last piece of bread and butter on a plate should be tossed before it is eaten to ward off bad luck. **1964** Girl, 15 [Epping, Essex] If you eat the last piece of bread on the plate without speaking you get a rich husband.

LAST FOOD/DRINK: 'Carling' peas divination

1895 J. HARDY *Denham Tracts* II 282. On Carling Sunday .. fried pease are served up on a dish. Every one .. is furnished with a spoon; they help themselves in regular succession and whoever gets the last will be first married. **1899** *Newcastle Weekly Chronicle* 11 Feb. 7 [Jesmond] On Passion or Carling Sunday, peas fried in butter are eaten with pepper and vinegar—special virtue attaches to the last pea.

LAST FOOD/DRINK: tea, wine, etc.

1849 BRAND *Antiquities* III 317. In some

parts of Oxfordshire it is believed that the last nine drops of tea poured from the teapot, after the guests are served, will cure the heartache. **1866** HENDERSON *Northern Counties* 55. The last glass of wine or spirits drained from the last bottle on New Year's Eve or Day is called the 'lucky glass'. It brings good fortune to whoever comes in for it, and if an unmarried person drinks it, he will be the first to marry among the company.

LAST PAYMENT to doctor/midwife

1881 W. PAUL *Aberdeenshire* 41. When the howdies [midwives] are paid the're aye ready oot wi' thar han's wi' a luckpenny. But dinna tak' it man; for if you do, ye'll soon see them back again at you. **1912** LEATHER *Herefordshire* 87. At Hay they say it is unlucky to pay the whole amount of a doctor's bill; anyone who does so is likely to require his services again soon, and therefore a small sum, if only a shilling, is sometimes left unpaid.

Cf. LUCK-PENNY.

LAST SHIFT

1962 Boy, 13 [Cumnock, Ayr.] Some miners refuse to work on the day before the holidays as they have a superstition that something will happen. **1974** *Yorkshire Post* 12 Mar. 6. A good many miners think that to work the first shift after a strike or a holiday, or the last shift before a break, is tempting Providence, that the accident all miners fear will happen to them that day only.

LAST WORDS OF PLAY

1910 T. SHARPER KNOWLSON *Superstitions* 225. Actors will not repeat the last lines of a play at rehearsals. **1922** LYND *Solomon* 157. It is unlucky during rehearsals to quote the catchword [last word] of a forthcoming play in casual conversation. **1933** J. B. BOOTH *Pink Parade* 97. A perfectly certain way to break a play's chance of success is to speak the 'tag'—the last lines—at rehearsal .. Any nonsense can be spoken, except the actual words of the author. **1950** *Everybody's* 18 Mar. 25. Talking of rehearsals .. it is bad luck to speak the tag of a play before the first night.

1965 BBC RADIO *Does the Team Think?* Jimmy Edwards said that in rehearsals whoever has the last line in a show does not speak it, they usually go 'Dumpty—dumpty—dumpty—dum'. **1984** Actress, 58 [London] You mustn't say the last line of the play till the opening night.

LAUGHING too much

1652 GAULE *Mag-astro-mances* 181. Superstitious ominations .. to be over merry on a suddain. **1959** [Bradley, Suffolk, *c.*1880] Laugh till you cry, Sorrow till you die. **1987** Woman, 58 [NE England] When we got too hilarious as children, my mother used to say, 'You've got a gale in your tail. You see, it'll end in a crying match.'

LEAD shapes in water: divination of cause of sickness

1486 SPRENGER & KRAMER *Malleus Maleficarum* (tr. Summers, 87) They hold molten lead over the sick man, and pour it into a bowl of water. And if the lead condenses into some image, they judge that the sickness is due to witchcraft. And when such men are asked whether the image so formed is caused by the work of devils, or is due to some natural cause, they answer that it is due to the power of Saturn over lead, the influence of that planet being in other respects evil. **1584** SCOT *Discoverie of Witchcraft* XII xviii. To learne how to know whether a sicke man be bewitched or no .. You must hold molten lead over the sicke bodie, and powre it into a porringer full of water; and then, if there appeare upon the lead, anie image, you may then knowe the partie is bewitched. **1643** Witchcraft trial, Orkney (*Abbotsford Club Misc.* I 184) Ye said that the child haid the hart cake; and that .. ye wold cast the hart cake, and sie what wold become of him .. Ye took ane pott with water in it, and laid the tonges athwart the mouth of the pott, and than laid ane codd [cushion] aboue the tonges, and set the child on it; thairefter ye took ane seif and set [it] on the childis head, and set ane cogge [pail] full of water in the seive, and then laid ane woll scheir on the coggis mouth, and then ye took lead and put it in ane iroun lamp, and meltit it, and powrit it throw the bowl of the scheir into the water threie severall tymes, devining throw the lead whither the child wold recover or not; and quhen ye haid done all, ye gaue the child ane drink of the said water, and said he wold be weill. **1874** *Journal Anthropological Inst.* III 267–8 [Banff.] A sudden fright was supposed to dislodge the heart. Slow disease followed .. Cure .. Casting the heart—The patient was seated. A sieve .. was put on the head, and in it .. in the form of a cross, a comb and a pair of scissors, and over them a 3-girdit-cog .. Into this cog water was poured. Melted lead was slowly dropped .. into the water. Search was then made among the pieces .. for one resembling .. a heart. If a piece of such a shape was found, it was .. sewed into a piece of cloth and given to the sufferer .. to carry constantly. **1909** J. GUNN *Orkney Book* 239. Another old man remembers having his side hurt as a boy, and going to a 'wise woman' to be cured. She told him he had been 'forespoken'—that is, bewitched .. She then put a hoop covered with a sheep's skin on his head, a basin of water on that, and poured melted lead through the head of a key into the water, giving the patient a piece of the lead in the form of a heart as a charm. The cure wrought by this modern Norma was not, however, effectual. **1932** J. M. E. SAXBY *Shetland Lore* 175–6. A good wise-woman could counteract suffering by 'rinnin' da hert'. The invalid was set in a tub near the fire. A 'blinnd sivv' (a sifter without holes in it) was set on his head and a bowl of water set in the sivv. Some lead was melted. Then two keys were held in the form of a cross, and the molten lead was poured through the 'bools' (finger-holes in key-handles) .. while .. the sick person was murmuring .. 'May Gude show His face And gie me His grace.' Then all the bits of lead were examined, and the bit most like a heart was tied up in a red rag and worn over the heart of the patient 'for three moons'. The water into which the lead had been run was taken in small doses.

LEAD shapes in water: divination of future spouse

1839 *Everlasting Fortune-Teller* 11 [Co.

Durham] On Midsummer eve, take a small lump of lead .. put it in your left stocking on going to bed, and place it under your pillow, the next day .. take a pail of water, and .. pour in your .. lead boiling hot; as soon as it is cold .. take it out, and you will find .. emblems of his trade; if a ship, he is a sailor, [if] a book, a parson .. and so on. **1893** *Folklore* 361–2 [Co. Leix] When we were children Hallow Eve was always an occasion for practising mysterious rites .. to foretell the future. The first .. was to get an old spoon, filled with lead in scraps; this was held over a hot fire till it melted [and] poured through the wards of the [hall-door] key, held over a tub of cold water .. The lead cooled .. and when it had all settled in the bottom of the tub, the old nurse proceeded to read its surface. **1909** M. TREVELYAN *Folk-Lore of Wales* 30. If a spinster on Christmas Eve pours melted lead into cold water, it will turn into the shape of the tools her future husband will use. A doctor will be represented by a lancet, and so on.

Cf. EGGS (whites of): shapes in water: divination.

LEATHER, burning

late **18th c.** J. RAMSAY (*Scotland in the Eighteenth Century*, 438–9) [St Kilda] On the evening before New Year's Day it is usual for the cowherd and the young people to meet together .. Each burns in the fire a little of the bit of hide which is tied to the end of the staff. It is applied to the nose of every person and domestic animal that belongs to the house. This, they imagine, will tend much to secure them from diseases and other misfortunes during the ensuing year. **1878** A. MACGREGOR *Brahan Seer* 137 'Superstitions of Highlanders'. On New Year's Eve .. they provide themselves with the flap .. of the hide on the cow's neck .. singed in the fire and presented to the .. family, one after another, to smell, as a charm against all injuries from fairies and spirits, [saying] 'Great good luck to the house, Good luck to the farm, Good luck to every rafter of it, And to every worldly thing in it.'

Cf. SHOES, old: burning; WASSAILING.

LEATHER in house

1923 T. G. CRIPPEN *Christmas Lore* 168. [At Christmas] to bring into the house anything made of leather was very unlucky.

Cf. SHOES, new: at Christmas.

LEAVES in house

1955 Man, 61 [Halifax, Yorks.] If leaves blow into the house it is a sign of good luck.

LEAVES, nine: divination

1866 HENDERSON *Northern Counties* 78–9. The leaves of the she-holly [smooth edged] are alone deemed proper for divination. These .. must be plucked, late on a Friday .. in a three-cornered handkerchief .. nine of them must be selected, tied with nine knots into the handkerchief, and placed beneath the pillow. Dreams [of future partner] will attend this rite. **1941** F. THOMPSON *Over to Candleford* XXIII. An ash leaf with nine leaflets had to be searched for, and, when found, placed in the seeker's bosom with the incantation: 'Here's an ash leaf with nine leaves on. Take it and press it to your heart And the first chap you meet'll be your sweetheart. If he's married let him pass by. If he's single, let him draw nigh.'

LEAVES: spell and divination

1507 *Gospelles of Dystaues* pt. 4 XXIII. Yf ony woman wyll that her husbande, or her paramoure loue her well, she ought to put in his shoo a lefe of brekens that had ben gadred on saynt Johans euen whyles that they rynge none, so that it be in the lefte shoo, and without faute he shall loue her meruaylously. **1884** JEFFERIES *Life of the Fields* 158. Here is a country recipe for discovering whether a lover is faithful or not. Take a laurel leaf, scratch his name on it, or the initials, and put it in the bosom of the dress. If it turns brown, he is true; if not, he'll deceive you. **1952** Girl, 12 [Swansea, Glam.] They scratch their boy's initials on a leaf, put it in their shoe, and wear it all day long, leaving the leaf in the shoe overnight. If, in the morning, the initials are plainer than they were, it is a sign that he will marry them; if they are fainter, he will not.

1974 M. BAKER *Customs of Love and Marriage* 7. Mr Cecil Atkins of Waddesdon [Bucks.], told the writer in 1968 that there, sixty years ago, boys pricked their sweethearts' initials upon laurel leaves which they put under their caps. If the letters turned red the suit would progress well.

LEAVES/PETALS, catching

1878 *Folk-Lore Record* 9 [Fittleworth, Sussex] If you catch a falling leaf, you will have twelve months of continued happiness. **1938** MACNEICE 'Autumn Journal' XIV. The plane-tree leaves come sidling down (Catch my guineas, catch my guineas). **1941** F. THOMPSON *Over to Candleford* XXII. The apple blossom was nearly over .. and they all tried to catch a petal or two because one of the cousins said that for every petal they caught they would have a happy month. **1948** [Romiley, Cheshire] If you can catch a leaf falling from a tree before it touches the ground, on Hallowe'en, you can have a wish. **1950** W. J. C. MURRAY *Copsford* 179. As a small boy I had whimsically been taught that there was magic in a falling leaf if you caught it before it touched the ground. **1953** Boy, 14 [Bucknell, Radnor.] For every leaf you catch you will have a lucky day. If you catch 365 leaves you will have a lucky year. **1957** UTTLEY *Year in the Country* XII. We try to catch a dancing leaf, for every leaf caught is a 'happy day', but how elusive they are, these fluttering alive things, which slip through the fingers and evade pursuit! **1968** *Sunday Express* 13 Oct. 4. It's an old saying that if you can catch a falling leaf in October you are sure of a lucky year to come. I have tried it and can assure you that it's not an easy task. **1986** Woman, c.60 [Northampton] If you catch twelve falling leaves during the autumn, you'll have a happy year.

LEFT FOOT unlucky

c. AD 65 PETRONIUS *Satyricon* XXX (tr. Mitchell) A slave, told off for this special duty, cried out: 'Right foot first, gentlemen' .. we all hesitated .. fearing lest one of us should cross the threshold with the wrong foot. *c.* AD 390 ST JOHN CHRYSOSTOM *Homilies on Ephesians* XII

(1879, 242) 'I myself in coming out set forth with the left foot foremost:' and this .. is a token of misfortune. **1652** GAULE *Mag-astro-mances* 181. To bode good or bad luck .. from lifting the left leg over the threshold, at first going out of doors. **1866** HENDERSON *Northern Counties* 86. If you enter another man's house, with your 'skir' [left] foot foremost, you draw down evil on its inhabitants. **1900** S. HEWETT *Nummits* 57 [Devon] It is unlucky .. to put the left foot first in starting to walk. **1962** *Scotsman* 9 May 11. The bride must step out of her front door putting her right foot first. **1967** M. WOODRUFF *Woody* 110. Some of my show-business friends always make sure that they make their entrance on the stage right foot first.

LEFT HAND unlucky

*c.*1650 DR WREN Note in Browne's *Vulgar Errors* IV v (1852, I 393) Wise men count them unlucky that use the left hand, as going contrary to the generall course of nature. **1866** HENDERSON *Northern Counties* 86 [Borders] Skir or kir-handed people, i.e. left-handed ones, are not safe for a traveller to meet on a Tuesday .. On other days it is fortunate. **1932** C. IGGLESDEN *Those Superstitions* 179. 'Are you left-handed?' hurriedly asked the ghillie .. 'Then don't hold the rod in your left hand, sir! If you do there'll be no luck today!' I had thought that the superstition was confined to the boatmen of the Kentish coast, but here I found it—in far off Perth.

Cf. BABY'S HAND: first one used.

LEFT HAND OF PRIEST unlucky

1630 DEKKER *Honest Whore* pt. 2 Fᵛ. I am the most wretched fellow: sure some left-handed Priest christned me, I am so vnlucky: I am neuer out of one puddle or another. **1852** *N & Q* 1st ser. VI 601 [Devon] The desire to have the bishop's right hand—at confirmation the right hand being thought lucky, the left unlucky. **1866** HENDERSON *Northern Counties* 20. Unfortunate recipients of the left hand are doomed .. to a life of single blessedness. **1873** HARLAND & WILKINSON *Lancashire Legends* 229–30. Those upon whom the bishop lays his right hand consider themselves most

fortunate, since they are .. insured of a prosperous career. **1883** BURNE *Shropshire* 269. A servant-girl from a village in Corve Dale received a special message from her mother before her confirmation, desiring her to be sure so to place herself as to avoid the touch of the left hand. **1895** S. O. ADDY *Household Tales* 95. When you are confirmed it is lucky to have the bishop's right hand on your head. **1959** OPIE *Lore and Language of Schoolchildren* 209. One wonders how many bishops are aware of the jockeying for places which goes on beforehand among the candidates for confirmation when word gets about that to be confirmed with the bishop's right hand is lucky, but to be confirmed with his left hand is bad luck.

LEMON PEEL: divination

*c.*1760 *Mother Bunch's Closet* 20. She who desires to be satisfied, whether she shall enjoy the man desired or no; Let her take two lemon peels in the morning, and wear them all day under her arm pits; then at night let her rub the four posts of the bed with them: which done, in your sleep he will seem to come and present you with a couple of lemons; but if not there is no hope.

LENT, marrying in

1850 *N & Q* 1st ser. II 259. If you marry in Lent, You will live to repent. **1876** MRS G. L. BANKS *Manchester Man* XVIII. The double fees of Lent, and the ill-luck supposed to follow a couple united during the penitential forty days. **1929** *Daily Mail* 6 Mar. 11. A London registrar told a *Daily Mail* reporter yesterday: 'The fixed idea that marriage should not take place in Lent seems to have disappeared.' **1953** Girl, 14 [Beguildy, Radnor.] If you marry in Lent it is bad luck.

Cf. MAY, marrying in.

LETTER, dropping

1732 DEFOE *Memoirs of Mr Campbell* 62. I have seen People, who, after writing a Letter, have prognosticated .. the ill Success of it, if, by any Accident, it happened to fall on the Ground. **1923** [Wellington, Som.] If you drop a letter, ill success will attend you.

LETTUCE detrimental to child-bearing

1578 DODOENS *Herball* 573–4. Letuce seede being often vsed to be eaten a long space, drieth vp the natural seede, and putteth away the desire to Lecherie .. The seede of the wilde Letuce also, abateth the force of Uenus. 1853 *N & Q* 1st ser. VII 152 [Richmond, Surrey] O'er much lettuce in the garden will stop a young wife's bearing. 1884 R. FOLKARD *Plant Lore* 157. Accordingly as plants .. exhibited peculiarities in their actions, so were they supposed to operate on man. Thus, sterile plants, such as Lettuce .. were believed to conduce to the procuring of sterility in men.

LIONESS etc. breeding

1872 GUBERNATUS *Zoological Mythology* II 158 n. The women of antiquity, when they met a lioness, considered it as an omen of sterility. 1879 HENDERSON *Northern Counties* 23–4 [East Grinstead, Sussex] A favourite sow had just brought into the world a litter of stillborn pigs and the man added it was only what he had looked for .. 'You see this be the year the lions breed. They breeds every seven years, and when the lions breed the young pigs be still-born.' 1884 *N & Q* 6th ser. IX 266–7 [Mexborough, Yorks.] Several women attended by a local midwife having died in child-bed, a neighbour of this woman assured me that she was not to blame .. because this was 'the Lion-year' .. that every seven years 'the lioness' had a litter .. and that if anything went wrong with either mother or cubs .. many lying-in women died during the year. Ibid. 337. In Cheshire .. in 1878 my son lost a litter of pigs, and several of my neighbours were equally unfortunate. The misfortune was gravely attributed by my farm man to the supposition that 'bears must be breeding this year'. He further explained .. that bears only breed every seventh year, and that their breeding affects prejudicially the breeding of domestic animals. 1895 ELWORTHY *Evil Eye* 76. The old women in Wellington Workhouse say: 'If a lioness dies in whelping, the year .. is a bad one for women to be confined in.' 1951 *Folklore* 327 [Spey valley, Inverness.] A midwife asserts as 'a very old saying handed down', that every seven years a peculiar year occurs, called an 'Elephant' Year. Any child born in this year is abnormal; and she instances two people in the district now about 35 years old, as proof of this. 1985 *Folklore* 283. In the village of Syresham [Northants.] a woman speaking of the death of a neighbour in childbirth, lately said, 'A lioness must have died this year.'

LIONS in Tower

1716 ADDISON *Free-Holder* 1 June. Our first visit was to the Lions. My Friend [the Tory fox-hunter] enquired very much after their Health, and whether none of them had fallen sick upon .. the Flight of the Pretender? .. He had learned from his Cradle, that the Lions in the Tower were the best Judges of the Title of our British Kings, and always sympathized with our Sovereigns. 1720 STRYPE *Stow's Survey of London* I 119. Here be [in the Tower] the Skins of Two dead Lions stuffed. One died two Days before K. Charles the Second. 1758 LORD CHESTERFIELD *Letters to his Son* 21 Nov. The King has been ill. It was generally thought that he would have died .. for the oldest lion in the Tower, much about the King's age, died a fortnight ago. This extravagancy .. was believed by many above *peuple*. So wild and capricious is the human mind!

LIZARD cures

AD 77 PLINY *Natural History* XXX xxx (1856, V 456) A green lizard, enclosed alive in a vessel .. and worn as an amulet; a method, it is said, by which recurrent fevers are often dispelled. 1873 *N & Q* 4th ser. XII 468–9 [Ireland] The person .. takes the lizard .. in his hand, licks the creature all over—head, feet, belly, legs, sides, tail; and the tongue of the person .. is said to possess the power, ever afterwards, of taking the sting and pain out of a burn.

Cf. FROG'S EYES; TOAD OR FROG cures.

LIZARD, meeting

1922 [Somerset] If you see a lizard running across the road you will have bad luck.

LOOKING BACK

*c.*1500 BC Genesis 19: 15–26. When the morning arose, then the angels hastened Lot, saying, Arise, take thy wife, and thy two daughters .. lest thou be consumed in the iniquity of the city .. And it came to pass, when they had brought them forth abroad, that [the Lord] said, Escape for thy life; look not behind thee, neither stay thou in all the plain .. lest thou be consumed .. But his wife looked back from behind him, and she became a pillar of salt. *c.*30 BC VIRGIL *Georgic* IV ll. 490–8 (tr. Way) He stopped: upon daylight's verge was Eurydice, almost his own! Forgetting, and heart-overmastered he looked back .. 'O Orpheus .. Farewell now! Compassed with limitless night am I swept away .. thine never more for aye!' *c.* AD 90 Luke 9: 62. And Jesus said unto him, No man, having put his hand to the plough, and looking back, is fit for the kingdom of God. 1818 *Edinburgh Magazine* Nov. 412 [Angus] [The bride] must not look behind her on the journey [to the church]. 1982 *Woman, c.*50 [Stockton-on-Tees, Co. Durham] The bridegroom must not see the bride before they are at the altar; and then he must not look back over his shoulder to see her coming up the aisle.

Cf. TURNING BACK.

LUCK, wishing

1883 *N & Q* 6th ser. VII 8. Some relations of mine were 'speeding the parting guest' the other day in the person of a sailor friend who was starting for Australia. One of them naturally proposed a bumper to a successful voyage. 'Stop, for Heaven's sake!' cried the sailor. 'Don't you know that is sure to bring ill luck?' 1909 *N & Q* 10th ser. XII 483 [Stromness, Orkney] Fishermen count it unlucky for any one to wish them good luck as they are putting out. 1922 LYND *Solomon* 156. To wish a man luck when on his way to a race-meeting is considered unlucky. Instead of saying 'Good luck!' you should say something insulting, such as, 'May you break your leg!' 1930 P. F. ANSON *East Coast of Scotland* 42. The Portessie fisherman would go so far as to beat anyone who

should wish him good luck (a sure sign that he will not catch fish!), and to draw blood so as to turn the ill luck. 1932 C. J. S. THOMPSON *Hand of Destiny* 282. Regarded as unlucky .. should anyone wish an actor .. 'good luck' on the first night or before a performance. 1970 Racing-driver, 34 [Sudbury, Suffolk] You must never say 'Good Luck' before a race. Say 'Break a leg' instead. 1986 Actress, 25, going for audition. Don't say that [good luck]! Say 'Break a leg', or 'Snap a wrist!'

LUCK-PENNY

1805 *Edinburgh Evening Courant* 28 Oct. 3. In the afternoon the drover received his payment from the butcher's wife, and not only went away content, but returned a shilling as luck-penny. 1808 JAMIESON *Scottish Dict. Luck-penny* .. from the superstitious idea of its ensuring good luck to the purchaser. It is now principally retained in selling horses and cattle. 1824 MACTAGGART *Gallovidian Encyclopedia. Luckpenny.* The cash which the seller gives back to the buyer after the latter has paid him; it is given back with the hope that it may prove a lucky bargain. 1876 F. K. ROBINSON *Whitby Glossary. Luck penny.* Thus what is given back to the buyer of a pig is termed 'penny-pig-luck'. 1877 *N & Q* 5th ser. VII 488. In all agricultural dealings connected with cattle or corn it is customary when receiving payments to return a small sum to the customer, which is termed 'luck money'. 1903 *N & Q* 9th ser. XI 127. A few years ago I sold a .. carriage .. to a young innkeeper in East Lancashire .. In handing me the money he asked me 'for something back "for luck"' .. When he received my florin he .. ceremoniously covered it with saliva before putting it in his pocket. 1917 J. C. BRIDGE *Cheshire Proverbs* 144. When a butcher pays for the cow he has bought, he expects a 'luck-penny' to be returned to him which .. is usually a shilling and is technically called 'tipping the cow's horn with silver'. 1962 *Daily Express* 15 May 4 [Welshpool, Montgomery.] He slipped a coin to the farmer who bought the sheep from him, in accordance with local custom which decrees it is bad luck not to do so. 1964

Daily Telegraph 8 June 19 [Appleby, Westmorland] Always there was an odd half-sovereign on the purchase price and .. the vendor handed this back to his client—just for luck. 1972 *Lore and Language* July 7 [Coalisland, Co. Tyrone] When selling animals the bargain is not finally sealed until both parties spit on their palms and shake hands and the buyer gives the seller back a 'luck-penny'.

Cf. HANDSEL; LAST PAYMENT to doctor/midwife.

LUCKY-BONE: T-shaped bone from sheep's head

1851 STERNBERG *Northamptonshire* 154. The lucky-bone .. is worn .. to produce good luck; and is .. an excellent protection against witchcraft. It is a bone taken from the head of a sheep, and its form, which is that of the T cross, may have, perhaps, originated the peculiar sanctity in which it is held. This form of the sacred symbol is frequently found on Druidical monuments. 1858 DENHAM *North of England* (1895, 58) Now seldom seen .. at least in the North .. this bone, which was worn as an amulet round the neck to ensure good luck, and protect the wearer from .. 'uncanny folk', was taken from the head of a Sheep. Its form was that of a T [tau] or cross. 1866 *N & Q* 3rd ser. IX 146. In some parts of Cornwall the little bone in a pig's skull is considered to possess peculiar virtues, and is carried about the person as a charm. 1869 J. P. MORRIS *Furness* [Lancs.] *Lucky-bone*. Children wear [it] in their clogs, or shoes, under the impression that it will bring them luck. 1894 R. O. HESLOP *Northumberland Words* II. *Lucky-byen*. A small bone found in a sheep's head, which people put in their pocket under the impression that good luck will attend them while they carry it. 1923 P. S. JEFFREY *Whitby Lore* 141. Many of the fishermen carry a 'lucky bone' called the Hammer of Thor, which can be found in a sheep's head, indeed there are two to each head. These small bones, roughly hammer shaped, are about an inch-and-a-half long, and can be carried in the waistcoat pocket. The writer has carried one with good results for some time.

M

MAGPIE bird of ill omen

1507 *Gospelles of Dystaues* pt. 2 VII. I assure you .. y[t] whan pyes chatter vpon a house it is synge of ryghte euyll tydynges. **1652** GAULE *Mag-astro-mances* 181. [among vain observations] The Pyes chattering about the House. **1725** BOURNE *Antiquitates Vulgares* 71. An omen of the Approach of some terrible Thing .. is the Chattering of a Mag-pye. **1763** J. COLLIER *Lancashire Dialect* 28. T: I saigh two rott'n Pynot .. os eh coom. M: Did ever! that wur o sign o bad Fartin [fortune]: Far I heard my Gronny sey, hoode os leef [she'd rather] o seen two owd Harries [devils] os two Pynots. **1818** *Edinburgh Mag.* Nov. 412. A magpie on flight crossing the way from right to left, or as some say, contrary to the sun, is the harbinger of bad luck, but if vice versa is reckoned harmless. **1824** CARR *Craven* pt. 1 8 [Yorks.] I thoute, forsure, when I gat up, that chatterin nanpie, peark'd i' th' ran-tree, betided naa good. **1825** JAMIESON *Scottish Dict.* Suppl. *Pyat.* It is when two magpies are picking on the top of a thatched roof, that death is to be dreaded, especially if one of its inmates be ailing or bed-rid at the time. **1838** A. E. BRAY *Devonshire* II 292. Our terror of meeting a single magpie crossing our path is very great. Sad must be the fortune of any person who has this mishap—sad .. then must be mine; for .. last .. year, never once did we ride .. along the Plymouth road .. without meeting a solitary magpie strutting or flying most ominously across the road. **1866** HENDERSON *Northern Counties* 95. A .. servant thus accounted for the unluckiness of the magpie .. It was, the girl said, the only bird which did not go into the Ark with Noah; it liked better to sit outside, jabbering over the drowned world. Ibid. When a boy .. driving an old lady in a pony-carriage .. the reins were suddenly snatched from my hand, and the pony brought to a stand .. I looked to my companion for some explanation .. and saw her gazing

.. on a magpie then crossing the road. After a pause .. she exclaimed .. 'Oh, the nasty bird! Turn back, turn back!' **1874** HARDY *Madding Crowd* VIII. What a night of horrors! .. I've seed a magpie all alone.

MAGPIE, chattering = stranger

1159 JOHN OF SALISBURY *Policraticus* (*Frivolities of Courtiers*, ed. J. B. Pike, 48) The chattering pie warns you to be cautious .. especially in the reception of strangers. **1303** MANNYNG *Handlyng Synne* (EETS 119 ll. 355–60) Beleue nou3t yn þe pyys cheteryng; Hyt ys no trouþe, but fals beleuyng. Many beleuyn yn þe pye: whan she comyþ lowe or hye Cheteryng, and haþ no reste, þan sey þey we shul haue geste. **1584** SCOT *Discoverie of Witchcraft* IX III. To prognosticate that ghests approach to your house, upon the chattering of pies .. is altogether vanitie and superstition. **1650** N. HOMES *Daemonologie* 59. By the chattering of Magpies, they know they shall have strangers. **1777** BRAND *Antiquities* 93. When the Pye chatters, we shall have Strangers. **1825** JAMIESON *Scottish Dict.* Suppl. *Pyat.* In Angus, if magpies be heard chattering from a tree, it is considered as a certain presage of the arrival of strangers at the adjoining house.

MAGPIE: divination rhyme

*c.*1780 T. PARK MS note in Brand's *Antiquities* 88. In Lincolnshire, Magpyes are held either good or bad omens according to the number seen .. 'One for sorrow, Two for mirth, Three for a wedding, And four for death.' But the prognostic of sorrow is thought to be averted by turning thrice round. **1825** JAMIESON *Scottish Dict.* Suppl. *Pyat.* In Roxburgh the following popular rhyme is repeated concerning the character of the omen; 'Ane's joy, Twa's grief; Three's a waddin', Four's death.' **1846** DENHAM *Proverbs* 35. According to the number of magpies you see at one and the same time when going on a journey, &., you may calculate your luck as follows:— 'One for sorrow, Two for luck (varia. mirth); Three for a wedding, Four for death (varia. birth); Five for silver, Six for gold; Seven for a secret, Not to be told; Eight for heaven, Nine for ——, And ten for the d---l's own sell!' 1849 J. O. HALLIWELL *Popular Rhymes* 168. In Lancashire they say: 'One for anger, Two for mirth, Three for a wedding, Four for a birth, Five for rich, Six for poor, Seven for a witch, I can tell you no more.' 1873 HARLAND & WILKINSON *Lancashire Legends* 219 [as 1849, but ending] 'Seven for a bitch; eight for a whore; Nine for a burying; ten for a dance; Eleven for England; twelve for France.' 1942 A. L. ROWSE *Cornish Childhood* 44. If [Uncle] saw a magpie he would say: 'Damn that bird! No luck today.' If .. two .. 'One for sorrow, two for mirth; Three for a wedding, four for a birth.' 1966 *Yorkshire Post* 6 June 10. Our version .. is 'One for sorrow, two for joy, Three for a letter, four for a boy, Five for silver, six for gold, Seven for a secret never to be told, Eight for a wish, nine for a kiss, Ten for a marriage never to be old.'

MAGPIE, harming

1932 C. IGGLESDEN *Those Superstitions* 54. Words cut on the barn of an old Tudor farmyard at Beaver, near Ashford [Kent]: 'He who takes a magpie's life Will rue the day he took a wife.'

MAGPIE, meeting: and actions to avert evil

1832 *Gents Mag.* pt. 1 593 [Scopwick, Lincs.] A single Magpie crossing your path is esteemed an evil omen, and I once saw a person actually tremble and dissolve into a copious perspiration, when one of these birds flitted chattering before him. But the evil influence may be averted by laying two straws across, or by describing the figure of a cross on the ground. 1850 N & Q 1st ser. II 512 [Devon] It is proper to make a low bow whenever a single magpie is seen. 1850 DENHAM *North of England* (1895, 20) The good folks in Westmoreland make use of the following charm to avert the

ill omen: 'Magpie, magpie, chatter and flee, Turn up thy tail and good luck fall me.' 1854 N & Q 1st ser. X 224. Can you tell me the origin of the superstition that taking off the hat, or kissing the hand to a magpie, will avert ill luck? 1872 *Bye-Gones* 18 Sept. 86 [Llansantffraid, Montgomery.] When a magpie crosses a road in advance it is customary for the person seeing the evil omen to make the form of a cross on the road .. spit on the cross, and say .. 'Satan, I defy thee!' 1888 S. O. ADDY *Sheffield Glossary* xviii. When a magpie crosses a man's path he will say: 'I crossed the pynot, and the pynot crossed me, The devil take the pynot, and God save me.' 1891 J. C. ATKINSON *Moorland Parish* 71 [Danby, Yorks.] A magpie flew across the line of our path. My friend, a solicitor in a large practice .. took off his hat with the greatest ceremony, and so saluted the bird in its passage. On my remarking on the circumstances, 'Oh,' said he, 'I always take off my hat to a magpie.' 1897 E. PHILLPOTTS *Lying Prophets* 59 [Dartmoor] I seed a maggotty-pie comin' along this marnin' .. Wan's .. a sign o' sorrer, but if you spits twice awver your left shoulder it doan't matter so much. 1899 *Newcastle Weekly Chronicle* 11 Feb. 7 [Jesmond] I cross the magpie, The magpie crosses me; Bad luck to the magpie, And good luck to me. 1969 M. HARRIS *A Kind of Magic* 125 [Ducklington, Oxon.] Speaking and bowing to magpies was quite a common thing and to this day I still nod my head and politely say 'Good morning, Sir,' when I catch sight of one. 1980 Primary schoolchildren [Dedham, Essex] If you see a magpie you don't need to worry, you just have to bow to him and say three times, 'Good day, your Lordship,' and you're OK. 1984 Woman, 26 [Wotton-under-Edge, Glos.] We say 'Good morning Mr Magpie' in the mornings—you only say it before mid-day.

MAIL VAN

1952 Schoolgirl, 11 [Swansea, Glam.] It is unlucky to see the back of a Royal Mail Van. 1952 Schoolgirl, 14 [Aberdeen] If a person touches the crown on the side of a royal mail van then she can have a wish. The second to touch it gets a kiss, and the third a disappointment. After you have wished you must run and touch something made of wood. **1954** Schoolboy, 13 [Liverpool, Lancs.] To see a mail van is lucky. **1974** *Mirror* 31 Oct. 20 [Brandon, Suffolk] A saying we had as youngsters after seeing a Royal Mail van was: 'Royal Mail, touch the ground, the first boy you speak to you love.' We would then spend ages avoiding boys we did not like!

MANDRAKE aids conception

10th c. BC Genesis 30: 14–16 [Jacob's wives were rivals; both wished to conceive, but Rachel was barren and Leah was past bearing.] Reuben .. found mandrakes in the field, and brought them unto his mother Leah. Then Rachel said to Leah, Give me, I pray thee, of thy son's mandrakes. And she said unto her, Is it a small matter that thou hast taken my husband? and wouldest thou take away my son's mandrakes also? And Rachel said, Therefore he shall lie with thee to night for thy son's mandrakes. [Both women conceived and bore sons.] **1542** BOORDE *Dyetary* XX (1870, 281) Mandragore doth helpe a woman to concepcion. **1597** GERARD *Herball* 281–2. The idle drones .. haue bestowed some of their time in caruing the rootes of Brionie, forming them into the shape of men & women; which falsifying practice hath confirmed the errour amongst the simple .. people, who haue taken them vpon their report to be true Mandrakes .. Great and strange effects are supposed to be in Mandrakes, to cause women to be fruitfull. **1633** DONNE *Poems* 'Song'. Goe, and catche a falling starre, Get with child a mandrake roote. **1646** BROWNE *Vulgar Errors* II vi. Many Mola's and false conceptions there are of Mandrakes .. The first .. a farre derived similitude, it holds with man; that is, in a byfurcation .. of the roote into two parts, which some are content to call thighes .. Many there are, in severall parts of Europe .. who .. sell rootes unto ignorant people .. to deceive unfruitfull women. **1936** E. H. RUDKIN *Lincolnshire* 28–9 [Willoughby] Black Briony [mandrake] and White Briony [womandrake]

.. 'Now, it's the root of these 'erbs as is useful—gurt big long 'uns they is, too! Take an' dry it .. When it's reeght dry, grate it up an' keep it in a tin .. You give Womandrake to a horse or man, and Mandrake to a mare.'

MANDRAKE, other powers of

*c.***1050** MS Cotton Vitell. C. iii (COCKAYNE *Leechdoms* I 249) If any see some heavy mischief in his home, let him take this wort mandragoras, into the middle of the house .. he compelleth all evils out of the house. **1507** *Gospelles of Dystaues* pt. 2 II. Who may fynde a true mandrake and ly hym bytwene a payre of whyte shetes & presente hym mete and drynke twyes a daye, notwithstandynge then he neyther eteth not drynketh, he that dothe it shal become ryche within shorte space. **1607** TOPSELL *Foure-footed Beastes* 424. In broken bones of a Horse .. what through the horses brutish vnrulinesse .. it is almost held incurable .. I haue not found for the purpose any thing so soueraine or absolut good, as oyle of Mandrag, which .. bindeth together any thing especially bones being either shiuered, or broken. **1623** WEBSTER *Duchess of Malfi* IV ii. Come violent death, Serue for Mandragora to make me sleepe. **1899** *Newcastle Weekly Chronicle* 11 Feb. 7 [Jesmond] The root of a white briony, falsely called 'mandrake', is held to be a specific for nearly all human ailments. **1925** E. LOVETT *Magic in London* 74. I have seen it cut up and sold in penny slices .. The vendor said: 'It cures everything.' **1966** BBC RADIO *Have a Go* [Wilfred Pickles interviewing a man who kept a herbalist's shop in the Old Kent Road, London] 'Do you sell anything to stop people smoking?' 'Well, we have Anti-smoking tablets, and one or two kinds of root that people chew, Mandrake, for instance.' 'Mandrake!' [said W.P. somewhat alarmed, and left it at that].

MANDRAKE, uprooting

1597 SHAKESPEARE *Romeo and Juliet* IV iii. Shrikes like Mandrakes torne out of the earth, That living mortalls hearing them, run mad. **1597** GERARD *Herball*

280–1. There have been many ridiculous tales brought vp of this plant, whether of olde wiues or some runnagate surgeons or phisickmongers, I know not. They adde further, that it is neuer or verie seldome to be founde growing naturally but vnder a gallows, where the matter that hath fallen from the dead bodie, hath giuen it the shape of a man .. They fable further and affirm, that he who woulde take vp a plant thereof must tie a dogge thereunto to pull it vp; otherwise if a man should do it, he should certainly die in short space after. 1646 BROWNE Vulgar Errors II VI. The roots of Mandrakes doe make a noyse or give a shreeke vpon eradication .. there followes an hazard of life to them that pull it up, that some evil fate pursues them, and they live not very long after. 1676 MARVELL General Councils (1875, IV 101) If they have a mind to pull up that mandrake, it were advisable .. to chuse out a dog for that imployment. 1791 E. DARWIN Loves of Plants 90 n. The Mandrake was said to utter a scream, when its root was drawn from the ground; and that the animal which drew it up, became diseased and soon died: on which account, when it was wanted for purpose of medicine, it was usual to loosen .. the earth about the root, and then to tie it .. to a dog's tail; who was whipped to pull it up, and was then supposed to suffer for the impiety of the action. 1910 HASTINGS Dict. of Bible. Mandrake .. It is a common plant in all parts of S. Palestine. Its long and branched root is very deeply imbedded in the earth, and an old superstition survives to-day that he who digs it up will be childless—but at the same time the effort of pulling it up will cure a bad lumbago. 1985 R. VICKERY Unlucky Plants 42–3. There used to be this chemist .. in Aberystwyth [Cardigan.] who had a mandrake plant in his garden. When he died, about ten years ago, he bequeathed it to the College Botanic Garden .. Quite a party of people gathered to remove the plant .. but they hesitated before digging it up, because it was supposed to be unlucky .. The College gardener said he didn't worry, so he dug it up, and is still alive and happy.

MARRIAGE: 'change the name'

1853 N & Q 1st ser. VIII 150. Is the following distich known in any part of England? 'To change the name but not the letter, Is to marry for worse, and not for better.' I met with it in an American book, but it was probably an importation. 1866 R. CHAMBERS Book of Days I 723. A common saying in East Anglia .. is 'To change the name, and not the letter, Is a change for the worst, and not for the better.' 1866 HENDERSON Northern Counties 26. It is unlucky for a woman to marry a man whose surname begins with the same letter as her own. c.1914 Woman, 20 [Bath, Som.] 'Change the name and not the letter, Change for worse and not for better,' as when a Miss Smith marries a Mr Stone. 1950 Woman, c.50 [Forfar, Angus] A change of name and not of letter Is a change for the worse and not the better.

MARRIAGE: dominant partner

1898 BLAKEBOROUGH Yorkshire Customs 103. Great care must be observed that the husband steps over the threshold in front of his bride, otherwise she will take the lead in all things through life. 1911 J. C. DAVIES Welsh Folk-Lore 36. When the bride .. reaches home after the wedding ceremony, she buys some small trifle, a pin or anything from her bridesmaid; and by .. buying something before her husband has a chance, she'll be master over him for life! Sometimes the newly-wedded couple resorted to a Wishing Well, and the first to drink .. became the master in their wedded life. 1923 [Martock, Som.] When a newly married couple first enter their new home, the one who gets left foot over the doorstep first will be boss of the show. 1978 Sussex Express 30 June 4 [Yorks.] If the wife has to help in putting on the wedding ring she will surely rule the home.

MARRIAGE, early

1615 The Cold Yeare A4. Early Bridals, make early Burials. 1840 STRICKLAND Queens of England III 400. The queen led the little bridegroom, who was not five, and her brother .. led the baby bride, scarcely three years old. The innocent and ill-fated infants, then married, verified the old English proverb, which says, 'Early wed, early dead.'

Cf. PRECOCIOUSNESS = early death.

MARRIAGE: younger before elder

10th c. BC Genesis 29: 26. It must not be so done in our country, to give the younger before the firstborn. *c.*1592 SHAKESPEARE *Taming of the Shrew* II i. She must have a husband, I must dance bare-foot on her wedding day. 1742 DELANY *Correspondence* (ed. Llanover, II 188) The eldest daughter was much disappointed that she should dance bare-foot, and desired her father to find out a match for her. 1787 GROSE *Provincial Glossary* Superstitions 62. If, in a family, the youngest daughter should be married before her elder sisters, they must all dance at her wedding without shoes: this will counteract their ill luck, and procure them husbands. 1863 R. CHAMBERS *Book of Days* I 723 [Suffolk] If a younger sister marries before the elder one, the elder must *dance in the hog's trough*. In the case to which I refer, a brother went through the ceremony also, and the dancers performed their part so well, that they danced both the ends off the trough, and the trough itself into two pieces. 1883 BURNE *Shropshire* 290–1. It is an old Shropshire custom, kept up in humble life, that if a younger sister should be married before the elders, the latter must dance at the wedding in their 'stocking-feet'. This was actually done at a wedding at Hodnet in 1881; and in the same year a maid-servant, who omitted to do so at a younger sister's wedding, was thus accosted by her aunt .. 'So I hear you didna dance barfut! I'm ashamed of you. If I'd 'a bin there I'd 'a made you do it' .. In the same year, a man in the Bridgnorth neighbourhood quite gravely observed, with reference to the marriage of the second son of the Squire of the place, that Mr M—— (the elder brother, still unmarried) would have to dance in a pig-trough on the wedding-day. 1899 J. SHAW *Schoolmaster* 32 [Tyron, Dumfries.] It is the correct thing to dance in stocking soles at the marriage of a sister or brother younger than yourself—the sister at the sister's, the brother at the brother's. 1932 WOMEN'S INSTITUTE

Worcestershire Book 35 [Hanbury] If a younger daughter in a family married before the eldest, the eldest was made to dance in a pig's trough on the wedding day.

MARRIAGE BANNS, hearing own

1856 *N & Q* 2nd ser. I 202 [Worcs.] She knew a young woman who would persist in going to church to hear her banns 'asked out', and whose six children were in consequence all deaf and dumb. 1873 HARLAND & WILKINSON *Lancashire Legends* 222. Should a young female attend church when her own banns are published, her children will be born deaf and dumb as a punishment for her want of decency. 1875 W. D. PARISH *Sussex Dialect. Church-cried.* Having the banns .. published in church. The tradition in Sussex is that if a person goes to church to hear himself cried, his children will be born deaf and dumb. 1898 BLAKE-BOROUGH *Yorkshire Customs* 95. The banns were published [and] the couple were said to be 'hanging in the bell-ropes'—no maiden would ever think of attending church during the time she was hanging in the bell-ropes. 1942 *Sussex County Mag.* 364. A curious tradition prevails in Sussex, that if a person goes to church to hear himself 'bawled' (his banns published) his children will be born deaf and dumb.

MARRIAGE BANNS: sequence broken

1795 *Stat. Acc. of Scotland* XV 258 [Monzie, Perth.] No person will be proclaimed for marriage in the end of one year .. and be married in the .. next. 1957 *Folklore* 503 [Clun Valley, Shrops.] Five years ago a relative had her banns called in a little village church [where] a visiting clergyman only came on alternate Sundays. On the intervening Sunday, the sexton-cum-verger insisted on calling the banns outside the church door .. as it was unlucky to break the sequence.

MARRIAGE SERVICE, baby cries during

1895 *N & Q* 8th ser. VII 145. To ensure domestic happiness it is necessary that a child's cry should be heard during the marriage ceremony; at least, they tell you so in Norfolk.

Cf. CHRISTENING, baby cries during.

MARRIAGE SERVICE in baptismal church

1900 *N & Q* 9th ser. V 54 [Derbys.] Women folks—especially those of country places .. used to consider their married life would be 'full of luck' if they were married at the church where they were baptized. My mother often spoke of this as being a common belief when she was a girl, and she was a "98' woman. With men it did not signify much, but women ought to be married, if possible, in the church in which they were baptized.

MARRIAGE SERVICE, reading

1861 *N & Q* 2nd ser. XII 490. The lady who reads the marriage service entirely through will never be married. 1923 [Taunton, Som.] Never read the wedding ceremony through at home, or you'll never get married.

MARRIAGES bring stormy weather

1885 *Folklore* 54 [Aberdeen.] It .is a common saying among the Rosehearty fisherfolks that marriages amongst them bring stormy weather. A very common season for marrying is immediately after the herring fishing is finished.

Cf. CHURCHING after marriage.

MARRIED COUPLE: first to die

1852 *N & Q* 1st ser. VI 312 [Hull, Yorks.] Whichever goes to sleep first on the marriage night, will be sure to die first; this is as true as scripture, at least they say so. 1866 HENDERSON *Northern Counties* 27. The first of the bridal pair to go to sleep on the wedding-night, will be the first to die. Ibid. 1879 ed., 42 [Barnoldby-le-Beck, Lincs.] They always say the one that kneels first at the marriage will die first. 1880 *N & Q* 6th ser. I 75. A few weeks ago .. in the south of Yorkshire .. when the bride was being decked for the ceremony her maid bid her remember not to speak too loud in church [because], 'Them 'at speaks loudest dies first.' 1883 BURNE *Shropshire* 294–5. It is said that if either the bride or bridegroom should let [the wedding ring] drop during the ceremony, he or she will be the first of the pair to die, I am told that 'Old Goff of

Westley' was very nervous, and dropped the ring, which rolled about merrily. He and his wife lived many years together, but he is gone, while she flourishes in Shrewsbury now. 1923 *Folklore* 236 [Connaught, Eire] It is unlucky .. for a newly married couple not to step over the chapel threshold together, otherwise the first to do it is soon dead. 1982 Woman, 20 [Yorks.] Whichever of the couple were the first to kneel down or rise from the altar, would be the first to die.

MARRIED COUPLE, touching

1866 HENDERSON *Northern Counties* 21. To rub shoulders with the bride or bridegroom is deemed an augury of speedy marriage. 1873 HARLAND & WILKINSON *Lancashire Legends* 222. Rubbing against a newly-married couple is said to be infectious. 1879 J. NAPIER *West of Scotland* 138. If, at a social gathering, a bachelor or maid were placed inadvertently betwixt a man and his wife, the person so seated would be married within a year. 1883 BURNE *Shropshire* 290. 'Mind you rub against the bride,' was the parting instruction of solicitous relatives to a young lady .. setting out to act as bridesmaid to a friend: the object being that she might catch the infection of matrimony. 1916 *N & Q* 12th ser. II 113 [Isle of Wight] At a wedding at Whippingham Church a few years ago, I saw the cottagers' children press forward as the bride passed down the churchyard, and heard them cry: 'I touched her. That's luck for me!' 1923 [Somerset] If a bachelor or a maid be accidentally placed between a married couple at supper they will be married before the year is up.

Cf. HAND, lucky.

MAY a dangerous month

1646 BROWNE *Vulgar Errors* IV XII. The like mistake there is in a tradition of our dayes; men conceiving a peculiar danger in the beginning dayes of May, which are set out as a fatall period unto consumption and Cronicall diseases. 1818 *Edinburgh Mag.* Nov. 410 [Angus] I have heard it said by the old women, that both fairies and witches have more influence, and take a greater delight in playing their pranks in the month of May, than at any other season. **1825** T. C. CROKER *Fairy Legends of S. Ireland* I 307. May-eve is considered a time of peculiar danger. The 'good people' are supposed then to possess the power and inclination to do all sorts of mischief .. The 'evil eye' is then also deemed to have more than its usual vigilance and malignity. **1846** DENHAM *Proverbs* 43. If he can climb over May-hill he'll do. **1887** F. T. HAVERGAL *Herefordshire Words* 49. March will search, April will try, May will tell if you'll live or die.

MAY, born in: baby

1853 *N & Q* 1st ser. VII 152. A May-baby's always sickly. You may try, but you'll never rear it. **1862** A. HISLOP *Proverbs of Scotland* 223. 'May birds are aye cheeping.' This refers to the popular superstition against marrying in .. May, the children of which marriages are said to 'die of decay'. **1895** S. O. ADDY *Household Tales* 116. Children born in the month of May require great care in bringing up, for 'May chickens come cheeping.' **1912** LEATHER *Herefordshire* 24. It is unlucky for a child to be born in May, and a frequent taunt is 'You're only a May cat.' **1923** [Bridgwater, Som.] Children born in May are very unlucky. **1957** *Folklore* 413. May-babies, like May kittens, are said to be weakly and unlikely to thrive. Whenever any misfortune befell my grandmother .. she never failed to remind us that she had been born in May. **1986** Woman, 57 [South Shields, Co. Durham] I used to be quite upset as a child when people said to me, when they heard that my birthday was in May, 'Oh, you're a May kitten—you should have been drowned!'

MAY, born in: cat

1851 *N & Q* 1st ser. III 20. In Wilts, and also in Devon, it is believed that cats born in the month of May will catch no mice nor rats, but will, contrary to the wont of all other cats, bring in snakes and slow-worms. Such cats are called 'May cats', and are held in contempt. Ibid. 516 [Lancs.] May cats are unlucky, and will suck the breath of children. **1853** *N & Q* 1st ser. VII 152

[Somerset] You should drown a May-kitten. It's unlucky to keep it. **1858** DENHAM *North of England* (1895, 55) Kittens born in May are, even still, proverbially spoken of .. as bad mousers. I only within the present year heard a female say that 'She wad nivver mair keep a May Kittling as lang as she lived, for they were just good for nought at all!' **1897** E. PHILLPOTTS *Lying Prophets* 209 [Dartmoor] Them chets had to go, missy. 'Tis a auld word, an'it ban't wise to take no count of sayings like that: 'May chets bad luck begets' .. Never let live no kittens born in May. They theer dead chets comed May Day. **1922** [Bridgwater, Som.] According to superstition cats born in the month of May will never make good mousers, and are unlucky to have about the house. **1957** R. M. LOCKLEY *Pembrokeshire* 42 [nr. Tenby] A 'maychate' he possessed .. brought many vipers from the hill into the house .. This apparently is a characteristic only of the maychate .. a cat born in the month of May. **1982** *Sunday Express* 9 May 4. It is unlucky to give or accept a kitten [in May].

MAY, born in: colt

1889 *Dorset Field Club* 26. Colts born in May have an awkward trick of lying down in water as you ride through.

MAY, born in: duckling

1889 *Dorset Field Club* 34. Ducks hatched in May are more liable to sprawl.

MAY, leaving off clothes in

1732 T. FULLER *Worthies of England* no. 6193. Leave not off a Clout, Till May be out. **1832** A. HENDERSON *Scottish Proverbs* 154. Cast ne'er a clout till May be out. **1852** *Englishwoman's Domestic Mag. Almanack* 13. We warn young persons during this month not to throw off their warm clothing too suddenly, as in this changeable climate we often have a day of sunshine followed by a day of rain and hail. Many are the deaths by consumption, the seeds of which have been sown by this pernicious practice. **1855** F. K. ROBINSON *Yorkshire Words* 41. Never think to cast a clout Until the month of May be out. **1886** F. T.

ELWORTHY *West Somerset* 467. If you would the doctor pay, Leave your flannels off in May. **1887** *Folk-Lore Record* 210 [Cornwall] It is unlucky to 'tuck' (short coat) children .. 'Tuck babies in May, You'll tuck them away.' **1923** [Wellington, Som.] Tuck a baby in May, You will tuck him away. **1962** Woman, 35 [Liss, Hants.] My mother says the rule is 'Tuck after three months', but if the baby is three months old during May, then wait until May is over. **1986** Woman, 64 [Blunham, Beds.] 'Ne'er cast a clout till May be out.' I've always kept to that, even if there's been a heatwave.

Cf. MAY, washing blankets in.

MAY, marrying in

c. AD 17 OVID *Fasti* V ll. 487–90 (tr. Riley, 198–9) That time, too, was not auspicious for the marriage torches of the widow or of the virgin. She who married then did not long remain a wife. For this reason, too, if proverbs have any weight with you, the common people say that 'bad prove the wives that are married in May.' **1675** *Poor Robin's Almanack* May. The proverb saies .. Of all the moneths 'tis worst to wed in May. **1796** *Stat. Acc. of Scotland* XVIII 122–3 [Gargunnock, Stirling.] Marriages usually happen in April and November. The Month of May is cautiously avoided. **1821** J. GALT *Annals of the Parish* VI. We were married on the 29th day of April, with some inconvenience to both sides, on account of the dread that we had of being married in May, for it is said, 'Of the marriages in May The bairns die of a decay.' **1879** J. NAPIER *West of Scotland* 43–4. Common alike to all classes .. and whose force is not yet spent, was the belief .. 'Marry in May, rue for aye' .. Judging from the statistics .. this .. has still a firm hold of the inhabitants of Glasgow .. During .. 1874 the marriages in May were only 204, against 703 in June. **1923** [Taunton, Som.] May—this month is still regarded as very unlucky for weddings. **1947** *Mirror* 5 Feb. 12. Parker suggested May. Miss Keble reminded him .. 'Marry in May, rue the day.' He replied: 'Very well, we'll get married in June.' **1952** Woman, *c.*50 [Forfar, Angus] May birds is aye

cheepin', May brides is aye greetin' [weeping]. **1959** *Journal of School of Scottish Studies* 197. Last year 42,672 marriages were registered in Scotland. The figure for the month of May was 1,164. The next lowest figure was for November—2,130 .. The figure for .. May has been constantly the lowest .. of any .. month. **1982** Female student, 20 [Sutton Coldfield, Warwicks.] 'Marry in May and rue the day' was a popular saying quoted by many on the questionnaire I conducted.

Cf. LENT, marrying in.

MAY, washing blankets in

1923 [Nynehead, Som.] 'If you wash blankets in May, You will wash one of the family away.' **1969** M. HARRIS *A Kind of Magic* 124 [Ducklington, Oxon, 1920s] There were, and still are, women who never dreamt of washing blankets during the month of May. 'Wash blankets in May, You'll soon be under clay.' **1978** *Bristol Folk News* Spring 8. From my family: 'Wash a blanket in May, Wash a loved one away.' **1987** Woman, 44 [Exmouth, Devon] Do not wash blankets in May, or you will wash a friend away.

MAY, weaning baby in

1818 *Edinburgh Mag.* Nov. 410 [Angus] As a woman will not marry in May, neither will she spean [wean] her child in that month.

MAY BLOSSOM in house

1850 *N & Q* 1st ser. II 5 [Suffolk] To sleep in a room with the whitethorn bloom in it during the month of May, will surely be followed by some great misfortune. **1868** *N & Q* 4th ser. I 550 [Yaxley, Suffolk] My servant saw that some white-thorn in bloom (provincially termed here 'May') had been brought into the room, and at once begged leave to remove it; giving as a reason .. that .. 'May' .. brought into a house .. brought with it misfortune or death. **1883** *Cornishman* 26 Apr. 4. You may bring the hawthorn (red or white) within doors, but not the blackthorn blossom, for with the last you introduce death. **1886** *N & Q* 7th ser. II 158. I have frequently heard that it is unlucky to bring hawthorn blossom (i.e. may) into a dwelling. I always warn my servants not to bring in any, and never do so myself. It portends, I have heard, a death in the house. **1910** *Folklore* 224. Essex people say, 'If you draw may into the house, you draw the head of the house out;' and this last spring (1909), when I was staying near Saffron Walden, I gave an old woman in the almshouse a piece of pink may .. and her rather sudden death the following week .. was attributed to this. **1923** [Cosham, Hants.] If into the house you bring the May, The head of the house will pass away. **1941** F. THOMPSON *Over to Candleford* XIX. Every pot and jug and vase was filled with hawthorn blossom. She was rather shocked at this, for .. she herself would not have brought may blossom indoors .. 'Aren't you afraid all this may'll bring you bad luck?' .. Mrs Merton smiled .. 'How can it?' she said. 'I've got nobody else to lose.' **1983** [Chelmondiston, Suffolk] When Mrs X. died, they said in the village, 'Well, she asked for it, didn't she? Her daughter brought a great big bunch of may into the house.' **1985** R. VICKERY *Unlucky Plants* 20 [Witham, Essex] May must not be brought into the house .. It was not lucky to even sit under a may hedge in flower, but quite safe otherwise.

MAY BLOSSOM smells of death

1627 BACON *Sylva Sylvarum* § 912. The Plague is many times taken without Manifest Sense .. And they report, that where it is found, it hath a Sent, of the Smell of a Mellow Apple; And (as some say) of May Flowers. **1866** *Gents Mag.* pt. 2 73. I have found it a popular notion among .. country cottagers, that the peculiar scent of the hawthorn is 'exactly like the smell of the Great Plague of London'. **1886** *N & Q* 7th ser. II 215 [Derbys.] If a child brought a may bough into a house some one would at once seize it and throw it out. The flowers 'smell like death' I have heard people say, and they .. said that if the may withered in the house the death of some one in the house would shortly follow. **1937** M. BUTTS *Crystal Cabinet* XXXVII. The hawthorn-jar gave out its scent, the scent one loved and was told was

dangerous; that Nurse had said would kill you if it slept beside you. **1965** S. PLATH *Ariel* 'Bee Meeting.' Is it the hawthorn that smells so sick? The barren body of hawthorn, etherizing its children. **1985** R. MABEY *Frampton Flora* 69. The blossoms of the woodland hawthorn smell strongly and sinisterly of rotten meat, which could explain its reputation as a harbinger of death.

MAY BOUGHS AND FLOWERS protect

1546 P. VERGIL *De Rerum Inventoribus* V II (tr. Langley) At the calends [first days] of Maie, the youthe aswell menne as women are wonte to go a maiying into the feldes and bryng home boughes and floures to garnishe their houses and gates, and in some places the churches. **1579** SPENSER *Shepheardes Calender* 'Maye'. Yougthes folke now flocken in every where, To gather May bus-kets [bushes] and smelling brere: And home they hasten the postes to dight, And all the Kirke pillours eare day light, With Hawthorne buds, and swete Eglantine, And girlonds of roses, and Sopps-in-wine. **1584** SCOT *Discoverie of Witchcraft* XII XVIII. The popish church .. to be delivered from witches .. hang in their entries .. haythorne, otherwise white [t]horne gathered on Maie daie .. Memorandum, that at the gathering .. the Credo is necessarie to be said .. and also the Pater Noster, for that is not superstitious. **1586** CAMDEN *Britannia* (tr. Gibson, II 380) [Limerick, Eire, c.1566] They [the Irish] think it foretells a plentiful dairy, if they set boughs of trees before their houses on May-day. **1600** NASHE *Summers Last Will* B3. The Palme and May make countrey houses gay. **1688** AUBREY *Remaines* (1881, 119 n.) At Woodstock in Oxen, they every May-eve goe into ye Parke, and fetch awa a number of Hawthorne-trees, wch they sett before their dores, 'tis pity that they make such destruction of so fine a tree. **1758** BORLASE *Natural History of Cornwall* 294. Among ancient customs still retained by the Cornish, may be reckoned that of decking their doors and porches on the first of May with green boughs of sycamore and hawthorn. **1770** C. VALLANCEY *De Rebus Hibernicis* I 123. On

May-Eve every family sets up before their door a green-bush ['May-bush' in margin]. **1771** PENNANT *Tour in Scotland* 159–60. A cross is cut on some sticks, which is dipped in pottage, and the Thursday before Easter one of each placed over the sheep-cot, the stable or the cow-house. On the 1st of May they are carried to the hill where the Bel-tain is celebrated, all decked with wild flowers, and after the feast is over, replaced over the spots they were taken from. These follies are now seldom practised. **1775** L. SHAW *History of Moray* 241. Upon Mandy Thursday, the several herds cut staves of Service Wood about three feet long, and put two cross sticks into clefts in one end of the staff: These staves they laid up till the First of May. On that day . . having adorned the heads of their staves with wild herbs, they fixed them on the tops, or above the doors of their several cotes; and this they fancied would preserve the Cattle from Diseases till next May. **1821** CLARE *Village Minstrel* I 11 [Helpston, Northants.]. And dear to him the rural sports of May, When each cot-threshold mounts its hailing bough, And ruddy milkmaids weave their garlands gay, Upon the green to crown the earliest cow. **1823** W. GRANT STEWART *Highlanders of Scotland* 260 [Belton Eve, i.e. 30 Apr.] Messengers are . . dispatched to the woods for cargoes of the blessed rowan tree . . Being formed into the shape of a cross, by means of a red thread, the virtues of which too are very eminent, those crosses are . . inserted in the different door lintels in the town . . Care should also be taken to insert one of them in the midden, which has at all times been a favourite site of *rendezvous* with the black sisterhood. **1845** J. TRAIN *Isle of Man* II 117. On May-eve, the juvenile branches of nearly every family in the Island gathered primroses, and strewed them before the doors of their dwellings, to prevent the entrance of the fairies on that night. **1854** BAKER *Northamptonshire* II 426. Formerly it was customary in the northern part of the county . . to place a large branch of white-thorn at the doors of most of the houses in the village; at the present time the young people in some places carry

about branches in their hands. **1862** *N & Q* 3rd ser. II 483 [Aberdeen.] On the 2nd of May, the eve of the Invention of the Holy Cross, it is customary to form crosses of twigs of the rowan tree, and to place them over the doors and windows, as a protection against evil spirits and witches. **1876** KILVERT *Diary* 25 Apr. [Monnington, Herefords.] Outside the door on the cottage wall hung the old dry withered birch and wittan twigs soon to be replaced on May Eve by new boughs 'to keep the old witch out' and counteract her spells during the coming year. **1886** *Folklore* 225. In West Cornwall it is the custom to hang a piece of furze to a door early in the morning of May-day. At breakfast-time the one who does this appears and demands a piece of bread and cream with a basin of 'raw-milk' [unskimmed milk]. **1887** 'SPERANZA' WILDE *Superstitions of Ireland* I 201. The marsh marigold . . is called 'the shrub of Beltaine'. Garlands are made of it for the cattle and the doorposts to keep off the fairy power. **1904** *Folklore* 457 [Co. Meath] On last May Eve . . I saw our cook coming in with a great bunch of May-flowers [marsh marigolds] which she . . intended strewing on the thresholds of all the entrance doors of the house, as, being May-Eve, the fairies would have great power, and the May-flowers are a potent charm to prevent their entering . . Whoever comes across the threshold, particularly that of the kitchen, must step on the flowers, and bring good luck and plenty of butter to the house. **1912** LEATHER *Herefordshire* 18. A tall birch tree, decorated with red and white rags, may still be seen occasionally, fastened near the door of the stable. It is placed there early on May day, and usually left up for the whole year. Its purpose is to avert ill-luck, and to prevent wicked fairies or witches from riding horses in the night, or plaiting their manes and tails so that waggoners cannot comb them. **1916** *Folklore* 262 [Ireland; May Eve and Day] There are herbs and dew to be gathered for charms, boughs and branches for protection—in the South they are placed not only on houses and sheds but on the railway engines, chestnut boughs for choice; flowers, especially primroses, or sometimes marsh marigolds—yellow, as best befits a butter festival—to be sprinkled on doorsteps and window-ledges, as offerings to the Good People. **1932** WOMEN'S INSTITUTE *Worcester Book* 32 [Three Hills] On the first of May an elm bough was put over the door for good luck, and on the 29th May a bough of oak, then a bough of each tree was placed on the bees, but not by the same person. **1937** *Folklore* 51 [Gwent] The commonest way of counteracting the witch's spell was by means of a white thorn or birch cross above the door. **1985** R. VICKERY *Unlucky Plants* 11. In Ireland it was thought unlucky to bring May Flowers (like buttercups) .. into the house before May. The old people used to say it was 'lucky' to .. place them in bunches on the outside of your win-dowsill, but not inside .. Sometimes we, as children, would gather them and bring them into the kitchen, and would be severely scolded .. Once when I cheekily asked why, I was told .. that 'they weren't lucky'. However once May had arrived, you could bring them in-doors without any misfortune threat-ening you.

Also see index: greenery.

MAY DAY, giving or selling on

1887 'SPERANZA' WILDE *Superstitions of Ireland* I 201. Neither fire, nor water, nor milk, nor salt, should be given away for love or money.

MAY DAY/EVE din

1686–7 AUBREY *Remaines* (1881, 18) At Oxford the Boyes doe blow Cows horns & hollow Caxes all night. **1724** T. HEARNE *Robert of Gloucester's Chronicle* xviii. Upon the Jollities on the first of May formerly the Custom of blowing with, and drinking in, Horns so much prevail'd which tho' it be now generally disus'd, yet the Custom of blowing them prevails, at that Season, even to this day, at Oxford. **1725** BOURNE *Antiquitates Vulgares* 200 [Northumb.] On the Cal-ends, or the first Day of May .. the juvenile Part of both Sexes, are wont to rise a little after Mid-night, and walk to some neighbouring Wood, accompany'd with Musick and the blowing of Horns. **1790** *Gents Mag.* 520 [Helstone, Corn-

wall] In the morning, very early, some troublesome rogues go round the streets with drums, or other noisy instruments, disturbing their sober neighbours, and singing parts of a song, the whole of which nobody now recollects, and of which I know no more than that there is mention in it of .. going to the 'green wood to bring home the summer and the May-o'. **1813** BRAND *Antiquities* I 184. The young chimney-sweepers, some of whom are fantastically dressed in girls' clothes, with a great profusion of brick-dust by way of paint, gilt paper, &c. making a noise with their shovels and brushes, are now the most striking objects in the celebrations of May Day in the streets of London.

Cf. NEW YEAR din.

MAY DEW auspicious

1825 JAMIESON *Scottish Dict.* Suppl. II 317. In Angus, the gathering of dew, on Rude-day [3 May] before dawn, has been reckoned an auspicious rite. **1827** HONE *Every-Day Book* II 609–10. Allow me .. to acquaint you with a custom of gathering the May-dew here in Ed-inburgh on the first of May. About four o'clock in the morning there is an unusual stir .. a hurrying of gay throngs of both sexes through the King's-park to Arthur's seat. In the course of half an hour the entire hill is a moving mass of all sorts and sizes. Ibid. 685. On the first morning [of May, in Falkirk] maidens rise early to gather May-dew, which they throw over their shoulder in order to propitiate fate in allotting them a good husband. *c.*1900 BANKS *Calendar Customs of Scotland* II 224 [Ross./Cromarty] On the first day of May girls went to wash their faces in the dew and wish before sunrise—while doing this they name some lad and wish in their own mind that he may become their sweetheart and they get their wish. **1952** Schoolgirl, 14 [Aberdeen] It is said to be lucky to wash your face in the early morning dew on the first of May. **1957** Schoolgirl, 11 [Penrith, Cumb.] On the first of May, if you wash your face in the dew, you are supposed to marry the first man you meet. **1961** *Glasgow Herald* 2 May 10. About 1,000 people climbed Arthur's Seat, Edinburgh, yesterday to take part in the twenty-first May Day sunrise service, and to follow the old tradition of washing their faces in the morning dew.

MAY DEW cosmetic

1667 PEPYS *Diary* 28 May. After dinner, my wife away down with Jane and W. Hewer to Woolwich in order to a little ayre and to lie there tonight, and so to gather May dew tomorrow morning, which Mrs Turner hath taught her as the only thing in the world to wash her face with, and I am contented with it. **1751** JOHNSON *Rambler* no. 130 5. I .. was never permitted to sleep till I had passed through the cosmetic discipline; in which was a regular lustration performed with bean-flower water and May-dews. **1778** W. HUTCHINSON *View of Northumberland* II app. 13. The young people of both sexes go out early in the morning of the 1st of May, to gather the flowering thorns and the dew of the grass .. The dew was considered as a grand cosmetic, and preserved the face from wrinkles, blotches, and the traces of old age. **1814** *Quarterly Review* XI XXII 282. The supposed cosmetic virtues of May dew, when gathered before sunrise, are pretty generally remembered in the country. **1869** W. C. HAZLITT *Proverbs* 367. The fair maid who, the first of May, Goes to the fields at break of day, And washes in dew from the hawthorn tree, Will ever after handsome be. **1879** HENDERSON *Northern Counties* 85–6. On May Day morning .. in Perth they climbed Kinnoul Hill .. with a lingering belief in the old saying—that those who wash their faces in May dew will be beautiful all the year. **1905** *Standard* 8 May 3. The quaint old custom of 'May-dewing', or washing the face in dew, on the first Sunday in May, in order to ensure lasting beauty, was observed yesterday by a large number of Blackburn girls and women, some of the latter being very elderly. **1952** *Schoolgirl*, 14 [Kirkcaldy, Fife] On the first of May you wash your face in the dew and have a good complexion all the year round.

MAY DEW/RAIN cures

1602 PLAT *Delights for Ladies* (1611,

H8b) Some commend May-dew gathered from Fennell and Celandine, to be most excellent for sore-eyes. **1626** BACON *Sylva Sylvarum* § 781. I suppose that he who would gather the best May-Deaw, for Medicine, should gather it from the Hills. **1661** M. STEVENSON *Twelve Moneths* 22. *May* .. Now .. the Apothecary gathers the Chrystal Dewy Drops for a Medicine. *c.*1691 AUBREY *Natural History of Wiltshire* (1847, 73) Maydewe is a very great dissolvent of many things with the sunne that will not be dissolved any other way: which putts me in mind of the rationality of the method used by Wm. Gore, of Clapton, Esq., for his gout, which was to walke in the dewe with his shoes pounced; he found benefit by it. I told Mr Wm. Mullens, of Shoe Lane, Chirurgion, this story, and he sayd this was the very method and way of curing that was used in Oliver Cromwell, Protectour. **1808** JAMIESON *Scottish Dict. Rude* [N. Scotland] Great virtue is ascribed to May-dew. Some, who have tender children, particularly on Rudeday [3 May], spread out a cloth to catch the dew, and wet them in it. **1846** DENHAM *Proverbs* 43. May rain kills lice. **1850** *N & Q* 1st ser. II 475 [Launceston, Cornwall] They say that a child who is weak in the back may be cured by drawing him over the grass wet with the morning dew. The experiment must be thrice performed, that is, on the mornings of the 1st, 2nd, and 3rd of May. **1883** BURNE *Shropshire* 190. I knew a little idiot boy whose mother (fancying it was weakness of the spine which prevented him from walking) took him into the fields 'nine mornings running' to rub his back with May-dew. **1901** *N & Q* 9th ser. VII 149. Rain which has fallen in May .. if caught in a clean vessel .. is an infallible remedy for sore eyes in man or beast. Such at least is the belief of our keeper, a Welshman.

Cf. ASCENSION DAY WATER.

May dew/rain: cf. WATER: first of year.

MEASURING child

1909 M. TREVELYAN *Folk-Lore of Wales* 268. If you measure a child for garments in the first six years of its life, it will often want clothes.

MEASURING cures

1911 *Folklore* 57 [Co. Clare] 'Head-measuring' to 'close the skull' and cure head ache was found .. in use near Corofin. **1926** *Folklore* 173 [Aberystwyth, Cardigan.] When people .. suffer from .. rheumatism they often go to a witch-doctor, a woman; she .. measures the affected parts with lengths of crimson wool, and then ties the wool round the arm [etc.]. The measuring is a very important part of the cure. **1946** M. SUMMERS *Witchcraft and Black Magic* 149. An old man, who lived at Traws-coed, in Cardiganshire, and who died in 1910, enjoyed a great reputation as a diviner and a healer. He worked cures with the spell of the scarlet yarn, commonly known as 'measuring the yarn'.

MEASURING two people

1899 *Newcastle Weekly Chronicle* 4 Feb. 7 [Jesmond] It is unlucky to measure two people's arms with the same string.

measuring: also see index: counting/measuring/weighing.

MEAT shrinks in pot

1876 *N & Q* 5th ser. VI 397 [Weardale, Co. Durham] If meat shrink in the pot when boiling, it is unlucky. **1948** E. & M. A. RADFORD *Superstitions* 171–2. If meat shrinks in the pot .. it is unlucky; if it swells, it is a sign of prosperity .. Still fervently believed by a number of people.
   Cf. MOON affects killing of livestock.

MENSTRUATING WOMAN defiles

*c.*580 BC Leviticus 15: 19. And if a woman have an issue, and her issue in her flesh be blood, she shall be put apart seven days: and whosoever toucheth her shall be unclean until the even. AD 77 PLINY *Natural History* VII XIII (1855 II 151) On the approach of a woman in this state, must will become sour, seeds .. sterile, grafts wither away, garden plants are parched up, and the fruit will fall from the tree .. Her very look, even, will dim the brightness of mirrors, blunt .. steel, and take away the polish from

ivory. A swarm of bees, if looked upon by her, will die. **1615** CROOKE *Body of Man* 667. A menstruous woman doth infect a looking glasse as it were with some materiall corruption. **1627** BACON *Sylva Sylvarum* § 923. It is an Ancient Tradition .. that a Menstruous Woman, looking upon a Glasse, doth rust it. Nay they have an Opinion, which seemeth Fabulous; That Menstruous Women, going over a Field, or Garden, doe Corne and Herbs good by Killing the Wormes. **1714** GAY *Shepherd's Week* 30. If e'er she brew'd, the drink wou'd strait grow sour, Before it ever felt the thunder's pow'r. **1922** JOYCE *Ulysses* (1960, 481) Wonder if it's bad to go with them then. Safe in one way. Turns milk, makes fiddlestrings snap. **1934** *Folklore* 267. Quite recently I have had reported to me the case of a servant girl who firmly refused to cut up .. some beef-steak for a pudding .. She explained that she was menstruating and that should she cut the steak it would undoubtedly go bad and be unfit to eat. **1941** *Folklore* 75. In my Fenland parish there is a very strong and general belief that a woman must not have anything to do with 'putting away' a pig during her monthly periods. **1956** G. E. EVANS *Ask the Fellows* XXIV [Stratford St Mary, Suffolk] While they were drying, the hams were to be locked in a room and there was a firm injunction that 'none of the girls should go near them'. It was believed .. that if a menstruating woman touched the hams they would 'go off'. **1982** Woman, *c.*60 [Leics.] Women menstruating should not milk cows or make butter. **1985** Woman, 62. I remember, during the war, the butcher at Hoddesdon, in Hertfordshire, told me it would be impossible to employ women as butchers—they would have to take a week off every month, or they would taint the meat.
   Cf. CHURCHING after childbirth.

MILK boils over into fire

1658 K. DIGBY *Late Discourse* 117–18. If it happen that in boyling the milk it swells so high that it sheds over the brim of the skillet, and so comes to fall into the fire, the good woman, or maid .. runs to the skillet, and she takes off the fire, and at the same time takes a handfull of salt .. and throws it upon the cinders whereon the milk was shed .. She will tell you, that it is to prevent, that the Cow who gave this milk may not have some hurt upon her udder, for without this remedy .. she would .. be in danger to die. **1881** W. GREGOR *North-East of Scotland* 193. For milk to boil over the edge of the pot and run into the fire was very unlucky, and diminished the quantity of milk given by the cow .. To counteract the evil consequences salt was immediately thrown into the fire.

Cf. BONES, burning; EGGSHELLS, burning.

MILK, giving or selling

1887 'SPERANZA' WILDE *Superstitions of Ireland* I 201. Milk .. is poured on the threshold [on May Day] though none would be given away. Neither fire, nor water, nor milk, nor salt, should be given away for love or money, and if a wayfarer is given a cup of milk, he must drink it in the house, and salt must be mixed with it. **1932** WOMEN'S INSTITUTE *Worcestershire Book* 42 [Hanbury] It used to be the custom for all Hanbury farmers to give milk to anyone who called for it on Whitsun Eve, and, as a result, everyone had baked custard on Whit Sunday. No milk was sold on that day, as ill luck came to anyone doing so.

Cf. DRINK, spilling; FIRE not allowed out of house.

MILK, spilling

1858 *N & Q* 2nd ser. V 209. The farmers in the West Riding of Yorkshire say that 'to spill new milk in any great quantity is a certain forerunner of misfortunes.' **1882** *N & Q* 6th ser. VI 63–4 [Fermoy, Co. Cork, family MS of 1832] 'Tis a bad thing to make waste wid new milk; 'tis a thing I never did myself nor ether I wouldn't like to see another do; nor I never saw any good come ov it. **1923** [Somerset] It is unlucky to spill milk.

MILLER cures whooping cough

1824 J. MACTAGGART *Gallovidian Encyclopedia* 293. *Kenkhoast*, the chincough. To cure this, the mothers put their children through the happers of mills, when they fancy it leaves them. **1862** *N & Q* 3rd ser. I 446 [childhood, in Co. Wexford] When the children of a family caught the 'chin cough', they were at once .. sent off to the nearest country mill, and dipped three times in the hopper. **1872** EWING *Jan of the Windmill* (1894–6, 84) For they do say .. that if a miller that's the son of a miller, and the grandson of a miller, holds a child, that's got the whooping-cough, in the hopper of a mill, whilst the mill's going, it cures them, however bad they be. **1912** LEATHER *Herefordshire* 83. When there was an epidemic of whooping cough at Blakemere, an old woman said to the Rector 'Lor bless you, Sir, when I was a girl we thought nothing of it, we never troubled the doctor. The child was taken to the mill, the miller set the mill going and said, "In the name of the Father, Son, and Holy Ghost grind away this disease," and it went, always.'

MINCE PIES = happy months

1853 DENHAM *Christmas* (1895, 91) As many mince pies as you taste at Christmas, so many happy months you will have .. General through .. Westmoreland and Cumberland—counties celebrated for their extreme hospitality. **1861** *N & Q* 2nd ser. XII 491. Eating mince-pies in different houses. This saying is so well known that I need not relate it at length. **1883** BURNE *Shropshire* 408. There is a 'luck' about mince-pies, and it is this. For every house in which any person eats a mince-pie during the Twelve Days, he will enjoy a happy month in the ensuing twelve months. **1908** BENNETT *Old Wives' Tale* I v. 'Now, Mr Scales, you must taste my mince. A happy month for every tart you eat, you know,' Mrs Baines reminded him. **1921** *N & Q* 12th ser. VIII 70. Fifty years ago I was taught that the first mince-pies should be eaten on 'Stirrup Sunday' and every one eaten between then and Twelfth Night, in a different house, meant one month of happiness in the New Year. **1923** [Martock, Som.] Even if only a currant of each, taste as many mince-pies and Christmas puddings as possible between

Christmas Day and 6 January—each is a happy month. **1960** Woman, 25 [Steep, Hants.] You get a happy month for each mince pie you eat, as long as you don't speak while you are eating it. **1985** Woman, 56 [Colchester, Essex] Every mince pie eaten in a different house during the twelve days of Christmas means a happy month in the coming year.

MINCE PIES, cutting

1966 Woman, 56 [Scarborough, Yorks.] You must never cut a mince pie, according to my aunt, or you will cut your luck. **1986** Woman, 57 [South Shields, Co. Durham] When I was a child they used to tell me, 'Never *cut* a mince pie, because you cut your luck.'
Cf. BREAD, cutting or pricking.

MINCE PIES eaten before Christmas

1922 UDAL *Dorsetshire* 51. Amongst strict observers of old customs .. no one would think of eating a mince-pie before Christmas Eve or later than Twelfth Night.
Cf. CHRISTMAS CAKE, cutting and eating.

MINCE PIES, opening: divination

1987 Man, 48 [Hoveringham, Notts.] When I was a child, when you opened a mince pie and there was a currant stuck to the lid it meant you were going to have a girlfriend—if there were two you'd have two, and so on.

MINCE PIES, wishing with

1923 [Somerset] When you eat the first mince pie you must wish. **1932** G. K. CHESTERTON *New Poems* 'Some Wishes at Xmas'. Mince-pies grant Wishes: let each name his Prize, But as for us, we wish for more Mince-Pies.
Cf. FIRST FRUITS AND FLOWERS.

'MINISTER' taboo word

1809 A. EDMONSTON *Zetland Islands* II 74. Certain names must not be mentioned while they are setting their lines, especially the minister .. and many others equally unmeaning. **1883** J. R. TUDOR *Orkneys and Shetland* 166 [Shetland] When setting their lines they avoided,

and do still, mentioning certain objects, except by certain special words. Thus .. a minister [is called] *upstanda, hoydeen,* or *prestingolva.* **1909** *N & Q* 10th ser. XII 483 [Stromness, Orkney] Fishermen count it unlucky to mention 'minister' or 'kirk' by these terms on board the boat. **1963** Man, c.40 [Aberdeen] The Shetland fishermen are wary of mentioning the word 'minister'. They refer to him as 'the upstander'.
Cf. 'CHURCH' taboo word; CLERGYMAN.

MIRROR, breaking

1777 BRAND *Antiquities* 91. The breaking a Looking Glass is accounted a very unlucky Accident. Mirrors were formerly used by Magicians in their superstitious and diabolical Operations; and there was an antient Kind of Divination by the Looking Glass. Hence it should seem the present popular Notion. **1787** GROSE *Provincial Glossary* Superstitions 48. Breaking a looking-glass betokens a mortality in the family, commonly the master. Ibid. 61. Extremely unlucky; the party to whom it belongs will lose his best friend. **1832** TENNYSON 'Lady of Shalott.' ll. 115–17. The mirror cracked from side to side; 'The curse has come upon me,' cried The Lady of Shalott. **1851** STERNBERG *Northamptonshire* 172. The breakage of [a mirror] portends death or bad luck, limited, according to some, for seven years. **1855** *N & Q* 1st ser. XII 38 [Cornwall] The breaking of a looking-glass entails 'seven years' trouble, but no want'. Ibid. 488. If a cat break a looking-glass .. one of the cats belonging to the house must pay the penalty .. If a child break one, some one of the children—or if a servant, one of the servants—must die within the year. **1861** C. C. ROBINSON *Dialect of Leeds* 296. It is about the unluckiest thing which can well befall a mortal this side the stars, to break a looking-glass, for it is a sure prognostic of family death; 'Ad raather thad done owt nah as that!' we have known a woman say to her child, to whom this misfortune had happened, weeping the while, in sheer expectation of what was to come. **1865** *Gents Mag.* pt. 2 700 [Ireland] Whoever breaks a looking-glass is supposed to incur some

future calamity. **1878** *Folk-Lore Record*
51 [Fittleworth, Sussex] To break a
looking-glass is accounted the greatest
of mishaps, because it portends the death
of some near and dear friend. **1883**
BURNE *Shropshire* 281. It adds to the bad
luck to preserve the broken pieces. **1900**
S. HEWETT *Nummits* 54 [Devon] To break
a looking glass .. brings seven years of
trouble, or the loss of one's best friend.
1960 *Yorkshire Post* 5 May 7. Two ..
schoolboys, aged 14 and 15 .. broke
everything they could in six railway
coaches—except the mirrors. 'We did
not break the mirrors because I was
superstitious,' one of the boys .. told
the police. **1966** J. HOLLOWAY *London
Childhood* 48 [1920s] My father .. was
in deep misery for a whole day or so ..
because my mother accidently broke a
mirror. **1982** Woman, 20 [Cleveland,
Yorks.] I have vivid recollections of
breaking a mirror when I was younger
and my mother saying that that would
mean seven years' bad luck. Since then,
I have frequently heard women who
have broken a small handbag mirror say
that the bad luck will not last a full
seven years because the mirror was so
small. **1983** Boy, 12 [Maldon, Essex] In
my home, if my mum breaks a mirror
she goes out into the garden, puts the
broken bits in a bag, and buries it. **1984**
Woman, 62 [Dockenfield, Surrey] My
mother used to get in a terrible state if
she found a mirror cracked, for instance
when she'd moved house. You know it
means seven years' bad luck. You know
why, don't you. It is because in the old
days mirrrors were so very expensive.
    Cf. GLASS, breaking.

MIRROR covered in sick room

1888 *Folklore* 145–6 [Midlands] When
a young girl, I was taken up to the
bedroom of an old maiden lady .. who
was suffering from .. paralysis .. and ..
in a state of semi-consciousness .. I was
much struck by seeing the looking-glass
on the toilet-table opposite the bed
covered with a large towel, and on
inquiring the reason I was told that it
was deemed unlucky that a sick person
should see their face in a glass. **1923**
[Bridgwater, Som.] It is very unlucky for
a sick person to look in a mirror.

MIRROR covered in the presence of death

1786 R. GOUGH *Sepulchral Monuments* II
pt. 1 205 [Orkney] I know not for what
reason they .. cover all looking glasses
as soon as any person dies. **1825** *Newcastle Mag.* Sept. 395. At a northern
latewake .. the looking-glass is muffled,
to intimate that all .. vanity .. is over
with the deceased. *c.*1828 Calvert MS,
Pickering, Yorks. (G. HOME *Evolution of
an English Town* 215) As soon as death
doth enter the chamber .. turn the
seeing glass to the wall. **1855** *N & Q*
1st ser. XI 215 [Scotland] In the room
of the house of the deceased where the
company met to attend the funeral,
every clear or shining object was covered
with white cloths, as looking-glasses,
pictures, &c. **1866** HENDERSON *Northern
Counties* 41 & n. In the chamber of death
.. a dread is felt of some spiritual being
imaging himself forth in the blank surface of the mirror .. I suspect that the
true reason for shrouding the looking-
glass .. is that given me in Warwickshire, that if you look into the mirror in
the death-chamber, you will see the
corpse looking over your shoulder. **1883**
BURNE *Shropshire* 299. The looking-glass
must be covered (lest an apparition
should be seen in it). **1888** *N & Q* 7th
ser. V 73 [Llanelli, Carmarthen.] A lady
who is wont to drape in white the
mirrors .. in the room where the departed lies, tells me it is done out of
respect for the dead. **1909** M. TREVELYAN
Folk-Lore of Wales 282. It is not good for
a corpse to be reflected in a glass or
mirror .. because the dead will not rest.
1911 FRAZER *Golden Bough* III 94. We
can now explain the widespread custom
of covering up mirrors or turning them
to the wall after a death has taken place
in the house. It is feared that the soul,
projected out of the person in the shape
of his reflection in the mirror, may be
carried off by the ghost of the departed,
which is commonly supposed to linger
about the house till the burial. **1922**
JOYCE *Ulysses* (1960, 243) Mother's
deathbed. Candle. The sheeted mirror.
1924 *N & Q* CXLVL 420. Nearly seventy
years since, in Durham, I remember
seeing my grandmother when laid out.
Mirror and pictures were covered with
white sheets. I was told then, or later,

that this was done lest persons seeing themselves reflected, the corpse should also be seen looking over their shoulders, and give them a fright. **1958** Woman, 48 [Edinburgh] I keep wondering if Paddy will observe the same practice as she remembers Aunt Jane observing when her grandmother died—the looking glasses were all covered with white cloths. **1960** Farmer & Stockbreeder 23 Feb. Suppl. 7. When Mrs Chandler came to lay him out she covered all the mirrors with sheets. **1978** J. D. RAYNER & B. HOOKER Judaism for Today 164 [London] During this period [seven days of mourning] many resort to the superstitious practice of covering mirrors. **1987** Woman, c.60 [Crewcatt, Co. Armagh] I can remember going over to our Catholic neighbours—their young daughter had died—I must have been a young teenager at the time, and all the mirrors were covered.

MIRROR covered in thunderstorm

1900 N & Q 9th ser. VI 7. A lady who lives near Buntingford, Herts., told me the other day that her servants always went round the house and covered the looking-glasses up whenever a thunderstorm occurred. **1954** Daily Express 10 Aug. 5 [Ripley, Derbys.] When the thunder and lightning began Violet was making up in front of a mirror for a visit to her fiancé. Her father said yesterday: 'I reminded her of the superstition that it is dangerous to look at lightning through a mirror .. But she laughed and told me not to be so old-fashioned.' Soon after Violet reached the home of her fiancé .. the lightning struck .. yesterday she was lying in hospital at Nottingham, in danger of losing her sight. **1969** S. MAYS Reubens Corner XIV [Essex] During thunderstorms .. Mirrors, pictures and photographs should be turned face to the wall. **1985** Man, c.60. My ancient aunts, who live in South London, always cover the mirrors in a thunderstorm.

MIRROR: divination

AD **54** I Corinthians 13: 9, 12. For we know in part, and we prophesy in part

.. For now we see through a glass, darkly. **1303** MANNYNG Handlyng Synne (EETS 119 ll. 351–4) Yf you yn swerd [sword], oþer yn bacyn [basin], Any chylde madyst loke þeryn, Or yn þumbe, or yn cristal,—wycchëcraft men clepyn hyt al. c.**1390** CHAUCER Squire's Tale ll. 132–40. This mirour eek, that I have in myn hond, Hath swich a myght that men may in it see Whan ther shal fallen any adversitee Unto youre regne or to youreself also, And openly who is youre freend or foo. And .. if any lady bright Hath set hire herte on any maner wight, If he be fals, she shal his tresoun see, His newe love, and al his subtiltee. c.**1566** BOAISTUAU Theatrum Mundi (tr. Alday, Svi[v]) A childe, who after he had looked in a glasse shewed him of hys destruction, and howe his enimies were coming. **1584** SCOT Discoverie of Witchcraft XIII XIX. The woonderous devises, and miraculous sights and conceipts made and conteined in glasse, doo farre exceed all other; whereto the art perspective is verie necessarie. For it sheweth the illusions of them, whose experiments be seene in diverse sorts of glasses .. for you may have glasses so made, as what image or favour soever you print in your imagination, you shall thinke you see the same therein. Others are so framed, as therein one may see what others doo in places far distant .. There are glasses also, wherein one man may see another mans image, and not his owne. **1606** SHAKESPEARE Macbeth IV i [A shew of eight Kings, and Banquo last, with a glasse in his hand] MACBETH .. What will the Line stretch out to'th'cracke of Doome? Another yet? A seaventh? Ile see no more: And yet the eight appeares, who beares a glasse, Which shewes me many more. **1621** A. MOLLE Living Librarie 2. In our time Coniurers vse Christall, calling the diuination Chrystallomantia, or Onychomantia, in the which, after they haue rubbed one of the nayles of their fingers, or a piece of Chrystall, they vtter I know not what words, and they call a boy that is pure .. to see therein that which they require. **1688** AUBREY Remaines (1881, 261) About 1649, one M[ris] Bodnam, of Fisherton Anger (a poor woman that taught children to reade) was tryed for a witch at Salisbury .. and was executed .. Evidence against her was that she did tell fortunes, and shewed people visions in a glasse, and that a maid saw the devill with her. 1691 R. BAXTER *Worlds of Spirits* 185 [Worcs.] When I lived at Kedderminster, one of my Neighbours affirmed, that having his Yarn stolen, he went to Hodges .. and he told him, that at such an Hour he should have it brought home again, and put in at the Window, and so it was; and as I remember, he showed him the Person's Face, in a Glass; yet I do not think that Hodges made any known Contract with the Devil, but thought it as any effect of Art. 1787 GROSE *Provincial Glossary* Superstitions 35. A speculator or seer .. to have a complete sight, ought to be a pure virgin, a youth who had not known woman, or at least a person of irreproachable life .. The conjuror having repeated the necessary charms and adjurations, with the Litany, or invocation peculiar to the spirits or angels he wishes to call .. the seer looks into a chrystal or berryl, wherein he will see the answer.

MIRROR: divination: to see future spouse

1660 BURTON *Anatomy of Melancholy* pt. 3 sect. 2 mem. 4 subs. 1. 'Tis their onely desire, if it may be done by Art, to see their husband's picture in a glass. 1787 BURNS *Poems* 163 [note to 'Halloween'] Take a candle, and go alone to a looking-glass; eat an apple before it, and some traditions say, you should comb your hair all the time; the face of your conjugal companion, to be, will be seen in the glass, as if peeping over your shoulder. 1883 BURNE *Shropshire* 381 [All Saints' Eve/St Thomas's Eve] Stand before a looking-glass, combing your hair with one hand and eating an apple held in the other, when the face of the man you are to marry will be seen in the glass looking over your shoulder. 1923 [Martock, Som.] First full moon of the year, place your mirror by the window to reflect it. Female, you gaze, and your sweetheart'll lookey auver your shoulder, and you'll see face in glass.

Cf. NEW MOON: divination by diffusion.

MIRROR in water

1697 J. POTTER *Antiquities of Greece* II 317. Sometimes they [ancient Greeks] dipp'd a Looking-glass into the Water [of a spring], when they had a desire to know what would become of a sick Person; for as he looked well or ill in the Glass, accordingly they presumed of his future Condition. 1912 LEATHER *Herefordshire* 87. It is held unlucky to place a mirror in water.

MIRROR, looking in

1486 SPRENGER & KRAMER *Malleus Maleficarum* (tr. Summers, 142) They [devils] entice young virgins and boys into their power .. by means of .. magic mirrors and the reflections seen in witches' finger-nails, and lure them on in the belief that they love chastity, whereas they hate it. 1691 *Athenian Mercury* 4 July. Quest. Some Years since I knew a very proud Maid in Cambridge, an Alderman's Daughter, who running to the Looking-Glass to View her self, as soon as ever she came home from hearing a Sermon upon a Sabbath-Day, she thought with her self that she saw the Devil in the Looking-Glass, and thereupon fell Distracted—Pray your Opinion of all this? Answ .. God does sometimes mark out and stigmatize a particular Example of his Justice, for the Admonition and Warning of others. 1883 *Folklore* 354. When a boy, one of my aunts who lived in Newcastle-on-Tyne used to tell me of a certain girl that she knew who was very vain and fond of standing before the looking-glass admiring herself. One night as she stood gazing, lo! all her ringlets were covered with dripping sulphur, and the devil appeared peeping over her shoulder. 1923 [Somerset] If you look in a looking glass too long you are sure to see the Devil. 1954 Girl, 14 [Newbridge, Monmouth.] I was looking in the mirror and my Gran said 'You'll see the Devil in the glass one day.' 1984 Woman, 56 [South Shields, Co. Durham] My great-aunt used to say that if anyone looked too long in a mirror, they would see the Devil. This was more frightening than my grandmother's 'something you don't want to see'.

Cf. MIRROR: divination.

MIRROR, looking in: baby

1851 STERNBERG *Northamptonshire* 172. It is .. considered highly injurious to let a child look in [a mirror] before it is one year old. **1858** DENHAM *North of England* (1895, 48) A child should not be suffered to look in a glass before it is xii months old. **1882** *People's Friend* 13 Sept. 580. If a child notices its own face in a looking-glass before it is a year old it will die before it comes to maturity. **1909** *Folklore* 218. A young woman here [Kirton, Lincs.] has been troubled because her baby might see itself in the looking-glass at the back of her sideboard before it was a year old. **1923** [Ruishton, Som.] A baby allowed to look into a mirror will have a troubled life. **1932** C. IGGLESDEN *Those Superstitions* 139–40. She was eighty .. she said 'A baby should never see itself in a looking-glass before it is four months old, otherwise rickets will follow.' From another old lady I gleaned the information that the tragic penalty .. was death within a year. **1953** Girl, 15 [Ipswich, Suffolk] Never show a baby itself in a glass, it will make it cross-eyed.

Cf. MIRROR: divination.

MIRROR, looking in: bride arrayed for wedding

1861 *N & Q* 2nd ser. XII 490. It is unlucky for a bride .. to look in the glass after she is completely dressed. In the south of England the greatest care is taken to put on a glove or some other article after the last look has been taken in the mirror. **1923** [Chard, Som.] If a bride looks at herself after she is dressed for her wedding she will be unlucky. **1962** *Yorkshire Post* 11 May 6. It is unlucky for the bride .. to look at herself in a mirror (cracked or uncracked) when she is ready to leave the house (even though this seems to be unavoidable).

Cf. BRIDE'S CLOTHES: wedding dress, bride tries on completed.

MIRROR, looking in: by candlelight/after dark

1630 B. HOLIDAY *Marriage of the Arts* M4b. I have often heard them say 'tis ill luck to see one's face in a glasse by candle-light. **1899** *Newcastle Weekly Chronicle* 4 Feb. 7 [Jesmond] If one look

into a mirror after dark, a face may appear looking over the shoulder. **1900** S. HEWETT *Nummits* 56–7 [Devon] It is unlucky .. to look into a mirror at dusk, or night-time .. there is a dread of something uncanny peeping over the shoulder; such an apparition would portend death. **1909** *N & Q* 10th ser. XII 484 [Stromness, Orkney] It is unlucky to look in a mirror after the lamp is lit. **1923** [Trowbridge, Wilts.] It is unlucky to look at yourself in a mirror by the light of a candle.

Cf. BRIDE'S CLOTHES: wedding dress by candlelight.

MIRROR, looking in: cat

1922 [Somerset] If we let a cat look in a looking glass it is unlucky.

MIRROR, looking in: in nightcap

1883 *N & Q* 6th ser. VII 398. A woman who ties her night-cap before the looking-glass will be an old maid.

MIRROR, looking in: two people

1923 [Ruishton, Som.] If two people look into a mirror together they risk a quarrel. **1954** Girl, 13 [Stoke-on-Trent, Staffs.] It is supposed to be unlucky for two people to look through a mirror at the same time. **1987** Man, *c.*65 [Newmarket, Suffolk] I'm not a very superstitious person—there is one thing though—two people looking into a mirror at the same time—that's very bad luck indeed.

MISTLETOE as protection

AD **77** PLINY *Natural History* XVI xcv (1855, III 435–6) The Druids .. held nothing more sacred than the mistletoe .. gathered with rites replete with religious awe .. offering up their prayers that God will render this gift of his propitious to those to whom he has so granted it. Ibid. XIII xxxix (III 203) Mistletoe .. is proof against all injury from either fire or water. **1640** J. PARKINSON *Theatrum Botanicum* 1394. Too superstitious .. is their conceit .. that it hath power against Witchcraft, and the illusion of Sathan, and for that purpose, use to hang a peece thereof at their children's neckes. **1656** W. COLES *Art of Simpling* 41. Mistletoe .. is carryed many miles to set up in Houses about Christmas time, when it is adorned with a white glistering berry.   1688 AUBREY *Remaines* (1881, 89) At Christmas [we] hange up in the Hall, or &c., a Misseltobough; 'tis obvious to ghesse how 'tis derived downe to us. 1719 J. COLBATCH *Dissertation Concerning Mistletoe* 3. Being one day upon a Journey, I saw some Hazle-Trees plentifully stock'd with Mistletoe. It .. enter'd into my Mind, that .. the Almighty had design'd it for farther and more noble Uses, than barely to feed Thrushes, or to be hung up superstitiously in Houses to drive away evil Spirits. 1805 J. E. SMITH *English Botany* XXI 1470. The Misseltoe is celebrated in story as the sacred plant of the Druids .. From some relics of such antient superstitions it is used, along with holly boughs, to dress up churches and houses at Christmas. In polite life it is as obsolete as some better things, and left to the kitchen. 1871 *N & Q* 4th ser. VIII 506 [Derbys.] It is considered very unlucky for a house unless some mistletoe is brought in at Christmas. 1883 BURNE *Shropshire* 245. Mistletoe .. is left hanging up till next year's mistletoe replaces it. 1887 F. T HAVERGAL *Herefordshire Words* 48. [Eardisland, *c.*1877] On the first of January .. it is customary to take down the mistletoe bough and hawthorn bush which have hung in the farm houses during the past year, and put fresh branches of each to remain for the next twelve months. 1954 Girl, 13 [Usk, Mon.] It is supposed to be lucky to keep the mistletoe from one Christmas to another till you get some more. 1955 *Trans. Devon. Ass.* 355. Mistletoe should always be kept hanging till the Christmas following. It is believed around the Chudleigh district that it will prevent the house from being struck by lightning. At Ottery, they say it will ensure that the house will never be without bread. 1968 *Daily Telegraph* 12 Dec. 23. Not only at Christmas, but throughout the year, if you look through the gates of the brewery of W. H. Brakspear and Sons Ltd. at Henley-on-Thames you will see .. a great bough of holly and a huge bunch of mistletoe, hanging from the eaves .. Every year .. on Christmas morning, fresh mistletoe and holly are ceremoniously chained in the place of last year's boughs .. in the belief that both boughs must hang there all the year, for should one fall the luck of the brewery might change.

Cf. CHRISTMAS LOG/ASHEN FAGGOT: piece kept for luck/protection; HOLLY protects.

MISTLETOE brings luck to farm

AD 77 PLINY *Natural History* XVI xcv (1855, III 436) It is the belief with them [Druids] that the mistletoe, taken in drink, will impart fecundity to all animals that are barren. 1857 *N & Q* 2nd ser. III 343. A Worcestershire farmer was accustomed to take down his bough of mistletoe, and give it to the cow that calved first after New Year's Day. This was supposed to ensure good luck to the whole dairy. 1909 M. TREVELYAN *Folk-Lore of Wales* 88. Welsh farmers used to say when mistletoe was scarce: 'No mistletoe, no luck.' They also said that mistletoe brought luck to the dairy .. a branch of mistletoe was .. placed beside the first cow that gave birth to a calf after the first hour of the New Year.

MISTLETOE cures

AD 77 PLINY *Natural History* XVI xcv (1855, III 436) Mistletoe .. is an antidote for all poisons. Ibid. XXIV VI (1856, V 6) Some .. have a notion that .. if it has not touched the ground, it will cure epilepsy. 1558 H. LLOYD *Treasvri of Helth* VIII. Mysceltowe layd to the head drawyth out the corrupt humores. 1578 DODOENS *Historie of Plantes* 747. They say .. that the wood of Misselto, that groweth vpon the Okes, and not vpon any other tree, is very good against the falling euyll .. to be hange about the necke of the Patient. 1652 CULPEPER *English Physitian* 83. The Misleto .. of the Oak (as the best) .. given in drinke to those that have the Falling-sickness, doth assuredly heal them .. Some .. have called it *Lignum Sanctae Crucis*, Wood of the holy Cross .. not only to be inwardly taken, but .. hung at their Necks. 1912 LEATHER *Herefordshire* 79. Old people used to say of an epileptic boy 'What a pity it was his mother did not give him mistletoe tea.' 1935 *I Walked by Night* (ed. L. Rider Haggard,

16) [Norfolk] The Misseltoe was a shure cure for the Hoping Cought.

MISTLETOE, kissing under

AD 77 PLINY *Natural History* XXIV VI (1856, V 6) Mistletoe .. will promote conception in females if they make a practice of carrying it about them. 1813 BRAND *Antiquities* I 408. I am of opinion .. the Misletoe .. never entered those sacred edifices [churches] but by mistake, or ignorance of the sextons; for it was the heathenish or profane plant .. of Druidism, and it therefore had its place assigned it in Kitchens, where it was hung up in great state with its white berries; and whatever female chanced to stand under it, the young man present either had a right or claimed one of saluting her, and of plucking off a berry at each kiss. I have made many diligent enquiries after the truth of this. I learnt at Bath that it never came into Churches there. An old Sexton at Teddington in Middlesex informed me that some Misletoe was once put up in the Church there, but was by the Clergyman ordered to be taken away. 1820 WASHINGTON IRVING *Sketch Book* II 63 n. The mistletoe is still hung up in farm-houses and kitchens at Christmas; and the young men have the privilege of kissing the girls under it, plucking each time a berry from the bush. When the berries are all plucked, the privilege ceases. 1822 NARES *Glossary. Misseltoe*. The custom longest preserved was the hanging up of a bush of it in the kitchen, or servants' hall, with the charm attached to it, that the maid, who was not kissed under it at Christmas, would not be married in that year. 1827 CLARE *Shepherd's Calender* 94. The shepherd now no more afraid, Since custom doth the chance bestow, Starts up to kiss the giggling maid Beneath the branch of misletoe That 'neath each cottage beam is seen, With pearl-like berries shining gay; The shadow still of what hath been, Which fashion yearly fades away. 1828 M. R. MITFORD *Our Village* III 53 [Three Mile Cross, Berks.] The ancient misletoe bough, on passing under which our village lads are apt to snatch a kiss from the village maidens. 1837 DICKENS *Pickwick Papers* XXVIII. Old Wardle had

just suspended, with his own hands, a huge branch of mistletoe, and this same branch of mistletoe instantaneously gave rise to a scene of general and most delightful struggling and confusion; in the midst of which, Mr Pickwick .. took the old lady by the hand, led her beneath the mystic branch, and saluted her in all courtesy and decorum. 1861 *Welcome Guest, Christmas Number* 3. Kissing a fair one under the mistletoe, and wishing her a happy new year, as you present her with one of the berries for luck, is the Christmas custom of our times; and in some places persons try lots for the bough with the most berries, by the crackling of leaves and berries in the fire. 1881 *N & Q* 6th ser. IV 509. In Derbyshire .. Lasses were sure of good luck if they were kissed under the mistletoe. If it was discovered that they had not been so kissed, the young men swept them down with a house brush or besom. 1892 C. M. YONGE *Old Woman's Outlook* December [Otterbourne, Hants.] The other peculiarly Christmas plant, Mistletoe (*Viscum album*), is banished from our churches on account of the associations, sometimes merely merry, but too often degenerating into vulgarity and rudeness, which make all the lads go about with a sprig of mistletoe in their hats. 1932 C. IGGLESDEN *Those Superstitions* 69–70. If mistletoe be not burned all couples who have kissed beneath it will be foes before the end of the year. 1987 *Woman*, 36 [Great Bentley, Essex] I always make a mistletoe ring and hang it up in the hall, just inside the front door. When you're under it you have to kiss, I don't know why.

Cf. NEW MOON, kissing under.

MISTLETOE, kissing under: divination/spell

1898 BLAKEBOROUGH *Yorkshire Customs* 69. Some maiden mayhap has retired to her chamber with a leaf and a berry plucked from the mistletoe under which she has been saluted. Having locked her door, the berry must be swallowed, whilst on the leaf she will prick the initials of him her heart loves best; this she will stitch in the inside of her corset, so that it rest near her heart, and thus bind his love to her so long as there it remains. 1909 M. TREVELYAN *Folk-Lore of Wales* 88. If an unmarried woman placed a sprig of mistletoe taken from the parish church under her pillow, she would dream of her future husband. 1961 *Folklore* 321 [Worcs.] The Christmas kissing-boss of mistletoe was often kept till the following year, and then burnt and a new one put up .. The unmarried girls would watch it for omens: a steady flame was a good sign, but if it spluttered it foretold cross and bad-tempered husbands.

Cf. FIRE, behaviour of: spits and roars; LEAVES: spell and divination.

MOLE as omen

AD 77 PLINY *Natural History* XXX VII (1856, V 429) Of all animals it is the mole that the magicians admire most .. There is no animal in the entrails of which they put such implicit faith, no animal .. better suited for the rites of religion. 1909 M. TREVELYAN *Folk-Lore of Wales* 280–1. If a molehill be found among the cabbages in the garden, the master of the house will die before the year is out. 1922 [Bridgwater, Som.] It is a very lucky thing to see a mole in the road. 1987 Woman, 58 [Petersfield, Hants.] I remarked to my neighbour that there were molehills all along the bank at the bottom of our garden, and he said, 'Oh, then we'll hear of a move for someone soon, and if they throw them up in a circle round the house, it means a death.'

MOLE: cures/spells

AD 77 PLINY *Natural History* XXX VII (1856, V 429) If a person swallows the heart of a mole, fresh from the body and still palpitating, he will receive the gift of divination .. and a foreknowledge of future events. Tooth-ache .. may be cured by taking the tooth of a live mole, and attaching it to the body .. One of the most probable of their assertions is, that the mole neutralizes the bite of the shrew-mouse. *ante* 1550 MS Ashmole 1378 (R. H. ROBBINS *Essays and Studies* 7) To make a woman daunce naked. Write thes name in a volume of pur parchment with the blode of an owle also mole vita vasta anima, and put it vnder the threshould of the dore or of

þe house where she is, and she shall bot in a whill daunce naked and take it awaye. 1684 H. WOOLLEY *Queen-like Closet* 14. For the Falling-Sickness. Take a live Mole, and cut the throat of it into a Glass of White-wine, and presently give it to the party to drink at the New and Full of the Moon (viz.) the day before the New, the day of the New, and the day after, and so at the Full. This will cure absolutely, if the Party be not above forty years of age. 1790 GROSE *Provincial Glossary* Superstitions 45. To make a sonsy hand; i.e. a healing hand: Hold a mole in your hand till it expires. 1866 *N & Q* 3rd ser. X 24 [Glos.] The mole must be cut in two, and the divided parts or halves fastened to the throat, so as to ensure the close application of the bleeding parts, while warm, to the sides of the tumour .. The mole .. must not be removed till decomposition is sufficiently advanced to become insufferably offensive to the patient. 1873 *N & Q* 4th ser. XI 499 [Glos.] Mole catcher. Against fits—A few drops of blood, got by pricking a live mole with a pin .. To be taken in a wineglassful of water. 1912 LEATHER *Herefordshire* 84. At Weobley, even nowadays, they catch a live mole, make its nose bleed, and cross the wen nine times with a finger dipped in the blood; then the mole is allowed to go, and should take the wen away with it. Or the mole may be cut in halves, applied to the wen all night, and buried afterwards; as it decays the wen should disappear. 1953 Woman, c.80 [Lostwithiel, Cornwall] A cure for goitre, which was tried on my own neck when I was a girl at school, is to get someone to catch a mole, skin it, and tie the skin on the swollen place. By the morning the swelling is some better, and in the end it goes away, but the smell is not very nice.

Cf. SHREW: cures/spells.

MOLE: moleskin purse

1861 A. STRICKLAND *Old Friends* 319 [Suffolk] The mole-catcher asked her if she would like to have a moleskin purse for luck. 1883 BURNE *Shropshire* 214. Whoever uses a moleskin purse will never want money to put in it. These purses are very common; they are made like a bag, terminated by the tail, tassel-wise. **1950** [Forfar, Angus] Lucky to possess a purse of moudie skin.

Cf. WEASEL-SKIN PURSE.

MOLE'S FEET cure

1854 *N & Q* 1st ser. X 6 [Staffs./Shrops.] A mole-trap must be watched, and the moment it is sprung, and whilst the poor mouldwarp is in extremis, but before life is extinct (for on this .. success .. depends) his hand-like paws are to be cut off, and worn by the patient. A dexter paw must be used should the offending tooth be on the right side .. and the contrary. **1867** *N & Q* 3rd ser. XII 197 [Worcs., late 18th c.] A mole was found one day in the garden, having had three of its legs cut off .. This cruel experiment had been tried upon the poor little animal as a charm for the toothache .. and one of the requisitions to make the charm work effectually was that the victim should be turned out alive. **1873** *N & Q* 4th ser. XI 500 [Glos.] In epilepsy, the 'pattes' of the mole are sewed up in a bag and worn round the neck. This custom obtains at Frampton, Cotterell, and in other parts of the county. **1877** T. BELL editorial note in White's *Natural History of Selborne* I XXVIII n. When I first became acquainted with Selborne, between thirty and forty years ago .. I remember a worthy and even kindly old man cutting off the feet of a mole and hanging them in a little bag round the neck of a child with the object of curing the 'king's evil' as it was called, and then letting the poor victim go, with the full conviction that as the maimed animal gradually died the child would be, *pari passu*, cured. **1887** F. T. HAVERGAL *Herefordshire Words* 46. A favourite remedy for tooth-ache is a little bag of unts feet .. hung up over the mantle-piece. Thence in case of tooth-ache they are fetched down and worn round the neck. **1933** *Folklore* 203 [Digby, Lincs.] A mole's foot worn on the watch-chain or carried in the pocket is a good preventive for rheumatism. **1972** *Sussex Express* 21 Apr. 10. Does anyone remember Tom Weller, peg-legged cattle tender on Ditchling Common? He sold moles' feet ('hands' to me) in pairs which, worn around the neck, would cure the tooth-ache. **1972** WOMEN'S INSTITUTE *Home and Country* May 225. When I lived in N. Kent on the Hoo Peninsula .. a silk bag containing mole's feet [was tied] round the neck of a teething baby to keep down the fever.

Cf. HARE'S OR RABBIT'S FOOT cures.

MOLES ON BODY, meaning of

1611 SHAKESPEARE *Cymbeline* V v. Guiderius had Upon his necke a Mole, a sanguine Starre, It was a marke of wonder. **1698** MISSON *Voyageur en Angleterre* (1719, 358) When Englishmen, i.e. the common people, have Warts or Moles on their Faces, they are very careful of the great Hairs that grow out of those Excrescences; and several have told me they look upon those Hairs as Tokens of good luck. **1777** BRAND *Antiquities* 95. Various and ridiculous are the Superstitions concerning Moles on different Parts of the Body. *c.*1797 H. MORE *Tawney Rachel* 6–7. She .. had consulted all the cunning women in the country to tell her whether the two moles on her cheek denoted that she was to have two husbands, or only two children. **1858** A. MAYHEW *Paved with Gold* 305. 'I never saw a man so completely in love as that dear captain,' [Mrs Hazlewood] said to Bertha. 'Something .. always convinced me that you were destined to be lucky. You have a mole on your left cheek, my dear, and that's considered a sign of luck.' **1866** HENDERSON *Northern Counties* 85. A mole at the back of the neck marks the bearer .. as in danger of hanging. **1889** *Folklore* 283 [NE Scotland] A mole 'abeen [above] the breath' in a woman shows she is a witch. *c.*1910 [Forfar, Angus] A mole above yer breath, Ye'll be rich afore yer death. A mole above yer glove, Ye'll marry the man you love. **1932** C. IGGLESDEN *Those Superstitions* 142–3. In Ireland .. a mole on the back of the neck betokens a future murderer, as the mole represents the knot of the hangman's rope. **1956** Woman, 46 [Scarborough, Yorks.] I cling firmly to the Scottish belief that with a mole above your breath you're sure to die rich, because I have one, right there just above my upper lip. **1965** Woman, 39 [Liss, Hants.] 'Three moles within a span, Marry a man with house and land,' my mother used to say. But it isn't true for me. **1986** Woman, 55 [Richmond, Yorks.] 'A mole on the back, Money by the sack.' My mother used to say that. She was from Somerset.

MOLUCCA BEAN amulet

1602 R. CAREW *Cornwall* 27. The sea strond is strowed with .. shels. With these are found .. certain Nuts, somewhat resembling a sheepes kidney, saue that they are flatter: the outside consisteth of a hard darke coloured rinde: the inner part, of a kernell voyd of any taste, but not so of vertue, especially for women trauayling in childbirth, if at least, old wiues tales may deserue any credit. **1703** M. MARTIN *Western Islands of Scotland* 38–9. There is a variety of Nuts [which drift from the Molucca Islands] called *Molluka* Beans .. used as Amulets against Witch-craft, or an Evil Eye, particularly the white one, and upon this account they are wore about Childrens Necks, and if Evil is intended to them, they say, the Nut changes into a Black colour: That they did change colour, I found true .. but cannot be positive as to the Cause of it. **1802** SCOTT *Minstrelsy of Scottish Border* II 172. The kidney shaped West Indian bean, which is sometimes driven upon the shore of the Feroes, is termed by the natives the Fairies' kidney. **1986** Woman, 57 [London] Would you like this [kidney-shaped nut, chestnut colour]? It's a 'lucky' bean. They sell them in a gift shop in Greenwich. The man said they're imported.

MONDAY auspicious/inauspicious

1000 ÆLFRIC (*Homilies*, ed. B. Thorpe, I 101) Many are .. possessed with such great error, that they .. will not undertake anything on Monday, because of the beginning of the week; though Monday is not the first day in the week, but is the second. **1641** H. BEST *Rural Economy of Yorkshire* (Surtees Soc. 135–6) Theire desire (hereaboutes) is to goe to theire newe masters eyther on a Tewsday or on a Thursday; for on a Sunday they will seldome remoove, and as for Munday, they account it ominous, for they say—Munday flitte, Neaver

sitte. late **18th c.** J. RAMSAY (*Scotland in the Eighteenth Century* II 448) In Mull, ploughing, sowing, and reaping are always begun on Tuesday, though the most favourable weather be in this way frequently lost. **1800** M. EDGEWORTH *Castle Rackrent* Gloss. (1895, 74) [Edgeworthstown, Co. Longford] No great undertaking can be auspiciously commenced in Ireland on any morning but *Monday morning*. 'Oh, please God we live till Monday morning, we'll set the slater to mend the roof of the house. On Monday morning we'll fall to, and cut the turf. On Monday morning we'll see and begin mowing. On Monday morning, please your honour, we'll begin and dig the potatoes.' **1825** JAMIESON *Scottish Dict.* Suppl. *Mononday* .. The idea is completely inverted in Ireland [as opposed to Scotland], Monday being accounted the most lucky day in the week .. undoubtedly a relique of the ancient pagan worship of the Moon. **1891**–3 *Proceedings Royal Irish Acad.* 3rd ser. II 820 [Aran Islands, Co. Galway] Some days are considered here unlucky upon which to begin any work of importance .. Monday is one of those days. **1909** M. TREVELYAN *Folk-Lore of Wales* 241. Work begun on Monday will never be a week old. **1930** P. F. ANSON *East Coast of Scotland* 42. Any job started on a Monday was always likely to be finished quickly.

MONDAY first mentioned by woman

1808 JAMIESON *Scottish Dict. Mononday* .. If Monday, be first mentioned in company by a female, of what age or rank soever, they [feeble-minded people] account it a most unlucky omen. But it gives relief to such minds, if the fatal term be first mentioned by a male. I know not, if this strange superstition be peculiar to the North of Scotland .. Why the power of dissolving the charm is ascribed to the male sex, it is not easy to imagine.

Cf. NEW MOON first mentioned by woman.

MONDAY, giving or receiving on

1825 JAMIESON *Scottish Dict.* Suppl. *Mononday* .. Some, who might well be supposed more enlightened, will not give away money on this day of the week, or on the first day of the Moon. 1893 *Folklore* 359 [Eire] In Tipperary and Limerick the country people object to giving away anything on a Monday. 1895 S. O. ADDY *Household Tales* 98. If a shopkeeper gives credit to his customers on Monday morning he will have no luck that week. 1898 *Weekly Scotsman Christmas Number* 6. In a Fife fishing village .. If one man was to ask a match from another on a Monday, the giver would break a bit off the end of it, so as not to part with his luck for the week. 1912 LEATHER *Herefordshire* 89. It is lucky to receive money on a Monday morning, and means money coming in all the week.

MONDAY, grave-digging on

1891–3 *Proceedings Royal Irish Acad.* 3rd ser. II 820 [Aran Islands, Co. Galway] Some days are considered here unlucky .. even to bury the dead. Monday is one of those days .. If they have occasion to bury a corpse .. they turn a sod on the grave the previous day. 1893 *Folklore* 358 [Co. Cork] No grave allowed to be dug on a Monday.

MONDAY, mending on

1923 [Bridgwater, Som.] Do not do any mending on a Monday, or you will be at it all the week.

MONDAY, visitors on

1912 LEATHER *Herefordshire* 89. If visitors come on Monday it is said the house will be full all the week. 1923 [Bridgwater, Som.] If the first person to come to your door on a Monday morning is dark, you will be lucky through the week. If fair, unlucky.

Cf. FIRST-FOOT at New Year/Christmas: dark man usually preferred.

Monday: also see index: first things/occasions; moon.

MONEY, dropping

1895 S. O. ADDY *Household Tales* 98. If a shopkeeper gives credit to his customers on Monday morning he will have no luck that week. 1936 E. H. RUDKIN *Lincolnshire* 20. If you drop money let someone else pick it up and give it to you—then money will come to you. 1954 Girl, 14 [Stoke-on-Trent, Staffs.] You should pick up a coin off the floor only after you have trod on it. 1962 Woman, 52 [Scarborough, Yorks.] I dropped sixpence on the floor of our neighbour's house this morning. 'Money on the floor, More at the door,' they said. 1987 Man, 50 [Waterlooville, Hants.] If anyone dropped any money we used to say, 'Money on the floor, Money to the door.' And you had to spit on it after you'd picked it up.

MONEY, finding

1591 R. GREENE *Art of Coney-Catching* B2ᵛ. Faith frend saith the verser [swindler], tis ill luck to keep founde mony, wele go spend it in a pottle of wine. 1617 T. COOPER *Mysterie of Witch-craft* 137. If silver be found, then it is euill. 1620 MELTON *Astrologaster* 46. It is a signe of ill lucke to finde money. 1668 W. RAMESEY *Elminthologia* 55. If they [devils] appear like *women* bringing money into their Chambers, Desks, Shoes, &c. they are called *Fayries.* 1691 *Athenian Mercury* II no. 20. Quest. I knew a young Man that often found Money, but it was observed that always some ill Accident followed it immediately; as the Breaking of a Leg, an Arm, or something else that was afflicting. 1873 HARLAND & WILKINSON *Lancashire Legends* 227. Bad luck soon follows the finding of a sixpence. 1909 M. TREVELYAN *Folk-Lore of Wales* 326. To find money in unexpected places is fortunate, and you will remain successful so long as you conceal it, and do not let anybody know you have found it. Ibid. 328. It is very unfortunate to find money on the highroad. 1911 J. C. DAVIES *West and Mid-Wales* 215. It is unlucky to find a coin in the road, but if the head and not the tail happens to be up it is a lucky omen. 1911 *N & Q* 11th ser. III 217. Spitting 'for luck' is still practised .. on money received or found. 1957 Student, c.18 [Beds.] Spit on money when found. 1957 Girl, 14 [Penrith, Cumb.] Unlucky to find a sixpence which someone or yourself has lost, but it stops the bad luck if you give it away. 1972 *Lore and Language* July 7 [Coalisland, Co. Tyrone] If you find sixpence leave it. It's unlucky and if you take it you'll hear of a death.

MONEY: having in purse etc.

1411–12 OCCLEVE *Regement of Princes* (EETS Extra Ser. 72: III ll. 685–6) þe feend, men seyn, may hoppen in a pouche Whan þat no croys [coin] þere-inne may a-pere. **1566** T. DRANT *Horace his Satyres* I A.iii. The deuille may daunce in crosslesse [penniless] purse when coyne hathe tooke his tyde. **1822** SCOTT *Pirate* I 142. I will .. keep it [the piece of gold] for a purse-penny .. and that's no using it in the way of spending-siller. **1876** *N & Q* 5th ser. VI 24. A nobleman, who has now been dead several years .. on leaving for a time his various houses in town and country .. placed some pieces of silver and copper in a drawer .. as he considered it very unlucky to return to a house in which there was not any money. **1882** *N & Q* 6th ser. VI 17. It is a common superstition in Sussex that unless you keep a halfpenny or other small coin always in a purse, cash-box, or other receptacle for money, the devil will get in, and it will never be full of money again. I know many cases, even among educated people, where this custom is rigidly observed. **1900** S. HEWETT *Nummits* 52 [Devon] It is unlucky .. to have an empty pocket (even a crooked coin keeps the devil away). **1957** *Folk-lore* 425 [Co. Durham] When the men were paid in gold, a gold coin was kept in the pocket for luck, in the belief that 'money begets money'.

Cf. CROOKED COIN; HANDSELLING new purse.

MONKEY PUZZLE TREE

1954 Boy, 13 [Forfar, Angus] A queer one is 'Never speak while passing a monkey puzzle tree.' **1960** Girl, 11 [Coulsdon, Surrey] If you talk as you go past a monkey puzzle tree it means you'll have bad luck for three years. **1969** E. PORTER *Cambridgeshire* 63. It was an old Fenland belief that if a Monkey Puzzle tree was planted on the edge of a grave-yard it would prove an obstacle to the Devil when he tried to hide in the branches to watch a burial. Many elderly .. people believe the tree is an unlucky one.

MOON affects birth/health/death

AD **77** PLINY *Natural History* II CII (1857, I 128–9) We may certainly conjecture, that the moon is not unjustly regarded as the star of our life. This it is that replenishes the earth; when she approaches it, she fills all bodies, while, when she recedes, she empties them. From this cause it is that shell-fish grow with her increase .. also, that the blood of man is increased or diminished in proportion to the quantity of her light. AD **731** BEDE *Historia Ecclesiastica* V III (tr. Sherley-Price, 1968) Archbishop Theodore, of blessed memory, said that it was very dangerous to bleed at a time when the light of the moon and the pull of the tide is increasing. *c.*1050 MS Cotton Calig. A. xv [and] Cotton Tib. A. iii (COCKAYNE *Leechdoms* III 157) If a man is born when the moon is one day old, he shall be long lived and wealthy. **1570** B. GOOGE *Popish Kingdome* IV 44. No vaine they pearse nor enter in the bathes at any day. Nor pare their nayles, nor from their hed do cut the heare away: They also put no childe to nurse, nor mend with doung their ground, Nor medicine do receyue to make their crased bodies sound, Nor any other thing they do, but earnestly before They marke the Moone how she is placde, and standeth euer more. **1584** SCOT *Discoverie of Witchcraft* IX III. One borne in the spring of the moone, shalbe healthie; in that time of the wane, when the moone is utterlie decaied, the child then borne cannot live; and in the conjunction, it cannot long continue. **1627** BACON *Sylva Sylvarum* §897. It may be, that Children, and Young Cattell, that are Brought forth in the Full of the Moone, are stronger, and larger, than those that are brought forth in the Wane. **1650** J. GREGORY *Opuscula, Assyrian Monarchy* 202. The most easie deliverie a woman can have, is alwaies in the increas, toward and in the full of the Moon, and the hardest labors in the new and silent Moon. **1661** M. STEVENSON *Twelve Moneths* 19. Be sure to put them [horses and mares] together in the encrease of the Moone, for foals got in the

Wane are not accounted strong and healthfull. **1664** S. BUTLER *Hudibras* pt. 2 III ll. 239–50. But with the Moon was more familiar Then e're was *Almanak-well-willer*. Her Secrets understood so clear, That some believ'd he had been there Knew when She was in fittest mood, For cutting Corns, or letting blood, When for anoynting Scabs or Itches: Or to the Bum applying Leeches; When Sows, and Bitches may be spade, And in what Sign best Sider's Made, Whether the *Wane* be, or *Increase*, Best to set, Garlick, or sow Pease. **1688** AUBREY *Remaines* (1881, 85) According to the Rules of Astrologie, it is not good to under-take any Businesse of importance .. in an Eclipse [of the moon]: and as to Nativities this is very remarkable. **1690** BROWNE *Letter to a Friend* (1852, III 68) I was not so curious to entitle the stars unto any concern of his death, yet could not but take notice that he died when the moon was in motion from the meridian. **1808** JAMIESON *Scottish Dict. Mone.* In Angus, it is believed that if a child be put from the breast during the waning of the moon, it will decay all the time that the moon continues to wane. **1878** HARDY *Return of the Native* I III. 'No moon, no man.' 'Tis one of the truest sayings ever spit out. The boy never comes to anything that's born at new moon. **1878** DYER *English Folk-Lore* 41. In Cornwall, when a child is born in the interval between an old moon and the first appearance of a new one, it is said that it will never live to reach the age of puberty. Hence the saying 'No moon, no man.' **1923** [Somerset] A baby born between the old moon and the new will need special care if he is to thrive. **1938** *Folklore* 225 [Shrops.] It is thought that people cannot die when the moon is rising, and watchers know well that a dying person cannot 'go' until the moon has passed the full.

Cf. TIDE affects birth and death.

MOON affects enterprises

*c.***1225** *Vices and Virtues* 27. 'I am afraid,' he said, 'that I have completely wasted my toil on you, who take heed of days, which one day can be better than another to begin something, or a new moon better than an old moon to go into a new house or lead home a wife' .. except it be sowing seeds because of the nature of these seeds of the earth. **15th c.** *Brut* (MS Univ. Lib. Camb. Hh 6. 9.: EETS 136: 441) In þis same yere (1422) .. was done the bataill of Vernoun [and] thanked be God! the victorie fell to þe Englishmen and þe moste vengeance fell vpon þe proude Scottes .. So that they may say wele 'In the croke of þe mone went thei thidre warde, And in the wilde wanyende come þei homewarde.' **1588** J. HARVEY *Discoursive Probleme* 98. Rest you merrie, O ye Colin clowtes .. For to a most plentiful and happy yeere awaiteth you: seeing this last Christmas day falleth whilest the moone increaseth, yea before she reacheth to the first quarter, which is all the luckier .. to make 88 a prosperous and gladsome yeere. **1775** L. SHAW *History of Moray* 249. They narrowly observe the Changes of the Moon, and will not fell wood, cut turf or fuel, or thatch for houses, or go upon an expedition of importance, but at certain periods of the revolution of that Planet. So the Druids avoided, if possible, to fight, till after the full moon. **1794** *Stat. Acc. of Scotland* XII 457 [Kirkmichael, Banff.] The moon in her increase, full growth, and in her wane, are with them the emblems of a rising, flourishing, and declining fortune. At the last period of her revolution, they carefully avoid to engage in any business of importance .. The love-sick swain and his nymph [watch] for the coming of the new moon to be noosed together in matrimony. Should the planet happen to be at the height of her splendour when the ceremony is performed, their future life will be a scene of festivity, and all its paths strewed over with rose-buds of delight. **1795** *Stat. Acc. of Scotland* XV 311 [Orkney] No couple chuses to marry except with a growing moon. **1825** JAMIESON *Scottish Dict. Mone* .. In Orkney, it is reckoned unlucky to flit .. during the waning of the moon. To secure a prosperous change of habitation .. requires the concurrence of three circumstances; that the moon be waxing, that the tide be flowing, and that the wind blow on the back of the person who removes. **1909** *N & Q* 10th ser. XII 484 [Stromness, Orkney] It is unlucky to marry when the moon is waning.

Cf. TIDE affects enterprises.

MOON affects growth of hair/nails/corns

AD 77 PLINY *Natural History* XVI LXXV (1855, III 417) The Emperor Tiberius used .. to observe the changes of the moon for cutting his hair. 1587 ARA-BELLA STEWART [aged 11] Letter 8 Feb. Good Lady Grandmother, I haue sent yoᵣ Laᵖ the endes of my heare, which was cutt the sixt day of the moone, on Saturday laste. *c.*1650 DR WREN Note in Browne's *Vulgar Errors* V XXIII (1852, II 84) They that would encrease the haire maye doe well to observe the increasing moone at all times .. And what is sayd of the haire may bee as fitly applied to the nayles. 1710 *British Apollo* 17 Apr. Q. Pray tell your Querest if he may Rely on what the Vulgar say, That when the Moon's in her Increase, If Corns be cut they'll grow apace; But if you always do take care, After the Full your Corns to pare, They do insensibly decay, And will in time wear quite away, If this be true, pray let me know, And give the reason why 'tis so. *A.* The Moon no more regards your Corns, Than Cits do one another's Horns .. Diversions better Phoebe knows, Than to consider your Gall'd Toes. 1717 N. BLUNDELL *Diary* 6 Oct. [Crosby, Lancs.] It being near Full Moon I cut my Wives Hair off. 1812 J. BRADY *Clavis Calendaria* I 111-12. The influence of the Moon was considered so very extraordinary, that few persons would kill their hogs but when the planet was on the increase, nor would any one .. dare to cut the corns on his feet, or pare his nails, at any other period. 1851 *N & Q* 1st ser. IV 99 [Devon] Hair and nails should always be cut during the waning of the moon. 1882 *N & Q* 6th ser. VI 416. The superstition .. about cutting an infant's hair, particularly in Sussex, is that the operation should be performed under the waxing moon, as it is unlucky to effect it when she is waning. 1884 *N & Q* 6th ser. IX 366. The other day .. a friend of mine told me that it was at least unwise, if not unlucky .. to have your hair cut at any other time than the new moon; because, if so, it would come out; instancing as proof his own beard (a very full one) which until he followed this recipe came away by handfuls. 1909 *Folklore* 342 [Hartlebury, Worcs.] Crop your hair in the moon's wax, Ne'er cut it in her wane, And then of a bald head You shall never complain. 1922 JOYCE *Ulysses* (1960, 453) Gerty's crowning glory was her wealth of wonderful hair .. She had cut it that very morning on account of the new moon. 1927 *Folklore* 37 n. Some women who shingle are careful to have their hair cut when the moon is not full, as at that time it is supposed to grow fast. 1956 G. E. EVANS *Ask the Fellows* [Blaxhall, Suffolk] XXIV. Some women believe that cutting their hair at the time of the new moon is a surety that their hair will grow thick—as the moon waxes, so is the belief, in like manner will their hair. 1987 [Liss, Hants.] Customer to hairdresser: 'Have you heard of the belief that hair grows faster if it's cut when the moon is waxing?' Hairdresser: 'Well, it's a scientific fact, isn't it?'

MOON affects killing of livestock (mainly pigs)

1529 BEN MS Insularum Orchadiarum Descriptio (DALYELL *Darker Superstitions of Scotland* 286 n.) [Orkney] Men heir keepe the observations of the moon, in sa fa that thay sla ther martes [cattle] at the vaxin thereof, affirming they grow in the barrell. 1673 *Husband-Man's Practice* H8. November .. kill swine in or near the full of the Moon, and flesh will the better prove in boyling. 1775 JOHNSON *Western Islands* 248. The moon has great influence in vulgar philosophy. In my memory it was a precept annually given in one of the English Almanacks, to kill hogs when the moon was increasing, and the bacon would prove the better in boiling. 1830 FORBY *East Anglia* 404. It is probably not a universal, but certainly a very general precaution, to kill hogs in the increase of the moon; because it is 'an admitted fact', that pork, killed in the wane of the moon, shrinks in boiling. 1875 *N & Q* 5th ser. III 84 [N. England] I tell you what it is, guv'nor, if you don't want to lose by your pig, you won't let me kill him when the moon's a going off. Better wait till she's getting near the full. 1882 *People's Friend* 13 Sept. 581. In the Isle of Skye they will neither kill a sheep nor stack peats when the moon is waning lest the mutton shrink in the pot and the peats in the fire. 1887 F. T. HAVERGAL *Herefordshire Words* 46. Never kill your pig in the waning of the moon, or the bacon will waste away with the moon. 1910 *N & Q* 11th ser. II 504 [Derbys.] It was most important to know all about the moon's phases, or, as some would have it, 'faces', on account of the 'pig-stickin' .. If by chance the killing had to be done on the wane, there was much anxiety following .. Special care had to be exercised .. or the portions would not take the salt, the crusts [of the Christmas pies] would be hard, and the 'minsh' [mincemeat] would turn sour. *c.*1950 [Spaldwick, Hunts.] Kill the pig in the waxing of the moon and it will 'fry bigger'.

MOON affects sowing and harvesting

AD 77 PLINY *Natural History* XVIII LXXV (1856, IV 111–12) All vegetable productions are cut, gathered, and housed to more advantage while the moon is on the wane .. It is generallly recommended, too .. to make seed-plots when the moon is above the horizon; to tread out the grape, to fell timber, [etc.], when the moon is below it. 1011 BYRHTFERTH *Manual* (EETS 177: I 159) Trees which are cut down at the full moon are harder against worm-eating, and more durable than those which are cut down at new moon. 1523 A. FITZHERBERT *Boke of Husbandrye* 8. Specially let [peas and beans] be sowen in the olde of the mone. For thopinyon of olde husbandes is that they shulde the better codde and ye soner be rype. 1557 TUSSER *Husbandrie* B1^v [Suffolk] Set gardeine beanes, after saint Edmonde the king: the Moone in the wane, theron hangeth a thing. Thencrease of one gallonde, well proued of some: Shall pleasure thy householde, ere peskod time come. 1573 TUSSER *Five Hundreth Points* XII 18^{v.} The Moone in the wane, gather fruit for to last. 1584 SCOT *Discoverie of Witchcraft* IX ii. The poore husbandman perceiveth that the in-

crease of the moone maketh plants and living creatures frutefull: so as in the full moone they are in best strength, decaieng in the wane, and in the conjunction doo utterlie wither and vade. Which when by observation, use and practise they have once learned, they distribute their business accordinglie; as their times and seasons to sowe, to plant, to proine, to let their cattell bloud, to cut [castrate], &c. 1682 C. RIDER *British Merlin* Oct. Sow Wheat and Rie .. about the New Moon. 1703 M. MARTIN *Western Islands of Scotland* 174 [Skye] The Natives are very much dispos'd to observe the influence of the Moon on humane Bodies, and for that cause they never dig their Peats but in the decrease, for .. if they are cut in the increase, they continue still moist, and never burn clear, nor are they without Smoak. 1748 S. WERENFELS *Dissertation upon Superstition* 6. He will not commit his Seed to the Earth, when the Soil, but when the Moon requires it. 1775 JOHNSON *Western Islands* 248. They [the islanders] expect better crops of grain, by sowing their seed in the moon's increase. 1813 RAY *Proverbs* 43 [Somerset] Sow or set beans in Candlemas waddle [wane of moon]. 1854 *N & Q* 1st ser. X 156. It is a very common custom among the farmers and peasantry of Devonshire, to gather in the hoard fruit at the 'shrinking of the moon'. 1927 *Observer* 21 Aug. 19 [Broadstairs, Kent] On inquiring for mushrooms recently at the local shops I was informed that none were to be obtained just then as it was nearing the full of the moon, and that they could only be gathered when the moon was young and rising. *Ibid.* 28 Aug. 10 [Kingston, Sussex] While I do not think that there is any definite evidence that mushrooms only grow when .. 'the moon is growing', it is a very widespread belief among countryfolk in general .. also carried out in other things. Many rustic gardeners never plant seeds except during this period even to-day. 1953 *Man*, 59 [Halifax, Yorks.] It is commonly believed that if you plant anything it will thrive if planted when the moon is increasing in light each day, and that it won't thrive if you plant when the moon is on the wane. 1954 Girl, 15 [Forfar,

Angus] To ensure a good crop of potatoes, plant them by the light of a full
moon. **1957** R. M. LOCKLEY *Pembrokeshire*
41 [nr. Tenby] A farmer [said] 'I'm not
superstitious. All the same I likes to sow
my corn and cure my bacon on a waxing
moon.' **1984** *Woman*, 67 [Liss, Hants.]
Don't plant anything until the waning
moon's gone, because it won't grow.

MOON, pointing at

1856 J. NOAKE *Worcestershire* 168. It is
unlucky to point at the moon, there
being a notion that the 'man' who was
transported to that satellite for stealing
sticks won't stand being pointed at.
1881 *N & Q* 6th ser. IV 407–8. In ..
East Lancashire, where I was brought
up, it is a common tradition that 'it is a
sin to point at the moon.' **1883** BURNE
Shropshire 258. A clergyman of Shrewsbury birth .. was instructed in his childhood that 'it is wicked to point the finger
at the moon.' **1895** S. O. ADDY *Household
Tales* 97 [Yorks.] If you point nine times
at the moon you will not go to heaven.
1902 *N & Q* 9th ser. IX 357. Fifty years
ago it was held to be unlucky to point
at the moon and count the stars. Derbyshire girls and boys 'dared' each other
to do it .. They might point six times
without ill effect, but at the seventh 'you
would be struck blind!' **1940** E. MUIR
Story and Fable 15 [Orkney, *c.*1895] To
us [Aunt Maggie] was merely odd, and
we teased her a great deal, especially
after we caught her one night trying to
get rid of a wart on her finger by pointing
a straw first at it and then at the moon,
and muttering something to herself.
Cf. STARS, pointing at/counting.

moon: also see NEW MOON.

MOON, MAN IN THE

*c.***1340** MS Harley 2253 (*Oxford Book
Med. Eng. Verse*, 132–3) [Herefords.]
Man in the moone stand and strit; On
his bot-forke his burthen he bereth ..
Wher he were o the feeld pichinde stake,
For hope of his thornes to dutten his
doren [to stop gaps in his hedge]?
*c.***1449** R. PECOCK *Repressor* pt. 2 IV (Rolls
I 155) A man which stale sumtyme a
birthan of thornis was sett in to the
moone, there forto abide for euere.

*c.***1595** SHAKESPEARE *Midsommer Nights
Dreame* V i. MOONSHINE. The Lanthorne
is the Moone; I, the man in the Moone;
this thorne bush, my thorne bush; and
this dog, my dog. DEMETRIUS. Why all
these should be in the Lanthorne: for
they are in the Moone. **1630** DEKKER
Honest Whore II D2. Thou art more
than the moone, for thou hast neither
changing quarters, nor a man standing
in thy circle with a bush of thornes.
1813 BRAND *Antiquities* II 476. This is
one of the most antient as well as one
of the most popular Superstitions. It
is supposed to have originated in the
account given in the Book of Numbers
.. of a Man punished with death for
gathering Sticks on the Sabbath Day.
1895 S. O. ADDY *Household Tales* 59 The
'man in the moon' is said to have a
bundle of sticks on his back, and it is
said that he was put there because
he gathered sticks on Sunday. **1963**
Hereford Times 2 Aug. 10. Old Mrs Nokes
will tell you that the face of the man in
the moon is the face of a man who 'went
hedgin' on Sunday'. **1969** *Times* 21
Nov. 11 [Berkhamsted, Herts.] When I
was a child I was told that the man in
the moon was sent there because he
gathered firewood on a Sunday.
Cf. SUNDAY: keeping Sabbath holy.

MOONLIGHT causes madness

1393 LANGLAND *Piers Plowman* C. text X
108. Lunatik lollers and leperes a-boute,
And mad as þe mone sitt more oþer
lasse [more or less mad according to
the moon's phases]. **1486** SPRENGER &
KRAMER *Malleus Maleficarum* (tr. Summers, 31) The stars can influence the
devils themselves. [As proof of this] certain men who are called Lunatics are
molested by devils more at one time
than at another; and the devils .. would
rather molest them at all times, unless
they themselves were deeply affected
by certain phases of the Moon. **1622**
SHAKESPEARE *Othello* V ii. It is the very
error of the Moone, She comes more
neerer Earth than she was wont, And
makes men mad. **1658** W. ROWLEY *Witch
of Edmonton* II I. When the Moon's in
the full, then's wit in the wane. **1674**
MILTON *Paradise Lost* XI ll. 480, 486. All
maladies of gastly Spasm, or racking

torture .. moaping Melancholie And Moon-struck madness. **1695** CONGREVE *Love for Love* IV iii. Oo'ns, that you cou'd not foresee that the Moon wou'd predominate, and my Son be mad. **1795** T. WILKINSON *Wandering Patentee* II 21. This was treatment 'horrible most horrible' for a lady .. whose spirits at certain times were under the controul of the moon. **1827** T. F. FORSTER *Pocket Encyclopædia* 43. When the moon is on the full, or new, people are more irritable than at other times .. Insanity at these times has its worst paroxysms. **1830** MARRYAT *King's Own* II II 20–1. 'I can .. state some other points, from observation, in which the moon has power.' 'Over lunatics, I presume?' 'Most certainly .. I believe that there is an ebb and flow of power in our internal mechanism, corresponding to the phases of the moon.' **1861** *N & Q* 2nd ser. XII 492. The full moon increases the symptoms of madness. **1940** *News of the World* 15 Dec. 3. 'Moon madness', which came over him with each full moon, was pleaded at Winchester Assizes in defence of .. a soldier .. charged with murdering a comrade. **1953** Man, 59 [Halifax, Yorks.] People say of an unstable character that 'he's ruled by t' moonin'. **1967** [Liss, Hants.] There's a woman lives near us who is not quite right in the head. You know there's been a full moon these last few days—well, this woman came up to Mrs ——, as she was standing talking to a friend in the street, and this woman whisked up her skirts and ripped down her knickers, and said, 'How's that, then!' **1987** Farmer, 65 [Devon] All the fluids in the body, including those in the brain, are controlled by the moon. I know a matron of a home for the elderly, she's Jewish by the way, in East London, who marked the full moon on the calendar to warn the staff. The patients always went slightly crazy at the full moon, she said.

MOONLIGHT, charm against baleful effects of

1873 HARLAND & WILKINSON *Lancashire Legends* 238. Should children observe the moon looking into their rooms, they are taught to avert her influence by repeating .. 'I see the moon; The moon sees me. God bless the priest That christened me.' **1876** F. K. ROBINSON *Whitby Glossary* xiii. We hear the children of this maritime part on moonlight nights, loudly reiterating the couplet— 'I see the moon and the moon sees me, God bless the sailors on the sea.' **1904** *N & Q* 10th ser. I 395. In Ireland, sixty years ago, children, at their first glimpse of the new moon, were taught, in order to escape bad luck or some dire calamity, to use the following invocation: 'I see the moon, And the moon sees me. God bless the moon, And God bless me.'

MOONLIGHT, sleeping in: dangerous

1621 *Help to Discourse* 8. When thou goest to thy bed .. draw close the curtaines to shut out the Moone-light, which is very offensive & hurtfull to the braine, especially to those that sleepe. **1830** MARRYAT *King's Own* II II 18–19. The moon, nearly at her full, was high in the heavens .. without one envious cloud to obscure the refulgence of her beams .. 'It would be as well,' observed the surgeon .. 'to request the officer of the watch not to permit the men to sleep on the upper deck. We shall have many of them moon blind.' **1857** LIVINGSTONE *Missionary Travels* 133. You may sleep out at night, looking up to the moon till you fall asleep, without a thought or sign of moon-blindness. **1867** W. H. SMYTH *Sailor's Word-Book. Moon-struck*, an influence imputed to the moon .. by which fish .. become .. spoiled. Human beings are also said to be injured by sleeping in the moon's rays. **1922** *N & Q* 12th ser. XI 355. As children we were cautioned against going to sleep with the moonlight shining on our faces. We were told that if we did, we should go blind. Ibid. 494. There is an old Irish superstition that to go to sleep with the moon shining on the face produces a form of blindness, and reduces the sleeper to a state of harmless idiocy .. generally alluded to as 'moonstruck', or as being 'loony'. **1982** Woman, *c.*55 [Stockton-on-Tees, Co. Durham] You mustn't go to sleep with the full moon shining in your face. If you wake up and it's shining in your face, get up quick and draw the curtains.

MOONLIGHT 'washes' warts away

AD 77 PLINY *Natural History* XXVIII XII
(1856, V 294) to get rid of warts, some
lie in a footpath with the face upwards,
when the moon is twenty days old at
least, and after fixing their gaze upon it
.. rub themselves with anything within
their reach. **1650** BROWNE *Vulgar Errors*
V XXII § 9. For Warts we rub our hands
before the Moon. **1658** K. DIGBY *Late
Discourse* 43. One would think it were a
folly that one should offer to wash his
hands in a well-polished silver-bason,
wherein there is not a drop of water, yet
this may be done by the reflexion of
Moonbeams onely, which will afford a
competent humidity to doe it .. This is
an infallible way to take away warts
from the hands, if it be often used.

MOONWORT loosens iron

1591 DU BARTAS *Divine Weeks* (tr. Sylvester, I III 763) Horse, that .. Tread
upon Moon-wort with their hollow
heels; Though lately shod, at night goe
bare-foot home. **1597** GERARD *Herball*
329. Small Moonewort .. hath beene
vsed among .. witches to do wonders
withall, who say, that it will loose locks,
and make them to fall from the feete of
horses that grase where it doth growe.
1646 BROWNE *Vulgar Errors* II VI. That
ferrum Equinum, or Sferra Cavallo hath
a vertue attractive of Iron, a power to
breake lockes, and draw off the shooes
of a horse that passeth over it. Whether
you take it for one kinde of Securidaca,
or will also take in Lunaria, we know
it to be false. **1653** CULPEPER *English
Physitian* 163. Moon-wort is an Herb
which they say wil open Locks, and
unshoo such Horses as tread upon it;
this some laugh to scorn, and those no
smal Fools neither: but Country people
that I know, cal it Unshoo the Horse:
Besides, I have heard Commanders say,
that on White Down in Devon-shire,
neer Tiverton, there was found thirty
Hors shoos, pulled off from the feet of
the Earl of Essex his Horses being there
drawn up in a Body, many of them being
but newly shod, and no reason known,
which caused much admiration: and
the Herb described usually grows upon
Heaths. **1657** W. COLES *Adam in Eden*
561. It is said, yea and believed by

many, that [moonwort] will open the
Locks, wherewith dwelling houses are
made fast, if it be put into the Keyhole,
as also that it will loosen the Locks,
Fetters and Shoos from those Horses
feet, that goe on the places where it
groweth. **1685** AUBREY *Natural History
of Wiltshire* (1847, XII) Sir Bennet
Hoskins, Baronet, told me that his keeper
.. did .. drive an iron naile thwert the
hole of the woodpecker's nest, there
being a tradition that the damme will
bring some leafe to open it .. They say
the moone-wort will doe such things.
1899 *Newcastle Weekly Chronicle* 11 Feb.
7 [Jesmond] The fern moonwort is said
to loosen horse shoes.

MOTH sign of letter coming

1869 *N & Q* 4th ser. IV 212 [Paisley,
Renfrew.] If a moth persists in flying
round about you it is said to be a sign
that you are about to receive a letter.
According to the size of the moth will
the letter be. **1922** [Taunton, Som.]
Sign that a letter is on its way to you if
a moth flies round you. **1922** [Bradford-
on-Tone, Som.] If a mother [*sic*] flies
round the lamp once, it is a sign of a
postcard, twice a letter, three a parcel.
1954 Girl, 14 [Newbridge, Monmouth.]
If a moth flies around the light at night
a letter will come in the morning.

MOTH/BUTTERFLY omen of death

*c.*1828 Calvert MS, Pickering, Yorks. (G.
HOME *Evolution of an English Town* 215)
It be an ill sign to the dying if a dark
winged moth make at the bed light and
fall at it, but it be a good sign should a
light winged one come thrice and go its
way unharmed. Even if it do fall at it, it
doth say nothing worse than the ailing
one will soon die but that the death shall
be the freeing of a happy soul. **1893**
QUILLER-COUCH *Green Bays* 'The White
Moth' [Cornwall] The light above the
poet's head Streamed on the pane and
on the cloth, And twice and thrice there
buffeted On the black pane a white-
winged moth: 'Twas Annie's soul that
beat outside And 'Open! open! open!'
cried. **1899** *Newcastle Weekly Chronicle*
11 Feb. 7 [Jesmond] Clothes moths are
called 'ghosts', and every time one is
killed there is a danger of injuring a

relative. **1909** M. TREVELYAN *Folk-Lore of Wales* 209. When they [witches] die their souls pass out of their bodies in the shape of a 'great big moth'. Ibid. 307. Aged people used to say that white moths were the souls of the dead, who in this form were allowed to take farewell of the earth. **1922** [Trowbridge, Wilts.] A large butterfly or moth seen in the room of a dying person is sometimes believed to be the soul quitting the body. It must not be killed. **1973** J. WYATT *Shining Levels* 153. In Lancashire big moths are known as 'night buggerts' . . I remember being told as a boy that if one came into the house there would be a death in the family.

Cf. SNAIL = spirit of the dead.

MOTHER-DIE

1878 *Folk-Lore Record* 158–9. In Cumberland, about Cockermouth for example, the red campion (*Lychnis diurna*) is called 'mother-dee', and there is a superstition among the children that if they pluck it some misfortune will happen to their parents. 'Death-come-quickly', a West Country name for the herb robert . . seems to point to some similar belief. **1886** R. HOLLAND *Cheshire Glossary. Mother dee*, the plant *Torilis anthriscus* [hedge parsley]. **1899** W. DICKINSON *Dialect of Cumberland* 203. A superstition exists that should a child pick the flowers of the red species [of campion] it will soon lose its father by death; if the white flowers be taken, then the mother will die. Hence the plants have been given the names of 'Fadder dees' and 'mudder dees'. **1922** A. S. MACMILLAN *Popular Names of Flowers. Mother Die*. A Bridgwater school-mistress gives me this as a local name for the 'Wild Parsley'. **1946** Girl, 12 [Watford, Herts.] Pick meadow sweet—break your mother's heart. **1957** UTTLEY *Year in the Country* IX. Several of the umbelliferae were debarred from entering our dwellings. These were called 'Mother-die' . . My little Cheshire maid . . was so upset when I brought some white flowers of the kex [hemlock] into the kitchen that she burst into tears. She implored me to throw them away. My mother or her mother would surely die very soon if I kept them.

1981 Woman, 63 [Coreley, Shrops.] Of course you never picked rose bay willow herb, that was a 'mother-die' flower. We used to call it 'mother-die'—means you think your mother would die. I wouldn't have picked them for anything. **1981** Woman, *c*.20 [Scarborough, Yorks.] Hogweed (also called 'mother-die'). If you bring it into the house, your mother will die. Source of knowledge—my mother.

MOTHER-OF-PEARL

c.**1945** Girl, 8 [Devon] Mother-of-pearl shells are lucky objects. **1975** Woman, 46 [Sudbury, Suffolk] When my man-friend gave me a birthday present of a mother-of-pearl cigarette lighter, he said, 'As long as you have that you'll be lucky, that pearly shell is very lucky.'

MOURNING CLOTHES unlucky to lovers

1925 D. R. PHILLIPS *Vale of Neath* 598. Young people who fall in love while dressed in mourning clothes are doomed never to marry.

Cf. GRAVE, meeting/parting at.

MOURNING NOTEPAPER etc. unlucky to keep

1880 *N & Q* 6th ser. I 55 [Ireland] It is very unlucky to keep black-edged paper in the house. Ibid. 212. A Cambridgeshire servant informs me that her mother enjoined her not to lay by some crape . . as if she did she would 'never have no more luck'. **1980** N. WOLLASTON *Man on the Icecap* 12. It was thought unlucky to keep a piece of crêpe in the house, so that at each death more supplies of it had to be bought.

MOUSE cures bed-wetting

AD 77 PLINY *Natural History* XXX XLVII (1856, V 466) Incontinence of urine in infants is checked by giving them boiled mice with their food. **1579** LUPTON *Thousand Notable Things* I § 40. A flayne Mouse rosted, or made in powder, & drunk at one tyme, doeth perfectly helpe such as can not holde or keepe their water: especially, if it be used three dayes in this order. This is verie true and often proued. **1607** TOPSELL *Foure-footed Beastes* 515. Sodden mice are exceeding good to restraine and hold in the vrine

of infants or children being too abound-
ant, if they be giuen in some pleasant
or delightsome drinke. **1661** R. LOVELL
Panzoologicomineralogia. Mouse .. Being
boiled and eaten they help childrens
pissing in bed. **1850** *N & Q* 1st ser. II
435. An old woman lately recommended
an occasional roast mouse as a certain
cure for a little boy who wetted his bed
at night. Her own son, she said, got over
this weakness by eating three roast mice.
I am told that the Faculty employ this
remedy, and that it has been prescribed
in the Oxford Infirmary. **1923** [Som-
erset] Mouse pie is a cure for a certain
childish ailment. **1943** F. THOMPSON
Candleford Green 119. Fried mice were
still given to children as a specific for
bed-wetting. The children were told the
mouse was meat and ate it without
protest, but with what result is
unknown. **1984** Man, 70. When I was
young in Lincolnshire, when children
used to wet their beds their parents gave
them roast mouse, fur and all, on toast
to eat, and that stopped the bed-wetting.

MOUSE cures whooping cough

1850 *N & Q* 1st ser. II 510. I was
stopping about three years ago in the
house of a gentleman whose cook had
been in the service of a quondam Canon
of Christ Church, who averred that she
roasted mice to cure her master's children. **1935** *I Walked by Night* (ed. L.
Rider Haggard, 16 n.) The local doctor
when he first came to South Norfolk was
completely at sea when informed that a
small patient continued to whoop .. in
spite of the fact that he had 'had his
mouse and all'. **1942** *Sussex County
Mag.* 53. 'Get three field mice, flaw them,
dry them, and roast one of them, and
let the party afflicted eat it; dry the other
two in the oven until they crumble to a
powder, and put a little of the powder
in what the patient drinks at night and
in the morning.' This is what Richard
Stapley, who lived at Twineham during
the reign of Queen Anne, advised as a
cure for the whooping cough. **1952** G.
RAVERAT *Period Piece* 57. And even in
the year 1947 *a fried mouse* was most
earnestly recommended to me. **1952**
Sunday Times 2 Mar. 8. A woman
brought her young son to see me for

some trivial ailment. She told me that
some weeks previously he had had
whooping cough, and that on the advice
of an old woman of the village she
caught a mouse in her kitchen, cooked
it and gave it to the boy, whereupon the
cough disappeared. **1986** *Daily Telegraph* 20 Jan. 8. Recent concern over
the number of whooping cough cases
this winter has reminded me of the time
when, as headmaster of a small village
school in East Suffolk, I sent home a boy
who was obviously suffering from this
disease. After two days absence he was
back, fit and well. He told me that he
had been sent straight to bed while his
father went out to fetch a fieldmouse.
This his mother had skinned and fried.
After his bed had been covered with
brown paper he had to eat the mouse.
He continued: 'I was terrribly sick, sir,
but in the morning I was all right again,'
and so he was. He stayed at school and
no one else caught the disease. I later
learned that his mother had been cured
in similar fashion when she was a small
child. Is there a lesson there for the
medical profession?

MOUSE, other cures using

AD **77** PLINY *Natural History* XXX xxx
(1856, V 454) In the treatment of quartain fevers .. amulets .. for instance ..
the muzzle of a mouse and the tips of
his ears, wrapped in red cloth. **1613**
BEAUMONT & FLETCHER *Knight of the Burning Pestle* III II. 'Faith, and those chilblains are a foul trouble. Mistress
Merrythought, when your youth comes
home, let him rub all the soles of his
feet, and his heels, and his ancles, with
a mouse-skin. **1909** M. TREVELYAN *Folk-
Lore of Wales* 319. Mouse-pie was to be
eaten by children who stammered. **1958**
[Heydon, Norfolk] A dead mouse rubbed
on the cheek will stop toothache.

mouse: also see 'RAT' AND 'MOUSE' taboo
words; RATS AND MICE.

MUGWORT against evil

late **10th c.** MS Harl. 585 (G. STORMS
Anglo-Saxon Magic 187) Remember,
Mugwort, what you made known .. You
were called Una, the oldest of herbs, you
have power against three and against

thirty, you have power against poison and against infection, you have power against the loathsome foe roving through the land. *c.*1050 MS Cotton Vitell. C. iii (COCKAYNE *Leechdoms* I 103) In the house in which he .. hath it within, it .. turneth away the evil eyes of evil men. 1578 DODOENS *Herball* 17. Whosoeuer shall carrie this herbe about him (as Plinie saieth) no venemous beast, or any like thing shall hurte him, and if he trauell vpon the way, he shall not be weary. 1845 J. TRAIN *Isle of Man* II 120 [St John's Eve] They gathered *barran fealoin* or mugwort as a preventive against the influence of witchcraft.

MUGWORT against tiredness on journeys

c. AD 950 MS Reg. 12 D. xvii (COCKAYNE *Leechdoms* II 155) For mickle travelling over land, lest he tire, let him take mugwort to him in hand, or put it into his shoe, least he should weary .. When he will pluck it .. let him say .. 'I will take thee, artemisia, lest I be weary on the way .. ' Sign it with the sign of the cross, when thou pullest it up. 1586 T. HILL *Natural and Artificial Conclusions* D7. That a man shall not be weary of going. Drinke the iuice of Mugworte, and beare the hearbe about him, with the hearbe Pedilion and Crowfoote. 1656 W. COLES *Art of Simpling* XXIII 68. If a Footman take Mugwort and put into his Shoos in the Morning, he may goe forty Miles before Noon and not be weary.

MUGWORT cures female ailments

1694 J. PECHEY *Compleat Herbal.* Mugwort, in Latin *Artemisia* .. 'Tis frequently used by Women, inwardly and outwardly, in all Diseases peculiar to them. 1842 R. CHAMBERS *Popular Rhymes of Scotland* 34. The funeral of a young woman who had died of consumption was passing along the high-road, on the margin of the Firth of Clyde, above Port-Glasgow, when a mermaid raised her head from the water, and .. uttered these words: 'If they wad drink nettles in March, And eat muggons in May, Sae mony braw maidens Wadna gang to the clay.' Muggons or mugwort .. [is] a favourite prescription for consumption amongst the common people. 1946 UTTLEY *Country Things* X [Cromford,

Derbys. *c.*1900] Wild wormwood, called mugwort, grows in the Buckinghamshire lanes and the silvery-grey leaves when rubbed in the hands give a pleasing smell. Perhaps the gipsies who live in the beech-woods near cure their ailments with it. 'If they'd eat nettles in March And mugwort in May, So many fine maids Wouldn't go to the clay.'

Cf. MAY a dangerous month.

mugwort: also see 'COAL' magic.

MURDER: blood indelible

10th c. BC Genesis 4: 9–10. The Lord said unto Cain .. the voice of thy brother's blood crieth unto me from the ground.   AD 731 BEDE *Historia Ecclesiastica* I XIX (tr. Sherley-Price) Germanus took away with him a portion of earth from the place where the blessed martyr's blood had been shed. This earth was seen to have retained the martyr's blood, which had reddened the shrine where his persecutor had grown pale with fear. As a result of these events, a great number of people were converted to our Lord on the same day. 1605 SHAKESPEARE *Macbeth* v i. Out damned spot: out I say .. What will these hands ne're be cleane? 1858 DENHAM *North of England* (1895, 60) Throughout the North .. stones are believed to have absorbed a portion of the blood of the murdered .. and it is said that nothing can remove it. 1890 J. C. COX *Derbyshire Annals* I 43. In the gaol at Derby, the block upon which these men [three leaders of a peasant uprising] were beheaded is still preserved .. The old warder drew our attention to the fact that, though the cell .. is very dry, the wood is still in places damp. It is a gaol tradition that the blood of these unhappy men, shed in 1817, has never and will never dry. 1894 N & Q 8th ser. V 85 [Lincoln Cathedral] There was death by violence, and the marks of a man's life-blood, which will never wash out, are still visible, although it is said they 'look a deal liker furniture polish than real blood'. 1910 *Folklore* 348 [Co. Clare] The house [where murder had been committed] brought misfortune on anyone who rented it .. One room was fastened up with iron clamps .. because its floor was soaked in ineffaceable blood.

MURDER: corpse bleeds

AD 972 (G. BUCHANAN *History of Scotland*, 1762, I 247) The executioners of the bloody fact were sent out of the way by Donald [who had planned the assassination], because there is an opinion, received from our ancestors, which as yet obtains amongst the vulgar, That blood will issue from a dead body many days after the party's being murdered, if the murderer be present, just as if the fact had been newly committed. 1579 LUPTON *Thousand Notable Things* X § 7. It is a manifest thing, and proued by dayly experience, that the bodies of them y[t] be murthred, when they be founde, if any of theyr kynred be then present, or the party or partyes that kylled or murthered them .. immediatly bloud wil burst forth suddenly, either out of the wound, or nose, or out of some other part of theyr body. 1584 SCOT *Discoverie of Witchcraft* XIII IX. I have heard by credible report .. that the wound of a man murthered reneweth bleeding; at the presence of a deere freend, or of a mortall enimie. *c.*1591 SHAKESPEARE *Richard the Third* I ii. See, see dead Henries wounds, Open their congeal'd mouthes, and bleed afresh. 1597 JAMES VI *Daemonologie* 136. In a secret murther, if the dead Carkasse be at any time thereafter handled by the Murtherer, it will gush out of blood, as if the Blood were crying to Heaven for revenge of the murtherer. 1627 BACON *Sylva Sylvarum* § 958. It is an usuall Observation, that if the Body of One Murthered, be brought before the Murtherer, the Wounds will bleed a-fresh .. It may be, that this participateth of a Miracle, by Gods Just Judgement, who usually bringeth Murders to Light: But if it be Naturall, it must be referred to Imagination. 1629 Witchcraft trial (*County Folk-Lore* III, ed. N. W. Thomas, 104) [Orkney] The cors having lyin ane guid space and not having bled any, Immediatlie bled mutch bluid as ane suir token that ye was the author of his death. *ante* 1672 BROWNE Commonplace book (*Works*, ed. Wilkin, 1852, III 352) Who can think that when 'tis said that the blood of Abel cried unto heaven, Abel fell a bleeding

at the sight of Cain, according to the observation of men slain to bleed at the presence of the murderer? 1691 *Athenian Mercury* 26 May. Quest. Why a dead corps should bleed when toucht by its Murtherer? Answ .. some Courts of Justice admit this Tryal of bleeding as a Proof to good purpose. 1787 GROSE *Provincial Glossary* Superstitions 59. The wounds of a murdered person will bleed afresh, on the body being touched, ever so lightly .. by the murderer. 1858 DENHAM *North of England* (1895, 49) The vulgar superstition .. of the corpse of a murdered person bleeding on being touched by the murderer, still pervades to a great extent. 1864 DICKENS *Our Mutual Friend* I III. Pity there was not a word of truth in that superstition about bodies bleeding when touched by the hand of the right person; you never got a sign out of bodies. 1910 *N & Q* 11th ser. II 498. An Irish peasant whom I met a few days ago told me that it is a very common belief in his country that the corpse bleeds afresh at the touch of the murderer. He said that he himself was fully convinced of its truth. 1978 N. MAYES *Nature Notebook* 88 [Cornwall] Where murder was concerned, folk believed that the body would bleed if the murderer touched it.

MURDER: earth remains barren

10th c. BC Genesis 4: 9–12. And the Lord said unto Cain .. And now art thou cursed from the earth, which hath opened her mouth to receive thy brother's blood from thy hand: When thou tillest the ground, it shall not from henceforth yield unto thee her strength. 1656 EVELYN *Diary* 8 July. To Colchester, a fine town, but now wretchedly demolished by the late siege .. It has six gates .. and some handsome churches. But what was showed us as a kind of miracle, at the outside of the Castle, [was] the wall where Sir Charles Lucas and Sir George Lisle, those valiant and noble persons .. were barbarously shot, murdered by Treton in cold blood, after surrendering .. The place was bare of grass for a large space, all the rest of it abounding with herbage. 1849 SOUTHEY *Common-Place Book* 2nd ser. 20–1. It would be worth your while to take a view of those wonderful marks of the Lord's hatred to duelling, called *The Brothers' Steps* .. The awful tradition concerning them is, that two brothers quarrelled about a worthless woman, and fought .. The prints of their feet are about the depth of three inches, and nothing will vegetate, so much as to disfigure them .. Each unhappy combatant wounded the other to death. And a bank on which the first .. died, retains the form of his agonizing couch, by the curse of barrenness, while grass flourishes all about it. **1851** DENHAM *North of England* (1895, 23–4) The popular belief of the earth no more growing grass where a foul and bloody murder has been committed is very common .. The exact spot whereon tradition says 'poor old Willy Robinson' was murdered on Holwick Fell, in Teesdale, in 1794, is positively asserted by a living eye witness to have remained a barren waste ever since. **1876** S. BARING-GOULD *Vicar of Morwenstow* 114. They turfed the grave, and they sowed the grass twenty times over, but 'twas all of no use, nothing would grow—he was hanged unjustly. **1878** *Folk-Lore Record* 17. We believe in Sussex that a curse lights upon the ground on which human blood has been shed .. that it will remain barren for ever. **1880** W. SIKES *British Goblins* 332 [Montgomery Castle] In his last speech .. he said .. 'I venture to assert that as I am innocent of the crime for which I suffer, the grass, for one generation at least, will not cover my grave.' For thirty years thereafter, the grave was grassless .. Then a sacrilegious hand planted the spot with turf; but it withered as if blasted by lightning; and the grave is still grassless. **1978** A. WRIGHT *Holderness* 17 [E. Yorks.] The piece of garden where nothing will grow is infertile because someone died a violent death on that spot at some time in the past.

MURDER: grass grows greener

AD **731** BEDE *Historia Ecclesiastica* III x (tr. Sherley-Price) Noticing that one spot was more green and beautiful than the rest of the field, he came to the wise conclusion .. that some person of greater sanctity than anyone else in the army

had been slain there. **1883** BURNE *Shropshire* 240 n. At a village near Eccleshall, in the year 1876, an old woman was found drowned in her well. A patch of peculiarly green turf long marked the spot where her body was laid on being taken out of the water, and the neighbours, who had suspicions of foul play, pointed to this as confirmation of their opinion.

MUSHROOM, looking at

1846 *Athenaeum* 17 Oct. 1069. We have, in Ireland, a strange idea that mushrooms never grow after they have been seen. **1911** *Folklore* 456 [Co. Clare] If you see a 'button mushroom' you should pluck it, as 'it will never grow any more once it is looked at.'

MYRTLE = love, peace, and happiness

1590 COUNTESS OF PEMBROKE *Antonie* 68. Since then the Baies so well thy forehead knewe To Venus mirtles yeelded haue their place. **1665** R. RAPIN *De Hortorum* (tr. Gardiner, 1706, 96) Venus this charming Green alone prefers, And this of all the verdant Kind is hers. Hence the Bride's Brow with Purple [myrtle] Wreaths is grac't, When the long wish'd for Night is come at last. **1671** *Westminster Drollery* 31. Beneath a Mirtle shade, Which none but Love for happy Lovers made. **1784** COWPER *Task* II ll. 229–30. Who sell their laurel for a myrtle wreath, And love when they should fight. **1884** R. FOLKARD *Plant Lore* 454–6. The Myrtle .. was, both by the Greeks and Romans, considered symbolic of love, and was appropriately consecrated to Venus .. around whose temples groves of Myrtle were planted .. The Roman bridegroom decked himself with Myrtle on his bridal day .. With the Jews, the Myrtle is a symbol of peace, and .. Jewish maidens were wont to be decked with a bridal wreath of Myrtle but this wreath was never worn by a widow, or by divorced women. **1909** M. TREVELYAN *Folk-Lore of Wales* 105–6. Myrtle is much esteemed .. they say if it grows on each side of the door the blessings of love and peace will never depart from the house. To destroy a myrtle is to 'kill' both love and peace. Sprigs of myrtle .. were not only used by brides, but .. worn in the girdle of young girls when going to their first Holy Communion. Sprigs were also placed in cradles to make babies happy. **1973** *Times* 15 Nov. 6 [Princess Anne's] bouquet, by Moyses Stevens, was all white and made with simple flowers: roses, lilies-of-the-valley and a sprig of myrtle from a bush at Osborne grown from the myrtle in Queen Victoria's wedding bouquet. **1973** *Woman*, 81 [Colchester, Essex] The piece of myrtle in a bride's bouquet, which is planted in the garden of her new home, is a very old custom. I have known of it all my life.

MYRTLE: divination

1839 *Everlasting Fortune-Teller* 8–9. Take from your bosom a sprig of myrtle, which you must have worn there all day, and fold it up in a piece of tissue paper, then light up a small chaffing dish of charcoal, and on it each maiden throw nine hairs from her head, [etc.]. Go to bed while the clock is striking twelve, place the myrtle exactly under your head, and you will be sure to dream of your future husband. **1895** S. O. ADDY

Household Tales 85. On Midsummer Eve let a girl take a sprig of myrtle and lay it in her Prayer Book upon the words of the marriage service, 'Wilt thou have this man to be thy wedded husband?' Then let her close the book, put it under her pillow, and sleep upon it. If her lover will marry her the myrtle will be gone in the morning.

MYRTLE, growing

1848 *Athenaeum* 5 Feb. 142 [Somerset] Speaking to a person the other day of the difficulty which I had always found in getting a slip of myrtle to grow, she directly accounted for my failure by observing that perhaps I had not spread the tail (or skirt) of my dress and *looked proud* during the time when I was planting it .. I find it is a popular belief that unless a slip of myrtle is so planted it will never take root. **1853** *N & Q* 1st ser. VII 152 [Somerset] Flowering myrtle [is] the luckiest plant to have in your window. Water it every morning, and be proud of it. **1887** *Folk-Lore Record* 216 [Cornwall] Only old maids can rear a myrtle.

N

NAILS driven in: cure

1579 LUPTON *Thousand Notable Things* II § 56. Three nayles made in the vigyll of the Natiuitie of Saint John Baptist, called Midsomer Eve, and driuen in so deepe that they can not be seene, in the place where the party doth fall that hath the falling sycknes, and naming the sayde parties name whyle it is a doing .. doth awaye the disease quyte. **1911** *Folklore* 56 [Co. Clare] I have noticed .. skulls with nails driven into them .. At Killone .. I was told by old people .. that this was secretly done by persons suffering from chronic headache.

Cf. TREE, disease transferred to.

NAILS left in floor

1923 [Taunton, Som.] It is not lucky to leave old tacks in the flooring before putting down new carpets or oilcloths.

NAILS: specks on finger nails: divination

1612 JONSON *Alchemist* I iii. H'is a fortunate fellow, that I am sure on .. And, in right way to'ward riches .. I knew't, by certaine spotts .. on the nayle of his Mercurial [little] finger. **1650** BROWNE *Vulgar Errors* V XII. We are not .. ready to admit sundry divinations vulgarly raised upon them .. that spots in the top of the nails doe signify things past; in the middle, things present; and at the bottome, events to come. That white specks presage our felicity, blue ones our misfortunes. **1708** *British Apollo* 7 Apr. Q. What is the Cause of little white Spots, which sometimes grow under the Nails of the Fingers? And what is the reason they say they are Gifts? **1755** *Connoisseur* 13 Mar. A white speck upon the nails made them as sure of a gift as if they had it already in their pockets. **1823** MOOR *Suffolk Words. Gifts.* The white spots on .. nails. Many of them give rise to certain hopes or expectations. **1829** BROCKETT *North Country Words. Gifts*, white specks on the finger nails— presages of felicity, not always realized. **1853** BAKER *Northamptonshire. Gifts.*

White specks on the finger nails; which .. are superstitiously believed to predict certain events, as indicated in the following couplet, which is repeated whilst touching the thumb and each finger in succession: 'A gift, a friend, a foe, A love to come, a journey to go.' Sometimes the augury is expressed in general positive terms; as, 'A gift on the thumb is sure to come: A gift on the finger is sure to linger.' **1882** *People's Friend* 8 Nov. 711. Those small white marks that come upon her nails when she happens to bruise them .. prognosticate presents; 'A present on the thumb is sure to come, A present on the finger is sure to linger.' **1899** *Newcastle Weekly Chronicle* 4 Feb. 7 [Jesmond] The white spots on the nails of your fingers indicate presents to be received when they reach the margin. **1950** Woman, *c.*50 [Forfar, Angus] A friend, a foe, A gift, a beau, A journey to go. **1969** Woman, 43 [Liss, Hants.] We always say you have a present when they [white specks] grow to the top.

Cf. HAND, yellow spots on.

NAILS AND HAIR: cures/spells

AD 77 PLINY *Natural History* XXVIII XXIII (1856, V 307) Take the parings of the toe-nails and finger-nails of a sick person, and mix them up with wax .. then stick this wax, before sunrise, upon the door of another person .. How highly criminal, if they really do thus transfer diseases from one person to another! **1579** LUPTON *Thousand Notable Things* IV § 46. Pare the nailes of one that hath the quarteyn ague, which being put into a lynnen cloath, and so tyed about the necke of a quicke Eele, and the same Eele put into the water: thereby the ague wyll be dryuen away. **1590** Witchcraft trial (R. PITCAIRN *Criminal Trials in Scotland* I pt. 2 201) Ye ar indytit and accusit .. that ye .. send for .. the notorious .. Wiches .. qua poillit [cut] the hair of Robert Munro, your brotheris heid, and plait the naillis of his fingeris, and tais, socht be their devilisch meanis to haif cureit him of his seiknes. **1590** SHAKE-SPEARE *Comedie of Errors* IV iii. Some divils aske but the parings of ones naile. **1673** *Depositions, York Castle* 21 Apr. (1861, 201) His mother Margaret Humble then lyeing not well, Isabell Thompson tooke some of her haire to medicine her. **1775** L. SHAW *History of Moray* 248. In Hectick and Consumptive Diseases, they [the Highlanders] pare the nails of the fingers and toes of the Patient, put these parings into a rag cut from his clothes, then wave their hand with the rag thrice round his head crying Deas-Soil, after which they bury the rag in some unknown place. I have seen this done. **1830** SCOTT *Demonology* 339–40. In a remote part of the Highlands, an ignorant and malignant woman .. meditated the destruction of her neighbour's property, by placing in a cowhouse .. a pot of baked clay, containing locks of hair, parings of nails, and other trumpery .. The formidable spell is now in my possession. **1866** HENDERSON *Northern Counties* 111. In Sunderland .. the crown of the head is shaved and the hair hung upon a bush .. in firm belief that the birds carrying it away to their nests will carry away the cough along with it. **1874** *Journal Anthropological Inst.* III 269 [Banff.] The parings of the nails and the cuttings of the hair, and ashes from the four corners of the hearth, were put three times round the *crook* [iron pot-hook]. A cock was buried alive along with these on the spot where the victim was first seized with the disease [epilepsy]. **1879** J. NAPIER *West of Scotland* 39. It was not necessary that the person possessed of the evil eye, and desirous of inflicting evil upon the child, should see the child. All that was necessary was that the person .. should get possession of something which belonged to the child, such as a fragment of clothing, a toy, hair, or nail parings. **1887** 'SPERANZA' WILDE *Superstitions of Ireland* II 101. Clippings of the hair and nails of a child tied up in a linen cloth and placed under the cradle will cure convulsions.

Also see index: body, parts or products of: may be used in cures/divination/spells.

NAILS AND HAIR, cutting: at sea

c. AD **65** PETRONIUS *Satyricon* CIV–V (tr. Mitchell) They say that no living man has a right to cut his nails or his hair on a ship; that is, unless the wind is blowing a hurricane .. Lichas went white with anger .. 'You don't say that somebody aboard this ship has had a crop .. Haul the villains aft at once, so that I may know whose blood I must shed to purify the vessel!' **1790** GROSE *Provincial Glossary* Superstitions 48. A principal passenger shaving himself at sea will procure a favourable change of wind.

NAILS AND HAIR, cutting: baby's

1851 *N&Q* 1st ser. IV 54. I always, when I cut the nails of my children, let the cuttings fall on the open Bible, that they may grow up to be honest. **1851** DENHAM *North of England* (1895, 24) If the finger or toe nails of an infant are cut previous to .. the age of xii months, it will prove a thief in mature age. Mothers and nurses beware; and mind you continue the good old-fashioned custom of 'nibbling'. **1865** *N&Q* 3rd ser. VIII 146 [nr. Bath, Som.] The poor woman assigned as a reason for their propensity to pilfer and steal, that their mothers must have cut their nails before they were a year old. She always bit her babies' nails. **1870** *N&Q* 4th ser. VI 204. In Cornwall and Devonshire .. children's nails are bitten instead of cut, to avert ill-luck. I have just been talking with a group of eight working men, from twenty-five to sixty years of age .. and found them all perfectly familiar with the usage. One of them added in confidence that, in his opinion, 'no one with a grain of common sense thought it anything but nonsense.' **1879** J. NAPIER *West of Scotland* 39. It was not considered lucky to pare the nails of a child under one year old, and when the operation was performed the mother was careful to collect every scrap .. and burn them. It was considered a great offence for any person, other than the mother or near relation, in whom every confidence could be placed, to cut a baby's nails; if some forward officious person should do this, and baby afterwards be taken ill, this would give rise to grave suspicions

of evil influence being at work. **1882**
N & Q 6th ser. VI 249 [nr. Lower
Heyford, Oxon.] A gardener's wife having an infant in arms with long hair . .
was desirous of improving the child's
appearance by cropping it, but as it is
said to be unlucky to cut a baby's hair,
she gained the desired end by biting it
off with her teeth. **1900** *N & Q* 9th ser.
V 375. Several people have told my wife
that 'if you cut the baby's nails he will
grow up a thief.' It appears that the
mother must bite them herself until the
child is short-coated. The nurse refused
to use the scissors until told she must
do so. Ibid. VI 173. As to the superstition
about 'cutting babies' nails', I have
lately had practical proofs of its prevalence among London people, who are
presumed to be less credulous in this
regard than provincials. **1973** *Trans.
Devon. Ass.* 213 [Bickleigh] Referring to
the custom of chewing young babies'
nails, a member said this holds good for
the first six months: if you use scissors
you risk making the baby 'light-fingered'
in later life. But Shillingford W.I. reckon
you must keep on chewing for a whole
year. **1982** Woman, 81 [London] A
baby's nails should not be cut before it
is one year old—otherwise it will steal.
1986 Woman, 62 [Liss, Hants.] I've
always heard that a baby's nails should
be nibbled by its mother, and not cut—
but that is so that they shouldn't have
sharp edges, or the baby would scratch
its face.

Cf. KNIFE taboo to pregnant woman.

NAILS AND HAIR, cutting: day important
c. AD **390** AUSONIUS *Eclogues* XXVI line
1. Clip nails on Tuesday, beards on
Wednesday, hair on Friday. **1594** NASHE
Terrors of the Night E4. I haue heard
aged mumping beldams . . bid yong folks
beware on what day they par'd their
nayles. **1603** W. PERKINS *Works* 39. It
is . . good lucke . . to pare our nayles on
some one day of the weeke. **1672**
BROWNE *Vulgar Errors* V XXII § 10. The
set and statary times of paring of nails,
and cutting of hair, is thought by many a
point of consideration; which is perhaps
but the continuation of an ancient superstition. For piaculous it was unto the
Romans to pare their nails upon the

Nundinae, observed every ninth day;
and was also feared by others in certain
daies of the week.

**NAILS AND HAIR, cutting: lucky on
Monday**
1596 LODGE *Wit's Miserie* (*Works*, 1887,
IV 12) He will not . . paire his nailes
while [until] Munday, to be fortunat in
his loue. **1688** AUBREY *Remaines* (1881,
196) Many are superstitious not to pare
their nailes (I thinke) on a monday.
1808 DUNCUMB *Herefordshire* I 208. Nails
of Fingers are supposed to be cut with
more propriety on Monday mornings
than on any other day. **1878** *Folk-Lore
Record* 8 [Fittleworth, Sussex] Should
you cut your nails on a Monday morning
without thinking of a fox's tail, you will
have a present made to you. **1887**
Folk-Lore Record 213 [Cornwall] Cut
them on Monday, before your fast you
break, And you'll have a present in less
than a week. **1952** *Woman's Illustrated*
23 Aug. 1 [Wolverhampton, Staffs.] Always remember to cut your nails before
twelve o'clock on Monday mornings.
When I do it, I always get a present . .
during the week—maybe a really big
one, or only a bar of chocolate.

NAILS AND HAIR, cutting: rhyme
1830 FORBY *East Anglia* 410–11. If we
are to believe an old rhyming saw . .
every day of the week is endowed with
its . . peculiar virtue . . Cut them on
Monday, you cut them for health; Cut
them on Tuesday, you cut them for
wealth; Cut them on Wednesday, you
cut them for news; Cut them on Thursday, a new pair of shoes; Cut them on
Friday, you cut them for sorrow; Cut
them on Saturday, see your true-love
to-morrow. Cut them on Sunday, the
devil will be with you all the week. **1848**
Athenaeum 142 [Herts.] Cut your nails
on a Sunday, you cut them for evil, For
all the next week you'll be ruled by the
devil. **1965** *Woman's Realm* 23 Oct. 6
[Chilham, Kent] Cut them on Monday,
cut them for health. Cut them on Tuesday, cut them for wealth. Cut them on
Wednesday, cut them for a letter. Cut
them on Thursday, cut for something
better. Cut them on Friday, you cut for
a wife. Cut them on Saturday, cut for

long life. Cut them on Sunday, you cut them for evil, For all of that week you'll be ruled by the devil. **1986** *Mirror* 3 July 24. The true saying for cutting nails .. was told me by my mother, who was born in the Fens before the century began: 'Cut on a Monday, cut for a gift. Cut on Tuesday, cut for thrift. Cut on Wednesday, cut for news. Cut on Thursday for a new pair of shoes. Cut on Friday cut for sorrow. Cut on Saturday, see your lover tomorrow. Cut your nails on Sunday, cut them for evil; All the week round you'll go to the devil.'

Cf. WEDDING, day of: divination rhyme.

NAILS AND HAIR, cutting: unlucky on Friday and Sunday

1621 T. MIDDLETON *Any Thing for a Quiet Life* IV. MRIS CHAMLET. What a curst wretch was I to pare my Nails to day, a Fryday too; I lookt for some mischief. **1678** RAY *Proverbs* 294. Friday's hair and Sunday's horn goes to the dule [devil] on Monday morn. **1695** CONGREVE *Love for Love* III iv. Thou'rt .. as melancholly as if thou hadst .. par'd thy Nails of a Sunday. **1824** T. HUDSON *Comic Songs* 9. But alas! who can look into fate's book of laws? Mr Lowe would have married Miss Cundy; He lost her! he lost her! and only because, He cut his toe nails on a Sunday! **1851** *N & Q* 1st ser. III 55 [Lancs.] Cutting or paring the nails of the hands or feet on a Friday or Sunday, is very unlucky. Ibid. 462 [Devon] Friday cut hair, Sunday cut horn, Better that man had never been born. **1882** *Folk-Lore Record* 81 [Co. Wexford] In cases of people losing cattle, no man in the owner's house shaves on a Sunday. **1889** *Folklore* 24. A lodging-house keeper in Macclesfield [Cheshire] had quite recently taken a girl from the workhouse as a servant. She caught her cutting her finger-nails one Friday; and, snatching the scissors from her shouted, 'Is that what I had you from the workhouse for; to cut your nails on a Friday, and bring bad luck to this house?' **1895** J. HARDY *Denham Tracts* 343 [Northumb.] Friday's hair and Sunday's horn, Ye'll meet the Black Man on Monanday morn. **1912** LEATHER *Herefordshire* 88. He that on the Sabbath Morn Cutteth either hair or horn Will

rue the day that he was born. **1954** Girl, 14 [Letham, Angus] It is unlucky to cut your nails on Sunday, and you will have sorrow if you cut your nails on Friday. **1975** C. COOKSON *Our Kate* 245 [Tyneside] As for cutting your nails on a Friday .. unthinking I took the scissors to them one Friday; I had just cut the thumbnail when the scissors went flying across the kitchen. **1983** Girl, 14 [Maldon, Essex] Just when I'd got the nail scissors out mum said 'What are you doing?' and I remembered the superstition 'Never cut your nails on a Friday or Sunday.'

NAMES, divination with

1755 *Connoisseur* 20 Feb. [St Valentine's Eve] We .. wrote our lovers' names upon bits of paper, and rolled them up in clay, and put them into water: and the first that rose up, was to be our valentine. **1776** STRUTT *Manners and Customs* III 180 [Midsummer Eve] Writing their names on a paper at twelve o'clock, burning the same, then carefully gathering up the ashes, and laying them close wrapp'd in a paper, upon a looking-glass, marked with a cross, under their pillows [to dream of lover]. **1832** HONE *Year Book* 8 Oct. A girl, on going to bed, is to write the alphabet on small pieces of paper, and put them into a bason of water with the letters downward; and it is said that in the morning she will find the first letter of her husband's name turned up, and the others as they were left. **1849** HALLIWELL *Popular Rhymes* 225. On a Friday morning, fasting, write on four pieces of paper the names of three persons you like best, and also the name of Death, fold them up, wear them in your bosom all day, and at night shake them up in your left shoe, going to bed backwards; take out one with your left hand, and the other with your right, throw three of them out of the shoe, and in the morning whichever name remains in the shoe is that of your future husband. If Death is left, you will not marry any of them. **1883** BURNE *Shropshire* 179. Write the initials of six young men of your acquaintance on six pieces of paper; in each paper wrap a bit of bread pinched into a soft mass. Put the six packets in a glass of water, and he whose name first rises to the surface will be the successful suitor. 1898 BLAKEBOROUGH *Yorkshire Customs* 79. There may be, here and there, a maiden left who, before retiring to rest, splits a holly twig and binds within the split part a small slip of paper, upon which she has written, with her heart's blood, the name of him she loveth best, and who places the same under her pillow, so that she may dream her fate.

NAMES, magical: married couple with same surname before marriage

1852 *N & Q* 1st ser. VI 71. The remedy [for whooping cough] consists in a plain currant cake, to be eaten by the afflicted child, the main virtue of which cake is, however, in its being made by a woman whose maiden name was the same as that of the man she married. 1867 *Gents Mag.* pt. 1 741 n. [Suffolk] An old woman, who boasts that she was 'born on the same day, and baptized on the same day, and married on the same day as her husband', and who did not change her name by marriage .. was much plagued afterwards by patients who came to consult her. 1887 'SPER-ANZA' WILDE *Superstitions of Ireland* II 92. A griddle cake made of meal, to be given, not bought or made; but a cake *given* of love or of charity, not for begging; a cake given freely, with a prayer and a blessing; and from the breakfast of a man and his wife who had the same name before marriage; this is the cure [for whooping cough]. 1893 *Folklore* 350 [Co. Donegal] For Erysipelas. Rub the part affected with butter made from the milk of the cows belonging to a married couple, who both had the same name before their marriage. [Or send their] son or daughter to the bog for bog-water, and bathe the part affected. 1912 LEATHER *Herefordshire* 83. A so-called infallible remedy [for whooping cough] is a piece of bread, received from a woman who has successively married two men of the same name being of different families.

NAMES, magical: married couple with special Christian names

1852 *N & Q* 1st ser. V 148. In Cornwall,

a slice of bread and butter or cake belonging to a married couple whose Christian names are John and Joan, is considered an efficacious remedy [for whooping cough] though of course not always readily found. 1883 W. G. BLACK *Folk-Medicine* 90. To the names of Joseph and Mary .. English peasants still bear special reverence when they send a child suffering from whooping-cough to a house where these are the names of the master and mistress. The child must ask [for] bread and butter. Joseph must cut the bread, and Mary butter it. 1932 WOMEN'S INSTITUTE *Worcestershire Book* 38. If a married couple with the names of Joseph and Mary, are told of anyone's illness, and send the sufferer a little gift, which must not be asked for, the gift will cure the sick person of any disease. Years ago a farmer and his wife bore these names at Abbot's Morton, and people came to them from miles around.

NAMES, magical: three with same initial

1877 *N & Q* 5th ser. VIII 182. At Youlgreave, Derbyshire, they say it is a sign of a wedding if three women with the same initial sit at the table together. 1923 [Ruishton, Som.] If three unmarried people who have the same Christian names meet at table, one of them will be married within the year.

NAMING baby after dead sibling

1858 DENHAM *North of England* (1895, 48) Many look upon it as a wicked piece of presumption .. to endeavour to perpetuate a .. baptismal name, when death has snatched away its first bearer. And should the 2nd, 3rd, or 4th of that name survive (.. rarely the case) he is sure to prove a 'graceless prodigal'. 1873 HARLAND & WILKINSON *Lancashire Legends* 220. Many persons consider it sinful to give a child the same Christian name as another who has died: one female remarked .. 'id wor gooin ageean God Omeety as hed ta'en t'other away.' 1886 M. LINSKILL *Haven under the Hill* XII [Whitby, Yorks.] John wants to have this one called Elsie, and I've given way to please him; but I don't like callin' a livin' child after a dead one; it's never lucky. 1888 *N & Q* 7th ser. VI 498. There was a very common feeling in the eastern counties against naming children after brothers or sisters .. who had previously died. My father was the third of his name in his family, and it was considered a proof of strong-mindedness in his parents going against the superstition. **1910** *N & Q* 11th ser. I 79. In Ireland it is regarded as a certain way of bringing .. early death to 'call a child for' a dead brother or sister. 'The name is already registered in heaven' used to be the solemn reply to the .. question 'Why is it so unlucky?' and fifty years ago both Catholics and Protestants shared in this 'freit'. **1923** [Ruishton, Som.] It is unlucky to christen a baby with the name of an older brother or sister who has died. **1956** Woman, *c*.55 [Eastbourne, Sussex] It is unlucky to name a later child in the family after one that has died. It will not live. **1986** *Sunday Telegraph* 23 Feb. 11 [Huddersfield, Yorks.] Criticism of the late Ben Hardwick's parents' choice of 'Ben' as a name for their prospective baby reveals a sad relic of illogical superstition .. If the late Ben does have a brother, the latter will surely be proud to bear a name so widely associated with courage and goodwill.

NAMING baby after living parent

1586 CAMDEN *Britannia* (tr. Gibson, II 378) [Limerick, Eire *c*.1566] It is looked upon as foreboding a speedy death to the parent, or other of the family then living, to give his or their names to any of the children; and therefore they avoid it as unlawful. When the father dies, the son takes his name, lest it should be forgotten. **1874** *N & Q* 5th ser. II 184 [Tiverton, Devon] If the son is called by the same name as the father, one of the two will be killed, or die suddenly. **1895** S. O. ADDY *Household Tales* 97. If the first children of a family take the names of their parents they will die before the parents.

NAMING baby after saint

1853 *N & Q* 1st ser. VII 128. In many country parishes the child is invariably called by the name of the saint on whose day he happens to have been born .. I lately baptized a child myself by the name of Benjamin Simon Jude. Sub-

sequently, on expressing some surprise at the strange conjunction, I was informed that he was born on the festival of SS. Simon and Jude, and that it was always very unlucky to take the day from a child. **1896** *N & Q* 8th ser. IX 5. A working man in Yorkshire was advised to call his child Giles or Michael, because of the dates of his birth and baptism; but he declined, saying 'the saints would want it' if he made it their namesake.

NAMING baby before christening

1853 *N & Q* 1st ser. VIII 468. In Scotland there is a superstition that it is unlucky to tell the name of infants before they are christened. **1878** *Folk-Lore Record* 11 [Fittleworth, Sussex] It is unlucky to divulge a child's intended name before its Baptism. **1879** J. NAPIER *West of Scotland* 31. When, before the child had been christened, any one asked the name of the baby, the answer generally was, 'It has not been out yet.' **1883** BURNE *Shropshire* 286–7. The Colliery people .. consider it extremely unlucky to mention a child's name before it is christened. The father always 'picks' the name, and often tells it to no one till he whispers it to the godmother on the christening day. **1898** BLAKE-BOROUGH *Yorkshire Customs* 151. When a child was born, and it proved unhealthy .. it was generally supposed some evil-disposed person must have pricked its name with pins on a pincushion. **1923** [Somerset] Never tell anyone a baby's 'chrissen' name until after its christening or the piskeys may hear it and harm the child.

Cf. BABY, referring to: before birth.

NAMING cows

1887 F. T. HAVERGAL *Herefordshire Words* 40. In the neighbourhood of Ledbury it is said that cows are never named until after the arrival of the first calf.

Cf. BOAT, new: naming before launching.

NEEDLE, breaking

1910 *Folklore* 89 [Argyll.] A needle broken in two while sewing brings good fortune to the wearer of the article sewn; if in three pieces an offer of marriage.

1923 [Taunton, Som.] For a needle to break when machining signifies that you will receive pleasant news from a distant relative regarding a small legacy. **1964** Girl, 15 [Woodford Green, Essex] If you break a needle you should bury it in the ground otherwise it would bring bad luck.

NEEDLE, dropping

1957 Girl, 12 [Langholm, Dumfries.] If you drop a needle and don't pick it up you will have bad luck. **1957** Girl, 11 [Swansea, Glam.] If you drop a needle and it lands with its head uppermost good times are coming.

Cf. PIN, finding; PIN points towards one.

NETTLE STING, charm for

*c.*1374 CHAUCER *Troilus* IV ll. 460–1. But kanstow playen raket, to and fro, Nettle in, dok out, now this, now that? **1546** HEYWOOD *Proverbs* (ed. Habernicht, 140) For in one state they twayne could not yet settyll. But waueryng as the wynde, in docke out nettyll. **1771** *North Briton* 20 Apr. 722. Hence even children, when they have stung their hands with nettle-tops, rub it [dock leaf] on the part affected, and, by singing the charm, 'In dock, out nettle', are immediately cured. **1820** R. WILBRAHAM *Cheshire Glossary* 26. Upon a person being stung with a nettle, the immediate application of the dock leaf to the aggrieved part, repeating the precise words, 'In dock out nettle', three times, (which constitute the charm) will mitigate the pain. **1842** AKERMAN *Wiltshire Glossary* 15. When a child is stung he plucks a dock-leaf, and, laying it on the part affected, sings—'Out 'ettle, In Dock, Dock zhall ha' A new smock; 'Ettle zhant Ha' narrun!' **1851** *N & Q* 1st ser. III 133 [Northumb.] The patient, while rubbing in the dock-juice, should keep repeating, 'Nettle in, dock out, Dock in, nettle out, Nettle in, dock out, Dock rub nettle out.' **1866** HENDERSON *Northern Counties* 17. Docken in and nettle out, Like an awde wife's dish-clout. **1895** S. O. ADDY *Household Tales* 92. Dock, go in, nettle, go out; Dock shall have a white smock, And nettle shall go without. **1957** Girl, 11 [Penrith, Cumb.] Dockin go in, nettle go out, Dockin go in and pull nettle out.

Cf. BURN OR SCALD, charm for.

NEW MOON and money

1507 *Gospelles of Dystaues* pt. 2 XIV. He that hathe no moneye in his purse ought to absteyne hym from lokynge on the newe mone, or elles he shall haue but lytell all alonge that mone. **1732** DEFOE *Memoirs of Mr Campbell* 62. To see a New Moon the first Time after her Change [and] to be without Gold in your Pocket at that Time, is of very bad Consequence. **1778** S. O'HALLORAN *History of Ireland* 113. Some remains of this worship [of the moon] may be traced, even at this day; as particularly borrowing, if they should not have it about them, a piece of silver on the first sight of a new moon, as an omen of plenty during the month .. saying 'as you have found us in peace and prosperity, so leave us in grace and mercy.' **1808** JAMIESON *Scottish Dict. Mone* .. Some deem it very unlucky to see the new moon for the first time, without having *silver* in one's pocket. Copper is of no avail. **1822** *Gents Mag.* pt. 2 603 [Forest of Dean, Glos.] At the new Moon they turn the money in their pockets, thinking it to be lucky. **1826** R. CHAMBERS *Popular Rhymes* 285 n. It is well known to be a prevalent custom or *freit*, on first seeing the new moon, to turn money in the pocket. **1826** HONE *Every-Day Book* I 26 Nov. [Newcastle upon Tyne] New moon customs, such as .. feeling for money in your pocket, to see if you will have a lucky month. **1827** Ibid. II 8 Jan. On the first day of the first new moon of the new year .. put your hand in your pocket, shut your eyes, and turn the smallest piece of *silver* coin .. upside down in your said pocket. This will ensure you .. throughout the whole year that 'summum bonum' of earthly wishes, a pocket never empty. **1838** A. E. BRAY *Devonshire* II 294. It is a prudent thing to shake your pockets .. likewise .. to pull out your money and let the new moon shine upon it. **1851** DENHAM *North of England* (1895, 240) I once saw an aged matron turn her apron to the new moon to ensure good luck for the ensuing month. **1882** *People's Friend*

13 Sept. 580. In the Highlands they believe that it is very lucky to have something in the hand on the first sight of the new moon. **1891** J. C. ATKINSON *Moorland Parish* 71. I was always in the habit of turning all the money I had in my pocket on the first sight of the new moon, until [a] friend of mine completely disillusioned me by remarking .. 'Why, what's the use of doing that? You always see the moon through glass,' in allusion to my invariably-worn spectacles. **1899** *Newcastle Weekly Chronicle* 4 Feb. 7 [Jesmond] If money be turned when the new moon is first seen, it will increase before the moon goes out. **1923** [Cosham, Hants.] Silver counted over when the new moon arrives will increase. **1957** Girl, 12 [Penrith, Cumb.] It is lucky if you see a new moon to turn your money over and make a wish and turn round three times and you should be standing on soft ground. **1984** Woman, 62 [Headley Down, Hants.] My mother always insisted on turning over her money at new moon.

NEW MOON, bowing etc. to

4th c. BC Job 31: 26–7. If I beheld .. the moon walking in brightness, And my heart hath been secretly enticed, or my mouth hath kissed my hand. **19** BC HORACE *Odes* (tr. Dunsany, III XXIII) If, Phidyle, thou lift thy hands To heaven when the moon is new .. Thy vine no pestilence shall know, Nor shall thy harvest blighted be. **1586** CAMDEN *Britannia* (tr. Gibson, II 380) [Limerick, Eire, *c*.1566] Whether or no they [the Irish] worship the moon, I know not; but, when they first see her after the change, they commonly bow the knee, and say the Lord's prayer; and, near the wane, address themselves to her with a loud voice after this manner, 'Leave us as well as thou foundest us.' **1686–7** AUBREY *Remaines* (1881, 37, 36) When I was a Boy before ye Civill warres 'twas the fashion to kisse ones hand, and make a legge [bow] .. In Scotland, (especially among the Highlanders) the woemen doe make a Curtsey to the New-moon. **1770–1804** C. VALLANCEY *De Rebus Hibernicis* XIII 91. The vulgar Irish at this day retain an adoration to the New Moon, crossing themselves and saying,

'May thou leave us as safe as thou found us.' **1812** J. BRADY *Clavis Calendaria* I 111. In some parts of England it is customary to bless the New Moon, while in Scotland they not only do so, but usually drop a courtsey at the same time. **1839** S. LOVER *Songs* 15 [Ireland] Bright was the omen, for love follow'd soon, And I bless'd as I gazed on the lovely new Moon. **1883** BURNE *Shropshire* 256–7. I was myself accustomed in my childhood, on the first sight of the new moon, to curtsey three times, turning round between each curtsey, in the expectation of receiving a present before the next new moon. **1889** *Scotsman* 27 Dec. 7. A few years ago, in Ayrshire, our housekeeper used to make obeisance several times to the new moon when first she observed it .. When I asked her why .. she replied that by doing so she would be sure to get a present before the next new moon appeared. **1899** J. SHAW *Schoolmaster* 30 [Tynron, Dumfries.] Turn your apron three times and look at the new moon, wishing for a present, and a present shall arrive to you ere it wain. **1946** [Lincs.] On seeing the new moon this rhyme is said three times, with a curtsey for each time: 'Welcome, new moon, I hope you bring me a present very soon.' **1973** Woman, 67 [Bradford, Yorks.] My only, and lifelong, superstition is that when I see the new moon .. I bow to it three times saying 'Lady Moon I hail thee.' **1984** Woman, 86. My father always went outside and bowed nine times to the new moon—he was quite unselfconscious about it. That was when we were living in Tunbridge Wells about 1903.

NEW MOON: divination

1685 *Mother Bunch's Closet* (1885, 19) The first change of the new moon in the new year; the first time you see, hold your hands across, saying this three times, 'New moon, new moon, I pray thee Tell me this night who my true love will be.' Then go to bed without speaking any more that night and you will certainly dream of the person you are to marry. **1686–7** AUBREY *Remaines* (1881, 36) Our English woemen in the Country doe retaine (some of them) a touch of this Gentilisme still, e.g. 'All haile to thee Moon, all haile to thee! I prithee good Moon, declare to me, This night, who my Husband must be.' This they doe sitting astride on a gate or stile the first evening the new moon appeares. **1805** J. NICOL *Poems* I 31–2 & n. As soon as you see the first new moon of the new year, go to a place where you can set your feet upon a stone naturally fixed in the earth, and lean your back against a tree; and in that posture hail, or address, the moon in the words . . 'O, new Moon, I hail thee! And gif I'm ere to marry man, Or man to marry me, His face turn'd this way fast's ye can, Let me my true love see, This blessed night!' If ever you are to be married, you will see an apparition exactly resembling the future partner of your joys and sorrows. **1824** MACTAGGART *Gallovidian Encyclopedia* 211. Young women . . sally out to the green braes in bevies, and there each pull a handful of grass, saying . . 'New moon, true moon, tell me if ye can, Gif I hae here a hair like the hair o' my gude man' . . and if a hair be found . . the colour of that hair determines the hue of the expected *gude man*'s. **1826** R. CHAMBERS *Popular Rhymes of Scotland* 287. The young women of the Lowlands, on first observing the new moon, exclaim as follows: 'New mune, true mune, Tell unto me, If —, my true-love, He will marry me. If he marry me in haste, Let me see his bonnie face; If he marry me betide, Let me see his bonnie side; Gin he marry na me ava, Turn his back and gae awa.' **1831** HONE *Year Book* 29 Feb. In Berkshire, at the first appearance of a new moon, maidens go into the fields, and, while they look at it, say, 'New moon, new moon, I hail thee! By all the virtue in thy body, Grant this night that I may see He who my true love is to be.' They then return home, firmly believing that before morning their future husbands will appear to them in their dreams. **1851** *N & Q* 1st ser. IV 99 [Devon] When you first see the new moon in the new year, take your stocking off from one foot, and run to the next stile; when you get there, between the great toe and the next, you will find a hair, which will be the colour of your lover's . . When you see the new

moon after midsummer, go to a stile, turn your back to it, and say: 'All hail, new moon, all hail to thee! I prithee, good moon, reveal to me This night who shall my true love be: Who he is, and what he wears, And what he does all months and years.' **1912** LEATHER *Herefordshire* 64. The first new moon in the year was formerly greeted by curious maidens in this fashion: 'All hail to thee, moon, all hail to thee, I prithee kind moon, reveal to me, Him who is my life partner to be.'

Cf. CUCKOO, first: divination with hair.

NEW MOON: divination by diffusion

1817 G. YOUNG *History of Whitby* II 881. The worshipper holds up a new black silk handkerchief between her and the [first new moon of the year] and . . pours out her prayer: 'New moon! new moon! I hail thee, This night my truelove for to see: Not in his best nor worst array, But his apparel for every day; That I to-morrow may him ken, From among all other men' [and] retires to bed backwards, without speaking a word to any one. **1826** HONE *Every-Day Book* I 26 Nov. [Newcastle upon Tyne] New moon customs, such as looking through a new silk handkerchief to ascertain the number of your lovers. **1853** *N & Q* 1st ser. VII 153 [Leics.] You may see as many new moons at once through a silk handkerchief as there are years before you will marry. Ibid. 177 [Yorks.] I was amused one evening to find the servants of the house excusing themselves for being out of the way when the bell rang, on the plea that they had been 'hailing the first new moon of the new year'. This . . was effected . . by means of a looking-glass, in which the first sight of the moon was to be had, and the object to be gained was the important secret as to how many years would elapse before the marriage of the observers. If one moon was seen in the glass, one year; if two, two years; and so on. In the case in question, the maid and the boy saw only one moon a-piece. **1883** BURNE *Shropshire* 257. There is . . an often-practised form of divination by the first new moon in the year . . by looking at it through a new silk handkerchief . . As many moons as the inquirer sees, so many years will it be before he or she is married. At Worthen the same thing has been practised by counting the reflections in a pail of water, and at Pulverbatch we hear of the reflections in a looking-glass cunningly placed. **1895** J. HARDY *Denham Tracts* II 280–1. On the appearance of the first moon after the new year, look through a black silk handkerchief unwashed [i.e. new] at it, and you will see by the number of moons visible the number of years that will elapse before you are married. **1978** A. WRIGHT *Holderness* [Yorks.] 12–13. A favourite way to find out when you would be married was to wait until full moon, go to a stream, or really any water would do, and hold a silk square over the water with the moon behind you. The silk diffused the light, and several little moon reflections appeared in the water. The number of moons denoted the number of months you must wait before becoming a bride.

Cf. MIRROR: divination: to see future spouse.

NEW MOON first mentioned by woman

1808 JAMIESON *Scottish Dict. Mone* .. With regard to the first mention of the term Moon by a woman, after this planet has made her first appearance .. some to prevent the dangerous consequences .. will anxiously inquire at any male, 'What is that which shines so clearly?'

Cf. MONDAY first mentioned by woman.

NEW MOON grants wishes

*c.*1050 MS Cotton Tib. A. iii (COCKAYNE *Leechdoms* III 177) When the moon is one day old, go to the king, and ask what you will, he shall give it. **1852** *N & Q* 1st ser. V 485–6. If, when you look at the new moon for the first time, you think of one particular thing which you greatly desire to have, or to have accomplished, your wishes .. will be realised before the close of the year.

NEW MOON, kissing under

1826 HONE *Every-Day Book* I 26 Nov. [Newcastle upon Tyne] The person, in a company, male or female, who first gets a glimpse of the new moon, immediately kisses some member of the company, and pronounces with a triumphant chuckle, 'Aha! Jane .. there's a pair of gloves for me!' **1861** C. C. ROBINSON *Dialect of Leeds* 301. Upon seeing the new moon, if a young man kisses the first fair maid he meets with, and without speaking before, he will receive a gift (which would be, no doubt, a pretty smart box on the ear). In the same way, if a maiden kisses the first young man she meets on this occasion, without speaking, *she* will receive a gift (which, we have little doubt of, would be a return of the compliment, if she was any bit like). **1883** BURNE *Shropshire* 257. It is lucky to get some one to kiss you when you see the new moon.

Cf. MISTLETOE, kissing under.

NEW MOON seen on left/right

1732 DEFOE *Memoirs of Mr Campbell* 62. To see a New Moon the first Time after her Change, on the Right-hand, or directly before you, betokens the utmost good Fortune that Month; as to have her on your Left, or behind you, so that in turning your Head back you happen to see her, foreshews the worst. **1830** FORBY *East Anglia* 415. It is lucky to see the moon over the left shoulder. **1838** A. E. BRAY *Devonshire* II 294. It is fortunate .. to see the new moon on the right hand. **1862** *N & Q* 3rd ser. II 485 [Oxon.] [She] could never be induced to look at the moon .. over her left shoulder. **1914** *Folklore* 247 [Jersey] Unlucky to see the moon [for the first time] over the left shoulder. **1923** [Stocklands, Som.] It is considered unlucky to see the new moon over the left, but lucky to see it over the right shoulder. **1953** *Folklore* 299 [Westmorland] You should try to see it over your left shoulder.

NEW MOON seen through glass (or tree)

1830 M. R. MITFORD *Our Village* IV 301. I had rather not see the new moon through a window. **1855** *Gents Mag.* pt. 2 384–5 [Shrops./Worcs.] To see the first of the new moon through a window, or glass of any sort, is unlucky. **1865** R. HUNT *West of England* 2nd ser. 236. To see the new moon for the first time, through glass, is unlucky; you may be certain that you will break glass before that moon is out. I have known persons whose attention has been called to a clear new moon, hesitate. 'Hev I seed her out a' doors afore?' if not, they will go into the open air, and if possible show the moon 'a piece of gold', or, at all events, turn their money. 1873 N & Q 4th ser. XI 141 [Kent/Sussex] Seeing the [new] moon through the boughs of a tree is supposed to be very unlucky, but the evil influence is broken by taking a piece of money from your pocket, and spitting on each side of the coin; a thing I have often seen done, as it is a ceremony which must be immediately performed. 1873 N & Q 4th ser. XI 53. A Rutland woman told me she had just been out of doors to look at the new moon .. 'because, if you look at it through glass, you will be sure to break glass.' And this saying had come true the previous month 'for I looked at the new moon through a window, and broke a tumbler that same evening.' 1878 A. MACGREGOR Brahan Seer 130 'Superstitions of Highlanders'. It is unlucky to catch sight of the new moon through a window. 1881 Punch 1 Jan. 310. It is most unlucky to look at the new moon through glass. Want of attention to this maxim is the reason why so many people who wear spectacles are short-sighted. 1895 S. O. ADDY Household Tales 59. It is often said of a man who is unlucky .. that he has looked at the new moon through a glass. The first new moon should be seen in the open air. 1914 Folklore 247 [Jersey] 'If the moon you see Neither through glass or tree, It shall be a lucky moon to thee.' 1952 Girl, 11 [Kirkcaldy, Fife] To look at the new moon through glass brings bad luck. 1963 Hereford Times 2 Aug. 10. Once Mollie saw the new moon through trees, but oh, dear, what a fuss there was! She was sure it boded some ill. 1984 Woman, 44 [Ruthin, Denbighs.] Don't look at a new moon through glass, it's bad luck.

Cf. FUNERAL seen through window or doorway.

new moon: also see index: first things/occasions; moon sacred and powerful.

NEW YEAR activities set precedent
c. AD 10 OVID Fasti I ll. 166–70 (1851,

tr. Riley, 14) Lest the whole year might be spent in idleness from a bad precedent .. each person takes a slight taste of his calling [on New Year's Day], but does no more than merely give evidence of his .. employment. 1831 HONE Year Book 29 Feb. Upon new year's day if you have not something new on, you will not get much all the year. 1858 G. P. W. SCOTT Tenby 8 [Pembroke.] To rise early on New Year's morning was generally considered 'lucky', on the principle that, as the year was begun, so it would be continued day by day till the next New Year's morn .. The good and thrifty housewife managed that a fresh loaf should be brought into the house [that morning]. 1891 A. W. MOORE Isle of Man 103. Nothing should be lent on this day, as anyone who does so will be lending all the year. In old times when tinder and flint were used, no one would lend them on this day. 1957 UTTLEY Year in the Country 11 [Cromford, Derbys., c.1900] 'If you cry on New Year's Day, you will cry all through the year,' said other children. 1960 Folklore 254 [Hartlepool, Co. Durham] There is still a widespread superstition that whatever one is doing when the bells ring in the New Year, one will be doing the same most of the year. Few people, therefore, go to bed, for obvious reasons, and even the old and infirm prefer to sit up. 1986 Man, 35 [Paisley, Renfrew.] All my grandmother's prejudices are kept up. You're strictly not allowed to break anything on New Year's Day.

NEW YEAR and house/home: bringing in the new year and expelling the old
1857 N & Q 2nd ser. III 343 [Worcs.] If the carol-singer who first comes to your door on New Year's morning is admitted at the front door, conducted all through the house, and let out at the back door, you will have good luck all through the year. 1875 N & Q 5th ser. III 6 [Worcester] The orthodox plan was for man or boy to enter at the back-door, go through the rooms on the ground floor, and go out by the front door. 1923 [West Malling, Kent] The first man to pass through the door on New Year's Day must be dark. He must ring the front door bell and the door must be

opened to him. He must walk through the house and out of the back door without holding conversation with anyone. **1953** Boy, c.15 [Rogart, Sutherland] On the stroke of twelve [on New Year's Eve] every door in the house has to be opened, to allow the old year to go out. A visitor arriving before twelve must not leave by the same door through which he came. **1953** Girl, c.14 [Brora, Sutherland] A few minutes before twelve o'clock all the doors of the house are opened to allow the spirit of the old year to depart. **1954** *Daily Telegraph* 31 Dec. 6 [Bradford, Yorks.] When I was a boy a few years before the war .. we 'let in' the New Year. One male member of the household crept out of the front door just before midnight, took a piece of coal from the outhouse, and having knocked loudly on the back door, shouted through the keyhole: 'I wish you a Happy New Year; please, may I come in?' The door was then opened by the lady of the house, who received the coal and a seasonable salutation from the visitor. He was given refreshment .. and left by the other door. **1954** Girl, 14 [Tunstall, Staffs.] A tall dark-haired man, with a glass of wine in one hand and a lump of coal in the other, must go out of one door, walk all the way round the house and in at the other door, to bring in the New Year. **1987** Man, 33 [Birmingham, Warwicks.] When it is exactly midnight, someone has to be outside the house, and they must go in by the back door and out through the front door, and round, and in again by the back. The family have done that as far back as I can remember.

Cf. DEATH: opening locks/doors and windows frees spirit; FIRST-FOOT at New Year/Christmas.

NEW YEAR and house/home: bringing things in before taking out

1849 BRAND *Antiquities* I 15. On New Year's Day they have a superstition in Lincoln and its neighbourhood, that it is unlucky to take anything out of the house before they have brought something in: hence you will see, on the morning of that day, the individual members of a family taking a small piece of coal, or any inconsiderable thing in

fact, into the house, for the purpose of preventing the misfortunes which would otherwise attach to them; and the rustics have a rhyme in which this belief is expressed: 'Take out, then take in, Bad luck will begin; Take in, then take out, Good luck comes about.' **1906** *N & Q* 10th ser. V 45. I remember as a lad in Derbyshire how .. when the old year passed away, the door was thrown open, and the head of the house stood bareheaded in the doorway, the rest of us standing behind, while one of the men .. brought something over the doorstone, before anything or anyone went out. Ibid. [Worksop, Notts.] The servant of one of my neighbours tied a piece of string to a lump of coal .. laid the string across the doorsill, and .. as the clock .. was striking .. twelve, opened the door. As soon as the last stroke sounded, she pulled the .. coal into the house, in this way making sure that something came into the house before anything was taken out. **1923** [Somerset] Allow nothing to go out of the house on New Year's Day until something has been brought in. **1955** *Trans. Devon. Ass.* 355 [Ottery St Mary] On New Year's Eve take a *silver* coin (usually a 3d piece), a piece of bread and a piece of coal, and place them outside on a window-sill or in the porch. Bring them in again next morning, and they will bring in luck. **1982** Woman, c.25 [E. Yorks.] Yes, we take out (each one of us) a piece of coal, a piece of bread and some coins. We take these out in the old year and we bring them in in the New Year. The coal is wrapped in cooking foil and the old piece we burn on New Year's Eve, or rather, after midnight New Year's Day.

Cf. FIRST-FOOT at New Year/Christmas.

NEW YEAR and house/home: nothing to be taken out

1664 PEPYS *Diary* 30 Dec. Made an end of looking over all my papers .. and taking everything out of my chamber to have all made clean. **1817** G. YOUNG *History of Whitby* II 880. On both days [Christmas and New Year's] it is exceedingly dangerous to give a light out of the house, nay, even to throw out the ashes, or sweep out the dust! **1845** J. TRAIN *Isle of Man* II 115. It would be considered a most grievous affair were the person who first sweeps the floor on New Year's morning to brush the dust to the door, instead of beginning at the door, and sweeping the dust to the hearth, as the good fortune of the family individually would thereby be considered to be swept from the house for that year. **1849** BRAND *Antiquities* I 20. Never throw any ashes, or dirty water, or any article, however worthless, out of your house on this day. It betokens ill-luck; but you may bring in as many honestly gotten goods as you can procure. **1866** HENDERSON *Northern Counties* 57. When a boy .. I remember accompanying the mistress of the house to her kitchen .. when she called together all her servants, and warned them, under pain of dismissal, not to allow anything to be carried out of the house on the following day .. All ashes, dish-washings, or potato-parings, and so forth, were retained in the house till the next day. **1883** BURNE *Shropshire* 402. [They] are to this day careful, after the ordinary custom in their youth, not to throw ashes out of the house on Christmas Day, 'for fear of throwing them in our Saviour's face', and one of them will not throw them away on Easter Day either, for the same reason. **1923** [Somerset] On New Year's Day, do not throw any ashes outside. **1955** *Trans. Devon. Ass.* 356. You must not sweep out of the door on New Year's Day. **1960** *Folklore* 254. At Hartlepool [Co. Durham] it was, and still is, customary to sweep the hearth and 'rake out the ashes' before 12.0 midnight on New Year's Eve. On no account must the old year's ashes be carried into the new. **1969** A. BARTON *Penny World* 145 [Tyneside, 1926] It was New Year's Eve .. we could hear people dumping their ashes and other refuse in bins and middens, for the tradition was still strong .. that nothing was ever taken out on New Year's Day. **1982** Woman, c.50 [Middlesborough, Teesside] Never throw anything out on New Year's Day.

Cf. DIRT lucky; NEW YEAR, working at.

NEW YEAR and money

c. AD 10 OVID *Fasti* I ll. 185–9. What means .. the white honey given as a present [and] the little coin also given [at New Year]? **1664** PEPYS *Diary* 30 Dec. Made an end of looking over all my papers .. After dinner forth to several places to pay away money, to clear myself in all the world. **1806** DOUGLAS *Poems* 68 [Fife] Granny, gie's oor hansel, It's new-year's day. **1822** *Time's Telescope* 3. In Cornwall, it is considered very unlucky to pay money on the first day of January, as it ensures a continuance of disbursements throughout the year. **1866** HENDERSON *Northern Counties* 55. Empty pockets or an empty cupboard .. portend a year of poverty. **1882** *N & Q* 6th ser. VI 186 [Worcs./Herefords.] 'Pay away money on New Year's Day, And all the year through you'll have money to pay.' **1923** [Wellington, Som.] If you have some money in your pocket on New Year's Day you will be lucky all the year. **1957** Woman, 20 [Shepshed, Leics.] If one had any unpaid bills on New Year's Day it was said one would owe money for the rest of the year. **1959** *Trans. Devon. Ass.* 202. My mother, who died in 1928 .. always put a small sum of money (it was always silver) out of the house before midnight and took it in again at some time on New Year's Day .. She said she had always been told that it would insure that during the year just beginning her 'incomings' would be more than her outgoings'. **1960** *Folklore* 254 [Hartlepool, Co. Durham] Money was placed in the pockets of even the smallest child to ensure money for the family during the ensuing year. **1971** Man, c.45 [London] If you are a Scot you think it right to settle all outstanding bills by December 31st. **1986** Man, 35 [Paisley, Renfrew.] I take it you know you should turn your money at Hogmanay.

Cf. HANDSEL MONDAY; MONEY, having in purse etc.; NEW MOON and money.

NEW YEAR din

late **18th c.** J. RAMSAY (*Scotland in the Eighteenth Century* II 438) [St Kilda, Outer Hebrides] It is usual for the cowherd and the young people to meet together [on New Year's Eve] and one of them is covered with a cow's hide. The rest of the company are provided with staves, to the end of which bits of raw hide are tied. The person covered with the hide runs thrice round the dwelling-house, *deiseil* . . the rest pursue, beating the hide with their staves, and crying . . 'Let us raise the noise louder and louder; let us beat the hide.' **1837** D. WALKER *Games and Sports* 204. In London at the present time, New-year's Eve is remarked . . by the horrid clang of the bells which bursts forth from every church tower and steeple at the hour of twelve. **1873** R. GRANT *Reminiscences* 26 [Bradford Abbas, Dorset] A custom obtains in this, as in most other parishes: viz., to ring out the old, and ring in the new, year, at midnight. **1878** A. MACGREGOR *Brahan Seer* 137 'Superstitions of Highlanders'. On New-Year's Eve, they surrounded each other's houses, carrying dried cow-hides, and beating them with sticks, thrashing the walls with clubs, all the time crying, shouting, and repeating rhymes . . as a charm against fairies, demons, and spirits of every order. **1957** L. PAUL *Boy Down Kitchener Street* 20 [SE London, *c.*1912] Armed with dustbin lids, bread bins, milk cans . . we would add our din to that of the neighbours, and beat the New Year in . . We could hear the hooters of trains and factory whistles. From the Surrey Docks came the trumpeting . . of the herd of ships penned among the streets there. **1957** J. KIRKUP *Only Child* 177 [South Shields, Co. Durham, 1929] Everyone sits up until after midnight 'to see the New Year in'. I was generally too sleepy to stay awake . . I would go to bed, to be awakened at midnight by bells and ma-roons and hooting sirens and laughter and shouting and singing in the streets. **1957** *Shrewsbury Chronicle* 4 Jan. 6. British Railways ushered in 1957 with an impressive salute of engine whistles . . When steam is replaced by Diesel Power . . there may be a few peeps . . but nothing to replace the full-throated chorus that greets the new year at present. **1961** *Glasgow Herald* 3 Jan. 7. At Kingsbarns, Fife . . one barrel of an old fowling piece was fired to send out the old year and another barrel to wel-come in the new—a ceremony they have performed for more than 100 years.

Cf. MAY DAY/EVE din; NEW YEAR and house/home: bringing in the new year and expelling the old.

NEW YEAR: speaking of the old year
1640 G. HERBERT *Outlandish Proverbs* (ed. Hutchinson, no. 297) Say no ill of the yeere, till it be past. **1732** T. FULLER *Gnomologia* no. 4071. Say not ill of the Year, till it be past.
Cf. CORPSE: speaking of the dead.

NEW YEAR, working at
1764 BURN *Poor Laws* 13. No labourer . . shall take any hire . . for the evens of feasts. **1838** A. E. BRAY *Devonshire* III 255–6. They [miners] regard it . . as unlucky to work either on Midsummer, or New-year's day, or on the eves of these days; and, formerly, all red-letter days were deemed sacred. **1877** *N & Q* 5th ser. VII 26 [Devon] It is . . unlucky to wash clothes on a New Year's Day . . it is thought that a member of the family will be . . washed out of existence before the close of the current year. Some persons will not even permit any dishes, plates, &c. to be cleaned on the first day of the year. **1887** F. T. HAVERGAL *Herefordshire Words* 47. It was the cus-tom to strike work on the afternoon of New Year's Day . . No one was permitted to carry on his avocations then. He who persisted was forcibly interfered with by the idle gang, raised on a ladder, and carried . . into the nearest public-house, where release was obtained by spending a fine of sixpence on drink. **1923** [Som-erset] Wash on New Year's Day, Wash one of the family away. **1934** *Times* 22 May 15. In South Worcestershire there is a saying that if you wash on New Year's Day you wash for the dead— i.e. that the person whose clothes are washed will die before the year is out. **1969** Gipsy woman [Liss, Hants.] Us people we won't do the wash on New Year's Day—I never have done it, and I never will. **1986** *Trans. Devon. Ass.* 246 [Broad Clyst] The jobbing gardener comes to my neighbour on Tuesdays and likes to have a nice leisurely talk. In an effort to get away on that particular Tuesday without causing umbrage, she said: 'Well, I must get along now. I've got some jerseys to wash.' 'That's right,

Ma'am,' was the rejoinder, 'Y'u du en now. For anything washed on a New Year's Day, y'u wash a member of the family away—they du say.'

New Year: also see index: first things/occasions; May-time.

NIGHTINGALE sings before cuckoo
ante **1391** or **1410** J. [OR T.] CLANVOWE *Cuckow and Nightingale* ll. 47–50. I thought how lovers had a tokeninge, And among hem it was a commune tale, That it were good to here the nightingale, Rather than the leud cuckow singe. **1629** MILTON 'To the Nightingale' ll. 5–7. O nightingale . . Thy liquid notes . . First heard before the shallow cuckoo's bill Portend success in love. **1923** [Somerset] To hear the nightingale before the cuckoo foretells success in love.

NORTH door of church
1891 DYER *Church-Lore* 116. Occasionally in old churches, as in that of Wellcombe [Devon], over against the font, and in the northern wall, there is an entrance named the 'Devil's Door'. This was thrown open at every baptism for the escape, as it was commonly said, of the fiend, while at other times it was carefully shut. **1984** C. F. TEBBUTT *Huntingdonshire Folklore* 12. At St Neots access to the church during weddings was by the south door only, use of the north door (the Devil's door) being considered unlucky.
Cf. BURIAL on north side of churchyard.

NORTH, first facing towards
1898 *N & Q* 9th ser. I 87. It is considered of great importance that the first journey of the new year should be towards the north. This year one member of the family who had to go down to the west on New Year's Day was obliged . . to go to Euston Square and travel to Willesden and back before taking the other journey. **1932** C. IGGLESDEN *Those Superstitions* 154. A girl is running the risk of spinsterhood should she fail to look towards the north when she goes out of the house before breakfast.

NOSE bleeds: ill omen
1180 NIGEL DE LONGCHAMPS *Mirror for Fools* (tr. Mozley, 96) From his left nostril gushing Cold blood in short and sudden spurt came rushing Then said Burnel [the donkey]: 'Something unfavourable This sign portends to me. I mind me well This happened on the night before that day when the four mastiffs bit my tail away.' **1587** GIFFORD *Subtill Practises of Devilles* C2. Heauvy newes is brought unto some, that her father, or her mother, or her brother is dead: I did euen looke for such a matter (saith she) for my nose this day did sodainly break forth a bleeding. **1594** NASHE *Terrors of the Night* D–D1. Wonderfull superstitious are such persons in obseruing euerie accident that befalls them . . if his nose bleede, some of his kinsfolkes is dead. *c.***1614** WEBSTER *Duchess of Malfi* II ii. How superstitiously we mind our evils! . . The . . Bleeding at nose [is] of powre To daunt whole man in us. **1620** MELTON *Astrologaster* 46. When a mans nose bleeds but a drop or two . . it is a signe of ill lucke. **1627** R. BERNARD *Guide to Grand-Jury Men* XIV 183. Dismayed at signes, as . . their bleeding suddenly at the nose. **1632** *Historie of Thomas of Reading* O4b. [shortly before he was murdered] When he came neere unto the Towne, his Nose burst out suddenly a bleeding. **1667** PEPYS *Diary* 6 July. Mr Rolt . . tells me that he is going Cornett under Collonell Ingoldsby . . and I think it is a handsome way for him. But it was an ominous thing methought, just as he was bidding me his last Adieu, his nose fell a-bleeding, which run in my mind a pretty while after. **1684** J. BANKS *Island Queens* 31–2. DOWGLAS. No sooner was I laid to rest, But just three drops of Blood fell from my Nose, and stain'd my Pillow. QUEEN MARY. That rather does betoken Some mischief to thy self. DOWGLAS. Perhaps to Cowards, Who prize their own base Lives, but to the Brave, 'Tis always fatal to the Friend they Love. **1709** *British Apollo* 30 Dec. Q. Gentlemen, I ask'd a young Woman whether She would have me, and She said Yes, and as soon as She had said the words my Nose drop'd several drops of Blood. I desire to know of You, whether you think my Life may attend

with Sorrow. **1787** GROSE *Provincial Glossary* Superstitions 47. A drop of blood from the nose, commonly foretells death, or a very severe fit of sickness: three drops are still more ominous. **1881** W. GREGOR *North-East of Scotland* 204. Three drops of cold blood falling from the nose was the sure indication of the death of one very nearly related.

NOSE bleeds: sign of affection

1592 T. LODGE *Euphues golden Legacie* K. He spyed where a man lay a sleepe, and .. as he stoode gazing, his nose on the sodaine bledde, which made him coniecture it was some friend of his. **1883** *N & Q* 6th ser. VII 238 [1710, MS account of recovery of Sir Cloudesley Shovell's body.] He was .. as if only asleep, his nose likewise bled as though alive, which Mr Paxton said was because of himself, for Sir C .. was his particular friend.

Cf. MURDER: corpse bleeds.

NOSE itches

1604 DEKKER *Honest Whore* II i. We shall ha' guests to day, I lay my little maidenhead; my nose itches so. **1620** MELTON *Astrologaster* 46. When a man's nose itcheth, it is a sign he shall drinke wine. **1738** SWIFT *Polite Conversation* I 87. My Nose itch'd, and I knew I should drink Wine, or kiss a Fool. **1755** *Connoisseur* 13 Mar. If your nose itches, you will shake hands with or kiss a fool, drink a glass of wine, run against a cuckold's door, or miss them all four. **1831** HONE *Year Book* 29 Feb. When your nose itches, you will be vexed. **1855** *Gents Mag.* pt. 2 385 [Shrops./ Worcs.] The itching of the nose is a sign of bad news. **1882** *People's Friend* 13 Sept. 580. An itch in the nose is, in the Highlands, considered the precursor of a stranger or letter. Ibid. In Yorkshire it is sensibly said to mean that the sufferer is to be kissed, cursed, or blessed. **1884** *N & Q* 6th ser. IX 247. Cook, who has been desired to consider herself disengaged, her ideas of honesty .. being incompatible with those of her employers: 'Well, I ain't surprised, not a bit .. This morning .. my nose itched .. so I made sure I should hear some news afore night.' **1885** *Folklore* 91. If your nose itches you are either going to be vexed or kissed by a fool. **1904** *Folklore* 461 [Abbeyleix, Co. Leix] They say that if .. your nose [itches] you will drink with strangers. **1913** *Folklore* 90 [Long Hanborough, Oxon.] If your nose itched it was a sign that you would be kissed, cursed, or vexed, run against a gatepost, or shake hands with a fool. **1932** C. IGGLESDEN *Those Superstitions* 228. If your nose itches, your mouth is in danger, You will see a fool, or kiss a stranger. **1954** Girl, 11 [Swansea, Glam.] If your nose itches you will be vexed. **1984** Woman, 37 [Harrow, Middx.] An itchy nose means a surprise. **1985** Woman, 57 [South Shields, Co. Durham] We always say if your nose itches, you're going to be angry.

NUNS, seeing

1926 *Folklore* 364 [London] My son Jim has never had more than two days' work the last seven weeks. Yesterday .. I see two nuns walking up the road .. I says, 'That's lucky. You'll have some work tomorrow. Come inside, and don't look at their backs.' Sure enough he has got some work today. **1952** Girl, 11. If you see a nun open your coat until you see a four-legged animal, then button your coat up again. It has something to do with letting in the Holy Ghost. **1954** Girl, 11 [Edinburgh] If you see three nuns walking together you might have luck. **1959** OPIE *Lore and Language of Schoolchildren* 218. In Ireland it has been noticed that children do not like seeing the back of a nun when she is walking away from them, and Catholic and Protestant children alike spit to ward off evil. **1968** *Observer* 10 Mar. 25. G. [a burglar] was superstitious about nuns. If he passed one on his way to commit a crime he would turn around and go home. **1968** *Observer* Suppl. 24 Nov. 10. Trawler skipper [Staithes, Yorks.] First thing on a morning when I'm going fishing .. I don't like to meet .. a nun. **1985** Woman, *c.*55 [London] You mustn't look at the back of a nun—it's bad luck.

Cf. CLERGYMAN, meeting.

NUTMEG in pocket: cures

1933 *Folklore* 203 [Digby, Lincs.] Backache, to cure, carry nutmegs in the pocket. **1957** UTTLEY *Year in the Country* III. My gardener has lumbago .. A nutmeg in the pocket is said to be a preventative. **1957** Woman, 47 [Scarborough, Yorks.] My aunt says the only sound cure [for rheumatism] is nutmeg in the pocket. **1959** *Trans. Devon. Ass.* 199 [North Bovey] The sufferer must be given a nutmeg by a member of the opposite sex. He places it in his pocket and nibbles a bit off it from time to time. When the nutmeg has quite disappeared the boils also will have vanished. **1966** [Liss, Hants.] The coalman had two nutmegs in his pocket. He'd had lumbago, and someone told him to carry a nutmeg on him, and he certainly hadn't had lumbago since he did.

NUTMEG in pocket: marriage prospects
1738 SWIFT *Polite Conversation* I 97. Have a care; for if you carry a Nutmeg in your Pocket, you'll certainly be marry'd to an old Man.

NUTMEG lucky
1965 *News of the World* 17 Oct. 6. When I've filled in my soccer coupon I .. sprinkle a little nutmeg powder on it. Then I leave it for 24 hours before posting it. This secret was told to me by a gipsy some years ago.

NUTS at wedding
*c.*40 BC VIRGIL *Eclogue* VIII (tr. Rieu) Fling nuts in the air, as bridegrooms do. **1648** HERRICK *Hesperides* 'An Epithalamie' st. 13. Now barre the doors, the Bridegroom puts The eager Boyes to gather Nuts. **1913** S. BARING-GOULD *Folk-Lore* 253. In Devonshire, as the bride leaves the church an old woman presents her with a little bag containing hazel nuts. These .. betoken fruitfulness.
Cf. WHEAT/RICE/CONFETTI thrown for luck.

NUTS: divination: burning
1714 GAY *Shepherd's Week* 35. Two Hazel-Nuts I threw into the Flame. And to each Nut I gave a Sweet-heart's Name. This with the loudest Bounce me sore amaz'd, That in a Flame of brightest Colour blaz'd. As blaz'd the Nut so may thy Passion grow, For 'twas thy Nut that did so brightly glow. **1787** BURNS

Poems 159–60 [note to 'Halloween'] Burning the nuts is a favourite charm. They name the lad and lass to each particular nut, as they lay them in the fire; and according as they burn quietly together, or start from beside one another, the course and issue of the Courtship will be. **1813** BRAND *Antiquities* I 302. It is a custom in Ireland, when the young women would know if their lovers are faithful, to put three nuts upon the bars of the grates, naming the nuts after the lovers. If a nut cracks or jumps, the lover will prove unfaithful; if it begins to blaze or burn, he has a regard for the person making the trial. If the nuts named after the girl and her lover, burn together, they will be married. **1863** R. CHAMBERS *Book of Days* I 550 [St Mark's Eve] A row [of nuts] being planted amongst the hot embers on the hearth, one from each maiden, and the name of the loved one being breathed, it was expected that if the love was .. to be successful, the nut would jump away; if otherwise, it would go on composedly burning till all was consumed: 'If you love me, pop and fly, If not lie there silently.' **1878** *Folk-Lore Record* 30 [Fittleworth, Sussex] Nuts are placed on a bright fire side by side, the one belonging to a youth, the other to a maiden, who .. repeat to themselves these words, varying the pronoun according to sex, 'If he loves me, pop and fly, If he hates me, lie and die.' **1946** UTTLEY *Country Things* XI [Cromford, Derbys., *c.*1900] The naming of chestnuts with boys' names as they are put on the hearth among the hot embers is still an All Hallows' Eve custom. The sweetheart was the one shot towards the girl sitting there. **1961** Woman, 58 [Eastbourne, Sussex, in girlhood] The first chestnut to burst meant its owner would be first to marry. We played the same game by putting chicken [small] potatoes in the oven—and what a mess they made!

NUTS: divination: tying knot
1883 BURNE *Shropshire* 243. A girl who can tie a knot in the fibre which encircles the kernel of a nut is sure to be married.

NUTS, double: eating
1883 BURNE *Shropshire* 243. A double

nut must never be eaten by one person; one of the kernels must be given to a friend—of the opposite sex no doubt! Most people prescribe secretly 'wishing a wish' at the same time. **1895** S. O. ADDY *Household Tales* 85. When you find two kernels inside a nut eat one of them, throw the other over your head, and wish something. After you have wished you must not speak to anybody until you can answer 'Yes' to a question. **1953** Girl, *c.*14 [Clun, Shrops.] If a girl cracks a nut with two kernels in it she gives one kernel away. If she ate both she would have twins.

NUTS, double: protect from toothache

1850 *N & Q* 1st ser. II 37 [Northants.] A double nut is . . sometimes worn in the pocket [for the toothache]. **1873** *Derbyshire Times* 24 May 6. Always wear in your pocket a double nut, and you will never be troubled with the toothache. **1878** *Folk-Lore Record* 40 [Fittleworth, Sussex] One of my grandchildren . . has been recommended by her nurse to hunt for a double hazel-nut, and to carry it in her pocket, and then she will never be troubled [with toothache] again.

NUTS, double: protect/lucky

1825 JAMIESON *Scottish Dict.* Suppl. I 636 [Dumfries./Perth.] To this day, young people are very happy if they can procure two nuts which grow together in one husk. This they call, but for what reason is not known, a St John's nut. The reason assigned . . is that it secures against the power of witchcraft. With this view, young people often carry one about with them . . In Perthshire . . it is believed, that a witch, who is proof against lead, may be shot by a St John's nut. **1978** [Stockton-on-Tees, Co. Durham] My son's got a lucky nut, which my father gave to him. It's polished, and he's still got it. A double hazel nut, it is.
Cf. SILVER BULLET.

NUTS, gathering

1670 *Poor Robin's Almanack* Sept. Let not thy son go a nutting on Holie-Rood day [14 Sept.], for fear he meet a tall man in black with cloven feet, which may scare him worse than a rosted shoulder of mutton will do a hungrie man. **1830** FORBY *East Anglia* 418. On Holy-Rood Day the Devil goes a nutting. *c.*1850 J. HUNTER MS note in Brand's *Antiquities* I opp. title page [nr. Sheffield, Yorks.] Persons who went a-nutting on Sundays, frequently were joined by an unknown companion & their wallets were soon filled, when casting a glance downwards they saw the cloven hoof, understood what their companion was, and fled in fear. **1894** A. J. C. HARE *Sussex* 43. If you go nutting on Sundays, the devil will come to help and hold the boughs for you.
Cf. SUNDAY: keeping Sabbath holy.

NUTS plentiful: children likewise

1668 *Poor Robin's Almanack* [end] Autumn . . Mars being in Conjunction copulative with Venus the beginning of this Quarter, it is probable that many a poor Countrey labouring man may be horrified this month, when their Wives go into the Wood, picking of Nuts, for opportunity has been the occasion of making many a man a Cuckold. **1823** COBBETT *Rural Rides* 30 Aug. This is a great nut year . . they put me in mind of the old saying, 'That a great nut year is a great year for that class whom the lawyers, in their Latin phrase, call the 'sons and daughters of nobody'. I once asked a farmer, who had often been overseer of the poor, whether he really thought that there was any ground for this old saying, or whether he thought it was mere banter? He said, that he was sure that there were good grounds for it; and he even cited instances in proof. **1855** *Gents Mag.* pt. 2 385 [Shrops./Worcs.] 'A great year for nuts, a great year for children', is a common saying. **1883** BURNE *Shropshire* 243. A plentiful nut year betokens the approaching birth of many children in the neighbourhood. **1925** D. R. PHILLIPS *Vale of Neath* 592. 'Collen lawn, cawell blawn'—a well-stocked hazel augurs a full cradle. **1968** Woman, 42 [Liss, Hants.] We say 'A good year for nuts, a good year for babies.' I was thinking of that when I was taking the baby for a walk yesterday, and the hedges were full of nuts. **1984** Woman, 65 [Llanrwst, Denbigh.] If it's a good year for cob nuts there will be a lot of babies born.
Cf. NUTS at wedding.

O

OAK TREE benign

1578 DODOENS *Herball* (tr. Lyte, 747) They say that the wood of Misselto, that groweth vpon the Okes, and not vpon any other tree, is very good against the falling euyll. 1584 SCOT *Discoverie of Witchcraft* XII XVIII. That neither hunters nor their dogs maie be bewitched, they cleave an oken branch, and both they and their dogs passe over it. 1776 PENNANT *Tour in Scotland* 46. A Highlander, in order to protect himself from any harms apprehended from the Fairy tribe, will draw round himself a circle with a sapling of the oak. 1879 *Herefordshire Times* 24 May 13. May-dew .. gathered under an oak was regarded as especially potent.

OAK TREE: divination with oak apple

1578 DODOENS *Herball* (tr. Lyte, 746) The Oke Apples .. being broken in sonder .. forshewe the sequell of the yeere, as the expert husbandmen of Kent haue obserued by the liuing thinges that are founde within them; as if they finde an Ante, they iudge plentie of grayne: if a white worme .. morreyne of beast: if a Spider, they presage pestilence .. among men. 1579 LUPTON *Thousand Notable Things* III § 7. If you take an Oake Aple from an Oake tree, and open the same: you shall finde a lytle woorme therin, which if it doth flye away, it sygnifies warres: if it creepe, it betokens scarcenes of Corne: if it run about, then it foreshewes the plague. This is the countrymans Astrologie: which they haue long obserued for trueth. 1710 *Athenian Oracle*, Suppl. 476. If a fly be found in an Oak-apple, 'tis believ'd that the year ensuing will be troubled with Wars .. If a Spider .. then a Pestilence is fear'd .. if a small worm .. plenty is prognosticated. 1909 M. TREVELYAN *Folk-Lore of Wales* 101. A worm in it was a sure sign of poverty.

OAK TREE, harming

c. AD 8 OVID *Metamorphoses* VIII (tr. Innes, 215–17) Erysichthon .. scorned the gods, and .. used his sacrilegious axe on the trees of Ceres' grove, violating .. a huge oak .. From the heart of the tree, a voice was heard saying: 'I who dwell within this tree am a nymph, whom Ceres dearly loves. I warn you with my dying breath, that punishment for your wickedness is at hand' .. But Erysichthon persisted. [The oak] was brought crashing down .. Ceres .. made the fields .. tremble, as she devised a punishment .. to torment him with deadly hunger. AD 77 PLINY *Natural History* XVI xcv (1855, III 435–6) The Druids .. held nothing more sacred than the mistletoe and the tree that bears it, supposing always that tree to be the [oak]. .. It is the notion with them .. that the mistletoe upon it is a proof that the tree has been selected by God himself as an object of his especial favour. 1665 R. RAPIN *De Hortorum* (tr. Gardiner, 1706, 70) No murd'ring Axes let 'em [oaks] feel. Nor violate the Groves with impious Steel .. Avenging Deities inhabit there: For Poets tell how wounded Oaks have bled .. Denouncing Terrors from their awful Head. And thence of old religiously rever'd, Their antient Groves our pious Fathers spar'd. 1673 Aubrey MSS (DICK *Brief Lives* lxxv) There was one Oak in the great Wood call'd Norwood, that had Miselto .. Some Persons cut this Missleto, for some Apothecaries in London .. and left only one Branch remaining for more to sprout out. One fell lame shortly after: Soon after, each of the others lost an Eye, and he that fell'd the Tree, about 1678 (tho' warned of these Misfortunes of the other Men) would not withstanding, adventure to do it, and shortly after broke his Leg. 1883 BURNE *Shropshire* 241. A ballad bewailing the destruction [of the Mile Oak near Oswestry], in 1824 was printed and circulated in the neighbourhood. In it occurs this noteworthy verse: 'To break a branch was deemed a sin, A bad-luck job for neighbours, For fire, sickness, or the like, Would mar their honest labours.'

oak tree: also see MISTLETOE.

OATS: divination

1787 BURNS *Poems* 159 [note to 'Halloween'] They go to the barn-yard, and pull each, at three several times, a stalk of Oats. If the third stalk wants the *top-pickle*, that is, the grain at the top of the stalk, the party in question will come to the marriage-bed any thing but a Maid. **1823** W. GRANT STEWART *Highlanders of Scotland* 231 [Hallowe'en] They .. pull each a stalk of oats, and according to the number of grains upon the stalk the puller will have a corresponding number of children. It may be observed, that it is essential to a female's good name that her stalk should have the top-grain attached to it.

ODD NUMBER lucky

*c.*40 BC VIRGIL *Eclogue* VIII (tr. Rieu) I walk round this altar with your effigy, three times. Odd numbers please the gods. AD **77** PLINY *Natural History* XXVIII v (1856, V 283) Why is it that we entertain the belief that for every purpose odd numbers are the most effectual? Ibid. XXVIII XIV (V 296) Rinse the mouth with cold water an odd number of times every morning, as a preservative against tooth-ache. *c.***1550** J. BALE *Comedye Concernynge Thre Lawes* B5ᵛ. For the cough take Judas eare, With the parynge of a peare, And drynke them without feare If ye wyll haue remedy, Thre syppes are for the hyckock, And vi. more for the chyckock. **1590** SPENSER *Faerie Queene* III III 50. Spitt thrise upon me, thrise upon me spitt; Th' uneven nomber for this business is most fitt. *c.***1597** SHAKESPEARE *Merry Wives* V i. This is the third time: I hope good lucke lies in odde numbers .. they say there is divinity in odde Numbers, either in nativity, chance, or death. **1615** J. STEPHENS *Essays* 379. Her [the witch's] best preseruatives be odde numbers. **1748** S. WERENFELS *Dissertation upon Superstition* 8. When he is sick, he will never swallow the Pills he is ordered to take, in an equal number. **1813** BRAND *Antiquities* II 574. Salutes with cannon

consist of an odd number. A Royal Salute is thrice seven, or twenty-one Guns. **1826** S. LOVER *Rory O'More* 'Then here goes another,' says he, 'to make sure, For there's luck in odd numbers,' says Rory O'More. **1880** *N & Q* 6th ser. I 193. The other day I was informed .. that unless pastry was rolled out an uneven number of times it was sure to be heavy and tough, and that this fact was well known to all cooks. **1948** E. & M. A. RADFORD *Superstitions* 183 [general] There is luck in odd numbers. **1965** *Observer* 7 Feb. I. The King's Troop, Royal Horse Artillery, fired a 41-gun salute for the thirteenth anniversary of the accession of the Queen. Surviving from an old superstition, such triumphal salutes are usually an odd number.

Cf. THREE: 'third time lucky'.

ODD NUMBER unlucky

*c.***1797** H. MORE *Tawney Rachel* 11. She .. would not stay in the kitchen, if there was not an even number of people. **1855** F. K. ROBINSON *Yorkshire Words* 29 [Whitby] Christmas eve at length arrives .. the family and friends assemble for supper, not in an odd but an even number .. for that would be an unlucky perpetration. **1861** C. C. ROBINSON *Dialect of Leeds* 300. There is the usual antipathy to odd numbers. A child is easily persuaded to give away a marble to make 'evven'. **1878** A. MACGREGOR *Brahan Seer* 128–9 'Superstitions of Highlanders'. It is unfortunate for an odd number to sit at table, such as 7, 9, 11; and 13 in particular. **1933** *Folklore* 191 [Trentside, Lincs.] On no account must there be an odd number in the funeral party, or soon the dead will call for a companion. **1983** Boy, 12 [Maldon, Essex] My lucky number is twenty-four because neither number is odd.

Cf. THIRTEEN unlucky number.

ONION: divination and spells

1570 B. GOOGE *Popish Kingdome* IV 44ᵛ. In these same dayes yong wanton Gyrles that meete for mariage bee, Doe search to know the names of them that shall their husbandes bee. Foure Onyons, fiue, or eight, they take and make in euery one, Such names as they do fancie most, and best do thinke vpon. Thus neere the Chimney them they set, and that same Onyon than, That first doth sproute, doth surely beare the name of their good man. **1660** BURTON *Anatomy of Melancholy* pt. 3 sect. 2 mem. 4 subs. 1. They'll give any thing to know when they shall be married, how many husbands they shall have, by *Cromnyomantia*, a kind of divination with Onions laid on the Altar on Christmas Eve. **1685** *Mother Bunch's Closet* (1885, 7) Take a St Thomas's onion, peel it, and lay it in a clean handkerchief and lay it under your head, and put on a clean smock .. and as soon as you be laid down .. say these words: 'Good St Thomas do me right, And bring my love to me this night, That I may look him in the face, And in my arms may him embrace.' Then .. in thy first sleep, thou shalt dream of him which shall be thy husband. *c.*1770 *Fortune-Book* 5. To know whom you shall Marry. Take an Onion call'd St Thomas's Onion, peel it and .. lay it under your head .. then lie down and .. say: St Thomas, pray do me right, And let my true Love come to Night [etc., as 1685]. **1821–4** CLARE 'St Martin's Eve' st. 13. (1935, I 396) Beneath her pillow lays an onion red, To dream on this same night with whom she is to wed. **1853** *N & Q* 1st ser. VII 153 [London] In buying onions always go in by one door of the shop, and come out by another. Select a shop with two doorways. These onions, placed under your pillow on St Thomas's Eve, are sure to bring visions of your true-love, your future husband. **1871** *N & Q* 4th ser. VIII 506 [Derbys.] On St Thomas's Eve there used to be a custom among girls to procure a large red onion, into which, after peeling, they would stick nine pins, and say—'Good Saint Thomas do me right, Send me my true love this night, In his clothes and his array Which he weareth every day.' Eight pins were stuck round one in the centre, to which was given the name of the swain .. and they were certain to dream of .. the desired person. **1872** *N & Q* 4th ser. X 24 [Co. Durham] If a lover does not come often enough, he may be brought by roasting an onion which has been stuck full of 'ounce' pins (they must not

have been through paper). The pins are to prick his heart. **1909** M. TREVELYAN *Folk-Lore of Wales* 235. Girls in some of the farm-houses take each an onion, and name it after a bachelor of their acquaintance. The onions are then put away in a loft. The man whose onion first 'begins to grow', or bud, will soon declare his love.

Cf. HEART stuck with pins: lover's spell.

ONION protects and cures

AD **77** PLINY *Natural History* XX xx (1856, IV 222) Fresh onions .. applied topically .. are good for the bites of dogs [and] for healing excoriations. *c.*1550 J. BALE *Comedye Concernynge Thre Lawes* B5. Geue onyons to saynt Cutlake, And garlyke to saynt Cyryake, If ye wyll shurne the head ake. **1616** SIR T. OVERBURY *Characters* (1630, M2) Hee cannot distinguish 'tweene onion seed and Gunpowder; if hee haue worne it in his hollow toothe for the Toothach, and so come to the knowledge of it, that's all. **1956** G. E. EVANS *Ask the Fellows* XXIV [Blaxhall, Suffolk] The onion is cut up and stood in an old tin-plate. Then you place it in the room where the sick child sleeps. The onion draws the complaint into itself, and when the child is better care must be taken to see that the onion is properly burnt. **1964** *West Sussex Gazette* 19 Mar. 8. When there's flu about, I puts a plate of cut up onion in every room. That's what keeps colds away .. All the cold germs goos into they. **1973** *Sunday Mirror* 15 Apr. 30. When I was a child over forty years ago we couldn't afford to visit the dentist so my grandmother used to cure toothache with a piece of cloth covered with raw onions. This was wrapped round the arm opposite to the side of the tooth that ached. **1973** *Woman*, *c.*60 [Scarborough, Yorks.] My mother always used to put an onion in our pockets when we went to school—a shallot—to ward off illness. **1977** *Woman*, 66 [Sheffield, Yorks.] I once had .. a mosquito bite .. and it began to fester and someone suggested putting a piece of onion on it as onion has good 'drawing power'. **1978** *Sun* 17 Oct. 18 [Lancs.] I fondly remember the smell of my mother's window sill adorned with half onions. She swore by the legend that the onions captured any incoming germs and purified the air.

ONION protects from effects of caning

1895 S. O. ADDY *Household Tales* 78. If you rub the schoolmaster's cane with an onion it will split when he strikes you. **1915** *N & Q* 11th ser. XI 409–10. The lads with whom I was at school held the belief that if the palm of the hand was rubbed with half of a freshly cut raw onion the effect would be to mitigate the pain, split the cane, and at the same time hurt the master's hand . . Once, to our intense joy, the master bound up his hand after giving a lade the cane, thus confirming the belief in the efficacy of onion juice. **1959** OPIE *Lore and Language of Schoolchildren* 375. Before the operation [being caned], it will mitigate the pain [if you] rub onion on hand (many give this).

ONION, raw and cut: unlucky in house

1855 *Gents Mag.* pt. 2 385 [Worcs.] To have a cut onion lying about in the house breeds distempers. **1891** *N & Q* 7th ser. XI 387. An old servant (Essex) . . recently complained that . . Spanish onions . . were too big. When an obvious method of getting over that difficulty was suggested, she replied, 'Oh, no! that would never do! It's so unlucky to have a cut onion in the house.' Ibid. 475. It is not safe to use an onion that has been cut and kept, because it absorbs impurities from the air. **1912** LEATHER *Herefordshire* 21. Onion peelings should be immediately and carefully destroyed; it is unlucky to keep part of an onion in the house. If all be not required, the rest is burnt or thrown away. I have had a . . cook who was most particular about this. **1923** [Trowbridge, Wilts.] For many people the keeping of a cut onion in the house is unlucky. **1958** *Woman*, c.50 [Bighton, Hants.] Special small onions are being grown for me as I am liable to keep half a cut onion from one meal to another, which I am assured is highly dangerous. **1986** *Woman*, c.60 [Petersfield, Hants.] I never keep half an onion, I always throw it away.

Cf. ONION protects and cures.

OPAL unlucky

1869 *N & Q* 4th ser. III 59. What is the origin of a superstition . . very generally believed in 'good society', as to opals being unlucky? **1875** *N & Q* 5th ser. IV 97. I have been assured that the luck depends upon the colour. In these days a white opal is considered unlucky, while a black opal, I am told, is held to be extremely lucky. **1890** *Young Ladies' Journal* XXXV 4. The lover will not give his sweetheart an opal ring, however pretty the stone may be. **1913** *Folklore* 90 [Long Hanborough, Oxon.] It was unlucky . . to have an engagement ring with an opal in it—an opal signified widowhood and tears. **1932** C. IG-GLESDEN *Those Superstitions* 71. The opal is . . commonly known as being unlucky to its owner, unless . . that individual was born in October, in which case it is definitely lucky. **1936** SASSOON *Sherston's Progress* 258 [France, 1918] 'And not a single casualty so far,' said Velmore. I didn't touch wood, but as tomorrow was the thirteenth I produced my fire-opal and touched that. 'Aren't opals supposed to be unlucky?' he enquired dubiously. **1970** *Mirror* 3 Sept. 16 [SE London] Recently I became engaged to the most wonderful girl in the world and I bought her an opal ring. Now every time she shows it to someone they exclaim with horror that 'An opal is unlucky for an engagement ring!' But my fiancée says that because she was born under the sign of Libra the stone is lucky for her.

OPPOSITE SEX lucky

1792 A. GEDDES *A Norfolk Tale* 30. On my approach, she stopt and said: 'Good morrow, sir!—I am afraid You'll think me pert—It is not so; But now to seek a place I go: And it is fortunate, they say, To meet a *man* at early day The first one meets.' I smil'd and said: 'God send thee luck, my pretty maid!' **1883** BURNE *Shropshire* 266. On the authority of a Shropshire coachman . . it is unlucky if the first person met by a man-servant going to a new place be a man, or if the first to meet a maidservant be a woman.

ORPINE: divination

1578 DODOENS *Herball* (tr. Lyte, 39) *Orpyne*. The people of the countrey delight much to set it in pots and shelles *on Midsummer Euen*, or vpon timber slattes, or trenchers, dawbed with Clay, and so to set, or hang it vp in their houses, where as it remayneth greene a long season and groweth, if it be somtimes ouer sprinckled with water. **1686–7** AUBREY *Remaines* (1881, 25–6) I remember, the mayds (especially the Cooke mayds & Dayrymayds) would stick-up in some chinkes of the joists or &c.: Midsommer-men, wch are slips of Orpins. they placed them by Paires, sc.: one for such a man, the other for such a mayd his sweet-heart, and accordingly as the Orpin did incline to, or recline from ye other, that there would be love, or aversion; if either did wither, death. **1755** *Connoisseur* 20 Feb. [Midsummer Eve] I .. stuck up two Midsummer Men, one for myself, and one for him. Now if his had died away, we should never have come together: but I assure you he blowed and turned to me. *c.***1797** H. MORE *Tawney Rachel* 7. She would never go to bed on Midsummer eve without sticking up in her room the well known plant called Midsummer-man, as the bending of the leaves to the right or to the left, would not fail to tell her whether Jacob .. was true or false. **1813** BRAND *Antiquities* I 263–4. On the 22d of January, 1801, a small gold ring .. was exhibited to the Society of Antiquaries .. It had been found .. in a ploughed field near Cawood, in Yorkshire, and had for a device two Orpine plants joined by a true-love knot, with this motto above: 'Ma fiance velt'; i.e. my sweet-heart wills, or is desirous. The stalks of the plants were bent to each other, in token that the parties represented by them were to come together in marriage .. From the form of the letters it appeared to have been a ring of the fifteenth century. **1873** KILVERT *Diary* 11 June. In Gander Lane we saw in the banks some of the 'Midsummer Men' plants which my Mother remembers the servant maids and cottage girls sticking up in their houses and bedrooms on Midsummer Eve, for the purpose of divining about their sweethearts. **1879**

Herefordshire Times 28 June 13. A piece of orpine (*sedum telephium*) was set in clay upon pieces of slate or potsherd, and placed in the house, being termed a 'Midsummer man'. As the stalk was found next morning to incline to the right or left, it was held to indicate to the maiden who gathered and placed it whether her lover would prove true to her or not. **1892** C. M. YONGE *Old Woman's Outlook* June. I have known an old woman who had duly, on St John's Eve, laid out nine pairs of Orpines, naming them after the couples thought to be courting. The pairs that kept together betokened a happy marriage, those that fell apart boded no good to the love affairs! **1926** W. RAYMOND *Verity Thurston* v. Now only to get back to her window-seat and before the stroke of midnight .. plant these precious orpines in her little teacup without a handle and the hornen cup that leaked. Thus she would learn for certain whether he loved her or not.

Cf. FLOWERS in pairs: divination.

OWL bird of ill omen

*c.***319** BC THEOPHRASTUS *Characters* (tr. Jebb, ed. Sandys, 143) If an owl is startled by him in his walk, he will exclaim 'Glory be to Athene!' before he proceeds. *c.* AD **15** OVID *Ibis* ll. 223–4. The owl of the night sat on an opposite house-top, and uttered his ill-boding notes with funereal voice. *c.***1250** *Owl and Nightingale* (ed. J. W. H. Atkins, 97–8) ll. 1150–2. Men beoþ of þe wel [owl] sore aferd. þu singst þar sum man shal be ded: euer þu bodest sumne qued [evil]. *c.***1374** CHAUCER *Parliament of Fowls* l. 343. The oule ek, that of deth the bode bryngeth. *c.***1595** SHAKESPEARE *Midsommer Nights Dreame* v i. Whil'st the scritch-owle, scritching loud, Puts the wretch that lies in woe, In remembrance of a shrowd. **1623** DELONEY *Thomas of Reading* XI. With that the scritch owle cried piteously .. Iesu haue mercy vpon me (quoth hee) what an ill fauoured cry doe yonder carrion birds make, and therewithall he laid him downe in his bed, from whence he neuer rose againe. **1725** BOURNE *Antiquitates Vulgares* 70–1. Omens and prognostications .. are still in the Mouths of all, tho' only observed by the Vulgar. In Country Places, especially they are in great Repute .. If an Owl, which they reckon a most abominable and unlucky Bird, sends forth its hoarse and dismal Voice, it is an Omen of the Approach of some terrible Thing; that some dire Calamity .. is near at Hand. **1773** WHITE *Selborne* 8 July. From this screaming probably arose the common people's imaginary species of screech-owl, which they superstitiously think attends the windows of dying persons. **1829** BROCK-ETT *North Country Words* 161. *Howlet,* the barn or white owl .. has the reputation of being the herald of horror and disaster. **1841** HARTSHORNE *Salopia Antiqua* 557. Screech Owl. *Strix flammea* of Jenyns: the common white owl. The singular cry or scream of this bird is considered ominous of death. **1872** *Bye-Gones* 18 Sept. 86 [Llansaintffraid-yn-Mechan, Monmouth.] Its visits and wild shriekings foretell the death of someone in the neighbourhood. It has thus gained the name of death-bird or 'Aderyn 'y corph'. **1887** RUSKIN *Praeterita* II 363. Whatever wise people may say of them, I at least myself have found the owl's cry always prophetic of mischief to me. **1936** W. J. BROWN *The Gods Had Wings* 16–17. In 1934, an old country-man .. told .. of the death of a common acquaintance. 'And .. it weren't no more nor I expected. I come past his house one night, and there

was a scret owl on his roof, scretting something horrible. I always reckon to take notice of them things.' **1967** S. MARSHALL *Fenland Chronicle* pt. 2 IX. If an owl sat on the roof, or flew up against a window at night, that meant a death actually in the house.

OWL seen in daytime

AD 77 PLINY *Natural History* X XVI (1855, II 492) It is looked upon as a direful omen to see it in the city, or .. in the day-time. **1599** SHAKESPEARE *Julius Caesar* I iii. Yesterday, the Bird of Night did sit, Even at Noone-day, upon the Market place, Howting and shreeking. When these Prodigies Doe so conjoyntly meet .. I beleeve, they are portentous things Unto the Clymate, that they point upon [an omen of Caesar's death]. **1850** *N & Q* 1st ser. II 164 [Northants.] When .. he [owl] exchanges the darkness of his ivy bush for the rays of the sun at noon-day, his presence is looked upon as indicative of bad luck. **1933** *Sussex County Mag.* 250. A large white owl sailed across the lane like an unnaturally solid ghost. 'Dear, dear,' lamented Mrs Bridger, 'that be a bad omen for sure.' **1981** *Woman,* 63 [Coreley, Shrops.] I was terrified of owls and since I've grown up they've become my favourite bird. To see an owl in the daytime was supposed to be most unlucky.

Cf. COCK crows unseasonably.

P

'PALM' protects

1584 SCOT *Discoverie of Witchcraft* XII xx. Such as observe dulie the rites and ceremonies of holie church .. by the lawfull use of .. greene leaves consecrated on Palm sundaie .. are preserved from witchcraft. **1600** NASHE *Summers Last Will* B3. The Palme and May make countrey houses gay. **1812** J. BRADY *Clavis Calendaria* I 256–7. Among our superstitious forefathers the palm tree, or its substitutes box and yew, were solemnly blessed and some of the branches burnt to ashes, and used by the priests on the Ash-Wednesday in the following year; while other boughs .. were distributed among the pious, who bore them about in .. processions .. The youth in many places yet preserve some vestiges of the custom of the day and gather willow flowers or buds, or such others as happen to be in a forward state of vegetation. **1858** DENHAM *North of England* (1895, 57) Palm Crosses .. are still often seen in the hands of children .. on Palm Sunday. The remaining portion of the year they hang upon a nail against the whitewashed wall of mayhap the poor man's only room .. In the triumphant days of popery they were considered indispensable in the hands of old and young, rich and poor. Hence the proverb, 'He that hath not a palm in his hands on Palm Sunday must have his hand cut off.' **1870** *N & Q* 4th ser. V 529. As real palms were not to be had, sprigs and branches of hazel, willow, etc. were substituted. These were used in the religious processions, and afterwards treasured by the people .. Branches gathered on Palm Sunday had peculiar virtues .. I have seen bunches of hazel and willow twigs so gathered preserved in constant verdure the year round by placing them in pots of water in cottage windows, and was once told by an aged granddame in South Lincolnshire that they were 'good against thunder and lightning'. **1873** J. B. BAGSHAWE *Threshold of the Catholic Church* 159 [Rich-

mond, Yorks.] In Mining districts, the Protestant miners come in crowds to get the 'blessed palms' on Palm Sunday, with the feeling that these will preserve them from danger at their work. **1950** Woman, 22 [Brighton, Sussex] When we went to Communion [Anglican] on Palm Sunday, we were given a cross made from a dried palm leaf. I've put mine on the wall of my bedroom and will keep it there till next year.

Cf. MAY BOUGHS AND FLOWERS.

'PALM' unlucky in house before Palm Sunday

1898 C. M. YONGE *John Keble's Parishes* XVI [Hursley & Otterbourne, Hants.] *Willow or Withy* (Salix caprea). Our yellow goslings in spring, as they shoot from their silver rabbit-tail catkins, and our palms on Palm Sunday, though it is unlucky to bring one home earlier. **1985** Woman, 79 [Fareham, Hants.] When I was a child, we thought it was unlucky to bring palm (I mean of course, pussy willow) into the house before Palm Sunday. It was perfectly all right afterwards.

Cf. MAY BLOSSOM in house.

PALM SUNDAY, sowing on

1849 BRAND *Antiquities* III 248 n. [Gloucester] A circumstance which occurred .. on Saturday evening last .. brought to my recollection a superstitious notion which I have often heard .. A lady (in the common acceptation of the term) requested of a seedsman that she might be furnished with various flower-seeds, 'for,' she added, 'I must not omit sowing them to-morrow .. Palm Sunday .. The advantage to be derived from sowing on that day is, that the flowers will be sure to come double.'

Cf. GOOD FRIDAY beneficial.

PANCAKES eaten on Shrove Tuesday

1857 *N & Q* 2nd ser. IV 25. If you eat pancakes on 'Goody Tuesday' (Shrove Tuesday), and grey peas on Ash Wednesday, you will have money in your purse all the year.

Cf. GOOSE eaten on Michaelmas Day.

PAPER BAG, bursting

1953 Schoolboy, 14. A lot of people are superstitious in Presteigne [Radnor.]. Blowing a paper bag up in the house and bursting it is a sign of a death. 1964 Girl, 15 [Chigwell, Essex] It is unlucky to burst a paper bag in the house.

Cf. PUDDING, bursting: divination.

PARISHES, three: beneficial

1787 BURNS *Poems* 170 [note to 'Hallowe'en'] You go out, one or more, for this is a social spell, to a south-running spring or rivulet, where 'three Lairds' lands meet', and dip your left shirt-sleeve. 1855 *N & Q* 1st ser. XI 239 [whooping cough] He told me she was 'no better, although he had carried her, fasting, on Sunday morning, into *three parishes*.' 1906 *Folklore* 206–7 [NW Ireland] Preparations for the cure [of a sick cow] are taken in hand .. A runner tears off for the 'three-mearne-water' .. running water taken from a spot at which three townlands meet. (I have noted many such eerie places, and in particular, one at the junction of three parishes, whose virtue was famed far and near.) Its influence is most powerful if .. dipped up before sunrise. 1909 M. TREVELYAN *Folk-Lore of Wales* 267. People formerly said if you wanted your children to attain a long age, you should see that the godparents come from three different parishes.

PARSLEY, devil controls

1883 BURNE *Shropshire* 248. Parsley is a decidedly uncanny herb .. There is a popular idea that it must be sown nine times before it will come up .. At Pulverbatch [they say] 'it goes to the devil nine times and very often forgets to come back again'. 1923 [Martock, Som.] Parsley seed is long germinating coz 'Goes to hell and back 'fore sprouts.' 1963 *Country Gents Estate Mag.* Apr. 142. Parsley goes nine times to the devil before it comes up. 1974 *Home & Country* July 344 [W.I., Cheshire] It's surprising parsley still exists, because according to an old-wives' tale only the

wicked can grow it. Rather embarrassing if you happen to have a healthy clump in your garden.

PARSLEY, giving

1873 *N & Q* 4th ser. XI 341. It is the belief of the peasantry in this part of the country [S. Hants.], that it is very unlucky to give parsley. 1954 A Swansea friend will not give a root away as doing so brings bad luck. 1957 Boy, 12 [Romford, Essex] It is unlucky to be given parsley. 1960 *Yorkshire Post* 29 Jan. 6. Some years ago she saw a woman from the village hovering over the parsley bed and carefully removing first one plant and then another .. 'I was utterly amazed,' says my correspondent, 'for I knew .. that she was the soul of honesty .. I would have given her all she wanted' .. And that, it seems, was just the difficulty, because parsley plants must not be given.

PARSLEY: mistress is master

1883 BURNE *Shropshire* 248. An informant at Longnor tells us that 'where parsley grows in the garden, the missis is master.' 1905 *Folklore* 67 [Monmouth.] Where the mistress is the master The parsley grows the faster. 1937 E. TALBOT *Sussex County Mag.* 571. 'Unless I plants our parsley bed I'll have wi' you no truck,' Ses I to him, 'for she,' I said 'Can give or take our luck. You, lad, may dig and hoe and weed The taters in their rows, But women-folk sow parsley seed, As all in Sussex knows. For parsley has a power, lad, That's old as histories, 'Twas guv her as a dower, lad, By Downland pharisees' [fairies]. 1969 PORTER *Cambridgeshire* 47. It is still a widely held .. belief that parsley .. flourishes best either when sown by the housewife rather than by her husband, or in gardens of homes where she is 'master'. 1987 Woman, 85 [South Petherton, Som.] Where the parsley grows strongly, the woman wears the trousers.

Cf. ROSEMARY: woman is master.

PARSLEY, moving/transplanting

1849 BRAND *Antiquities* III 113. At Islip, Co. Oxon., It is reckoned very unlucky to transplant parsley. 1864 R. WHATELY *Misc. Remains* 270–1. The vulgar account it very unlucky to transplant parsley. A gentleman's gardener in Yorkshire being desired to do so, insisted on sowing a bed instead; assuring his master that nothing would thrive with him if he planted it. **1912** *Folklore* 350 [Bampton, Devon] I never didn't transplant pars'ley. That's the worst thing you can go for to do. You sow some on a bed and lets it grow there, and that's all right, but if you digs it up and goes for to transplant it someone in the family's sure to die. **1955** *Sunday Times* 6 Mar. 2 [Guildford, Surrey] Parsley should not be transplanted, it means a death in the family. **1978** *Folklore* 158 [Thorncombe, Dorset] Parsley plants were among those moved, and, as she transplanted these, my mother lightheartedly said: 'Transplant parsley, transplant death.' These words were remembered a few days later when an elderly uncle of my father died. **1986** Woman, 30 [Colchester, Essex] My mother told me that it was very unlucky to plant parsley when she saw me planting some in our new garden. I said, 'What a lot of rubbish!' But I had the worst year of my life afterwards and superstitious or not, I'll never plant parsley again!

PARSLEY planted by stranger

1890 *North-Country Lore* 474 [Blackburn, Yorks.] If a stranger plants parsley in a garden, great trouble will befall the owner.

PARSLEY, pregnancy caused by

1933 *Folklore* 198 [Navenby, Lincs.] If a young woman sows parsley-seed she will have a child. **1936** *N & Q* CLXXI 33. The planting of parsley in Surrey is frequently considered to mean an addition to the family. **1951** Woman, *c.*50 [Oxford] When a woman wants a baby, she should go out and pick some parsley.

Cf. PARSLEY BED, babies found in.

PARSLEY, pregnancy prevented by

1707 *Aristotle's Last Legacy* 96. Take Parsley, bruise it, and press out the Juice, and put it (being so dipp'd) into the Mouth of the Womb, and it will presently cause the Child to come away,

tho' it be dead, and the After-burden also. **1939** *Folklore* 187 [Cambridge] Parsley is believed to prevent a pregnancy, and .. is sometimes eaten as a salad by young married women who do not desire to have a family. **1982** Woman, *c.*20 [London] If you want to bring on your period put a sprig of parsley inside your vagina for 12 hours—your period should start 24 hours later.

PARSLEY BED, babies found in

1622 MABBE tr. *Aleman's Guzman d'Alfarache* I 25 *margin*. That phrase which we vse to little children, when we tell them they were borne in their mothers Parsly-bed. **1640** R. BROME *Antipodes* I IV. For I am past a child My selfe to thinke they are found in parsley beds. **1659** *London Chaunticleres* 6. My mother indeed used to say that I was born to be a Gardiners wife as soon as ever I was taken out of her parsley-bed. **1690** LOCKE *Concerning Human Understanding* II XXVIII. If I believe that Sempronia digged Titus out of the parsley-bed (as they used to tell children). **1726** GAY Riddle 'recipe', in letter to Swift, 22 Oct. (*Poems*, ed. Faber, 213) Some sprigs of that bed Where children are bred. **1796** PEGGE *Anonymiana* I 91 (1809, 52) The child, when new-born, comes out of the persley bed, they will say in the North. **1852** *N & Q* 1st ser. VI 517. I was told that little girls came out of a parsley-bed, and little boys from under a goose-berry bush. **1875** *N & Q* 5th ser. III 325. In England every little girl knows that male babies come from the nettle-bed, and the female ones from the parsley bed. **1886** ELWORTHY *West Somerset Word-Book* 557. *Parsley-bed* .. the source whence children are told that the little girls come. **1903** *N & Q* 9th ser. XII 496. In Derbyshire new babies come from under the gooseberry bushes; from nettle and parsley beds also—boys from the nettles, and girls from the parsley. They are 'dug up', wrapped in a white cloth.

Cf. GOOSEBERRY BUSH; PARSLEY, pregnancy caused by.

PARTING at gate or stile

1895 *Folklore* 305 [Worcs.] To say goodbye over a stile brings bad luck. **1953**

Girl, 14 [Llangunllo, Radnor.] It is bad luck to part at a gate.

PARTING: saying 'Goodbye' more than once

1898 BLAKEBOROUGH *Yorkshire Customs* 133. Remember it is unlucky to say goodnight three times to the girl you love, without returning to the house and starting the whole thing over again. **1923** [Martock, Som.] Don't 'ee say goodbye and shake hands twice or you'll not again tosh [be on good terms]. **1927** *N & Q* CLIII 137. Why is it supposed to be not lucky to say 'goodbye' twice to the same person?

Cf. TURNING BACK unlucky.

PARTING: watching out of sight

1866 HENDERSON *Northern Counties* 88. It is unlucky to watch anyone out of sight; if you do so you will never see that person again. **1912** LEATHER *Herefordshire* 87. It is very unlucky to stand and watch out of sight a person who is going away from home. **1924** F. M. FORD *Some Do Not* pt. 2 VI. She said: 'I won't watch you out of sight .. It is unlucky to watch anyone out of sight.' **1932** C. IGGLESDEN *Those Superstitions* 111. I learned .. that in this part of the country [Berks.] it is unlucky to wave your hand at departing friends till they are out of sight. **1953** Boy, *c.*15 [Isle of Portland] If by some mis-chance they have to sail on Friday then no relative of the crew will watch the ship sail out of sight for fear it will not return. **1954** Girl, 13 [Perth] If your husband is in the airforce never watch his take-off or you will get bad luck. **1968** BBC RADIO 5 Feb. At Hull [Yorks.] wives never see their husbands off when a trawler sails, for it would be bad luck. **1982** Female student, 20 [Cleveland, Yorks.] It also used to be thought that it was unlucky to watch a departing guest till they were out of sight, because this meant that they would never re-visit the house. However, the number of people who stand waving from their gates or doorsteps until their guests have departed seems to suggest that this superstition is no longer followed.

PAVEMENT, stepping on lines/cracks in

*c.***1890** [Kennington, SE London] Ill for-

tune was thought to come from treading on these cracks—or it was thought one's mother would turn black. *c.***1910** [Cardiff, Glam.] Tread on a line and you'll marry a negro and have a black baby. **1924** MILNE *When We Were Very Young* 'Lines and Squares'. The masses of bears, Who wait at the corners all ready to eat The sillies who tread on the lines in the street. **1952** Girl, 14 [Aberdeen] The number of lines one walks on, that is how many of their mother's best china dishes they are going to break. **1953** Girl, 12 [Aberystwyth, Cardigan.] If you step on a line in the pavement you will have a black baby. **1954** LORD ELTON *General Gordon* 108 [Weymouth, Dorset, 1868] Gordon's cousin remembered .. at this time nothing would persuade Gordon to step on the cracks, and his usual rapid gait was diversified by the frequent hops and strides with which he avoided them. **1984** Man, 51 [Gloucester] I don't step on the lines on pavements—still.

PEACOCK bird of ill omen

1660 LUPTON *Thousand Notable Things* § 311. This Bird doth by his loud and harsh clamor, Prophesie, and foretell rain .. And Paracelsus saies, if a Peacock cries more than usuall, or out of his time, it foretels the death of some in that family to whom it doth belong. **1968** *Observer* Suppl. 24 Nov. 12 [Peter Bull, actor] Anything to do with peacocks is fatal .. I put on a play called 'Cage me a Peacock' which lost me every penny I had.

PEACOCK FEATHERS

1586 HOLINSHED *Chronicles* (1808, VI 251–2) [Kilkenny, Eire, 1323] The ladie Alice Kettle .. was charged to haue nightlie conference with a spirit .. to whome she sacrificed in the high waie nine red cocks, and nine peacocks eies. **1865** *N & Q* 3rd ser. VIII 332. Can anyone inform me the origin of the theory, that the possession of peacocks' feathers brings ill luck to the owner? **1866** *N & Q* 3rd ser. IX 187. I can vouch for a superstitious feeling regarding peacocks' feathers being general in Derbyshire and the surrounding counties.

It is considered extremely unlucky to have them in the house, and they are believed to bring losses and various misfortunes, including illness and death, to the inmates. I have seen people perfectly horrified when a child or other person has unwittingly brought into the house one of these feathers. **1881** *N & Q* 6th ser. III 339. A servant hailing from March, Cambridgeshire, seeing peacocks' feathers brought into her master's house for decorative purposes, remarked, 'We shall never have no more luck now.' **1883** *Folklore* 93. I have met various people who object to have the peacock's-feather fans, &c., now so much in vogue, in the house because they consider them unlucky. **1883** BURNE *Shropshire* 230. The good folk of a certain Nottinghamshire village, near Southwell, wondered at their clergyman's wife for allowing peacock's feathers to be set up in her little daughters' nursery. The young ladies would never be married if she did. *c.***1890** [Bristol, Glos.] A peacock feather in the house makes old maids. **1893** *N & Q* 8th ser. IV 531. Some eight or ten years ago a gentleman well known to me went to call on a baronet, an intimate friend of his. Unfortunately .. he had the eye of a peacock's feather in his hat. When the lady of the house saw it, she snatched it from him, and threw it out of the hall door. **1899** *Newcastle Weekly Chronicle* 11 Feb. 7 [Jesmond] It is lucky to have a live peacock on a farm, but very unlucky to have peacock feathers in the house. **1968** *Sunday Express* 11 Aug. 4. Recently I was presented with a bunch of peacock tail feathers. My husband eyed them with dismay and said: 'That means bad luck.' I am not superstitious but within three days a fox had killed several of our hens .. and a marauding gull stole 23 of our goldfish. **1977** R. C. SCRIVEN *Edge of Darkness, Edge of Light* 85 [Yorks., *c.*1910] I took into the kitchen a long, lovely tail-plume Pharaoh [the peacock] had moulted. Ann boxed my ears. 'I'll learn thi to bring t'evil eye int' t' house,' she said. **1984** *Observer Suppl.* 29 Jan. 32. In a corner of the room, there is a large collection of peacock feathers .. 'They're supposed to be terribly unlucky in the house

.. But, really, we've been fortunate' [Christina Foyle said].

PEARL under pillow

1963 *New Society* 3 Aug. 23. Within the last year .. a married couple sought expert medical advice because they were childless; but they also slept with a pearl under their pillow to make sure they were doing everything possible to remedy their childless condition.

PEARLS = tears

*c.***1623** WEBSTER *Duchess of Malfi* III v. DUCHESS. I had a very strange dreame tonight .. Me thought I wore my Coronet of State, And on a sudaine all the Diamonds Were chang'd to Pearles. ANTONIO. My Interpretation Is, you'll weepe shortly .. the pearles Doe signifie your teares. **1641** KILLIGREW *Parson's Wedding* II v. The captain sad! 'tis prophetic: I'd as lieve have dreamt of pearl. **1937** H. A. VACHELL *Golden House* 293. The ring had been chosen by Dawn; a pearl surrounded with brilliants. Humphry had said that pearls brought tears. He recalled Dawn's reply: 'To the men who buy them, perhaps, not to the women who wear them.' **1966** B. MESSENGER *Guide to Etiquette* 38. Any girl who is unable to make up her mind about the gem for her engagement ring might like to choose her birthstone .. June— moonstone or pearls (considered by many to be unlucky, however). **1984** [Cambridge] At a wedding here last June, the bride and bridesmaids were all festooned in long strings of pearls. The bride said she knew of the superstition about pearls, but had decided to have them all the same.

PEAS, nine: divination

1654 DOROTHY OSBORNE Letter to William Temple, 22 July (1928, 175–6) I could not forbeare layeing a Pescod with nine Pease in't under the doore Yesterday and was informed by it that my husbands name should bee Thomas, how doe you like that? but what Thomas I cannot imagine. **1714** GAY *Shepherd's Week* 35. As Peascods once I pluck'd, I chanc'd to see One that was closely fill'd with three times three, Which when I crop'd I safely home convey'd And o'er my Door the Spell in secret laid. *c.*1760 *Mother Bunch's Closet* 20. If any one .. desires to know the name of the man whom she shall marry, let her .. seek a green peascod, in which there are full nine peas; which done, either write or cause to be written, on a small slip of paper, these words. 'Come in my dear, and do not fear.' Which writing you must enclose within the aforesaid peascod, and lay it under the door, then mind the next person who comes in, for you'll certainly marry one of the same name. 1824 MACTAGGART *Gallovidian Encyclopedia* 384. A bean podd, that holds five beans, and a pea podd, which contains nine peas, are considered to be sonsy [lucky], and put up above the lintle of the door by maidens, and the first male that enters after they are so placed will either be their husband, or like him. 1830 FORBY *East Anglia* 424. The mode of discovering the sweetheart, by laying a peascod with nine peas in it over the door, is common to us with most other parts of the country. 1849 BRAND *Antiquities* II 99. The kitchenmaid, when she shells green peas, never omits, if she finds one having nine peas, to lay it on the lintel of the kitchen-door, and the first clown who enters it is infallibly to be her husband, or at least her sweetheart. 1878 *N & Q* 5th ser. X 494. A pod with nine peas in it should always be hung on the handle of the front door of the house. The first dark man who passes through the door will marry one of the heiresses of the family. 1923 [Ruishton, Som.] If a girl hangs a pod containing nine peas over the door the first single man to enter will be her husband. 1946 UTTLEY *Country Things* 134. Nine peas in a pod was an omen I much desired, and I always counted my peas.

Cf. LEAVES, nine: divination.

PENDULUM: divination

1584 SCOT *Discoverie of Witchcraft* XVI v. You shall knowe what it is a clocke, if you hold betweene your finger and your thumbe a thred of six or seven inches long, unto the other end whereof is tied a gold ring, or some such like thing: in such sort as upon the beating of your pulse, and the mooving of the

ring, the same may strike upon either side of a goblet or glasse. 1620 MELTON *Astrologaster* 45. A man may know whats a clocke, onely by a Ring and a silver Beaker. 1697 J. POTTER *Antiquities of Greece* II 317–18. Sometimes they [ancient Greeks] fill'd a Bowl with Water, and let down into it a Ring, equally poised on each side and hanging by a Thread tied to one of the Fingers: then in a form of Prayer requested of the Gods to declare, or confirm the Question in dispute; where upon, if the thing proposed was true, the Ring of its own accord would strike against the side of the Bowl a set number of Times. 1851 *N & Q* 1st ser. III 517. *Od* [a hypothetical force]. One of the experiments by which the existence of this agency is tested, consists in attaching a horsehair to the first joint of the forefinger, and suspending to it a smooth gold ring. When the elbow is rested on the table, and the finger held in a horizontal position, the ring begins to oscillate in a plane of the direction of the finger; but if a female takes hold of the left hand of the person thus experimenting, the ring begins .. to oscillate in a plane at right angles to that of its former direction .. For this purpose .. it is essential .. that the ring be a wedding-ring, and of course the lady towards whom it oscillates is set down as the future spouse of the gentleman experimenting. 1853 *Pictorial Juvenile Mag.* II 158. If you tie a shilling .. to a piece of thread, and .. suspend the shilling within a tumbler .. it will .. begin to swing backwards and forwards .. until the shilling will strike the side of the glass. It will strike .. just so many times as will indicate the nearest hour. 1866 HENDERSON *Northern Counties* 82. Take a tumbler of 'south running water' .. borrow the wedding ring of some gudewife, and suspend it by a hair of one's head over the glass .. If the ring hit against the side of the glass, the holder of it will die an old maid; if it turn quickly round she will be married once—if slowly, twice. 1878 *Folk-Lore Record* 31 [Hallowe'en] A ring, or piece of money, is suspended by a thread or hair, and held as steadily as may be within a glass .. When it begins to oscillate it will strike the number of years that are to pass before the holder of the thread is married. **1928** A. R. WRIGHT *English Folklore* 36 [Norfolk, 'during the war'] His landlady wanted to separate hen eggs for setting from cock eggs for immediate consumption, and suspended a small cork by a thread .. over the egg to be tested. The sex was announced by the cork oscillating from side to side or moving in a circle .. This .. is now chiefly practised as a Christmas game, with a thread, a shilling, and a wine-glass, to answer questions, tell a lady's age, and so on. **1950** Unpublished diary. Cousin Mildred earnestly hopes her next baby will be a girl. 'Why not try the test?' said Adelaide, our Bradford [Yorks.] aunt. 'You suspend your wedding ring on a hair from your own head and if, as you hold it, it turns clockwise then it's going to be a daughter.' **1955** Bookseller, *c.*50 [Kensington, London] I always test any medicine which is prescribed for me, to see if it's good for me. I place the bottle on a white sheet of paper and then hang a pendulum over it. When the pendulum starts moving, I place my hand between it and the bottle. If the pendulum moves in a clockwise manner, all's well, if anti-clockwise then there's an evil influence, and if in no certain manner, the medicine will not be actively good or bad. If the medicine is for my wife, I do the same thing, but hold her hand in my other hand. **1961** *Weekend* 17 Dec. 18. Many readers described how they had regularly used a 'magic' pendulum—either a wedding ring on a silken strand, or a darning needle on a thread, or a simple bead to foretell 'with invariable success' the sex of babies. **1973** *Annabel* Oct. 4 [Cumnock, Ayr.] When my young sister-in-law was pregnant she tied a length of thread through her wedding ring and held it over her bare tummy. Seemingly, if it moved straight up and down it would be a girl; if it moved round in a circle it would be a boy. The ring moved up and down. Sure enough, five months later she had a baby girl.

PEONY protects

*c.*1050 MS Cotton Vitell. C. iii (COCKAYNE *Leechdoms* I 303) If any one suffer stormy weather, in rowing, let him take this [peony], set ablaze for incense; the rough weather will be countermanded. For cramps, and for quiverings, let the patient .. have it with him; then if any one beareth it with him, all evil ones will dread him. **1579** LUPTON *Thousand Notable Things* IV § 100. If the roote of Pyony (especialy, of the male Pyony) be hangde at the necke of a chylde or a boye, that hath the falling sycknes: it doth helpe very much. **1621** BURTON *Anatomie of Melancholy* pt. 2 sect. 5 mem. 1 subs. 5. Amulets .. are not altogether to be rejected, Piony doth help Epilepsie. **1627** BACON *Sylva Sylvarum* § 966. It hath beene long received, and confirmed by divers Trialls; That the Root of the Male-Piony, dried, tied to the Necke, doth help the Falling-Sicknesse; And likewise the Incubus, which we call the Mare. **1640** J. PARKINSON *Theatrum Botanicum* 1382. I saw a childe freed from that disease [epilepsy], that had for eight whole moneths together, worne a good peece of the roote about him. **1791** E. DARWIN *Loves of Plants* 90 n. Even at this day bits of dried root of Peony are rubbed smooth, and strung, and sold under the name of Anodyne necklaces, and tied round the necks of children, to facilitate the growth of teeth! **1878** *Folk-Lore Record* 44 [Fittleworth, Sussex] A necklace made of beads turned from the root of the peony is worn by children to prevent convulsions, and to aid dentition.

PETTICOAT showing

1864 R. CHAMBERS *Book of Days* II 322 [Suffolk] If a girl's petticoats are longer than her frock, that is a sign that her father loves her better than her mother does—perhaps because it is plain that her mother does not attend so much to her dress as she ought to do. **1879** J. NAPIER *West of Scotland* 137. If a daughter's petticoat was longer than her frock, it shewed that her father loved her better than her mother did. **1959** Woman, 51 [Oxted, Surrey] If any of the staff are showing a petticoat they are accused of husband hunting, but when I was a child in London it was always 'Your father loves you better than your mother.'

PETTING STONE, bride steps or leaps over

1824 G. ALLAN *Durham* 207. Ethelwold caused a ponderous Cross of stone .. to be erected in the ground adjoining Lindisfarne Abbey .. The socket-stone .. is now called the Petting Stone. Whenever a marriage is solemnized at the church, after the ceremony the bride is to step upon it, and if she cannot stride to the end thereof, it is said the marriage will prove unfortunate. **1858** DENHAM *North of England* (1895, 67) The Petting Stone. Marriages celebrated at the church of Lindisfarne, in Holy Island [Northumb.] are said to be unfortunate if the bride, on making the essay, cannot step the length of it. This stone is supposed to be the pedestal of St Cuthbert's Cross, anciently held in superstitious veneration. **1879** HENDERSON *Northern Counties* 38 [Northumb.] At the village of Belford .. the bridal pair with their attendants leap over a stone placed in their path at the outside of the church porch. This is called the louping stone or petting stone .. In the year 1868 .. in .. High Coquetdale .. a stick was held .. for the bride to jump over. Had she .. stumbled the worst auguries as to her temper would have been drawn. **1901** *N & Q* 9th ser. VII 135. In 1874 .. I assisted in jumping the bride over the jumping-stone .. at the entrance .. of the church at Woodhorn, Northumberland. This .. took place as the bridal party were leaving the church. Its omission would have been considered very unlucky. **1902** *Folklore* 227 [Whittingham, Northumb.] Directly the wedding party was safely within the church .. the young men of the village proceeded to erect the 'Petting Stone' within the porch, which .. consisted of three short stone pillars .. at one time .. the supports of an old 'trough' tombstone. These were placed 'Stonehenge' fashion .. in front of the church door, and two .. young men .. were told off to 'jump' the bride over. **1953** *Sunday Times* 6 Sept. 8 [Holy Island] The bride .. was 'handed' over the 'petting-stone' .. 'for luck' by her great-uncle of 88 and her second-cousin of 87 .. The petting-stone is the worn base of a Saxon cross set among the grave stones. **1962** *Times* 6 Mar. 7 [Tewin, Herts.] As she leaves

the church [the bride] will hold her bridegroom's hand and jump over a 'petting stool' .. symbolizing her husband's promise to help her through life .. The wooden stool was used by her mother in 1933 [at her wedding in Northumberland].

Cf. BRIDE lifted over threshold.

PICTURE falls

1668 P. HEYLIN *Life of William Laud* 451. Going into his upper study .. he [Laud] found his Picture at full Length, and taken as near unto the life as the Pensil was able to express it, to be fallen on the Floor, and lying flat upon its face, the string being broke by which it was hanged against the wall. At the sight whereof .. he began to fear it as an *Omen* of that ruine which was coming toward him [he was executed]. **1692** *Athenian Mercury* VIII no. 6. We read in many very good Authors, and I my self have known it, it being so common a thing, that before a King, or some great Man dyes, or is beheaded, &c. his Picture .. suffers some considerable Damage, as falling from the place where it hung, the string breaking by some strange invisible touch. **1774** BOSWELL *For the Defense* (1960, 303) Edinburgh, 30 Aug. Here is a man sitting for his picture who is to be hanged this day eight days .. When it was finished and hung upon a nail to dry, it swung, which looked ominous, and made an impression on my fancy. **1874** KILVERT *Diary* 15 Jan. Mrs Knight told me she had been taken over Wraxall House and shown the doorway where the great picture fell down and broke the neck of the wicked Lady Long when she came back from her second marriage, after having promised her deceased husband she would not marry again. **1883** BURNE *Shropshire* 280. A picture falling is very unlucky, 'especially on a wedding-day', adds one. If a family portrait falls, it is a sign of death. **1899** *N & Q* 9th ser. IV 6. As we reached the door, a large portrait of my stepmother fell .. Neither the glass nor the cord of the picture was broken, and the nail from which it had been suspended remained firmly in the wall .. My father was greatly perturbed, and telegraphed for news of his wife. **1923**

[West Malling, Kent] If a picture falls from the wall without apparent reason it foretells a death in the house. **1932** C. IGGLESDEN *Those Superstitions* 213. Should the portrait of a man or woman fall it is said that that person's death will follow within a month, but to ensure the death penalty the glass must be broken. **1975** C. COOKSON *Our Kate* 247. When a picture dropped from the wall you waited day-in, day-out for someone to die .. I have known Kate coddle me granda with hot whisky and extra care after a picture fell. **1986** Woman, *c*.50 [Leics.] I've never known a picture fall, without someone in the family dying soon after.

Cf. MIRROR, breaking.

PICTURE over door or bed

1932 C. IGGLESDEN *Those Superstitions* 234. Pictures may not be hung over the [theatrical] dressing-room door. **1933** *Folklore* 193 [Digby, Lincs.] Bad luck .. to hang a picture over a doorway. **1984** Woman, 56 [South Shields, Co. Durham] Pictures were never hung over the bed-head in our house. It was considered very unlucky.

PICTURE, taking

1879 J. NAPIER *West of Scotland* 142. I know of several persons who refuse to have their likeness taken lest it prove unlucky; and give as instances the cases of several of their friends who never had a day's health after being photographed. **1880** F. H. GROOME *Gipsy Tents* 337–8. She clutched my sketch-book with one hand and sent it spinning along the road, while with the other she seized poor Sinfi .. and lugged her up .. 'How dare you let a man put you in his book, to .. steal the blood from your face? .. I won't have her drawed out .. I know there's a *fiz* (a charm) in it. There was my youngest, that the gorja [man] drawed out on Newmarket Heath, she never held her head up after, but wasted away, and died.' **1887** F. T. HAVERGAL *Herefordshire Words* 43. To illustrate the popular prejudice against .. photography, 'It's all a charm.' **1916** *Folklore* 308. An old couple from Sopworth, Wilts., drove over to see some friends near Stroud. The master of the house

wanted to take their photograph, in the cart, but they begged him not to think of such a thing, as their last horse died very soon after having had his photograph taken. This was in **1910** or **1911**. **1932** H. V. MORTON *In Search of Wales* 231. 'Why did the old women hide their faces in their shawls when they saw a camera?' 'Oh, it is bad luck to have your photograph taken,' said the old lady. **1958** *Trans. Devon. Ass.* 246. On Saturday, 8 March **1958**, there was a soccer match between Beer and Dawlish. Before the match began, a press photographer approached the teams and asked to be allowed to take a picture. Both teams flatly refused on the ground that it is unlucky to have a picture taken before a match. **1968** *Observer* Suppl. 24 Nov. 12 [Peter Bull, actor] I've got a marvellous magic tie which brings one extraordinarily good luck .. it would lose all its magic if I was photographed with it.

PIEBALD HORSE cures whooping cough

1850 *N & Q* 1st ser. I 397. I did every thing that every body teld me. One teld me to get him breathed on by a pie-bald horse. I took him ever such a way .. and put him under the horse's mouth; but he was no better. **1855** *N & Q* 1st ser. XII 37 [Cornwall] If a piebald horse is to be found .. the child is taken to it, and passed thrice under its belly. **1887** 'SPERANZA' WILDE *Superstitions of Ireland* II 92. The touch of a piebald horse. Even a piebald horse pawing before the door helps the cure. **1899** *Newcastle Weekly Chronicle* 11 Feb. 7 [Jesmond] A hair from a piebald horse will cure whooping cough. **1912** LEATHER *Herefordshire* 82 [She] cured her grandson of whooping cough by holding him up to inhale the breath of a piebald horse. **1954** Girl, 14 [Newbridge, Monmouth.] There is a superstition about a little boy going out into the field where there were a number of horses grazing, and the little boy went through one of the horses' legs to cure the whooping cough.

PIEBALD HORSE cures whooping cough via its rider

c.**1780** T. PARK MS Note in Brand's *Antiquities* 97. In Yorkshire, if a child has the Chin-Cough .. and a man happens to pass on a piebald horse, if .. the relatives run after him, and desire him to say, what will cure the chincough? Whether his reply is, to give the child a glass of water, or to draw it thro' a hedge, the recipe is believed to be infallible. **1813** BRAND *Antiquities* II 581. There is a vulgar Superstition still remaining in Devonshire and Cornwall, that any person who rides on a pye-balled Horse can cure the Chin-cough. **1825** JAMIESON *Scottish Dict.* Suppl. II 209. That absurd idea, so generally prevailing among the vulgar .. that one who rides a pyat-horse has power to prescribe an infallible remedy for the chin-cough .. A worthy friend of mine .. told me, that he used to be pursued by people running after him out of every village .. bawling, 'Man wi' the pyatie horse, what's gude for the kink-host?' **1831** HONE *Year Book* 29 Feb. Country women travel the road to meet a man on a piebald horse, and ask him what will cure hooping cough .. A young mother made an enquiry .. as directed; he told her to put her finger, to the knuckle joint, down the child's throat, and hold it there twenty minutes by the church clock. She went home, and did so, and it never coughed again. **1863** R. CHAMBERS *Book of Days* I 733 [Suffolk] My grandfather at one time always used to ride a piebald horse, and he has frequently been stopped by people asking for a cure for whooping-cough. His invariable answer was, 'Patience and water-gruel'. **1882** *Folk-Lore Record* 83 [Co. Wexford] [They] watch on the roads for the first man they meet riding a piebald horse, and accost him thus: 'Hallo, man on the piebald horse, what is good for the whooping cough?' And they are supposed to be cured by whatever he may prescribe.

PIEBALD HORSE, meeting

1882 *N & Q* 6th ser. VI 357. I remember a tradition of my childhood that if you could touch a piebald horse with a man on it, accidentally met, or else curtsey nine times backwards, whatever you wished for while doing so would come to pass. It required some dexterity to perform either feat unremarked while

taking a constitutional in Hyde Park. **1911** *N & Q* 11th ser. III 217–18. Spitting 'for luck' is still practised .. on a finger, and touching the toes of the boots when a black-and-white horse is espied. **1931** *Folklore* 293. An Oxfordshire girl .. says .. if you see a piebald horse, you should cross your fingers till you see a dog, and then you will have some luck. **1950** *Woman*, 20 [Bath, Som.] A piebald horse is lucky. If you see one you should cross your fingers and wish, spit over your left shoulder and say 'Shakespeare come true.'

PIEBALD HORSE, seeing tail of

1965 *Woman*, 40 [London] A piebald horse is very lucky, I know; but you mustn't see its tail. **1983** Doctor, *c.*60 [Colchester, Essex] There's one thing I still do, and that's if I see a piebald horse, I must not see its tail or I would be unlucky.

PIG dies

1913 E. M. WRIGHT *Rustic Speech* 216. Just twenty years ago, when an old cook .. inquired after my brother who was then recovering from a severe attack of scarlet-fever, she concluded .. 'I knew quite well that there would be a serious illness in your family, because you told me that one of the pigs had died suddenly.'

PIG, disease transferred to

1887 'SPERANZA' WILDE *Superstitions of Ireland* II 95. Wrap the child in a blanket, take it to a pigsty, rub the child's head to the back of a pig, and the mumps will leave it and pass from the child to the animal.

PIG, meeting

1787 GROSE *Provincial Glossary* Superstitions 61–2. If .. a sow cross the road, you will probably meet with a disappointment, if not a bodily accident, before you return home .. If the sow is attended with her litter of pigs, it is lucky, and denotes a successful journey. *c.***1816** Wilkie MS (HENDERSON *Northern Counties* 1879, 21) It is unlucky for swine to cross the path in front of a wedding-party. Hence the old adage 'The swine's run through it.' **1852**

N & Q 1st ser. V 5 [Prestonpans, East Lothian] If, on their way to their boats [the fishermen] meet a pig, they at once turn back and defer their embarkation. **1861** E. B. RAMSAY *Scottish Life* 30–1. Among the many superstitious notions . . prevalent among the lower orders of the fishing towns on the east coast of Fife, till very recently, that class entertained a great horror of swine . . If that animal crossed their path when about to set out on a sea voyage, they considered it so unlucky an omen that they would not venture off. Ibid. 30 n. I recollect an old Scottish gentleman, who shared this horror, asking very gravely, 'Were not swine forbidden under the law, and cursed under the gospel?' **1895** F. T. ELWORTHY *Evil Eye* 31 [SW England] The writer knows people . . who are terrified if a . . sow cross their path, and fully expect some misfortune presently to happen. **1899** *Newcastle Weekly Chronicle* 11 Feb. 7 [Jesmond] It is unlucky to meet a pig when on the way to a wedding, a funeral, or a christening. **1909** *N & Q* 10th ser. XII 483 [Stromness, Orkney] Sailors count it unlucky to see a pig on land when about to set sail. **1923** [Lyng, Som.] It is unlucky to have a pig cross your path when walking along a country lane.

PIG, nose of

1887 *Folklore* 195 [Summercourt, Cornwall] The lady took the nose of a pig, that was killed the day before, in her right hand; stood with her back to the house, and threw the nose over her head, and over the house, into the back garden. Had she failed in the attempt her luck was supposed to be bad.

PIG, taboo on flesh of

*c.***600** BC Deuteronomy 14: 7–8. Ye shall not eat . . the swine . . it is unclean unto you: ye shall not eat of their flesh, nor touch their dead carcase. **1831** J. LOGAN *Scottish Gael* (1876, II 61) The Scots retain an antipathy to pork; whether derived from the ancient Celts, or the early Christians, is difficult to determine, and although the aversion is disappearing, it is far from being eradicated. In the Agricultural Report for the county of Banff, it is stated that live swine have never yet been sold in any of the fairs of the north. **1878** A. MACGREGOR *Brahan Seer* 108 [*c.*1840, Skye] 'Superstitions of Highlanders'. Farquhar had a superstitious dislike to bacon or pork . . The servants . . prepared lean parts of the meat . . which they passed off as mutton [of which, while eating], he frequently said, to no small amusement and tittering of the domestics . . 'Thou art the good, right meat, and not the filthy, unclean pig.' **1885** *Folklore* 182 [St Combs, Aberdeen.] The flesh of the pig was not used as food by many. I was told lately by a St Combs man that his father . . had occasion to borrow a pot in which to cook his dinner . . of pork. When it came to the knowledge of the man that had given the pot in loan that pork had been cooked in it, he was in a great rage, and the pot underwent a great deal of scrubbing to purify it. There are some yet that will not taste the flesh of pig. **1898** *Aberdeen Weekly Free Press* 29 Oct. 3. I remember . . going on board a steam trawler . . and asking the cook . . what sort of fishing they had been having. 'Very poor, miss . . we've had no luck since that thing came on board,' he said, pointing to a partly consumed ham . . 'I'm going to throw it overboard as soon as we get outside the bar.' **1904** *Folklore* 96. On the Fifeshire coast the pig is par excellence the unlucky being. 'Soo's tail to ye!' is the common taunt of the (non-fishing) small boy . . One informant told me that some years ago he flung a pig's tail aboard a boat passing outwards at Buckhaven, and that the crew turned and came back. **1924** *N & Q* CXLVII 159. It is a well-known fact that some fishermen will not carry pork to sea, especially the Brixham [Devon] smacks. **1956** [Scarborough, Yorks.] The fishermen's families here will have a joint of pork on Sundays, but of course they won't take it on board. They won't have anything to do with a pig on their boats.

Cf. HARE, eating: taboo.

'PIG' taboo word

1726 C. ELLISON *Benwell Village* 20 [Northumb.] Neither did here, In sight appear Of Swine, foul, dreadful Nomen;

Which common Fame, Will oft proclaim Of Luck, dire, wretched Omen. **1861** E. B. RAMSAY *Scottish Life* 31–2 [E. coast, Fife] It was arranged that his friend [a visiting minister who could not believe the taboo] was to read the chapter relating to the herd of swine into which the evil spirits were cast. Accordingly, when the first verse was read .. a slight commotion was observable among the audience, each one of them putting his or her hand on any piece of iron—on a nail on the seat or back-board, or to the nails on their shoes. At the repetition of the word again and again, more commotion was visible, and the words 'cauld airn' .. were heard issuing from various corners of the church. And finally, on his coming over the hated word again, the alarmed parishioners .. rose and all left the church in a body. **1875** *N & Q* 5th ser. III 204 [Flamborough Head, Yorks.] The fishermen would not go out if any one mentioned a pig in any way when they were baiting their lines. **1898** A. C. HADDON *Study of Man* 420. In Sunderland [Co. Durham] the pig is known by fisherfolk as 'the queer fellow', it bringing bad luck for [it] to be called by [its] proper designation. **1930** P. F. ANSON *East Coast of Scotland* 43 [St Monans, *c.*1884] A minister came to preach .. and chose for his text the parable of the prodigal son .. His astonishment was extreme when on reading the words 'and he sent him into the fields to feed swine', a simultaneous mutter of 'Touch cauld iron', accompanied by a general bowing down towards cuddy heels and heads of nails in the pews, took place. **1952** Girl, 14 [Aberdeen] It is unlucky for someone to speak about a pig without touching cold iron. **1964** *Folklore* 39. The formula 'cauld iron' must be used if the ill-omened name is inadvertently blurted out. Indeed this has gone so far that on the Fifeshire coast, the ordinary word for a pig is 'cauldie', i.e. cauld iron, and in Ross-shire pigs are called collectively simply 'themselves'. **1986** Woman, 56 [South Shields, Co. Durham] It was unlucky to say the word 'pig' on a Friday. We used to spell it out, or if we said it by mistake we turned up our thumbs and said 'Thumbs up!' Come to

think of it, my mother *never* said 'pig'— it was always 'porker'.

Cf. 'HARE' OR 'RABBIT' taboo word.

PIGEON, live: used in cures

1627 BACON *Sylva Sylvarum* § 96. The Soales of the Feet have great Affinity with the Head .. Pigeons bleeding, applyed to the Soales of the Feet, ease the Head. **1660** J. TAYLOR *Rule of Conscience* II II rule 2 (ed. Heber, XXI, 290) Cruelty to beasts is innocent when it is charity to men: and therefore though we do not eat them, yet we cut living pigeons in halfs and apply them to the feet of men in fevers. **1668** PEPYS *Diary* 21 Jan. Comes news from Kate Joyce that if I would see her husband alive, I must come presently .. his breath rattled in his throate and they did lay pigeons to his feet while I was in the house. **1678** W. SALMON *London Dispensatory* 224. A Live Pigeon .. cut in the middle and laid to the feet, abates the heat of burning Feavers .. and so laid to the Head, takes away Head aches, Frenzy, Melancholy, and Madness. **1874** *Journal Anthropological Inst.* III 269 [Banff.] Cure for any disease .. Two live pigeons were .. ripped up, and tied to the soles of the patient's feet. A near relative .. removed the pigeons and carried them to a place which the dead and the living did not cross, that is .. a precipice, and left them. Some who have gone through this rite are still alive. **1900** *N & Q* 9th ser. VI 306–7. Some forty years ago, a farmer living in the Isle of Axholme [Lincs.] was asked by a woman .. to give her one of [his tame pigeons]. Her husband was ill, and she desired to cut it open alive and put it on his breast to cure him .. The farmer disregarded the woman's petition, and used strong language at being thought capable of lending countenance to such a horrible rite. Ibid. 12. Within the last few weeks this remedy was applied by a lady in Deptford [London] to her .. son .. The remedy did not succeed. The infant died of pneumonia the next night.

Cf. SHEEP cures: organs and skin.

PIGEON, longing for = death omen

1851 *N & Q* 1st ser. III 517. On applying .. to a highly respectable farmer's wife to know if she had any pigeons ready to eat, as a sick person had expressed a longing for one, she said 'Ah! poor fellow! is he so far gone? A pigeon is generally almost the last thing they want; I have supplied many a one for the like purpose.' **1919** *Folklore* 157 [Llanilar, Cardigan.] If a rich man asks for a pigeon-pie or a pigeon in any other form, it is a sign that his death is near.

PIGEON settles = death omen

1861 *N & Q* 2nd ser. XII 492. Pigeons coming into a house [are] unlucky. If they settle on a table, a sign of sickness; if on a bed, of death. **1899** *Newcastle Weekly Chronicle* 11 Feb. 7 [Jesmond] A strange pigeon, especially if white, alighting on the house or flying in front of one indicates death. **1925** D. R. PHILLIPS *Vale of Neath* 598. A pigeon perched on the top of a coal pit . . is usually called '*Aderyn y Corff*' or corpse bird and prognosticates death. **1926** *Folklore* 364 [London] A pigeon . . settled on the wash-house where I was working, and the woman's old man died. **1953** Girl, 15 [Knighton, Radnor.] If a white pigeon lands on top of a chimney there will be a death in the house.

Cf. DOVE sign of peace to departing soul.

PIGEONS' FEATHERS, lying on

*c.***1607** SHAKESPEARE *Tymon of Athens* IV iii. Plucke stout mens pillowes from below their heads. **1617** FYNES MORYSON *Itinerary* pt. 3 I 34. The Italian Sansovinus grossely erreth in this kinde . . who affirmes that Parents in England take the pillowes from the heads of their children ready to die, out of tender pitty and charity, to putt them out of their paine. **1684** H. WOOLLEY *Queen-like Closet* Suppl. 11. A Man taken suddenly with an Apoplex . . I being called unto him, chanced to come just when they had taken the Pillow from his Head, and were going to strip him . . but he lived above ten hours after. **1710** *British Apollo* 25 Jan. *Q.* I have heard, that if any body be sick and lye a dying, if they lye upon Pigeon's Feathers they will lye Languishing and never Dye, but be in Pain and Torment. *A.* This is an Old Woman's Story. But the Scent of Pigeons

Feathers are so strong, that they are not fit to make Beds with. **1787** GROSE *Provincial Glossary* Superstitions 69. It is impossible for a person to die while resting on a pillow stuffed with the feathers of a dove; but they will struggle with death in a most exquisite torture. The pillows of dying persons are therefore frequently taken away, when they appear in great agonies, lest they may have pigeons feathers in them. **1847** E. BRONTË *Wuthering Heights* XII. Ah, they put pigeons' feathers in the pillows— no wonder I couldn't die! **1861** C. C. ROBINSON *Dialect of Leeds* 298. A person can't die on a feather bed. We know of one or two in a dying state who were removed from their beds upon this account, and being laid on the floor, died, of course, 'nat'rally'. **1888** S. O. ADDY *Sheffield Glossary* xx. It is commonly said in this neighbourhood that people cannot die easily on feather beds, and that if a dying person is lying upon a feather bed it should be changed to a flock bed. Old nurses . . used to take the pillows, if stuffed with feathers, from the heads of people who were about to die. **1899** *Newcastle Weekly Chronicle* 11 Feb. 7 [Jesmond] Game feathers should not be put in a bed, because no one can die on them. **1938** *Folklore* 225 [Shrops.] A woman at Ford . . related that her husband just couldn't go. Then she remembered that there were some pigeon's feathers in the bed. So she pulled the poor old man off the bed on to the floor, 'and then . . he went off as nice and easy as you please.'

PIN as present

1711 *Spectator* 14 July. This very old woman had the reputation of a witch . . There was not a maid in the parish that would take a pin of her, though she should offer a bag of money with it. **1755** *Connoisseur* 13 Mar. The old woman had very often asked them for a pin, but they took care never to give her anything that was sharp, because she should not bewitch them. *c.***1797** H. MORE *Tawney Rachel* 7. She would rather have gone with her gown open than have taken a pin of an old woman, for fear of being bewitched. **1866** HENDERSON *Northern Counties* 88. Many . .

people would not . . lend another a pin. They will say, 'You may take one, but, mind, I do not give it.' **1912** *N & Q* 11th ser. V 157. Having been commissioned by the members of a mother's meeting to spend some collected money on a present for a conductor of the meeting, who was about to leave, she bought a brooch. This . . was objected to because of the pin; and it had to be exchanged for a pendant before the mothers were content. **1912** LEATHER *Herefordshire* 86. It is very unlucky to say 'thank you' for a pin. **1923** [Bridgwater, Som.] It is very unlucky to receive a knife, brooch or anything with a pin in it, unless you pay a penny or two for the gift. **1968** *Observer* Suppl. 24 Nov. 8 [John McCormack, boxing champion] If you give a safety-pin never give it direct or you'll sever your friendship. Always pin it on his jacket. **1981** *Woman*, 20 [Sheffield, Yorks.] When a pin or needle is passed from one person to another it must always be in a piece of cloth.

Cf. KNIFE as present.

PIN, finding

1668 PEPYS *Diary* 2 Jan. I see your Majesty do not remember the old English proverb, 'He that will not stoop for a pin, will never be worth a pound.' **1842** HALLIWELL *Nursery Rhymes* 98. See a pin and pick it up, All the day you'll have good luck; See a pin and let it lay, Bad luck you'll have all the day! **1883** BURNE *Shropshire* 279–80. Salopians say, 'Pick up pins, pick up sorrow.' But side by side with this we have the thrifty maxim—'See a pin and let it stay (or 'lie'), You'll want a pin another day (or 'before you die'). See a pin and pick it up, All the day you'll have good luck.' **1922** JOYCE *Ulysses* (1960, 214) Women won't pick up pins. Say it cuts to [love]. **1954** Girl, 15 [Forfar, Angus] The discovery of a bright new pin means a new and staunch friend. **1956** Girl, *c.*18 [Brierley Hill, Staffs.] Good luck to find a safety pin in the street. **1969** S. MAYS *Reuben's Corner* [Essex] 164. Never should dropped pins be disregarded . . 'See a pin and let it lie, Before the evening you will cry.' **1983** Girl, 13 [Maldon, Essex] See a pin, pick it up, All the day you'll have good luck. **1987** *Woman*, *c.*40 [Waterlooville, Hants.] My husband's terrible. If he sees a pin he'll grovel in the gutter to pick it up. He'd go to any length rather than leave it lying.

Cf. IRON, finding.

PIN points towards one

1824 MACTAGGART *Gallovidian Encyclopedia* 210. A preen [pin], if the broadside is not found lying towards the face, will not be touched. **1865** *Gents Mag.* pt. 2 700 [Ireland] It is regarded unlucky to find a pin with the point turned towards you. **1873** *Chambers' Journal* 809. To pick up a pin lying with its head towards you . . is matter for rejoicing. **1904** *Folklore* 462 [Abbeyleix, Co. Leix] If you see a pin on the floor with the point towards you, do not lift it or you will have great 'sharpness' and disappointment; but if the pin's head is towards you, lift it, and you will have good luck and never want for a pin. **1924** *Folklore* 352 [Westleton, Suffolk] The old woman suddenly 'turned back in a circle', and retraced her steps. Asked why . . she replied 'I saw a pin on the road with its point towards me, and I could not go near it or go on because of getting bad luck.'

Cf. KNIFE, spinning: points towards one.

PINS, bride's

1565 (D. H. FLEMING *Mary Queen of Scots* 348) [after the Queen's marriage to Darnley on 29 July] She suffreth them that stood by, everie man that coulde approche to take owte a pyn [from her wedding gown] and so being commytted unto her ladies changed her garments. **1698** MISSON *Voyageur en Angleterre* (1719, 352 n.) They must throw away, and lose all the Pins. Woe be to the Bride if a single one is left about her; nothing will go right. Woe also to the Bridemaids, if they keep one of them, for they will not be marry'd before Easter. **1878** *Folk-Lore Record* 33 [Fittleworth, Sussex] A bride, on her return from church, is often robbed of all the pins about her dress by the single women present, from the belief that whoever possesses one of them will be married in the course of a year. **1909** M. TREVELYAN *Folk-Lore of Wales* 270–1. A bride must not keep the pins that fasten her wedding dress .. The pins must be thrown over her left shoulder, or into the fire for luck. **1959** *Woman* 14 Mar. 6. If she wears a pin used in the making of a bridal gown, an old superstition says she'll be a bride herself within the next twelve months. **1962** *Folklore* 134. A dressmaker of her acquaintance always keeps the pins she uses when making a wedding-dress, and gives them to her friends for use in picking out horses before betting in a horse-race.

PINS, corpse's

1878 *N & Q* 5th ser. X 49 [Lavant, Sussex] The undertaker tells me that the pins employed on a corpse for any purpose are never used again, but are always deposited in the coffin and buried with the dead body. **1899** *Newcastle Weekly Chronicle* 4 Feb. 7 [Jesmond] A pin left in a shroud causes the dead to walk in the night.

Cf. KNOTS in shroud/clothes of dead.

PINS cure warts

1866 HENDERSON *Northern Counties* 109. Boys take a new pin, cross the warts with it nine times, and fling it over the left shoulder. **1870** *N & Q* 4th ser. VI 340. In Essex a pin is stuck in the ground and as that rusts, so will the wart disappear. **1883** BURNE *Shropshire* 201 n. Take a pin, score it with a knife in several directions, then move it slowly and mysteriously over and around the wart, muttering mysterious and inaudible words. Then the pin is given to the afflicted one, and placed away carefully in some one of his garments, and always worn till the wart disappears.

Cf. NAILS driven in: cure.

PINS defend against corpse

AD **77** PLINY *Natural History* XXXIV XLIV (1857, VI 210) If nails .. that have been extracted from a tomb, are driven into the threshold of a door, they will prevent night-mare. **1824** *Gents Mag.* pt. 2 112 [nr. Rochester, Kent] A superstitious practice of sticking pins in a stile whenever a corpse is taken over it, prevails in these parts. **1870** *N & Q* 4th ser. V 119. An old lady who died in the early part of the present century was in the habit of taking a store of pins in her carriage when she drove out, and whenever she met a funeral would throw some of them out of the carriage window. **1873** *N & Q* 4th ser. XII 44 [Lincs.] A lady told me the other day that when she was a girl, say forty years ago, she and other girls used to go and peep into the scawp-house [charnel-house], belonging to Grantham church; and that every time they did so they threw therein a pin .. to prevent bad luck. **1878** *N & Q* 5th ser. X 49 [Lavant, Sussex] The undertaker promised to stick half-a-dozen black pins in the gate-post of the meadow through which the funeral cortege passed. He tells me he himself did so, and thus the path was not made common. **1932** C. IGGLESDEN *Those Superstitions* 200–1 [Isle of Oxney, Kent] The burial ground is still on the mound, with no approach by road. I am told that years ago when the mourners returned from the burial each one stuck a pin into the gate through which the body had passed. This was to guard against evil which might befall them had they neglected to carry out this primitive protection from the devil. This .. is probably reflected in the custom of a gamekeeper who, in the event of an accident occurring, always sticks a pin in a stile over which the victim may have been carried. **1933** *Folklore* 291 [Willoughton, Lincs.] Some forty-five or fifty years ago .. a bowl was set on the chest of the deceased, and those that went to 'view the corpse' placed pins in the bowl.

Cf. IRON, food pricked with; SALT protects at death.

PINS on ship

1887 *The People* 5 June 5 [Lowestoft, E. Suffolk, fishing smack] A large .. apple tart, wrapped in a clean white napkin fastened with pins .. was handed on board [and] I could see there was something amiss. One man held it, and the captain cautiously took out each pin, and with arm extended to the uttermost, carefully dropped them over the counter into the sea to drown .. The captain then slowly, seriously, and solemnly assured me that pins were spiteful witches, and ought never to be brought on board a vessel. **1923** P. S. JEFFREY *Whitby Lore* 141. To have a pin about you on board ship is considered very foolish, but no one can tell me why. **1938** M. LANE *Edgar Wallace* III [Lincs.] He had outraged their superstitions by bringing a paper of pins on board [a Grimsby trawler, 1890], and this bad impression was not easy to dissipate.

PINS: pinning by another person

1912 LEATHER *Herefordshire* 114. If a village dressmaker accidentally pin a dress to a girl's underclothing when fitting she will say, 'There now, you won't be married this year.' **1957** London tailor, *c.*50. If a tailor pins the garment being fitted onto the customer's own clothes, one pin so pinned means a happy month (two pins two months, and so on) and the customer will return.

Cf. CLOTHES: mending while wearing.

PINS: pinning the Devil

1979 *Mirror* 9 Nov. 24. There is a Greek superstition which is .. remarkable. Suppose you mislay some article in your house and cannot find it. Well, you then stick a pin in the padding of your chair or settee and say: 'I pin the Devil.' Before you know it, you have found the lost article. **1983** Girl, 13 [Maldon, Essex] If you lose something get a pin and stick it in a cushion and say 'I pin you my devil.' I done this when I lost my badge and I found it.

PLANTAIN: divination

1866 HENDERSON *Northern Counties* 77 n. [Berwicks.] A divination is practised by means of 'kemps'. Two spikes must be taken in full bloom, and being bereft of every appearance of blow, they are wrapped in a dock-leaf and laid beneath a stone. If the next morning the spikes appear in blossom, then there will be 'aye love between them twae'. **1899** *Newcastle Weekly Chronicle* 11 Feb. 7 [Jesmond] Ribwort heads are plucked and concealed in the bosom; if they blow [put out stamens] one's lover is thinking of the experimenter. **1910** *Folklore* 91 [Castle Douglas, Kirk-

cudbright.] It is believed that if two plants of cock's head are put by a happy lover under a stone, and flower thereafter, he or she will be married, if not, not. Ibid. 92. A woman divines with the dark, and a man with the light variety. The plant is pulled up by the root, laid under a .. flat stone, and left all night. Next morning, if the root be examined, the initial letter will be found .. of the future husband or wife. **1956** U. VENABLES *Life in Shetland* 68. It was now nearly Johnsmas (25th June) and Lizzie .. insisted we should look for Johnsmas flowers, the ribwort plantain .. We picked them in pairs, stripped off the stamens, named them after a loving couple and bundled them in a dockleaf blanket till morning .. If the stamens are back next day your love will prosper—and I have never known them to fail.

Cf. KNAPWEED: divination.

PLANTS put into mourning

1838 A. E. BRAY *Devonshire* II 295. Mary observed in the cottage window several beautiful plants, each having a small piece of black crape .. tied around it .. The poor woman told her .. that she had very lately buried her husband, and if she had not put the plants into mourning they would have died too. **1855** *N & Q* 1st ser. XII 38 [Cornwall] In cases of death, the in-door plants are also put in black; for if this is omitted, they soon droop and die. **1887** *Folklore* 193. When, some years since, the landlady of the First and Last Inn, at the Land's End, died, the bird-cages and flower-pots were .. tied with crape, to prevent the birds and plants from dying.

Cf. BEES take part in funeral/wedding.

PLATE on top of another = death

1936 E. H. RUDKIN *Lincolnshire* 17. To eat off a plate with another plate beneath it .. foretells death. **1982** Woman, 20 [Cleveland, Yorks.] Death is imminent if a meal is eaten from a plate resting on another plate.

PLOUGH, crossing path of

1887 'SPERANZA' WILDE *Superstitions of Ireland* II 103. If a man is ploughing, no one should cross the path of the horses.

POINTING AT

1881 W. GREGOR *North-East of Scotland* 200. It was not lawful in some of the villages to point with the finger to the boats when at sea; if such a thing had to be done, the whole hand had to be used .. Nothing aroused the indignation of a company of fishwomen .. more than to point towards them with the finger. **1901** J. RHYS *Celtic Folklore* I 346. Novices in the Manx fisheries have to learn not to point to anything with one finger: they have to point with the whole hand or not at all. **1948** E. & M. A. RADFORD *Superstitions* 192 [Norfolk] If you point at a ship, you will bring bad luck to it.

POKER against grate

1731 *Round about our Coal Fire* 22. Witch-dealers .. take their Magick chiefly from setting up Pokers against a decaying Fire. **1778** MRS THRALE *Diary* Mar.–Apr. (ed. Balderston, I 251) Why do the Maids set the Poker and Tongs across one another to make the Fire burn? they themselves have forgotten why; the young ones probably never heard: but the Reason originally was, to bless the Fire by the form of the Cross, & so induce it to blaze. **1779** BOSWELL *Life of Johnson* 10 Oct. BOSWELL. 'Why, Sir, do people play this trick which I observe now, when I look at your grate, putting the shovel against it to make it burn?' JOHNSON. 'They play the trick, but it does not make the fire burn. *There* is a better; (setting the poker perpendicularly up at right angles with the grate.) In the days of superstition they thought, as it made a cross with the bars, it would drive away the witch.' **1813** BRAND *Antiquities* II 606 n. Whatever may be the reason, it is a certain fact that setting up a Poker before a Fire has a wonderful effect in causing it to burn. **1821** GALT *Ayrshire Legatees* IV. What would ye think of buying coals by the stimpert, for any thing that I know, and then setting up the poker afore the ribs, instead of blowing with the bellies to make the fire burn? **1864** R. CHAMBERS *Book of Days* II 104 [Suffolk] You should set the poker across the hearth, with the fore part leaning across the top bar of the grate, and you will have a good fire .. but you must not be unreasonable, and refuse to give time for the charm to work. For a charm it is, the poker and top bar combined, forming a cross. **1873** HARLAND & WILKINSON *Lancashire Legends* 238. Almost every housewife will place the poker against the bars .. so as to form a cross, in full confidence that the fire will soon burn briskly. **1879** J. NAPIER *West of Scotland* 135. This practice is still followed by many, but being compelled now to give an apparently scientific reason for their conduct, they say that it is so placed to produce a draught. But this it does not do. The practice originated in the belief that the fire [slow to kindle] was spell-bound by witchcraft, and the poker was so placed that it would form the shape of a cross with the front bar of the grate .. In early times .. the person who placed it repeated an *Ave Marie* or *Paternoster*. **1913** E. M. WRIGHT *Rustic Speech* 230. People who do it tell you in all seriousness that it draws the fire by creating a draught. **1915** *Folklore* 210 [Weybourne, Norfolk] To make the fire burn up our landlady placed the poker .. horizontally across the top bar, resting on the coals .. A cross is thus formed which is visible from up the chimney .. thus keeping off any evil thing which may attack .. from that quarter. **1916** JOYCE *Portrait of the Artist* 71. The parlour fire would not draw that evening and Mr Dedalus rested the poker against the bars of the grate to attract the flame. **1923** [Bridgwater, Som.] Putting a poker against the grate to make a bad fire burn, thus making a cross with poker and bars, drives the divil out of the chimney so that the fire can burn. **1980** Woman, 59 [South Shields, Co. Durham] Grandma, she used to take the poker and put it across the fire in a deliberate cross—like a cross in a church. **1983** Woman, 81 [Liss, Hants.] I put a poker up against the fire to draw it up. I done it hundreds of times—and a bit of paper over the poker.

POKER on table

1923 [Taunton, Som.] It is unlucky to put the poker on the table.

poker: also see FIRE, poking; IRON.

POSTHUMOUS CHILD cures

1855 *N & Q* 1st ser. XII 37 [Cornwall] If the infant suffers from the thrush, it is taken, fasting, on three following mornings, 'to have its mouth blown into' by a posthumous child. 1893 *Folklore* 351 [Co. Donegal] A posthumous child will cure a sore mouth. 1898 BLAKEBOROUGH *Yorkshire Customs* 161. Witches held in great aversion posthumous children, more especially male children. 1909 M. TREVELYAN *Folk-Lore of Wales* 225. A posthumous child, by putting its hands on a tumour, could charm it away. 1957 *Folklore* 413. In Cheshire between the two wars, posthumous children were supposed to have healing powers.

POTATO cures rheumatism

1868 *N & Q* 4th ser. I 362. I have heard of a man who belongs to what he would consider the educated classes, and who nevertheless wears a potato in each of his trowsers' pockets as a cure for rheumatism. As the vegetables diminish .. he believes that they are absorbed into his system, and .. that he is much benefited thereby. 1873 HARLAND & WILKINSON *Lancashire Legends* 226–7. Those who suffer from rheumatic pains are advised to carry small potatoes in their pockets, which are held not only to cure, but to prevent a return of the disease. 1875 W. D. PARISH *Sussex Dialect* 95. For my part, if ever I be troubled with the rheumattics (and I be quite eat-up otherwhile) I goos out and steals a tater, and carries it in my pocket till the rheumatittics be gone. 1922 JOYCE *Ulysses* (1960, 557) Spud again the rheumatiz? All poppycock, you'll scuse me saying. For the hoi polloi. 1932 *Folklore* 104 [Naphill, Bucks., 1911] Grannie carries about a whole potato in her pocket, so that the rheumatism may go into that instead of into her. 1933 *Sussex County Mag.* 801. A curious belief still lingers in some country districts, as to the efficacy of wearing a potato somewhere about the body as a cure for rheumatism. Little by little these .. shrivel till hard as a stone, and are then said to have absorbed and become full

of the uric acid drawn from the patient's body. 1943 *Folklore* 238. Potatoes .. against rheumatism. Some examples, used by Oxford citizens about 1900, can be found in the Pitt Rivers Museum together with the names of their owners, which I do not like to reveal, because the potatoes had to be stolen, if they were to prove curative .. Atropine, a reputed cure for rheumatism, is found in potato 'Eyes', which renders some justification for the belief. 1968 J. K. STANFORD *Keeper's Country* 178. 'Have you got a potato?' 'I always hev,' said the man from Swaffham [Norfolk], 'a master good cure agin the rheumatics.'

Cf. ONION protects and cures.

POURING backwards

1865 R. HUNT *West of England* 2nd ser. 241. To pour gravy out of a spoon backwards (or back-handed) is unlucky, and leads to quarrels. 1899 J. SHAW *Schoolmaster* 33 [Tynron, Dumfries.] It is dangerous for future welfare to pour out any liquid turning your hand backwards. 1966 B. MESSENGER *Guide to Etiquette* 65. It is unlucky to pour wine backwards over the wrist. (This is a breach of wine etiquette, too.)

PRAISING dangerous

c.1350 HIGDEN *Polychronicon* (MS Harl. 2261, tr. Trevisa: Rolls II 187–8) In Affrica beeþ meyneys þat haueþ wycchen [witching] tonges, so þat þinges þat þey preiseþ þey schendeþ and sleep [slayeth] wiþ hire preisynge. So þat trees þat þey preiseþ waxen drie and children deyeþ. 1579 LUPTON *Thousand Notable Things* IV § 81. There are found in Africke families of men, that if they chaunce exceedingly to prayse, fayre Trees, pure seedes, goodly chyldren, excellent horsses, fayre and well-lyking cattell, soone after they wyll wyther and pyne away, & so dye. (No cause or hurt knowne of their withering or death.) Thereupon the custome came, that when any do praise any thing, that we should say God blesse it or keepe it. 1586 CAMDEN *Britannia* (tr. Gibson, II 380) [Limerick, Eire, *c.*1566] If one praise a horse, or any other creature, he must cry, 'God save him,' or spit upon him; and, if any mischief befalls the horse within three days, they find out the person who commended him, who is to whisper the Lord's prayer in his right ear. **1774** G. LOW *Tour through Orkney* (1879, 7) Nobody must praise a child or anything they set a value on, for if anything evil afterwards befals it, these poor ignorant creatures will be sure to attribute to the tongue that spoke of it. This they call forspeaking, and pretend to cure persons so forspoken by washing them with a water compounded with great ceremony. **1795** *Stat. Acc. of Scotland* XIV 541 n. [Banff.] To prevent what is called forespeaking, they say of a person, God save them; of a beast, Luck sair it. **1811** A. GRANT *Highlanders of Scotland* I 167–8. There was .. an indistinct notion, that it was impious .. to boast of the health or beauty of any creature, which seemed to belong to us .. An infant, in short, was not to be praised at all, without a previous invocation of the Deity. **1811** SCOTT *Letters* (Cent. edn. III 33) To obviate the risque of forspeaking the gossips usually add some little ejaculation expressive of deference to heaven or fortune, as 'It's a well natured bairn God bless it'—or 'a braw cow Luck sair her!' **1841** C. OTWAY *Erris and Tyrawly* 379 [Connaught, Eire] [A schoolmistress praised a boy without adding a blessing, and he took ill.] She was .. sent for .. and was to spit three times on the boy and accompany each expectoration by a 'God bless you'. **1868** *N & Q* 4th ser. I 193 [Co. Galway] Mrs R's nurse happened to meet Mrs E's .. with 'the baby', and as nurses do, she kissed the child, and praised its good looks .. but unfortunately forgot to say 'God bless it', or to make the gesture of spitting on the child .. An attack of convulsions .. proved fatal .. Both mother and nurse were .. convinced that its death was .. owing to .. omitting the proper ceremonies when praising it. **1879** J. NAPIER *West of Scotland* 34. It was unsafe to be lavish in praise of the child's beauty .. for the *well faured* ran the greatest risk from evil influences .. There was also the .. danger of the mother forgetting God, who then in jealousy and mercy would remove it from her. **1887** *Journal of Anthropological Inst.* III 267 [Banff.]

Forespeaking. Praise beyond measure—praise accompanied with a sort of amazement or envy—was followed by disease or accident. **1887** 'SPERANZA' WILDE *Superstitions of Ireland* I 38. A woman in the County Galway had a beautiful child, so handsome, that all the neighbours were careful to say 'God bless it' when they saw him, for they knew the fairies would desire to steal the child. **1895** F. T. ELWORTHY *Evil Eye* 12–13 [SW England] A few weeks ago a .. farmer had a very nice-looking horse in his cart, which the writer .. admired .. The owner began to expatiate on the good qualities of the animal, but suddenly stopped and said: 'But there .. mustn' zay too much for fear o' bad luck.' **1946** M. SUMMERS *Witchcraft and Black Magic* 163. In the Scottish Highlands, should a stranger praise a fine cow too admiringly, and keep gazing at her, it is thought the animal will waste away from the evil eye, and the spell must be broken at once by offering the visitor some of her milk to drink, after which no ill result can ensue. **1953** *Nat. Scottish Dict.* [Shetland, Orkney, Caithness, Aberdeen.] *Forespeak*. To bewitch, cast an evil spell over, especially by praising unduly. **1972** *Lore and Language* July 7 [Coalisland, Co. Tyrone] Never admire a beautiful child unless you put a spittle on his forehead and say: 'God bless him.' If someone admires your child and fails to do [this], then do it yourself or the child will be blinked.

PRAM, buying

1955 MISS READ *Village School* 224. 'Defying Providence!' she boomed. 'Never does to order the pram or cot till the little stranger's in the house. Times without number I've seen things go awry within the last three months. Seems to be the most dangerous time—particularly with the first.' **1957** *Folklore* 503 [Clun Valley, Shrops.] I have heard .. that it is unlucky to have the cradle in the house before a birth. [Here] it took the more modern form of the perambulator. **1960** *News Chronicle* 21 Jan. 4. The Queen has already chosen the pram she wants, but she is superstitious about some things. It will not be delivered to the palace until after the baby is born.

1984 Woman, 57 [South Shields, Co. Durham] One of my mother's superstitions was only recalled to mind by the preparations for Prince Henry, that it is unlucky to buy the pram before the baby is born. **1987** Woman journalist, 32 [London, expecting first child] I don't mind looking at prams, but I'd rather not have it in the house until after the baby is born.

Cf. CRADLE, buying.

PRAM, pushing

1959 *Trans. Devon. Ass.* 201 [Newton Abbot, Devon] If you push an empty pram, you will always have a full one. **1982** Girl, *c.*15 [Herts.] If you push a pram with someone else's baby in it you will soon get pregnant.

Cf. CRADLE, rocking empty.

PRAYERS said backwards = witchcraft

c. AD **200** (B. CUNLIFFE *Aquae Sulis*, 1971, 12–13) [found in sacred spring, Bath] Small lead sheet .. upon which had been scratched a curse backwards .. 'May he who carried off Vilbia from me become as liquid as the waters' and then, for the goddess' information, a list of the possible culprits. **1584** SCOT *Discoverie of Witchcraft* XII XVI. To be utterlie rid of a witch .. you must prepare an image [etc.] then these psalmes read backward: *Domine Dominus noster*, *Dominus illuminatio mea* [etc.] **1619** MS Univ. Lib. Camb. Bz/37 f. 78 [Ely Diocesan Records] Margarett the wife of Henry Edwarde to her infame and greate disgrace [is accused]. It was accoordinge to her deserte [for though she says many prayers] they be naught for she prayghte backward. **1663** BUTLER *Hudibras* I iii l. 344. He that gets her by heart must say her The back-way, like a Witches prayer. **1673** *Depositions, York Castle* 21 Apr. (1861, 197) The said Jane allighted .. and she and the rest had drawne their compasse nigh to a brig end, and the devil placed a stone in the middle of the compasse, they sett themselves downe and bending towards the stone, repeated the Lord's prayer backwards. And when they had done, the devill, in the forme of a little black man and black cloaths, calld of one Isabell Thompson, of Slealy, widdow, by name, and required of her

what service she had done him. **1711** *Spectator* 14 July. This very old woman had the reputation of a witch .. If she made a mistake at church .. they never failed to conclude that she was saying her prayers backwards. *c.*1850 J. HUNTER MS note in Brand's *Antiquities* I opp. title page. In the parts of Yorkshire in which I lived there were .. occasions in which he [the Devil] was visible .. When *evoked*. This was to be done by drawing a circle on the pavement, placing within it a broken tobacco pipe and a bad halfpenny, saying the Lords Prayer backwards, & perhaps some words of invoking. Then it was understood he rose in the middle of the circle in smoke. I never saw it attempted; but we had a persuasion in our school that it was done, & that particularly it had been done in the Free School at Sheffield. **1851** *N & Q* 1st ser. IV 53. School superstition .. If you say the Lord's Prayer backwards, the devil would come up. **1871–2** ELIOT *Middlemarch* VII LXIII. A man will not be tempted to say the Lord's Prayer backward to please the devil, if he does not want the devil's services. **1959** OPIE *Lore and Language of Schoolchildren* 1. To a child it can be a 'known fact' that the Lord's Prayer said backwards raises the devil.

PRAYERS: saying at foot of bed

1861 *N & Q* 2nd ser. XII 491. It is unlucky to say your prayers at the foot of the bed. They should always be said at the side.

PRAYERS, stopping/stumbling while saying

1590 Witchcraft trial (R. PITCAIRN *Criminal Trials in Scotland* II pt. 2 232) Sche [the Wise Wife of Keith] had foirknawledge be hir Wichcraft of diseasit persounes, gif thay wald leue or nocht; or quha wes wichit [bewitched] persounes. To wit, That gif sche stopit anis [once] in hir prayer, the seik persoun wes bewichit; and gif the prayer stoppit twyis, the diseasit persoune wald die. **1700** *Protestant Mercury* 10–12 July (J. HUNTER MS note in Brand's *Antiquities*) A Brewer's servant in Southwark, having lately had his head turned awry, made out this week before a Justice, that he was bewitched by an old woman, upwards of 80 years of age, who being sent for, she was ordered to say the Lord's prayer and Creed, the first she did tolerably well, but could not do the latter, upon which she was committed to the Marshalsea; and tomorrow it is said they will try the experiment of swimming her. **1893** *N & Q* 8th ser. III 209. From Wiltshire I hear that a notion exists that if a clergyman makes a mistake in reading prayers there will be a death during the week. Ibid. 272. This notion exists in Worcestershire .. but I think the death is supposed to follow after three mistakes, and not after a single slip.

PRECOCIOUSNESS = early death

AD 77 PLINY *Natural History* VII LII (1855, II 209) Precocity in youth is a sign of an early death. **1576** G. PETTIE *Petite Pallace* (1908, II 160) Those children which are destined to death in the prime time of their life, are far more witty, discreet, and perfect every way, than those who have long time granted them to live on earth. **1586** BRIGHT *Melancholie* (1940, 54) Whereupon I take it, the prouerbe ariseth: that they be of short life, who are of wit so pregnant: because their bodies do receaue by nature so speedie a ripenesse, as thereby age is hastened. **1591** SHAKESPEARE *Richard the Third* III i. So wise, so young, they say doe never live long. **1607** MIDDLETON *Phoenix* I i. A little too wise, a little too wise to live long. **1738** SWIFT *Polite Conversation* I 385. I fear Lady Answerall can't live long, she has so much wit. **1787** GROSE *Provincial Glossary* Superstitions 51. Children prematurely wise are not long-lived, that is, rarely reach maturity. **1850** *Life of Robert Southey* (ed. C. C. Southey, II 70) He was in more danger on account of his being handsome and quick; as we say, a child is too clever to live. **1873** HARLAND & WILKINSON *Lancashire Legends* 221. Precocious children are seldom long-lived; they are often reminded that they 'are too fause [wise] to live'. **1923** [Bridgwater, Som.] If a baby a few weeks old takes a lot of notice he won't live to see his twenty-first birthday.

Cf. PRAISING dangerous.

PREGNANCY, cravings during

1507 *Gospelles of Dystaues* pt. I XVII. They sholde not speke afore a woman .. grete with chylde of ony maner of mete that for the present and at a nede may not be founde, to the ende that the fruyte that she bereth haue not a marke upon his body. **1691** *Athenian Mercury* 11 May. *Quest.* What is the Reason that when Women with Child long for Fruits, &c. the Mark of that which they long for is often Imprinted in some part of the child's Body? *Answ.* The Imaginations of pregnant Women, their Humours being extreamly stirr'd and disturb'd, must needs be very strong and lively. **1708** *British Apollo* Supernumerary no. 3 for June. It being usual for a Woman with Child, disappointed of her Longing, to mark the Child with what she had Long'd for; I desire to know, if She long'd for a Kiss, what Mark the Child wou'd have? **1727** *Strength of Imagination in Pregnant Women* 10–11. What I deny, is .. that her strong Desire of a Peach, or of an Apricock can cause the Colour and Shape of a Peach, or of an Apricock upon a Determined part of the Child's Body. **1778** WHITE *Selborne* 8 Jan. The good women, who love to account for every defect in children by the doctrine of longing, said that his mother felt a great propensity for oysters, which she was unable to gratify; and that the black, rough scurf on his hands and feet were the shells of that fish. **1923** [Martock, Som.] Her'd a turble wish for liver and the child have a-got a slice marked pon's shoulder. **1954** *News of the World* 22 Aug. 2. When I was expecting her I craved for black currants and from birth she has carried the imprint of a bunch of the fruit on her instep. Every year when black currants begin to ripen the birthmark turns a darker colour.

PREGNANCY, influences during

1579 LUPTON *Thousand Notable Things* II § 24. If a Ratte, Mouse, or Wesell, or any other thing sodenlye leape or fall on the body of a Woman with chyld, or else any Cheryes, or a cluster of Grapes, or other thing whatsouer chance to fal or hyt any part of her body: by and by it haps that the chylde is marked with some speciall noate or marke on that part. **1584** SCOT *Discoverie of Witchcraft* XIII XVI. We read of a woman that brought foorth a yoong blacke Moore, by meanes of an old blacke Moore who was in hir house at the time of her conception, whome she beheld in phantasie, as is supposed: howbeit, a gelous husband will not be satisfied with such phantasticall imaginations. **1668** W. RAMESEY *Elminthologia* 262. No less common are the Instances of the Mothers Imagination on the Child in her womb, every house affording one or more .. One .. brought forth a Blackemoor, only by looking on such a Picture, at such a time. **1672** BROWNE *Vulgar Errors* V XXIII § 9. If a woman with child looketh upon a dead body, her child will be of a pale complexion. **1844** DICKENS *Martin Chuzzlewit* XLVI. Her husband's brother bein' six foot three, and marked with a mad bull in Wellington boots upon his left arm, on account of his precious mother havin' been worrited by one into a shoemaker's shop, when in a sitivation which blessed is the man as has his quiver full of sech. **1939** *Folklore* 117. A short time ago I heard a Hitchin midwife recount how a patient of hers brought forth a child with a wing instead of an arm because the mother had previously been frightened by a bird. **1962** M. B. TELLING *Over My Shoulder* 10. My left ear has a bit cut out of the lobe .. Mother [was] quite certain of the cause. Some months before I was born, all the boys in the house were having their hair cut .. My youngest brother .. rushed, yelling loudly, with a clipped ear. Mother, who had a peculiar horror of blood, fainted .. and so, according to the old wives' tale—the mischief was done. **1967** S. MARSHALL *Fenland Chronicle* pt. 2 II. I know all these birthmarks are laughed at nowadays .. but we believed in such things. When I were a child, I had a white lock down the back o' my head .. because my mother were frightened by a white bear at Peterborough Fair. **1983** *Farmers Weekly* 26 Aug. 100. A neighbour once rang the police when she heard piercing screams from my property. I had arrived home to find an adder coiled on the slate-stone doorstep .. I'm glad I wasn't pregnant;

folklore has it that the unborn child would have had a flat head.

PREGNANT WOMAN as godmother or taking oath

*c.***1535** Letter from Ralph Sadler to Secretary Cromwell (H. ELLIS *Original Letters* 3rd ser. II 226) I wold also be right glad to have Mr Richards wyf or my Lady Weston to be the godmother. Ther is a certen superstycious opynyon and vsage amongst women, which is, that in case a woman go with childe she may chrysten no other mannes childe as long as she is in that case: and therfore not knowing whether Mr Rychards wyf be with childe or not, I do name my Lady Weston. **1851** *Times* 28 May 8. Mrs F. was called upon to give evidence, and upon the book being tendered to her said she could not be sworn [and] intimated that it must be evident to the magistrate that she could not take an oath. The usher .. said the woman was pregnant, and that low women who were in that situation entertained an absurd superstition that it was unlucky to take an oath. **1880** *N & Q* 4th ser. I 392. In Holderness, a woman being asked to stand as godmother, refused, on the ground that she was about to become a mother, and if she stood while in that condition the child for whom she stood would soon die. This is commonly believed in the East Riding of Yorkshire. **1893** *Folklore* 357 [Connemara, Co. Galway] A pregnant woman will not take an oath in a Court of Justice. This custom is recognised by the local magistrates.

PREGNANT WOMAN causes pregnancy

1972 *Lore and Language* July 7 [Coalisland, Co. Tyrone] If you are in the company of two pregnant women slap your backside three times or you too will become pregnant. **1982** Woman, *c.*35 [Beds.] If you sit in a chair recently occupied by a pregnant woman, you will soon get pregnant. Also, if you wear a pregnant woman's coat, you will soon be pregnant.

PREGNANT WOMEN, two

1881 W. GREGOR *North-East of Scotland* 4. On the occasion of a birth .. a woman with child was not allowed to be in the room; and if two women with child happened to be living in the same house when one felt the pains of labour, they took a straw, or a stalk of grass .. and broke it, each repeating .. 'Ye tak yours, an I tak mine.'

PRIMROSES etc.: first of the year

1853 *N & Q* 1st ser. VII 201. In East Norfolk some old women are still found who believe that if a less number of primrosen than thirteen be brought into a house on the first occasion of bringing any in, so many eggs only will each hen or goose hatch that season .. My gravity was sorely tried by being called on to settle a quarrel between two old women, arising from one of them having given one primrose to her neighbour's child, for the purpose of making her hens hatch but one egg out of each set of eggs. And it was seriously maintained that the charm had been successful. 1868 *N & Q* 4th ser. I 550. A certain fowl-woman .. is always very particular that none of her friends .. should enter her cottage bringing a *small* posy, either of violets, primroses, cowslips, or any other flower .. Her explanation is, that *few* flowers mean *few* chickens. 1892 C. M. YONGE *Old Woman's Outlook* February. If you find a stray primrose or two, beware of bringing them home, for the first brood of chickens will be of the same scanty numbers. 1923 [Trowbridge, Wilts.] Never bring fewer than thirteen primroses or daffodils into a house, for the first time in a season, for the geese find out and regulate the number of the eggs they lay during the year. 1985 R. VICKERY *Unlucky Plants* 48 [Dorset] Never look for early primroses, because .. it affects the fertility of the eggs the hens are sitting on at the time, and however many primroses .. you pick that is the number of chicks (ducks or whatever) that will hatch out of each clutch. She has had many a 'clout around the yer' for that, but if her sister and her wanted to please their mother they would hunt around and try to find a nice lot (say a dozen or more).

Cf. DAFFODIL in house.

PROSTITUTE, meeting

c. AD 388 ST JOHN CHRYSOSTOM *Baptismal Instructions* (ed. Harkins, 190) If you happen to meet a prostitute, the day is lucky and filled with an abundance of business. 1159 JOHN OF SALISBURY *Policraticus* (*Frivolities of Courtiers*, ed. J. B. Pike, 50) A woman walking with uncovered head is to be regarded as bringing ill luck unless .. she be a woman of the street or is notorious for numerous liaisons. 1584 SCOT *Discoverie of Witchcraft* XI xv. Marrie if they had used venerie with a beggar, they should win all the monie they plaied for that daie at dice. 1652 GAULE *Mag-astromances* 181. To bode good or bad luck .. from .. the meeting of .. a Harlot first [in a morning]. 1886 *Folklore* 13 [Buckie, Banff.] Some people are .. regarded as carrying luck with them. Such as have led an immoral life, whether man or woman, are those that bring success, and the name of such a one is used as a talisman. Thus when beginning to shoot the lines one of the crew will say, 'We'll try in ——'s name for luck.'

PROSTITUTE on ship causes storm

1688 AUBREY *Remaines* (1881, 67) Thus much Superstition they [seamen] still retain, that they will not endure a whore on Shipboard; w^h (they doe believe) does cause a storme; and they will then make bold to throw her overboard, as it were a sacrifice to Neptune.

PUDDING, naming: divination

1969 M. BRAGG *Hired Man* II. Alice .. took down a black pudding and set it in the oven. John blushed once more, for he knew that she had 'likened' it to Emily and himself—as was done with newly married couples—and that she would believe that their life would be happy if the skin held, disrupted if it burst.

PUDDING, naming: prevents bursting

1895 J. HARDY *Denham Tracts* 365 [Northumb.] The peasant women believe that the 'black and white puddings' made at a pig-killing will certainly burst while boiling if the cook does not, when putting each string of puddings into the pot, mentally dedicate it to some one who is not present. This has nothing to do with the subsequent disposal of the delicacy.

PURSE, string kept in

1952 Woman, *c.*50. When I was married in Dundee thirty years ago my mother slipped a purse in my hand, and in it a length of string tied in a circle. She said as long as I had purse and string I would always have friends and money. It has been true up to now.

1969 Woman, 43 [Liss, Hants.] Some people put small bits of string in their handbags. They say it brings luck.

Cf. MONEY, having: in purse etc.

R

rabbit: see HARE OR RABBIT.

RACING CAR, going in front of

1955 Man, *c.*30 [Swansea, Glam.] Racing drivers will go in front of their cars only once before a race. Every other time they go round at the back.

RAILWAY BRIDGE/TUNNEL, passing under/over

1932 C. IGGLESDEN *Those Superstitions* 229. To talk when passing under a railway bridge brings bad luck. This superstition was observed during the war, especially by Welsh regiments. **1954** Girl, 14 [Newbridge, Monmouth.] There is a superstition more children than grown-ups believe in, and that is if you walk under a tunnel while a train is going over it is bad luck—people say you should cross your fingers. **1954** Boy, [Shoreham-by-Sea, Sussex] An old superstition is if you speak under a tunnel or a bridge you must touch a green object or you will get bad luck. It is still believed now. **1957** Boy, 12 [Patterdale, Cumb.] If you cross a railway bridge while there is a train going under you can have a wish. **1988** Man, 45 [Liss, Hants.] My mother would never drive under a bridge when a train was going over the top. **1988** Woman, 60 [South Shields, Co. Durham, *c.*1938] When we saw a train coming, we used to rush up the steps on to the iron foot-bridge, and stand in the smoke that billowed up from the engine. We thought it was lucky in some way.

Cf. LADDER, walking under.

RAILWAY TUNNEL cures whooping cough

1883 BURNE *Shropshire* 190. I was once travelling from Whitchurch to Tutbury .. when at the Harecastle Tunnel I pulled up the window (third-class); on which a respectable woman opposite to me, with a child in her arms, pulled it down again hastily, and lifted the child to the open window. When we got out of the tunnel she explained that she had been advised that the air of the tunnel was good for whooping-cough! **1962** *South Wales Evening Post* 15 Dec. 4. Every mother in the Valley held a fixed notion that if you stuck a child's head out of the window and made him breathe the air of the tunnel it was a certain cure for whooping cough. **1982** *Times* 1 Oct. 11. The sufferer was taken by train on the Great Western line from Dovey Junction to Aberdovey and back. There are a number of short tunnels on this section of the line. We were made to stand at the open carriage window, alternatively exposed to the cold sea air from Cardigan Bay and the hot sulphurous fumes trapped in the tunnels from the coal driven railway engine. Any child foolish enough to whoop once more at the end of the journey had to undergo it all over again.

Cf. CAVE cures whooping cough.

RAIN, charm against

1659 J. HOWELL *Proverbs* 20. Raine, raine, goe to Spain: faire weather come againe. **1688** AUBREY *Remaines* (1881, 180) Little children have a custome, when it raines to sing, or charme away the Raine; thus they all joine in a Chorus, and sing thus, viz: 'Raine, raine, goe away, Come againe a Saterday.' **1851** DENHAM *North of England* (1895, 22) There are several infantile Rhymes, used as charms .. against rain, viz. 'Rain, rain, go away, Come again another day' .. 'Rain, rain, pour down, And come na' mair to our towne' etc. **1866** HENDERSON *Northern Counties* 15. Does rain threaten to spoil a holiday, let him chant out .. 'Rain, rain, go to Spain; Fair weather come again' .. If there be a rainbow the .. devotee must look at it all the time. **1899** *Newcastle Weekly Chronicle* 11 Feb. 7 [Jesmond] The children's charm to drive away rain is to join hands and sing: 'Rain, go away, And don't come back till another day.' **1959** OPIE *Lore and Language of*

Schoolchildren 218. 'Rain, rain, go away, Come again another day,' or variations thereof, is still commonly repeated.

RAINBOW, charm against

1856 G. HENDERSON *Popular Rhymes of Berwick* 135. 'Rainbow, rainbow, haud away hame, A' your bairns are dead but ane, And it lies sick at yon grey stane, And will be dead ere ye win hame; Gang owre the Drumaw and yont the lea, And down by the side o' yonder sea, Your bairn lies greetin' like to die, And the big tear-drop is in his ee.' This is a very popular rhyme among boys and girls in the country who run about repeating it on seeing a rainbow.

Cf. LADYBIRD, killing.

RAINBOW, 'crossing out'

1858 DENHAM *North of England* (1895, 58) When a schoolboy I recollect that we were wont, on the appearance of a rainbow, to place a couple of straws or twigs on the ground in the form of a +, in order to dispel the sign in the heavens, or, as we termed it, to 'cross out the rainbow'. **1890** *N & Q* 7th ser. X 366. You can cross them out .. make them go away by making a cross on the ground, like what Christ's cross was .. We used to do it when we were children; but I don't do it now. I'm afraid it's wicked. **1948** E. & M. A. RADFORD *Superstitions* 197. In Leeds .. our search discovered that there was among the old people this recipe for 'driving away a rainbow': Make a cross of two sticks and lay four pebbles on it, one at each end of the cross. **1985** Man, *c*.75 [Eire] If you make a cross with two straws, it breaks the rainbow.

RAINBOW over house = death

1932 J. M. E. SAXBY *Shetland Lore* 183. If a rainbow arched over a house a death was to be in it soon, or some relation at a distance was to die.

RAINBOW, pointing at

1912 LEATHER *Herefordshire* 16. A lady at Monkland, teaching her Sunday School class in the garden, pointed with her finger to show the children a beautiful rainbow. They all cried out 'Oh don't, teacher, don't!' [and] explained that it was 'dreadful bad luck to point at a rainbow'. **1953** Boy, 14 [Knighton, Radnor.] To point at a rainbow brings the rain back again. **1985** Girl, 16 [Matlock, Derbys.] If you see a rainbow you must draw a person's attention to it by any means other than pointing at it—that would be unlucky.

Cf. THUNDER AND LIGHTNING, drawing attention to.

RAINBOW, stepping on

1959 OPIE *Lore and Language of Schoolchildren* 218 [Girl, 15, Ipswich, Suffolk] Oil .. marks on a wet road are sometimes held to be spots where a rainbow has stood. 'It is said that if one walks over an oily patch in the road one will get one's sums wrong.' **1985** Woman, *c*.50 [Colchester, Essex] When we were children, and saw those coloured oil marks in water on the ground, we used to put our foot on it and say, 'Rainbow, rainbow, bring me luck. If you don't, I'll break you up.'

Cf. CIGARETTE PACKET, stepping on.

'RAT' AND 'MOUSE' taboo words

1886 *Folklore* 13 [Crovie, Banff.] The rat [is a] bringer of bad luck, and the word was never uttered during the time the lines were being baited. **1901** J. RHYS *Celtic Folklore* I 345 [Isle of Man] The unluckiness of mentioning .. a mouse on board a fishing boat. **1953** Girl, 14. I have heard many people in East Anglia who will not say the word 'rat' but will call it some other name like Joseph. They say it is unlucky.

RATS AND MICE gnawing = death

c.**319** BC THEOPHRASTUS *Characters* (tr. Jebb, ed. Sandys, 143) 'The Superstitious Man'. If a mouse gnaws through a meal-bag, he will go to the expounder of sacred law and ask what is to be done; and, if the answer is, 'give it to a cobbler to stitch up', he will disregard this counsel .. and expiate the omen by sacrifice. AD **77** PLINY *Natural History* VIII LXXXII (1855, II 350) By gnawing the silver shields at Lanuvium, mice prognosticated the Marsian war; and the death of our general, Carbo, at Clusium, by gnawing the latchets with which he fastened his shoes. *c*. AD

396 ST AUGUSTINE OF HIPPO *De Doctrina Christiana* I xx (tr. Robertson, 56) Similar [superstitious] practices are .. when your clothes are torn by mice, to dread more the omen of a future evil than the actual damage. Whence that elegant saying of Cato, who, when consulted by a man whose shoes had been gnawed by mice, observed that there was nothing strange about the fact, but that it would have been strange indeed if the shoes had gnawed the mice. *c.***1395** CHAUCER *Parson's Tale* l. 604. Hem that bileeven on divynailes .. by gnawynge of rattes. **1620** MELTON *Astrologaster* 46. It is a great signe of ill lucke, if Rats gnaw a mans cloathes. **1648** J. TURNER *Memoirs* (1829, 61) I have often heard that the eating or gnauing of cloths by rats is ominous, and portends some mischance to fall on these to whom the cloths belong. I thank God I was never addicted to such divinations, or heeded them. **1787** GROSE *Provincial Glossary* Superstitions 48. Rats gnawing the hangings of a room, is reckoned the forerunner of a death in the family. **1909** M. TREVELYAN *Folk-Lore of Wales* 283. If a mouse nibbles any part of a person's clothing, he or she will surely die soon. **1909** *Folklore* 344 [Worcs.] Death omen .. rats nibbling furniture.

RATS AND MICE, influx of: ominous

*c.***1682** W. BEDELL *Life of William* (1872, 63) [Kilmore, Co. Wexford] There wanted not some forerunning tokens of this calamity [rebellion, Oct. 1641]. A strange multitude of ratts .. overrunning the houses and so bold as to .. gather the crumbs and bones under the table .. so much the more remarkable because .. for many years space, seldom any rat was to be seen in the countrey. And the elder Irishwomen would say often .. that these rats were a signe of war. **1793** *Every Lady's Fortune Teller* 85. To dream you are attacked by rats .. shews that somebody will endeavour .. to injure you .. Mice are pretty much of the same nature, but not in so high a degree. **1850** *N & Q* 1st ser. II 164 [Northants.] A sudden influx of mice into a house .. denotes approaching mortality among its occupants. A mouse running over a person is considered to be an infallible sign of death, as is also the squeaking of one behind the bed of an invalid. **1872** *N & Q* 4th ser. IX 402. In 1849, during an impending visitation of cholera, I was at a village on the Cornish coast .. A woman of about thirty-five .. expressed her apprehension of the cholera proving fatal to her. She being then, apparently, in perfect health .. I inquired the reason for her expectation, and .. she informed me 'she had seen some mice'. **1882** *People's Friend* 8 Nov. 712 [Scotland] Mice are extremely unlucky. **1885** *Folklore* 182 [Aberdeen.] In Broadsea the animals which are looked upon as unlucky are .. the hare, and the rabbit and the 'rottin' (rat) .. In St Combs, on the other hand, the rat is looked on as lucky, and the arrival of rats in a house is regarded as the harbinger of money. The idea of rats leaving a house or a ship foreboding disaster is quite general. *c.***1915** [Newcastle upon Tyne, Northumb., miner's song.] There's a moose run up the waal, Pit lie idle! Pit lie idle! **1923** [Somerset] If mice come into a house .. it is a sign of sickness. If they are seen in a bedroom—death. **1932** J. M. E. SAXBY *Shetland Lore* 191. I don't really believe some old notions, but well—a mouse ran across me road, and the men [the other fishermen] said I must not come with them after that.

Cf. CRICKET as omen.

RATS AND MICE, riddance to

1st c. AD *Geoponika* XIII 5 (T. Owen, 1805, II 141) Take some paper and write these words on it: 'I adjure the mice taken in this place, that you do me no injury yourselves, nor suffer another to do it; for I give you this ground (and you mention which); but if I again take you on this spot, I take the mother of the Gods to witness, I will divide you into seven parts' .. Fasten the paper in the place where the mice are, before the rising of the sun. **1584** SCOT *Discoverie of Witchcraft* III xv. They [Irishmen] will not sticke to affirme, that [the eye-biting witches] can rime either man or beast to death. **1600** SHAKESPEARE *As You Like It* III ii. I was never so berim'd since Pythagoras time that I was an Irish Rat, which I can hardly remember. **1603** W.

PERKINS *Works* 39. The like superstition, is to surmise that beasts may be tamed by verses, praiers, or the like. **1869** R. CHAMBERS *Popular Rhymes of Scotland* 339. When these creatures become superabundant in a house of the humbler class, a writ of ejectment .. is served upon them, by being stuck up legibly written on the wall: 'Ratton and mouse, Lea' the puir woman's house; Gang awa' owre by to 'e mill, And there ane and a' ye'll get your fill.' **1962** *Daily Express* 31 Jan. 7. [When the maid complained of mice in the kitchen Lady Dowding got rid of them by talking to them in a kindly way.] She sat on the stairs under the hole and just .. said 'You are spoiling my home. It wouldn't be safe for you to come down because we have a big cat. So do you think you could find somewhere else to live?'

RAVEN ominous

*c.*40 BC VIRGIL *Eclogue* IX (tr. Rieu) If a timely raven on my left hand .. had not warned me at all costs to cut short this last dispute, neither your friend Moeris nor Menalcas himself would be alive today. AD 77 PLINY *Natural History* X xv (1855, II 492) Ravens .. are of the very worst omen when they swallow their voice, as if they were being choked. **1507** *Gospelles of Dystaues* pt. 3 v. Whan the lorde or the lady of a house is seke, and that a rauen cometh and cryeth vpon the chambre where as the pacyent lyeth it is synge that he shall deye of that sykenes. **1587** GIFFORD *Subtill Practises of Devilles* C1ᵛ–2. The raven he sitteth upon the steeple and cryeth: which way doth he looke sayth one, from thence ye shal haue an eie ere it be long. **1587** PEELE *David and Bethsabe* IV D1. Like as the fatall Rauen, that in his voice Carries the dreadful summons of our deaths. **1606** SHAKESPEARE *Macbeth* I v. The Raven himselfe is hoarse, That croakes the fatall entrance of Duncan Under my battlements. *c.*1650 DR WREN Note in Browne's *Vulgar Errors* V XXIII (1852, II 79) The raven, by his accute sense of smelling, discerns the savour of the dying .. and that makes them flutter about the windows, as they use to doe in the searche of a carcasse .. thence ignorant people counte them

ominous, as foreboding deathe, and in some kind as causing deathe. **1652** A. ROSS *Arcana Microcosmi* 220. A young gentleman .. my intimate friend, who about five or six years ago, being then in the flower of his age, had on a sudden .. ravens in his chamber, which had been quarrelling upon the top of the chimney; these he apprehended as messengers of his death, and so they were; for he died shortly after. **1693** *Athenian Mercury* 1 Apr. There's a Raven has built a Nest in the North-west Pinnacle of Louth Church .. the like has not been remember'd of 60 years, and above. Some People look upon it as Ominous. **1748** SMOLLETT *Roderick Random* XIII. At that instant a monstrous, overgrown raven entered our chamber .. and made directly towards our bed. As this creature is reckoned in our country a common vehicle for the devil and witches to play their pranks in, I verily believed we were haunted, and, in a violent fright, shrunk under the bed-clothes. **1799** SOUTHEY *Poems* II 'Old Woman of Berkeley'. The Raven croak'd as she sate at her meal, And the Old Woman knew what he said, And she grew pale at the Raven's tale, And sicken'd and went to her bed. **1853** *N & Q* 1st ser. VII 496. At an ordinary meeting of the guardians of the poor .. the officer stated that the applicant's inability to work was owing to depressed spirits, produced by the flight of a croaking raven over her dwelling on the morning of his visit. **1873** KILVERT *Diary* 26 May. John Vincent said that a man was sick at Derry Hill. Two ravens flew over the house crying 'Corpse, Corpse'. The man died the next day. **1899** *Newcastle Weekly Chronicle* 11 Feb. 7 [Jesmond] The Cheviot shepherds say they hear the raven laugh when some one is about to die. **1910** HUDSON *Shepherd's Life* X. He had much to say about the old belief that the raven 'smells death', and when seen hovering over a flock, uttering its croak, it is a sure sign that a sheep is in a bad way and will shortly die. **1922** R. KEARTON *At Home with Wild Nature* 58–9. In the Highlands of Scotland even educated people appear to have a dread of the bad luck a raven is likely to bring them. I remember .. entering a friend's house with the wing quill of one of these birds in my hand, and being seriously entreated to dispose of it at once lest it should bring one of us misfortune. **1932** J. M. E. SAXBY *Shetland Lore* 123. No raven had croaked within hearing [of the bridal party]. The young couple were to be happy all their lives! **1971** *Trans. Devon. Ass.* 268 [Stockleigh Pomeroy] A croaking raven (not a rook) was a sign of coming bad luck. Mr Brown adds that he has found this to be true.

Cf. CROWS OR RAVENS ominous.

RED lucky to card players

1953 *Reveille* 2 Oct. 2. The women [at whist drives] insist on marking their score cards with red pencils.

RED unlucky to lovers

*c.***1797** H. MORE *Tawney Rachel* 12. She recollected that red was an unlucky colour, and changed it for a blue ribbon, tied in a true lover's knot. **1923** [Lyng, Som.] It is considered very unlucky to write a love letter with red ink. **1981** *Mirror* 6 Apr. 24 [Merseyside] Can you please tell me why one should not write personal letters in red ink? I can find no real reason for it, except, perhaps, superstition.

RED CARS lucky

1969 *Folklore* 244. The belief, reported to me on several occasions within the last three years, that red cars are lucky .. seems to have developed from a road safety report which showed that fewer red-painted cars were involved in accidents than cars of other colours.

RED FLOWERS unlucky

1839 *Life of M. G. Lewis* I 20. Mrs Lewis happened to make some remark on a beautiful rose which Miss Ray wore in her bosom. Just as the words were uttered, the flower fell to the ground .. as she picked it up, the red leaves scattered themselves on the carpet, and .. the poor girl .. said .. 'I trust I am not to consider this as an evil omen!' [Later that evening Miss Ray was murdered at the entrance of Covent Garden Theatre.] **1889** *N & Q* 7th ser. VIII 265. I have always understood that a red rose was considered unlucky. **1890** *N & Q* 7th

ser. X 485. A gentleman whom I know had a full-blown rose given to him. As he was putting it into his button-hole the leaves fell to the ground. He picked up two, and, having put them apart, placed his hat over them, and then jumped over his hat twice, backwards and forwards. He did this so that he should not have bad luck all day. **1955** *Woman's Illustrated* 16 Apr. 13. Her grandmother .. believed the old superstition that if you picked a red poppy and one of the petals fell off and dropped on your hand you would be struck by lightning.

Cf. FLOWERS: red and white together.

RED HAIR unlucky

*c.***1200** *Proverbs of Alfred* (*Rel. Ant.* I 188) The rede mon he is a quet [wicked man]; for he wole the thin uvil red [will give thee evil counsel]. **1422** *Secreta Secretorum* (EETS Extra Ser. 74: 229) Tho that bene rede men, bene .. trechurus, and full of queyntise [artfulness], i-likenyd to Foxis. *c.***1430–40** CAXTON *Boke of Curtesye* (ed. Halliwell, Percy Soc., 12) In no kyn house that rede-mon is, Ne women of tho same colour y-wys, Take neuer thy innes for no kyn nede, ffor those be folke that ar to drede. **1607** G. CHAPMAN *Bussy D'Ambois* III 1. Worse than the poison of a red-hair'd man. **1652** GAULE *Mag-astro-mances* 183–4. Physiognomical ominating .. a red hair, trecherous. **1654** E. GAYTON *Festivous Notes on Don Quixote* (1768, 146) Black-beards are bad, brown dangerous, yellow worse, and red worst of all. **1853** *N & Q* 1st ser. VII 616. In every part of England I have visited, there appears to be a deep-rooted prejudice .. against people with red hair .. Tradition .. assigns to Absalom's hair a reddish tinge; and Judas .. is ever painted with locks of the same unhappy colour. **1865** *Gents Mag.* pt. 2 700 [Ireland] A red-haired woman, if met first in the morning, betokens something unlucky falling out during the day. **1873** HARLAND & WILKINSON *Lancashire Legends* 225. Red-haired children are supposed to indicate infidelity on the part of the mother; they are consequently looked upon as unlucky and are not wanted in a neighbour's house on the morning of

New Year's Day .. Red-haired persons .. are not infrequently reproached with having descended from the Scots and Danes. 1875 *N & Q* 5th ser. III 465 [Shrops.] It's not lucky for .. a red-haired man to come in your house first on a New Year's Day; there'll be a death in it afore the year's out. 1882 *People's Friend* 13 Sept. 581. A person setting out on a journey will have good luck if he first meets a black-haired person, who is a friend, and bad luck if he meets a red-haired person, or an enemy. 1885 *Folklore* 308 [Pittulie, Aberdeen.] A person with red hair is by some looked upon as having 'an ill fit' [unlucky foot]. 1891–3 *Proceedings Royal Irish Acad.* 3rd ser. II 818 [Aran Islands, Co. Galway] The meeting of a red-haired woman [brings ill-luck to the fishing]. 1930 P. F. ANSON *East Coast of Scotland* 38. It was .. unlucky to meet a red-haired person. 1960 *Folklore* 252 [Hartlepool, Co. Durham] Before the ship was due to sail, I became aware of a muttering outside my door. I asked the Captain what it was all about and, after some hesitation, he replied that the fo'castle did not want to sail with a strange red-haired woman aboard, especially as the cargo was iron ore.

Cf. FIRST-FOOT at New Year/Christmas: dark male usually preferred.

RED THREAD cures

*c.*1040 MS Harl. 55 (COCKAYNE *Leechdoms* II 307) If a man ache in .. his head .. delve up waybroad without iron, ere the rising of the sun, bind the roots about the head .. by a red fillet, soon he will be well. 1314 JOHN OF GADDESDEN *Rosa Angelica* (tr. Wulff, 315) Take a scarlet or other red cloth, and put it about the pox; as I did to the King of England's son when the disease [smallpox] seized him, and I permitted only red things to be about his bed, by the which I cured him. 1607 TOPSELL *Foure-footed Beastes* 536. The Shrew which dyeth in the furrow of a cart-wheele, being .. rowled in .. scarlet-wollen-cloth, and three times marked about the impostumes .. effectually .. cure the same. 1858 DENHAM *North of England* (1895; 48) Red garters are considered by certaine laydies an effectual charm against the

'rheumatiz'. But, I believe to act properly .. they should be stolen. 1861 ELIOT *Silas Marner* II. The Wise Woman had words that she muttered to herself, so that you couldn't hear what they were, and if she tied a bit of red thread round the child's toe the while, it would keep off the water in the head. 1872 *N & Q* 4th ser. X 83. I was told on July 18, in the country town of Rutland, by a woman who kept a small shop, the following infallible remedy to stop nose-bleeding in an unmarried female: 'Tie a new piece of red ribbon round her neck.' 1880 W. SIKES *British Goblins* 251 [Wales] Tie a red string about the neck to cure nose-bleed. 1887 'SPERANZA' WILDE *Superstitions of Ireland* II 92. The child to be passed seven times under and over an ass, while a red string is tied on the throat of the patient [for whooping cough]. 1909 M. TREVELYAN *Folk-Lore of Wales* 311. Even in the present day the peasantry of Wales cling very closely to the old superstition about a bit of red flannel as a preventative against fever, smallpox, and rheumatism. 1910 *Folklore* 223 [Saffron Walden, Essex] One day, the rector—it must have been in the sixties or seventies—called at some cottages .. In one house the woman said her baby had been very bad with the teething, but she had been to Walden and got a skein of red silk to put round its neck. 1926 *Folklore* 173 [Aberystwyth, Cardigan.] When people .. suffer from .. rheumatism they often go to a witch-doctor, a woman; she .. measures the affected parts with lengths of crimson wool, and then ties the wool round the arm [etc.] The ministers object to this, but the people go after dark and on the sly. 1933 *Folklore* 203 [Willoughton, Lincs.] Nose-bleeding—tie a red cotton or ribbon round the neck of the patient. 1954 Girl, 13 [Forfar, Angus] When someone has a sore throat, it is a usual thing to bandage it in red flannel. This is meant to keep the heat in. The flannel *must* be red, or no good is done.

RED THREAD protects

c. AD 390 ST JOHN CHRYSOSTOM *Homilies on Corinthians* XII (1839, I 164). What shall we say about the amulets and the bells .. and the scarlet woof, and the other things full of such extreme folly; when they ought to invest the child with nothing else save the protection of the Cross. *c.* AD 1050 MS Cotton Vitell. C. iii (COCKAYNE *Leechdoms* I 101) For a lunatic, take [clove wort] and wreathe it with a red thread about the man's swere [neck] when the moon is on the wane . . soon he will be healed. 1814 J. TOLAND *History of Druids* (ed. Huddleston) 283. Roan tree and red thread, Put the witches to their speed. 1814 J. TRAIN *Mountain Muse* 27. Lest witches should obtain the power Of hawkie's milk . . She winds a red thread round her horn. 1827 HONE *Every-Day Book* II 20 May. The reputed consequences of the blink of an ill-ee, are either death, or some horrible debility; for which there are some preventatives, such as rolling a red silk thread round the finger or the neck. 1851 *N & Q* 1st ser. IV 380. It is a common practice with the housewives [in Buchan, Aberdeen.] to tie a piece of red worsted thread round their cows' tails, previous to turning them out to grass for the first time in the spring. It secures their cattle, they say, from an evil eye. 1852 DENHAM *Fairies, Witches* (1895, 82) I have seen a twig of Rowan-tree . . gathered on the ii of May . . wound round with some dozens of yards of reed threed . . placed visibly in the window, to act as a Charm in keeping Witches and Boggleboes from the house. 1972 *Lore and Language* July 7 [Coalisland, Co. Tyrone] To prevent a cow being blinked tie a red rag on its front left leg.

Cf. THREAD tied round.

RING made of blessed money/silver: cures
1323 *Household Ordinance of York* June (T. F. TOUT *Edward II in Eng. Hist.* 317) Item the king must offer without fail on Good Friday to the cross Vs [5 shillings] to make of them rings to give for medicine to various persons, and to replace with other Vs. *c.*1400 MS Arundel 276 (BLOCH *The Royal Touch* 330 n.) For the Crampe . . Tak . . on Gude Friday, at fyfe parisch kirkes, fife of the first penyes that is offerd at the crose . . and say v. pater noster in the worschip of fife wondes [wounds] and than gar mak a

ryng ther of . . and vse it alway aftirward. 1550 BOORDE *Introduction of Knowledge* Biᵛ–Bii. The Kynges of Englande doth halowe euery yere Crampe rynges, ye whyche rynges worne on ones fynger dothe helpe them the whyche hath the Crampe. 1794 *Gents Mag.* 433. A notion that prevails in Berkshire [is] that a ring made from a piece of silver collected at the communion, is a cure for convulsions and fits of every kind. A woman in my parish . . applied to me for a shilling on Easter Sunday . . As I was convinced she was not influenced by any mercenary motive . . I took care not to deprive her of such benefit, at least, as she might derive from her imagination. 1849 BRAND *Antiquities* III 280 [Sowerby, Yorks.] He was to obtain thirty pennies from thirty different people [and] after receiving them to get them exchanged for a half-crown of sacrament money, which was to be fashioned into a ring and worn by the patient. 1903 *Southern Daily Mail* 22 Jan. 4. On a recent Sunday a farm labourer stood in the porch of the parish church of a village on the banks of the Tamar [Devon], and collected half-a-crown in coppers from different members of the congregation, the thirtieth donor giving the half-crown and taking the twenty-nine pence . . From the consecrated coin thus quaintly acquired the labourer has manufactured a silver ring, which he will wear as an infallible remedy for epilepsy.

RING made of money/silver given by bachelors/spinsters: cures
1794 *Gents Mag.* 598 [Bourton, Glos.] She said that her daughter . . was very much troubled with convulsion fits . . 'Sir . . I came to beg . . five sixpences of five different bachelors . . to make a ring for my daughter, to cure her fits' . . It was to be kept a profound secret . . I did as desired; and, behold! it cured the girl. 1850 *N & Q* 1st ser. II 5 [Suffolk] If a young woman has fits, she applies to ten or a dozen unmarried men (if the sufferer be a man, he applies to as many maidens) and obtains from each of them a small piece of silver of any kind, as a piece of a broken spoon, or ring, or brooch, buckle, and even sometimes a

small coin, and a penny; the twelve pieces of silver are taken to a silversmith .. who forms therefrom a ring, which is to be worn by the person affected. **1852** *N & Q* 1st ser. VI 50. The following charm was practised a few weeks since in the village of Newport, Essex, on a poor lad subject to epileptic fits. Nine sixpences were procured from nine virgins ('for which they were neither to be asked nor thanked'); the money was then made into a ring, which the child wore; but with no satisfactory result, possibly from some flaw in the primary condition. **1881** *N & Q* 6th ser. IV 106. On July 15 .. I observed a broad silver ring on the middle finger of the left hand of a man, formerly of Chudleigh [Devon], a painter .. working at my house .. He .. had worn the ring about seven years for the purpose of protecting himself from fits .. The ring .. was made of nine sixpences, given to him .. by nine unmarried females .. The givers and receivers of the sixpences must be of different sexes. **1943** *Sussex N & Q* Aug. 158–9 [West Hoathly, 1929] Mrs Pellatt was in despair till she remembered a cure for fits which she had heard of as a girl .. 'You must get seven threepenny bits from seven strange men, not saying who you are or what you want them for, and put them in a bag and tie them secretly round the child's neck, never letting them leave her, and the fits will die away.'

Cf. SILVER protects; VIRGIN heals.

RINGWORM, charm for

1826 R. CHAMBERS *Popular Rhymes of Scotland* 283. Charm used in Galloway for curing scorbutic spots on the skins of children: 'Ringwood, ringwood, roon, I wish ye may neither spread nor spring, But aye grow less and less, Till ye fa' i' e' ase [ashes] and burn.' Ibid. 1842 ed., 37. The person afflicted with ringworm takes a little ashes between the forefinger and thumb, three successive mornings, and before having taken any food, and holding the ashes to the part affected, says 'Ringworm! ringworm red! Never mayest thou either spread or speed; But aye grow less and less, And die away among the ase.'

ROBIN = death

1829 BROCKETT *North Country Words. Robin* .. about Heworth, near Newcastle, it is looked upon as a bird of bad omen. I am also told that among the lower classes in Northumberland and Scotland, it is considered the harbinger of death. **1850** *N & Q* 1st ser. II 165 [Northants.] Before the death of a person, a robin is believed, in many instances, to tap thrice at the window of the room in which he or she may be. **1868** *N & Q* 4th ser. I 87. In the north of Devon .. it is .. believed that, when a robin perches on the top of a cottage and utters its plaintive 'weet', the baby in the cottage will die. **1879** HENDERSON *Northern Counties* 50 [Suffolk] An old woman expressed her dismay at having a robin come 'weeping, weeping', as she called it, to her door, and related two instances in her own family in which it had been a warning of death. **1892** C. M. YONGE *Old Woman's Outlook* February. Perhaps the story has been told before of the Devon doctor who was summoned in haste to a farm-house on the moor. He found an old man in bed, but in perfect health, and could only ask why he had been called in. 'Why, sir,' said the daughter-in-law, 'there came a little robin about the door. We knowed it was a call, and we thought it must be for granfer; so we put 'im to bed and sent for you.' **1913** E. M. WRIGHT *Rustic Speech* 216 [Oxon.] Any bird pecking at the window announces death, but the robin is the chief harbinger .. whether .. by tapping at the window, chirping on the sill, or by hopping into the room. In the winter of 1910, a tame robin used to cause considerable uneasiness in this household by coming into the house. **1918** A. CLARKE *Diary* 19 Nov. (J. MUNSON *Echoes of Great War*) Theophilus Fuller .. has died after a very short illness. Great Leighs [Essex] villagers have a strong belief that attention from a robin is a sign of death. They are now saying that before T.F. took ill, a robin followed him about in his garden for two days. **1932** C. IGGLESDEN *Those Superstitions* 76. One day a robin hopped into the hall of my house, and one of the maids became hysterical. 'A death within a month,' she kept moaning. But someone contradicted her, and said: 'Not within a month, but within a year.' **1932** *Sussex County Mag.* 91 [nr. Midhurst, 1926] When they sings mournful 'weep, weep' that's when 'tis unlucky .. that means death. **1943** Woman, 20 [Thurso, Caithness.] I'll not have to do with a robin in the house, oh no! A robin is an omen of death. **1971** Woman, *c.*70 [Liss, Hants.] Don't be surprised if you hear some bad news today. A robin come right into the house this morning! **1984** Man, 31 [Pewsey, Wilts.] My grandmother has just gone into hospital to have an ulcer in her throat treated. I sent her a printed Get-Well-Soon card, the picture on the front of which was a robin on its nest. My mother later drew my attention to this awful *faux pas*—my grandmother had been clearly uneasy on receipt of the card due to her belief in the superstition. **1986** *Mirror* 2 May 20 [Chelmsford, Essex] I made friends with a robin, so tame it would sit on the edge of the draining board and peck at biscuits .. My sister says the robin brought death to the house, hence my husband's death.

ROBIN protects the dead

1606 SHAKESPEARE *Cymbeline* IV ii. The Raddocke [robin] would With Charitable bill .. bring thee all this, Yea, and furr'd Mosse besides. When Flowres are none To winter-ground thy Coarse. **1612** WEBSTER *White Devil* V iv. Call for the Robin-Red-brest and the wren, Since ore shadie groves they hover, And with leaves and flowres doe cover The friendlesse bodies of unburied men.

ROBIN AND NEST, harming

1709 *British Apollo* 2 Mar. Q. The Robin Red Breast is as malicious and Envious a Bird as any that flies .. I desire to know why many People should have so good an Esteem of this Bird, as to account it a Crime to do it any Injury. **1713** *Guardian* 21 May. As for Robin-red-breasts .. 'tis not improbable they owe their Security to the old Ballad of *the Children in the Wood* [in which robins cover the bodies of the dead children]. *c.*1780 T. PARK MS note in Brand's *Antiquities* 92. There is .. a popular belief in many Country places, that it is

unlucky either to kill or keep Robins. **1838** A. E. BRAY *Devonshire* I 67. The boys will pelt any one of their companions who may steal but an egg from 'poor Cock Robin's' nest. Ibid. II 289–90 [Tavistock; Garland Day, 29 May] The garlands are .. strung with birds' eggs .. every egg being held allowable, save that of the redbreast .. Very few children in this town would hurt a redbreast, as it is considered unlucky to do so; this bird being entitled to kindness .. above every other. **1868** *N & Q* 4th ser. I 193–4 [Yorks.] In the neighbourhood of Boro'bridge .. a young woman .. told .. of .. a cow .. giving bloody milk after one of the family had killed a robin .. A male cousin of hers, disbelieving the tale .. shot a robin purposely. Next morning her uncle's best cow .. gave half a canful of this 'bloody' milk .. The matter furnished talk to the village. **1871** *N & Q* 4th ser. VIII 505 [Yorks.] From the mouth of a young miner: 'My father killed a robin .. He had at that time a pig which was ready for pigging; she had a litter of seven, and they all deed.' **1887** 'SPERANZA' WILDE *Superstitions of Ireland* II 64. Whoever kills a robin redbreast will never have good luck were they to live a thousand years. **1889** *Dorset Field Club* 40. It used to be said to children that if they ever took robins' eggs .. their little fingers would be sure to grow crooked. **1906** E. THOMAS *Heart of England* XI [Hants.] Yonder .. goes a boy birdnesting in a double hedge .. He will not take the robin's eggs, 'or I shall get my arm broken,' he says. **1932** *Folklore* 107 [Naphill, Bucks., 1910] They say .. that if you break a robin's leg, your leg will be broken; and if you break a robin's wing, your arm will be broken. **1972** *Farmers Weekly* 58. Pull out a robin's nest or break one of their eggs and you'll end up with a broken leg or arm. This superstition .. is still found in East Anglian villages. **1974** Ted Edgar, international show-jumper, asked why he was not doing so well this season, said 'I must have shot a robin, mustn't I?'

ROBIN AND WREN sacred

1773 *Poetical Description of Song Birds*

(1787, 40) Whoe'er has mix'd in child-ish play, Must sure have heard the children say, The Robin and the Jenny Wren Are God Almighty's cock and hen. *c.*1780 T. PARK MS note in Brand's *Antiquities* 92. When a boy, I remember it was said .. that Tom Tit and Jenny Wren Were God Almighty's cock and hen, and therefore to be held sacred. 1838 W. HOLLOWAY *Provincialisms* 90. In Hampshire we have this couplet, 'Little Cock Robin and Little Jenny Wren, Are God Almighty's little Cock and Hen.' And agreeably to this these birds are held sacred, no boys, however daring, venturing to take their nests or to kill them. 1839 W. HOWITT *Boy's Country Book* 60. It is a very ancient adage— Robinets and Jenny Wrens, Are God Almighty's cocks and hens. 1842 R. CHAMBERS *Popular Rhymes of Scotland* 41. Birds whose nests it is deemed unlucky to molest .. The robin and the wren; If ye harry their nests, Ye'll never thrive again. 1883 BURNE *Shropshire* 216. Mrs Dudley, in her childhood at Clee St Margaret, learnt to believe that if any-body robbed the nest of either robin or wren, his hand would presently drop off. 1900 S. BARING-GOULD *Book of Dartmoor* 252 [Devon] There is a saying among the country folk: 'Kill a robin or a wren, Never prosper, boy or man.' 1970 [Liss, Hants.] A robin was on the roof, and the gypsy girl said: 'The robin and the wren are God's best friend.' 'Why?' asked Gwen. 'How should I know?' replied the seventeen-year-old.

Cf. WREN.

ROBIN/WREN/MARTIN/SWALLOW
sacred

1826 HONE *Every-Day Book* 11 May [Warwicks.] The robin and the wren Are God Almighty's cock and hen; The martin and the swallow Are God Almighty's bow and arrow. 1826 R. WIL-BRAHAM *Cheshire Glossary* 105. The following .. is common in Cheshire: The Robin and the Wren Are God's cock and hen, The Martin and the Swallow Are God's mate and marrow. 1830 FORBY *East Anglia* 409. The robin-redbreast and the wren, Are God Almighty's cock and hen; The martin and the swallow Are the next two birds that follow. 1849

HALLIWELL *Popular Rhymes* 164. A robin and a titter-wren Are God Almighty's cock and hen; A martin and a swallow Are God Almighty's shirt and collar! Ibid. 165 [Essex] The robin and the red-breast, The robin and the wren; If ye take out o' their nest, Ye'll never thrive agen! The robin and the red-breast, The martin and the swallow; If ye touch one o' their eggs, Bad luck will surely follow! 1875 W. D. PARISH *Sussex Dialect* 100. The Sussex small boys have a Small Birds Act of their own, which is found sufficient for the protection of all birds which they consider entitled to protection, and commands much more respect and obedience than a recent Act of Parliament: 'Robins and wrens Are God Almighty's friends; Martins and swallers Are God Almighty's scholars.' 1939 F. THOMPSON *Lark Rise* 170. No boy would rob a robin's nest; nor would they have wrecked a swallow's nest if they could have reached one, for they believed that: 'The robin and the wrens Be God Almighty's friends. And the martin and the swallow Be God Al-mighty's birds to follow.' And those four were safe from molestation.

Cf. SWALLOW AND MARTIN.

ROLLING-PIN, glass

1899 *N & Q* 9th ser. III 245. I find the following .. in a catalogue of curios .. 'Sailor's Charm, Glass Rolling-Pin for hanging in a Ship's Cabin .. with in-scription 'A Present from Newcastle'.' Ibid. 337 [Worksop, Notts.] In the Mid-lands [rolling-pins] were given for luck, as a rule. One which hangs in a cottage near me bears the words 'I wish you well!' It was sent to the owner on her wedding-day fifty years ago .. used on special occasions in preparing pastry for weddings and birthdays only. This rolling-pin was sent .. filled with the best tea .. of the old 'gunpowder' sort .. It is filled with salt at the present time. 1900 *N & Q* 9th ser. IV 154–5 [Guernsey] In 1878 .. I .. saw one of these rolling-pin charms .. It is of pale blue clouded glass .. at one end [is] a ship under full sail; at the other—'From rocks and sands and barren lands Kind fortune keep me free, And from great guns and women's tongues Good Lord deliver me.' Reflecting on my experience [in fog at sea], and on the near approach of my marriage, I thought the legend not inappropriate, so purchased the pin. **1988** Woman, 59 [Co. Durham] I have a glass rolling-pin. It's about nine inches long, and made of solid dark blue glass. I always took it to be a sample from the Sunderland glassworks. It used to hang on the wall in my grandmother's house in South Shields, but whether for decoration or good luck, I don't know.

ROOKS = death

*c.*1816 Wilkie MS (HENDERSON *Northern Counties*, 1866, 90) When rooks haunt a town or village, mortality is supposed to await its inhabitants. **1887** 'SPERANZA' WILDE *Superstitions of Ireland* II 64. A flight of rooks over an army betokens defeat; if over a house, or over people when driving or walking, death will follow. **1977** H. DOUGLAS-HOME *Birdman* 144. Rooks were always said to be ominous birds. In the last century there was a rookery near the castle at Douglas, and when my great-grandfather was fairly young he got irritated by their cawing and ordered the keepers to get rid of them .. about three hundred nests .. An old crone bawled him out for banishing the rooks .. 'You wait, they'll be back the day you die!' .. The time came when he was slipping away and suddenly, to his horror, all the rooks came cawing into the trees around Douglas Castle. 'God rooks!' he exclaimed and .. subsided into his pillows. 'That means I'm going to die today.' And he did.

ROOKS informed of a death

1883 BURNE *Shropshire* 218. If the master of the house dies, they must be told of it, like bees, or they will go away.

Cf. BEES, news told to.

ROOKS leave after a death

1879 *N & Q* 5th ser. XI 506 [Lincs.] A singular circumstance is reported in connexion with the recent suicide of Mr Graves, of Linwood Grange. Near the house a colony of rooks had established themselves, and on the day of the funeral, immediately on the appearance of the hearse, the birds left the locality in a body, deserting their nests. **1909** M. TREVELYAN *Folk-Lore of Wales* 328. A deserted rookery means misfortune and probably death in the mansion. **1936** E. H. RUDKIN *Lincolnshire* 21 [Grayingham] On the death of a head of a house rooks will desert the rookery for a year.

ROOKS nesting near house: lucky

1830 FORBY *East Anglia* 414. Rooks building near a house are a sign of prosperity. **1872** *Bye-Gones* 18 Sept. 86 [Llansantffraid-yn-Mechain, Monmouth.] Rooks nesting near a house are said to be a sign of good luck, and their forsaking a rookery .. a warning of coming evil. **1922** R. KEARTON *At Home with Wild Nature* 58. The establishment of a new rookery round one's house is considered a harbinger of good luck, just as the forsaking of an old one by its inhabitants is accepted as an omen of evil. **1971** G. SNAGGE *More Letters from Longstock* 129. There is the comfortable tradition that a house with a rookery is a happy one.

ROOK'S EGG, finding broken

1966 MASEFIELD *Grace Before Ploughing* 41 [Ledbury, Herefords., *c.*1884] I was told that if I found a broken rook's egg in January in any year, I should have a happy year.

ROOM, UPPER: unlucky

c. AD 70 Mark 14: 14–18. Say ye to the goodman of the house, The Master saith, Where is the guest-chamber, where I shall eat the passover with my disciples? And he will shew you a large upper room furnished and prepared; there make ready for us .. And in the evening he cometh with the twelve. And as they sat and did eat, Jesus said, Verily I say unto you, One of you which eateth with me shall betray me. **1872** *N & Q* 4th ser. IX 36. In the past Christmas I was helping in some decorations for a village church in Rutland, and was at work upon them in a first-floor room of a house. I was told that it was a very unlucky thing to make in an upper room anything .. for a church.

ROPE CIRCLE, boat passed through

1881 W. GREGOR *North-East of Scotland*

199–200. When it was suspected that the boat had been forespoken . . it was put through the halyards . . by making a noose . . on the halyards large enough to allow the boat to pass through . . This noose was put over the prow . . and pushed under the keel, and the boat sailed through . . The evil was taken off the boat.

ROSE: divination

1648 HERRICK *Hesperides* 61 'Epithalamie' st. 12. She must no more . . by Rose-buds devine, Who'l be her Valentine. **1755** *Connoisseur* 20 Feb. Our maid Betty tells me, that if I go backwards without speaking a word into the garden upon Midsummer Eve, and gather a Rose, and keep it in a clean sheet of paper, without looking at it, till Christmas Day, it will be as fresh as in June; and if I then stick it in my bosom, he that is to be my husband will come and take it out. **1787** *Gents Mag.* pt. 2 719 [Midsummer Eve] She bids it [the moss-rose] Await the new-year's frolic wake: When, faded, in its altered hue, She reads, the rustic is untrue. **1838** A. E. BRAY *Devonshire* II 287. It is here said, that if a young woman, on Midsummer-day, plucks a full-blown rose, blindfolded, while the chimes are playing twelve, and folds it up in a sheet of white paper, and does not open it till Christmas day, it will then be found as fresh as when gathered; and if she places it in her bosom, the young man to whom she is to be married will come and snatch it away. **1862** *N & Q* 3rd ser. II 62 [Devon] On Midsummer Day pluck a rose; fold it up in paper, and put it by till Christmas Day. On that day wear it at church; and . . the man who comes and takes it from you will be your husband. **1912** LEATHER *Herefordshire* 61. Gather a rose on Midsummer Eve, and carry it home, walking backwards, and not speaking a word. It must be carefully preserved in clean white paper, till the following Christmas Day, and then the girl must wear it; it will be taken from her by her future husband.

Cf. SAGE: divination.

ROSE-GALL cures

1878 *Folk-Lore Record* 38 [Fittleworth]

Hang round the patient's neck the excrescence often found upon the briarrose, and called here in Sussex by the name of Robin Redbreast's Cushion; it is the finest thing known for the whooping-cough. **1883** BURNE *Shropshire* 194. The wild-rose gall is . . considered good for toothache. 'If you light on a briar-boss *accidental* w'en yo' 'an the tuthache, an' wear it in yore boasom, it'll cure it,' said Isabella Pearce of the Twitchen. **1909** M. TREVELYAN *Folk-Lore of Wales* 98–9. On the wild-rose brambles and the whitethorn there is often a moss-like excrescence. In Wales they say if this is placed under the pillow of a person who cannot sleep, it will perfectly restore him. **1912** LEATHER *Herefordshire* 82. A gall of the wild rose is frequently carried in the pocket, as a preventive of toothache. **1932** *Folklore* 105. In Derbyshire . . when children are affected [with whooping cough] they hang in the house the 'pin-cushions' from wild rose-trees. 'I sent my boy 5 miles to get one, and as soon as I hung it up, she got better.'

ROSEMARY at funerals

1584 C. ROBINSON *Handefull of pleasant delites* Aijb. Rosemarie is for remembrance. *c.***1595** SHAKESPEARE *Romeo and Juliet* IV v. Drie up your teares, and sticke your Rosemarie On this faire Coarse, and as the custome is, And in her best array beare her to Church. **1648** HERRICK *Hesperides* 273 'The Rosemarie branch'. Grow for two ends, it matters not at all, Be't for my Bridall, or my Buriall. **1698** MISSON *Voyageur en Angleterre* (1719, 91) They nail up the Coffin, and a Servant presents the Company with Sprigs of Rosemary: Every one takes a Sprig, and carries it in his Hand 'till the Body is put into the Grave, at which Time they all throw their Sprigs in after it. **1708** *British Apollo* 20 Oct. Q . . Whence proceeds that so constant formality of such Persons bearing a sprig of Rosemary in their hand when Accompanying the Obsiquies of a Deceas'd Person? *A.* That Custom ('tis like) had its Rise from a Notion of a . . preservative Vertue in that Herb against Pestilential Distempers. **1714** GAY *Shepherd's Week* 49. Upon her Grave their

Rosemary they threw. **1880** W. SIKES *British Goblins* 336 [Wales] By a most graceful custom which . . prevailed until recently, each mourner at a funeral carried in his hand a sprig of rosemary, which he threw into the grave. **1883** BURNE *Shropshire* 304. The ancient custom of the mourners carrying sprigs of rosemary . . which after the burial service they cast into the grave . . is still practised . . in 1879, at all funerals of the lower and middle classes around Market Drayton. **1890** *North-Country Lore* 474 [Blackburn, Yorks.] A bunch of rosemary thrown into a grave will make the spirit rest. **1987** *Times* 16 Apr. 24. Two survivors from the crew [of the Zeebrugge ferry] laid a wreath of golden carnations and rosemary before the nave altar while the congregation stood in silence.

Cf. YEW at funerals.

ROSEMARY protective/lucky

1658 LEMNIUS *Secret Miracles of Nature* 391. Rosemary purgeth howses, and a branch of this hung at the entrance of howses drives away devills and contagions of the Plague. **1871** *N & Q* 4th ser. VIII 506 [Derbys.] Rosemary worn about the person . . will give success in love and other undertakings. **1900** S. HEWETT *Nummits* 23 [Devon] It is necessary to carry sprigs of . . rosemary . . in the pocket, to enhance the felicity of the pair [at wedding]. **1969** M. HARRIS *A Kind of Magic* 49 [Northleach, Glos., 1920s] 'Never give a bunch of flowers away unless you slips a sprig of rosemary in, my dear,' she once told me. 'It'll bring the receiver good luck, and bad to you if you forgets.' **1971** *Trans. Devon. Ass.* [Stockleigh Pomeroy] If you had a rosemary bush growing near the cottage, no witch could harm you.

ROSEMARY: woman is master

1708 *British Apollo* 8 Dec. Pray tell me the Reason, that where the Rosemary grows, there it is said the Woman Reigns. **1832** HONE *Year Book* 4 Jan. It is a jocular saying, among country people, that where the rosemary-bush flourishes in a cottage garden, 'the grey mare is the better horse'; that is, the wife manages the husband. **1852** *N & Q*

1st ser. VI 123. 'That be rosemary, sir,' said the worthy cottager, 'and they do say that it only growis where the missis is master, and it do grow here like wildfire.' **1875** W. D. PARISH *Sussex Dialect* 73. They say in Sussex that the rosemary will never blossom except where 'the mistus' is master. **1890** *North-Country Lore* Oct. 474 [Blackburn, Yorks.] If rosemary flourishes in a garden, the wife will be master; if it dies, the master will.

Cf. PARSLEY: mistress is master.

ROWAN protects

*c.***1000** MS Harl. 585 (COCKAYNE *Leechdoms* III 15) Pour the salve in . . then put in the gums above named . . then stir with a spoon of quickbeam [rowan]. **1597** JAMES I *Daemonologie* 11–12. Charmes as commonlie dafte wiues vses . . for preseruing them [cattle] from euill eyes, by knitting roun-trees . . to the haire or tailes of the goodes [cattle]. **1674** *Depositions, York Castle* 26 Aug. (1861, 209) Shee heard the said Susan say to the said Ann [both accused of witchcraft] 'I think I must give this Thomas Bramhall some, for they tye soe much whighen [rowan] about him, I cannot come to my purpose, else I could have worn him away once in two yeares.' **1685** AUBREY *Natural History of Wiltshire* (1847, IX) Whitty-tree . . In Herefordshire . . they used, when I was a boy, to make pinnes for the yoakes of their oxen of them, believing it had vertue to preserve them from being forespoken [bewitched], as they call it; and they use-to plant one by their dwelling-house, believing it to preserve from witches and evill eyes. **1768** A. ROSS *Fortunate Shepherdess* 12. Gryt was the care an' tut'ry that was ha'en, Baith night an' day, about the bony wean [child]. The jizzen-bed wi' rantree leaves was sain'd [blessed], An' sicklike craft as the auld grandys kend. late **18th c.** J. RAMSAY (*Scotland in the Eighteenth Century* II 454) On Hallowday and Beltane the people of Strathspey make a hoop of rowan-tree, through which all the sheep and lambs are forced to pass evening and morning. **1793** *Stat. Acc. of Scotland* IX 328 [Tongland, Kirkcudbright, *c.*1730] The lower class . .

were tainted strongly with superstitious sentiments .. They fixed branches of mountain ash, or narrow leaved service-tree above the stakes of their cattle, to preserve them from the evil effects of elves and witches. **1827** HONE *Every-Day Book* 20 May. The reputed consequences of the blink of an ill-ee, are either death, or some horrible debility; for which there are some preventitives .. such as .. keeping a slip of rowntree .. in the bonnet. **1827** HONE *Table Book* I 674–5 [Witherslack, Lancs.] To prevent the old beldam introducing herself into the churn, the churn-staff must be made of the 'Wiggen Tree' .. All honest people .. take special care to have a branch .. at their bed heads. This has been the practice of my mother ever since I can remember. **1832** *Gents Mag.* pt. 2 493 n. A seaman belonging to one of the Grimsby Greenland whalers, applied to my servant the night before the vessel sailed .. for a small branch of wicken-tree, several of which grew in my garden, as a preservative against witchcraft. **1882** *Folk-Lore Record* 81 [Co. Wexford] Cows going out on May morning are struck with a quicker-berry switch, which prevents any person putting any evil on them or taking their

profit or butter. **1888** S. O. ADDY *Sheffield Glossary* xxii. In Bradfield people nail sprigs of wiggin, witchen, or mountain ash upon their 'leaven-kits', or vessels for leavening oat-cake, 'to keep out the witch' .. Fifty years ago [they] liked to have cups, bowls, &c., made of this wood for the same reason. The Old Norse *reynir* was a holy tree, consecrated to Thor. **1934** *Folklore* 344. Here on the Tweed, the Rowan tree is still cherished. Further north .. the tree is seen planted close beside the farm-house or byre, which it protects.

Cf. MAY BOUGHS AND FLOWERS protect.

RUST = money

1873 *Chambers' Journal* 810 [Scotland] Steel belongings .. get rusty .. when some kind-hearted soul is laying up riches for their owner's benefit. **1876** *N & Q* 5th ser. VI 397 [Weardale, Co. Durham] If the good wife's keys persist in getting rusty, some friend is laying up money for her. **1948** E. & M. A. RADFORD *Superstitions* 207 [Wales] If, without any neglect on your part, articles made of iron or steel, such as keys, knives, etc., continually become rusty, somebody is laying up money for you.

S

SAGE: divination

1883 BURNE *Shropshire* 177. On all Saints' Eve, a young woman must go out into the garden alone at midnight, and while the clock strikes twelve she must pluck nine sage-leaves, one at every stroke up to the ninth. Then, if she is destined to be married, she will see the face of her future husband; if not, she will see a coffin. **1915** J. A. PENNY *Horncastle* 76 [Lincs.] If a girl picks twelve sage leaves as the clock strikes 12 at mid-day on St Mark's Day, one leaf for each, and at each strike of the clock, she will see her future husband, if she is to have one.

Cf. ROSE: divination.

SAILOR, touching: lucky

1916 *N & Q* 12th ser. I 430. In a Birmingham factory, on the appearance of a sailor, the hands crowd round the visitor and touch him 'for luck'. **1923** [Exeter, Devon] It is very lucky to touch a sailor, especially his collar. I have heard of a sailor walking through the streets of Taunton, being absolutely jostled by people trying to touch him. **1932** C. IGGLESDEN *Those Superstitions* 129. It is lucky for a girl to touch a sailor's collar—one of those superstitions which the sailor is never tired of emphasising! **1953** Girl, 15 [Loughton, Essex] Touch a sailor's collar and you'll have good luck. **1972** E. BLISHEN *Cackhanded War* 28 [Essex coast, 1940] George was on leave .. a sailor .. those bell-bottomed trousers, the collar round his neck that the children reached up to touch for luck. **1984** Man, 70. I used to return to the Lincolnshire fens near Billinghay each year. The local people asked me to bring my son with me in his sailor's uniform, and when we went into a pub they all asked if they could touch his collar, and then they each bought him a pint because they said that it had brought them luck.

ST AGNES'S EVE/DAY: divination

1603 JONSON 'Satyr' ll. 50–3. On sweet St Anna's [St Agnes's] night Feed them with a promised sight, Some of husbands, some of lovers, Which an empty dream discovers. **1660** BURTON *Anatomy of Melancholy* pt. 3 sect. 2 mem. 4 subs. I. They'll give any thing to know when they shall be married .. by fasting on St Agnes Eve, or night, to know who shall be their first husband. **1696** AUBREY *Miscellanies* (1890, 131) On St Agnes night, 21st day of January, take a row of pins, and pull out every one, one after another, saying a Pater Noster .. sticking a pin in your sleeve, and you will dream of him, or her, you shall marry. **1711** *Aristotle's Last Legacy* 50. On St Agnes Day. Take a Sprigg of Rosemary, and another of Time, sprinkle them with Urine thrice .. put one into one Shooe, and the other into the other; place your Shooes on each side your Beads-head, and going to Bed, say .. St Agnes, that's to Lovers kind, Come ease the Trouble of my Mind .. You will dream of your Lover. **1734** *Poor Robin's Almanack* Jan. Saint Agnes Day comes by and by, When pretty Maids do fast to try Their Sweet hearts in their Dreams to see, Or know who shall their Husbands be. **1832** *Time's Telescope* 15 [Scotland] A number of young lads and lasses [meet] together on the eve of St Agnes, and at the hour of twelve, one by one, go to a certain corn-field and throw in some grain, after which they pronounce—'Agnes sweet, and Agnes fair, Hither, hither, now repair; Bonny Agnes, let me see The lad who is to marry me' .. The shadow of the destined bride or bridegroom is seen in a mirror on this very night. **1880** *Routledge's Every Girl's Annual* 43–4. There is scarcely a young girl who is not acquainted, I imagine, with the superstition attached to St Agnes' Eve. The maiden who goes to bed fasting will dream of her future husband—at least this is the popular belief. **1898** BLAKE-

BOROUGH *Yorkshire Customs* 73. On the day of the eve of St Agnes .. fast from the time of rising, eating only a little stale bread and drinking parsley tea. On retiring to rest, remake your bed, putting thereon clean sheets and pillow-cases, remembering to repeat as you lay on each cover: 'St Agnes, I pray unto thee, I, a maid, would married be, So thou my husband show to me.'

ST CATHERINE patron saint of spinsters

1586 CAMDEN *Britannia* (tr. Gibson, II 378–9) [Limerick, Eire *c.* 1566] The very women and maidens fast every Wednesday and Saturday, the year round; also upon St Catharine's day [25 Nov.]; and never omit, though it fall on a birthday, or though themselves be ever so sick; to the end, some say, that the virgins may get good husbands, and that the wives may become happier in a married state, either by the death or desertion of their husbands, or else by their reformation and amendment. **1865** *Family Herald* 16 Sept. 319 [visit of the Archaeological Institute to the Norman chapel of St Catherine at Milton Abbey, Dorset] The legend was that on a certain day in the year the young women of Abbotsbury used to go up to St Catherine's Chapel, where they made use of the following prayer: 'A husband, St Catherine; a handsome one, St Catherine; A rich one, St Catherine; a nice one, St Catherine; and soon, St Catherine!' **1907** H. PENTIN *Old Dorset* 105–6 [Milton Abbey] St Catherine is the patron-saint of spinsters, and in days gone by she was supposed to have the power of finding a husband for those who sought her aid. The following .. rhymes [are] in use to-day .. 'St Catherine, St Catherine, O lend me thine aid, And grant that I never may die an old maid. A husband, St Catherine, A good one, St Catherine; But arn-a-one [any] better than Narn-a-one [none], St Catherine.'

ST CHRISTOPHER protects travellers

c. **1386** CHAUCER *Tales* Prol. ll. 111–15. He baar .. A Cristopher on his brest of silver sheene. **1488** *Will of Scotte* (Somerset Ho.) A Tabulet of goold with a cristofre. **1526** ERASMUS *Familiar Colloquies* (tr. Bailey, 406) A Mariner when in a Storm is more ready to invoke St Christopher, or some one or other of the Saints, than Christ himself. **1646** BROWNE *Vulgar Errors* V XVI. Christopher .. before his Martyrdom .. requested of God, that where ever his body were, the places should be freed from pestilence and mischiefs .. And therefore his picture or pourtract, was usually placed in publick waies, and at the entrance of Towns and Churches, according to the received Distich, *Christophorum videas, postea tutus eris* [after seeing Christopher you will be safe]. **1962** *Sunday Times* 16 Dec. 19. Donald Campbell .. leaves at the end of the month [for his attempt on the land speed record] taking with him .. a gold St Christopher. **1965** D. ATTWATER *Dict. of Saints* 85. It was a common medieval belief that he who looked on an image of St Christopher would suffer no harm that day, which led to the painting of large pictures of him on church walls; he is the patron saint of wayfarers, and now of motorists. **1981** *Sunday Times* 22 Mar. 32 [Clare Francis, yachtswoman] I suppose that I am very superstitious and would get nervous if I lost my St Christopher.

ST JOHN'S EVE, born on

1894 *Times* 30 June 6. While so many are rejoicing at the safe arrival of the little Prince on Saturday evening, it may interest your readers to be reminded of the old saying—'Under the stars, on the Eve of St John, Lucky the babe that those stars shine on!'

ST JOHN'S WORT protects

15th c. MS Digby 164 [Bodleian Lib.] f. 72. If anyone carries hypericon or St John's wort, the Devil cannot approach within the space of nine paces. **1603** STOWE *Survey of London* (1908, I 101) On the Vigil of St Iohn Baptist, and on Saint Peter and Paule the Apostles, euery mans doore [was] shadowed with greene Birch, long Fennel, Saint Iohns wort, Orpin, white Lillies, and such like, garnished vpon with Garlands of beautiful flowers. **1660** BURTON *Anatomy of Melancholy* pt. 2 sect. 5 mem. 1 sub. 5. S. Johns wort, gathered on a friday .. and .. hung about the neck, it mightily helps [melancholy] and drives away all phantastical spirits. **1696** AUBREY *Miscellanies* (1890, 139–40) A house (or chamber) somewhere in London, was haunted; the curtains would be rashed at night, and awake the gentleman that lay there, who was .. a familiar acquaintance of Henry Lawes. Henry Lawes to be satisfied did lie with him; and the curtains were rashed so then. The gentleman grew lean and pale with the frights; one Dr —— cured the house of this disturbance, and Mr Lawes said, that the principal ingredient was *Hypericon* put under his pillow. **1703** M. MARTIN *Western Isles of Scotland* 334. John Morison who lives in Bernera of Harries, wears the Plant call'd *Fuga Demonum* sew'd in the neck of his Coat, to prevent his seeing of Visions, and says he never saw any since he first carried that Plant about him. **1777** J. LIGHTFOOT *Flora Scotica* 417. The superstitious in Scotland carry this plant about them as a charm against the dire effects of witchcraft and enchantment. They also cure, or fancy they cure their ropy milk, which they suppose to be under some malignant influence, by putting this herb into it, and milking afresh upon it. **1800** W. BINGLEY *Tour round North Wales* II 237. On the eve of St John the baptist, they fix sprigs of the plant .. over their doors .. in order to purify their houses, and by that means drive away all fiends, and evil spirits. **1802** J. LEYDEN Editorial note in Scott's *Minstrelsy* II 371. The author recollects a popular rhyme, supposed to be addressed to a young woman by the devil, who attempted to seduce her in the shape of a handsome young man: 'Gin ye wish to be leman [lover] mine, Lay off the St John's wort, and the vervine.' **1815** SCOTT *Guy Mannering* III. Trefoil, vervain, John's wort, dill, Hinders witches of their will.

Cf. MAY BOUGHS AND FLOWERS protect; VERVAIN, powers of.

ST SWITHIN = rain

c.**1125** WILLIAM OF MALMESBURY *Gestis Pontif. Angl.* (ed. Hamilton, 162) [Bishop Swithin, renowned for his humility] ordered his household that they should inter his corpse outside the cathedral, where the feet of passers by and rain dripping from the eaves would beat upon it. early **14th c.** MS Emmanuel Coll. Camb. 27 f. 163. In the daye of seynte Svithone rane ginneth rinigge Forti dawes mid ywone. [On St Swithin's day it begins raining and usually continues 40 days.] *c*.**1336** ROBERT DE GRAYSTANE (Surtees Soc. IX 96) In 1315 .. on the day after the anniversary of the moving of St Swithin's body [into the church] namely the 15th of July, such was the deluge of rain, that rivers overflowed their banks to an awesome degree, submerging crops .. and rushing through houses, drowning men, women and children. No survivor could recall such a flood, nor such a famine that followed .. A quartern of grain was selling at 40 shillings. **1600** JONSON *Every Man out of his Humour* I III [Sordido, looking at an almanack] O heare, S. Swithens, the xv day .. for the most part raine; Why, it should raine fortie daies after .. it was a rule helde afore I was able to holde a plough, and yet here are two daies no raine. **1697** *Poor Robin's Almanack* July. In t'is Month is S. Swithen's day, On which, if that it Rain, they say Full forty Days after it will, Or more or less, some Rain distill. **1716** GAY *Trivia* 12–13. If on Swithin's Feast the Welkin lours, And ev'ry Penthouse streams with hasty Show'rs, Twice twenty Days shall Clouds their Fleeces drain, And wash the Pavements with incessant rain. **1812** J. BRADY *Clavis Calendaria* II 97–8. Swithin, at his own .. solicitation, was buried in the common .. church-yard of Winchester, instead of the chancel of the Minster, as .. other bishops .. His grave was soon marked as peculiarly efficacious to the suffering Christians, and miracles out of number were recorded .. An order was obtained to remove the holy reliques into the choir, as better suiting their merits .. A most violent rain shower, however, fell on the destined day, and continued for 39 .. in consequence .. the idea of a removal was abandoned, as displeasing to St Swithin .. The vulgar adage, that we shall have forty days .. of wet weather whenever rain falls on St Swithin's Festival, no doubt, arose from this presumed supernatural circumstance. **1813** *Gents Mag.* pt. 2 35–6. One of the most popular notions .. relied upon by the superstitious is, 'that when it rains on St Swithin's Holiday, we shall have .. wet weather for 40 days'; and this conceit has received considerable encouragement this year .. there having .. been constant .. heavy showers, commencing from the festival of that 'Watery Saint'. **1813** BRAND *Antiquities* I 272 n. In Mr Douce's interleaved copy of the Popular Antiquities is the following note: 'I have heard these lines upon St Swithin's Day: "St Swithin's Day, if thou dost rain, For forty days it will remain: St Swithin's Day, if thou be fair, For forty days 'twill rain na mair".' **1832** A. HENDERSON *Scottish Proverbs* 157. If St Swithin greets [weeps], the proverb says, The weather will be foul for forty days. **1882** *People's Friend* 8 Nov. 711. People not ordinarily superstitious are still to be found who cling to the old belief 'If on St Swithin's it does rain, For forty days it will remain.' **1892** C. M. YONGE *Old Woman's Outlook* 169. If Swithin's day be fair and clear, It betides a happy year; If Swithin's day be dark with rain, Then will be dear all sorts of grain. **1986** Man, c.50 [Richmond, Yorks.] If it rains on St Swithin's Day it will rain for forty days and forty nights—I've known that since childhood.

Cf. EXHUMATION.

'SALMON' taboo word

1881 W. GREGOR *North-East of Scotland* 146. If there was occasion to speak of a salmon, a circumlocution was used, and it was often named after the tax-man of the fishings nearest the villages .. Sometimes it was called 'The beast'. **1898** A. C. HADDON *Study of Man* 419–20. A fisherman told me that in Aberdeen the salmon is called 'the red fish' .. it bringing bad luck for [it] to be called by [its] proper designation. **1930** P. F. ANSON *East Coast of Scotland* 40. I was on a Buckie drifter on Loch Ness when one of the crew .. asked me if I did much fishing there. Without thinking, I replied: 'Oh yes, plenty of .. ' But before I had time to utter the fatal word 'salmon', he had pushed his hand in front of my mouth, remarking nervously: 'Na. Ye dinna say yon word! I

ken vat fish ye mean.' **1964** *Folklore* 39. On the East coast [of Scotland] the salmon is the red fish, the liberty fish, the foul fish, or simply the fish. **1969** [Aberdeen] Fishermen's superstitions are still very much observed here .. You must never mention salmon by name.

SALMON unlucky first catch

1898 *Weekly Scotsman Christmas Number* 7 [Buckie, Banff.] The first draw of the pump brought up a fine young salmon which [was] considered so unlucky .. the crew determined not to shoot their nets that night and they accordingly put round their boat.

Cf. FISHING: first catch.

SALT as propitiation/for luck and prosperity

c.800 BC HOMER *Iliad* IX (tr. Rieu, 166–7) Patroclus .. scattered the embers and laid the spits above them .. after he had sprinkled the meat with holy salt .. to sacrifice to the gods. *c*.585 BC Leviticus 2: 13. With all thine offerings thou shalt offer salt. AD 77 PLINY *Natural History* XVIII 11 (1856, IV 4) Numa first established the custom of offering corn to the gods, and of propitiating them with the salted cake. **1586** CAMDEN *Britannia* (tr. Gibson, II 380) [Limerick, Eire] Before they sow their field, the wife sends salt to it. **1787** *Historical Guide to Scarborough* 62. A most whimsical superstitious rite is often secretly performed .. with a view to appease the angry waves and obtain a propitious breeze favourable to the voyager's safe return. His fair spouse, (or other anxious *female* friend,) proceeds, unaccompanied, about 40 paces along the pier. Here a small circular cavity among the stones .. receives a saline .. libation, which is poured into it, while the sacrificer, muttering her tenderest wishes, looks towards that quarter from whence the object of her anxiety, is expected to arrive. **1886** *Folklore* 16 [Portessie, Banff.] Another custom to secure a fishing, if it is poor .. is to throw a handful of salt after the skipper, or any of the crew, as he is leaving the house, or to throw salt over the boat. **1937** *N & Q* CLXXIII 459. 'I don't like to be short of salt,' a woman said to me recently. 'They

say "Short of salt, short of money".'
1967 M. WOODRUFF *Woody* 109. Mother
always kept a lot of salt in the house.
'Where there is salt in a house,' she
would say, 'money will come.' I always
keep a stack of salt in my London house
and at my cottage in the country. Some
of my friends never arrive .. without
bringing me a gift of salt; to others I
frequently give a packet as they leave.
Peter Sellers always asks for his.

Also see HOUSE, moving.

SALT as protection against witch or evil spirits/for luck

1486 SPRENGER & KRAMER *Malleus Maleficarum* (tr. Summers, 228) The Judge
and all his assessors [at a witch trial]
must not allow themselves to be touched
.. by the witch .. but they must always
carry about them some salt consecrated
on Palm Sunday .. enclosed together in
Blessed Wax and worn round the neck
.. The Church exorcizes and blesses such
objects .. for the banishing of all power
of the devil. **1584** SCOT *Discoverie of
Witchcraft* XII xx. Such as observe dulie
the rites .. of holie church .. through
receiving consecrated salt .. are preserved from witchcraft. Ibid. XV xxvii.
A conjuration written in the masse booke.
I conjure thee O creature of salt .. by
the God that liveth .. that thou be to all
that take thee, health both of bodie
and soule; and let all phantasies and
wickednesse, or diabolical craft or de-
ceipt, depart from the place whereon it
is sprinkled. **1586** CAMDEN *Britannia* (tr.
Gibson, II 380) [Limerick, Eire] In towns,
when any magistrate enters upon his
office, the wives in the streets, and the
maidens out of the windows, strew him
and his retinue with wheat and salt.
1688 AUBREY *Remaines* (1881, 121)
That Salt is inimique to the Evill spirits
is agreed upon by the writers of Magick
.. Holy water is water wherein fine
white Salt hath been dissolved. **1744** G.
W. WALDRON *Isle of Man* 143. No Person
will go out on any material Affair without taking some [salt] in their Pockets,
much less remove from one House to
another [or marry]. Nay, tho' a poor
Creature be almost famished in the
Streets, he will not accept any Food ..
unless you join Salt to the rest of your

Benevolence. **1846** *Athenaeum* 988 [W.
Scotland] An *old* sixpence is borrowed
from some neighbour, without telling
the object to which it is to be applied:
as much salt as can be lifted upon the
sixpence is put into a tablespoonful of
water and melted; the sixpence is then
put into the solution, and the soles of
the feet and palms of the hands of the
patient are moistened three times with
the salt water; it is then tasted three
times, and the patient afterwards 'scored
aboon the breath', that is, by the operator dipping the forefinger into the salt
water, and drawing it along the brow.
When this is done, the contents of the
spoon are thrown behind and right over
the fire, the thrower saying at the same
time, 'Lord preserve us frae a' scathe!'
If recovery follow this, there is no doubt
of the individual having been under the
influence of an evil eye. **1849** *Norfolk
Archaeology* II 299 [Irstead] A complaint
was made to her that the linen which
she sent home, after washing it, was
damp .. She maintained, she was sure
it was wholesome; for she put plenty of
salt in, to keep the thunder out. There
is reason to believe from some hints
which she let fall as to 'bad things being
about', that the salt was employed by
her to avert foul spirits, as well as to
counteract the ill effects of the atmo-
sphere. **1850** *N & Q* 1st ser. II 150. This
custom I have frequently observed, of
taking a pinch of salt without any
remark, and flinging it over the shoulder.
I should be glad to know its origin. **1879**
J. NAPIER *West of Scotland* 36–7. I have
.. a vivid remembrance of being myself
believed to be the .. victim of an evil
eye .. To remove this .. the soles of my
feet and the palms of my hands were
bathed with this solution [salt and
water] thrice, and .. I was made to taste
the solution three times. The .. contents
of the spoon she then cast .. into the
hinder part of the fire, saying .. 'Guid
preserve frae a' skaith [harm].' **1909**
N & Q 10th ser. XII 484. [Stromness,
Orkney] To keep a visitor away for a
long time, spill salt on the doorstep as
he leaves. **1954** Girl, 12 [Dungworth,
Yorks.] Throw salt over your left shoulder for luck. **1986** Woman, 45. In South
Wales, where I grew up, if you weren't

too sure about somebody who came to your house, you threw some salt after them as they left—at their backs, see? Cf. WATER, holy.

SALT, being helped to

1830 M. R. MITFORD *Our Village* IV 299. Who shrinks from being helped to salt as if one were offering him arsenic? **1849** *Norfolk Archaeology* II 296 [Irstead] The offer to help to salt would be rejected: 'Help me to salt, Help me to sorrow.' **1855** *N & Q* 1st ser. XII 200. I offered to help an old Highland lady .. to some salt .. she gravely put back my hand, and drew away her plate, saying at the same time, with a kind of shudder, between her teeth: 'Help me to saut! Help me to sorrow!' **1881** *Punch* 1 Jan. 310. If you help your neighbour to salt, you and she are certain to quarrel if, at the time of your uncalled-for politeness, she is eating ham, bacon, meringues, or ice-puddings. **1943** F. THOMPSON *Candleford Green* 119. No one would at table spoon salt on to another person's plate, for 'Help you to salt, help you to sorrow.' **1983** Scotsman, 78. It's unlucky to give anyone the salt. I have a friend in Perth who still believes that. **1984** Woman, 37 [Harrow, Middx.] Pass the salt, pass the sorrow.

SALT, borrowing or lending

1866 HENDERSON *Northern Counties* 179. He added a warning on giving salt out of the house, a most dangerous thing. **1883** BURNE *Shropshire* 278. If you borrow salt it is unlucky to pay it back. **1898** *Weekly Scotsman Christmas Number* 6 [Fife fishermen] They will on no account part with salt, especially at sea, as to part with salt is to part with luck. **1910** *N & Q* 11th ser. II 150. On Bank Holiday .. the shops being closed, I proposed to borrow some from a neighbour. One of my servants, a girl from Stockton Heath, close to Warrington [Lancs.], expressed a hope that this would not be done, saying, 'If you ask for salt, you ask for sorrow.' **1922** *N & Q* 12th ser. XI 217. It is extremely unlucky to return borrowed salt; a disruption of friendship will ensue .. During the war, when salt was valued by British housewives .. there was no idea of

returning even a packet of table salt. **1953** Boy, 15 [Nottingham] To borrow salt is to borrow trouble: always pay for it with a copper coin. **1972** *Lore and Language* July 7 [Coalisland, Co. Tyrone] Don't borrow or lend salt at any time but particularly not on New Year's Day. You'll give your luck away with it. Anyone who borrows salt from you on New Year's Day is deliberately wishing bad luck on your house.

SALT, burning, in spell or to counteract witchcraft

1832 *Gents Mag.* pt. 2 494 [Lincs.] To neutralize the evil influence of witchcraft .. when good housewives put their cream into the churn, they sometimes cast a handful of salt into the fire. **1838** W. HOWITT *Rural Life of England* II 220. He [a shoemaker in Nottingham] had standing regularly by his fire-side a sack-bag of salt .. and of this he frequently took a handful, with a few horsenail stumps, and crooked pins, and casting them into the fire together, prayed to the Lord to torment all witches and wizards in the neighbourhood. **1850** *N & Q* 1st ser. II 259. It is not salt I mean to burn, But my true lover's heart I mean to turn; Wishing him neither joy nor sleep, Till he come back to me and speak. **1872** W. CHAMBERS *Memoir* 23 [Peebles, c.1810] I remember seeing salt thrown on the fire .. when aged women, suspected of not being quite *canny*, happened to call at a neighbour's dwelling. **1873** HARLAND & WILKINSON *Lancashire Legends* 235. The power of a witch is supposed to be destroyed by sprinkling salt into the fire nine mornings in succession. The person who sprinkles the salt .. must repeat 'Salt! salt! I put thee into the fire, and may the person who has bewitched me neither eat, drink, nor sleep, until the spell is broken.' **1879** HENDERSON *Northern Counties* 176. The 'salt spell' of the southern counties .. A pinch of salt must be thrown into the fire on three successive Friday nights while these lines are repeated: 'It is not this salt I wish to burn, It is my lover's heart to turn, That he may neither rest nor happy be Until he comes and speaks to me.' **1923** [Nynehead, Som.] If somebody comes into the house you don't care about, you must sprinkle salt where they have been, sweep it up and burn it, and they'll never come again. **1955** [Scarborough, Yorks.] The old idea of burning letters to Santa Claus on the fire along with a pinch of salt may save the Post Office work, but it is by no means as satisfying for the child as posting the letter to Santa Claus at his Danish address.

Cf. SALT as protection against witch or evil spirits/for luck; TEETH, disposing of.

SALT protects at death

1648 HERRICK *Hesperides* 5 'To Perilla'. Dead when I am, first cast in salt .. Then shall my Ghost not walk about, but keep Still in the coole, and silent shades of sleep. **1771** PENNANT *Tour in Scotland* 92. Friends lay on the breast of the deceased a wooden platter, containing a small quantity of salt and earth .. the earth, an emblem of the corruptible body; the salt, an emblem of the immortal spirit. **1785** *Gents Mag.* pt. 2 603. It was a custom in Leicester and its shire, yet continued, to place a dish .. of salt on a corpse, to prevent its swelling and purging. **1824** MAC-TAGGART *Gallovidian Encyclopedia* 210. *A cup o' saut* is yet put on a corpse, from the time it is *straughted* until it be coffined. *c.*1828 Calvert MS, Pickering, Yorks. (G. HOME *Evolution of an English Town* 215) Many there be who yet do grace their dead with a salt platter putten upon the breast of the corpse, and all those friends who do view the dead .. do first touch the corpse .. and then lay their own hands upon the platter first having full and free forgiven the dead any fault or ill-feeling they had in life held as a grudge again the dead. **1830** FORBY *East Anglia* 426. The practice of setting a plate of salt on the breast of a corpse prevails generally in East Anglia .. but tradition furnishes no account of the origin of the custom. **1851** *N & Q* 1st ser. IV 163. The custom of placing a plate of salt on .. the dead is very general in Wales. I remember, when a child, inquiring the reason .. and being told by an old woman that it was to prevent the body from swelling.

My remark, that *any* weight might answer the same purpose, was met by the reply; 'there's no weight so heavy as salt gets when it is on the dead.' This proves that some feeling of superstition mingles with the custom. **1854** *N & Q* 1st ser. X 395. The custom .. is .. of general practice .. in Ireland .. The superstitious .. regard it as the means of frightening away evil spirits. **1882** *N & Q* 6th ser. VI 335. I saw it done in this village [Selmeston, Sussex] a day or two ago, and was told it was to prevent the corpse swelling. **1920** *Folklore* 154 [Cumberland coroner] Almost universal amongst the poorer classes in the country, is the placing .. of a saucer of salt on a dead man's breast .. An undertaker told me it was done for hygienic reasons, but I doubt this. **1956** G. E. EVANS *Ask the Fellows* [Blaxhall, Suffolk] XXIV. The placing of a dish of salt either on the corpse or underneath the coffin .. makes sure you have a good corpse; it makes sure that it doesn't start rising. **1974** A. MACVICAR *Heather in my Ears* 44 [Southend, Kintyre] [My father] was called to the death-bed of an old man, whose daughter of nearly seventy was .. there. The old man .. trying to speak .. 'The earth, Phemie. The Earth' .. The daughter took the saucer of earth and salt and laid it on her father's breast. And as the padre prayed .. the shallow breathing stopped.

SALT protects baby/child

*c.*580 BC Ezekiel 16: 4–5. In the day thou wast born .. thou wast not salted at all .. None eye pitied thee .. to have compassion upon thee; but thou wast cast out in the open field. **1551** J. HAMILTON *Catechisme* 131 [At baptism] the minister puttis Salt in ye barnis mouth, quhilk .. suld keip him fra the corruption and stink of dedlie syn. **1744** G. W. WALDRON *Isle of Man* 143. No Person will .. put out a Child, or take one to nurse, without Salt being mutually interchanged. **1768** A. ROSS *Fortunate Shepherdess* 6. Gryt was the care an' tut'ry that was ha'en, Baith night an' day about the bony wean .. Jane's paps wi' sa't and water washen clean, For fear her milk gat wrang fan it was green. **1857** *N & Q* 2nd ser. III 59 [Ayr.] It was not an unusual sight, some sixty or seventy years ago .. to see a quantity of common table salt carried withershins round the baby before the baptismal company left the parental dwelling. This done, no harm .. would befall the little stranger in its unchristened state. **1879** J. NAPIER *West of Scotland* 30. Immediately after birth, the newly-born child was bathed in salted water, and made to taste of it three times. **1887** 'SPERANZA' WILDE *Superstitions of Ireland* II 103. Unbaptised children are readily seized by the fairies. The best preventive is a little salt tied up in the child's dress when it is laid to sleep in the cradle. **1950** *Sunday Times* 19 Feb. 5. In Wales .. when a child leaves its mother's house for the first time .. salt [is put] in its pockets.

Cf. BABY, gifts to.

SALT protects cow and calf

1795 *Stat. Acc. of Scotland* XVI 121–2 [Killearn, Stirling] Superstition yet continues to operate so strongly on some people, that they put a small quantity of salt into the first milk of a cow, after calving, that is given any person to drink. This is done with a view to prevent *skaith* (harm), if it should happen that the person is not *cany* [is a witch]. **1895** J. HARDY *Denham Tracts* 365 [Northumb.] Only five years ago I had a cow that took milk-fever after calving. An elderly woman immediately asked if we had been careful to rub a pinch of salt along her back at the moment she calved.

SALT, spilling, and countercharm

1584 SCOT *Discoverie of Witchcraft* XI xv. Amongst us there be manie women, and effeminat men .. that make great divinations upon the shedding of salt. **1587** GIFFORD *Subtill Practises of Devilles* C2. Frends meet together & make mery: some one at unwares doth turn down the salt: the man or the woman towards who it falleth, doth blush and take little comfort of the dainty banquet. For that is taken to be a grieuous euil sign of mishap that will follow. **1594** NASHE *Terrors of the Night* D. If the salt fall right against him, all the starres cannot saue him from .. misfortune. **1652** GAULE *Mag-astro-mances* 320. He knew a young

Gentleman, who by chance spilling the salt of the Table, some that sate with him said merrily to him, that it was an ill omen, and wisht him take heed to himselfe that day; of which the young man was so superstitiously credulous that it would not goe out of his mind; and going abroad that day, got a wound of which he died not long after. **1668** W. RAMESEY *Elminthologia* 271. If the salt fall but towards them .. then they expect Anger. **1711** *Spectator* 8 Mar. She desired me to reach her a little salt upon the point of my knife, which I did in such trepidation .. that I let it drop by the way; at which she immediately started, and said it fell towards her .. and she said to her husband, with a sigh, 'My dear .. Do you not remember .. that the pigeon-house fell the very afternoon that our careless wench spilt the salt upon the table?' **1738** SWIFT *Polite Conversation* II 148–9. LADY SMART. Mr Neverout, you have overturn'd the Salt, and that's a Sign of Anger: I'm afraid, Miss and You will fall out. LADY ANSWERALL. No, no; throw a little of it into the Fire, and all will be well. **1771** PENNANT *Journey from Chester to London* 31. The dread of spilling salt is a known superstition among us .. being reckoned a presage of some future calamity, and particularly that it foreboded domestic feuds; to avert which it is customary to fling some salt over the shoulder into the fire. **1777** BRAND *Antiquities* 95. The Observation on the falling of Salt, proceeds from the antient Opinion that Salt was incorruptible; it had therefore been made the Symbol of Friendship; and if it fell casually, they thought their Friendship would not be of long Duration. **1787** GROSE *Provincial Glossary* Superstitions 65–6. To scatter salt, by overturning the vessel in which it is contained, is very unlucky, and portends quarrelling with a friend, or fracture of a bone [etc.]. This may in some measure be averted, by throwing a small quantity of it over one's head. **1823** MOOR *Suffolk Words* 384. This ominous accident is still felt in its full force among us; but the threatened result may be in part averted by throwing a little of the spilled article over your left shoulder .. Salt .. has been long

held in .. some superstitious regard ..
The earliest allusion to it that I can call
to mind is in the Last Supper by Leonardo
da Vinci, where Judas is heedlessly upsetting the salt-cellar. **1832** S. LOVER
Legends of Ireland 121. I spilt the salt ..
and was certain something unlucky was
going to happen. **1849** *Norfolk Archaeology* II 296 [Irstead] Every grain
spilt represents a tear you will shed.
1881 *Punch* 1 Jan. 310. The Folk-Lore
with regard to salt is conflicting. If you
have spilt salt on the table, and have
then thrown a handful over your left
shoulder, the servant who receives this
in his eyes seldom considers that ill-luck
has been averted. **1914** *Folklore* 365
[Newmarket, Cambs.] When salt is spilt,
nothing must be said until it has been
thrown over the shoulder. **1923** [Mar-
tock, Som.] Throw over left shoulder
saying: 'With this cast, May ill-luck
pass.' **1951** M. M. HUTCHINGS *Walnut
Tree* 128 [Wales] One must never spill
the salt without taking the precaution
to blind the Devil by throwing a pinch
at him over the left shoulder. **1987**
Woman, 58. You know if you spill salt
you have to throw some over your left
shoulder with the right hand, and make
a cross in what's left. That's from my
father, in a parsonic household in
Nottingham.

Cf. SALT as protection against witch
or evil spirits/for luck.

'SALT' taboo word

1930 P. F. ANSON *East Coast of Scotland*
38. In many districts the word salt could
never be mentioned when at sea. A story
is told that an Eyemouth boat ran short
of salt in the autumn of 1905 when
fishing. Hailing a Yarmouth drifter, the
skipper called out: 'We need something
that we dinna want tae speak aboot.'
Whereupon the English skipper shouted
back: 'Is it salt ye want?' The salt
was handed over, but the Englishmen
remarked that all the .. Scottish crew
disappeared below rather than hear the
terrible word.

SALT CELLAR, breaking

1861 C. C. ROBINSON *Dialect of Leeds*
296. To break a salt-cellar, or pot, is
accounted, too, a certain omen of im-

pending misfortune even by those who
do not credit other common superstitions. **1909** *N & Q* 10th ser. XII 66
[nr. Exeter, Devon] It is unlucky to break
a salt cellar. **1923** [Taunton, Som.] If
you break a salt cellar it is a sign of
death.

Cf. SALT, spilling: and countercharm.

SALT CELLARS, two

1923 [West Malling, Kent] It is unlucky
to leave two salt cellars in front of one
person.

SALT HERRING: divination

1861 C. C. ROBINSON *Dialect of Leeds* 302.
Take as many herrings as there are
persons (servants generally perform
these feats in company), throw them
into the fire and roast them very dry,
then eat them, skin, bones, and all, go
backwards-way to bed, each and all,
and the man who is to be the sweetheart
of anyone, will bring the one water in
her dreams. **1866** HENDERSON *Northern
Counties* 70. A raw red herring, swallowed bones and all .. is very pro-
vocative of dreams .. Swains sometimes
adopt this plan to get a glimpse of their
future wives. **1898** *Weekly Scotsman
Christmas Number* 6 [Fogo, Berwick.]
Take a salt-herring out of the brine,
roast it and eat it without the accompaniment of bread or water, speak
nothing, drink nothing before going to
bed, and some one is sure to appear in
a dream-vision offering the much-
longed-for drink. That one .. is the
future help-mate. **1901** J. RHYS *Celtic
Folklore* I 320. The Manx girl has only
to eat a salt herring .. without drinking
or uttering a word, and to retire backwards to bed. When she .. dreams, she
will behold her future husband approaching to give her a drink.

SALT IN EGG: divination

1688 AUBREY *Remaines* (1881, 62) A
magiall Receipt to know whom one shall
marry. Egges roasted hard, and the yelke
taken out and salt putt in its sted, sc.
filled up: to be eaten fasting without
supper, when you goe to bed. I thinke
only one egge. **1755** *Connoisseur* 20
Feb. [St Valentine's Eve] I boiled an egg
hard, and took out the yolk, and filled

it up with salt; and when I went to bed, eat shell and all, without speaking or drinking after it. **1827** HONE *Every-Day Book* 19 Nov. [St Agnes's Eve] After fasting the whole of the day, upon going to bed an egg must be filled with salt, and eaten, which occasions a great thirst. The vessel the female dreams of drinking from, according to situation and circumstances, denotes who will be her husband. **1869** *N & Q* 4th ser. IV 505 [Dublin serving-woman] On Hallowe'en .. women take the yolk from eggs boiled hard, fill the eggs with salt, and eat egg, shell, and salt. They are careful not to quench their thirst till morning. If .. they dream that their lovers are at hand with water, they believe they will be jilted. **1912** LEATHER *Herefordshire* 62. Mrs A——, being anxious, when a young girl, to discover her future husband, once took the first egg laid by a pullet and boiled it hard. She cut it in halves, and put one half beneath her pillow. As she did so she said: 'I put this under my head, To dream of the living and not of the dead, To dream of the young man that I am to wed, Not in his apparel nor in his array, but in the clothes he will wear every day.' Then she had to eat the other half of her egg, but before doing so, took out the yolk and filled the cavity with salt. She got into bed without speaking a word [and] dreamed of a young man wearing a white 'apurn'.

SATURDAY, beginning on: unlucky

1551 J. HAMILTON *Catechisme* pt. 1 22^v [Scotland] Certane craftis men .. will nocht begin thair Warke on the Saterday, certane .. marinars will nocht begin to sail on the Satterday, certane trauelars will nocht begin thair iornay on ye Satterday, quhilk is plane superstition. **1851** STERNBERG *Northamptonshire* 169. Saturday and Sunday are unlucky days for servants to go to their places: thus the saying—'Saturday servants never stay, Sunday servants run away.' **1854** BAKER *Northants Glossary. Flit.* 'Saturday's flit will never sit' is a proverb of prediction with superstitious servants, who reluctantly enter upon a new service on that day. **1899** J. SHAW *Schoolmaster* 30 [Tynron, Dumfries.] It is

not well to change situations on a Saturday. 'Saturday's enter is a short residenter.' **1901** *N & Q* 9th ser. VII 337–8. I recollect, when I was a boy in Norfolk, thirty-five years ago, hearing old labourers say that it was bad luck to put in a crop on a Saturday. **1909** M. TREVELYAN *Folk-Lore of Wales* 242. A Welshman of the past would not begin a new undertaking on a Saturday if he could possibly avoid it. **1923** [Wellington, Som.] If you start work on a Saturday you will either marry or run away. **1930** P. F. ANSON *East Coast of Scotland* 40–2. Work begun on a Saturday was sure to 'see seven Saturdays before completion.' **1943** *Woman*, 20 [Thurso, Caithness] I'd move house any day but a Saturday, because 'Saturday flittin's short sittin'.'

SATURDAY, working on: unlucky

AD **958** (BRAND *Antiquities* 1813, I 458) King Edgar .. made an Ecclesiastical Law that the Sabbath or Sunday should be observed on Saturday at noon, till the light should appear on Monday morning. **1586** CAMDEN *Britannia* (tr. Gibson, II 380) [Limerick, Eire *c.*1566] It is thought unlawful to clean their horses feet, or curry them, or gather grass for them, on a Saturday; though all this may be done upon their highest festivals. **1725** BOURNE *Antiquitates Vulgares* 116 [Northumb.] We find a great Deference paid to Saturday Afternoon, above the other worky Days of the Week: Then the Labours of the Plough ceast, and Refreshment and Ease are over all the Village. *c.*1850 J. HUNTER MS note in Brand's *Antiquities* I 458. Saturday Afternoon. Always a holiday at school. In serious families, in which evening amusements were not encouraged on Saturdays, which marks the cessation from labour as having a religious allusion. **1887** O. J. BURKE *South Isles of Aran* 101 [Co. Galway] The spinning-wheel in Aran, the old crones say, should never spin on a Saturday. **1909** M. TREVELYAN *Folk-Lore of Wales* 201. She that makes butter on a Monday or Saturday is a 'witch for sure and certain'. Ibid. 242. It was unlucky to do any laundry-work on Saturday, or to do any kind of labour after sunset on that day. **1909** *N & Q*

10th ser. XII 484 [Stromness, Orkney] It is unlucky to wash on Saturday.

Cf. SUNDAY: keeping Sabbath holy.

SCISSORS as present

1654 DOROTHY OSBORNE Letter 13–15 Jan. Did not you say once you knew where good french tweeses were to bee had? Send mee a payer, they shall Cutt noe Love. **1707** Feb. Letter from Elizabeth Wentworth (*Wentworth Papers*, ed. Cartwright, 76) Dearest Brother, I give you a grate many thanks for the siszers you sent me by Mr Shokman. I gave him sixpencs for fear tha should cute love one your side: but for mine 'tis to well gronded to fear ather siszers ar knifs cuting of it. **1861** C. C. ROBINSON *Dialect of Leeds* 299. It is unlucky to give a pair of scissors to a friend, as the friendship will be cut thereby. **1861** *Welcome Guest* 5 Oct. 48. 'Notices to Correspondents'. Jessie is sad at heart for a cause which, we trust, she will speedily be able to remove. Her lover has left her in a 'tiff' for this simple reason. He presented her with a pair of silver-handled scissors, which she declined, considering it unlucky to accept cutlery, lest it should 'sever their love'. Her lover was incensed at the rejection of his gift, and we are afraid called Jessie 'a little fool'. Since then she has not seen him. **1866** EWING *Mrs Overtheway's Remembrances* (1894–6, 35) I had found half a rusty pair of scissors in the summer-house. Perhaps some fair lady of former days had lost them here . . Perhaps they were a present, and she had given a luck-penny for them, lest they should cut love. **1952** Girl, 14 [Aberdeen] Never give a pair of scissors as a present as it will cut the knot of friendship. **1979** WOMEN'S INSTITUTE *Home & Country* May 235. After cutting the ribbon to open the new Home Economics Centre, Her Majesty handed back the scissors with a traditional small gift to show no malice is meant by passing a sharp object. The parcel contained a 1966 sixpenny piece. **1983** *Woman*, 24 [Kent] If you give something sharp, like scissors, you must receive payment, otherwise the friendship will be cut.

Cf. KNIFE as present.

SCISSORS fall

1882 *Folk-Lore Record* 83 [Co. Wexford] If a person lets a pair of scissors fall and they stick in the ground it is a sign that he or she will be leaving the house, and any wish expressed while it is in the ground will be fulfilled. **1883** BURNE *Shropshire* 280. An Oswestry dressmaker says that if a pair of scissors falls so that the points stick into the floor, it is a sign of more work coming in. **1909** *Folklore* 344 [Worcs.] If you drop a pair of scissors and they stand up on their double point, you will hear of a wedding, but, if only on one point, it is a sign of a death. **1912** LEATHER *Herefordshire* 87. If a pair of scissors be dropped on the floor they should be closed before picking them up. **1923** [Bridgwater, Som.] Drop your scissors on Sunday and it betokens a strange visitor. If on any other day of the week—more work is coming to you. **1932** C. IGGLESDEN *Those Superstitions* 209. Never pick up a pair of scissors [yourself]. If you are alone and must needs pick them up, warm the scissors with your hands before using them. **1967** M. WOODRUFF *Woody* 108. If she [his mother] dropped a pair of scissors she would always wait for someone else to pick them up. If there was no one in the house, she would tread on the scissors before bending down to retrieve them from the floor.

Cf. KNIFE falls.

SEAGULL AND STORMY PETREL

1878 A. MACGREGOR *Brahan Seer* 31 'Superstitions of Highlanders'. Sailors . . greatly dread the stormy petrel, or Mother Carey's chickens, as they flutter at night around their masts and yards. These birds are regarded as objects of superstitious fear, believing that they are possessed of supernatural agency in creating danger for the . . mariner. **1885** *Folklore* 306. In Macduff and Pennan [Aberdeen.] it is believed that the seagulls cry before any disaster. **1886** *Folklore* 14 [Portessie, Banff.] It is unlucky to catch a sea-gull when out fishing, and keep it on board. My informant told me that one day he caught a gull . . One of the old men in the boat . . ordered him to set it adrift, which was done at once. **1969** C. WOODFORD *Sussex*

Ways 60. Old Captain Mockett had a real fear of seagulls and declared them to be souls of the dead, and if three flew overhead, he proclaimed a warning of death. **1969** R. GODDEN *House of Brede* 275. The seagulls . . wheeling round the tower with their cries. She remembered how sailors say they are the souls of Liverpool seamen—Liverpool men, because, legend says, they are the worst and so their souls are lost. **1987** Man, *c*.60 [London] Seagulls? They're supposed to be the souls of departed sailors, and you should never shoot them. Or is that albatrosses?

Cf. ALBATROSS.

SEAWEED in house

1948 E. & M. A. RADFORD *Superstitions* 215 [Devon fishing villages] Dried seaweed (known as Lady's Trees) if kept . . on the mantelpiece, will prevent the house catching fire. **1961** *Reveille* 24 Aug. 16 [Swindon, Wilts.] An elderly woman always brings a piece of seaweed for me after her day at the seaside. She says you will never be without a friend as long as you have a bit of seaweed about the place.

SELLING cures various ills

11th c. *Lacnunga* (GRATTAN & SINGER *Anglo-Saxon Magic* 191) The woman who cannot nourish her child [in the womb]: Let her herself take a piece of her own child's grave, then wrap it up in black wool and sell it to traders, and then say: 'I sell it; buy ye it, This black wool, and seeds of this sorrow.' **1895** S. O. ADDY *Household Tales* 91. People sometimes sell their coughs and colds for a small sum of money. **1953** *Folklore* 202 [Castlethorpe, Lincs.] Superfluous flesh can be got rid of by 'selling', like warts. You sell 3 lbs. or 7 lbs. or as much as you will. **1988** Woman, 68 [E. London] When I was thirteen I was very ill and they thought I was going to die, so my mother sold me to a neighbour for a penny and after a year she bought me back again. That was to confuse the evil spirits so that they wouldn't get me.

Cf. WARTS 'sold'.

SEVENTH CHILD, powers of

c.1250 *Physicians of Myddvai* (tr. Pughe,

456) Wash the warts with the water from a font in which the seventh son of the same man and wife is baptized. **1579** LUPTON *Thousand Notable Things* II § 2. It is manifest by experience that the seuenth Male Chyld by iust order (neuer a Gyrle or Wench being borne betweene) doth heele onely with touching through a naturall gyft, the Kings Euyll. **1663** *Depositions, York Castle* 17 Oct. (1861, 101) [in trial 'for seditious words'] What is the Kinge better than another man? for Robin Bulman . . a seaventh sonne, can cure seaven evills, and the Kinge can but cure nine. **1691** R. KIRK *Secret Commonwealth* (1815, 16) [Scottish–Irish] It may seem alike strange . . in such as Seventh-sons . . that cure the King's Evill, and chase away Diseases and Pains, with only stroaking of the affected Part. **1708** *British Apollo* Supernumerary no. 5, for Aug. *Q.* Gentlemen, it being a General Notion in this Nation, that the Seventh Son, is blest with an Uncommon Vertue in the Cure of Maladies, I Beg you'll . . *A.* . . our Opinion is, that the Seventh Son receives his healthy Attribute only from the Old Superstitious Notion of the Number 7. *c*.1730 *Round about our Coal-Fire* 15. Wizards or Conjurers . . such as . . seventh Sons. **1807** SOUTHEY *Letters from England* L. The favourite assertion formerly in all countries was, that of an innate gift as a seventh son, I know not on what superstition founded, and of course augmented seven fold in due proportion, if the father had been a seventh son also, or even the mother a seventh daughter, for in this case there is no Salic law. **1849** BRAND *Antiquities* III 333. The person who generally practises this divination boasts himself to be the seventh son of a seventh son. The twig of hazel bends in his hands to the conviction of the miners that ore is present. **1850** T. KEIGHTLEY *Fairy Mythology* 411 n. Jones was their name, and they lived at a place called Muddfi. In them was said to have originated the tradition of the seventh son, or Septimus, being born for the healing art; as for many generations seven sons were regularly born in each family, the seventh of whom became a doctor, and wonderful in his profession. **1852** *N & Q* 1st ser.

V 572. In Saltash Street, Plymouth, my
friend copied . . the following inscription
on a board, indicating the profession and
claims of the inhabitant: A. SHEPHERD,
THE THIRD SEVENTH DAUGHTER,
DOCTRESS. Ibid. 617. At my father's
school was a Yorkshire lad . . intended
for the medical profession . . he was the
seventh son of a seventh son; and the
seventh son of a seventh son 'maks
the bigg'st o' doctors'. 1866 HENDERSON
Northern Counties 177–8. The wise man
of Stokesley . . was at once resorted to
in cases of sickness, distress, or loss of
property, and this not by the lower
orders alone . . He owed his powers to
his being the seventh son of a seventh
daughter [he said]. 1879 *N & Q* 5th ser.
XII 466 [Somerset] I had a family in my
parish which numbered seven daughters, and people came from far and near
to be touched by the youngest of them for
the king's evil. 1895 J. HARDY *Denham
Tracts* 273. It is a belief . . in the North
of England . . that the seventh son . . is
destined to be a skilful and eminent
physician . . A representation of 'the
seven starns' is believed to be impressed
on his side or his breast . . If the seventh
daughter appeared in uninterrupted succession, she was to be a witch. 1914
N & Q 11th ser. X 135. In Ulster it is
truly no joke to be a seventh son, for I
knew in my childhood of small traders
in country towns who were pestered
by patients, to the great hurt of their
business. They could not refuse their
aid to those who had been brought in
springless carts some thirty miles of
mountain road, but they detested their
own celebrity. My impression is that
they dealt chiefly with erysipelas and
such diseases, and that they professed
to cure by prayers and in the name of
God. 1986 Woman, 45. My mother
was considered to be a white witch
because she was a seventh daughter,
and her birthday was the seventh day
of the seventh month. She lived in Ash-
combe, Devon, then. 1988 *Times* 28
May 2 [E. London] Bernard Ward, aged
6, who is believed by gypsies to have
psychic and healing powers because he
is the seventh son of a seventh son, has
been kidnapped for the second time this
year.

SHADOW, headless

1898 BLAKEBOROUGH *Yorkshire Customs*
69 n. Before retiring to rest the older
and more superstitious look round to see
if there is a shadowless head [sic] thrown
on the wall; should anyone cast such a
shadow, it is held they will die ere next
Christmas Eve comes round. 1909 M.
TREVELYAN *Folk-Lore of Wales* 30. When
the Christmas log is burning you should
notice the people's shadows on the wall
. . Shadows that appear without heads
belong to the persons who are to die
within the year. 1948 S. M. LEHRMAN
Jewish Customs (1964, 149) Q. What
part do shadows play in our folklore? A.
. . The absence of a shadow altogether,
or a headless shadow on the night of
Hoshana Rabba [Jewish New Year] is
supposed to be an omen of ill-luck, for
it forebodes death in the course of the
year.

SHAKING HANDS across people

1883 BURNE *Shropshire* 269. Some people
say it is very unlucky for four persons
to shake hands across each other at the
same time . . if accidentally such a thing
happens, each of the four offenders must
immediately cross himself to avert the
bad omen . . Some . . aver that shaking
hands across is a sign of a wedding.
1895 *Folklore* 305 [Worcs.] If four persons cross arms when shaking hands,
one of the four will shortly be married.

SHAKING HANDS across table

1872 H. CULLWICK *Diary* 6 Nov. She held
her hand out over the big table, but as
I'd heard that's bad luck I said, 'I won't
shake hands over the table, ma'am,' &
run round to her. 1883 BURNE *Shropshire*
269. There is no disagreement as to the
ill omen of two persons shaking hands
over a table—that is very unlucky, but
who shall say why? 1914 M. JAGGER
History of Honley 120 [Yorks.] It is
unlucky . . to shake hands across a table
or person.

SHEEP cures: organs and skin

1507 *Gospelles of Dystaues* pt. 6 IX. Yf a
woman haue the smal pockes, it be-
houeth that her husbande bye her a
blacke lamb of the same yere, and after

bynde her in the skynne, and then let hym make hys pylgrymage and offrynge to saynt Arragonde, and for a trouthe she shall hele. **1638** J. PRIMROSE *De vulgi erroribus in medicina* (tr. Wittie, 398) The moderne Physicians use .. the lungs of a Ramme yet warme. **1808** SCOTT (LOCKHART *Life* I 16) Among the old remedies recurred to aid my lameness, some one had recommended that so often as a sheep was killed .. I should be stripped, and swathed up in the skin warm as it was flayed from the carcass of the animal. **1863** *The Book and its Missions* Mar. 69 [Leicester] The mother informed me that a neighbour had told her to get a sheep's melt and put it to the soles of the child's feet, and that would save its life if anything would. **1866** *N & Q* 3rd ser. X 307. A Huntingdonshire woman has been telling me of her sister's recovery from typhus fever. She said that they placed 'the skirt' of a sheep to the soles of her feet. **1895** *Folklore* 167 [Lewis, Outer Hebrides, 1825] When a man was afflicted with pains in his joints, a black sheep, still living, was placed over the rheumatic limbs of the patient. **1912** LEATHER *Herefordshire* 77. Riding across Eywas Harold Common [*c.*1840] he came on a group of people surrounding something on the ground. At first he took it to be a dead sheep, but .. it was but the skin of one, inside of which was the body of a child .. only its head visible. [The] little one had been bitten by an adder [and] the best cure .. was the pelt warm and reeking from the body of a sheep. **1925** [Abergavenny, Monmouth.] The child had pneumonia, and her grandmother .. tied raw sheep's lights on the soles of her feet. She said that as the inflammation went from her, holes would appear in the lights. And this is what happened. **1929** *N & Q* CLVII 15. The sheep's melts .. had to be buried, the belief being that the ailment is buried with them. **1957** A doctor friend of mine, practising in Yorkshire in the 1920s, went to visit a child who had measles. He wondered what the stench was, and when he pulled back the bedclothes he found a still-born lamb had been placed at the patient's feet. The same lamb had been used for two other children in the family. **1968** A. FRANCIS *Guinea a Box* 23–4 [Curbridge, Oxon., 1920s] In country logic, wool being thought to absorb infection .. when the Prince of Wales contracted typhoid fever, it was seriously opined that healing could be hastened by wrapping him in a sheepskin still warm from the animal.

Cf. PIGEON, live: used in cures.

SHEEP, flock of: cures

1851 *N & Q* 1st ser. III 320 [Somerset] A child in my parish has been for some time afflicted with disease of some of the respiratory organs. The mother was recommended to have it carried through a flock of sheep as they were let out of the fold in the morning. The time was considered to be of importance. Ibid. 367–8. The attempted cure of consumption, or some complaints, by walking among a flock of sheep, is not new. The present Archbishop of Dublin was recommended it .. when young. **1887** 'SPERANZA' WILDE *Superstitions of Ireland* II 100. When a family has been carried off by fever, the house where they died may be again inhabited with safety if a certain number of sheep are driven in to sleep there for three nights. **1925** W. JOHNSON *Talks with Shepherds* 113. There was a spot on the lew side of Easdon Tor, where the sheep used to huddle together for shelter .. and they used to think that the smell of the sheep would cure [whooping cough]. So they carried the youngsters up there to stay awhile. **1936** *Sussex County Mag.* 122. An old .. shepherd recently informed a newspaper interviewer that 'penned sheep are good for consumption'. **1966** C. WOODFORD *Sip from Any Goblet* 23. She [author's grandmother] would hold the sufferer [from whooping cough] before a sheep whose breath would have the desired effect. **1968** A. FRANCIS *Guinea a Box* 23–4 [Curbridge, Oxon., 1920s] Remedies for respiratory complaints, including consumption, were often attempted by making the invalid walk about amongst a flock, or even driving a few sheep into the house for several nights, and sleeping near them.

Cf. COW cures consumption.

SHEEP, flock of: lucky

1874 *N & Q* 5th ser. II 184 [Tiverton, Devon] If you meet a flock of sheep, it is lucky to part them. **1923** [Somerset] A flock of sheep met when on a journey is considered lucky, especially if you overtake them and wend your way through the middle of the flock.

SHEEP, greeting: brings luck

1953 *Woman's Illustrated* 1 Aug. 1 [Glasgow] If you say 'Good morning, Mr Sheep,' to the first sheep you meet, you somehow or other receive a surprise parcel.

Cf. MAGPIE, meeting.

SHEPHERD'S PURSE: divination

1890 *North-Country Lore* 474 [Blackburn, Yorks.] On finding a plant of shepherd's purse, open a seed vessel; if the seed is yellow, you will be rich; if green you will be poor.

SHIFT/SMOCK etc., apparition turns

1685 G. SINCLAIR *Satans Invisible World Discovered* 215 [Highlands] I heard of a Woman, who dipt her smock in South-running-water, on that night [Hallowe'en] and hanged it up before the fire to dry. One comes in, in the likness of the man, who was to be her husband, and turns it, and went immediately to the Bed, where she was attending the event, and kist her. It seems she did not believe it was the Devil. **1685** *Mother Bunch's Closet* (1885, 17) [Midsummer Eve] Three or four of you .. must take your smocks and dip them in fair water, then turn the wrong side outwards, and hang them on chairs before the fire, and have by you a vessel with drink in it and lay some salt in another before the fire, and be sure not to speak whatever you hear or see. In a little time the likeness of those persons you shall marry will come and turn your smocks, and drink to you; now if there be any of you that will never marry, they will hear a bell. **1755** *Connoisseur* 20 Feb. [Midsummer Eve] I took a clean shift, and turned it, and hung upon the back of a chair; and very likely my sweetheart would have come and turned it right again, (for I heard his step) but I was frightened, and could not help speaking, which broke the

charm. **1770** *Poor Robin's Almanack* Apr. On St Mark's Eve, at Twelve o'Clock, The Fair Maid she will watch her Smock; To find her Husband in the Dark, By praying unto good St Mark. **1783** C. VALLANCEY *De Rebus Hibernicis* III 459–60 [Hallowe'en] They hang a smock before the fire .. and sit up all night .. convinced that his apparition will come down the chimney, and turn the smock. **1790** BURNS 'Tam Glen'. The last Halloween I was waukin [watching] My droukit [wetted] sark-sleeve, as ye ken—His likeness came up the house staukin, And the very grey breeks o' Tam Glen. **1838** HOLLOWAY *Provincialisms* 128 [Sussex, *c.*1815] On Midsummer night young servant girls try the experiment of seeing their future husbands .. they hang their under garments down by a fire to air, and at midnight the predestined lovers come and turn them. *c.*1845 (*Trans. Devon. Ass.*, 1976, 189) [Upton] One of the sisters turned her chemise inside out and hung it on the hedge, then ran indoors and watched from a small window under the eaves to see who would come along and turn the garment to its right side. If a man should do this he would be her future husband according to the local superstition. **1878** *Folk-Lore Record* 33 [Fittleworth, Sussex] Simple maidens have confessed in my hearing to their having just before midnight [on St John's Eve] washed their sarks, and hung them out to dry before the kitchen fire, and waited to see who would come in and turn them. The kitchen door must be set wide open or the charm will not work. **1887** 'SPERANZA' WILDE *Superstitions of Ireland* I 209. All the spells worked on November Eve are performed in the name of the devil .. The most usual .. is to wash a garment in a running brook, then hang it on a thorn bush, and wait to see the apparition of the lover, who will come to turn it. **1898** BLAKEBOROUGH *Yorkshire Customs* 83–4 [Midsummer Eve] Near one end of the room a basin half full of water must be placed, in which each maiden has dropped a handful of red-rose leaves; the three sprigs of rosemary must now be laid on the rose leaves; next, fix a line across the room, over which each must throw .. a chemise of her own make, but she has never worn .. A few moments after twelve o'clock the husband of each will appear .. will seize a sprig of rosemary and sprinkle the chemise of the girl he loves. **1932** J. M. E. SAXBY *Shetland Lore* 178. The sark-sleeve dipped in water three times where three lairds' lands meet shewed a girl the face of her future husband.

Cf. SUPPER, apparition comes to share.

SHOELACE breaks

45 BC CICERO *De Divinatione* II 40. Stumbling, breaking a shoe-latchet, and sneezing, were [superstitiously] noted. **1159** JOHN OF SALISBURY *Policraticus* (*Frivolities of Courtiers*, ed. J. B. Pike, 57) The apostle Mark, setting out for Alexandria to spread the gospel, when on disembarking he burst the latchets of his shoe offered thanks that his journey had been unimpeded. **1652** GAULE *Mag-astro-mances* 181. Superstitious ominations .. the bursting of the shooe latchet. **1909** *N & Q* 10th ser. XII 484 [Stromness, Orkney] It is unlucky to break your shoe-lace. **1954** Schoolgirl, 13 [Pontnewydd, Monmouth.] If you break your shoelaces it means bad luck.

SHOELACE comes untied

1898 BLAKEBOROUGH *Yorkshire Customs* 150. When you discover your shoe-lace is loose, walk nine paces before tying it, otherwise you will tie ill-luck to you for that day.

SHOELACE, giving

1932 C. IGGLESDEN *Those Superstitions* 221 [Surrey] It is very unlucky to give a new bootlace to a friend unless he gives you a broken one in return.

SHOES as present

1984 Woman, 57 [Petersfield, Hants.] I gave the slippers to him and got my halfpenny. You must get money for a present of shoes or they walk away.

SHOES, new: at Christmas

1875 *N & Q* 5th ser. III 7. A small Herefordshire farmer some time since made lamentation .. that a pair of new shoes had been unwittingly received into his house on Christmas morning, and

he said it was 'a bad job', for he 'had lost a sight of cattle that year'. **1912** LEATHER *Herefordshire* 109. It is unlucky to receive new shoes, or untanned leather, into the house on Christmas Day, or some say during Christmas week.

Cf. LEATHER in house.

SHOES, new: on table

1869 *N & Q* 4th ser. IV 307. In Shropshire, about Shiffnal, it is thought very unlucky to place a pair of .. new boots on a table. If you do so, there will certainly be a quarrel in the household. **1884** *N & Q* 6th ser. IX 66. Whilst staying in some apartments in London, I placed for a moment on the table my boots, which the servant had just brought up. She .. rushed at them, and said, 'Oh, sir, we shall have ill luck in the house.' **1909** *N & Q* 10th ser. XII 484 [Stromness, Orkney] It is unlucky to put shoes on the table: there will be thunder and lightning, or you will quarrel with some one. **1932** C. IGGLESDEN *Those Superstitions* 225. The dread of placing boots on a table .. The Duke of Wellington instantly discharged an old servant because he placed his Grace's boots on a table. **1946** UTTLEY *Country Things* 127 [Derbys., c.1895] Shoes must never be put on the table. It was considered extremely unlucky, and I was so deeply impressed by the seriousness of this that even now I cannot resist removing shoes placed there. **1984** Woman, 26 [Wotton-under-Edge, Glos.] Never put new shoes on a table— I'd *never* do that.

SHOES, new: squeaking

1849 *Norfolk Archaeology* II 45 [Irstead] If your new boots creak, the shoemaker is still unpaid. *c.*1910 [Eastbourne, Sussex] Squeaking shoes meant that they had not been paid for. *c.*1930 [Middlesbrough, Teesside] If a person walks down the aisle in church with squeaking shoes it is said: 'They are not paid for yet.' And the remedy is first to pay for them, and then, 'Steep the soles in the pot [chamber pot].' **1952** Girl, 14 [Aberdeen] When someone gets a pair of shoes and they creak when they walk, people say that the shoes are not paid for. **1987** Woman, *c.*60 [Great Ayton, Teesside] John had a very creaky pair of boots. When we were in Switzerland last year, and I was walking behind him, I'd be thinking, 'he hasn't paid for those'.

Cf. CLOTHES, tacking thread/pins left in.

SHOES, new: trodden on

1959 OPIE *Lore and Language of School-children* 303. When anybody receives a new pair of shoes the custom is to stand on her toes for luck.

SHOES, old: burning

1884 *N & Q* 6th ser. IX 49. A woman residing at Hamble, Hants., who was lately taken ill very suddenly, said to a person who called to inquire after her, 'Ah! I be ill all over; and no wonder; it as good as serves me right, for I burnt a pair of old shoes yesterday.' **1895** S. O. ADDY *Household Tales* 92. In Nottinghamshire they say that to prevent infection from fevers and other diseases you should burn an old shoe. **1900** J. G. CAMPBELL *Superstitions of the Highlands* 36 [Hebrides] Most frequently it was women, not yet risen from childbed, and their babes that the Fairies abducted .. Various .. precautions were taken .. an old shoe was put in the fire. **1912** LEATHER *Herefordshire* 258. It is lucky to burn any old boots available, before starting on a journey. A Herefordshire servant told her mistress she had seen the hop-pickers, who were to leave next day, with such funny old boots laid out all round their fire. 'They [are] sure to be going to burn them,' she said, 'Mother always does before going away anywhere; she says its *such* a lucky thing to do!' **1958** *Trans. Devon. Ass.* 246 [Exmouth] If you burn a boot on Christmas Eve, it will keep you in shoe leather all next year.

Cf. LEATHER, burning.

SHOES, old: pass on left of

1898 BLAKEBOROUGH *Yorkshire Customs* 150–1. Always pass an old shoe so as to have it on your right hand; and don't move it, lest you should help some unknown person on in the world, which would only be done to the detriment of yourself, for just as much as you advanced them, to that extent you would be the loser.

SHOES, old: thrown etc. for luck

1546 J. HEYWOOD *Proverbs* I IX C2. For good lucke, cast an olde shoe after mee. **1621** JONSON *Gipsies* (1890, 264) Hurle after an old shooe, I'le be merry what e'er I doe. **1777** BRAND *Antiquities* 94. It is accounted lucky to throw an old Shoe after a Person, when we wish him to succeed in what he is going about. **1827** HONE *Table Book* II 348. A custom prevalent in different parts of Yorkshire .. called 'trashing', which signifies pelting people with old shoes on their return from church on their wedding day. **1849** DICKENS *David Copperfield* x. I found that Mr Peggotty was prepared with an old shoe, which was to be thrown after us [wedding party] for luck. **1850** *N & Q* 1st ser. II 197. Some years ago, when the vessels engaged in the Greenland whale-fishery left Whitby [Yorks.] I observed the wives and friends of the sailors to throw old shoes at the ships as they passed the pier-head. **1855** QUEEN VICTORIA *Journal* 7 Sept. At a quarter-past seven o'clock we arrived at dear Balmoral [Aberdeen.] The new house looks beautiful .. An old shoe was thrown after us into the house, for good luck, when we entered the hall. **1861** C. C. ROBINSON *Dialect of Leeds* 445–6. It is usual here, as in other places, to fling the shoe after the bridal conveyance, or in the wake of the blissful couple, if they are obliged to trudge afoot, 'for good luck'. At the sight of a wedding-party, children may be heard calling out, 'A wedding a woo, A clog an' a shoe', and make feint of taking off their shoes and throwing them at or after the couple. **1873** KILVERT *Diary* 1 Jan. [Bredwardine, Herefords.] The bride went straight away to her carriage. Someone thrust an old white pair of satin shoes into my hand with which I made an ineffectual shot at the post boy, and someone else behind me missed the carriage altogether and gave me with an old shoe a terrific blow on the back of the head. **1873** *Chambers' Journal* 810 [Scotland] There is nothing like well-worn leather to propitiate fate .. The time-honoured custom of throwing an old shoe after a departing friend, in order that his journey may have a prosperous issue, is so ancient and so common, that we .. only mention it here to remind intending throwers that the shoe should belong to the left foot—there is no virtue in its fellow. 1910 *N & Q* 11th ser. II 509. Can any of your readers give me the .. explanation of luck being considered an attribute of old shoes? 1923 [Castle Cary, Som.] An old shoe tied on a wedding carriage, means good luck. 1928 E. LOVETT *Surrey and Sussex* 8–9. An old shoe hung up at the side of the fire-place 'for luck' .. is a very common practice. 1952 Boy, 12 [Sale, Cheshire] When I have an exam they throw a slipper after me as I leave the house. 1963 M. LAWRENCE *Wedding Etiquette* 144. While they [bride and groom] have been away there will probably have been a certain amount of skylarking with the car in which they are to depart—old shoes tied on, at the very least.

Cf. BABY protected by 'something old'; BRIDE'S CLOTHES: 'something old'.

SHOES, old: thrown over beam/house: divination

1340 HIGDEN MS Speculum Curatorum (OWST, in *Studies*, ed. J. Conway Davies, 1957, 288) Some .. on the night of the Circumcision .. throw their shoes over the tie-beams to discover whether they ought to stay in the house for another year or not [i.e. according to the direction in which the fallen shoes point, e.g. towards the door]. 1616 Witchcraft trial, Orkney (C. ROGERS *Social Life in Scotland* III 303) Peter Hollandis wyfe come to the said Helen, the said Petter being seik, and askit at hir quidder or nocht hir husband wald die or leive. The said Helen commandit hir to tak his left fute shoe and cast it ouir the hous, and said gif the mouth of it fell vp he wald leive, and gif doun he wald die.

SHOES placed in form of a T

1831 HONE *Year Book* 9 Oct. [Dorset, Midsummer Eve] If, at going to bed, she put her shoes at right angles with each other .. and say, 'Hoping this night my true love to see, I place my shoes in the form of a T,' they say she will be sure to see her husband in a dream, and perhaps in reality, by her bed-side. 1862 *N & Q* 3rd ser. II 62 [Devon] Retiring to bed on Midsummer Eve, when you take your shoes off, place them in the form of a letter T, and repeat these lines—'I place my shoes like a letter T, In hopes my true love I shall see, In his apparel and his array, As he is now and every day.' Then change the shoes, so as to make the down stroke with the one that was the top stroke before, and repeat the lines again. Reverse them, and say the lines for the third time. Having written a letter of the alphabet on so many little pieces of paper, throw them all into a basin under the bed. Then go to bed, but be sure not to speak .. or the charm will be broken .. In the morning examine the basin. If any of the letters have turned over, face upwards, they will indicate the name of your future husband. 1896 *N & Q* 8th ser. X 214. The custom in Yorkshire is, or used to be, to place one shoe at right angles to the other on the floor by the side of the bed and to say 'I set my shoes in the form of a T, Hoping my true-love for to see, Not in his riches or his array, But in the clothes he wears every day.' 1913 *Folklore* 79–80 [Barnard Gate, Oxon., *c.*1840, similar description].

Cf. SHOES/STOCKINGS in form of cross.

SHOES, turned: cure cramp

1852 *N & Q* 1st ser. VI 601 [Cornwall] In the neighbourhood of Penzance the following is considered an infallible cure for cramp: 'On going to rest, put your slippers under the bed and turn the soles upwards.' 1895 *Folklore* 126 [Suffolk] Cramp is easily cured. You will never have it again if you put your shoes outside your bedroom door every night 'coming and going', i.e. with the toe of one pointing towards, and the other away from, the room. 1971 *Farmers Weekly* 1 Jan. 55 [East Grinstead, Sussex] At our women's meeting the other day .. remedies [for night cramp] were suggested by the audience of country women .. For the pure superstitious, turn your slippers upside-down before retiring.

SHOES, turned: prevent nightmare

1945 *Folklore* 270 [Suffolk] Shoes placed

at a door, one going in, one out, will prevent nightmare.

SHOES, turned: stop dog howling

1849 *Norfolk Archaeology* II 302–3 [Irstead] 'Pull off your left-foot shoe, and turn it; and it will quiet him [howling dog]. They won't howl three times after.' 'What do you do when you are in bed, and have no shoe on?' 'I turn the shoe upside down, by the bed's side; and that stops the dog.' 1878 DYER *English Folk Lore* (1880, 101–2) [Staffs.] When you hear a dog howl, take off your shoe from the left foot, and spit upon the sole, place it on the ground bottom upwards, and your foot upon the place you spat upon, which will not only preserve you from harm, but stop the howling of the dog.

SHOES/STOCKINGS in form of cross

1831 HONE *Year Book* 29 Feb. Stockings are hung crosswise at the foot of the bed, with a pin stuck in them, to keep off the nightmare. 1850 *N & Q* 1st ser. II 37 [Northants.] A very common charm for the cramp consists in the sufferer's always taking care, when he pulls off his shoes and stockings, to place them .. to form a resemblance to the 'holy sign'. 1866 HENDERSON *Northern Counties* 27. There is no chance at all of a family, unless, when she retires on the wedding-night, her bridesmaids lay her stockings across. 1878 *Folk-Lore Record* 39 [Fittleworth, Sussex] She couldn't no way understand her rheumatis being so uncommon bad, for she had put her shoes in the form of a cross every night by the side of her bed, ever since she felt the first twinge. 1938 *Folklore* 229 [Shrops.] A doctor of Church Stretton .. was called for to a man who was ill. He asked the man's wife what she had already done. She replied, 'Oh, doctor, there be naught that I 'unna done. I've even crossed 'is stockins under 'is bed.' 1976 *Sun* 27 Feb. 16 [Holbeach, Lincs.] To avoid having cramp during the night, leave your stockings in the form of a cross when you take them off.

SHOES/STOCKINGS, putting on: left/right

c. AD 390 ST JOHN CHRYSOSTOM *Homilies on Ephesians* XII (1879, 242) The wretch of a servant in giving me my shoes, held

out the left shoe first. 1507 *Gospelles of Dystaues* pt. 4 XVI. Whan ony woman bereth her capons to the good towne for to sell .. yf by aduenture she dothe on her ryght sho fyrste in the mornynge it is good hap for to sell well. 1627 W. HAWKINS *Apollo Shroving* IV I. I haue heard you often tell of a man that brake his legge because hee pul'd on his left stocking first on one of the dogge dayes. 1827 R. BERNARD *Guide to Grand-Jury Men* XIV 183. Dismayed at signes, as .. when they put on 1 hose or shoo before another, as the left before the right. 1878 *Folk-Lore Record* 12 [Fittleworth, Sussex] To put on the left shoe before the right is a sign of evil to come. 1909 *N & Q* 10th ser. XII 484 [Stromness, Orkney] It is unlucky to put on the left boot first. 1910 *Folklore* 226 [Yorks To put the right boot on first is unlucky 1954 *Daily Express* 13 Aug. 4. Her mother in Scotland never steps out of bed without putting on her left stocking and shoe. She says 'I would not dream of breaking this habit—just to be on the safe side!' 1983 Primary headmaster, *c.*45 [Dedham, Essex] I'm not superstitious, but I always put my left shoe on first, particularly football boots before a match.

Cf. LEFT FOOT unlucky.

SHOES/STOCKINGS, putting on: spitting

AD 77 PLINY *Natural History* XXVIII VII (1856, V 290) Among the counter-charms [is] reckoned, the practice of .. spitting into the shoe of the right foot before putting it on. 1584 SCOT *Discoverie of Witchcraft* XII XVIII. Spet into the shoo of your right foote, before you put it on.

SHOES/STOCKINGS, putting on: to prevent toothache

1875 *N & Q* 5th ser. III 465 [Shrops.] If you always put your left stocking and shoe on first, it prevents toothache. 1960 *Radio Times* 27 May 25. How comes Ned Larkin (of 'The Archers') with toothache? As a countryman surely he should know that if he put his left stocking on first every morning he would never get toothache. I suggest he try it.

SHOES/STOCKINGS, putting on: wrongly

1585 SCOT *Discoverie of Witchcraft* XI

xv. He that receiveth a mischance, wil consider whether he .. put not .. his left shoo on his right foote. **1603** W. PERKINS *Works* 39. That it is vnluckie for one in the morning to put on his shooe awrie, or to put the left shooe on the right foote. **1652** GAULE *Mag-astro-mances* 181. To bode good or bad luck .. from putting on the hose uneven or a crosse, and the shooe upon the wrong foot. *c.*1700 W. PAUL *Aberdeenshire* 18–19. Alex. Thomson, minister of Peterculter .. is guilty of superstitious observances .. saying that he knew some evil would befall that day that he fell and hurt his leg, for his right foot shoe would not go on, and he was going to burn it. **1910** *Folklore* 226 [Pontefract, Yorks.] Huntsmen in the district believe that .. to put a riding boot on the wrong foot, foretells a mishap in the hunting field. **1923** [Wellington, Som.] To put your shoes on wrong feet, it is unlucky. **1982** Woman, *c.*50 [Middlesbrough, Teesside] Unlucky to put shoes on wrong feet.

shoes/stockings, putting on: also *see* SNEEZING: divination: time of day.

SHOES/STOCKINGS, wearing out: divination

1888 *Household Words* 29 Sept. 435. Tread at the toe, live and see woe; Tread at the heel, live and get a deal; Tread at the side, friends will abide; Tread at the ball, you will lose them all. **1903** LEAN *Collectanea* II 43. To wear out shoes and stockings on the ball or sole of the foot indicates long life and prosperity. 'Wear on the ball, you'll live to spend all.' **1909** M. TREVELYAN *Folk-Lore of Wales* 329. Those who tread their heels inward will be rich; if outward, they will be poor. **1923** [Somerset] To wear a hole in the middle of your shoe, you will be lucky. **1956** [nr. London] Wear at the toe, Spend as you go. Wear at the ball, You'll live to spend all. **1986** *Mirror* 7 July 20. My mother-in-law claimed she could tell what people were like merely by looking at their feet and reciting: 'Wear out the toe, live to know woe. Wear out the ball, live to spend all. Wear at the heel, ne'er do we'al.'

SHREW an evil creature

AD 77 PLINY *Natural History* VIII LXXXIII (1855, II 353) The bite of the shrew-mouse is venomous. **1535** COVERDALE *Ecclesiasticus* XXXI 12. Remembre, that an euell eye is a shrew. **1620** T. GRANGER *Divine Logike* 223. Enmitie, hatred, and ill will is a shrew. **1850** *N & Q* 1st ser. II 164 [Northants.] To meet with a shrew-mouse, in going a journey, is reckoned ominous of evil. **1883** BURNE *Shropshire* 213. An old man of Ruyton-of-the-Eleven-Towns, avers that if you see a Shrew-mouse, you must cross your foot or you will suffer for it.

SHREW causes lameness

1545 T. ELYOT *Dictionary*. *Mus Araneus*, a kynde of myse called a shrew, whyche yf it goo ouer a beastes backe, he shall be lame in the chyne. **1579** LUPTON *Thousand Notable Things* X § 11. If *Musaraneus*, called a Shrew, (I take it to be the blinde Mowse,) doth chaunce to go ouer any part of any Beast: that part of the Beast wyll after be lame. **1722** W. GIBSON *Farrier's Guide* 61. Many of the Country People .. when they see a Horse or a Bullock have his Limbs suddenly taken from him .. believe him to be either Planet-Struck or Shrow-run. **1776** WHITE *Selborne* 8 Jan. It is supposed that a shrew-mouse is of so baneful and deleterious a nature, that wherever it creeps over a beast, be it horse, cow, or sheep, the suffering animal is afflicted with cruel anguish, and threatened with the loss of the limb. **1889** *Dorset Field Club* 41. If a shrew-mouse runs over a man's foot it will make him lame. **1899** *Newcastle Weekly Journal* 11 Feb. 7 [Jesmond] A shrew mouse running over the foot will cause the toes to turn in. **1971** *Trans. Devon. Ass.* 268 [Stockleigh Pomeroy] If a shrew mouse ran over your foot, you would go lame and walk with a bad limp all your life.

SHREW crosses road or path

AD 77 PLINY *Natural History* VIII LXXXIII (1855, II 353) The shrew-mouse .. always dies immediately if it goes across the rut made by a wheel. **1607** TOPSELL *Foure-footed Beastes* 536. The Shrew, which falling by chaunce into a Cart-roade or tracke doth die vpon the same.

1883 BURNE *Shropshire* 214. The shrew-mouse, in Shropshire and elsewhere, is popularly supposed to be unable to cross a road, and must therefore remain all his life within the compass of the roads surrounded by which he was born. If he attempts to cross one, he dies in the middle of it; hence the numbers of these mice which are found lying dead in country roads and paths. **1923** [Somerset] Shrews cannot cross a path, and die if they attempt to do so.

SHREW: cures/spells

AD **77** PLINY *Natural History* XXIX XXVII (1856, V 402) Where a shrewmouse has bitten beasts of burden .. the shrewmouse itself .. split asunder and applied to the wound, is a cure for its bite .. The best plan is to apply the mouse itself which has inflicted the bite, but others are commonly kept for this purpose .. coated with clay .. Another remedy .. is the earth taken from the rut made by a cart-wheel; for this animal, it is said .. will never cross a rut made by a wheel. **1579** LUPTON *Thousand Notable Things* VII § 52. To keepe Beastes safe that the blynde mowse, called a Shrew, do not byte them. Enclose the same Mowse quicke in chalke, which when it is hard, hang the same about the necke of the Beast .. and it is most certayne, that he shall nor be toucht not bitten. **1607** TOPSELL *Foure-footed Beastes* 536. The Shrew which dyeth in the furrow of a cart-wheele, being .. rowled in potters clay .. and three times marked about the impostumes .. effectually .. cure the same. Ibid. 541. Against the bitings of Shrewes .. keepe her .. till she dye, and waxe stiffe, then hang her about the necke of the beast .. and there wil not any Shrew come neare them. **1898** C. M. YONGE *John Keble's Parishes* XVI [Hursley & Otterbourne, Hants.] Dead shrews bestrew the paths though the magic effects of having a 'sherry mouse' die in one's hand and thus being enabled to stroke cattle and cure them, have never been experienced. **1972** G. SUMMERS *Lure of the Falcon* 48 [Horam, Sussex, 1936] He [farmer, in his 80s] was as superstitious as an African tribesman. He believed .. that to prevent the onset of rheumatism all one had to do

was to carry a dead shrew in one's pocket.

Cf. MOLE: cures/spells.

SHREW-ASH cures

1686 R. PLOT *Staffordshire* 222. To make any tree, whether Oak, Ash, or Elm (it being indifferent which) a Nursrow-tree [shrew tree] they catch one or more of these mice (which they fancy bite their Cattle, and make them swell), and having bored a hole to the center in the body of the tree, they put the mice in, and then drive a pegg in after them of the same wood, where they starving at last, communicat forsooth such a virtue to the tree, that Cattle thus swoln being whipt with the boughs of it, presently recover: of which trees they have not so many neither (though so easily made) but that at some places they goe 8 or 10 miles to procure this remedy. **1776** WHITE *Selborne* 8 Jan. A shrew-ash is an ash whose twigs or branches, when gently applied to the limbs of cattle, will immediately relieve the pains which a beast suffers from the running of a shrew-mouse over the part affected .. Against this accident, to which they were continually liable, our provident forefathers always kept a shrew-ash at hand, which, when once medicated, would maintain its virtue for ever. A shrew-ash was made thus:—Into the body of the tree a deep hole was bored with an auger, and a poor devoted shrew-mouse was thrust in alive, and plugged in, no doubt, with several quaint incantations long since forgotten. **1829** BROCKETT *North Country Words*. *Shrew*, a field mouse .. It was customary to close up the shrew alive in a hole bored in an ash, elm, or willow-tree; and afterwards to whip the cattle .. with one of the boughs, which was considered an efficacious cure. **1834** A. E. BRAY *Warleigh* XIII [Devon] So long as I hold in my hand this wand of shrew ash there is nothing to fear. You are safe from the spirit of this chamber. **1860** ELIOT *Mill on the Floss* I I. Tom was in a state of as blank unimaginativeness concerning the cause and tendency of his sufferings, as if he had been an innocent shrew-mouse imprisoned in the split trunk of an ash-tree in order

to cure lameness in cattle. **1872**
Routledge's Every Boy's Annual 131. The
curative power which alone could heal
the Shrew-stroke lay in the branches of
a Shrew-ash.

Cf. TREE, disease transferred to.

SHUDDER

1738 SWIFT *Polite Conversation* I 84.
MISS. [*shuddering*] Lord! there's somebody walking over my Grave. **1755**
Connoisseur 13 Mar. If you shiver, somebody is walking over the place of your
grave. **1787** GROSE *Provincial Glossary*
Superstitions 59. A person being suddenly taken with a shivering, is a sign
that some one has just then walked over
the spot of their future grave. **1848**
DICKENS *Dombey and Son* XXIV. Florence
was seized with such a shudder .. that
Sir Barnet, adopting the popular superstition, supposed somebody was passing over her grave. **1886** C. E. DIXON
Chimneypiece of Bruges 9. Good lack! this
spring air has a chill today, Or some one
is too active o'er my grave! Twice I have
shivered as with wintry cold. **1897** E.
PHILLPOTTS *Lying Prophets* 291 [Corn-
wall] Joan shivered with a sudden sense
of chill .. 'Goose-flaish down the spine
do mean as theer's feet walkin' on my
graave.' **1909** M. TREVELYAN *Folk-Lore
of Wales* 281. When people experience
a cold shiver they say: 'A donkey is
walking over my grave,' or, 'Death is
picking my grave.' **1922** UDAL *Dorsetshire* 285. If you shiver involuntarily
somebody is said to be walking over
your grave. **1978** J. GARDNER *Dancing
Dodo* 350. As they stood there, a chill
gust of wind came in over the Marsh
from the Channel. Dobson shivered.
Someone walking over his grave? **1987**
Woman, 32 [London] When I shudder
without any reason, I always think it's
a goose running over my grave, and I
connect it with the goose pimples.

SIEVE AND SHEARS: divination

*c.*275 BC THEOCRITUS *Idylls* III (tr. Creech)
When I design'd to prove Whether I
should be happy in my Love .. To Aggrio
too I made the same demand, A cunning
Woman she .. She turn'd the Sieve and
Sheers, and told me true, That I should

love, but not be lov'd by you. **1584** SCOT
Discoverie of Witchcraft XII XVII. Sticke a
paire of sheeres in the rind of a sive, and
let two persons set the top of each of
their forefingers upon the upper part of
the sheeres, holding it with the sive up
from the ground steddilie, and aske *Peter*
and *Paule* whether A. B. or C. hath stolne
the thing lost, and at the nomination of
the guiltie person, the sive will turne
round. **1598** Nottingham Archdeaconry Papers (*Trans. Thoroton Soc.* XXX
51) John Casson .. admitted 'that ..
a weather [sheep] beinge loste in their
parishe .. there was a device used to
knowe what was become of the said
weather by takynge a Syve and a payre
of Sheeres and sayeinge, In the name of
the father and of the sonne and of the
holie ghoste, after which wordes the
Syve would tourne aboute, which devise
he and his Syster Dorothie Devell once
without anie yll intent made triall of.'
1620 MELTON *Astrologaster* 45. If anything be lost amongst a company of
seruants, with the tricke of the Sive and
the Sheeres, it may be found out againe,
and who stole it. **1686–7** AUBREY *Remaines* (1881, 25) The Sheers are stuck
in a Sieve, and two maydens hold up y^e
sieve with the top of their fingers by the
handle of the shiers: then say, By St
Peter & St Paule such a one hath stoln
(such a thing), the others say, By St
Peter & St Paule He hath not stoln it.
After many such Adjurations, the Sieve
will turne at ye name of ye Thiefe. **1695**
CONGREVE *Love for Love* II i. I saw you
together .. turning the sieve and shears,
and pricking your thumbs to write poor
innocent servants' names in blood,
about a little nutmeg-grater, which she
had forgot in the caudle-cup. **1787**
GROSE *Provincial Glossary* Superstitions
54–5. To discover a thief by the sieve
and sheers: Stick the points of the sheers
in the wood of the sieve, and let two
persons support it, balanced upright,
with their two fingers: then read a
certain chapter in the Bible, and afterwards ask St Peter and St Paul, if A.
or B. is the thief, naming all the persons
you suspect. On naming the real thief,
the sieve will turn suddenly round about.
1829 BROCKETT *North Country Words.
Riddle*, a coarse sieve .. The vulgar,

in many parts, have an abominable practice of using a riddle and a pair of shears in divination. If they have any thing stolen from them, the riddle and shears are sure to be resorted to .. In Northumberland young people *turn the riddle* for the purpose of amusing themselves with the foolish idea of raising their lovers. **1892** N & Q 8th ser. II 305 [Yorks.] He says .. he remembers the household of the hall being gathered together, and some one .. taking a sieve in which a pair of shears had been stuck upright, and going round to each person, and repeating .. 'Bless St Peter, Bless St Paul, Bless the God that made us all. If so-and-so [naming the person he stood before] stole this money, turn sieve.'

Cf. BIBLE AND KEY: divination.

SILVER, crossing palm with

*c.***275** BC THEOCRITUS Idylls III (tr. Creech) When I design'd to prove Whether I should be happy in my Love .. To *Aggrio* too I made the same demand, A cunning Woman she, I crost her hand. **1621** JONSON *The Gipsies* (1890, 264) I prythee dispose some small peece of siluer; it shalbe no losse but onlie to make the syne of the Crosse. If your hand you hallowe Good fortune will followe. I sweare by theise ten You shall haue it agen—I do not say when. **1711** ADDISON *Spectator* 30 July. An honest Dairy-maid who crosses their [gipsies'] Hands with a Piece of Silver every Summer, and never fails being promised the handsomest young Fellow in the Parish. **1755** *Connoisseur* 20 Feb. The love-sick girl runs to the cunning man, or crosses the gipsy's hand with her last sixpence to know when she shall be married. **1766** GOLDSMITH *Vicar of Wakefield* X. The tawny sibyl no sooner appeared, than my girls came running to me for a shilling a-piece, to cross her hand with silver. **1838** D. JERROLD *Men of Character* I 137. Every domestic .. had crossed her [the fortune-teller's] hand and looked on future life.

SILVER protects

1822 SCOTT *The Pirate* I 142 [Shetland] Ye had muckle better say an *oraamus* to Saint Roland, and fling a sixpence ower

your left shouther. **1883** BURNE *Shropshire* 165. A goodwife at Moreton Say is accustomed to put a silver coin into the churn when the cream swells instead of turning into butter. **1899** J. SHAW *Schoolmaster* 30 [Tynron, Dumfries.] Silver is lucky. A father gave a lucky shilling to his daughter at her marriage. **1923** *Folklore* 92 [Skye] A silver coin put under the threshold when a house is built brings good luck. **1942** A. L. ROWSE *Cornish Childhood* IX. [re-taking Oxford scholarship] I hoped the three-penny bit I had carried round in my pocket for weeks would counteract the ill-luck. It did. **1952** *Folklore* 49 [Beauly, Inverness.] She seeks to remind me that a piece of silver suspended round the neck is still regarded in the Scottish Highlands as a charm against witchcraft, and as a means of effecting a cure for various ailments such as the King's Evil. **1953** Girl, 12 [Aberystwyth, Cardigan.] You might keep a silver sixpence in your pocket, so you might pass the exam. Some people say it should be a very new sixpence, new from the bank. **1968** *Observer* Suppl. 24 Nov. 10 [Staithes, Yorks.] At a wedding .. there was scrambling silver; throwing it at the women and children for good luck. **1969** E. PORTER *Cambridgeshire* 15. As soon as the baby arrived the old woman .. would snatch up the child, breathe down its throat and then lay it face downwards on her lap. With the words 'Devil away!' she would place the sixpence on the child's buttocks.

Cf. BABY, gifts to; 'GOLD AND SILVER WATER'.

SILVER protects: in shoe

1774 PENNANT *Tour in Scotland* 232 [Islay, Hebrides] The bridegroom to avert the harm [of his rival's spell] puts a sixpence beneath his foot. **1814** J. TRAIN *Mountain Muse* 9–10 [Scottish Highlands] It is deemed necessary for a young woman, who has had many suitors, to wear a piece of silver in one of her shoes from the time of her marriage till after she is kirked, lest the malignant glance of a disappointed lover's eye should have a physical effect on her constitution. **1939** S. O'CASEY *I Knock at the Door* 103 [Dublin] [On her wedding morning] she was ready for any emergency, so she was, having with her something old and something new, something borrowed and something blue, and a lucky sixpence in her shoe. **1946** *Mirror* 29 Aug. 6. 'Something old, Something new, Something borrowed, Something blue, And a silver sixpence In your shoe.' The coin should be worn in the left shoe and will then bring luck. **1958** Girl, 18 [New Malden, Surrey] My mother comes from Stornoway [Outer Hebrides] and she put sixpence in my shoe for my 11-plus exam.

Cf. BRIDE'S CLOTHES: shoe, gold coin in.

SILVER BULLET

*c.***1700** W. KENNETT Note to Aubrey's *Remaines* (1881, 154) They say that a silver bullet will kill any Hardman .. The Elector Palatine, Prince Roberts Brother, did not believe at all that any man could make himself hard. **1810** R. H. CROMEK *Nithsdale Song* 281 [Dumfries.] Tradition has arrayed the brave persecutor Claverhouse in a lead proof jacket. He rode through the hail of bullets unhurt .. but at length .. his charmed fecket [jacket] could not resist a 'silver sixpence' from the mouth of a Cameronian's fusee. **1816** SCOTT *Old Mortality* XVI. Many a whig that day loaded his musket with a dollar cut into slugs, in order that a silver bullet .. might bring down the persecutor of the holy kirk, over whom lead had no power. **1893** STEVENSON *Catriona* XV. My grandsire gied Sandie a siller tester to pit in his gun wi' the leid draps, bein' mair deidly again the bogles. **1898** BLAKEBOROUGH *Yorkshire Customs* 203. Some one suggested silver shot; this was duly made, and the hare shot dead. Afterwards, on comparing the times, it was found that Mrs —— had thrown up her arms the very moment when the hare was shot, ejaculating 'They have killed my familiar spirit;' uttering these words, she fell dead on her kitchen floor. **1902** *People's Friend* 15 Sept. 656 [Aberdeenshire, 1863] John .. rammed a sixpence down on the top of his charge of lead. The hare came as usual, and John fired .. the hare tumbled over, and when she got up one leg, a hind one, hung useless .. Next

day .. the suspected witch was confined to her bed a helpless cripple.

SILVER 'GARLAND'

1546 P. VERGIL *De Rerum Inventoribus* I IV (tr. Langley) In Rome, the maner was that two chyldren should leade the bryde and another bare afore her a torche of whyte thorne .. Whiche maner is vsed in Englande, sauyng in steade of the torche, there is borne here a basen of siluer or golde before. **1698** MISSON *Voyageur en Angleterre* (1791, 307) On the first of May and the five or six days following, all the pretty young Country Girls that serve the Town with Milk, dress themselves up very neatly, and borrow abundance of Silver Plate, whereof they make a Pyramid, which they adorn with Ribbands and Flowers, and carry upon their head, instead of their common Milk-Pails. *c.***1850** J. HUNTER MS note in Brand's *Antiquities* I 203. I have seen Plate Garlands .. At Sheffield on the 29th of May is what is called Scotland-Feast .. celebrated in a street called Scotland Street which may be seen with large garlands suspended on ropes stretched from one house to the opposite. These garlands are formed of leaves & flowers, with as much silver plate brightly polished as the parties have of their own or can borrow of their neighbours. **1872** A. HARE *Memorials of a Quiet Life* I 245 [Stoke-upon-Tern, 1829] The walk through the churchyard was lined with the school-children, with wreaths of flowers in their hands; one went before us strewing flowers in our path; and all the silver spoons, tankards, watches, and ornaments of the neighbouring farmers were fastened on white cloths drawn over hoops, so as to make a sort of trophy on each side the church gate, which is, I understand, a Shropshire custom.

SINGING before breakfast

1530 PALSGRAVE *La langue francoyse* (1852, 776) You waxe mery this morning. God gyve grace you wepe nat or nyght. **1855** *N & Q* 1st ser. XI 416. If you sing before breakfast, you'll cry before night. **1866** HENDERSON *Northern Counties* 85 [Co. Durham] If you sing before breakfast you will cry before supper. **1881** W. GREGOR *North-East of Scotland* 31. It was accounted unlucky to sing before breakfast. Hence the saying: 'Sing afore breakfast, Greet aifter 't.' **1887** *Folk-Lore Record* 220 [Cornwall] If you sing afore bite, You'll cry before night. **1923** [Somerset] Sing before breakfast you will cry before night. **1932** C. IGGLESDEN *Those Superstitions* 177. Do not burst into song before breakfast lest you have bad luck at the close of day. **1950** Woman, *c*.50 [Forfar, Angus] Sing afore ye eat Ye'll greet afore ye sleep.

SINGING during meal

1923 [Wellington, Som.] To sing during a meal means a disappointment. **1950** Woman, *c*.50 [Forfar, Angus] Sing at yer meat, Ye'll die ee puir house.

SKIRT turned up

1914 *Folklore* 372 [Herts.] It is a common belief that if the lower edge of a woman's skirt has become turned up so as to form a kind of pocket, some good fortune, such as a present of a new dress, will come to the owner. **1915** *Folklore* 210 [Glos.] If the hem of a woman's skirt turns up behind, forming a sort of bag, she will receive a present, and ought not to turn the skirt down again for fear of annulling the omen.

Cf. CLOTHES inside out.

SKULL cures

1584 SCOT *Discoverie of Witchcraft* XII XIV. *Against the biting of a mad dog*. Take pilles made of the skull of one that is hanged. **1858** *Stamford Mercury* 8 Oct. 3. A collier's wife recently applied to the sexton of Ruabon [Denbighs.] church for ever so small a piece of a 'human skull' for the purpose of grating it similar to ginger, to be afterwards added to some mixture which she intended giving to her daughter as a remedy against fits. **1887** 'SPERANZA' WILDE *Superstitions of Ireland* II 95. Take nine pieces of a dead man's skull, grind them to powder, and then mix with a decoction of wall rue. Give the patient [epileptic] a spoonful of this mixture every morning fasting, till the whole potion is swallowed. None must be left, or the dead man would come to look for the pieces of his skull.

Cf. CORPSE'S HAND cures.

SKULL, eating or drinking from: cures

AD **77** PLINY *Natural History* XXVIII II (1856, V 277) For epilepsy, Artemon has prescribed water drawn from a spring in the night, and drunk from the skull of a man who has been slain, and whose body remains unburnt. *c*.1350 HIGDEN *Polychronicon* (MS Harl. 2261, tr. Trevisa: Rolls V 371) þis Albuinus had .. overcome þe kyng of Gispides, and i-made hym a cuppe of his skulle forto drinke of. **1584** SCOT *Discoverie of Witchcraft* XII XIV. For the falling evill .. Drinke in the night at a spring, water out of a skull of one that hath been slaine. **1836** *Perthshire Courier* 11 Aug. 3. In a parish to the northward of Dunkeld .. two junior members [of a particular family] had been subject to epileptic fits, and the mother, impressed with belief in .. a barbarous superstition, viz., that food prepared *in a human skull* was an unfailing remedy for that disease—had .. procured one for the purpose of proving its efficacy .. It was a principal of the charm that the mess should be boiled upon fire raised upon the march between two large properties .. Oatmeal porridge was boiled at the proper time and .. place, a human skull forming the pot! .. The operation was performed with all due secrecy—for the charm was imperfect if the patient was made aware of the circumstances. **1851** *N & Q* 1st ser. IV 227–8 [Drumcondra, Dublin] On the borders of this churchyard there is a well .. resorted to by the folks of the village afflicted with toothache, who, on their way across the graves pick up an old skull, which they carry with them to drink from .. which they assert to be an infallible cure. **1962** A. ROSS *Listener* 30 Aug. 314. In certain areas of the .. Highlands it was believed, until recent times, that well water drunk from the skull of an ancestor was a certain cure for epilepsy.

SKULL, moss from: cures

AD **77** PLINY *Natural History* XXVIII XI (1856, V 293) Any plant which may happen to have grown there [in a human skull], if chewed, will cause the [aching] teeth to come out. *c*.1620 *Arcana Fairfax* (1890, 61) Magneticall cure of a Wound .. Take of the mosse of the skull of a

strangled man 2 ounces. **1627** BACON
Sylva Sylvarum § 980. It is approved,
that the Mosse, which groweth upon
the Skull of a Dead Man, unburied, will
stanch Bloud Potently. *ante* **1646** J.
GREGORY *Posthuma* (1649, 63) The Principal Ingredient of the weapon-Salv, is
the Moss of a dead Man's-skul. *c.***1665**
(*Archaeologia* XXXVII 4) One Shoesmith
. . was requested by a London correspondent to collect and send [as medicine for the plague] some of the 'moss
that grows on dead men's sculls and
bones', since his 'father saith he has
formerly seen a greate deale at Win-
chelsea [Sussex] in or neare the church.'
1744 R. BOYLE *Works* IV 212 'Porousness
of Animal Bodies'. Having been one
summer frequently subject to bleed at
the nose, and reduced to employ several
remedies . . I found the most effectual to
stanch the blood, was some moss of a
dead man's skull, (sent for a present
out of Ireland). **1787** GROSE *Provincial
Glossary* Superstitions 56. Moss growing
on a human skull, if dried, powdered,
and taken as snuff, will cure the headach. **1911** *Folklore* 56 [Co. Clare] There
is some belief relating to moss upon
skulls which I could not get explained,
but I was asked not to pull it off.

SKULL, tooth from: cures

AD **77** PLINY *Natural History* XXVIII 11
(1856, V 277) Apollonius . . informs us
. . that the most effectual remedy for
tooth-ache is to scarify the gums with
the tooth of a man who has died a
violent death. **1579** LUPTON *Thousand
Notable Things* X § 15. The toothe of a
man hanged at the necke of the partye
that is tormented with toothe ache, doth
take away the payne therof, especially:
if a Beane be put therto, wherin there is
a hoale bored, and a lowse put therin,
and ye same beane wrapt in a peece of
sylk, and then hanged about the parties
neck, as is before sayde. **1688** AUBREY
Remaines (1881, 164–5) [Bristol] I remember at Bristow (when I was a boy)
it was a common fashion for the
woemen, to get a Tooth out of a Sckull
in ye ch: yard, wch they wore as a preservative against the Tooth-ach. **1838**
A. E. BRAY *Devonshire* II 292. Here is the
cure . . if the sufferer have a tooth left

sufficiently whole to enable him to use
it. 'Take an old skull found in the churchyard, bite a tooth out of it, and keep it
in your pocket all the year round.' **1851**
N & Q 1st ser. IV 227–8 [Drumcondra,
Dublin] The folks of the village afflicted
with toothache . . resort to . . pulling a
tooth from a skull, which they place on
or over the hole or stump of the grown
tooth, and they affirm that . . the pain
ceases. **1867** *Trans. Devon. Ass.* 39. The
tooth ache is cured, and . . exemption
from it for the future is supposed to be
attained, by biting out a tooth from a
corpse or skull; and very recently, a
skeleton having been discovered at
Croyde, the jaws were quickly denuded
of all their teeth by the number of
persons who hastened to the spot to bite
them out. **1872** *N & Q* 4th ser. IX 257
[West Auckland, Co. Durham] The aged
sexton . . engaged in digging a grave . .
threw up a skull . . and remarked . .
that if he was ever troubled with the
toothache he was only to pull one of the
teeth out with his own, and he would
be cured on the spot. **1909** M. TREVELYAN
Folk-Lore of Wales 321. To bury an old
tooth in the churchyard will relieve the
owner of toothache.

SKULL unlucky to move

1831 J. ROBY *Traditions of Lancs.* II 285.
Wardley Hall is an ancient building
about seven miles west from Manchester
. . A human skull was formerly shown
here . . which the occupiers would not
permit to be removed. This grim fixture,
it was said . . never failed to punish the
individual . . who should dare to lay
hands on it. **1872** *N & Q* 4th ser. X
183. At a farmhouse in [Bettiscombe]
Dorsetshire at the present time is carefully preserved a human skull . . The
peculiar superstition attaching to it is,
that if it be brought out of the house, the
house itself would rock to its foundation,
whilst the person by whom such an act
of desecration was committed, would die
within the year. It is . . suggestive of the
power of this superstition, that through
many changes of tenancy . . the skull
still holds its 'accustomed place'. **1873**
N & Q 4th ser. XI 64. There are the
remains of a skull . . at Tunstead, a
farmhouse about a mile and a-half from

Chapel-en-le-Frith [Cheshire]. It is said that if this skull is removed everything on the farm will go wrong . . I saw this skull about six weeks ago, and many of the country people still believe that it has these magic powers.

Cf. EXHUMATION.

SLEEPING north/south

1646 BROWNE *Vulgar Errors* 69. Eusebius Nierembergius . . a Jesuit of Spain delivers, that the body of man is magneticall . . If this be true, the bodies of Christians doe lye unnaturally in their graves, and the Jews have fallen upon the natural position, who in the reverence of their Temple, do place their beds from North to South. 1648 HERRICK *Hesperides* 188 'Observation'. Who to the North, or South, doth set His Bed, Male children shall beget. 1887 'SPERANZA' WILDE *Superstitions of Ireland* II 98. A sick person's bed must be placed north and south, not crossways. 1923 [Trowbridge, Wilts.] If you put bedsteads with the heads to the north and the feet to the south you will sleep better on them than if you placed them from east to west. 1927 E. GLYN *Wrinkle Book* 9–10. While we are on the subject of rejuvenation . . always sleep with your head to the Magnetic North, because there are strong currents which rush through the earth, from the North Pole to the South Pole, and . . receptivity to them is a good thing for elimination of impurities . . This rule makes all the difference to the growth and health of children. 1953 Man, *c.*40 [London] It is healthy to sleep with your head towards the north and your feet towards the south.

SLEEPING: young and old together

*c.*900 BC I Kings I: 1–2. Now king David was old and stricken in years; and they covered him with clothes, but he gat no heat. Wherefore his servants said unto him, Let there be sought for my lord the king a young virgin; and let her . . lie in thy bosom, that my lord the king may get heat. 1973 B. SLEIGH *The Smell of Privet* 22 [Birmingham] Slept with her [great-aunt] because of the grisly theory that the old absorb vitality from the young if they sleep together.

SNAIL = spirit of the dead

1954 Teacher, *c.*25 [Ballingry, Fife] The most interesting superstition I discovered from the children—for I had practised it myself in Cowdenbeath, *c.*1944—bespeaks of a rudimentary belief in reincarnation. 'If you see a large black snail, spit on it and say "It's no ma Dye [Grandad], an' it's no ma Grannie".'

Cf. MOTH/BUTTERFLY omen of death.

SNAIL: divination

1714 GAY *Shepherd's Week* 34 [May Day] I seiz'd the vermine, home I quickly sped, And on the hearth the milk-white embers spread. Slow crawl'd the snail, and if I right can spell, In the soft Ashes mark'd a curious L. 1827 HONE *Every-day Book* II 20 May [Falkirk, Stirling. May Day] If it is placed on a slate, then . . it will describe by its turning, the initials of their future husband's name. 1876 *N & Q* 5th ser. VI 158 [Ireland] On May Eve the young people used to go into the fields . . and collect snails. The creature was placed on a dinner-plate covered pretty thickly with flour, and . . on the morning of May Day the marks made on the flour by the crawling of the snail were interpreted as the initials of the girl's future husband. 1883 BURNE *Shropshire* 179. Take a black snail by the horns, and throw it over your shoulder on to the hearth at night. In the morning, its slimy trail among the ashes will show the initials of your future husband. 1916 *Folklore* 262. I myself know of a comparatively recent case in Co. Cork, where the little slug was hunted for and found early on May morning, placed on a plate sprinkled with flour, and baked alive in an oven that its writhings might trace in the flour the initials of the future lucky man. 1923 [Martock, Som.] Bring a snail indoors and watch its trail for your sweetheart's initial. 1954 Woman, 47 [Hallowe'en] When I was young, in Hay, Brecon, we used to catch snails and put them under a cover or box-lid to prevent them crawling away. By the morning they were supposed to have traced out in their slime the initials of one's future husband. My snail always crawled up on to the underside of the lid and remained there. **1957** Teacher [Swansea, Glam.] Margaret says she was talking to her grandmother about Hallowe'en customs and her grandmother had just learnt about the snail divination from a London friend. So Margaret got a snail and placed it under an ash-bin lid. But nothing happened and she has not tried since. Another girl has a friend who told her that to find your sweetheart's name you must place a snail against a wall, blocking it in with the inner part of a matchbox. Then in the morning you follow the trail to see if the slime has formed the shape of a letter.

SNAIL indoors

1922 [Bridgwater, Som.] When snails come in the dairy it is a sign of death. **1922** [Bradford-on-Tone, Som.] If a snail comes into your house it is unlucky.

SNAIL, live: cure

1867 *Gents Mag.* pt. I 730 [Suffolk] I have heard of a woman who obtained a certain number of 'hodmidods', or small snails. These were passed through the hands of the invalids, and then suspended in the chimney on a string, in the belief that as they died, the hooping-cough would leave the children.

Cf. WARTS cured with snail.

SNAIL, live: thrown for luck

1827 HONE *Every-Day Book* II 20 May [Falkirk, Stirling. May Day] If they can succeed by the way in catching a snail by the horns, and throwing it over their shoulder, it is an omen of good luck. **1851** *N & Q* 1st ser. III 56 [Lancs.] If black snails are seized by the horn and tossed over the *left* shoulder, the process will insure good luck. **1898** BLAKEBOROUGH *Yorkshire Customs* 133. If you can, within three days after becoming engaged, seize a snail by its horns and throw it over your left shoulder, you will .. reduce the roughness of the road which true love is said to journey along.

SNAIL, meeting

1887 *Folklore* 186. Miners .. had some superstition in regard to snails, known in Cornwall as 'bulhorns', for if they met one on their way to work they always dropped a bit of their dinner or some grease from their lanthorn before him for good-luck. **1900** S. HEWETT *Nummits* 55 [Devon] It is unlucky .. for a miner to meet a snail when entering a mine.

SNAKE buried alive in bottle

1851 *N & Q* 1st ser. III 405 [Withyham, Sussex] For the cure of a common complaint, called 'large neck' .. a common snake, held by its head and tail, is slowly drawn .. nine times across the front part of the neck .. the reptile being allowed, after every third time, to crawl about for a while. Afterwards the snake is put alive into a bottle, which is corked tightly and then buried in the ground. The tradition is, that as the snake decays the swelling vanishes.

SNAKE, first: killed

1855 *N & Q* 1st ser. XII 38 [Cornwall] The killing the first adder you see predicts that you will triumph over your enemies. **1878** *Folk-Lore Record* 9 [Fittleworth, Sussex] To kill the first snake you see in any year will give you power over your enemies for the rest of the twelvemonth. **1923** [Somerset] Kill the first snake you see in the year and put its head in a matchbox, and you will be free from enemies all the year.

SNAKE, meeting or dreaming of

1608 J. HALL *Characters* 88. If hee see a snake vnkilled, he feares a mischiefe. **1895** S. O. ADDY *Household Tales* 67. It is unlucky to dream about snakes, which are your enemies. If in your dream you get safely past them you will overcome all your enemies. **1922** [Martock, Som.] If a snake or a viper do cross your path, watch out for false friends.

SNAKE SLOUGH/SKIN eases childbirth

1579 LUPTON *Thousand Notable Things* IV § 27. Let the Woman that trauels of her chylde, (or is in her labour,) be gyrded with the skynne that a Serpent or Snake castes off: and then she will quickly be delyuered. *c.***1740** *Aristotle's Midwife* 52–3. If it happens .. that the Waters break away too long before the Birth .. there are many .. Things .. Physicians affirm are good in this Case: among which [is] the Skin which a Snake has cast off, girt about the Middle next the Skin. **1897** E. PHILLPOTTS *Lying Prophets* 287 [Cornwall] She picked up the adder's slough, designing to sew it upon a piece of flannel and henceforth wear it against her skin until her baby should be born . . When night came, Joan slept within the mystic circumference of the glen-ader.

SNAKE SLOUGH/SKIN preserves health

1627 BACON *Sylva Sylvarum* § 969. The Writers of Naturall Magick, commend the Wearing of the Spoile of a Snake, for Preserving of Health. I doubt it is but a Conceit; For that the Snake is thought to renue her Youth, by Casting her Spoile. **1685** AUBREY Royal Soc. MS, Nat. Hist. of Wilts. (*Remaines* 1881, 224) For the prick of a thorne . . a piece of the slough of an adder . . tye it to the wrong side of the finger or, &c. that is prick't with a thorne: it will open the orrifice that you may pluck it forth. From Mrs Markey, Sir Jo. Hoskyn's aunt. **1686–7** AUBREY *Remaines* (1881, 38) The Sussexians doe weare them for Hatt-bands, wch they say doe preserve them from the gripeing of the Gutts. **1797** Swete MS XV [Devon Record Office] I saw an old Rustic with the exuviae, or skin, of a large snake wreathed as a band round his hat; I had the curiosity to enquire whether he thus wore it for ornament or use; he replied that he never went without it for that, if by accident he had taken into his flesh a thorn, or prickle, the application of this Snake-skin would operate as a charm, and instantly extract it. **1877** JEFFERIES *Gamekeeper at Home* II [nr. Swindon, Wilts.] She has had snakes' skins, or more properly sloughs, for the curious . . Some country folk put them in their hats to cure headache, which is a very old superstition, but more in sport than earnest. **1912** LEATHER *Herefordshire* 81. The folk at Westhope search for the cast adder-skins on Birley Hill in the spring . . They say, 'If you have a thorn in your hand, apply the adder-skin to the other side, and the thorn will come out.' **1935** *I Walked by Night* (ed. L. Rider Haggard, 15–16) [Norfolk] The

cure for Head acke was to get the skin of the Viper and sew it in to the lining of the hat . . people would hunt many miles for these skins in the month of April wen the Vipers shot there skin, and any one finding one could make a good price of it for that purpose.

Cf. EEL-SKIN GARTERS prevent cramp/ rheumatism.

SNAKE SLOUGH/SKIN protects house

1853 *N & Q* 1st ser. VII 152 [Leics.] It'll bring you good luck to hang an ether [adder] skin o'er the chimbly. **1855** *N & Q* 1st ser. XII 38 [Cornwall] The slough of an adder, hung on the rafters, preserves the house against fire. **1922** R. KEARTON *At Home with Wild Nature* 60–1. The slough, or discarded skin, of the adder suspended from a beam in the house was, in the days of unclouded faith, considered as efficacious against fire as any of our up-to-date precautionary measures.

SNAKE STONE

AD **77** PLINY *Natural History* XXIX XII (1856, V 389–90) In summer time . . on a certain day of the moon . . numberless snakes become . . entwined together, and form rings around their bodies with the viscous slime which exudes from their mouths . . The Druids tell us, that the serpents eject these eggs . . by their hissing . . I . . have seen one . . it was round, and about as large as an apple of moderate size . . It is held in high estimation among the Druids. The possession of it is marvellously vaunted as ensuring success in law-suits, and a favourable reception with princes. **1602** R. CAREW *Survey of Cornwall* 21^v. The countrey people retain a conceite, that the Snakes, by their breathing about a hazell wand, doe make a stone ring of blew colour, in which there appeareth the yellow figure of a Snake, & that beasts which are stung, being giuen to drink of the water wherein this stone hath been soked, will therethrough recouer. **1695** E. LHWYD in Camden's *Britannia* (tr. Gibson, 1772, II 683) In most parts of Wales we find it a common opinion of the vulgar, that about Midsummer-Eve . . 'tis usual for snakes to meet in companies, and that by joyning heads together and hissing, a kind of Bubble is form'd like a ring about the head of one of them, which the rest by continual hissing blow on till it comes off at the tail, and then it immediately hardens, and resembles a glass ring; which whoever finds (as some old women and children are perswaded) shall prosper in all his undertakings. The rings .. are call'd *Gleineu Nadroeth*, i.e. *Gemmae Anguinae*. 1753 T. RICHARDS *Antiquae Linguae Britanniae. Glain y nadraedd* .. Snake-stones .. call'd also Maen magl, because accounted good for a web in the eye. 1855 *N & Q* 1st ser. XI 345. All that I have seen were merely blue, green, or striped glass beads. They are still used as charms to assist dentition, cure ague and whooping cough. The querist will be very likely to find one in some of the London curiosity shops. 1865 *Gents Mag.* pt. 2 699 [Ireland] Glein Naidr or 'the adder stone'—ensures good luck for the owner. 1865 R. HUNT *West of England* 2nd ser. 220 [Land's End, Cornwall] It was not safe [because of the adders] to venture amongst the furze .. without a milpreve .. a beautiful ball of coralline lime-stone, the section of the coral being thought to be entangled young snakes. 1909 M. TREVELYAN *Folk-Lore of Wales* 170–1 [Glam.] I have before me .. a Maen Magi of a soft pink shade blended with lilac. The tints resemble those of the opal. It is over two hundred years old, and feels extremely cold to touch .. The owner of the bead states that for inflammation of the eyes, ulceration of the eye-lids, and for sties, it is a never-failing cure if held or rubbed upon the affected part .. Several persons .. said they were eye-witnesses of the great snake congress in the spring [on May Eve]. One of them states that it is the time when the snakes select a new king, and the old colony rises up in arms against the younger generation. The newly chosen monarch and his party are victorious. Some of my informants have seen in the midst of the snake froth the Maen Magi. 1983 *Folklore* 184. The snakestone was in considerable demand in the neighbourhood [Llansamlet, Glam., until 1914] for all kinds of eye ailments. The water in which it had been soaked might be used, but most commonly it was revolved several times on the eyelid.

SNEEZE, baby's first

1855 *N & Q* 1st ser. XII 200. A new-born child is in the fairy spells until it sneezes .. I once overheard an old .. dame .. crooning over a new-born child; and then watching it intently .. for nearly a minute, she said, taking a huge pinch of snuff, 'Och! oich! No yet—no yet.' Suddenly the youngster exploded into a tremendous sneeze; when the old lady .. drew her forefinger across the brows of the child .. and joyfully exclaimed, 'God sain the bairn, it's no a warlock.'

SNEEZING: 'bless you'

AD 77 PLINY *Natural History* XXVIII v (1856, V 283) Why is it that we salute a person when he sneezes, an observation which Tiberius Caesar, they say, the most unsociable of men, as we all know, used to exact, when riding in his chariot even? *c.* AD 150 APULEIUS *Golden Ass* (tr. Graves, XIII) 'Bless you, my dear!' he said, and 'bless you, bless you!' at the second and third sneeze. *ante* AD 500 *Greek Anthology* (1874, 181) Dick cannot blow his nose whene'er he pleases, His nose so long is, and his arm so short; Nor ever cries, God bless me! when he sneezes—He cannot hear so distant a report. 1483 *Golden Legend* 22. Our lord was meuyd ayenst them [the Christian Romans] and sente to them a grete pestelence .. that was cruell & sodayne, and caused peple to dye in goyng by the waye, in playeng, in beying atte table, and in spekyng one with another sodeynly they deyed. In this manere somtyme snesynge they deyed, so that whan ony persone was herd snesyng anone they that were by said to hym, god helpe you, Or Cryst helpe, and yet endureth the custome. 1526 ERASMUS *Familiar Colloquies* (1725, 4) Forms of well-wishing .. To one that Sneezes. May it be lucky and happy to you. God keep you. May it be for your Health. God bless it to you. 1608 J. HALL *Characters* 88. When hee neeseth, thinks them not his friends that vncouer not. 1618 J. HARRINGTON *Epigrams* I no. 83 (1930, 180) If one had sneez'd, to say (as is the fashion) Christ help, 'twas witch-craft and deserv'd damnation. **1646** BROWNE *Vulgar Errors* IV ix. Concerning Sternutation or Sneezing, and the custome of saluting or blessing upon that motion, it is .. generally beleeved to derive its originall from a disease, wherein Sternutation proved mortall, and such as Sneezed dyed. **1652** A. ROSS *Arcana Microcosmi* 222. Prometheus was the first that wisht wel to the sneezer, when the man which he had made of clay, fell into a fit of Sternutation upon the approach of that celestiall fire which he stole from the Sun. This gave originall to that custome among the Gentiles in saluting the sneezer. They used also to worship the head in sternutation, as being a divine part. **1688** AUBREY *Remaines* (1881, 103) We have a Custome, that when one sneezes, every one els putts off his hatt, and bowes, and cries God bless ye S^r. I have heard, or read a Story that many yeares since, that Sneezing was an Epidemical Disease and very mortal, wch caused this yet received Custome. **1738** SWIFT *Polite Conversation* I 59 [*Neverout sneezes.*] MISS. God bless you, if you ha'n't taken Snuff. **1753** *Scots Magazine* Nov. 544. They bowed with a graceful simper to a lady who sneezed. **1830** MITFORD *Our Village* IV 299. Who if his neighbour chance to sneeze thinks it a bounden duty to cry God bless him? **1866** HENDERSON *Northern Counties* 106. Nurses in Durham, not to say mothers, still invoke a blessing on children when they sneeze; indeed some extend the practice to adults. **1875** *Monthly Packet* Jan. 9. It is strange how many educated people will persist in dating the national 'God bless you!' from the time of the Great Plague; though we have clear proof to the contrary in *The Golden Legend* .. printed by Caxton in 1483. **1892** *N & Q* 8th ser. I 106. At the Asylum for Fatherless Children at Reedham [Norfolk] a custom prevails amongst the girls of solemnly rising and saying 'God bless you, miss!' whenever a mistress sneezes in their presence. **1934** *N & Q* CLXVII 158. In my youth one often heard a person say 'God bless you! to a child when it sneezed, but I never heard it said to an adult. **1985** Woman, *c.*60 [London] I always say

'Bless you' when I hear someone sneeze—even if they are at the other end of a bus.

Cf. YAWNING: crossing the mouth.

SNEEZING: divination: 'days' rhyme
1848 *Athenaeum* 142 [Herts.] If you sneeze on a Monday, you sneeze for danger; Sneeze on a Tuesday, kiss a stranger; Sneeze on a Wednesday, sneeze for a letter; Sneeze on a Thursday, something better; Sneeze on a Friday, sneeze for sorrow; Sneeze on a Saturday, see your sweetheart tomorrow. Sneeze on a Sunday, and the devil will have domination over you all the week! **1867** HARLAND & WILKINSON *Lancashire Folk-Lore* 68. [As 1848, but ends] 'Sneeze on a Sunday, your safety seek, The Devil will have you the whole of the week.' **1950** Woman, 40 [Scarborough, Yorks.] Sneeze on Monday, sneeze for danger; Sneeze on Tuesday, kiss a stranger; Sneeze on Wednesday, sneeze for a letter; Sneeze on Thursday, something better; Sneeze on Friday, sneeze for woe; Sneeze on a Saturday, a journey to go; Sneeze on Sunday, your safety seek, For Satan will have you the rest of the week.

SNEEZING: divination: number of times
*c.*800 BC HOMER *Odyssey* XVII (tr. Rieu) As she finished, Telemachus gave a loud sneeze, which echoed round the house . . Penelope laughed . . 'Do go,' she said eagerly, 'and bring this stranger here to me. Didn't you notice that my son sneezed a blessing on all I had said?' *c.*275 BC THEOCRITUS *Idylls* XVIII (tr. Creech) O happy Bridegroom! Thee a lucky sneeze to Sparta welcom'd. **1584** SCOT *Discoverie of Witchcraft* XI XIII. A great matter is made of neezing, wherein the number of neezings .. is greatly noted. *Ibid.* XI XIX. But sure it is meere casual, and also very foolish and incredible, that by two neezings, a man should be sure of good luck or successe in his businesse. *c.*1600 MS Lansdowne 121 [British Lib.] 146. Yf a man sneese once or iij tymes lett hym proceade no further in eny matter butt lett all a lone for hit wyll com to nought .. to sneese twise is a good syne but to sneese once or iij tymes is an yll syne ..

if y^t eny man sneese twyse iij nyghtes together it is a tokyn y^t one of ye house shall dye. **1855** *N & Q* 1st ser. XI 17. As I have long understood, to sneeze once is considered lucky; twice in succession unlucky. **1923** [Cosham, Hants.] First a wish, second a kiss, third a letter. **1984** Woman, 37 [Harrow, Middx.] Once a wish, twice a kiss, Three times a letter, Four times something better.

SNEEZING: divination: on left or right

ante **50** BC CATULLUS *Poems* (tr. Michie, XLV) Love, who had before Sneezed on the left-hand side, now sneezed On the right, to show that he was pleased. *c.* AD **110** PLUTARCH *Lives* (tr. North, 1928, II 22) Euphrantides the soothsayer had seen them [the prisoners] and at their arrival observed there rose a great bright flame out of the sacrifice, and at the very self same instant that one on his right hand had sneezed: he took Themistocles by the hand, and willed him to sacrifice all those three prisoners [so that] the Grecians .. should have the victory over their enemies. **1909** M. TREVELYAN *Folk-Lore of Wales* 326. To sneeze to the right is lucky, to the left unfortunate; right in front of you, good news is coming.

SNEEZING: divination: time of day

c. AD **396** ST AUGUSTINE OF HIPPO *De Doctrina Christiana* I xx (tr. Robertson, 56) Similar [superstitious] practices are .. to go back to bed if anyone sneezes while you are putting on your shoes. **1584** SCOT *Discoverie of Witchcraft* XI XIII. A great matter is made of neezing, wherein .. the time thereof is greatly noted. Ibid. xv. Many will go to bed againe, if they neeze before their shooes be on their feet. **1603** W. PERKINS *Works* 39. It is vnluckie for one in the morning .. to sneeze in drawing on his shooes. **1848** *Athenaeum* 142. If you sneeze any morning before breakfast, you will have a present before the week is out. **1851** *N & Q* 1st ser. IV 99 [Devon] If you sneeze on a Saturday night after the candle is lighted, you will next week see a stranger. **1880** *N & Q* 4th ser. I 42. Whoever sneezes at an early hour either hears some news or receives some present the same day. **1923** [Lyng, Som.] It is unlucky to sneeze on a Sunday night after the lamp or gas is lit. **1982** Woman, 20 [Cleveland, Yorks.] A gift is said to be predicted if somebody sneezes before breakfast.

Cf. SHOES/STOCKINGS, putting on.

SOAP breaks

1923 [Rowbarton, Som.] If soap breaks in two—it's a true sign of parting.

Cf. BREAD: loaf, cake, etc. breaks.

SOAP falls from hands

1875 *N & Q* 5th ser. IV 9. A friend of mine .. was washing his hands .. when the soap, as it often does, slipped out of his hand into the basin. 'Dear me,' he cried, 'that means a death!' **1876** *N & Q* 5th ser. VI 323. A woman in the Highlands, named Kate Elshender, went to a quarry hole to wash her clothes. As she passed the village shop she went in and bought half a pound of soap, and proceeded to wash; the soap slipped out of her hands, and she went back and bought another half pound. The shop keeper warned her to be careful, remembering the old superstition .. It again slipped from her hands, and she returned for a third half pound .. This time the old woman in the shop was thoroughly frightened, and begged .. her not to go back again; but she would go .. Shortly after the old woman .. went away to the quarry .. found no one there .. gave the alarm, and .. the said Kate Elshender was discovered, drowned, at the bottom of the quarry hole. **1909** M. TREVELYAN *Folk-Lore of Wales* 7. Soap frequently falling means 'fresh work'.

SOAP, giving or lending

1909 M. TREVELYAN *Folk-Lore in Wales* 210. If a woman borrows soap and thanks you for it, she is a witch. **1912** LEATHER *Herefordshire* 87. Two persons, more especially if they are sisters, must not pass soap from hand to hand; it should be put down by the first, so that the other can take it up. **1980** Woman, 52 [Colchester, Essex] It's unlucky to give soap as a present. It will wash the friendship away.

SOAP left behind in theatre

1932 C. IGGLESDEN *Those Superstitions* 234 [in theatre] When moving from one room to another soap must never be left behind. **1952** W. GRANVILLE *Theatrical Terms* 179. To leave soap behind when on tour is considered an ill-omen. **1968** *Observer* Suppl. 24 Nov. 13 [Peter Bull, actor] You must never leave your bit of soap at the end of a run; you must take it or you'll never get another job. **1984** Ex chorus-girl, 37 [Harrow, Middx.] If I ever leave a piece of soap somewhere I never go back there—it's happened time and again.

SOOT, fall of

*c.*1828 Calvert MS, Pickering, Yorks. (G. HOME *Evolution of an English Town* 214) It be held to be a sure sign that an ailing body will die if there be a downcome of soot. **1948** E. & M. A. RADFORD *Superstitions* 223 [Scotland] If during a wedding breakfast, a clot of soot should come down the chimney, it is a sign of bad luck for those married. **1988** *Woman*, 60. At home in South Shields [Co. Durham] my mother always said a fall of soot was 'a bad sign'.

SOUL CAKE

1817 G. YOUNG *History of Whitby* II 882. The custom of making soul mass loaves, on the day of all-souls, Nov. 2, is kept up to a certain extent: they are small round loaves, sold by the bakers at a farthing each, chiefly for presents to children. In former times it was usual to keep one or two of them for good luck: a lady in Whitby has a soul mass loaf about 100 years old. **1851** DENHAM *North of England* (1895, 26) A few thrifty, elderly housewives, still practice the old custom of keeping a soul mass-cake (2 November), for good luck.

Cf. GOOD FRIDAY, bread made on: protects.

SOWING: part missed out

1853 *N & Q* 1st ser. VII 353. In Norfolk .. labourers generally believe that if a drill go from one end of a field to the other without depositing any seed—an accident which may result from the tubes and coulters clogging with earth—some person connected with the farm will die before the year expires, or before the crop then sown is reaped. **1856** *Gents Mag.* pt. 1 39 [Worcs.] At Mathon, some people believe that if land is left unsown in a field there will be a death in the family within the year, and when the accident is discovered they never sow it again. **1883** BURNE *Shropshire* 296–7. A 'butt' of land accidentally missed in sowing a field [is a death-token]. **1912** LEATHER *Herefordshire* 118. It is an omen of death if a 'reeve' or ridge be missed when sowing the corn; this sometimes happened before the introduction of machine drills.

SOWING postponed

1881 W. GREGOR *North-East of Scotland* 181. When the seed was once taken to the field, it must on no account be taken back to the barn, if the weather broke, and prevented it from being sown. It lay on the field till .. the soil became fit for being sown, however long the time might be.

SPADE etc.: on shoulder in house

1855 *N & Q* 1st ser. XII 488. Nothing more presages a death in the family, than for a labourer to enter his cottage with a mattock, shovel, or spade (the sexton's implements) on his shoulder. **1883** BURNE *Shropshire* 280. It is most unlucky to carry an axe, or any sharp tool, on your shoulder through the house, as it is a sign of the death of one or more of the inmates. Some extend this omen to *any* tool carried on the shoulder through a house. At Pulverbatch and Wenlock a spade is the fatal implement; it is a certain sign that a grave will shortly be dug for some member of the household. **1912** LEATHER *Herefordshire* 119. If a man come into the house with a shovel or any edged tool on his shoulder it is 'terrible bad luck', or a sign of a death. 'I've seen mother sit down and cry over it.' **1922** UDAL *Dorsetshire* 286. It is unlucky to carry a spade into the house on your shoulder.

Cf. BOOTS on shoulder.

SPEAKING at same time

1738 SWIFT *Polite Conversation* 1 30. Colonel, you shall be married first, I was just going to say that. **1755** *Connoisseur* 20 Feb. If she happens to bring out any thing in conversation which another person was about to say, she comforts herself that she shall be married before them. **1887** *Folk-Lore Record* 215 [Cornwall] When two people accidentally say the same thing at the same time the one who finishes first will be married first. **1895** S. O. ADDY *Household Tales* 95. If two people say the same thing at the same time they should lock their little fingers together and wish, and the wish will come true. **1909** M. TREVELYAN *Folk-Lore of Wales* 282. If two people express the same thought at the same moment, one of them will die before the year is out. *c.***1914** [Swansea, Glam.] If two people utter the same word simultaneously they link little fingers, wish, and then pronounce a poet's name—but not Shakespeare's, that would destroy the wish. **1923** [West Malling, Kent] If two persons say the same thing at the same time, the one who refrains longest from speaking again will receive a letter. **1935** Girl, 13 [Bath, Som.] When two people say the same thing at the same moment without saying anything further, they hook right-hand little fingers, say the name of a poet (not Shakespeare or Burns, which spears or burns your wish), silently make a wish, and then one says, 'I wish, I wish your wish come true,' and the other replies, 'I wish, I wish the same to you.' But if you both said the same poet that invalidated the whole thing. **1952** [Glasgow] Children link their little fingers and say, 'Pinkety, pinkety, thumb to thumb, wish a wish, and it's sure to come.' **1953** Girl, 15 [Ipswich, Suffolk] If two people say exactly the same, at exactly the same time, touch wood, touch knee, and whistle, and this is supposed to bring the first one to do so a letter.

SPEAKING first and last words

*c.***1816** Wilkie MS (HENDERSON *Northern Counties* 1866, 143) It .. is unlucky to be praised by a witch, or indeed to hold any conversation with her, and our only safety consists in having the last word. **1886** *Folklore* 13 [Fraserburg, Aberdeen.] Another mode of counteracting the evil of an 'ill fit' [unlucky foot] is to have 'the first word o' the one that has the evil power', that is, to be the first to speak. **1903** *N & Q* 9th ser. XI 208. When a boy on Deeside, forty years ago, I knew an old woman who was reputed to be 'uncanny' .. I was told, when I met her, always to speak to her before she could speak to me, as that would counteract her 'ill ee'.

SPEAKING in rhyme

1912 LEATHER *Herefordshire* 86. If a rhyme be made in talking, without intention, it is a sign that the speaker will have a present before the end of the month.

SPECTACLES, distrust of

1868 *N & Q* 4th ser. II 202. When I first came to London, I was constantly annoyed by a certain class of persons 'spitting aside' when they passed me. I one day asked a servant girl, who by accident spat upon my foot, what she meant by it, and the reply was, 'I should have bad luck if I didn't spit at a gentleman in spectacles.' **1954** *Daily Sketch* 22 Sept. 24. Tom Smith, the gipsy, finally consented .. His .. daughter could marry Norman, even though he did wear glasses .. Said Emily: 'Dad did not like Norman's glasses. Gipsies don't believe in them.' Grannie .. had the last word: 'We don't like four-eyes,' she said.

Cf. EYES, peculiar.

SPEEDWELL, picking

1878 *Folk-Lore Record* 159. In some parts of Yorkshire it is said that if a child gathers the germander speedwell .. its mother will die during the year. **1923** [Somerset] If you pick the blue speedwell birds will pick your eyes out. **1947** Girl, 11 [Brierley Hill, Staffs.] If one picks bird's-eye flowers, the birds will pick your eyes out. **1985** R. VICKERY *Unlucky Plants* 79 [Wigston Magna, Leics.] As a small child, I believed that if I picked the small blue flower—speedwell?—birds would come and peck my eyes out .. we used to call the flower 'Bird's eye'.

SPIDER, big = death

1923 [Somerset] If a big black spider comes into the house it is a sure sign of death. **1957** Girl, 11 [Swansea, Glam.]

To see big spiders is a sign of death; middle sized, means illness. **1975** Woman, 63 [Sheffield, Yorks.] If a very tiny spider landed on you it was considered very good luck when I was a child . . But children were usually scared or disgusted with a *big* spider.

SPIDER, 'money spinner'

1507 *Gospelles of Dystaues* pt. 2 XVI. Whan a man fyndeth a spyder vpon his gowne it is a synge to be that daye ryght happye. **1594** NASHE *Terrors of the Night* D1. If a spinner creepe vppon him, hee shall haue golde raine downe from heauen. **1662** FULLER *Worthies* pt. 2 58. When a Spider is found upon our clothes, we use to say, some money is coming towards us. The Moral is this, such who .. imitate the industry of that contemptible creature .. may by Gods blessing weave themselves into wealth and procure a plentiful estate. **1732** DEFOE *Memoirs of Mr Campbell* 60. Others have thought themselves secure of receiving Money, if .. by chance, a little Spider fell upon their Cloaths. *c.*1780 T. PARK MS note in Brand's *Antiquities* 93. Small spiders termed Money-Spinners are held by many to prognosticate good luck if they are not destroyed or injured or removed from the person on whom they are first observed. *c.*1816 Wilkie MS (HENDERSON *Northern Counties* 1866, 83) A spider descending upon you from the roof is a token that you will soon have a legacy from a friend. **1831** HONE *Year Book* 29 Feb. To always have money in your pocket, put into it small spiders, called money spinners. **1850** *N & Q* 1st ser. II 165 [Northants.] The small spiders called 'money spinners' prognosticate good luck .. to propitiate which, they must be thrown over the left shoulder. **1851** *N & Q* 1st ser. III 3 [Northants.] When a spider is found upon your clothes, or about your person, it signifies that you will shortly receive some money. **1899** *Newcastle Weekly Chronicle* 11 Feb. 7 [Jesmond] A spider on a coat indicates that we are about to get a new one. **1914** *Folklore* 365 [Newmarket, Cambs.] If you catch the spider known as 'a money-spinner', wave it round your head three times and then let it crawl on the top of your

head, it brings money. **1922** [Trowbridge, Wilts.] If a small red spider (called by some the 'money spinner') is on your clothes you will receive money. **1942** A. L. ROWSE *Cornish Childhood* IX. I took a money-spider which crawled over my arm while working for the County Scholarship as a good omen. It was. **1961** Boy, 13 [Norwich, Norfolk] Little red spiders are called 'Money Spiders'. If you find one put it on your hand, whirl it round your head three times, and flick it off. This should bring you some money. **1983** Woman, 21 [Yorks.] It is lucky to find a money spider, the very small spider, on you, and if you swallow it, it will bring you money. **1983** Girl, 13 [Maldon, Essex] My sister and I think that money spiders are good luck if you twirl your spider round your head three times.

SPIDER, 'ticking'

1923 [Somerset] If you hear a ticking spider in the wall it is a sign of death. **1967** S. MARSHALL *Fenland Chronicle* pt. 2 IX. A ticking-spider was a sure sign of death.

Cf. DEATH-WATCH BEETLE.

SPIDER OR SPIDER'S WEB cures ague as amulet

AD 77 PLINY *Natural History* XXX xxx (1856, V 456) In cases of tertian fever .. it may be worth while to make trial whether the web of the spider called 'lycos' is of any use, applied, with the insect itself, to the temples .. in a compress .. or the insect .. attached to the body in a reed .. is said to be highly beneficial for other fevers. **1597** GERARD *Herball* 1006 [Such cures] are .. vaine .. as my selfe haue prooued .. hauing a most greeuous ague and of long continuance; notwithstanding .. spiders put into a walnut shell, and diuers such foolish toies that I was constrained to take by fantasticke peoples procurement. **1660** BURTON *Anatomy of Melancholy* pt. 2 sect. 5 mem. 1 subs. 5. Being in the Country in the vacation time not many years since at Lindley in Leicestershire, my Father's house, I first observed this Amulet of a Spider in a nut-shell lapped in silk, &c. so applied for an Ague by my Mother .. this

methought was most absurd and ridiculous, I could see no warrant for it
.. till at length, rambling among authors
(as often I do) I found this very medicine
in Dioscorides, approved by Matthiolus,
repeated by Aldrovandus .. I began to
have a better opinion of it, and to give
more credit to Amulets, when I saw it
in some parties answer to experience.
1678 W. SALMON *London Dispensatory*
256. The Spider being made into a
plaster and laid to the Wrists and
Temples cures Agues .. So also if they
be put into a nutshell, and hung about
the neck. **1681** ASHMOLE *Diary* 11 Apr.
I took early in the Morning a good dose
of Elixir, and hung three Spiders about
my Neck, and they drove my Ague
away—Deo gratias. **1736** E. ALBIN *Natural History of Spiders* 3–4. In the cure
of intermitting fevers, when the bark
and other remedies have failed .. I have
.. cured several children .. by hanging
a large Spider confined alive in a box
about their neck. **1850** *N & Q* 1st ser. II
130 [Somerset] One of my parishioners,
suffering from ague, was advised to
catch a large spider and shut him up in
a box. As he pines away, the disease
is supposed to wear itself out. **1923**
[Somerset] Three spiders in a bag hung
round the neck is a remedy for the
'aigey'.

SPIDER OR SPIDER'S WEB cures ague as medicine

1678 W. SALMON *London Dispensatory*
257. The Spiders Web .. some use it
outwardly against Agues .. others adventure to give it inwardly. **1736** E.
ALBIN *Natural History of Spiders* 3–4. I
will now publish [a cure for fevers] for
the benefit of poor and country people,
who are remote from the help of physicians .. As much of the clean web of
the house Spider as the weight of two
scruples [etc.] Give to the patients the
night before the fit .. after the second
dose it will leave them. **1747** J. WESLEY
Primitive Physick 26. For an Ague .. six
middling Pills, of Cobwebs .. I never
knew this fail. **1757** S. HARRISON *Housekeepers Pocket-Book* pt. 2. For an Ague ..
Take a Spider alive, cover it with new,
soft, crummy Bread .. let the Patient
swallow it fasting. **1850** *N & Q* 1st ser.

II 259. A lady in the south of Ireland
was celebrated far and near .. for the
cure [of ague]. Her universal remedy
was a large house-spider alive, and en-
veloped in treacle or preserve. Of course
the parties were carefully kept in ignorance of what the wonderful remedy
was. **1867** *Gents Mag*. pt. 1 731 [Suffolk]
To swallow a spider, or its web, when
placed in a small piece of apple, is an
acknowledged cure for ague .. It is
employed not only by the poor, but
by the better-informed. **1894** A. HARE
Sussex 171. Mr Warter, the vicar of West
Ferring, has testified to the prevalence
among the peasantry thereabouts of
such superstitions as the following. Pills
made of spiders' webs are prescribed by
unqualified practitioners as a remedy for
ague. **1902** F. A. KNIGHT *Sea-Board of
Mendip* 296. There are people in Brean
[Som.] who still, it is said, consider
spiders as efficacious remedies for ague
.. Sometimes the spider is .. made into
a pill with bread. Sometimes a live spider
is put in water, and when 'he do curly
up', both water and spider are swallowed. **1904** *N & Q* 10th ser. I 317–18.
In the spring of 1871 I was staying at
Wakefield [Yorks.], in the house of the
Rev. Thomas Pearson, an old West Indian missionary. I was making merry
over Wesley's 'Primitive Physic', and
particularly over cobweb pills as a remedy for ague, or for anything. Mrs Pearson quietly observed, 'You may laugh,
but I have many times cured Mr Pearson
of ague with cobweb pills, when we
were abroad' .. Mrs Pearson swept down
the cobwebs, and with bread mixed them
into pills. **1912** *Folklore* 353. When,
about 1897, a man of my acquaintance,
living near Dartford [Kent], was ill of
ague, one of the old women visiting him
suggested that he should swallow a live
spider, which would cause the ague
egg to be vomited. **1922** [Trowbridge,
Wilts.] A live spider swallowed in water
will cure the ague.

SPIDER OR SPIDER'S WEB cures bleeding

AD **77** PLINY *Natural History* XXIX xxxvi
(1856, V 410) For fractures of the cra-
nium, cobwebs are applied, with oil and
vinegar .. Cobwebs are good, too, for
stopping the bleeding of wounds made

in shaving. *c.*1240 BARTHOLOMAEUS *De Proprietatibus Rerum* (tr. Trevisa, XVIII 314) Thoughe the spinner be venemous, yet the webbe that commethe oute of the guttes therof is not venemouse but is acounted full good and profitable to the vse of medycyne. And as Dyoscorides sayth the coppe webbe that is whyte & clene .. hath vertue to .. joyne .. and to restreyne. And therefore it stauncheth bloud .. and healeth a newe wounde, if it be layed therto. 1579 LUPTON *Thousand Notable Things* VIII § 88. If a Spider be put in a lynnen cloath a lytle brused, and holden to the nose that bleedes .. by & by the bloud wil stay, and the nose wil leave bleeding .. The venemous Spyder is so contrary, and such an enemie to mans bloud, that the bloud drawes backe. *c.*1595 SHAKESPEARE *Midsommer Nights Dreame* III i. I shall desire you of more acquaintance, good Master Cobweb: if I cut my finger, I shall make bold with you. 1678 W. SALMON *London Dispensatory* 257. The Spiders Web helps Haemorrhages. 1736 E. ALBIN *Natural History of Spiders* 4. Their web .. is a most excellent styptick for bleeding at the nose, or any slight wound .. With this remedy I saved a gentleman of worth in Lincolns-Inn-Fields, who had bled at the nose several hours. 1774 L. SHAW (PENNANT *Tour in Scotland* app. 2 I 272–3) When one is bit by a mad dog .. he with a razor .. cuts out the flesh .. sucks the blood .. and covers the wound with a handful of cobwebs. 1969 E. PORTER *Cambridgeshire* 79 [Man, 53, Comberton, 1964] If ever he cut himself when working in a barn, stable or cowshed and there was a cobweb handy [he] applied it to the wound. He admitted, though, that on returning home he took the precaution of cleansing the cut and applying a patent germicidal ointment .. 'My old dad never did that, though,' he said, 'nor his dad neither, and they never came to no harm.'

SPIDER OR SPIDER'S WEB cures whooping cough

1856 *N & Q* 2nd ser. I 386 [Reepham, Norfolk] He caught a common housespider, which he tied up in muslin, and pinned over the mantlepiece .. when it died the cough went away. 1867 *Gents Mag.* pt. I 731 [Suffolk] Procure a live spider, shut it up between two walnutshells, and wear it on your person. As the spider dies, the cough will go away. 1951 *Trans. Devon. Ass.* 75 [Budleigh Salterton] Catch a spider and place in a bag round the neck. When the spider dies the whooping cough will go.

SPIDER OR SPIDER'S WEB, harming

1777 BRAND *Antiquities* 93. It is vulgarly thought unlucky to kill Spiders .. it serves in many Places for an Apology for the Laziness of Housewives, in not destroying the Cobwebs. 1853 *N & Q* 1st ser. VII 152 [Essex] The harvest-man [harvest spider] has got four things on its back—the scythe, the rake, the sickle, and (Query the fourth?). It's most unlucky for the reaper to kill it on purpose. 1863 *N & Q* 3rd ser. III 262. In this county [Kent] I have often heard the following couplet: 'If you wish to live and thrive, Let a spider run alive.' 1866 HENDERSON *Northern Counties* 267. About nine years ago, my friend the Rev. J. B. Dykes .. while visiting an old woman .. observed a spider near her bed, and attempted to destroy it. She at once .. told him .. that spiders ought not to be killed; for .. when our Blessed Lord lay in the manger .. the spider .. spun a beautiful web, which protected the innocent Babe. 1895 S. O. ADDY *Household Tales* 66. In the East Riding they say, 'Never kill a spider; there is room in the world for us and it.' 1900 S. HEWETT *Nummits* 58 [Devon] Who kills a spider, Bad luck betides her. 1909 *N & Q* 10th ser. XII 484 [Stromness, Orkney] If you wish to thrive, Let the spider go alive. 1923 [Rowbarton, Som.] Never kill a spider, but sweep them out of doors, or you'll lose your luck. 1933 J. B. BOOTH *Pink Parade* 97. You should never destroy a cobweb you may find behind the scenes [in a theatre]. 1957 *Woman's Own* 2 Oct. 7 [Battle, Sussex] I was taking down the cobwebs in a stable preparatory to whitewashing it when one of the milk roundsmen told me that if cobwebs were taken down in a stable a horse would go lame. Sure enough, a few days later, one of the horses was lame. 1965 [Scarborough, Yorks.] Peggy frequently quotes 'If you wish to live and thrive, Let a spider run alive.' **1982** Woman, 57 [Poole, Dorset] I brushed aside a spider's web on our sailing boat, when I was a child, and my father exploded. He was Scottish, and he thought it terribly unlucky to break a spider's web.

SPINNING WHEEL on ship

1909 M. TREVELYAN *Folk-Lore of Wales* 4. The old Welsh sea-captains would not allow spinning-wheels on board, for they brought disaster.

Cf. PINS on ship.

SPITTING for luck

c. AD **60** PETRONIUS *Satyricon* sect. 74. She will not spit in her bosom for luck. **1911** *N & Q* 11th ser. III 217–18. Spitting 'for luck' is still practised .. on marbles or buttons whilst playing games with them. **1919** *Morning Post* 9 June 3. Nearly every sailor spits in his boat for luck, and in the North Sea every fisherman spits into his trawl or dredge before lowering it into the sea. **1953** Boy, 9 [Sale, Cheshire] You spit on a marble to change your luck.

SPITTING for luck: on money

*c.***1816** Wilkie MS (HENDERSON *Northern Counties* 1866, 143–4) Should you receive money from a witch, put it at once into your mouth, for fear the donor should spirit it away, and supply its place with a round stone .. Old people constantly put into their mouths the money which is paid them. **1861** C. C. ROBINSON *Dialect of Leeds* 301. When a coin has been given, or come, somewhat unexpectedly, it is spit upon 'for luck' before it goes into the pocket. **1864** DICKENS *Our Mutual Friend* I. He chinked it once, and he blew upon it once, and he spat upon it once—'for luck', he hoarsely said—before he put it in his pocket. **1883** BURNE *Shropshire* 272. An old woman at Donington .. receiving a gift of a shilling from an unexpected quarter, was observed to gaze earnestly at it and spit on it with much gravity before putting it into her pocket. **1895** F. T. ELWORTHY *Evil Eye* 412. The .. habit of spitting on a coin is very common also by the receiver when won in a bet. **1903** *N & Q* 9th ser. XI 358. Last Derby

Day, standing on an elevation overlooking the road that crosses Wimbledon Common, I saw several children .. pursuing the vehicles [carriages] for largess. The custom of spitting on the coin given is universal as a specific against every species of fascination. **1954** Woman, 47. My friend remembers workmen in Gowerton [Glam.] about forty years ago being paid in gold coins and holding them up to their mouths as if to spit on them, without actually doing so. It was supposed to bring luck. **1954** [Alton, Hants.] In the post office, the man next in the queue spat twice on the postal order before sending it off with his football coupon.

Cf. HANDSEL (first sale of day); MONEY, finding.

SPITTING into one's hand

AD **77** PLINY *Natural History* XXVIII VII (1856, V 289) Some persons .. before making an effort, spit into the hand .. in order to make the blow more heavy. **1577** J. GRANGE *Golden Aphroditis* Hjb. If I haue anoynted your palmes with hope, spitte on your handes and take good holde. **1613** W. BROWNE *Britannia's Pastorals* I V 98. To clappe a well-wrought shooe (for more then pay) Vpon a stubborne Nagge of Galloway .. The swarty Smith spits in his Buckehorne fist. **1688** AUBREY *Remaines* (1881, 197) Countrey boyes & fellowes (I believe all England over) when they prepare themselves to goe to cuffs (boxes): before they strike, they doe spitt in their hands, sc. for good luck to their endeavours. *c.***1700** W. KENNETT Note to Aubrey's *Remaines* (1881, 197) I remember in Kent, when a person in a declining condition recovers and is likely to live longer, it is a proverb to say of him that he has spit in his hand, and will hold out the nother year. **1738** SWIFT *Polite Conversation* I 28. I warrant, Miss will spit in her Hand, and hold fast. **1813** BRAND *Antiquities* II 571. Spitting, according to Pliny, was superstitiously observed in averting Witchcraft, and in giving a shrewder Blow to an Enemy. Hence seems to be derived the Custom our Bruisers have of spitting in their Hands before they begin their barbarous diversion, unless it was originally done for luck's sake. **1946**

UTTLEY *Country Things* XI [Cromford, Derbys. *c.*1900] Men spat on their hands before they attempted work needing great strength, a custom one can see every day, and it was not only to get a good grip of a tool. **1948** E. & M. A. RADFORD *Superstitions* 225. It is a very curious thing that today when two men, or even boys, prepare to engage in a bout of fisticuffs, they invariably . . begin by spitting on their hands. **1957** Boy, 13 [Upminster, Essex] Spitting on the hand gives the idea of courage. **1969** s. MAYS *Reuben's Corner* 20 [Essex] Before he took his sharp chisels or planes to oak or elm he would spit on his hands, clasp them in prayer and thank God for the smell of the wood and the work he was about to perform.

SPITTING to avert evil

*c.*319 BC THEOPHRASTUS *Characters* (tr. Jebb, ed. Sandys, 147) If he sees a maniac or an epileptic man, he will shudder and spit into his bosom. *c.*275 BC THEOCRITUS *Idylls* VI. To avoid the evil eye, I spat thrice in my breast. AD 77 PLINY *Natural History* XXVIII VII (1856, V 288) We are in the habit of spitting [to] repel contagion. **1508** DUNBAR *Tua Mariit Wemen* 396. I spittit quhen I saw That super spendit euill spreit. **1657** T. M. *Life of a Satirical Puppy Called Nim* 35. One of his Guardians (being fortifi'd with an old charm) marches crosse-legg'd, spitting three times, East-South-West: and afterwards prefers his vallor to a Catechising office. **1800** COLERIDGE *Annual Anthology* II 63–4. According to the superstition of the West Countries, if you meet the Devil, you may . . cause him instantly to disappear by spitting over his horns. **1841** LANE *Arabian Nights* I 68. When any of you has a bad dream, spit three times over your left shoulder. **1882** *N & Q* 6th ser. VI 178 [Oxon.] I remember an old nurse of ours who, if in the course of our walks we had to pass a house where any one was ill with an infectious disease, always enforced this precaution [spitting] upon us to keep off infection. **1885** *Folklore* 181 [St Combs, Aberdeen.] In hauling the line a hook at times gets fixed . . in the rocky bottom. It is supposed to be held by some one that had been met when

going to the boat. The man who hauls, lifts any little bit of sea-weed or piece of shell that may be lying in the boat, spits on it, throws it overboard, and again spits to counteract the power of the ill-wisher. **1952** Girl, 12 [Aberystwyth, Cardigan.] We spit and say, 'No fever in my bed tonight.' **1952** Girl, 14 [Aberdeen] If we imagine that somebody knocked at the door, and we go and see and there is no-one there we spit, because if we don't it is considered bad luck. **1957** Boy, *c.*12 [Brentwood, Essex] If you want to bring a person bad luck, you spit behind his back.

Cf. SPITTLE protects baby.

SPITTLE cures (usually 'fasting spittle')

c. AD 70 Mark 7: 32–5. And they bring unto him one that was deaf, and had an impediment in his speech . . And he took him aside from the multitude, and put his fingers into his ears, and he spit, and touched his tongue; and saith unto him, Ephphatha, that is, Be opened. AD 77 PLINY *Natural History* XXVIII VII (1856, V 289) Ophthalmia may be cured by anointing . . the eyes every morning with fasting spittle. Ibid. XXII (304) A woman's fasting spittle is generally considered highly efficacious for bloodshot eyes. *c.*1000 MS Harl. 585 (COCKAYNE *Leechdoms* III 11) This . . charm a man may sing against a penetrating worm [ache or pain], sing it frequently upon the wound and smear it with thy spittle. **1579** LUPTON *Thousand Notable Things* I § 57. The fasting spytle of a whole and sounde personne, doth quyte take awaye all scuruines . . And . . puts away . . all painefull swellinges. **1597** ARISTOTLE *Problemes* B7ᵛ. Why doth the spettle of one who is fasting, heale an impostume? **1678** *Yea and Nay Almanack* C7ᵛ. A good Medicine for the Eyes. In the morning as soon as you rise, instead of fasting Spittle . . rub your eyes with . . Gold. **1748** *Gents Mag.* 413. The following . . appear'd in the News-papers. Middlewych in Cheshire, Aug. 28. There is risen up . . a great doctress . . resorted to by people of all ranks . . to be cured of ALL diseases . . I went to see her yesterday out of curiosity, and believe near 600 people were with her. I believe all the country are gone stark mad. The chief thing she cures with is fasting spittle, and God bless you with faith. Ibid. Old Bridget Bostock fills the country with as much talk as the rebels did .. She cures .. almost every thing, except the French disease .. All the means she uses .. are fasting spittle, and praying. **1855** J. BOSTOCK Note to Pliny's *Natural History* II 126. The saliva of a person who has fasted for some time, is still, in this country, a popular remedy for ophthalmia. It contains a greater proportion of saline matter than saliva under ordinary circumstances. **1865** *N & Q* 3rd ser. VII 275. One of my children being badly cut on his forehead, a Huntingdonshire woman told his nurse that if she wished the wound not to leave a scar, she must wet it every morning with her spittle before she had eaten or drunk. **1912** LEATHER *Herefordshire* 78. A mother complained that her baby had a large birthmark that threatened to be permanent: 'I've licked it all over for nine mornings, too,' she said. **1913** E. M. WRIGHT *Rustic Speech* 236. Not many months ago my gardener's little girl .. fell out of bed, and grazed her back .. by way of remedy, she was told to wet her finger with spittle, and apply it to the wound. **1946** UTTLEY *Country Things* XI. The eyes of new-born children were touched by a licked finger, to ensure good sight. **1949** E. TAYLOR *Wreath of Roses* XIV. That's a teething-rash .. There's one cure for that .. that's fasting-spittle .. In the morning, madam, as soon as you wake up, just give your hand a good lick and put it to baby's neck. The poison that's collected in your mouth all night will kill the rash. **1954** Girl, 13 [Forfar, Angus] One cure is to put your first spittle on the wart, as it is said to be poisonous. **1957** *Folklore* 415. Lick the mark [birthmark] all over every morning, beginning as soon as possible after the birth and continuing until the blemish is gone. I know of three babies who have been successfully treated in this way within the last ten years.

SPITTLE kills snakes

AD 77 PLINY *Natural History* VII 11 (1855, II 126) All men possess in their bodies a poison which acts upon serpents, and the human saliva, it is said, makes them take to flight [and] destroys them the moment it enters their throat, and more particularly so, if it .. be the saliva of a man who is fasting. *c.*1400 J. MIRK *Festial* (EETS Extra Ser. 96: 83) The spittle of a fasting man can kill an adder. **1650** BROWNE *Vulgar Errors* III XXVII. Whether the fasting spittle of man be poison unto Snakes and Vipers?

SPITTLE protects baby

ante AD 62 PERSIUS *Satires* II ll. 31–6 (tr. Gifford, ed. Warrington, 201) From his little crib the granny hoar (Or auntie) versed in superstitious lore, Snatches the babe, in lustral spittle dips Her middle finger, and anoints the lips And forehead. 'Charms of potency,' she cries, 'To break the influence of evil eyes!' **1893** *Folklore* 357 [Co. Cork] Immediately after birth the child is sometimes spat on by the father.

Cf. SPITTING to avert evil.

SPOON, wooden

1900 *N & Q* 9th ser. V 112. Wooden spoons are given to brides for luck. **1988** *Woman*, 55 [Bramshott, Hants.] I saw a woman go up to the bride as she came out of church and give her a wooden spoon—'For good luck,' she said.

SPOONS, two

1872 *N & Q* 4th ser. X 495. If single persons happen to have two spoons in their cup, it is a sign that they will figure prominently at a wedding before the year is out. **1883** BURNE *Shropshire* 279. Two spoons in a cup or basin are accounted a sign of a wedding; some say, the wedding of the person who inadvertently added the second spoon. If two spoons are accidently handed to anybody with a cup of tea, he or she will be married shortly; or, some say, will be married twice. **1902** *N & Q* 9th ser. IX 357 [Worksop, Notts.] In my young days .. if spoons were found crossed that was considered to be a sign of a wedding. **1923** [Bradford-on-Tone, Som.] If there are two spoons in a cup, sign of marriage. **1952** Girl, 14 [Aberdeen] If two teaspoons are crossed it means a wedding soon. **1954**

Girl, 15 [Newbridge, Monmouth.] Two spoons on one saucer, there will be a marriage or a birth in the family. **1979** Woman, 21. A Hertfordshire variant is that if two spoons are set in a girl's saucer she will marry twice. **1981** Woman, 20 [Wilts.] Two spoons in a cup is a sign of ginger twins. **1982** Woman, 20 [Cleveland, Yorks.] Having two teaspoons in a saucer can mean either a wedding or twins.

STAIRS, bride goes up

1923 [Cosham, Hants.] The first person who goes upstairs after a bride has come down, will be the next to marry.

Cf. MARRIED COUPLE, touching; STAIRS, stumbling going up.

STAIRS, crossing on

1865 R. HUNT *West of England* 2nd ser. 239. It is considered unlucky to meet on the stairs, and often one will retire to his or her room rather than run the risk of giving or receiving ill luck. **1890** *N & Q* 7th ser. IX 397. While staying in the house of a friend in Scarborough [Yorks.] the hostess and myself happening to meet on the stairs, she exclaimed, 'It's unlucky to meet on the stairs' [and] would not pass. **1912** LEATHER *Herefordshire* 87. It is undesirable to meet or pass a person on the stairs. **1928** *Folklore* 95 [Kensington, London] I was going down the lowest stairs in this block when a girl, who had .. begun to come up, suddenly jumped back and stood at the foot of the stairs. I thanked her .. and suggested that there might have been room for us both—but she replied 'Yes! But it is unlucky to cross another on the stairs.' **1960** Boy, 10 [Selborne, Hants.] When you are going downstairs and you meet somebody coming up the stairs if you cross you get bad luck. **1982** Woman, 20 [Cleveland, Yorks.] Even normally unsuperstitious people will not cross on the stairs. **1985** My ancient aunts, who live in South London, will not cross on the stairs.

Cf. STILE, two going through or over.

STAIRS, stumbling going down

1695 CONGREVE *Love for Love* II i. I stumbled coming down stairs .. bad omen. **1777** BRAND *Antiquities* 95. Stumbling in going down Stairs is held to be [a] bad [omen]. **1808** *Gents Mag.* pt. I 342. And didst thou not mark the warnings dark? 'Twas all on a Friday morn— She tripp'd unawares as she hurried downstairs, And thrice was her kirtle torn. **1870** *N & Q* 4th ser. VI 211 [Walton-le-Dale, Lancs., *c.*1820] It was accounted unlucky to tumble downstairs: hence when [it] occurred within the hearing of another person, it was usual for the latter to divert the omen by calling out .. 'Tumble up!' **1952** Girl, 13 [Swansea, Glam.] If you trip coming downstairs a funeral is imminent.

STAIRS, stumbling going up

1755 *Connoisseur* 20 Feb. If she tumbles as she is running up stairs [she] imagines she shall go to church with her sweetheart before the week is at an end. **1787** GROSE *Provincial Glossary* Superstitions 63. It is lucky to tumble up stairs: probably this is a jocular observation, meaning, it was lucky the party did not tumble down stairs. **1861** C. C. ROBINSON *Dialect of Leeds* 301. If you stumble upstairs it is the sign of a wedding. **1866** HENDERSON *Northern Counties* 85. If you stumble upstairs (by accident), you will be married the same year. **1883** BURNE *Shropshire* 283. Tripping in going upstairs is a sign of a wedding, either that of the person who stumbles or of the one who next goes up the staircase afterwards. *c.*1914 Girl, 11 [Eastbourne, Sussex] Fall upstairs, and the next person going up will be married within a year. **1923** [Martock, Som.] To stumble upstairs is good; some say, 'sign of a wedding'.

STAIRS, turning on

1890 *N & Q* 7th ser. IX 486 [Fareham, Hants.] If you forget anything .. on the stairs, do not stop to rectify mistake, but go to the top of the flight, sit down to consider before you turn back, or ill-luck will follow. **1923** [Wellington, Som.] If you turn back when you are going upstairs it is very unlucky. **1953** Girl, 14 [Llangunllo, Radnor.] If you walk upstairs and turn back before you get to the top you will have bad luck. **1962**

Daily Express 17 July 11 [Quorn, Leics.] 68-year-old Charles .. couldn't bear to turn round when he was on them .. He would either carry on walking until he reached the top, then .. come down again .. or .. stop halfway up and then walk down backwards. **1964** Girl, 15 [Chigwell, Essex] You must whistle if you turn round on the stairs.

Cf. TURNING BACK.

STAR, falling/shooting = birth

c. AD **80** Matthew 2: 1–9. Now when Jesus was born in Bethlehem of Judæ, in the days of Herod the king, behold, there came wise men from the east .. Saying, Where is he that is born King of the Jews? for we have seen his star in the east .. Then Herod .. sent them to Bethlehem; and said, Go and search diligently for the young child .. and, lo, the star .. went before them, till it came and stood over where the young child was. **1824** L. HAWKINS *Anecdotes* II 74. There's a child born, when a star shoots: it is supposed to fall over the spot. **1876** *N & Q* 5th ser. VI 506. In Yorkshire, when folks see shooting stars, they say, 'They are babies' souls coming down from heaven.' **1923** [Castle Cary, Som.] A shooting star means a baby born. **1955** Woman, 52 [Nutfield, Surrey] A shooting star means a new baby born.

STAR, falling/shooting = death or disaster

AD **77** PLINY *Natural History* II VI (1855, I 25–6) They have neither come into existence, nor do they perish in connexion with particular persons, nor does a falling star indicate that any one is dead. *c.* AD **80** Matthew 24: 29. Immediately after the tribulation of those days shall the sun be darkened, and the moon shall not give her light, and the stars shall fall from heaven, and the powers of the heavens shall be shaken. **1595** SHAKESPEARE *Richard the Second* II iv. Meteors fright the fixed Starres of Heaven .. These signes fore-run the death of Kings. **1690** T. BURNET *Theory of the Earth* III 98. The last sign we shall take notice of [at the end of the world] is that of Falling Stars. **1711** *Spectator* 8 Mar. I have known the shooting of a star spoil a night's rest. **1838** GASKELL (*Letters*, ed. Chapple & Pollard, 31) A

shooting star is unlucky to see. I have so far a belief in this that I always have a chill in my heart when I see one, for I have often noted them when watching over a sick-bed and very very anxious. **1866** *N & Q* 3rd ser. X 25. A Huntingdonshire woman was telling me of the death of her baby .. She said: 'I had a warning that it was to go. The night before it was took I was passing your gate, Sir, and a great star fell from the sky plump afore me.' **1883** BURNE *Shropshire* 258 n. Every time a star rolls or changes places, a soul ascends. **1907** *N & Q* 10th ser. VII. 196–7 [Worksop, Notts.] I remember that on one occasion, when a shooting star burst with a report, it was said by one present, 'Ah! we shall hear of some big man's death.' **1953** Girl, 14 [Knighton, Radnor.] If you see a star falling it means someone is dying.

STAR, falling/shooting = wish granted

1839 S. LOVER *Songs* 21 [Ireland] I saw a star that was falling, I wish'd the wish of my soul. **1851** *N & Q* 1st ser. IV 99. Whatever you think of when you see a star shooting, you are sure to have. **1887** *Folk-Lore Record* 218–19 [Cornwall] You may .. wish when you see a falling star, and if you can succeed in framing it before it disappears your wish will be granted. **1953** *Folklore* 295 [Westmorland] Wish quickly while the star falls. **1957** Girl, *c.*18 [Pontypool, Mon.] See a shooting star, have a wish.

STAR, first: wishing on

1958 B. KOPS *Hamlet of Stepney Green* I. SAM: Ah, there it is, the evening star. Starlight. Starbright, first star I've seen tonight, wish I may, wish I might, grant this wish. [*He closes his eyes and makes a wish.*] **1964** Woman, *c.*60. In Essex half a century ago we always looked for a solitary star at twilight and said 'Star light, star bright, first star I've seen tonight, Wish I may, wish I might, have the wish I wish tonight.'

Cf. NEW MOON grants favours.

STARS, nine: wishing on

1952 Girl, 12 [Swansea, Glam.] Count nine stars nine nights running and wish.

STARS, pointing at/counting

1866 HENDERSON *Northern Counties* 88. It is thought sinful .. to point at the stars, or to try and count them .. Many, they say, have been struck dead for so doing. **1882** *N & Q* 6th ser. V 14 [Selmeston, Sussex] I find a superstition prevalent here .. that it is a sin to count the stars. **1902** *N & Q* 9th ser. IX 357–8. Fifty years ago it was held unlucky to .. count the stars. Derbyshire girls and boys 'dared' each other to do it .. It was bad luck to count .. up to one hundred, and 'you might be struck down dead' for it. Generally the counting stopped at ninety-nine, only a few venturing beyond in fear and trembling. **1953** Girl, 15 [nr. Ipswich, Suffolk] Never point at a star.

Cf. MOON, pointing at.

STEPPING OVER

1507 *Gospelles of Dystaues* pt. I XXIV. If it happen that some body stryde ouer a lytell chylde, knowe ye for certayne that he shall neuer growe more but yf they stryde backewarde ouer it agayne. Glose. Certaynly sayd Sebylle of such thynge cometh dwerfes and lytel women. **1846** BROCKETT *North Country Words. Crile*, to pass the leg over the head of a child, vulgarly supposed to *crile* or stop its growth. **1880** [Hay-on-Wye, Herefords.] If anyone cocks his leg over you while you are bending down you will not grow any more. **1892** HESLOP *Northumberland Words. Creel.* To throw the leg over the head of another person. This is generally practised by children, who say after doing it, 'There noo, aa've creeled thoo an thoo'll nivver grou ne bigger.' **1908** *N & Q* 10th ser. IX 494 [Yorks., *ante* 1829] I remember my mother telling me how frightened she was, as a child, by her elder brother suddenly throwing one of his legs over her head, and assuring her she would grow no more. Ibid. X 36 [St Andrews, Fife] In other days I have myself frequently lifted a conveniently elastic limb over the head of a junior .. with the disconcerting assurance that the victim's further development in stature was extremely improbable.

Cf. CAT endangers health of unborn child.

STILE lucky

1883 BURNE *Shropshire* 367. In Condover Park there was formerly a turnstile known as the Wishing Gate. A wish formed at this turnstile at midnight on Midsummer Eve was certain to be obtained. **1887** *Folk-Lore Record* 217 [Cornwall] A foolish warning says, 'Go thro' a gate when there's a stile hard by You'll be a widow before you die.' **1953** Girl, 14 [Stowe, Herefords.] This will bring you luck—Kiss on a stile in the dark.

STILE, nail driven into: cure

1867 *Gents Mag.* pt. I 731 [Suffolk] When I was suffering from ague a few years ago, I was strongly urged to go to a stile .. and to drive a nail into that part over which foot-passengers travel.

STILE, two going through or over

1883 BURNE *Shropshire* 276. I saw a party of little girls passing through the turnstile beside the churchyard gate at Eccleshall, one of whom was urgent with her companions only to go through the stile one at a time. 'One at once!' she cried distractedly, tugging at the skirts of those who pressed forward too fast; 'one at once! It's bad luck, it's bad luck!' **1912** LEATHER *Herefordshire* 87. It is unlucky for two persons to get over a stile together; perhaps because Herefordshire stiles are ill-adapted for trying this experiment. **1985** Woman, 50 [Dedham, Essex] If you're coming up to a stile—the sort where two people can get through at the same time—and somebody is coming up to it in the opposite direction, you mustn't cross on it (get over at the same time) it's unlucky.

Cf. STAIRS, crossing on.

STOCKING, left: cures

1912 LEATHER *Herefordshire* 81. Tie a stocking which has been worn on the *left* foot round the patient's throat on going to bed: his [sore] throat will be well in the morning. **1923** [Wellington, Som.] If you have a sore throat take off your left stocking, and put it round your neck, it will be sure to ease it. **1965** [Wrecclesham, Surrey] When Mother had a sore throat her mother used to tell her to take her left stocking off and tie it round her neck (with the foot next to the throat). In the morning it was replaced on the foot.

STOCKING, left: divination

1883 BURNE *Shropshire* 179. A fellow-servant .. every Friday night before getting into bed drew her left stocking into her right, saying 'This is the blessed Friday night; I draw my left stocking into my right, To dream of the living, not of the dead, To dream of the young man I am to wed.' After this she would not speak again that night. **1895** G. HARDY *Denham Tracts* 281. At Wooler servant girls tie their left-leg stocking round their neck in order to dream of him whom they were to get for a husband. **1899** *Newcastle Weekly Chronicle* 4 Feb. 7 [Jesmond] To induce favourable dreams .. the left stocking is put round the neck.

STOCKING: spell

1901 P. H. DITCHFIELD *Old English Customs* 198 [Bucks.] Girls .. are wont to pin their woollen stockings to the wall, and repeat .. 'I hang my stocking on the wall, Hoping my true love for to call; May he neither rest, sleep, nor happy be, Until he comes and speaks to me.'

STONE with hole

*c.*1425–50 MS Bodleian Rawlinson C. 506 f. 297 [charm against nightmare] Take a flynt stone that hath an hole thorow of hys owen growyng, & hange it ouer the stabill dore, or ell ouer horse, and ell writhe this charme: In nomine Patris &c. Seynt Iorge, our lady knygth, he walked day, he walked nygth, till that he fownde that fowle wygth; & whan that he here fownde, he here bete & he here bownde, till trewly ther here trowthe sche plygth that sche sholde not come be nygthe, With-Inne vij rode [seven rods] of londe space ther as Seynt Ieorge i-namyd was. In nomine Patris &c. & wryte this in a bylle & hange it in the hors' mane. **1566** T. BLUNDEVILL *Fowerchiefystoffices of Horsemanshippe* 'Horses Diseases' 17 [Norfolk] A disease [nightmare] oppressing eyther man or beast, in the nighte season .. an olde

English wryter .. teacheth howe to cure it with a fonde foolishe charme, which bicause it may perhappes make you gentle reader to laugh, as well it did me .. will here rehearse it. Take a Flynt Stone that hath a hole of his owne kynde, and hang it ouer hym [goes on to give word charm 'St George' etc.] **1584** SCOT *Discoverie of Witchcraft* IV XI. Item, hang a stone over the afflicted persons bed, which stone hath naturallie such a hole in it, as wherein a string may be put through it, and so be hanged over the diseased or bewitched partie; be it man, woman or horsse. **1650** BROWNE *Vulgar Errors* V XXII. To prevent the Ephialtes or night-Mare we hang up an hollow stone in our stables. **1686–7** AUBREY *Remaines* (1881, 28) In the West of England (& I beleeve, almost everywhere in this nation) the Carters, & Groomes, & Hostlers doe hang a flint (that has a hole in it) over horses that are hagge-ridden for a Preservative against it. **1777** BRAND *Antiquities* 97. They are usually called in the North, Holy Stones. **1787** GROSE *Provincial Glossary* Superstitions 57. A stone with a hole in it, hung at the bed's head, will prevent the night-mare: it is therefore called a hag-stone, from that disorder, which is occasioned by a hag, or witch, sitting on the stomach of the party afflicted. It also prevents witches riding horses; for which purpose it is often tied to a stable key. **1823** *Gents Mag.* pt. I 17 [Ipswich, Suffolk] Some stable-keepers in this neighbourhood hang up a flint stone, with a natural hole through it, in the stable, to prevent the Devil riding the horses in the night. **1824** CARR *Craven Dialect* [Yorks.] *Holy-staan*. A stone with a natural hole .. suspended by a string from the roof of a cowhouse, or from the tester of a bed, as an infallible prevention of injury from witches. **1827** HONE *Table Book* II 538 [Bridlington, Yorks.] Having a small, smooth lime-stone, picked up on the beach, with .. a natural hole through it, tied to the key of a house, ware-house, barn, stable, or other building, prevented the influence of witches over whatever the house &c. contained. **1889** *Longman's Mag.* XIII 519. Around Poole [Dorset, *c.*1820] perforated pebbles are not uncommon, and

.. considered 'lucky' .. The stone was
.. spat upon, and thrown backward over
the head of the fortunate finder with ..
'Lucky stone! Lucky stone! go over my
head, And bring me some good luck
before I go to bed.' **1896** *N & Q* 8th ser.
VIII 52 [Dorset] When I was a boy it was
common enough to see 'holy stones',
sea-rolled flints with a natural bore, tied
as charms inside the bows of Weymouth
boats. **1906** *Proceedings Soc. Antiquaries*
8 Feb. 82. In some parts of Bedfordshire
it is still believed that a suspended holed
stone will prevent illness in cows, and
prevent the entry of the 'night-hag'.
1924 *N & Q* CXLVI 96. Only the other
day I was told of a farm near Morpeth
[Northumb.], every outhouse around
which is protected by a holy (or 'limmel')
stone. **1928** E. LOVETT *Surrey and Sussex*
38. Holed stones are in most cases on
a loop of red ribbon .. hooked on to
one of the knobs of the bedstead. **1932**
C. J. S. THOMPSON *Hand of Destiny* 286.
In the Metropolis .. many people carry
holed-flints .. in their pockets, in the
firm belief that they will protect them
from rheumatism and bad luck. **1942**
Folklore 96. While touting for fire-
watchers the other day I was pleased to
find .. two holed-stones hung up over
the door of a house I visited. I asked,
'Are these for luck?' and was told ..
'They were there when we came, we've
only been here a month; but we've got
two holed-stones inside that we picked
up ourselves for luck!' **1948** Girl, 11
[Watford, Herts.] A lucky object—a
stone with a hole in it. **1984** Woman,
55 [Colchester, Essex] I still keep stones
with holes in them on my window-sill
for luck. I used to pick them up as a
child from the beach in South Shields
[Co. Durham], and all my family still
pick them up—because we think they're
lucky.

STORK brings babies

1937 *N & Q* CLXXII 283. The idea that
the stork has brought a new child is, I
believe, Dutch and German nursery lore.
Is there any special significance in the
choice of the bird? **1956** *Listener* 21
June 842. It is odd .. that that delightful
myth about babies being brought by
storks should have such a firm hold in

Britain, where, so far as we know, there
never have been any breeding storks.
1987 Woman, 32 [Bermondsey, E. Lon-
don] When I took my baby to the Clinic,
I asked about the red marks on the
back of her neck and the assistant said,
'They're 'stork' marks, where the stork
holds the baby in its beak. Don't worry,
they go in about a year.'

STRAW, animal brings a

1711 *Aristotle's Last Legacy* 53. To meet
a Swine the first thing in a Morning,
carrying a Straw in its Mouth, denotes
a Maid, or a Widow, shall soon be
married, and very fruitful in Children.
1807 HOGG *Mountain Bard* Note 6. If a
feather, a straw, or any such thing, be
observed hanging at a dog's nose or
beard, they call that a guest, and are
sure of the approach of a stranger. **1882**
Folk-Lore Record 83 [Co. Wexford] A
dog coming into a house with straws
attaching to his tail is a sign of a visitor
coming. **1904** *Folklore* 462 [Abbeyleix,
Co. Leix] If a hen comes into the house
with a straw sticking to her tail, and if
she drops it in the house, it is a sign
that a stranger will be coming to stay;
but if the hen goes out again with the
straw .. still in her tail, it only means a
call from a stranger. **1923** [Bradford-
on-Tone, Som.] To find a piece of straw
in your room means a visitor coming.

STRAW magic

1800 COLERIDGE *Annual Anthology* [note
to 'Recantation'] According to the superstition of the West-Countries, if you
meet the Devil, you may .. cut him in
half with a straw. **1852** W. R. WILDE *Irish
Superstitions* 55. Those who adhered to
the remnants of the .. customs of their
Celtic ancestors, put a *soogaun* of straw
round the neck of each cow upon May
Eve .. to preserve it from ill luck. **1941**
M. BANKS *British Calendar Customs: Scotland* 111. An old man, a native of
Ross-shire, lived in Corgarff. If a 'rape',
a rope made of straw, was laid across
the road before him when he set out to
the hills for the first load of peats for the
winter fuel, he turned at once, and
would not drive a single load till after
Halloway. **1984** C. F. TEBBUTT *Huntingdonshire Folklore* 84–5 (*Peterborough*

Advertiser, 1927) [Upwood] A man was bringing home a load of wheat when the horses stopped suddenly and were unable to draw the wagon any further. The old witch came out of her cottage and picked up a straw across the road, saying 'There my man, the horses are not likely to draw the load while that straw was in the way.' The horses then proceeded without difficulty.

Cf. CROSS, witch unable to pass.

STUMBLING = ill omen

c. AD 110 PLUTARCH *Life of Tiberius Gracchus* (tr. North, 1928, VIII 99) As he went out [on the day of his death] he hit his foot such a blow against the stone at the threshold of the door, that he brake the nail of his great toe, which fell in such a bleeding, that it bled through his shoe. *c.* AD 396 ST AUGUSTINE OF HIPPO *De Doctrina Christiana* I xx (tr. Robertson, 56) Similar [superstitious] practices are .. to return to the house if you stumble going out. 1180 NIGEL DE LONGCHAMPS *Mirror for Fools* (tr. Mozley, 26) Hurrying away he stumbled at the gate; Some laughed, and neighbours said: 'Unfortunate! This shows you'd best turn back.' 1579 SPENSER *Shepheardes Calender* May 21. Tho went the pensife Damme out of dore, And chaunst to stomble at the threshold flore: Her stombling steppe some what her amazed, (For such, as signes of ill luck, bene dispraised). 1584 SCOT *Discoverie of Witchcraft* XI xv. If one chance to take a fall from a horse, either in a slipperie or a stumbling waie, he will note the daie and houre, and count that time unluckch for a journie. Otherwise, he that receiveth a mischance, wil consider whether he .. stumbled not at the threshold at his going out. 1593 SHAKESPEARE *3 Henry the Sixth* IV vii. Many men that stumble at the Threshold, Are well fore-told, that danger lurkes within. 1608 J. HALL *Characters* 88. He returnes .. if hee stumbled at the threshold. *c.*1614 WEBSTER *Duchess of Malfi* II ii. How superstitiously we mind our evils! .. the stumbling of a horse [is] of powre To daunt whole man in us. 1620 MELTON *Astrologaster* 46. If a man stumbles in a morning as soone as he comes out of dores [or] if a horse stumble

on the high way, it is a signe of ill lucke. 1652 GAULE *Mag-astro-mances* 181. To bode good or bad luck .. from .. the stumbling at first going about an enterprise. 1686–7 AUBREY *Remaines* (1881, 20) If .. one stumble at the threshold goeing-out: it is still held ominous among some countrey people. 1778 MRS THRALE *Diary* (ed. Balderston, I 338) When I myself was at Lisle in Flanders in the Year 1775, I walked with Mr Johnson & Mr Thrale round the great Church there, and in one of the Chapels I observed myself to stumble in an odd manner, so as to give me uncommon Pain, & at the same time to excite strange Ideas of Terror, wholly unaccountable to me, who am neither timorous nor even delicate: I looked at the Altar-piece & saw it was the figure of an Angel protecting a boy about twelve Years old as it should seem, & somehow the Child struck me with a Resemblance to my own, and alarmed me in an unusual Manner [not long after her return her eldest son died suddenly]. *c.*1840 *Mother Bunch's Golden Fortune-Teller* 22. It is very unlucky to stumble .. on the road to the church to be married. 1889 *Folklore* 46. The fishermen and seamen .. on Yule Night, Old Style [carry a burning barrel through Burghead, Moray.]. Should the bearer stumble or fall the consequences would be unlucky for the town and to himself. 1923 [Trowbridge, Wilts.] Should a stranger fall down on entering your house for the first time, ill-luck will be on your dwelling connected with that visitor .. Such an accident has twice happened in my house, and each time certainly very ill luck has followed my connection with the victim of it.

STUMBLING in graveyard

1592 SHAKESPEARE *Romeo and Juliet* v iii. How oft to night have these aged feete Stumbled at graves .. my minde presageth ill. 1824 MACTAGGART *Gallovidian Encyclopedia* 210. If at the funeral one of the handspakes [coffin bearers] misses his foot, and falls beneath the bier, he will soon be in a coffin himself. 1887 'SPERANZA' WILDE *Superstitions of Ireland* I 154. If any one stumbles at a grave it is a bad omen; but if he falls and touches the clay, he will assuredly die before the year is out. **1968** C. WOODFORD *Sussex Ways* 59–60 [Newhaven] It was especially ominous to stumble at a graveside .. But grandmother only believed what she chose to believe .. that a stumble foretold a wedding.

STUMBLING reveals guilt

1982 Woman, 20 [Yorks.] If the bride or groom were to stumble or make a false step when approaching the altar rail, then this was believed to be a sure sign that some unconfessed moral wrong had been committed.

SUGAR, spilling

1923 [Rowbarton, Som.] If you spill sugar you spill joy. **1982** Woman, *c.*55 [Middlesbrough, Teesside] If you spill sugar, sign of joy.

Cf. SALT, spilling.

SUN, pointing at

1988 Woman, 68 [E. London] I remember when I must have only been about four, playing in the street and being told by the other children that if I pointed at the sun, I'd be struck dead.

Cf. MOON, pointing at.

SUN puts out fire

1261 *Flores Historiarum* (Rolls I 472–3) On July 27, during a violent storm, the church at Evesham was struck by a thunderbolt .. whereupon a fire immediately broke out on the roof of the tower, spreading some thirty feet downwards .. The monks and people came running .. and made a courageous attempt to put out the fire .. with water. But all .. to no avail, till at length Phoebus's rays, shining on the blaze, extinguished it completely by God's will. **1583** *The Schoolemaster* A4v. Externall heat weakeneth naturall heat, lyke as the shining of the Sunne putteth out the fire if it come to it. *c.***1608** SHAKESPEARE *Coriolanus* IV vii. One fire drives out one fire. **1853** *N & Q* 1st ser. VII 285–6. There is a current and notorious idea, that the admission of the sun-light into a room puts the fire out; and, after making every deduction for an apparent effect in this matter, I confess I am disposed to think that the notion is not

an erroneous one. Can any of your correspondents account for it on philosophical principles? Ibid. 439–40. The relative quantities of .. rays in sun-light varies .. Where the luminous and heating rays are most abundant, the proportion of chemical rays is least .. The combustion of an ordinary fire, being strictly a chemical change, is retarded whenever the sun's heating and luminous rays are most powerful, as during bright sunshine. **1895** *N & Q* 8th ser. VIII 148. Does the sun put out the fire? Most servants, and probably all their mistresses, say that it does, and carefully screen the fire from the solar ray. **1956** Man, *c.*70. My Irish nanny used to say 'The sun puts the fire out.' She would hang a towel on the nursery guard to keep it off. **1983** Woman, 63 [Colchester, Essex] My mother believed that the sun put the fire out.

SUN, rising and declining

1584 SCOT *Discoverie of Witchcraft* XI VII. *The times and seasons to exercise augurie.* They [the Roman augurs] must beginne at midnight, and end at noone, not travelling therein in the decaie of the day, but in the increase of the same. **1688** AUBREY *Remaines* (1881, 121) Mariage is celebrated in the Fore-noon by the Canons of the Church; some hold that 'tis not so lucky to undertake any serious affaire *declinante Sole*. **1967** S. MARSHALL *Fenland Chronicle* pt. I XIII. The old saying says 'Always be born in the morning.'

Cf. MOON affects enterprises.

SUNDAY, born on

*c.***1120** MS Junius 23 (COCKAYNE *Leechdoms* III 163) Who ever is born on Sunday .. shall live without anxiety, and be handsome. *c.***1850** *True Fortune Teller* 21. The child born on a Sunday shall be of a long life and obtain riches. **1866** HENDERSON *Northern Counties* 2. 'Sunday children' are in Yorkshire deemed secure from the malice of evil spirits. **1904** E. V. LUCAS *Highways .. in Sussex* 76. A Sussex child born on Sunday can neither be hanged nor drowned. **1957** *Folklore* 413. A child born on Sunday .. is commonly expected to be lucky in life.

Cf. BIRTH, day of: divination rhyme.

SUNDAY, convalescing on

1867 *Gents Mag.* pt. I 740–1 [Suffolk] Sunday being the day of His resurrection, is regarded as auspicious; and if persons have been ill .. they almost always .. get up for the first time on Sunday. 1878 *N & Q* 5th ser. X 24 [Dorset] Everybody do know .. when you do up for the first time after sickness, should always be a Sunday.

SUNDAY, courting on

1832 A. HENDERSON *Scottish Proverbs* 9. Sunday's wooing draws to ruin.

SUNDAY, crying on

1839 C. BARON-WILSON *Harriot, Duchess of St Albans* II 134 [They] endeavoured to bear, without sobbing, the soap smarting in their eyes, because the nursemaid said it was 'unco bad to cry o' the Sabbath mornin'.

SUNDAY, darning, sewing, or knitting on

1841 DICKENS *Old Curiosity Shop* XXVIII. 'That,' said Mrs Jarley .. 'is an unfortunate Maid of Honour in the Time of Queen Elizabeth, who died from pricking her finger in consequence of working upon a Sunday.' 1909 M. TREVELYAN *Folk-Lore of Wales* 243. Whoever sews any bed-linen or clothing on Sunday, if taken ill, she cannot die until it is unpicked. 1923 *Folklore* 328 [Northleigh, Oxon.] If you sewed on Sunday, the Devil would thread the needle. 1954 *Girl*, 15 [Tunstall, Staffs.] Another way to bring bad luck to oneself is by darning or sewing on a Sunday. 1984 Man, *c.*60 [Ockham, Surrey] My mother used to say that if you knit on a Sunday you have to unpick it with your nose on the last day.

SUNDAY, getting married on

1900 S. HEWETT *Nummits* 22 [Devon] Sunday is an exceptionally fortunate day upon which to enter the holy state.

SUNDAY, going to sea on

1608 J. HALL *Characters* 89. Hee will neuer set to Sea but on a Sunday. 1808 SCOTT (LOCKHART *Life* I 29–30) We had a tutor at home, a young man .. bred to the Kirk .. he resigned an excellent living in a seaport town, merely because he could not persuade the mariners of the guilt of setting sail of a Sabbath—in which, by the by, he was less likely to be successful, as, *caeteris paribus*, sailors, from an opinion that it is a fortunate omen, always choose to weigh anchor on that day. 1823 *Gents Mag.* pt. I 17 [Ipswich, Suffolk] Sailors .. have their lucky and unlucky days. Sunday is the most fortunate: whatever voyage is begun on that day is sure to be prosperous. 1852 *N & Q* 1st ser. V 5 [Prestonpans, East Lothian] It is a favourite custom to set sail on the Sunday for the fishing grounds. A clergyman of the town is said to pray against their sabbath-breaking; and to prevent any injury accruing from his prayers, the fishermen make a small image of rags, and burn it on top of their chimneys. 1930 P. F. ANSON *East Coast of Scotland* 42. Sunday was a lucky day, but no ship would ever put to sea 'until a blessing had been pronounced', i.e. until after morning service.

SUNDAY: keeping Sabbath holy: transgressors punished

5th c. BC Numbers 15: 32–6. While the children of Israel were in the wilderness, they found a man that gathered sticks upon the sabbath day .. And the Lord said unto Moses, The man shall be surely put to death: all the congregation shall stone him with stones without the camp. And all the congregation brought him without the camp, and stoned him .. and he died. 1303 MANNYNG *Handlyng Synne* (EETS 119 ll. 4305–16) 3yf hyt be nat þan redy, hys dyner, Take furþe þe chesse or þe tabler; so shal he pley tyl hyt be none, And Goddys seruysse be al done .. Swyche a lyfe þan shal he lede, Noght þat he shal haue to mede; yn alle hys lyfe shal he [nat] fynde Oght þat may hym to syne vnbynde. 1662 M. HALE *Letter to his Children on Keeping the Lords Day* (1762, 106–7) In all your .. actions of this day, let there be no lightness nor vanity; use no running, nor leaping, nor playing, nor wrestling; use no jesting, nor telling of tales or foolish stories, no talk about worldly business. Ibid. 98. I have found .. that a due observation of the duty of the day, hath ever had joined to it, a blessing upon the rest of my time; and the week that hath been so begun, hath been blessed and prosperous to me; and on the other side, when I have been negligent of the duties of the day, the rest of the week hath been unsuccessful and unhappy. **1697** W. TURNER *Remarkable Providences* CVII 18. A certain Nobleman, profaning the Sabbath, usually in Hunting, had a Child by his Wife, with a Head like a Dog, and with Ears and Chaps, crying like a Hound. **1782** W. COWPER *Letters* 7 Mar. The Duke of Gloucester's rout on a Sunday! 'May it please your R.H.! I am an Englishman, and must stand or fall with the nation .. Sin ruins us .. especially the violation of the Sabbath .. For shame, Sir!—if you wish well to your brother's arms, and would be glad to see the kingdom emerging again from her ruins, pay more respect to an ordinance that deserves the deepest!' **1798** R. WARNER *Walk Through Wales* 21 [Llanvair Kilgeddin, Monmouth.] We .. were leaving the church-yard, when our attention was caught by the following admonitory stanza, engraven on a stone placed as a style into it .. 'Who Ever hear on Sonday Will Practis playing At Ball it May be beFore Monday The Devil will Have you all.' **1807** SOUTHEY *Letters from England* LXVII. Half the people seriously believe that were they to touch a card on a Sunday, they should immediately find the devil under the table. **1838** A. E. BRAY *Devonshire* III 260. Three men were at work late on the Saturday night .. when .. they saw issue from the rock a large ball of fire, which .. rolled on towards them .. The men were dreadfully terrified, and calling to their recollection that the Sunday had commenced, they fully believed they .. were pursued by the devil. **1910** *N & Q* 11th ser. II 388. A Sunday well spent Brings a week of content, And health for the toils of the morrow; But a Sabbath profaned, Whatsoe'er may be gained, Is a certain forerunner of sorrow. **1923** [Castle Cary, Som.] If you keep a person's birthday festivities on a Sunday—they will sure die before another birthday. **1923** [Ruishton, Som.] It is unlucky to

wash your doorstep on a Sunday. **1965** [Yorks.] A farmer's wife was telling me they had an old chap over from Farndale way to look at some beasts on Sunday but he didn't seem a bit interested. Then yesterday he rang up and said, 'I do want the beasts, only I didn't want to buy them a'Sunda.' **1968** LORD TWEEDSMUIR *One Man's Happiness* 161. The old Tay Bridge .. was blown down in 1879. And the loss of the train that went with it was a story that chilled us in childhood. It was said that my Grandfather, who was at that time a minister at Kirkcaldy, had held up my four-year-old father to look at that 'wicked Sunday train'. It was at that moment on its way to pay for its wickedness. **1983** Boy, 12 [Maldon, Essex] My Dad says never work on a Sunday because nearly every time you do something goes wrong. **1987** Woman, *c.*70 [Scarborough, Yorks.] My old granny used to say, 'Work done on a Sunday will come undone on the Monday.'

Cf. MOON, MAN IN THE.

SUNDAY: keeping Sabbath holy: transgressors turned to stone

1602 R. CAREW *Cornwall* 129ᵛ. Not far [from Liskeard] in an open plaine, are to be seen certaine stones .. termed, The hurlers .. The countrey peoples report [is] that once they were men, and for their hurling vpon the Sabboth, so metamorphosed. **1900** S. BARING-GOULD *Book of Dartmoor* 59 [nr. Penzance, Cornwall] A tradition or fancy relative to more than one of these circles is that the stones represent maidens who insisted on dancing on a Sunday, and were, for their profanity, turned into stone when the church bells rang for divine service.

SUNSET, after

1868 *N & Q* 4th ser. I 193 [Yorks.] It is very unlucky to go out of doors in the dark, lest some misfortune happen to you.

Also see index: night.

SUNWISE as 'sacred' ritual

1608 J. HALL *Characters* 91. He [the superstitious man] knowes not why, but his custome is to goe a little about, and to leaue the crosse stil on the right hand. 1703 M. MARTIN *Western Islands of Scotland* 140 [Skye] Several of the common People oblige themselves by a Vow to come to this Well, and make the ordinary Touer about it, call'd *Dessil* .. thus; they move thrice round the Well proceeding Sunways. Ibid. 247–8. The Natives of Collonsay, are accustomed after their arrival in Oronsay Isle, to make a Tour Sunways about the Church, before they enter any kind of Business. *c.*1740 TOLAND *History of the Druids* 142–4 [Hebrides] The vulgar in the Islands do still show a great respect for the Druids' Houses, and never come to the antient .. Carns, but they walk three times round them from east to west, according to the course of the Sun. This sanctified tour .. by the south, is call'd *Deiseal* .. from *Deas*, the right, understanding, *hand*, and *Soil* .. the Sun, the right hand in this round being ever next the heap [of stones, i.e. Carn].

SUNWISE, boat goes

1703 M. MARTIN *Western Islands of Scotland* 16 [Lewis] When they go to Sea, they .. make towards the Islands with an East Wind; but if .. the Wind turn Westerly, they hoist up Sail and steer directly home again .. When they are got up into the Island, all the crew uncover their Heads, and make a turn Sun-ways round, thanking God for their Safety. 1793 *Stat. Acc. of Scotland* VII 560 [Kirkwall, Orkney] On going to sea, they would reckon themselves in the most imminent danger, were they by accident to turn their boat in opposition to the sun's course. 1900 S. HEWETT *Nummits* 58 [Devon] Fishermen .. would never think of turning a craft against the sun. 1962 Man, 55 [Loch Clash, Sutherland] My old gillie brought me up to take the boat out of the harbour clockwise, even if the tide was wrong.

SUNWISE, bride goes

1744 WALDRON *Isle of Man* 120. When they [wedding party] arrive at the Church-Yard, they walk three times round the Church, before they enter it. 1775 L. SHAW *History of Moray* 230. I have often seen at Marriage and Church-ing of women .. such a tour [deas-soil] made about the Church. 1794 *Stat. Acc.* of *Scotland* XI 621 n. [Callander, Perth.] The bride is conducted to her future spouse .. in the course of the sun. This is called, in Gaelic, going round the right, or lucky way. 1878 A. MACGREGOR *Brahan Seer* 129. 'Superstitions of High-landers'. It is unlucky .. to commence a procession at a marriage or funeral, but to the right.

SUNWISE, corpse goes

1744 WALDRON *Isle of Man* 121–2. The Procession of carrying the Corps to the Grave is in this manner: When they come within a Quarter of a mile of the Church, they are met by the Parson, who walks before them, singing a Psalm .. In every Church-Yard there is a Cross, round which they go three times before they enter the Church. 1775 L. SHAW *History of Moray* 230. I have often seen at .. Burials, such a tour [deas-soil] made about the Church. 1838 *Hereford Times* 20 Mar. 3. When we reached the Wall of the church-yard, we were led all the way round it, it being the custom to carry the corpse round the church-yard the way of the sun. The Clergyman, a very young man, was about to enter the burial-ground in another direction, it being the nearest, and he being the head of the procession, when some one cried out, 'Sir, you are going the wrong way: it is the other.' 1877 *N & Q* 5th ser. VIII 182 [Worksop, Notts.] Many persons in this neighbourhood consider it very bad luck if, when a body is taken to be buried, the funeral procession proceeds to the churchyard by a way which will make them meet the sun in its course. They call this going to be buried 'the back way'; and I know of people who would do almost anything .. rather than not follow the sun. 1887 'SPERANZA' WILDE *Superstitions of Ireland* I 155. When the grave is dug, a cross is made of two spades, and the coffin is carried round it three times before being placed in the clay. 1900 S. BARING-GOULD *Book of Dartmoor* 92. Sometimes the dead is carried rapidly three or four times round the house so as to make him giddy and not know in which dir-ection he is carried. [Footnote] This was done at Manaton at every funeral, the only difference being that he was carried round and round the cross. A former rector, Rev. C. Carwithen, destroyed the cross so as to put a stop to this practice. **1959** *Journal of School of Scottish Studies* 197 [S. Uist and Arisaig, Inverness.] The sunwise, *deiseal*, approach to the graveyard is still observed.

SUNWISE cures

1814 SCOTT *Waverley* XXIV. The surgeon—or he who assumed the office—appeared to unite the characters of a leech and a conjuror .. He observed great ceremony in approaching Edward; and though our hero was writhing with pain, would not proceed .. until he had perambulated his couch three times, moving from east to west, according to the course of the sun .. which both the leech and the assistants seemed to consider of the last importance to the accomplishment of a cure. **1894** *Folklore* 224 [Isle of Man, ash-tree well] The patients who came to it took a mouthful of water, retaining it in their mouths till they had walked round the well sunways twice.

SUNWISE, laying table

1988 Woman, 58 [Cheltenham, Glos.] I was laying the table towards the right, because it was the easiest way, and she said 'You must *never* lay a table that way round, that's against the sun.' She came from Bawtry, in Yorkshire.

SUNWISE, passing drink

1708 *British Apollo* 16 Apr. Q. Say whence, Great Apollo, The Custom We follow, When drinking brisk Liquors per Bumper: In a Circular pass, We quaffe e'ry glass; And Why is it o'er the left Thumb Sir? A. When Mortals with Wine Make their Faces to shine, 'Tis to look like Apollo in Luster; And Circulatory, To follow thy Glory, Which over the left Thumb they must Sir. *c.*1740 TOLAND *History of Druids* 142, 143–4. This sanctified tour .. by the south, is call'd *Deiseal* .. It is perhaps from this .. that we retain the custom of drinking over the left thumb, or as others express it, according to the course of the Sun; the breaking of which order, is reckon'd no small impropriety .. in Great Britain and Ireland. **1822** J. H. ALLAN *Bridal of*

Caölchairn 312 [Argyll.] The rotation of the whiskey bottle is as regular as the sun which it follows. **1878** A. MACGREGOR *Brahan Seer* 129. 'Superstitions of Highlanders'. It is unlucky to drink the health of a company, or to serve them round a table, except from left to right, as the sun goes in the firmament, or the hands on the dial-plate of a watch. **1932** C. IGGLESDEN *Those Superstitions* 190. Percy Chapman, the England captain, tells me he believes in none of them [superstitions], but port certainly must go the right way round. **1965** W. GRAEBNER *My Dear Mister Churchill* 60. At a meal .. Churchill always poured for everyone within reach. Then he would pass the bottle along and ask the others to help themselves. He took great care to see that the bottle was always passed to the left. Passing to the right was bad luck, and Churchill was very superstitious. **1966** B. MESSENGER *Guide to Etiquette* 63. The port decanter is brought with the glasses and the guest on the host's right is served first. The port must circulate clockwise and is *never* reversed.

SUNWISE, rope coiled

1885 *Folklore* 310 [Macduff, Banff.] It is the common practice to coil a rope according to the course of the sun. **1988** Captain, Merchant Navy, 67 [Chelmondiston, Suffolk] You always coil rope clockwise. Of course that's the natural way for it to go, as the strands are woven together that way in ropemaking.

SUNWISE round farm

1924 J. A. EGGAR *Remembrances* 149 [Binstead, Hants.] When conducting farm valuations some valuers will on no account go round the farm except by following the sun, and will only measure a rick by the same rule. I follow the same rule by habit. **1932** WOMEN'S INSTITUTE *Worcestershire Book* 34 [Cotheridge] Never ride round a farm starting away from the sun.

SUNWISE round house

1970 J. MCPHEE *Crofter and Laird* 150 [Colonsay, Hebrides] Walking around a house you were about to enter—you went to the right. You did all such things in the direction that corresponded to the course of the sun.

SUNWISE, stirring

1928 *Folklore* 174 [Cardigan.] Cakes must be stirred the same way as the clock; if you stir the other way the cake will be spoilt in the baking. 1965 *Folklore* 46. Even in the middle of the twentieth century girls in Portnahaven [Islay] were urged to stir food in a clockwise direction only; otherwise the mixture would go wrong or, worse, some unrelated evil might occur. 1982 Female student, 20 [Cleveland, Yorks.] Stirring the tea in the pot widdershins [anticlockwise] was said to cause a quarrel.

SUPPER, apparition comes to share

1684 R. BOVET *Pandaemonium* 221. We had been told divers times, that if we fasted on Midsummer Eve, and then at 12 a Clock at night laid a cloath on the Table; with Bread, and Cheese, and a cup of the best Beer, setting ourselves down, as if we were going to eat, & leaving the door of the Room open; we should see the Persons whom we should afterwards Marry, come into the Room, and drink to us. 1796 *Hull Advertiser* 14 May 3. On Friday morning a girl living at a public house .. in this town, was seized with an illness .. she died early on Saturday morning. Thursday evening, being what is called St Mark's eve, the above girl in company with two others sat up to observe a custom of the most dangerous and ridiculous nature, which they called watching their suppers; in doing which it is supposed this girl heard some noise, or fancied she saw some object, which had such a terrible effect on her mind, as to produce the fatal consequences abovementioned. We hope her awful example will be a warning to the thoughtless observances of such superstitious and impious practices. c.1840 *Mother Bunch's Golden Fortune-Teller* 11. Any unmarried woman fasting on Midsummer Eve, and at midnight laying a clean cloth, with bread, cheese, and ale .. the street door being left open, the person whom she is afterwards to marry will come into the room, and drink to her by bowing. 1872 HARDY *Under the Greenwood Tree* pt. I VIII. Never was I in such a taking as on that Midsummer-eve! I sat up .. I put the bread-and-cheese and cider quite ready, as the witch's book ordered, and I opened the door, and I waited till the clock struck twelve, my nerves all alive .. and when the clock had struck, lo and behold! I could see through the door a little small man in the lane wi' a shoe-maker's apron on. 1880 W. SIKES *British Goblins* 302–3 [Wales] One known as the Maid's Trick is thus performed; and none must attempt it but true maids, or they will get themselves into trouble with the fairies: On Christmas eve, or on one of the Three Spirit Nights, after the old folks are abed, the curious maiden puts a good stock of coal on the fire, lays a clean cloth on the table, and spreads thereon such store of eatables and drinkables as her larder will afford. Toasted cheese is considered an appropriate luxury for this occasion. Having prepared the feast, the maiden then takes off all her clothing, piece by piece, standing before the fire the while, and her last and closest garment she washes in a pail of clear spring water, on the hearth, and spreads it to dry across a chair-back turned to the fire. She then goes off to bed, and listens for her future husband, whose apparition is confidently expected to come and eat the supper. If her lover come, she will be his bride that same year. 1915 J. A. PENNY *Horncastle* 75 [Lincs.] An old woman of nearly 80 told me her aunt and other girls, who wanted husbands, set a supper for them on St Mark's Eve, leaving a vacant chair between them for the husbands, and sat looking at the supper .. waiting for the spirits of their future husbands to come and sit down at table as soon as they had returned from Church at midnight. At 10 minutes to 12 they heard such a dreadful noise .. they all rushed off to bed .. and so .. neither her aunt nor any of the other girls ever got any husbands.

Cf. SHIFT/SMOCK etc., apparition turns.

SWALLOW AND MARTIN, harming

1650 BROWNE *Vulgar Errors* V XXII.

Though uselesse unto us and rather of molestation, we commonly refrain from killing Swallows, and esteem it unlucky to destroy them. 1713 *Guardian* 21 May. Some Advantage might be taken of the common Notion, that 'tis ominous or unlucky to destroy some sorts of Birds, as Swallows and Martins; this Opinion might possibly arise from the Confidence these Birds seem to put in us by building under our Roofs, so that it is a kind of Violation of the Laws of Hospitality to murder them. 1777 BRAND *Antiquities* 92. It is accounted unlucky to destroy Swallows;—This is probably a Pagan Relique. We read in Ælian, that these Birds were sacred to the *Penates*, or household Gods of the Antients, and therefore were preserved. 1826 HONE *Every-Day Book* I 23 Apr. Children of all ages in .. Berkshire, Buckingham, and Oxford, repeat the following couplet, which if not taught, is always sanctioned by their parents: 'The Martin and the Swallow, Are God Almighty's birds to hollow [hallow].' 1858 *N & Q* 2nd ser. VI 522. One day in my childhood while playing with a bow and arrows, I was going to shoot at a swallow that was sitting on a paling. An old woman who was near me exclaimed, 'Oh! Sir, don't shoot a swallow; if you do the cows will milk blood.' 1895 S. O. ADDY *Household Tales* 67. It is lucky to have swallows' nests about your house, and boys who throw stones at them must be punished. These birds mourn for Our Lord. They are sacred and must not be destroyed. Cats will not eat .. swallows. 1900 S. HEWETT *Nummits* 54 [Devon] It is unlucky .. to kill a swallow.

SWALLOW AND MARTIN, harming nests of

1625 T. JACKSON *Originall of Vnbeliefe* 177–8. To robbe a Swallowes nest built in a fire-house, is from some old bell-dames Catechismes, held a more fearfull sacrilege, than to steale a chalice from out of a Church .. The prime cause of this superstitious feare, or hope of good lucke by their kinde vsage, was that these birds were accounted sacred amongst the Romanes, to their houshold gods, of which number Venus the especiall patronesse of swallowes was one.

1734 POPE *Second Satire of Second Book of Horace* Till of late .. children sacred held a Martin's nest. 1864 *N & Q* 3rd ser. V 237 [Sheringham, Norfolk] The superstition that it is unlucky to interfere with swallows' nests is .. universal [but] I should .. add that in Upper Sheringham they explain it by saying that when the birds gather .. and sit in long rows along the leads of the church, they are settling who is to die before they come again. 1866 HENDERSON *Northern Counties* 91. A farmer's wife near Hull told .. how some young men, sons of a banker in that town, had pulled down all the swallows' nests about a little farm which he possessed. 'The bank broke soon after .. and .. the family have had nought but trouble since.' 1878 *N & Q* 5th ser. X 65. There is a curious superstition in Cheshire that if a martin's nest is destroyed on a farm the cows will give milk tainted with blood. 1882 *Folk-Lore Record* 83 [Co. Wexford] If swallows build in an outhouse and are routed out, the cows will give bloody milk during the year. 1888 S. O. ADDY *Sheffield Glossary* xix. If one robs a swallow's nest .. it is said that the cows will give blood in their milk. 1928 E. LOVETT *Surrey and Sussex* 16. It is unlucky to destroy martins' nests on a house. 1938 *Folklore* 91 [Shelfanger, Norfolk] The farmer's wife wanted some house-martins' nests removed, as they were soiling the window-sills. The man employed in painting, however, said his master had warned him not to injure the nests as it was very unlucky, and he had known a man break his leg after having done so. 1953 *Folklore* 293 [Westmorland] If you rob a swallow's nest the cows will give blood in their milk. 1954 Boy, 10 [Etton, Yorks.] It is bad luck to rob a swallow's nest. 1969 R. BLYTHE *Akenfield* xiv. Each house seems to have so many people in it and so many martins. You must never bang their mud nests down or make them unwelcome, it is very unlucky. It is thought poor manners to destroy a martin's nest while he is abroad.

SWALLOW AND MARTIN: nests lucky

1507 *Gospelles of Dystaues* pt. 2 VII. Whan .. swalowes chatter or make their nestes it is synge of good ayre and good fortune. **1787** GROSE *Provincial Glossary* Superstitions 65. It is deemed lucky to have martins or swallows build their nests in the eaves of a house, or on the chimneys. *c.***1816** Wilkie MS (HENDERSON *Northern Counties* 1866, 90) It is a very good omen for swallows to take possession of a place, and build their nests around it. **1827** HONE *Every-Day Book* II 19 Nov. It is considered a presage of good, for [a martin] to build its nest in the corner of the bedroom-window; and particularly so, should the first inhabitants return in the season. **1863** R. CHAMBERS *Book of Days* I 678 [Suffolk] It is lucky for you that martins should build against your house, for they will never come to one where there is strife. Soon after setting up housekeeping for myself, I was congratulated on a martin having built its nest in the porch over my front door. **1899** J. SHAW *Schoolmaster* 34 [Tynron, Dumfries.] Swallows building in your eaves is lucky. **1923** [Somerset] Swallows bring good luck to a house on which they build. *c.***1940** [Great Paxton, Hunts.] Swallows only build under the eaves of houses where there is money. **1954** [Forfar, Angus] Lightning never strikes a barn where swallows nest. **1968** Woman, 29 [Fringford, Oxon.] The baker said that when he retired the swallows no longer nested under his eaves because swallows only do so when there is money in the house. **1978** A. WRIGHT *Holderness* 14 [E. Yorks.] If housemartins build on your home, a baby will come.

Cf. SWIFT unlucky.

swallow and martin: also see ROBIN/WREN/MARTIN/SWALLOW sacred.

SWAN unlucky

1986 *Scots Mag.* July 440 [Sutherland] In the Dornoch Firth area, fishermen regard the swan as a portent of bad luck.

Cf. ALBATROSS.

SWIFT unlucky

1867 *N & Q* 3rd ser. XII 203 [Isle of Thanet, Kent] The farmer said .. 'Knock them black swifts down, sir; they are regular limbs of the devil .. The martins and swallows .. bring good luck. Them black imps always bring the contrary.'

Ibid. 273. Almost all the provincial names of the Swift seem to indicate something unholy, as Devling, Devilet, Sker-devil, Screech-devil. **1883** *Folklore* 394 [Hants.] A farmer who made light of popular superstition went out one day and, by way of bravado, shot seventeen swifts. He was the owner of seventeen fine cows; but before seven weeks were over every one of his cows died. **1885** SWAINSON *British Birds* 95 [Yorks.] It is called .. Devil bird. **1889** *Folklore* 44 [Advie, Moray.] If the 'black swallows' .. are out, there will be no luck.

SWORD falls from scabbard

*c.***1816** Wilkie MS (HENDERSON *Northern Counties* 1866, 30) On the Border .. swords falling out of their scabbards .. are tokens of approaching death.

Cf. KNIFE falls; UMBRELLA/WALKING STICK, dropping.

SWORD AND SCABBARD: divination

1685 *Mother Bunch's Closet* (1885, 18) You that dare venture yourselves into a church-yard just as it strikes twelve, take there a naked sword in your hand, and go nine times about the church, saying only thus, 'Here's the sword, but where's the scabbard?', and the ninth time the person you are to marry will meet you with a scabbard, and so kiss you. **1828** HONE *Table Book* II 159. In Chancery, Aug. 2, 1827. In a cause, 'Barker *v.* Ray', a deponent swore, that a woman, named Ann Johnson, and also called 'Nanny Nunks', went to the deponent, and said to her, 'I'll tell you what I did to know if I could marry Mr Barker. On St Mark's night I ran round a haystack nine times, with a ring in my hand, calling out, 'Here's the sheath, but where's the knife?' and, when I was running round the ninth time, I thought I saw Mr Barker coming home; but he did not come home that night, but was brought from the Blue Bell, at Beverley, the next day.' **1880** W. SIKES *British Goblins* 305 [Wales] Enter the church-yard at midnight, carrying a *twca*, which is a sort of knife made out of an old razor, with a handle of sheep or goat-horn, and encircle the church edifice seven times, holding the *twca* at arm's length, and saying, 'Dyma'r twca, p'le mae'r wain?'

(Here's the *twca*—where's the sheath?). 1883 BURNE *Shropshire* 177. A young man wishing to know who should be his future wife, was advised to walk three times round the church at midnight, and each time he passed the porch to put his sword through the key-hole and say, 'Here is the sword, but where is the sheath?' As he returned home he would meet the woman he was destined to marry.

T

TABLE, extra place at

1972 *Lore and Language* July 7 [Coalisland, Co. Tyrone] When there has been a recent death in the family, continue to set a place for that person until his month's mind has been read. During the period after death his spirit is still very close. **1986** [London] Her husband had this awful habit of laying an extra place at table for every meal. He said it would ensure that he would never go hungry, and also that a long absent friend would return. It drove her to distraction, and she cited it as one of the grounds for divorce. **1986** Man, *c.*45 [Scone, Perth.] You know you should always lay an extra place at table? My mother said, and I believe, it is in case our Lord returns as he said he would.

TABLE, sitting on

1910 *Folklore* 89 [Argyll.] A girl who sits on a table will never be married. **1914** *Folklore* 364 [Newmarket, Cambs.] When I was sitting one day on a table in her house, a labourer's wife said that I must be wanting to get married. **1923** [Bradford-on-Tone, Som.] For a single person to sit on the edge of the table, it is a sign that he or she wants to get married. **1932** C. IGGLESDEN *Those Superstitions* 154. If a girl sits on a table while she is talking to a man she will never be married. **1953** Girl, 15 [Ipswich, Suffolk] They say if you sit upon a table you will never get married. **1955** Woman, 52 [Redhill, Surrey] To sit on a table is a sign of wanting a young man. **1982** Female student, 20 [Cleveland, Yorks.] An engaged girl who sits on a table talking to her fiancé runs the risk of losing him.

TABLE, two people sitting on

1962 Woman, 52 [Scarborough, Yorks.] If two people sat on a table it meant a quarrel.

table: also see index: table, sacred/magical.

TABLECLOTH/SHEET, creases in

1868 *N & Q* 4th ser. I 193. In folding up a table-cloth, if there happen to be a crease in the middle of diamond shape, it is the sign of a death. **1912** LEATHER *Herefordshire* 118. It is an omen of death if the tablecloth be folded with the middle doubled up, so that the octagonal crease resembles the shape of a coffin, in the centre, when it is opened. **1936** E. H. RUDKIN *Lincolnshire* 17. To find a diamond in a freshly unfolded sheet—it denotes 'death in the bed' that it is used on. **1956** Woman, 46 [Scarborough, Yorks.] Diamond-shaped creases in tablecloths and sheets are sure signs of death—or bad ironing, of course. **1967** S. MARSHALL *Fenland Chronicle* pt. 2 IX. Signs when anybody were a-going to die .. like finding a coffin-shaped crease in a sheet when you unfolded it. **1982** Female student, 20 [Cleveland, Yorks.] If a diamond or coffin-shaped crease appears in a table cloth as it is unfolded, this is seen as an omen of death.

TABLE-NAPKIN, folding

1923 [Martock, Som.] Don't 'ee mean to come agean? *That's* why you folded up your table napkin so neatly. **1948** E. & M. A. RADFORD *Superstitions* 180. A guest who folds his napkin after a first meal in any house, will never go to the house again.—General. **1982** Female student, 20 [Cleveland, Yorks.] There is a relic of the old hospitality lore in the belief that if a guest making a single visit to one's home folds his own serviette, he has virtually fore-ordained the 'folding up' of the friendship.

Cf. CHAIR put back in place.

TEA, bubbles on

1831 HONE *Year Book* 29 Feb. Bubbles upon tea, denote kisses. **1867** HARLAND & WILKINSON *Lancashire Folk-Lore* 228. Young persons may occasionally be detected in the act of stirring a cup of tea

.. so as to .. produce a circle of foam .. The quantity of foam indicates the amount of money which will ultimately be bequeathed.   1882 *People's Friend* 13 Sept. 580. If, after the tea has been stirred, a little foam remains on the surface, it means that money will soon be received by the person whose cup it is.   1923 [Somerset] Bubbles in the middle of your cup, sign of some money coming. Bubbles at the side, sign of kisses.   1970 Woman, *c.*60 [Pontypridd, Glam.] We used to say the bubbles meant money—but that's when you put sugar in, and I haven't taken sugar for years. 1984 Woman, 57 [South Shields, Co. Durham] If your tea is 'frothy' on top, there is 'money in the cup'.

Cf. URINE, bubbles on; WELL: divination.

TEA, making

1868 *N & Q* 4th ser. II 553 [N. England] To put milk into one's tea before sugar, is to 'cross' the love of the party so doing. 1883 *N & Q* 6th ser. VIII 226. A woman in a Rutland village on returning from a visit brought with her a teapot, which she gave as a present to a young woman friend .. 'because no one had good luck until she had made tea out of her own teapot.'   1923 [Trowbridge, Wilts.] If water is put into a tea-pot and the tea forgotten, it is a sign of a coming misfortune.   1953 Girl, 15 [Ipswich, Suffolk] If you make the tea weaker than usual without meaning to do so, a friend is turning away from you. To make the tea too strong, a new friendship for you.   1985 [Taunton, Som.] To spill a spoonful of tea when you are making it, is a lucky omen for the mother of the house.

TEA, stirring

1900 S. HEWETT *Nummits* 54 [Devon] It is unlucky .. to stir the leaves in the teapot before pouring.   1923 [Chard, Som.] It is unlucky to stir your tea with anything else but a spoon.   1975 Woman, 72 [Sudbury, Suffolk] Stirring someone else's tea means stirring up strife.

TEA, two people pouring

1885 *N & Q* 6th ser. XII 466. This evening as I was about to take the teapot from 'the neat-handed Phyllis' who looks after my wants, she—then pouring the hot water from it—said, 'It's bad luck for two to pour out of a pot, isn't it, sir?' .. My Phyllis hails from Evesham [Worcs.].   1932 C. IGGLESDEN *Those Superstitions* 155–6 [Romney Marsh, Kent] A parson told me that in his parish there existed a belief that if a man and woman poured out a cup of tea from the same pot a child would be born to them. 1939 *Folklore* 185 [Cambs.] A woman may not pour out tea or any drink in another woman's house especially after the hostess has started doing so [or] the woman would become pregnant.   1940 *Folklore* 117. I have often heard .. that two women should not catch hold of a teapot at once or one of them will have gingerheaded twins within the year.   1983 Woman, 24 [Kent] If you change the pourer, you'll have twins.

TEA/COFFEE CUP, 'reading'

1726 *Dublin Weekly Journal* 11 June 4. Advice is hereby given, That there is lately arrived in this City, the Famous Mrs Cherry, the only Gentlewoman truly Learned in that Occult Science of Tossing of Coffee Grounds; who has .. for some time past, practiced, to the General Satisfaction of her Female Visitants .. Her Hours are after prayers are done at St Peter's Church, till Dinner. 1731 *Round about our Coal-Fire* 21. We have a sort of Mother Witch .. which are the Coffee and Tea Throwers to tell People's Fortunes.   1755 *Connoisseur* 17 Feb. I have seen him [future husband] several times in coffee-grounds, with a sword by his side; and he was once at the bottom of a tea-cup, in a coach and six, with two footmen behind it.   1766 GOLDSMITH *Vicar of Wakefield* x. The girls themselves had their omens .. true-love knots lurked in the bottom of every tea-cup. 1811 *Ora & Juliet* I 205. She tossed the cup after breakfast, and read the fortunes of the maid-servants.   1854 *N & Q* 1st ser. X 534. The divination by 'coffee-grounds' appears to be the same as that still practised by young females in Scotland out of frolic, called 'reading the cups'. In any of the residuum of the tea leaves .. at the bottom of the cup ..

there is fancied .. representations of utensils in trade, horses, cows, coaches, houses, castles, &c., from which are prognosticated the station, occupation, &c., of the future husband. **1883** BURNE *Shropshire* 277. In my childish days, the nurses .. by a dextrous sort of circular jerk, emptied the last remains of the tea in such a manner as to leave the dregs scattered well over the bottom and sides of the cup. Some were more skilful (or more imaginative) in their interpretations than others. **1884** *Harper's Mag.* Nov. 889. In a sort of Oriental divination they always turned their tea-cups .. after tea-drinking. **1911** J. C. DAVIES *Welsh Folk-Lore* 14 [Pontshan, Cardigan.] There was a woman, who only died a few years ago .. who was considered an expert in the art of fortune telling by a tea cup .. Having emptied the cup, it is turned round three times in the left hand .. If the leaves are scattered evenly round the sides .. it is .. a very good sign; if .. the bottom of the cup appears very black with leaves, it is a very bad sign' [etc.]. *c.***1939** *Book of Fortune* 61–2. The ritual traditionally associated with divination by tea-leaves .. The inquirer drinks from the cup until about one teaspoonful of liquid only is left .. The cup is then held in the left hand and moved three times in a circular, anti-clockwise direction .. then slowly inverted on the saucer .. Glancing into the cup .. pictures and symbols will begin to appear, and each will have some specific meaning. **1953** Girl, 14 [Aberdeen] Leaves in the shape of a heart means future happiness. If there are dots .. one may expect some money. If two hearts .. a marriage. **1957** Girl, 12 [Penrith, Cumb.] One way some people tell fortunes is to read a tea cup. When someone finishes their tea the person empties the cup and just leaves the leaves. Then they turn the cup upside down and turn it round about three times. Then they look at the leaves and tell you your fortune. **1971** *Evening Standard* 29 Nov. 21 [cartoon] 'Now let me see! What do my tea leaves say?'

TEA-LEAF OR STALK

1854 *N & Q* 1st ser. X 534 [Scotland]

A piece of the woody fibre .. swimming in the liquid, is named a 'stranger' .. if found to be hard, it is a male; if soft, a female; and if large or small, indicates the tallness .. of some person expected to visit that day. **1865** R. HUNT *West of England* 2nd ser. 234. Stems of tea floating in that beverage indicate strangers .. The time of the stranger's arrival may be known by placing the stem on the back of one hand, and smacking it with the other; the number of blows given before it is removed indicates the number of days before his arrival. **1882** *People's Friend* 8 Nov. 711. If a 'stranger' floats to the top of her cup of tea she has only to bite it to tell you whether her visitor is to be a lady or gentleman—the tenderness of the stalk indicating a lady. **1883** BURNE *Shropshire* 277. A stalk or long tea-leaf floating in the tea was .. at once taken out and laid on the back of one hand, which was then struck sharply with the palm of the other, in order to see whether the 'chap' would come to the back door or the front, according to whether, after this, the stalk was found on the back of the hand or the palm. Then the stalk was placed on the palm of one hand and the hands were clapped. If it remained adhering to the hand on which it was placed, the 'chap' was 'faithful', if not, he was 'fickle'. **1923** [Taunton, Som.] If a tea leaf floats on your cup of tea, take it, place on your hand and bang with the other hand. Count the bangs, and each is a day before a stranger comes. If a hard leaf a man, if a soft one a woman. 'There's a stranger in your tea' is a common saying. **1939–40** MACNEICE 'Prognosis.' Goodbye, Winter, The days are getting longer, The tea-leaf in the teacup Is herald of a stranger. **1983** Woman, 21 [Yorks.] The 'stranger' is a piece of stalk which floats on top of the tea. You should .. place it on the back of your hand and hit it with the palm of the other hand. At the same time, say the days of the week, and when the 'stranger' sticks to the other hand this shows the day he will come: 'Then you put him under the table, And he'll come if he's able.' Of course, this ritual for removing tea stalks is not necessary if you use tea bags.

TEA-LEAVES, disposing of

1982 Female student, 20 [Cleveland, Yorks.] It is considered extremely unlucky to throw tea leaves away, as they should always be laid on the back of the fire to keep poverty away.

Cf. WASHING WATER, throwing out.

TEAPOT LID

1855 *Gents Mag.* pt. 2 385 [Shrops./Worcs.] To leave a tea-pot lid open undesignedly is an indication that a stranger is coming. **1875** *N & Q* 5th ser. III 465 [Shrops.] If the tea-pot lid is accidentally left up, it's a sure sign of a stranger coming. **1936** E. H. RUDKIN *Lincolnshire* 18. To leave the lid off the teapot (accidentally) when mashing the tea denotes the coming of a stranger. **1983** Woman, 60 [Colchester, Essex] 'Oh look, I've left the lid off the teapot—there'll be a stranger coming.'

TEETH, born with

AD 77 PLINY *Natural History* VII xv (1855, II 153) Some infants are even born with teeth .. When this .. happened in the case of a female, it was looked upon .. as an omen of some inauspicious event. **1593** SHAKESPEARE *3 Henry the Sixth* v vi. Teeth had'st thou in thy head, when thou wa't borne, To signifie, thou cam'st to bite the world. **1957** *Folklore* 413. To be born with teeth is an extremely bad sign .. One midwife informed me .. that it means the child will grow up to be a murderer .. In some districts it has been watered down to .. simple ill-luck. **1965** *Scarborough News* 29 Mar. 4. Freddie Trueman, Junior (born on Saturday) will be lucky .. He was born with two front teeth. **1987** *Mirror* 28 Aug. 20 [Stepney, London] I have heard of two superstitions about babies born with a tooth or teeth and am puzzled because they seem to be contradictory. One is that the child will be extremely clever, the other, which is quite horrendous, is that the child is born to be hanged.

TEETH, cutting early = another baby

1858 DENHAM *North of England* (1895, 48) Soon teeth—soon toes. This means that if your baby's teeth begin to sprout early, you will soon have .. another

baby. **1873** HARLAND & WILKINSON *Lancashire Legends* 221. When children cut their teeth early, their mothers are supposed to be prolific .. 'Soon with goom; quick with woom.'

TEETH, cutting early = death

1659 HOWELL *Proverbs* 4a. Soon todd [toothed], soon with God. A Northern Proverb when a child hath teeth too soon. **1670** RAY *Proverbs* 52. Some have it quickly to'd, quickly with God, as if early breeding of teeth, were a sign of a short life. **1888** *N & Q* 7th ser. V 285. I was speaking to a woman in this parish [Knightwick, Worcs.], a few days ago, of a baby which was nine months old and still toothless. 'Then she will live all the longer,' was her reply; 'for my mother used always to say "soon toothed, soon turfed".'

TEETH, cutting upper first

1849 BRAND *Antiquities* II 87. If a child tooths first in the upper jaw, it is considered ominous of its dying in its infancy. **1858** DENHAM *North of England* (1895, 75) If a child 'tooths downbank' (i.e. has its first teeth in the upper jaw), it won't live long. **1891** *N & Q* 7th ser. XI 305 [Worksop, Notts.] A baby in which I have an interest was found to have cut its first tooth the other day. It was a bottom tooth, and the servant exclaimed 'A long life! A long life!' **1895** *Folklore* 395 [Tyrie, Aberdeen.] If ye cut yir first teeth abeen, Ye winna dance i' yir marriage sheen [shoes]. **1957** Man, 63 [Halifax, Yorks.] They used to say that a child who cut the first tooth upward (that is a bottom tooth) was almost sure to live. If the first tooth was cut downward it was not so sure to live.

TEETH, disposing of

1686–7 AUBREY *Remaines* (1881, 11) When Children shaled their Teeth the women use to wrap, or put salt about the tooth, and so throw it into a good fire. **1830** FORBY *East Anglia* 414. You should always burn a tooth when it is drawn; because, if a dog should find it and eat it, you would have dog's teeth that come in its place. **1858** DENHAM *North of England* (1895, 48) Fill the cavities of extracted teeth with salt and burn them in the fire saying the while: 'Fire, fire, burn baan, God send me my tuthe again.' 1869 *N & Q* 4th ser. IV 212 [Paisley, Renfrew.] When .. a tooth falls out .. go to some retired spot .. and throw it with your left hand over your right shoulder .. When you again visit the place, you will find a treasure. 1870 *N & Q* 4th ser. VI 131 [Lancs./Yorks.] When a boy I remember being told .. that the penalty for not burning an extracted tooth is to search for it in a pail of blood in hell after death. 1878 *Folk-Lore Record* 44 [Fittleworth, Sussex] Should they be found, and gnawed by any animal, the child's new teeth would be .. like the animal's that had bitten the old one. Master Simmons .. had a very large pig's tooth in his upper jaw .. that he averred was caused by his mother's having thrown one of his cast teeth away by accident in the hog-trough. 1895 F. T. ELWORTHY *Evil Eye* 437. At Westleigh [Devon] it was up to a recent time the custom carefully to preserve all teeth extracted; women used to hide them in their back hair. This was done to prevent enemies or dogs getting hold of them. 1953 Girl, 12 [Aberystwyth, Cardigan.] When you have a tooth out, you must sprinkle it with salt and throw it over your left shoulder, for luck. 1954 Girl, 14 [Tunstall, Staffs.] If a child's tooth came out I would not think of burning it without smothering it in salt first. 1954 Girl, 14 [Stoke-on-Trent, Staffs.] Put a tooth under your pillow and a fairy will give you sixpence for it. 1973 A. TIBBLE *Greenhorn* 30 [Rounton, Yorks., c.1915] Mother .. told us to put the tooth into the flame of the fire. Then she taught us: 'Fire, fire, burn a bone, God send another tooth again: A straight one, A white one, And in the same place.' 1987 Boy, 8 [Manchester, Lancs.] You put it under your pillow, and then you write a message, 'Dear Tooth Fairy, would you leave my tooth?' And in the morning you find the tooth still there, and you find 20p—or 50p if you're lucky.

TEETH, dreaming about

c.1050 MS Cotton Tib. A. iii (COCKAYNE *Leechdoms* III 203) If a man's teeth seem to drop out [in a dream], one of his relatives will die. 1641 T. KILLIGREW *Parson's Wedding* II v. The Captain sad? 'tis prophetick, I'de as live have dreamt of .. the loss of my teeth. 1646 BROWNE *Vulgar Errors* IV v. To dream of the losse of right or left tooth presageth the death of male or female kindred. 1708 *Aristotle's New Book of Problems* 89. *Q.* What to dream that one's Teeth or Eyes drop out? *A.* The loss of Children, near Relations, or other Friends. c.1816 Wilkie MS (HENDERSON *Northern Counties* 1866, 84) If a man dream that his teeth fall out, he will hear next day of the death of a friend. 1878 *Folk-Lore Record* 14 [Fittleworth, Sussex] To dream about your teeth is a warning that sorrow of some kind is near at hand. 1895 J. HARDY *Denham Tracts* II 272 [Scottish Border] If one dreams that a tooth is out it is a sign of a relative's death. 1985 Woman, 57. I still hate to dream of my teeth falling out. My mother used to say it meant sickness for yourself or one of the family. That was in South Shields [Co. Durham].

TEETH, gap between

1387 CHAUCER *Tales* Prol. ll. 467–8. She koude muchel of wandrynge by the weye; Gat toothed was she, soothly for to seye. 1861 C. C. ROBINSON *Dialect of Leeds* 297. When the teeth are wide apart, it is the sign of being rich at a future time, or, according to another interpretation, of travel. 1883 BURNE *Shropshire* 268. A person whose teeth are far apart is born to travel, says one (Ellesmere), but such an one will die rich, says another (Pulverbatch). 1895 S. O. ADDY *Household Tales* 94. If you can get a threepenny piece between the two front teeth in your top jaw you will be rich. 1909 M. TREVELYAN *Folk-Lore of Wales* 268. The old women say: 'Watch well when the child has finished cutting its first teeth, for if there is a parting between the two front teeth to admit .. a sixpenny piece [he] will have riches and prosperity through life.' 1953 Boy, 15 [Felindre, Radnor.] If you have a wide parting between your teeth you are going to be rich. 1964 *Woman* 9 May 5 [Cheadle, Cheshire] My first even teeth were followed by a set of all shapes and sizes. The wide gap between the two front ones I was told (maybe for consolation) meant I should marry riches.

TEETHING amulet

AD 77 PLINY *Natural History* XXVIII LXXVIII (1856, V 364) A wolf's tooth, attached to the body .. acts as a preservative against the maladies attendant upon dentition .. The first teeth shed by a horse, attached as an amulet to infants, facilitate dentition, and are better still, when not allowed to touch the ground. 1688 AUBREY *Remaines* (1881, 204) Coralls are worne by children still: but in Ireland they value the fang-tooth (holder) of an wolfe before it: which they set in silver and gold as we doe ye Coralls. 1713 *Wentworth Papers* (1883, 332 n.) On April 10 Lady Wentworth wrote [to her son] that she had sent to Ireland for a wolf's tooth, for her granddaughter Lady Anne—'none ever breeds their teeth ill that has a wolf's tooth. I had one for all you.'

TELEPHONE, ringing

1982 Female student, 20 [Cleveland, Yorks.] It is thought that a telephone ringing at intermittent intervals with no call following it is an omen of death.

   Cf. KNOCKING = death omen.

THATCH: piece stolen to destroy witch's power

1586 CAMDEN *Britannia* (tr. Gibson, II 380) [Limerick, c.1566] If their butter be stolen, they fancy they shall recover it, if they take some of the thatch that hangs over the door, and throw it into the fire. 1618 W. PERKINS *Works* III 643. The burning of the thatch of the suspected parties house .. is thought to bee able to cure the party bewitched, and to make the Witch to bewray her selfe. c.1623 DEKKER *Witch of Edmonton* IV i. What hast got there? A handful of Thatch pluck'd off a Hovel of hers; and they say, when 'tis burning, if she be a Witch, she'll come running in. 1671 BLAGRAVE *Astrological Practice* 154. To afflict the Witch, causing the evil to return back upon them .. take some of her thatch from over the door .. wet .. it over with the patients water .. then let it burn .. through a trivet. 1877 E.

PEACOCK *Lincolnshire Glossary* 252. If you are bewitched, and steal some thatch off the house of the person who bewitches you, it is almost certain that his or her power will cease from that moment. 1892 *Folklore* 84 [Isle of Man] A fisherman on his way in the morning to the fishing, and chancing to pass by the cottage of another fisherman who is not on friendly terms with him, will pluck a straw from the thatch of the latter's dwelling. Thereby he is supposed to rob him of luck in the fishing for that day. 1934 *Folklore* 249 [Willoughton, Lincs.] If you pluck a straw from the thatch of a witch's house and hold it in your hand, a witch can't harm you.

THEATRE: bouquet

1879 *Folk-Lore Record* 204. To receive a bouquet at the stage-door before the play begins is an omen of failure.

   Cf. LUCK, wishing.

THEATRE: colours

1879 *Folk-Lore Record* 204. Blue is an unlucky colour among players, all the world over, silver being its only saving relief. 1910 T. SHARPER KNOWLSON *Superstitions* 226. Certain shades of yellow in a tie, or vest, or hat, are thought to exert an injurious influence. Even the orchestra leader would not allow a musician to play a yellow clarionet. 1933 J. B. BOOTH *Pink Parade* 97. A yellow clarinet in the orchestra [is unlucky].

THEATRE: curtain

1910 T. SHARPER KNOWLSON *Superstitions* 226-7. The looping of a drop curtain is the certain forerunner of evil [and] nearly every actor and manager believes it is bad luck to look at the audience from the wrong side [of the drop curtain] when it is down. 1984 Dancer, 37 [Harrow, Middx.] You mustn't peep through the curtains at the audience, that's *very* unlucky.

THEATRE, knitting in

1932 C. J. S. THOMPSON *Hand of Destiny* 282. Knitting on the side of the stage is regarded as unlucky. 1952 W. GRANVILLE *Theatrical Terms* 179. Knitting on the stage by actresses is taboo. 1987 Actress, 58 [Cheltenham, Glos.] We went on tour with *Daddy Long-Legs*, and it folded after six weeks. The older character-actress turned to me and said 'It's all your fault, you knitted at rehearsals.'

THEATRE: *Macbeth*

1910 T. SHARPER KNOWLSON *Superstitions* 225. Old actors believe the witches' song in *Macbeth* to possess the uncanny power of casting evil spells, and the majority of them strongly dislike to play in the piece. Hum the tune in the hearing of an old actor and the chances are you will lose his friendship. **1922** LYND *Solomon* 156. Actors .. have .. a number of professional superstitions. It is unlucky, they say .. to quote *Macbeth*. Actors dare not say to each other at parting: 'When shall we three meet again?' **1924** *Morning Post* 31 Jan. 4. The Fellowship of Players .. are avoiding Matthew Locke's music for 'Macbeth', for the reason that an old stage superstition that its use is disastrous to any company which adopts it .. Mr Harry Nelson, an octogenarian actor .. says that thirty years ago the superstition was very strong, and received confirmation on one occasion at the old City of London Theatre, when a repertory company he was in played 'Macbeth' to Locke's music. At the end of the week when the company was to be paid the treasury was found to be bare; someone had absconded with all the available cash. Thereafter, anyone who dared to whistle or hum the music in the theatre was immediately suppressed .. The 'Macbeth' music of Locke was really supplied for Davenant's altered version of 'Macbeth', produced at Dorset Garden in 1672. **1933** J. B. BOOTH *Pink Parade* 97. If you wish to bring about calamity on a wholesale scale you must whistle one or two bars of Locke's music to 'Macbeth'. **1936** *Folklore* 108 [letter from Sybil Thorndike] I have always heard that the superstition about quoting 'Macbeth' arose from the old days of stock companies, when this play was always put on when business was bad (being a favourite, so that it often presaged the end of a season). **1961** *Guardian* 7 Jan. 3. The Old Vic company .. left four days

behind schedule .. A spokesman for the company said: 'We blame it all on "Macbeth". There is a tradition .. that a performance of "Macbeth" always brings ill-fortune.' **1966** *Observer* 6 Nov. 12. 'I've met an enormous amount of people who are constantly quoting Shakespeare—especially Macbeth, though it's supposed to be unlucky—just to show they know all about the bloody play.'—Simone Signoret, actress. **1984** Actress, 58 [London] Oh! I nearly quoted the Scottish play, I just stopped myself in time.

THEATRE: make-up

1910 T. SHARPER KNOWLSON *Superstitions* 226. The upsetting of a make-up box is the certain forerunner of evil. **1922** LYND *Solomon* 157. It is unlucky to carry a make-up box, like an amateur actress. **1932** C. J. S. THOMPSON *Hand of Destiny* 283. To make up with a new set of grease paints on an opening night .. is .. unlucky. **1952** W. GRANVILLE *Theatrical Terms* 115. Make-up boxes should never be 'cleaned out', as this is said to bring bad luck. Ibid. 179. Powder, if dropped, should be danced upon (chorus girls' superstition) to bring luck. **1984** Actress, 58 [London] You must never clean out your make-up box.

THEATRE, new: coal thrown for luck

1933 J. B. BOOTH *Pink Parade* 96. To ensure a successful career [for the new theatre], you must stand on the stage and throw a piece of coal into the gallery.

Cf. FIRST-FOOT at New Year/Christmas: ritual of gifts.

THEATRE: pinch for luck

1968 *Daily Express* 16 Jan. 4. Christine Curtis .. stepped last night into a leading role—her first in the West End. As she stood nervously waiting to go on the stage, Robert Morley, the star of the show, gave her the traditional pinch for luck.

THEATRE: real flowers on stage

1928 A. R. WRIGHT *English Folklore* 36. Real flowers must not be used [on stage]. **1952** W. GRANVILLE *Theatrical Terms* 179. Real flowers are barred .. for stage decorations. **1968** *Observer* Suppl. 24

Nov. 12 [Peter Bull, actor] Real flowers are frightfully bad luck. 1985 Actor, 58 [Colchester, Essex] We never put real flowers on the stage in a play.

THEATRE: real things on stage

1961 *Daily Express* 9 Nov. 16. Actors think it unlucky .. to use real mirrors. 1968 *Observer* Suppl. 24 Nov. 12 [Peter Bull, actor] A lot of people won't wear real jewellery [on the stage].

Cf. THEATRE: real flowers on stage.

THEATRE, stumbling in

1879 *Folk-Lore Record* 204. In the English theatres, to trip on entering on the scene on the first night of a play is a sure sign of success. 1932 C. J. S. THOMPSON *Hand of Destiny* 283. If a heel comes off a girl's shoe, or if she stumbles during a dance, it is said to be a lucky omen. 1962 BBC RADIO 17 June. Kaye Webb said if an actress trips over the hem of her dress she picks it up and kisses it. This will bring a contract.

Cf. STUMBLING.

THEATRE: thread

1952 W. GRANVILLE *Theatrical Terms* 179. To find a piece of cotton which will wind round a finger without breaking indicates a contract with a management bearing the initial suggested by the number of times the cotton went round the finger. 1962 BBC RADIO 17 June. Kaye Webb said .. picking a length of cotton from off another actor and winding it round your finger will bring a contract.

Cf. THREAD on clothes: divination.

THEATRE: unlucky tunes

1932 C. J. S. THOMPSON *Hand of Destiny* 282. At one time .. to hum 'I Dreamt that I Dwelt in Marble Halls' or 'The Dead March', was to court disaster. 1938 *Oxford Companion to Music* 934. 'Three Blind Mice' .. has an absurd reputation of being very 'unlucky' .. were it played in a circus no performer would dare to do his 'turn'. 1952 W. GRANVILLE *Theatrical Terms* 179. Certain tunes are considered unlucky, especially the Barcarolle from *The Tales of Hoffmann* and the nursery rhyme *Three Blind Mice*. 1955 *Daily Express* 24 Jan. 6. I came across a musicians' superstition yes-

terday. It seems they dislike playing 'I Dreamt that I Dwelt in Marble Halls' from 'The Bohemian Girl'. It is supposed to presage a death. 1956 *Mirror* 28 Nov. 18. I was once threatened with the sack at the West End club where I worked as resident pianist .. because I played a tune from 'The Bohemian Girl'. 1975 TV Director. They say it's bad luck if anyone whistles 'I Dreamt I Dwelt in Marble Halls' on the set.

Cf. THEATRE: *Macbeth.*

THIMBLE

1923 [Bridgwater, Som.] If you have three thimbles given to you, you will never be married. 1929 E. MARJORIBANKS *Marshall Hall* 89 [London, 1894] Mrs Bricknell had helped her to get the body into the box, and had, from some strange superstition, thrown in a thimble. 1974 *People's Friend* 12 Jan. 45 [St Boswells, Roxburgh.] Forty years ago, a very old beggar regularly called at my door. [One day he said] 'I don't think I'll be on the roads much longer, but take this thimble for good luck.'

THIRTEEN in company or at table

c. AD 100 John 6: 70–1. Jesus answered them, Have I not chosen you twelve, and one of you is a devil? He spake of Judas Iscariot .. for he it was that should betray him, being one of the twelve. 1711 *Spectator* 8 Mar. On a sudden an old woman unluckily observed there were thirteen of us in company. This remark struck a panic terror into several who were present, insomuch that one or two of the Ladies were going to leave the room: but a friend of mine, taking notice that one of our female companions was big with child, affirmed there were fourteen in the room, and that, instead of portending one of the company should die, it plainly foretold one of them should be born. 1787 GROSE *Provincial Glossary* Superstitions 69. Notwithstanding .. opinions in favour of odd numbers, the number thirteen is considered as extremely ominous; it being held that, when thirteen persons meet in a room, one of them will die within the year. 1788 MRS THRALE *Diary* 8 Sept. (ed. Balderston, II 720) Why is the number 13 reckoned unlucky? Is it not because when our Saviour sate down to his last Supper—Judas Iscariot—the 13th of the Company, was a Traitor & a Devil? 1796 *Gents Mag.* 573. Dining lately with a friend, our conviviality was suddenly interrupted by the discovery of a maiden lady, who observed that our party consisted of thirteen. Her fears, however, were not without hope, till she found, after a very particular enquiry, that none of her married friends were likely to make any addition to the number. She was then fully assured that one of the party would die within the twelvemonth. 1808 JAMIESON *Scottish Dict. De'il's Dozen.* Many will not sail in a vessel, when this is the number of persons on board; and it is believed that some fatal accident must befal one of them .. Whence this strange superstition could originate, it is impossible to say. But it evidently includes the idea, that the thirteenth is the *devil's* lot. 1823 MOOR *Suffolk Words* 384. I have known, and now know, persons in genteel life, who did, and do, not sit down to table unmoved with twelve others. And so far is this feeling carried that one of the thirteen is requested to dine at a side table! The last sad supper .. may have furnished materials for this superstition. Our notion is that one of thirteen so partaking, will die ere the expiry of the year. The manner of the death .. is not necessarily Iscariotish. 1839 C. BARON-WILSON *Harriot, Duchess of St Albans* II 135–6. The old story runs, that the last individual of the thirteen who takes a seat has the greatest chance of being the 'doomed one'; but Miss Mellon always gave the last comer an equal chance with the rest for life .. she used to rise and say, 'I will not have any friend of mine sit down as the thirteenth; you must all rise, and we will then sit down again together.' 1865 S. EVANS *Brother Fabians MSS and other Poems* 'Charm'. If thirteen sit down to sup And thou first have risen up, Goodman, turn thy money! 1883 BURNE *Shropshire* 262. Every one knows that to sit down thirteen to table is a most unlucky omen, sure to be followed by the death of one of the party within the year .. Some say, however, that the evil will only befall the first who leaves the table, and may be averted if the whole company are careful to rise from their seats at the same moment. 1890 *Young Ladies' Journal* XXXV 4. The days of superstition are by no means over. There are women, not over conscientious in the discharge of religious observances, who would sooner disconcert a hostess .. than sit down with twelve others at the dinner table. 1899 J. SHAW *Schoolmaster* 34 [Tynron, Dumfries.] Thirteen at table is unlucky. He who rises first runs most risk. 1930 E. RAYMOND *Jesting Army* 12. He was resolved that they should sit down thirteen at a table and defy the Luck of Gallipoli. 1932 C. IGGLESDEN *Those Superstitions* 58. I once asked J. E. Mollison, the young Scotsman who broke the record flight from Australia to England, if he was superstitious. 'No,' was his reply, 'but I prefer not to sit with thirteen at the table.' 1970 S. JACKSON *The Great Barnato* 235. At a farewell dinner-party at the Savoy, thirteen guests had sat down, one having fallen out at the last minute. Woolf was so upset .. that he almost cancelled his passage and finally insisted on his wife and baby son following him by a different boat. 1983 K. ROSE *King George V* IV. The King .. was less superstitious than his father, who would never .. willingly sit down thirteen to dinner. 1985 Woman, 42 [Glasgow] I was serving everybody—dodging round—and he said 'I realize why you're not sitting down, because then we'd be thirteen.'

THIRTEEN unlucky number
1893 *Westminster Gazette* 3 Nov. 1. 'Look at that,' said Parnell, pointing to the number on his door. It was No. 13! 'What a room to give me! They are Tories, I suppose, and have done it on purpose.' 1923 [Castle Cary, Som.] Thirteen is a very unlucky number. 1927 *Folklore* 306–7. For some time before the late War I went almost daily to the British Museum reading room .. I gave some attention to the desks left to the last comers .. there was a very marked preference of any other desk to that numbered '13'. 1930 WAUGH *Vile Bodies* x. The mechanic helped him get out [of racing car]. 'May as well scratch,'

he said. 'He won't be good for anything more this afternoon. It's asking for trouble having a No. 13.' **1951** W. H. THOMPSON *Churchill's Shadow* 153. Invariably the two berths allotted to us seemed to be numbered 12 and 13 .. He [Churchill] always took 12 and left me with 13. **1959** *Journal of School of Scottish Studies* 198. At a recent piping competition in Scotland's third city the thirteenth piper bore the number 12A. **1960** *Sunday Times* 30 Oct. 11. Although this splendid hotel [Carlton Tower, in Knightsbridge, London] is described as having eighteen storeys, there are only seventeen floors. Number 13 is missing. **1961** *Woman's Mirror* 4 Feb. 55 [Hove, Sussex] How superstitious can some people get? After the shop assistant had carefully wrapped some material and rung up the charge on the till, her customer refused the material because the bill came to 13s. **1964** *Daily Sketch* 1 June 6. Thirty-four years ago, when Princess Margaret was born in Glamis Castle, the registration of her birth was delayed so that her number on the register wouldn't be the unlucky 13. **1968** *Times* 23 Oct. 2. Mr Jack Ellis, mineworker, of Hucknall, Nottinghamshire, who claims he has had three years of bad luck, is to be allowed to change the number of his council house from 13 Arden Close to 11A. **1983** Girl, 14 [Maldon, Essex] Down our road the builder has done houses 11, 12, 14, 15 and so on: he has missed out 13. **1985** Man, *c.*70 [London] I'm a hard-headed type: my sole exception is that when I shave and count the strokes, to make sure I have covered the ground, I always take care not to end at thirteen or any multiple of thirteen. **1985** Man, 69 [London] I never go out with £13 in my pocket—I always check.

THORN in flesh: charm

1583 H. HOWARD *Defensative against Supposed Prophecies* Oo4. What godly reason can any man alyve alledge, why mother Joane of Stowe, speaking these wordes, and neyther more nor lesse: Our Lord was the fyrst man, that euer thorne prickt vpon. It neuer blysted nor it neuer belted, and I pray God, nor this not may, Should cure eyther beastes, or men and women from diseases. **1664** PEPYS *Diary* 31 Dec. This Christmas I [looked] over all my papers .. to tear all that I found .. not to be worth keeping. [The following charms survived.] 'A Thorne. Jesus, that was of a virgin born Was pricked both with nail and thorn; It neither wealed, nor belled [festered], rankled, nor boned; In the name of Jesus no more shall this.' Or thus—'Christ was of a virgin born, And he was pricked with a thorn; And it did neither bell, nor swell; And I trust in Jesus this never will.' **1804** MS charmer's book (LEATHER *Herefordshire* 73) At Bethlehem our Saviour Jesus Christ was born, and at Jeruzalem was crucified with a cround of thorns and it did neither wrinkel nor swell and I trust in and through the name of our Lord and Savour this thorn it will go well. **1846** *Athenaeum* Sept. 956 [Wilts.] When I came home from birds-nesting, with my hands, and sometimes my face, well studded with thorns they were extracted with a needle, and the finger passed over the wound, with these words: 'Unto the Virgin Mary our Saviour he was born, And on his head he wore a crown of thorn; If you believe this true, and mind it well, This hurt will never fester, nor yet swell.' **1887** *Folklore* 200 [Cornwall] Christ was of a virgin born: And he was pricked by a thorn, And it did never bell, And I trust in Jesus this never will.' **1900** *Trans. Devon. Ass.* 91. For a Thorn in the Flesh. Christ met His disciples, and asked where they were going. They said they were going into the garden to gather the precious herb for the prick of a thorn. Christ said it should neither wrink (*sic*) nor fester. In the Name, etc.

THORN TREE, harming

AD **77** PLINY *Natural History* XV XVII (1855, III 302) It is not permitted to graft upon the thorn, for .. we are told that as many as are the kinds of trees that have been engrafted on the thorn, so many are the thunderbolts that will be hurled against that spot in a single flash. **1792** *Stat. Acc. of Scotland* III 609–10 [New Parish] There is a quick thorn, of a very antique appearance, for which the people have a superstitious veneration. They have a mortal dread to lop off, or cut any part of it, and affirm, with a religious horror, that some persons, who had the temerity to hurt it, were afterwards severely punished for their sacrilege. **1850** W. ALLINGHAM *Poems* 'The Fairies'. They have planted thorn-trees, For pleasure, here and there. Is any man so daring As dig them up in spite, He shall find their sharpest thorns In his bed at night. **1865** *Gents Mag.* pt. 2 700 [Ireland] To pluck a fairy hawthorn-tree is supposed to be extremely dangerous . . as it provokes elfin resentment and bodes ill-luck. **1882** *Folk-Lore Record* 168–9. A man near Kilmaganny, Co. Kilkenny, came to me in a great state of mind . . as the previous night some one had cut a thorn-tree in a rath on his land, and some ill luck must come to him before the end of the year . . curiously enough before Christmas he buried a fine girl of a daughter. **1887** 'SPERANZA' WILDE *Superstitions of Ireland* II 107. A white-thorn stick is a very unlucky companion on a journey. **1904** *Folklore* 460. 'A protestant man', living in Co. Meath, was about to cut down one of these 'lone thorn' . . trees, and was cautioned that if he did so evil would befall him. He ridiculed the idea, but as he was cutting down the tree he got a thorn in his hand . . got blood-poisoning . . and he died . . soon afterwards. This happened about the year 1877. **1941** *N & Q* CLXXXI 320 [Dorset] The following story is extant in the village of Berwick St John, a mile due south of which is a large old encampment called Winklebury, in the middle of which there used to stand an old thorn-tree or scrag. The whole property around belonged to Sir Thomas Grove, whose son, Walter Grove, lived in the Manor House of Berwick. One day, when short of firewood, he went up with a horse and axe, cut down the scrag and hauled it back. The result of this in the village was that no chicken would lay eggs, no cow would have a calf, and no women would have babies. [He planted another, and the village became productive once more.] **1985** R. VICKERY *Unlucky Plants* 18–19. When I moved to . . rural Cheshire, the farmer from whom I bought the house mentioned [that May flower] should never

be cut . . because if you did you would not get an apple crop . . It seemed to be the actual cutting which did the damage. Ibid. 21. I was brought up on a farm in southern Ireland (Longford) . . As I remember from preparing May Altars, cutting a lone hawthorn bush [meant] death/illness.

THORN TREE protects

AD **77** PLINY *Natural History* XVI xxx (1855, III 372) The thorn . . affords the most auspicious torches of all for the nuptial ceremony. **1563** J. PILKINGTON *Burnynge of Paules Church* sig. 3. Al the popes creatures therfore be supersticious . . They . . be superstycious that put holinesse in . . thorne bushes for light-nings. **1579** LUPTON *Thousand Notable Things* V § 86. It is the opinion of many, that an hearbe (called Leucacanthus) that is Whyt thorne . . is neuer strucken nor touched with lyghtning, nor is not touched with any euyl from heauen. **1878** *Folk-Lore Record* 43 [Fittleworth, Sussex] Mothers teach their children to say—'Beware of an oak, It draws the stroke; Avoid an ash, It courts the flash; Creep under the thorn, It can save you from harm.' **1883** BURNE *Shropshire* 244. An old woman, Mrs W—— . . told a friend of mine that 'if you gather a piece of hawthorn on Holy Thursday and keep it in your house, the house will never be struck by lightning, because "Under a thorn Our Saviour was born".' **1912** LEATHER *Herefordshire* 91–2. The 'Bush' is a globe made of hawthorn, which is hung up in the kitchen of the farmhouse with the mistletoe, after the bush-burning ceremony each New Year's morning; it hangs there till the day comes round again, when it is taken out to be burnt, and a new one is made. **1935** *N & Q* CLXVIII 457 [Spennymoor, Co. Durham] When caught in a thunder-storm: 'Beware of an oak, It draws the stroke. Take care of the ash, It courts the crash. Creep under the thorn, It will save you from harm.' **1938/9** *Sussex N & Q* VII 218. Readers may be interested in the following account . . from a note, written, I think, by my grandfather, the Rev. Henry Hoper, Vicar of Portslade 1815–59. 'Singular superstition exists at Portslade . . and has been entertained within the memory of man .. that a dying person can be recovered if thrice carried round, and thrice bumped against, a thorn of great antiquity, which stands on the down, ever ready to dispense its magic power to all believers. A few years ago a medical attendant gave up all hopes of his patient. The Goodies of the village obtained the Doctor's and sick man's consent to restore him to health, and having carried him round the tree bumped the dying man and had the mortification of carrying him back a corpse.' 1943 *Folklore* 365. To this day, it is an established .. belief in .. West Sussex .. that thorn-trees afford certain protection from lightning.

Cf. MAY BOUGHS AND FLOWERS protect.

THREAD, first: divination

1507 *Gospelles of Dystaues* pt. I VI. A mayden that wyll knowe ye name of her to comynge husbande, ought to hange before her dore the fyrst threde that she spynneth that daye, and the fyrst man that passeth therby aske his name and knowe for certayne that the same name shall her husbande haue. 1909 M. TREVELYAN *Folk-Lore of Wales* 235. When spinning of yarn and flax was general in Welsh homesteads, the girls stretched the first piece of yarn or thread they spun on Christmas Eve or the day of the Twelfth Night outside the door of the house. The first man who passed over it would bear the same Christian name as the future husband.

THREAD on clothes: divination

1923 [Somerset] When cotton is on your frock you will have a present. 1948 Woman, 20 [Kent] A piece of cotton picked off a dress and dropped on the floor forms the initial of your boyfriend's name. 1935 Girl, 12 [Parkstone, Dorset] At school, if we pick a bit of thread off someone's clothes, we wind it round our finger and say a letter for each turn, to find out the initial of the man we're going to marry. 1955 Woman, c.50 [Norwich, c.1910] After picking a piece of cotton off someone's clothes, hold both ends between wet finger tips, twist hard, drop, and the letter formed is the initial of the person from whom one is

about to receive a letter. 1956 Teacher, 49 [Swansea, Glam.] I had known before only the belief that whoever takes a thread from off someone else will receive a letter, but a second-form child told me that she always wound the thread [round her finger] to discover the sender's name. 1959 Woman, 56 [Nutfield, Surrey] If you take a white cotton off somebody's clothes you'll have a letter, but if they take it off the letter is for them.

THREAD on distaff

1507 *Gospelles of Dystaues* pt. 2 XI. Who that leueth on the saterdaye to make an ende of ye flackes on her rocke [distaff] all that she spynneth on mondays after shall neuer do good. 1841 HAMPSON *Medii Ævi Kalendarium* I 90–1. With regard to Christmas Eve, the vulgar entertain numerous ridiculous notions .. Women will not venture to leave any flax or yarn on their wheels, under an apprehension that the evil one would assuredly cut it for them before morning. Those who are in a single state, assign another reason for this custom; that their rocks would otherwise follow them to church on their marriage. If any flax be left on their rock, they salt it, in order to preserve it from Satanic power. 1909 M. TREVELYAN *Folk-Lore of Wales* 242. In the days of old they said if a woman had not cleared her distaff by Saturday night, the threads would never bleach white.

THREAD tied round

1833 W. CARLETON *Irish Peasantry* 2nd ser. II 5. When the cows happened to calve, this good woman tied, with her own hands, a woollen thread about their tails, to prevent them from being overlooked by evil eyes. 1850 *N & Q* 1st ser. II 36–7 [Northants.] If it be a man who suffers [from nose-bleeding] he asks a female to buy him a lace, (if a female she asks a man), without either giving money, saying what it is wanted for, or returning thanks when received. The lace .. must be worn round the neck for the space of nine days. 1893 *Folklore* 363 [Dublin] A thread is sometimes tied round the toe of a corpse. 1913 E. M. WRIGHT *Rustic Speech* 248. I knew a baby that always wore a mysterious black velvet band round its neck, which the mother said was a certain preventive against teething troubles. **1959** *Journal of School of Scottish Studies* III 193–4 [Highlands] The engine appeared to be in perfect order but would not start again. The driver was at his wit's end, when who should come by .. but the district nurse .. They came to the conclusion that some malignant eye must have lighted on the new lorry. The nurse, although she had become slightly too sophisticated to believe in charms .. went as stealthily as she could to the old lady's house and got the charmed thread. As soon as it was wound round the radiator-cap .. the engine started up again and off it went. **1966** BBC RADIO *World at One*. 31 Aug. Asked if sailors were superstitious, the naval submarine officer said, 'One has heard of men who put twine round their toe to ward off the Devil.' **1969** M. HARRIS *A Kind of Magic* 112 [Ducklington, Oxon., *c*.1925] Our next-door neighbour's daughter was supposed to be 'weak in the chest' and she was never seen without her 'velvety band' as her mother called it. It was a narrow, black velvet band fastened tightly round her neck, and this was only taken off when she washed.

Cf. RED THREAD protects.

THREAD: winding after sunset

1855 F. K. ROBINSON *Yorkshire Words* [Whitby] *Wossit*. Housewives tell us, it is not good to wind worsted or thread from the skein into a ball by candle light, 'for it raffles the sailors in steering their course at sea.' **1910** *Folklore* 227 [Yorks.] Wives of fishermen will not wind wool after sundown, for, if they do, they will soon be making their husbands' winding sheets.

THREAD, winding: divination

1780 J. MAYNE *Ruddiman's Weekly Mercury* Nov. Some i' the kiln-pat thraw a clue, At whilk, bedeen, Their sweethearts at the far-end pu', At Hallowe'en. **1783** C. VALLANCEY *De Rebus Hibernicis* III 459–60 [Hallowe'en] They throw a ball of yarn out of the window, and wind it in on the reel within, convinced, that if they repeat the Pater Noster

backwards, and look at the ball of yarn without, they will .. see his sith or apparition. **1787** BURNS *Poems* 162 [note to 'Halloween'] Whoever would, with success, try this spell, must strictly observe these directions: Steal out, all alone, to the kiln, and, darkling, throw into the *pot* a clew of blue yarn; wind it in a new clew off the old one; and, towards the latter end, something will hold the thread: demand, *Wha hauds?* i.e. who holds? and answer will be returned from the kiln-pot, by naming the Christian and Sirname of your future Spouse. **1865** *Gents Mag.* pt. 2 702 [Ireland, All-Hallows Eve] Young females go out at midnight and cast a ball of yarn into .. a lime-kiln, whilst holding on by a thread. If the girl wind on, and if nothing hold the yarn, it is a sign that the winder will die unmarried. If she feel it pulled from her, she asks: 'Who pulls my yarn?' when it is supposed her future husband will give his name, or appear to her. **1887** 'SPERANZA' WILDE *Superstitions of Ireland* I 267–8. If a ball of worsted is thrown into a lime-kiln and wound up till the end is caught by invisible hands, the person who winds calls out 'Who holds the ball?' and the answer will be the name of the future husband or wife. But the experiment must be made only at midnight, and in silence and alone. **1904** C. ROEDER *Manx N & Q* 17. On Holy Eve the girls used to go at 12 o'clock at night and carry a ball of woollen yarn in their hand, and steal to a barn without anyone knowing anything about it, and twisting the end of it round their wrist threw the ball in the darkness as far as they could; then after a little while they began to wind it up, beginning at the end twined round their wrist. If the thread was held they would cry out: 'Who is holding the thread?' and they expected whoever held it to say who he was; and if there was no answer they were to be old maids.

thread: also see index: knots in garments/ knitting/sewing.

THREE accidents

1849 *Norfolk Archaeology* II 47 [Irstead] A boy who cuts his hand expects to do so other twice. **1864** R. CHAMBERS *Book* *of Days* II 104 [Suffolk] A neighbour saw one of her servants take up a coarse earthenware basin, and deliberately throw it down upon the brick floor. 'What *did* you do that for?' asked the mistress. 'Because, ma'am, I'd broke tew things,' answered the servant, 'so I thout the third'd better be this here.' 1891 *N & Q* 7th ser. XII 489. One of my servants having accidentally broken a glass shade, asked for two other articles of little value, a wine bottle and jam crock, that she might break them, and so prevent the two other accidents .. which would otherwise follow. 1912 LEATHER *Herefordshire* 87. When servants break glass or china I have frequently seen them carry out two broken pieces and smash them. They think if they break one thing they must break three. 1923 [Somerset] Never two but three, is most firmly believed in here, in connection with accidents, breakages, etc. Another version is 'Once, twice, beware of the third.' 1983 Woman, 21 [Kent] If you break two things, you must break a matchstick to prevent a third.

THREE deaths

1858 *N & Q* 2nd ser. V 209. The inhabitants of Keighley [Yorks.] say, 'If the coroner once enter the town, he is sure to be required other twice in a very short time.' 1866 HENDERSON *Northern Counties* 46. Three funerals constantly follow one another in quick succession. 1878 KILVERT *Diary* 26 Dec. Lizzie Abberley told me the other day that there is an idea in Bredwardine [Herefords.] that 3 deaths generally happen together. 1895 J. HARDY *Denham Tracts* II 271–2. In North Northumberland it is said that 'the coroner never comes once but he comes twice.' 1953 Girl, 14 [Knighton, Radnor.] If you hear of a death you're supposed to hear of three. 1962 *Daily Herald* 19 Oct. 9. A member of the .. committee said at Cirencester [Glos.] yesterday: 'There are people who honestly believe death goes in threes and they are scared to go on with the exercise' [after two deaths]. 1964 L. BECKWITH *Loud Halo* 172–3 [Hebrides] Murdoch's been taken awful bad .. What I'm after wonderin' now is whether the third one's not goin' to be

Willy as we've all been expectin'.' Erchy was .. referring to the old belief that graves were always required in threes. 'Once you've opened up the burial ground you'll need to open it up twice more.' Although it was uncanny how often it came true it was a cruel superstition for once the first cycle of deaths had occurred the old folks in the village would begin to show distinct signs of uneasiness, even panic, until the third grave was satisfactorily filled. 1982 B. COLLOMS *Victorian Visionaries* 185 [Hants., 1859] To the sorrowing horror of the Kingsleys the very first burial in the new churchyard was that of Fanny's sister .. Eversley villagers waited knowingly for another fatality, telling each other that deaths come in threes. 1984 Woman, 47 [Chichester, Sussex] When my father died and an old neighbour died someone said to me 'There'll be another death soon, they always go in threes.'

THREE: 'third time lucky'

c.1380 *Sir Gawain and the Green Knight* (ed. Tolkien & Gordon, 1967, ll. 1679–80) For I haf fraysted þe twys, and faythful I fynde þe. Now 'þrid tyme þrowe best.' 1574 J. HIGGINS *First parte of Mirour for Magistrates* I 24. The thirde payes home, this prouerbe is to true. 1599 *Warning for Fair Women* E3. Haue you forgot what the old prouerbe is, The third time payes for all? 1601 SHAKESPEARE *Twelfe Night* v i. The olde saying is, the third payes for all: the triplex sir, is a good tripping measure, or the belles of *S. Bennet* sir, may put you in minde, one, two, three. 1721 KELLY *Scotish Proverbs* 26. All things thrive at thrice .. An Encouragement .. to try the third time. They will say the third's a Charm. 1909 M. TREVELYAN *Folk-Lore of Wales* 326. They say 'Three chances for a Welshman', and if he is successful the third time, he will be very fortunate afterwards. 1987 TV CHANNEL 4 *Fish 'n Ships.* 2 Sept. Seaman's wife. My husband's been washed overboard and back three times. I don't worry about him any more because they say if it happens three times and you're not drowned, the sea doesn't want you. 1987 Man, 29 [Birmingham] 'Third time lucky'—that's such a worn out phrase, you don't believe it any more.

Cf. ODD NUMBER lucky.

THRESHOLD

c. AD 396 ST AUGUSTINE OF HIPPO *De Doctrina Christiana* I xx (tr. D. W. Robertson, 56) Similar [superstitious] practices are .. to step on the threshold when you leave your house by the front door. **1865** *Gents Mag.* pt. 2 289 [Ireland] It is considered inhuman to strain potatoes or spill hot water on or over the threshold of a door, as thousands of spirits are supposed to congregate invisibly at such a spot. **1890** *N & Q* 7th ser. X 126. In Ireland the peasants in the south and west regard that portion of the earthen floor of their poor homes just inside the threshold—'the welcome of the door', as it is called, where he who enters pauses to say, 'God bless all here'—as sacred, and the clay taken from this spot is frequently given medicinally, with full faith in its curative qualities.

THRUSH (ulcers in mouth) cured with psalm

1838 A. E. BRAY *Devonshire* II 293. Reading of the eighth psalm ['Out of the mouths of babes and sucklings hast thou ordained strength, because of thine enemies; that thou mightest still the enemy and the avenger.'] over the heads of infants three times three days in the week, for three following weeks, will .. prevent babes having the thrush. **1853** *N & Q* 1st ser. VIII 146 [Devon] Visiting one of my parishioners, whose child was ill with the thrush, I asked her what medicine she had given the child [and] found that her cure was to repeat the eighth Psalm over the infant three times, three days running. **1953** *Trans. Devon. Ass.* 218. To cure what he calls 'white mouth' .. this charmer says the patient must have verses 2 and 3 of Psalm 8 read silently over him.

THUMB, holding

c. AD 17 OVID *Fasti* V ll. 433–6 (tr. Gower) Then points with his clos'd fingers, and his thumb Put in the midst, lest ghosts should near him come. *c.* AD 396 ST AUGUSTINE OF HIPPO *De Doctrina Christiana* I xx (tr. D. W. Robertson, 55)

Among superstitious things .. belong those .. remedies which medical science .. condemns .. Of this type [is] the practice of telling a person with hiccups to hold his left thumb in his right hand. *c.***1350** MS Douce 52 (*Ox. Dict. Eng. Proverbs,* 342) Holde þy thombe in thi fyst, And kepe þe welle fro 'Had I wyst'. **1605** SHAKESPEARE *Macbeth* IV i. By the pricking of my Thumbes, Something wicked this way comes. **1778** W. HUTCHINSON *View of Northumberland* II app. 4. Children, to avoid approaching danger, are taught to double the thumb within the hand. This was much practised whilst the terrors of witchcraft remained .. it was a custom to fold the thumbs of dead persons within the hand, to prevent the power of evil spirits over the deceased. **1787** GROSE *Provincial Glossary* Superstitions 29–30. On meeting a supposed Witch, it is advisable .. whilst passing her, to clench both hands, doubling the thumbs beneath the fingers: this will prevent her having a power to injure the person so doing. **1826** R. CHAMBERS *Popular Rhymes* 278 n. In the author's boyhood, and so late as within the last twelve years, there resided at Peebles several old women who had the credit of being witches .. One .. in particular .. I remember perfectly well, that no boy ever went past her door .. without laying his thumb into the palm of his hand and closing down the fingers. **1828** HONE *Table Book* II 583 [Bridlington, Yorks.] On meeting a suspected witch the thumb of each hand was turned inward, and the fingers firmly closed upon it. **1858** DENHAM *Fairies, Witches* (1895, 82) 'Witchy, Witchy, I defy thee! Four fingers round my thumb, Let me go quietly by thee!!'—The anti-Witch rhyme used in Teesdale some lx or lxx years ago. **1879** *Folk-Lore Record* 205 [Weardale, Co. Durham] In passing a witch, doubling the thumbs under the fore-fingers was considered a preventive to being bewitched. **1883** BURNE *Shropshire* 273–4. It is considered lucky for friends to pinch the thumb of a person setting out on a journey, lest otherwise, I suppose, their farewells should accidentally 'ill-wish' him. **1954** Boy, 12 [Brixton, London] Hold your thumbs. This is very lucky. **1986** G. AVERY Letter 7 Nov. On Monday John Patten MP and Klaus Moser, Warden of Wadham, are going to see Paul Hamlyn on behalf of the Opie Appeal; hold your thumbs! **1987** Actress, 58 [Cheltenham, Glos.] My mother always used to say she'd hold her thumbs for me, on a first night.

Cf. CROSSED FINGERS; HICCUP, cures for.

THUNDER AND LIGHTNING, drawing attention to

AD **77** PLINY *Natural History* II LV (1855, I 85) There are some kinds of thunder which it is not thought right to speak of, or even to listen to. **1862** *N & Q* 3rd ser. II 342 [Taunton, Som., *c*.1815] It is wicked to point towards the part of the heavens from which lightning is expected. I have seen a little boy, for this offence, made to kneel blindfold on the floor, to teach him how he would feel if the lightning came and blinded him. **1890** *N & Q* 7th ser. IX 244. When I lived in the village of Bierley [Yorks.] the boys of the place believed that if they made any mention of the lightning, immediately after the flash 'the seat of their trousers would be torn out.' **1915** *N & Q* 11th ser. XII 257. Among the children in Devonshire thirty years ago it was regarded as unlucky to draw one another's attention to lightning. **1969** S. MAYS *Reuben's Corner* XIV [Essex] Never count between lightning's flash and thunder's peal, to determine if the storm is arriving or departing.

Cf. RAINBOW, pointing at.

THUNDER AND LIGHTNING, interpretation of: direction, day, or season

c.800 BC HOMER *Iliad* IX (tr. Rieu, 167) Zeus .. has encouraged them [Trojan army], with lightning flashes on the right. Hector .. triumphant .. trusts in Zeus, and fears neither man nor god. AD **77** PLINY *Natural History* II LIV (1857, I 84) In the interpretation of thunder .. it enables us to predict what is to happen on a certain day .. or it discloses events which are concealed from us; as is proved by an infinite number of examples, public and private. Ibid. II LV (I 85) Thunder on the left is supposed to be lucky, because the east is on the left side of the heavens. Ibid. II LII (I

51) Among the prognostics .. at the time of Catiline's conspiracy .. a magistrate .. was struck by lightning when the sky was without clouds. **1556** L. DIGGES *Prognostication* 6ᵛ. Somme wryte (their ground I see not) that Sondayes Thundre, shoulde brynge the death of learned men, Judges & others: Mondayes Thundre, the death of women: Tuesdayes Thundre, plentie of grayne: Wednesdayes Thundre, the deathe of Harlottes, & other blodshede: Thursdayes Thundre, plentie of Shepe, and Corne: Frydaies Thundre, the slaughter of a great Man, and other horrible murders: Saturdayes Thundre, a generall pestilent plage and great deathe. **1605** R. VERSTEGAN *Restitvtion of Decayed Intelligence* VII 199. Wee say, Winters thunder is summers wunder. **1658** T. WILLSFORD *Natures Secrets* 113. Thunder and lightning in Winter .. is held ominous, portending factions, tumults, and bloody wars, and a thing seldome seen, according to the old Adigy, Winters thunder, is the Sommers wonder. **1853** *N & Q* 1st ser. VII 81 [Ingatestone, Essex] I was conversing the other day with a very old farmer .. he told me .. 'Winter thunder and summer flood Bode England no good.' **1909** M. TREVELYAN *Folk-Lore of Wales* 282. If there is sudden thunder in mid-winter, the most important person for twenty miles around will die. **1922** *N & Q* 12th ser. XI 25 [Bedale, Yorks., 1875] When it thunners on God's day, amang high larned staups [stalks] death, An' some great judge or general 'll soon lack for breath. Monday's thunner, 'fore midmeal, ho'ds great ladies i' thrall. But a crack gi'en at sunset brings a king's miss ti fall. Tuesday's thunner is luck, may it thunner amain, It brings us mair gear, an' biggens all grain. Wednesday's thunner comes black, loud an' lang, An' Hell's deeath geckens [grins] all harlots amang. Thosday's thunner at t'backend, when t'tups [rams] plaay ther part, Gi'es good ho'd o' t'yows [ewes] an' ti t'corn a soond heart. Friday's thunner frae Hellwards diz bring a black pall, Ower coonvil an' King-slafterin' all. An' should t'storm hing on while Setterda' morn Then plagues of great death of no dread shall be shorn. **1957** M. STEWART

Thunder on the Right XVII. 'Thunder—on the right,' said Stephen. 'There's your omen, Jenny, and not on the sinister side. Thunder on the right—the best of omens! A happy ending!'

THUNDER AND LIGHTNING, interpretation of: voice and weapon of God

AD 77 PLINY *Natural History* II XVIII (1857, I 51) Thunder-bolts are darted by Jupiter. Ibid. XXVIII IV (1856, V 280) King Tullus H .. while attempting to summon Jupiter .. was struck by lightning in consequence of his omission to follow certain forms with due exactness. *c.* AD 100 John 12: 28–9. There came a voice from heaven .. The people .. that stood by, and heard it, said that it thundered: others said, An angel spake to him. *c.* AD 120 TACITUS *Annals* XIV XXII. As Nero sat at meat in a villa called Sublaqueum .. the viands were struck by lightning and the table overthrown; and, as this .. took place in the neighbourhood .. whence the patronal ancestors of Plautus sprang, they [the populace] believed this was the man predestined for empire by the decree of the deities. *c.*1530 MS Balliol 354 (*Early Eng. Carols*, ed. Greene, no. 163) Howge was the erthquak, horyble was the thonder; I loked on my swet Son on the crosse that I stode vnder. 1661 HENRY BOLD 'On the Thunder, happening after the Solemnity of the Coronation of Charles II'. Heavens! we thank you, that you Thunder'd so! As We did here, you Cannonado'd too .. Thus mighty Jove, Copartner in our Joy, Out-sounded, what we cry'd, Vive le Roy! 1825 *Newcastle Mag.* Sept. 391. It was a beautiful afternoon .. contradicting all their traditions .. The little clouds .. were watched, therefore, with intense interest, as if they were expected .. to burst in thunder and lightning round the death-scene of the witch. 1922 *N & Q* 12th ser. XI 25 [Bedale, Yorks., 1875] When thunner's loud crack shaks t'Heavenly vau'ts, It's the Lord wo is callin' ti men o' their fau'ts. 1963 *Man*, 83 [Finchdean, Hants.] When Sir Jervoise died I went to the funeral. I looked down into the vault and I saw the casket and I well remember the terrific clap of thunder that seemed to

come out of nowhere. It didn't seem like thunder weather then. 1984 Letter to *Times* 11 July 11 [after the fire at York Minster] 'Just lightning,' says the Bishop dismissively. To those as old-fashioned as I, lightning is the wrath of God.

Cf. WEATHER linked with lives of the great.

THUNDER AND LIGHTNING: tree struck by lightning cures toothache

AD 77 PLINY *Natural History* XXVIII XI (1856, V 293) To bite off a piece from wood that has been struck by lightning .. and then to apply it to the tooth, is a sure remedy, they say, for tooth-ache. 1884 *Electrician* 18 Oct. 505. Chewing the splinters from a tree struck by lightning will cure the toothache.

TIDE affects birth and death

AD 77 PLINY *Natural History* II CI (1857, I 128) Aristotle adds, that no animal dies except when the tide is ebbing .. The observation has been often made on the ocean of Gaul; but it has only been found true with respect to man. 1557 TUSSER *Good Husbandrie* XIV st. 4. Tyde flowing is feared for many a thing, Great danger to such as be sick it doth bring. 1600 SHAKESPEARE *Henry the Fifth* II iii. A parted ev'n just betweene Twelve and One, ev'n at the turning o' th' Tyde. 1830 MARRYAT *King's Own* II II 21. Dr Mead has observed, that of those who are at the point of death, nine out of ten quit this world at the ebb of the tide. 1849 DICKENS *David Copperfield* XXX. 'People can't die, along the coast,' said Mr Peggotty, 'except when the tide's pretty nigh out. They can't be born, unless it's pretty nigh in—not properly born, till flood. He's a going out with the tide .. If he lives 'till it turns, he'll hold his own till past the flood, and go out with the next tide.' 1855 *N & Q* 1st ser. XII 38 [Cornwall] Death is .. thought to be delayed until the ebb of the tide. 1866 HENDERSON *Northern Counties* 41. It is a common belief along the east coast .. from Northumberland to Kent, that deaths mostly occur during the falling of the tide. 1957 *Folklore* 413. In coastal areas, the old notion still lingers that life comes in with the flowing tide and goes out with the ebb, and consequently a birth at ebb-tide is ill-omened. **1978** N. MAYES *Nature Notebook* 88 [Cornwall] The fishermen believed that death could only occur at ebb tide. If the dying survived one ebb tide, they would live at least till the next.

TIDE affects enterprises

1886 *Folklore* 9–10. At Portessie [Banff.] the fisher folks do not begin any piece of work, such as barking nets, baiting lines, &c., except when the tide is 'flou-win' .. When a new boat was to be brought home (Crovie), those that were to do so set out when the tide was 'flouwin'.

TIDE cures

1887 'SPERANZA' WILDE *Superstitions of Ireland* II 106. To cure fever, place the patient on the sandy shore when the tide is coming in, and the retreating waves will carry away the disease and leave him well. **1909** M. TREVELYAN *Folk-Lore of Wales* 320. One of the most popular remedies for whooping cough was to take the sufferers daily to the edge of the tide at low-water mark, and allow them to walk up and down before the flowing sea. **1956** *Manchester Guardian* 13 Oct. 5. I don't remember the details of my cure, but I do know that an aunt, an uncle, one set of grandparents, and my parents walked in solemn procession at seven thirty a.m., clad in I know not what, out with Morecambe's tide, bearing one whooping infant, like an offering to the sea gods. My mother is now strangely reticent about this episode, but as my grandmother tartly puts it: 'Ah, but it cured you!' **1978** A. WRIGHT *Holderness* 18 [E. Yorks.] A child with whooping cough would be taken down to the beach at the turn of the tide and be made to vomit by drinking sea-water. As the outgoing sea washed the vomit away, so the disease would be carried away too.

Cf. WATER, running: cures.

tide: also see index: moon.

TOAD OR FROG cures

AD 77 PLINY *Natural History* XXXII XXIV (1856, VI 32) The right eye of a frog, suspended from the neck .. is a cure for ophthalmia in the right eye; and the left .. similarly suspended, for ophthalmia in the left. Ibid. XXXII xxv (33) The fat of frogs, injected into the ears, instantly removes all pains in these organs. Ibid. XXXII xxvi (34) For Tooth-Ache .. A decoction is made of a single frog boiled in .. vinegar, and the teeth are rinsed with it. Ibid. XXXII xxix (39) There is a small frog .. which .. if a person suffering from cough spits into its mouth and then lets it go, he will experience a cure, it is said. **1658** SIR K. DIGBY *Discourse on Sympathy* 76–7. In time of common contagion, they use to carry about them the powder of a toad, and sometimes a living toad or spider shut up in a box; or else they carry arsnick, or some other venomous substance, which draws unto it the contagious air, which otherwise would infect the party. **1665** J. ALLIN *Letter* 24 Aug. (*Archaeologia* XXXVII 8) The sicknes yet increaseth: this bill is 249 more than ye last, viz .. of the Plague, 4,237 .. Here are many who weare amulets made of the poison of the toad, which, if there be no infection, workes nothing, but, upon any infection invadeing .. raise a blister, wch a plaister heales, and so they are well. **1678** W. SALMON *London Dispensatory* 201. A dried Toad steept in Vinegar .. smelt to it stops bleeding at Nose, especially laid to the forehead .. or hung about the Neck. **1823** *Gents Mag.* pt. 1 214 [Worcs.] A cunning man of high reputation .. caught a frog .. and with his knife inflicted a wound on that part of its neck, corresponding exactly with the seat of disease in the patient's, and then suffered the animal to escape. 'If (said he) it lives, the disease will gradually waste away, and your daughter recover; but if the creature dies .. there is then no hope' .. Some time after .. the maid no longer suffered; the disease had dispersed. **1850** *N & Q* 1st ser. II 36 [Northants.] For stopping or preventing bleeding at the nose, a toad is killed by transfixing it with some sharp pointed instrument, after which it is inclosed in a little bag and suspended round the neck. **1855** *Gents Mag.* pt. 2 385–6 [Worcs.] In the neighbourhood of Hartle-bury [and also in Tenbury] they break the legs of a toad, sew it up in a bag alive, and tie it round the neck of the patient .. the life or death of the patient being supposed to be shadowed forth by the survival or death of the poor animal. 1857 *N & Q* 2nd ser. IV 486 [Chirnside, Berwick.] Scottish reapers .. believe that if a sprained wrist is rubbed with a live toad it will effect a cure. I have often seen this operation performed in the early part of my life. 1869 *N & Q* 4th ser. III 238. An old woman, whom I well remember, always carried in her pocket a dried toad, as a preservative from small-pox. One day .. she went into the village .. without her toad. The small-pox prevailed in the place at the time, and the old woman caught it. 1875 *N & Q* 5th ser. IV 83. In the month of July, 1822, she was staying at Haselbury Brian, near Blandford [Dorset], and .. a man came in a gig, who was known as 'the toad doctor'. He brought with him a number of small bags, and the people flocked to him from far and near with toads. The 'doctor' cut off the hind legs of these toads and put the severed portions into the bags, and hung them around the necks of his patients, the newly cut off limbs quivering on their naked chests. This was held to be a certain remedy for the king's evil. Ibid. 184 [Camelford, Cornwall] A 'wise woman' .. prescribed for him as follows: 'Get a live toad, fasten a string round its throat, and hang it up till the body drops from the head; then tie the string round your own neck, and never take it off, night or day, till your fiftieth birthday. You'll never have quinsy again.' 1883 BURNE *Shropshire* 194. A particularly barbarous cure for whooping-cough, recommended to a clergyman's wife in the Clun neighbourhood, is to draw three yards of narrow black ribbon three times through the body of a live frog, and to let the patient wear the ribbon round his neck. 1892 M. C. F. MORRIS *Yorkshire Folk-Talk* 247 [for whooping cough] Catch a frog, and put it into a jug of water; make the patient cough into the jug; this *smits* the frog, and the patient is cured. 1912 LEATHER *Herefordshire* 74. Thomas Whittington, of Walford, suffered from an abscess in his arm .. A gypsy woman told him how to cure it

by wearing the leg of a toad. 'One day when I was a hedgin',' he said, 'I found un and put un in a wheelbarra and looked at un a good while, and thinking how I cud cut a leg off the poor creetur, so as un cud walk, 'thout it.' In the end he decided that the toad could dispense with a hind leg .. A turf was next cut from under the hedge, and carefully replaced, with the unfortunate toad, still living, beneath it .. 'I was to wear [the leg] round me neck, in a silk bag .. and to look next morning if the toad was gone, and a was, and me arm was well in three wiks.'

TOAD OR FROG in house

1834 G. ROBERTS *Lyme Regis and Charmouth* 262. Toads that gained access to .. a house were ejected with the greatest care, and no injury was offered, because these were regarded, as being used as familiars by witches, with veneration or awe. 1876 *Trans. Devon. Ass.* 52 [Ashburton] He had a heart to work, but no strength .. One evening on entering his door, he saw a great toad, which he killed with a pitchfork, and threw into the fire. The next evening he saw another .. and did the same .. He believes they were witches. Soon recovered, and has not suffered the like since. 1922 [Bradford-on-Tone, Som.] When a frog comes in your house it is lucky. 1922 [Creech St Michael, Som.] If a toad crawls into the house it is an enemy for you, and if you kill it you overcome your enemy, also thwart them as it were. 1922 [Trowbridge, Wilts.] For a toad to be found in the house is unlucky, foreshadowing a death in the family. 1923 [Somerset] If a toad comes into your house you must never turn it out or else the worst of luck will follow you and your family for a whole year. 1935 *I Walked by Night* (ed. L. Rider Haggard, 18) [Norfolk] If a Toad come onto the Threshold, and .. if it come in and sit down that ment that an Enemy was tryen to hurt one of the household.

TOAD OR FROG, meeting

1180 NIGEL DE LONGCHAMPS *Mirror for Fools* (tr. Mozley, 97) May .. a .. toad in all his body manifest Cross leftward on their [his enemies'] path. 1584 SCOT

Discoverie of Witchcraft XI xix. Sure it is meere casual, and also very foolish and incredible, that . . by meeting of a toade, a man should escape a danger, or atchieve an enterprise. **1818** *Edinburgh Magazine* Nov. 412. A toad crawling over the path she [the bride] has to pass is a good omen. **1871** *Good Words for the Young* Sept. 630. The child's big sister, who had charge of her, came up, and seizing her by the hand, pulled her away [from the toad] exclaiming, 'Don't go near the nasty thing, it'll spit at you, and kill you!' **1889** *Dorset Field Club* 44. It is considered very unlucky if a toad goes over your foot . . Whenever you see [one] you should always spit . . at it, in order to ward off any evil effects the sight of it would otherwise cause you. **1900** S. HEWETT *Nummits* 23 [Devon] Should [the bride and groom] encounter a toad, frog, or other reptile, then terrible misfortunes will follow them. **1922** [Creech St Michael, Som.] They say it is good luck to see a frog crossing the road or path at the same time you are walking there. **1922** [Taunton, Som.] It is a sign of good luck if a toad hops across your path when you are going for a walk. But never frighten it, as if a toad springs from your path, death follows.

TOAD OR FROG, meeting = money

1159 JOHN OF SALISBURY *Policraticus* (*Frivolities of Courtiers*, ed. J. B. Pike, 50) Meeting with a toad announces success to come, though for myself I can scarcely bear the sight of one. late **14th** c. R. RYPON MS Harl. 4894 (OWST, in *Studies*, ed. J. Conway Davies, 1957, 297) A toad . . affords [a] lucky meeting. **1496** H. PARKER *Dives & Pauper* 1st com. XLVI. Some man hadde leuer for to mete with a froude or a frogge in the waye than to mete with a knyght or squyre . . for than they . . byleue that they shall haue golde. **1922** [Trowbridge, Wilts.] To meet a frog is lucky: you will have money given you.

TOAD'S OR FROG'S BONE

AD **77** PLINY *Natural History* XXXII xviii (1856, VI 22) 'Rubetae', or 'bramble-frogs' . . are the largest [probably the toads of the ancients]. By throwing into boiling water a small bone . . found in their right side, the water will immediately cool . . This bone . . may be found by . . letting ants eat away the flesh . . Another bone . . has the property of assuaging the fury of dogs, and, if put into the drink, of conciliating love and ending discord . . Worn, too, as an amulet, it acts as an aphrodisiac, we are told. **1584** SCOT *Discoverie of Witchcraft* VI VII. A frogs bones, the flesh being eaten off round about with ants, whereof some will swim, and some will sinke: those that sinke, being hanged up in a white linnen cloth, ingender love, but if a man be touched therewith, hate is bred thereby. **1835** *Country Horse-Doctor* (1959, 27) [Swaffham, Norfolk] To make a horse lay down. Get some grey toads—hang them up on a White thorn bush till they are Dead, then lay them into an Ant hill, then . . put them into a stream . . then dry them and beat them to a powder, touch a Horse on the Shoulder to jade him and on the rump to draw him. **1901** *Folklore* 168–9 [Lincoln] Take the breast-bone of a toad and bury it in an ant-hill till the ants have eaten all the flesh from it. Then throw it into a running stream. Whichever way the water goes it will float up against it, and you will find that however often you fling that bone away it will always return into your pocket, and give you power over horses, cattle, and people. **1914** *Folklore* 363–4. Grooms [at Newmarket, Cambs.] catch a frog and keep it in a bottle or tin until nothing but the bones remains. At the new moon they draw these up stream in running water; one of the bones which floats is kept as a charm in the pocket or hung round the neck. This gives the man power to control any horse. **1936** E. H. RUDKIN *Lincolnshire* 24. You take a *black* toad, an' put it in an ant-'ill, an' leave it there while bones is all cleaned. Then take the bones and go down to a good stream of *runnin'* water at midnight an' throw the bones i' the stream. All the bones *but one* will go down stream, an' that one as wont go downstream is the breast-bone. Now, *you* must get 'old of this 'ere bone afore the Devil gets it, an' if you get it an' keep it allus by you— in your pocket, or wear it—then *you* can *witch*; as well as that, you'll be safe from bein' witched yourself.

TOADSTONE

1488 *Inventory of Royal Wardrobe* (1815, 10) Item a ring with a paddockstane, with a charnale [hinge]. *c.***1495** BARTHOLOMAEUS *De Proprietatibus Rerum* (tr. Trevisa, XVI 70) Noset orapondien is a precyous stoon somdeale whyte: other of dyuers colours. It is sayd y^t this stone is take oute of a toodes heed .. This stone helpith ayenst bytyng of serpentis & of crepying wormes: & ayenst venym. For in presence of venym, y^t stoon warmyth & brennyth his fyngre y^t towchyth hym. **1558** Gift to Queen Elizabeth (NICHOLS *Progresses* II 539) A iewell containing a Crapon or Toade stone set in golde. **1569** E. FENTON *Secret Wonders of Nature* 42^v In an other cuntrie of the Indians is founde a stone in the heades of olde and greate toades, which they call Borax or Stelon, which Brasauolus approueth, is most commonly founde in the head of a hee toade, and yet is of opinion that it is rather a boane than a stone, which some affirme to be of power to repulse poysons, and that it is a moste soueraigne medecine for the stone. **1579** LUPTON *Thousand Notable Things* I § 52. A Tode stone (called Crapandina) touching any part be venomed, hurte or stung with Ratte, Spider, Waspe, or any other venomous Beast, ceases the paine or swelling thereof. Ibid. VII § 18. A Good waye to get the stone called Craupaundina, out of the Tode. Put a great or ouergrowne Tode, (fyrst brused in dyvers places) into an earthen potte, and put the same in an Antes hyllocke, & couer the same with earth, which Tode at length ye Antes wyll eate: So that the bones of the Tode and stone, wyll be left in the potte. **1627** BACON *Sylva Sylvarum* § 968. To procure easie Travailes of Women .. the best Help is, to stay the Comming downe too Fast: Whereunto they say, the Toad-Stone likewise helpeth. **1700** E. LHWYD in Rowlands' *Mona Antiqua* 338. Besides the Snakestones .. the Highlanders have their Snail-Stones, Paddoc-Stones .. etc. to all which they attribute their several Virtues. **1776** PENNANT *Zoology* III 15.

It [the toad] was believed by some old Writers to have a Stone in its head, fraught with great Virtues, medical and magical. It was .. called the Toad Stone, but all its fancied powers vanished on the discovery of its being nothing but the fossile Tooth of the Sea-Wolf, or some other flat-toothed Fish. **1802** SCOTT *Minstrelsy of Scottish Border* II 219 n. The editor [i.e. Scott himself] is possessed of a small relique, termed by tradition a toad-stone, the influence of which was supposed to preserve pregnant women from the power of daemons, and other dangers incidental to their situation. It has been carefully preserved for several generations, was often pledged for considerable sums of money, and uniformly redeemed from a belief in its efficacy. **1873** *Trans. Devon. Ass.* 200–1. The toad-stone .. now exhibited belonged to the late Mr Blaydon, of Puddington .. Persons from different parishes used to come to his house to borrow it to cure fits .. and king's evil or scrofula. [It] is evidently of considerable antiquity .. probably .. the fourteenth century .. Dr Grey of the Zoological Department of the British Museum [said] it was the tooth of a fossil fish. Ibid. 201. When I was a boy I was told how to obtain the toad-stone. The toad was to be killed and buried in an ant-hill, and the flesh would be eaten by them.

TONGUE: signs of lying

*c.***275** BC THEOCRITUS *Idylls* XII (tr. Creech, 1684) Thee I'le sing; Thee sweet, nor midst my Song Shall tell-tale Blisters rise, and gall my Tongue. **1611** SHAKESPEARE *Winters Tale* II ii. These dangerous, unsafe Lunes i'th' King, beshrew them: He must be told on't, and he shall .. Ile take't upon me, If I prove hony-mouth'd, let my tongue blister. **1686–7** AUBREY *Remaines* (1881, 28) [blister on tongue = sign of lying] This was doctrine when I was a little boy. **1948** E. & M. A. RADFORD *Superstitions* 241. If you bite your tongue while eating, it is because you have told a falsehood. **1987** Woman, *c.*60 [Great Ayton, Teesside] Spots on the tongue? That means that you've been telling lies. My mother always used to say that.

TONGUE, tip of: 'lucky bit'

1851 STERNBERG *Northamptonshire* 172–3. In the pocket of a rustic will be frequently found a small piece of dried flesh: this .. is the tip of a calf's tongue, and is called a 'lucky bit'. He considers it to be wonderfully efficacious in all cases of assault and battery, ensuring to its possessor the privilege of coming out unscathed [and] there is a saying that the pocket which contains it will never be without money. **1884** *N & Q* 6th ser. IX 185. There was a cold tongue on the breakfast table. An elderly clergyman, who was a guest, said, 'Will you allow me to cut off the tip? .. If you carry about with you the tip of a cow's tongue it will bring you good luck.' **1917** *Folklore* 315 [Clifton, Glos.] When cold tongue was carved at table, the extreme tip was sliced off and presented to one of the company. 'Keep that in your purse, and then you will never be without something in it.' **1932** C. IGGLESDEN *Those Superstitions* 146. The tip of a human tongue is .. effective in warding off bad luck, and I know one of the greatest surgeons in Harley Street who treasured one of these ghastly possessions. He secured it while a medical student, and religiously carried it in his pocket every day of his life.

TOOTHACHE, charm for

*c.*1000 MS Harl. 585 (COCKAYNE *Leechdoms* III 64) Christus super marmoreum sedebat; Petrus tristis ante eum stabat, manum ad maxillum tenebat; et interrogabat eum Dominus, dicens, 'Quare tristis es, Petre?' Respondit Petru set dixit, 'Domine, dentes mei dolent.' Et Dominus dixit. 'Adjuro te, migranea, uel gutta maligna, per Patrem et Filium et Spiritum Sanctum, et per celum et terram, et per xx ordines angelorum, &c .. ut non possit diabolus nocere ei, nec in dentes, nec in aures, nec in palato, famulo Dei.' *c.*1250 *Physicians of Myddvai* (tr. Pughe, 453–4) Saint Mary sat on a stone, the stone being near her hermitage, when the Holy Ghost came to her, she being sad. Why art thou sad, mother of my Lord, and what pain tormenteth thee? My teeth are painful, a worm called megrim has penetrated them, and I have masticated, and swal-

lowed it. I adjure thee *daffin o negrbina* by the Father, and the Son, and the Holy Ghost, the Virgin Mary, and God, the munificent Physician, that thou dost not permit any disease, dolour, or molestation to affect this servant of God here present, either in tooth, eye, head, or in the whole of her teeth together. So be it. Amen. **1691** *Athenian Mercury* III no. 22. I remember one particular instance of a Charm for the Tooth Ach, which after a sort of a Dialogue between our Saviour and Peter upon the Tooth Ach, it ended thus, 'In the Name of the Father, of the Son, and of the Holy Ghost', and this Charm had effects according to the belief of such persons as made use of it. **1696** AUBREY *Miscellanies* (1890, 135) To cure the Tooth-Ach: out of Mr Ashmole's manuscript writ with his own hand. '*Mars, hur, abursa, aburse.* Jesu Christ for Mary's sake, Take away this Tooth-Ach.' Write the words three times; and as you say the words, let the party burn one paper, then another, and then the last. He says he saw it experimented, and the party 'immediately cured'. **1851** *N & Q* 1st ser. III 20. To be written on a piece of parchment, and worn round the neck next to the skin: 'When Peter sat at Jerusalems gate His teeth did most sorely eake (ache) Ask counsel of Christ and follow me Of the tooth eake you shall be ever free Not you a Lone but also all those Who carry these few Laines safe under clothes In the name of the Father Son and Holy Ghoste.' **1883** BURNE *Shropshire* 183. To be written out, and carried about the person of the sufferer. 'As Jesus passed through Jerusalem He saw Peter standing at the gates and saith unto him, What aileth thee, Peter? Peter saith, Lord, I have the toothache that I can neither walk, lie, nor stand. He saith unto him, Follow Me, and thou shalt not have the toothache any more.' 'I never could find that verse in the Bible [said the owner of the charm] but it *is* there, *somewhere*.' **1900** *Trans. Devon. Ass.* 92. Teeth Charm. Pitter [Peter] lying at the gate of Sodom, Jesus passeth by saith unto him 'What aileth thee?' Pitter said unto Him, 'I am sorely tempted with the Pain of the Teeth.' Jesus saith unto him, 'Rise up and follow

Me, and whosoever keepeth this saying in memory or in writing shall never be troubled with the Pain of the Teeth.' In the Name, etc. Amen. 1937 *Folklore* 54 [Gwent] One which his old mother used .. was written on the front leaf of her Bible .. 'Jesus came to Peter as he stood at the gate of Jerusalem, and said unto him, "What doest thou here?" Peter answered and said unto Jesus, "Lord, my teeth do ache." Jesus answered and said unto Peter, "That whosoever carry these words in memory with them, or near them, shall never have the teeth ache any more".' 1957 *East Anglian Mag.* 274. The wise woman would .. rub the gums with a stone, chanting .. 'As Thomas sat upon a marble stone Jesus came to him all alone And said, "Thomas, swear now for My sake And you shall never have toothache".'

TREE, disease transferred to

*c.*1250 *Physicians of Myddvai* (tr. Pughe, 454) Get an iron nail and engrave .. thereon, + agla + Sabaoth + athanatos + and insert the nail under the affected tooth. Then drive it into an oak tree, and whilst it remains there the toothache will not return. *c.*1640 MS Bodleian Add. c. 287 (G. GREGORY SMITH *Poems of Robert Henryson* xcvii) [Sir Francis Kinaston tells the story of Robert Henryson's death in 1506 of a 'diarrhea or fluxe'.] All phisitians hauing giuen him ouer & he lying drawing his last breath there came an old woman vnto him, who was held a witch, & asked him whether he would be cured, to whome he said very willingly, then quod she there is a whikey [rowan] tree in the lower end of your orchard, & if you will goe and walke but thrice about it, & thrice repeate theis wordis whikey tree whikey tree take away this fluxe from me you shall be presently cured. 1668 SIR K. DIGBY *Receipts* 45. A Sympathetic cure for the Tooth-ach. With an Iron-nail .. cut the gum from about the Teeth, till it bleed, and that some of the blood stick upon the nail; then drive it into a woodden beam up to the head; After this .. you never shall have the tooth-ach in all your life. (But whether the man used any Spell, or said any Words while he drove the nail, I know

not; only I saw done all that is said above). 1671 BLAGRAVE *Astrological Practice* 158–9. To cure a .. wasting Limb. Bore a hole in a Willow-tree .. take the parings of the nails, with some hair .. from the limb .. put all these into the hole of the tree, and stop them up close. 1790 GROSE *Provincial Glossary* Superstitions 40. In Scotland, nails are driven into oaks, as a preventative and cure for the tooth-ach. 1849 HALLIWELL *Popular Rhymes* 208. Whoever will charm away a wart must take a pin and go to an ash-tree. He then crosses the wart with the pin three times, and, after each crossing, repeats: 'Ash-tree, ashen-tree, Pray buy this wart of me!' After which he sticks the pin in the tree, and the wart soon disappears, and grows on the tree instead. This must be done secretly. 1850 *N & Q* 1st ser. I 482 [Sussex] The nails are cut, the cuttings carefully wrapped in paper, and placed in the hollow of a pollard ash, concealed from the birds; when the paper decays, the warts disappear. 1852 *N & Q* 1st ser. VI 5 [nr. Berkhampstead, Herts.] Aguish patients used to .. peg a lock of their hair into one of these oaks, then, by a sudden wrench, transfer the lock from their heads to the tree, and return home with the full conviction that the ague had departed with the severed lock .. The frequency of failure, however, to cure the disease, and the unpleasantness of the operation, have entirely destroyed the popular faith in this remedy. 1854 *N & Q* 1st ser. X 505. My old clerk in Wiltshire, whenever he was afflicted [with the toothache] had the singular habit of driving a nail into an oak tree. 1866 HENDERSON *Northern Counties* 119 [Lincs.] [For the ague.] Thou mun .. cut off a long lock o' thy heer .. and then thou mun gan to t'espin-tree, and thou mun tak a greet pin and wrap thy heer around it, and .. pin it t'it bark o' t'espin-tree; and .. say, 'Espin-tree, espin-tree, I prithee to shak an shiver insted o' me.' 1884 *N & Q* 6th ser. X 18. [Winchester, Hants.] The village schoolmaster .. had long been afflicted with ague. Being popular with his children and their parents, he received .. many remedies .. One .. was .. that he should, with a ceremony .. insert some of the parings of his finger-nails in the hole of a tree. **1889** *Dorset Field Club* 39. Go to a young oak-tree, cut a slit in the tree, cut off a bit of your hair, put it under the rind, put your hand up to the tree, and say, 'This [toothache] I bequeath to the oak-tree, in the name of the Father' [etc.]. **1909** M. TREVELYAN *Folk-Lore of Wales* 225. For ague the sufferer was to go silently, without crossing water, to a hollow willow-tree. He was to breathe into the hole three times, then stop the aperture as quickly as possible, and go home without looking round or speaking a word. **1912** LEATHER *Herefordshire* 82–3. In Oaker Coppice, Eyton, is a curious ash tree growing out of the stump of an oak. Its trunk is covered with hairs, small locks of human hair placed in notches made in the bark. Eyton folk believe that an offering of child's hair to this tree will cure the [whooping] cough, and an old keeper stated that people from Eyton living in London had sent him locks of hair, requesting him to fasten them in the bark of the tree. **1914** *Folklore* 365 [Suffolk] Clasp a birch tree in your arms. Then cut a slit in it, and sever a piece of hair with your left hand from behind your ear. Bury it in the slit, and when the hair has disappeared so will the toothache. **1945** *Folklore* 307 [Silsoe, Beds.] Until thirty or forty years before .. people .. suffering from ague would nail strands of their hair or toe nail clippings to the tree, to effect a cure.

Cf. NAILS driven in: cure; SHREW-ASH.

TRUNK, unlucky to lock

1885 *Folklore* 309–10. The practice of not locking the trunks of those going from home to prosecute the fishing is followed in Macduff [Aberdeen.] The trunk is packed .. and the key put in the lock. It is turned when set outside the door. My informant .. has himself been forbidden to lock the trunk, while it stood inside the house.

TURNING BACK unlucky

c. AD **60** Luke 17: 29–32. The same day that Lot went out of Sodom it rained fire and brimstone from heaven, and destroyed them all. Even thus shall it be in the day when the Son of man is revealed. In that day, he which shall be upon the housetop, and his stuff in the house, let him not come down to take it away: and he that is in the field, let him likewise not return back. Remember Lot's wife. **1159** JOHN OF SALISBURY *Policraticus* (*Frivolities of Courtiers*, ed. J. B. Pike, 57) If one is called back as he starts on a journey he should not on that account, if he has set out with the blessing of the Lord, give it up. **1678** BUNYAN *Pilgrim's Progress* 3–4. Then said Evangelist, Keep that light in your eye, and go up directly thereto .. The Man began to run; Now he had not run far from his own door, but his Wife and Children .. began to cry after him to return: but the Man put his fingers in his Ears .. The Neighbours also cried after him to return .. but he said, That can by no means be: You dwell .. in the City of Destruction .. and dying .. you will sink lower than the Grave. **1824** MACTAGGART *Gallovidian Encyclopedia* 210. If we are on the way to rid an errand, yet forget something, we will have no luck that day. **1865** R. HUNT *West of England* 2nd ser. 241. If you are going on an errand, never turn back to your house, it presages ill luck to do so. If, however, you are compelled to it, fail not to sit down. **1866** HENDERSON *Northern Counties* 87 [Yorks.] Grandfather, though anything but a weak man, would never turn back when he had once started on an expedition: he has been known to stand on horseback at the end of his grounds, shouting to the house for something that he had forgotten, rather than turn back for it. **1883** BURNE *Shropshire* 274. A wedding party on their way to church missed meeting one of the company who was to have joined them on the road, and turned back to look for him. This excited much comment. **1890** *N & Q* 7th ser. IX 486 [Fareham, Hants.] If you forget anything, never turn back, or misfortune will overtake you. **1899** J. SHAW *Schoolmaster* 30 [Tynron, Dumfries.] It bodes ill to turn when you are setting out on a journey. **1900** S. HEWETT *Nummits* 54 [Devon] It is unlucky .. to return, or to look back when leaving the house .. If compelled to return one should sit down .. for a few minutes

before making a fresh start. **1912**
LEATHER *Herefordshire* 87. If starting on
a journey it is very unlucky to turn
back; should anything be forgotten it is
better to sit down and try and think of
it; if it be something left behind, one
may be gravely told still that it would
be better to go on without it if possible.
1922 A. L. ROWSE *Cornish Childhood* IX.
I was to go in for the Christ Church
Scholarship .. On the morning I left
home .. I found half-way down the road
to the station that I had forgotten my
shaving gear. I ran back, and was almost
pushed away from the door by mother,
who said it was the unluckiest thing
possible to come back. **1968** *Observer*
Suppl. 24 Nov. 8 [John McCormack,
boxing champion.] Once Young John
has left his home for a fight it would be
terrible bad luck to return for anything
he forgets: he sends his companion or
waits for a passer-by. **1978** *Woman*,
67 [Sheffield, Yorks.] If a miner forgot
his 'snap' [lunch] and went back home
to fetch it he would not cross the threshold but waited for someone to fetch it
and hand it out to him. **1984** *Woman*,
62 [Headley Down, Hants.] If she had to

return home after forgetting something
my mother used to sit down and lift her
feet in the air.
Cf. LOOKING BACK.

TWIN, surviving

1878 *Folk-Lore Record* 47–8 [Fit-
tleworth, Sussex] The child that has
out-lived its fellow twin is always called
a left twin, and .. it's faith that works
the cure. A young woman .. had the
black thrush so bad that she could
neither eat nor drink, but a young man,
which was a left twin, came and blew
in her mouth three times, and the thrush
left her. It must be one of the male sex
that blows into the mouth of a woman,
and a female into that of a man.

TWIN ANIMALS

1904 *N & Q* 10th ser. II 406 [Llangybi,
Cardigan.] A farmer's wife .. informed
me that one of the cows had twin calves,
and that she was very anxious to sell
the animal at once, as such an incident
was considered an omen of .. very great
misfortune to the family or the owner. I
find that this superstition is very general,
even at the present day.

U

UMBRELLA as present
1982 Female student, 20 [Cleveland, Yorks.] It is considered unlucky to give an umbrella as a gift.

UMBRELLA on bed
1923 [Martock, Som.] You must never lay an umbrella or sunshade on the bed, or tragedy follows. **1982** Woman, 20 [Cleveland, Yorks.] Most people are aware that it is unlucky to put up an umbrella in the house. It is also unlucky to put one on a bed.

UMBRELLA on table
1883 BURNE *Shropshire* 280. It is unlucky .. to put an umbrella upon [a table]. **1890** *N & Q* 7th ser. IX 486 [Fareham, Hants.] Umbrella laid on the table, quarrel will ensue. **1933** J. B. BOOTH *Pink Parade* 97. If you really want to damn a play's chance utterly, place an umbrella on the prompter's table. **1937** *Newcastle Weekly Chronicle* 8 May 3 [Yorks.] Only a day or two ago, on my entry into a house, someone took my umbrella and coat and was about to deposit them for the moment on a table. Then—'Oh, but I mustn't put your umbrella on a table.'

UMBRELLA opened indoors
1883 BURNE *Shropshire* 280. It is unlucky to open an umbrella in the house, especially if it is held over the head, when it becomes a sign of death. **1909** *N & Q* 10th ser. XII 484 [Stromness, Orkney] It is unlucky to open an umbrella in the house. **1909** *Folklore* 345 [Hartlebury, Worcs., 1900] If you open an umbrella in the house and hold it over your head, there will be a death in the house before the year is out. **1932** C. IGGLESDEN *Those Superstitions* 210. An umbrella should not be put up indoors. **1961** Woman, *c.*60 [Redhill, Surrey] A local woman visiting my office today put up her umbrella to show us that it was 'quite all right so long as you don't hold it over your head.' **1983** Girl, 14 [Maldon, Essex] My family is not really su-

perstitious although we don't put up umbrellas inside. **1985** Man, 57 [London] I notice the typists coming into the office and drying their umbrellas, open, indoors, and I don't like it!

UMBRELLA/WALKING-STICK, dropping
1895 S. O. ADDY *Household Tales* 102. If you let your stick fall you will be sure to meet a friend immediately afterwards. **1899** J. SHAW *Schoolmaster* 33–4 [Tynron, Dumfries.] To drop your umbrella or walking-stick shows that your mind is likely to give way. **1909** *N & Q* 10th ser. XII 484 [Stromness, Orkney] It is unlucky to pick up your umbrella yourself if you let it fall. **1910** *Folklore* 226 [Pontefract, Yorks.] To pick up someone else's umbrella is lucky. **1911** J. C. DAVIES *West and Mid-Wales* 215. To drop your stick or your umbrella on your journey is unlucky. **1914** *N & Q* 11th ser. X 196 [Bury, Lancs.] Not so long since, in one of the principal streets, I heard a young shop-woman exclaim to a sceptical female friend who was standing smilingly by a fallen umbrella, 'Oh, do pick it up, please! I am so superstitious. I am frightened something will happen if I pick it up.' **1936** E. H. RUDKIN *Lincolnshire* 17. Bad luck .. to drop an umbrella. You must not pick it up, as a quarrel .. will ensue, but let some one else pick it up for you to avert the evil omen. **1952** Boy, 15 [Golspie, Sutherland] If a man is going somewhere to receive a decision and should drop his walking stick, he must not pick it up himself or the decision is bound to be given against him.

Cf. SWORD falls.

URINATING: must not offend divine powers
AD **77** PLINY *Natural History* XXVIII XIX (1856, V 301) The adepts in magic expressly forbid a person, when about to make water, to uncover the body in the face of the sun or moon, or to sprinkle with his urine the shadow of

any object whatsoever. Hesiod gives a precept, recommending persons to make water against an object standing full before them, that no divinity may be offended by their nakedness being un-covered. **1886** *Folklore* 15 [Portknockie, Banff.] If one of the crew makes his water over the boat's side before casting the nets, the boat would have been brought back at once without the nets having been shot.

URINATING together

1688 AUBREY *Remaines* (1881, 99) 'Tis an old reciev'd opinion, That if two doe p—— together they shall quarrell.

URINE, bubbles on

1922 JOYCE *Ulysses* (1960, 915) [Molly sits on the chamber and thinks] 'how noisy I hope theyre bubbles on it for a wad of money from some fellow.'

Cf. TEA, bubbles on; WELL: divination.

URINE in cake to detect witch

1648 HERRICK *Hesperides* 336 'Another to bring in the Witch'. To house the Hag, you must doe this; Commix with Meale a little Pisse Of him bewicht; then forthwith make A little Wafer or a Cake: And this rawly bak't will bring The old Hag in. No surer thing. **1683** REVD. O. HEYWOOD (*Autobiography etc.*, ed. Horsfall Turner, IV 53–4) [Northowram, Yorks.] May 7. Came to my house—Judith Higson and because I was not at home she writ down her business . . which was to desire my advice in a weighty case . . She . . hath a son . . who hath lyen long under a strange & sad hand of God in his body; he lyes in his bed, hath swelling in his throat, hand, cannot stirre . . about 12 years of age . . That day, May 7, came to their house . . one Dr Thornton who . . saith [her son's illness] is not a naturall distemper, that he is troubled with, but he hath had some hurt by an evil tongue, he saith he will not prescribe any medicine for him, until his water haue been tryd by fire—i.e. they must take his water and make a cake or loaf of it with wheat meal and put some of his hair into it, and horse-shooe stumps, and then put it in the fire; and till she or he or some one doe this he will prescribe nothing for him—not that he

bids her [the mother] say any words, yet she fears it may be some kind of charm, and as she piously expressed herself (for I hope she is a good woman) I being afraid to offend God by such a tryall as he prescribes, I came purposely to you and Mr Dawson to get your judgement . . I went to Halifax that day . . called of her, told her our thoughts, and then perceived their imagination, that upon their using these means, the witch that had hurt him would come and discover all . . I utterly dislik'd it, so did her husband and she . . I told them the right way was to goe to god by fasting and prayer. **1693** I. MATHER *Cases of Conscience* 29. Many Su-perstitious and Magical experiments have been used to try Witches by: Of this sort is . . seething the Urine of the bewitched Person, or making a Witch-cake with that Urine.

URINE: iron nails etc. in patient's urine to detect witch

1593 GIFFORD *Dialogue concerning Witches* G2ᵛ. The cunning man biddeth, set on a posnet or some pan with nayles, and saeth them [in the urine], and the witch shal come in while they be in saething, and within a fewe dayes after, her face will be all bescratched with the nailes. **1671** BLAGRAVE *Astrological Practice* 138. To afflict the Witch, caus-ing the evil to return back upon them . . Get two new horseshooes, heat one of them red hot, and quench him in the patients urine; then . . nail him on the inside of the threshold of the door. Ibid. 154. Stop the urine of the Patient, close up in a bottle, and put into it three nails, pins, or needles, with a little white Salt, keeping the urine alwayes warm: If you let it remain long in the bottle, it will endanger the witches life: for I have found by experience, that they will be grievously tormented making their water with great difficulty, if any at all. **1681** J. GLANVILL *Sadducismus Tri-umphatus* 206–8 [Suffolk, *c.*1630] He . . advised him to take a Bottle, and put his Wife's Urine into it, together with Pins and Needles and Nails, and Cork them up, and set the Bottle to the fire . . The Man followed the prescription . . but at last . . the Cork bounced out, and the

Urine, Pins, Nails and Needles all flew up . . and his Wife continued in the same trouble and languishment still. Not long after, the Old Man came to the house again, and inquired . . how his Wife did . . Ha, quoth he . . now I will put you in a way that will make the business sure. Take your Wife's Urine as before, and cork it in a Bottle with Nails, Pins and Needles, and bury it in the Earth . . The Man did accordingly. And his Wife began to mend . . and in a competent time was finely well recovered. But there came a Woman from a Town some miles off to their house, with a lamentable Out-cry, that they had killed her Husband . . that . . Husband was a Wizzard and had bewitched this Mans Wife. **1696** AUBREY *Miscellanies* (1890, 140) Mr Sp. told me that his horse which was bewitched, would break bridles and strong halters, like a Samson. They filled a bottle of the horse's urine, stopped it with a cork . . and then buried it under ground: and the party suspected to be the witch, fell ill, that he could not make water, of which he died. **1731** *Daily Journal* 15 Jan. (*Gents Mag.* 1731, 29) [Frome, Som.] A child of one Wheeler, being seized with strange fits, the mother was advised, by a Cunning Man, to hang a Bottle of the child's water, mix'd with some of its hair, close stop'd, over the fire, that the witch would thereupon come and break it. **1787** GROSE *Provincial Glossary* Superstitions 29. Some hair, the parings of the nails, and urine, of any person bewitched . . being put into a stone bottle with crooked nails, corked close, and tied down with wire, and hung up the chimney, will cause the Witch to suffer the most acute torments imaginable, till the bottle is uncorked, and the mixture dispersed; insomuch that they will even risk a detection, by coming to the house, and attempting to pull down the bottle. **1856** *N & Q* 2nd ser. I 415 [Lincs.] A man digging in his garden in the village of Yaddlethorpe came upon a skeleton of a horse or ox . . and near to it two bottles containing pins, needles, human hair, and a stinking fluid, probably urine. **1887** *Hull Daily Mail* 25 Feb. 3 [North Frodingham, E. Yorks.] The other day, while some men were removing the foundation and

débris of [an] old house a small stone bottle was found, sealed up with black pitch or wax, and when it was broken it was found to be filled with pins and needles and half horse shoe nails, and some wickin tree, *alias* mountain ash. **1955** *Folklore* 201. It is significant that in addition to such ingredients as nails or human hair, commonly found in later witch-bottles, at least two of the London bellarmines [jugs] contained a recognisable representation of a human heart, carefully cut from a piece of cloth or felt, and pierced with bent pins. **1971** *Trans. Devon. Ass.* 270 [Stockleigh Pomeroy] A witch story my father told me. A farmer near Torrington kept losing his calves (stillborn). He went to a white witch, and she told the farmer to hang a calf over the fire on the chimney crook, slowly burning it, also to sneak into the witch's house, and catch three fleas from her bed, put them in a bottle and cork them in. The witch after four or five days would *have* to pass his window and look in the room. The spell would be over then because so long as the fleas were corked up in the bottle (and the calf burning slowly) the witch would never 'beable' (spend a penny) until she showed up and broke the spell.

Cf. CATTLE: burning entrails gives power over witch.

URINE protects

late **18th c.** J. RAMSAY (*Scotland in the Eighteenth Century* II 454–5) Human urine is supposed to be endued with hidden virtues. Thus in Breadalbane, when the plough is first yoked, it is the custom yearly to sprinkle the horses and then the coulter with it . . In Glenlyon, the landlady takes care to rise early on the morning of New Year's Day. She ties together some straw in the form of a brush, and sprinkles urine with it upon the whole family as they are getting out of bed. In Morven and Breadalbane, the old woman who officiates as midwife commonly sprinkles the bed of the lying-in woman, and sometimes every person in the room, with the same liquor. **1900** J. G. CAMPBELL *Superstitions of the Highlands* 36. Various precautions were taken [at childbirth] . . The door posts were sprinkled with *maistir*, urine kept for washing purposes—a liquid extremely offensive to the Fairies.

URINE, spitting into

AD 77 PLINY *Natural History* XXVIII VII (1856, V 290) Among the counter-charms are reckoned, the practice of spitting into the urine the moment it is voided. **1584** SCOT *Discoverie of Witchcraft* XII XVIII. To unbewitch the bewitched .. you must spet into the pissepot, where you have made water.

V

VALENTINE, drawing lots for

*c.*1430 J. LYDGATE (*Minor Poems*, 1911, I 305) Saynt Valentyne, of custume yeere by yeere, Men haue an vsavnce in this Regyoun To looke and serche Cupydes Kalundere .. Taking theyre choyse, as theyre soort dothe falle. 1596 RALEIGH *Discoverie of Guiana* 23. After the Queens haue chosen, the rest cast lottes for their Valentines. 1667 PEPYS *Diary* 16 Feb. To Mrs Pierce's, where I took up my wife and there find that Mrs Pierce's little girl is my Valentine, she having drawn me—which I was not sorry for, it easing me of something more that I must have given to others. 1712 WOODES ROGERS *Voyage round the World* 359. That same Day, in Commemoration of the antient Custom .. of chusing Valentines, I drew up a list of the fair Ladies in Bristol .. and sent for my Officers into the Cabbin, where every one drew. 1725 BOURNE *Antiquitates Vulgares* 174. It is a Ceremony, never omitted among the Vulgar, to draw Lots, which they Term Valentines, on the Eve before Valentine-day. The Names of a select Number of one Sex, are by an equal Number of the other put into some Vessel; and after that, every one draws a Name, which .. is called their Valentine, and is also look'd upon as a good Omen of their being Man and Wife afterwards. 1790 BURNS 'Tam Glen'. Yestreen at the valentines' dealing, My heart to my mou gied a sten, For thrice I drew ane without failing, And thrice it was written 'Tam Glen'. 1866 HENDERSON *Northern Counties* 73 [S. Scotland, St Valentine's Eve] Young people .. write .. names .. on slips of paper, placing those of lads and lasses in separate bags apart. The maidens draw from the former, the young men from the latter, three times in succession .. If one person takes out the same name three times .. it is .. that of the future husband or wife.

VALENTINE: first person seen

1654 DOROTHY OSBORNE Letter 19 Feb. I was up Early but with noe desig[n]e of getting another Valentine and goeing out to walk in my Nightcloths and Nightgowne I mett Mr Fish. goeing a hunting I think hee was, but hee stayed to tell mee I was his Valentine, and I should not have bin rid on him quickly if hee had not thought himself a litle too Necgligeé his haire was not pouderd and his Cloths were but ordinary. 1698 MISSON *Voyage en Angleterre* (1719, 321) There is another kind of Valentine; which is the first young Man or Woman that Chance throws in your way, in the Street, or elsewhere on that Day. 1755 *Connoisseur* 20 Feb. Mr Blossom was my man: and I lay a-bed and shut my eyes all the morning [Valentine's Day], till he came to our house; for I would not have seen another man before him for all the world. 1812 J. BRADY *Clavis Calendaria* I 212–13. The first person of the opposite sex who is seen, is generally esteemed the Valentine for the year, whether consonant to 'choice', or not .. Some young gentlemen and ladies, in order to remedy this uncertainty, contrive to be brought together blindfold. 1828 MITFORD *Our Village* III 72. Our country maidens .. hold, that the first man whom they espy in the morning .. is to pass for their Valentine during the day; and, perhaps .. to prove their husband for life. It is strange how much faith they put in this kind of *sortes virgilianæ*. 1872 *Punch* 17 Feb. 69. The belief is universal .. that if you are single, the first unmarried person you meet outside the house on St Valentine's Day will exercise an important influence over your future destiny. Fortunately there is a simple way of evading the hand of Fate, open to those who desire a greater freedom in their choice of a partner in wedlock—at least, if they are willing to remain indoors till the expiration of the spell at twelve p.m. 1923 [Wincanton, Som.] The first person you see of the opposite sex on St Valentine's Day will become your husband or wife as the case may be. **1933** *Folklore* 280 [Gainsborough, Lincs.] The first dark man you meet on Valentine's Day is your Valentine.

VERVAIN, powers of

AD **77** PLINY *Natural History* XXV LIX (1856, V 121–2) There is no plant that enjoys a more extended renown than .. 'verbenaca' .. It is .. borne by envoys when treating with the enemy .. with this houses are purified and due expiation made .. The people in the Gallic provinces make use of it .. for the prediction of future events .. Persons .. rub themselves with it .. to gain .. their desires; and they assure us that it .. conciliates friendship, and is a cure for every possible disease [and] for the stings of serpents. *c.*1050 MS Cotton Vitell. C. iii (COCKAYNE *Leechdoms* I 93) For bite of adder, whatsoever man hath on him, this wort verbenaca, with its leaves and roots, he will be firm against all snakes. *c.*1250 *Physicians of Myddvai* (tr. Pughe, 314, 338) If one goes to battle let him seek the vervain, and keep it in his clothes (on his person) and he will escape from his enemies .. To prevent dreams. Take the vervain, and hang about a man's neck, or give him the juice in going to bed. **1579** LUPTON *Thousand Notable Things* II § 58. The roote of Varuayn hanged at the necke of such as haue the Kings Euyll: it brings a maruelous and an unhoped helpe. **1584** SCOT *Discoverie of Witchcraft* XII XVIII. The popish church .. to be delivered from witches .. hang in their entries .. verven .. Memorandum, that at the gathering [of it] the Credo is necessarie to be said .. for that is not superstitious. **1608** J. WHITE *Way to the Trve Chvrch* pref. 13. Many .. weare Veruein against blastes .. first they crosse the herbe .. and blesse it, thus: 'Hallowed be thou Veruein, as thou growest on the ground, For in the mount of Calvary there thou was first found: Thou healedst our Sauiour Iesus Christ, and stanchedst his bleeding wound.' **1625** T. JACKSON *Originall of Vnbeliefe* XIX 175–7. Of wearing medicines [for] no reason, saue onley .. of lucke good or bad to follow .. Such is the vse of Vervine, of our Ladies gloues, and S. Johns grasse at this day

.. amongst some rude and ignorant Christians .. A tradition [there] was of a maid that liked well of the devil making love to her in the habit of a gallant young man, but could not enjoy his company, nor he hers, so long as she had Vervine and S. Johns grass about her. **1627** DRAYTON *Nimphidia* ll. 389–92. She Night-shade strawes to work him [Puck] ill, Therewith her Vervayne and her Dill, That hindreth Witches of their will, Of purpose to dispight him. **1813** BRAND *Antiquities* II 598 n. Squire Morley of Essex used to say a prayer which he hoped would do no harm when he hung a bit of vervain-root from a scrophulous person's neck. **1878** *Folk-Lore Record* 38 [Fittleworth, Sussex] Its dried leaves, 'worn in a black silk bag', are recommended as a cure for weakly children. **1884** R. FOLKARD *Plant Lore* 575. In many rural districts, Vervain is still regarded as a plant possessing magical virtues as a love philtre.

Cf. ST JOHN'S WORT protects.

VIRGIN first to hold baby

1866 HENDERSON *Northern Counties* 5. An old belief in Yorkshire enjoins that a new-born child be laid in the arms of a maiden before anyone else holds him. **1898** BLAKEBOROUGH *Yorkshire Customs* 106. When possible, a new arrival, before being laid by its mother's side, or even touched by her, is placed in the arms of a maiden.

VIRGIN has power of divination

1621 J. MOLLE *Living Librarie* 2. The Magicians .. maintaine, that Angels and Spirits loue maides and boyes that are not corrupted, for the agreement and conformitie that is betweene them. For likenesse causeth loue .. Some .. (being curious to finde out by the helpe of a looking-glasse, or a glasse-viall full of water, a theefe that lies hidden) make choyce of young Maides or Boyes vnpolluted, to discerne therein those Images or sights which a person defiled cannot see.

VIRGIN heals

AD **77** PLINY *Natural History* XXVIII x (1856, V 292) A virgin should touch the patient with her right thumb—a circumstance that has led to the belief that persons suffering from epilepsy should eat the flesh of animals in a virgin state. *c*.1000 MS Harl. 585 (COCKAYNE *Leechdoms* III 43) Against a warty eruption, one must . . sing the charm which is hereinafter mentioned . . then let one who is a maiden . . hang it upon his neck. *c*.1050 MS Cotton Vitell. C. iii (COCKAYNE *Leechdoms* I 219) That . . a woman, may quickly bring forth, take seed of . . coriander . . knit them . . on a clean linen cloth; let then . . a person of maidenhood, a boy or a maiden . . hold this at the left thigh, near the natura. 1486 SPRENGER & KRAMER *Malleus Maleficarum* (tr. Summers, 179) We hear of a certain poor and very devout virgin, one of whose friends had been grievously bewitched in his foot, so that it was clear to the physicians that he could be cured by no medicines. But it happened that the virgin went to visit the sick man, and he at once begged her to apply some benediction to his foot. She consented, and did no more than silently say the Lord's Prayer . . at the same time making . . the sign of the life-giving Cross. The sick man then felt himself at once cured. 1548 SCOT *Discoverie of Witchcraft* XII XIV. To heale the Kings or Queenes evill, or any other sorenesse in the throte . . Let a virgine fasting laie hir hand on the sore, and saie; Apollo denieth that the heate of the plague can increase, where a naked virgine quencheth it: and spet three times upon it. 1704 T. D'URFEY *Tales, Tragical and Comical* 191. She starts from Bed, spins round the House . . Drops in her haste, when up she got, Green Stockings in the Chamber-Pot, Where she did Virgin-Amber make, A Sovereign Cure for Teeth that ake. 1855 F. K. ROBINSON *Yorkshire Words* 96 [for whooping cough] Great faith is put in a piece of bread and butter which shall be the gift of an unmarried female.

VIRGIN, meeting

c. AD 388 ST JOHN CHRYSOSTOM *Baptismal Instructions* (ed. Harkins, 190) If a virgin chances to meet you, you say the day is an unsuccessful one. 1652 GAULE *Mag-astro-mances* 181. To bode good or bad luck . . from . . the meeting of a Virgin . . first [in a morning].

Cf. PROSTITUTE, meeting.

VIRGIN'S GRAVE

1862 *N & Q* 3rd ser. II 483 [Aberdeen.] A little fresh earth taken from the open grave of a child, who has been baptised within a twelve-month of death, is regarded—if sprinkled on the flower-pot—as calculated to make the blossoms of the plants large and handsome. 1898 BLAKEBOROUGH *Yorkshire Customs* 139 [for worms] A bunch of fine yarrow gathered from off a maiden's grave, had to be boiled in water, and a wineglassful of the liquor, with . . as much finely powdered glass as would lie on a groat, had to be taken fasting for six alternate mornings. 1909 M. TREVELYAN *Folk-Lore of Wales* 319. A stone from a virgin's grave was formerly tied to any person who had been bitten by an adder. 1984 Woman, *c*.70 [Liss, Hants.] My mother always used to say that the grass grows greener on a virgin's grave.

Cf. GRAVE cures.

VOLUNTEERING for a job

1934 E. RIDDELL & M. C. CLAYTON *The Cambridgeshire—1914–19* 216. It was unlucky to volunteer for a job.

W

WALKING backwards

1851 *N & Q* 1st ser. III 55 [Lancs.] Children are frequently cautioned by their parents not to walk backwards when going an errand; it is a sure sign that they will be unfortunate in their objects. 1861 C. C. ROBINSON *Dialect of Leeds* 300. Children are cautioned never to walk backwards way upon being sent on errands, as it is 'unlucky'. 1867 HARLAND & WILKINSON *Lancashire Folk-Lore* 220. Young children are often re-minded that they ought not to walk backwards [or] death will soon deprive them of their mothers.

WARTS cured with bean pod

1849 HALLIWELL *Popular Rhymes* 208. Take a bean-shell, and rub the wart with it; then bring the bean-shell under an ash-tree, and repeat: 'As this bean-shell rots away, So my wart shall soon decay.' This must be done secretly. 1852 *N & Q* 1st ser. VI 519–20. They dis-appeared in less than a fortnight, after being well rubbed with a bean swad, and the pod thrown away. 1870 *N & Q* 4th ser. VI 69. She charmed hern off with a broad bean shell—that is, to rub the warts well wi' the inside (9 times, I think) and then bury the shell, and tell no one where, and as it rots so the warts die. 1954 [Swansea, Glam.] Rub wart with the inside of a broad bean. Then bury the bean in the garden, or, throw it in the rubbish bin. 1969 M. HARRIS *A Kind of Magic* 114 [Ducklington, Oxon., 1920s] One old lady could charm them away simply by rubbing them .. with the inside of a broad-bean pod.

WARTS cured with elder wood

1627 BACON *Sylva Sylvarum* § 997. The Rubbing of Warts with a Green Elder Sticke, and then Burying the Stick to Rot in Muck. 1850 *N & Q* 1st ser. II 150 [Somerset] The village-charmer .. cut off a slip of elder-tree, and made a notch in it for every wart. He then rubbed the elder against each, strictly enjoining me to think no more about it, as if I looked often at the warts the charm would fail. 1883 BURNE *Shropshire* 199. She had been cured by taking as many sprigs of elder as she had warts; with each sprig she touched a wart, saying, 'Here's a wart,' then she touched a place where there was not one, saying, 'but here's none'; and then buried the sprigs. 1946 UTTLEY *Country Things* x [Crom-ford, Derbys., *c.*1900] Every old man seemed to have his particular cure, which was secret. One touched the warts with elder-wood, murmured an in-cantation over them, and buried the wood. 1954 Girl, 15 [Newbridge, Mon-mouth.] My grandfather told me to put a small twig of elderberry down the toilet, and say, 'Wart, wart, on my knee, please go, one, two, three.'

Cf. ELDER protects against and cures disease.

WARTS cured with meat

*c.*1250 *Physicians of Myddvai* (tr. Pughe, 337) Take an eel and cut its head off, anoint the parts, where the warts are situated, with the blood, and bury the head deep in the earth; as the head rottens, so will the warts disappear. 1579 LUPTON *Thousand Notable Things* VI § 59. Wartes rubbed with a peece of rawe Beefe, and the same Beefe being buryed within the grounde: the Wartes wyll weare and consume, as the Beefe doth rotte in the ground. Proued. 1627 BACON *Sylva Sylvarum* § 997. The English Embassadours Lady, who was a Woman farre from Superstition, told me, one day; She would helpe me away with my Warts: Whereupon she got a Peece of Lard, with the Skin on, and rubbed the Warts all ouer with the Fat Side .. Then she nailed the Peece of Lard, with the Fat towards the Sunne, upon a Poast of her Chamber Window, which was to the South. The Successe was, that within five weekes space, all the Warts went quite away. 1769 *Poor Robin's Almanack* 'Prognostication' (last page) The second is a Butcher's Daughter [who] once buried a Bit of Beef in the Ground, as a known Receipt to cure warts on her hands. **1787** GROSE *Provincial Glossary* Superstitions 57. Steal a piece of beef from a butcher's shop, and rub your warts with it; then throw it down the necessary house, or bury it; and, as the beef rots, your warts will decay. **1850** *N & Q* 1st ser. II 68 [Burnley, Lancs.] Steal a piece of meat from a butcher's stall or his basket, and after having well rubbed the parts affected with the stolen morsel, bury it under a gateway, at a four lane ends, or .. in any secluded place. All this must be done so secretly as to escape detection .. This .. is very prevalent in Lancashire and some parts of Yorkshire. **1882** *People's Friend* 8 Nov. 711 [Scotland] The person suffering [from a sty] *stole* a morsel of raw flesh, rubbed with it the part affected, and thereafter hid the flesh in the ground. As it decayed away, the stye gradually disappeared. The odd part of the business is, that the bit of flesh must be obtained and hid surruptitiously, else no cure. Warts were removed in a manner very similar. **1946** UTTLEY *Country Things* x [Cromford, Derbys., *c*.1900] One old man .. rubbed them with a piece of leaf-lard. The lard was hung in the sun and as it melted the warts vanished. **1954** Girl, 14 [Newbridge, Monmouth.] I have also tried putting a piece of bacon on the clothes line. **1983** Woman, *c*.60 [Colchester, Essex] I had warts all my life and then one day I heard on the radio you could cure them by rubbing them with raw meat and burying it in the garden. You mustn't tell anyone. It worked for me.

WARTS cured with snail
1826 CULPEPER *Herbal* 221. Take a black snail, and rub them with the same nine times one way, and then nine times another, and then stick that said snail upon a black-thorn, and the warts will waste. **1851** *N & Q* 1st ser. III 56 [Lancs.] Warts are cured by being rubbed over with a black snail, but the snail must afterwards be impaled upon a hawthorn. **1893** *Folklore* 356 [Glenavy, Co. Antrim] If you happen on a big black snail, rub it across your wart an' stick

it on a thorn, an' as the snail withers, so will the wart. **1912** LEATHER *Herefordshire* 84. Take a live snail, rub the warts with it, bury it alive, or stick it on the black thorn; this must be done secretly, and as the snail shrivels up the warts will disappear. **1922** [Trowbridge, Wilts.] A snail must be pricked as many times as you have warts and then stuck on a thorn by the wayside. As it dies so will your warts disappear. Should anyone take the snail from the thorn, on him will the warts appear. **1935** *I Walked by Night* (ed. L. Rider Haggard, 17) [Norfolk] There is a certain snail .. that must be rubbed on the wharts and then stuck on a White thorn bush and as the snail wasted so did the wharts. **1954** Girl, 14 [Llandrindod Wells, Radnor.] He rubbed her hands with a snail and hung it on a thorn bush .. Aunty says she has never had a wart since.

WARTS 'given' to corpse
1850 *N & Q* 1st ser. II 226. In some parts of Ireland .. they place great faith in the following charm. When a funeral is passing by, they rub the warts and say three times, 'May these warts and this corpse pass away and never more return.' **1878** *Folk-Lore Record* 223 [Donegal, Eire, in childhood.] If a corpse is passing who was no near relative or 'sib', get a stone, and throw it in the name of the Father, the Son, and the Holy Ghost after the corpse; and, while you mention the name and surname of the deceased, say you 'force your warts on him'; as the dead body decays, so will the warts. **1887** 'SPERANZA' WILDE *Superstitions of Ireland* II 93. On meeting a funeral, take some of the clay from under the feet of the men who bear the coffin and apply it to the wart, wishing strongly at the same time that it may disappear; and so it will be. **1893** *Folklore* 355-6 [Old beggar woman, Co. Derry] If you see a funeral passing, stoop down an' lift some clay from under your right foot, an' throw it in the same road that the funeral is going, an' say, 'Corpse of clay, carry my warts away', an' do this three times, an' as the corpse decays in the grave, your warts will go away. **1960** Girl, 11 [SE London] When you

see a funeral, look at your wart and say 'Wart, wart, follow the corpse', and it's supposed to go. And my mum knows a person who done that and it went.

WARTS 'sold'

1579 LUPTON *Thousand Notable Things* VI § 59. If one doth buye Wartes of them that haue them, and geue them a pin therfore: if the party that hath the Warts, pricke the same pyn upon some garment that he weares .. commonly .. the Wartes without doubte wyll demynish and weare away priuely, and be cleane gone in short time. This was tolde me for an often tryed and prooued thing: yea, and by such a one as had seene the experyence therof. **1648** HERRICK *Hesperides* 193 'Oberons Palace'. Those warts, Which we to others (from our selves) Sell. **1969** S. MAYS *Reuben's Corner* [Essex] 165. Warts could be purchased away: 'I'll give ye a tanner forrit, then it's MY. Don't think about it till it's gone. Then you gits yer tanner back.' **1969** *Sunday Express* 25 May 4 [Lancing, Sussex] My little son had several warts on his hands and we tried various remedies. Then one day an elderly lady in a bus noticed them and said: 'I'll buy them off you'—and gave him a penny. Lo and behold the warts disappeared never to return.

Cf. SELLING cures various ills.

WARTS 'thrown away'

AD **77** PLINY *Natural History* XXII LXXII (1856, IV 451) On the first day of the moon, each wart must be touched with a single chickpea, after which, the party must tie up the pease in a linen cloth and throw it behind him. **1807** SOUTHEY *Letters from England* L. Stealing dry peas or beans, and wrapping them up, one for each wart, he carries the parcel to a place where four roads meet, and tosses it over his head, not looking behind to see where it falls; he will lose the warts, and whoever picks it up will have them. **1851** *N & Q* 1st ser. III 56 [Lancs.] If a bag containing as many small pebbles as a person has warts, be tossed over the left shoulder, it will transfer the warts to whoever is unfortunate enough to pick up the bag. **1912** LEATHER *Herefordshire* 83. Make a packet of as

many grains of wheat as there are warts. These are to be thrown over the shoulder without looking round, where four roads meet, in the hope of transferring them to the finder of the packet. **1953** Girl, 14 [Norton, Yorks.] Take a stick and cut notches in it, then rub the warts in the notches and throw the stick down, someone will pick it up and get the warts and yours will go. **1960** Boy, 11 [SE London] You put four pebbles in a matchbox and you go to a crossroad and drop them in the middle .. it worked with my sister.

Cf. COUNTING cures warts.

WASHING as ritual

c. 200 BC Psalms xxvi 6. I will wash my hands in innocency: so will I compass thine altar, O Lord. AD **77** PLINY *Natural History* XXXIV LXII (1856, V 42) The clothing .. must be white, the feet bare and washed clean, and a sacrifice of bread and wine must be made before gathering it [the herb]. **1648** HERRICK *Hesperides* 310 'Another to the Maids'. Wash your hands, or else the fire Will not teend to your desire; Unwasht hands, ye Maidens, know, Dead the Fire, though ye blow. **1775** L. SHAW *History of Moray* 242–3. The Scots Highlanders, not only put on clean clothes on the Sabbath day, as others do; but in the morning of that day, they wash (not in the house, but *Flumine vivo*) in running water, and they call it *Uisg Domhnich*, i.e. 'Aqua Dominica'. **1855** *N & Q* 1st ser. XII 489 [Worcs.] La, bless me, mum! why, don't you know as you can't kill any living thing, unless you've washed your face first? I'm sure that I tried for full ten minutes to wring this 'en's neck, and I couldn't kill her; and all because I hadn't time to wash my face this morning. **1866** HENDERSON *Northern Counties* 85 [Leeds, Yorks.] Before you kill anything it is necessary to wash your face. **1907** *Folklore* 435 [Norfolk] Unless the hands of the milker were washed before and after milking the cow would become dry.

WASHING clothes: day of sailing

1956 'Please don't wash tomorrow,' said the Humber pilot's wife, 'He'll be going to sea tomorrow and I never wash when he's going off .. You may wash them away, you know.' **1978** A. WRIGHT *Holderness* 18 [E. Yorks.] She [seaman's wife] would not wash on the day she [his ship] set sail, because the rushing away of the washday water might wash his ship away.

WASHING clothes: drying
1954 [Swansea/Aberdeen] If you manage to dry your washing in between showers, 'your man loves you.'

WASHING clothes: sloppily
1895 S. O. ADDY *Household Tales* 100. If you splash yourself .. very much when you wash clothes you will have a drunken husband. **1909** M. TREVELYAN *Folk-Lore of Wales* 6. The woman who wets her apron very much, or splashes the water much about, will have a drunken husband. **1982** Female student, 20. Yorkshire country women still remember that a woman who spills a large amount of water over herself when doing the washing, will have a drunken husband. 'A sloppy washer will have a drunken husband.'

WASHING HANDS together
1584 SCOT *Discoverie of Witchcraft* XII xviii. *Charme for the ague.* Wash with the partie [i.e. the patient], and privilie saie this psalme, *Exaltabo te Deus meus, rex &c.* **1652** GAULE *Mag-astro-mances* 181. To bode good or bad luck .. to wash in the same water after another. **1688** AUBREY *Remaines* (1881, 99) If two doe wash their hands together, they will quarrel. **1787** GROSE *Provincial Glossary* Superstitions 65. Washing hands in the same bason, or with the same water, as another person has washed in, is extremely unlucky, as the parties will infallibly quarrel. **1852** *N & Q* 1st ser. VI 193 [Plymouth, Devon] For two persons to wash their hands in the same water is deemed a cause of strife, unless the second person spits in the water. **1867** *N & Q* 3rd ser. XII 477 [Ramsgate, Kent] A custom prevailing among the lower classes, that anyone wishing to wash their hands in water that some one else has previously used for that purpose, he or she must first make the sign of the cross on the water

with their forefinger, to avert misfortune. **1872** *N & Q* 4th ser. IX 45 [Worksop, Notts.] If you wipe your hands on the same towel, and at the same time with another person, you and that person will, at some time in life, go a-begging together. **1881** *Punch* 1 Jan. 310. If you dip your hands into a basin where even your best friend has cleansed his face, you and he will quarrel. **1896** *N & Q* 8th ser. IX 425. The other day a little niece (from Wales), after 'helping' me in the garden, came to wash her hands in water I had just used for the same purpose. She said: 'Make a cross in the water first, or we shall quarrel.' **1932** C. IGGLESDEN *Those Superstitions* 189–90. Just before .. a cricket match a man was washing his hands when another member of the eleven also plunged his hands in the water. 'That means a duck for both of us,' exclaimed the first man. **1968** M. H. BELL *What Shall We Do Tomorrow* 92. Sonia spat into the water and crossed it. 'Mustn't wash in the same basin without doing that.' **1983** Woman, 76 [Bentworth, Hants.] When you wash your hands in the same water as someone else, make the sign of the Cross on the water. We've always done that.

WASHING UP together
1982 Female student, 20 [Cleveland, Yorks.] If both partners assist each other with the washing up, the marriage will be happy: 'Wash and wipe together, Live in peace together.'

WASHING WATER, throwing out
1648 HERRICK *Hesperides* 383 'Another [charm]'. In the morning .. Wash your hands, and cleanse your eyes. Next .. disperse the water farre. For as farre as that doth light, So farre keepes the evill Spright. **1873** *N & Q* 4th ser. XI 53. While staying at Deeside last summer, I noticed my host drop a hot cinder into the water in which he had just bathed his feet, before it was thrown out. This .. he adheres to at all such lavations .. I may mention that my host was of the Roman Catholic persuasion. **1878** A. MACGREGOR *Brahan Seer* 129 'Superstitions of Highlanders'. It is unlucky to throw out water after sunset, and

before sunrise. **1909** M. TREVELYAN *Folk-Lore of Wales* 5. People were warned not to spurt or scatter the water from their hands after washing the first thing in the morning, else they would scatter their good luck for the day. **1923** *Folklore* 235 [Connaught, Eire] It is unlucky .. to throw out water after dark.

WASP, first: killed

AD **77** PLINY *Natural History* XXX xxx (1856, V 453–4) In the treatment of quartain fevers, clinical medicine is .. pretty nearly powerless; for which reason we shall insert .. remedies .. of the magic art .. amulets .. for instance .. the first wasp that a person sees in the current year [caught with the left hand and attached beneath the patient's chin]. **1850** *N & Q* 1st ser. II 165 [Northants.] The first wasp seen in the season should always be killed. By doing so you secure to yourself good luck and freedom from enemies throughout the year. **1922** [Taunton, Som.] Always kill the first queen wasp you see and you will overcome your enemies.

WASSAILING cornfields and cattle

1686–7 AUBREY *Remaines* (1881, 40) In Somersetshire when they Wassaile (which is on .. I think Twelfe-eve) the Plough-men have their Twelve-cake, and they go into the Ox-house to the oxen, with the Wassell-bowle and drink to the ox w. the crumpled horne that treads out the corne; they have an old conceived Rythme. **1771** PENNANT *Tour in Scotland* 91 n. [Glos.] On the twelfth day .. in the evening: all the servants of every particular farmer assemble together in one of the fields that has been sown with wheat [and] in the most elevated place they make twelve fires of straw, in a row; around one of which, made larger than the rest, they drink a chearful glass of cyder to their master's health, success to the future harvest, and then returning home they feast on cakes, made of carraways, &c. soaked in cyder, which they clame as a reward for their past labours in sowing the grain. **1873** *N & Q* 4th ser. XII 466 [Herefords., 1830] On the eve of old Christmas-day there are thirteen fires lighted in the corn fields of many of the farms, twelve

.. in a circle and one .. much .. higher than the rest, in the centre .. While they are burning the labourers retire into some shed .. where .. they lead a cow, on whose horn a plum-cake has been stuck .. The oldest labourer takes a pail of cider, and .. the following .. is chaunted .. by all present: 'Here's to thy pretty face and thy white horn, God send thy master a good crop of corn, Both wheat, rye and barley, and all sorts of grain, And next year, if we live, we'll drink to thee again.' He then dashes the cider in the cow's face, when, by a violent toss of her head, she throws the plum-cake on the ground; and, if it falls forward, it is an omen that the next harvest will be good; if backward, that it will be unfavourable. **1887** F. T. HAVERGAL *Herefordshire Words* 48. Twelfth Night Custom at Eardisland .. A cake was placed on a bullock's horn .. A bucket of cider was then drunk .. each drinking the master's health .. 'Here's to the champion, to the white horn [etc.]'. Another toast, 'Here's to the plough, the fleece, and the pail, May the landlord ever flourish, And the tenant never fail.' Sometimes the cake would be placed on a heifer's horn, then the verse ran: 'Here's a health to the heifer, And to the white teat, Wishing the mistress a house full of meat, With cruds, milk and butter fresh every day, And God grant the young men keep out of her way.' **1923** [Somerset] The health of the cattle must be drunk in the cowshed on Old Christmas Day. Give your cattle extra rations on Christmas Day, or rain will spoil your corn and hay.

Cf. FIRE protects cattle and crops.

WASSAILING fruit trees

1648 HERRICK *Hesperides* 311 'Another [to the Maids]'. Wassaile the Trees, that they may beare You many a Plum, and many a Peare: For more or lesse fruits they will bring, As you doe give them Wassailing. **1787** GROSE *Provincial Glossary. Watsail.* [Exmoor] A drinking song, sung on twelfth-day eve, throwing toast to the apple-trees, in order to have a fruitful year, which seems to be a relic of the heathen sacrifice to Pomona. **1791** *Gents Mag.* pt. 1 403. In the

Southhams of Devonshire, on the eve of Epiphany, the farmer, attended by his workmen, with a large pitcher of cyder, goes to the orchard, and there, encircling one of the best bearing trees, they drink the following toast three several times: 'Here's to thee, old apple-tree, Whence thou may'st bud, and whence thou may'st blow! And whence thou may'st bear apples enow! Hats full! caps full! And my pockets full too! Huzza!' .. Some are so superstitious as to believe that, if they neglect this custom, the trees will bear no apples that year. 1838 A. E. BRAY *Devonshire* I 335. On Christmas-eve, the farmers .. often take a large bowl of cider with a toast in it, and .. salute the apple-trees .. in order to make them bear well the next season. This salutation consists in throwing some of the cider about the roots .. placing bits of the toast on the branches; and then forming .. a ring, they .. sing a song. 1902 *N & Q* 9th ser. IX 287. Wassailing or toasting the apple-trees, is still observed in .. North Devon and Somerset, and probably nowhere with more ceremony .. than at Wootton Basset .. Old Twelfth-eve .. is the usual day .. and in the evening well-nigh all the folk of the parish .. start in procession for the nearest orchard .. The 'master' walks in front .. whilst .. men with guns, old muzzle-loaders .. or anything that will make a noise, form the rearguard .. At the orchard, the party all form a ring .. and .. holloa, shout, or sing: 'Hatfuls, capfuls, [etc.]' .. The 'butler' takes a piece of toast, and, pouring cider over it .. hands it to the master, who sticks it up in the tree .. in the hope that it will bring luck. 1954 *Girl,* 15 [Forfar, Angus] To make sure of a fruit tree bearing well pour a drop of wine at the foot. 1970 *English Dance and Song* XXXII 138 [Old Twelfth Night, i.e. 17 Jan.] Ten years ago .. wassailing the apple trees in the tiny village of Carhampton [Som.] was just celebrated by a family and their friends. Today, as for centuries, men with shot guns go out into the orchard behind the village pub, and the trees are toasted in cider and .. urged .. to bring forth a good crop .. 'Apples, hatfuls, capfuls, three bushel bagfuls, And a little heap under

the stairs' .. Evil spirits and witches are warded off by firing shots through the boughs .. The custom has become a popular entertainment .. There is a queue of photographers and television cameramen—and a few hopeful preservationists. 1981 *Western Morning News* 16 Jan. 3. To ensure a fruitful year .. the cider queen soaks toast in cider and places it into a tree to encourage good spirits .. Any evil spirits .. are soon seen off .. with shotgun pellets.

WASSAILING sea

1703 M. MARTIN *Western Islands of Scotland* 28–9. The Inhabitants .. had an ancient Custom to sacrifice to a Sea God .. at Hallow-tide .. One of their number was pickt out to wade into the Sea .. carrying a Cup of Ale. [He] cry'd out in a loud Voice .. 'I give you this Cup of Ale, hoping that you'll be so kind as to send us plenty of Sea-ware, for inriching our Ground' .. and so threw the Ale into the Sea .. They believ'd [this] a powerful means to procure a plentiful Crop .. Ministers in Lewis, told me .. this ridiculous piece of Superstition .. is quite abolish'd for these 32 Years past. 1904 E. V. LUCAS *Highways and Byways in Sussex* 173 [Brighton] It was once the custom .. for these men, when casting their nets for mackerel or herring, to stand with bare heads repeating in unison these words: 'There they goes then. God Almighty send us a blessing it is to be hoped.' As each barrel, (which is attached to every two nets out of the fleet, or 120 nets) was cast overboard they would cry: 'Watch, barrel, watch! Mackerel for to catch, White may they be, like a blossom on a tree. God send thousands, one, two, and three, Some by their heads, some by their tails, God sends thousands, and never fails.'

WATER, buying and selling

1909 M. TREVELYAN *Folk-Lore of Wales* 6. It was unlucky to take any pay for water. Those who did so would have to cry in torment for a few drops.

WATER: first of year

1648 HERRICK *Hesperides* 5 'To Perilla'. Dead when I am .. bring Part of the creame from that Religious Spring; With which (Perilla) wash my hands and feet. **1804** DUNCOMB *Herefordshire* I 206. A well in the parish of Dindor excites much emulation on each New-year's Day, in a contest for the first pail-full of water, which is termed *the cream of the well*, and is presented to some neighbour as a mark of respect, and a pledge of good fortune; a pecuniary compliment is expected in return. **1841** R. T. HAMPSON *Medii Ævi Kalendarium* I 129–30. In the south of Scotland . . the instant the clock has struck the midnight hour, one of the family goes to the well as quickly as possible, and carefully skims it . . this Flower of the Well signifies the first pail of water, and the girl who is so fortunate as to obtain the prize, is supposed to have more than a double chance of obtaining the most accomplished young man in the parish. **1848** *Athenaeum* 5 Feb. 142. Before dawn on the first day of the New Year, it is the custom in South Wales for the poor children to carry about a jug full of water drawn that morning from the well. This they call 'New Year's Water'; and with a sprig of box or other evergreen they sprinkle it on those they meet, at the same time wishing them the compliments of the season. In order to pay their respects to those not abroad at this early hour, they serenade them . . under their windows: 'Here we bring new water From the well so clear, For to worship God with This happy New Year. Sing levy dew, sing levy dew, The water and the wine; The seven bright gold wires And the bugles they do shine. Sing reign of Fair Maid, With gold upon her toe, Open you the west door, And turn the Old Year go. Sing reign of Fair Maid With gold upon her chin Open you the east door, And let the New Year in.' **1872** *N & Q* 4th ser. X 408 [Scotland] One of the family goes to the village well at twelve o'clock on the last night of the year, draws water from it, plucks a little grass, throws it into the water . . and carefully carries the water and the grass home. If there is more than one well, it has been known that one of the family went to each well . . If the drawer of the water has cows, all the dairy utensils are washed with part of it, and the remainder is given in drink to the cows.

The cream of the cows of those who are in the habit of frequenting the well to draw water is thus secured to the midnight drawer. **1880** *Arch. Aeliana* VIII 67. On New Year's morning, within memory, each of these wells [at Wark, Northumb.] was visited by the villagers in the hope of their being the first to take what was called the 'Flower of the Well' . . Whoever first drank of the spring would obtain, it was believed, marvellous powers throughout the next year . . At Birtley [Northumb.] the fortunate first visitant . . who should fill his flask with the water would find that it retained its freshness . . throughout the whole year, and also brought good luck to the house in which it remained. **1886** *Folklore* 17 [Portessie, Banff.] It was a custom to go to the sea, and draw a pailful of water, and take it along with a little seaweed to the house on the morning of New Year's Day. **1888** *Bye-Gones* 138. At Tenby there is a very curious custom carried on on New Year's Day . . The 'New Year Waterers' . . The people who have been sprinkled are supposed to be 'lucky' during the year. **1899** *Newcastle Weekly Chronicle* 11 Feb. 7 [Jesmond] The country girls strive to get the cream of the well and sing: 'The cream of the well goes to our house, and I'll get the bonniest lad.' **1912** LEATHER *Herefordshire* 91. It was formerly the custom . . for the servants to sit up to see the New Year in, and at midnight to rush for the 'cream o' the well', the first water drawn from the well in the year, which was thought to be beautifying and lucky. The maid who succeeded in getting it would take it to the bedroom of her mistress, who would give a present for it. 'My missus always had the cream o' the well to wash in on New Year's morning,' said Mrs M——, 'and she always put a shilling under the basin for me, too.' **1944** *Country Life* 14 Jan. 77 [Tenby, Pembroke.] On New Year's morning the children go round the streets calling at the houses to offer all New Year's water, which they bring with them in cups, with sprinklers of . . sea spurge . . A penny or two is expected before the sprinkling is given. No doubt if asked, the object would be called 'For Luck'. **1965** P. F. ANSON *Fisher Folk-Lore*

78 [Buckie] On the Banffshire coast the fisher folk about the middle of the last century went down to the shore [on New Year's Day], filled a jug with salt water and carried it home with a certain kind of seaweed. They sprinkled the water over the fire, and put the seaweed above the doors and corners of their houses. Having done this they felt sure of good luck for the rest of the year.

WATER, holy

731 BEDE *Historia Ecclesiastica* V iv (tr. Sherley-Price) The bishop had sent the sick woman some of the holy water that he had blessed for the dedication of the church, telling him to give her some of it to drink and to apply some as a lotion to the place where the worst pain lay. *c.*1000 MS Harl. 585 (COCKAYNE *Leechdoms* III 15) Then take nine cloves of hallowed garlic, pound in wine .. shive the wort myrrhis into it, and holy water from the fount .. Be the sore where it may, let one smudge on the salve. AD 1220 Conc. Dunelm (WILKINS *Concilia* I 576) Fonts are kept locked to prevent [the water being used for the purposes of] magic. **1486** SPRENGER & KRAMER *Malleus Maleficarum* (tr. Summers, 89, 91) There are .. men blessed by God, whom that detestable race [witches] cannot injure with their witchcraft .. Those who .. make lawful use of .. Holy Water .. It is lawful in any decent habitation of men or beasts to sprinkle Holy Water for the safety and security of men and beasts, with the invocation of the .. Trinity and a Paternoster. For it is said in the Office of Exorcism, that wherever it is sprinkled .. all harm is repelled, and no pestilent spirit can abide there. **1584** SCOT *Discoverie of Witchcraft* XII xx. Such as observe dulie the rites and ceremonies of holie church .. through the sprinkling of holie water .. are preserved from witchcraft. **1790** GROSE *Provincial Glossary* Superstitions 53. Water preserved in fonts, was by the common people supposed to have a mystic virtue .. to heal diseases, &c. wherefore there was a lock and key to most fonts, to prevent the water from being stolen. **1813** BRAND *Antiquities* II 264. Old Women are very fond of washing their Eyes with

the water after Baptism. **1854** *N & Q* 1st ser. IX 536 [Somerset] Water from the font is good for ague and rheumatism. **1874** *N & Q* 5th ser. I 383. Within the recollection of the present vicar of the parish of Churcham, Gloucestershire, after public baptism, the .. parish monthly nurse invariably washed out the mouth of the recently regenerated infant with the remaining sanctified water. She assured the vicar it was a safeguard against toothache. **1878** A. MACGREGOR *Brahan Seer* 132 'Superstitions of Highlanders'. It was once prevalent when a child was baptised, that the infant was neither washed nor bathed that night, for fear of washing off the baptismal water before it had slept under it .. The water used in baptism was bottled up as an effectual recipe for various disorders.

WATER, running: crossing over

1686–7 AUBREY *Remaines* (1881, 27) Mat. Nayler was advised by the Wizard of Feversh. in Kent to leap three times over a small running streame, to prevent her being taken, when she escaped out of prison. **1791** BURNS *Tam o' Shanter* l. 208 [of the pursuing witches] A running stream they dare na cross. **1865** *Gents Mag.* pt. 2 702. Still prevalent in most districts of Ireland [the belief that] spirits cannot cross running water. **1909** M. TREVELYAN *Folk-Lore of Wales* 6. Very old people always spat thrice on the ground before crossing water after dark, to avert the evil influence of spirits and witches.

WATER, running: cures

*c.*1000 MS Harl. 585 (COCKAYNE *Leechdoms* III 11–13) This is the holy drink against one full of elfin tricks. Bid an immaculate person fetch in silence against the stream half a sextarius of running water; then take and lay all the worts in the water. *c.*1570 Durham Ecclesiastical Court (C. L. EWEN *Witchcraft* 1933, 447) Deponent went to Jenkyn Pereson's wife who said the child 'was taken with the farye and bad hir sent 2 for southrowninge water, and theis 2 shull not speke by the waye, and that the child shuld be washed in that water, and dib the shirt in the water, and so hang it upon a hedge all that night, and that on the morowe the shirt shuld be gone and the child shuld recover health.' 1625 T. JACKSON *Originall of Vnbeliefe* XIX 179–80. This vpon mine owne knowledge .. I can relate; of two, sent more than a mile, after the Sun-setting, to fetch South-running Water [for a cure], with a strict injunction, not to salute any either going or comming. 1746 *Gents Mag.* pt. 2 645. A charm for the Boneshave (as the Exmoorians .. call the Sciatica). The patient must lie on his back on the bank of a river or brook of water, with a straight staff by his side, between him and the water; and must have the following words repeated over him: 'Bone-shave right; Bone-shave straight; As the water runs by the stave Good for Bone-shave. In the name, &c.' 1837 SCOTT (LOCKHART *Life* IV 243–4) Abbotsford, 15th April, 1819 .. The most extraordinary recipe [to cure Scott's stomach pains] was that of my Highland piper, John Bruce, who spent a whole Sunday in selecting twelve stones from twelve *south-running* streams, with the purpose that I should sleep upon them, and be whole. 1850 *N & Q* 1st ser. II 512. Cure for Thrush. Take a child to a running stream, draw a straw through its mouth, and repeat the verse 'Out of the mouth of babes and sucklings, &c.' 1853 *N & Q* 1st ser. VIII 265 [Devon] Take three rushes from any running stream, and pass them separately through the mouth of the infant; then plunge the rushes again in the stream, and as the current bears them away, so will the thrush depart from the child. 1866 HENDERSON *Northern Counties* 110 [Stamfordham, Northumb.] Several cures for whooping-cough are practised .. such as .. making porridge over a stream running from north to south. 1883 *Folklore* 396 [Highlands] Her friends .. set her illness down to witchcraft .. The treatment consisted in taking water, before sunrise, from a stream running south, and immersing a piece of silver in it, and liberally splashing the patient in the face with it. 1887 'SPERANZA' WILDE *Superstitions of Ireland* II 94. Take three green stones, gathered from a running brook, between mid-

night and morning, while no word is said. In silence it must be done. Then uncover the limb and rub each stone several times closely downwards from the hip to the toe, saying in Irish— 'Wear away, wear away, There you shall not stay, Cruel pain—away, away.' 1895 J. HARDY *Denham Tracts* 326. All the cows' milk of a place in Northumberland was once bewitched .. To remedy this the cows were milked in a south-running stream. 1906 *Folklore* 206–7 [Co. Cavan] [for an elf-struck cow] He is strictly charged to scoop up the water against the stream, and on no account to speak to any one .. The messenger is usually a .. young lad .. In a pail are put .. the 'erribs' [herbs, etc.] and .. the water. 1932 *Folklore* [Naphill, Bucks., 1910] Her mother told her that in the old time they used to carry children across running water as a cure [for whooping cough]. 1951 *Trans. Devon. Ass.* 75 [Budleigh Salterton; for whooping cough] Take five green-slimed stones from a brook and boil them, pouring the liquid over the left shoulder.

Cf. 'GOLD AND SILVER WATER'.

WATER, running: ford 'where dead and living cross'

1841 R. T. HAMPSON *Medii Ævi Kalendarium* I 129. Among the Strathdown highlanders, early in the morning [of New Year's Day], the Usque Cashrichd, or water drawn from the Dead and the Living Ford .. is drunk as a potent charm against .. the activity of all infernal agency. 1874 *Journal of Anthropological Inst.* III 267 [Banff.] [to counter effects of evil eye] Go to a ford where the dead and living cross, draw water from it, pour it .. over a *crosst shilling*, and then sprinkle the water over the patient in the name of the Father, the Son, and the Holy Ghost.

WATER, sprinkling: brings rain

1486 SPRENGER & KRAMER *Malleus Maleficarum* (tr. Summers, 135) When a woman dips a twig in water and sprinkles the water in the air to make it rain .. she has entered into a pact with the devil by which she can do this as a witch, although it is the devil who causes the rain. **1584** SCOT *Discoverie of Witchcraft* III XIII. She .. wetteth a broome sprig in water, and sprinkleth the same in the aire: [a thing] confessed by witches, and affirmed by writers to be the meanes that witches use to moove extraordinary tempests and raine.

WATER under bed

1856 *N & Q* 2nd ser. I 386. I have heard that a basin of cold water put under the bed of the person liable to cramp, is an effectual preventive of it. **1913** E. M. WRIGHT *Rustic Speech* 236–7. Five or six years ago, in a country vicarage in the Midlands, a girl I knew was nursing her brother in the last stages of consumption .. every day she placed [two buckets filled with fresh spring-water] under the patient's bed, to ward off bed-sores. **1923** [Somerset] To cure cramp, keep a basin of cold water always under the bed. **1968** A. FRANCIS *Guinea a Box* 23–4 [Curbridge, Oxon., 1920s] A dish of water placed under the bed effectively removed cramp.

Cf. WATER, running: cures; WELL cures.

WEASEL

*c.*319 BC THEOPHRASTUS *Characters* (tr. Jebb, ed. Sandys, 141) If a weasel run across his path, he will not pursue his walk until someone else has traversed the road, or until he has thrown three stones across it. **1587** G. GIFFORD *Discourse of the Subtill Practises of Devilles* IX G4ᵛ. Euery body sayth .. that mother W is a witch in deede .. It is out of all doubt: for there were which saw a weasil runne from her housward into his yard euen a little before hee fell sicke. **1695** CONGREVE *Love for Love* II i. I stumbled coming down stairs, and met a weasel; bad omens those. **1710** *British Apollo* 9 Jan. Q. Why .. Weasels do come more common against Death than any other time? **1732** DEFOE *Memoirs of Mr Campbell* 60. I have known People who have been put into .. terrible Apprehensions of Death by the squeaking of a Weazel. **1777** BRAND *Antiquities* 95. Meeting a weasel [is] held to be [a] bad [omen]. **1898** BLAKEBOROUGH *Yorkshire Customs* 150. A weasel crossing your path is most unlucky: it speaks of treach-

ery .. Drop a coin on the road where you saw the weasel cross, and the evil .. will cling to those who are unlucky enough to find it. **1911** *Folklore* 456 [Co. Clare] The stoat is always called 'weazel' [and] was equally disliked and respected. It is wished 'Good morning, ma'am,' by some, and generally saluted by raising the hat on meeting; but others spit and cross themselves. **1912** LEATHER *Herefordshire* 23. An old farmer who lived near Longtown was once taking his cattle to market; they had travelled some miles .. when a stoat [? weasel] crossed in front of them. 'Turn 'em back boys,' he shouted to the drovers. 'Turn 'em back, no luck today.' **1954** Girl, 11 [Perth] If a weasel crosses your path you'll get bad luck.

WEASEL-SKIN PURSE

1799 GOLDSMITH *Vicar of Wakefield* XII. My wife was usually fond of a weasel-skin purse, as being the most lucky. **1887** 'SPERANZA' WILDE *Superstitions of Ireland* II 103. A purse made from a weasel's skin will never want for money; but the purse must be found, not given or made.

Cf. MOLESKIN: moleskin purse.

WEATHER linked with deaths of criminals

1854 *N & Q* 1st ser. II 494 [Grantham, Lincs.] A remark by a labouring man .. is to the following effect .. When the judges are on circuit, and when there are any criminals to be hanged, there are always winds .. and roaring tempests. **1858** R. S. HAWKER Letter 26 Dec. (*Life*, ed. Byles, 313) [Morwenstow, Cornwall] The whole country side is excited by these storms, and the people connect them with the death of a Mr ——, a notorious wrecker .. On Sunday evening this day week [he] was seen watching the sea, it is supposed for Wreck. He returned quite well .. At Six O'Clock next morning the Servants knocked— no answer .. They went in, and there he lay quite dead .. Ever since .. the storms have been continual .. while I now write my Table trembles with the wind. **1890** *N & Q* 7th ser. X 145. Remarking, recently, to an old man that, though it rained, it did not appear warmer, he replied, 'We shan't have fine weather till after tomorrow .. tomorrow is "hanging day".' Three men were to be hung the next day at Worcester. 1967 S. MARSHALL *Fenland Chronicle* pt. I xv. One o' his beliefs were that it allus blowed a gale on a day anybody were hung for a crime, to show God A'mighty's displeasure at the takin' o' a human life by other human beings.

WEATHER linked with lives of the great

c. AD 90 Luke 23: 44–6. And it was about the sixth hour, and there was a darkness over all the earth until the ninth hour. And the sun was darkened, and the veil of the temple was rent in the midst. And when Jesus had cried with a loud voice .. Father, into thy hands I commend my spirit .. he gave up the ghost. *c.*1142 WILLIAM OF MALMESBURY *Hist. of Own Times* (1854, tr. J. Sharpe, III pt. I 387) In 1133 .. Henry .. set sail for Normandy .. The providence of God, at that time, bore reference in a wonderful manner to human affairs .. that he should embark, never to return alive .. The elements manifested their sorrow at this great man's last departure. For the sun on that day, at the sixth hour, shrouded his glorious face .. in hideous darkness, agitating the hearts of men by an eclipse. 1534 P. VERGIL *English History* (tr. Ellis, IV 140) This most jentil prince [Ethelbertus] was feared with manie .. wonderus tokens as semed to portende som infortunate ende of his life; for when he tooke horsse the earthe .. trembled under his feete; and while he jornied in the midfst of the day hee was soe beeset with a clowde that for a season hee sawe nothinge. 1663 PEPYS *Diary* 19 Oct. Waked with a very high winde, and said to my wife, 'I pray God I hear not of the death of any great person, this wind is so high'; fearing that the Queen might be dead. [The Queen was ill at this time.] 1664 K. PHILIPS *Poems* 'On the Fair Weather just at Coronation' [of Charles II] So clear a season, and so snatch'd from storms, Shews Heav'n delights to see what Man performs .. He [the sun] therefore check'd th' invading Rains we feared, And a more bright Parenthesis appeared. So that we knew not which look'd most content, The King, the

People, or the Firmament. 1668 P. HEYLIN *Life of William Laud* 450–1 [27 Dec. 1640] There was raised a violent Tempest .. at the Metropolitical Church in .. Canterbury .. one of the Pinacles .. which carried a vane, with this Archbishops Arms upon it, was violently struck down .. and gave occasion unto one who loved him not, to collect this Inference, that the Arms of the present Archbishop of Canterbury [Laud] .. portended his own fall. 1711 G. HICKES Letter to Dr Charlett, 23 Jan. (MS Bodl. Ballard 12) Omens that happened at the Coronation of .. James II w[ch] I saw, viz .. the rent flag hanging upon the white tower overag[t] my door, when I came home from the Coronation. It was torn by the wind at the same time the signal was given to the tower that he was crown'd: I put no great stresse upon omens, but I cannot despise them; most of them I believe, come by chance, but some from superior Intellectual Agents, especially those, w[ch] regard the fate of kings, and nations. 1852 *N & Q* 1st ser. VI 531. A superstition prevails among the lower classes of many parts of Worcestershire, that when storms, heavy rains, or other elemental strifes take place at the death of a great man, the spirit of the storm will not be appeased till the moment of burial. This superstition gained great strength on the occasion of the Duke of Wellington's funeral, when, after some weeks of heavy rain .. the skies began to clear, and both rain and flood abated .. It was a common observation hereabout in the week before the interment of his Grace, 'Oh, the rain won't give over till the Duke is buried.' 1880 *N & Q* 6th ser. I 212. His charwoman .. likes to take it [her holiday] on a day when the Queen is going somewhere, because then the elements are most likely to be favourable to 'an outing'. 1911 *N & Q* 11th ser. III 207. An odd belief .. among the Warwickshire peasantry .. is that the death of the sovereign brings on a flood, as witness the highest flood recorded in 1901, and the last serious one in 1910. 1952 O. SWIRE *Skye* [Hebrides] 69–70 [During George V's illness in 1928] an old man .. every night .. walked down to us for news .. Then came the great storm .. Our usual visitor arrived [and asked] 'Is my King still alive?' We said that he was. [He] stopped his visits of inquiry [saying] quite simply 'That was a Royal storm. It came for my King but he did not go with it. When a Royal storm is sent back empty, my mother told me, the one for whom it came would live and do well ..' He himself had seen the one that came for Lord Kitchener, but Kitchener went with it.

WEDDING, day of: divination rhyme

1850 *N & Q* 1st ser. II 515. Monday for wealth, Tuesday for health, Wednesday the best day of all; Thursday for crosses, Friday for losses, Saturday no luck at all. 1867 HARLAND & WILKINSON *Lancashire Folk-Lore* 223. Monday for health, Tuesday for wealth, Wednesday best day of all; Thursday for losses, Friday for crosses, Saturday no luck at all.

Cf. NAILS AND HAIR, cutting: rhyme.

WEDDING: flight of birds

1923 [Somerset] If you see a flight of birds on your wedding morning it means a long family.

WEDDING follows burying

1937 D. L. SAYERS *Busman's Honeymoon* x. Well, well, after a buryin' comes a weddin'. Tell us w'en it's to be, Frank.

WEDDING, guns fired at

1818 *Edinburgh Magazine* Nov. 413 [Angus] When arrived within a short distance of [the bridegroom's] home, there are always some young men and boys secreted behind hedges, cornstacks, or whatever may screen them .. who pop off their rusty muskets when least expected, as a *feu de joye*. 1822 J. H. ALLAN *Bridal of Caölchairn* 309–10 [Argyll.] The bridegroom arrives: his approach is announced at a distance by a continual and running discharge of fire-arms from his party. These signals are answered by the friends of the bride, and when at length they meet, a general but irregular *feu de joie* announces the arrival. [During the march to the church] the parties of the bride and bridegroom endeavour to emulate each other in the discharge of their fire-arms. 1866 HENDERSON *Northern Counties* 24.

In rural parts .. guns are fired over the heads of the newly-married couple all the way from church. 1898 BLAKE-BOROUGH *Yorkshire Customs* 101. In days past it was usual in Great Ayton to discharge firearms over the bridal party as they proceeded both to and from the church. The firing of the stithy .. was never omitted; i.e. a charge of powder poured into a hole in the anvil .. this, when fired, went off with the report of a cannon. 1935 *N & Q* CLXVIII 394. Firing the anvils .. was familiar to me in the eighties of the last century. In the village of Merrington [Co. Durham] where I was born and reared, the .. smithy faced one side of the .. village green. On the occasion of a marriage the smith took his anvil .. and placed it in the centre of the green, and fired the charge as the bridal procession came from the church, situated not far away. It is some years now since this custom was discontinued. *Ibid*. CLXIX 141 [Satley, Co. Durham] The firing of guns over the heads of the bridal pair, or near the churchyard gates, was also a common custom, now almost obsolete .. The noises were .. believed to drive away all evil spirits from the bridal party. 1953 *Sunday Times* 6 Sept. 8 [Holy Island, Northumb.] At the church-yard gate .. the bridegroom paid the toll: then the shot-guns, wielded by every wildfowler on the island, roared their salute and blew one of the island's few telephone lines into a tangled heap in the roadway. 1963 *Yorkshire Post* 7 Oct. 8 [Holy Island, Northumb.] Shotguns were used to fire a salute as the couple left the church.

WEDDING: 'one brings on another'

c.1634 M. PARKER *Wooing Maid* (*Roxburgh Ballads* III 54) 'Tis said that one wedding produceth another. 1713 GAY *Wife of Bath* 1 i. One Wedding, the Proverb says, begets another. 1848 DICKENS *Dombey and Son* XXXI. The cook says at breakfast-time that one wedding makes many. 1929 *Daily Mail* 19 Sept. 10. It is apparent that weddings do breed weddings, and that bridesmaids are particularly apt to find themselves early involved in matrimony.

WEDDING postponed

1793 *Stat. Acc. of Scotland* VII 560–1 [Kirkwall and St Ola, Orkney] [The inhabitants] would consider it an unhappy omen, were they, by any means, disappointed in getting themselves married .. on the very day which they had previously fixed in their mind for that purpose. **1957** Woman, 54 [Redhill, Surrey] It's bad luck to postpone a wedding.

WEDDING: route changed

1909 *N & Q* 10th ser. XII 484 [Stromness, Orkney] It is unlucky for the newly married couple to go home from church the same road they came.

Cf. FUNERAL: route changed.

WEDDING CAKE, cutting

1898 BLAKEBOROUGH *Yorkshire Customs* 94. It would be a most unlucky omen, should anyone but the bride cut the first piece from the bride's cake. **1905** *Folklore* 66 [Penallt, Mon.] When they arrive at the house, before taking her hat off, the bride is led by her husband to the breakfast table, where (with his sword if he has one, or, if not, with the best knife in the house) she makes one cut in the cake, he then takes the knife and makes a cut the other way, thus finishing the slice. **1944** *Folklore* 28 [Lincs.] The bride .. should not take any active part in the social proceedings, except for cutting the cake, during which she forms a silent wish.

WEDDING CAKE: divination

1733 *Palace Miscellany* 30 'Progress of Matrimony'. But, Madam, as a Present take This little Paper of Bride-Cake: Fast any Friday in the Year, When Venus mounts the starry Sphere, Thrust this, at Night, in Pillowber. In Morning Slumber, you will seem T' enjoy your Lover in a Dream. **1755** *Connoisseur* 20 Feb. Cousin Debby was married a little while ago, and she sent me a piece of Bride-Cake to put under my pillow; and I had the sweetest dream—I thought we were going to be married together. **1765** W. COLLINS *Gents Mag.* 231. Written on a paper, which contained a piece of Bride Cake given to the author by a lady. 'This precious relick, form'd by magick pow'r,

Beneath her shepherd's haunted pillow laid, Was meant by love to charm the silent hour, The secret present of a matchless maid.' **1793** Correspondent [Brampton, Cumb.] (J. HUNTER MS note in Brand's *Antiquities* II 85) Cake [is] passed nine times through the Ring, a number of pieces are passed through, put in the bride's apron, hid, and who gets the piece on which the Ring is left, will be first married. Any one of these pieces will make you dream of your future *marrow* [partner]. **1813** BRAND *Antiquities* I 32. In the North, slices of the bridecake are put through the wedding ring: they are afterwards laid under pillows, at night, to cause young persons to dream of their Lovers .. Douce [in a MS note] says this custom is not peculiar to the North of England, it seems to prevail generally. The pieces of the Cake must be drawn nine times through the Wedding Ring. **1821** Letter from Archdeacon Wraugham 26 Apr. (*Trans. Bibliog. Soc.* no. 12, Suppl.) This day dear Phil has left us, after a brilliant marriage .. and I am left with a houseful of young Ladies .. they are just gone upstairs backward to bed, with bridecake passed through the ring to place under their pillows. **1832** *Gents Mag.* pt. 2 492 [Lincs.] The bride holds the ring between the fore-finger and thumb of her right hand, through which the groom passes each portion of the cake nine times .. These he delivers .. to the bride-maids .. If the fair idolatress deposit one .. in the foot of her *left* stocking .. and place it under her pillow, she will dream of .. her partner for life. **1879** J. NAPIER *West of Scotland* 52. Young girls still put a piece [of bridecake] under their pillows in order to obtain prophetic dreams. In some cases, this is done by a friend writing the names of three young men on a piece of paper, and the cake, wrapped in it, is put under the pillow .. Should the owners of the cake have dreamed of one of these young men .. it is regarded as a sure proof that he is to be her future husband. **1923** *Folklore* 324–5 [Northleigh, Oxon.] She took a piece of wedding cake, which must consist of both cake and icing, the cake representing the man and the icing the girl, and got into bed backwards, repeating the while .. 'I put this cake under my head, To dream of the living and not of the dead, To dream of the man that I am to wed; Not in his best or Sunday array, But in the clothes he wears every day.' On no account must the girl speak after repeating this rhyme. **1954** Girl, 14 [Stoke-on-Trent, Staffs.] Put a piece of wedding cake under your pillow to dream of your future husband or wife.

Cf. WEDDING CAKE/PLATE broken over bride.

WEDDING CAKE, making

1887 *Folk-Lore Record* 216 [Cornwall] It is considered extremely unlucky here .. for a wedding-cake to crack after baking. **1963** Baker, c.50 [Liss, Hants.] Some people won't allow me to put any colour [icing] on a wedding cake because they say it's unlucky. **1966** C. WOODFORD *Sip From Any Goblet* 22. No girl would [c. 1860] bake her own wedding cake, for fear she worked hard all her life. **1983** Woman, 54 [Colchester, Essex] When I told a woman I was making my daughter's wedding cake, she said 'If it turns out well, so will the marriage, and vice versa.' What a responsibility!

WEDDING CAKE: part kept

1953 Unpublished letter to *Woman* [Horsham, Sussex] My grandmother told me that unless a piece of wedding cake was saved for the first christening then it was a sure thing that the bride would be barren. **1986** Woman, c.50 [Petersfield, Hants.] We kept the top tier of my wedding cake for the first christening— but we had to re-ice it of course.

WEDDING CAKE/PLATE broken over bride

1771 SMOLLETT *Humphry Clinker* (1943, 332) A cake being broken over the head of Mrs Tabitha Lismahago, the fragments were distributed among the bystanders, according to the custom of the antient Britons, on the supposition that every person who ate of this hallowed cake, should that night have a vision of the man or woman whom Heaven designed should be his or her wedded mate. **1818** *Edinburgh Magazine* Nov. 413 [Angus] When they reach the bridegroom's door, the bride is met by his mother, or one deputed to fill her place; some cakes of shortbread are broken over the bride's head, and distributed among the spectators; this is most anxiously sought after, and, if the company is large, it is a peculiar favour to obtain the smallest crumb of this cake, which is known by the name of dreaming bread, as it possesses the talismanic virtue of favouring such as lay it below their pillow with a nocturnal vision of their future partner for life. **1813** BRAND *Antiquities* I 32. In Yorkshire [the wedding cake] is cut into little square pieces, thrown over the bridegroom's and bride's head, and then put through the ring. The cake is sometimes broken over the bride's head, and then thrown away among the crowd to be scrambled for. **1822** J. H. ALLAN *Bridal of Caölchairn* Note [Loch Awe, Argyll.] Before [the bride] crosses the threshold, an oaten cake is broken over her head by the bridesman and bridesmaid, and distributed to the company, and a glass of whiskey passes round. **1829** BROCKETT *North Country Words* 48. In some places in the North, it is customary, after the bridal party leave the church, to have a thin currant-cake, marked in squares, though not entirely cut through. A clean cloth being spread over the head of the bride, the bridegroom stands behind her, and breaks the cake. Thus hallowed, it is thrown up and scrambled for by the attendants, to excite prophetic dreams of love and marriage, and is said, by those who pretend to understand these things, to have much more virtue than when it is merely put nine times through the ring. **1853** *N & Q* 1st ser. VII 545 [Yorks.] On the bride alighting from her carriage at her father's door, a plate covered with morsels of bride's cake was flung from a window of the second story upon the heads of the crowd congregated in the street below .. If it reach the ground in safety, without being broken, the omen is a most unfavourable one. If .. the plate be shattered to pieces .. the auspices are looked upon as most happy. **1898** BLAKEBOROUGH *Yorkshire Customs* 96. [The bride] was met on the doorstep, and presented with a small cake on a plate. A little of this she would eat, throwing the remainder over her head, typical of the hope that they might always have plenty and something to spare. She then handed the plate to her husband; this he threw over his head, their future happiness depending upon its being broken. **1929** J. M. MCPHERSON *Primitive Beliefs* 121 [NE Scotland] As she approached the threshold, she was met by her mother and one or two of her relatives, carrying a napkin with pieces of shortbread or oatmeal cake, the infar-cake, which was thrown over her head .. If the bread was not broken over the bride's head, she would come to poverty. **1953** *Sunday Times* 6 Sept. 8 [Holy Island, Northumb.] Between the church and the village hall a napkin was put over the bride's hair and an island maiden threw a plate over her head 'for luck' and the plate smashed to pieces, which should mean years of wedded bliss. **1962** *Times* 6 Mar. 7 [Tewin, Herts., observing an old Northumbrian custom] At the reception her mother will throw the wedding cake plate over [the bride's] head so that it can crash into 'little pieces of happiness'.

Cf. WHEAT/RICE/CONFETTI thrown for luck.

WEDDING CARRIAGE, galloping

1824 CARR *Craven Dialect* 61–2 [Yorks.] Nothing is deemed more unlucky than for the bride and bridegroom to gallop [home after the ceremony].

WEDDING CARRIAGE turns back

1883 BURNE *Shropshire* 294. When carriages are used at a wedding it is considered very unlucky to turn the horses' heads round at the church door. **1909** *N & Q* 10th ser. XII 484 [Stromness, Orkney] It is unlucky for the newly married couple to go home from church the same road they came. **1959** *Yorkshire Post* 20 Nov. 12. Although their home .. is less than 30 yards from Mexborough Parish Church, the Victorian landau .. will take a circular route .. When a horse-drawn landau is used to take the bride to church it should never be turned round, otherwise it brings bad luck.

Cf. HEARSE turns back.

WEDDING RING

1711 *Aristotle's Last Legacy* 46. To Dream a Gold Ring breaks and falls from off your Finger, denotes the loss of a Lover. *c.*1763 *Weekly Amusement* 8 June (T. PARK MS note in Brand's *Antiquities*, front flyleaf) Elegy from honest Country Woman on her Husband who was killed by the Wheel of a Cart. 'Twas on the twentieth of September I lost my dear good man .. That day off dropt my wedding ring. **1813** BRAND *Antiquities* I 35. Many married Women are so rigid, not to say superstitious, in their notions concerning their Wedding Rings, that neither when they wash their Hands, nor at any other time, will they take it of from their Finger, extending, it should seem, the expression of 'till Death us do part' even to this golden circlet, the token and pledge of Matrimony. **1831** HONE *Year Book* 29 Feb. If a married woman loses her wedding ring, it is a token that she will lose her husband's affections. **1834** DALYELL *Darker Superstitions of Scotland* 288. It is considered ominous in Scotland ever to part with the marriage ring. **1861** C. C. ROBINSON *Dialect of Leeds* 301. If the woman's ring falls off on the day of marriage, the couple wedded will be parted afterwards. **1866** *N & Q* 3rd ser. X 469 [Essex] My sister .. lost her husband after breaking her ring—it is a sure sign. **1882** *N & Q* 6th ser. VI 9. A Yorkshire lady told me that, having lost her wedding ring .. she had been told by the wise people of the place that she must on no account permit her husband to buy her a new one, but that her nearest male relatives must pay for the fresh ring and give it to her. **1883** BURNE *Shropshire* 294–5. It is of course considered most unlucky to take it off .. If it should come off accidentally, the lady's husband must put it on again, or the misadventure will prove unlucky. **1896** 'Sunlight' *Almanac* 335. If a married person dreams she breaks her wedding ring it is a sign she will soon be a widow. **1898** BLAKEBOROUGH *Yorkshire Customs* 103. It is considered unlucky to remove the wedding ring before the birth of the first child. **1933** *Folklore* 193 [Digby, Lincs.] To remove your wedding ring means seven years' bad luck. **1981** Female student, 20 [S. England] It is unlucky to take off your wedding ring, partly for the practical reason that you might lose it, but mainly because it is tempting fate to come and remove the ring permanently, by way of ending the marriage.

wedding: also see BRIDE.

WEIGHING

1709 *British Apollo* 7 Sept. *Q*. I have heard several say it is Unlucky for a Man to weigh himself. I desire your Opinion. *A*. We believe it is no more Unlucky to weigh a Gander than to weigh a Goose. **1864** R. CHAMBERS *Book of Days* II 39 [Suffolk] It is unlucky to weigh [newborn children]. If you do, they will probably die, and, at anyrate, will not thrive. I have caused great concern in the mind of a worthy old monthly nurse by insisting on weighing mine. **1878** A. MACGREGOR *Brahan Seer* 130 'Superstitions of Highlanders'. It is unlucky to weigh infants; they are sure to die. **1882** *People's Friend* 8 Nov. 711 [Scotland] Servants are exceedingly superstitious. Nurse will tell you .. how unlucky it is to weigh baby. **1883** BURNE *Shropshire* 285. 'How are your daughter and her husband?' I asked a well-to-do yeoman's wife. 'Very well, thank you,' was the answer, 'but I'm very angry with them, for they've weighed the baby.' **1957** *Folklore* 414. The prejudice against weighing babies before they are twelve months old is dying out fast under the influence of health visitors and clinics.

Cf. COUNTING; MEASURING.

WELL: ceremonies

10th c. Canon enacted under King Edgar (THORPE *Ancient Laws of England* 396) We enjoin that every priest .. totally extinguish every heathenism; and forbid .. well-worshipings, and the vain practices which are carried on with various spells. **1581** *Acts of Parliament of Scotland* (THOMSON & INNES, III 212) The dregges of Idolatrie git remanis in diuers pairtes of þe realme, be vsing of pilgramage to sum chappellis [and] wellis .. It is statut and ordanit .. that nane of his hines lieges presume .. in tyme cuming to

hant, frequent, or vse þe saidis pilgramages. **1703** M. MARTIN *Western Islands of Scotland* 140 [Skye] Several of the common People oblige themselves by a Vow to come to this Well, and make the ordinary Touer about it, call'd *Dessil* .. thus; they move thrice round the Well proceeding Sunways .. After drinking of the Water .. it's a never failing custom, to leave some small offering on the Stone which covers the Well. **1810** C. O'CONOR *Columbanus's Third Letter* 83 [Castlerea area, Co. Roscommon] When I pressed a very old man, Owen Hester, to state what possible advantage he expected to derive from the singular custom of frequenting .. such wells as were contiguous to an old blasted oak, or an upright unhewn stone, and what the meaning was of the yet more singular custom of sticking rags on the branches of such trees, and spitting on them, his answer was, that their ancestors always did it; that it was a preservative against Gaesa-Draoidecht, i.e. the sorceries of Druids; that their cattle were preserved by it from infectious disorders; that .. the fairies were kept in good humour by it .. They would travel .. from ten to twenty miles for the purpose of crawling on their knees round these wells and upright stones, and oak trees, westward, as the Sun travels, some three times, some six, some nine, and so on in uneven numbers, until their voluntary penances were completely fulfilled. **1904** A. GEIKIE *Scottish Reminiscences* 112. The well of Craiguck, parish of Avoch, has long been a place of annual resort on the first Sunday of May, old style. The water used to be taken in a cup and spilt three times on the ground before being tasted, and thereafter a rag or ribbon was hung on the bramble bush above the spring.

WELL cures, and ensures good fortune

AD **77** PLINY *Natural History* XXVIII XI (1856, V 293) Mix water in equal proportions from three different wells, and, after making a libation with part of it in a new earthen vessel, administer the rest to patients suffering from tertian fever. *c.***1390** CHAUCER *Tales* Pardoner's Prologue ll. 361–5. If that the good-man that the beestes oweth Wol every wyke, er that the cok hym croweth, Fastynge, drynken of this welle a draughte .. His beestes and his stoor shal multiplie. **1774** PENNANT *Additions to Tour in Scotland* 18. They visit the well of Spey for many distempers, and the well of Drachaldy for as many, offering small pieces of money and bits of rags. **1789** BRAND *Newcastle upon Tyne* II 54. About a mile to the west of Jarrow there is a well still called Bede's Well, to which as late as the year 1740, it was a prevailing custom to bring children troubled with any disease or infirmity; a crooked pin was put in, and the well laved dry between each dipping. **1813** BRAND *Antiquities* II 269-70. I have formerly frequently observed Shreds or Bits of Rag upon the Bushes that overhang a Well in the road to Benton [nr. Newcastle upon Tyne], which .. is now or was very lately called The Rag-Well. **1850** *N & Q* 1st ser. II 514. The holy well .. near Pont yr allt Gôch .. has .. the reputation of curing lameness .. Welsh people still come .. miles over the hills to this holy spring. A whole family was there when I visited its healing waters last month. **1854** *N & Q* 1st ser. X 398. Near Polperro [Cornwall] the spring .. is still resorted to by those afflicted with inflamed eyes and other ailments .. It must be visited on three mornings before sunrise, fasting. **1881** W. GREGOR *North-East of Scotland* 40. A rag torn from the patient's clothing was hung on one of the neighbouring trees .. Strict charge was laid not to touch or carry any of them off. Whoever carried off one of such relics contracted the disease of the one who left it. **1899** *Daily Mail* 8 May 3. In Scotland old customs die hard, especially in the Highlands, as was evidenced yesterday, the first Sunday in May .. Young and old journeyed from Inverness .. to St Mary's Well, which is situated near to blasted Culloden Heath, and after drinking the water a coin was dropped into the well. This act is supposed to be an earnest of good health and success during the year. **1957** *Times* 25 May 8. This year I joined in the pilgrimage [first Sunday in May] .. to Culloden .. The ritual .. has survived the centuries: first a coin must be thrown into the well .. then a sip

taken of the water .. after the wish, a 'clootie', or small rag, must be tied to the branch of an over-hanging tree .. This wishing-well .. is now known .. as the Clootie Well .. Rags there were of all colours .. they must hang until .. winter has rotted them away; to remove them would bring bad luck, if not a transfer of the very afflictions of which the .. owners had been trying to rid themselves.

WELL: divination

*c.*1605 MS Cotton, Julius f. 6 (GROSE *Provincial Glossary* Superstitions 71-2) [Yorks.] Between the towns of Aten and Newton .. there is a well dedicated to St Oswald. The neighbours have an opinion, that a shirt, or shift, taken off a sick person, and thrown into that well, will shew whether the person will recover, or die: for if it floated, it denoted the recovery of the party; if it sunk, there remained no hope of their life: and, to reward the Saint for his intelligence, they tear off a rag of the shirt, and leave it hanging on the briars thereabouts; 'where', says the writer, 'I have seen such numbers, as might have made a fayre rheme in a paper myll'. **1703** M. MARTIN *Western Islands of Scotland* 7 [Lewis] St Andrew's Well in the Village of Shadar, is by the vulgar Natives made a Test to know if a sick Person will die .. They send one with a wooden Dish to bring some water to the Patient, and if the Dish which is laid softly upon the surface of the water turn round Sun-ways, they conclude that the Patient will recover .. but if otherwise, that he will die. **1758** BORLASE *Natural History of Cornwall* 31 [Maddern Well] Hither .. come the uneasy, impatient, and superstitious, and by dropping pins or pebbles into the Water, and by shaking the ground round the Spring, so as to raise bubbles from the bottom, at a certain time of the year, Moon, and day, endeavour to settle such doubts and enquiries as will not let the idle and anxious rest. **1955** Woman, 47 [Lampeter, Cardigan.] The Divinity students turn their backs to an ornamental pool in the grounds. Whoever throws in a coin that lands heads up will pass his exam, but if tails, he will fail.

WELL: propitiating for luck

c. AD 61 PLINY, YOUNGER *Epistles* VIII viii (tr. J. D. Lewis, 263–4) The spring emerges .. and .. opens out to the view with broad expanse, clear and transparent, so that you are able to count the small coins thrown into it. 1824 F. HITCHINS *Cornwall* I 534 [Menacuddle Grove] Each visitor, if he hoped for good luck through life, was expected to throw a crooked pin into the water; and it was presumed that the other pins which had been deposited there by former devotees, might be seen rising from their beds to meet it before it reached the bottom. 1854 *N & Q* 1st ser. X 397 [Pelynt, Cornwall] In the basin of the well may be found a great number of pins, thrown in .. 'to get the good will of the piskies'. 1883 BURNE *Shropshire* 433–4. The 'Halliwell Wakes' .. was celebrated on Ascension Day at the 'Halliwell' or Holy Well at Rorrington Green .. The people .. threw pins into the well, an offering which one old man .. says was supposed to bring good luck to those who made it, and to preserve them from being bewitched. 1953 *Mass Observation* 1 May [London Zoo] The object of throwing coins into the pond is to try and get one to land on a crocodile .. This is held to bring good luck. 1964 *Sheffield Telegraph* 25 Sept. 10. The great British public are so anxious to throw coins into the nearest well or fountain in the hope that it will bring them luck. 1983 *Woman*, 53. At Stratford, in the Royal Shakespeare Theatre foyer, there's a small pool into which people were throwing coins for luck—there was a whole layer of coins.

WELL, wishing at

c. AD 200 Curse (*Britannia* XII 372) [inscription in Latin on lead tablet found in hot spring at Bath, *Aquae Sulis*] Docilianus .. to the most holy goddess Sulis. I curse him who has stolen my hooded cloak, whether man or woman, slave or free, that the goddess Sulis [will] not allow [the thief] sleep or children .. until he has brought the cloak to the temple of her divinity. 1792 J. MOORE *Monastic Remains* I 2 [Walsingham, Norfolk] The wishing wells still remain .. where the pilgrims used to kneel and throw in a piece of gold, whilst they prayed for the accomplishment of their wishes. 1830 FORBY *East Anglia* 401–2. [Walsingham] Amongst the slender remains of this once celebrated seat of superstitious devotion, are two small circular basons of stone, a little to the north-east of the site of the conventual church (exactly in the place described by Erasmus in his 'Peregrinatio religionis ergo') .. The water of these wells had at that time a miraculous efficacy in curing disorders of the head and stomach, the special gift, no doubt, of the Holy Virgin .. The waters have no such quality now. She has substituted, however, another of far more comprehensive virtue. This is nothing less than the power of accomplishing all human wishes. 1883 BURNE *Shropshire* 422–3. At Rhosgoch on the Long Mountain .. is a famous wishing-well .. The bottom was bright with pins .. you could get whatever you wished for the moment the pin you threw in touched the bottom. 'It was mostly used for wishing about sweethearts.' 1895 J. HARDY *Denham Tracts* 151. Resort to the Fairy Well is still a favourite pastime in holiday times with young people at Wooler [Northumb.]. They express a secret wish and drop in a crooked pin. 1899 *Newcastle Weekly Chronicle* 4 Feb. 7 [Jesmond] Pins are dropped into the Maiden Well at Wooler and a wish expressed. The Worm Well, Lambton, Co. Durham, and the well at Keyheugh, Eisdon, are also used as wishing wells. 1905 *Folklore* 166 [Trelleck, Cornwall] The Virtuous Wells .. are about a mile outside the village .. The water of the main spring contains iron, and very nasty it is, as I know from sad experience, having tasted it under the impression that that was the right way to wish. I afterwards learnt that I ought to have dropped in a pebble and wished as it fell through the water. 1956 *Sunday Times* 12 Aug. 8 [London] Fountains round the Victoria Memorial .. are benefiting from the growing habit of visitors who 'wish' on coins before throwing them into the water. 1987 *Woman*, *c.*45 [Liss, Hants.] My neighbour's just built what she calls a 'wishing well' in her garden. It's *so* out of character, she's such a practical woman—she's a nurse. She's going to fill it with flowers, I think.

WHEAT/RICE/CONFETTI thrown for luck

1486 LELAND (S. SEYER *Memoirs of Bristol* XXII 6) The King [Henry VII] proceeded toward the Abbey of Saint Austeyn's; and by the way there was a baker's wife, who cast out of a window a great quantity of wheat, crying, *welcome* and *good luck*. **1546** P. VERGIL *De Rerum Inventoribus* I IV (tr. Langley) In Rome .. when [the bride] came home wheate was scatered abroade ouer her heade in tokenyng of plentie and fruitfulnesse. **1586** CAMDEN *Britannia* (tr. Gibson, II 380) [Limerick, Eire] In towns, when any magistrate enters upon his office, the wives in the streets, and the maidens out of the windows, strew him and his retinue with wheat and salt. **1648** HERRICK *Hesperides* 129 'Nuptiall Song' st. 5. Some repeat Your praise, and bless you, sprinkling you with Wheat. **1655** MOUFET *Healths Improvement* 130. English people, when the Bride comes from Church, are wont to cast wheat upon her head. **1796** H. ROWE *Poems* I 113. The wheaten ear was scatter'd near the porch. **1873** *N & Q* 4th ser. XII 396. In some North Notts villages, corn is thrown [at weddings] with this exclamation, 'Bread for life, and pudding for ever!' **1874** KILVERT *Diary* 11 Aug. Our dear little bride went off with her husband happy and radiant amid blinding showers of rice and old shoes. **1880** *Folk-Lore Record* 133. This morning, April 10th, 1880, girls and women were rushing into grocers' shops in the locality of the Broad Quay [Bristol] to buy each a quarter of a pound of rice, with which to salute a quay lumper and his bride as they came out of church. Yesterday the newspaper recounting certain ceremonies connected with a fashionable wedding at Clifton states that rice was freely thrown over the bridal party as they left the church. **1881** W. GREGOR *North-East of Scotland* 197. On the arrival of a new boat at its home the skipper's wife, in some of the villages, took a lapful of corn or barley, and sowed it over the boat. **1883** BURNE *Shropshire* 293. The horrid modern fashion of throwing handfuls of rice upon

the party within the very walls of the church itself. **1896** A. CHEVIOT *Proverbs* 285 [Scotland] 'Rice for good luck, and bauchles for bonny bairns' .. Refers to the custom of throwing rice and old shoes after a newly married couple. **1904** *Newcastle Daily Journal* 11 Apr. 6. At the Parish Church, Eglingham .. on leaving the church the newly-wedded couple were met with the usual shower of rice and confetti. **1911** J. C. DAVIES *Welsh Folk-Lore* 36. It is still very general to throw rice at the bride and bridegroom. **1923** BENNETT *Riceyman Steps* V [Clerkenwell, London, 1919] Elsie [the maidservant] flung a considerable quantity of rice on to the middle-aged persons of the married .. 'I had to do it, because it's for luck,' Elsie amiably explained. **1927** MRS MASSEY LYON *Etiquette* 126. Nowadays no confetti, rice or their equivalents are thrown at the church door. That is left for those of humbler rank. **1987** [Bristol] [bridegroom's mother, distributing handfuls of paper rose-petals after wedding] 'Have some confetti, and be ready to throw it over them when they come out.'

WHISTLING = magical activity

1555 Articles objected against Bishop Ferrar, martyr (FOXE *Acts and Monuments*, 1965, VII 8–9) Item, He daily useth whistling of his child; and saith that he understood his whistle, when he was but three days old .. and so whistleth him daily, all friendly admonition neglected. Item .. among other his surveys he surveyed Milford Haven, where he espied a seal-fish tumbling. And he crept down the rocks to the water-side, and continued there whistling by the space of an hour, persuading the company that laughed fast at him, that by his whistling he made the fish to tarry there.

WHISTLING after dark

*c.*1605 MS Cotton, Julius f. 6 (GROSE *Provincial Glossary* Superstitions 70) [Guisborough, Yorks.] Any one whistling, after it is dark, or day-light is closed, must go thrice about the house, by way of penance. **1865** R. HUNT *West of England* 2nd ser. 239. To whistle by night is one of the unpardonable sins amongst the fishermen of St Ives .. 'I would no more dare go among a party of fishermen at night whistling a popular air than into a den of untamed tigers.'

WHISTLING at sea

1686-7 AUBREY *Remaines* (1881, 21) Mdm. The seamen will not endure to have one whistle on ship-board: believing that it rayses winds. **1763** *Gents Mag.* pt. I 14-15. Our sailors, I am told, at this very day, I mean the vulgar sort of them, have a strange opinion of the devil's power and agency in stirring up winds, and that this is the reason why they so seldom whistle on ship-board, esteeming that to be a mocking, and consequently an enraging of the devil. **1777** BRAND *Antiquities* 98. Sailors .. have various puerile Apprehensions concerning whistling on Shipboard .. all which are Vestiges of the old Woman in human Nature. **1787** GROSE *Provincial Glossary* Superstitions 66. Whistling at sea is supposed to cause an increase of wind, if not a storm, and therefore much disliked by seamen; though, sometimes, they themselves practise it when there is a dead calm. **1835** H. MILLER *Scenes of North Scotland* 109 [Ross./Cromarty] Thoughtlessly beginning to whistle one evening about twelve years ago .. I was instantly silenced by one of the fishermen with a 'Whisht, whisht, boy, we have more than wind enough already.' **1866** HENDERSON *Northern Counties* 28. A few years ago, when a party of friends were going on board a vessel at Scarborough, the captain astonished them by declining to allow one of them to enter it. 'Not that young lady,' he said, 'she whistles.' **1909** *N & Q* 10th ser. XII 483 [Stromness, Orkney] Sailors count it unlucky to whistle on board ship; it will bring wind. **1930** P. F. ANSON *East Coast of Scotland* 42. The Caithness fishermen shared the almost universal superstition among sailors that wind can be produced by whistling; while no Caithness wife would ever dare to blow on the oat-cakes when baking, or a hurricane would arise and her husband's boat would be in danger. **1977** *Daily Mirror* 7 Nov. 22. In 1955, as a cabin boy just recuperating from my first week at sea, I was amazed when our Scots cook marched into the pantry ordering me to stop whistling. 'Why?' I asked. 'Because,' he replied, 'whistlin' summons up the bad weather, yuh cheeky wee upstart!' **1985** Ex-Naval man, *c.*60 [Goldhanger, Essex] You're not allowed to whistle on a ship—that's the signal for a mutiny.

Cf. WIND, whistling for.

WHISTLING down mine

1815 J. VAREY *Agriculture and Minerals of Derbyshire* I 316-17. By which class of persons [miners] whistling in a mine was supposed to frighten away the ore or lessen its chance of continuance; and hence they say arose the custom that, however miners may sing or halloo when at their work, no boy or man is to whistle, under pain of severe chastisement from his fellow-miners. **1838** A. E. BRAY *Devonshire* III 255. The miners have invariably a great horror .. at whistling underground, believing it to be very unlucky. **1852** *N & Q* 1st ser. VI 601. Amongst the miners in Cornwall a superstition greatly prevails .. that whistling below ground brings 'evil spirits' amongst them, and for that reason you never hear a miner whistling whilst under ground. **1855** *N & Q* 1st ser. XII 201 [Allendale, Northumb.] Can any reason be assigned for the prevailing antipathy which lead-miners have to whistling in the mine? **1873** HARLAND & WILKINSON *Lancashire Legends* 239. No one will whistle when he is working in the mine, under the idea that the roof may fall upon and smother him. **1984** BBC RADIO *Underground Britain* 11 Sept. [miner] I don't think you'd find a man whistling underground. You can sing, but you mustn't whistle.

WHISTLING in theatre

1910 T. SHARPER KNOWLSON *Superstitions* 225. To whistle in a theatre is a sign of the worst luck in the world, and there is no offence for which the manager will scold an employee more quickly. **1932** C. J. S. THOMPSON *Hand of Destiny* 282. It is considered of evil portent to whistle in an actor's dressing room, and those who .. do so are made to go outside and turn round three times. **1933** J. B. BOOTH *Pink Parade* 97. If .. you wish to make yourself thoroughly unpopular you have only to whistle in a dressing-room, for then the person who happens to be nearest to the door is absolutely certain to be attacked by a serious illness. **1952** W. GRANVILLE *Theatrical Terms* 179. To whistle in the dressing-room [is considered an ill omen], the belief being that the artiste nearest to the door will be 'whistled out' (i.e. sacked). **1984** Dancer, 37 [Harrow, Middx.] On my first theatre job I was told never to whistle in the dressing-room and if anyone did they had to go out, turn round three times, knock, and wait to be told to enter—and if they didn't like you you had to wait a long time. **1985** Actor, 28. I've been told several times that it's whistling in the wings that's unlucky—that's because, before there was a Tannoy system, whistling was the signal to change the scenery. **1987** Actress, 58. If you whistle in a dressing room you've got to go out, turn round three times, spit, and come in and swear.

WHISTLING WOMAN AND CROWING HEN

1721 KELLY *Scotish Proverbs* 33. A crooning cow, a crowing hen, and a whistling maid boded never luck to a house. *c*.**1810** S. SIBBALD (*Memoirs*, ed. Hett, 238) My Grandmother once told me that 'a whistling woman and a crawing hen were na canny.' **1850** *N & Q* 1st ser. II 226. A whistling wife and a crowing hen, Will call the old gentleman out of his den. **1855** *N & Q* 1st ser. XII 37 [Cornwall] An old proverb in use here says: 'A whistling woman and a crowing hen, are two of the unluckiest things under the sun.' **1891** J. L. KIPLING *Beast and Man* 40. 'A whistling woman and a crowing hen are neither fit for God nor men,' is a mild English saying. **1943** F. THOMPSON *Candleford Green* 119 [Oxon.] If a girl began to whistle a tune, those near her would clap their hands over her mouth, for 'A whistling maid and a crowing hen is no good either to gods nor men.' **1972** *Lore and Language* July 7 [Coalisland, Co.Tyrone] A whistling woman and a crowing hen Will bring no luck to the house of men. **1988** [Matlock, Derbys.] Sitting in a pub the other lunchtime I fell into conversation

with a woman of 45 who came out with: 'A whistling woman and a crowing hen, Is enough to make the Devil come out of his den.'

WHITE unlucky

1959 OPIE *Lore and Language of Schoolchildren* 215. In Sale, Cheshire .. the boys spit on seeing anything white, whether it be white horse, white cat, white flannels, or white straw hat.

Cf. BLACK.

WHITE APRON

1849 *Norfolk Archaeology* II 46 [Irstead] On our coast, if fishermen meet a woman with a white apron, when they are going to sea, they will turn back and wait a tide. **1883** *Folklore* 355 [Staffs.] If a collier on his way to work meet a woman wearing a white apron, he will not go to work. Ibid. [Holderness, Yorks.] The fishermen when going to sea will turn back and wait a tide if they meet a woman wearing a white apron.

WHITE BIRD

1885 *N & Q* 6th ser. XII 489. If miners see white birds about the gearing of mine-shafts they consider them to be harbingers of disaster. **1957** Boy, 11 [Beccles, Suffolk] To see a white bird is unlucky.

Cf. DOVE sign of peace to departing soul; PIGEON settles = death omen.

WHITE CAT

1889 *N & Q* 7th ser. VIII 464. I have a little white cat, which I am begged to get rid of, 'as white cats are so unlucky in a house, and everything had been going wrong since it came.' **1899** *Newcastle Weekly Chronicle* 11 Feb. 7 [Jesmond] It is unlucky to meet a black cat, but lucky to meet a white one. **1922** [Somerset] If a white cat crosses your path, cross your fingers or you will have bad luck. **1973** *Annabel* Oct. 4. I saw a white cat this morning. Since then the milk has boiled over, I've had to pay 5p on a letter somebody posted and forgot to stamp, a friend I wanted to see called while I was out and the head came off the hammer.

WHITE COW

1853 *N & Q* 1st ser. VII 153 [Wilts.] A child that sucks a white cow will thrive better. 1923 [Somerset] When you see a white cow spit three times. 1927 *N & Q* CLIII 443. White cows are thought unlucky by farmers in Wales, and they sell £10 to £15 cheaper than other cows. The assumption is that they are too like the Fairy Cow—'the milk white milch cow' of tradition, in Wales. 1946 UTTLEY *Country Things* 130 [Cromford, Derbys., *c*.1900] White cattle were not liked, and when a white calf was born, it was sold. There was an old prejudice against them.

WHITE DOG

1952 Girl, 11 [Swansea, Glam.] Three white dogs together brings good luck. 1961 Woman, 67 [Exmouth, Devon] To see a white dog before noon is lucky.

WHITE FEET, horse's

15th c. Bodleian MS Wood empt. 18. If your horse has four white feet, Give him to your foe, And if he has three, Do even so. If he has two, Give him to your friend, But if he has just one, Keep him till the end. *ante* 1672 BROWNE Commonplace book (*Works*, ed. Keynes, 1964, III 282) Why they are good signs to have one foot white before or 2 before & one behind & not the left foot. One or 2 white feet & none in their left behind. 1797 URE *Agriculture of Kinross* 34. If he has one foot buy him, If he has two you may try him, If he has three look shy at him, But if he has four go by him. 1858 T. HUGHES *Scouring of White Horse* 11. Gently, my beauty! if it wasn't for the blaze in her face, and the white feet, the Squir'd give me one hundred pounds for her to-morrow. 1877 *N & Q* 5th ser. VII 64. One white foot—buy a horse; Two white feet—try a horse; Three white feet—look well about him; Four white feet—do without him. Ibid. 299 [Stoke-in-Teignhead, Devon] If you have a horse with four white legs, Keep him not a day; If you have a horse with three white legs, Send him far away; If you have a horse with two white legs, Sell him to a friend; If you have a horse with one white leg, Keep him to his end. 1901 *N & Q* 9th ser. VII 193. In the magnificent animals yoked to the lorries in Glasgow streets white faces and white stockings are at present .. in the majority. The same thing was observable among the .. horses .. at a show of Clydesdales .. on 6 February .. The modern expert would appear to ignore the old scruples as to white faces and stockings, four of the latter being now no rarity whatever. 1955 Man, 61 [Halifax, Yorks.] If it has one, buy it, If it has two, try it; If it has three respect it, If it has four, reject it. 1986 Girl, 15 [Exmouth, Devon] If a horse has one, two or three white 'socks', he is all right, but if he has four, he 'has a will of his own'.

WHITE FLOWERS = death/misfortune

1922 LYND *Solomon* 161. Some .. will put the blame of their misfortunes on a friend .. who has sent them a gift of white flowers without a mixture of other colours. 1931 *N & Q* CLX 195. I have heard from a social worker in London that it is most unlucky .. to give any white flowers .. to sick people. Apparently some implication that, being white, they would be suitable for the funeral, is involved. 1981 Woman, 63 [Coreley, Shrops.] You didn't take white flowers into the house, unless it was sweet peas and they were mixed up with others—and I think marguerites were acceptable—but mostly white flowers were banned.

Cf. FLOWERS, red and white.

WHITE FLOWERS: arum lily

1954 N. FAIRBROTHER *Children in the House* pt. 3 131. I bought this morning at a market stall a great armful of white lilies for a shilling. No one will buy them, they said, because they bring death into the house. 1960 *Folklore* 205. Some people dislike lilies .. refusing them house-room on the grounds that they are associated with funerals.

WHITE FLOWERS: lilac

1960 *Folklore* 205. In the Midlands lilac, especially the white variety, is sometimes regarded as a death omen. Florists .. advise their customers against it, if they know that it is intended as a gift for someone who is ill. 1969 M.

HARRIS *A Kind of Magic* 125. Some people still think that having lilac indoors or white flowers of any sort will bring bad luck. **1983** Girl, 13 [Maldon, Essex] My mum won't let us bring lilac indoors.

WHITE FLOWERS: lily of the valley

1850 *N & Q* 1st ser. II 512 [Devon] It is not considered safe to plant a bed of lilies of the valley; the person doing so will probably die in the course of the next twelve months. **1954** Girl, 11 [Luncarty, Perth.] It is unlucky to bring lily of the valley into the house. **1970** A. GILBERT *Death Wears a Mask* 132-4. Mr Crook . . asked for a silk scarf . . 'How about this one with lilies-of-the-valley?' Mr Crook thought not the lilies-of-the-valley, his auntie was superstitious.

WHITE FLOWERS: snowdrop

1821 T. D. FOSBROKE *Ariconensia* 70 [Herefords.] Wild Flowers, especially Snow-drops, brought into the house, prevent the first brood of chickens. **1856** J. NOAKE *Worcestershire* 170. The first snowdrop brought into the house betokens the death of the gatherer. **1875** *N & Q* 5th ser. III 465 [Shrops.] It's bad luck to bring snowdrops into the house. **1878** *Folk-Lore Record* 52 [Fittleworth, Sussex] The snowdrop [is] dreaded, if one only is brought into the house when they first appear. **1895** *N & Q* 8th ser. VII 167 [Stourbridge, Worcs.] Snowdrops should, to prevent ill luck, always be presented by one of the opposite sex. **1913** E. M. WRIGHT *Rustic Speech* 217. When a school-fellow of mine died of typhoid fever, the lady Principal of the boarding-school wrote to my parents, charging them with being the authors of the calamity, in that they had a short time before sent me a box of snowdrops. **1931** *N & Q* CLX 160. Many people . . think it is unlucky to take snowdrops into a house, because 'a snowdrop looks like a corpse in a shroud,' and because they are used in funeral wreaths, and placed on graves, especially of young people. **1966** *Times* 15 Feb. 12. We called them 'corpses in shrouds' when we were little and we never took them indoors at all. All white flowers is unlucky. **1985** R. VICKERY *Unlucky Plants*

33. I hate and detest them . . My mother started it all by saying never pick them and take them indoors they are bad luck. When my brother-in-law died . . at the age of 35, as we were following the coffin . . both sides of the road were white with snowdrops.

WHITE HARE/RABBIT/WEASEL/MOLE

1893 *Folklore* 258 [Droitwich, Worcs.] Tharr was some lads in an arrchard . . and says they, 'Let's have a bit o them apples!' So up tha climbs, an tharr tha was, a settin in the tree . . when 'Lor bless us,' says one, 'tharr's a tame rabbit, a white 'n!'—an the rabbit run right under the tree. An 'twas a token of thurr master's death, an die a did. **1909** M. TREVELYAN *Folk-Lore of Wales* 78 [Glam./Cardigan.] The white hare, white weasel, and white mole were . . regarded . . as heralds of misfortune. **1959** OPIE *Lore and Language of School-children* 215 [Knighton, Radnor.] If you see a white hare you are unlucky, but if you see a black hare you will have luck.

WHITE HORSE

1850 *N & Q* 1st ser. I 451 [Midlands] It is believed a sign of 'bad luck' to meet a white horse, unless the person spits at it. **1861** *N & Q* 2nd ser. XII 490-1. Grey horses at a wedding lucky. This probably is simply because white is considered the wedding colour. **1861** C. C. ROBINSON *Dialect of Leeds* 316. 'Good luck for a grey horse!'—A common expression of children, accompanied by the act of spitting over their little finger, at the sight of a grey horse, an action supposed to bring good luck, and . . they congregate at places where a long line of road is before the eye, and at the first glimpse of such an animal perform this ceremony. **1882** *N & Q* 6th ser. VI 9 [Oxon.] Walking the other day . . with some of my schoolchildren, we were met on the road by a carriage and pair of greys. Some of the children at once spat on the ground . . I was told that it was very bad luck to meet a pair of white or grey horses, and that one's bad luck could only be averted by at once spitting on the ground. **1884** *N & Q* 6th ser. IX 266. An old carter . . talking about some local races [said] that he had never known a grey horse to be much good; it was an unlucky colour for a horse; they never won in a race. **1887** 'SPER-ANZA' WILDE *Superstitions of Ireland* II 118 [Western Islands] It is ill luck when going with a funeral to meet a man on a white horse. No matter how high the rank of the rider may be, the people must seize the reins and force him to turn back and join the procession at least for a few yards. **1890** J. NICHOLSON *East Yorkshire* 43. Schoolboys .. will spit when they meet a white horse, to avoid the ill consequences of such an unlucky meeting. After which operation, the following rhyme is said: 'Good luck to you, good luck to me, Good luck for every white horse I see.' **1909** M. TREVELYAN *Folk-Lore of Wales* 183. Whenever a pure snow-white horse .. passes through some of the villages in West Glamorgan, Carmarthen, and Pembrokeshire, people say there will be a death in the parish. **1933** *N & Q* CLXV 305. I can recall in London, among boys, fifty years or so ago, the practice of making the sign of a cross, on the toe of a boot or shoe, with the finger moistened with spittle .. with the object of dispelling bad luck arising from having sighted a white or partly white horse. **1949** Woman, *c.*35 [Sheffield, Yorks.] Upon seeing a white horse: 'White horse, white horse, Bring me good luck. Good luck to you, Good luck to me, Good luck to every one I see.' **1956** Girl, 11 [Gloucester] If you see a white horse to bring luck you must spit on the sole of your shoe and then rub it on the ground. **1985** Woman, 48 [Carmarthen] My husband has to spit three times over his left shoulder whenever he sees a white horse.

WHITE STONE

1885 *Folklore* 308 [Macduff, Banff.] A white stone is not used as a 'lug-steen'; that is, the stone tied to the lower corner of the herring-net to sink it. **1901** J. RHYS *Celtic Folklore* I 344 [Isle of Man] Another of the unlucky things is to have a white stone in the boat, even in the ballast. **1911** J. C. DAVIES *West and Mid-Wales* 216. People in Montgomeryshire .. consider it unlucky to pick up or carry white stones in their pockets.

WHITSUN: new clothes

1626 T. DELONEY *Jack of Newbery* 64–5. 'My french-hood is bought already, and my silke gowne is a making' .. 'And when doe you meane to weare them Gossip?' 'At Whitsontide (quoth shee) if God spare mee life.' **1864** R. CHAMBERS *Book of Days* II 322. If you would have good-luck, you must wear something new on Whitsun-Sunday' (pronounced Wissun-Sunday). More generally, Easter Day is the one thus honoured, but a glance round a church or Sunday-school in Suffolk, on Whitsunday, shews very plainly that it is the one chosen for beginning to wear new 'things'. **1878** *N & Q* 5th ser. X 287 [Yorks.] On Whitsunday, if you don't put on at least one brand-new article of dress, the birds will be sure to come and 'drop' on you. **1957** HOGGART *Uses of Literacy* 11. The 'best clothes' newly bought at Whitsun and the round tour on Whit Sunday morning to show these clothes to relatives and receive a present of money. **1985** Woman, 61. Traditionally in Manchester the children had to have new clothes at Whitsun—everything, from top to bottom, right down to the liberty bodice. The parents would run into debt to do it.

WIDOW unlucky at wedding

1883 BURNE *Shropshire* 292. It is considered unlucky for a widow to attend a wedding. **1984** *Sunday People* 2 Dec. 36. When my youngest child married in July .. I gave her away, because her father died suddenly a year ago. It wasn't until after the wedding that I was told it is unlucky for a woman to do this.

WIDOW'S (OR WIDOWER'S) PEAK

1620 MELTON *Astrologaster* 45. By a certaine tuft of haire growing on the foremost part of a man's forehead, it may be knowne whether he shall bee a widdower or no. **1861** *N & Q* 2nd ser. XII 492. If, when a lady parts her hair, a very small lock remains at the extremity, forming a sort of peak on her forehead, it is a sign she will outlive her husband and be a widow. **1879** HENDERSON *Northern Counties* 42. When a woman's hair grows in a low point on the forehead, it is supposed to presage widowhood, and is called a 'widow's peak'. **1896** NORTHALL *Warwickshire*. *Widow's-lock*, a small lock or fringe growing apart from the hair above the forehead. Credulous persons believe that a girl so distinguished will become a widow after marriage. **1933** *Folklore* 196 [Scawby, Lincs.] As she dusted the mirror she caught sight of herself; she seemed 'somehow different' and paused to look at herself more closely. She saw .. a curl over each temple .. and knew quite well what this omen meant. Within the fortnight her husband was brought home ill, and died soon after. **1964** Woman, 36 [South Shields, Co. Durham] If your hair grows to a point in the middle of your forehead, you will be a widow. I used to look at my hair to see if I had one, but stopped when my husband died.

WIFE, unfaithful

1911 *Folklore* 58 [Co. Clare] Difficult childbirth could be aided by hanging on the sufferer's bed the clothing of a man whose wife was reputed to have been unfaithful to him.

WILL, making

1748 S. WERENFELS *Dissertation upon Superstition* 7. He could wish indeed, that his Estate might go to his next and best Friends after his Death, but he had rather leave it to any body than make his Will, for fear least he should presently die after it. **1937** SAYERS *Busman's Honeymoon* VIII. There's some people won't ever make a will—say it's like signing their own death-warrant. And they ain't so far out.

WILLOW, burning

1969 E. PORTER *Cambridgeshire* 63. Few fenmen cared to bring willow wood into the house for firing or to use the sawn-off limbs of the trees for fencing. When the willows were felled for cricket-bat wood it was difficult to get rid of the tops of the trees even as fire kindling for the poorest families. **1985** R. VICKERY *Unlucky Plants* 60 [Accrington, Lancs.] Twelve children mentioned that willow should not be burnt on Bonfire Night.

WILLOW BLOSSOMS in house

1883 BURNE *Shropshire* 250. The strongest condemnation of all lights on willow catkins. The soft round yellowish blossoms are considered to resemble young goslings, and [none] may be brought into the house, for if they be, no feathered goslings will be hatched. **1912** LEATHER *Herefordshire* 17. It is held unlucky to bring .. into the house .. the catkins of the round-leaved sallow, which are known to all as 'gulls' (goslings); this would be fatal to the real goslings. **1955** Man, 52 [Alton, Hants.] Pussy willow should not be brought into the house.

WILLOW STICK

1883 BURNE *Shropshire* 248. If yo' drive a 'orse with a withy-stick, 'e'll sure to 'a the bally-ache. **1912** LEATHER *Herefordshire* 19. It is believed that any young animal or child struck by a willow rod, usually called 'withy-stick' or 'sally twig', will cease to grow afterwards. A woman at Pembridge said, 'I've never hit nothing with a sally twig, never, nor shouldn't like to either.' **1932** WOMEN'S INSTITUTE *Worcestershire Book* 34 [Cotheridge] No animal should be hit with a willow stick.

Cf. ELDER malevolent.

WIND: coin thrown into sea

1861 PHILO SCOTUS *Reminiscences of Scottish Gentleman* 15 [Pentland Firth, 1804] Soon after we entered the Frith, the wind entirely failed .. and many a 'whistle and blow, good breeze' was uttered .. but all seemed in vain. At length I tried the experiment which sailors consider the last resource .. but in which they have great faith, of throwing a sixpence overboard; and, strange to say, the enchantment seemed to work. **1961** *Times* 18 Jan. 12. It was in Halfway Reach that he decided we must buy a penn'orth of wind .. The penny was thrown into the water with the incantation: 'Blow a little breeze, please, Father,' and immediately Father Neptune .. sent the breeze.

WIND, undoing knots for

*c.*1350 HIGDEN *Polychronicon* (MS Harl. 2261, tr. Trevisa: Rolls II 43) In whiche yle [Isle of Man] wycchecrafte ys exercisede moche, for women þer be wonte to selle wynde to the schippemen commenge to that cuntre, as includede vnder thre knottes of threde, so that thei wylle vnloose the knottes lyke as thei wylle haue the wynde to blawe. **1594** NASHE *Terrors of the Night* D2. Three knots in a thread, or an odde grandams blessing in the corner of a napkin, will carrie you all the worlde ouer. **1631** DRAYTON *Battaile of Agincourt* 'Moone-Calfe' ll. 865–7. She could sell windes to any one that would, Buy them for money, forcing them to hold What time she listed, tye them in a thrid. **1822** SCOTT *The Pirate* I 158 [Shetland] Does she get rich by selling favourable winds to those who are port-bound? **1880** W. JONES *Credulities* 71 [Kintyre] Old John McTaggart was a trader .. Wishing to get a fair wind to waft his bark across to the Emerald Isle, he applied to an old woman [and] received from her two strings, on each being three knots. He undid the first knot, and there blew a fine breeze. On opening the second, the breeze became a gale. On nearing the Irish shore he loosed the third, and such a hurricane arose, that some of the houses on shore were destroyed. **1902** *Irish Times* 19 Apr. 7. It seems incredible, but is nevertheless a fact, that as late as the year 1814 an old woman named Bessie Millie of Pomona, in the Orkney Islands, sold favourable winds to seamen at the small price of 6d a vessel. The old woman .. used to knit three magical knots; the buyer was told he would have a good gale when he untied the first knot, the second knot would bring a strong wind, and the third a severe tempest.

WIND, whistling for

*c.*1510 *Cock Lorel's Boat* 344. Some whysteled after the wynde. **1823** *Gents Mag.* pt. 1 17 [Ipswich, Suffolk] Sailors .. in calm weather [whistle] the wind to induce it to blow—and many of them believe it to be a very powerful charm. **1832** *Gents Mag.* pt. 1 592 [Scopwick, Lincs.] Seamen whistling for a wind, which I have repeatedly seen practised on board of the passage boats plying between Grimsby and Hull .. was a direct invocation to 'the prince of the power of the air' to exert himself in their behalf. **1869** *N & Q* 4th ser. IV 131 [Scarborough, Yorks.] One old man said, 'We only whistle when the wind is asleep, and then the breeze comes.' **1885** *Folklore* 54 [NE Scotland] When it is calm, sailors and fishermen whistle, for the most part softly, to make the wind blow; hence the phrase .. 'Fussle t'raise the win'.' **1913** M. ROBERTS *Salt of the Sea* 452. 'I could whistle for a good wind, sir,' said Wilde. ''Tis a superstition,' said the captain severely. 'It works if you whistle long enough,' cried the mate, smiling. **1936** E. H. RUDKIN *Lincolnshire* 22 [Kirton] You must whistle for the wind.

Cf. WHISTLING at sea.

WINDOW-BLIND falls

1899 J. SHAW *Schoolmaster* 33 [Tynron, Dumfries.] If a window blind fall of its own accord, it is unlucky. **1923** [Taunton, Som.] If the blind suddenly unrolls without being touched you will shortly have to pull them down through death.

WINNOWING CORN: divination

1787 BURNS *Poems* 167–8 [note to 'Halloween'] This charm must .. be performed unperceived and alone. You go to the barn, and open both doors, taking them off the hinges, if possible: for there is danger, that the being, about to appear, may shut the doors, and do you some mischief. Then take that instrument used in winnowing the corn, which, in our country-dialect we call a *wecht*, and go through all the attitudes of letting down corn against the wind. Repeat it three times, and the third time, an apparition will pass through the barn, in at the windy door, and out at the other, having both the figure in question, and the appearance or retinue, marking the employment or station in life. [*wecht*, a close sieve, the bottom covered with leather] **1865** *Gents Mag.* pt. 2 702 [Ireland, All-Hallows Eve] Sometimes girls take a riddle, and collect a quantity of thrashed grain, which they winnow, believing they shall see a future spouse before their work is ended. **1898** BLAKEBOROUGH *Yorkshire Customs* 81. At midnight, with the barn doors thrown wide open, a quantity of chaff had to be riddled, those taking part in the ceremony riddling in turn; should a coffin pass the door whilst any one was working the sieve, that person would die within the year.

WISHBONE

1688 AUBREY *Remaines* (1881, 92) 'Tis common for two to breake the Merry-thought of a chicken, or wood-cock, &c., the Anatomists call it Clavicula; 'tis called the merrythought, because when the fowle is opened, dissected, or carv'd, it resembles the pudenda of a woman. The manner of breaking it, as I have it from the woemen, is thus: viz. One puts ye merrithought on his nose (slightly) like a paire of spectacles, and shakes his head till he shakes if off his nose, thinking all the while his Thought; then he holds one of the legs of it between his forefinger and Thumbe, and another hold the other in like manner, and breake it; he that has the longer part, has got the Thought; then he that has got the thought putts both parts into his hand, and the other drawes (by way of Lott), and then they both Wish, and he that lost his Thought drawes; if he drawes the longest part, he has his wish, if the shorter he looses his Wish. **1708** *British Apollo* 26 Nov. *Q.* Gentlemen, For what Reason is the Bone next the Breast of a Fowl, &c. Called the Merry-thought? And when was it first Called so? *A.* The Original of that Name was doubtless from the Pleasant Fancies, that commonly arise upon the Breaking of that Bone. **1711** *Spectator* 8 Mar. I .. have seen a man in love grow pale and lose his appetite, upon the plucking of a merry thought. **1843** C. J. LEVER *Jack Hinton* II. Simpering old maids cracked merry thoughts with gay bachelors. **1861** C. C. ROBINSON *Dialect of Leeds* 409. The 'skip-jack' of a goose is always preserved, and the younger members of a family, or the servants, break it, by one taking hold of each end. The one retaining the longest piece will be the first to be married. **1901** MACLAGAN *Games of Argyleshire* 6. At a marriage in Islay .. M. got me to break a *cnamh posaidh* (marriage-bone) with him. I got the longest piece. I was then instructed

to break it in two and offer both pieces as in drawing lots .. and M. got the longest piece. This he broke and offered me my choice, which resulted in my getting the longer piece .. so I am to be first married. **1923** [Ruishton, Som.] When pulling apart a fowl's wishbone, the wish of the person left holding the biggest part will come true. **1986** Man, 55 [Richmond, Yorks.] Oh yes, we always do it—and the one who gets the longest piece has the wish.

WOMAN crosses water

1587 HOLINSHED *Chronicles* (1808, V 16) [Hebrides] Ouer against Rosse, in an Ile named Lewis, 60 miles in length, in this Ile is but one fish riuer, it is said that if a woman wade through the same at the spring of the yeere, there shall no samon be seene there for a twelue month after. **1703** M. MARTIN *Western Islands of Scotland* 7 [Lewis] The Natives .. retain an ancient Custom of sending a Man very early to cross Barvas river, every first day of May, to prevent any Females crossing it first; for that they say would hinder the Salmon from coming into the River all the year round. **1775** JOHNSON *Western Islands* 157 [Skye] It is held that .. if any woman crosses the water to the opposite Island, the herrings will desert the coast.

Cf. FIRST-FOOT at New Year/Christmas: female unlucky.

WOMAN, meeting

1691 *Hist. Athenian Society* pt. 2 16. I cannot but wonder to find Tycho Brahe, running back to his House with no small consternation .. if the first thing in a Morning, he met an old Woman. **1813** BRAND *Antiquities* II 404. In Northumberland, I found a reputed witch in a lonely cottage .. where the parish had placed her, to .. keep her out of the way .. I was told .. that everybody was afraid of her cat, and that she herself was thought to have the evil eye, and that it was accounted dangerous to meet her in a morning. **1874** N & Q 5th ser. I 383 [*Oswestry Advertiser* May] A strange tale comes to us from Cefn [Denbigh.] A woman is employed as messenger at one of the collieries .. and meets .. great numbers of colliers going to their work.

numbers of colliers going to their work. Some of them .. consider it a bad omen to meet a woman first thing in the morning, and .. waited upon the manager and declared that they should remain at home unless the woman was dismissed. **1874** *N & Q* 5th ser. II 184 [Staithes, Yorks.] If a fisherman happens to meet a female first on leaving his cottage to put out to sea, he will turn back again, as he firmly believes that all his luck would be spoiled for the day. **1883** BURNE *Shropshire* 266. If on putting her head out of doors the first time in the morning she saw one of her own sex, she would shut herself within doors for the day. **1909** M. TREVELYAN *Folk-Lore of Wales* 327. It is bad to meet an old woman early in the morning, or to pass between two old women in the forenoon. **1952** Boy, 12 [Lydney, Glos.] If you see a lady driver you cross your fingers and wait till you see a dog and then uncross them. **1957** *Folklore* 424 [Co. Durham] A miner in first shift would return home if he met a woman before he got to the lamp cabin [and] some still do. **1968** *Observer* Suppl. 24 Nov. 10 [Staithes, Yorks.] The men didn't like to see a woman when they were going fishing: Mrs Stornhouse, she was allus up early and out at the tap and if they saw her they'd say 'It's no use to go to work today.'

Cf. FIRST-FOOT: animal or person first encountered.

WOMAN on ship

1965 J. INGRAM *The World's My University* 101. The donkey-engine boiler blew up .. This seemed to confirm the truth of the old sea superstition that women aboard a windjammer are unlucky, for the Heryokin Cecilie carried five. **1969** *Daily Express* 29 Oct. 1. Princess Anne broke a superstition yesterday and became the first woman to visit a North Sea natural gas .. rig. **1980** Sea captain's wife, 59 [South Shields, Co. Durham] No woman was encouraged to go in a fishing vessel. **1985** Ex-Navy man, *c.*60 [Goldhanger, Essex] I don't like women on boats—but they've forgotten all that sort of thing nowadays.

WOOD creaks and cracks

c. AD **388** ST JOHN CHRYSOSTOM *Baptismal Instructions* (tr. Harkins, 39) I exhort both men and women to shun altogether omens and superstitions .. this meddling of yours with the cawing of crows, the squeaking of mice, the creaking of beams. *c.***1395** CHAUCER Parson's Tale l. 604. What seye we of hem that bileeven on divynailes, as by .. chirkynge [creaking] of dores, or crakkynge of houses? **1861** C. C. ROBINSON *Dialect of Leeds* 299. When the furniture of the house cracks it is regarded as a sign of death. **1876** S. BARING-GOULD *Vicar of Morwenstow* 165. He was staying with a friend. Suddenly the table gave a crack. Mr Hawker started, and laying his hand on the table said, 'Mark my words, there has been a death in the family.' By next post came news of the death of one of the Miss I'ans. **1909** M. TREVELYAN *Folk-Lore of Wales* 328. Creaking rafters and squeaking tables foretoken disaster or death.

WOOD: going against grain

1895 S. O. ADDY *Household Tales* 94 [Yorks.] When you are playing at cards on a wooden table do not play against the grain of the wood.

WOOD, touching

1805 R. ANDERSON *Ballads in Cumberland Dialect* 35. Tig-touch-wood. **1828** *Boy's Own Book* 24. Touch .. is sometimes called Touch-iron or Touch-wood; in these cases, the players are safe only when they touch iron or wood. **1877** *N & Q* 5th ser. VII 163-4 [Uppingham, Rutland] Sitting by a school-fellow in form the other day, he remarked he had not been put to construe for some days; immediately after saying this he rapped underneath the form on which he was sitting .. He said it was an old superstition, possibly in Kent or Lincolnshire, that when anybody said that something—invariably something not wished for—had not happened to him lately, rapping underneath anything near would prevent its fulfilment. **1906** *N & Q* 10th ser. VI 130. 'Touching wood' after boasting of one's exemption from ill fortune—a species of 'absit omen' practised in Shropshire and

Cheshire, and probably in many other parts of England. The procedure is of this kind: 'I'm thankful to say I never broke a bone .. well, I'd better touch wood'; and a chair or table, or anything near that is wooden, is touched. Can the custom come from some lingering memory of the veneration attached to relics of the true Cross? Ibid. 174. I have heard and seen—but it is long ago—persons express themselves and touch wood on it .. and in particular upon an occasion when a man had made an assertion he touched wood, placing his thumb on a table. Ibid. 231 [London] This custom, as well as that of saying 'Unberufen' ['Heaven preserve us'] to ward off future evil, is by no means extinct. Both are, I should say, very prevalent in this country, either alone or in combination. Many people seem to employ them habitually. I have had patients who never answer a question in the negative without this accompaniment—as 'Have you had cough?' 'No, unberufen.' 'Any headache?' 'No, unberufen.' 1908 *Westminster Gazette* 30 Dec. 2. On the next occasion when we read of Christmas with spring weather or of the changing seasons we shall 'touch wood'. 1911 *Folklore* 203 [Co. Clare] Rub your hand on wood .. after a boastful speech or speaking too confidently of the future; in east Clare you touch wood twice, with the phrase, 'Good word (*or* time) be it spoken,' after an imprudent expression. 1913 E. M. WRIGHT *Rustic Speech* 230. Many educated people habitually 'touch wood' if they have given vent to some expression of satisfaction over their own health or fortune, or that of any member of their family .. If the trick were omitted, the speaker would probably feel uncomfortable. 1915 *T.P.'s Weekly* 4 Dec. 563. When Mr Asquith referred in his great war speech in the House of Commons the other week to the insignificant number of British losses .. the First Lord of the Admiralty leant forward and gravely touched the wood of the Clerk's table. 1930 N & Q CLIX 213. We had in common use before the World War the German form 'unberufen', but it is not now fashionable; the Latin 'absit omen'

is too pedantic .. A French form, easily said and remembered, might be an addition to our parlance. 1934 SAYERS *Nine Tailors* 69. 'Mrs Wallace is a funny woman; she takes offence rather easily, but so far—touch wood'—(Mrs Venables performed this ancient pagan rite placidly on the oak of the [church] screen)—'so far, I've managed to work in quite smoothly with her over the Women's Institute.' 1959 *Journal of School of Scottish Studies* III 199. We need only consider how often in our daily lives we use such expressions as 'Touch wood'. 1987 Woman, 60 [London] Touching wood is absolutely *basic*. I go scurrying around looking for a piece of wood. You feel if you don't touch wood, the gods will wreak vengeance on you.

Cf. IRON, touching.

WOODEN LEG

1923 [Lyng, Som.] It is considered very lucky to walk out of your house in the morning and see a man with a wooden leg. Never look back after having passed him however, for that would bring a disappointment during the day. 1926 *Folklore* 364 [London] If a man with a wooden leg walks in front of you, there will be a surprise in store for you. 1954 Girl, 13 [Stoke-on-Trent, Staffs.] Some people believe that it is bad luck to see the back of a wooden leg before you see the front. 1982 Woman, c.55 [Middlesbrough, Teesside.] Unlucky to see the back of a wooden leg.

WORK, new place of: time of arrival

1883 BURNE *Shropshire* 274. It is unlucky for a maid to arrive at a new place as long as there is light enough to see to hang her bonnet up. So the most respectable young women are in the habit of trudging through dark muddy lanes to arrive at their destination just before the house is shut up for the night. 1932 C. IGGLESDEN *Those Superstitions* 169 [Sussex] [The new servant] seated herself stolidly on the box, just outside the front door, and on no account would she enter the house until the clock had struck twelve. To do so would bring disaster to the family as well as herself.

WOUND healed by tending weapon

1584 SCOT *Discoverie of Witchcraft* XII xx. They [witches] can remedie anie stranger, and him that is absent, with that verie sword wherewith they are wounded. Yea and that which is beyond all admiration, if they stroke the sword upwards with their fingers, the partie shall feele no paine: whereas if they drawe their finger downewards thereupon, the partie wounded shall feele intollerable paine. **1621** DEKKER *Witch of Edmonton* III iii. This follows now, To heal her wounds by dressing of the weapon. **1627** BACON *Sylva Sylvarum* § 998. It is constantly Received, and Avouched, that the Anointing of the Weapon, that maketh the Wound, will heale the Wound it selfe. **1640** GLAPTHORNE *Hollander* E4ᵛ–Fᵛ. This same salve will cure At any distance (as if the person hurt Should be at Yorke) the weapon, dress'd at London, On which the blood is. Tis the blood sticking to the sword atchieves The Cure; there is a reall simpathy Twixt it, and that which has the juyce of life, Moystens the body wounded. **1748** S. WERENFELS *Dissertation upon Superstition* 8. If the superstitious person be wounded by any chance, he applies the Salve, not to the Wound, but .. to the Weapon by which he received it. **1830** FORBY *East Anglia* 415. If a horse gets a nail in his foot, it must be kept bright after it is taken out, or the horse will not recover from his lameness. **1855** *N & Q* 1st ser. XII 37 [Cornwall] The fisherman, whose hand is wounded by a hook, is very careful to preserve that hook from rust during the healing of the wound. **1866** HENDERSON *Northern Counties* 125. When a Northumbrian reaper is cut by his sickle, it is not uncommon to clean and polish the sickle. Lately, in the village of Stamfordham, a boy hurt his hand with a rusty nail. The nail was immediately taken to a blacksmith to file off the rust, and was afterwards .. rubbed every day, before sunrise and after sunset .. thus the injured hand was perfectly healed. **1889** *N & Q* 7th ser. VIII 238. One of my brothers .. had the misfortune to have a hay-fork run through his arm. His old nurse .. fetched away the fork, that she might keep it bright until the wound healed; for she said if the fork got rusty the wound would 'take bad ways'. **1929** *Folklore* 120 [Norfolk] Another patient of his injured his hand on one of the spikes of a straw elevator; as he did not know which spike injured him, he greased them all. **1969** E. PORTER *Cambridgeshire* 78 [woman, 65, Cambridge; man, 73, Barrington] Whenever they cut, scratched or grazed themselves they always applied some iodine or a patent skin ointment to the wound, but, at the same time, never failed to apply it also to the knife, barbed wire or whatever was the cause of the trouble.

WREN, dead

1824 MACTAGGART *Gallovidian Encyclopedia* 157. Manx herring-fishers dare not go to sea without one of these birds, taken dead with them, for fear of disasters and storms. Their tradition is of a 'sea-sprit', that haunted the 'herring-tack', attended always by storms, and at last it assumed the figure of a wren and flew away. So they think when they have a dead wren with them, all is snug. **1911** J. CLAGUE *Manx Reminiscences* 13–15. The man who caught it [the wren] would be the great man of the day [St Stephen's Day], and it brought him good luck the whole year. The little bird was carefully kept, and brought on board the boat to the herrings (herring fishing) for good luck. Some of the feathers were given to other people, and some kept a feather in their purse.

WREN sacred

AD **77** PLINY *Natural History* X xcv (1855, II 551) There are antipathies between .. the eagle and the trochilus [golden-crested wren] because the latter has received the title of the 'king of the birds'. *c.***1508** SKELTON *Philip Sparowe* ll. 598–601. That Phyllyp may .. treade the prety wren, That is our Ladyes hen. **1770** G. SMITH *Pastorals* 30. And in the Barn a Wren has young ones bred, I never take away their Nest, nor try To catch the old ones, lest a Friend should die. Dick took a Wren's Nest from his Cottage side, And, ere a Twelvemonth past, his Mother dy'd! **1842**

R. CHAMBERS *Popular Rhymes of Scotland* 41. The puerile malediction upon those who rob the nest of the wren . . 'Malisons, malisons, mair than ten, That harry the Ladye of Heaven's hen!' **1951** *Sussex County Mag.* 75. He told me that if I ever took a Juggie's [wren's] egg I would be sure to get a crooked finger.

Also see ROBIN AND WREN sacred; ROBIN/WREN/MARTIN/SWALLOW sacred.

WREN'S NEST

1889 *Dorset Field Club* 28. Good luck if a 'cutty' [wren] builds in your hayrick.

WYCH ELM protects

1716 ADDISON *Drummer* II ii. He [the conjuror] had a long white Wand in his Hand. I fancy 'tis made out of Witch Elm. **1771** SMOLLETT *Humphry Clinker* (1943, 292) As for me, I put my trust in the Lord; and I have got a slice of witch elm sewed in the gathers of my under petticoat. **1958** *Farmer & Stockbreeder* 18 Mar. Suppl. N. 'The butter wunna come in that,' she said firmly. 'There's no wych elm in it, and anybody in their right senses knows as butter wunna gather unless there's wych elm in the churn.'

Y

YARROW: divination

1849 HALLIWELL *Popular Rhymes* 223. An ounce of yarrow, sewed up in flannel, must be placed under your pillow when you go to bed, and having repeated the following words, the required dream will be realized: 'Thou pretty herb of Venus' tree, Thy true name it is yarrow; Now who my bosom friend must be, Pray tell thou me to-morrow.' **1851** *N & Q* 1st ser. IV 99. Pluck yarrow from a young man's grave, saying as you do so— 'Yarrow, sweet yarrow, the first that I have found, And in the name of Jesus I pluck it from the ground. As Joseph loved sweet Mary, and took her for his dear, So in a dream this night, I hope my true love will appear.' Sleep with the yarrow under the pillow. **1869** *N & Q* 4th ser. IV 505 [Dublin serving-woman] On May Day, or on the preceding night, women put a stocking filled with yarrow under their pillow and recite .. 'Good morrow, good yarrow, good morrow to thee; I hope 'gain [by] the morrow my lover to see, And that he may be married to me; The colour of his hair, and the clothes he does wear; And if he be for me may his face be turned to me; And if he be not, dark and surly he may be, And his back be turned to me.' **1884** *Folklore* 90 [Co. Donegal] On May Eve the boys and girls cut out a square sod in which grows a yarrow, and put it under their pillow; if they have not spoken between the time of cutting the sod and going to sleep they will dream of their sweetheart. **1887** *Folk-Lore Record* 215 [Cornwall] Go into the fields at the time of the new moon and pluck a piece of herb yarrow; put it .. under your pillow, saying: 'Good night, fair yarrow, Thrice good night to thee; I hope before tomorrow's dawn My true love I shall see.' **1942** S. O'CASEY *Pictures in the Hallway* 42 [Dublin, *c*.1894] Jennie was bringing back with her a bundle of yarrow stalks .. He an' Jennie were to put nine of them under their pillows, and throw one over their left shoulders so he'd dream of his future wife and she'd dream of her future husband .. And when he was throwin' the yarrow stalk over his shoulder, he'd say, sing-song like, 'Good-morrow, good-morrow, fair Yarrow, Thrice good-morrow to thee! I hope, before this time tomorrow, You'll show my thrue to me.'

YARROW: nosebleed divination

1597 GERARD *Herball* 615. The leaves of yarrow being put into the nose do cause it to bleede, and easeth the pain of the megrim. **1616** Witchcraft trial, Orkney (*Maitland Club Misc.* II 189) Be plucking of the herb callit Merefow quhilk causis the nose bleid He [the Devil] haid taucht hir to tell quhatsoever sould be speirit at hir. **1830** FORBY *East Anglia* 424. Another plant of omen is the yarrow, called by us yarroway. The mode of divination is this: you must take one of the serrated leaves of the plant, and with it tickle the inside of the nostrils, repeating at the same time the following lines: 'Yarroway, yarroway, bear a white blow, If my love love me, my nose will bleed now.' **1878** *Folk-Lore Record* 156 [Suffolk] A leaf is placed in the nose, with the intention of making it bleed, while the .. lines are recited: 'Green 'arrow, green 'arrow, you bears a white blow, If my love love me, my nose will bleed now; If my love don't love me, it o'nt bleed a drop; If my love do love me, 'twill bleed every drop.'

Cf. NOSE bleeds: sign of affection.

YARROW protects

1872 *N & Q* 4th ser. X 25 [Ireland] I received .. a little packet from an old woman .. with an assurance that .. it would assuredly bring me luck, and I should escape the wiles of my enemies .. I found that the packet contained some dried yarrow .. I inquired .. in what its virtue consisted? She whispered .. that 'it was the first herb our Saviour put in his hand when a child.' **1969** E. PORTER *Cambridgeshire* 49. Old people ..

still [*c.*1900] credited yarrow with the power of averting evil spells; if the plant was strewn on the doorstep, no witch dared enter the house.

YAWN, last one to

1861 C. C. ROBINSON *Dialect of Leeds* 301. If two persons are seen to yawn one after the other, it is said that the one who yawned last bears no malice towards the one who yawned first.

YAWNING: crossing the mouth

1546 P. VERGIL *De Rerum Inventoribus* VI x (tr. Langley) Crossyng of our mouth. Alike deadly plage was sometyme in yawnyng, wherfore menne vsed to fence them selues with the signe of y[e] crosse .. which[e] custome we reteyne styl at this day. **1887** 'SPERANZA' WILDE *Superstitions of Ireland* II 104. When yawning make the sign of the cross instantly over the mouth, or the evil spirit will make a rush down and take up his abode within you. **1985** Woman, *c.*55 [London] You put your hand over your mouth when you yawn to stop the Devil getting in. That's why you always close a baby's mouth when it yawns.

Cf. SNEEZING: 'bless you'.

YEW at funerals

*c.*1601 SHAKESPEARE *Twelfe Night* II iv. Come away death .. My shrowd of white, stuck all with Ew, O prepare it. **1610** BEAUMONT & FLETCHER *Maid's Tragedy* II i. Lay a garland on my hearse, Of the dismal yew. **1648** HERRICK *Hesperides* 126 'To the Yew and Cypresse to Grace his Funerall'. Both you two have relation to the grave: And where The Fun'rall-Trump sounds, you are there. **1791** COLLINSON *History of Somersetshire* I 13. Our forefathers were particularly careful in preserving this funeral tree whose branches it was usual for mourners to carry in solemn procession to the grave, and afterwards to deposit therein under the bodies of their departed friends.

Cf. ROSEMARY at funerals.

YEW unlucky

1616 T. SCOT *Philomythie* pt. 2 B4b. The cursed Eldar and the fatall Yewe. **1663** COWLEY *Verses* 52. Beneath a Bow'r for sorrow made .. Of the black Yew's unlucky green. **1830** FORBY *East Anglia* 413. If you bring yew into the house at Christmas, amongst the other evergreens used to dress it, you will have a death in the family before the end of the year. **1923** [Somerset] Never take yew in a house, it is unlucky.

Select Bibliography

Books were published in London unless otherwise stated.

Abbotsford Club, Miscellany of the, Edinburgh, vol. 1, 1837.

Addy, Sidney Oldall. *Household Tales: with other traditional remains, collected in the Counties of York, Lincoln, Derby, and Nottingham*, 1895.

Allan, John Hay. *The Bridal of Caõlchairn and other poems*, 1822.

Archaeologia or, miscellaneous tracts relating to antiquity, Society of Antiquaries, 1773– .

Athenaeum, The. Articles and correspondence on folklore appeared in the volumes for 1846–9.

Athenian Mercury. The Athenian Gazette, no. 1, 17 Mar. 1690. Continued as *Athenian Mercury*, no. 2, 21 Mar. 1690–14 June 1697. Suppls.

Atkinson, J. C. *Forty Years in a Moorland Parish: reminiscences and researches in Danby in Cleveland*, 1891.

Aubrey, John. *Remaines of Gentilisme and Judaisme 1686–88*, ed. and annotated James Britten, 1881.

—— *Miscellanies*, 1696; 5th edn, enlarged 1890.

—— *The Natural History of Wiltshire 1656–91*, ed. John Britton, 1847.

Augustine, St, of Hippo. *De Doctrina Christiana*, tr. D. W. Robertson, 1958.

Bacon, Francis. *Sylva Sylvarum: or a naturall historie*, 1627.

Baker, Anne Elizabeth. *Glossary of Northamptonshire Words and Phrases*, 2 vols., 1854.

Baring-Gould, S. *The Vicar of Morwenstow*, new and revised edn., 1876.

—— *A Book of Dartmoor*, 1900.

—— *A Book of Folk-Lore*, Nation's Library series, 1913.

Bartholomaeus Anglicus. *De Proprietatibus Rerum*, tr. John Trevisa, c.1495.

Baxter, Richard. *The Certainty of the Worlds of Spirits*, 1691.

Bede, The Venerable, Saint. *Historia Ecclesiastica*, AD 731, tr. as *A History of the English Church and People*, by L. Sherley-Price, 1955.

Black, W. G. *Folk-Medicine: a chapter in the history of culture*, 1883.

Blagrave, Joseph. *Astrological Practice of Physick*, 1671.

Blakeborough, Richard. *Wit, Character, Folklore, and Customs of the North Riding of Yorkshire*, 1898.

Booth, J. B. *Pink Parade*, 1933.

Borlase, William. *Observations on the Antiquities, Historical and Monumental, of the County of Cornwall*, Oxford, 1754; 2nd edn., London, 1769.

—— *Observations on the Ancient and Present State of the Islands of Scilly*, Oxford, 1756.

—— *The Natural History of Cornwall*, Oxford, 1758.

Bourne, Henry. *Antiquitates Vulgares; or, the antiquities of the common people*, Newcastle, 1725.

Brady, John. *Clavis Calendaria: or, a compendious analysis of the calendar, illustrated with ecclesiastical, historical, and classical anecdotes*, 2 vols., 1812.

Brand, John. *Observations on Popular Antiquities: including the whole of Mr Bourne's Antiquitates Vulgares, with addenda to every chapter of that work: as also, an appendix, containing such articles on the subject as have been omitted by that author,* 1777.

—— *Observations on Popular Antiquities, chiefly illustrating the origin of our vulgar customs, ceremonies, and superstitions,* arranged and revised, with additions, by Henry Ellis, 2 vols., 1813; new edn. with further additions, 3 vols., 1849.

Bray, Mrs A. E. *Traditions, Legends, Superstitions, and Sketches of Devonshire ... in a series of letters to Robert Southey, Esq.,* 3 vols., 1838.

British Apollo or, curious amusements for the ingenious, 13 Feb. 1708–11 May 1711.

Brockett, John Trotter. *A Glossary of North Country Words,* Newcastle, 1825; repr. 1829; enlarged, 2 vols., 1846.

Browne, Sir Thomas. *Pseudodoxia Epidemica [Vulgar Errors]: or, enquiries into very many received tenets and commonly presumed truths,* 1646; enlarged 1650, 1658 (repr. 1669), 1672.

—— *Works,* ed. Simon Wilkin, 3 vols., 1852; ed. Geoffrey Keynes, 4 vols., 1964.

Burne, Charlotte Sophia. *Shropshire Folk-Lore: a sheaf of gleanings,* ed. from the collections of Georgina F. Jackson, 1883.

Burns, Robert. Notes to 'Halloween', in *Poems, chiefly in the Scottish dialect,* 1787.

Burton, Robert. *The Anatomy of Melancholy,* Oxford, 1621; augmented 1628, etc.; repr. London, 1652, 1660, etc.; repr. of 1660 edn. in 3 vols., 1893.

Butler, Samuel. *Hudibras.* The first part, 1663. The second part, 1664. The third and last part, 1678.

Bye-Gones, relating to Wales and the Border Countries, reprinted from Oswestry Advertiser, vols. 1–9, 1871–88; new series 1889–1913.

Calvert MS, *c.*1828, used by G. Home in *Evolution of an English Town* [Pickering, Yorkshire], 1915.

Camden, William. *Britannia,* 1586; tr. of the 1607 edn. by Richard Gough, enlarged, 3 vols., 1789.

Carew, Richard. *The Survey of Cornwall,* 1602.

Carleton, William. *Traits and Stories of the Irish Peasantry,* 2 vols., 1830; 2nd ser., 3 vols., 1833.

Celtic Magazine, Inverness, 13 vols., 1875–88.

Chambers, Robert. *The Popular Rhymes of Scotland,* Edinburgh, 1826; enlarged 1842, enlarged 1869.

—— *The Book of Days: a miscellany of popular antiquities, in connection with the calendar,* 2 vols., 1863, 1864.

Chrysostom, St John. *Baptismal Instructions,* ed. Paul W. Harkins, Ancient Christian Writers Series, 31, 1963.

—— *Homilies,* Library of the Fathers, 1842; repr. in 2 vols., 1851, 1852.

—— *Commentary on the Epistle to the Galatians and Homilies on the Epistle to the Ephesians,* Library of the Fathers, new edn., 1879.

Clare, John. *Poems Descriptive of Rural Life and Scenery,* 1820.

—— *The Shepherd's Calendar with village stories, and other poems,* 1827.

—— *The Poems of John Clare,* ed. J. W. Tibble, 2 vols., 1935.

Cockayne, Revd Oswald. *Leechdoms, Wortcunning, and Starcraft of Early England: being a collection of documents, for the most part never before printed, illustrating the history of science in this country before the Norman Conquest,* 3 vols., 1864–6.

Coleridge, Samuel Taylor. *The Notebooks of Samuel Taylor Coleridge,* ed. Kathleen Coburn *et al.,* 2 vols., 1957, 1961.

Coles, William. *The Art of Simpling,* 1656.

—— *Adam in Eden: or, Natures Paradise,* 1657.

Connoisseur, The. Ed. G. Colman and B. Thornton, 31 Jan. 1754–30 Sept. 1756; 1757; 1793.

Culpeper, Nicholas. *The English Physitian or an astrologo-physical discourse of the vulgar herbs of this nation*, 1652; enlarged 1653.

Dalyell, Sir John Graham. *The Darker Superstitions of Scotland, Illustrated from History and Practice*, Edinburgh, 1834.

Davies, J. Ceredig. *Folk-Lore of West and Mid-Wales*, 1911.

[Defoe, Daniel.] *History of the Life and Adventures of Mr Duncan Campbell*, 1720.

—— *Secret Memoirs of the late Mr D. Campbell*, 1732.

Denham, M. A. *Proverbs and Popular Sayings Relating to the Seasons*, 1846.

—— *The Denham Tracts 1846–59*, ed. J. Hardy, 2 vols., 1892, 1895.

Depositions and other Ecclesiastical Proceedings from the Courts of Durham from 1311 to the Reign of Elizabeth, Surtees Society no. 21, ed. J. Raine, 1845.

Depositions from the Castle of York to Offences in the Northern Countries in the seventeenth century, Surtees Society no. 40, ed. J. Raine, 1861.

Devonshire Association for the Advancement of Science, Literature, and Art, Transactions of the, 1862– .

Digby, Sir Kenelm. *A Late Discourse ... Touching the Cure of Wounds by the Powder of Sympathy*, 2nd edn. corrected and augmented, 1658.

—— *Choice and Experimented Receipts in Physick and Chirugery: translated out of several languages by G. H.*, 1668.

Dodoens, Rembert. *A Niewe Herball or Historie of Plantes*, tr. H. Lyte, 1578.

Dorset Natural History and Antiquarian Field Club, Proceedings of the, Sherborne, 1875–1928.

Drayton, Michael. *Poly-olbion: Or A Chorographicall Description of ... this renowned Isle of Great Britaine, With intermixture of the most Remarquable Stories, Antiquities ... of the same*, 1622.

—— [*Nymphidia.*] *The History of Queen Mab: or the court of fairy*, 1751.

Duncumb, John. *Collections towards the History and Antiquities of the County of Hereford*, 2 vols., 1804, 1812.

Dyer, T. F. Thiselton. *English Folk-Lore*, 1878; 2nd edn., 1880.

—— *Folk Lore of Shakespeare*, 1883.

—— *Church-lore Gleanings*, 1891.

Edinburgh Magazine, Edinburgh, 1818, Oct. pp. 326–7, Nov. pp. 410–14.

Elworthy, F. T. *The Evil Eye*, 1895.

Evans, George Ewart. *Ask the Fellows who Cut the Hay*, 1956.

—— and Thomson, David. *The Leaping Hare*, 1972.

Everlasting Fortune-Teller, The, Durham, 1839.

Folkard, Richard. *Plant Lore, Legends, and Lyrics*, 1884.

Folklore, the journal of the Folklore Society, 1878– . First published as *The Folk-Lore Record*, 5 vols., 1878–82.

Forby, Robert. *The Vocabulary of East Anglia*, 1830. Appendix, 'Popular Superstitions'.

Fosbroke, Revd T. D. *Ariconensia: or, archaeological sketches of Ross, and Archenfield*, 1821.

Frazer, Sir James George. *The Golden Bough: a study in comparative religion*, 2 vols., 1890; 2nd edn., 3 vols., 1900; 3rd edn., 12 vols., 1907–15. *Aftermath*, a supplement to *The Golden Bough*, 1936.

Gaule, John. *The Mag-astro-mances: or, the magicall- astrologicall-divines posed, and puzzled*, 1652.

Gay, John. *The Shepherd's Week: in six pastorals*, 1714.

—— *Fables*, 1727.

Gentleman's Magazine, The, 1731–1907.

Gerard, John. *The Herball, or Generall Historie of Plantes*, 1597; enlarged and amended by T. Johnson, 1633.

Gifford, George. *A Discourse of the Subtill Practises of Devilles by Witches and Sorcerers*, 1587.

—— *A Dialogue Concerning Witches*, 1593.

Gospelles of Dystaues, The, 1507.

Granville, Wilfred. *A Dictionary of Theatrical Terms*, 1952.

Gregor, Revd Walter. *Notes on the Folk-Lore of the North-East of Scotland*, 1881.

Grigson, Geoffrey. *The Englishman's Flora*, 1958.

Grose, Francis. *A Provincial Glossary; with a Collection of Local Proverbs, and Popular Superstitions*, 1787; 2nd edn., 1790.

—— *A Classical Dictionary of the Vulgar Tongue*, 2nd edn., 1788.

Hall, Joseph. *Characters of Vertues and Vices*, 1608.

Hampson, R. T. *Medii Ævi Kalendarium: or dates, charters, and customs of the Middle Ages*, 2 vols., 1841.

Harland, J., and Wilkinson, T. T. *Lancashire Folk-Lore*, 1867.

—— ——*Lancashire Legends, Traditions, Pageants, Sports, etc.*, 1873.

Hastings, James. *Encyclopaedia of Religion and Ethics*, 13 vols., 1908–26.

Havergal, F. T. *Herefordshire Words and Phrases*, 1887.

Hawker, Revd R. S., Vicar of Morwenstow, *see* Baring-Gould.

Henderson, William. *Notes on the Folk Lore of the Northern Counties of England and the Borders* [incorporating the Wilkie MS], 1866; new edn. with additions, 1879.

Herrick, Robert. *Hesperides: or, the works both humane & divine of Robert Herrick (His Noble Numbers ...)*, 1648.

Hewett, Sarah. *Nummits and Crummits: Devonshire customs, characteristics, and folklore*, 1900.

Higden, Ranulphus. *Polychronicon*, tr. John Trevisa *et al.*, *c.*1350. Rolls ser., 41.

Hill, Thomas. *Naturall and Artificiall Conclusions*, 1586; enlarged, 1650.

Homes, Nathaniel. *Daemonologie ... and Theologie*, 1650.

Hone, William. *The Every-Day Book*, 2 vols., 1826, 1827.

—— *The Table Book*, 1827.

—— *The Year Book*, 1831.

Hospinian, Rudolph. *Festa Christianorum*, 2nd edn., 1612.

Hunt, Robert. *Popular Romances of the West of England: or, the drolls, traditions, and superstitions of old Cornwall*, 2nd ser., 1865.

Hunter, Revd Joseph. MS notes in Brand's *Observations on Popular Antiquities*, 1813, 2 vols., British Library Addit. MSS 24544, 24545.

Hutchinson, William. *A View of Northumberland*, 2 vols., Newcastle, 1778.

I Walked by Night: being the life & history of the king of the Norfolk poachers written by himself, ed. L. Rider Haggard, 1935.

Igglesden, Sir Charles. *Those Superstitions*, 1932.

Jackson, Thomas. *A Treatise Containing the Originall of Unbeliefe, Misbeliefe or Misperswasions Concerning the ... Deitie*, 1625.

James I. *Daemonologie: in forme of a dialogue*, Edinburgh, 1597.

Jamieson, John. *An Etymological Dictionary of the Scottish Language*, 2 vols., 1808; Supplement, 2 vols., 1825.

Jefferies, Richard. *The Game Keeper at Home*, 1878.

—— *The Life of the Fields*, 1884.

Jeffrey, P. Shaw. *Whitby Lore and Legend*, 2nd edn., 1923; 3rd edn. revised, 1952.

John of Salisbury. *Frivolities of Courtiers and Footprints of Philosophers* [1st, 2nd, and 3rd books, and selections from 7th and 8th books, of the *Policraticus* of John of Salisbury], ed. Joseph B. Pike, 1938.

Jones, William. *Credulities Past and Present*, 1880.

Kearton, Richard. *At Home with Wild Nature*, 1922.

Kirk, Robert. *Secret Commonwealth: or, a treatise displaying the chiefe curiosities ... in use among ... the people of Scotland to this day*, etc., 1691; repr. in Edinburgh, 1815.

Knowlson, T. Sharper. *The Origins of Popular Superstitions, Customs, and Ceremonies*, 1910.

Lean, Vincent Stuckey. *Lean's Collectanea*, 4 vols., 1902–4.

Leather, Ella Mary. *The Folk-Lore of Herefordshire*, 1912.

Lemnius, Levinus. *The Secret Miracles of Nature*, 1658. First published in Antwerp in 1559.

Leofric Missal, The: as used in the Cathedral of Exeter, during the episcopate of its first Bishop, AD 1050–1072, Oxford, 1883.

Lore and Language, the journal of the Centre for English Cultural Tradition and Language, Sheffield, 1969– .

Lovett, Edward. *Magic in Modern London*, 1925.

—— *Folk-Lore & Legend of the Surrey Hills and of the Sussex Downs & Forest*, 1928.

Lupton, Thomas. *A Thousand Notable Things, of Sundry Sortes*, 1579; enlarged 1660.

Macgregor, Alexander. *The Prophecies of the Brahan Seer ... with an appendix on the superstition of the Highlanders*, Inverness, 1878.

Mactaggart, John. *The Scottish Gallovidian Encyclopedia: or, the original, antiquated, and natural curiosities of the south of Scotland*, 1824.

Maitland Club, Miscellany of the, Glasgow, 1834–47.

Mannyng, Robert, of Brunne. *Handlyng Synne*, ed. F. J. Furnivall, 2 vols., EETS original ser., 119 & 123, 1901, 1903.

Martin, Martin. *A description of the Western Islands of Scotland*, 1703.

Mather, Increase. *Cases of Conscience concerning Evil Spirits Personating Men*, 1693.

Melton, John. *Astrologaster, or the Figure-Caster*, 1620.

Miller, Hugh. *Scenes and Legends of the North of Scotland*, Edinburgh, 1835.

Misson, Henri. *Memoires et observations faites par un voyageur en Angleterre*, tr. J. Ozell, 1719.

Mitford, Mary Russell. *Our Village: sketches of rural character and scenery*, 5 vols., 1824–32.

Molle, John. *The Living Librairie*, 1621.

Moor, Edward. *Suffolk Words and Phrases*, 1823.

More, Hannah. *Tawney Rachel, or, the Fortune Teller: with some account of dreams, omens and conjurers*, by 'Z', Cheap Repository, c.1797.

Moresinus, Thomas. *Papatus: seu, depravatae religionis origo et incrementum*, Edinburgh, 1594.

Mother Bunch's Closet Newly Broke Open, 1685, ed. G. L. Gomme, 1885.

Mother Bunch's Golden Fortune-Teller, c.1840.

Myddvai, see *Physicians of Myddvai*.

N & Q, see *Notes and Queries*.

Napier, James. *Folk Lore: or, superstitious beliefs in the West of Scotland within this century*, Paisley, 1879.

Nigel de Longchamps. *A Mirror for Fools*, ed. J. H. Mozley, 1961.

Norfolk Archaeology, Norfolk and Norwich Archaeological Society, 1847– .

Notes and Queries: a medium of communication for literary men, artists, antiquaries, genealogists, etc., 1849– .

O'Halloran, Sylvester. *A General History of Ireland: from the earliest accounts to the close of the twelfth century*, 1778.

Opie, Iona and Peter. *The Lore and Language of Schoolchildren*, Oxford, 1959.

Ovid. *Ovids Festivalls, or Romane Calendar*, tr. J. Gower, 1640.

Oxford Dictionary of English Proverbs, compiled W. G. Smith, 3rd edn. ed. F. P. Wilson, 1970.

Parish, W. D. *A Dictionary of the Sussex Dialect*, 1875.

Park, Thomas, FSA. MS notes and additions in J. Brand's *Observations on Popular Antiquities*, 1777, British Library 810.e.4.

Parker, Henry. *A Compendyouse Treatyse Dyalogue of Dives and Pauper: that is to saye, the riche & the poore*, 1496.

Pennant, Thomas. *A Tour in Scotland*, 1769, Chester, 1771; 2nd edn., 1772.

—— *The Additions to the quarto edition of the Tour in Scotland, 1769, and the new appendix. Reprinted for the purchasers of the first and second editions*, 1774.

—— *A Tour in Scotland and Voyage to the Hebrides*, 2 vols., 1774–6. (The *Tour in Scotland* is as 1771. The *Voyage to the Hebrides*, which he undertook in the summer of 1772, occupies pp. 157–369 of vol. I.)

Pepys, Samuel. *The Diary of Samuel Pepys*, ed. R. Latham and W. Matthews, 11 vols., 1970–83 (vol. 11 is the Index).

Perkins, William. *Works*, 3 vols., 1616–18.

Pettigrew, Thomas Joseph. *On Superstitions Connected with the History and Practice of Medicine and Surgery*, 1844.

Physicians of Myddvai; Meddygon Myddfai: or the medical practice of ... Rhiwallon and his sons, tr. J. Pughe, Llandovery, 1861.

Pitcairn, Robert. *Criminal Trials in Scotland, from AD 1488 to AD 1624 ... compiled from the original records and MSS*, Edinburgh, 3 vols., 1833.

Pliny, the Elder. *The Natural History of Pliny*, tr. J. Bostock and H. T. Riley, 6 vols., 1855–7.

Poor Robin's Almanack, ed. William Winstanley and others, 1664–1776.

Porter, Enid. *Cambridgeshire Customs and Folklore*, 1969.

Radford, E. and M. A. *Encyclopaedia of Superstitions*, 1948; ed. and revised by Christina Hole, 1961.

Ramesey, William. *Elminthologia: or, some physical considerations of the matter, origination and several species of wormes*, 1668.

Ramsay, John. *Scotland and Scotsmen in the Eighteenth Century from the MSS of John Ramsay*, ed. A. Allardyce, 2 vols., 1888.

Reliquiæ Antiquæ, see Wright, Thomas.

Rhys, John. *Celtic Folklore: Welsh and Manx*, Oxford, 2 vols., 1901.

Robinson, C. C. *The Dialect of Leeds, and its Neighbourhood*, 1861.

Robinson, F. K. *A Glossary of Yorkshire Words and Phrases: collected in Whitby and the neighbourhood*, 1855.

Rogers, Charles. *Social Life in Scotland*, Edinburgh, 3 vols., 1884–6.

Royal Anthropological Institute of Great Britain and Ireland, Journal of the, 1871– .

Royal Irish Academy, Proceedings of the, Dublin, 1837–70.

Rudkin, Ethel H. *Lincolnshire Folklore*, 1936.

Salmon, William. *Pharmacopoeia Londinensis, or the New London Dispensatory*, tr. W. Salmon, 1678.

Saxby, Jessie M. E. *Shetland Traditional Lore*, 1932.

Scot, Reginald. *The Discoverie of Witchcraft*, 1584.

Scott, Sir Walter. *Letters on Demonology and Witchcraft*, 1830.

Scottish Studies, Journal of the School of, University of Edinburgh, 1957– .

Shaw, James, of Tynron, Dumfriesshire. *A Country Schoolmaster, James Shaw*, ed. R. Wallace, Edinburgh, 1899.

Shaw, Lachlan. 'Of Elgin and the Shire of Murray', in T. Pennant's *Additions to ... the Tour in Scotland, 1769, 1774*, appendix 2.

—— *The History of the Province of Moray*, Edinburgh, 1775.

Sikes, William Wirt. *British Goblins: Welsh Folk-Lore, Fairy Mythology, Legends and Traditions*, 1880.

Sinclair, George. *Satans Invisible World Discovered*, Edinburgh, 1685.

Southey, Robert. *Letters from England*, 3 vols., 1807.

Sprenger, J., and Kramer, H. *Malleus Maleficarum*, tr. Montague Summers, 1928.

Statistical Account of Scotland: drawn up from the communications of the ministers of the different parishes, Sir John Sinclair, Edinburgh, 21 vols., 1791–9.

Swift, Jonathan. [*Polite Conversation.*] *A Complete Collection of Genteel and Ingenuous Conversation ... in three dialogues*, by 'Simon Wagstaff Esq.', 1738.

Theocritus. *The Idylliums of Theocritus*, tr. T. Creech, 1684.

Theophrastus. *The Characters of Theophrastus*, ed. R. G. Ussher, 1960.

Thomas, Keith. *Religion and the Decline of Magic: studies in popular beliefs in sixteenth- and seventeenth-century England*, 1971.

Thompson, C. J. S. *The Hand of Destiny: the folk-lore and superstitions of everyday life*, 1932.

Thompson, Flora. *Lark Rise*, 1939.

—— *Over to Candleford*, 1941.

—— *Candleford Green*, 1943.

Thrale, Mrs. *The diary of Mrs H. L. Thrale*, ed. K. C. Balderston, 2 vols., 1951.

Time's Telescope: or a complete guide to the almanack, 23 vols., 1814–34.

Toland, John. *Critical History of the Celtic Religion ... containing an account of the Druids, c.*1740; ed. R. Huddleston, 1814.

Topsell, Edward. *The Historie of Foure-footed Beastes*, 1607.

Train, Joseph. *Strains of the Mountain Muse*, Edinburgh, 1814.

—— *An Historical and Statistical Account of the Isle of Man*, Douglas: Isle of Man, 2 vols., 1845.

Trevelyan, Marie. *Folk-Lore and Folk-Stories of Wales*, 1909.

Turner, William. *A Compleat History of the most Remarkable Providences*, 1697.

Tusser, Thomas. *A Hundreth Good Pointes of Husbandrie*, 1557.
—— *Five Hundreth Points of Good Husbandry*, 1573.

Uttley, Alison. *Country Things*, 1946.
—— *A Year in the Country*, 1957.
—— *The Swans Fly Over*, 1959.

Vallancey, Charles. *Collectanea de Rebus Hibernicus*, Dublin, 6 vols., 1770–1804.
Vergil, Polydore. *Three Books of Polydore Vergil's English History*, ed. Sir H. Ellis, 1844.
—— *An Abridgement of the Notable Worke of Polidore Vergile*, tr. T. Langley, 1546. Includes *De Rerum Inventoribus*.
Vickery, Roy. *Unlucky Plants: a folklore survey*, 1985.
Virgil. [*Eclogues.*] *The Pastoral Poems*, tr. E. V. Rieu, 2 vols., Harmondsworth, 1949.

Waldron, George. *The History and Description of the Isle of Man*, 1744.
Werenfels, Samuel. *A Dissertation upon Superstition in Natural Things*, 1748.
White, Gilbert. *The Natural History of Selborne*, ed. R. Jefferies, 1887.
Wilde, Lady 'Speranza' [mother of Oscar Wilde]. *Ancient Legends, Mystic Charms, and Superstitions of Ireland*, 2 vols., 1887.
Wilkie MS, *c.*1816. A collection of Border customs, legends, and superstitions. *See* Henderson.
Wright, A. R. *English Folklore*, 1928.
Wright, Ann. *Folk Lore of Holderness*, Hedon and District Local History Society, N. Humberside, 1978.
Wright, Elizabeth Mary. *Rustic Speech and Folk-Lore*, 1913.
Wright, Thomas, and Halliwell, James Orchard. *Reliquiæ Antiquæ: scraps from ancient manuscripts, illustrating chiefly early English literature and the English language*, 2 vols., 1841, 1843.

Yonge, Charlotte Mary. *An Old Woman's Outlook in a Hampshire Village*, 1892.
—— *John Keble's Parishes: a history of Hursley and Otterbourne*, 1898.
Young, Revd George. *A History of Whitby and Streoneshalh Abbey*, Whitby, 2 vols., 1817.

Analytical Index

THE Index is composed of two sorts of entry: (i) Cross references to entries in the Dictionary (which are distinguished by small capitals) or to the Index itself. (ii) Thematic entries in which the superstitions are grouped according to an underlying concept which they share. This concept is briefly stated in the heading after the colon, e.g. touching: magic transmitted by contact. Attention is also directed, at the end of the lists, to related themes within the Index.

The thematic entries are intended to show how superstitions, often concerning different subjects and circumstances, are linked by these concepts, and also the relationships that exist among the themes themselves. There are also some cross-references within the text of the Dictionary where these were felt to be helpful.

adder see SNAKE
adder stone see SNAKE STONE
ague see fevers etc.
altar see COMMUNION table/altar; KNEE itches; MARRIED COUPLE: first to die; STUMBLING reveals guilt. Cf. church building; table, sacred
amulets see wearing/carrying things
anger see quarrels/anger
animals/reptiles/fishes and parts or products of: magical see ANIMAL; ASH TREE protects against snakes; BAT; BLACK Devil's colour; BLACK SHEEP; BLADE-BONE; BRIDE feeds cat; CAT; CAT OR DOG; CLERGYMAN'S WIFE gives luck in horses; CLOVER as protection; COW; CRAMP BONE; DALMATIAN DOG; DEATH: dying creature; DOG; DONKEY; EEL-SKIN; EGGS dangerous to horses; ELEPHANT; EXCREMENT; FERRET; FIRST ANIMALS; FIRST ANIMALS/ BIRDS; FIRST-FOOT: animal or person first encountered; FISH; FISHING; FOOD, giving away; FROG; GOAT; HARE; HARE OR RABBIT; HARE-LIP; HEART stuck with pins; HERRING(S); HORSE/HORSEMAN; LEATHER; LIONESS etc.; LIONS; LIZARD; LUCKY-BONE; MAY, born in; MIRROR, looking in: cat; MOLE; MOONWORT; MOUSE; NEW YEAR din; NUNS; PIEBALD HORSE; PIG; PLOUGH, crossing path of; 'RAT' AND 'MOUSE'; RATS AND MICE; SALMON; SHEEP; SHOES, old: burning; SHOES, turned: stop dog howling; SHREW; SNAIL; SNAKE; SPITTLE kills snakes; STONE with hole; STRAW, animal brings a; TEETH, disposing of; TEETHING amulet; TOAD OR FROG; TOADSTONE; TONGUE, tip of; URINE: iron nails etc. in patient's urine to detect witch; WARTS cured with meat; WARTS cured with snail; WEASEL; WHISTLING WOMAN AND CROWING HEN; WHITE; WOMAN crosses water. Also see bones; livestock; pied; transference
anticipating/tempting fate: unlucky see BABY,

referring to; BOAT, new: naming before launching; BRIDE not to be seen by bridegroom; BRIDE'S CLOTHES: wedding dress, bride tries on completed; BRIDE'S CLOTHES: wedding dress not to be seen by bridegroom; BRIDESMAID too many times; CALENDAR showing future date; CHRISTENING ROBE, buying; CHRISTMAS CAKE, cutting and eating; CHRISTMAS CANDLE; CHRISTMAS DECORATIONS (evergreens): bringing in before Christmas; CRADLE; EASTER: new clothes; ENGAGED COUPLE; ENGAGEMENT RING; MARRIAGE BANNS, hearing own; MARRIAGE SERVICE, reading; MINCE PIES eaten before Christmas; 'PALM' unlucky in house before Palm Sunday; PRAM; SINGING before breakfast; THEATRE: bouquet; THEATRE: curtain. Cf. unseasonableness/untimeliness
anvil see blacksmith
apparitions see BLADE-BONE: spell; BURIAL: last person buried; CABBAGE STALK: divination; CANDLE burns blue; CANDLE, pricking: spell; CHIME CHILD; CHRISTMAS, born at; CHURCH PORCH, watching in; CORPSE carried feet first; CORPSE: speaking of the dead; DISHES, three: divination; DOOR, changing; DUMB CAKE; FIRST-BORN; FUNERAL: room rearranged; FUNERAL: route changed; HAIR thrown into fire: divination of future husband; HEMP SEED: divination; KNOTS in shroud/clothes of dead; MIRROR; MOTH/BUTTERFLY omen of death; NEW MOON: divination; PINS, corpse's; ROSE: divination; SAGE: divination; ST JOHN'S WORT; SALT protects at death; SHIFT/SMOCK etc., apparition turns; SKULL cures; SUPPER, apparition comes to share; THREAD, winding: divination; WINNOWING CORN: divination. Also see Devil/demons/evil spirits; spirit/soul of dead
APRON also see clothes/bedclothes

arching over *see* stepping/treading on, or stepping/leaping/arching over

ASHES *also see* DIRT lucky; NEW YEAR and house/home: nothing to be taken out

B

babies/children: *see* ASH TREE, child passed through; BABY; BIBLE protects; BIRCH TREE; BREAD cures and protects; BROOM (plant), whipping with; BUCKET, jumping over; CAT endangers health; CHILDREN; CHRISTENING; CORAL; CRADLE; DOOR, front; EXCREMENT, baby's first; FIRE protects child; FIRST-BORN; FIRST-FOOT on way to christening; FRIDAY butter and eggs; FROG, live: in patient's mouth; GODPARENTS; GOOD FRIDAY beneficial; GOOSEBERRY BUSH, babies found under; GRAVE: treading on grave of stillborn/unchristened child; GROANING CHEESE; GROANING CHEESE OR CAKE; IRON in cradle or childbed; MARRIAGE BANNS, hearing own; MARRIAGE SERVICE, baby cries during; MAY; MEASURING child; MIRROR, looking in: baby; MOON affects birth; MOONLIGHT, charm against baleful effects of; MOTHER-DIE; NAILS AND HAIR: cures/spells; NAILS AND HAIR, cutting: baby's; NAMING baby; PARSLEY BED, babies found in; PENDULUM: divination; POSTHUMOUS CHILD; PRAISING; PRAM; PRECOCIOUSNESS; SALT protects baby/child; SEVENTH CHILD; SLEEPING north/south; SNEEZE, baby's first; SPITTLE protects baby; STEPPING OVER; STORK; TEETH, born with; TEETH, cutting; TEETH, disposing of; TEETHING; THRUSH (ulcers in mouth); VIRGIN first to hold baby; WALKING backwards; WATER, holy; WEDDING CAKE: part kept; WEIGHING; WILLOW STICK; YAWNING: crossing the mouth. *Also see* birth, predictions; childbirth; church ceremonies/sacraments; clothes/bedclothes; divination (love/marriage/children); pregnancy

back/front or tail/head of magical creature/object: inauspicious/auspicious *see* CAT, black: seeing back of; CHIMNEY SWEEP, meeting; DAFFODIL, head of; ELEPHANT ORNAMENT must face door; FIRST ANIMALS in spring: facing observer; FIRST PLOUGH in spring: coming towards one; HAY, load of; MAIL VAN; MONEY, finding; NEEDLE, dropping; NEW MOON: divination; NUNS; PARTING: watching out of sight; PIEBALD HORSE, seeing tail of; WOODEN LEG. *Cf.* finishing/not finishing

backache *see* rheumatism/gout/lumbago

backwards (doing things in contrary way): associated with witchcraft *see* BABY looks between legs; BED, getting out of: backwards; BIRTH, breech; BLADE-BONE: spell; DISHES, three: divination; DUMB CAKE; GRAVE cures incontinence; HEART stuck with pins: lover's spell; KNOTS in garters: divination; NAMES, divination with; NEW MOON: divination by diffusion; PIEBALD HORSE, meeting; POURING; PRAYERS said backwards; ROSE: divination; SALT HERRING: divination; THREAD, winding: divination; WALKING backwards; WEDDING CAKE: divination. *Cf.* sunwise/anti-sunwise; throwing/spitting backwards; turning/looking back

barefoot *see* FOOT, bare

beans/peas: associated with magic *see* BEAN: divination; BEAN BLOSSOMS; LAST FOOD/DRINK: 'Carling' peas; MOLUCCA BEAN; MOON affects sowing and harvesting; PANCAKES; PEAS, nine: divination; WARTS cured with bean pod; WARTS 'thrown away'

BED *also see* DEATH: standing in front of the dying; PIGEON'S FEATHERS, lying on; UMBRELLA on bed. *Also see* clothes/bedclothes; sleep; sleeping

bed-wetting *see* GRAVE cures incontinence; MOUSE cures bed-wetting

bee, bumble *see* BUMBLE BEE

BEES *also see* insects; livestock

beginning: vulnerable to evil influences *see* BROOM thrown for luck; CHILDERMAS DAY; FRIDAY, beginning anything on; MONDAY auspicious/inauspicious; SATURDAY, beginning on; SHOES, old: thrown etc. for luck; STUMBLING ominous; TURNING BACK; WORK, new place of: time of arrival. *Cf.* first things/occasions

bell *see* CHURCH BELL. *Also see* church building/appurtenances; noise/din

Beltane *see* May-time

BIBLE *also see* church building/appurtenances

birds and eggs: sacred/magical/ominous *see* ALBATROSS; ASCENSION DAY, egg laid on; BIRD, dead; BIRDS' EGGS; COCK; COCK AND HEN; CROWS OR RAVENS; CUCKOO; DOVE; DUCK OR GOOSE; EAGLE-STONE; EASTER: new clothes; EGG[S]; EGGSHELL[S]; EXCREMENT: birds' droppings; FEATHER; FEVER cured by transference; FIRST ANIMALS/BIRDS; GABRIEL'S HOUNDS/SEVEN WHISTLERS; GOOD FRIDAY, egg laid on; GOOSE; GUINEA FOWL; HAIR: disposing of combings/cuttings; HEN; HERON; JACKDAW; KINGFISHER; LARK; MAGPIE; MAY, born in: duckling; NIGHTINGALE; OWL; PEACOCK; PENDULUM: divination; PIGEON; RAVEN; ROBIN; ROBIN AND WREN; ROBIN/

C

cakes/puddings/pies: used in magic *see* BABY, referring to; BREAD: loaf, cake, etc. breaks; BURIAL CAKE; CANDLE, failing to blow out (on birthday-cake); CHARMS in food; CHRISTENING CAKE; CHRISTMAS CAKE; CHRISTMAS DECORATIONS (evergreens): burning on Shrove Tuesday; CHRISTMAS PUDDING; CROOKED STICK; DUMB CAKE; FIRST-FOOT on way to christening; FRIDAY butter and eggs; MINCE PIES; PANCAKE; PUDDING; SOUL CAKE; SUNWISE, stirring; URINE in cake; WASSAILING cornfields and cattle; WEDDING CAKE. *Cf.* bread; food/drink. *Also see* divination (love/marriage/children); wishing

CANDLE *cf.* fire

candlelight *see* night

car *see* BABY: bringing home in car; CAT, black: meeting; EXCREMENT: birds' droppings; GREEN unlucky; RACING CAR; RED CARS lucky; THREAD tied round; WOMAN, meeting

cards *see* CARDS; CHAIR turned or changed for luck; CROOKED PIN; CROSSING LEGS for luck; HANGMAN'S ROPE lucky to card players; RED lucky to card players; SUNDAY: keeping Sabbath holy: transgressors punished; WOOD: going against grain

changing *see* turning round/over, or changing

charms, verbal *see* AMBULANCE, seeing; APPLE PIPS, squeezing: divination; ASH TREE protects against snakes; BLADE-BONE: spell; BLEEDING, charm to staunch; BURN OR SCALD, charm for; BUTTER, charm for; CANDLE, pricking: spell; CIGARETTE PACKET; CRAMP, verbal charm for; CROSS, making sign of: cures and protects; FEVER, verbal charm for; HICCUP, cures for; IVY LEAF: divination; KNOTS in garters: divination; LADYBIRD flies to lover; MAGPIE, meeting: and actions to avert evil; MOONLIGHT, charm against baleful effects of; NETTLE STING, charm for; PIEBALD HORSE, meeting; PREGNANT WOMEN, two; RAIN, charm against; RAINBOW, charm against; RATS AND MICE, riddance to; RINGWORM, charm for; ST AGNES'S EVE/DAY; ST CATHERINE; SALT, burning; SPEAKING at same time; STONE with hole; TEETH, disposing of; THORN in flesh; THRUSH (ulcers in mouth) cured with psalm; TOOTHACHE; VERVAIN, powers of; VIRGIN heals; WATER, running: cures; WHITE HORSE. *Cf.* speaking

chilblains/corns *see* HOLLY cures chilblains; MOON affects growth: hair/nails/corns; MOUSE, other cures using

childbirth/labour *see* AFTERBIRTH, burning:

divination; BABY protected by parent's garment; BED-MAKING: turning mattress/changing sheets at 'dangerous' times; BIRDS' EGGS in house; BIRTH, breech; BIRTH, opening locks eases; CAUL, possession of: lucky; CHURCH BELL cures; CHURCHING after childbirth; CORAL; CROSSING LEGS hinders birth; EAGLE-STONE; HORSE'S [OR DONKEY'S] HOOF; KNOTS hinder birth; LIONESS; MOLUCCA BEAN; MOON affects birth; PREGNANT WOMEN, two; SNAKE SLOUGH/SKIN eases childbirth; TIDE affects birth; TOADSTONE; URINE protects; WIFE, unfaithful

CHILDREN *also see* babies/children; marriage/courtship/children

chimney/chimney place *see* fire; threshold

CHRISTENING *also see* babies/children; church ceremonies/sacraments

CHRISTMAS *also see* New Year/Christmas

church building/appurtenances: magical associations *see* BIBLE; BOOK: opening at random; CHRISTMAS DECORATIONS (evergreens) from church; CHURCH; CLOCK strikes during hymn; CLOCK strikes while church bells are ringing; CROSS cures; HAT worn in church; HOUSE, moving; IRON taboo on sacred occasions; IVY picked off church; KNEE itches; MISTLETOE, kissing under; MISTLETOE protects; NAILS AND HAIR, cutting: baby's; NEW YEAR din; NORTH door of church; ONION: divination and spells; PETTING STONE; ROOM, upper; SUNWISE as 'sacred' ritual; SWORD AND SCABBARD: divination; WATER, holy

church ceremonies/sacraments: magical power *see* BLOOD: shedding at funeral; BREAD cures and protects; CHRISTENING; CHURCHING; COMMUNION; CONFIRMATION; CORPSE, unburied; FIRST-FOOT on way to christening; GODPARENTS, healing powers of; GRAVE: treading on grave of stillborn/unchristened child; MARRIAGE SERVICE; NAMING baby before christening; RING made of blessed money/silver: cures; SALT protects against witch or evil spirits. *Cf.* blessing; corpse; cross; marriage/wedding

church festivals/holy days: influence for good or ill *see* ASCENSION DAY; ASHES, footprint in; BLACKBERRIES not to be eaten after Michaelmas; BURIAL, symbolic: counteracts Whitsuntide birth; CANDLE, holy: cures and protects; CHARMS in food; CHILDERMAS DAY; CHRISTMAS; CHRISTMAS DECORATIONS (evergreens): burning on Shrove Tuesday; CHRISTMAS DECORATIONS (evergreens etc.), taking down; CUCKOO, first: on Easter morning; DUMB CAKE; EASTER; EGG, first; GOOD FRIDAY; GOOSE eaten on Michaelmas Day;

strike together; CONVERSATION, lull in; NAMES, magical: married couple with same surname; SPEAKING at same time

coins see money/coins

colds see fevers etc.

colours: significant/magical see AURORA BOREALIS; BLUE protects; BRIDE'S CLOTHES: 'something blue'; BRIDE'S CLOTHES: wedding dress, colour of; BUMBLE BEE in house = stranger; BUTTERFLY, first: colour of; CANDLE burns blue; CORAL; CUCKOO, first: divination with hair; EGG, first; FIRE, behaviour of: blue flames in; FLOWERS: red and white together; GREEN; HAND, yellow spots on; IONA STONE; IVY LEAF: divination; KNOTS in garters; LEAVES: spell and divination; MAY BLOSSOM in house; MEASURING cures; MOLUCCA BEAN; MOTHER-DIE; NAILS: specks on finger nails; OPAL; PLANTAIN: divination; RED; ROSE: divination; SHEPHERD'S PURSE; THEATRE: colours; WEDDING CAKE, making. Also see black; pied; white

COMMUNION also see church ceremonies/sacraments

confetti see WHEAT/RICE/CONFETTI thrown for luck

CONFIRMATION also see church ceremonies/sacraments

consumption see BURIAL, symbolic: cure; CHURCHYARD, grass etc. from; COW cures consumption; DONKEY cures: passing under; GREENERY, circle of; MAY a dangerous month; MAY, leaving off clothes in; MUGWORT cures female ailments; NAILS AND HAIR: cures/spells; SHEEP, flock of: cures

continuity/preservation: of sacred/protective object see 'BUSH', burning; CATTLE: carcass hung in chimney to protect livestock; CHAMPAGNE CORK; CHRISTMAS CANDLE; CHRISTMAS LOG/ASHEN FAGGOT: piece kept for luck/protection; CORN DOLLY hung up in house; CROOKED COIN; EGG, first; GOOD FRIDAY, bread made on: protects; HANDSEL MONDAY; HOPS kept for luck; MAY BOUGHS AND FLOWERS; MISTLETOE protects; MONEY, having: in purse etc.; 'PALM' protects; SKULL unlucky to move; SOUL CAKE; THORN TREE protects; WEDDING CAKE: part kept. Cf. interruption/impediment; wearing/carrying

convulsions see epilepsy/fits/convulsions

cooking see burning/boiling/melting/roasting

CORAL also see stones/beads

corns see chilblains/corns

corpse: the dead are feared/revered see ASHES, footprint in; BED: foot towards door; BEES, lifting/turning; BLOOD: shedding at funeral; BODY: locating in water; BRIDE, sun shines on; BURIAL; CANDLE, funeral: cures and protects; CAT OR DOG passes over corpse; CHURCHING after funeral; CLOCK is stopped at death; CLOTHES of the dead; COFFIN; CORPSE; DEATH: opening locks/doors frees spirit; DISHES, three: divination; DOOR, back; DOOR, front; EXHUMATION; FIRE extinguished in presence of corpse; FUNERAL; GALLOWS; GRAVE; HANGMAN'S ROPE; HEARSE; KNOTS in shroud/clothes of dead; MIRROR covered in sick room; MURDER; PINS, corpse's; ROOKS leave after a death; ROSEMARY at funerals; ST SWITHIN; SALT protects at death; SKULL; SUNWISE, corpse goes; THIMBLE; WARTS 'given' to corpse; WATER, running: ford 'where dead and living cross'; YEW accompanies corpse. Also see church ceremonies/sacraments; death/dying

countercharms (defenses against evil) see blessing; cross; propitiation; spittle/spitting; stepping/treading on, or stepping/leaping/arching over; throwing at/after/over; throwing/ spitting backwards, over shoulder; touching; turning round/over, or changing; wearing/carrying

counting/measuring/weighing: magical/dangerous effects see BALL: divination; BUTTONS OR FRUIT STONES: divination; CHURCH BELL foretells length of incumbency; CLERGYMAN: divination; COUNTING; CUCKOO; MEASURING; STARS, pointing at/counting; TEA-LEAF OR STALK; THUNDER AND LIGHTNING, drawing attention to; WARTS 'thrown away'; WEIGHING. Also see divination (multiple/other); numbers; pointing

courtship see marriage/courtship/children

cowslip ball see BALL, cowslip: divination

CRADLE also see BABY'S CLOTHES/CRADLE; IRON in cradle. Also see sleep

cramp/stitch/pins and needles see COFFIN, parts of; CORK cures cramp; CRAMP; CRAMP BONE; CROSS, making sign of: cures; EEL-SKIN GARTERS prevent cramp/rheumatism; HARE'S OR RABBIT'S FOOT cures; IRON cures; IVY-WOOD CUP; RING made of blessed money; SHOES, turned: cure cramp; SHOES/STOCKINGS in form of cross; WATER under bed. Also see rheumatism/gout/lumbago etc.

crookedness: protective/lucky see CROOKED. Cf. turning round/over, or changing

crops, success of see BLOOD, shedding first; 'BUSH', burning; CHRISTMAS DECORATIONS (evergreens): burning; CORN DOLLY; CROOKED FURROW; FIRE protects cattle and crops; FIRST FRUITS AND FLOWERS; FIRST FURROW; GOOD FRIDAY, ploughing on; GUINEA FOWL; HAY, load of; HOPS kept for luck; LUCK-PENNY;

crops (*cont.*):

MONDAY auspicious/inauspicious; MOON affects sowing and harvesting; PALM SUNDAY; PLOUGH; SALT as propitiation; SOWING; STRAW; SUNWISE round farm; WASSAILING. *Also see* fertility

creases: in linen *see* TABLECLOTH/SHEET, creases in

cross: power to cure/protect, frequently made by crossing fingers *see* ASH TREE protects against storm and witchcraft; BAY/LAUREL LEAVES: divination; BIRCH TREE; BREAD cures and protects; CHRISTENING: unchristened baby dangerous; CORN DOLLY; CROSS; CROSSED FINGERS; CROSSING LEGS; DALMATIAN DOG; DONKEY; EGGSHELL, piercing or crushing; ELDER protects against lightning; 'FAIRY' taboo word; FIRE blackens chalk mark: cure for ague; FUNERAL, meeting: and actions to avert evil; GOOD FRIDAY, bread made on; GRAVE, pregnant woman treads on; HARE OR RABBIT, meeting; HICCUP, cures for; IRON taboo on sacred occasions; LADDER, walking under; LEAD shapes in water: divination of cause of sickness; LUCKY-BONE; MAGPIE, meeting; MAY BOUGHS AND FLOWERS; MOLE: cures/spells; MONEY, having: in purse etc.; NEW MOON: divination; 'PALM' protects; PETTING STONE; PIEBALD HORSE, meeting; PINS get rid of warts; POKER against grate; RAILWAY BRIDGE/TUNNEL; RAINBOW, 'crossing out'; SHAKING HANDS across people; SHOES/STOCKINGS in form of cross; SHREW an evil creature; SILVER, crossing palm with; SNAKE, meeting; SPOONS, two; SUNWISE as 'sacred' ritual; WASHING HANDS together; WEASEL; WHITE CAT; WOMAN, meeting; YAWNING: crossing the mouth. *Cf.* church building/appurtenances

cross eyes *see* EYES, peculiar

crossing/across (path/road, beams/floorboards, knives, etc.): ominous *see* ANIMAL, four-legged: meeting; BED across floorboards or ceiling-beam; BEES cross running water; CAT = witch; CAT, black: meeting; CHURCHING after childbirth: woman must not cross road; CRIPPLE, meeting; CROWS OR RAVENS ominous; FOOT, bare; GABRIEL'S HOUNDS/SEVEN WHISTLERS; HARELIP; HARE OR RABBIT, meeting; KNIFE laid across; LIZARD, meeting; MAGPIE, meeting; PAVEMENT, stepping on lines/cracks in; PIG, meeting; PLOUGH, crossing path of; RACING CAR; RATS AND MICE, influx of; SHAKING HANDS across people; SHREW crosses road or path; SLEEPING north/south; STAIRS, crossing on; STILE, two going through; STRAW magic; TOAD OR FROG,

meeting; WATER, running: crossing over; WATER, running: ford 'where dead and living cross'; WEASEL; WHITE CAT; WOMAN crosses water. *Cf.* ground/earth; stepping/treading on, or stepping/leaping/arching over

crossroads/boundaries: strategic places, associated with magic *see* DONKEY cures: passing under; EARTH, hole in: divination; FEVER cured by transference and decay; FIRE protects cattle and crops; PARISHES; SKULL, eating or drinking from: cures; WARTS cured with elder wood; WARTS 'thrown away'. *Cf.* ground/earth

crying/tears *see* BIRD sings unseasonably; BIRTHDAY, crying on; BRIDE cries on wedding day; CHRISTENING, baby cries during; tears falling on; EYE itches; HANDKERCHIEF = tears; LAUGHING too much; MARRIAGE SERVICE, baby cries during; NEW YEAR activities set precedent; PEARLS = tears; PIN, finding; SALT, spilling; SINGING before breakfast; SUNDAY, crying on

cure-alls *see* AMBER; ASH TREE benign; BLACKSMITH; BLUE protects; BRAMBLE ARCH; BURIAL, symbolic: cure; CAT, black: cures; CHRISTENING as protection for baby; CHURCH, dust from; CHURCHYARD, grass etc. from; 'COAL' magic; COFFIN, parts of; COMMUNION; CORPSE'S HAND cures; CROSS cures; CAT OR DOG, disease transferred to; DONKEY; ELDER protects against and cures disease; FISH, live; FROG[S]; GOAT on farm; GOLD; 'GOLD AND SILVER WATER'; GOOD FRIDAY, bread made on: cures; GRAVE cures; GREENERY, circle of; HANGMAN'S ROPE cures/protects; IRON cures; KNOTS used in cures; LIZARD cures; MANDRAKE, other powers of; MAY DEW cures; MEASURING; MOLE: cures/spells; MOUSE; MUGWORT; NAILS AND HAIR: cures/spells; NAILS driven in; NAMES, magical; ONION protects and cures; PEONY protects; PIGEON, live: used in cures; POSTHUMOUS CHILD; RED THREAD cures; SEVENTH CHILD; SHEEP; SKULL; SNAKE STONE; SPIDER OR SPIDER'S WEB cures; SPITTLE cures; SUNWISE cures; THREAD tied round; THRESHOLD; TOAD OR FROG cures; TOAD'S OR FROG'S BONE; TOADSTONE; TREE, disease transferred to; VERVAIN, powers of; VIRGIN heals; WATER, holy; WATER, running: cures; WELL

cures *see* cure-alls; diseases/infirmities. *Also see* charms, verbal; passing through/under/over; transference

curtseying *see* propitiation

D

days of the week: auspicious/inauspicious *see* BED-MAKING: turning mattress/changing sheets at 'dangerous' times; BIRTH, day of: divination rhyme; CHILDERMAS DAY; CLOTHES, clean/new; CORPSE, unburied: over Saturday/Sunday; DREAM, telling: Friday night's; DUMB CAKE; EGGS, setting: Friday and Sunday; FRIDAY; GRAVE open on Sunday; HANDSEL MONDAY; LAST SHIFT; LEAVES, nine; LEFT HAND; MONDAY; MOON, MAN IN THE; NAILS AND HAIR, cutting: day important; NAILS AND HAIR, cutting: lucky on Monday; NAILS AND HAIR, cutting: rhyme; NAILS AND HAIR, cutting: unlucky on Friday and Sunday; 'PIG' taboo word; ST JOHN'S WORT protects; SATURDAY; SCISSORS fall; SNEEZING: divination: 'days' rhyme; SUNDAY; THREAD on distaff; THUNDER AND LIGHTNING, interpretation of: direction, day, or season; WEDDING, day of: divination rhyme. *Cf.* birth (day/time); church festivals/holy days; saints/saints' days

deas-soil (in accordance with the course of the sun) *see* sunwise/anti-sunwise

death/dying (process/circumstances) *see* BED across floorboards or ceiling-beam; BEES take part in funeral/wedding; BEES, news told to; CAT OR DOG passes over corpse; CLOCK stops at moment of death; DEATH; KNOTS in shroud/clothes of dead; MIRROR covered in sick room; MOON affects birth/health/death; PIGEON; PIGEONS' FEATHERS, lying on; PLANTS put into mourning; ROOKS informed of a death; TIDE affects birth and death; WEATHER. *Also see* corpse; divination: life or death; grave/graveyard; spirit/soul of dead

death/sickness/disaster (omens/predictions) *see* AMBULANCE; APPLE BLOSSOM in house; ASH TREE keys: divination; AURORA BOREALIS; BAT; BAY/LAUREL withers; BED: foot towards door; BED, sitting on; BED-MAKING: three people; BEES leave hive; BEES, swarming; BIRD, dead; BIRD in house; BLACK SHEEP; BLADE-BONE; BLOSSOM unseasonable; BOAT, changing name of; BOAT, new: delivery postponed; BONES, burning; BREAD, hole in; BREAD: loaf, cake, etc. breaks; BREAD: loaf upside-down; BRIDE married after sunset; BROOM: buying in May or at Christmas; BROOM (plant); BUMBLE BEE in house = death; BURIAL, symbolic: counteracts Whitsuntide birth; BUTTERFLIES, three; CANDLE alone in room; CANDLE, failing to blow out; CANDLE, lighting third; CANDLE, signs in:

winding sheet; CARDS, unlucky; CAT: drowning at sea; CAT endangers health; CHAINLETTER; CHAIR falls over; CHAIR, sitting in someone else's; CHILDREN, dreaming of; CHRISTENING, baby cries during; CHRISTMAS, working at; CHRISTMAS CANDLE; CHRISTMAS DECORATIONS (evergreens): burning; CHRISTMAS DECORATIONS (evergreens etc.), taking down; CHURCH, illness in; CHURCH BELL omen of death; CHURCH DOOR/GATE rattles/clicks; CHURCH PORCH, watching in; CIGARETTE, lighting third; CINDERS: divination; CLOCK; CLOTHES: mending while wearing; COCK; COFFIN, sound of earth on; COFFIN SUPPORTS turned over; COMET; CORPSE; COUNTING/MEASURING ancient stones; COW trespasses; CRICKET as omen; CROWS OR RAVENS ominous; DAFFODIL; DEATH: opening locks/doors and windows frees spirit; DEATH-WATCH BEETLE; DIRT lucky; DISHES, three: divination; DOG, howling; DOOR, front; DOVE sign of peace to departing soul; DROWNING STRANGER; EAR, ringing in: ill omen; EGG: double yolk; EGG, last; ELDER, burning; ELDER malevolent; EXHUMATION; FAIRY RINGS; FIRE, behaviour of: burns hollow; FIRE, behaviour of: burns on one side; FIRE, behaviour of: fails to go out; FIRE not allowed out of house; FLOWERS; FUNERAL: divination; FUNERAL: sun shines on mourner's face; FUNERAL FEES; GABRIEL'S HOUNDS/SEVEN WHISTLERS; GLASS, breaking; GOOD FRIDAY, ploughing on; GOOD FRIDAY, washing on; GORSE in house; GRAVE open on Sunday; GRAVE, possession falls into; GREEN; HAIR: combing after sunset; HAIR: disposing of combings/cuttings; HAIR falling out; HAIR, keeping; HAND, yellow spots on; HEARSE; HEN crows; HERON ominous; HOUSE, new: fatal; INK, spilling; IRON, food pricked with; IVY; KNIFE falls; KNIFE, spinning: points towards one; KNOCKING; LADDER, walking under; LANTERN on table; LIONESS; LOOKING BACK; MAGPIE ominous; MANDRAKE, uprooting; MARRIAGE, early; MARRIED COUPLE: first to die; MAY; MAY BLOSSOM; MIRROR; MOLE as omen; MONEY, finding; MOONLIGHT; MOTH/BUTTERFLY; MOTHER-DIE; NAMING baby; NEW YEAR, working at; NOSE bleeds; OAK TREE, harming; OPAL; OWL; PAPER BAG, bursting; PARSLEY, moving/transplanting; PEACOCK; PEACOCK FEATHERS; PICTURE; PIG dies; PIGEON; PLANTS put into mourning; PLATE on top of another; PRAISING; PRAYERS, stopping/stumbling while saying; PRECOCIOUSNESS; PREGNANT WOMAN as godmother; RAINBOW; RATS AND MICE death/sickness/disaster (*cont.*):

gnawing; RATS AND MICE, influx of; RAVEN; RED unlucky to lovers; RED FLOWERS unlucky; RED HAIR unlucky; ROBIN; ROOKS; ROSEMARY: woman is master; SALT CELLAR, breaking; SCISSORS fall; SEAGULL AND STORMY PETREL; SHADOW, headless; SHREW; SKULL unlucky to move; SNAIL indoors; SOAP falls; SOOT, fall of; SOWING: part missed out; SPADE; SPEEDWELL, picking; SPIDER, big; SPIDER, 'ticking'; STAIRS, stumbling going down; STAR, falling/shooting = death; STARS, pointing at/counting; STEPPING OVER; STUMBLING; SUNDAY, darning, sewing, or knitting on; SUNDAY: keeping Sabbath holy; SWALLOW AND MARTIN, harming; SWIFT; SWORD falls from scabbard; TABLECLOTH/SHEET; TEETH, born with; TEETH, cutting; TEETH, dreaming about; TELEPHONE, ringing; THEATRE: unlucky tunes; THIRTEEN in company or at table; THORN TREE, harming; THREAD, winding: after sunset; THREE DEATHS; THUNDER AND LIGHTNING; TIDE affects birth and death; TOAD OR FROG in house; UMBRELLA on bed; UMBRELLA opened indoors; WALKING backwards; WEASEL; WEDDING RING; WEIGHING; WHITE; WIDOW'S [OR WIDOWER'S] PEAK; WILL, making; WINDOW-BLIND falls; WOOD creaks and cracks; WREN sacred; YEW unlucky

demons *see* Devil/demons/evil spirits

departure *see* PARTING. *Also see* breaking; last

Devil/demons/evil spirits *see* BLACK; BLACKBERRIES not to be eaten after Michaelmas; BLOSSOM unseasonable; BREAD; BURIAL: first in churchyard; CARDS, unlucky; CHRISTENING, baby cries during; CHRISTMAS LOG/ASHEN FAGGOT: piece kept for luck/protection; CHURCH BELL drives away devils and storms; CLERGYMAN on ship; COFFIN LID undone; CROOKED FURROW; CROSS, making sign of; 'DEVIL' taboo word; DOOR, changing; DOORSTEP PATTERNS; EGG, last; ELDER, burning; FERN, harming; HOLLY protects; IMAGE/PICTURE used to injure or kill; IRON; KNOTS hinder conception; LEAD shapes in water: divination of cause of sickness; MAGPIE; MIRROR covered in the presence of death; MIRROR: divination; MIRROR, looking in; MISTLETOE protects; MONEY: having in purse etc.; MONKEY PUZZLE TREE; MOONLIGHT causes madness; NAILS AND HAIR, cutting: Friday and Sunday; NEW YEAR din; NORTH door of church; NUTS, gathering; PARSLEY; PINS: pinning the Devil; PRAYERS said backwards; RAVEN; ST JOHN'S WORT protects; SALT as protection; SALT protects at death; SALT, spilling; SHIFT/SMOCK etc., apparition turns;

SNEEZING divination: 'days' rhyme; SPITTING to avert evil; STRAW magic; SUNDAY, born on; SUNDAY: keeping Sabbath holy; SWIFT; THREAD on distaff; WEDDING, guns fired at; WHISTLING; WIND, whistling for; YARROW: nosebleed divination; YAWNING: crossing the mouth. *Cf.* fairies; witches/witchcraft

dew *see* MAY DEW/RAIN. *Also see* water

diarrhoea/stomach disorders *see* GOOD FRIDAY, bread made on: cures

dirt/dust/ashes/earth/muck/mud/sweepings: bring good fortune, often money *see* BABY'S HANDS, washing; CABBAGE STALK: divination; COW'S DUNG; DIRT lucky; EXCREMENT; NEW YEAR and house/home: nothing to be taken out

disaster *see* death/sickness/disaster

diseases/infirmities (cures and charms) *see* BURN OR SCALD: RINGWORM. *Also see* bed-wetting; bleeding; chilblains/corns; consumption; cramp/stitch/pins and needles; diarrhoea/stomach disorders; epilepsy/fits/convulsions; eye ailments; fevers etc.; headache; rheumatism/gout/lumbago; rickets; rupture; shingles/erysipelas/other rashes; sprain; swelling/goitre/king's evil/scrofula/tumour/wen/boils/mumps/sore throat; thrush (ulcers in mouth); toothache/teething troubles; warts; whooping cough; wounds/bites/thorns in flesh

divination (of life or death) *see* AFTERBIRTH, burning; ASHES, footprint in; BALL; CUCKOO: divination of years till death; CUCKOO, first: where standing when heard; DISHES, three: divination; FIRE divination: stones in bonfire; FLOWERS in pairs; HAIR thrown into fire: divination of life or death; IVY LEAF in water; LEAD shapes in water: divination of cause of sickness; LIONESS; WELL: divination; WINNOWING CORN. *Also see* divination (multiple/other); itching/sneezing/other involuntary actions

divination (love/marriage/children) *see* AFTERBIRTH, burning; APPLE PEEL; APPLE PIPS; APPLE STALK; ASH TREE: even ash-leaf; ASHES, streaks in; BACHELOR'S BUTTON; BALL; BAY/LAUREL LEAVES; BEAN; BIBLE AND KEY; BLADEBONE: spell; BUTTONS OR FRUIT STONES; CABBAGE STALK; CANDLE burns blue; CARDS, lucky at; CHARMS in food; CHRISTENING CAKE; CHURCHING after childbirth: divination; CLERGYMAN: divination; CLOVER, two-leaved; 'COAL' magic; COCK AND HEN; CUCKOO: divination of years till marriage; CUCKOO, first: divination with hair; DAISY; DANDELION OR HAWKWEED SEEDS; DISHES, three: divination; DUMB CAKE; EAR, ringing in:

divination; EARTH, hole in; EGG, first; EGGS (whites of): shapes in water; FERN STALK; FINGERS, cracking joints of; FIRE, poking: divination; FIRST-FOOT on way to christening; FLOWERS in pairs; GATE; GRASS; HAIR thrown into fire: divination of future husband; HEMP SEED; HERRING MEMBRANE; IVY LEAF; KNAPWEED; KNIFE, spinning; KNOTS in garters; KNOTS in grass; LADYBIRD; LAST FOOD/DRINK: 'Carling' peas; LEAD shapes in water: divination of future spouse; LEAVES, nine; LEAVES: spell and divination; LEMON PEEL; MINCE PIES, opening; MISTLETOE, kissing under; MYRTLE; NEW MOON: divination; NUTS: divination; OATS; ONION: divination and spells; ORPINE: divination; PEAS; PLANTAIN: divination; PUDDING; ROSE; SAGE; ST AGNES'S EVE/DAY; SALT HERRING; SALT IN EGG; SHIFT/SMOCK etc., apparition turns; SHOES placed in form of a T; SNAIL: divination; STOCKING, left: divination; SWORD AND SCABBARD; TEA/COFFEE CUP, 'reading'; TEA-LEAF OR STALK; THREAD, first; THREAD, winding: divination; VALENTINE; WEDDING CAKE: divination; WINNOWING CORN; YARROW. *Also see* apparitions; divination (multiple/other); marriage/courtship/children: predictions; sleeping; wearing/carrying things
divination (multiple/other than the above) *see* ASHES, pictures in; BIBLE AND KEY; BIRTH, day of: divination rhyme; BLADE-BONE; BOOK: opening at random; BREAD: loaves joined; BUS TICKETS; CHARMS in food; CINDERS; CLOVER, four-leaved; CROWS, two or more; CUCKOO, first; DIMPLES; FINGERS: divination; FIRE, behaviour of; FIRE: divination: sparks from burning brand; FIRST ANIMALS/BIRDS in spring; HAIR, strand of; MAGPIE; MIRROR: divination; MOLES ON BODY, meaning of; NAILS: specks on finger nails; NAILS AND HAIR, cutting: rhyme; NEEDLE, breaking; NEW MOON; OAK TREE: divination with oak apple; PENDULUM; PINS: pinning the Devil; SHEEP, greeting; SHEPHERD'S PURSE; SHOES, old: thrown over beam/house; SHOES/STOCKINGS, wearing out; SIEVE AND SHEARS; SKIRT turned up; SNEEZING: divination: 'days' rhyme; SPEAKING in rhyme; TEA/COFFEE CUP, 'reading'; THREAD on clothes; THUNDER AND LIGHTNING, interpretation of: direction, day, or season; VIRGIN has power of divination; WASSAILING cornfields and cattle. *Also see* dreams; letter/news; quarrels/anger; stranger/strange
DONKEY *Also see* HORSE'S [OR DONKEY'S] HOOF
doors/locks: supernatural/magical associations *see* BABY: bringing home in car; BED: foot towards door; BIRTH: opening locks eases; CATTLE: burning entrails gives power over witch; CHRISTMAS, first to open door at; CHURCH DOOR/GATE rattles/clicks; COFFIN LID undone; CORPSE carried feet first; DEATH: opening locks/doors and windows frees spirit; DEATH: opening locks/doors and windows eases; DIRT lucky; DOOR; DOORS AND WINDOWS opened in thunderstorm; MOONWORT; NEW YEAR and house/home: bringing in the new year; NORTH door of church; ONION: divination and spells; SUPPER, apparition comes to share; TRUNK, unlucky to lock; WINNOWING CORN: divination. *Cf.* knots; threshold
double/two: magical/ominous *see* APPLE CROP; BELT twisted; BREAD: loaves joined; CLOCKS: two strike together; CLOVER, two-leaved: divination; COCK AND HEN; EGG: double yolk; EGGS: two laid; EYES, peculiar; HAIR: double crown; NUTS, double; PALM SUNDAY; PLATE on top of another; SALT CELLARS, two; SPOONS, two; TWIN. *Also see* two people
dreams *see* CHILDREN, dreaming of; COAL, dreaming of; DREAM; FLOWERS: red and white together; GREEN; PEARLS = tears; SNAKE, meeting or dreaming of; TEETH, dreaming about. *Also see* nightmare; sleep; sleeping
DRINK *also see* food/drink
dropping *see* falling/dropping/spilling
drowning *see* BODY: locating in water; CAUL, possession of: lucky; DROWNING STRANGER; GOLD EAR-RINGS prevent drowning; HAIR: double crown; IONA STONE; THREE: 'third time lucky'. *Also see* sea/seamen
druids *see* IRON taboo on sacred occasions; LOOKING BACK; LUCKY-BONE; MISTLETOE; MOON affects enterprises; OAK TREE, harming; SNAKE STONE; WELL ceremonies
dust *see* dirt/dust etc.
dying *see* death/dying

E

ear-rings *see* GOLD EAR-RINGS
earth *see* ground/earth
EASTER *also see* church festivals/holy days
EGG[s] *also see* birds and eggs
epilepsy/fits/convulsions *see* BAY/LAUREL protects; CHURCH, lead from; 'COAL' magic; COFFIN, parts of; COMMUNION table/altar; CORAL; CORPSE'S WASHING WATER cures; ELDER protects against and cures disease; HOLE in stone, passing through; MISTLETOE

epilepsy/fits/convulsions (*cont.*):
cures; MOLE: cures/spells; MOLE'S FEET cure; NAILS driven in: cure; NAILS AND HAIR: cures/spells; OAK TREE benign; PEONY protects; RING made of blessed money/silver; RING made of money/silver given by bachelors/spinsters; SKULL, eating or drinking from: cures

erysipelas *see* shingles/erysipelas/other rashes

evil spirits *see* Devil/demons/evil spirits

eye ailments *see* ASCENSION DAY WATER; CAT, black: cures; FROG'S EYES; GOLD cures sore eyes; GOLD EAR-RINGS good for eyes; GOOSEBERRY THORN; MAY DEW/RAIN: cures; SNAKE STONE

eyes: power to injure *see* BABY looks between legs; CORPSE, eyes of; 'DEVIL' taboo word; EYES; MIRROR, looking in: baby; MUGWORT against evil; MUSHROOM, looking at; SPECTACLES. *Cf.* speaking: magical/dangerous connotations; witches/witchcraft

F

fairies: feared and propitiated *see* BABY, referring to; CHRISTMAS DECORATIONS (evergreens etc.), taking down; CLOTHES inside out; CLOVER, four-leaved: opens eyes to fairy deceptions; COW'S DUNG; CROOKED FURROW; EGGSHELL, piercing or crushing; ELF-SHOT; FAIRY RINGS; 'FAIRY' taboo word; FIRE protects child; FOOD left out overnight; IRON deters evil; IRON in cradle or childbed; KNIFE edge upwards; LEATHER, burning; MAY a dangerous month; MAY BOUGHS AND FLOWERS; MONEY, finding; NAMING baby before christening; NEW YEAR din; OAK TREE benign; PRAISING dangerous; ROWAN protects; SNEEZE, baby's first; TEETH, disposing of; URINE protects; WATER, running: cures. *Cf.* Devil/demons/evil spirits; witches/witchcraft

falling/dropping/spilling: significant, usually unlucky *see* BIBLE, treatment of; BOILING WATER spills over; CHAIR falls over; CLOCK falls down; CUTLERY, dropping; DRINK, spilling; DROPPING THINGS; FIRE TONGS fall; FLOWERS, picking up; GLOVE, dropping; GRAVE, possession falls into; HAIRPIN falls out; HANDKERCHIEF, dropping; KEY, dropping; KNIFE falls; LEAVES/PETALS, catching; LETTER, dropping; MARRIED COUPLE: first to die; MILK, spilling; MISTLETOE protects; MONEY, dropping; NEEDLE, dropping; PICTURE falls; RED FLOWERS unlucky; SALT, spilling; SCISSORS, dropping; SOAP falls; SOOT; STAIRS,

stumbling going down; STAR, falling/shooting; STUMBLING; SUGAR, spilling; SWORD falls from scabbard; TEETH, dreaming about; THEATRE: make-up; THREAD on clothes: divination; UMBRELLA/WALKING STICK, dropping; WEDDING RING; WELL cures, and ensures good fortune; WINDOW-BLIND falls. *Also see* ground/earth; thanking: magical implications

farm *see* crops; livestock

fasting: magical condition *see* BRAMBLE ARCH cures; CHRISTENING CAKE; CUCKOO, first: hearer will do same thing all year; DREAM, telling; DUMB CAKE; NAILS AND HAIR, cutting: on Monday; NAMES, divination with; PARISHES; POSTHUMOUS CHILD; RINGWORM; ST AGNES'S EVE/DAY; SALT HERRING; SALT IN EGG; SINGING before breakfast; SPITTLE cures; WELL. *Cf.* secrecy/stealth/silence

fate, tempting *see* anticipating/tempting fate

feet: transmit good or evil *see* ground/earth

fertility: motive for magical practices/beliefs *see* APPLE CROP; ASH TREE keys: divination; BIRTH, contact with; CHURCHING after childbirth; CORPSE defiles: makes earth barren; EGGS carried over running water; EGGS, setting; EXCREMENT, baby's first; HAY RICK; HOLE in stone: passing through; KNOTS hinder conception; LETTUCE detrimental to childbearing; LIONESS; MANDRAKE aids conception; MENSTRUATING WOMAN; MISTLETOE brings luck to farm; MISTLETOE, kissing under; MURDER: earth remains barren; NUTS at wedding; PARSLEY, pregnancy prevented by; PEARL under pillow; PRIMROSES; SHOES/STOCKINGS in form of cross; THORN TREE, harming; WEDDING CAKE: part kept; WHEAT/RICE/CONFETTI thrown for luck. *Also see* crops; livestock

fevers etc. *see* 'COAL' magic; COMMUNION; CROOKED COIN; CAT OR DOG, disease transferred to; DONKEY cures; EGG, first; FEVER; FIRE blackens chalk mark: cure for ague; GALLOWS, chips of: cure; GREENERY, circle of; HOLLY prevents fever; KNOTS used in cures; MOUSE, other cures using; NAILS AND HAIR: cures/spells; SPIDER OR SPIDER'S WEB cures; STILE, nail driven into; TIDE cures; TREE, disease transferred to; WASHING HANDS together. *Also see* diseases/infirmities

finding by chance: ominous *see* BUTTON, four-holed; CLOVER, four-leaved: lucky to find; COAL, finding; CROOKED PIN; HORSESHOE, lucky to find; HORSE'S TOOTH; IRON, finding; KNIFE, finding; MONEY, finding; PIN, finding; ROOK'S EGG; WEASEL-SKIN PURSE. *Also see* ground/earth fingers/thumb: significant *see* BLACK INSECT; FINGERS; NAILS: specks on finger nails: divination; THUMB, holding; VIRGIN heals; WOOD, touching. *Also see* cross; pointing

finishing/not finishing: feared *see* BABY'S CLOTHES/CRADLE given away; BEDSPREAD, making; BREAD AND BUTTER on plate; BRIDE'S CLOTHES: wedding dress, bride tries on completed; BUILDING left unfinished; CHAIR put back in place; CHRISTMAS DECORATIONS (evergreen, etc.), taking down; FIREWOOD: faggot band; FISHING: fish scales not to be cleaned off; FOOD left unfinished; LAST PAYMENT; MARRIAGE SERVICE, reading; MIRROR, looking in: bride arrayed for wedding; TABLE-NAPKIN, folding; THEATRE: make-up; TRUNK, unlucky to lock. *Cf.* anticipating/tempting fate; back/front; interruption/impediment; last things/ occasions

fire (outbreaks of): precautions/predictions *see* lightning/fire

fire: sacred/powerful *see* ASHES, footprint in; BABY, gifts to; BELLOWS; BOILING; CANDLE; CAT, behaviour of: sits with back to fire; CATTLE: carcass hung in chimney to protect livestock; CATTLE: one sacrificed to protect rest of herd; CHIMNEY; CHRISTMAS CANDLE; CHRISTMAS LOG; CHRISTMAS LOG/ASHEN FAGGOT; CIGARETTE, lighting third; CINDERS; CLOCK facing fire; CORPSE'S HAND holding candle; DISHES, three: divination; DUMB CAKE; FAIRY LOAF; FENDER; FEVER: word charm; FIRE; FIRST-FOOT at New Year/ Christmas: ritual of gifts; GOOD FRIDAY, egg laid on; HAIR thrown into fire: divination; HOLLY, sweeping chimney with; HOPS kept for luck; IRON cures; IRON in churn; IRON: ironing shirt-tail; IRON taboo on sacred occasions; MAY DAY, giving or selling on; MOON affects sowing and harvesting; NAILS AND HAIR: cures/spells; NEW YEAR and house/ home: nothing to be taken out; PINS, bride's; POKER against grate; RINGWORM; SALT; SALT HERRING; SHADOW; SHIFT/SMOCK etc., apparition turns; SOOT; SUN puts out fire; WASHING as ritual; WASHING WATER, throwing out; WASSAILING cornfields and cattle; WATER, first of year. *Also see* burning; lightning/fire

fire irons: doubly powerful *see* fire: sacred/ powerful; iron

first things/occasions: significant/magical/ affect future *see* ASH TREE benign; ASH TREE: even ash-leaf: divination; BABY; BABY'S CLOTHES put over head; BABY'S HAND[S]; BABY'S NAPPY: first; BEGGAR, meeting; BLACK SHEEP; BLOOD, shedding first: brings success;

BOOK: opening at random; BREAD, cutting or pricking; BREAD: upper crust; BRIDE lifted over threshold; BUMBLE BEE, first: killed; BURIAL: first in churchyard; BUTTERFLY, first: killed; BUTTONS OR FRUIT STONES; CAROL SINGERS; CHAMPAGNE CORK; CHIMNEY SWEEP, meeting; CHRISTENING CAKE; CHRISTENING CLOTHES, baby must sleep first night in; CHRISTMAS, first to open door at; CHURCH BELL foretells length of incumbency; CHURCHING after childbirth: divination; CLOTHES, clean/ new; CLOTHES: first time worn; CLOVER, two-leaved: divination; CUCKOO, first; DAFFODIL, head of; DOOR, front; EGG, first; EXCREMENT, baby's first; EYEBROWS; FIRE, newcomer gives priority to; FIRST; FIRST-FOOT; FISHING: first catch; FISHING HOOK: first baited; FUNERAL: divination; GRAVE, meeting/parting at; HANDSEL; HANDSELLING; HARE OR RABBIT, meeting; 'HARE' OR 'RABBIT': saying at change of month; HAY RICK; HORSE/ HORSEMAN lucky to meet; HOUSE, moving; LEFT FOOT; MARRIAGE: dominant partner; MARRIED COUPLE: first to die; MAY; MINCE PIES, wishing with; MISTLETOE brings luck to farm; MONDAY; NEW MOON; NEW YEAR; NORTH; OPPOSITE SEX; PRIMROSES; RED HAIR unlucky; RING made of blessed money/silver; SALMON unlucky first catch; SHOES/ STOCKINGS, putting on: left/right; SNAKE, first: killed; SNEEZE, baby's first; SPEAKING first and last words; STAR, first; SUNDAY, convalescing on; TABLE-NAPKIN; TEETH: cutting upper first; THIRTEEN in company or at table; THREAD, first; VALENTINE: first person seen; VIRGIN first to hold baby; VIRGIN, meeting; WASP, first: killed; WATER: first of year; WEDDING CAKE, cutting; WOMAN, meeting; YARROW: divination. *Cf.* beginning; last things/occasions

fishermen *see* sea/seamen

fishes *see* animals/reptiles/fishes and parts or products of

fits *see* epilepsy/fits/convulsions

flour *see* bread/wheat/flour etc.

flowers: significant/magical *see* APPLE BLOSSOM; BACHELOR'S BUTTON; BALL, cowslip: divination; BEAN BLOSSOMS; BROOM (plant); DAFFODIL; DAISY; DANDELION OR HAWKWEED SEEDS; DOG-ROSE; FIRST FRUITS AND FLOWERS; FLOWERS; GORSE; GRAVE, picking leaves/ flowers from; HEATHER, white; KNAPWEED; MAY BLOSSOM; MAY BOUGHS AND FLOWERS; MOONWORT; MOTHER-DIE; PEONY; PLANTAIN: divination; PRIMROSES; RED FLOWERS unlucky; ROSE; SPEEDWELL; THEATRE: bouquet; THEATRE: real flowers on stage; WHITE

flowers: significant/magical (*cont.*):
FLOWERS; WILLOW BLOSSOMS in house. *Cf.* greenery
font *see* WATER, holy
food/drink: associated with magic *see* BABY, eating and drinking to; BOILING continues off fire; CHAMPAGNE CORK; CHRISTMAS LOG: stirring fire during supper; CHURCHING after childbirth; COMMUNION chalice/wine; CROSS, making sign of: on other food; DOG, hair of; DRINK; DRINKING; EGG[S]; EGGSHELL, piercing or crushing; FAIRY LOAF; FERRET cures whooping cough; FIRE protects child; FIRST-FOOT; FIRST FRUITS AND FLOWERS; FIRST FURROW; FLY in drink; FOOD; GOOSE eaten on Michaelmas Day; HARE, eating: taboo; IRON, food pricked with; IVY-WOOD CUP; LAST FOOD/DRINK; LUCK, wishing; MEAT shrinks in pot; MENSTRUATING WOMAN defiles; MIRROR: divination: to see future spouse; MOON affects killing of livestock; MOUSE; NAMES, magical: married couple; PIGEON, longing for; PIG, taboo on flesh of; PLATE on top of another; POURING; PREGNANCY, cravings during; SALT HERRING; SALT IN EGG; SINGING during meal; SKULL, eating or drinking from: cures; SPIDER OR SPIDER'S WEB cures ague as medicine; SPOONS, two; SUGAR; SUNWISE, passing drink; SUNWISE, stirring; SUPPER; TABLE-NAPKIN; TEA; TEA/COFFEE CUP, 'reading'; WASSAILING. *Also see* bread; cakes/puddings/pies; milk/butter; propitiation
forespeaking/forespoken *see* PRAISING
fortune-telling *see* divination; omens
fossil *see* FAIRY LOAF
front *see* back/front or tail/head of magical creature/object
fruit stones *see* BUTTONS OR FRUIT STONES
FUNERAL *also see* church ceremonies/sacraments; corpse; death/dying
furrow *see* crops

G

gate *see* stile/gateway
ghosts *see* apparitions
giving/accepting, lending/borrowing: bring good/bad luck *see* BABY, gifts to; BELLOWS as present; BELLOWS, borrowing or lending; BIBLE as present; BORROWING AND LENDING; BRIDE'S CLOTHES: 'something borrowed'; CAT, buying; CATTLE: burning entrails gives power over witch; CHAMBER POT; CORPSE'S LINEN lucky; FIRE not allowed out of house; FIRST-FOOT; FOOD, giving away; GLOVES as

present; HANDKERCHIEF = tears; HANDSEL MONDAY; HANDSELLING new purse; 'HARE' OR 'RABBIT': saying at change of month; HOUSE, new: visitor brings present; KNIFE as present; LAST FOOD/DRINK: bite of apple; MAY DAY, giving or selling on; MILK, giving or selling; MONDAY, giving or receiving on; NAMES, magical: married couple; NEW YEAR; PARSLEY, giving; PIG, taboo on flesh of; PIN as present; RING; SALT as protection against witch; SALT, being helped to; SALT, borrowing or lending; SCISSORS as present; SHOE-LACE, giving; SHOES as present; SOAP as present; THEATRE: bouquet; UMBRELLA as present; WHITE FEET, horse's. *Also see* buying/selling; propitiation
GODPARENTS *also see* ENGAGED COUPLE as godparents; KNOTS used in cures; PARISHES; PREGNANT WOMAN as godmother
goitre *see* swelling
gold *see* silver/gold
GOOD FRIDAY *also see* FRIDAY; church festivals/holy days
'good people'/'good neighbours' *see* fairies
GOOSE *also see* DUCK OR GOOSE; GABRIEL'S HOUNDS/SEVEN WHISTLERS
gout *see* rheumatism/gout/lumbago etc.
grandparents *see* parents/grandparents
grave/graveyard *see* BABY, stillborn; BURIAL; CHURCHYARD, grass etc. from; GRAVE; HAND above grave; MONDAY, grave-digging on; MONKEY PUZZLE TREE; MURDER: earth remains barren; SHUDDER; STUMBLING in graveyard; VIRGIN'S GRAVE; YARROW: divination. *Also see* corpse
GREEN *also see* colours; greenery
greenery (vegetation in general, and particular herbs and plants): magical/protective or dangerous *see* BAY/LAUREL; Baby's nappy: first; BRAMBLE ARCH cures; BROOM [plant]; 'BUSH', burning; CHRISTMAS DECORATIONS (evergreens); CHURCHYARD, grass etc. from; CLOVER; CUCKOO, first: where standing when heard; FAIRY RINGS; FERN; FIRST-FOOT at New Year/Christmas: ritual of gifts; GOOSEBERRY BUSH, babies found under; GRASS; GRAVE, picking leaves/flowers from; GREEN; GREENERY; HEMP SEED: divination; HOLLY; HOLLY AND IVY; HOUSELEEK; HYDRANGEA; IRON taboo on sacred occasions; IVY; KNOTS in grass; LEAVES; LETTUCE; MANDRAKE aids conception; MAY BOUGHS AND FLOWERS; MENSTRUATING WOMAN defiles; MISTLETOE; MOON affects sowing and harvesting; MUGWORT; MURDER: grass grows greener; MYRTLE; NETTLE STING; NEW MOON: divination; ONION; ORPINE: divination; 'PALM'; PARSLEY; PLAN-

TAIN: divination; PLANTS; RAILWAY BRIDGE/TUNNEL; ROSEMARY at funerals; ST AGNES'S EVE/DAY; ST JOHN'S WORT; SAGE; SEAWEED; VERVAIN, powers of; VIRGIN'S GRAVE; WATER: first of year; WATER, sprinkling: brings rain; YARROW. *Also see* flowers; house: creatures/plants; thorns; trees/wood

ground/earth (path/road/field/stairs/stile/threshold): influence for good or evil, reflected in significance and vulnerability of feet *see* ANIMAL, four-legged: meeting; ASHES, footprint in; BED, getting out of: on right side; BIRTH, breech; CATTLE: one sacrificed to protect rest of herd; CHURCHING after childbirth: woman must not cross road; CORPSE defiles; CRAMP BONE; CRIPPLE, meeting; CUCKOO, first: divination with hair; CUCKOO, first: where standing when heard; DONKEY cures: passing under; EARTH, hole in: divination; ELDER protects against and cures disease; FAIRY RING; FEATHER stuck in ground; FEVER cured by transference; FIRE protects cattle and crops; FIRST FURROW; FIRST-FOOT; FOOT; GOOD FRIDAY, ploughing on; GRAVE, earth/dew from: cures; KNIFE laid across; LEAVES/PETALS, catching; LEFT FOOT; MAIL VAN; MARRIAGE: younger before elder; MISTLETOE cures; MURDER; NAILS left in floor; NEEDLE, breaking; NEW MOON and money; NEW MOON: divination; PIGEON, live: used in cures; PINS cure warts; SCISSORS fall; SHEEP cures: organs and skin; SHREW cures/spells; SOWING; STILE, nail driven into; TEETHING; THRESHOLD; URINE: iron nails etc. in patient's urine to detect witch; WARTS 'given' to corpse; WHITE FEET, horse's. *Also see* crossroads/boundaries; falling; finding; threshold

guns fired *see* noise/din

H

hair/nails *see* BREAD, kneading; BRIDE'S CLOTHES: wedding dress, hair sewn into; BUTTER, charm for; CAT, black: cures; CAT OR DOG, disease transferred to; CHRISTENING boys before girls; CUCKOO, first: divination with hair; DOG, hair of; DONKEY cures; EYEBROWS; EYELASH; FIRST-FOOT at New Year/Christmas: dark male usually preferred; HAIR; HAND, yellow spots on; HORSE'S HAIR cures; MIRROR divination: to see future spouse; MOLES ON BODY, meaning of; MOON affects growth of hair/nails/corns; MYRTLE: divination; NAILS: specks on finger nails; NAILS AND HAIR; NEW MOON: divination; PENDULUM; PIEBALD HORSE

cures whooping cough; RED HAIR unlucky; TEA, two people pouring; TREE, disease transferred to; URINE: iron nails etc. in patient's urine to detect witch; WIDOW'S [OR WIDOWER'S] PEAK. *Also see* body, parts or products of; transference

Hallowe'en (All-Hallows' Eve, 31 Oct.): associated with magic, witchcraft, and the dead *see* CABBAGE STALK: divination; CANDLE, pricking: spell; DISHES, three: divination; DUMB CAKE; EARTH, hole in: divination; EGGS (whites of): shapes in water: divination; FIRE: divination: stones in bonfire; FIRE not to die out; FIRE protects cattle and crops; GARLIC protects from evil; HEMP SEED: divination; IVY in house; IVY LEAF in water: divination; KNOTS in garters: divination; LEAD shapes in water: divination of future spouse; LEAVES/PETALS, catching; MIRROR: divination: to see future spouse; NUTS: divination: burning; OATS: divination; ROWAN protects; SALT IN EGG; SHIFT/SMOCK etc., apparition turns; SNAIL: divination; THREAD, winding: divination; WASSAILING sea; WINNOWING CORN: divination. *Cf.* church festivals/holy days; saints/saints' days

HAND *also see* fingers/thumb; left/right; touching

HANDSEL/HANDSELLING *also see* buying/selling; first things/occasions; giving/accepting; money/coins

hat, doffing *see* propitiation

hawkweed *see* DANDELION OR HAWKWEED SEEDS: divination

hawthorn/hawthorn blossom *see* 'BUSH', burning; MAY BLOSSOM; MAY BOUGHS AND FLOWERS; THORN TREE. *Cf.* thorns/prickles

head/tail *see* back/front or tail/head of magical creature/object

headache *see* CORPSE'S LINEN cures; HAIR, disposing of; HANGMAN'S ROPE cures/protects; MEASURING cures; NAILS driven in; SNAKE SLOUGH/SKIN preserves health

healers *see* people with special powers

heavenly bodies *see* weather/heavenly bodies

hole, magical *see* circle/ring; passing through/under/over

HOLLY *also see* CHRISTMAS DECORATIONS. *Cf.* thorns/prickles

holy days *see* church festivals/holy days

Holy Innocents' Day *see* CHILDERMAS

home *see* house/home

honeymoon *see* DESTINATION, unlucky to be asked one's

Hot Cross Buns *see* GOOD FRIDAY, bread made on

house: creatures/plants etc. coming into or out of, ominous *see* APPLE BLOSSOM in house; BAT;

I

left/right (*cont.*):
    see north/south; sunwise/anti-sunwise;
    throwing/spitting backwards
letter/news (predictions of/about) *see* BEES,
    news told to; BUTTON, four-holed; CANDLE,
    signs in: letter; CANDLE, ringing in: ill omen;
    FIRE, behaviour of: sends out sparks; FRIDAY,
    hearing news on; HAIRPIN falls out; MOTH
    sign of letter coming; NOSE itches; SPEAKING
    at same time. *Also see* divination (multiple/
    other). *Cf.* stranger/strange
lightning/fire (precautions/predictions) *see* AS-
    CENSION DAY, egg laid on; BAT; BAY/LAUREL
    protects; CANDLE, holy: cures and protects;
    CHRISTMAS LOG/ASHEN FAGGOT: piece kept for
    luck/protection; CHURCH BELL drives away
    devils and storms; CLOCK strikes while
    church bells are ringing; COCK crows = ill
    omen; CORAL; DOORS AND WINDOWS opened in
    thunderstorm; EAGLE-STONE; ELDER protects
    against lightning; 'FIRE' taboo word; GOOD
    FRIDAY, bread made on: protects; HARE por-
    tends fire; HOLLY protects; HOUSELEEK pro-
    tects; KNIFE dangerous in thunderstorm;
    MIRROR covered in thunderstorm; MISTLETOE
    protects; MOON, pointing at; 'PALM' protects;
    RED FLOWERS unlucky; SALT as protection
    against witch; SHOES, new: on table; SNAKE
    SLOUGH/SKIN protects house; STARS, pointing
    at/counting; SWALLOW AND MARTIN: nests
    lucky; THORN TREE protects; THUNDER AND
    LIGHTNING. *Also see* weather/heavenly bodies
lilac *see* WHITE FLOWERS: lilac
livestock: *see* ANIMAL, buying and selling;
    BEES; BLACK SHEEP; BLADE-BONE medicates
    well-water; BURIAL, symbolic: counteracts
    Whitsuntide birth; CATTLE; CHRISTMAS DEC-
    ORATIONS (evergreens) fed to cattle; CHRIST-
    MAS LOG/ASHEN FAGGOT: piece kept for
    luck/protection; COW'S DUNG; DAFFODIL in
    house; CAT OR DOG, disease transferred to;
    DONKEY with cows; EGGS; EGGSHELLS; ELF-
    SHOT; FAIRY RINGS; FERN protects; FIRE not
    allowed out of house; FIRE protects cattle
    and crops; FOOD, giving away; GOAT on
    farm; 'GOLD AND SILVER WATER'; GUINEA
    FOWL; HEART stuck with pins; IRON cures;
    IRON deters evil; KNOTS used in cures; LAN-
    TERN on table; LEATHER, burning; LIONESS;
    LUCK-PENNY; MAY BOUGHS AND FLOWERS;
    MILK; MISTLETOE brings luck to farm; MOON
    affects birth/health/death; MOON affects kill-
    ing of livestock; NAMING COWS; PRAISING
    dangerous; PRIMROSES; RED THREAD protects;
    ROWAN; SALT protects cow/calf; SHREW;
    SHREW-ASH; THREAD tied round; TOAD'S OR

FROG'S BONE; TWIN ANIMALS; WASHING as
ritual; WASSAILING cornfields and cattle;
WILLOW BLOSSOMS in house; WILLOW STICK.
Also see animals; birds and eggs; fertility
locks *see* doors/locks
LOOKING BACK *also see* turning back/looking
back
love *see* divination (love/marriage/children);
    marriage/courtship/children
lucky-bird *see* FIRST-FOOT at New Year/
    Christmas: dark male usually preferred
lucky-bit *see* TONGUE, tip of
lumbago *see* rheumatism/gout/lumbago etc.
lying, sign of *see* CHAIR falls over; CLOTHES:
    mending while wearing; TONGUE: signs of
    lying. *Cf.* speaking

M

Macbeth *see* THEATRE: *Macbeth*
madness *see* MOONLIGHT
marriage/courtship/children   (predictions/
    spells) *see* APRON comes untied; BEDSPREAD,
    making; BELT twisted; BREAD: loaves joined;
    BREAD AND BUTTER on plate; BRIDE: threshold
    washed; BRIDE'S BOUQUET; BRIDESMAID too
    many times; BUTTER will not come; CANDLE,
    lighting third; CANDLE, signs in: ring or
    sweetheart; CHAIR falls over; CHRISTMAS PUD-
    DING, stirring; CROOKED PIN; EGG: double
    yolk; ENGAGED COUPLE; ENGAGEMENT RING;
    FIRE, behaviour of: burns on one side;
    FRIDAY, courting on; GARTER; GRAVE,
    meeting/parting at; HAIR, long; HEART stuck
    with pins: lover's spell; HORSESHOE NAIL;
    HYDRANGEA; LADDER, walking under; LAST
    FOOD/DRINK: bread etc. on plate; LAST FOOD/
    DRINK: tea, wine, etc.; PEACOCK FEATHERS;
    PETTICOAT showing; PETTING STONE; PIN,
    finding; PINS, bride's; RED unlucky to lovers;
    ST CATHERINE; SCISSORS fall; SHAKING HANDS
    across table; SILVER, crossing palm with;
    SNAIL, live: thrown for luck; SPEAKING at
    same time; SPOONS, two; STAIRS, bride goes
    up; STAIRS, stumbling going up; STILE lucky;
    STOCKING: spell; STRAW, animal brings a;
    STUMBLING reveals guilt; SUNDAY, courting
    on; TABLE, sitting on; TEA, bubbles on;
    THIMBLE; TOAD'S OR FROG'S BONE; VERVAIN,
    powers of; WISHBONE. *Also see* divination
    (love/marriage/children); quarrels/anger
marriage/wedding   (ceremony/celebrations/
    institution of) *see* BEES, news told to; BEES take
    part in funeral/wedding; BETWEEN, coming;
    BONE: side-bone of fowl; BRIDE; BRIDESMAID;

CHAMBER POT; CHIMNEY SWEEP, meeting; CHURCHING after marriage; CLOCK strikes during marriage ceremony; DOOR; EXCREMENT; FIRST-FOOT on occasion of wedding; FRIDAY, getting married on; FUNERAL, meeting: unlucky for bridal party; GREEN; HEN cackles; HOLLY indicates dominant partner; HOLLY AND IVY = male and female; HORSE/ HORSEMAN lucky to meet; KNOTS hinder conception; LEFT FOOT; LENT, marrying in; LOOKING BACK; MARRIAGE; MARRIED COUPLE; MAY, marrying in; MIRROR, looking in: bride; MOON affects enterprises; MYRTLE = love; NAMES, magical: married couple; NUTS at wedding; PARSLEY: mistress is master; PEARLS = tears; PETTING STONE; PIG, meeting; PINS, bride's; ROSEMARY protective/ lucky; ROSEMARY: woman is master; SHOES, old: thrown etc. for luck; SHOES/STOCKINGS in form of cross; SILVER protects; SILVER 'GARLAND'; SPOON, wooden; SUNDAY, getting married on; SUNWISE, bride goes; THREAD on distaff; TOAD OR FROG, meeting; WASHING clothes: drying; WASHING UP together; WEDDING; WHEAT/RICE/CONFETTI thrown for luck; WIDOW unlucky at wedding; WIDOW'S [OR WIDOWER'S] PEAK. Also see church ceremonies/sacraments; circle/ring; marriage/courtship/children

martin see SWALLOW AND MARTIN

May-time: season of rebirth, associated with magic and witchcraft see BROOM, buying: in May; BROOM (plant) in house; BROOM (plant), sweeping with; CATTLE: one sacrificed to protect rest of herd; CHARMS in food; ELDER protects against evil; FIRE not allowed out of house; FIRE not to die out; FIRE protects cattle and crops; HARE = witch; HORSESHOE at threshold; IRON taboo on sacred occasions; MAY; MILK, giving or selling; MUGWORT cures female ailments; ROWAN protects; SILVER 'GARLAND'; SNAIL: divination; SNAKE STONE; WELL; WOMAN crosses water; YARROW: divination. Cf. Easter; New Year/Christmas

MAY DEW/RAIN also see water

measuring see counting/measuring/weighing

melting see burning/boiling/melting/roasting

mending see knots in garments/knitting/ sewing

meteor see COMET; STAR, falling/shooting

midsummer-men see ORPINE: divination

Midsummer/St John's Day: survival of pagan summer solstice beliefs and practices see ASH TREE benign; CATTLE: one sacrificed to protect rest of herd; 'COAL' magic; DISHES, three: divination; DUMB CAKE; EARTH, hole

in: divination; EGGS (whites of): shapes in water: divination; FERN LEAF in shoe; FERN SEED makes invisible; FIRE not to die out; FIRE protects cattle and crops; HEMP SEED: divination; LEAD shapes in water: divination of future spouse; NAILS driven in: cure; NAMES, divination with; NEW YEAR, working at; ORPINE: divination; ROSE: divination; ST JOHN'S EVE; ST JOHN'S WORT; SHIFT/SMOCK etc., apparition turns; SHOES placed in form of a T; STILE lucky; SUPPER, apparition comes to share. Cf. saints/saints' days

milk/butter: sacred, must be protected see BUTTER; CORPSE'S HAND gives power over butter; COW'S DUNG; FIRE not allowed out of house; FRIDAY butter and eggs; HOLLY-WOOD CUP; IRON in churn; MAY BOUGHS AND FLOWERS protect; MAY DAY, giving or selling on; MILK; MISTLETOE brings luck to farm; ROBIN AND NEST, harming; ST JOHN'S WORT; SILVER 'GARLAND'; SWALLOW AND MARTIN, harming; SWALLOW AND MARTIN, harming nests; WYCH ELM protects. Also see animals; food/drink; livestock

MINISTER also see churchmen/women

MIRROR also see image/picture/reflection/ shadow

MISTLETOE also see CHRISTMAS DECORATIONS.

money/coins see BABY, gifts to; BABY'S HANDS, washing; BLADE-BONE: divination; BRIDE'S CLOTHES: shoe, gold coin in; BUMBLE BEE, first: killed; CHAMPAGNE CORK; CHARMS in food; CIGARETTE PACKET, stepping on; CLOTHES: first time worn; COAL, dreaming of; COIN; COMMUNION table/altar; CROOKED COIN; CROWN (five-shilling piece); CUCKOO, first: money in pocket; DIRT lucky; FIRST-FOOT at New Year/Christmas: ritual of gifts; FIRST-FOOT on way to christening; GOOSE eaten on Michaelmas Day; HAIR: double crown; HAND itches; HAND, lucky; HANDSEL; HANDSELLING; IRON: ironing shirt-tail; LAST FOOD/DRINK: bread etc. on plate; LAST PAYMENT; LUCK-PENNY; MOLE: moleskin purse; MONDAY, giving or receiving on; MONEY; NEW MOON and money; NEW YEAR and money; NUTMEG lucky; PANCAKES eaten on Shrove Tuesday; PURSE, string kept in; RING; RUST = money; SALT as propitiation; SPIDER, 'money spinner'; SPITTING for luck; SWALLOW AND MARTIN: nests lucky; TEA, bubbles on; TEETH, gap between; TOAD OR FROG, meeting = money; TONGUE, tip of; URINE, bubbles on; WEASEL-SKIN PURSE; WELL; WIND: coin thrown into sea; WREN, dead. Also see buying/selling; divination (multiple/other); propitiation; silver/gold

after sunset; KNOTS in shroud/clothes of dead; MAY DAY/EVE din; MIRROR, looking in: by candlelight; MOTH/BUTTERFLY; NAILS AND HAIR: cures/spells; OWL; ROSE: divination; ST AGNES'S EVE/DAY; SHADOW, headless; SHIFT/SMOCK etc., apparition turns; SNEEZING: divination: time of day; STILE lucky; SUPPER, apparition comes to share; SWORD AND SCABBARD: divination; TEETH, disposing of; THREAD ON DISTAFF; THREAD, winding; WASHING WATER, throwing out; WATER, running: cures; WHISTLING after dark; WORK, new place of: time of arrival. Cf. black/dark; sleep: vulnerable state; sleeping; sun

nightmare (causes/cures) see BEAN BLOSSOMS; BED-MAKING: turning mattress/changing sheets at 'dangerous' times; COFFIN, parts of; CORPSE, touching; IRON deters evil; PEONY protects; SHOES, turned: prevent nightmare; SHOES/STOCKINGS in form of cross; STONE with hole. Cf. night; sleep: vulnerable state

nine see three

noise/din (bells, guns, etc.): drives away evil see CHURCH BELL drives away devils and storms; MAY DAY/EVE din; NEW YEAR din; WASSAILING fruit trees; WEDDING, guns fired at

north/south: significance of orientation see BURIAL on north side of churchyard; NORTH; PARISHES; SLEEPING north/south; SUNWISE; WATER, running: cures. Cf. left/right; sunwise/anti-sunwise

numbers: significant/magical see ASH TREE: even ash-leaf: divination; BLACKSMITH; BREAD: loaves joined; BUS TICKETS; BUTTON, four-holed; CARDS, unlucky; CAT, black: cures; CLOVER, four-leaved; CONVERSATION, lull in; CROWS, two or more; DANDELION OR HAWKWEED SEEDS: divination; DONKEY cures: hair from 'cross'; EAR, ringing in: divination; EGGS: breaking accidentally; EGGS, setting: odd number; ELDER protects against and cures disease; FINGERS, cracking joints of; FIRE, poking someone else's; FIRE protects cattle and crops; FRIDAY THE THIRTEENTH; GABRIEL'S HOUNDS/SEVEN WHISTLERS; GATE: divination; GLASS, breaking; HORSESHOE NAIL; LIONESS; MAGPIE: divination rhyme; MINCE PIES = happy months; MIRROR, breaking; MOON, pointing at; MOTH sign of letter; NEEDLE, breaking; NEW MOON: divination by diffusion; NUNS; ODD NUMBER; PINS: pinning by another person; PRAYERS, stopping/stumbling while saying; PRIMROSES; RING; SEVENTH CHILD; SNEEZING: divination: number of times; SWORD AND SCABBARD: divination; THEATRE: thread; THIRTEEN;

WASSAILING cornfields and cattle; WATER, running: cures; WHITE FEET, horse's. Also see double/two; three; two people. Cf. counting/measuring/weighing

NUN also see churchmen/women

O

odd/even see numbers; three

old/used objects: significance see clothes/bedclothes. Cf. cleanliness/newness

omens: of things feared see death/sickness; lightning/fire; quarrels/anger; stranger/strange; weather/heavenly bodies

opposite sex/same sex: requirement in magic see BABY protected by clothes of opposite sex; BLEEDING, charm to staunch; BRIDE'S CLOTHES: stocking, throwing; CANDLE burns blue; CHRISTENING CAKE: divination; CHURCHING after childbirth: divination; CORPSE'S HAND cures; DONKEY cures: hair from 'cross'; EYES, peculiar; FIRST-FOOT on way to christening; FUNERAL: divination; GLOVES as present; GRAVE cures; GRAVE open on Sunday; KNOTS used in cures; MANDRAKE aids conception; NEW MOON, kissing under; NUTMEG in pocket: cures; NUTS, double: eating; OPPOSITE SEX; RING made of money/silver given by bachelors/spinsters: cures; SALT as propitiation; THREAD tied round; TWIN, surviving; WHITE FLOWERS: snowdrop. Cf. sexuality

opposite side/same side: requirement in magic see ELBOW, knocking; MOLE'S FEET cure; ONION protects and cures; SNAKE SLOUGH/SKIN preserves health; TOAD OR FROG cures

P

parents/grandparents: sacred/protective see BABY protected by parent's garment; HAND above grave; HARE, eating: taboo; MOTHER-DIE; NAMING baby: after living parent; NOSE bleeds: ill omen; PAVEMENT, stepping on lines/cracks; PETTICOAT showing; SKULL, eating or drinking from: cures; SNAIL = spirit of the dead; SPEEDWELL, picking; WALKING backwards

PARTING also see breaking; last

passing through/under/over: curative/magical/protective see ASH TREE, child passed through; BABY protected by parent's garment; BLACKSMITH; BRAMBLE ARCH cures;

ANALYTICAL INDEX

Q

quarrels/anger (predictions/effects) *see* BEES dislike bad behaviour; BELLOWS on table; BETWEEN, coming; BOILING WATER spills over; BREAD: loaf, cake, etc. breaks; CHAIR passed over table; CHAIR turned round = quarrel; COOKING: two together; FIRE, behaviour of: burns badly, FIRE, behaviour of: spits and roars; FIRE, two people making; GLOVES as present; HERRINGS dislike quarrels; IRON, touching; KNIFE as present; KNIFE falls; KNIFE laid across; KNIFE, stirring with; MIRROR, looking in: two people; MISTLETOE, kissing under; NOSE itches; PIN; POURING backwards; SALT, spilling; SCISSORS as present; SHOES, new: on table; SUNWISE, stirring; TABLE, two people sitting on; TEA, making; TEA, stirring; UMBRELLA on table; UMBRELLA/ WALKING STICK, dropping; URINATING together; WASHING HANDS together

R

rabbit *see* HARE OR RABBIT

rag well *see* WELL

RAIN *also see* water; weather/heavenly bodies

reflection *see* image/picture/reflection/shadow

reptiles *see* animals/reptiles/fishes and parts or products of

rheumatism/gout/lumbago etc. *see* BELLOWS cure; BIRTH, breech; BRAMBLE ARCH; COFFIN, parts of; CONFIRMATION good for rheumatism; CAT OR DOG, disease transferred to; EEL-SKIN GARTERS prevent cramp/ rheumatism; ELDER protects against and cures disease; HARE'S OR RABBIT'S FOOT cures; IRON cures; MAY DEW cures; MEASURING cures; MOLE'S FEET cure; NUTMEG in pocket: cures; POTATO cures rheumatism; SHOES/ STOCKINGS in form of cross; WATER, running: cures. *Also see* cramp/stitch/pins and needles

rice: thrown for luck *see* WHEAT/RICE/CONFETTI thrown for luck

rickets *see* ASH TREE, child passed through; BLACKSMITH; DONKEY cures: passing under; HOLE in stone: passing through; MAY DEW cures

right *see* left/right

RING *also see* circle/ring

road *see* crossing/across; crossroads/boundaries; ground/earth

roasting *see* burning/boiling/melting/roasting

rupture *see* ASH TREE, child passed through

S

saints/saints' days: associated with magic *see* BAY/LAUREL LEAVES: divination; BLEEDING, charm; BUTTER, charm for; CANDLE burns blue; CHURCH PORCH, watching in; COCK AND HEN on St Valentine's morning; CRAMP, verbal charm for; DUMB CAKE; FEVER, verbal charm for; LEAVES: spell and divination; MUGWORT against evil; NAMES, divination with; NAMES, magical: married couple with special Christian names; NAMING baby: after saint; NUTS, double: protect/lucky; ONION: divination and spells; PLANTAIN: divination; SAGE: divination; ST AGNES'S EVE/DAY; ST CATHERINE; ST CHRISTOPHER; ST JOHN'S EVE; ST JOHN'S WORT; ST SWITHIN; SALT IN EGG: divination; SHIFT/SMOCK etc., apparition turns; SIEVE AND SHEARS; SUPPER, apparition comes to share; SWORD AND SCABBARD: divination; TOOTHACHE, charm for; VALENTINE; WELL: divination; WREN, dead. *Cf.* church festivals/holy days; days of the week; Midsummer/St John's Day

salt: sacred/magical/protective *see* BABY, gifts to; CHAMBER POT; DISHES, three: divination; DUMB CAKE; FEVER cured by transference; HOUSE, moving; MAY DAY, giving or selling on; MILK boils over; SALT; TEETH, disposing of; THREAD on distaff; URINE: iron nails etc. in patient's urine to detect witch

same sex/side *see* opposite sex/same sex; opposite side/same side

scald *see* BURN OR SCALD

sciatica *see* rheumatism/gout/lumbago etc.

SCISSORS *also see* knives/scissors

scrofula *see* swelling

scythes *see* knives/scissors

sea/seamen: sea feared/revered, as controlling life/livelihood *see* ALBATROSS; BALLAST; BIRD on ship; BLOOD, shedding first; BOAT; BOOTS on shoulder; BOWL overturned; BREAD: loaf upside-down; BROOM: losing at sea; BROOM thrown for luck; BUCKET: losing at sea; BUCKET upturned; CAT: drowning at sea; CAT, shutting up: raises wind; 'CAT' taboo word; CAUL, possession of: lucky; CHILDREN on ship; 'CHURCH' taboo word; CLERGYMAN; COAL carried for luck; COIN for luck in fishing; CORPSE defiles ship; COUNTING dangerous/ unlucky; DESTINATION, unlucky to be asked one's; DROWNING STRANGER; EGG on board ship; 'EGG' taboo word; EGGSHELL, piercing or crushing; FIRE protects fishing line; FISHING; FRIDAY, beginning voyage on; GLASS, ringing; GOAT at mast; GOLD EAR-RINGS prevent

485

sea/seamen (*cont.*):

drowning; GOOD FRIDAY, bread made on: protects; HARE OR RABBIT on ship; 'HARE' OR 'RABBIT' taboo word; HERRINGS dislike quarrels; HORSE/HORSEMAN lucky to meet; HORSESHOE on ship; KNIFE in mast; 'KNIFE' taboo word; 'LAST' taboo word; LUCK, wishing; MARRIAGES bring stormy weather; 'MINISTER' taboo word; NAILS AND HAIR, cutting: at sea; PIG; PINS on ship; POINTING AT; PROSTITUTE on ship; 'RAT' AND 'MOUSE' taboo words; RED HAIR unlucky; ROLLING-PIN; ROPE CIRCLE, boat passed through; SAILOR; ST CHRISTOPHER; 'SALMON' taboo word; SALT as propitiation; 'SALT' taboo word; SATURDAY, beginning on; SEAGULL AND STORMY PETREL; SEAWEED in house; SHOES, old: thrown etc. for luck; SPINNING WHEEL on ship; SUNDAY, going to sea on; SUNWISE, boat goes; SUNWISE, rope coiled; SWAN unlucky; THREAD, winding: after sunset; TIDE; TRUNK, unlucky to lock; URINATING: must not offend divine powers; WASHING clothes: day of sailing; WASSAILING sea; WHEAT/RICE/CONFETTI thrown for luck; WHISTLING at sea; WHITE APRON; WHITE STONE; WIND; WOMAN on ship; WREN, dead. *Also see* weather/heavenly bodies

sea urchin *see* FAIRY LOAF

secrecy/stealth/silence (not speaking): requirements for, and precautions against, magic *see* ADULTERER cures warts; ASH TREE: even ash-leaf: divination; BABY, referring to; BIBLE AND KEY: divination; BLACKSMITH; BLADE-BONE: spell; CANDLE burns blue; CANDLE, failing to blow out; CHARMS in food; CHRISTENING CAKE: divination; CLOVER, four-leaved: lucky to find; 'COAL' magic; COUNTING; DESTINATION, unlucky to be asked one's; DIRT lucky; DONKEY cures: passing under; DUMB CAKE; FIRE, newcomer gives priority to; FLOWERS in pairs; FROGS, nine: in soup; HAIR thrown into fire: divination of future husband; IRON, finding; IRON taboo on sacred occasions; IVY LEAF: divination; KNOTS in garters; KNOTS used in cures; LAST FOOD/DRINK: bread etc. on plate; MINCE PIES = happy months; MONEY, finding; MONKEY PUZZLE TREE; NAILS driven in: cure; NAMING baby before christening; NAMING COWS; NEW MOON: divination; NEW MOON, kissing under; NEW YEAR and house/home: bringing in the new year; NUTS, double: eating; PEAS, nine: divination; PINS cure warts; POTATO cures rheumatism; RAILWAY BRIDGE/TUNNEL, passing under/over; RED THREAD cures; RING made of money/silver given by bachelors/

spinsters: cures; ROSE: divination; SALT HERRING; SALT IN EGG; SHIFT/SMOCK etc., apparition turns; SHOES placed in form of a T; SKULL, eating or drinking from: cures; SPEAKING at same time; STOCKING, left: divination; THATCH: piece stolen to destroy witch's power; THREAD tied round; THREAD, winding: divination; TREE, disease transferred to; WARTS cured with [stolen] meat; WASHING HANDS together; WATER, running: cures; WINNOWING CORN: divination; YARROW: divination. *Also see* speaking

selling *see* buying/selling

seven: magical/lucky *see* numbers

Seven Whistlers *see* GABRIEL'S HOUNDS/SEVEN WHISTLERS

sewing *see* knots in garments/knitting/sewing; pins/needles/nails

sexuality: powerful/lucky *see* ADULTERER cures warts; BASTARD lucky; HAY RICK; OPPOSITE SEX; PROSTITUTE lucky; WIFE, unfaithful. *Cf.* fertility; opposite sex/same sex; virginity

SHAKING HANDS *also see* TABLE, shaking hands across

shamrock *see* CLOVER

shears *see* knives/scissors

sheet *see* clothes/bedclothes

shingles/erysipelas/other rashes *see* BLACKSMITH; CAT, black: cures; CHURCH BELL cures; ELDER protects against and cures disease; GRAVE, treading on; IRON cures; NAMES, magical: married couple with same surname before marriage; RINGWORM; SEVENTH CHILD

shoes/stockings: significant because of contact with feet/ground *see* clothes/bedclothes; ground/earth

shoulder, behind *see* throwing/spitting backwards

shroud *see* corpse

sickles *see* knives/scissors

sickness *see* death/sickness/disaster; diseases/infirmities; divination (of life or death)

silver/gold: magical/protective *see* BABY, gifts to; BEES, buying and selling; BRIDE'S CLOTHES: shoe, gold coin in; CROOKED COIN; GOLD; 'GOLD AND SILVER WATER'; GOLD EAR-RINGS; PENDULUM; RING; SILVER; WEDDING RING. *Also see* money/coins

sixpence *see* CHARMS in food; CROOKED COIN; SILVER; SILVER BULLET

SKULL *also see* bones; corpse

sleep: vulnerable state *see* BED; BONES, sleeping on; BIBLE protects; BREAD cures and protects; CAT endangers health; CHRISTENING CLOTHES, baby must sleep first night in; CLOVER as protection; CORK cures cramp; CORPSE'S HAND holding candle; FAIRY RINGS; IRON cures;

IRON deters evil; IRON in cradle or childbed; MARRIED COUPLE: first to die; MAY BLOSSOM; MOONLIGHT; PICTURE over door or bed; ST AGNES'S EVE/DAY; ST JOHN'S WORT; SHOES, turned; SHOES/STOCKINGS in form of cross; SLEEPING north/south; STOCKING, left; UMBRELLA on bed; WATER under bed. Cf. night; nightmare

sleeping: preceded by preparations for divination see BAY/LAUREL LEAVES: divination; BLADE-BONE: spell; CHRISTENING CAKE: divination; 'COAL' magic; DIAMOND; DUMB CAKE; EGG, first; KNOTS in garters; LEAD shapes in water: divination of future spouse; LEAVES, nine; LEMON PEEL; MISTLETOE, kissing under: divination; MYRTLE; NAMES, divination with; NEW MOON: divination; ONION: divination and spells; PEARL under pillow; SALT HERRING; SALT IN EGG; SHOES placed in form of a T; WEDDING CAKE: divination; YARROW. Also see divination (love, marriage, and children)

smallpox see fevers etc.

SNEEZING also see itching/sneezing/similar involuntary actions

soul see spirit/soul of dead

speaking: magical/dangerous connotations see ASH TREE: even ash-leaf: divination; BEES, news told to; CLOCK strikes, speaking while; CONVERSATION, lull in; CORPSE: speaking of the dead; CRICKET as omen; DREAM, telling; EAR OR CHEEK tingles = someone talking about you; EYELASH, wishing on; EYES, peculiar; 'HARE' OR 'RABBIT': saying at change of month; LAST WORDS OF PLAY; LUCK, wishing; MARRIED COUPLE: first to die; MONDAY first mentioned by woman; NEW MOON first mentioned; NEW YEAR: speaking of the old year; PARTING: saying 'Goodbye'; PRAISING dangerous; PRAYERS; RAILWAY BRIDGE/TUNNEL; ROOKS informed of a death; SPEAKING; STAIRS, stumbling going down; THUNDER AND LIGHTNING, drawing attention to; TONGUE: signs of lying; WARTS cured with elder wood; WARTS 'given' to corpse. Also see charms, verbal; lying; secrecy/stealth/silence; taboo words; thanking

spells see charms, verbal; divination

spilling see falling/dropping/spilling

spinning see knots in garments/knitting/sewing

spirit/soul of dead: takes form of living creature see HARE, eating: taboo; MOTH/BUTTERFLY omen of death; SEAGULL AND STORMY PETREL; SNAIL = spirit of the dead

spittle/spitting: power to cure/protect see BIRD, dead; CAT, black: meeting; CLERGYMAN,

meeting; COAL, finding; COAL in Christmas stocking; CROSS, making sign of: cures; 'DEVIL' taboo word; EYES, peculiar; FIRE, behaviour of: spits and roars; FIRST VISIT; FISHING HOOK: first baited; FUNERAL, meeting: and actions to avert evil; HANDSEL (first sale of day); HAY, load of; IRON, finding; LADDER, walking under; LUCK-PENNY; MAGPIE, meeting; MONEY; NUNS, seeing; PIEBALD HORSE, meeting; PRAISING; SHOES, turned: stop dog howling; SHOES/STOCKINGS, putting on: spitting; SNAIL = spirit of the dead; SPECTACLES, distrust of; SPITTING; SPITTLE; TOAD OR FROG, meeting; URINE, spitting into; WASHING HANDS together; WATER, running: crossing over; WEASEL; WHITE HORSE. Also see fasting; throwing/spitting backwards

spirits see apparitions

SPOON(S) also see CUTLERY, dropping

sprain see BIRTH, breech; KNOTS used in cures; TOAD OR FROG cures

springs see water

squint see EYES, peculiar

stairs see ground/earth

STAR(S) also see weather/heavenly bodies

stealing see secrecy/stealth/silence; thieves

stepping/treading on, or stepping/leaping/arching over: magic power of see BUCKET, jumping over; CAT endangers health of unborn child; CAT OR DOG passes over corpse; CATTLE: one sacrificed to protect rest of herd; CHAMBER POT; CIGARETTE PACKET, stepping on; DIRT lucky; FIRE TONGS, treading on; FISHING LINE etc., walking over; HANDSEL (first sale of day); HARE-LIP; KNIFE falls; LADDER, walking under; LADYBIRD, killing; MONEY, dropping; PETTING STONE; RAILWAY BRIDGE/TUNNEL; RAINBOW over house; RAINBOW, stepping on; RATS AND MICE, influx of; RED FLOWERS unlucky; SCISSORS fall; SHOES, new: trodden on; SHREW causes lameness; SHREW-ASH; SHUDDER; STEPPING OVER; THEATRE: make-up; THRESHOLD. Cf. crossing; passing through/under/over

stile/gateway: associated with magic see GATE: divination; NEW MOON: divination; PARTING at gate or stile; PINS defend against corpse; STILE. Cf. threshold

stirring: magical/potentially dangerous see CHRISTMAS LOG: stirring fire during supper; CHRISTMAS PUDDING, stirring; COOKING: two together; CORPSE'S HAND gives power over butter; DUMB CAKE; FIRE, newcomer gives priority to; FIRE, poking; KNIFE, stirring with; TEA, bubbles on; TEA, stirring; SUNWISE, stirring

stitch (i.e. pain) *see* cramp/stitch/pins and needles

stoat *see* WEASEL

STOCKING *also see* shoes/stockings

stones, ancient: magical nature/power *see* COUNTING/MEASURING ancient stones; HOLE in stone, passing through; IRON taboo on sacred occasions; PETTING STONE; SUNDAY: keeping Sabbath holy: transgressors turned to stone; WELL ceremonies

stones/beads: magical nature/power *see* AMBER cures/protects; BALLAST; BLUE protects; CORAL; DIAMOND; EAGLE-STONE; ELF-SHOT; FAIRY LOAF; FIRE: divination in bonfire; IONA STONE; MOTHER-OF-PEARL; OPAL; PEARL; PLANTAIN: divination; SNAKE STONE; STONE with hole; TOADSTONE; WHITE STONE. *Also see* colours; touching; wearing

stormy petrel *see* SEAGULL AND STORMY PETREL

stranger/strange (people/places/objects): ominous/magical *see* BIBLE AND KEY: divination; BROOM ominous; BUMBLE BEE in house = stranger; BURIAL on north side of churchyard; BUTTER, stranger helps to churn; CANDLE, signs in: stranger; CAT, behaviour of: washes behind ear = stranger; CHRISTMAS PUDDING, stirring; COCK crows on doorstep; COOKING: two together; CUTLERY falls = visitor; DOG, followed by; DROWNING STRANGER; ELBOW itches; FIRE, behaviour of: blazes suddenly; FIRE, behaviour of: 'stranger' on grate; FIRE, poking someone else's; FIRE TONGS fall; FISHING LINE, baiting; FOOT: sole itches; HAIR: double crown; HOUSE, new: visitor brings present; IRON in cradle or childbed; KNEE itches; KNIFE falls; KNOTS in garters; MAGPIE, chattering = stranger; MONDAY, visitors on; NOSE itches; PARSLEY planted by stranger; RING made of money/silver given by bachelors/spinsters: cures; SCISSORS fall; STRAW, animal brings a; TEA/LEAF OR STALK; TEAPOT LID; TEETH, gap between

streams *see* water

STUMBLING *also see* interruption/impediment

suicide *see* BURIAL on north side of churchyard

sun: sacred/beneficent/powerful *see* ASH TREE benign; BLADE-BONE: divination; BRIDE, sun shines on; EASTER: sun dancing, or Lamb seen in sun; EGGS (whites of): shapes in water; FUNERAL: sun shines on mourner's face; RATS AND MICE, riddance to; SUN; SUNDAY; SUNSET. *Cf.* morning; night; north/south; sunwise/anti-sunwise

sunwise/anti-sunwise (circling/turning with/against the course of the sun) *see* BLACK Devil's colour; BUTTER, charm for; CAT OR

DOG, disease transferred to; CHURCHING after childbirth; CROSS cures; FIRE protects cattle and crops; HOLE in stone: passing through; NEW YEAR din; PENDULUM; SALT protects baby/child; SUNWISE; TEA/COFFEE CUP, 'reading'; WELL. *Also see* left/right; north/south; sun; turning round

sweeping/sweeping brush *see* BROOM; BROOM (plant); DIRT lucky; NEW YEAR and the house/home: nothing to be taken out

swelling (usually in neck, such as goitre/king's evil/scrofula/tumour/wen/boils/mumps/sore throat) *see* BRAMBLE ARCH cures; CORPSE'S HAND cures; CORPSE'S LINEN cures; GRAVE cures; HOLE in stone: passing through; HORSE'S HAIR cures; IRON cures; KING touches for evil; MOLE: cures/spells; MOLE'S FEET cure; NUTMEG in pocket; PIG, disease transferred to; POSTHUMOUS CHILD; SEVENTH CHILD; SNAKE buried alive in bottle; STOCKING, left

swords *see* knives/scissors

T

table: sacred/magical through associations with holy table or altar *see* BELLOWS on table; BILLHOOK on table; BROOM on table; CAT on table; CHAIR; CONVERSATION, lull in; FIRE TONGS on table; KNIFE laid across; LANTERN on table; NAMES, magical: three; PIGEON settles; POKER on table; SHAKING HANDS across table; SHOES, new: on table; SUNWISE, laying table; TABLE; THIRTEEN in company or at table; UMBRELLA on table; WOOD, touching. *Cf.* iron; trees

taboo words *see* 'CAT'; 'CHURCH'; 'DEVIL'; 'EGG'; 'FAIRY'; 'FIRE'; 'HARE' OR 'RABBIT'; 'KNIFE'; 'LAST'; 'MINISTER'; 'PIG'; 'RAT' AND 'MOUSE'; 'SALMON'; 'SALT'; THEATRE: *Macbeth. Cf.* speaking

tail *see* back/front or head/tail of magical creature/object

tears *see* crying/tears

TEETH *also see* body, parts or products of; toothache/teething troubles

thanking: magical implications *see* DROPPING THINGS; ENGAGEMENT RING; GLOVE, dropping; HORSE'S HAIR cures; PIN as present; RING made of money/silver given by bachelors/spinsters: cures; SOAP, giving or lending; THREAD tied round. *Also see* giving/accepting; speaking

THEATRE *also see* CANDLE, lighting third; LAST WORDS OF PLAY; LEFT FOOT; LUCK, wishing;

SOAP left behind in theatre; SPIDER OR SPIDER'S WEB, harming; UMBRELLA on table; WHISTLING in theatre

thieves *see* BEES dislike bad behaviour; BIBLE AND KEY: divination; COAL carried for luck; CORPSE'S HAND holding candle; EXCREMENT; MOON, MAN IN THE; NAILS AND HAIR, cutting: baby's; SIEVE AND SHEARS. *Also see* divination (multiple/other)

thorns/prickles: used to injure/protect *see* BRAMBLE ARCH; 'BUSH', burning; DOG-ROSE; GOOSEBERRY THORN; HEART stuck with pins etc. and burned to detect witch; HOLLY; MAY BOUGHS AND FLOWERS; ROSE-GALL; SHIFT/ SMOCK etc., apparition turns; THORN TREE; WARTS cured with snail. *Also see* greenery; pins/needles/nails; wounds/bites/thorns in flesh

three (and multiples, mainly nine): powerful/ ominous *see* APPLE PEEL; ASH TREE, child passed through; BAT; BED-MAKING: three people; BEES, news told to; BEETLE cures; BIBLE protects; BIRTH, breech; BLACKSMITH; BLADE-BONE: spell; BORROWING AND LENDING; BRAMBLE ARCH cures; BRIDESMAID too many times; BURIAL of woman; BURIAL, symbolic: cure; BURN OR SCALD, charm for; BUTTER, charm for; BUTTERFLIES, three; CANDLE, lighting third; CAT, black: cures; CAT: nine lives; CHAIN-LETTER; CHIMNEY SWEEP, meeting; CHRISTMAS PUDDING, stirring; CHURCH, lead from; CHURCH BELL cures; CHURCH PORCH, watching in; CIGARETTE, lighting third; CLOVER; COFFIN, parts of; COMMUNION; CORPSE'S HAND gives power over butter; CROWS OR RAVENS ominous; DISHES, three; DONKEY cures: hair from 'cross'; DONKEY cures: passing under; DUCK OR GOOSE; DUMB CAKE; FEVER, verbal charm for; FROGS, nine: in soup; GOLD cures sore eyes; GOOSEBERRY THORN; GRAVE cures; HICCUP, cures for; HOLE in stone: passing through; HORSE'S HAIR cures; IRON cures; IRON in churn; KNIFE falls; KNOCKING; KNOTS; LADDER, walking under; LARK; LAST FOOD/DRINK: tea, wine, etc.; LEAD shapes in water: divination of cause of sickness; LEAVES, nine; MAY DEW cures; MILLER; MOLE: cures/spells; MOLES ON BODY, meaning of; MOTH/BUTTERFLY; MOUSE cures; NAILS AND HAIR: cures/spells; NAILS driven in: cure; NAMES, magical: three; NETTLE STING; NEW MOON; OATS; ODD NUMBER lucky; ONION: divination and spells; PAR-ISHES, three; PARSLEY, Devil controls; PEAS, nine: divination; PIEBALD HORSE cures; PIE-BALD HORSE, meeting; PREGNANT WOMAN causes pregnancy; RINGWORM; SAGE; SEA-

GULL AND STORMY PETREL; SHOELACE comes untied; SNAKE, live; SPIDER, 'money spinner'; SPITTING to avert evil; STARS, nine; SUNWISE as 'sacred' ritual; SWORD AND SCAB-BARD: divination; TEA/COFFEE CUP, 'reading'; THIMBLE; THREE; THRUSH (ulcers in mouth); TREE, disease transferred to; WARTS cured with snail; WARTS 'given' to corpse; WEDDING CAKE: divination; WELL: ceremonies; WHISTL-ING after dark; WHISTLING in theatre; YAR-ROW: divination. *Also see* numbers

threshold (including window-sill/chimney): of strategic significance as entrance to house, church, etc. *see* BRIDE lifted over threshold; BRIDE: threshold washed; BROOM protects house; BUCKET, jumping over; CABBAGE STALK: divination; CAROL SINGERS; CATTLE: burning entrails; CATTLE: one sacrificed; CHRISTMAS, first to open door at; CHURCH PORCH, watching in; COCK crows on doorstep = stranger; CORPSE defiles: threshold washed; DIRT lucky; DOORSTEP PATTERNS; EXCREMENT; FIRST-FOOT at New Year/ Christmas; HEART stuck with pins etc. and burned to detect witch; HORSESHOE; IRON deters evil; LEFT FOOT; MARRIAGE: dominant partner; MARRIED COUPLE: first to die; MAY BOUGHS AND FLOWERS; MILK, giving or selling; NAILS AND HAIR: cures/spells; ONION protects and cures; PEAS, nine: divination; PETTING STONE; PICTURE over door or bed; ST CHRIS-TOPHER; ST JOHN'S WORT; SALT as protection against witch; STUMBLING ominous; THREAD, first: divination; THRESHOLD; URINE: iron nails etc. in patient's urine to detect witch. *Cf.* ground/earth; house/home; stile/gateway

throwing at/after/over: averts evil/for luck *see* BRIDE'S CLOTHES: shoe, throwing; BROOM thrown for luck; CAT OR DOG, disease trans-ferred to; EGG, last; FIRE protects fishing line; NUTS at wedding; NUTS, double: eating; PIG, nose of; PINS defend against corpse; ROSEMARY at funerals; ST AGNES'S EVE/DAY; SALT; SHOES, old: thrown etc. for luck; THEATRE, new: coal thrown for luck; THREAD, winding: divination; WASSAILING; WEDDING CAKE/PLATE broken over bride; WHEAT/RICE/CONFETTI thrown for luck. Cf. stepping/treading on, or stepping/leaping/ arching over

throwing/spitting backwards, over shoulder: averts evil/for luck *see* APPLE PEEL: div-ination; BEETLE cures; BRIDE crosses running water; BRIDE'S BOUQUET; BRIDE'S CLOTHES: stocking, throwing; CATERPILLAR, hairy: lucky; COAL, finding; EGG, last; ELDER pro-

U

V

W

wounds/bites/thorns in flesh (*cont.*):
via cause of wound *see* BLEEDING, charm to staunch; CANDLE, holy: cures and protects; DOG, hair of; ELF-SHOT; FINGERS: power for good/evil; IRON cures; NETTLE STING, charm for; ONION protects and cures; SHREW cures/spells; SKULL, moss from; SNAKE SLOUGH/SKIN preserves health; SPIDER OR SPIDER'S WEB cures bleeding; THORN in flesh: charm; TOAD-STONE; WOUND healed by tending weapon

WREN *also see* ROBIN AND WREN; ROBIN/WREN/MARTIN/SWALLOW

wresting thread *see* KNOTS used in cures